L. L. C... Henry D. Th...

E. Plome... Countee Cullen D.H. Lawrence

Charles Dickens Jonathan Swift Daniel Defoe

G. Bernard Shaw Phillis Wheatley Stephen Crane

Langston Bret Harte Henry W. Longfellow

Oscar Wilde Thornton Wilder Edgar A Poe

Ernest Hemingway J. Austen

Sinclair Lewis Herman Melville R Eme...

Juan Turgeneur A Bradstreet

T.S. Eliot Jack London Thomas Hardy

SCRIBNER LITERATURE SERIES

Signature Edition

INTRODUCING LITERATURE

ENJOYING LITERATURE

UNDERSTANDING LITERATURE

APPRECIATING LITERATURE

AMERICAN LITERATURE

ENGLISH LITERATURE
WITH WORLD MASTERPIECES

COVER: The central image is an original woodcut of William Shakespeare. The woodcut is framed by handmade marbleized paper. The combination of these two art forms suggests the sources of the finest literature—imaginative power and delicate craft.

GENERAL ADVISERS

READING AND INSTRUCTIONAL METHODS

Jack Cassidy
Professor of Education
Millersville University
Millersville, Pennsylvania

TEACHER'S PROFESSIONAL RESOURCES

Robert DiYanni
Professor of English
Pace University
Pleasantville, New York

SPEAKING AND LISTENING SKILLS

R. Brian Loxley
Communications Consultant
New York, New York

THINKING SKILLS

Eric Cooper
Director, Comprehension and Cognition Project
The College Board
New York, New York

LITERATURE AND CURRICULUM

George Kearns
Associate Professor of English
Rutgers University
New Brunswick, New Jersey

CONSULTANTS

Elizabeth Ackley, Teacher, Indian Hill High School, Cincinnati, Ohio

Wanda N. Cain, English Department Head and Teacher, Waxahachie High School, Waxahachie, Texas

Paula A. Calabrese, Principal, Espe School, North Allegheny School District, Pennsylvania

Sandra A. Cavender, English Teacher and Former Chairperson, Nathan Hale High School, West Allis, Wisconsin

Meg Durham, English Department Chairman, South Houston High School, South Houston, Texas

Robert Flores, California Assessment Program–Language Arts: Mentor Teacher, San Diego, California

Carolyn Dennis Jones, Chairperson, Martin Luther King, Jr., National Network of Schools, Englewood, New Jersey

Beverly Merrill, Language Program Specialist, Mesa Unified School District, Arizona

Sonya Pohlman, Rangeview High School, Aurora Public Schools, Aurora, Colorado

Judi Purvis, Secondary Language Arts Appraiser, Carrollton–Farmers Branch Independent School District, Texas

Robert S. Ranta, Supervisor of Languages, Lacey Township High School, Lanoka Harbor, New Jersey

Pearl Thomas, NYC Board of Communication Arts—Adviser (Martin Luther King, Jr., Network of Schools)

Ruth Townsend, Teacher, Yorktown High School, Yorktown Heights, New York

Kathleen M. Keitert Wilkinson, Department Chair, Judson High School, Judson Independent School District, Texas

Marjory Carter Willis, Teacher, Midlothian High School, Midlothian, Virginia

WRITERS

Instructional Text

Brenda Aronowitz, Teacher and Assistant Headmaster

Cosmo F. Ferrara, Writer and Consultant, Former Department Chair

Gale Cornelia Flynn, Poet and Writer, Former English Teacher

Philip McFarland, English Teacher

Gail Mack, Educational Writer

Eileen Hillary Oshinsky, Educational Writer

Julie Stone Peters, Educational Writer

Barbara King-Shaver, Writer

David Wanzer, Educational Writer

Marjory Carter Willis, English Teacher

Thinking Skills Handbook

Beau F. Jones-Davis, North Central Regional Educational Laboratory, Elmhurst, Illinois

Susan Sardy, Yeshiva University, New York, New York

John Sherk, University of Missouri, Kansas City, Missouri

Writing About Literature Handbook

Catherine Sagan, English Department Chair

Research Paper Casebook

Sharon Shaloo, Educational Writer, Boston, Massachusetts

Teacher's Classroom Resources

Stanlee Brimberg, Bank Street School for Children, New York, New York

Ellen Davis, Friendswood Independent School District, Texas

Judith H. McGee, Coordinator of Secondary Education, Athens Independent School District, Texas

David Nicholson, Riverdale Country School, Bronx, New York

The publisher is grateful for assistance and comments from the following people:

Jack V. Booch, Theatre Guild, New York, New York

Mrs. Rosalie Clark, Austin High School, Decatur, Alabama

Harry James Cook, Ozerlea High School, Baltimore, Maryland

Mr. Albert G. Craz, Northport–East Northport High School, Northport, New York

Gerald Dwight, Cherry Hill High School West, Cherry Hill, New Jersey

José Flores, Center for Mexican American Studies, University of Texas, Austin

Mrs. Doris E. R. Gilbert, Syracuse City Schools, Syracuse, New York

William Ince, Stuyvesant High School, New York, New York

Sister Edna Lutton, West Windsor–Plainsboro High School, Princeton Junction, New Jersey

Francisco Jiménez, Santa Clara University, Santa Clara, California

Iris Gates McAnear, Austin High School, Decatur, Alabama

SCRIBNER LITERATURE SERIES

ENGLISH LITERATURE

WITH WORLD MASTERPIECES

Signature Edition

Glencoe
a division of Macmillan Publishing Company
Mission Hills, California

Glencoe Publishing Company
15319 Chatsworth Street
Mission Hills, California 91345
Collier Macmillan Canada, Inc.

Printed in the United States of America

Pupil's Edition ISBN 0-02-195490-9
Teacher's Annotated Edition ISBN 0-02-195550-6

3 4 5 6   92 91 90 89

ACKNOWLEDGMENTS

Grateful acknowledgment is given authors, publishers, and agents for permission to reprint the following copyrighted material. Every effort has been made to determine copyright owners. In the case of any omissions, the Publisher will be pleased to make suitable acknowledgments in future editions.

Aitken & Stone
V. C. NAIPAUL: "B. Wordsworth" from *Miguel Street* (pp. 45–52). Copyright © V. S. Naipaul, 1959. All rights reserved. By permission of Aitken & Stone.

Edward Arnold Ltd.
E. M. FORSTER: "The Beauty of Life" from *Albergo Empedocle and Other Writings by E. M. Forster* edited by George H. Thomson. Copyright © 1972 by George H. Thomson. Reprinted by permission of the publisher.

1964 by the University of Nebraska Press. Reprinted by permission of University of Nebraska Press.

Viking Penguin Inc.

MIGUEL DE CERVANTES (SAAVEDRA): From *The Ingenious Gentleman Don Quixote de la Mancha* translated by Samuel Putnam. Translation copyright 1949 by Samuel Putnam. Copyright renewed 1976 by Hilary Putnam.

NADINE GORDIMER: "The Train From Rhodesia" from *The Soft Voice of the Serpent.* Copyright 1951, 1952, 1953, by Nadine Gordimer.

GRAHAM GREENE: "A Shocking Accident" from *Collected Stories.* Copyright © 1957 by Graham Greene.

JAMES JOYCE: "Araby" from *Dubliners.* Originally published by B. W. Huebsch in 1916. Definitive text copyright © 1967 by the Estate of James Joyce.

D. H. LAWRENCE: "Goose Fair" from *The Complete Short Stories, Vol. I.* Copyright 1934 by Frieda Lawrence. Copyright renewed 1962 by Angelo Ravagli and C. Montague Weekly, Executors of the Estate of Frieda Lawrence Ravagli.

SIEGFRIED SASSOON: "Everyone Sang" from *Collected Poems.* Copyright 1918 by E. P. Dutton Co. Copyright renewed 1946 by Siegfried Sassoon.

The preceding selections were reprinted by permission of Viking Penguin Inc.

A. P. Watt Ltd.

NADINE GORDIMER: "The Train From Rhodesia" from *Selected Stories.* Reprinted by permission of Nadine Gordimer, Jonathan Cape Ltd., and A. P. Watt Ltd.

ROBERT GRAVES: "Song: Sullen Moods" from *Collected Poems.* Reprinted by permission of Robert Graves and A. P. Watt Ltd.

W. B. YEATS: "Down by the Salley Gardens," "An Irish Airman Foresees His Death," "The Lake Isle of Innisfree," "Sailing to Byzantium," "The Second Coming," and "The Wild Swans at Coole" from *Collected Poems of W. B. Yeats.* Reprinted by permission of Michael Yeats, Anne Yeats, Macmillan London Limited, and A. P. Watt Ltd.

CREDITS

Cover: David Frampton
Illustration Credits: Lynn Adams, 454: Linda Benson, 707; Robert Byrd, 897, 901; William Cigliano, 6, 7: Kenneth Dewy, 392, 393, 490, 491, 566, 567; Leo and Diane Dillon, 806, 813; Donald Gates, 727; Jerry Harston, 244, 245, 314, 315; Tom Herbert, 766–767; David Johnston, 549–552; Bob Masheris, 714, 715; Alexis Oussenko, 368–369; Bob Pepper, 129, 130; Steve Schindler, 445, 446–447; Richard Waltz, 513; Larry Winborg, 50, 51, 112, 113, 784, 785.

Photo Credits: Albright-Knox Art Gallery, Buffalo, N.Y.: Room of Contemporary Art Fund, 953. ALDUS ARCHIVE/BPCC,: 546; Collection Bodleian Library, 114; © Manchester City Art Gallery,

526. American Repertory Theatre: Richard Feldman, photographer, 905, 909. ART RESOURCE/SCALA: 233, 238BL; Biblioteca Nazionale Marciana, Venezia, 778 BL, 882; Bridgeman Art Library, 525; Library of Congress, Washington, D.C., 377, 378L; Hirschhorn Museum and Sculpture Garden, Smithsonian Institution, Joseph Martin, 398; Louvre, Paris, 555; Musei Capitolini, Roma, 804; Museo de Belle Arti, 673; N.Y.P.L. Picture Collection, Joseph Martin, 386BL; Victoria and Albert Museum, London, 3387B. © Ashmolean Museum, Oxford, 3C. Ayer Press: Arno Press, Mayflower Books, New York, 1979, 386BR, 415. BBC Hulton Picture Library: 510, 657, 658. THE BETTMANN ARCHIVE: 524B, 528, 548, 702, 862, 878; Corcoran Gallery, 864; by Francis Dodd, 1936, 554; © Muray, 717. Bibliothèque Nationale, Paris, France, 99. BLACK STAR: British Museum, London, 4; © Ted Spiegel, 13, 14, 15B; Historical Museum, Oslo, Norway, 12; Viking Ship Museum, Norway, © Ted Spiegil, 11. THE BODLEIAN LIBRARY, OXFORD: Bede, Initial from his "Life of St. Cuthbert," 12th c. Ms Digby 20, fol. 194, Initial D, 2BC, 35; Ms Rawlinson, FR. 55F. 132V., 44BL. THE BRIDGEMAN ART LIBRARY, London: 106TL, 390; Bodleian Library, Oxford, 308C, 322; Courage Brewery, Southwark, 308BR; Greater London Council, 484BL; The Guildhall, London, 387T, detail 485C; Roy Miles Gallery, London, 400; National Portrait Gallery of Scotland, Edinburgh, 308TL, TR, 345; Ben Nicholson © Estate of Artist, 560TR; Phillips, Son & Neale, London, 402–3. Courtesy of The Trustees of The British Museum, 52. CULVER PICTURES, INC.: 56, 120, 243, 291, 432, 441, 449, 461, 466, 484, T, L, C, 492, 508, 560TC, BL, BR, 561B, 570, 573L, C, R, 579, 589, 611, 627, 641, 684, 689, 699, 712, 725, 778C, 894, 904, 934. By Kind Permission of the Dickens House, 485B. E.T. ARCHIVE, LONDON: 386TC, 561T; British Museum, London, 110, 308CL; Garrick Club, 146; London Museum, 303, 311; National Maritime Museum, London, 106CL; Parliamentary Library Victoria, 484CL; Tate Gallery, 360; George Walker, 389. MARY EVANS PICTURE LIBRARY, London: 239T, 241, 374, 386TR, 484TR, 484CR; Elliott & Fry Photo, 535; R. Sack ARA, 562; Tenniel, 488. Courtesy, Farrar, Straus, & Giroux: Alan Hillyer, 682. THE FOLGER SHAKESPEARE LIBRARY, WASHINGTON, D.C.: 106TC, BL, 107T, 108, 109, 145, 238TR, 261. THE FOTOMAS INDEX, LONDON: 44TL, 58, 106BR, 232, 324. © Guy Gladwell, 950. THE GRANGER COLLECTION: 2TC, CL, BR, 3B, 5, 10, 16–17, 23, 24, 29, 44TR, BC, BR, 46, 47, 49, 70, 106BC, 107C, B, 115, 117, 128T, 128B, 132, 228, 238CL, 238C, 239B, 240, 242, 246, 256, 258, 267, 274, 287, 299, 308BL, C, 309B, 316, 317, 318–19, 322, 332T, B, 340, 353, 359, 366, 386TL, 386CL, 387C, 388, 391, 407, 470, 477, 484C, 486, 493, 502, 515, 522, 524T, 531, 541, 651, 665, 674, 706, 732, 778TL, TR, BR, 826, 918, 930, 938, 946. Sonia Halliday Photographs, 252, 533. HAMLYN GROUP PICTURE LIBRARY: Bodleian Library 45B; British Museum, 238BR; British National Trust, 664; © Ethel Hurwics, 309T; Museum of London, 308TC, 337L, R, 484BR; Science Museum, London, 310; Statens Historiska Museum, Stockholm, 2TR, 39; Victoria and Albert Museum, 106TR, 485T. Hirschhorn Museum and Sculpture Garden, Smithsonian Institution, © Lee Boltin, 560BC. HUNTINGTON LIBRARY, Art Collections and Botanical Gardens, San Marino: 59, 60, 62, 64, 71, 72, 81, 84. THE IMAGE BANK: © L. Fried, 680–81; © Nick Nicholson, 772–73; © Robert Philips, 693; © Peter Thomann, 740; © Pete Turner, 935; © Frank Whitney, 644–5. © Bord Failte/Irish Tourist Board: photograph by Brian Lynch, 564. © Karsh, 745. © Francene Keery, 687. Kobal Collection,

A LETTER TO THE STUDENT

Imagine a traveler in a foreign land without maps or guidebooks. So many enjoyable and worthwhile sights would be missed entirely or only partially appreciated. For these reasons wise travelers rely on the advice and guidance of those who have traveled those lands before.

English Literature with World Masterpieces is a kind of traveler's guide. Along the way you will encounter fiction, poetry, drama, and nonfiction that countless readers have judged to be among the best ever written—best not only in terms of their artistic beauty but also in terms of the sheer enjoyment they give and the insights they provide into different cultures.

Like any good traveler's guide, this anthology is designed to help you use your time efficiently. It does so not by telling you what to think about literature but by giving you practice in how to think logically and creatively about what you read.

Each unit introduction and each author biography is written to help you focus your thinking as you read the literary selections. The Study Questions after each selection guide your thinking in an organized way: *Recalling* questions lay the groundwork of the selection's important facts, *Interpreting* questions help you discover the significance of those facts, *Extending* questions help you relate the selection to your own experience. Other special features—such as Viewpoint, Comparing Writers, and Model for Active Reading—will also help you think critically as you read.

Near the back of this book you will find a special section called "Student's Resources: Lessons in Active Learning." The handbooks that make up this section are practical guides for responding to literature by speaking, thinking, researching, and writing. Each handbook lesson is designed to help you grow as an active, independent reader and thinker. The Research Paper Casebook offers you both instruction and sources for writing a full-fledged literary research paper.

English Literature with World Masterpieces was created to guide you through an extraordinary experience of the mind and imagination. As you continue to think about literature, that experience will grow all the more enjoyable.

CONTENTS

STUDENT'S RESOURCES

LESSONS IN ACTIVE LEARNING

Literary Map of Britain

This map, with current borders, identifies
locales associated with many of the authors
and selections included in this book.
As you read more English literature,
you will be able to place other
authors and literary works in
correct geographic locations.

HIGHLANDS

SCOTLAND

Aberdeen
Sir Patrick
Spens
drowns

BIRNAM
WOODS
DUNSINANE

NORTH
SEA

Glasgow
Burns statue

Edinburgh
Boswell born

ATLANTIC
OCEAN

Heaney's
Death of a Naturalist

Burns
writes

Yeats's
Innisfree

NORTHERN
IRELAND

Belfast
MacNeice born

Kelloe
E. B. Browning born

Whitby
Caedmon a monk

IRELAND

IRISH
SEA

LAKE
DISTRICT
POETS

Croft
Carroll boyhood

ENGLAND

Dublin
Beckett, Joyce, Shaw, Steele, Wilde, Yeats born
Hopkins teaches
Swift preaches

York
Auden born

Haworth
Brontës write

Winstead
Marvell born

Newstead Abbey
Byron home

Eastwood
Lawrence born

Surrey's
Kenninghall

Kilcolman
Spenser writes *Faerie Queene*

Cork
O'Connor, O'Faolain born

WALES

Housman's
Shropshire Lad

Lichfield
Dr. Johnson born

Rugby
Brooke at
school

Aldwinkle
Dryden born

Lowestoft
Conrad lands
in England

Stratford
Shakespeare born,
lives

Swansea
Thomas born

Wordsworth's
Tintern Abbey

● OXFORD

● CAMBRIDGE

Bedford
Bunyan jailed

Canterbury
Chaucer's *Tales*
Lovelace home
Marlowe born

Westward Ho!
Kipling attends school

Bath
Austen lives

Chalfont St. Giles
Milton writes

LONDON

Thames

Nether Stowey
Coleridge writes *Mariner*

WESSEX
Hardy's fiction

Stoke Poges
Gray's Churchyard

Arnold's
Dover Bea

Tintagel
King Arthur
born

Dean Prior
Herrick a rector

Bury
Galsworthy home

Sidney's
Penshurst
Place

STRAIT
OF DOVE

East Budleigh
Raleigh born

Portsmouth
Dickens born

West Grinstead
Pope begins *Lock*

Bournemouth
Mary Shelley buried

Maidstone
Tennyson writes

ENGLISH   CHANNEL

FRANCE

⊛ **London**
Caxton publishes Malory's tales
Bacon, Defoe, Jonson, Keats, Lamb born
Blake prints
Donne preaches
Eliot publishes periodical
Lessing, Mansfield, Naipaul, Pepys write
Shakespeare's Globe Theatre
Tatler and *Spectator* published
Pre-Raphaelite Brotherhood formed
Bloomsbury Group congregates

English Literature

A few basic facts about England will be helpful to you as you begin your study of English literature. First of all, modern-day England is actually one division of the United Kingdom of Great Britain and Northern Ireland, often called simply Great Britain. The other divisions are Wales, Scotland, and Northern Ireland. When we refer to English literature in this book, however, we speak in broad terms about literature from all these areas, as well as English-language literature from Ireland or other independent nations that were once part of the British Empire.

The British have had a monarch, or hereditary royal sovereign, for more than a thousand years. The powers of the monarch have gradually declined over these years, and today Great Britain is a constitutional monarchy, in which the sovereign serves as the head of state but does not actually rule. A cabinet of government officials called ministers and headed by the prime minister actually rules the country. The Parliament is the lawmaking body, consisting of the House of Lords and the House of Commons. The House of Lords is composed of nobility, most of whom have inherited their titles.

Much of the literature you will be reading contains titles of royalty and nobility. Royalty includes the king (the male sovereign) and the queen (the female sovereign or the wife of the king). Other members of the royal family include princes (the sons of the sovereign, the sons of a son of the sovereign, or the husband of the queen) and princesses (the daughters of the sovereign, the daughters of a son of the sovereign, or the wives of princes). The upper nobility consists of dukes and duchesses, marquesses and marchionesses, earls and countesses, viscounts and viscountesses, and barons and baronesses.

Sovereigns of England and Great Britain

Anglo-Saxons and Danes

Kingdom of Kent
Ethelbert, 560–616

Kingdom of Northumbria
Ethelfrith, 593–617
Edwin, 617–633
Oswald, 635–642
Oswy, 642–670
Ecgfrith, 670–685

Kingdom of Mercia
Penda, 626–655
Ethelbald, 716–757
Offa II, 757–796
Cenulf, 796–821

Kingdom of Wessex
Ine, 688–726
Egbert, 802–839
Ethelwulf, 839–858
Ethelbald, 858–860
Ethelbert, 860–866
Ethelred I, 866–871
Alfred the Great, 871–899
Edward, 899–924
Athelstan, 924–939

Edmund I, 939–946
Edred, 946–955
Edwy, 955–959
Edgar, 959–975
Edward, 975–978
Ethelred II, 978–1016
Edmund II, 1016
Canute, 1016–1035
Harold I, 1035–1040
Hardecanute, 1040–1042
Edward the Confessor, 1042-1066
Harold II, 1066

Normans
William I, 1066–1087
William II, 1087–1100
Henry I, 1100–1135
Stephen, 1135–1154

House of Plantagenet
Henry II, 1154–1189
Richard I, 1189–1199
John, 1199–1216
Henry III, 1216–1272
Edward I, 1272–1307
Edward II, 1307–1327
Edward III, 1327–1377
Richard II, 1377–1399

House of Lancaster
Henry IV, 1399–1413
Henry V, 1413–1422
Henry VI, 1422–1461

House of York
Edward IV, 1461–1483
Edward V, 1483
Richard III, 1483–1485

House of Tudor
Henry VII, 1485–1509
Henry VIII, 1509–1547
Edward VI, 1547–1553
Mary I, 1553–1558
Elizabeth I, 1558–1603

House of Stuart
James I (James VI of Scotland), 1603–1625
Charles I, 1625–1649

Interregnum (1649–1659)
Oliver Cromwell, 1653–1658
Richard Cromwell, 1658–1659

House of Stuart
Charles II, 1660–1685
James II, 1685–1688

House of Orange
William III and Mary II, 1689–1702

House of Stuart
Anne, 1702–1714

House of Hanover
George I, 1714–1727
George II, 1727–1760
George III, 1760–1820
George IV, 1820–1830
William IV, 1830–1837
Victoria, 1837–1901

House of Saxe-Coburg-Gotha (from 1917, Windsor)
Edward VII, 1901–1910
George V, 1910–1936
Edward VIII, 1936 (abdicated)
George VI, 1936–1952
Elizabeth II, 1952–

The Bodleian Library, Oxford, Ms. Digby 20, folio 194

Key to Illustrations appears on page 43.

THE ANGLO-SAXON PERIOD

449–1066

English literature may be said to begin when the Angles, the Saxons, and a closely related tribe called the Jutes left northern Europe and began invading the island of Britain in A.D. 449. The ancient Germanic dialects spoken by these tribes, now separated by water from the European mainland, would evolve as a separate language called English (from "Angleish") and thereby give rise to *English* literature. Today we call the language of this period **Old English,** or **Anglo-Saxon,** to distinguish it from our very different modern form.

Although English literature begins with the Anglo-Saxon era, the Anglo-Saxons were not the first people, nor indeed the most civilized people, to invade Britain. Some centuries before their arrival, Britain was invaded by the Romans, who by 250 B.C had conquered most of the then-known world. It is in the annals of Roman history—composed in Latin, the language of ancient Rome—that Britain makes its first appearance in written literature.

Before the Anglo-Saxons

The first Roman general to visit Britain was Julius Caesar, who led his army from what was then Gaul and is now France across the English Channel to the island of Britain, some twenty miles off the European coast. In his *Commentaries,* an early Latin history, Caesar described Britain and the two tribes who then inhabited it. One tribe was the Picts, a Roman name suggesting "painted faces"; the other was the Britons, or Celts of Britain, whose Celtic language had given the island its name. A second group of Celts, the Gaels, lived on a smaller island to the west of Britain, which they called Eire and today we call Ireland (from Eireland).

Caesar remained in Britain only a short time, but in A.D. 43 the Romans returned in earnest and stayed for more than three hundred years. They drove the belligerent Picts far to the north, but they worked with the Britons, introducing a standard of living more advanced than any the Celtic tribes had ever known. When the Roman Empire adopted Christianity in the fourth century, so did the Britons; in fact St. Patrick, who brought Christianity to the Gaels of Ireland a century later, was probably a Romanized Celt of Britain.

Unfortunately, the Britons came to rely too heavily on Roman military protection. Early in the fifth century, when the Roman Empire began to fall, the Roman legions left Britain to defend Rome, their capital, and the Britons became easy prey to invaders.

Anglo-Saxon Invasions

Not long afterward, the Angles, the Saxons, and the Jutes began invading Britain's eastern shores. The Britons—led, legends tell us, by a Christian king

named Arthur—won a few victories against the Saxon forces, but gradually the invaders pushed them from the central portion of their island—the area that would now become known as England (from "Angleland"). Many fleeing Britons settled in Wales, an isolated region on Britain's west-central coast. Others settled in Ireland, from where groups of Celts traveled back to northern Britain, near the Picts, and brought to the area a new name, Scotia—or, as the Anglo-Saxons called it, Scotland. In Wales, Ireland, and Scotland, the Celtic languages flourished, as did the Christianity that the Romans and St. Patrick had introduced. In Ireland, Celtic monks created one of the most beautiful early Bible manuscripts, the Book of Kells; off Scotland's coast, Irish monks built the monastery on Iona; and in Wales, displaced Britons, now called the Welsh, preserved tales of their leader Arthur. Nevertheless, though Celtic legends and practices did later influence

English literature, we must look to the new Anglo-Saxon society—and its language—for the roots of English literature in these early times.

Anglo-Saxon Civilization

The Angles, Saxons, and Jutes who invaded Britain were seafaring warriors who at first fought often among themselves. The brutalities of sea and of battle led to short life expectancies and a bleak, gloomy outlook on life in which one's fate, which they called *wyrd,* was unavoidable; all roads led inescapably to death. With time, however, the less violent agricultural life style of the settler began to make its impression. By the end of the seventh century, Christianity had become firmly established, and it too served as a peace-keeping force. A more unified civilization emerged— one that we usually call **Anglo-Saxon civilization**—and the seven kingdoms by now established in England were allied in the so-called Heptarchy: Northumbria and Mercia, the kingdoms of the Angles, in the north; Kent, the kingdom of the Jutes, in the southeast; and Essex, Middlesex, Sussex, and Wessex, the kingdoms of the Saxons, in the south and west.

Christianity also brought the beginnings of education and culture. At first Northumbria and Kent were the chief centers of learning, Northumbria because Celtic monks established England's first monastery on the island of Lindisfarne off its coast, and Kent because the Roman missionary St. Augustine founded another early monastery in the village of Canterbury. By the eighth century, Anglo-Saxon culture reached its peak in the Northumbrian monasteries that produced the Venerable Bede, the greatest European scholar of his day, and such beautifully decorated Bible manuscripts as the Lindisfarne Gospels.

Around the turn of the ninth century, however, new Germanic tribes of northern Europe—variously called Danes, Vikings, and Norsemen—began to attack Britain's eastern shores. With Northumbria and Kent devastated, it became the task of the Saxon king of Wessex to repel the invaders. That king was called Alfred the Great, in part because he halted the Danish incursions, but also because he was able to salvage much of Anglo-Saxon civilization. Under his sponsorship Exeter, the capital of Wessex, became the new center of Anglo-Saxon learning, and the monks of Exeter Cathedral gathered together the largest collection of Anglo-Saxon scholarship to survive the Danish invasions.

The Beginnings of English Literature

The first English literature was oral, not written. Songs and poems were sung or recited by traveling minstrels known as **scops,** who composed or memorized oral literature and passed it down from generation to generation. To celebrate a battle or the return of a hero, people

Dover Castle, constructed during the Anglo-Saxon Period.

would gather in the large communal banquet halls of Anglo-Saxon castles and listen to the scops as part of the evening's festivities. The scops served as keepers of tribal history, and their earliest poems recount great battles and the feats of important heroes.

The earliest English story-poem to come down to us is about a hero named Beowulf. *Beowulf* is an example of an **epic,** a long narrative (storytelling) poem that recounts, in grave and stately language, the achievements of a hero who usually embodies his civilization's ideals. The Anglo-Saxons also composed **lyric poems,** shorter verse whose chief purpose is not to tell a story but to express personal thoughts and feelings. Many Anglo-Saxon lyrics are religious in nature, revealing the deep faith and devotion of these early Christian times. Others describe tribal wanderings on land or sea and lament the tragedy of war and emigration. Still others are poetic riddles, showing the Anglo-Saxon fondness for imaginative use of language.

It was not until Bede's day that Anglo-Saxon monks working as **scribes,** or writers of handwritten manuscripts, began to record the scops' oral compositions. Bede himself preserved some lines by a religious poet named Caedmon, the first English poet that we know by name. After the Danish attacks, monks at Exeter Cathedral recopied damaged older manuscripts in a collection called *The Exeter Book,* in which a number of Anglo-Saxon lyric poems have been preserved.

Bede and other monks also composed their own scholarly literature, which represents the first *written* literature in England. The earliest important work of this kind was Bede's *Ecclesiastical History of the English People,* which offers a remarkably complete picture of early Anglo-Saxon life and times. However, like most monastic scholars of the era, Bede composed his *History* in Latin, the language of Church scholarship. It was Alfred the Great, the era's most important political leader, who first encouraged the widespread use of Old English in written literature. Alfred's greatest achievement in this regard was *The Anglo-Saxon Chronicle,* an Old English history in prose and poetry that Alfred initiated in 892 and that was continued as a sort of yearly record book until well after the Normans invaded England in 1066 and the Anglo-Saxon era had come to its close.

TIME LINE

449   Germanic tribes cross the North Sea to England, and Anglo-Saxon rule begins

c. 537   King Arthur, legendary king of Britain and hero of English literature, dies

563   Establishment of Iona monastery, one of earliest centers of Christianity in Britain

597   St. Augustine, missionary, establishes monastery in Canterbury

c. 658   Caedmon's *Hymn*

c. 673   Birth of Venerable Bede, earliest English historian and earliest important prose writer

c. 700   Book of Kells, decorated manuscript of the four gospels

c. 460   Mexico: Peak of Mayan culture

476   End of western Roman Empire

c. 500   China: Tea brought from India

517   China: Buddhism introduced

542   Europe: Bubonic plague spreads through Europe, killing about half the population

550   India: Beginnings of chess game

552   Europe: Beginning of silk industry

560   Japan: Buddhism introduced

c. 570   Arabia: Mohammed born, founder of Islam

630   Arabia: Cotton introduced

700   Easter eggs come into use among Christians

China: Population explosion

c. 700   *Beowulf* by anonymous
         author, oldest epic poem
         composed in English.

787   Danish invasions

771   Charlemagne becomes ruler
         of Frankish kingdom

810   Persia: Term *algebra* coined

861   Iceland discovered by
         Vikings

871   Alfred the Great begins rule
         (until 899)

878   Alfred defeats Danish
         invaders

892   *Anglo-Saxon Chronicles*
         initiated by Alfred the Great,
         first historic record to be
         kept in English

895   Holy Land: Earliest Hebrew
         manuscript of Old Testament

900   Beginnings of Arabian tales
         "A Thousand and One
         Nights"

         Greenland discovered by
         Vikings

         Europe: Emergence of feudal
         system

975   *The Exeter Book,* group of
         short meditative poems,
         including "The Seafarer"

1000   North America discovered by
         Leif Ericsson

1040   The real Macbeth kills King
         Duncan

1042   Edward the Confessor begins
         rule (until 1066), last English
         king descended from Alfred
         the Great

1045   Spain: Birth of The Cid

1066   The Norman Conquest of
         England

Anglo-Saxon Epic Poetry

When the Angles, Saxons, and Jutes invaded Britain from the European mainland, they introduced a new language, the ancestor of modern English that today we call **Old English** or **Anglo-Saxon**. They also brought legends of traditional heroes who would become the subjects of the first English literature.

Because of constant intertribal warfare and the primitive state of science and medicine, life in early Anglo-Saxon times was strife-ridden and brief. As a result, the early Anglo-Saxons believed that fate, which they called *wyrd,* controlled human destiny and that one's ultimate and inescapable fate was death. However, they also believed that a person could attain a degree of immortality by winning fame and being remembered for heroic deeds. It is thus not surprising that the earliest Anglo-Saxon literature told tales of heroes and the great feats they performed. These tales took the form of poetry known as heroic poetry, or epics. An **epic** is a long narrative (storytelling) poem that records, in grave and stately language, the exploits of a larger-than-life hero who usually embodies the ideals of the culture that produced him.

The Anglo-Saxon epic hero displays the qualities that were highly valued by the Anglo-Saxon tribes who settled on Britain's shores. Courage was an important virtue since, by demonstrating courage, fame and immortality could be achieved. Loyalty to one's tribal lord or king was also important, as was wisdom in making decisions and guiding others. Boasting was a hero's dare to destiny and a commitment to courageous action. Physical strength was crucial to overcoming one's enemies.

In the primitive and harsh environment of the early Anglo-Saxons, the hero occupied a place of great importance, for his qualities of strength, wisdom, and courage might save the people from the evils that threatened them. Stories of epic heroes were passed down orally from generation to generation, recited by wandering minstrels called **scops**, who usually could not write, to audiences of listeners who usually could not read. Because of the oral tradition of Anglo-Saxon epic poetry, most of the early epics have not survived, and others exist only in tiny fragments. One Anglo-Saxon epic, however, survives almost in its entirety, the story of the great hero Beowulf.

Introducing **Beowulf**

Beowulf is the oldest of the surviving national epics produced in western Europe in the centuries after the fall of Rome. It is one of Europe's first literary works to be composed in the **vernacular**, the language of the people, rather than in Latin, the language of Church scholarship. Like other national epics—Spain's *Poem of the Cid,* for example, and France's *Song of Roland—Beowulf* tells of a great national hero—in this case, a hero named Beowulf, who flourished in the Anglo-Saxons' ancestral home on the European mainland.

Beowulf himself is a Geat, a member of an ancient tribe in what is today southern Sweden, and many of his adventures take place among the Danes, who—along with the Angles, Saxons, and Jutes—inhabited the nearby European region that is today Denmark and northern Germany. In the closely related Germanic languages of these tribes, the name *Beowulf* means "bear," and it is likely that legends of a bearlike hero were told long before the Anglo-Saxon invasions of Britain. However, the legends that involve Beowulf with the Geat king Higlac and the Danish king Hrothgar must have come later, for Higlac and Hrothgar were real-life sixth-century kings.

Our version of the *Beowulf* epic was composed in Britain early in the eighth century, by which time the Anglo-Saxons had converted to Christianity. The anonymous author was clearly a Christian, for his *Beowulf* contains references to the Bible and many expressions of a deep religious faith. He was also rather well educated, displaying knowledge of Greek and Roman mythology and familiarity with the *Aeneid,* the great Latin epic by the ancient Roman poet Virgil (see page 862).

The author composed his *Beowulf* epic in the oral tradition, but at some point it was written down, and a copy was made by Christian scribes in the late tenth century. It is their manuscript that has survived over the years, despite various misadventures, including a fire that destroyed some of the lines. Today the *Beowulf* manuscript is carefully preserved by the British Museum in London.

The surviving *Beowulf* manuscript consists of about 3,200 lines, or eighty or ninety printed pages. It recounts three principal episodes in the life of its hero: Beowulf's battle with the monster Grendel, his battle with Grendel's mother, and a fight with a fire-breathing dragon that results in Beowulf's death. All three of those episodes are presented in the portion of *Beowulf,* in modern translation from Old English, that appears on the upcoming pages.

We enter the perilous world of *Beowulf* with a description of the deadly monster Grendel. Hrothgar, king of the Danes, has built a great hall called Herot, where he and his people celebrate. The Danes lead a happy and peaceful existence until Grendel, who hates their noisy celebrations, invades Herot late one night and murders the Danes as they sleep.

■ Beowulf's heroism was so great that he has been remembered for almost 1300 years. What qualities and achievements do you think might contribute to such enduring fame?

Shoulder clasp from the Sutton Hoo Ship Burial, c. 625.

from **Beowulf**

Translated by Burton Raffel

CHARACTERS

Danes

HROTHGAR [hroth′gär]: king of the Danes and builder of the great hall of Herot [hā′rot]
WELTHOW [wāl′thō]: Hrothgar's wife and queen
ESHER: Hrothgar's closest friend and adviser
UNFERTH: one of Hrothgar's courtiers and his chief spokesman

Geats [gā′ats]

BEOWULF [bā′ə woolf′]: nephew of Higlac, king of the Geats; later he succeeds to the Geat
  throne
WIGLAF: one of Beowulf's kinsmen

Monsters

GRENDEL: the first of the monsters to attack Herot
GRENDEL'S MOTHER: the second of the monsters to attack Herot
THE FIRE-BREATHING DRAGON: the last monster that Beowulf faces

The Battle with Grendel

A powerful monster, living down
In the darkness, growled in pain, impatient
As day after day the music rang
Loud in that hall, the harp's rejoicing
5 Call and the poet's clear songs, sung
Of the ancient beginnings of us all, recalling
The Almighty making the earth, shaping
These beautiful plains marked off by oceans,
Then proudly setting the sun and moon
10 To glow across the land and light it;
The corners of the earth were made lovely with trees
And leaves, made quick with life, with each
Of the nations who now move on its face. And then
As now warriors sang of their pleasure:
15 So Hrothgar's men lived happy in his hall
Till the monster stirred, that demon, that fiend,
Grendel, who haunted the moors, the wild
Marshes, and made his home in a hell
Not hell but earth. He was spawned in that slime,
20 Conceived by a pair of those monsters born
Of Cain, murderous creatures banished
By God, punished forever for the crime
Of Abel's death.[1] The Almighty drove
Those demons out, and their exile was bitter,
25 Shut away from men; they split
Into a thousand forms of evil—spirits
And fiends, goblins, monsters, giants,
A brood forever opposing the Lord's
Will, and again and again defeated.

30   Then, when darkness had dropped, Grendel
Went up to Herot, wondering what the warriors
Would do in that hall when their drinking was done.
He found them sprawled in sleep, suspecting
Nothing, their dreams undisturbed. The monster's
35 Thoughts were as quick as his greed or his claws:
He slipped through the door and there in the silence
Snatched up thirty men, smashed them
Unknowing in their beds and ran out with their bodies,
The blood dripping behind him, back

---

1. Cain . . . Abel's death: In the Bible (*Genesis* 4), Cain (Adam and Eve's eldest son) murders his brother Abel and is banished from Eden.

40 To his lair, delighted with his night's slaughter.
     At daybreak, with the sun's first light, they saw
   How well he had worked, and in that gray morning
   Broke their long feast with tears and laments
   For the dead. Hrothgar, their lord, sat joyless
45 In Herot, a mighty prince mourning
   The fate of his lost friends and companions,
   Knowing by its tracks that some demon had torn
   His followers apart. He wept, fearing
   The beginning might not be the end. And that night
50 Grendel came again, so set
   On murder that no crime could ever be enough,
   No savage assault quench his lust
   For evil. Then each warrior tried
   To escape him, searched for rest in different
55 Beds, as far from Herot as they could find,
   Seeing how Grendel hunted when they slept.
   Distance was safety; the only survivors
   Were those who fled him. Hate had triumphed.
     So Grendel ruled, fought with the righteous,
60 One against many, and won; so Herot
   Stood empty, and stayed deserted for years,
   Twelve winters of grief for Hrothgar, king
   Of the Danes, sorrow heaped at his door
   By hell-forged hands. His misery leaped
65 The seas, was told and sung in all
   Men's ears: how Grendel's hatred began,
   How the monster relished his savage war
   On the Danes, keeping the bloody feud
   Alive, seeking no peace, offering
70 No truce, accepting no settlement, no price
   In gold or land, and paying the living
   For one crime only with another. No one
   Waited for reparation from his plundering claws:
   That shadow of death hunted in the darkness,
75 Stalked Hrothgar's warriors, old
   And young, lying in waiting, hidden
   In mist, invisibly following them from the edge
   Of the marsh, always there, unseen.
     So mankind's enemy continued his crimes,
80 Killing as often as he could, coming
   Alone, bloodthirsty and horrible. Though he lived
   In Herot, when the night hid him, he never
   Dared to touch king Hrothgar's glorious
   Throne, protected by God—God,
85 Whose love Grendel could not know. But Hrothgar's
   Heart was bent. The best and most noble
   Of his council debated remedies, sat

Gold brooch from the Viking
Age.

In secret sessions, talking of terror
And wondering what the bravest of warriors could do. . . .

Carved head from the Viking Age unearthed with the Oseberg Ship.

90   In his far-off home Beowulf, Higlac's
Follower[2] and the strongest of the Geats—greater
And stronger than anyone anywhere in this world—
Heard how Grendel filled nights with horror
And quickly commanded a boat fitted out,
95 Proclaiming that he'd go to that famous king,
Would sail across the sea to Hrothgar,
Now when help was needed. None
Of the wise ones regretted his going, much
As he was loved by the Geats: the omens were good,
100 And they urged the adventure on. So Beowulf
Chose the mightiest men he could find,
The bravest and best of the Geats, fourteen
In all, and led them down to their boat;
He knew the sea, would point the prow
105 Straight to that distant Danish shore.
    Then they sailed, set their ship
Out on the waves, under the cliffs.
Ready for what came they wound through the currents,
The seas beating at the sand, and were borne
110 In the lap of their shining ship, lined
With gleaming armor, going safely
In that oak-hard boat to where their hearts took them.
The wind hurried them over the waves,
The ship foamed through the sea like a bird
115 Until, in the time they had known it would take,
Standing in the round-curled prow they could see
Sparkling hills, high and green,
Jutting up over the shore, and rejoicing
In those rock-steep cliffs they quietly ended
120 Their voyage. Jumping to the ground, the Geats
Pushed their boat to the sand and tied it
In place, mail[3] shirts and armor rattling
As they swiftly moored their ship. And then
They gave thanks to God for their easy crossing.

Beowulf is met by a Danish watchman, who asks Beowulf to identify himself. Beowulf explains his mission, and the watchman directs him to the king. Beowulf then meets with King Hrothgar and outlines his plan for battling Grendel: That night, Beowulf and his warriors will sleep in Herot and wait for Grendel's return.

---

2. Higlac's follower: Beowulf, who is a loyal follower, or subject, of his uncle Higlac, king of the Geats.
3. mail: flexible armor made of interlinked metal rings.

125 And Beowulf was ready, firm with our Lord's
High favor and his own bold courage and strength.
    He stripped off his mail shirt, his helmet, his sword
Hammered from the hardest iron, and handed
All his weapons and armor to a servant,
130 Ordered his war-gear guarded till morning.
And then, standing beside his bed,
He exclaimed:
                "Grendel is no braver, no stronger
Than I am! I could kill him with my sword; I shall not,
Easy as it would be. This fiend is a bold
135 And famous fighter, but his claws and teeth
Scratching at my shield, his clumsy fists
Beating at my sword blade, would be helpless. I will meet him
With my hands empty—unless his heart
Fails him, seeing a soldier waiting
140 Weaponless, unafraid. Let God in His wisdom
Extend His hand where He wills, reward
Whom He chooses!"
                    Then the Geats' great chief dropped
His head to his pillow, and around him, as ready
As they could be, lay the soldiers who had crossed the sea
145 At his side, each of them sure that he was lost
To the home he loved, to the high-walled towns
And the friends he had left behind where both he
And they had been raised. Each thought of the Danes
Murdered by Grendel in a hall where Geats
150 And not Danes now slept. But God's dread loom[4]
Was woven with defeat for the monster, good fortune
For the Geats; help against Grendel was with them,
And through the might of a single man
They would win. Who doubts that God in His wisdom
155 And strength holds the earth forever
In His hands? Out in the darkness the monster
Began to walk. The warriors slept
In that gabled hall where they hoped that He
Would keep them safe from evil, guard them
160 From death till the end of their days was determined
And the thread should be broken.[5] But Beowulf lay wakeful,
Watching, waiting, eager to meet
His enemy, and angry at the thought of his coming.

Silver coin from the Viking Age.

---

4. God's dread loom: the loom on which fate is woven. The image goes back to
ancient Greek mythology, in which the Fates were three weaver-goddesses who
wove in cloths on their loom the destiny of every individual.
5. the thread should be broken: Breaking the thread on the loom of fate would
end the weaving of the cloth of a person's destiny and therefore would mean the
end of his or her life.

Out from the marsh, from the foot of misty
165 Hills and bogs, bearing God's hatred,
Grendel came, hoping to kill
Anyone he could trap on this trip to high Herot.
He moved quickly through the cloudy night,
Up from his swampland, sliding silently
170 Toward that gold-shining hall. He had visited Hrothgar's
Home before, knew the way—
But never, before nor after that night,
Found Herot defended so firmly, his reception
So harsh. He journeyed, forever joyless,
175 Straight to the door, then snapped it open,
Tore its iron fasteners with a touch
And rushed angrily over the threshold.
He strode quickly across the inlaid
Floor, snarling and fierce: his eyes
180 Gleamed in the darkness, burned with a gruesome
Light. Then he stopped, seeing the hall
Crowded with sleeping warriors, stuffed
With rows of young soldiers resting together.
And his heart laughed, he relished the sight,
185 Intended to tear the life from those bodies
By morning; the monster's mind was hot
With the thought of food and the feasting his belly
Would soon know. But fate, that night, intended
Grendel to gnaw the broken bones
190 Of his last human supper. Human
Eyes were watching his evil steps,
Waiting to see his swift hard claws.
Grendel snatched at the first Geat
He came to, ripped him apart, cut
195 His body to bits with powerful jaws,
Drank the blood from his veins and bolted
Him down, hands and feet; death
And Grendel's great teeth came together,
Snapping life shut. Then he stepped to another
200 Still body, clutched at Beowulf with his claws,
Grasped at a strong-hearted wakeful sleeper
—And was instantly seized himself, claws
Bent back as Beowulf leaned up on one arm.
    That shepherd of evil, guardian of crime,
205 Knew at once that nowhere on earth
Had he met a man whose hands were harder;
His mind was flooded with fear—but nothing
Could take his talons and himself from that tight
Hard grip. Grendel's one thought was to run
210 From Beowulf, flee back to his marsh and hide there:
This was a different Herot than the hall he had emptied.

The prow of the Oseberg
Ship. *Foreground:* silver
coin from the Viking Age.

But Higlac's follower remembered his final
Boast and, standing erect, stopped
The monster's flight, fastened those claws
215 In his fists till they cracked, clutched Grendel
Closer. The infamous killer fought
For his freedom, wanting no flesh but retreat,
Desiring nothing but escape; his claws
Had been caught, he was trapped. That trip to Herot
220 Was a miserable journey for the writhing monster!
   The high hall rang, its roof boards swayed,
And Danes shook with terror. Down
The aisles the battle swept, angry
And wild. Herot trembled, wonderfully
225 Built to withstand the blows, the struggling
Great bodies beating at its beautiful walls;
Shaped and fastened with iron, inside
And out, artfully worked, the building
Stood firm. Its benches rattled, fell
230 To the floor, gold-covered boards grating
As Grendel and Beowulf battled across them.
Hrothgar's wise men had fashioned Herot
To stand forever; only fire,
They had planned, could shatter what such skill had put
235 Together, swallow in hot flames such splendor
Of ivory and iron and wood. Suddenly
The sounds changed, the Danes started
In new terror, cowering in their beds as the terrible
Screams of the Almighty's enemy sang
240 In the darkness, the horrible shrieks of pain
And defeat, the tears torn out of Grendel's
Taut throat, hell's captive caught in the arms
Of him who of all the men on earth
Was the strongest.

245   That mighty protector of men
Meant to hold the monster till its life
Leaped out, knowing the fiend was no use
To anyone in Denmark. All of Beowulf's
Band had jumped from their beds, ancestral
250 Swords raised and ready, determined
To protect their prince if they could. Their courage
Was great but all wasted: they could hack at Grendel
From every side, trying to open
A path for his evil soul, but their points
255 Could not hurt him, the sharpest and hardest iron
Could not scratch at his skin, for that sin-stained demon
Had bewitched all men's weapons, laid spells
That blunted every mortal man's blade.

Replica of a Viking helmet
from the Sutton Hoo Ship
Burial, c. 625.

And yet his time had come, his days
260 Were over, his death near; down
To hell he would go, swept groaning and helpless
To the waiting hands of still worse fiends.
Now he discovered—once the afflictor
Of men, tormentor of their days—what it meant
265 To feud with Almighty God: Grendel
Saw that his strength was deserting him, his claws
Bound fast, Higlac's brave follower tearing at
His hands. The monster's hatred rose higher,
But his power had gone. He twisted in pain,
270 And the bleeding sinews deep in his shoulder
Snapped, muscle and bone split
And broke. The battle was over, Beowulf
Had been granted new glory: Grendel escaped,
But wounded as he was could flee to his den,
275 His miserable hole at the bottom of the marsh,
Only to die, to wait for the end
Of all his days. And after that bloody
Combat the Danes laughed with delight.
He who had come to them from across the sea,
280 Bold and strong-minded, had driven affliction
Off, purged Herot clean. He was happy,
Now, with that night's fierce work; the Danes
Had been served as he'd boasted he'd serve them; Beowulf,
A prince of the Geats, had killed Grendel,
285 Ended the grief, the sorrow, the suffering
Forced on Hrothgar's helpless people
By a bloodthirsty fiend. No Dane doubted
The victory, for the proof, hanging high
From the rafters where Beowulf had hung it, was the monster's
290 Arm, claw and shoulder and all.

And then, in the morning, crowds surrounded
Herot, warriors coming to that hall
From faraway lands, princes and leaders
Of men hurrying to behold the monster's
295 Great staggering tracks. They gaped with no sense
Of sorrow, felt no regret for his suffering,
Went tracing his bloody footprints, his beaten
And lonely flight, to the edge of the lake
Where he'd dragged his corpselike way, doomed
300 And already weary of his vanishing life.
The water was bloody, steaming and boiling
In horrible pounding waves, heat
Sucked from his magic veins; but the swirling
Surf had covered his death, hidden
305 Deep in murky darkness his miserable
End, as hell opened to receive him.

STUDY QUESTIONS

Recalling

1. According to the opening lines, from what Bible figure does Grendel descend? In addition to *monster,* name two nouns used to identify Grendel.
2. According to lines 53–62, what is the only course of action that allows some Danes of Herot to survive Grendel's attacks? For how many years does Grendel terrorize the Danes?
3. According to lines 125–126, what are two qualities that Beowulf displays in battle? From whose "high favor" does Beowulf gain his superior fighting ability?
4. For what reason does Beowulf decide not to use weapons in fighting Grendel (lines 132–140)? For what reason do the weapons of the other Geats prove ineffective (lines 248–258)?
5. Briefly summarize how Beowulf succeeds in mortally wounding Grendel.

Interpreting

6. Based on details in the selection, what contrasting forces do Beowulf and Grendel seem to represent? What universal battle might their battle represent?
7. Contrast the Geats' behavior when they arrive at Herot with the Danes' behavior after Grendel's earlier attacks. In what way are Beowulf's expectations of the upcoming battle with Grendel different from the expectations of his Geat comrades?
8. Based on the character of Beowulf, identify at least three qualities that you can conclude the early Anglo-Saxons admired.
9. What Anglo-Saxon belief is illustrated by the reference to Grendel in lines 188–190? Find one additional passage that illustrates this belief.

Extending

10. Do you think it is better to confront a problem immediately or to move with deliberation and thus perhaps give the problem time to solve itself or be solved by others? Why?

VIEWPOINT

We can often increase our pleasure in a work of literature by consulting the opinion of an expert on the author's writing. Throughout this book in each section titled "Viewpoint," you will find a quotation about the author or selection you have read. Most of these quotations come from literary critics; some come from the authors themselves. Each quotation is followed by questions that will ask you to consider the quoted opinion in light of your own reactions to the literature.

The literary historian David Daiches reminds us that the world of *Beowulf*

> is certainly not uncivilized, though the civilization it reflects is primitive enough. There is a genuine ideal of nobility underlying its adventure stories.

■ Through what evidence in "The Battle with Grendel" can we conclude that the world of *Beowulf* was primitive yet civilized? How would you distinguish between the two? Cite examples from the selection to support Daiches' claim that "a genuine ideal of nobility" underlies the story.

LITERARY FOCUS

Foreshadowing

Foreshadowing is the use of clues by an author to prepare readers (or listeners) for events that will happen in a narrative. Foreshadowing often helps to build suspense or interest by making us predict what will happen from the clues provided and then keep reading to see if our predictions are correct. An example of foreshadowing occurs in lines 188–190 of "The Battle with Grendel," when the author tells us "But fate, that night, intended/Grendel to gnaw the broken bones/Of his last human supper." From this foreshadowing we can predict that Grendel is likely to be defeated.

Thinking About Foreshadowing

■ Find one more example of foreshadowing in "The Battle with Grendel." What can you predict from this foreshadowing?

The Battle with Grendel's Mother

With the departure of Grendel, the Danes are able to return to Herot to celebrate. Hrothgar gives Beowulf many fine gifts, and also extends his generosity to the other Geats. The court poet sings as the Danes and Geats feast. Finally they disperse, leaving behind a multitude of Danish warriors to sleep in Herot once again. None suspect that a second vengeful monster is headed toward Herot.

They sank into sleep. The price of that evening's
Rest was too high for the Dane who bought it
With his life, paying as others had paid
When Grendel inhabited Herot, the hall
5 His till his crimes pulled him into hell.
And now it was known that a monster had died
But a monster still lived, and meant revenge.
She'd brooded on her loss, misery had brewed
In her heart, that female horror, Grendel's
10 Mother, living in the murky cold lake
Assigned her since Cain had killed his only
Brother, slain his father's son
With an angry sword. God drove him off,
Outlawed him to the dry and barren desert,
15 And branded him with a murderer's mark.[1] And he bore
A race of fiends accursed like their father;
So Grendel was drawn to Herot, an outcast
Come to meet the man who awaited him.
He'd snatched at Beowulf's arm, but that prince
20 Remembered God's grace and the strength He'd given him
And relied on the Lord for all the help,
The comfort and support he would need. He killed
The monster, as God had meant him to do,
Tore the fiend apart and forced him
25 To run as rapidly as he could toward death's
Cold waiting hands. His mother's sad heart,
And her greed, drove her from her den on the dangerous
Pathway of revenge.
           So she reached Herot,
Where the Danes slept as though already dead;
30 Her visit ended their good fortune, reversed
The bright vane of their luck. No female, no matter
How fierce, could have come with a man's strength,
Fought with the power and courage men fight with,
Smashing their shining swords, their bloody,

Viking warrior's head made of horn.

---

1. a murderer's mark: in the Bible (*Genesis* 4), the mark with which God branded Cain to warn those who might have slain the outcast that the murder would not go unpunished.

35 Hammer-forged blades onto boar-headed helmets,[2]
Slashing and stabbing with the sharpest of points.
The soldiers raised their shields and drew
Those gleaming swords, swung them above
The piled-up benches, leaving their mail shirts
40 And their helmets where they'd lain when the terror took hold
  of them.
To save her life she moved still faster,
Took a single victim and fled from the hall,
Running to the moors, discovered, but her supper
Assured, sheltered in her dripping claws.
45 She'd taken Hrothgar's closest friend,
The man he most loved of all men on earth;
She'd killed a glorious soldier, cut
A noble life short. No Geat could have stopped her:
Beowulf and his band had been given better
50 Beds; sleep had come to them in a different
Hall. Then all Herot burst into shouts:
She had carried off Grendel's claw. Sorrow
Had returned to Denmark. They'd traded deaths,
Danes and monsters, and no one had won,
Both had lost!

  Hrothgar is devastated by this new attack, which has claimed the life of Esher, his closest friend. He implores Beowulf to help the Danes once more.

55   Beowulf spoke:
"Let your sorrow end! It is better for us all
To avenge our friends, not mourn them forever.
Each of us will come to the end of this life
On earth; he who can earn it should fight
60 For the glory of his name; fame after death
Is the noblest of goals. Arise, guardian
Of this kingdom, let us go, as quickly as we can,
And have a look at this lady monster.
I promise you this: she'll find no shelter,
65 No hole in the ground, no towering tree,
No deep bottom of a lake, where her sins can hide.
Be patient for one more day of misery;
I ask for no longer."
      The old king leaped
To his feet, gave thanks to God for such words.
70 Then Hrothgar's horse was brought, saddled
And bridled. The Danes' wise ruler rode,
Stately and splendid; shield-bearing soldiers
Marched at his side. The monster's tracks

---

2. boar-headed helmets: The boar, a wild hog known for fighting ability, was often depicted on the fighting gear of the Danes and other Germanic tribes.

Led them through the forest; they followed her heavy
75 Feet, that had swept straight across
The shadowy waste land, her burden the lifeless
Body of the best of Hrothgar's men.
The trail took them up towering, rocky
Hills, and over narrow, winding
80 Paths they had never seen, down steep
And slippery cliffs where creatures from deep
In the earth hid in their holes. Hrothgar
Rode in front, with a few of his most knowing
Men, to find their way. Then suddenly,
85 Where clumps of trees bent across
Cold gray stones, they came to a dismal
Wood; below them was the lake, its water
Bloody and bubbling. And the Danes shivered,
Miserable, mighty men tormented
90 By grief, seeing, there on that cliff
Above the water, Esher's bloody
Head. They looked down at the lake, felt
How its heat rose up, watched the waves'
Blood-stained swirling. Their battle horns sounded,
95 Then sounded again. Then they set down their weapons.
    They could see the water crawling with snakes,
Fantastic serpents swimming in the boiling
Lake, and sea beasts lying on the rocks
—The kind that infest the ocean, in the early
100 Dawn, often ending some ship's
Journey with their wild jaws. They rushed
Angrily out of sight, when the battle horns blew.
Beowulf aimed an arrow at one
Of the beasts, swimming sluggishly away,
105 And the point pierced its hide, stabbed
To its heart; its life leaked out, death
Swept it off. Quickly, before
The dying monster could escape, they hooked
Its thrashing body with their curved boar-spears,
110 Fought it to land, drew it up on the bluff,
Then stood and stared at the incredible wave-roamer,
Covered with strange scales and horrible. Then Beowulf
Began to fasten on his armor,
Not afraid for his life but knowing the woven
115 Mail, with its hammered links, could save
That life when he lowered himself into the lake,
Keep slimy monsters' claws from snatching at
His heart, preserve him for the battle he was sent
To fight. Hrothgar's helmet would defend him;
120 That ancient, shining treasure, encircled
With hard-rolled metal, set there by some smith's

Long dead hand, would block all battle
Swords, stop all blades from cutting at him
When he'd swum toward the bottom, gone down in the surging
125 Water, deep toward the swirling sands.
And Unferth helped him, Hrothgar's courtier
Lent him a famous weapon, a fine,
Hilted old sword named Hrunting; it had
An iron blade, etched and shining
130 And hardened in blood. No one who'd worn it
Into battle, swung it in dangerous places,
Daring and brave, had ever been deserted—
Nor was Beowulf's journey the first time it was taken
To an enemy's camp, or asked to support
135 Some hero's courage and win him glory. . . .

Then Edgetho's brave son[3] spoke:
                                        "Remember,
Hrothgar, Oh knowing king, now
When my danger is near, the warm words we uttered,
And if your enemy should end my life
140 Then be, oh generous prince, forever
The father and protector of all whom I leave
Behind me, here in your hands, my belovèd
Comrades left with no leader, their leader
Dead. And the precious gifts you gave me,
145 My friend, send them to Higlac. May he see
In their golden brightness, the Geats' great lord
Gazing at your treasure, that here in Denmark
I found a noble protector, a giver
Of rings[4] whose rewards I won and briefly
150 Relished. And you, Unferth, let
My famous old sword stay in your hands:
I shall shape glory with Hrunting, or death
Will hurry me from this earth!"
                                        As his words ended
He leaped into the lake, would not wait for anyone's
155 Answer: the heaving water covered him
Over. For hours he sank through the waves;
At last he saw the mud of the bottom.
And all at once the greedy she-wolf
Who'd ruled those waters for half a hundred
160 Years discovered him, saw that a creature
From above had come to explore the bottom

---

3. Edgetho's brave son: Beowulf. Beowulf's father, Edgetho, was the brother-in-law of Higlac, king of the Geats.
4. giver of rings: a lord; a protector. Typically, in the tribal rituals in which one swore allegiance to a lord or a king, the lord or king bestowed a golden ring as a token of his acceptance and promise of protection.

Of her wet world. She welcomed him in her claws,
Clutched at him savagely but could not harm him,
Tried to work her fingers through the tight

165 Ring-woven mail on his breast, but tore
And scratched in vain. Then she carried him, armor
And sword and all, to her home; he struggled
To free his weapon, and failed. The fight
Brought other monsters swimming to see

170 Her catch, a host of sea beasts who beat at
His mail shirt, stabbing with tusks and teeth
As they followed along. Then he realized, suddenly,
That she'd brought him into someone's battle-hall,
And there the water's heat could not hurt him,

175 Nor anything in the lake attack him through
The building's high-arching roof. A brilliant
Light burned all around him, the lake
Itself like a fiery flame.

Then he saw

The mighty water witch, and swung his sword,

180 His ring-marked blade,[5] straight at her head;
The iron sang its fierce song,
Sang Beowulf's strength. But her guest
Discovered that no sword could slice her evil
Skin, that Hrunting could not hurt her, was useless

185 Now when he needed it. They wrestled, she ripped
And tore and clawed at him, bit holes in his helmet,
And that too failed him; for the first time in years
Of being worn to war it would earn no glory;
It was the last time anyone would wear it. But Beowulf

190 Longed only for fame, leaped back
Into battle. He tossed his sword aside,
Angry; the steel-edged blade lay where
He'd dropped it. If weapons were useless he'd use
His hands, the strength in his fingers. So fame

195 Comes to the men who mean to win it
And care about nothing else! He raised
His arms and seized her by the shoulder; anger
Doubled his strength, he threw her to the floor.
She fell, Grendel's fierce mother, and the Geats'

200 Proud prince was ready to leap on her. But she rose
At once and repaid him with her clutching claws,
Wildly tearing at him. He was weary, that best
And strongest of soldiers; his feet stumbled
And in an instant she had him down, held helpless.

205 Squatting with her weight on his stomach, she drew

Detail of lyre ornaments from the
Sutton Hoo Ship Burial, c. 625.

---

5. ring-marked blade: a blade with ringlike patterns etched onto it,
as described in lines 126–30.

A scepter, or symbol of royal authority, from the Sutton Hoo Ship Burial, c. 625.

A dagger, brown with dried blood, and prepared
To avenge her only son. But he was stretched
On his back, and her stabbing blade was blunted
By the woven mail shirt he wore on his chest.
210 The hammered links held; the point
Could not touch him. He'd have traveled to the bottom of the earth,
Edgetho's son, and died there, if that shining
Woven metal had not helped—and Holy
God, who sent him victory, gave judgment
215 For truth and right, Ruler of the Heavens,
Once Beowulf was back on his feet and fighting.
　　Then he saw, hanging on the wall, a heavy
Sword, hammered by giants, strong
And blessed with their magic, the best of all weapons
220 But so massive that no ordinary man could lift
Its carved and decorated length. He drew it
From its scabbard, broke the chain on its hilt,
And then, savage, now, angry
And desperate, lifted it high over his head
225 And struck with all the strength he had left,
Caught her in the neck and cut it through,
Broke bones and all. Her body fell
To the floor, lifeless, the sword was wet
With her blood, and Beowulf rejoiced at the sight.
230 　　The brilliant light shone, suddenly,
As though burning in that hall, and as bright as Heaven's
Own candle, lit in the sky. He looked
At her home, then following along the wall
Went walking, his hands tight on the sword,
235 His heart still angry. He was hunting another
Dead monster, and took his weapon with him
For final revenge against Grendel's vicious
Attacks, his nighttime raids, over
And over, coming to Herot when Hrothgar's
240 Men slept, killing them in their beds,
Eating some on the spot, fifteen
Or more, and running to his loathsome moor
With another such sickening meal waiting
In his pouch. But Beowulf repaid him for those visits,
245 Found him lying dead in his corner,
Armless, exactly as that fierce fighter
Had sent him out from Herot, then struck off
His head with a single swift blow. The body
Jerked for the last time, then lay still.
250 　　The wise old warriors who surrounded Hrothgar,
Like him staring into the monsters' lake,
Saw the waves surging and blood
Spurting through. They spoke about Beowulf,

All the graybeards, whispered together
255 And said that hope was gone, that the hero
Had lost fame and his life at once, and would never
Return to the living, come back as triumphant
As he had left; almost all agreed that Grendel's
Mighty mother, the she-wolf, had killed him.
260 The sun slid over past noon, went further
Down. The Danes gave up, left
The lake and went home, Hrothgar with them.
The Geats stayed, sat sadly, watching,
Imagining they saw their lord but not believing
They would ever see him again.
265   —Then the sword
Melted, blood-soaked, dripping down
Like water, disappearing like ice when the world's
Eternal Lord loosens invisible
Fetters and unwinds icicles and frost
270 As only He can, He who rules
Time and seasons, He who is truly
God. The monsters' hall was full of
Rich treasures, but all that Beowulf took
Was Grendel's head and the hilt of the giants'
275 Jeweled sword; the rest of that ring-marked
Blade had dissolved in Grendel's steaming
Blood, boiling even after his death.
And then the battle's only survivor
Swam up and away from those silent corpses;
280 The water was calm and clean, the whole
Huge lake peaceful once the demons who'd lived in it
Were dead.
                Then that noble protector of all seamen[6]
Swam to land, rejoicing in the heavy
Burdens he was bringing with him. He
285 And all his glorious band of Geats
Thanked God that their leader had come back unharmed;
They left the lake together. The Geats
Carried Beowulf's helmet, and his mail shirt.
Behind them the water slowly thickened
290 As the monsters' blood came seeping up.
They walked quickly, happily, across
Roads all of them remembered, left
The lake and the cliffs alongside it, brave men
Staggering under the weight of Grendel's skull,
295 Too heavy for fewer than four of them to handle—
Two on each side of the spear jammed through it—

Viking weathervane.

---

6. that noble protector of all seamen: Beowulf, whose burial tower will serve as
a navigational guide to sailors.

Yet proud of their ugly load and determined
That the Danes, seated in Herot, should see it.
Soon, fourteen Geats arrived
300 At the hall, bold and warlike, and with Beowulf,
Their lord and leader, they walked on the mead-hall
Green.⁷ Then the Geats' brave prince entered
Herot, covered with glory for the daring
Battle he had fought; he sought Hrothgar
305 To salute him and show Grendel's head.
He carried that terrible trophy by the hair,
Brought it straight to where the Danes sat,
Drinking, the queen among them. It was a weird
And wonderful sight, and the warriors stared.

7. **mead-hall green:** the lawn of Herot. Mead, a beverage made from fermented honey, water, and spices, was often drunk in the tribal banquet halls.

STUDY QUESTIONS

Recalling

1. For what two reasons does Grendel's mother attack the Danes?
2. According to lines 55–68, what is better than mourning a friend's death?
3. Summarize the two requests that Beowulf makes of Hrothgar before entering the lake.
4. What two things protect Beowulf (lines 212–214)? What weapon does Beowulf use to kill Grendel's mother (lines 217–220)?
5. What does Beowulf bring back? What does he leave behind (lines 273–275)?

Interpreting

6. Explain the role of revenge in motivating the killings in this section.
7. What quality does the desire for fame inspire in Beowulf?
8. Is Beowulf concerned with gold and other treasures because of those treasures' monetary worth? If not, what do the treasures symbolize, or represent, to Beowulf?

LITERARY FOCUS

Old English Poetry

Old English poetry was based on oral tradition. Since very few people could read or write, the **scop,** or minstrel, chanted memorized poetry to an assembled group. Many devices of Old English verse serve to aid the poet's memory and make the shaping of his poetry easier.

Alliteration. Like later poetry the verse of the Anglo-Saxons makes use of repetition, but instead of repeating vowel sounds at the ends of lines (as in rhyme), Old English poetry employs **alliteration,** the repetition of identical consonant sounds at the beginning of words in the same lines. One consonant will be alliterated, or repeated, in one line, another in the next, and so on. For this reason, it is called alliterative verse.

Caesura [si zhoor′ə]. Old English verse is characterized by a strong rhythm in which a pronounced pause, or **caesura,** occurs in the middle of each line. On either side of the caesura are two stressed syllables, though the number of unstressed syllables varies:

And *Un*ferth *helped* him, / / *Hroth*gar's *cour*tier

Kennings. Yet another device characteristic of Old English poetry is the use of **kennings,** imaginative metaphorical phrases used in place of a simple noun. For example, the sea may be called the "whale-road" or the "swan's riding"; the sun is often called "heaven's candle."

Thinking About Old English Poetry

Mark the caesura and stresses in any ten successive lines of *Beowulf*. First copy the lines, and divide the words into syllables. Then mark stressed syllables with an accent and the caesura with two diagonal lines. Also identify the different sounds that are alliterated in the passage.

The Death of Beowulf

Once again Hrothgar praises Beowulf and rewards him with treasures; once again the Danes and the Geats celebrate in Herot. The next morning Beowulf and his warriors depart, and Beowulf promises to return whenever the Danes need him. At home Beowulf recounts the events of his journey and is praised by his king.

Eventually Beowulf himself becomes king of the Geats and reigns peaceably until a fire-breathing dragon that has been guarding a treasure becomes enraged when a poor man steals a jeweled chalice. The dragon seeks revenge by killing the Geats and devastating their country.

Vomiting fire and smoke, the dragon
Burned down their homes. They watched in horror
As the flames rose up: the angry monster
Meant to leave nothing alive. And the signs
5 Of its anger flickered and glowed in the darkness,
Visible for miles, tokens of its hate
And its cruelty, spread like a warning to the Geats
Who had broken its rest. Then it hurried back
To its tower, to its hidden treasure, before dawn
10 Could come. It had wrapped its flames around
The Geats; now it trusted in stone
Walls, and its strength, to protect it. But they would not.
Then they came to Beowulf, their king, and announced
That his hall, his throne, the best of buildings,
15 Had melted away in the dragon's burning
Breath. Their words brought misery, Beowulf's
Sorrow beat at his heart: he accused
Himself of breaking God's law, of bringing
The Almighty's anger down on his people.
20 Reproach pounded in his breast, gloomy
And dark, and the world seemed a different place.
But the hall was gone, the dragon's molten
Breath had licked across it, burned it
To ashes, near the shore it had guarded. The Geats
25 Deserved revenge; Beowulf, their leader
And lord, began to plan it, ordered
A battle-shield shaped of iron, knowing that
Wood would be useless, that no linden shield[1]
Could help him, protect him, in the flaming heat
30 Of the beast's breath. That noble prince
Would end his days on earth, soon,
Would leave this brief life, but would take the dragon
With him, tear it from the heaped-up treasure

---

1. **linden shield:** a shield made of linden wood.

It had guarded so long. And he'd go to it alone,
35 Scorning to lead soldiers against such enemy:
An enemy: he saw nothing to fear, thought nothing
Of the beast's claws, or wings, or flaming
Jaws—he had fought, before, against worse
Odds, had survived, been victorious, in harsher
40 Battles, beginning in Herot, Hrothgar's
Unlucky hall. He'd killed Grendel
And his mother, swept that murdering tribe
Away. . . .

Then Beowulf rose, still brave, still strong,
And with his shield at his side, and a mail shirt on his breast,
45 Strode calmly, confidently, toward the tower, under
The rocky cliffs: no coward could have walked there!
And then he who'd endured dozens of desperate
Battles, who'd stood boldly while swords and shields
Clashed, the best of kings, saw
50 Huge stone arches and felt the heat
Of the dragon's breath, flooding down
Through the hidden entrance, too hot for anyone
To stand, a streaming current of fire
And smoke that blocked all passage. And the Geats'
55 Lord and leader, angry, lowered
His sword and roared out a battle cry,
A call so loud and clear that it reached through
The hoary[2] rock, hung in the dragon's
Ear. The beast rose, angry,
60 Knowing a man had come—and then nothing
But war could have followed. Its breath came first,
A steaming cloud pouring from the stone,
Then the earth itself shook. Beowulf
Swung his shield into place, held it
65 In front of him, facing the entrance. The dragon
Coiled and uncoiled, its heart urging it
Into battle. Beowulf's ancient sword
Was waiting, unsheathed, his sharp and gleaming
Blade. The beast came closer; both of them
70 Were ready, each set on slaughter. The Geats'
Great prince stood firm, unmoving, prepared
Behind his high shield, waiting in his shining
Armor. The monster came quickly toward him,
Pouring out fire and smoke, hurrying
75 To its fate. Flames beat at the iron
Shield, and for a time it held, protected
Beowulf as he'd planned; then it began to melt,

---

2. **hoary:** grayish white.

And for the first time in his life that famous prince
Fought with fate against him, with glory
80 Denied him. He knew it, but he raised his sword
And struck at the dragon's scaly hide.
The ancient blade broke, bit into
The monster's skin, drew blood, but cracked
And failed him before it went deep enough, helped him
85 Less than he needed. The dragon leaped
With pain, thrashed and beat at him, spouting
Murderous flames, spreading them everywhere.
And the Geats' ring-giver[3] did not boast of glorious
Victories in other wars: his weapon
90 Had failed him, deserted him, now when he needed it
Most, that excellent sword. Edgetho's
Famous son stared at death,
Unwilling to leave this world, to exchange it
For a dwelling in some distant place—a journey
95 Into darkness that all men must make, as death
Ends their few brief hours on earth.
　　Quickly, the dragon came at him, encouraged
As Beowulf fell back; its breath flared,
And he suffered, wrapped around in swirling
100 Flames—a king, before, but now
A beaten warrior. None of his comrades
Came to him, helped him, his brave and noble
Followers: they ran for their lives, fled
Deep in a wood. And only one of them
105 Remained, stood there, miserable, remembering,
As a good man must, what kinship should mean. . . .

Waves of fire swept at his shield
And the edge began to burn. His mail shirt
Could not help him, but before his hands dropped
110 The blazing wood Wiglaf jumped
Behind Beowulf's shield; his own was burned
To ashes. Then the famous old hero, remembering
Days of glory, lifted what was left
Of Nagling,[4] his ancient sword, and swung it
115 With all his strength, smashed the gray
Blade into the beast's head. But then Nagling
Broke to pieces, as iron always
Had in Beowulf's hands. His arms
Were too strong, the hardest blade could not help him,

Dragon shield ornament
from the Sutton Hoo Ship
Burial, c. 625.

---

3. **Geats' ring-giver:** Beowulf, who as king would now be the one
to bestow golden rings on those who swear allegiance to him.
4. **Nagling:** a name meaning "nailer" or "that which nails."

120 The most wonderfully worked.[5] He carried them to war
But fate had decreed that the Geats' great king
Would be no better for any weapon.
    Then the monster charged again, vomiting
Fire, wild with pain, rushed out
125 Fierce and dreadful, its fear forgotten.
Watching for its chance it drove its tusks
Into Beowulf's neck; he staggered, the blood
Came flooding forth, fell like rain.

    And then when Beowulf needed him most
130 Wiglaf showed his courage, his strength
And skill, and the boldness he was born with. Ignoring
The dragon's head, he helped his lord
By striking lower down. The sword
Sank in; his hand was burned, but the shining
135 Blade had done its work, the dragon's
Belching flames began to flicker
And die away. And Beowulf drew
His battle-sharp dagger: the blood-stained old king
Still knew what he was doing. Quickly, he cut
140 The beast in half, slit it apart.
It fell, their courage had killed it, two noble
Cousins had joined in the dragon's death.
Yet what they did all men must do
When the time comes! But the triumph was the last
145 Beowulf would ever earn, the end
Of greatness and life together. The wound
In his neck began to swell and grow;
He could feel something stirring, burning
In his veins, a stinging venom, and knew
150 The beast's fangs had left it. He fumbled
Along the wall, found a slab
Of stone, and dropped down; above him he saw
Huge stone arches and heavy posts,
Holding up the roof of that giant hall.
155 Then Wiglaf's gentle hands bathed
The blood-stained prince, his glorious lord,
Weary of war, and loosened his helmet.
    Beowulf spoke, in spite of the swollen,
Livid wound, knowing he'd unwound
160 His string of days on earth, seen
As much as God would grant him; all worldly
Pleasure was gone, as life would go,
Soon:
        "I'd leave my armor to my son,
Now, if God had given me an heir,

---

5. **worked:** here, molded; carved; designed.

165 A child born of my body, his life
Created from mine. I've worn this crown
For fifty winters: no neighboring people
Have tried to threaten the Geats, sent soldiers
Against us or talked of terror. My days
170 Have gone by as fate willed, waiting
For its word to be spoken, ruling as well
As I knew how, swearing no unholy oaths,
Seeking no lying wars. I can leave
This life happy; I can die, here,
175 Knowing the Lord of all life has never
Watched me wash my sword in blood
Born of my own family. Belovèd
Wiglaf, go, quickly, find
The dragon's treasure: we've taken its life,
180 But its gold is ours, too. Hurry,
Bring me ancient silver, precious
Jewels, shining armor and gems,
Before I die. Death will be softer,
Leaving life and this people I've ruled
185 So long, if I look at this last of all prizes."

Then Wexstan's son[6] went in, as quickly
As he could, did as the dying Beowulf
Asked, entered the inner darkness
Of the tower, went with his mail shirt and his sword.
190 Flushed with victory he groped his way,
A brave young warrior, and suddenly saw
Piles of gleaming gold, precious
Gems, scattered on the floor, cups
And bracelets, rusty old helmets, beautifully
195 Made but rotting with no hands to rub
And polish them. They lay where the dragon left them:
It had flown in the darkness, once, before fighting
Its final battle. (So gold can easily
Triumph, defeat the strongest of men,
200 No matter how deep it is hidden!) And he saw,
Hanging high above, a golden
Banner, woven by the best of weavers
And beautiful. And over everything he saw
A strange light, shining everywhere,
205 On walls and floor and treasure. Nothing
Moved, no other monsters appeared;
He took what he wanted, all the treasures
That pleased his eye, heavy plates
And golden cups and the glorious banner,

---

6. **Wexstan's son:** an epithet for Wiglaf, whose father was named Wexstan.

210 Loaded his arms with all they could hold.
Beowulf's dagger, his iron blade,
Had finished the fire-spitting terror
That once protected tower and treasures
Alike; the gray-bearded lord of the Geats
215 Had ended those flying, burning raids
Forever.
            Then Wiglaf went back, anxious
To return while Beowulf was alive, to bring him
Treasure they'd won together. He ran,
Hoping his wounded king, weak
220 And dying, had not left the world too soon.
Then he brought their treasure to Beowulf, and found
His famous king bloody, gasping
For breath. But Wiglaf sprinkled water
Over his lord, until the words
225 Deep in his breast broke through and were heard.
Beholding the treasure he spoke, haltingly:
   "For this, this gold, these jewels, I thank
Our Father in Heaven, Ruler of the Earth—
For all of this, that His grace has given me,
230 Allowed me to bring to my people while breath
Still came to my lips. I sold my life
For this treasure, and I sold it well. Take
What I leave, Wiglaf, lead my people,
Help them; my time is gone. Have
235 The brave Geats build me a tomb,
When the funeral flames have burned me, and build it
Here, at the water's edge, high
On this spit of land, so sailors can see
This tower, and remember my name, and call it
240 Beowulf's tower, and boats in the darkness
And mist, crossing the sea, will know it."
   Then that brave king gave the golden
Necklace from around his throat to Wiglaf,
Gave him his gold-covered helmet, and his rings,
245 And his mail shirt, and ordered him to use them well:
   "You're the last of all our far-flung family.
Fate has swept our race away,
Taken warriors in their strength and led them
To the death that was waiting. And now I follow them."
250   The old man's mouth was silent, spoke
No more, had said as much as it could;
He would sleep in the fire, soon. His soul
Left his flesh, flew to glory. . . .

            Then Wiglaf commanded
The wealthiest Geats, brave warriors
255 And owners of land, leaders of his people,

To bring wood for Beowulf's funeral:
    "Now the fire must feed on his body,
Flames grow heavy and black with him
Who endured arrows falling in iron
260 Showers, feathered shafts, barbed
And sharp, shot through linden shields,
Storms of eager arrowheads dropping."
    And Wexstan's wise son took seven
Of the noblest Geats, led them together
265 Down the tunnel, deep into the dragon's
Tower; the one in front had a torch,
Held it high in his hands. The best
Of Beowulf's followers entered behind
That gleaming flame: seeing gold
270 And silver rotting on the ground, with no one
To guard it, the Geats were not troubled with scruples
Or fears, but quickly gathered up
Treasure and carried it out of the tower.
And they rolled the dragon down to the cliff
275 And dropped it over, let the ocean take it,
The tide sweep it away. Then silver
And gold and precious jewels were put
On a wagon, with Beowulf's body, and brought
Down the jutting sand, where the pyre waited.

280   A huge heap of wood was ready,
Hung around with helmets, and battle
Shields, and shining mail shirts, all
As Beowulf had asked. The bearers brought
Their belovèd lord, their glorious king,
285 And weeping laid him high on the wood.
Then the warriors began to kindle that greatest
Of funeral fires; smoke rose
Above the flames, black and thick,
And while the wind blew and the fire
290 Roared they wept, and Beowulf's body
Crumbled and was gone. The Geats stayed,
Moaning their sorrow, lamenting their lord:
A gnarled old woman, hair wound
Tight and gray on her head, groaned
295 A song of misery, of infinite sadness
And days of mourning, of fear and sorrow
To come, slaughter and terror and captivity.
And Heaven swallowed the billowing smoke.
    Then the Geats built the tower, as Beowulf
300 Had asked, strong and tall, so sailors
Could find it from far and wide; working
For ten long days they made his monument,
Sealed his ashes in walls as straight

Viking picture stone, eighth century.

And high as wise and willing hands
305 Could raise them. And the riches he and Wiglaf
Had won from the dragon, rings, necklaces,
Ancient, hammered armor—all
The treasures they'd taken were left there, too,
Silver and jewels buried in the sandy
310 Ground, back in the earth, again
And forever hidden and useless to men.
And then twelve of the bravest Geats
Rode their horses around the tower,
Telling their sorrow, telling stories
315 Of their dead king and his greatness, his glory,
Praising him for heroic deeds, for a life
As noble as his name. So should all men
Raise up words for their lords, warm
With love, when their shield and protector leaves
320 His body behind, sends his soul
On high. And so Beowulf's followers
Rode, mourning their belovèd leader,
Crying that no better king had ever
Lived, no prince so mild, no man
325 So open to his people, so deserving of praise.

STUDY QUESTIONS

Recalling

1. What causes the fire-breathing dragon to attack the Geats? At the time of the attack, for how many years had Beowulf ruled peacefully?
2. Who is the only Geat to help Beowulf fight the dragon (lines 104–111)? Summarize the outcome of the battle.
3. What does Beowulf tell the Geats to do with the dragon's treasure (lines 180–185)? What do they actually do with the treasure (lines 305–311)?
4. What reason does Beowulf give for wanting the Geats to build a high tower at the water's edge (lines 234–240)? What opinion of Beowulf do the Geats express in the final lines of the poem?

Interpreting

5. Why would Beowulf take responsibility for the dragon's reawakening even though Beowulf himself has not awakened the dragon? What do this detail and other details in the section reveal about the kind of king Beowulf was?
6. What qualities valued by the Anglo-Saxons does Wiglaf display?
7. In general, what attitude toward God and religion is reflected in the poem? Explain the double meaning of "flew to glory" in line 253.
8. In what sense might the navigational assistance provided by Beowulf's memorial tower symbolize, or represent, the effects of Beowulf's life, reign, and memory?
9. Briefly explain the view of gold and other worldly treasures suggested by the details of this section. Cite specific details to support general statements.

Extending

10. What opportunities for individual heroic behavior exist in our own age?

Bede *673?–735*

The Venerable Bede is considered the father of English history. During his lifetime he was without doubt the most learned scholar in all of western Europe. Bede, who was a monk, passed his days teaching in the monasteries of Wearmouth and Jarrow in northeast Britain, where he had been sent at the age of seven to study. There he wrote his famous *Ecclesiastical History of the English People,* which he completed in 731.

The *History* is our most valuable record of the earlier Anglo-Saxon period. Composed in Latin (Bede knew Greek and Hebrew as well), it provides many fascinating glimpses of the people of the time. One such glimpse is of Caedmon, the earliest known poet in English literature. Caedmon's *Hymn,* written sometime between 658 and 680 at Whitby Abbey in Northumbria, is the oldest English poem to have been preserved. The following excerpt from Bede's *History* relates the story of Caedmon's miraculous composition of this Old English poem.

■ Do you think that it is possible for a single idea to transform a person's life? What might such an idea be?

Bede

from Ecclesiastical History of the English People

Translated by J. A. Giles

Caedmon of Whitby

There was in this abbess's[1] monastery a certain brother, particularly remarkable for the grace of God, who was wont to make pious and religious verses, so that whatever was interpreted to him out of Scripture he soon after put the same into poetical expressions of much sweetness and humility in English, which was his native language. By his verses the minds of many were often excited to despise the world and to aspire to heaven. Others after him attempted, in the English nation, to compose religious poems, but none could ever compare with him, for he did not learn the art of poetry from men, but from God; for which reason he never could compose any trivial or vain poem, but only those which relate to religion suited his religious tongue; for having lived in a secular habit[2] till he was well advanced in years,

---

1. **abbess's:** referring to St. Hilda, who had founded the monastery in 658.

2. **secular habit:** nonreligious dress. In other words, Caedmon had been a layman, not a monk.

he had never learned anything of versifying; for which reason being sometimes at entertainments, when it was agreed for the sake of mirth that all present should sing in their turns, when he saw the instrument[3] come towards him, he rose up from table and returned home.

Having done so at a certain time, and gone out of the house where the entertainment was, to the stable, where he had to take care of the horses that night, he there composed himself to rest at the proper time; a person appeared to him in his sleep, and saluting him by his name, said, "Caedmon, sing some song to me." He answered, "I cannot sing; for that was the reason why I left the entertainment and retired to this place, because I could not sing." The other who talked to him replied, "However you shall sing." "What shall I sing?" rejoined he. "Sing the beginning of created beings," said the other. Hereupon he presently began to sing verses to the praise of God, which he had never heard, the purport whereof[4] was thus: We are now to praise the Maker of the heavenly kingdom, the power of the Creator and his counsel, the deeds of the Father of glory. How he, being the eternal God, became the author of all miracles, who first, as almighty preserver of the human race, created heaven for the sons of men as the roof of the house, and next the earth. This is the sense, but not the words in order as he sang them in his sleep; for verses, though never so well composed,[5] cannot be literally translated out of one language into another, without losing much of their beauty and loftiness. Awaking from his sleep, he remembered all that he had sung in his dream, and soon added much more to the same effect in verse worthy of the Deity.

In the morning he came to the steward, his superior, and having acquainted him with the gift he had received, was conducted to the abbess, by whom he was ordered, in the presence of many learned men, to tell his dream and repeat the verses, that they might all give their judgment what it was, and whence his verse proceeded. They all concluded that heavenly grace had been conferred on him by our Lord. They expounded to him a passage in holy writ, either historical or doctrinal,[6] ordering him, if he could, to put the same into verse. Having undertaken it, he went away, and returning the next morning, gave it to them composed in most excellent verse; whereupon the abbess, embracing the grace of God in the man, instructed him to quit the secular habit and take upon him the monastic life; which being accordingly done, she associated him to the rest of the brethren in her monastery, and ordered that he should be taught the whole series of sacred history. Thus Caedmon, keeping in mind all he heard, and as it were chewing the cud,[7] converted the same into most harmonious verse; and sweetly repeating the same, made his masters in their turn his hearers. He sang the creation of the world, the origin of man, and all the history of Genesis; and made many verses on the departure of the children of Israel out of Egypt, and their entering into the land of promise, with many other histories from holy writ; the incarnation, passion, resurrection of our Lord, and his ascension into heaven; the coming of the Holy Ghost, and the preaching of the apostles; also the terror of future judgment, the horror of the pains of hell, and the delights of heaven; besides many more about the Divine benefits and judgments, by which he endeavored to turn away all men from the love of vice, and to excite in them the love of, and application to, good actions; for he was a very religious man, and humbly submissive to regular discipline, but full of zeal against those who behaved themselves otherwise; for which reason he ended his life happily.

---

3. **instrument:** presumably a harp.
4. **purport whereof:** meaning of which.
5. **though . . . composed:** no matter how well they are written.

6. **doctrinal:** having to do with church principles or teachings.
7. **cud:** grass that a cow rechews before converting it into milk.

Caedmon's *Hymn*

Praise we the Lord
Of the heavenly kingdom,
God's power and wisdom,
The works of His hand;
5 As the Father of glory,
Eternal Lord,
Wrought the beginning
Of all His wonders!
Holy Creator!
10 Warden of men!
First, for a roof,
O'er the children of earth,
He stablished the heavens,
And founded the world,
15 And spread the dry land
For the living to dwell in.
Lord Everlasting!
Almighty God!

—*Translated by*
Charles W. Kennedy

Two scenes of Creation, from the Junius Manuscript, 1025–1050.

The Bodleian Library, Oxford, Ms. Junius 11, P. 84

STUDY QUESTIONS

Recalling

1. According to paragraph 1, what influence did Caedmon's religious verses have upon his listeners?
2. According to paragraph 2, where did Caedmon have his famous dream? What work did he have to do that night?
3. What did the learned men conclude had been "conferred" on Caedmon and by whom, according to paragraph 3?
4. According to Caedmon's *Hymn,* why did God create the "heavens"? Why did he create "dry land"?

Interpreting

5. What change in stature does Caedmon undergo? In light of this change, why might the place in which Caedmon had his dream be especially significant?
6. How would you characterize the kind of world God created, according to Caedmon's *Hymn*?

Extending

7. What can we conclude about Caedmon's significance to the people, and especially to the scholars, of his own time from the fact that he is included in Bede's *Ecclesiastical History of the English People*? Explain why poets of all eras may be highly esteemed by their contemporaries.

Anglo-Saxon Lyric Poetry

In addition to epics like *Beowulf,* which are **narrative** (storytelling) poems, the Anglo-Saxons composed shorter poems whose chief purpose was not to tell a story but to communicate personal thoughts and feelings. Such poems are called **lyric** poems. As the name suggests, lyric poems were originally written for musical accompaniment, much as song lyrics of today. In ancient Greece the accompaniment was usually on a harplike instrument called a *lyre,* from which the word *lyric* comes. In Anglo-Saxon times the scops continued to accompany their poetry recitations with music, usually strummed on primitive harps.

Much of the Anglo-Saxon lyric poetry that has come down to us is religious poetry, expressions of the deep faith and devotion characteristic of the era's early Christians. Among the most famous examples of Anglo-Saxon religious verse is Caedmon's *Hymn,* which appears on page 37. Of the secular, or nonreligious, verse that has survived, many of the poems are **elegies,** or poems of lament, mourning not only the deaths of individuals but the tragedies of war and emigration that touched so heavily on early Anglo-Saxon experience. A poem called "The Wanderer," for example, expresses the deep sorrow and confusion of a warrior exiled from his homeland following the death of his lord in battle; a poem called "The Wife's Lament" expresses a woman's loneliness and grief after her husband has gone off to war.

"The Seafarer" is one of the most famous of Anglo-Saxon lyric poems. An anonymous poem included in *The Exeter Book,* the collection of Anglo-Saxon poetry compiled by tenth-century monks at Exeter Cathedral, "The Seafarer" is especially noted for its musical style and its powerful expression of deeply felt emotion. Like many Anglo-Saxon secular poems, it is an elegy, an old sailor's lament for a way of life that is lost to him and a typically Anglo-Saxon expression of life's sadness, harshness, and brevity.

■ Do our feelings remain static or do they evolve over time? Why do you think so?

Model for Active Reading

In this selection, as in one selection in each unit, you will find notes in the right-hand margin that highlight parts of the selection. These notes point out important ideas of the literary period and draw your attention to literary elements and techniques covered in the Literary Focuses. Page numbers in the notes refer you to more extensive discussions of these important ideas and elements.

Detail of Viking picture stone, eighth century.

from **The Seafarer**

Translated by Burton Raffel

This tale is true, and mine. It tells
How the sea took me, swept me back
And forth in sorrow and fear and pain,
Showed me suffering in a hundred ships,
5 In a thousand ports, and in me. It tells
Of smashing surf when I sweated in the cold
Of an anxious watch, perched in the bow
As it dashed under cliffs. My feet were cast
In icy bands, bound with frost,
10 With frozen chains, and hardship groaned
Around my heart. Hunger tore
At my sea-weary soul. No man sheltered
On the quiet fairness of earth can feel
How wretched I was, drifting through winter
15 On an ice-cold sea, whirled in sorrow,
Alone in a world blown clear of love.

. . . And yet my heart wanders away,
My soul roams with the sea, the whales'
Home, wandering to the widest corners

Alliteration (p. 26):
Alliteration was an important
tool for the Anglo-Saxon poet.
Here, the repeated *s* sounds
capture the harsh music of the
sea.

Kenning (p. 26): In the oral
literature of the Anglo-Saxons,
the sea was often called "the
whales' home" or "whale-road."

20 Of the world, returning ravenous with desire,
Flying solitary, screaming, exciting me
To the open ocean, breaking oaths
On the curve of a wave.
                        Thus the joys of God
Are fervent with life, where life itself
25 Fades quickly into the earth. The wealth
Of the world neither reaches to Heaven nor remains.
No man has ever faced the dawn
Certain which of Fate's three threats
Would fall: illness, or age, or an enemy's
30 Sword, snatching the life from his soul.

. . . Fate is stronger
And God mightier than any man's mind.
Our thoughts should turn to where our home is,
Consider the ways of coming there.

Anglo-Saxon idea: Belief in fate, or *wyrd*, and religious faith were strong (p. 4).

STUDY QUESTIONS

Recalling

1. According to lines 4–5, where did the speaker see suffering?
2. Name three hardships that the speaker endured at sea, according to stanza 1.
3. According to stanza 2, what does the speaker's soul do?

Interpreting

4. What are the speaker's two conflicting attitudes toward the sea? Which attitude seems stronger? Why do you think this is so?
5. According to line 33, "Our thoughts should turn to where our home is." Where is home, according to the speaker? How do you know?
6. In your own words, how would you characterize the speaker's view of his life? In what tone is that view expressed?

LITERARY FOCUS

Old English

The language spoken by the Germanic tribes of Angles, Saxons, and Jutes who invaded Britain in the fifth century is called either **Anglo-Saxon** or **Old English.** While the terms are synonymous, the latter is used to distinguish that language from Middle English, which developed from it after the Norman Conquest of the eleventh century, and from modern English, which was established by the beginning of the sixteenth century.

Old English ("Angleish"), then, is the Germanic speech spoken in England before the invasion of the French-speaking Normans in 1066. The speech of the Germanic tribes that remained on the Continent developed into languages now spoken in northern Europe. Thus, the roots of English are closely intertwined with those of other modern Germanic languages: specifically, of Dutch, Danish, Swedish, Norwegian, and, especially, German.

Early Anglo-Saxons used an alphabet consisting of characters called *runes.* Runic writing was used for inscriptions carved in wood or stone, the chief purpose for which written language was used outside the monasteries. Eventually it was replaced by the Latin alphabet used by Christian missionaries and monks for writing English.

With only a little practice you can learn to read the Middle English that developed after the Norman Conquest (see page 96). Old English, however, must be learned like a foreign language, and a difficult one at that. Here, for example, are two lines of *Beowulf* in the original Old English:

þa com of móre under mist-hleóþum
Grendel gongan godes yrre bær.

They might be translated literally as: "Then came from moor under misty hills Grendel going, God's anger bore." (þ is the Old English letter *thorn*, pronounced *th*.) Compare the original with the modern translation on page 15, lines 164–166. Despite all the differences, you will recognize similarities between current English and its distant ancestor.

Old English is a highly *inflected* language—in other words, the forms of words change to indicate different meanings and usages such as tense, case, gender, and number. Over several centuries the grammar has become simpler and most inflections have been weakened.

The chart below outlines some of the inflections of the word *ship* in Old English.

	singular	*plural*
Subject	scip	scipu
Object	scip	scipu
Possessive	scipes	scipa
Indirect Object	scipe	scipum

Modern English has grown out of the Old English that the Anglo-Saxons spoke. Later both French and Latin were added, from the influence of the Norman invaders and the medieval Christian church, respectively. Of these three languages, Old English contributes about twenty-five percent of the vocabulary we now use, including many of our modern English connectives, pronouns, prepositions, and common nouns and verbs. While French has given English its precision and grace, the language of the Anglo-Saxons has given it much of its strength and durability.

Thinking About Old English
◼ Which words in the following passage derive from Old English? Check your guesses with a good dictionary.

Once upon a time in medieval days a poor widow lived in a little cottage standing in a dale near a grove of trees. Her life was a very simple one, with only one dog and no children. One day she was surprised by the arrival of a knight in armor. He had been wounded in battle and was far from home.

COMPOSITION

Writing About Character
◼ Write a description of the speaker of "The Seafarer." First describe his age and physical appearance as you imagine them based on information given in the poem. Then describe his personality, including evidence from the poem to support your assertions.

Writing a Description
◼ Early lines of "The Seafarer" create a sense of intense discomfort in freezing weather. Imagine a comparable discomfort from heat, cold, thirst, or hunger. Then, using vivid details, write a descriptive paragraph to convey that feeling to your reader.

COMPARING WRITERS

◼ For the Anglo-Saxons fate, or *wyrd*, was an important factor believed to rule human destiny. Compare the role of fate in the lives of two or more of the following characters: Beowulf, Caedmon, and the seafarer. Be sure to support your assertions with specifics from the selections.

ACTIVE READING

Significant Detail

A great work of literature is made of countless details. Like a classic painting, a medieval cathedral, a symphony, or a satellite, a great story or poem is constructed with the closest attention to detail. Every element, large or small, matters.

Usually the larger elements—the characters, the plot, the setting—first attract us to a story or a narrative poem. We wonder, "Who are these characters? Where are they? What is going to happen to them?" Yet we have probably heard stories in the past that followed a similar pattern or plot line; the characters may very well be similar to others we have known; the setting or even the theme may not be particularly surprising. What then makes the work unique? What gives it its individuality, its own particular texture? The answer lies in details.

In literature a writer provides readers with a world full of details, and, as we read, we re-create that world in our imaginations. To do that imaginative work, to give body to that world, we absorb details that appeal to our senses, our minds, and our hearts. We see the color of a landscape, hear the tone of a bell, feel the warmth of a fire. We understand a motivation or an allusion; we feel an emotion.

We can of course simply enjoy the details that a writer provides; it is easy to note them and pass them by. However, we can go further and think about the *selection* of details that the writer has made. We can increase our enjoyment and appreciation of a work of literature if we think about *why* a particular detail was included and why another was not. To do so, we must look closely at every sentence, keep alert, be aware of this dimension of reading literature.

In *Beowulf,* for example, we are immediately aware of its heroic characters, harsh setting, and adventure-filled plot. Reading in this way, however, we must be sure not to overlook details. Consider the lines in which the author of *Beowulf* sings:

The high hall rang, its roof
  boards swayed,
And Danes shook with terror.
  Down
The aisles the battle swept, angry
And wild.

We hear that the benches in the hall

            . . . rattled, fell
To the floor, gold-covered
  boards grating
As Grendel and Beowulf battled
  across them.

The details in this scene are more than enough to enable us to visualize the titanic struggle taking place in the hall "of ivory and iron and wood." The hall *rang* and its roof *swayed:* As if it were a gigantic iron bell, the hall reverberates with the sound of the battle. It trembles and rocks just as the very kingdom of the Danes is trembling, rocking on its foundation, knowing it will face extinction if Grendel defeats Beowulf. The heavy wooden benches *rattled* and *fell:* We can only wonder at the stupendous crashing it would take to rattle those benches in the hall.

Later, after defeating the dragon, the fatally wounded Beowulf

            . . . fumbled
Along the wall, found a slab
Of stone, and dropped down;
  above him he saw
Huge stone arches and heavy
  posts,
Holding up the roof of that
  giant hall.

The beast is dead, but Beowulf knows that his own kingdom—the arches and posts of *his* hall, the support of *his* people—still stands. This perfectly selected, significant detail enables us to imagine one of the final satisfactions of the epic hero.

REVIEW: THE ENGLISH VOICE
Fate and Fame

The lives of the Anglo-Saxons were given shape and meaning by the vital ideas of *fate* and *fame*. Fate was unchangeable, universal, inescapable. Every man, woman, and child was subject to it. A hero, an artist, a common man—as we see in Beowulf, in Caedmon, and in the seafarer—all bowed down before *wyrd,* or destiny.

Fame was the only means of transcending fate, enduring it, and rising above it. Individual greatness, achievement, loyalty, or courage—the sources of fame—gave people one small measure of power over fate.

Beowulf

>   . . . *I will meet him*
> *With my hands empty—unless his heart*
> *Fails him, seeing a soldier waiting*
> *Weaponless, unafraid. Let God in His wisdom*
> *Extend His hand where He wills, reward*
> *Whom He chooses!*
>
> *I've never known fear; as a youth I fought*
> *In endless battles. I am old, now,*
> *But I will fight again, seek fame still,*
> *If the dragon hiding in his tower dares*
> *To face me.*

>   *My days*
> *Have gone by as fate willed, waiting*
> *For its word to be spoken.*

Bede

Others after him [Caedmon] attempted, in the English nation, to compose religious poems, but none could ever compare with him, for he did not learn the art of poetry from men, but from God.

The Seafarer

>   *The wealth*
> *Of the world neither reaches to Heaven nor remains.*
> *No man has ever faced the dawn*
> *Certain which of Fate's three threats*
> *Would fall: illness, or age, or an enemy's*
> *Sword, snatching the life from his soul.*
>   . . . *Fate is stronger*
> *And God mightier than any man's mind.*

Slaying a dragon and composing a great poem were both heroic acts, worthy of fame. The deep underlying lament of the lonely seafarer is that he has suffered heroically without anyone knowing about it. For the Anglo-Saxons fame meant that a person would remain alive in the minds of those who came after.

Key to Illustrations on Pages 2–3.

1. The Gundestrap cauldron, depicting the Celtic god Cernunnos, c. third century.
2. Detail, the Saxons, Jutes, and Angles arriving in Britain, from an English manuscript, c. 1130.
3. Detail, Viking picture stone, eighth century.
4. Detail, the Book of Kells, c. 800.
5. Viking helmet, seventh century.
6. Detail, the manuscript of Bede's *Life of St. Cuthbert,* twelfth century.
7. Roman silver coin with the head of Julius Caesar.
8. Carved head from a sledge unearthed with a Viking ship at Oseberg, Norway.
9. The Alfred Jewel, gold filigree, enamel, and rock crystal, used as either an ornament or a pointer, ninth century.
10. Detail, the Book of Lindisfarne, late seventh century.

43

The Bodleian Library, Oxford, Ms. Rawlinson, folio 132v

Key to Illustrations appears on page 105.

THE MEDIEVAL PERIOD

1066–1485

In England the Medieval Period, also called the Middle Ages, began in a year that has become famous—1066. In that year the Normans, who had settled in what is now western France, defeated the Anglo-Saxons at the Battle of Hastings and earned for their leader the title William the Conqueror. Now England had a Norman king.

Norman Rule in England

William bestrode the English Channel like a colossus, with one court in England and one in Normandy. The Anglo-Saxon character and culture, solid and civilized, did not give way before the more stylized, older culture of the Norman conquerors. Instead, the two cultures seemed to blend into a truly English culture that retained—and still does—some values from each source.

Norman kings ruled England for less than a hundred years, but during that time the Normans brought England closer to the mainstream of European society. William introduced in England the European social, economic, and political system called feudalism. Under **feudalism,** land (the real wealth of the nation) was divided among noble overlords, or barons. Lesser lords, called knights, pledged their wealth and services to the overlords. The overlord, in

The murder of Thomas à Becket in 1170. Illumination from an English Psalter, or the Book of Psalms, c. 1200.

return, provided use of the land. At the lowest end of the social scale were the serfs, peasants pledged to the lord of the manor and bound to the land. William and the Norman kings who followed him (William II, Henry I, and Stephen of Blois) had feudal domains—land, lords, knights, and serfs—on the Continent, in what is now France. Similarly, some French rulers had, or claimed to have, feudal rights in England.

The Royal Houses of Plantagenet, Lancaster, and York

In 1154 the Norman line was at an end. The royal houses, or families, of Plantagenet, Lancaster, and York would carry England through the Middle Ages.

Beginning with Henry II's reign in 1154, we find upon the throne of England a series of kings whose lives were filled with drama enough to fill the stages of the world. In fact, in Shakespeare's series of great historical dramas, they do just that. Almost all of these kings were strong, interesting people living troubled, dangerous, complex lives in their search for power.

Among the eight Plantagenet kings, Henry II has gone down in history for increasing royal power at the expense of the nobles. His desire to control the Roman Catholic Church in England led to the murder of Thomas à Becket, the Archbishop of Canterbury.

Henry's son, Richard I, called Richard the Lion-Hearted, has become a model of a true knight. Richard was away from England for all but five months of his ten-year reign, traveling across the world, giving his riches to the poor and seeking holy relics. John, Henry II's other son, who succeeded Richard I, gained a reputation as a weak, even villainous ruler. But John, too, had a moment of high drama when in 1215, a year before his death, he was forced to sign the Magna Carta (Latin for "Great Charter"). By this document he agreed not to raise taxes without the consent of the barons. Many see in this curtailment of royal power the beginning of constitutional government in England, including the right to trial by jury. Most of the remaining Plantagenet kings— Edward I, especially—provided strong leadership for England, despite family troubles over succession, trouble with Scotland, trouble with France, trouble with Ireland, and near revolution at home. However, when the young Richard II took the throne, he was plagued by power-hungry relatives and was eventually forced to abdicate. The Lancaster line came to power.

The first of the three kings of the House of Lancaster, Henry IV (1399–1413), survived many crises and was succeeded by his more powerful son, Henry V, fondly known among his followers as Prince Hal. Henry V led his armies to a dramatic and memorable victory over the French in the Battle of Agincourt in 1415. It was one of the high points of the so-called Hundred Years' War with France, waged from 1337 to 1453 in England's attempt to keep its French lands. Henry V's men turned back the French army with a newly fashioned weapon, the longbow, which was able to pierce armor.

Henry VI, next in line, went insane for a brief period and left the throne in the hands of an uncle, the Duke of York. When Henry's health returned and he sought to retrieve his authority, the Duke of York rallied forces against him. Thus in 1455 began thirty years of civil strife, known as the Wars of the Roses, between the House of Lancaster (whose symbol was a red rose), and the House of York (whose symbol was a white rose). The Lancasters never returned to the throne.

Edward IV, the first of the Yorkist kings, can be thanked for encouraging William Caxton to

Sir Gawain. Miniature from a manuscript of Arthurian romances, c. 1400.

set up a printing press with movable type, capable of printing in quantities large enough to bring the printed word to the general public. After this notable event, the drama of the Yorkist kings turns dark. When in 1483 Edward V succeeded to the throne, he was only twelve years old. At this point another story-book figure, Edward V's Uncle Richard, steps onto the stage of history. Richard had Edward V and his younger brother imprisoned in the Tower of London. He then assumed the throne as Richard III. When it was rumored that he had had the two little boys murdered in the tower, rebellion broke out. In the end, Richard III himself was killed in battle, and Henry Tudor, a distant descendant of the Lancaster kings, assumed the throne. With the beginning of Tudor rule in 1485, the story of the Middle Ages in England, so far as kings are concerned, is over.

Chivalric Life in Medieval England

The feudalism that the Normans brought to England was not just an economic and political system, a means of dividing up land and power. Feudalism was also a social system. The feudal manor— the home of the lord and the lands around it—was self-sufficient and in many ways like a small city. To the serfs in the small cottages on the estate, feudalism meant complete dependence upon the overlord. Social life, at least outside of the big towns and cities, was limited to hard work at farming or herding and a bit of amusement provided by the local church. In the royal courts and in the manor houses of the overlords, life was more sophisticated. Though the lord had responsibilities to the welfare of his estate, knights and serfs freed him from the demands of daily struggle.

The English kings and barons from 1066 to 1485 played their roles against a backdrop of glory and violence that spread from the royal courts and Roman ruins near London northward into Scotland, west into Wales and Ireland, across the English Channel into France, and southeast into what was called the Holy Land—the city of Jerusalem, then in Moslem hands. This was the period when knighthood flourished in England, when knights went on local quests, or across the sea to fight the French, or on what could be a life-time journey to the Holy Land. It was also the period when knights jousted in tournaments or upon a chance meeting on the road while fair ladies watched and waited.

With feudalism and knighthood the Normans brought to England the code of chivalry. **Chivalry** was an ideal that all knights must try to attain: to be honorable, courteous, generous, brave, skillful in battle, respectful to women, and helpful to the weak. This romantic attitude would affect much of the literature of the period, especially the songs and stories.

Religious Life in Medieval England

The Roman Catholic Church was also a powerful force in the England of the Middle Ages. Never had so many people been more totally and unquestioningly at one with a single institutional church and with the faith that church professed. Kings, courts, knights, and common people down to the lowliest serf all practiced a belief in the church on earth and in the afterlife that it proclaimed. Knights were willing to die for their religious belief, as witnessed in particular by their ardent desire to join in the **Crusades,** which were military expeditions undertaken to recapture the city of Jerusalem from the Moslems.

In the years between 1096 and 1270, knights in full regalia, armor bright, with footsoldiers and all the paraphernalia that an

A view of Canterbury Cathedral, Kent, England.

army needs—almost a traveling city—plundered their way to the Holy Land. They were never successful—some never even reached Jerusalem—but they left a violent and bloody trail behind them.

Back in England the Normans strengthened the physical domain of the Church, building stone monasteries and abbeys. Like the feudal manor, each monastery or abbey was a small, self-sufficient city. They also continued to be centers of learning and of literature. Latin was the language of the Church and was known to all educated people in England. Thus, much of the literature of the time was written in Latin, particularly the more scholarly histories. The Crusaders straggling back from Jerusalem would contribute to the learning of these centers some of the more advanced knowledge that distinguished the Moslem world, including Arabic numerals, algebra, and Arab medicine.

Churches and cathedrals, perhaps the most dramatic and beautiful legacy of the period, were another product of religious faith and energy. Church bells pealed messages almost hourly, and every town, it seems, had a towering, stone cathedral. By 1200 the still-small city of London, with a population of no more than 40,000 people, had 120 churches in addition to the giant cathedral that was dedicated to the city's patron saint, St. Paul.

City Life in Medieval England

By all reports, London remained a merry town with children playing ball games in the streets and wealthy merchants, now on horseback, hunting wild boar and deer in nearby park-land. In winter when the marshes froze, people skated happily across the flats on skates of sheep bone. Sickness and death were never very far away, however. In 1348 and 1349 the dreadful Black Death, a form of the bubonic plague, killed at least a third of the English population.

In spite of plague and warfare, England prospered during the later Middle Ages. People began to move from castle towns to villages and cities, and cities had sprung up in the north as well as on the southern plains. Guilds—organizations not unlike modern-day trade unions—developed in the cities, and an apprentice moved through an elaborate hierarchy before becoming a master craftsman. Also during this time herding became more

important than farming. British wool became famous; cottages were turned into small mills; and the famous textile industry—the carding, combing, spinning, and weaving of sheep's wool—began.

Even more important than the end of knighthood (mostly due to the invention of gunpowder) and the beginning of the textile industry toward the end of the Middle Ages was the development of printing. William Caxton established his printing press in England in 1476. Up until this time literature existed in England only in manuscript, copied out by hand for the very few. When Caxton introduced to England the invention of printing that had begun to spread through Europe in the late 1400s, the written word in English began to reach a much wider audience.

Caxton was a fine editor as well as a printer. He played a very important role in bringing the two great literary works of this period—Chaucer's *Canterbury Tales* and Malory's *Morte d'Arthur*—to light.

Storytelling in the Middle Ages

Although printing was now available, it would be centuries before storytelling would take the form of novels. Nevertheless, the seeds of the novel and short story find rich ground in this period. Geoffrey Chaucer told

King Arthur. Detail from a French tapestry, c. 1450.

short stories in verse, using a bright, new kind of English poetry influenced by European models as well as hewed from his own genius. Thanks to Thomas Malory, the great English literary legend of King Arthur was printed in a version heavily influenced by the romantic notions of French storytellers. When the Anglo-Saxon soldiers at the beginning of this period marched against the Normans, they carried from England songs about King Arthur. During the Norman Period the French added their own special notes to Arthur's story and created the **romance,** a blend of chivalry with touches of love, magic, and marvels. Malory stresses the romantic aspect of the Arthur legend, but his portrait of Arthur still retains some of the real flesh-and-blood Celtic warrior-king that Arthur had once been.

The folk ballads in the pages ahead are also a form of storytelling, although, unlike the writings of Chaucer and Malory, they were still composed orally. These ballads were not the work of professional poets—minstrels who performed for the entertainment of courts—but rather stories sung by common people gathering among friends and family in their cottages in the evening. These ballads contain storytelling techniques that, centuries later, would be used by novelists; the use of dialogue to tell a story is the most important of these techniques.

Drama in the Middle Ages

Drama is a form of storytelling that seems to have a life of its own. The idea of telling a story by acting it out seems to be a very ancient one, perhaps appealing to an instinct of human nature: the desire to imitate another human being. Some of us like to act out the part. Some of us prefer to see and hear a part acted out by another. In theater (a name we give to drama that is produced on a stage) a simple, perhaps penniless baker, for example, can become for a few moments a heroic king, and his audience can lose itself in the story that unfolds.

Drama as public entertainment began in England in the Medieval Period as religious ritual, in the form of **mystery plays,** or **miracle plays,** as they are usually called. The miracle play was developed by the Church in an attempt to instruct the illiterate in the miraculous stories. To celebrate a feast day,

the Church would often have common people, members of a bakers' guild, for example, dress up like characters in the Bible. The plays were very well attended. They eventually moved from the cathedral to the village green and finally to pageant wagons, ox-drawn wagons that brought this early form of theater to neighboring towns and villages. The actors were amateurs, technically speaking, but they were paid for their work, the actor playing God getting more than the others. Rehearsals were frequent, and if one did not go well, the actors would be fined.

The miracle play was followed by a somewhat different development—the **morality play,** in which actors played the roles of virtues and vices—patience, greed, and so on. The most significant aspect of the morality play was that the conflict between virtue and vice, good and evil, was not external (a good king and a bad king, for example) but took place in the heart of a single hero.

All in all, the literature of the Medieval Period carries us back into a colorful and exciting world as reported by the poets, storytellers, and dramatists of that time and forward into other ages in which knights, crusaders, monks, and fine ladies would continue to inspire writers. Indeed, the Medieval Period is at once very far away and very close at hand.

TIME LINE

1066 Anglo-Saxons defeated by the Norman William the Conqueror at Battle of Hastings

1086 *Domesday Book,* first official record of property owners in England

1096 Crusades, attempts to rescue Jerusalem from Moslems (until 1270)

Battle of Hastings

1151 Game of chess arrives in England

1154 House of Plantagenet rules England (until 1399)

1167 Oxford University founded

1170 Murder of Thomas à Becket, Archbishop of Canterbury

Oxford University

1215 Magna Carta, signed by King John

1265 First Parliament

1296 Wars between England and Scotland (until 1328)

King John signs the Magna Carta

1337 Beginning of Hundred Years' War, series of wars between England and France

1125 France: Beginning of troubadour music

1170 France: Chrétien de Troyes, "Lancelot"

1191 Japan: Tea arrives from China

1204 Holland: Founding of Amsterdam

1211 China: Invasion by Genghis Khan

1241 Korea: Movable metal type first used

1271 China: Exploration by Marco Polo

1307 Italy: Dante begins *Divine Comedy*

1325 Italy: Beginning of the Renaissance

Japan: Development of *No* drama

Aztec Empire: Establishment of capital on site of modern Mexico City

1348 Black Death, series of plagues

1375 Earliest part of *Sir Gawain and the Green Knight,* verse romance in English about knights at King Arthur's court

1377? William Langland, *The Vision of Piers the Plowman,* a protest on behalf of the common people

1386 Geoffrey Chaucer, *The Canterbury Tales*

1388 John Wycliff's translation of Bible into English

1399 House of Lancaster rules England (until 1461)

1455 Beginning of thirty-year Wars of the Roses, civil war between House of York and House of Lancaster

1461 House of York rules England (until 1485)

1469 Sir Thomas Malory, *Le Morte d'Arthur*

1476 William Caxton establishes first printing press in England

1485 King Henry VII (of House of Tudor) begins reign

1341 Italy: Petrarch crowned with laurel wreath

1348 Italy: Boccaccio, *Decameron*

1368 China: Beginning of Ming Dynasty

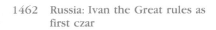

1431 France: Joan of Arc burned at stake

1452 Italy: Birth of Leonardo da Vinci

1453 Germany: The Gutenberg Bible, thought to be the first European book printed from movable type

1462 Russia: Ivan the Great rules as first czar

English Literature: The Medieval Period **51**

Folk Ballads

Although most people in the British Isles were unable to read or write for centuries after the Norman Conquest in 1066, they, like human beings everywhere, told stories to one another. We have inherited their **folk ballads**, the stories they told in verse and usually sang. Transmitted orally from generation to generation, most of the English and Scottish ballads we know date from the fourteenth and fifteenth centuries but were not collected and printed until the eighteenth century.

Love, adventure, courageous feats of daring, and sudden disaster are frequent topics of folk ballads. Folk ballads relate out-of-the-ordinary incidents—ones that might make headlines now, such as a shipwreck or an accidental death. Despite such tragic subjects, ballads rarely contain opinions on what has happened. The narrative usually dramatizes a single incident with little attention to characterization, background, or description. Why do the characters act as they do? How did they get into such a plight? We must read between the lines and supply our own answers as we hear the little dramatic scenes unfold. Indeed, the ballad presents action as sparsely as possible, often through **dialogue**—the speech of the characters involved. We should not, however, think that ballads are simple or shallow. They may be brief and sparse—economic—but they contain sharp psychological portraits and much folk wisdom.

The original authors of ballads are unknown; in fact, a given ballad may exist in several versions, because many different people told and revised the ballad as it traveled from village to village. It is important to remember that most ballads were originally sung. But even when read—preferably aloud—enough remains to place the best of the folk ballads among the most haunting narrative poems in British literature.

■ What haunting and dramatic songs have you recently heard? What events did they narrate?

Medieval gittern, an instrument similar to a guitar.

Sir Patrick Spens

The king sits in Dumferling[1] toune,
    Drinking the blude-reid[2] wine:
"O whar will I get a skilly[3] skipper,
    To sail this new schip of mine?"

5 O up and spak an eldern knicht,[4]
    Sat at the kings richt[5] kne:
"Sir Patrick Spens is the best sailor,
    That ever sailed the sea."

The king has written a braid[6] letter,
10   And sealed it wi' his hand,
And sent it to Sir Patrick Spens,
    Was walking on the strand.[7]

The first line that Sir Patrick red,
    A loud lauch[8] lauched he;
15 The next line that Sir Patrick red,
    The teir blinded his ee.[9]

"O wha[10] is this has don this deid,
    And told the king o' me,
To send us out at this time o' the yeir,
20   To sail upon the sea!

"Mak ready, mak ready, my mirry men all,
    Our guid schip sails the morne."
"Now, ever alake,[11] my master deir,
    I feir a deadlie storme.

25 "I saw the new moone late yestreen,[12]
    Wi' the auld[13] moone in hir arme,
And if we gang to sea, master,
    I feir we'll cum to harme."

O laith, laith[14] wer our guid Scots lords
30   To weet[15] their cork-heild schoone;[16]
Bot lang owre a'[17] the play was playd,
    They wat their hats aboone.[18]

O lang, lang may their ladies sit,
    Wi' their fans into their hand;
35 Before they se Sir Patrick Spens
    Cum sailing to the strand.

And lang, lang may their maidens sit,
    Wi' their gold kems[19] in their hair,
All waiting for their ain[20] deir loves,
40   For thame they'll se na mair.[21]

Haf owre, haf owre to Aberdour,[22]
    'Tis fiftie fadom[23] deip,
And thair lies guid Sir Patrick Spens,
    Wi' the Scots lords at his feit.

---

1. **Dumferling** [dum fur'ling]: a town in Scotland.
2. **blude-reid**: blood red.
3. **skilly**: skillful.
4. **eldern knicht**: elderly knight.
5. **richt**: right.
6. **braid**: broad (this may refer to a long sheet of paper or may mean "commanding").
7. **strand**: seashore.
8. **lauch**: laugh.
9. **ee**: eye.
10. **wha**: who.
11. **alake**: alack.

12. **yestreen**: yesterday evening.
13. **auld**: old; sailors thought that a thin crescent moon meant storms at sea.
14. **laith**: loath; very unwilling.
15. **weet**: wet.
16. **schoone**: shoes.
17. **lang owre a'**: long before all.
18. **aboone**: above.
19. **kems**: combs.
20. **ain**: own.
21. **na mair**: no more.
22. **haf owre to Aberdour**: halfway over to Aberdeen (in Scotland).
23. **fadom**: fathoms. A fathom is six feet.

The Wife of Usher's Well

There lived a wife at Usher's Well,
  And a wealthy wife was she;
She had three stout[1] and stalwart sons,
  And sent them o'er the sea.

5 They hadna' been a week from her,
  A week but barely ane,[2]
When word came to the carlin[3] wife
  That her three sons were gane.[4]

They hadna' been a week from her,
10   A week but barely three,
When word came to the carlin wife
  That her sons she'd never see.

"I wish the wind may never cease,
  Nor fashes in the flood,[5]
15 Till my three sons come hame[6] to me,
  In earthly flesh and blood."

It fell about the Martinmas,[7]
  When nights are lang and mirk,[8]
The carlin wife's three sons came hame,
20   And their hats were o' the birk.[9]

It neither grew in sike[10] nor ditch,
  Nor yet in ony sheugh,[11]
But at the gates o' Paradise
  That birk grew fair eneugh.

25 "Blow up the fire, my maidens,
  Bring water from the well:
For a'[12] my house shall feast this night,
  Since my three sons are well."

And she has made to them a bed,
30   She's made it large and wide,
And she's ta'en her mantle[13] her about,
  Sat down at the bedside.

Up then crew the red, red cock,
  And up and crew the gray.
35 The eldest to the youngest said,
  " 'Tis time we were away."

The cock he hadna' crawed but once,
  And clapped his wings at a',
When the youngest to the eldest said,
40   "Brother, we must awa'.[14]

"The cock doth craw, the day doth daw,[15]
  The channerin'[16] worm doth chide:
Gin[17] we be missed out o' our place,
  A sair pain we maun bide.[18]

45 "Fare ye weel,[19] my mother dear,
  Fareweel to barn and byre.[20]
And fare ye weel, the bonny[21] lass
  That kindles my mother's fire."

---

1. **stout:** brave.
2. **ane:** one.
3. **carlin:** old.
4. **gane:** gone.
5. **fashes . . . flood:** disturbances at sea.
6. **hame:** home.
7. **Martinmas:** November 11.
8. **lang and mirk:** long and dark.
9. **o' the birk:** of the birch tree. It was believed that people who returned from the dead wore plant life on their heads.
10. **sike:** field.
11. **sheugh:** furrow.

12. **a':** all.
13. **ta'en her mantle:** taken her cloak.
14. **must awa':** must go away, leave. Spirits of the dead had to return to their graves at cockcrow.
15. **daw:** dawn.
16. **channerin':** complaining.
17. **Gin:** If.
18. **A sair . . . bide:** A sore pain we must abide; we must endure great pain.
19. **weel:** well.
20. **byre:** cow shed.
21. **bonny:** pretty.

STUDY QUESTIONS

Sir Patrick Spens
Recalling
1. According to stanza 2, what recommendation is made to the king and by whom?
2. How does Sir Patrick Spens react in stanzas 4 and 5 to the letter from his king? After reading the letter, what does he nevertheless tell his men to do?
3. According to lines 23–28, why are Sir Patrick's sailors reluctant to obey the king's order?
4. What are the king's nobles who sail on Sir Patrick's ship worried about, according to lines 29–30? What happens instead in lines 31–32?
5. Where do Sir Patrick and his nobles "lie"?

Interpreting
6. What internal conflict do you suppose Sir Patrick feels in stanzas 4 and 5?
7. What are we led to understand happens to Sir Patrick, his sailors, and the king's nobles on the voyage? Give four specific references in the ballad that support this conclusion.
8. Why is the last line fitting or just?

The Wife of Usher's Well
Recalling
1. What news of her three sons does the old wife receive in stanzas 2 and 3?
2. According to lines 20–24, what kind of hats are the sons wearing when they return to visit?
3. According to stanzas 10 and 11, when do the sons realize they must leave? What will happen to them if they don't go?

Interpreting
4. Based on the "birk" the sons are wearing, what might we surmise about the sons?
5. What might be the "place" referred to in line 43 from which the sons will be missed?
6. Why might the sons have come back to their mother's fireside?

LITERARY FOCUS

The Folk Ballad
Folk ballads are anonymous narrative verses intended to be sung and passed on by oral tradition. The folk ballad is a *popular* literary form; that is, it comes from unlettered people rather than from professional minstrels or scholarly poets. Thus, the ballad tends to express its meaning in simple language (although the centuries-old dialect of many folk ballads may make that language seem complex at first). The narrative style of the typical ballad is straightforward as well, relying heavily on dialogue and moving quickly from scene to scene.

The so-called **ballad stanza** consists of four lines (a quatrain), rhyming *abcb,* with four accented syllables within the first and third lines and three in the second and fourth lines.

a There lived a wife at Usher's Well,

b And a wealthy wife was she;

c She had three stout and stalwart sons

b And sent them o'er the sea.

Some folk ballads make use of **refrains,** repetitions of a line or lines in every stanza without variation. Refrains add emphasis and a note of continuity to the ballads.

Thinking About Folk Ballads
Demonstrate your understanding of the traditional ballad stanza by transcribing and marking the stress of one stanza from "Sir Patrick Spens." Indicate which lines rhyme.

COMPOSITION

Developing a Thesis About Folk Ballads
Develop an idea about the structure of folk ballads. Before you begin to write, review how they begin, how they develop, and how they end. State your thesis about the parts of a folk ballad. Support your idea about each part with examples. You may want to devote one paragraph to each part. *For help with this assignment, refer to Lesson 1 in the Writing About Literature Handbook at the back of this book.*

Writing a Folk Ballad
Try writing two or three stanzas of a folk ballad. Choose an appropriate subject and follow the form of the traditional ballad stanza (see the preceding Literary Focus). Use dialogue, repetition, and archaic (old-fashioned) diction to make your stanzas sound authentic.

Geoffrey Chaucer   1343?–1400

Along with William Shakespeare and John Milton, Geoffrey Chaucer comes to most scholars' minds when they list the three greatest poets of the English language. Chaucer's most important work, *The Canterbury Tales,* vividly demonstrated the literary potential of the English language in the 1300s. It also preserved for all future ages a realistic, detailed, and comprehensive panorama of daily life at that time.

Like Shakespeare the actor and Milton the public servant, Chaucer led an extremely busy life. The son of a wealthy London wine merchant, Chaucer had the good fortune to serve as a page in the royal household while in his early teens. Later he married one of the queen's ladies-in-waiting, was sent as the king's emissary to France and Italy, and held various positions in the home government. Despite these responsibilities, Chaucer somehow found time to produce an astonishing body of prose and poetry. He died while still at work on his poems and was buried in Westminster Abbey in London. Around his burial spot has grown up the famous Poets' Corner.

Chaucer's poetry is generally divided into three periods. The earliest poetry is in the artificial manner of medieval French poets and includes the dream vision *The Romaunt of the Rose.* This French period was followed by an Italian period, inspired by the poet's own journeys to Italy as a royal emissary. Influenced by the vigor of three great Italian writers—Dante, Petrarch, and Boccaccio—Chaucer brought to his own verse a new strength. During this phase he produced one of his two masterpieces, *Troilus and Criseyde,* a long narrative poem based on Boccaccio's retelling of an ancient love story set during the legendary Trojan War. The greatest of Chaucer's achievements—and one of the glories of all literature—was a product of his final, English period: *The Canterbury Tales.* At last Chaucer broke away from French and Italian models and fully realized his own style.

Chaucer's works are written in the Middle English of London in the 1300s. Middle English did not have the prestige of the French language introduced to England by the Normans or of the Latin used by the Church. Chaucer changed all that.

Introducing **The Canterbury Tales**

The Canterbury Tales is a long poem made up of a general introduction ("The Prologue") and a series of stories, told in verse, by a cross section of English men and women. They tell their stories as they travel one April from an inn in a London suburb southeastward for fifty miles to the cathedral city of Canterbury. They are on a pilgrimage, a journey to a sacred place; Canterbury Cathedral is where Archbishop Thomas à Becket had been killed by order of King Henry II in 1170, to the shock of the religious world. The pilgrims' stories are framed by the narrative of the journey. That is, the tales are connected by links that relate what happens among the pilgrims traveling together.

The individual stories are of many different kinds: religious stories, legends, fables, fairy tales, sermons, and courtly romances. Short story writers in the following centuries learned much about their craft from the poet Geoffrey Chaucer.

In "The Prologue," which begins on the following page, the narrator introduces us to the pilgrims who gather at the Tabard Inn at the start of the journey. The pilgrims fall into the three dominant groups that made up medieval society in England: the feudal group, the church group, and the city group. In the excerpt from "The Prologue," we will meet representatives of each group:

The Feudal Group	The Church Group	The City Group
Knight	Nun	Merchant
Squire	Monk	Sergeant at the
Yeoman	Friar	Law (Judge)
Franklin	Cleric	Five Tradesmen
Plowman	Parson	Cook
Miller	Summoner	Skipper
Reeve	Pardoner	Doctor
		Wife of Bath
		Manciple
		Host (Innkeeper)

The famous opening lines of "The Prologue" appear first in the original Middle English (page 58). A modern translation of those lines and of the remainder of "The Prologue" follows. The Middle English contains many words with two dots over the *e*. The dots remind us that we should pronounce every syllable in Middle English. Thus *bathëd* (line 3) has two syllables, not one as in the modern English *bathed,* and the original line of poetry consequently has the ten syllables of iambic pentameter verse.

◼ If Chaucer were writing his tales today, what kinds of people might some of his pilgrims be? Where might their journey take them?

Geoffrey Chaucer

The Prologue to The Canterbury Tales

Translated by Nevill Coghill

Geoffrey Chaucer. Chaucer and the pilgrims who appear on the following pages are details from the Ellesmere Manuscript.

    Whan that Aprill with his shourës sootë
The droghte of March hath percëd to the rootë
And bathëd every veyne in swich licour
Of which vertu engendrëd is the flour,
5 Whan Zephirus eek with his sweetë breeth
Inspirëd hath in every holt and heeth
The tendrë croppës, and the yongë sonnë
Hath in the Ram his half cours y-ronnë,
And smalë fowelës maken melodyë
10 That slepen al the nyght with open eyë,
So priketh hem Nature in hir corages,
Than longen folk to goon on pilgrymages,
And palmeres for to seken straungë strondës,
To fernë halwës kouthe in sondry londës.
15 And specially, from every shirës endë
Of Engelond, to Caunterbury they wendë,
The holy, blisful martir for to sekë
That hem hath holpen whan that they were seekë.

    When in April the sweet showers fall
And pierce the drought of March to the root, and all
The veins are bathed in liquor of such power
As brings about the engendering of the flower,
5 When also Zephyrus[1] with his sweet breath
Exhales an air in every grove and heath
Upon the tender shoots, and the young sun
His half-course in the sign of the *Ram*[2] has run,
And the small fowl are making melody
10 That sleep away the night with open eye
(So nature pricks them and their heart engages)
Then people long to go on pilgrimages
And palmers[3] long to seek the stranger strands[4]
Of far-off saints, hallowed in sundry lands,
15 And specially, from every shire's end
Of England, down to Canterbury they wend
To seek the holy blissful martyr,[5] quick
To give his help to them when they were sick.
    It happened in that season that one day
20 In Southwark,[6] at The Tabard,[7] as I lay
Ready to go on pilgrimage and start
For Canterbury, most devout at heart,

1 **Zephyrus** [zef'ər əs]: the west wind, which brings mild weather.

2 **Ram:** the constellation Aries and first sign of the zodiac. Evidence suggests that the pilgrimage began on April 11, 1387.

3 **palmers:** pilgrims who wore palm leaves as a sign that they had visited the Holy Land.
4 **strands:** shores.

5 **martyr:** Thomas à Becket.

6 **Southwark** [suth'ərk]: area just across the River Thames from London; today, part of Greater London.
7 **The Tabard** [ta'bərd]: an inn in Southwark.

The opening lines of the *Prologue to The Canterbury Tales,* from the Ellesmere Manuscript, an original manuscript of Chaucer's work.

At night there came into that hostelry
Some nine and twenty in a company
25 Of sundry folk happening then to fall
In fellowship, and they were pilgrims all
That toward Canterbury meant to ride.
The rooms and stables of the inn were wide;
They made us easy, all was of the best.
30 And, briefly, when the sun had gone to rest,
I'd spoken to them all upon the trip
And was soon one with them in fellowship,
Pledged to rise early and to take the way
To Canterbury, as you heard me say.
35 But nonetheless, while I have time and space,
Before my story takes a further pace,
It seems a reasonable thing to say
What their condition was, the full array
Of each of them, as it appeared to me,
40 According to profession and degree,
And what apparel they were riding in;
And at a Knight I therefore will begin.
There was a *Knight,* a most distinguished man,
Who from the day on which he first began
45 To ride abroad had followed chivalry,
Truth, honor, generousness, and courtesy.
He had done nobly in his sovereign's war
And ridden into battle, no man more,
As well in Christian as in heathen places,
50 And ever honored for his noble graces.
When we took Alexandria,[8] he was there.
He often sat at table in the chair
Of honor, above all nations, when in Prussia.
In Lithuania he had ridden, and Russia,
55 No Christian man so often, of his rank.
When, in Granada, Algeciras sank
Under assault, he had been there, and in
North Africa, raiding Benamarin;
In Anatolia he had been as well
60 And fought when Ayas and Attalia fell,
For all along the Mediterranean coast
He had embarked with many a noble host.[9]
In fifteen mortal battles he had been
And jousted[10] for our faith at Tramissene
65 Thrice in the lists,[11] and always killed his man.
This same distinguished knight had led the van
Once with the Bey of Balat,[12] doing work
For him against another heathen Turk;

The Knight.

8 **Alexandria:** This and the place names that immediately follow are sites of wide-ranging campaigns and Crusades by medieval Christians against the Moslems.

9 **host:** army.

10 **jousted:** fought in formal combat as part of a knightly tournament.
11 **lists:** the fenced area where jousts were held.
12 **Bey of Balat:** a Turkish ruler.

He was of sovereign value in all eyes.
70 And though so much distinguished, he was wise
And in his bearing modest as a maid.
He never yet a boorish thing had said
In all his life to any, come what might;
He was a true, a perfect gentle-knight.
75   Speaking of his equipment, he possessed
Fine horses, but he was not gaily dressed.
He wore a fustian[13] tunic stained and dark
With smudges where his armor had left mark;
Just home from service, he had joined our ranks
80 To do his pilgrimage and render thanks.

    He had his son with him, a fine young *Squire*,
A lover and cadet, a lad of fire
With locks as curly as if they had been pressed.
He was some twenty years of age, I guessed.
85 In stature he was of a moderate length,
With wonderful agility and strength.
He'd seen some service with the cavalry
In Flanders and Artois and Picardy[14]
And had done valiantly in little space
90 Of time, in hope to win his lady's grace.
He was embroidered like a meadow bright
And full of freshest flowers, red and white.
Singing he was, or fluting all the day;
He was as fresh as is the month of May.
95 Short was his gown, the sleeves were long and wide;
He knew the way to sit a horse and ride.
He could make songs and poems and recite,
Knew how to joust and dance, to draw and write.
He loved so hotly that till dawn grew pale
100 He slept as little as a nightingale.
Courteous he was, lowly and serviceable,
And carved to serve his father at the table.

    There was a *Yeoman*[15] with him at his side,
No other servant; so he chose to ride.
105 This Yeoman wore a coat and hood of green,
And peacock-feathered arrows, bright and keen
And neatly sheathed, hung at his belt the while
—For he could dress his gear in yeoman style,
His arrows never drooped their feathers low—
110 And in his hand he bore a mighty bow.
His head was like a nut, his face was brown.
He knew the whole of woodcraft up and down.
A saucy brace[16] was on his arm to ward
It from the bowstring, and a shield and sword

13 **fustian:** coarse, heavy fabric of cotton and linen.

14 **Flanders . . . Picardy:** historic regions of Belgium, Holland, and northern France.

15 **Yeoman** [yō'mǝn]: nobleman's attendant.

16 **brace:** leather guard worn on the archer's forearm.

115 Hung at one side, and at the other slipped
    A jaunty dirk,[17] spear-sharp and well-equipped.
    A medal of Saint Christopher[18] he wore
    Of shining silver on his breast, and bore
    A hunting horn, well slung and burnished clean,
120 That dangled from a baldrick[19] of bright green.
    He was a proper forester, I guess.

    There also was a *Nun,* a Prioress,[20]
    Her way of smiling very simple and coy.
    Her greatest oath was only "By Saint Loy!"[21]
125 And she was known as Madam Eglantyne.
    And well she sang a service,[22] with a fine
    Intoning through her nose, as was most seemly,
    And she spoke daintily in French, extremely,
    After the school of Stratford-atte-Bowe;[23]
130 French in the Paris style she did not know.
    At meat her manners were well taught withal;
    No morsel from her lips did she let fall,
    Nor dipped her fingers in the sauce too deep;
    But she could carry a morsel up and keep
135 The smallest drop from falling on her breast.
    For courtliness she had a special zest,
    And she would wipe her upper lip so clean
    That not a trace of grease was to be seen
    Upon the cup when she had drunk; to eat,
140 She reached a hand sedately for the meat.
    She certainly was very entertaining,
    Pleasant and friendly in her ways, and straining
    To counterfeit a courtly kind of grace,
    A stately bearing fitting to her place,
145 And to seem dignified in all her dealings.
    As for her sympathies and tender feelings,
    She was so charitably solicitous
    She used to weep if she but saw a mouse
    Caught in a trap, if it were dead or bleeding.
150 And she had little dogs she would be feeding
    With roasted flesh, or milk, or fine white bread.
    And bitterly she wept if one were dead
    Or someone took a stick and made it smart;
    She was all sentiment and tender heart.
155 Her veil was gathered in a seemly way,
    Her nose was elegant, her eyes glass-gray;
    Her mouth was very small, but soft and red,
    Her forehead, certainly, was fair of spread,
    Almost a span[24] across the brows, I own;
160 She was indeed by no means undergrown.
    Her cloak, I noticed, had a graceful charm.

17 **dirk:** small dagger.

18 **Saint Christopher:** patron saint of foresters and travelers.

19 **baldrick:** shoulder belt.

20 **Prioress:** the nun ranking next below the head nun in an abbey.

21 **Saint Loy:** Saint Eligius, who would not swear upon holy relics.

22 **service:** daily prayers.

23 **Stratford-atte-Bowe:** a nunnery not far from London.

The Nun.

24 **span:** nine inches. A broad forehead was a sign of beauty in Chaucer's day.

She wore a coral trinket on her arm,
A set of beads, the gaudies[25] tricked in green,
Whence hung a golden brooch of brightest sheen
165 On which there first was graven a crowned *A*,
And lower, *Amor vincit omnia.*[26]
    Another *Nun,* the secretary at her cell,
Was riding with her, and three *Priests* as well.

    A *Monk* there was, one of the finest sort
170 Who rode the country; hunting was his sport.
A manly man, to be an Abbot[27] able;
Many a dainty horse he had in stable.
His bridle, when he rode, a man might hear
Jingling in a whistling wind as clear,
175 Aye, and as loud as does the chapel bell
Where my lord Monk was Prior of the cell.[28]
The Rule of good Saint Benet or Saint Maur[29]
As old and strict he tended to ignore;
He let go by the things of yesterday
180 And took the modern world's more spacious way.
He did not rate that text at a plucked hen
Which says that hunters are not holy men
And that a monk uncloistered is a mere
Fish out of water, flapping on the pier,
185 That is to say a monk out of his cloister.
That was a text he held not worth an oyster;
And I agreed and said his views were sound;
Was he to study till his head went round
Poring over books in cloisters? Must he toil
190 As Austin[30] bade and till the very soil?
Was he to leave the world upon the shelf?
Let Austin have his labor to himself.
    This Monk was therefore a good man to horse;
Greyhounds he had, as swift as birds, to course.[31]
195 Hunting a hare or riding at a fence
Was all his fun, he spared for no expense.
I saw his sleeves were garnished at the hand
With fine gray fur, the finest in the land,
And on his hood, to fasten it at his chin
200 He had a wrought-gold cunningly fashioned pin;
Into a lover's knot it seemed to pass.
His head was bald and shone like looking-glass;
So did his face, as if it had been greased.
He was a fat and personable priest;
205 His prominent eyeballs never seemed to settle.
They glittered like the flames beneath a kettle;
Supple his boots, his horse in fine condition.

25 **gaudies:** large beads used in counting prayers.

26 **Amor vincit omnia** [ä môr' wink'it om'nē ä]: Latin for "Love conquers all."

27 **Abbot:** the head of a monastery.

28 **Prior of the cell:** head of a subordinate monastery.
29 **Saint Benet or Saint Maur:** French versions of Saint Benedict, who established the rules of European monasticism, and Saint Maurice, one of his followers. Monastic life is governed by strict rules requiring poverty, chastity, and obedience.

30 **Austin:** English version of Saint Augustine (A.D. 354–430), famous Church scholar who criticized lazy clerics (not the Saint Augustine [?–A.D. 604?] who founded Canterbury Cathedral).
31 **to course:** for hunting.

He was a prelate[32] fit for exhibition,
He was not pale like a tormented soul.
210 He liked a fat swan best, and roasted whole.
His palfrey[33] was as brown as is a berry.

There was a *Friar,* a wanton[34] one and merry,
A Limiter,[35] a very festive fellow.
In all Four Orders[36] there was none so mellow,
215 So glib with gallant phrase and well-turned speech.
He'd fixed up many a marriage, giving each
Of his young women what he could afford her.
He was a noble pillar to his Order.
Highly beloved and intimate was he
220 With County folk[37] within his boundary,
And city dames of honor and possessions;
For he was qualified to hear confessions,
Or so he said, with more than priestly scope;
He had a special licence from the Pope.
225 Sweetly he heard his penitents at shrift[38]
With pleasant absolution,[39] for a gift.
He was an easy man in penance-giving
Where he could hope to make a decent living;
It's a sure sign whenever gifts are given
230 To a poor Order that a man's well shriven,[40]
And should he give enough he knew in verity
The penitent repented in sincerity.
For many a fellow is so hard of heart
He cannot weep, for all his inward smart.
235 Therefore instead of weeping and of prayer
One should give silver for a poor Friar's care.
He kept his tippet[41] stuffed with pins for curls,
And pocketknives, to give to pretty girls.
And certainly his voice was gay and sturdy,
240 For he sang well and played the hurdy-gurdy.[42]
At sing-songs he was champion of the hour.
His neck was whiter than a lily flower
But strong enough to butt a bruiser down.
He knew the taverns well in every town
245 And every innkeeper and barmaid too
Better than lepers, beggars, and that crew,
For in so eminent a man as he
It was not fitting with the dignity
Of his position, dealing with a scum
250 Of wretched lepers; nothing good can come
Of commerce with such slum-and-gutter dwellers,
But only with the rich and victual sellers.
But anywhere a profit might accrue
Courteous he was and lowly of service too.

32 **prelate:** high-ranking clergy-man.

33 **palfrey:** saddle horse.

34 **wanton:** playful.

35 **Limiter:** begging friar limited to a certain district in which to beg.
36 **Four Orders:** referring to the four orders of begging friars: Dominicans, Franciscans, Carmelites, and Augustinians.

37 **County folk:** the wealthy and socially prominent rural landowners.

38 **shrift:** confession.

39 **absolution:** formal forgiveness.

40 **well shriven:** completely forgiven, through confession, of his sins.

41 **tippet:** hood.

42 **hurdy-gurdy:** stringed instrument played by turning a hand crank.

The Friar.

255 Natural gifts like his were hard to match.
He was the finest beggar of his batch,
And, for his begging district, paid a rent;
His brethren did no poaching where he went.
For though a widow mightn't have a shoe,
260 So pleasant was his holy how-d'ye-do
He got his farthing[43] from her just the same
Before he left, and so his income came
To more than he laid out. And how he romped,
Just like a puppy! He was ever prompt
265 To arbitrate disputes on settling days[44]
(For a small fee) in many helpful ways,
Not then appearing as your cloistered scholar
With threadbare habit hardly worth a dollar,
But much more like a Doctor or a Pope.
270 Of double-worsted was the semi-cope[45]
Upon his shoulders, and the swelling fold
About him, like a bell about its mold
When it is casting, rounded out his dress.
He lisped a little out of wantonness
275 To make his English sweet upon his tongue.
When he had played his harp, or having sung,
His eyes would twinkle in his head as bright
As any star upon a frosty night.
This worthy's name was Hubert, it appeared.
280 There was a *Merchant* with a forking beard
And motley dress; high on his horse he sat,
Upon his head a Flemish[46] beaver hat
And on his feet daintily buckled boots.
He told of his opinions and pursuits
285 In solemn tones, he harped on his increase
Of capital; there should be sea police
(He thought) upon the Harwich–Holland[47] ranges;
He was expert at dabbling in exchanges.
This estimable Merchant so had set
290 His wits to work, none knew he was in debt,
He was so stately in administration,
In loans and bargains and negotiation.
He was an excellent fellow all the same;
To tell the truth I do not know his name.

295 An *Oxford Cleric,* still a student though,
One who had taken logic long ago,
Was there; his horse was thinner than a rake,
And he was not too fat, I undertake,
But had a hollow look, a sober stare;
300 The thread upon his overcoat was bare.
He had found no preferment[48] in the church

43 **farthing:** British coin used in former times.

44 **settling days:** days on which disputes could be settled out of court.

45 **semi-cope:** cape. A cape using doubled worsted, a woolen fabric, would be rather luxurious.

46 **Flemish:** from Flanders, a region of northwestern Europe.

47 **Harwich–Holland ranges:** North Sea shipping lanes between Harwich [har'ij], an English port, and Holland.

48 **preferment:** promotion; sponsorship.

And he was too unworldly to make search
For secular employment. By his bed
He preferred having twenty books in red
305 And black, of Aristotle's[49] philosophy,
Than costly clothes, fiddle or psaltery.[50]
Though a philosopher, as I have told,
He had not found the stone for making gold.[51]
Whatever money from his friends he took
310 He spent on learning or another book
And prayed for them most earnestly, returning
Thanks to them thus for paying for his learning.
His only care was study, and indeed
He never spoke a word more than was need,
315 Formal at that, respectful in the extreme,
Short, to the point, and lofty in his theme.
A tone of moral virtue filled his speech
And gladly would he learn, and gladly teach.

A *Sergeant at the Law*[52] who paid his calls,
320 Wary and wise, for clients at Saint Paul's[53]
There also was, of noted excellence.
Discreet he was, a man to reverence,
Or so he seemed, his sayings were so wise.
He often had been Justice of Assize[54]
325 By letters patent,[55] and in full commission.
His fame and learning and his high position
Had won him many a robe and many a fee.
There was no such conveyancer[56] as he;
All was fee-simple[57] to his strong digestion,
330 Not one conveyance could be called in question.
Though there was nowhere one so busy as he,
He was less busy than he seemed to be.
He knew of every judgment, case, and crime
Ever recorded since King William's[58] time.
335 He could dictate defenses or draft deeds;
No one could pinch a comma from his screeds[59]
And he knew every statute off by rote.
He wore a homely particolored coat,
Girt with a silken belt of pin-stripe stuff;
340 Of his appearance I have said enough.

There was a *Franklin*[60] with him, it appeared;
White as a daisy petal was his beard.
A sanguine man, high-colored and benign,
He loved a morning sop[61] of cake in wine.
345 He lived for pleasure and had always done,
For he was Epicurus'[62] very son,
In whose opinion sensual delight

49 **Aristotle's:** referring to the Greek philosopher (384–322 B.C.).
50 **psaltery** [sôl'tə rē]: stringed instrument played by plucking.
51 **stone . . . gold:** Medieval alchemists believed that there existed a "philosopher's stone" capable of turning ordinary metals into gold.

52 **Sergeant at the Law:** lawyer appointed by the king to serve as a judge.
53 **Saint Paul's:** London cathedral outside which lawyers often met clients when the courts were closed.

54 **Assize:** traveling law court.

55 **letters patent:** royal documents commissioning Assize judges.

56 **conveyancer:** The Sergeant specializes in deeds (conveyances) and property disputes.
57 **fee-simple:** property owned outright.

58 **King William's:** referring to William the Conqueror, king from 1066 to 1087.
59 **screeds:** long, tiresome writing.

60 **Franklin:** wealthy landowner.

61 **sop:** piece.
62 **Epicurus':** referring to the Greek philosopher (341?–270 B.C.) who held that pleasure should be one's life goal.

Was the one true felicity in sight.
As noted as Saint Julian[63] was for bounty
350 He made his household free to all the County.
His bread, his ale were finest of the fine
And no one had a better stock of wine.
His house was never short of bake-meat pies,
Of fish and flesh, and these in such supplies
355 It positively snowed with meat and drink
And all the dainties that a man could think.
According to the seasons of the year
Changes of dish were ordered to appear.
He kept fat partridges in coops, beyond,
360 Many a bream and pike[64] were in his pond.
Woe to the cook unless the sauce was hot
And sharp, or if he wasn't on the spot!
And in his hall a table stood arrayed
And ready all day long, with places laid.
365 As Justice at the Sessions none stood higher;[65]
He often had been Member for the Shire.[66]
A dagger and a little purse of silk
Hung at his girdle, white as morning milk.
As Sheriff[67] he checked audit, every entry.
370 He was a model among landed gentry.

A *Haberdasher,* a *Dyer,* a *Carpenter,*
A *Weaver,* and a *Carpet-maker* were
Among our ranks, all in the livery
Of one impressive guild-fraternity.[68]
375 They were so trim and fresh their gear would pass
For new. Their knives were not tricked out with brass
But wrought with purest silver, which avouches
A like display on girdles and on pouches.
Each seemed a worthy burgess,[69] fit to grace
380 A guildhall with a seat upon the dais.
Their wisdom would have justified a plan
To make each one of them an alderman;[70]
They had the capital and revenue,
Besides their wives declared it was their due.
385 And if they did not think so, then they ought;
To be called "Madam" is a glorious thought,
And so is going to church and being seen
Having your mantle[71] carried, like a queen.

They had a *Cook* with them who stood alone
390 For boiling chicken with a marrowbone,
Sharp flavoring-powder and a spice for savor.
He could distinguish London ale by flavor,
And he could roast and seethe and broil and fry,

63 **Saint Julian:** patron saint of hospitality.

64 **bream and pike:** kinds of fishes.

65 **Justice . . . higher:** When Justices of the Peace heard a case, he was the presiding judge.
66 **Member . . . Shire:** representative to Parliament from his county.

67 **Sheriff:** royal tax collector.

68 **livery . . . guild-fraternity:** The five tradesmen all belong to the same fraternal organization and wear its livery, or identifying uniform.

69 **burgess:** citizen or freeman of a British borough; townsman.

70 **alderman:** high-ranking member of the town council.

71 **mantle:** cloak; cape.

Make good thick soup and bake a tasty pie.
395 But what a pity—so it seemed to me,
That he should have an ulcer on his knee.
As for blancmange,[72] he made it with the best.

There was a *Skipper* hailing from far west;
He came from Dartmouth, so I understood.
400 He rode a farmer's horse as best he could,
In a woolen gown that reached his knee.
A dagger on a lanyard[73] falling free
Hung from his neck under his arm and down.
The summer heat had tanned his color brown,
405 And certainly he was an excellent fellow.
Many a draft of vintage, red and yellow,
He'd drawn at Bordeaux,[74] while the trader snored.
The nicer rules of conscience he ignored.
If, when he fought, the enemy vessel sank,
410 He sent his prisoners home; they walked the plank.
As for his skill in reckoning his tides,
Currents and many another risk besides,
Moons, harbors, pilots, he had such dispatch
That none from Hull to Carthage[75] was his match.
415 Hardy he was, prudent in undertaking;
His beard in many a tempest had its shaking,
And he knew all the havens as they were
From Gotland to the Cape of Finisterre,
And every creek in Brittany and Spain;
420 The barge he owned was called the *Maudelayne*.

A *Doctor* too emerged as we proceeded;
No one alive could talk as well as he did
On points of medicine and of surgery,
For, being grounded in astronomy,[76]
425 He watched his patient closely for the hours
When, by his horoscope, he knew the powers
Of favorable planets, then ascendant,
Worked on the images for his dependant.
The cause of every malady you'd got
430 He knew, and whether dry, cold, moist or hot;[77]
He knew their seat, their humor and condition.
He was a perfect practicing physician.
These causes being known for what they were,
He gave the man his medicine then and there.
435 All his apothecaries[78] in a tribe
Were ready with the drugs he would prescribe
And each made money from the other's guile;
They had been friendly for a goodish while.

72 blancmange: here, a kind of chicken stew.

73 lanyard: cord worn around the neck and used for carrying small objects.

74 vintage . . . Bordeaux: Bordeaux [bôr dō'], France, was famous for its red and white (here, "yellow") wine.

75 Hull to Carthage: These and the place names that immediately follow indicate how widely the Skipper has traveled.

76 astronomy: in Chaucer's day, astrology. The planets' positions supposedly determined the best time to treat a patient.

77 dry, cold, moist, or hot: In Chaucer's day people believed that the body was composed of four elements: earth (said to be dry and cold), water (cold and moist), air (hot and moist), and fire (hot and dry). Excess of one element could lead to illness; it also affected one's personality, or "humor" (line 431).
78 apothecaries: druggists.

He was well-versed in Aesculapius[79] too
440 And what Hippocrates and Rufus knew
And Dioscorides, now dead and gone,
Galen and Rhazes, Hali, Serapion,
Averroes, Avicenna, Constantine,
Scotch Bernard, John of Gaddesden, Gilbertine.
445 In his own diet he observed some measure;
There were no superfluities for pleasure,
Only digestives, nutritives, and such.
He did not read the Bible very much.
In blood-red garments, slashed with bluish gray
450 And lined with taffeta, he rode his way;
Yet he was rather close as to expenses
And kept the gold he won in pestilences.[80]
Gold stimulates the heart, or so we're told.
He therefore had a special love of gold.

455　A worthy *woman* from beside *Bath*[81] city
Was with us, somewhat deaf, which was a pity.
In making cloth she showed so great a bent
She bettered those of Ypres and of Ghent.[82]
In all the parish not a dame dared stir
460 Toward the altar steps in front of her,
And if indeed they did, so wrath was she
As to be quite put out of charity.
Her kerchiefs were of finely woven ground;[83]
I dared have sworn they weighed a good ten pound,
465 The ones she wore on Sunday, on her head.
Her hose were of the finest scarlet red
And gartered tight; her shoes were soft and new.
Bold was her face, handsome, and red in hue.
A worthy woman all her life, what's more
470 She'd had five husbands, all at the church door,
Apart from other company in youth;
No need just now to speak of that, forsooth.
And she had thrice been to Jerusalem,[84]
Seen many strange rivers and passed over them;
475 She'd been to Rome and also to Boulogne,
Saint James of Compostella and Cologne,
And she was skilled in wandering by the way.
She had gap-teeth, set widely, truth to say.
Easily on an ambling horse she sat
480 Well wimpled[85] up, and on her head a hat
As broad as is a buckler[86] or a shield;
She had a flowing mantle that concealed
Large hips, her heels spurred sharply under that.
In company she liked to laugh and chat

79 **Aesculapius:** This and the names that immediately follow identify medical experts from ancient times to Chaucer's day.

80 **pestilences:** plagues.

81 **Bath:** city in southwestern England.

82 **Ypres . . . Ghent** [ē′pr(ə); gent]: Flemish cities known for weaving and wool making.

83 **ground:** a composite fabric.

84 **Jerusalem:** This and the place names immediately following were famous pilgrimage sites during the Middle Ages.

85 **wimpled:** wearing a cloth covering the head, neck, and chin.
86 **buckler:** small round shield.

Geoffrey Chaucer **69**

Canterbury pilgrims as depicted in a fourteenth-century illuminated manuscript.

485 And knew the remedies for love's mischances,
An art in which she knew the oldest dances.

A holy-minded man of good renown
There was, and poor, the *Parson* to a town,
Yet he was rich in holy thought and work.
490 He also was a learned man, a clerk,
Who truly knew Christ's gospel and would preach it
Devoutly to parishioners, and teach it.
Benign and wonderfully diligent,
And patient when adversity was sent
495 (For so he proved in much adversity)
He hated cursing to extort a fee,
Nay rather he preferred beyond a doubt
Giving to poor parishioners round about
Both from church offerings and his property;
500 He could in little find sufficiency.[87]
Wide was his parish, with houses far asunder,
Yet he neglected not in rain or thunder,
In sickness or in grief, to pay a call
On the remotest, whether great or small,
505 Upon his feet, and in his hand a stave.
This noble example to his sheep he gave
That first he wrought, and afterward he taught;
And it was from the gospel he had caught
Those words, and he would add this figure too,
510 That if gold rust, what then will iron do?
For if a priest be foul in whom we trust
No wonder that a common man should rust; . . .
The true example that a priest should give
Is one of cleanness, how the sheep should live.

87 **He . . . sufficiency:** He required little to satisfy his own needs.

515 He did not set his benefice to hire[88]
And leave his sheep encumbered in the mire
Or run to London to earn easy bread
By singing masses for the wealthy dead,
Or find some Brotherhood and get enrolled.
520 He stayed at home and watched over his fold
So that no wolf should make the sheep miscarry.
He was a shepherd and no mercenary.
Holy and virtuous he was, but then
Never contemptuous of sinful men,
525 Never disdainful, never too proud or fine,
But was discreet in teaching and benign.
His business was to show a fair behavior
And draw men thus to Heaven and their Savior,
Unless indeed a man were obstinate;
530 And such, whether of high or low estate,
He put to sharp rebuke, to say the least.
I think there never was a better priest.
He sought no pomp or glory in his dealings,
No scrupulosity[89] had spiced his feelings.
535 Christ and His twelve apostles and their lore
He taught, but followed it himself before.

There was a *Plowman* with him there, his brother;
Many a load of dung one time or other
He must have carted through the morning dew.
540 He was an honest worker, good and true,
Living in peace and perfect charity,
And, as the gospel bade him, so did he,
Loving God best with all his heart and mind
And then his neighbor as himself, repined
545 At no misfortune, slacked for no content,
For steadily about his work he went
To thrash his corn, to dig or to manure
Or make a ditch; and he would help the poor
For love of Christ and never take a penny

550 If he could help it, and, as prompt as any,
He paid his tithes[90] in full when they were due
On what he owned, and on his earnings too.
He wore a tabard[91] smock and rode a mare.

There was a *Reeve,*[92] also a *Miller,* there,
555 A College *Manciple* from the Inns of Court,[93]
A papal *Pardoner*[94] and, in close consort,[95]
A Church-Court *Summoner,*[96] riding at a trot,
And finally myself—that was the lot.

The Parson.

88 **set . . . hire:** pay someone else to perform his clerical duties.

89 **scrupulosity:** here, overly careful attention to social niceties.

90 **tithes** [tīthz]: payments made to the Church and consisting of one-tenth of a person's income.
91 **tabard smock:** loose jacket of heavy fabric.

92 **Reeve:** manager of a landowner's estate.
93 **Manciple . . . Court:** administrator in charge of providing food for the lawyers who lived and trained at London's Inns of Court.
94 **Pardoner:** official authorized to sell people indulgences, or Church pardons, for their sins.
95 **consort:** accompaniment.
96 **Summoner:** layman charged with summoning sinners before a Church court.

The *Miller* was a chap of sixteen stone,[97]
560 A great stout fellow big in brawn and bone.
He did well out of them, for he could go
And win the ram at any wrestling show.
Broad, knotty, and short-shouldered, he would boast
He could heave any door off hinge and post,
565 Or take a run and break it with his head.
His beard, like any sow or fox, was red
And broad as well, as though it were a spade;
And, at its very tip, his nose displayed
A wart on which there stood a tuft of hair
570 Red as the bristles in an old sow's ear.
His nostrils were as black as they were wide.
He had a sword and buckler at his side,
His mighty mouth was like a furnace door.
A wrangler and buffoon, he had a store
575 Of tavern stories, filthy in the main.
His was a master-hand at stealing grain.
He felt it with his thumb and and thus he knew
Its quality and took three times his due—
A thumb of gold, by God, to gauge an oat!
580 He wore a hood of blue and a white coat.
He liked to play his bagpipes up and down
And that was how he brought us out of town.

     The *Manciple* came from the Inner Temple;[98]
All caterers might follow his example
585 In buying victuals; he was never rash
Whether he bought on credit or paid cash.
He used to watch the market most precisely
And got in first, and so he did quite nicely.
Now isn't it a marvel of God's grace
590 That an illiterate fellow can outpace
The wisdom of a heap of learned men?
His masters—he had more than thirty then—
All versed in the abstrusest legal knowledge,
Could have produced a dozen from their College
595 Fit to be stewards in land and rents and game
To any Peer in[99] England you could name,
And show him how to live on what he had
Debt-free (unless of course the Peer were mad)
Or be as frugal as he might desire,
600 And make them fit to help about the Shire
In any legal case there was to try;
And yet this Manciple could wipe their eye.[100]

     The *Reeve* was old and choleric and thin;

The Miller.

97 **sixteen stone:** 224 pounds. A stone is a British unit of weight equal to 14 pounds.

98 **Inner Temple:** one of the four Inns of Court.

99 **stewards . . . to any Peer:** estate managers for any nobleman.

100 **wipe their eye:** steal their thunder; knock the conceit out of them.

His beard was shaven closely to the skin,
605 His shorn hair came abruptly to a stop
Above his ears, and he was docked on top
Just like a priest in front; his legs were lean,
Like sticks they were, no calf was to be seen.
He kept his bins and garners[101] very trim;
610 No auditor could gain a point on him.
And he could judge by watching drought and rain
The yield he might expect from seed and grain.
His master's sheep, his animals and hens,
Pigs, horses, dairies, stores, and cattle pens
615 Were wholly trusted to his government.
He had been under contract to present
The accounts, right from his master's earliest years.
No one had ever caught him in arrears.
No bailiff, serf, or herdsman dared to kick,
620 He knew their dodges, knew their every trick;
Feared like the plague he was, by those beneath.
He had a lovely dwelling on a heath,
Shadowed in green by trees above the sward.[102]
A better hand at bargains than his lord,
625 He had grown rich and had a store of treasure
Well tucked away, yet out it came to pleasure
His lord with subtle loans or gifts of goods,
To earn his thanks and even coats and hoods.
When young he'd learned a useful trade and still
630 He was a carpenter of first-rate skill.
The stallion-cob he rode at a slow trot
Was dapple-gray and bore the name of Scot.
He wore an overcoat of bluish shade
And rather long; he had a rusty blade
635 Slung at his side. He came, as I heard tell,
From Norfolk, near a place called Baldeswell.
His coat was tucked under his belt and splayed.
He rode the hindmost of our cavalcade.

There was a *Summoner* with us at that Inn,
640 His face on fire, like a cherubin,[103]
For he had carbuncles.[104] His eyes were narrow,
He was as hot and lecherous as a sparrow.
Black scabby brows he had, and a thin beard.
Children were afraid when he appeared.
645 No quicksilver, lead ointment, tartar creams,
No brimstone, no boracic, so it seems,
Could make a salve that had the power to bite,
Clean up or cure his whelks[105] of knobby white
Or purge the pimples sitting on his cheeks.

101 **garners:** buildings for storing grain.

102 **sward:** grassland; lawn.

103 **cherubin:** one of the angels who, in medieval art, usually had flame-colored faces.
104 **carbuncles:** large pimples.

105 **whelks:** pustules.

650 Garlic he loved, and onions too, and leeks,
    And drinking strong red wine till all was hazy.
    Then he would shout and jabber as if crazy,
    And wouldn't speak a word except in Latin
    When he was drunk, such tags as he was pat in;
655 He only had a few, say two or three,
    That he had mugged up[106] out of some decree;
    No wonder, for he heard them every day.
    And, as you know, a man can teach a jay
    To call out "Walter" better than the Pope.
660 But had you tried to test his wits and grope
    For more, you'd have found nothing in the bag.
    Then *"Questio quid juris"*[107] was his tag.
    He was a noble varlet[108] and a kind one,
    You'd meet none better if you went to find one. . . .
665 He wore a garland set upon his head
    Large as the holly bush upon a stake[109]
    Outside an alehouse, and he had a cake,
    A round one, which it was his joke to wield
    As if it were intended for a shield.

670   He and a gentle *Pardoner* rode together,
    A bird from Charing Cross[110] of the same feather,
    Just back from visiting the Court of Rome.
    He loudly sang *"Come hither, love, come home!"*
    The Summoner sang deep seconds to this song,
675 No trumpet ever sounded half so strong.
    This Pardoner had hair as yellow as wax,
    Hanging down smoothly like a hank of flax.
    In driblets fell his locks behind his head
    Down to his shoulders which they overspread;
680 Thinly they fell, like rattails, one by one.
    He wore no hood upon his head, for fun;
    The hood inside his wallet[111] had been stowed,
    He aimed at riding in the latest mode;
    But for a little cap his head was bare
685 And he had bulging eyeballs, like a hare.
    He'd sewed a holy relic on his cap;
    His wallet lay before him on his lap,
    Brimful of pardons come from Rome, all hot.
    He had the same small voice a goat has got.
690 His chin no beard had harbored, nor would harbor,
    Smoother than ever chin was left by barber. . . .
    There was no pardoner of equal grace,
    For in his trunk he had a pillowcase
    Which he asserted was Our Lady's veil.
695 He said he had a gobbet[112] of the sail

106 **mugged up:** memorized.

107 *Questio quid juris:* Latin for "The question is, what part of the law applies?"
108 **varlet:** rascal.

109 **holly bush . . . stake:** A holly wreath on a pole commonly signaled a tavern.

110 **Charing Cross:** a district of London.

111 **wallet:** pack; knapsack.

112 **gobbet:** piece.

Saint Peter had the time when he made bold
To walk the waves, till Jesu Christ took hold.[113]
He had a cross of metal set with stones
And, in a glass, a rubble of pigs' bones.
700 And with these relics, any time he found
Some poor up-country parson to astound,
In one short day, in money down, he drew
More than the parson in a month or two,
And by his flatteries and prevarication
705 Made monkeys of the priest and congregation.
But still to do him justice first and last
In church he was a noble ecclesiast.
How well he read a lesson or told a story!
But best of all he sang an Offertory,[114]
710 For well he knew that when that song was sung
He'd have to preach and tune his honey-tongue
And (well he could) win silver from the crowd.
That's why he sang so merrily and loud.

Now I have told you shortly, in a clause,
715 The rank, the array, the number and the cause
Of our assembly in this company
In Southwark, at that high-class hostelry
Known as the Tabard, close beside the Bell.[115]
And now the time has come for me to tell
720 How we behaved that evening; I'll begin
After we had alighted at the inn,
Then I'll report our journey, stage by stage,
All the remainder of our pilgrimage.
But first I beg of you, in courtesy,
725 Not to condemn me as unmannerly
If I speak plainly and with no concealings
And give account of all their words and dealings,
Using their very phrases as they fell.
For certainly, as you all know so well,
730 He who repeats a tale after a man
Is bound to say, as nearly as he can,
Each single word, if he remembers it,
However rudely spoken or unfit,
Or else the tale he tells will be untrue,
735 The things pretended and the phrases new.
He may not flinch although it were his brother,
He may as well say one word as another.
And Christ Himself spoke broad[116] in Holy Writ,
Yet there is no scurrility[117] in it,
740 And Plato[118] says, for those with power to read,
"The word should be as cousin to the deed."

113 **Saint Peter . . . hold:** In the Bible (Matthew 14:29–31), Jesus extended a helping hand to Peter when Peter walked on the water and became afraid.

114 **Offertory:** song accompanying the collection of the offering in church.

115 **the Bell:** another inn.

116 **broad:** bluntly; plainly.

117 **scurrility:** coarseness; indecency.

118 **Plato:** Greek philosopher (427?–347? B.C.).

Geoffrey Chaucer **75**

Further I beg you to forgive it me
If I neglect the order and degree
And what is due to rank in what I've planned.
745 I'm short of wit as you will understand.
    Our *Host* gave us great welcome; everyone
Was given a place and supper was begun.
He served the finest victuals you could think,
The wine was strong and we were glad to drink.
750 A very striking man our Host withal,
And fit to be a marshal in a hall.
His eyes were bright, his girth a little wide;
There is no finer burgess in Cheapside.[119]
Bold in his speech, yet wise and full of tact,
755 There was no manly attribute he lacked,
What's more he was a merry-hearted man.
After our meal he jokingly began
To talk of sport, and, among other things
After we'd settled up our reckonings,
760 He said as follows: "Truly, gentlemen,
You're very welcome and I can't think when
—Upon my word I'm telling you no lie—
I've seen a gathering here that looked so spry,
No, not this year, as in this tavern now.
765 I'd think you up some fun if I knew how.
    And, as it happens, a thought has just occurred
To please you, costing nothing, on my word.
You're off to Canterbury—well, God speed!
Blessed Saint Thomas[120] answer to your need!
770 And I don't doubt, before the journey's done
You mean to while the time in tales and fun.
Indeed, there's little pleasure for your bones
Riding along and all as dumb as stones.
So let me then propose for your enjoyment,
775 Just as I said, a suitable employment.
And if my notion suits and you agree
And promise to submit yourselves to me
Playing your parts exactly as I say
Tomorrow as you ride along the way,
780 Then by my father's soul (and he is dead)
If you don't like it you can have my head!
Hold up your hands, and not another word."
    Well, our opinion was not long deferred,
It seemed not worth a serious debate;
785 We all agreed to it at any rate
And bade him issue what commands he would.
"My lords," he said, "now listen for your good,
And please don't treat my notion with disdain.

119 **Cheapside:** area of London that, in Chaucer's day, was the main business district.

120 **Saint Thomas:** here, Saint Thomas à Becket.

This is the point. I'll make it short and plain.
790 Each one of you shall help to make things slip
By telling two stories on the outward trip
To Canterbury, that's what I intend,
And, on the homeward way to journey's end
Another two, tales from the days of old;
795 And then the man whose story is best told,
That is to say who gives the fullest measure
Of good morality and general pleasure,
He shall be given a supper, paid by all,
Here in this tavern, in this very hall,
800 When we come back again from Canterbury.
And in the hope to keep you bright and merry
I'll go along with you myself and ride
All at my own expense and serve as guide.
I'll be the judge, and those who won't obey
805 Shall pay for what we spend upon the way.
Now if you all agree to what you've heard
Tell me at once without another word,
And I will make arrangements early for it."
    Of course we all agreed, in fact we swore it
810 Delightedly, and made entreaty too
That he should act as he proposed to do,
Become our Governor in short, and be
Judge of our tales and general referee,
And set the supper at a certain price.
815 We promised to be ruled by his advice
Come high, come low; unanimously thus
We set him up in judgment over us.
More wine was fetched, the business being done;
We drank it off and up went everyone
820 To bed without a moment of delay.
    Early next morning at the spring of day
Up rose our Host and roused us like a cock,
Gathering us together in a flock,
And off we rode at slightly faster pace
825 Than walking to Saint Thomas' watering place;[121]
And there our Host drew up, began to ease
His horse, and said, "Now, listen if you please,
My lords! Remember what you promised me.
If evensong and matins will agree[122]
830 Let's see who shall be first to tell a tale.
And as I hope to drink good wine and ale
I'll be your judge. The rebel who disobeys,
However much the journey costs, he pays.
Now draw for cut and then we can depart;
835 The man who draws the shortest cut shall start."

121 **Saint Thomas' watering place:** a brook two miles from London.

122 **If evensong . . . agree:** If what you said last night is what you mean this morning. Matins are morning songs.

STUDY QUESTIONS

Recalling

1. Where are the pilgrims gathered, and for what purpose? What time of year is it?
2. What code of behavior does the Knight (lines 43–80) follow? Who are the other two characters in his party?
3. Of the Nun, the Monk, and the Friar (lines 122–279), who takes money from poor widows? Who hunts instead of studying? Who is kind to animals?
4. Of the Merchant, the Cleric, the Sergeant at the Law, and the Franklin (lines 280–370), who is most obsessed with food? With books? Which two serve as judges? Which one is secretly in debt?
5. What rules does the Skipper (lines 398–420) ignore? What does the Doctor (lines 421–454) not often read? In what "art" does the Wife of Bath (lines 455–486) know "the oldest dances"?
6. What does the Parson (lines 487–536) prefer to extorting fees from parishioners? What does his brother the Plowman (lines 537–553) do "for love of Christ"?
7. Of the Miller, the Manciple, and the Reeve (lines 559–638), which two are thrifty shoppers? Which one earns money by overcharging?
8. Explain the professional duties of the Summoner and the Pardoner (lines 639–713). For what reason does the Pardoner "tune his honey-tongue"?
9. What contest does the Host propose over dinner? How will the winner be determined? What will the prize be?

Interpreting

10. What does the narrator think of the Knight, the Parson, and the Plowman? What do the three have in common?
11. What is the narrator's attitude toward the Nun? Toward the Monk? In addition to their high rank in the clergy, what do these two have in common? By contrasting them to the low-ranking Parson and Cleric, what generalization can you make about the clergy in Chaucer's day?
12. What do the Friar and the Pardoner have in common? Why is it significant that the Summoner and the Pardoner work together?
13. Based on the portraits of the city dwellers, what qualities seem to have been needed for business success in Chaucer's day? In what way is the basis of the Manciple's financial success different from that of the Miller and the Skipper?
14. Based on the Host's proposal, what seems to be Chaucer's idea of good literature? Does "The Prologue" fit that definition? Why or why not?

Extending

15. Describe what might be the modern-day equivalent of the Merchant, the Manciple, and the Cleric.

VIEWPOINT

In his "Preface to the *Fables*," seventeenth-century writer John Dryden calls Chaucer "the father of English poetry" and continues:

He is a perpetual fountain of good sense; learned in all sciences; and, therefore, speaks properly on all subjects. As he knew what to say, so he knows also when to leave off, a continence which is practiced by few writers.

■ Identify three examples of Chaucer's "good sense" and three passages where he shows knowledge of geography or other sciences. Do you agree that Chaucer "knew what to say" and "when to leave off"? Why or why not?

LITERARY FOCUS

Characterization

Chaucer describes his pilgrims so well that, after six hundred years, they still stand vividly before us as round characters, or complete and complex people. An important technique that Chaucer uses to create round characters is the mixture of both direct and indirect characterization. Most later writers follow Chaucer's lead. Chaucer uses **direct characterization** when the narrator explicitly tells us something about a pilgrim's personality. For example, he explicitly says of the Squire, "Courteous he was, lowly and serviceable." He uses **indirect characterization** when he provides details that force us to draw our own conclusions about a character's personality. For example, in describing the Merchant, he makes us form our own conclusion about someone who "told of his opinions and pursuits / In solemn tones" and "harped on his increase / Of capital."

Chaucer also succeeds in presenting vivid characters by selecting **significant details**—not every detail about the characters but those details that count: the Nun's golden brooch, the Friar's double-worsted cape, the Knight's armor-smudged tunic. Moreover, the details appear to be random, as they would be remembered in real life. When we meet a group of people for the first time, we usually remember some details about them and forget others. Similarly, the narrator recalls where the Reeve comes from but not what his name is—although he does recall the name of the Reeve's horse. The effect is to create a sense of **verisimilitude,** a sense that what he is narrating is true, that it really happened.

Chaucer adds to the verisimilitude by convincing us that his characters have **motivations,** reasons underlying their behavior. For instance, we see that the Pardoner is motivated by love of money and the Parson by love of Christianity.

Thinking About Characterization

1. In the portrait of the Cleric (lines 295–318), what character traits are stated directly? What do the Cleric's actions in lines 309–312 suggest about his character and motivation?
2. What seems to motivate the Doctor (lines 421–454)? What do the details about his reading matter suggest about his character?
3. Based on the details provided about the Wife of Bath (lines 455–486), list five adjectives describing her personality.

4. In the portrait of the Reeve (lines 603–638), how do the details about the Reeve's physical appearance help support the details about his behavior?

COMPOSITION

Writing About Characterization

Choose one character in "The Prologue" and write a composition in which you explain how Chaucer succeeds in making that character come alive. First take notes on direct and indirect characterization, significant details, motivation, and other means by which Chaucer achieves verisimilitude in portraying the character. Use your prewriting notes as the basis of a composition that opens with a general statement about Chaucer's success in portraying the character and then demonstrates that success with specific details from "The Prologue."

Writing a Character Portrait

Write a brief prose character portrait about a twentieth-century intruder into Chaucer's fourteenth-century world: a musician, a student, an actor, or any other character you choose to accompany the pilgrims to Canterbury. In the Chaucerian manner (1) use direct and indirect characterization, (2) select significant details that make your character come to life, and (3) make your character's motivation clear.

Geoffrey Chaucer

The Wife of Bath's Tale (slightly abridged)

*Perhaps Chaucer's most remarkable gift was his ability to create
suitable stories for narrators from all different walks of medieval
life. One of those narrators is the devout but worldly Wife of Bath,
described in lines 455–486 of the Prologue. She tells a story about a
knight in King Arthur's day. The knight has been condemned to die
because he treated a woman most cruelly; however, on the eve of his
execution, he is given a chance to live by Arthur's queen, who summons the knight to an interview and addresses him.*

"You stand, for such is the position still,
In no way certain of your life," said she,
"Yet you shall live if you can answer me:
What is the thing that women most desire?
5 Beware the axe and say as I require.
   "If you can't answer on the moment, though,
I will concede you this: you are to go
A twelvemonth and a day to seek and learn
Sufficient answer, then you shall return.
10 I shall take gages[1] from you to extort
Surrender of your body to the court."
   Sad was the knight and sorrowfully sighed,
But there! All other choices were denied,
And in the end he chose to go away
15 And to return after a year and day
Armed with such answer as there might be sent
To him by God. He took his leave and went.
   He knocked at every house, searched every place,
Yes, anywhere that offered hope of grace.
20 What could it be that women wanted most?
But all the same he never touched a coast,
Country or town in which there seemed to be
Any two people willing to agree.
   Some said that women wanted wealth and treasure,
25 "Honor," said some, some "Jollity and pleasure." . . .
And some that what most mattered
Was that we should be cosseted and flattered.
That's very near the truth, it seems to me;
A man can win us best with flattery.
30 To dance attendance on us, make a fuss,
Ensnares us all, the best and worst of us.
   Some say the things we most desire are these:

1 **gages:** pledges.

In tholde dayes of king Arthour,
Of which that Britons speken greet honour,
Al was this land fulfild of fairye.
The Elf queene, with hir joly compaignye,
Daunced ful ofte in many a grene mede.
This was the olde opinion, as I rede;
I speke of manye hundred yeres ago.
But now kan no man se none elves mo,
For now the grete charitee and prayeres
Of lymytours and othere hooly freres,
That serchen every lond and every streem,
As thikke as motes in the sonne beem,
Blessynge halles, chambres, kichenes, boures,
Citees, burghes, castels, hye toures,
Thropes, bernes, shipnes, dayeryes,
This maketh that ther been no fairyes.
For ther as wont to walken was an elf,
Ther walketh now the lymytour hym self
In undermeles and in morwenynges,
And seyth his matyns and his hooly thynges
As he gooth in his lymytacioun.
Wommen may go saufly up and doun
In every bussh or under every tree
Ther is noon oother incubus but he,
And he ne wol doon hem but dishonour.
And so bifel that this kyng Arthour
Hadde in his hous a lusty bacheler,
That on a day cam ridynge fro ryver;
And happed that, allone as he was born,
He saugh a mayde walkynge hym biforn

The Wife of Bath's Tale, from the Ellesmere Manuscript.

Freedom to do exactly as we please,
With no one to reprove our faults and lies,
35 Rather to have one call us good and wise.
Truly there's not a woman in ten score
Who has a fault, and someone rubs the sore,
But she will kick if what he says is true;
You try it out and you will find so too.
40 However vicious we may be within
We like to be thought wise and void of sin.
Others assert we women find it sweet
When we are thought dependable, discreet
And secret, firm of purpose and controlled,
45 Never betraying things that we are told.
But that's not worth the handle of a rake;
Women conceal a thing? For Heaven's sake!
Remember Midas?[2] Will you hear the tale?
　　Among some other little things, now stale,
50 Ovid[3] relates that under his long hair
The unhappy Midas grew a splendid pair
Of ass's ears; as subtly as he might,
He kept his foul deformity from sight;
Save for his wife, there was not one that knew.
55 He loved her best, and trusted in her too.
He begged her not to tell a living creature
That he possessed so horrible a feature.
And she—she swore, were all the world to win,
She would not do such villainy and sin
60 As saddle her husband with so foul a name;
Besides to speak would be to share the shame.
Nevertheless she thought she would have died
Keeping this secret bottled up inside;
It seemed to swell her heart and she, no doubt,
65 Thought it was on the point of bursting out.
　　Fearing to speak of it to woman or man,
Down to a reedy marsh she quickly ran
And reached the sedge.[4] Her heart was all on fire
And, as a bittern bumbles in the mire,[5]
70 She whispered to the water, near the ground,
"Betray me not, O water, with thy sound!
To thee alone I tell it: it appears
My husband has a pair of ass's ears!
Ah! My heart's well again, the secret's out!
75 I could no longer keep it, not a doubt."
And so you see, although we may hold fast
A little while, it must come out at last,
We can't keep secrets; as for Midas, well,
Read Ovid for his story; he will tell.
80 　　This knight that I am telling you about

2 **Midas:** king of ancient Greek legends.

3 **Ovid** [äv'id]: Roman poet (43 B.C.–A.D. 17?) who retold Midas' story in the *Metamorphoses*. Actually, according to Ovid, it was Midas' barber, not his wife, who told the secret of Midas' long ears.

4 **sedge:** grasslike marsh plant.

5 **as a bittern . . . mire:** as a bittern booms in the swamp. The bittern, a wading bird, is noted for its echoing, thumping call.

Perceived at last he never would find out
What it could be that women loved the best.
Faint was the soul within his sorrowful breast,
As home he went, he dared no longer stay;
85 His year was up and now it was the day.
      As he rode home in a dejected mood
Suddenly, at the margin of a wood,
He saw a dance upon the leafy floor
Of four and twenty ladies, nay, and more.
90 Eagerly he approached, in hope to learn
Some words of wisdom ere he should return;
But lo! Before he came to where they were,
Dancers and dance all vanished into air!
There wasn't a living creature to be seen
95 Save one old woman crouched upon the green.
A fouler-looking creature I suppose
Could scarcely be imagined. She arose
And said, "Sir knight, there's no way on from here.
Tell me what you are looking for, my dear,
100 For peradventure[6] that were best for you;
We old, old women know a thing or two."
      "Dear Mother," said the knight, "alack the day!
I am as good as dead if I can't say
What thing it is that women most desire;
105 If you could tell me I would pay your hire."
"Give me your hand," she said, "and swear to do
Whatever I shall next require of you
   —If so to do should lie within your might—
And you shall know the answer before night."
110 "Upon my honor," he answered, "I agree."
"Then," said the crone, "I dare to guarantee
Your life is safe; I shall make good my claim.
Upon my life the queen will say the same.
Show me the very proudest of them all
115 In costly coverchief[7] or jeweled caul[8]
That dare say no to what I have to teach.
Let us go forward without further speech."
And then she crooned her gospel[9] in his ear
And told him to be glad and not to fear.
120   They came to court. This knight, in full array,
Stood forth and said, "O Queen, I've kept my day
And kept my word and have my answer ready."
      There sat the noble matrons and the heady
Young girls, and widows too, that have the grace
125 Of wisdom, all assembled in that place,
And there the queen herself was throned to hear
And judge his answer. Then the knight drew near
And silence was commanded through the hall.

6 **peradventure:** perhaps; possibly.

7 **coverchief:** kerchief.
8 **caul:** elaborate, decorative hairnet.

9 **gospel:** here, truth.

The queen gave order he should tell them all
130 What thing it was that women wanted most.
He stood not silent like a beast or post,
But gave his answer with the ringing word
Of a man's voice and the assembly heard:
"My liege and lady, in general," said he,
135 "A woman wants the self-same sovereignty
Over her husband as over her lover,
And master him; he must not be above her.
That is your greatest wish, whether you kill
Or spare me; please yourself. I wait your will."
140   In all the court not one that shook her head
Or contradicted what the knight had said;
Maid, wife and widow cried, "He's saved his life!"
    And on the word up started the old wife,
The one the knight saw sitting on the green,
145 And cried, "Your mercy, sovereign lady queen!
Before the court disperses, do me right!
'Twas I who taught this answer to the knight,
For which he swore, and pledged his honor to it,
That the first thing I asked of him he'd do it,
150 So far as it should lie within his might.
Before this court I ask you then, sir knight,
To keep your word and take me for your wife;
For well you know that I have saved your life.
If this be false, deny it on your sword!"
155   "Alas!" he said, "Old lady, by the Lord
I know indeed that such was my behest,
But for God's love think of a new request,
Take all my goods, but leave my body free."
"A curse on us," she said, "if I agree!
160 I may be foul, I may be poor and old,
Yet will not choose to be, for all the gold
That's bedded in the earth or lies above,
Less than your wife, nay, than your very love!"
    "My love?" said he. "By heaven, my damnation!
165 Alas that any of my race and station
Should ever make so foul a misalliance!"
Yet in the end his pleading and defiance
All went for nothing, he was forced to wed. . . .
    Now peradventure some may well suspect
170 A lack of care in me since I neglect
To tell of the rejoicings and display
Made at the feast upon their wedding day.
I have but a short answer to let fall;
I say there was no joy or feast at all,
175 Nothing but heaviness of heart and sorrow.
He married her in private on the morrow

The Wife of Bath.

And all day long stayed hidden like an owl,
It was such torture that his wife looked foul. . . .
     "Bless us! Is this, my dear,
180 How knights and wives get on together here?
Are these the laws of good King Arthur's house?
Are knights of his all so contemptuous?
I am your own beloved and your wife,
And I am she, indeed, that saved your life;
185 And certainly I never did you wrong. . . .
You're carrying on as if you were half-witted.
Say, for God's love, what sin have I committed?
I'll put things right if you will tell me how."
     "Put right?" he cried. "That never can be now!
190 Nothing can ever be put right again!
You're old, and so abominably plain,
So poor to start with, so low-bred to follow;
It's little wonder if I twist and wallow!
God, that my heart would burst within my breast!"
195   "Is that," said she, "the cause of your unrest?"
     "Yes, certainly," he said, "and can you wonder?"
     "I could set right what you suppose a blunder,
That's if I cared to, in a day or two,
If I were shown more courtesy by you.
200 Just now," she said, "you spoke of gentle birth,
Such as descends from ancient wealth and worth.
If that's the claim you make for gentlemen
Such arrogance is hardly worth a hen.
Whoever loves to work for virtuous ends,
205 Public and private, and who most intends
To do what deeds of gentleness he can,
Take him to be the greatest gentleman.
Christ wills we take our gentleness from Him,
Not from a wealth of ancestry long dim,
210 Though they bequeath their whole establishment
By which we claim to be of high descent.
Our fathers cannot make us a bequest
Of all those virtues that became them best
And earned for them the name of gentlemen,
215 But bade us follow them as best we can.
     "Thus the wise poet of the Florentines,[10]
Dante[11] by name, has written in these lines,
For such is the opinion Dante launches:
'Seldom arises by these slender branches
220 Prowess of men, for it is God, no less,
Wills us to claim of Him our gentleness.'
For of our parents nothing can we claim
Save temporal things, and these may hurt and maim.
     "But everyone knows this as well as I;

10 **Florentines:** people of Florence, a city in Italy.
11 **Dante:** Italian poet (1265–1321) whose masterpiece, *The Divine Comedy,* appeared a few decades before *The Canterbury Tales* was written.

Geoffrey Chaucer **85**

A Flemish tapestry depicting a hawking party, sixteenth century.

225 For if gentility were implanted by
The natural course of lineage down the line,
Public or private, could it cease to shine
In doing the fair work of gentle deed?
No vice or villainy could then bear seed.

230   "Take fire and carry it to the darkest house
Between this kingdom and the Caucasus,[12]
And shut the doors on it and leave it there,
It will burn on, and it will burn as fair
As if ten thousand men were there to see,

235 For fire will keep its nature and degree,
I can assure you, sir, until it dies.
    "But gentleness, as you will recognize,
Is not annexed in nature to possessions.
Men fail in living up to their professions;

240 But fire never ceases to be fire.
God knows you'll often find, if you inquire,
Some lording[13] full of villainy and shame.
If you would be esteemed for the mere' name
Of having been by birth a gentleman

245 And stemming from some virtuous, noble clan,

12 **Caucasus:** mountain range located between the Black Sea and the Caspian Sea and today part of the Soviet Union.

13 **lording:** lord.

And do not live yourself by gentle deed
Or take your father's noble code and creed,
You are no gentleman, though duke or earl.
Vice and bad manners are what make a churl.[14]

250   "Gentility is only the renown
For bounty that your fathers handed down,
Quite foreign to your person, not your own;
Gentility must come from God alone.
That we are gentle comes to us by grace

255 And by no means is it bequeathed with place.
   "Reflect how noble (says Valerius)
Was Tullius surnamed Hostilius,[15]
Who rose from poverty to nobleness.
And read Boethius,[16] Seneca[17] no less,

260 Thus they express themselves and are agreed:
'Gentle is he that does a gentle deed.'
And therefore, my dear husband, I conclude
That even if my ancestors were rude,
Yet God on high—and so I hope He will—

265 Can grant me grace to live in virtue still,
A gentlewoman only when beginning
To live in virtue and to shrink from sinning.
   "As for my poverty which you reprove,
Almighty God Himself in whom we move,

270 Believe and have our being, chose a life
Of poverty, and every man or wife—
Nay, every child—can see our Heavenly King
Would never stoop to choose a shameful thing.
No shame in poverty if the heart is gay,

275 As Seneca and all the learned say.
He who accepts his poverty unhurt
I'd say is rich although he lacked a shirt.
But truly poor are they who whine and fret
And covet what they cannot hope to get.

280 And he that, having nothing, covets not,
Is rich, though you may think he is a sot.[18]
   "True poverty can find a song to sing.
Juvenal[19] says a pleasant little thing:
'The poor can dance and sing in the relief

285 Of having nothing that will tempt a thief.'
Though it be hateful, poverty is good,
A great incentive to a livelihood,
And a great help to our capacity
For wisdom, if accepted patiently.

290 Poverty is, though wanting in estate,[20]
A kind of wealth that none calumniate.[21]
Poverty often, when the heart is lowly,

---

14 **churl:** a low-class person.

15 **Valerius . . . Hostilius:** Valerius Maximus, first-century Roman historian, wrote about Tullius Hostilius, legendary Roman king.
16 **Boethius** [bō ē′thē əs]: Roman philosopher (A.D. 480?–524?).
17 **Seneca:** Roman philosopher, playwright, and politician (4? B.C.–A.D. 65).

18 **sot:** here, a foolish person.

19. **Juvenal:** Roman satirical poet (A.D. 60?–140?)

20 **estate:** pomp; showy display.
21 **calumniate:** slander.

Brings one to God and teaches what is holy,
Gives knowledge of oneself and even lends
295 A glass by which to see one's truest friends.
And since it's no offense, let me be plain;
Do not rebuke my poverty again.
    "Lastly you taxed me, sir, with being old.
Yet even if you never had been told
300 By ancient books, you gentlemen engage
Yourselves in honor to respect old age.
To call an old man 'father' shows good breeding,
And this could be supported from my reading. . . .
    "You have two choices; which one will you try?
305 To have me old and ugly till I die,
But still a loyal, true, and humble wife
That never will displease you all her life;
Or would you rather I were young and pretty
And chance your arm[22] what happens in a city
310 Where friends will visit you because of me,
Yes, and in other places too, maybe.
Which would you have? The choice is all your own."
    The knight thought long, and with a piteous groan
At last he said, with all the care in life,
315 "My lady and my love, my dearest wife,
I leave the matter to your wise decision.
You make the choice yourself, for the provision
Of what may be agreeable and rich
In honor to us both, I don't care which;
320 Whatever pleases you suffices me."
    "And have I won the mastery?" said she,
"Since I'm to choose and rule as I think fit?"
"Certainly, wife," he answered her, "that's it."
"Kiss me," she cried. "No quarrels! On my oath
325 And word of honor, you shall find me both,
That is, both fair and faithful as a wife;
May I go howling mad and take my life
Unless I prove to be as good and true
As ever wife was since the world was new!
330 And if tomorrow when the sun's above
I seem less fair than any lady love,
Than any queen or empress east or west,
Do with my life and death as you think best.
Cast up the curtain, husband. Look at me!"
335   And when indeed the knight had looked to see,
Lo, she was young and lovely, rich in charms.
In ecstasy he caught her in his arms,
His heart went bathing in a bath of blisses
And melted in a hundred thousand kisses.

22 **chance your arm:** take your chance.

STUDY QUESTIONS

Recalling

1. To what question must the knight find an answer in order to save himself? How long does he have to seek the answer?
2. Describe the woman who provides the answer. What does she make the knight promise?
3. What *is* the answer? After the knight provides it to the queen and her court, what must he do to fulfill his promise?
4. Summarize the knight's four complaints about his wife. After the wife refutes his complaints, what does he agree that she has won? What happens when he kisses her?

Interpreting

5. What is the relationship between the question the knight must answer and the crime he committed? Between the answer and the knight's behavior after marriage?
6. In refuting her husband's complaints, what Christian values does the wife express? What social attitudes does she contradict?
7. What central message does this tale express about the way people should treat those they love?

Extending

8. Examine the character of the Wife of Bath as described in lines 455–486 of "The Prologue." Why is this tale a suitable one for the Wife of Bath to tell?
9. In what ways are the ideas expressed in this story still relevant today?

LITERARY FOCUS

Motif

A **motif** is an event, an idea, or another element that occurs again and again in a particular type of literature. One motif of medieval romances is the quest, in which the knight-hero embarks on a search for an object, a person, or anything else whose pursuit will lead to adventure. In *Sir Gawain and the Green Knight*, a verse romance written by a contemporary of Chaucer's, Sir Gawain, a knight of King Arthur's court, rides off on a yearlong quest for the mysterious Green Knight who has challenged him to battle; in French versions of the Arthurian romances, Arthur's knights are often involved in the quest for the Holy Grail, the cup or platter that Christ used at the Last Supper.

One motif of fairy tales is the metamorphosis, in which someone or something is magically transformed into something entirely different. In "The Frog Prince," for example, a maiden's kiss transforms an ugly frog into a handsome prince; in "Cinderella," a pumpkin is transformed into an elegant coach with the wave of the Fairy Godmother's wand.

Thinking About Motif

1. Explain how both the quest and the metamorphosis motifs are employed in "The Wife of Bath's Tale."
2. What are some motifs of science-fiction stories and films? Of adventure tales and films?

VOCABULARY

Synonyms

Synonyms are words that have the same or nearly the same meanings; for example, *dine* and *eat* are synonyms. The words in capitals are from "The Wife of Bath's Tale." Choose the word that is *nearest* the meaning of the word in capitals, *as the word is used in the selection.* Write the number of each item and the letter of your choice on a separate sheet.

1. COSSETED: (a) controlled (b) pampered (c) insulted (d) tossed
2. REPROVE: (a) recheck (b) research (c) glorify (d) criticize
3. DEJECTED: (a) depressed (b) cheerful (c) emitted (d) unfriendly
4. CRONE: (a) maiden (b) hag (c) heiress (d) angel
5. COVET: (a) conceal (b) achieve (c) envy (d) utilize

The Pardoner's Tale, from the Ellesmere Manuscript.

Most important, there were fewer inflectional endings in Middle English. As an example, notice that there were only two forms of the noun in Middle English:

	Singular	Plural
Subject		
Object	ship	
Indirect Object		shipes
Possessive	shipes	

A number of notable features make Middle English, nevertheless, a different language from modern English. Pronunciation is the most obvious difference—especially, pronunciation of vowels. Speakers of Middle English pronounced vowels in the French manner (the letter *a* as *ah*; a long *e* as long *a*; a long *i* or *y* as long *e*; and so on).

When English people began to pronounce the vowels as we do, English experienced a phenomenon so important that it is now called the Great Vowel Shift. Another pronunciation difference of note is that speakers of Middle English pronounced every vowel, unlike speakers of modern English, who acknowledge the "silent *e*." For example, in Middle English *eyë* has two syllables, whereas the modern English *eye* has only one.

Thinking About Middle English

1. Looking again at the Middle English sample on page 58, what would be the plural of *breeth* in line 5?
2. How would a speaker of Middle English pronounce *breeth*?
3. From the sample find the Middle English equivalent of the modern English noun *end*. How many syllables are in the older form?

VOCABULARY

Word Origins

As the conquering Normans and their descendants established themselves in England and became a part of the life there, they lent medieval English words from Old French. Many of these French words have endured right up to the English we now speak, although their spelling and pronunciation may have changed along the way.

French importations from 1250 to the end of the Medieval Period reached astonishing propor-

tions and affected all walks of life. For example, French gave English the words basic to government, which are now *crown, state,* and *prince,* among dozens of others. The words *fashion* and *dress* are French in origin, as are *gown, veil, kerchief,* and *galoshes.* French also entered the English vocabularies particular to religion, the military, the arts, and medicine. In addition, adjectives from the French were very important for description in Chaucer's day and included *amiable, courteous, gentle, gracious, honest, rude, treacherous,* and nearly a thousand others.

Using a good dictionary, explain the changes in meaning or spelling that have occurred in each of the following words since they entered our language as Old French. The words are presented in modern English, but Chaucer used them in Middle English in *The Canterbury Tales.*

1. engender
2. tender
3. devout
4. company
5. degree
6. poison
7. chivalry
8. courtesy
9. sovereign
10. gentle

COMPOSITION

Citing Evidence

In a brief essay persuade your reader that "The Pardoner's Tale" has an absorbing plot. To be persuasive you will need to cite evidence—specific details to support your opinions. You may want to comment on the flow of events, suspense, foreshadowing, and outcome. *For help with this assignment, refer to Lesson 3 in the Writing About Literature Handbook at the back of this book.*

Writing a Moral Tale

Try your hand at writing a moral tale. Begin with the moral—some bit of popular wisdom that can be expressed in a sentence such as "The early bird gets the worm" or "Never trust flatterers" or "Better late than never." Then devise a brief story that illustrates the point. Several paragraphs should be sufficient, though you will want to include enough appropriate detail to make your story vivid and memorable.

Sir Thomas Malory   1405–1471

Although several Englishmen named Thomas Malory lived during the 1400s, most evidence suggests that the writer Sir Thomas Malory was the same hot-blooded Thomas Malory who had represented Warwickshire in Parliament in 1455. Those were troubled times, and the Member of Parliament had found himself supporting the wrong side—the Lancasters—in the war to determine which family would rule England, the War of the Roses. Charged with various crimes, he spent much of his later life in jail. He may have been a political prisoner rather than an actual perpetrator, but he nevertheless died in jail. It was in there that the "knyght presoner," as the author called himself, composed the great English prose work that related the heroic adventures of King Arthur and his Knights of the Round Table.

Malory's account of the legend is a reworking from English, French, and Latin sources. In this narrative Malory translated and gave order to that diverse body of Arthurian romance that had grown up in England and France since Anglo-Saxon times. William Caxton, the first English printer, published Malory's work in 1485 as *Le Morte d'Arthur,* French for "The Death of Arthur."

Did King Arthur really exist? When the Anglo-Saxons invaded Britain in the fifth century, they pushed the inhabitants of that island northward into present-day Scotland and westward into Ireland and Wales. Those older, displaced inhabitants were the Celts. Arthur was presumably a sixth-century chieftain of one of those Celtic tribes, fighting from Wales against the invading Germanic tribes. Hundreds of years later, that primitive chieftain caught the imagination of the Middle Ages. Indeed, the nonreligious literature of the Middle Ages from the twelfth century onward—on the European continent even more than in England itself—was filled with the tales of King Arthur, around whom the medieval ideal of chivalry flourished. Malory, it would seem, wanted to recapture the Arthurian romantic ideals that his age was already losing, for as he wrote, knighthood was coming to an end.

■ What knightly virtues—loyalty, honor, generosity, courtesy—do you see in Americans today? Are these traits as important now as they were in medieval times?

Model for Active Reading

In this selection, as in one selection in each unit, you will find notes in the right-hand margin that highlight parts of the selection. These notes point out important ideas of the literary period and draw your attention to literary elements and techniques covered in the Literary Focuses. Page numbers in the notes refer you to more extensive discussions of these important ideas and elements.

Illustration from a medieval manuscript of Malory's *Morte d'Arthur.*

Sir Thomas Malory

from **Le Morte d'Arthur**

Modern Idiom by Keith Baines

One day a squire arrived at the court, supporting his master, Sir Myles, who had been mortally wounded. He described to Arthur how he had been attacked by King Pellinore[1] at the well, and then begged that he should be buried, and that one of Arthur's knights should avenge his death. After the burial a squire named Gryfflette pleaded with Arthur to make him a knight; he was the same age as Arthur.

"You are too young to be a knight," Arthur said gravely.

"Sire, but I beg you," said Gryfflette.

"It would be a shame," said Merlin,[2] "to lose Gryfflette. He will make an excellent knight when he is older, but at the moment he would be no match for King Pellinore."

"I will make you a knight," said Arthur, "if you will swear not to joust with King Pellinore more than once, and then return to me."

"I swear it," said Gryfflette; so Arthur dubbed[3] him.

Sir Gryfflette ran happily to his armor, and when he was clad and mounted, set off at a gallop for the well. He found there a brilliantly decorated pavilion,[4] and outside it a horse, already harnessed. A multicolored shield hung from a tree, and resting against it was a spear. Sir Gryfflette struck the shield a ringing blow, and it fell to the ground. King Pellinore appeared at the entrance to his pavilion. "Sir, why do you strike my shield?" he asked.

"Because I wish to joust with you," Sir Gryfflette replied.

"You are but newly knighted, and too young," said the king. "Tell me, where do you come from?"

"I come from the court of King Arthur, and still I mean to joust with you."

Medieval idea: Loyalty to one's master was important in the feudal hierarchy (p. 45).

---

1. **King Pellinore:** one of the many rulers of the kingdoms that made up Arthurian Britain; probably a fictitious name.
2. **Merlin:** magician and counselor to King Arthur.
3. **dubbed:** made a knight by tapping on the shoulders with a sword. Once knighted, a person is addressed as "Sir."
4. **pavilion** [pə vil′yən]: tent.

"Very well, then; but I am reluctant to do so," the king rejoined.

The two knights met at full gallop: Sir Gryfflette's spear was broken, and the shaft driven deeply into his side; he lost consciousness and fell to the ground. King Pellinore swiftly ran over to him and loosened his armor. Sir Gryfflette recovered his wind slowly, and when he had done so, King Pellinore lifted him gently onto his horse. "God's speed, young knight," he said.

At King Arthur's court Sir Gryfflette collapsed once more; however, he was placed in the hands of a surgeon by whose skillful treatment the wound was eventually healed.

Meanwhile, twelve aged ambassadors had come from Rome, and in the name of the Emperor Lucius, demanded tribute.[5] "Since you are only ambassadors," Arthur said, "we shall not put you to death for your insolent words; but tell your Emperor that if he tries to win tribute from us, that will be his fate."

The ambassadors withdrew angrily, and Arthur himself was doubly grieved: by the Emperor's message and by Sir Gryfflette's injury. He decided to avenge Sir Gryfflette secretly, so he commanded the chamberlain[6] to take his horse and armor to the outskirts of the city at dawn the following day.

When Arthur was armed and mounted, he instructed the chamberlain to await his return, and then galloped off toward the well. He had not gone far when he saw Merlin being chased by three ruffians; he galloped up to them and the ruffians fled in terror.

"Your magic did not save you that time," said Arthur.

"It could have," Merlin replied, "had I so wished, whereas your anger will certainly not save you from the superior strength of King Pellinore, whom you are about to challenge."

Merlin accompanied Arthur to the well, and when they arrived they found King Pellinore seated outside his pavilion. "Sir," said Arthur, "it would seem that no knight can pass this well without your challenging him."

"That is so," said King Pellinore.

"I have come to force you to change this custom of yours, so defend yourself!"

They jousted three times, each time breaking their spears, until the third time, when Arthur was flung from his horse. "Very well," said Arthur, "you have won the advantage jousting; now let us see what you can do on foot." King Pellinore was reluctant to dismount and lose the advantage he had won; however, when Arthur rushed at him boldly with drawn sword, he grew ashamed and did dismount.

Verisimilitude (p. 79): Malory selects details that make life in a medieval court seem real.

Motivation (p. 79): Arthur has reason for seeking King Pellinore.

---

5. **tribute:** money paid by one ruler to another to acknowledge submission or for protection.
6. **chamberlain:** officer in charge of a ruler's household.

They fought until both collapsed from pain and exhaustion; their armor was splintered and the blood flowed from their wounds. They fought again, until Arthur's sword broke in his hand. "Now," said King Pellinore, "you shall yield to me, or die."

"Not so!" Arthur shouted as he sprang at him, and grabbing him around the waist, threw him to the ground. Arthur was unlacing his helmet when, with a sudden fearful effort, King Pellinore overturned Arthur and clambered on top of him. King Pellinore had loosened Arthur's helmet and raised his sword to strike off his head when Merlin spoke.

"Hold your hand!" he said; "you will endanger the whole realm. You do not realize who it is you are about to kill."

"Who is it, then?"

"King Arthur."

Hearing this, King Pellinore feared that he would receive little mercy from Arthur if he spared him—so he raised his sword once more. Merlin adroitly put him to sleep with a magic spell.

"You have killed him with your magic," said Arthur hotly. "I would rather that my whole realm were lost, and myself killed; he was a magnificent fighter."

> **Medieval idea:** Skill in battle was worthy of great praise (p. 47).

"He is more whole than you are," Merlin replied. "He will not only live, but serve you excellently. It is to him that you will give your sister in marriage, and she will bear two sons—Sir Percivale and Sir Lamerok—who will be two of the most famous of the Knights of the Round Table."

They mounted, and Merlin led the way to a hermit, who treated Arthur's wounds, and in whose dwelling they rested for three days. They resumed their journey, which was to the Lake of Avalon,[7] and as they were approaching the lake, Arthur said, "How sad that I broke my magic sword!"

"You shall have another one," Merlin replied.

Just then Arthur saw that in the center of the lake the surface was broken by an arm, clothed in white samite,[8] and that the hand grasped a finely jeweled sword and scabbard.

"That is the magic sword Excalibur," said Merlin, "and it will be given to you by the Lady of the Lake, who is now crossing the water in her bark.[9] She comes from her castle, which is hewn in the rock, and more beautiful than any earthly dwelling. You must address her courteously, and do as she directs you."

> **Romance** (p. 49): Magic was an important element of most medieval romances.

The Lady of the Lake appeared before them. "My lady," said Arthur, "I beg you to make me a gift of the sword Excalibur."

"King Arthur," she replied, "Excalibur shall be yours, if you

> **Medieval idea:** Knights were expected to treat women with respect at all times (p. 47).

---

7. **Lake of Avalon:** the lake in which is situated Avalon, the legendary rock island inhabited by a race of women who know all the world's magic.
8. **samite:** a heavy silk worn in the Middle Ages.
9. **bark:** boat.

consent now to granting me whatever gift I shall ask of you in my own time."

"I swear," said Arthur, "whatever gift is in my power to grant."

"Even so," said the Lady of the Lake. "Now use my bark and row yourself to the sword, and take it, together with the scabbard."

Arthur and Merlin tethered their horses to two trees, and boarded the bark. When Arthur had taken the sword and scabbard the arm disappeared into the water.

On the homeward journey they repassed King Pellinore's pavilion, and Arthur asked Merlin why King Pellinore was not there. "He has been fighting Sir Egglame, and has chased him nearly all the way into Caerleon,"[10] Merlin replied.

"What a pity!" said Arthur. "Because now that I have this beautiful sword I should like to fight him again, and perhaps this time have my revenge."

"That you shall not do," said Merlin. "King Pellinore is already tired from his fight with Sir Egglame. To win would bring you no honor, to lose would be to increase your shame. And lose you might, because he is still stronger than you are."

Medieval idea: Honor was an important part of the code of knighthood (p. 47).

"I will do as you advise," said Arthur, as he examined his sword once more, admiring its beauty and temper. "Tell me," said Merlin, "do you prefer the sword or the scabbard?"

"The sword," said Arthur.

"You are a fool," said Merlin. "The scabbard is worth ten of the sword, because while you wear it, regardless of how seriously you are wounded, you will lose no blood."

They were drawing close to Caerleon when they passed King Pellinore; he appeared not to see them. "Why," asked Arthur, "did King Pellinore not speak to us?"

"Because he did not see us," Merlin replied. "I cast a spell over him; had he done so, you would not have escaped so lightly."

When Arthur and Merlin arrived at the court, they were questioned eagerly on all that had happened; and when the story was told, Arthur's knights rejoiced in the boldness of their king.

---

10. **Caerleon:** Arthur's residence.

STUDY QUESTIONS

Recalling

1. On what condition does Arthur make Gryfflette a knight? What reasons does King Pellinore give for his initial reluctance to joust with Sir Gryfflette?

2. Why does Arthur decide to fight with Pellinore? How is Arthur's life saved during his combat with Pellinore?

3. After Arthur's sword is broken in the combat, how does he get his new sword and scabbard? Why is the scabbard more valuable than the sword Excalibur itself?

4. What reason does Merlin give to dissuade Arthur from fighting Pellinore again after Pellinore chases Sir Egglame? Why does King Pellinore not see Arthur and Merlin when they pass him on their way to Caerleon?

Interpreting

5. What qualities about Pellinore does King Arthur value highly? Why does Arthur react angrily when he thinks Merlin has slain Pellinore?
6. In general, what is Merlin's role in this selection? What is ironic about the knights' reaction to King Arthur at the end?
7. Besides the points noted in the margin of the selection, what medieval ideals and characteristics do the actions of Gryfflette, Merlin, and Arthur celebrate?

Extending

8. According to the modern American novelist John Steinbeck, the story of King Arthur "continues even into the present day." He suggests that the television western, for example, bears many similarities to the world of King Arthur. What similarities do you see between the two worlds?

VIEWPOINT

The scholar Derek Brewer has noted that *Le Morte d'Arthur* expresses

the enduring contemporary need to reconcile the individual's demands with those of society, to recognize and cherish personal integrity and true love, and to create a good society.

Brewer is reminding us that while the knights are individuals, they are also members of a larger group to which they owe service. In this selection in what ways do the individual characters attempt to improve the society in which they live?

LITERARY FOCUS

Myth, Legend, and Literature

A **myth** is an anonymous traditional story with its roots in cultural or national folk beliefs that rely on the supernatural to explain the mysteries of the world. A **legend** is also a traditional tale handed down from generation to generation, but unlike a myth, a legend is believed to be based on history. Usually, a legend celebrates the heroic qualities of a national leader.

The world that Malory created for Arthur is far from the primitive world of the Celts and Anglo-Saxons. Rather, it is the world of chivalry—a world of elaborate courtesy and high ideals, in which the knights devote their formidable skills to making life better for the poor and oppressed, thereby ridding society of many of its dangers. Thus, the historic Arthur becomes a legendary figure.

Thinking About Myth, Legend, and Literature

Find at least two details in this selection that contribute to the picture of King Arthur as a legendary hero.

COMPOSITION

Writing About Character

Write an essay that presents Pellinore's character clearly, with his strengths as well as his defects. Consider first what we are directly told about him by Malory. Then explain what we indirectly learn from what he says and does and from what others say about him. Support each assertion with specific evidence from the selection.

Writing a Description

Use your imagination to describe one of Arthur and Pellinore's jousts as vividly as you can. Choose vivid details and action words to create a clear impression of the sight, sound, and movement of the struggle.

COMPARING WRITERS

1. The ballads, Chaucer, and Malory all present medieval knights and heroes. Select a knight or a hero from two of the selections in this unit, and explain in which ways the two figures are similar and in which respects they are different.
2. In "The Prologue" to *The Canterbury Tales,* the Host specifies that a good story must entertain and contain a moral. The ballads, "The Wife of Bath's Tale," "The Pardoner's Tale," and the excerpt from *Le Morte d'Arthur* are all examples of medieval storytelling. Which do you think comes closest to meeting the Host's conditions for a good story?

ACTIVE READING

Details of Characterization

Earlier in this book (page 79), we talked about the vital importance of details in a work of literature. Details enrich and deepen a work; they give substance to a setting, fill out the turns of a plot, lend plausibility to an action.

Details, then, are crucial to a literary work overall and especially important in characterization. Often what we remember best about a novel is a certain character whom we feel we have come to know deeply. The novelist's art has rendered that character strong, complex, fascinating—*believable.* A good deal of that believability, that art, comes from the author's selection of revealing details.

Consider for a moment some of the other arts. Good sculptors and portrait painters seek to distill and capture in a single frozen image the truth about the character of the individual being portrayed. In the same way, good writers strive for truth, depth, and distinctiveness in the characters they create. For sculptors, painters, and writers alike the most effective way to achieve this genuineness and individuality is through the imaginative and artistic choice of telling details.

In the Prologue to *The Canterbury Tales,* Chaucer introduces us to the pilgrims who will journey together to Canterbury in the course of the poem. One by one, he identifies the pilgrims, then describes them with numerous details that distinguish each portrayal.

First we meet the Knight, who, we are told at the outset, has fought hard and nobly and has lived chivalrously, honorably, and wisely: "He was a true, a perfect gentle-knight." Chaucer simply states these things, but notice how he ends this portrayal:

> . . . he possessed
> Fine horses, but he was not gaily
> dressed.
> He wore a fustian tunic stained
> and dark
> With smudges where his armor
> had left mark.

These details, placed near the end of the description, leave us with our sharpest impression of the Knight. Although he owns fine horses (an indication of high stature), he is himself unpretentious. Rather than fancy dress, as befits a man of his position, he chooses a rough tunic that even bears the old dark stains of the armor he used to wear. The implication in these details is that the Knight is both proud of his accomplishments and humble in the face of them.

Of course, writers are not restricted to details of physical appearance. They can also build a characterization through details of physical *action.* A little later in the Prologue we encounter the Nun, an exemplar of proper behavior and good manners:

> No morsel from her lips did she
> let fall,
> Nor dipped her fingers in the
> sauce too deep . . .
> And she would wipe her upper
> lip so clean
> That not a trace of grease was to
> be seen
> Upon the cup when she had
> drunk.

Through the accumulation of these amusing details, observed in a series of intense "close-ups"—from the morsel of meat to her lips to her fingers to the rim of her cup—the poet creates a picture of the Nun as a woman pristine, angelically graceful, and altogether pure. However, we can detect in this depiction of her rigorous cleanliness a certain extremism.

Why do both of these portraits leave an indelible impression? In each case Chaucer endows the characterization with precise, affectionate, revealing details, and these details help create for us a distinct and definitive image of the character.

REVIEW:
THE ENGLISH VOICE

Order

When we think of the Middle Ages, we think of knights in shining armor. These battling lords and wandering heroes were actually a very small part of the population, but they remain the essential image of medieval adventure and romance. Yet knights were part of the complicated chivalric system just as the code of chivalry itself was part of the larger way of life called feudalism. As a part of feudalism, chivalry was not just a set of rules for good behavior: It was an *order*. Everyone—king, knight, lady, friar, squire, serf—knew his or her place. Everyone commanded and obeyed, served and was served, according to the ladder of society.

Sir Patrick Spens
*"O wha is this has don this
    deid,
    And told the king o' me,
To send us out at this time o'
    the yeir,
    To sail upon the sea!*

*"Mak ready, mak ready, my
    mirry men all,
    Our guid schip sails the
    morne."*

Chaucer
*There was a Knight, a most dis-
    tinguished man,
Who from the day on which he
    first began*

*To ride abroad had followed
    chivalry,
Truth, honor, generousness, and
    courtesy.
He had done nobly in his sov-
    ereign's war
And ridden into battle, no man
    more.*

*He had his son with him, a
    fine young Squire,
A lover and cadet, a lad of
    fire. . . .
He'd seen some service with the
    cavalry
In Flanders and Artois and Pic-
    ardy
And had done valiantly in little
    space
Of time, in hope to win his la-
    dy's grace.*

Malory
*"Hold your hand!" he said;
"you will endanger the whole
realm. You do not realize who
it is you are about to kill."
    "Who is it, then?"
    "King Arthur."*

A lord's command or a lady's grace had the power to send someone into a ferocious storm at sea or into a distant desert. Any harm to the king meant harm to the whole realm—not because the king was powerful or rich or symbolic but because the king and the people were part of the vast medieval order.

1. Detail, engraving of Geoffrey Chaucer from the Ellesmere Manuscript of *The Canterbury Tales.*
2. Detail, stained glass window, Canterbury, England.
3. Detail, *The Elephant and Castle*, twelfth-century bestiary.
4. Detail, thirteenth-century French manuscript depicting an Old Testament battle.
5. Detail, the shop of a dealer in art objects, altarpiece, Konrad Witz, c. 1440.
6. Detail, the court of King Arthur at dinner, from a medieval manuscript.
7. Fourteenth-century English ivory hunting horn.
8. Fifteenth-century playing card, Milan.
9. Castle, Sussex, England, built 1385.

105

Key to Illustrations appears on page 237.

THE ELIZABETHAN AGE

1485–1625

When Henry VII, a Tudor, became king of England in 1485, he was starting a new royal line. His defeat of Richard III and his marriage to a member of the House of York had ended the civil war known as the Wars of the Roses, and he could perhaps predict the time of peace and progress that his reign would bring to England until 1509. No one, however, could have predicted the events and forces that reshaped Henry's kingdom before the Tudor line ran out over a century later. Henry VII could not foresee his son Henry VIII marrying six wives and breaking with the Roman Catholic Church over a question of divorce and succession. Nor could Henry VII imagine his granddaughter Elizabeth's reign (1558–1603)—so long and illustrious that the whole period of history and the magnificent literature it produced came to be named for her.

The Growth of English Power

Luck, wisdom, and monumental forces were at work to produce the golden age that was to come to England by the late 1500s. To begin with, feudalism had collapsed. A new economy took shape and brought great prosperity to the island. Money as well as land became a source of power; banking became a business. Secondly, overseas commerce helped to make the nation rich. Henry VII had been king for only seven years when Columbus landed in the New World. A few years later the explorer John Cabot sailed his ships along the coast of North America, establishing British claims to Newfoundland and New England.

During this time (the early 1500s) a religious revolution that had begun in central Europe was spreading across the Continent. It was called the Protestant Reformation, a protest against the powerful Roman Catholic Church. Until the Reformation the only form of Christianity in western Europe was Roman Catholicism. The German monk Martin Luther and the French-born theologian John Calvin both criticized the established Church, disagreeing with its actions, its conduct, and even many of its beliefs. By the 1530s Henry VIII had reasons to align himself and England with the Protestants. He wanted his marriage to Catherine of Aragon annulled because she had not given him a male heir. When the Pope in Rome refused, Henry VIII broke with the Roman Catholic Church. He established the Church of England (the Anglican Church) and made himself its powerful head, initiating factional fighting among different religious groups that would

Miniature of Queen Elizabeth I, after a portrait by John de Critz, seventeenth century.

plague England until the end of the 1600s. It lasted even longer in Scotland and Ireland.

In 1588, during the reign of Elizabeth I, England became one of the great sea powers of the world. In that year Philip II, king of Spain and the most powerful ruler on the Continent, sent his renowned Spanish Armada to fight England's small navy. The fight seemed unequal; Philip should easily have invaded England, occupied it, and restored the supremacy of the Roman Catholic Church on the island. Yet the English navy won an amazing victory, aided by the inhospitable climate of the English seas. After this victory England forgot that it was a little island and became a great sea power. On December 31, 1599, the East India Company was chartered; world trade and colonization had begun. Nothing, not even the opening of the American frontier or our recent exploration of space, would ever match the explosion of energy in England in those days.

When Elizabeth I died in 1603, the throne of England went to her cousin James, king of Scotland and a member of the Stuart family that would rule England through most of the 1600s. Thus James VI of Scotland became James I of England, and the old island of Britain (England, Scotland, and Wales) was at last ruled by one monarch. Yet, as powerful as it became from 1485 to 1625, Great Britain, as we call it now, was still a small country, not only in area (smaller than Oregon) but also in population (probably at this time fewer than four million people).

Life in Elizabethan England

What kinds of people would you be likely to meet if you traveled along the narrow, winding, country trails of Elizabethan England? In the first place, if you were like most travelers, you would go miles without seeing anyone at all. Then you would probably get lost following the wrong trail through uncut forests. You would be fortunate if you did not meet a highwayman or two—cutthroats and robbers were numerous and dangerous—and you would most probably encounter a beggar. On the other hand, you could meet farmers and shepherds, prosperous-looking merchants, scholars, clerics, and nobles.

In London and in other cities, life was not so lonely. London was now one of the

Costume from the time of King James I.

great capitals of Europe, with a population of over 100,000. It was not free of poverty: Records indicate the presence of about 12,000 "begging poor." Nevertheless, especially when Elizabeth held her court there, the city seemed to sparkle with new wealth and energy. The Thames, the famous river that slides by London and then winds into the countryside, was both a thoroughfare for commerce and a playground for city residents. During the day it was filled with boats and barges of every size and shape; and as evening fell, pageants, music, and fireworks could be enjoyed by rich and poor alike.

The Influence of the Renaissance

While England was becoming an economic, religious, and naval power, it was also being influenced by a cultural movement, the Renaissance. Beginning in Italy in the early years of the fourteenth century, the **Renaissance** was a flowering of learning that swept into France, Holland, and the other nations of western Europe, including England. Basically the Renaissance (French for "rebirth") was a period that saw reborn in Europe the interest in science, art, and all learning that had flourished in ancient Greece and Rome. People became excited rather than frightened by unknown lands across the sea and by the unknown in religion, in science, and in art. Europeans

"discovered" new lands in America and the Pacific. They painted, sculpted, and composed music as never before. They tested outmoded learning in science, studied and created new forms of literature, and as explained in the discussion of the Protestant Reformation, questioned religious principles that had not been questioned for centuries. This exploration led to some great achievements.

All this flurry and creativity made its way to the court of Elizabeth I. When not involved with statecraft, the queen often occupied herself by giving new life and style to literature. She enjoyed it. She also enjoyed flattery (for chivalry was far from dead). Playwrights would dedicate their works to her, and often she was the direct subject of a piece of poetry, for writers sought her sponsorship and her favor. Responding to the new interest in learning of all kinds, the queen in 1571 reorganized and chartered the universities of Oxford and Cambridge. These

centers of learning, along with the court, the presence of printing, and the new-found wealth and consequently wider leisure for many helped to create an era of English literature that has never been surpassed. We judge its greatness not only in the works of Shakespeare but also in the new forms of literature that it explored successfully and in its abundance of talented poets and playwrights.

Elizabethan Poetry and Drama

Shakespeare and his work deserve and receive separate discussion in the pages ahead. Here we add only that he brought to its fullest flowering two new forms of written English literature: the lyric poem in sonnet form and the poetic drama.

The Elizabethan Age is an age of poetry. Except for philosopher and essayist Sir Francis Bacon and satirist Thomas Nashe, few writers of the period concentrated their efforts on the production of prose literature. Late in the era the translation of the Bible at the direction of King James I would do much to raise the low estate of prose writing; but, generally speaking, the literature of the age is the product of poets. Some Elizabethan writers dealt exclusively in lyric poetry, but many were also playwrights writing in verse.

One new and crucial fact about these poets and playwrights is that almost all of them saw the writing of literature as their primary work in life and expected some financial reward for their efforts. In the Elizabethan Age there flourished three institutions that actively helped to support writing as a legitimate profession: acting companies, the universities, and the court.

An Elizabethan playwright made a very small amount of money for each play, not enough to support himself. Since actors and other members of the theatrical profession might make a better living, being a member of an acting company could give a playwright means to support himself and his work. And so, for example, Shakespeare was a professional actor, and playwright John Lyly for a short time gained control of Blackfriars Theatre, where his early plays were produced by a company in which all the actors were boys. (He later went into debt.)

Many Elizabethan writers or their families were associated with universities or the royal court, both of which encouraged writers. Thomas Campion, a notable writer of Elizabethan songs, began his career as a student at Cambridge; Samuel Daniel, who often wrote patriotic verse, was the son of a well-educated music teacher. Both Edmund Spenser and Christopher Marlowe wrote extensively while students at Cambridge. Sir Thomas Wyatt and

Globe Theatre, based on Visscher's view of London, 1616.

Henry Howard, Earl of Surrey, were high-ranking courtiers of King Henry VIII; Sir Philip Sidney and Sir Walter Raleigh were high-born gentlemen and favorites of Queen Elizabeth.

At the same time that new and professional talent appeared, the form of poetry and drama changed. Unlike the long, story-telling poems of the Middle Ages, lyric poetry—poetry dealing with the emotions of the poet—was short, intricate, intellectual, and rigorous in form. The sonnet, which had its pedigree in Italy, was a popular form, and love was a popular topic. The poetic drama was also very different from the simple morality plays that were written in the Middle Ages.

Poetry and drama are not inseparable. To be sure, the great tragedies of ancient Greece—one of which, *Antigone,* begins on page 829 of this book—were written in verse, as were the great dramas of European countries. Most modern playwrights do not write in verse, however. The meeting of

poetry and drama in English literature—in the plays of William Shakespeare, Christopher Marlowe, John Lyly, Ben Jonson, and John Dryden, to name just a few—was glorious but relatively brief. It was glorious in its poetry and in the fact that poets produced plays that endure to this day. Yet after Shakespeare, Jonson, and Dryden, the poetic drama becomes very rare in English literature.

That the Elizabethan playwrights were skilled as poets may account for the magnificent language of their plays. It cannot account, however, for the distance covered between the medieval morality play and an Elizabethan drama such as *Macbeth.* Drama, poetic or otherwise, had obviously developed in many ways.

When we left drama in the villages of medieval England, it had by that time reached out beyond the confines of the church, both physically and intellectually. With the Renaissance, interest in ancient Greece and Rome led to the study of the works of Greek and Roman playwrights, especially the comedies of Plautus and Terence and the tragedies of Seneca. These plays often explored complex characters and themes, and they were widely imitated. Translators played a major part in the development of Elizabethan drama. It was not just coincidence that George Chapman, another famous playwright of the time, is even better known as a translator of the

William Shakespeare's home at Stratford-on-Avon.

works of the ancient Greek poet Homer.

The schools and universities contributed not only their scholarship but also an atmosphere in which drama served as entertainment. Students and teachers enjoyed working together to produce brief comedies and dialogues called **interludes** as campus entertainment. A new form of drama, of more historical than literary interest, was developing meanwhile at the court. This was the **masque,** a very stylized form of drama that involved dancing.

Ralph Roister Doister (1534) was the first true comedy of the period. It was written by Nicholas Udall, a headmaster at the Westminster School, a school for high-born boys in the borough of Westminster, within London. The comedy was about a braggart warrior whose bravery, as Alan Downer of Princeton puts it, is "purely verbal, and whose love affairs are inspired by an empty pocket rather than a warm heart." A few years later *Gammer Gurton's Needle,* a comedy by an unknown author, was produced at Cambridge University. Out of a simple comic situation

(a woman loses her sewing needle while sewing her husband's trousers and then "finds" the needle again when her husband sits down), this play stretches into a delightful entertainment, moving comedy closer to the traditional five-act form used by Shakespeare.

Meanwhile, two young playwrights, Thomas Sackville and Thomas Norton, wrote and produced *Gorboduc, or Ferrex and Porex,* a tragedy that followed the lines of an ancient Roman tragedy by Seneca. This play won the praise of Sir Philip Sidney, and the queen herself was so inspired that she tried her own hand at translating Seneca.

These years saw a happy combination of the great literary accomplishments of ancient Greece and Rome, the soaring poetry of Elizabethan England, the young professional playwrights, and a new, cheering, theater-going public.

Queen Elizabeth I died in 1603, a convenience for historians who can end the sixteenth century more or less with her death and start talking about the Stuart kings of the seventeenth century. For the student of literature, however, 1603 is not quite so neat an end date. After all, some of the towering figures of what we think of as Elizabethan literature simply kept on writing after the queen's death. Shakespeare did not write *Macbeth* and other masterpieces in Elizabeth's lifetime, although he had the grace to retire happily to his home town, Stratford-on-Avon, soon after the turn of the century. Sir Walter Raleigh, Francis Bacon, and Ben Jonson—to name just a few "Elizabethans"—outlived and outwrote their queen. Literary historians would prefer, therefore, to give James I to the Elizabethan Age and to extend that period to 1625, the year in which King James died.

TIME LINE

1485   Henry VII begins reign (until 1509)

King Henry VII

1496   Scottish Parliament requires schooling for eldest sons

1503   Canterbury Cathedral (begun 1070) completed

1509   Henry VIII begins reign (until 1547)

1512   English navy builds double-deck ships with seventy guns

English seventy-gun ship

1516   Sir Thomas More, *Utopia,* statement of the ideal society

1524   Soap first made in London

1527   Sonnet form introduced

1534   Henry VIII breaks with Roman Catholic Church

   Ralph Roister Doister, first comedy of period

Sir Thomas More

1547   Edward VI begins reign (until 1553)

1492   North America: Columbus reaches New World

1497   North America: Italian John Cabot explores East Coast for the English

1501   Italy: Michelangelo begins to sculpt *David*

1503   Italy: Leonardo da Vinci paints *Mona Lisa*

1512   Poland: Copernicus' theory that earth and other planets revolve around sun

1513   North America: Spaniard Balboa discovers Pacific Ocean; Spaniard Ponce de León discovers Florida

1514   Europe: Pineapples introduced

1517   Germany: Martin Luther, *Ninety-Five Theses,* declaring objections to abuses in the Church

   Europe: Coffee introduced

Copernicus' theory

1535   Canada: Frenchman Jacques Cartier sights St. Lawrence River, Quebec, and Montreal

1547   Russia: Ivan the Terrible crowned czar

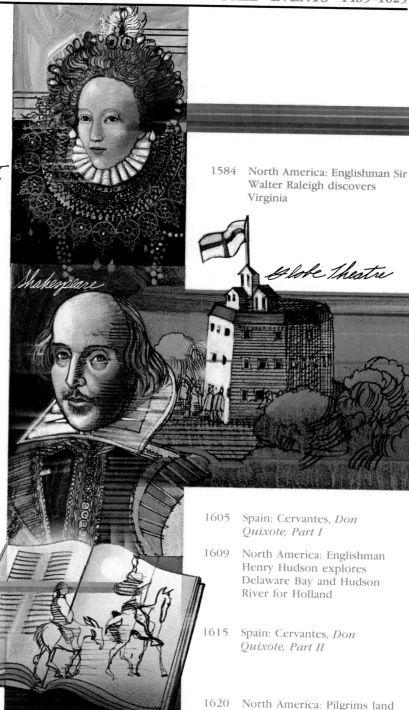

1553   Mary I begins reign (until 1558)

1558   Elizabeth I begins reign (until 1603)

1577   *Tottel's Miscellany,* containing posthumous poems of Wyatt and Surrey

c.1582   Sidney, *Astrophel and Stella*

Elizabeth I

1587   Marlowe, *Doctor Faustus*

1588   Defeat of Spanish Armada by English ships

1590   First part of Spenser's *Faerie Queene*

1594   Shakespeare, *Romeo and Juliet*

1597   Bacon's first essays published

1599   Globe Theatre, home of Shakespeare's company, founded

      East India Company chartered

      Marlowe, "The Passionate Shepherd to His Love"

1601   Thomas Campion and Philip Rosseter, *A Book of Airs*

1603   James I begins reign (until 1625)

1606   Shakespeare, *Macbeth*

1611   King James Bible

Don Quixote

1616   Shakespeare dies

Shakespeare

Globe Theatre

1584   North America: Englishman Sir Walter Raleigh discovers Virginia

1605   Spain: Cervantes, *Don Quixote, Part I*

1609   North America: Englishman Henry Hudson explores Delaware Bay and Hudson River for Holland

1615   Spain: Cervantes, *Don Quixote, Part II*

1620   North America: Pilgrims land at Plymouth

Sir Thomas Wyatt   *1503?–1542*

Thomas Wyatt is England's first important poet after the death of Chaucer. A member of a high-ranking family, Wyatt served on a number of overseas diplomatic missions for the court of Henry VIII. He died before reaching his fortieth birthday, of a fever contracted while traveling abroad on a royal errand.

Wyatt's diplomatic service took him to Italy, where he witnessed the Italian Renaissance firsthand. On returning to England, he brought back fashions in Italian poetry that would influence the direction Elizabethan verse would take. Most importantly, he introduced England to the **sonnet**, a fourteen-line lyric poem first popularized by the Italian poet Petrarch around the middle of the fourteenth century. The following sonnet, modeled on one by Petrarch, appeared in 1557 in *Tottel's Miscellany* as "The Lover Compareth His State to a Ship in Perilous Storm Tossed on the Sea."

■ In what ways might a person react to a love that seems hopeless?

Sir Thomas Wyatt

My Galley

My galley, chargèd with forgetfulness,[1]
Thorough[2] sharp seas in winter nights doth pass
'Tween rock and rock; and eke[3] mine enemy, alas!
That is my lord, steereth with cruelness;
5 And every oar a thought in readiness,
As though that[4] death were light in such a case.
An endless wind doth tear the sail apace
Of forcèd sighs, and trusty fearfulness;
A rain of tears, a cloud of dark disdain,
10 Hath done the wearied cords[5] great hinderance,
Wreathèd with error and eke with ignorance.
The stars be hid that led me to this pain.
Drownèd is reason that should me consort,
And I remain despairing of the port.

---

1. **chargèd with forgetfulness:** that is, so weighted with love that I am oblivious to all other things.
2. **Thorough:** through.
3. **eke:** also.
4. **As though that:** as if.
5. **cords:** ropes used in the ship's rigging.

Henry Howard, Earl of Surrey   *1517?–1547*

Henry Howard, Earl of Surrey, belonged to one of Tudor England's most powerful families. Like his father, one of Henry VIII's most capable generals, Surrey fought for his king and won fame for bravery. Nevertheless, when Henry VIII split with Rome, Surrey earned royal displeasure by refusing to disavow his Roman Catholicism. He was executed for treason when he was barely thirty.

Well read in Latin and Italian, Surrey translated into English portions of the *Aeneid,* the epic by the poet Virgil (see page 862). In doing so, he introduced to English literature the use of blank verse, or unrhymed ten-syllable lines of poetry, that would become the hallmark of the great verse dramas of the Elizabethan stage.

What are some associations that spring has for you?

Henry Howard, Earl of Surrey

Description of Spring

The soote[1] season, that bud and bloom forth brings,
With green hath clad the hill and eke the vale;
The nightingale with feathers new she sings;
The turtle to her make[2] hath told her tale.
5 Summer is come, for every spray now springs;
The hart hath hung his old head on the pale,[3]
The buck in brake[4] his winter coat he flings,
The fishes float with new repairèd scale,
The adder all her slough[5] away she slings,
10 The swift swallow pursueth the flies smale,[6]
The busy bee her honey now she mings.[7]
Winter is worn, that was the flowers' bale:[8]
And thus I see among these pleasant things,
Each care decays—and yet my sorrow springs.

---

1. **soote:** sweet.
2. **turtle to her make:** turtle dove to her mate.
3. **The hart . . . pale:** The hart, who grows new antlers each year, has rubbed off his old ones on the fence of the enclosure in which he is kept.
4. **brake:** thicket.
5. **slough:** outer layer of a snake's skin, which is periodically shed.
6. **smale:** small.
7. **mings:** mingles; mixes.
8. **bale:** woe; disaster; sorrow.

STUDY QUESTIONS

My Galley

Recalling

1. Through what kind of seas, and at what time of day and year, does the galley pass? With what does "mine enemy . . . that is my lord" steer the galley?
2. What rips the galley's sails? What hinders the worn cords of the rigging?
3. According to the last lines, of what does the speaker "remain despairing"?

Interpreting

4. What personal state or condition is the speaker comparing to the storm-tossed ship's perilous condition? Given that comparison, to whom or what is the speaker referring when he speaks of "mine enemy . . . that is my lord"? To whose tears does line 9 refer?
5. What physical feature of his beloved might the speaker have in mind when he speaks of the "stars . . . that led me to this pain"?
6. With the nouns in line 11 and the image in line 13, what does the speaker recognize about his love?

Extending

7. What advice would you give to the speaker?

Description of Spring

Recalling

1. What does spring "bring forth" in line 1? With what does it clothe "hill" and "vale"?
2. List five occurrences in the animal world that the poem details.
3. In the final lines, what does the speaker observe to be decaying? What nevertheless "springs"?

Interpreting

4. How, in general, do the images in lines 1–11 depict spring?
5. What contrast is presented in the last two lines? What pun, or play on words, do these lines contain?

Extending

6. What do this poem and the depiction of spring in the opening of The Canterbury Tales (page 58) have in common?

LITERARY FOCUS

The Speaker

The **speaker** of a lyric poem is the voice that communicates the poem's thoughts or feelings to us. The speaker is not necessarily the poet; sometimes the poet adopts a voice or a personality that is actually quite different from his or her own. This is especially true of Elizabethan poetry, in which conventions often dictated who the speaker would be.

The conventional speaker in love sonnets, established in the sonnets of the Italian poet Petrarch, is the *unrequited lover,* or lover whose feelings are not returned. The speaker of "My Galley" is just such a lover. He feels quite miserable; his fate is even worse than death (line 6).

Is this unrequited lover actually Sir Thomas Wyatt? Like most people, Wyatt at one time may have experienced unrequited love; in fact, there were rumors that he was once in love with Anne Boleyn, a lady of the court who later became Henry VIII's second queen. Nevertheless, it is unlikely that Wyatt was deep in the throes of passion and despair when he wrote this carefully crafted love poem. Rather, he probably adopted the voice of an unrequited lover because his poem is modeled on one of Petrarch's and because the voice helps strengthen the feelings that the poem expresses.

Thinking About the Speaker

■ *Tottel's Miscellany* first printed Surrey's poem with the title "Description of Spring, Wherein Each Thing Renews, Save Only the Lover." Using this information and the details of the poem, briefly describe the poem's speaker. Does it seem likely that the speaker is Surrey himself? Why or why not?

Sir Philip Sidney   *1554–1586*

A "Renaissance man" is someone who can do a variety of things exceptionally well, as so many great personalities of the Renaissance seemed able to do. The Italian Leonardo da Vinci, for example, was an architect, a scientist, and an inventor, as well as one of the world's greatest painters. Similarly, Sir Philip Sidney excelled in many ways during his brief life. Sidney was a courtier and a high-born attendant at court whose refined, aristocratic behavior made him a particular favorite of Queen Elizabeth's. A student at Oxford, he was a great traveler who met many important teachers, writers, and statesmen during his sojourns on the Continent. Sidney was a noted patron of the arts, encouraging other writers in their work. He was also a man of convictions and a brave soldier, who gave his life on a battlefield while fighting for the Protestant cause in Holland.

Finally, Sir Philip Sidney was a gifted writer. His *Arcadia,* a story of romance, intrigue, and politics, is probably the finest imaginative prose work of the Elizabethan era, and his *Defense of Poesy* is the outstanding piece of literary criticism of the age. He is perhaps best noted, however, as the author of *Astrophel and Stella,* a sequence of mostly sonnets that began a tradition in English lyric poetry that others have followed to the present time. *Astrophel and Stella* is a series of 110 brief poems that develop a single subject, love. The poems do not tell a story. Instead, they examine love from many different perspectives. The two poems that follow are representative.

▪ The speaker in the following poems is an unrequited lover. How would you advise him to win his love's favor?

Sir Philip Sidney

Loving in Truth

Loving in truth, and fain[1] in verse my love to show,
That the dear she might take some pleasure of my pain,
Pleasure might cause her read, reading might make her know,
Knowledge might pity win, and pity grace[2] obtain,
5 I sought fit words to paint the blackest face of woe;
Studying inventions fine, her wits to entertain,
Oft turning others' leaves[3] to see if thence would flow
Some fresh and fruitful showers upon my sunburned brain.
But words came halting[4] forth, wanting Invention's stay;[5]
10 Invention, Nature's child, fled stepdame Study's blows;
And others' feet still seemed but strangers in my way.
Thus, great with child to speak, and helpless in my throes,
Biting my truant pen, beating myself for spite:
"Fool," said my Muse[6] to me, "look in thy heart, and write!"

---

1. **fain:** wanting, desiring.
2. **grace:** favor.
3. **leaves:** pages of books or manuscripts.
4. **halting:** limping.

5. **wanting . . . stay:** lacking the support of inspiration.
6. **Muse:** source of poetic inspiration. In Greek mythology muses presided over the various arts and sciences.

Sonnet 31

With how sad steps, Oh Moon, thou climb'st the skies!
How silently, and with how wan a face!
What, may it be that even in heavenly place
That busy archer[1] his sharp arrows tries?
5 Sure, if that long-with-love-acquainted eyes
Can judge of love, thou feel'st a lover's case,
I read it in thy looks; thy languished grace,
To me, that feel the like, thy state descries.[2]
Then, even of fellowship,[3] Oh Moon, tell me,
10 Is constant love deemed there but want of wit?[4]
Are beauties there as proud as here they be?
Do they above love to be loved, and yet
Those lovers scorn whom that love doth possess?
Do they call virtue there ungratefulness?[5]

---

1. **That . . . archer:** Cupid, god of love.
2. **descries:** reveals.
3. **even of fellowship:** that is, because we both know what it is to be in love.

4. **wit:** intelligence.
5. **Do . . . ungratefulness:** Is to be ungrateful to one who loves you called a virtue?

STUDY QUESTIONS

Loving in Truth

Recalling

1. According to the first two lines, what is the speaker trying to show in his poems? According to line 4, what is his ultimate goal?
2. According to lines 6−7, where does the speaker look for help? Which lines indicate that these two sources prove unsatisfactory?
3. What does the speaker's "Muse" finally tell him?

Interpreting

4. According to line 6, what sort of poem does the speaker seem to think his love will like? Do lines 2−4 reflect that kind of poem? Why or why not?
5. What does the speaker finally conclude he must write to his love? How does his conclusion contradict what he seems to think in lines 1−8?

Extending

6. Think of a difficult assignment or project that you have done in the past. Did some kind of inspiration help you to complete it? Where did you find that inspiration?

Sonnet 31

Recalling

1. How does the speaker describe the moon's "face" in line 2? What question does he ask in lines 3−4?
2. According to lines 5−9, what do the speaker and the moon have in common?
3. In your own words, tell what the speaker asks in lines 10−14.

Interpreting

4. What does the description of the moon in lines 1−8 suggest about the speaker's emotions when he is in love?
5. What do the questions that conclude the poem imply about the object of the speaker's love?

Extending

6. In Sidney's title *Astrophel and Stella* the first word is Greek for "starlover," and the second word is Latin for "star." What might Sidney be saying by thinking of himself as Astrophel and his love as Stella?

LITERARY FOCUS

The Italian Sonnet

Although Elizabethan poets produced some of the world's finest sonnets, the sonnet was not originally an English form. The conventions of sonnets were established by Petrarch, the great lyric poet of the Italian Renaissance. A **sonnet** (from the Italian for "little song") is a fourteen-line lyric poem with a fixed rhyme pattern and a regular rhythm, or **meter.** Its usual meter is **iambic pentameter;** that is, each line has five feet (*pentameter*), and each foot is made up of an *iamb,* an unstressed syllable (marked ˘) followed by a stressed syllable (marked ′):

$$\breve{}\quad ′\; /\; \breve{}\quad ′\; /\; \breve{}\quad ′\; /\; \breve{}\quad ′\; /$$
Are beau / ties there / as proud / as they /
$$\breve{}\quad ′\; /$$
here be? /

Sonnet form is also characterized by its pattern of end-of-line rhymes, or **rhyme scheme.** The **Italian,** or **Petrarchan, sonnet** is divided into two parts in which the first eight lines, or **octave,** use one set of end rhymes and the last six lines, or **sestet,** use another. This change in end rhymes helps reflect the poem's content: Usually the octave presents a question or a problem, and the sestet answers the question or draws a conclusion.

In analyzing a poem's rhyme scheme, we use letters of the alphabet to represent each new end rhyme. The typical Italian sonnet uses the rhyme scheme *abbaabba* for the octave and *cdecde, cdccdc,* or *cdedce* for the sestet, but there are variations. Sidney's "Sonnet 31," for example, illustrates the typical Italian octave but modifies the sestet to rhyme *cdcdee.* Nevertheless, it is considered an Italian sonnet because it maintains the octave / sestet division: an octave with one set of end rhymes and a sestet with another.

Thinking About the Italian Sonnet

1. Copy line 5 of "Loving in Truth," and mark the stressed and unstressed syllables. In what way does the poem vary typical sonnet meter?
2. Why is "Description of Spring" (page 115) not an *Italian* sonnet? Study the group of lines with one set of end rhymes and the group with another. How does the rhyme scheme reflect the poem's content?

Edmund Spenser   *1552–1599*

Known as the "prince of poets" in his time, Edmund Spenser is generally regarded as the greatest nondramatic poet of the Elizabethan Age. He was born in London to a poor family and was educated at Cambridge on a scholarship. In 1580 he became secretary to the governor of Ireland, where he lived until a year before his death. One of his visitors in Ireland was Sir Walter Raleigh, who helped him publish *The Faerie Queene,* an adventure-packed epic that won him a lasting place on the roster of Britain's great poets. Spenser was also a master of pastoral verse, poems that portray the simple beauties of rural life; his works in the pastoral tradition include *The Shepherd's Calendar* (1579) and two poems celebrating a rural wedding, *Prothalamion* (1594) and *Epithalamion* (1594). To mourn the death of his friend Sir Philip Sidney, Spenser wrote a number of elegies, or poems of lament, including the famous *Astrophel* (1586). Finally, like other great lyric poets of the day, Spenser created a sonnet sequence, which he called *Amoretti* (1594).

Introducing The Faerie Queene

The Faerie Queene is an **epic** that, like *Beowulf,* depicts heroism in an enchanted world of dragons, monsters, and other marvels. A long poem, it is divided into books, which are further divided into **cantos** (from the Latin *cantus,* meaning "song"). Spenser had planned twelve books for *The Faerie Queene,* but he completed only six, publishing the first three in 1589 and the last in 1596. Each book has as its hero a knight who performs noble deeds for a glorious fairy queen whom Spenser intentionally associates with Queen Elizabeth. The knight in each book represents a different moral virtue: justice, courtesy, and so on. Obstacles the knight encounters stand for evils and temptations that must be overcome. Such a work—in which characters, events, and settings all represent abstract moral qualities—is called an **allegory.**

In the following segment from Book I, Canto I, the Red Cross Knight, who represents holiness, is bound on a mission for the Faerie Queene. The episode opens with a warning from Lady Una, who represents truth, a warning echoed by her companion the Dwarf, who represents prudence, or sound judgment.

■ What are some evils that a monster might represent?

Edmund Spenser

from **The Faerie Queene**

from **Canto I**

Saint George and the Dragon,
Roger van der Weyden, c. 1432.

12

"Be well aware," quoth then that Lady mild,
  "Lest sudden mischief ye too rash provoke;
  The danger hid, the place unknown and wild,
  Breeds dreadful doubts: oft fire is without smoke,
5 And peril without show; therefore your stroke,
  Sir knight, withhold, till further trial made."
  "Ah, Lady," said he, "shame were to revoke
  The forward footing for a hidden shade:[1]
Virtue gives herself light, through darkness for to wade."

1 **shade:** shadow (of danger).

13

10 "Yea, but," quoth she, "the peril of this place
  I better wot[2] than you, though now too late
  To wish you back return with foul disgrace,
  Yet wisdom warns, whilst foot is in the gate,
  To stay the step, ere forced to retrate.[3]
15 This is the wandering wood, this Error's den,
  A monster vile, whom God and man doth hate:
  Therefore I read[4] beware." "Fly, fly," quoth then
The fearful Dwarf: "this is no place for living men."

2 **wot:** know.

3 **retrate:** retreat.

4 **read:** advise; counsel.

14

But full of fire and greedy hardiment,[5]
20 The youthful knight could not for aught be stayed,
  But forth unto the darksome hole he went,
  And looked in: his glistering armor made
  A little glooming light, much like a shade,
  By which he saw the ugly monster plain,
25 Half like a serpent horribly displayed,
  But th' other half did woman's shape retain,
Most loathsome, filthy, foul, and full of vile disdain.

5 **greedy hardiment:** eager boldness.

15

And as she lay upon the dirty ground,
  Her huge long tail her den all overspread,
30 Yet was in knots and many boughtes[6] upwound,
  Pointed with mortal sting. Of her there bred
  A thousand young ones, which she daily fed,

6 **boughtes:** coils.

Sucking upon her poisonous dugs, each one
Of sundry shapes, yet all ill favored:
35   Soon as that uncouth[7] light upon them shone,
Into her mouth they crept, and sudden all were gone.

7 **uncouth:** unfamiliar.

16

Their dam upstart, out of her den affrayed,[8]
And rushed forth, hurling her hideous tail
About her cursed head, whose folds displayed
40   Were stretched now forth at length without entrail.[9]
She looked about, and seeing one in mail
Armed to point,[10] sought back to turn again;
For light she hated as the deadly bale,[11]
Ay wont[12] in desert darkness to remain,
45 Where plain none might her see, nor she see any plain.

8 **affrayed:** frightened.

9 **entrail:** coiling.

10 **to point:** completely.

11 **bale:** disaster; destruction.

12 **wont:** accustomed.

17

Which when the valiant Elf[13] perceived, he leapt
As lion fierce upon the flying prey,
And with his trenchant blade her boldly kept
From turning back, and forced her to stay:
50   Therewith enraged she loudly 'gan to bray,
And turning fierce, her speckled tail advanced,
Threatening her angry sting, him to dismay:
Who naught aghast, his mighty hand enhanced:[14]
The stroke down from her head unto her shoulder glanced.

13 **Elf:** the knight, who is of "faerie" birth.

14 **enhanced:** raised.

18

55 Much daunted with that dint,[15] her sense was dazed,
Yet kindling rage, herself she gathered round,
And all at once her beastly body raised
With doubled forces high above the ground:
Then wrapping up her wreathèd stern around,
60   Leaped fierce upon his shield, and her huge train[16]
All suddenly about his body wound,
That hand or foot to stir he strove in vain:
God help the man so wrapped in Error's endless train.

15 **dint:** blow.

16 **train:** tail.

19

His Lady sad to see his sore constraint,
65   Cried out, "Now, now, Sir knight, show what ye be.
Add faith unto your force, and be not faint:
Strangle her, else she sure will strangle thee."
That when he heard, in great perplexity,
His gall did grate for grief[17] and high disdain,
70   And knitting all his force got one hand free,

17 **for grief:** because of pain.

Wherewith he gripped her gorge[18] with so great pain,
That soon to loose her wicked bands did her constrain.

20

Therewith she spewed out of her filthy maw[19]
  A flood of poison horrible and black,
75 Full of great lumps of flesh and gobbets[20] raw,
  Which stunk so vilely, that it forced him slack
  His grasping hold, and from her turn him back:
  Her vomit full of books and papers was,
  With loathly frogs and toads, which eyes did lack,
80 And creeping sought way in the weedy grass:
Her filthy parbreake[21] all the place defiled has.

21

As when old father Nilus 'gins to swell
  With timely pride above the Egyptian vale,
  His fatty waves do fertile slime outwell,
85 And overflow each plain and lowly dale;
  But when his later spring 'gins to avale,[22]
  Huge heaps of mud he leaves, wherein there breed
  Ten thousand kinds of creatures, partly male
  And partly female of his fruitful seed;
90 Such ugly monstrous shapes elsewhere may no man reed.[23]

22

The same so sore annoyèd has the knight,
  That well nigh chokèd with the deadly stink,
  His forces fail, nor can no longer fight.
  Whose courage when the fiend perceived to shrink,
95 She pourèd forth out of her hellish sink
  Her fruitful cursèd spawn of serpents small,
  Deformèd monsters, foul, and black as ink,
  Which swarming all about his legs did crawl,
And him encumbered sore, but could not hurt at all.

23

100 As gentle Shepherd in sweet eventide,
  When ruddy Phoebus 'gins to welke[24] in west,
  High on an hill, his flock to viewen wide,
  Marks which do bite their hasty supper best;
  A cloud of cumbrous gnats do him molest,
105 All striving to infix their feeble stings,
  That from their 'noyance he nowhere can rest,
  But with his clownish hands their tender wings
He brusheth oft, and oft doth mar their murmurings.

18 **gorge:** throat.

19 **maw:** stomach.

20 **gobbets:** pieces (of flesh).

21 **parbreake:** vomit.

22 **spring . . . avale:** flood begins to subside.

23 **reed:** perceive; see.

24 **ruddy Phoebus . . . welke:** the red sun begins to set. Apollo, often called Phoebus Apollo, was the Greek god of the sun.

24

Thus ill bestead,[25] and fearful more of shame
110   Than of the certain peril he stood in,
Half furious unto his foe he came,
Resolved in mind all suddenly to win,
Or soon to lose, before he once would lin;[26]
And struck at her with more than manly force
115   That from her body full of filthy sin
He reft[27] her hateful head without remorse;
A stream of coal-black blood forth gushèd from her corse.[28]

25 **bestead:** situated.

26 **lin:** stop.

27 **reft:** took away with violence.
28 **corse:** body.

25

Her scattered brood, soon as their Parent dear
They saw so rudely falling to the ground,
120   Groaning full deadly, all with troublous fear,
Gathered themselves about her body round,
Weening[29] their wonted entrance to have found
At her wide mouth: but being there withstood
They flockèd all about her bleeding wound,
125   And suckèd up their dying mother's blood,
Making her death their life, and eke[30] her hurt their good.

29 **Weening:** thinking; believing.

30 **eke:** also.

26

That detestable sight him much amazed,
To see th' unkindly Imps of heaven accursed,
Devour their dam; on whom while so he gazed,
130   Having all satisfied their bloody thirst,
Their bellies swollen he saw with fullness burst,
And bowels gushing forth: well worthy end
Of such as drunk her life, the which[31] them nursed:
Now needeth him no longer labor spend,
135 His foes have slain themselves, with whom he should contend.

31 **the which:** who.

27

His Lady seeing all that chanced, from far
Approached in haste to greet his victory,
And said, "Fair knight, born under happy star,
Who see your vanquished foes before you lie:
140   Well worthy be you of that Armory,[32]
Wherein you have great glory won this day,
And proved your strength on a strong enemy,
Your first adventure: many such I pray,
And henceforth ever wish, that like succeed it may."

32 **Armory:** the armor of a Christian.

Spenser's skill as a lyric poet is nowhere more apparent than in his sonnet sequence *Amoretti,* from which the following three sonnets come. *Amoretti* means "little love songs," and the sonnets that comprise it recount a courtship, probably Spenser's courtship of Elizabeth Boyle, whom he married in 1594.

Edmund Spenser

Sonnet 15

Ye tradeful merchants, that with weary toil
Do seek most precious things to make your gain;
And both the Indias[1] of their treasure spoil;
What needeth you to seek so far in vain?
5 For lo, my love doth in herself contain
All this world's riches that may far be found:
If sapphires, lo, her eyes be sapphires plain;
If rubies, lo, her lips be rubies sound;
If pearls, her teeth be pearls, both pure and round;
10 If ivory, her forehead ivory ween;[2]
If gold, her locks are finest gold on ground;[3]
If silver, her fair hands are silver sheen;[4]
But that which fairest is, but few behold,
Her mind, adorned with virtues manifold.

1. **both the Indias:** both the East and West Indies, sources of precious metals and other valuable goods.
2. **ween:** imagined.
3. **ground:** earth.
4. **sheen:** shining.

Edmund Spenser

Sonnet 26

Sweet is the rose, but grows upon a briar;
Sweet is the juniper, but sharp his bough,
Sweet is the eglantine,[1] but pricketh near;
Sweet is the fir bloom, but his branch is rough;
5 Sweet is the cypress, but his rind is tough;
Sweet is the nut, but bitter is his pill;[2]
Sweet is the broom flower, but yet sour enough;
And sweet is moly,[3] but his root is ill.
So every sweet with sour is tempered still,[4]
10 That maketh it be coveted the more:
For easy things, that may be got at will,
Most sorts of men do set but little store.
Why then should I account of little pain,
That endless pleasure shall unto me gain!

---

1. **eglantine:** European rose with hooked
spines; sometimes called sweetbrier.
2. **pill:** core; center.
3. **moly:** wild garlic with white flowers.
4. **still:** always.

Sonnet 75

One day I wrote her name upon the strand,[1]
But came the waves and washèd it away;
Again I wrote it with a second hand,
But came the tide, and made my pains his prey.
5 "Vain man," said she, "that dost in vain assay,[2]
A mortal thing so to immortalize,
For I myself shall like to this decay,
And eke[3] my name be wipèd out likewise."
"Not so," quod[4] I, "let baser things devise
10 To die in dust, but you shall live by fame:
My verse your virtues rare shall eternize,[5]
And in the heavens write your glorious name.
Where whenas death shall all the world subdue,
Our love shall live, and later life renew."

---

1. **strand:** seashore.
2. **assay:** try.
3. **eke:** also
4. **quod:** said.
5. **eternize:** make eternal.

A Vase with Flowers, Jacob Vosmer, 1615.

STUDY QUESTIONS

The Faerie Queene

Recalling

1. Summarize Lady Una's advice in stanza 12 and the knight's response.
2. What monster must the knight face (stanzas 13–14)? Briefly describe the monster and the creatures whom she feeds daily (stanza 15).
3. In what "endless train" is the knight wrapped in stanza 18? What does the knight hear that gives him courage?
4. By what means does the knight kill the monster? What causes the deaths of the monster's children? According to stanza 26, why need the knight no longer labor?
5. In the final stanza, of what does Lady Una say the knight is "well worthy"?

Interpreting

6. Since the knight represents holiness, what sort of error might the monster represent? What message about this sort of error is suggested by the behavior of the monster's children after their mother is killed? What message is suggested in line 135?
7. Explain the symbolic situation that the events in stanzas 18–19 represent. Keep in mind that Lady Una represents truth.
8. What typical heroic qualities does the knight display?

Sonnet 15

Recalling

1. What people, seeking what things, does the speaker address directly? What question does he ask these people in line 4?
2. What does the speaker say his beloved "doth in herself contain"? List three examples he uses to support this statement.
3. Of all his beloved's attributes, which does the speaker find "fairest"? With what is this attribute "adorned"?

Interpreting

4. Does "mind" in line 14 refer merely to intelligence? Explain your answer.
5. In what way do the qualities of the beloved discussed in lines 7–12 contrast with the qualities discussed in lines 13–14? What general message about love is implied?
6. What general message does the poem suggest about the riches the merchants pursue?

Sonnet 26

Recalling

1. Summarize the point that the speaker makes about each flower or plant in lines 1–8.
2. What effect does the "sour" aspect of things have on people (lines 9–12)? What does the speaker say about "easy things"?
3. In lines 13–14, of what should the speaker not take account? What will he gain?

Interpreting

4. To what specific personal experience might lines 13–14 refer?
5. An analogy explains something unfamiliar by comparing it to something familiar. What central analogy does the poem make to explain the experience of lines 13–14?

Sonnet 75

Recalling

1. Where does the speaker write the name of his beloved? What happens to the writing?
2. What reason does the beloved give for calling the speaker vain (lines 5–8)? What does she say will happen to her?
3. In response, what does the speaker say his verse will do? What does he say will live after "death shall all the world subdue"?

Interpreting

4. What occupation of the speaker might his activities in lines 1–4 represent?
5. To what time is the speaker referring in the last two lines? What sort of love is he therefore describing?
6. What kind of poetry does this sonnet suggest might be immortal?

LITERARY FOCUS

The Spenserian Stanza

For *The Faerie Queene* Spenser invented a new stanza form, a nine-line stanza rhyming *ababbcbcc*. The first eight lines are iambic pentameter; the last line has six iambic feet (iambic *hexameter*) instead of five and is called an **alexandrine**. Known now as the **Spenserian stanza**, this nine-line format was used by such later British poets as Robert Burns, Lord Byron, Percy Bysshe Shelley, and John Keats.

Thinking About the Spenserian Stanza

■ Examine the alexandrines in stanzas 12, 18, and 26. Why do you think Spenser put these ideas in the alexandrine of each stanza?

Christopher Marlowe 1564–1593
Sir Walter Raleigh 1552–1618

Christopher Marlowe.

Born in the same year as Shakespeare, Christopher Marlowe was killed in a brawl when he was just twenty-nine. Some maintain the brawl erupted from an argument over paying the bill. Others think that Marlowe was killed as a result of espionage work he had done for the government.

If Shakespeare had died at twenty-nine, his greatest plays would have remained unwritten, and we would scarcely recognize his name. Yet Marlowe, by the time of his death, had already established himself as a powerful dramatist—earning the title "father of English tragedy." His tragedies *Tamburlaine, The Jew of Malta,* and *Dr. Faustus* place him second only to Shakespeare himself as the greatest playwright of the time.

In addition to his plays, Marlowe wrote one of the most famous of Elizabethan lyric poems, "The Passionate Shepherd to His Love." The poem is an invitation to the pastoral life, the happy peaceful life of country shepherds.

Sir Walter Raleigh.

Soldier, explorer, courtier, poet, and historian—Sir Walter Raleigh is one of the most colorful figures in English history. He founded the colony of Virginia, introduced tobacco to Europe, and fought the Spanish Armada. A famous story also has gallant Sir Walter removing his cloak and dropping it to the ground so that Queen Elizabeth could navigate a puddle without wetting her royal feet. Raleigh was also a great help to other artists of Elizabethan times. A friend of Marlowe and Spenser, he managed to obtain royal aid to help publish the first three books of Spenser's *Faerie Queene.*

James I, Elizabeth's successor, feared and distrusted Raleigh. During James's reign Raleigh was charged with treason and was convicted and sentenced to death. He was imprisoned instead in the Tower of London, where for twelve years he lived with his family and servants and wrote his *History of the World.* After a failed quest to South America for gold that was to buy his release, Raleigh was executed in 1618. Maintaining his equanimity until the end, Raleigh is said to have composed one of his best poems, "The Author's Epitaph, Made by Himself," the night before he died.

Much of Raleigh's poetry has been lost, but one gem that has survived is "The Nymph's Reply to the Shepherd," which appears on page 130. In it Raleigh's speaker, a young woman, replies to Marlowe's famous "passionate shepherd."

▨ What are the consequences of making a promise that is impossible to keep?

Christopher Marlowe

The Passionate Shepherd to His Love

Come live with me and be my love,
And we will all the pleasures prove[1]
That valleys, groves, hills, and fields,
Woods, or steepy mountain yields.

5 And we will sit upon the rocks,
Seeing the shepherds feed their flocks,
By shallow rivers to whose falls
Melodious birds sing madrigals.[2]

And I will make thee beds of roses
10 And a thousand fragrant posies,
A cap of flowers, and a kirtle[3]
Embroidered all with leaves of myrtle;

A gown made of the finest wool
Which from our pretty lambs we pull;
15 Fair lined slippers for the cold,
With buckles of the purest gold;

A belt of straw and ivy buds,
With coral clasps and amber studs:
And if these pleasures may thee move,
20 Come live with me, and be my love.

The shepherds' swains[4] shall dance and sing
For thy delight each May morning:
If these delights thy mind may move,
Then live with me and be my love.

---

1. **prove:** experience.
2. **madrigals:** here, harmonious songs.
3. **kirtle:** dress.
4. **swains:** country youths.

Sir Walter Raleigh

The Nymph's Reply to the Shepherd

If all the world and love were young,
And truth in every shepherd's tongue,
These pretty pleasures might me move
To live with thee and be thy love.

5　Time drives the flocks from field to fold[1]
When rivers rage and rocks grow cold,
And Philomel[2] becometh dumb;
The rest complains of cares to come.

The flowers do fade, and wanton[3] fields
10　To wayward winter reckoning yields;
A honey tongue, a heart of gall,[4]
Is fancy's spring, but sorrow's fall.

Thy gowns, thy shoes, thy beds of roses,
Thy cap, thy kirtle, and thy posies
15　Soon break, soon wither, soon forgotten—
In folly ripe, in reason rotten.

Thy belt of straw and ivy buds,
Thy coral clasps and amber studs,
All these in me no means can move
20　To come to thee and be thy love.

But could youth last and love still breed,[5]
Had joys no date[6] nor age no need,
Then these delights my mind might move
To live with thee and be thy love.

---

1. **fold:** enclosure or pen for sheep.
2. **Philomel:** According to Greek myth, the princess Philomela's tongue was cut out to prevent her from revealing a scandal. Later the gods turned Philomela into a nightingale.
3. **wanton:** here, profuse or ample.
4. **gall:** bitterness.
5. **still breed:** always thrive.
6. **date:** ending.

The Passionate Shepherd to His Love

Recalling

1. What does the shepherd entreat his love to do in the first stanza? What pleasures does he say he and his love will "prove"?
2. Name three things that the shepherd claims he will do for his love.

Interpreting

3. Which of the speaker's promises seem unrealistic? Why would the speaker make these promises?
4. What is the effect of the repetition of line 1 in lines 20 and 24? Does the entreaty become more or less persuasive with each repetition? Does the speaker sound more or less confident than earlier in the poem? Explain.

The Nymph's Reply to the Shepherd

Recalling

1. According to the first stanza, what would make the nymph accept the shepherd's offer?
2. What does the nymph say will happen to the flowers and fields promised by the shepherd (stanza 3)? What does she say will happen to the gown, shoes, rose beds, cap, kirtle, and posies (stanza 4)?
3. According to the last stanza, what would make the nymph accept the shepherd's offer?

Interpreting

4. What do all the predictions in stanzas 3 and 4 have in common? Basically, why does the speaker find the shepherd's offer unimpressive?
5. How are the views expressed in the first and last stanzas similar? Is the speaker saying there is a possibility she will accept the shepherd's offer, or is her answer a definite "no"? Explain.

LITERARY FOCUS

The Pastoral

A **pastoral** (from the Latin *pastor,* meaning "shepherd") is a work that depicts the simple pleasures of rural life. The typical pastoral is a lyric poem, like Marlowe's "Passionate Shepherd"; however, narrative poems like Spenser's *Shepherd's Calendar* and even dramas like Shakespeare's *As You Like It* are also considered pastorals. What all these works have in common is their idealized portrayal of rustic life, a portrait that is not grounded in reality but instead exaggerates rural innocence and splendor, often to make a point about the value of innocent simplicity in a world different from the writer's own.

Thinking About the Pastoral

1. List four phrases or lines in Marlowe's poem that exaggerate rural innocence or splendor, and underline the word or words that make each an exaggeration.
2. How was Marlowe different from the speaker in his poem? Use the author biography on page 128 to help you answer this question.

COMPOSITION

Developing a Thesis Statement

Develop a thesis statement about what Raleigh's poem adds to your reaction to Marlowe's poem, and in a brief essay defend your thesis with examples from the two poems. Before you write, first consider what you thought of Marlowe's poem when you initially read it. Then consider your impression of Marlowe's poem after reading Raleigh's response to it. *For help with this assignment, refer to Lesson 1 in the Writing About Literature Handbook at the back of this book.*

Writing a Letter

Write your own reply in the form of a letter to the shepherd in Marlowe's poem. Like Raleigh, you might pretend to be the woman whom the shepherd addresses. Explain why you accept or refuse his offer. If you prefer, pretend to be another suitor for the lady's hand, and explain why you can offer her a better life than the shepherd can. Your letter may be serious or humorous, but it should refer to the specific promises that the shepherd makes as well as to the general picture he paints.

William Shakespeare   *1564–1616*

William Shakespeare, poet and playwright, is said to be the world's favorite author. No other writer's plays have been produced so often and read so widely in so many different countries. Shakespeare's contemporaries first admired him for his long narrative poems *Venus and Adonis* (1593) and *The Rape of Lucrece* (1594). In the latter half of the seventeenth century and in the eighteenth century, he was revered for his dramas. Poets and critics in the nineteenth century considered him the "genius of the English race," and in the twentieth century he is regarded as the greatest of all writers for the stage.

Not much is known about Shakespeare's early life. He was born in 1564, probably on April 23, in the small country town of Stratford-on-Avon. His father was a prosperous glove maker and held several important positions in the town government. His mother, Mary Arden, was the daughter of a wealthy landowner. By the age of seven, Shakespeare was probably attending the local grammar school.

In 1582, when he was eighteen, Shakespeare married Anne Hathaway, the twenty-six-year-old daughter of a farmer who lived about a mile from Stratford. Over the next three years the couple had a daughter, Susanna, and twins, Hamnet and Judith. From 1585 to 1592, a period some scholars call "the lost years," virtually nothing is known about Shakespeare's life. From 1592 on, however, the records are much fuller. Sometime during the lost years Shakespeare moved to London and became part of the city's busy theatrical life. By 1594 he was a shareholder, or part owner, in one of London's most popular acting companies, the Lord Chamberlain's Men, and at least six of his plays had been produced. (Each shareholder contributed in some way to the company. Shakespeare was both a writer and actor; he is said to have played the ghost in *Hamlet*. The more popular his plays, the larger his share of the company's income.) In 1599 the company built the Globe Theatre, the most famous of Elizabethan theaters.

After Queen Elizabeth's death in 1603, the Lord Chamberlain's Men were sponsored by King James I and became known as the King's Men. In 1608 the company acquired a second theater in Blackfriars, a fashionable district of London. Shakespeare seems to have retired from acting about this time; his name does not appear in the lists of players after 1607. Between 1608 and 1613 Shakespeare wrote his last five plays: *Pericles, Cymbeline, The Winter's Tale, The Tempest,* and *Henry VIII.* While he was writing these plays, Shakespeare lived mostly in Stratford, where he was regarded as one of the town's most important citizens. He died on April 23, 1616, and is buried in Holy Trinity Church in Stratford.

What makes Shakespeare the world's favorite author? No other writer—playwright, poet, or novelist—has seen more deeply into the many manifestations of human nature. In an uncanny way Shakespeare understands why people behave the way they do. Young and old, women and men, good and evil, beggars and kings: All live in his plays. All speak in voices so right and so true that again and again they emerge as solid as life, as much at home in our time as in Shakespeare's own.

In addition to his plays and two narrative poems, Shakespeare wrote a sequence of 154 sonnets. It was probably written in the 1590s, when Sir Philip Sidney's sequence, *Astrophel and Stella,* was so popular. Unlike most other sequences of his day, Shakespeare's cycle seems to tell a story. The plot is vague and fragmentary, involving a young nobleman, a "dark lady," a poet, and a rival poet. However, the "plot" of the "story" is not as important as Shakespeare's themes regarding life, love, beauty, and friendship.

■ In what ways might someone today celebrate the themes of life, love, beauty, and friendship?

William Shakespeare

Sonnet 18

Shall I compare thee to a summer's day?
Thou art more lovely and more temperate.
Rough winds do shake the darling buds of May,
And summer's lease[1] hath all too short a date.[2]
5 Sometime too hot the eye of heaven shines,
And often is his gold complexion dimmed;
And every fair from fair[3] sometime declines,
By chance or nature's changing course untrimmed;[4]
But thy eternal summer shall not fade,
10 Nor lose possession of that fair thou ow'st,[5]
Nor shall Death brag thou wand'rest in his shade,
When in eternal lines[6] to time thou grow'st.
So long as men can breathe or eyes can see,
So long lives this, and this gives life to thee.

1. **lease:** allotted time.
2. **date:** duration.
3. **fair . . . fair:** beautiful thing from beauty.
4. **untrimmed:** stripped of beauty.
5. **thou ow'st:** you possess.
6. **lines:** lines of poetry.

William Shakespeare

Sonnet 29

When, in disgrace[1] with Fortune and men's eyes,
I all alone beweep my outcast state,
And trouble deaf heaven with my bootless[2] cries,
And look upon myself and curse my fate,
5 Wishing me like to one more rich in hope,
Featured like him, like him with friends possessed,
Desiring this man's art[3] and that man's scope,[4]
With what I most enjoy contented least;
Yet in these thoughts myself almost despising,
10 Haply[5] I think on thee, and then my state,
Like to the lark at break of day arising
From sullen earth, sings hymns at heaven's gate;
   For thy sweet love remembered such wealth brings,
   That then I scorn to change my state with kings.

1. **disgrace:** disfavor.
2. **bootless:** useless, futile.
3. **art:** skill.
4. **scope:** mental power.
5. **Haply:** by chance.

Sonnet 30

When to the sessions[1] of sweet silent thought
I summon up remembrance of things past,
I sigh the lack of many a thing I sought,
And with old woes new[2] wail my dear time's waste.
5 Then can I drown an eye, unused to flow,
For precious friends hid in death's dateless[3] night,
And weep afresh love's long since canceled[4] woe,
And moan th' expense[5] of many a vanished sight;
Then can I grieve at grievances foregone,[6]
10 And heavily from woe to woe tell[7] o'er
The sad account of fore-bemoanèd moan,
Which I new pay as if not paid before.
   But if the while I think on thee, dear friend,
   All losses are restored and sorrows end.

1. **sessions:** that is, sittings of a law court.
2. **new:** again.
3. **dateless:** endless.
4. **canceled:** that is, because paid in full.
5. **expense:** loss.
6. **grievances foregone:** earlier griefs.
7. **tell:** count.

Sonnet 55

Not marble, nor the gilded monuments
Of princes, shall outlive this pow'rful rhyme,
But you shall shine more bright in these contents
Than unswept stone, besmeared with sluttish time.[1]
5 When wasteful war shall statues overturn,
And broils[2] root out the work of masonry,
Nor Mars his sword nor[3] war's quick fire shall burn
The living record of your memory.
'Gainst death and all-oblivious enmity[4]
10 Shall you pace forth; your praise shall still find room
Even in the eyes of all posterity
That wear this world out[5] to the ending doom.
    So, till the judgment that yourself arise,[6]
    You live in this, and dwell in lovers' eyes.

---

1. **Than . . . time:** than in a stone tomb or on a memorial
tablet, worn down by time and covered with dust.
2. **broils:** skirmishes, battles.
3. **Nor Mars . . . nor:** neither the Roman war god's sword nor . . .
4. **oblivious enmity:** enmity, or hostility, that brings oblivion,
causing us to be forgotten.
5. **wear . . . out:** outlast this world.
6. **So . . . arise:** so until you rise from the dead on Judgment Day.

Sonnet 73

That time of year thou mayst in me behold
When yellow leaves, or none, or few, do hang
Upon those boughs which shake against the cold,
Bare ruined choirs,[1] where late the sweet birds sang.
5 In me thou see'st the twilight of such day
As after sunset fadeth in the west;
Which by and by black night doth take away,
Death's second self[2] that seals up all in rest.
In me thou see'st the glowing of such fire,
10 That on the ashes of his youth doth lie,
As the deathbed whereon it must expire,
Consumed with that which it was nourished by.[3]
    This thou perceiv'st which makes thy love more strong,
    To love that well which thou must leave ere long.

---

1. **choirs:** choir lofts; parts of church interiors occupied by choirs.
2. **Death's . . . self:** that is, sleep.
3. **Consumed . . . by:** choked by the ashes of the wood that previously
fueled its flame.

William Shakespeare **135**

In this selection, as in one selection in each unit, you will find notes in the right-hand margin that highlight parts of the selection. These notes point out important ideas of the literary period and draw your attention to literary elements and techniques covered in the Literary Focuses. Page numbers in the notes refer you to more extensive discussions of these important ideas and elements.

William Shakespeare

Sonnet 116

Let me not to the marriage of true minds
Admit impediments.[1] Love is not love
Which alters when it alteration finds
Or bends with the remover to remove.[2]
5 Oh, no, it is an ever-fixèd mark[3]
That looks on tempests and is never shaken;
It is the star to every wand'ring bark,[4]
Whose worth's unknown, although his height[5] be taken.
Love's not Time's fool,[6] though rosy lips and cheeks
10 Within his bending sickle's compass[7] come;
Love alters not with his[8] brief hours and weeks,
But bears it out even to the edge of doom.[9]
    If this be error and upon[10] me proved,
    I never writ, nor no man ever loved.

English Sonnet (p. 139): The English, or Shakespearean, sonnet consists of three quatrains *(abab cdcd efef)* and a rhymed couplet *(gg).*

Elizabethan idea: The definition of *love* reflects the intellectual side of Elizabethan poetry (p. 109).

Figurative language (p. 139): Shakespeare uses a variety of metaphors to make the abstract *love* more concrete.

Elizabethan idea: Lyric poetry expressed human emotions as well as intellect (p. 110).

---

    1. **impediments:** reasons for preventing a marriage. Compare the Marriage Service: "If any of you know cause or just impediment why these persons should not be joined together . . ."
    2. **Or . . . remove:** or withdraws when the object of its love leaves.
    3. **an . . . mark:** a permanent beacon.
    4. **star . . . bark:** that is, the North Star, used by sailors in barks, or boats, for navigation.
    5. **height:** altitude.
    6. **fool:** plaything.
    7. **compass:** circle, range.
    8. **his:** that is, Time's.
    9. **doom:** Judgment Day.
    10. **upon:** against.

Sonnet 130

My mistress'[1] eyes are nothing like the sun;
Coral is far more red than her lips' red;
If snow be white, why then her breasts are dun;[2]
If hairs be wires, black wires grow on her head.
5 I have seen roses damasked,[3] red and white,
But no such roses see I in her cheeks;
And in some perfumes is there more delight
Than in the breath that from my mistress reeks.[4]
I love to hear her speak, yet well I know
10 That music hath a far more pleasing sound;
I grant I never saw a goddess go;[5]
My mistress, when she walks, treads on the ground.
And yet, by heaven, I think my love as rare
As any she belied with false compare.

---

1. **mistress':** sweetheart's.
2. **dun:** dull grayish-brown.
3. **damasked:** spotted and streaked pink and white.
4. **reeks:** emanates.
5. **go:** walk.

Portrait of a Man and Woman at a Casement, Fra Filippo Lippi (c. 1406–1469).

William Shakespeare **137**

STUDY QUESTIONS

Sonnet 18

Recalling

1. According to lines 1−8, in what ways is the speaker's friend unlike a summer's day?
2. What will prevent the friend's eternal summer from fading, according to lines 9−12?

Interpreting

3. What does "this" refer to in the last line?
4. What is the speaker's purpose in writing his "eternal lines," and what conditions are necessary for his purpose to be carried out?

Sonnet 29

Recalling

1. List the speaker's catalogue of complaints in the first eight lines.
2. What does the speaker remember in line 10? What image describes his mood in lines 11 and 12?

Interpreting

3. Compare the speaker's thoughts in the first eight lines of the sonnet to his thoughts in the last six lines. How has his perspective changed, especially in the last two lines?

Extending

4. Is the transition in the speaker's mood realistic or insincere? Why or why not?

Sonnet 30

Recalling

1. Of what does the speaker think in the first four lines, and what does that thought lead him to express in the next four lines?
2. As a result of his thoughts in lines 4−8, what does the speaker reexperience in lines 8−12?
3. Of whom does the speaker think in the final lines? How does this thought affect his mood?

Interpreting

4. What do the last two lines, coming after twelve lines that express a contrasting point of view, add to the overall effect of the poem?
5. Besides the image of a court session in lines 1−2, what other image does the sonnet introduce in line 7 with "canceled" and continue in lines 10−12? Why is the image appropriate?

Sonnet 55

Recalling

1. In lines 1−4 what does the speaker say will not outlive the poem?
2. In lines 5−8 what cannot destroy the poem?
3. Therefore, what will find room "in the eyes of all posterity"?

Interpreting

4. Whose eyes is the phrase "lovers' eyes" referring to?

Extending

5. Do you think this poem has accomplished its purpose? Give reasons for your answer.

Sonnet 73

Recalling

1. The speaker associates himself with what time of year in lines 1−2? With what time of day in lines 5−6? With what kind of fire in lines 9−10?
2. What does the friend, addressed in lines 13−14, "perceiv'st"?

Interpreting

3. How does the speaker take the image in lines 1−2 and expand it in lines 3−4? Show that the speaker makes a similar expansion for the images in lines 5−6 and 9−10.
4. What do all the images in lines 1−12 symbolize?
5. According to the last two lines, for what is the speaker praising his friend? How does the couplet tie in emotionally with the first twelve lines?

Sonnet 116

Recalling

1. List three or four things that love is *not,* according to Sonnet 116.
2. List several things that love *is,* according to Sonnet 116.

Interpreting

3. What is the meaning of the image of the star in lines 7−8? How does this image apply to love?

Extending

4. Do you agree or disagree with the speaker's interpretation of love? Why or why not?

Sonnet 130

Recalling

1. Summarize the contrasts that the speaker makes in lines 1–10. With whom does he contrast his beloved in lines 11–12?
2. According to the last lines, what does the speaker nevertheless think about his love?

Interpreting

3. What does line 12 suggest about the sort of person the speaker's beloved is? What sort of person is she to the speaker?
4. What sort of poetry does this poem mock or criticize? What message about love is implied with this criticism?

Extending

5. Contrast the physical description of the beloved in this sonnet with the description of the beloved in Spenser's Sonnet 15 (page 125). Despite the contrast, what idea about love do the two poems have in common?

VIEWPOINT

In praising Shakespeare's sonnets in a sonnet of his own, the Victorian poet and critic Matthew Arnold concludes:

All pains the immortal spirit must endure,
All weakness which impairs, all griefs which bow,
Find their sole speech in that [Shakespeare's] victorious brow.

■ What are some of the spiritual pains and human griefs or weaknesses that Shakespeare describes in the sonnets you have read? What human mood or condition does he describe in the first eight lines of Sonnet 29? Examine the specific details that Shakespeare provides about that mood or condition. Do you find the description accurate and moving? Why or why not?

LITERARY FOCUS

The English Sonnet

The various adaptations that English poets made to the Italian or Petrarchan sonnet (see page 119) resulted in what is called the **English sonnet**—or sometimes the **Shakespearean sonnet,** since Shakespeare was the master of this sonnet form. Unlike the Italian sonnet, in which ideas divide into an octave and a sestet, the English sonnet divides into three **quatrains,** or groups of four lines, and a rhymed **couplet,** or pair of lines, that usually draws a conclusion or presents a solution to the problems outlined earlier in the poem. In the typical English sonnet, each quatrain has its own set of end rhymes and the couplet introduces yet another rhyme; the usual rhyme scheme is *abab cdcd efef gg.* The seven sonnets by Shakespeare on the preceding pages all illustrate this format.

As with the Italian sonnet, the English sonnet has variations. Henry Howard, Earl of Surrey, who composed some of the first English sonnets, often used the rhyme scheme *abab abab abab cc;* his "Description of Spring" on page 115 is an example. Edmund Spenser tended to use the rhyme scheme *abab bcbc cdcd ee;* his version of the English sonnet, often called the **Spenserian sonnet,** is illustrated on pages 125–126.

Thinking About the English Sonnet

■ Examine the organization of Shakespeare's ideas in Sonnets 30, 55, 73, and 116. Choose two of these sonnets, and identify the main idea of each quatrain and the solution or conclusion presented in the final couplet.

Figurative Language

All words have a literal or matter-of-fact meaning. Yet words can be used in such a way that something beyond their literal meaning is implied. **Figurative language**—language using figures of speech—cannot be taken literally. For instance, Shakespeare's Sonnet 18 speaks of "the eye of heaven," but the poet does not expect us to imagine a great eye in the sky. He is using a **metaphor,** an implied comparison between two dissimilar things, in order to make us see the sun in an unusual and vivid way.

A **simile** is a figure of speech in which the comparison is made directly, most often by the use of the word *like* or *as.* If Shakespeare had written, "the sun is like the eye of heaven," his figure of speech would have been a simile.

Thinking About Figurative Language

■ Choose at least two similes and two metaphors from the Shakespeare sonnets you have read. Decide what they refer to, and explain what you think they add to the poem as a whole.

Modern English

Both the English of four hundred years ago and the English we speak and write today are referred to as **modern English.** We should discuss the pronunciation, spelling, and grammar of modern English during Elizabethan times.

Pronunciation and spelling. Three important pronunciation features of Chaucer's day had changed by Elizabethan times: (1) Elizabethans, unlike medieval Englishmen, pronounced vowels as we do. (2) Elizabethans pronounced some consonants differently from medieval Englishmen. (3) Elizabethans did *not* pronounce the final e at the ends of words. (For more information about Middle English, see page 96.)

The popularity of printing in the 1500s had a good deal to do with stabilizing spelling so that the English of today looks so close to Elizabethan English. But not all modern English words seem to be spelled as they are pronounced, and the reason for the discrepancy rests with the early English printers. Although pronunciations had already changed, these printers picked up and standardized medieval spellings. As a result, we have the silent consonants in *knight* and the spelling *gh* for the sound *f* in words such as *tough.*

Grammar. Elizabethan English differs from twentieth-century English in fewer ways than it differed from Middle English, but there are still enough differences in pronouns, verbs, and prepositions to remind us that all language changes over time. For one thing, Elizabethan English still uses some pronouns that sound antiquated to our ears: *thou* for *you* in the subject position; *thee* for *you* in the object position; and *thy* and *thine* for possessives. In addition, with *thou* we find certain outdated verb forms: *thou climbst, thou art.* Elizabethan English verb forms are different in another important way. We are used to using *do* with *not* as in "They do not know what they are doing." In Elizabethan English a writer would say, "They know not what they do."

One other difference between Elizabethan English and our English concerns prepositions. Old English and Middle English (see pages 40 and 96) did not rely heavily on prepositions because words had inflections, or endings, that often carried with them meanings such as "to," "for," or "by." In Shakespeare's day writers began to experiment to make up for the disappearance of inflections from words. Some of the prepositions Shakespeare used are not the ones we would use today. For example, he says, "Haply I think *on* thee," where we would say *of* or *about.* It took a while for the system of English prepositions to become polished.

Thinking About Modern English

1. From Shakespeare's sonnets or from poems by Wyatt, Surrey, Sidney, Spenser, Marlowe, or Raleigh, find one more example each of *thou, thee,* and *thy* or *thine.*
2. From a Shakespeare sonnet find a verb expressing the negative without *do* before *not.*

COMPARING WRITERS

1. How is time pictured in the seven sonnets by Shakespeare? What is the relationship between time, love, and art in these sonnets?
2. Compare and contrast one of Shakespeare's sonnets with Sidney's Sonnet 31. First discuss the rhyme scheme of each sonnet. Then discuss the tone of Shakespeare's speaker and of Sidney's speaker. Consider how each speaker suffers and what solace, if any, each finds in the course of the poem.
3. Of all the Elizabethan poems you have read by Wyatt, Surrey, Sidney, Spenser, Marlowe, Raleigh, and Shakespeare, which one do you find most moving? Most humorous? Why?

Music was a popular part of Elizabethan theater, and Shakespeare's plays are filled with some of the finest songs ever written. The first of the songs that follow is from *As You Like It,* a comedy that was probably first performed in 1599; the second is from *Cymbeline,* a romance that dates from 1609.

■ What are the themes of two of your favorite songs?

William Shakespeare

Blow, Blow, Thou Winter Wind

Blow, blow, thou winter wind,
Thou art not so unkind
   As man's ingratitude;
Thy tooth is not so keen,
5   Because thou art not seen,
   Although thy breath be rude.[1]
Heigh-ho! sing, heigh-ho! unto the green holly:
Most friendship is feigning, most loving mere folly.
   Then, heigh-ho, the holly!
10   This life is most jolly.

Freeze, freeze, thou bitter sky,
That dost not bite so nigh
   As benefits forgot:
Though thou the waters warp,[2]
15   Thy sting is not so sharp
   As friend remembered not.
Heigh-ho! sing, heigh-ho! unto the green holly:
Most friendship is feigning, most loving mere folly.
   Then, heigh-ho, the holly!
20   This life is most jolly.

---

1. **rude:** harsh.
2. **warp:** make rough by freezing.

William Shakespeare

Fear No More the Heat o' the Sun

Fear no more the heat o' the sun,
  Nor the furious winter's rages;
Thou thy worldly task hast done,
  Home art gone, and ta'en[1] thy wages.
5 Golden lads and girls all must,
As chimney-sweepers, come to dust.

Fear no more the frown o' the great;
  Thou art past the tyrant's stroke;
Care no more to clothe and eat;
10 To thee the reed is as the oak:
The scepter,[2] learning, physic, must
All follow this, and come to dust.

Fear no more the lightning flash,
  Nor the all-dreaded thunder stone;[3]
15 Fear not slander, censure rash;
  Thou hast finished joy and moan:
All lovers young, all lovers must
Consign[4] to thee, and come to dust.

No exorciser harm thee!
20 Nor no witchcraft charm thee!
Ghost unlaid[5] forbear thee!
Nothing ill come near thee!
Quiet consummation[6] have;
And renownèd be thy grave!

---

1. **ta'en:** taken.
2. **scepter:** staff carried as a badge of royalty.
3. **thunder stone:** stone or missile once thought to be hurled to earth in a lightning's flash.
4. **consign:** give themselves over.
5. **unlaid:** troubled and wandering.
6. **consummation:** ending, completion.

STUDY QUESTIONS

Blow, Blow, Thou Winter Wind

Recalling

1. According to the song, what is more unkind than the winter wind? What has a sharper sting than the winter sky?
2. According to the refrain, what is most friendship? Most loving? What is "this life"?

Interpreting

3. Why is the metaphor about the tooth (line 4) appropriate in describing the wind? In describing human ingratitude?
4. What kind of attitude toward life is expressed in line 8? Does line 10 mean what it says? Explain.

Fear No More the Heat o' the Sun

Recalling

1. According to the first stanza, what should the person addressed "fear no more"? What has this person done (line 3)?
2. According to the song, what do all "golden lads and girls," "the scepter, learning, physic," and all lovers come to?

Interpreting

3. What has happened to the person addressed? What comforting message does the singer have for this person?

LITERARY FOCUS

Elizabethan Songs

The England of Queen Elizabeth's day was full of music. The queen herself inspired composers and musicians—as she did poets and playwrights—and was generous in rewarding their efforts. London was so full of pipers and fiddlers that an observer in 1587 notes that it was impossible for someone to enter a tavern without having "two or three of them hang at his heels, to give him a dance before he depart."

Song writing reached its peak in Elizabethan times, and lyrics often overshadowed music. Elizabethan **madrigals**—lyric poems designed to be sung without instrumental accompaniment—spoke of love and the joys of pastoral life; street jingles spread the news; ballads told exciting stories.

In Shakespeare's plays songs of all kinds augment the dramatic action by evoking emotions in the audience. The songs may make what is merry merrier or what is sad sadder. They include love songs, nonsense songs, and dirges, songs mourning a death. Although most of the original music accompanying Shakespeare's songs has been lost, traditional renditions in most modern productions of his plays probably "descend" from the original tunes.

Thinking About Elizabethan Songs

What moods or emotions do the two songs from Shakespeare's plays intensify? Which is a dirge, and why?

COMPOSITION

Analyzing the Use of Images

Write a brief essay in which you explain how Shakespeare uses images from nature in one of the songs. First describe the picture of nature he paints. Then describe the function of the natural images in the context of the song: Do they make a comparison, illustrate an idea, or what? Finally, explain how the portrait of nature is related to the mood or emotion expressed in the song.

Writing Figuratively

In the first song Shakespeare uses figurative language to express the effects of a freezing winter's day. Briefly describe another phenomenon—a rainstorm, a snowfall, or a heat wave, for example—by using figurative language. You might begin by writing a literal description of the phenomenon, using adjectives and verbs like *wet* and *rains,* and then rewrite your description with similes, metaphors, and specific verbs that make it more vivid.

SHAKESPEAREAN THEATER

Although there is no precise record of when Shakespeare wrote each of his thirty-seven plays, it is likely that by 1600 he had completed *The Taming of the Shrew, Romeo and Juliet, A Midsummer Night's Dream, The Merchant of Venice,* and *Julius Caesar,* as well as twelve or thirteen others. But even greater work lay before him: *Twelfth Night, Hamlet, Othello, King Lear, Macbeth, Antony and Cleopatra*—all masterpieces written from 1600 to 1607.

Shakespeare's plays are divided into three groups—comedies, histories, and tragedies. Most of the comedies are romantic fantasies, designed to delight and amuse their audiences. The histories illustrate the moral lessons to be learned from the crimes of ambitious and treacherous leaders of state. In his later histories Shakespeare combined sober events with lively comedy. The tragedies deal with death, morality, and destruction and show how the breaking of a moral law inevitably leads to disaster.

Most of Shakespeare's plays were first performed at the Globe, a theater located across the Thames River from London in the suburb of Southwark. The Globe was an octagonal building, with a thatched roof covering only the perimeter of the area. Under the roof were three levels of galleries that surrounded a yard about sixty-five feet in diameter. The galleries looked down on the stage, a rectangular platform of twenty-seven by forty-three feet that occupied about a third of the yard at one end. The main stage had a large trap door through which actors who played the parts of ghosts and spirits could rise and disappear. At the back of the main stage was a small curtained inner stage used for indoor scenes. Above the inner stage were two galleries. The first level could be used as a balcony, bedroom, or castle wall. Musicians performed from the second level, and sound effects, such as thunder or the ringing of a bell, came from a hut on top of the stage roof.

Those who could afford it watched the plays from seats in the galleries. For a penny, less wealthy spectators, called groundlings, could stand in the yard. The yard was open to the sky, and the stage was lit by daylight. Performances were given in midafternoon before an audience of about two thousand. No curtain rose to indicate the start of the play or fell to signal the close of an act. To begin the play, actors entered by one of two doors at the rear of the stage, and when they left the stage, the scene was over. Within seconds the next scene would begin, with new actors appearing to describe the new setting.

Costumes in the Shakespearean theater were always colorful and elaborate versions of Elizabethan "modern dress," whether they were for *Macbeth,* set in the eleventh century, or for *Julius Caesar,* in 44 B.C. Scenery was almost nonexistent. One tree might signify a forest; a chair might represent a throne room. Shakespeare compensated for the lack of scenery by giving his characters beautiful descriptive passages to speak, and Elizabethan audiences listened closely to the actors' words.

The plays moved at a rapid speed, advancing from scene to scene with scarcely an interruption. Elizabethan actors probably performed much as actors do today, but they spoke their lines much more quickly than modern performers. Presenting a sixteen- to twenty-thousand-word play in about two hours left no time for dawdling.

Elizabethan audiences were accustomed to several dramatic conventions of the time. No women appeared on the stage; women's and children's roles were played by boys who, although they were apprentices to the company, were skillful and highly trained. Soliloquies and asides were two other conventions. In a **soliloquy** the actor is alone on stage, speaking to himself and revealing to the audience his inner thoughts and feelings. In an **aside** the actor speaks words that the other characters on stage are not supposed to hear.

As you read *Macbeth,* imagine from time to time that you are attending a performance at the Globe. The presentation would at first seem noisy and crude, but after a time you would get used to the trumpet calls and lack of scenery, the crowded theater, and the rapid rate of speech, and you would probably join the Elizabethan spectators who are responding to the action with displays of grief, joy, and amusement.

Model of the Globe Theatre by John Cranford Adams. Courtesy of the Folger Shakespeare Library, Washington, D.C.

The Tragedy of Macbeth

The Tragedy of Macbeth was probably written in 1606 and was performed that summer at Hampton Court Palace to celebrate the state visit of Christian IV of Denmark, King James's brother-in-law. The play touches on many topics—including witchcraft, the ideals of kingship, and special curative powers—that would have appealed to James and to other Elizabethans whose interest both in the king and in Scotland blossomed when James assumed the throne in 1603. James was already king of Scotland when he became king of England. His family was descended from a line of Scottish kings dating back to the eleventh century, when *Macbeth* takes place.

For the basic story of this play, Shakespeare turned to one of the most popular books of the times, Raphael Holinshed's *Chronicles of England, Scotland, and Ireland,* where he read about the real-life Macbeth. Shakespeare often consulted histories and stories of his own and earlier eras for the plots of his plays. He then amplified, altered, and combined incidents and personalities to serve his own dramatic purposes and to shape his own creations.

In *Macbeth,* for example, he invented the banquet scene, the ghost of Banquo, the sleepwalking scene, and the death of Lady Macbeth. History's Banquo is a traitor and an accomplice in the murder of Duncan, whereas Shakespeare's Banquo is honorable and loyal. In the *Chronicles* Duncan is a younger, feeble king, "a faint-hearted milksop," but in *Macbeth* he is an older, benevolent ruler. King James claimed Banquo as his Stuart ancestor, and he appears in *Macbeth* as a character above reproach.

Shakespeare fashioned the story of Macbeth into one of the best-known tragic patterns—the rise and fall of a powerful but flawed individual. In Elizabethan tragedies the main character, or **tragic hero,** is generally a high-ranking person, distinguished by such admirable traits as integrity, bravery, and strength. The hero's personality, however, also includes a fatal weakness, or **tragic flaw,** that causes his eventual decline from success to destruction.

Shakespeare's tragedy focuses on the downfall of Macbeth. At the start of the play, Macbeth is a brilliant and courageous general who unstintingly serves Duncan, his king. Macbeth is a noble Scot who commands great respect. As the play progresses, Macbeth's hunger for more and greater power provokes increasingly reckless and violent actions. Joined in his crimes by his wife, Macbeth rushes along a desperate course of terror and destruction, and by the play's conclusion he is a broken man.

In many ways the faraway, dark, and murderous world of *Macbeth* is strangely current, in part because the people in the play are so vividly alive, in part because issues in the play—loyalty, fate, quenchless ambition—are timeless.

■ What recent events exemplify one or more of these issues?

Mrs. Siddons as Lady Macbeth, G. H. Harlow, early nineteenth century. (See William Hazlitt's description of Mrs. Siddons' performance as Lady Macbeth, page 464.)

Key Ideas in *Macbeth*

As you read *Macbeth,* look for references to each of the following topics. If you keep track of what the work says about these subjects, you will grasp the most important themes of the play.

- Appearance versus reality
- Reason versus desire
- The importance of loyalty
- Attempts to control the future
- Responses by humans to supernatural powers
- Responses by nature to human actions
- Violence and its outcome

Key Quotations from *Macbeth*

As you read *Macbeth,* you will come across some of the most famous lines in English drama. Here are a few examples.

Fair is foul, and foul is fair.

　　　　　—Three Witches, Act I, Scene i, 10.

There's no art
To find the mind's construction in the face:

　　　　　—Duncan, Act I, Scene iv, 11–12

Yet do I fear thy nature;
It is too full o' th' milk of human kindness

　　　　　—Lady Macbeth, Act I, Scene v, 15–16

Will all great Neptune's ocean wash this blood
Clean from my hand?

　　　　　—Macbeth, Act II, Scene ii, 59–60

Where we are
There's daggers in men's smiles;

　　　　　—Donalbain, Act II, Scene iii, 126–127

Things without all remedy
Should be without regard: what's done is done.

　　　　　—Lady Macbeth, Act III, Scene ii, 11–12

Double, double, toil and trouble;
Fire burn and caldron bubble.

　　　　　—Three Witches, Act IV, Scene i, 20–21

Out, out, brief candle!
Life's but a walking shadow, a poor player
That struts and frets his hour upon the stage
And then is heard no more.

　　　　　—Macbeth, Act V, Scene v, 23–26

Left: Maggie Smith. Douglas Rain. *Right:* Jack Wetherall. Stephen Russell. Maurice Good. Photos courtesy of Stratford Festival, Canada, 1978.

Lady Macbeth and Macbeth.

Malcolm, Macduff, and Ross.

William Shakespeare

The Tragedy of Macbeth

CHARACTERS

DUNCAN: King of Scotland

MALCOLM: his elder son and heir to the throne

DONALBAIN: his younger son

MACBETH: Thane of Glamis, a Scottish nobleman and general in King Duncan's army

LADY MACBETH: his wife

BANQUO: Scottish nobleman and general in King Duncan's army

FLEANCE: his son

MACDUFF: Thane of Fife, a Scottish nobleman

LADY MACDUFF: his wife

LENNOX, ROSS, ANGUS, MENTEITH, CAITHNESS: noblemen of Scotland

SIWARD: Earl of Northumberland, general of the English forces

YOUNG SIWARD: his son

THREE WITCHES

A PORTER

AN OLD MAN

THREE MURDERERS

HECATE: leader of the Witches

APPARITIONS

AN ENGLISH DOCTOR

A GENTLEWOMAN: attending Lady Macbeth

SEYTON: an officer attending Macbeth

Other **LORDS, OFFICERS, SOLDIERS, ATTENDANTS, MESSENGERS**

ACT I

Scene i. *Scotland. An open place.*

[*In the midst of a great storm of thunder and lightning,* THREE WITCHES *appear in a deserted, outdoor place. They are plotting to meet* MACBETH, *a nobleman and general in* KING DUNCAN'*s army, when he returns from battle.*]

FIRST WITCH. When shall we three meet again?
In thunder, lightning, or in rain?

SECOND WITCH. When the hurlyburly's[1] done,
When the battle's lost and won.

5 **THIRD WITCH.** That will be ere the set of sun.

FIRST WITCH. Where the place?

SECOND WITCH   Upon the heath.

THIRD WITCH. There to meet with Macbeth.

FIRST WITCH. I come, Graymalkin.[2]

SECOND WITCH. Paddock[3] calls.

THIRD WITCH.   Anon![4]

10 **ALL.** Fair is foul, and foul is fair.
Hover through the fog and filthy air.

[*The* WITCHES *leave.*]

1 **hurlyburly:** uproar and confusion of battle.

2 **Graymalkin:** a common name for a gray cat. In Shakespeare's time cats and toads were believed to be witches' familiars, or helpers.
3 **Paddock:** the second witch's familiar, a toad.
4 **Anon:** at once.

Scene ii. *A camp.*

[*The setting is a military camp near Forres, a town about a hundred miles north of Edinburgh in Scotland. From off-stage come the sounds of men fighting, weapons clashing, and trumpets blaring.* DUNCAN, *King of Scotland, enters with his two teenage sons.* MALCOLM, *the elder, who is heir to the throne, and* DONALBAIN, *the younger. With them are a Scottish nobleman,* LENNOX, *and other attendants. They meet a* CAPTAIN *bleeding from wounds received in battle between the king's army and the forces of his two rivals, Macdonwald and the Thane of Cawdor.* DUNCAN *learns of the battle's progress from the wounded sergeant.*]

KING. What bloody[1] man is that? He can report,
As seemeth by his plight, of the revolt
The newest state.

MALCOLM.   This is the sergeant[2]
Who like a good and hardy soldier fought

1 **bloody:** the atmosphere of violence and horror is increased by images of blood throughout the play. The word *blood* is used over one hundred times in *Macbeth*.
2 **sergeant:** in Shakespeare's time *sergeant* and *captain* were interchangeable.

5   'Gainst my captivity.[3] Hail, brave friend!
     Say to the king the knowledge of the broil[4]
     As thou didst leave it.

     CAPTAIN.   Doubtful it stood,
     As two spent swimmers, that do cling together
     And choke their art.[5] The merciless Macdonwald—
10   Worthy to be a rebel for to that
     The multiplying villainies of nature
     Do swarm upon him[6]—from the Western Isles[7]
     Of kerns and gallowglasses[8] is supplied;
     And Fortune, on his damnèd quarrel smiling,
15   Showed like a rebel's wench:[9] but all's too weak:
     For brave Macbeth—well he deserves that name—
     Disdaining Fortune, with his brandished steel,
     Which smoked with bloody execution,
     Like valor's minion[10] carved out his passage
20   Till he faced the slave;[11]
     Which nev'r shook hands, nor bade farewell to him,
     Till he unseamed him from the nave to th' chops,[12]
     And fixed his head upon our battlements.

     KING. O valiant cousin![13] Worthy gentleman!

25   CAPTAIN. As whence the sun 'gins his reflection[14]
     Shipwracking storms and direful thunders break,
     So from that spring whence comfort seemed to come
     Discomfort swells. Mark, King of Scotland, mark:
     No sooner justice had, with valor armed,
30   Compelled these skipping kerns to trust their heels
     But the Norweyan lord,[15] surveying vantage,[16]
     With furbished arms and new supplies of men,
     Began a fresh assault.

     KING.   Dismayed not this
     Our captains, Macbeth and Banquo?

     CAPTAIN.   Yes;
35   As sparrows eagles, or the hare the lion.
     If I say sooth,[17] I must report they were
     As cannons overcharged with double cracks;[18]
     So they doubly redoubled strokes upon the foe.
     Except[19] they meant to bathe in reeking wounds,
40   Or memorize another Golgotha,[20]
     I cannot tell—
     But I am faint; my gashes cry for help.

     KING. So well thy words become thee as thy wounds;
     They smack of honor both. Go get him surgeons.

3 **captivity:** capture.
4 **broil:** battle.

5 **choke their art:** The image is of two exhausted swimmers, who by clinging to each other prevent each other from swimming.

6 **Worthy . . . him:** suited to be a rebel because nature has given him many evil qualities.
7 **Western Isles:** Ireland and the Hebrides, off Scotland.
8 **kerns and gallowglasses:** light-armed foot soldiers and horsemen armed with axes, both from Ireland.
9 **Fortune . . . wench:** Fortune appeared to favor the rebel Macdonwald.

10 **minion:** favorite.
11 **slave:** Macdonwald.
12 **unseamed . . . chops:** cut him open from the navel to the jaw. *Unseamed* is one of the many sewing metaphors in the play.

13 **cousin:** often a term of courtesy between noblemen. Duncan and Macbeth actually are first cousins.
14 **As . . . reflection:** as from the same place from which the sun rises.

15 **Norweyan lord:** Sweno, King of Norway.
16 **vantage:** seeing an opportunity for attack.

17 **sooth:** truth.

18 **double cracks:** double explosives.

19 **Except:** unless.

20 **memorize . . . Golgotha** [gol'gə thə]: make the place as memorable for slaughter as Golgotha, the place where Christ was crucified.

[*As the* CAPTAIN *leaves with the help of attendants, noblemen* ROSS *and* ANGUS *arrive with more news of the fighting.*]

Who comes here?

45 **MALCOLM.**   The worthy Thane[21] of Ross.

LENNOX. What a haste looks through his eyes! So should he
       look
    That seems to[22] speak things strange.

ROSS.   God save the king!

KING. Whence cam'st thou, worthy Thane?

ROSS.   From Fife, great King;
    Where the Norweyan banners flout the sky
50 And fan our people cold.[23]
    Norway[24] himself, with terrible numbers,
    Assisted by that most disloyal traitor
    The Thane of Cawdor, began a dismal[25] conflict;
    Till that Bellona's bridegroom, lapped in proof,[26]
55 Confronted him with self-comparisons,[27]
    Point against point, rebellious arm 'gainst arm,
    Curbing his lavish[28] spirit: and, to conclude,
    The victory fell on us.

KING.   Great happiness!

ROSS.   That now
    Sweno, the Norways' king, craves composition;[29]
60 Nor would we deign him burial of his men
    Till he disbursèd, at Saint Colme's Inch,[30]
    Ten thousand dollars[31] to our general use.

KING. No more that Thane of Cawdor shall deceive
    Our bosom interest:[32] go pronounce his present[33] death,
65 And with his former title greet Macbeth.

ROSS. I'll see it done.

KING. What he hath lost, noble Macbeth hath won.

    [*They leave.*]

Scene iii. *A heath.*

[*It is thundering as the* THREE WITCHES *wait on a desolate heath for* MACBETH *and* BANQUO. *The two generals are on their way to* KING DUNCAN*'s palace at Forres. As they wait, the*

21 **Thane:** a Scottish title of nobility, similar to an English earl.

22 **seems to:** seems about to.

23 **flout . . . cold:** The invading banners filled the Scots with a cold fear.
24 **Norway:** the King of Norway.
25 **dismal:** ominous.
26 **Bellona's . . . proof:** Macbeth is referred to as the mate of Bellona, Roman goddess of war, dressed in tested armor (proof).
27 **Confronted . . . self-comparisons:** faced him with equal courage and skill.
28 **lavish:** arrogant.

29 **craves composition:** desires terms of peace.

30 **Saint Colme's Inch:** Isle of St. Columbia near Edinburgh, Scotland.
31 **dollars:** Dollars were first coined in 1518, about five hundred years after Macbeth's time.
32 **bosom interest:** vital and confidential concerns.
33 **present:** immediate.

witches speak of their evil powers. They greet the two men with strange prophecies of future glory, saying that MACBETH *will ultimately be King of Scotland and that* BANQUO *will be a father of kings.*]

FIRST WITCH. Where hast thou been, sister?

SECOND WITCH. Killing swine.[1]

THIRD WITCH. Sister, where thou?

FIRST WITCH. A sailor's wife had chestnuts in her lap,
And mounched, and mounched, and mounched.
5   "Give me," quoth I.
"Aroint thee,[2] witch!" the rump-fed ronyon[3] cries.
Her husband's to Aleppo[4] gone, master o' th' Tiger:
But in a sieve I'll thither sail,
And, like a rat without a tail,[5]
10   I'll do, I'll do, and I'll do.

SECOND WITCH. I'll give thee a wind.[6]

FIRST WITCH. Th' art kind.

THIRD WITCH. And I another.

FIRST WITCH. I myself have all the other;
15   And the very ports they blow,
All the quarters that they know
I' th' shipman's card.[7]
I'll drain him dry as hay:
Sleep shall neither night nor day
20   Hang upon his penthouse lid;[8]
He shall live a man forbid:[9]
Weary sev'nights[10] nine times nine
Shall he dwindle, peak,[11] and pine:
Though his bark cannot be lost,
25   Yet it shall be tempest-tossed.
Look what I have.

SECOND WITCH. Show me, show me.

FIRST WITCH. Here I have a pilot's thumb,[12]
Wracked as homeward he did come.

[*The sound of a drum is heard offstage.*]

30   **THIRD WITCH.** A drum, a drum!
Macbeth doth come.

ALL. The weird[13] sisters, hand in hand,
Posters[14] of the sea and land,

1 **Killing swine:** It was commonly believed that witches killed or bewitched domestic animals.

2 **Aroint thee:** Go away!
3 **rump-fed ronyon:** fat-rumped, shabby creature.
4 **Aleppo:** The captain of the ship *Tiger* is sailing to Aleppo, then a city in Syria.
5 **sieve . . . tail:** According to popular belief, a witch often used a sieve as a boat and could assume the shape of any animal, but the tail would always be missing.
6 **wind:** Witches were thought to sell winds.

7 **shipman's card:** circular piece of cardboard on which the thirty-two points of the compass are marked.
8 **penthouse lid:** the eyelid, which overhangs the eye like a penthouse. A penthouse was originally a shed with a roof that sloped down from the main building.
9 **forbid:** cursed.
10 **sev'nights:** weeks.
11 **peak:** waste away.

12 **thumb:** Parts of corpses were used to create spells.

13 **weird:** As a noun this word once meant fate or destiny. As an adjective it indicates that the witches can foresee people's destinies.
14 **Posters:** swift travelers.

Richard Curnock as the first witch. Karen Austin as the second witch. Douglas Rain as Macbeth. Lewis Gordon as Banquo. Bernard Hopkins as the third witch. Photo courtesy of Stratford Festival, Canada, 1978.

Thus do go about, about:
35 Thrice to thine, and thrice to mine,
And thrice again, to make up nine.
Peace! The charm's wound up.

[MACBETH *and* BANQUO *enter.*]

MACBETH. So foul and fair a day I have not seen.[15]

BANQUO. How far is 't called to Forres? What are these
40 So withered, and so wild in their attire,

15 **So . . . seen:** foul because of the storm; fair because of his victory. (Compare with Act I, scene i, line 10.)

That look not like th' inhabitants o' th' earth,
And yet are on 't? Live you, or are you aught
That man may question? You seem to understand me,
By each at once her choppy[16] finger laying
45   Upon her skinny lips. You should be women,
And yet your beards[17] forbid me to interpret
That you are so.

MACBETH.   Speak, if you can: what are you?

FIRST WITCH. All hail, Macbeth! Hail to thee, Thane of Glamis!

SECOND WITCH. All hail, Macbeth! Hail to thee, Thane of
   Cawdor!

50   **THIRD WITCH.** All hail, Macbeth, that shalt be King hereafter!

[MACBETH *is startled by the* WITCHES' *greeting;* BANQUO
notices and addresses him.]

BANQUO. Good sir, why do you start, and seem to fear
   Things that do sound so fair? [*To the* WITCHES.] I' th' name
     of truth,
   Are ye fantastical,[18] or that indeed
   Which outwardly ye show? My noble partner
55   You greet with present grace and great prediction
   Of noble having[19] and of royal hope,
   That he seems rapt withal:[20] to me you speak not.
   If you can look into the seeds of time,
   And say which grain will grow and which will not,
60   Speak then to me, who neither beg nor fear
   Your favors nor your hate.

FIRST WITCH. Hail!

SECOND WITCH. Hail!

THIRD WITCH. Hail!

65   **FIRST WITCH.** Lesser than Macbeth, and greater.

SECOND WITCH. Not so happy,[21] yet much happier.

THIRD WITCH. Thou shalt get kings, though thou be none.
   So all hail, Macbeth and Banquo!

FIRST WITCH. Banquo and Macbeth, all hail!

70   **MACBETH.** Stay, you imperfect[22] speakers, tell me more:
   By Sinel's[23] death I know I am Thane of Glamis;
   But how of Cawdor? The Thane of Cawdor lives,
   A prosperous gentleman; and to be King
   Stands not within the prospect of belief,
75   No more than to be Cawdor. Say from whence

16 **choppy:** chapped.

17 **beards:** According to popular belief, witches often had beards.

18 **fantastical:** imaginary.

19 **having:** possession, fortune.

20 **rapt withal:** entranced.

21 **happy:** fortunate.

22 **imperfect:** because their predictions have been so puzzling.

23 **Sinel's** [si'nəlz]: referring to Macbeth's father.

You owe this strange intelligence?[24] Or why
Upon this blasted heath you stop our way
With such prophetic greeting? Speak, I charge you.

[*The* WITCHES *vanish.*]

BANQUO. The earth hath bubbles as the water has,
80   And these are of them. Whither are they vanished?

MACBETH. Into the air, and what seemed corporal[25] melted
As breath into the wind. Would[26] they had stayed!

BANQUO. Were such things here as we do speak about?
Or have we eaten on the insane root[27]
85   That takes the reason prisoner?

MACBETH. Your children shall be kings.

BANQUO   You shall be King.

MACBETH. And Thane of Cawdor too. Went it not so?

BANQUO. To th' selfsame tune and words. Who's here?

[ROSS *and* ANGUS, *two Scottish noblemen, arrive with a
message from* KING DUNCAN.]

ROSS. The King hath happily received, Macbeth,
90   The news of thy success; and when he reads[28]
Thy personal venture in the rebels' fight,
His wonders and his praises do contend
Which should be thine or his.[29] Silenced with that,
In viewing o'er the rest o' th' selfsame day,
95   He finds thee in the stout Norweyan ranks,
Nothing afeard of what thyself didst make,
Strange images of death.[30] As thick as tale
Came post with post,[31] and every one did bear
Thy praises in his kingdom's great defense,
And poured them down before him.

100 ANGUS.   We are sent
To give thee, from our royal master, thanks;
Only to herald thee into his sight,
Not pay thee.

ROSS. And for an earnest[32] of a greater honor,
105   He bade me, from him, call thee Thane of Cawdor;
In which addition,[33] hail, most worthy Thane!
For it is thine.

BANQUO. [*Aside.*] What, can the devil speak true?

MACBETH. The Thane of Cawdor lives: why do you dress me
In borrowed robes?[34]

---

24 **owe . . . intelligence:** where you got this strange information.

25 **corporal** [kôr′pər əl]: flesh and blood, real.
26 **Would:** I wish.

27 **insane root:** A number of plants, such as henbane and hemlock, were believed to cause insanity.

28 **reads:** thinks about.

29 **His . . . his:** His amazement at the victory struggles with his desire to praise Macbeth.

30 **Nothing . . . death:** killing, yet not afraid of dying.
31 **post with post:** message after message.

32 **earnest:** pledge.

33 **In which addition:** with this new title.

34 **why . . . robes:** The idea that Macbeth's honors are ill-fitting occurs several times in the play.

ANGUS.   Who was the thane lives yet,
110   But under heavy judgment bears that life
           Which he deserves to lose. Whether he was combined
           With those of Norway, or did line[35] the rebel
           With hidden help and vantage, or that with both
           He labored in his country's wrack,[36] I know not;
115   But treasons capital, confessed and proved,
           Have overthrown him.

MACBETH. [*Aside.*]   Glamis, and Thane of Cawdor:
           The greatest is behind.[37] [*Addressing* ROSS *and* ANGUS.]
               Thanks for your pains.
           [*Aside to* BANQUO.] Do you not hope your children shall be
               kings,
           When those that gave the Thane of Cawdor to me
           Promised no less to them?

120   **BANQUO.** [*Aside to* MACBETH.] That, trusted home,[38]
           Might yet enkindle you unto[39] the crown,
           Besides the Thane of Cawdor. But 'tis strange:
           And oftentimes, to win us to our harm,
           The instruments of darkness tell us truths,
125   Win us with honest trifles, to betray's
           In deepest consequence.
           Cousins, a word, I pray you.

           [BANQUO *speaks privately to the two noblemen while* MAC-
           BETH *expresses his thoughts in an aside.*]

      MACBETH.   Two truths are told,
           As happy prologues to the swelling act
           Of the imperial theme.[40]—I thank you, gentlemen—

           [MACBETH *interrupts himself to speak to* ROSS *and* BANQUO;
           he then continues his aside.]

130   This supernatural soliciting[41]
           Cannot be ill, cannot be good. If ill,
           Why hath it given me earnest of success,
           Commencing in a truth? I am Thane of Cawdor:
           If good, why do I yield to that suggestion[42]
135   Whose horrid image doth unfix my hair
           And make my seated[43] heart knock at my ribs,
           Against the use of nature?[44] Present fears
           Are less than horrible imaginings.[45]
           My thought, whose murder yet is but fantastical,
140   Shakes so my single state of man that function
           Is smothered in surmise, and nothing is
           But what is not.[46]

35 **line:** support, strengthen.

36 **wrack:** ruin.

37 **behind:** still to come.

38 **trusted home:** fully believed.
39 **enkindle you unto:** encourage you to hope for.

40 **swelling . . . theme:** stately idea of becoming king.

41 **supernatural soliciting:** consulting the witches.

42 **suggestion:** thought of murdering Duncan.
43 **seated:** firmly placed.
44 **Against . . . nature:** contrary to my normal state.
45 **Present fears . . . imaginings:** Although Macbeth is unafraid of the real dangers of battle, his courage is sapped by his supernatural thoughts.
46 **function . . . is not:** I am so unnerved by my imaginings that my ability to act is stifled. The only things that are real to me now are unreal.

BANQUO. [*Speaking to* ROSS *about* MACBETH.] Look
    how our partner's rapt.

MACBETH. [*Aside.*] If chance will have me King, why, chance
    may crown me,
    Without my stir.[47]

BANQUO.   New honors come upon him,
145   Like our strange garments, cleave not to their mold
    But with the aid of use.[48]

MACBETH. [*Aside.*]   Come what come may,
    Time and the hour runs through the roughest day.

BANQUO. Worthy Macbeth, we stay upon your leisure.[49]

MACBETH. Give me your favor.[50] My dull brain was wrought
150   With things forgotten.[51] Kind gentlemen, your pains
    Are registered where every day I turn
    The leaf to read them. Let us toward the King.
    [*Aside to* BANQUO.] Think upon what hath chanced, and at
      more time,
    The interim having weighed it,[52] let us speak
    Our free hearts[53] each to other.

155 BANQUO.   Very gladly.

MACBETH. Till then, enough. Come, friends.

    [*They all leave together.*]

Scene iv. The palace at Forres.

[*At* KING DUNCAN'*s palace at Forres, the king and his two
sons,* MALCOLM *and* DONALBAIN, *enter to a fanfare of trumpets.
They are accompanied by* LENNOX *and other attendants. They
discuss the execution of the treacherous Thane of Cawdor
and praise* MACBETH *and* BANQUO *for their valor.*]

KING. Is execution done on Cawdor? Are not
    Those in commission[1] yet returned?

MALCOLM.   My liege,
    They are not yet come back. But I have spoke
    With one that saw him die, who did report
5   That very frankly he confessed his treasons,
    Implored your Highness' pardon and set forth
    A deep repentance: nothing in his life
    Became him like the leaving it. He died
    As one that had been studied[2] in his death,
10   To throw away the dearest thing he owed[3]
    As 'twere a careless[4] trifle.

47 **stir:** without an effort on my part.

48 **Like...use:** like new clothes that do not fit comfortably until worn for a while.

49 **we stay . . . leisure:** we are waiting for you at your convenience.
50 **Give . . . favor:** Pardon me.
51 **wrought . . . forgotten:** Macbeth pretends to be distracted by things he says he has forgotten.

52 **The interim . . . it:** having had time to consider it.
53 **Our free hearts:** our minds freely.

1 **Those in commission:** those charged with the duty of the execution.

2 **studied:** a theatrical term meaning "learned by heart." Cawdor died as if he had carefully rehearsed his execution.

3 **owed:** owned.

4 **careless:** worthless.

KING.   There's no art
To find the mind's construction in the face:[5]
He was a gentleman on whom I built
An absolute trust.

[MACBETH, BANQUO, ROSS, *and* ANGUS *join them. The* KING *addresses* MACBETH.]

                                        O worthiest cousin!
15   The sin of my ingratitude even now
Was heavy on me: thou art so far before,[6]
That swiftest wing of recompense is slow
To overtake thee. Would thou hadst less deserved,
That the proportion both of thanks and payment
20   Might have been mine! Only I have left to say,
More is thy due than more than all can pay.[7]

MACBETH. The service and the loyalty I owe,
In doing it, pays itself. Your Highness' part
Is to receive our duties: and our duties
25   Are to your throne and state children and servants;
Which do but what they should, by doing every thing
Safe toward[8] your love and honor.

KING.   Welcome hither.
I have begun to plant thee, and will labor
To make thee full of growing. Noble Banquo,
30   That hast no less deserved, nor must be known
No less to have done so,[9] let me enfold thee
And hold thee to my heart.

BANQUO.   There if I grow,
The harvest is your own.

KING.   My plenteous joys,
Wanton[10] in fullness, seek to hide themselves
35   In drops of sorrow. Sons, kinsmen, thanes,
And you whose places are the nearest, know,
We will establish our estate upon
Our eldest,[11] Malcolm, whom we name hereafter
The Prince of Cumberland: which honor must
40   Not unaccompanied invest him only,
But signs of nobleness, like stars, shall shine
On all deservers. From hence to Inverness,[12]
And bind us further to you.

MACBETH. The rest is labor, which is not used for you.[13]
45   I'll be myself the harbinger,[14] and make joyful
The hearing of my wife with your approach;
So, humbly take my leave.

5 **There's . . . face:** There is no way to know what a person is thinking by looking at his face.

6 **so far before:** so far ahead.

7 **Would . . . pay:** If you had been less worthy, I could have repaid you what you deserve. You deserve more than anyone could pay.

8 **Safe toward:** with sure regard for.

9 **That . . . so:** who is just as deserving as Macbeth.

10 **Wanton:** unrestrained.

11 **establish . . . eldest:** I will settle the succession of the throne upon my oldest son. The throne of Scotland was not hereditary then. Macbeth now realizes that chance will not crown him. (Compare with Act I, Scene iii, line 143.)

12 **Inverness** [in vər nes′]: Macbeth's castle, about twenty-five miles away.

13 **The rest . . . you:** Anything not done for you is a burden.
14 **harbinger** [här′bin jər]: officer who precedes royalty to arrange reception for a visit.

KING.   My worthy Cawdor!

MACBETH. [*Aside.*] The Prince of Cumberland! That is a step
On which I must fall down, or else o'erleap,
50   For in my way it lies. Stars, hide your fires;
Let not light see my black and deep desires:[15]
The eye wink at the hand;[16] yet let that be
Which the eye fears, when it is done, to see.

[MACBETH *leaves.*]

KING. True, worthy Banquo; he is full so valiant,
55   And in his commendations I am fed;
It is a banquet to me. Let's after him,
Whose care is gone before to bid us welcome.
It is a peerless kinsman.

[*They all leave to a flourish of trumpets.*]

Scene v. *The castle at Inverness.*

[*In* MACBETH's *castle at Inverness,* LADY MACBETH *appears
alone, reading a letter from her husband.*]

LADY MACBETH. [*Reads.*] "They met me in the day of success; and
I have learned by the perfect'st report they have more in
them than mortal knowledge. When I burned in desire to
question them further, they made themselves air, into
5   which they vanished. Whiles I stood rapt in the wonder of
it, came missives[1] from the King, who all-hailed me 'Thane
of Cawdor'; by which title, before, these weird sisters
saluted me, and referred me to the coming on of time, with
'Hail, King that shalt be!' This have I thought good to
10 deliver thee, my dearest partner of greatness, that thou
mightst not lose the dues of rejoicing, by being ignorant of
what greatness is promised thee. Lay it to thy heart, and
farewell."

Glamis thou art, and Cawdor, and shalt be
15   What thou art promised. Yet do I fear thy nature;
It is too full o' th' milk of human kindness[2]
To catch the nearest way.[3] Thou wouldst be great,
Art not without ambition, but without
The illness[4] should attend it. What thou wouldst highly,
20   That wouldst thou holily; wouldst not play false,
And yet wouldst wrongly win. Thou'dst have, great Glamis,
That which cries "Thus thou must do" if thou have it;
And that which rather thou dost fear to do
Than wishest should be undone.[5] Hie thee hither,

15 **Stars . . . desires:** Macbeth calls on darkness to obscure his action. This is one of many images of darkness in the play.
16 **The eye . . . hand:** Let my eyes be blind to my hand's deed.

1 **missives:** messengers.

2 **th' milk . . . kindness:** sentimentality.

3 **To catch . . . way:** the quickest way to the throne—killing Duncan.

4 **illness:** wickedness.

5 **Thou'dst . . . undone:** What you want, Glamis, requires you to do certain things in order to get it. You are afraid to do these things, but you would rather do them than not get what you want.

25 That I may pour my spirits in thine ear,
And chastise[6] with the valor of my tongue
All that impedes thee from the golden round[7]
Which fate and metaphysical[8] aid doth seem
To have thee crowned withal.

[A MESSENGER arrives.]

What is your tidings?

MESSENGER. The King comes here tonight.

30 **LADY MACBETH.**   Thou'rt mad to say it!
Is not thy master with him, who, were 't so,
Would have informed for preparation?

MESSENGER. So please you, it is true. Our thane is coming.
One of my fellows had the speed of him,[9]
35 Who, almost dead for breath, had scarcely more
Than would make up his message.

LADY MACBETH.   Give him tending;
He brings great news. [The MESSENGER leaves.]
                        The raven[10] himself is hoarse
That croaks the fatal entrance of Duncan
Under my battlements. Come, you spirits
40 That tend on mortal[11] thoughts, unsex me here,
And fill me, from the crown to the toe, top-full
Of direst cruelty! Make thick my blood,
Stop up th' access and passage to remorse,[12]
That no compunctious visitings of nature[13]
45 Shake my fell[14] purpose, nor keep peace between
Th' effect[15] and it! Come to my woman's breasts,
And take my milk for gall,[16] you murd'ring ministers,
Wherever in your sightless substances
You wait on[17] nature's mischief! Come, thick night,
50 And pall thee in the dunnest smoke[18] of hell,
That my keen knife see not the wound it makes,
Nor heaven peep through the blanket of the dark,
To cry "Hold, hold!"

[MACBETH enters.]

                        Great Glamis! Worthy Cawdor!
Greater than both, by the all-hail hereafter!
55 Thy letters have transported me beyond
This ignorant present, and I feel now
The future in the instant.[19]

MACBETH.   My dearest love,
Duncan comes here tonight.

6 **chastise:** reprimand.
7 **golden round:** the crown.
8 **metaphysical:** supernatural.

9 **had . . . him:** overtook him.

10 **raven:** traditionally a bird of ill omen.

11 **mortal:** murderous.

12 **remorse:** compassion.
13 **compunctious . . . nature:** natural feelings of pity.
14 **fell:** deadly.
15 **effect:** fulfillment.
16 **And . . . gall:** change any kindness to bitter hatred, murdering agents.
17 **in your sightless . . . on:** in your invisible forms you are ready to bring out the evil in nature.
18 **pall . . . smoke:** enshroud yourself in the darkest smoke.

19 **in the instant:** at this very moment.

LADY MACBETH.   And when goes hence?

MACBETH. Tomorrow, as he purposes.

LADY MACBETH.   O, never
60 Shall sun that morrow see!
Your face, my Thane, is as a book where men
May read strange matters. To beguile the time,
Look like the time;[20] bear welcome in your eye,
Your hand, your tongue: look like th' innocent flower,
65 But be the serpent under 't. He that's coming
Must be provided for: and you shall put
This night's great business into my dispatch;[21]
Which shall to all our nights and days to come
Give solely sovereign sway and masterdom.

MACBETH. We will speak further.

70 **LADY MACBETH.**   Only look up clear.[22]
To alter favor ever is to fear.[23]
Leave all the rest to me.

[*They leave.*]

Scene vi. Outside the castle at Inverness.

[*Outside* MACBETH's *castle oboes sound to announce the arrival of royalty.* KING DUNCAN *and his sons enter with a group of Scottish noblemen, including* BANQUO, LENNOX, MACDUFF, ROSS, *and* ANGUS. *It is nighttime, and they are attended by servants with torches.*]

KING. This castle hath a pleasant seat;[1] the air
Nimbly and sweetly recommends itself
Unto our gentle senses.

BANQUO.   This guest of summer,
The temple-haunting martlet, does approve
5 By his loved mansionry that the heaven's breath
Smells wooingly here.[2] No jutty,[3] frieze,
Buttress, nor coign of vantage,[4] but this bird
Hath made his pendent bed and procreant cradle.[5]
Where they most breed and haunt, I have observed
The air is delicate.

[LADY MACBETH *enters to welcome her guests.*]

10 **KING.**   See, see, our honored hostess!
The love that follows us sometime is our trouble,
Which still we thank as love.[6] Herein I teach you

20 **To beguile . . . the time:** To deceive observers, imitate their expressions.

21 **my dispatch:** Lady Macbeth plans to manage the whole affair.

22 **look up clear:** appear innocent.
23 **To . . . fear:** To change your usual appearance will reveal your fear and arouse suspicion.

1 **seat:** location.

2 **temple-haunting . . . here:** The house martin, a swallowlike bird, usually nests in churches. The presence of its nests (mansionry) at Macbeth's castle indicates that this is a pleasant place. In Shakespeare's time *martin* was a slang term for dupe.
3 **jutty:** projection.

4 **coign of vantage:** advantageous corner.
5 **procreant** [prō′krē ənt] **cradle:** nest for the young.

6 **The love . . . love:** Duncan means that since his visit to Macbeth and his wife is prompted by his love for them, they should forgive him for the great trouble he is causing.

How you shall bid God 'ield us for your pains
And thank us for your trouble.[7]

LADY MACBETH.   All our service
15 In every point twice done, and then done double,
Were poor and single business[8] to contend
Against those honors deep and broad wherewith
Your Majesty loads our house: for those of old,
And the late dignities heaped up to them,
We rest your hermits.[9]

20 **KING.**   Where's the Thane of Cawdor?
We coursed him at the heels,[10] and had a purpose
To be his purveyor:[11] but he rides well,
And his great love, sharp as his spur, hath holp[12] him
To his home before us. Fair and noble hostess,
We are your guest tonight.

25 **LADY MACBETH.**   Your servants ever
Have theirs, themselves, and what is theirs, in compt,
To make their audit at your Highness' pleasure,
Still to return your own.[13]

KING.   Give me your hand.
Conduct me to mine host: we love him highly,
30 And shall continue our graces towards him.
By your leave, hostess.

[LADY MACBETH *and the* KING *go into the castle.*]

Scene vii. The castle at Inverness.

[*In a torch-lit room in* MACBETH*'s castle, music is heard. A
steward, followed by other servants carrying dishes of food,
crosses the stage. As they leave,* MACBETH *enters. He is trying
to make up his mind about murdering* DUNCAN, *who is still
in the banquet room. It is the likelihood of punishment, not
the moral consequences of the crime, that discourages* MAC-
BETH *from proceeding with the murder.*]

MACBETH. If it were done when 'tis done, then 'twere well
It were done quickly.[1] If th' assassination
Could trammel up the consequence, and catch,
With his surcease, success; that but this blow
5 Might be the be-all and the end-all—here,
But here, upon this bank and shoal of time,
We'd jump the life to come.[2] But in these cases
We still have judgment[3] here; that we but teach
Bloody instructions, which, being taught, return
10 To plague th' inventor:[4] this even-handed justice

---

7 **bid God 'ield us . . . trouble:** Ask
God to reward me for the pains I
have caused and thank me for the
trouble I have caused—all has been
brought about by my love for you.

8 **single business:** feeble service.

9 **We . . . hermits:** We (as hermits)
will pray for you. Hermits were often
paid to pray for another's soul.

10 **coursed . . . heels:** pursued him
closely.

11 **purveyor:** advance supply
officer.
12 **holp:** helped.

13 **Have . . . own:** Have themselves
and everything that is theirs in trust
for you, to be rendered to you at your
wish.

1 **If . . . quickly:** If the murder itself
would put an end to this whole
situation, then it would be best to do
it quickly.
2 **If . . . come:** If the murder could
be done without consequence and
if his death would achieve my
objective, I would risk life in the world
to come.
3 **still . . . judgment:** receive
sentence.
4 **that we . . . inventor:** we teach
others how to commit evil acts that
they may in turn inflict on us.

Commends[5] th' ingredients of our poisoned chalice[6]
To our own lips. He's here in double trust:
First, as I am his kinsman and his subject,
Strong both against the deed; then, as his host,
15 Who should against his murderer shut the door,
Not bear the knife myself. Besides, this Duncan
Hath borne his faculties[7] so meek, hath been
So clear[8] in his great office, that his virtues
Will plead like angels trumpet-tongued against
20 The deep damnation of his taking-off;
And pity, like a naked newborn babe,
Striding the blast, or heaven's cherubin[9] horsed
Upon the sightless couriers of the air,[10]
Shall blow the horrid deed in every eye,
25 That tears shall drown the wind. I have no spur
To prick the sides of my intent, but only
Vaulting ambition, which o'erleaps itself
And falls on th' other—

[LADY MACBETH *joins him.*]

How now! What news?

LADY MACBETH. He has almost supped. Why have you left the
chamber?

MACBETH. Hath he asked for me?

30 LADY MACBETH.   Know you not he has?

MACBETH. We will proceed no further in this business:
He hath honored me of late, and I have bought[11]
Golden opinions from all sorts of people,
Which would be worn now in their newest gloss,
Not cast aside so soon.

35 LADY MACBETH.   Was the hope drunk
Wherein you dressed yourself? Hath it slept since?
And wakes it now, to look so green and pale
At what it did so freely? From this time
Such I account thy love. Art thou afeard
40 To be the same in thine own act and valor
As thou art in désire? Wouldst thou have that
Which thou esteem'st the ornament of life,[12]
And live a coward in thine own esteem,
Letting "I dare not" wait upon "I would,"
Like the poor cat i' th' adage?[13]

45 MACBETH.   Prithee, peace!
I dare do all that may become a man;
Who dares do more is none.

---

5 **commends:** offers.
6 **chalice:** cup.

7 **borne . . . faculties:** used his powers.
8 **clear:** blameless, free from reproach.

9 **cherubin:** angels.

10 **sightless . . . air:** invisible runners (the wind).

11 **bought:** acquired.

12 **ornament of life:** the crown.

13 **poor . . . adage:** An old proverb tells of the cat who holds back from catching fish because it is afraid of getting its feet wet.

LADY MACBETH.   What beast was 't then
That made you break[14] this enterprise to me?
When you durst do it, then you were a man;
50 And to be more than what you were, you would
Be so much more the man. Nor time nor place
Did then adhere,[15] and yet you would make both.
They have made themselves, and that their fitness now
Does unmake you.[16] I have given suck, and know
55 How tender 'tis to love the babe that milks me:
I would, while it was smiling in my face,
Have plucked my nipple from his boneless gums,
And dashed the brains out, had I so sworn as you
Have done to this.

MACBETH.   If we should fail?

LADY MACBETH.   We fail?
60 But screw your courage to the sticking-place,[17]
And we'll not fail. When Duncan is asleep—
Whereto the rather shall his day's hard journey
Soundly invite him—his two chamberlains
Will I with wine and wassail[18] so convince,[19]
65 That memory, the warder of the brain,
Shall be a fume, and the receipt of reason
A limbeck only:[20] when in swinish sleep
Their drenchèd natures lies as in a death,
What cannot you and I perform upon
70 Th' unguarded Duncan, what not put upon
His spongy[21] officers, who shall bear the guilt
Of our great quell?[22]

MACBETH.   Bring forth men-children only;
For thy undaunted mettle[23] should compose
Nothing but males. Will it not be received,
75 When we have marked with blood those sleepy two
Of his own chamber, and used their very daggers,
That they have done 't?

LADY MACBETH.   Who dares receive it other,[24]
As[25] we shall make our griefs and clamor roar
Upon his death?

MACBETH.   I am settled, and bend up
80 Each corporal agent to this terrible feat.
Away, and mock the time[26] with fairest show:
False face must hide what the false heart doth know.

[*They leave.*]

---

14 **break:** disclose.

15 **Did then adhere:** was then appropriate (for murder).

16 **They . . . unmake you:** Now that time and place are right, their very convenience has made you less of a man.

17 **screw . . . sticking-place:** as in preparing a crossbow, screw the bowstring tight into the notch (sticking-place) where it will not slip before firing.

18 **wassail** [wos'əl]: carousing, merrymaking.
19 **convince:** overpower.

20 **memory . . . only:** Memory, the guardian of the brain, shall become only a vapor, and the brain only a still (limbeck) into which the fumes pass.

21 **spongy:** sodden.
22 **quell:** murder.

23 **mettle:** spirit.

24 **receive it other:** take it otherwise.
25 **As:** seeing that.

26 **mock the time:** mislead the world; mislead all observers.

STUDY QUESTIONS

Recalling

1. After the brief Act I, Scene i, what does the captain in Scene ii tell Duncan that Macbeth did to the rebel Macdonwald? What does Ross report about Macbeth's confrontation with the Thane of Cawdor? How does Duncan reward Macbeth?

2. In Scene iii what do the witches predict for Macbeth and for Banquo? In lines 143–144 what does Macbeth decide to do about his horrible imaginings?

3. In Scene iv what obstacle does King Duncan place between Macbeth and the throne of Scotland? In lines 48–50 what does Macbeth say about the king's proclamation?

4. At the end of Scene v, how does Lady Macbeth advise Macbeth to behave toward the guests who will be arriving shortly?

5. In his speech at the beginning of Scene vii, what misgivings does Macbeth voice about killing King Duncan?

6. At the end of Scene vii, what plan does Lady Macbeth propose to Macbeth?

Interpreting

7. What kind of man is Macbeth? Base your answer on what you have learned about him from the reports of the captain and Banquo in Scene ii and from his association with the witches in Scene iii. How does Macbeth's reaction to the witches differ from Banquo's?

8. What additional character traits does Shakespeare reveal through Macbeth's aside at the end of Scene iii? How do these traits relate to the weaknesses of character that Lady Macbeth, in her speech at the beginning of Scene v, fears will prevent her husband from securing the Scottish throne?

9. What kind of woman is revealed in Lady Macbeth's speeches in Scene v? How does she feel about her husband? What motivates her to help Macbeth plan a course of action?

10. In Scene vii how does Lady Macbeth make Macbeth pledge every effort to bring about Duncan's death?

11. Reread King Duncan's speeches in Scenes ii, iv, and vi. What are several adjectives that might describe him? What kind of character is Shakespeare trying to create?

Extending

12. What do you think the witches represent? What is their effect on Macbeth? How do you think he would behave if he had never met them?

LITERARY FOCUS

Blank Verse

Shakespeare's plays are written largely in **blank verse**—unrhymed lines of iambic pentameter. Each line is divided into five units, or feet, with the stress falling on every second syllable. Blank verse is a versatile meter and comes closest of all metrical patterns to everyday speech. It can be used for description, as in the captain's report of the battle and Macbeth's bravery (Act I, Scene ii). It can be used for conversations of all kinds—for exhortation or rebuke, as in Lady Macbeth's chastisement of Macbeth (Act I, Scene vii), or for introspection, as in Macbeth's soliloquy over the murder of Duncan (Act I, Scene vii). Shakespeare is so skillful in the variation of rhythms, stresses, and caesura (page 20) in his blank verse that he can convey a speaker's every mood.

Thinking About Blank Verse

Read aloud Macbeth's aside at the end of Act I, Scene iii, lines 127–142. Emphasize the stresses so that you are aware of the basic iambic pattern. Analyze eight to ten lines of the passage and discuss how Shakespeare varies rhythms, stresses, and caesuras (page 26) to create a particular mood. Identify the mood you think he creates.

ACT II

Scene i. *The castle at Inverness.*

[*It is late at night as* BANQUO *and his son,* FLEANCE, *both guests of* MACBETH's, *enter the courtyard of the castle.* FLEANCE *carries a torch to light the way.*]

BANQUO. How goes the night, boy?

FLEANCE. The moon is down; I have not heard the clock.

BANQUO. And she goes down at twelve.

FLEANCE.   I take't, 'tis later, sir.

BANQUO. Hold, take my sword. There's husbandry[1] in heaven.
5   Their candles are all out. Take thee that[2] too.
A heavy summons[3] lies like lead upon me,
And yet I would not sleep. Merciful powers,
Restrain in me the cursèd thoughts that nature
Gives way to in respose!

[MACBETH *and a servant carrying a torch appear.*]

                                        Give me my sword!
10   Who's there?

MACBETH. A friend.

BANQUO. What, sir, not yet at rest? The King's a-bed:
He hath been in unusual pleasure, and
Sent forth great largess to your offices:[4]
15   This diamond he greets your wife withal,
By the name of most kind hostess; and shut up[5]
In measureless content.

MACBETH.   Being unprepared,
Our will became the servant to defect,
Which else should free have wrought.[6]

BANQUO.   All's well.
20   I dreamed last night of the three weird sisters:
To you they have showed some truth.

MACBETH.   I think not of them.
Yet, when we can entreat an hour to serve,[7]
We would spend it in some words upon that business,
If you would grant the time.

BANQUO.   At your kind'st leisure.

25   **MACBETH.** If you shall cleave to my consent, when 'tis,[8]
It shall make honor for you.

1 **husbandry:** thrift. The stars are not shining.

2 **that:** probably his sword belt.

3 **summons:** weariness.

4 **largess** [lär′jis]...**offices:** gifts to your servants' quarters.

5 **shut up:** retired.

6 **Being . . . wrought:** Our lack of preparation hindered our will to entertain more lavishly.

7 **entreat . . . serve:** find a free hour.

8 **cleave . . . 'tis:** join my cause when the time comes.

BANQUO.   So[9] I lose none
          In seeking to augment it, but still keep
          My bosom franchised[10] and allegiance clear,
          I shall be counseled.[11]

MACBETH.   Good repose the while!

30 BANQUO. Thanks, sir. The like to you!

          [BANQUO *and* FLEANCE *leave.*]

     MACBETH. [*To the servant.*] Go bid thy mistress, when my
          drink is ready,
          She strike upon the bell. Get thee to bed.

          [*The servant leaves.* MACBETH, *alone, imagines that he sees
          a bloody dagger.*]

          Is this a dagger which I see before me,
          The handle toward my hand? Come, let me clutch thee.
35   I have thee not, and yet I see thee still.
          Art thou not, fatal vision, sensible
          To feeling[12] as to sight, or art thou but
          A dagger of the mind, a false creation,
          Proceeding from the heat-oppressèd[13] brain?
40   I see thee yet, in form as palpable
          As this which now I draw.
          Thou marshal'st me[14] the way that I was going;
          And such an instrument I was to use.
          Mine eyes are made the fools o' th' other senses,
45   Or else worth all the rest.[15] I see thee still;
          And on thy blade and dudgeon[16] gouts[17] of blood,
          Which was not so before. There's no such thing.
          It is the bloody business which informs[18]
          Thus to mine eyes. Now o'er the one half-world
50   Nature seems dead, and wicked dreams abuse
          The curtained sleep;[19] witchcraft celebrates
          Pale Hecate's offerings;[20] and withered murder,
          Alarumed by his sentinel, the wolf,
          Whose howl's his watch, thus with his stealthy pace,
55   With Tarquin's[21] ravishing strides, towards his design
          Moves like a ghost.[22] Thou sure and firm-set earth,
          Hear not my steps, which way they walk, for fear
          Thy very stones prate of my whereabout,
          And take the present horror from the time,
60   Which now suits with it.[23] Whiles I threat, he lives:
          Words to the heat of deeds too cold breath gives.

          [*A bell rings,* LADY MACBETH'S *signal for* MACBETH *to go to*
          DUNCAN'S *room.*]

9 **So:** provided that.

10 **My . . . franchised:** my heart free from guilt.
11 **I . . . counseled:** I will be ready to listen to you.

12 **sensible . . . feeling:** capable of being perceived by senses—in this case, by touch.
13 **heat-oppressèd:** fevered.

14 **marshal'st me:** leads me (to King Duncan's room).

15 **Mine eyes . . . the rest:** If the dagger is a vision, my eyes are misled by my other senses. If it is real, my eyes are worth all my other senses put together.
16 **dudgeon:** hilt, handle.
17 **gouts:** large drops.
18 **informs:** takes shape.

19 **curtained sleep:** sleeper enclosed by the curtains of his bed.
20 **Hecate's offerings:** rituals dedicated to Hecate, the Greek goddess of witchcraft.
21 **Tarquin:** infamous sixth-century Roman tyrant.
22 **withered . . . ghost:** murder, called to action by the wolf whose howl tells him of the progress of the night, moves toward his victim as silently as a ghost.

23 **take . . . it:** do not let noise deprive this awful silence of any of its horror.

I go, and it is done: the bell invites me.
Hear it not, Duncan, for it is a knell
That summons thee to heaven, or to hell.

[MACBETH *leaves.*]

Scene ii. *The castle at Inverness.*

[*Later the same night* LADY MACBETH *enters the empty courtyard of the castle. She is waiting for* MACBETH *to return from
his murderous errand.*]

LADY MACBETH. That which hath made them drunk hath made
   me bold;
  What hath quenched them hath given me fire. Hark!
  Peace!
  It was the owl that shrieked, the fatal bellman,[1]
  Which gives the stern'st good night. He is about it.
5 The doors are open, and the surfeited grooms[2]
  Do mock their charge[3] with snores. I have drugged their
   possets,[4]
  That death and nature do contend about them,
  Whether they live or die.

MACBETH. [*Calling from within.*] Who's there? What, ho?

LADY MACBETH. Alack, I am afraid they have awaked
10 And 'tis not done! Th' attempt and not the deed
  Confounds[5] us. Hark! I laid their daggers ready;
  He could not miss 'em. Had he not resembled
  My father as he slept, I had done 't.

[MACBETH *enters, his hands covered with blood.*]

               My husband!

MACBETH. I have done the deed. Didst thou not hear a noise?

15 **LADY MACBETH.** I heard the owl scream and the crickets cry.
  Did not you speak?

MACBETH.   When?

LADY MACBETH.   Now.

MACBETH.   As I descended?

LADY MACBETH. Ay.

MACBETH. Hark!
  Who lies i' th' second chamber?

LADY MACBETH.   Donalbain.

1 **fatal bellman:** It was the custom in
London for the bellman to toll the bell
outside a condemned person's cell
the night before his execution.
2 **surfeited grooms:** overfed
servants.
3 **mock their charge:** make a
mockery of their duty.
4 **possets:** hot, spiced bedtime
drinks.

5 **Confounds:** ruins, destroys.

20 **MACBETH.** [*Looking at his hands.*] This is a sorry[6] sight.

LADY MACBETH. A foolish thought, to say a sorry sight.

MACBETH. There's one did laugh in 's sleep, and one cried "Murder!"
That they did wake each other. I stood and heard them.
But they did say their prayers, and addressed them[7]
Again to sleep.

25 **LADY MACBETH.**   There are two[8] lodged together.

MACBETH. One cried "God bless us!" and "Amen" the other,
As[9] they had seen me with these hangman's hands:
List'ning their fear, I could not say "Amen,"
When they did say "God bless us!"

LADY MACBETH.   Consider it not so deeply.

30 **MACBETH.** But wherefore could not I pronounce "Amen"?
I had most need of blessing, and "Amen"
Stuck in my throat.

LADY MACBETH.   These deeds must not be thought
After these ways; so,[10] it will make us mad.

MACBETH. Methought I heard a voice cry "Sleep no more!
35 Macbeth does murder sleep"—the innocent sleep,
Sleep that knits up the raveled sleave[11] of care,
The death of each day's life, sore labor's bath,
Balm of hurt minds, great nature's second course,[12]
Chief nourisher in life's feast—

LADY MACBETH.   What do you mean?

40 **MACBETH.** Still it cried "Sleep no more!" to all the house:
"Glamis hath murdered sleep, and therefore Cawdor
Shall sleep no more: Macbeth shall sleep no more."

LADY MACBETH. Who was it that thus cried? Why, worthy Thane,
You do unbend[13] your noble strength, to think
45 So brainsickly of things. Go get some water,
And wash this filthy witness from your hand.
Why did you bring these daggers from the place?
They must lie there: go carry them, and smear
The sleepy grooms with blood.

MACBETH.   I'll go no more.
50 I am afraid to think what I have done;
Look on 't again I dare not.

LADY MACBETH.   Infirm of purpose!

6 **sorry:** miserable, pitiable.

7 **addressed them:** prepared themselves.

8 **two:** King Duncan's sons, Malcolm and Donalbain.

9 **As:** as if.

10 **so:** if we do so.

11 **knits . . . sleave:** straightens out the tangled threads.
12 **second course:** the main and most nourishing course of an Elizabethan feast.

13 **unbend:** relax.

Give me the daggers. The sleeping and the dead
Are but as pictures. 'Tis the eye of childhood
That fears a painted devil. If he do bleed,
55 I'll gild[14] the faces of the grooms withal,
For it must seem their guilt.

[*As* LADY MACBETH *leaves, knocking is heard offstage.*]

MACBETH.   Whence is that knocking?
How is 't with me, when every noise appalls me?
What hands are here? Ha! They pluck out mine eyes!
Will all great Neptune's ocean wash this blood
60 Clean from my hand? No; this my hand will rather
The multitudinous seas incarnadine,[15]
Making the green one red.

[LADY MACBETH *returns.*]

LADY MACBETH. My hands are of your color, but I shame
To wear a heart so white. [*Knocking within.*] I hear a
        knocking
65 At the south entry. Retire we to our chamber.
A little water clears us of this deed:
How easy is it then! Your constancy
Hath left you unattended.[16] [*Knock.*] Hark! more knocking.
Get on your nightgown, lest occasion call us
70 And show us to be watchers. Be not lost
So poorly in your thoughts.

MACBETH. To know my deed, 'twere best not know myself.[17]
[*Knock.*]
Wake Duncan with thy knocking! I would thou couldst!

[*They leave.*]

Scene iii. The castle at Inverness.

[*The setting is the same as above, except that now it is early
morning and a drunken* PORTER, *or doorkeeper, enters. Talking to himself as he goes to open the castle gate, he imag-
ines that he is a porter at the gates of hell who is admitting
various lost souls. Finally he lets in* MACDUFF *and* LENNOX,
two noblemen who have been staying in another part of
MACBETH's *castle.*]

PORTER. Here's a knocking indeed! If a man were porter of
hell gate, he should have old[1] turning the key. [*Knocking
is heard offstage.*] Knock, knock, knock! Who's there, i'
th' name of Beelzebub?[2] Here's a farmer, that hanged
5   himself on th' expectation of plenty.[3] Come in time! Have

14 **gild:** paint.

15 **incarnadine** [in kär′nə din]:
redden, color red.

16 **Your constancy . . .
unattended:** Your firmness of
purpose has deserted you.

17 **To . . . myself:** If I am to
acknowledge what I've done, it would
be better for me to remain "lost" in
my thoughts.

1 **should have old:** old was a
colloquialism for "plenty of."
2 **Beelzebub:** the devil's helper.
3 **Here's . . . plenty:** a farmer who
hoarded grain, expecting a poor
harvest to raise prices.

napkins enow[4] about you; here you'll sweat for 't. [*Knock.*] Knock, knock! Who's there, in th' other devil's name? Faith, here's an equivocator, that could swear in both the scales against either scale;[5] who committed treason enough for God's sake, yet could not equivocate to heaven. O, come in, equivocator. [*Knock.*] Knock, knock, knock! Who's there? Faith, here's an English tailor come hither for stealing out of a French hose:[6] come in, tailor. Here you may roast your goose.[7] [*Knock.*] Knock, knock; never at quiet! What are you? But this place is too cold for hell. I'll devil-porter it no further. I had thought to have let in some of all professions that go the primrose way to th' everlasting bonfire. [*Knock.*] Anon, anon! [*The* PORTER *opens the gate.*] I pray you, remember the porter.

[MACDUFF *and* LENNOX *come in.*]

20 MACDUFF. Was it so late, friend, ere you went to bed,
That you do lie so late?

PORTER. Faith, sir, we were carousing till the second cock:[8] and drink, sir, is a great provoker.

MACDUFF. I believe drink gave thee the lie[9] last night.

25 PORTER. That it did, sir, i' the very throat on me: but I requited[10] him for his lie, and, I think, being too strong for him, though he took up my legs sometime, yet I made a shift to cast[11] him.

MACDUFF. Is thy master stirring?

[MACBETH *enters in his dressing gown.*]

30 Our knocking has awaked him; here he comes.

LENNOX. Good morrow, noble sir.

MACBETH.   Good morrow, both.

MACDUFF. Is the king stirring, worthy Thane?

MACBETH.   Not yet.

MACDUFF. He did command me to call timely[12] on him:
I have almost slipped the hour.

MACBETH.   I'll bring you to him.

35 MACDUFF. I know this is a joyful trouble to you;
But yet 'tis one.

MACBETH. The labor we delight in physics pain.[13]
This is the door.

4 **napkins enow:** handkerchiefs enough.

5 **equivocator . . . scale:** person who, under oath, can give two contradictory answers and still claim not to have violated his oath.

6 **tailor . . . hose:** He stole some cloth from the hose as he was making them.
7 **goose:** pressing iron.

8 **second cock:** 3:00 A.M.

9 **gave . . . lie:** laid you out (as in wrestling).

10 **requited:** repaid.

11 **cast:** a pun on the double meaning of the word—to throw (as in wrestling) and to vomit.

12 **timely:** early.

13 **The labor . . . pain:** The labor we enjoy cures any discomfort associated with it.

MACDUFF   I'll make so bold to call,
For 'tis my limited service.[14]

[MACDUFF *goes to wake* KING DUNCAN.]

LENNOX. Goes the king hence today?

40 **MACBETH.**   He does: he did appoint so.

LENNOX. The night has been unruly. Where we lay,
Our chimneys were blown down, and, as they say,
Lamentings heard i' th' air, strange screams of death,
And prophesying with accents terrible
45 Of dire combustion[15] and confused events
New hatched to th' woeful time: the obscure bird[16]
Clamored the livelong night. Some say, the earth
Was feverous and did shake.[17]

MACBETH.   'Twas a rough night.

LENNOX. My young remembrance cannot parallel
50 A fellow to it.

[MACDUFF *returns, appearing very shaken.*]

MACDUFF. O horror, horror, horror! Tongue nor heart
Cannot conceive nor name thee.

MACBETH and LENNOX.   What's the matter?

MACDUFF. Confusion[18] now hath made his masterpiece.
Most sacrilegious murder hath broke ope
55 The Lord's anointed temple,[19] and stole thence
The life o' th' building.

MACBETH.   What is 't you say? The life?

LENNOX. Mean you his Majesty?

MACDUFF. Approach the chamber, and destroy your sight
With a new Gorgon:[20] do not bid me speak;
60 See, and then speak yourselves. Awake, awake!

[MACBETH *and* LENNOX *rush off.* MACDUFF *comes forward,
still upset and shouting.*]

Ring the alarum bell. Murder and Treason!
Banquo and Donalbain! Malcolm! Awake!
Shake off this downy sleep, death's counterfeit,
And look on death itself! Up, up, and see
65 The great doom's image![21] Malcolm! Banquo!
As from your graves rise up, and walk like sprites,[22]
To countenance[23] this horror. Ring the bell.

[*A bell begins to ring offstage as* LADY MACBETH *enters.*]

14 **limited service:** assigned duty.

15 **combustion:** confusion, especially political.

16 **obscure bird:** bird of darkness, the owl, because he is nocturnal.

17 **the earth . . . shake:** There was a popular belief that nature was unruly when there was unrest in the state.

18 **Confusion:** destruction.

19 **The Lord's anointed temple:** the King's body.

20 **Gorgon:** Medusa, a mythological monster whose appearance was so terrible that those who looked at her turned to stone.

21 **great doom's image:** likeness of Judgment Day, doomsday.

22 **sprites:** ghosts, spirits.

23 **countenance:** look upon.

LADY MACBETH. What's the business,
    That such a hideous trumpet calls to parley[24]
    The sleepers of the house? Speak, speak!

70 **MACDUFF.**   O gentle lady,
    'Tis not for you to hear what I can speak:
    The repetition, in a woman's ear,
    Would murder as it fell.

    [BANQUO *enters.*]

                  O Banquo, Banquo!
    Our royal master's murdered.

LADY MACBETH.   Woe, alas!
    What, in our house?

75 **BANQUO.**   Too cruel anywhere.
    Dear Duff, I prithee, contradict thyself,
    And say it is not so.

    [MACBETH *and* LENNOX *return with* ROSS.]

MACBETH. Had I but died an hour before this chance,
    I had lived a blessèd time; for from this instant
80   There's nothing serious in mortality:[25]
    All is but toys.[26] Renown and grace is dead,
    The wine of life is drawn, and the mere lees[27]
    Is left this vault[28] to brag of.

    [MALCOLM *and* DONALBAIN *appear confused as they enter. Having just come from bed, they are still in their nightclothes.*]

DONALBAIN. What is amiss?

MACBETH.   You are, and do not know 't.
85   The spring, the head, the fountain of your blood
    Is stopped; the very source of it is stopped.

MACDUFF. Your royal father's murdered.

MALCOLM.   O, by whom?

LENNOX. Those of his chamber, as it seemed, had done 't:
    Their hands and faces were all badged[29] with blood;
90   So were their daggers, which unwiped we found
    Upon their pillows. They stared, and were distracted.
    No man's life was to be trusted with them.

MACBETH. O, yet I do repent me of my fury,
    That I did kill them.

MACDUFF.   Wherefore did you so?[30]

95 **MACBETH.** Who can be wise, amazed, temp'rate and furious,
Loyal and neutral, in a moment? No man.
The expedition[31] of my violent love
Outrun the pauser,[32] reason. Here lay Duncan,
His silver skin laced with his golden blood,
100 And his gashed stabs looked like a breach in nature
For ruin's wasteful entrance: there, the murderers,
Steeped in the colors of their trade, their daggers
Unmannerly breeched with gore.[33] Who could refrain,
That had a heart to love, and in that heart
Courage to make 's[34] love known?

105 **LADY MACBETH.**   Help me hence, ho!

[LADY MACBETH *faints.*]

MACDUFF. Look to the lady.

MALCOLM. [*Aside to* DONALBAIN.] Why do we hold our
tongues,
That most may claim this argument for ours?[35]

DONALBAIN. [*Aside to* MALCOLM.] What should be spoken here,
Where our fate, hid in an auger-hole,[36]
110 May rush, and seize us? Let's away:
Our tears are not yet brewed.

MALCOLM [*Aside to* DONALBAIN.] Nor our strong sorrow
Upon the foot of motion.[37]

BANQUO.   Look to the lady.

[LADY MACBETH, *faint, is carried out.*]

And when we have our naked frailties[38] hid,
That suffer in exposure, let us meet
115 And question[39] this most bloody piece of work,
To know it further. Fears and scruples[40] shake us.
In the great hand of God I stand, and thence
Against the undivulged pretense I fight
Of treasonous malice.[41]

MACDUFF.   And so do I.

ALL.   So all.

120 **MACBETH.** Let's briefly put on manly readiness,
And meet i' th' hall together.

ALL.   Well contented.

[*Everyone leaves except* MALCOLM *and* DONALBAIN.]

MALCOLM. What will you do? Let's not consort with them.

31 **expedition:** haste.
32 **pauser:** delayer.

33 **breeched with gore:** covered with blood, as with breeches (trousers that end just below the knee).

34 **make 's:** make his.

35 **That . . . ours?:** who are the most concerned with this topic under discussion.

36 **auger-hole:** a very small hole made by a carpenter's tool. Because it is so small, an improbable hiding place.

37 **Upon . . . motion:** yet begun to express itself.

38 **naked frailties:** they are still in their nightclothes.

39 **question:** investigate.
40 **scruples:** doubts.

41 **Against . . . malice:** I fight against the reason, as yet unknown, for this treasonous act.

To show an unfelt sorrow[42] is an office[43]
Which the false man does easy. I'll to England.

125 **DONALBAIN.** To Ireland, I; our separated fortune
Shall keep us both the safer. Where we are
There's daggers in men's smiles; the near in blood,
The nearer bloody.[44]

MALCOLM.   This murderous shaft that's shot
Hath not yet lighted,[45] and our safest way
130 Is to avoid the aim. Therefore to horse;
And let us not be dainty of leave-taking,
But shift away.[46] There's warrant in that theft
Which steals itself when there's no mercy left.[47]

[*They leave.*]

Scene iv. *The castle at Inverness.*

[*The nobleman* ROSS *and an* OLD MAN *meet outside* MACBETH's
*castle. They discuss the terrible storm and other unnatural
phenomena that accompanied the murder of* DUNCAN.]

OLD MAN. Threescore and ten I can remember well:
Within the volume of which time I have seen
Hours dreadful and things strange, but this sore[1] night
Hath trifled former knowings.

ROSS.   Ha, good father,
5 Thou seest the heavens, as troubled with man's act,
Threatens his bloody stage.[2] By th' clock 'tis day,
And yet dark night strangles the traveling lamp:[3]
Is 't night's predominance, or the day's shame,
That darkness does the face of earth entomb,
When living light should kiss it?

10 **OLD MAN.**   'Tis unnatural,
Even like the deed that's done. On Tuesday last
A falcon, tow'ring in her pride of place,[4]
Was by a mousing owl hawked at and killed.

ROSS. And Duncan's horses—a thing most strange and
certain—
15 Beauteous and swift, the minions[5] of their race,
Turned wild in nature, broke their stalls, flung out,
Contending 'gainst obedience, as they would make
War with mankind.

OLD MAN.   'Tis said they eat[6] each other.

42 **unfelt sorrow:** an indication that Malcolm and Donalbain suspect the sorrow of one of the onlookers is false.
43 **office:** duty.

44 **The near . . . bloody:** The more closely we are related to Duncan, the greater our chance of being murdered.
45 **lighted:** reached its target.

46 **And . . . away:** Let's not worry about the particulars of saying goodbye, but slip away quickly.
47 **There's . . . left:** There's justification in stealing away in these merciless times.

1 **sore:** terrible, grievous.

2 **bloody stage:** the earth.
3 **traveling lamp:** the sun.

4 **tow'ring . . . place:** soaring as high as it could before swooping down on its prey.

5 **minions:** favorites; best of their breed.

6 **eat:** ate.

Macbeth Act II, Scene iv **175**

ROSS. They did so, to th' amazement of mine eyes,
That looked upon 't.

[MACDUFF *enters.*]

20   Here comes the good Macduff.
How goes the world, sir, now?

MACDUFF.   Why, see you not?

ROSS. Is 't known who did this more than bloody deed?

MACDUFF. Those that Macbeth hath slain.

ROSS.   Alas, the day!
What good could they pretend?[7]

MACDUFF.   They were suborned:[8]
25 Malcolm and Donalbain, the king's two sons,
Are stol'n away and fled, which puts upon them
Suspicion of the deed.

ROSS.   'Gainst nature still.
Thriftless ambition, that will ravin up[9]
Thine own life's means! Then 'tis most like
30 The sovereignty will fall upon Macbeth.

MACDUFF. He is already named, and gone to Scone
To be invested.[10]

ROSS.   Where is Duncan's body?

MACDUFF. Carried to Colmekill,
The sacred storehouse of his predecessors
And guardian of their bones.

35 **ROSS.**   Will you to Scone?

MACDUFF. No, cousin, I'll to Fife.[11]

ROSS.   Well, I will thither.

MACDUFF. Well, may you see things well done there. Adieu,
Lest our old robes sit easier than our new![12]

ROSS. Farewell, father.

40 **OLD MAN.** God's benison[13] go with you, and with those
That would make good of bad, and friends of foes!

[*They leave.*]

7 **pretend:** intend, hope for.

8 **suborned:** bribed.

9 **ravin up:** swallow greedily.

10 **already named . . . invested:** already chosen (king) and gone to Scone, the traditional site of the coronation of Scottish kings, to be crowned.

11 **Fife:** Macduff is Thane of Fife.
Also: Barney

12 **Lest . . . new:** Lest the old rule suits us better than the new. Another image of clothing.

13 **benison:** blessing.

STUDY QUESTIONS

Recalling

1. What does Macbeth imagine he sees as he begins his soliloquy near the end of Act II, Scene i? Where is Macbeth going at the end of the scene?

2. In Scene ii what does Lady Macbeth do with the bloody daggers that Macbeth has brought with him from the king's rooms? Why does Macbeth not deal with the daggers himself?

3. What two things does Lady Macbeth tell Macbeth to do at the end of Scene ii? What does Macbeth say when he hears the knocking at the end of the scene?

4. Why has Macduff come to Macbeth's castle in Scene iii? Who discovers the body of the king?

5. In Scene iii how does Macbeth justify his killing of the king's servants?

6. What unnatural events do the Old Man and Ross describe at the beginning of Scene iv?

7. Where is Macbeth and what is he doing as Scene iv is taking place? As the scene ends, where does Macduff tell Ross he has decided to go?

Interpreting

8. What kind of mood or atmosphere does Macbeth's soliloquy create at the end of Scene i, lines 33–64? Mention three or four images in support of your answer.

9. In Scene iii who seems more genuinely excited and troubled by the death of King Duncan, Macbeth or Macduff?

10. In Scenes ii and iii who seems better able to maintain emotional control, Macbeth or Lady Macbeth? Do you think Lady Macbeth's fainting is genuine or deliberate? Build a case for both possibilities.

11. In Scene iii what reasons do Donalbain and Malcolm give for not consorting with Banquo, Macduff, and Macbeth? Specifically, whom do they mistrust and why?

12. How do the unnatural events described by the Old Man and Ross in Scene iv relate to the violence that has taken place in Macbeth's castle?

Extending

13. For what reasons do you imagine Macbeth kills Duncan? Are his actions based on practicality or emotion? Do you think Macbeth will achieve his goals?

LITERARY FOCUS

Imagery

Through the use of **imagery,** writers expand and enhance the basic literal meaning of their words. **Imagery** is language that appeals to the senses. Although *visual imagery* (appealing to the sense of sight) is most common, an image may appeal to any of the five senses and often may involve more than one at a time. For example in Act I, Scene v, when Lady Macbeth says "The raven himself is hoarse/That croaks the fatal entrance of Duncan," we see a black bird of ill omen; at the same time we feel in our throats the raspy cry that rings in our ears.

Imagery that evokes a particular dramatic mood was especially important to Shakespeare because his plays were performed in daylight without benefit of elaborate scenery. The "temple-haunting martlet" soars on "heaven's breath" when the gentle, unsuspecting Duncan arrives at Macbeth's castle (Act I, Scene vi), but on the day of the king's murder "darkness does the face of earth entomb."

Thinking About Imagery

■ Examine Macbeth's speech in Act II, Scene ii, lines 56–62. What image does he use to convey his emotion? What feelings is he expressing? What kind of mood does the image create?

ACT III

Scene i. *The palace at Forres.*

[BANQUO *is alone in a room in the royal palace at Forres. He is recalling all that the witches prophesied.*]

BANQUO. Thou hast it now: King, Cawdor, Glamis, all,
As the weird women promised, and I fear
Thou play'dst most foully for 't. Yet it was said
It should not stand¹ in thy posterity,

5   But that myself should be the root and father
Of many kings. If there come truth from them—
As upon thee, Macbeth, their speeches shine—
Why, by the verities on thee made good,
May they not be my oracles as well

10 And set me up in hope? But hush, no more!

[*A trumpet sounds as* MACBETH, *the new king, and* LADY
MACBETH *enter. They are accompanied by* LENNOX, ROSS,
other LORDS, LADIES, *and attendants.*]

MACBETH. Here's our chief guest.

LADY MACBETH.   If he had been forgotten,
It had been as a gap in our great feast,
And all-thing² unbecoming.

MACBETH. Tonight we hold a solemn supper,³ sir,
And I'll request your presence.

15 **BANQUO.**   Let your Highness
Command upon me, to the which my duties
Are with a most indissoluble tie
For ever knit.

MACBETH. Ride you this afternoon?

BANQUO.   Ay, my good lord.

20 **MACBETH.** We should have else desired your good advice
(Which still hath been both grave and prosperous⁴)
In this day's council; but we'll take tomorrow.⁵
Is 't far you ride?

BANQUO. As far, my lord, as will fill up the time

25 'Twixt this and supper. Go not my horse the better,⁶
I must become a borrower of the night
For a dark hour or twain.

MACBETH.   Fail not our feast.

BANQUO. My lord, I will not.

1 **stand:** continue.

2 **all-thing:** altogether.

3 **solemn supper:** formal banquet.

4 **still . . . prosperous:** always has been weighty and profitable in its result.

5 **we'll . . . tomorrow:** tomorrow will do just as well.

6 **Go . . . better:** unless my horse goes faster than I expect.

MACBETH. We hear our bloody cousins are bestowed
30   In England and in Ireland, not confessing
      Their cruel parricide, filling their hearers
      With strange invention.[7] But of that tomorrow,
      When therewithal we shall have cause of state
      Craving us jointly.[8] Hie you to horse. Adieu,
35   Till you return at night. Goes Fleance with you?

BANQUO. Ay, my good lord: our time does call upon 's.[9]

MACBETH. I wish your horses swift and sure of foot,
      And so I do commend you to their backs.
      Farewell. [BANQUO leaves.]
40   Let every man be master of his time
      Till seven at night. To make society
      The sweeter welcome, we will keep ourself
      Till suppertime alone. While[10] then, God be with you!

      [Everyone leaves except MACBETH and a SERVANT.]

      Sirrah,[11] a word with you: attend those men
45   Our pleasure?

ATTENDANT. They are, my lord, without the palace gate.

MACBETH. Bring them before us.

      [The SERVANT leaves. MACBETH, alone, realizes that he will
      never feel safe on the throne as long as BANQUO—promised
      by the WITCHES to be father of kings—is alive.]

      To be thus is nothing, but to be safely thus[12]—
      Our fears in Banquo stick deep,
50   And in his royalty of nature reigns that
      Which would be feared. 'Tis much he dares;
      And, to[13] that dauntless temper of his mind,
      He hath a wisdom that doth guide his valor
      To act in safety. There is none but he
55   Whose being I do fear: and under him
      My genius is rebuked,[14] as it is said
      Mark Antony's was by Caesar. He chid[15] the sisters,
      When first they put the name of King upon me,
      And bade them speak to him; then prophetlike
60   They hailed him father to a line of kings.
      Upon my head they placed a fruitless crown
      And put a barren scepter in my gripe,[16]
      Thence to be wrenched with an unlineal hand,
      No son of mine succeeding. If 't be so,
65   For Banquo's issue have I filed[17] my mind;
      For them the gracious Duncan have I murdered;
      Put rancors in the vessel of my peace

7 **invention:** lies.

8 **cause . . . jointly:** matters of state requiring the attention of both of us.

9 **our . . . upon 's:** time is short, urging us to depart.

10 **While:** until.

11 **Sirrah:** a form of address to an inferior.

12 **To . . . thus:** To be king is nothing, unless I can rule in safety.

13 **And, to:** in addition to.

14 **genius is rebuked:** spirit is cowed.

15 **chid:** scolded.

16 **gripe:** grip.

17 **filed:** defiled, corrupted.

Only for them, and mine eternal jewel[18]
Given to the common enemy of man,[19]
70 To make them kings, the seeds of Banquo kings!
Rather than so, come, fate, into the list,[20]
And champion me to th' utterance![21] Who's there?

[*The* SERVANT *returns with two* MURDERERS, *and* MACBETH
addresses the SERVANT.]

Now go to the door, and stay there till we call.

[*The* SERVANT *leaves.*]

Was it not yesterday we spoke together?

MURDERERS. It was, so please your Highness.

75 **MACBETH.**   Well then, now
Have you considered of my speeches? Know
That it was he[22] in the times past, which held you
So under fortune,[23] which you thought had been
Our innocent self: this I made good to you
80 In our last conference; passed in probation[24] with you,
How you were born in hand,[25] how crossed; the
        instruments,
Who wrought with them, and all things else that might
To half a soul[26] and to a notion[27] crazed
Say "Thus did Banquo."

FIRST MURDERER.   You made it known to us.

85 **MACBETH.** I did so; and went further, which is now
Our point of second meeting. Do you find
Your patience so predominant in your nature,
That you can let this go? Are you so gospeled,[28]
To pray for this good man and for his issue,
90 Whose heavy hand hath bowed you to the grave
And beggared yours for ever?

FIRST MURDERER.   We are men, my liege.

MACBETH. Ay, in the catalogue ye go for[29] men;
As hounds and greyhounds, mongrels, spaniels, curs,
Shoughs, water-rugs[30] and demi-wolves,[31] are clept[32]
95 All by the name of dogs: the valued file[33]
Distinguishes the swift, the slow, the subtle,
The housekeeper, the hunter, every one
According to the gift which bounteous nature
Hath in him closed,[34] whereby he does receive
100 Particular addition,[35] from the bill
That writes them all alike: and so of men.
Now if you have a station in the file,[36]

18 **eternal jewel:** soul.

19 **common . . . man:** devil.

20 **list:** lists, the field of combat, tournament ground.

21 **champion . . . utterance:** fight me to the very death.

22 **he:** Banquo.

23 **held . . . fortune:** thwarted your good fortune.

24 **passed in probation:** reviewed the proofs.
25 **born in hand:** deceived.

26 **half a soul:** half-wit.
27 **notion:** mind.

28 **so gospeled:** ready to forgive.

29 **go for:** pass as.

30 **Shoughs, water-rugs:** shaggy, long-haired water dogs.
31 **demi-wolves:** half-wolf, half-dog.
32 **clept:** called.
33 **valued file:** list of valuable traits that distinguish each breed.

34 **in him closed:** enclosed him.
35 **Particular addition:** a name or title that distinguishes him (from the other dogs).
36 **file:** ranks.

Not i' th' worst rank of manhood, say 't,
And I will put that business in your bosoms
105 Whose execution takes your enemy off,
Grapples you to the heart and love of us,
Who wear our health but sickly in his life,[37]
Which in his death were perfect.

SECOND MURDERER.   I am one, my liege,
Whom the vile blows and buffets of the world
110 Hath so incensed that I am reckless what
I do to spite the world.

FIRST MURDERER.   And I another
So weary with disasters, tugged with fortune,
That I would set[38] my life on any chance,
To mend it or be rid on 't.

MACBETH.   Both of you
Know Banquo was your enemy.

115 BOTH MURDERERS.   True, my lord.

MACBETH. So is he mine, and in such bloody distance[39]
That every minute of his being thrusts
Against my near'st of life:[40] and though I could
With barefaced power sweep him from my sight
120 And bid my will avouch[41] it, yet I must not,
For certain friends that are both his and mine,
Whose loves I may not drop, but wail his fall[42]
Who I myself struck down: and thence it is
That I to your assistance do make love,
125 Masking the business from the common eye
For sundry weighty reasons.

SECOND MURDERER.   We shall, my lord,
Perform what you command us.

FIRST MURDERER.   Though our lives—

MACBETH. Your spirits shine through you. Within this hour at
    most
I will advise you where to plant yourselves,
130 Acquaint you with the perfect spy o' th' time,[43]
The moment on 't; for 't must be done tonight,
And something[44] from the palace; always thought[45]
That I require a clearness:[46] and with him—
To leave no rubs[47] nor botches in the work—
135 Fleance his son, that keeps him company,
Whose absence is no less material to me[48]
Than is his father's, must embrace the fate
Of that dark hour. Resolve yourselves apart:[49]
I'll come to you anon.

37 **wear . . . life:** I am a sick man as long as he (Banquo) lives.

38 **set:** risk.

39 **distance:** disagreement.

40 **near'st of life:** most vital parts.

41 **avouch:** justify.

42 **wail his fall:** (I must) bewail his death.

43 **perfect . . . time:** exact information of the exact moment.

44 **something:** some distance.
45 **always thought:** being understood.
46 **I . . . clearness:** I must remain above suspicion.
47 **rubs:** flaws, imperfections.

48 **Whose . . . me:** whose death is no less important to me.

49 **Resolve . . . apart:** Make up your minds privately.

BOTH MURDERERS.   We are resolved, my lord.

140 **MACBETH.** I'll call upon you straight.[50] [*The* MURDERERS *leave.*]
Abide within.
It is concluded: Banquo, thy soul's flight,
If it find heaven, must find it out tonight. [MACBETH
leaves.]

50 **straight:** immediately.

Scene ii. The palace at Forres.

[LADY MACBETH *and a* SERVANT *are in another room in the palace. She is concerned about what has happened and sends
for* MACBETH *to discuss recent events with him.*]

LADY MACBETH. Is Banquo gone from court?

SERVANT. Ay, madam, but returns again tonight.

LADY MACBETH. Say to the King, I would attend his leisure
For a few words.

SERVANT.   Madam, I will. [*The* SERVANT *leaves to
summon* MACBETH.]

LADY MACBETH.   Nought's had, all's spent,

5 Where our desire is got without content:
'Tis safer to be that which we destroy
Than by destruction dwell in doubtful[1] joy.

1 **doubtful:** apprehensive.

[MACBETH *enters.*]

How now, my lord! Why do you keep alone,
Of sorriest[2] fancies your companions making,

10 Using those thoughts which should indeed have died
With them they think on? Things without all remedy
Should be without regard: what's done is done.

2 **sorriest:** most miserable.

MACBETH. We have scorched[3] the snake, not killed it:
She'll close[4] and be herself, whilst our poor[5] malice

15 Remains in danger of her former tooth.[6]
But let the frame of things disjoint, both the worlds
suffer,[7]
Ere we will eat our meal in fear, and sleep
In the affliction of these terrible dreams
That shake us nightly: better be with the dead,

20 Whom we, to gain our peace, have sent to peace,
Than on the torture of the mind to lie
In restless ecstasy.[8] Duncan is in his grave;
After life's fitful fever he sleeps well.
Treason has done his worst: nor steel, nor poison,

3 **scorched:** slashed, wounded.

4 **close:** heal.
5 **poor:** ineffective.

6 **in . . . tooth:** in as much danger
as before.

7 **But . . . suffer:** Let the universe
fall apart, and let both heaven and
earth perish.

8 **ecstasy:** frenzy, madness.

25   Malice domestic, foreign levy,[9] nothing,
    Can touch him further.

    LADY MACBETH.   Come on.
    Gentle my lord, sleek o'er your rugged looks;
    Be bright and jovial among your guests tonight.

    MACBETH. So shall I, love; and so, I pray, be you:
30   Let your remembrance apply to Banquo;
    Present him eminence,[10] both with eye and tongue:
    Unsafe the while, that we must lave
    Our honors in these flattering[11] streams
    And make our faces vizards[12] to our hearts,
    Disguising what they are.

35   **LADY MACBETH.**   You must leave this.

    MACBETH. O, full of scorpions is my mind, dear wife!
    Thou know'st that Banquo, and his Fleance, lives.

    LADY MACBETH. But in them nature's copy's not eterne.[13]

    MACBETH. There's comfort yet; they are assailable.
40   Then be thou jocund.[14] Ere the bat hath flown
    His cloistered[15] flight, ere to black Hecate's summons
    The shard-borne[16] beetle with his drowsy hums
    Hath rung night's yawning peal, there shall be done
    A deed of dreadful note.

    LADY MACBETH.   What's to be done?

45   **MACBETH.** Be innocent of the knowledge, dearest chuck,[17]
    Till thou applaud the deed. Come, seeling[18] night,
    Scarf up[19] the tender eye of pitiful day,
    And with thy bloody and invisible hand
    Cancel and tear to pieces that great bond[20]
50   Which keeps me pale! Light thickens, and the crow
    Makes wing to th' rooky[21] wood.
    Good things of day begin to droop and drowse,
    Whiles night's black agents to their preys do rouse.
    Thou marvel'st at my words: but hold thee still;
55   Things bad begun make strong themselves by ill:
    So, prithee, go with me. [*They leave together.*]

Scene iii. *Outside the palace at Forres.*

[*About a mile from the palace, the two assassins wait to attack* BANQUO *and* FLEANCE. *They are joined by a mysterious* THIRD MURDERER *who is probably a spy sent by* MACBETH *to make sure the other murderers carry out his orders.*]

---

9 Malice . . . levy: civil and foreign war.

10 Present him eminence: Assign to him the highest distinction.
11 Unsafe . . . flattering: We are not safe so long as we must bathe our honors in a stream of flattery.
12 vizards [viz'ərdz]: masks.

13 in . . . eterne: they do not have eternal life.
14 jocund: merry.
15 cloistered: Bats live in cloisters (covered walks along the walls of a monastery, usually built around a courtyard) and belfries, or bell towers.
16 shard-borne: borne on scaly wings.

17 chuck: a term of endearment.

18 seeling: eye-closing. The term comes from falconry. Night is like the falconer who sometimes sewed his hawk's eyes closed in order to tame it.
19 Scarf up: blindfold.

20 that great bond: between Banquo and fate.
21 rooky: black and full of rooks (crowlike birds).

FIRST MURDERER. But who did bid thee join with us?

THIRD MURDERER.   Macbeth.

SECOND MURDERER. He needs not our mistrust; since he
     delivers
     Our offices[1] and what we have to do
     To the direction just.[2]

FIRST MURDERER.   Then stand with us.
5   The west yet glimmers with some streaks of day.
     Now spurs the lated traveler apace[3]
     To gain the timely inn,[4] and near approaches
     The subject of our watch.

THIRD MURDERER.   Hark! I hear horses.

BANQUO. [*Calls from offstage.*] Give us a light there, ho!

SECOND MURDERER.   Then 'tis he. The rest
10   That are within the note of expectation[5]
     Already are i' th' court.

FIRST MURDERER.   His horses go about.[6]

THIRD MURDERER. Almost a mile: but he does usually—
     So all men do—from hence to th' palace gate
     Make it their walk.

     [BANQUO *and* FLEANCE, *carrying a torch, enter on foot.*]

SECOND MURDERER. A light, a light!

THIRD MURDERER.   'Tis he.

15 FIRST MURDERER.   Stand to 't.

BANQUO. It will be rain tonight.

FIRST MURDERER.   Let it come down.

     [*They attack* BANQUO.]

BANQUO. O, treachery! Fly, good Fleance, fly, fly, fly!

     [FLEANCE *escapes.*]

     Thou mayst revenge. O slave! [BANQUO *dies.*]

THIRD MURDERER. Who did strike out the light?

FIRST MURDERER.   Was 't not the way?[7]

20 THIRD MURDERER. There's but one down; the son is fled.

SECOND MURDERER. We have lost best half of our affair.

1 **offices:** duties.
2 **To . . . just:** in exact detail.

3 **apace:** speedily.
4 **To gain . . . inn:** to reach an inn in good time.

5 **within . . . expectation:** on the list of the expected guests.

6 **His . . . about:** His horses have been taken around to the stable.

7 **Was 't . . . way:** Was this not the way we were told to do it?

FIRST MURDERER. Well, let's away and say how much is done.

[*The* MURDERERS *leave.*]

Scene iv. The palace at Forres.

[*A banquet has been prepared in a hall of the royal palace.*
MACBETH *and* LADY MACBETH *enter with their guests,* ROSS, LEN-
NOX, *and other* LORDS *and their attendants.*]

MACBETH. You know your own degrees;[1] sit down:
At first and last, the hearty welcome.

LORDS. Thanks to your Majesty.

MACBETH. Ourself will mingle with society
5   And play the humble host.
Our hostess keeps her state,[2] but in best time
We will require her welcome.[3]

LADY MACBETH. Pronounce it for me, sir, to all our friends,
For my heart speaks they are welcome.

[*The first* MURDERER *enters and stands near the door.*]

10 **MACBETH.** See, they encounter thee with their hearts' thanks.
Both sides are even: here I'll sit i' th' midst:[4]
Be large in mirth; anon we'll drink a measure[5]
The table round. [*He goes to the* MURDERER *at the door.*]
There's blood upon thy face.

MURDERER. 'Tis Banquo's then.

15 **MACBETH.** 'Tis better thee without than he within.[6]
Is he dispatched?

MURDERER. My lord, his throat is cut; that I did for him.

MACBETH. Thou art the best o' th' cutthroats.
Yet he's good that did the like for Fleance;
20 If thou didst it, thou art the nonpareil.[7]

MURDERER. Most royal sir, Fleance is 'scaped.

MACBETH. [*Aside.*] Then comes my fit[8] again: I had else been
    perfect,
Whole as the marble, founded as the rock,
As broad and general as the casing air:[9]
25 But now I am cabined, cribbed, confined, bound in
To saucy[10] doubts and fears. [*To the* MURDERER.]—But
    Banquo's safe?

MURDERER. Ay, my good lord: safe in a ditch he bides,

---

1 **You . . . degrees:** You know your ranks. At state banquets guests were seated according to rank.

2 **keeps her state:** sits apart on her throne.
3 **in . . . welcome:** When the proper time comes, we will ask her to join us.

4 **Both . . . midst:** There are equal numbers on both sides of the table, and Macbeth sits at the head.

5 **measure:** toast.

6 **'Tis better . . . within:** It is better on your face than in his body.

7 **nonpareil** [non′pə rəl′]: one without equal.

8 **my fit:** my torment.

9 **As . . . air:** as free and unrestrained as the surrounding air.

10 **saucy:** insolent.

With twenty trenchèd gashes[11] on his head,
The least a death to nature.[12]

MACBETH.   Thanks for that.
30 [*Aside.*] There the grown serpent lies; the worm that's fled
Hath nature that in time will venom breed,
No teeth for th' present. [*To the* MURDERER.]—Get thee gone.
Tomorrow
We'll hear ourselves[13] again. [*The* MURDERER *leaves.*]

LADY MACBETH.   My royal lord,
You do not give the cheer.[14] The feast is sold
35 That is not often vouched, while 'tis a-making,
'Tis given with welcome.[15] To feed were best at home;
From thence, the sauce to meat is ceremony;[16]
Meeting were bare without it.

[*The* GHOST OF BANQUO *enters and sits in* MACBETH'*s place.*]

MACBETH.   Sweet remembrancer!
Now good digestion wait on appetite,
And health on both!

40 **LENNOX.**   May 't please your Highness sit.

MACBETH. Here had we now our country's honor roofed,[17]
Were the gracèd person of our Banquo present—
Who may I rather challenge for unkindness
Than pity for mischance![18]

ROSS.   His absence, sir,
45 Lays blame upon his promise. Please 't your Highness
To grace us with your royal company?

[MACBETH *looks at his chair and sees the* GHOST.]

MACBETH. The table's full.

LENNOX.   Here is a place reserved, sir.

MACBETH. Where?

LENNOX. [*Indicating the empty place where* MACBETH *sees the*
GHOST.] Here, my good lord. What is 't that moves your
Highness?

MACBETH. Which of you have done this?

50 **LORDS.**   What, my good lord?

MACBETH. Thou canst not say I did it. Never shake
Thy gory locks at me.

ROSS. Gentlemen, rise, his Highness is not well.

LADY MACBETH. Sit, worthy friends. My lord is often thus,

11 **trenchèd gashes:** deep cuts.
12 **death to nature:** enough to kill a man.

13 **hear ourselves:** talk it over.

14 **cheer:** make the company welcome.
15 **The feast . . . welcome:** A feast where guests are not made welcome is no more than a tavern-bought meal.
16 **To feed . . . ceremony:** When not eating at home, ceremony adds a pleasant flavor to the meal.

17 **our . . . roofed:** the most honorable men in the country under one roof.

18 **I . . . mischance:** I would rather reproach him for being absent due to discourtesy than because of some accident.

55 And hath been from his youth. Pray you, keep seat.
The fit is momentary; upon a thought[19]
He will again be well. If much you note him,
You shall offend him and extend his passion.[20]
Feed, and regard him not. [*To* MACBETH.]—Are you a man?

60 MACBETH. Ay, and a bold one, that dare look on that
Which might appall the devil.

LADY MACBETH.   O proper stuff![21]
This is the very painting of your fear.
This is the air-drawn dagger which, you said,
Led you to Duncan. O, these flaws[22] and starts,
65 Impostors to true fear, would well become
A woman's story at a winter's fire,
Authorized by her grandam.[23] Shame itself!
Why do you make such faces? When all's done,
You look but on a stool.

MACBETH.   Prithee, see there!
70 Behold! Look! Lo! [*To the* GHOST.] How say you?
Why, what care I? If thou canst nod, speak too.
If charnel houses[24] and our graves must send
Those that we bury back, our monuments
Shall be the maws of kites.[25] [*The* GHOST *vanishes.*]

LADY MACBETH.   What, quite unmanned in folly?

MACBETH. If I stand here, I saw him.

75 LADY MACBETH.   Fie, for shame!

MACBETH. Blood hath been shed ere now, i' th' olden time,
Ere humane statute purged the gentle weal;[26]
Ay, and since too, murders have been performed
Too terrible for the ear. The times has been
80 That, when the brains were out, the man would die,
And there an end; but now they rise again,
With twenty mortal murders on their crowns,[27]
And push us from our stools. This is more strange
Than such a murder is.

LADY MACBETH.   My worthy lord,
Your noble friends do lack you.

85 MACBETH.   I do forget.
Do not muse at me, my most worthy friends;
I have a strange infirmity, which is nothing
To those that know me. Come, love and health to all!
Then I'll sit down. Give me some wine, fill full.

[*The* GHOST *reappears, but* MACBETH *does not notice him at once.*]

19 **upon a thought:** in a moment.

20 **passion:** suffering.

21 **proper stuff!:** Nonsense!

22 **flaws:** literally, sudden gusts of wind; outbursts of emotion.

23 **Authorized . . . grandam:** given on the authority of her grandmother.

24 **charnel houses:** buildings where bones dug up from old graves were stored.
25 **our . . . kites:** our tombs will be the bellies of birds of prey.

26 **Ere . . . weal:** before human laws civilized the state and made it peaceful.

27 **mortal . . . crowns:** deadly wounds on their heads.

90 I drink to th' general joy o' th' whole table,
And to our dear friend Banquo, whom we miss;
Would he were here! To all and him we thirst,[28]
And all to all.

LORDS.   Our duties, and the pledge.

MACBETH. [*To the* GHOST.] Avaunt![29] and quit my sight! Let
the earth hide thee!
95 Thy bones are marrowless, thy blood is cold;
Thou hast no speculation[30] in those eyes
Which thou dost glare with.

LADY MACBETH.   Think of this, good peers,
But as a thing of custom; 'tis no other.
Only it spoils the pleasure of the time.

100 MACBETH. What man dare, I dare.
Approach thou like the rugged Russian bear,
The armed rhinoceros, or th' Hyrcan tiger;[31]
Take any shape but that,[32] and my firm nerves
Shall never tremble. Or be alive again,
105 And dare me to the desert[33] with thy sword.
If trembling I inhabit then, protest me
The baby of a girl.[34] Hence, horrible shadow!
Unreal mock'ry, hence! [*The* GHOST *vanishes again.*]
            Why, so: being gone,
I am a man again. Pray you, sit still.

LADY MACBETH. You have displaced the mirth, broke the good
110   meeting,
With most admired disorder.[35]

MACBETH.   Can such things be,
And overcome us[36] like a summer's cloud,
Without our special wonder? You make me strange
Even to the disposition that I owe,[37]
115 When now I think you can behold such sights,
And keep the natural ruby of your cheeks,
When mine is blanched with fear.

ROSS.   What sights, my lord?

LADY MACBETH. I pray you, speak not: he grows worse and
    worse;
Question enrages him: at once, good night.
120 Stand not upon the order of your going,[38]
But go at once.

LENNOX.   Good night; and better health
Attend his Majesty!

28 **thirst:** drink.

29 **Avaunt!:** Be gone!

30 **speculations:** sights.

31 **Hyrcan** [hər′kən] **tiger:** Hyrcania was located south of the Caspian Sea in ancient Asia. Hercules was said to have killed the Hyrcan tiger.
32 **that:** Banquo's shape.

33 **desert:** inescapable place.

34 **If . . . girl:** If I tremble, then call me a baby girl.

35 **admired disorder:** amazing lack of self-control.

36 **overcome us:** come over us.

37 **disposition . . . owe:** my own nature, myself.

38 **Stand . . . going:** Do not wait to leave in order of your rank.

LADY MACBETH.   A kind good night to all!

[*Everyone leaves except* MACBETH *and* LADY MACBETH.]

MACBETH. It will have blood, they say: blood will have blood.
Stones have been known to move and trees to speak;
125 Augures and understood relations[39] have
By maggot-pies and choughs[40] and rooks brought forth[41]
The secret'st man of blood.[42] What is the night?

LADY MACBETH. Almost at odds[43] with morning, which is
which.

MACBETH. How say'st thou, that Macduff denies his person
At our great bidding?

130 **LADY MACBETH.**   Did you send to him, sir?

MACBETH. I hear it by the way, but I will send:
There's not a one of them but in his house
I keep a servant fee'd.[44] I will tomorrow,
And betimes[45] I will, to the weird sisters:
135 More shall they speak, for now I am bent[46] to know
By the worst means the worst. For mine own good
All causes shall give way. I am in blood
Stepped in so far that, should I wade no more,
Returning were as tedious as go o'er.
140 Strange things I have in head that will to hand,
Which must be acted ere they may be scanned.[47]

LADY MACBETH. You lack the season of all natures,[48] sleep.

MACBETH. Come, we'll to sleep. My strange and self-abuse[49]
Is the initiate fear that wants hard use.[50]
145 We are yet but young in deed.

[*They leave.*]

Scene v. A heath.

[*There is thunder and lightning on a heath as the* THREE
WITCHES *enter and meet* HECATE, *the goddess of witchcraft.*]

FIRST WITCH. Why, how now, Hecate! you look angerly.

HECATE. Have I not reason, beldams[1] as you are,
Saucy and overbold? How did you dare
To trade and traffic with Macbeth
5 In riddles and affairs of death;
And I, the mistress of your charms,

---

39 **Augures . . . relations:** omens and the relationship between the omens and what they signify.
40 **maggot-pies and choughs** [chufs]: magpies and crows.
41 **brought forth:** revealed.
42 **man of blood:** murderer.

43 **at odds:** disputing (it is almost midnight).

44 **fee'd:** in my pay as a spy.
45 **betimes:** early in the morning.
46 **bent:** eager.

47 **scanned:** examined.

48 **season . natures:** that which keeps fresh all living things.
49 **My . . . self-abuse:** my strange delusion.
50 **initiate . . . use:** beginner's fear that will toughen with more experience.

1 **beldams:** old hags.

The close contriver[2] of all harms,
Was never called to bear my part,
Or show the glory of our art?
10 And, which is worse, all you have done
Hath been but for a wayward son,
Spiteful and wrathful; who, as others do,
Loves for his own ends, not for you.
But make amends now: get you gone,
15 And at the pit of Acheron[3]
Meet me i' th' morning: thither he
Will come to know his destiny.
Your vessels and your spells provide,
Your charms and everything beside.
20 I am for th' air; this night I'll spend
Unto a dismal[4] and a fatal end:
Great business must be wrought ere noon.
Upon the corner of the moon
There hangs a vap'rous drop profound;
25 I'll catch it ere it come to ground:
And that distilled by magic sleights[5]
Shall raise such artificial sprites[6]
As by the strength of their illusion
Shall draw him on to his confusion.[7]
30 He shall spurn fate, scorn death, and bear
His hopes 'bove wisdom, grace, and fear:
And you all know security[8]
Is mortals' chiefest enemy.

[*Music and a song are heard offstage.* HECATE *is called away.*]

Hark! I am called; my little spirit,[9] see,
35 Sits in a foggy cloud and stays for me.

[HECATE *leaves.*]

FIRST WITCH. Come, let's make haste; she'll soon be back
again.

[*The* WITCHES *leave quickly.*]

Scene vi. The palace at Forres.

[LENNOX *and another* LORD *enter a room in the palace and discuss the recent deaths of* DUNCAN *and* BANQUO *and* MAC-DUFF'S *mission to the court of King Edward of England to enlist the king's aid against* MACBETH.]

LENNOX. My former speeches have but hit[1] your thoughts,
Which can interpret farther.[2] Only I say

2 **close contriver:** secret inventor.

3 **Acheron** [ak'ə ron']: hell; in Greek mythology, a river of Hades.

4 **dismal:** disastrous.

5 **sleights:** devices, arts.
6 **artificial sprites:** spirits created by magic.

7 **confusion:** ruin, destruction.

8 **security:** overconfidence.

9 **my little spirit:** her familiar, or helper.

1 **hit:** agreed with.
2 **Which . . . farther:** from which you can draw your own conclusions.

Things have been strangely borne.[3] The gracious Duncan
Was pitied of Macbeth: marry,[4] he was dead.
5 And the right-valiant Banquo walked too late;
Whom, you may say, if 't please you, Fleance killed,
For Fleance fled. Men must not walk too late.
Who cannot want the thought,[5] how monstrous
It was for Malcolm and for Donalbain
10 To kill their gracious father? Damnèd fact![6]
How it did grieve Macbeth! Did he not straight,
In pious rage, the two delinquents tear,
That were the slaves of drink and thralls[7] of sleep?
Was not that nobly done? Ay, and wisely too;
15 For 'twould have angered any heart alive
To hear the men deny 't. So that I say
He has borne all things well:[8] and I do think
That, had he Duncan's sons under his key—
As, an 't[9] please heaven, he shall not—they should find
20 What 'twere to kill a father. So should Fleance.
But, peace! for from broad words,[10] and 'cause he failed
His presence at the tyrant's feast, I hear,
Macduff lives in disgrace. Sir, can you tell
Where he bestows himself?

LORD.   The son of Duncan,
25 From whom this tyrant holds the due of birth,[11]
Lives in the English court, and is received
Of the most pious Edward[12] with such grace
That the malevolence of fortune nothing
Takes from his high respect.[13] Thither Macduff
30 Is gone to pray the holy King, upon his aid[14]
To wake Northumberland and warlike Siward;[15]
That by the help of these, with Him above
To ratify the work, we may again
Give to our tables meat, sleep to our nights,
35 Free from our feasts and banquets bloody knives,
Do faithful homage and receive free honors:[16]
All which we pine for now. And this report
Hath so exasperate the King that he
Prepares for some attempt of war.

LENNOX.   Sent he to Macduff?

40 LORD. He did: and with an absolute "Sir, not I,"
The cloudy[17] messenger turns me his back,
And hums, as who should say "You'll rue the time
That clogs[18] me with this answer."

LENNOX.   And that well might
Advise him to a caution, t' hold what distance
45 His wisdom can provide. Some holy angel

---

3 **strangely borne:** oddly managed.

4 **marry:** indeed; a mild oath, originally, "By the Virgin Mary!"

5 **Who . . . thought:** who cannot help thinking.

6 **fact:** act, deed.

7 **thralls:** slaves.

8 **He . . . well:** He has managed things cunningly.

9 **an 't:** if it.

10 **broad words:** free, unguarded speaking.

11 **holds . . . birth:** withholds his birthright—that is, the throne.

12 **Edward:** Edward the Confessor, King of England 1042–1066.

13 **That . . . respect:** His misfortune does not lessen the high respect he is given.
14 **his aid:** on Malcolm's behalf.
15 **To wake . . . Siward:** to call to arms the Earl of Northumberland, general of the English forces, and his son, Siward. Northumberland is a part of England close to the Scottish border.

16 **free honors:** honors given to free men.

17 **cloudy:** disturbed.

18 **clogs:** burdens.

Fly to the court of England and unfold
His message ere he come, that a swift blessing
May soon return to this our suffering country
Under a hand accursed!

LORD.   I'll send my prayers with him.

[*They leave.*]

STUDY QUESTIONS

Recalling

1. In Act III, Scene i, just before the murderers enter, what reasons does Macbeth give for wanting to have Banquo killed? At the end of Scene i, whom else does Macbeth tell the murderers to kill?

2. At the beginning of Scene ii, what does Lady Macbeth say that reveals her feelings about being queen of Scotland?

3. What happens to Banquo and Fleance in Scene iii?

4. In Scene iv why does Macbeth refuse to sit at the table with his guests? What explanation do Lady Macbeth and Macbeth give for his strange behavior?

5. At the end of Scene iv, why does Macbeth decide to seek the advice of the weird sisters?

6. At the end of her speech in Scene v, what effect does Hecate say the witches' predictions will have on Macbeth?

7. In Scene vi what reason are we given for Macduff's trip to the king of England? What does Macbeth do when he learns of Macduff's mission?

Interpreting

8. In Scene i how does Macbeth manipulate the murderers into doing what he wants them to do?

9. How has Macbeth's attitude toward murder changed? Compare his state of mind as he arranges Banquo's assassination in Act III, Scene i, with his emotional state in Act II, Scene i, as he prepares to murder King Duncan.

10. Examine Macbeth's speeches in Scene ii. What do they show about how his relationship with his wife has changed?

11. In what ways do the events in Scene iv change Macbeth's personality? At this point could he stop killing even if he wanted to?

12. What are your impressions of Macduff from what you learn about him in Scene vi? What importance do you think he will have in Acts IV and V?

Extending

13. Imagine that you are a guest at Macbeth's banquet. How would you react to the new king's behavior? How would you explain it?

VIEWPOINT

According to Mark Van Doren, the world of *Macbeth*

can be most easily described as "strange." The word, like the witches, is always somewhere doing its work. Even in the battle which precedes the play the Thane of Glamis [Macbeth] has made "strange images of death" (Act I, Scene iii, line 97), and when he comes home to his lady his face is "as a book where men may read strange matters" (Act I, Scene v, lines 61– 62). . . . Nothing is as it should be in such a world. . . . There is a drift of disorder in all events, and the air is murky with unwelcome miracles.

■ What "unwelcome miracles" can you cite in support of Van Doren's observation? What else seems strange about the world the play creates? Is the word *strange* used elsewhere?

ACT IV

Scene i. *A deserted place.*

[*It is thundering as the* THREE WITCHES *enter and stand around a large caldron, or pot, in their deserted meeting place.*]

FIRST WITCH. Thrice the brinded[1] cat hath mewed.

SECOND WITCH. Thrice and once the hedge-pig[2] whined.

THIRD WITCH. Harpier[3] cries. 'Tis time, 'tis time.

FIRST WITCH. Round about the caldron go:
5   In the poisoned entrails throw.

[*The* WITCHES *circle the caldron, and as each mentions an item, she throws it into the pot.*]

  Toad, that under cold stone
  Days and nights has thirty-one
  Swelt'red venom sleeping got,[4]
  Boil thou first i' th' charmèd pot.

10 **ALL.** Double, double, toil and trouble;
  Fire burn and caldron bubble.

SECOND WITCH. Fillet of a fenny snake,[5]
  In the caldron boil and bake;
  Eye of newt and toe of frog,
15   Wool of bat and tongue of dog,
  Adder's fork[6] and blindworm's[7] sting,
  Lizard's leg and howlet's[8] wing,
  For a charm of pow'rful trouble,
  Like a hell-broth boil and bubble.

20 **ALL.** Double, double, toil and trouble;
  Fire burn and caldron bubble.

THIRD WITCH. Scale of dragon, tooth of wolf,
  Witch's mummy, maw and gulf[9]
  Of the ravined[10] salt-sea shark,
25   Root of hemlock digged i' th' dark,
  Slivered in the moon's eclipse,
  Nose of Turk and Tartar's lips,
  Finger of birth-strangled babe
  Ditch-delivered[11] by a drab,
30   Make the gruel thick and slab:[12]
  Add thereto a tiger's chaudron,[13]
  For th' ingredients of our caldron.

1 **brinded** [brin′did]: striped.

2 **hedge-pig:** hedgehog, a witch's familiar, like the brinded cat.

3 **Harpier:** one of the familiar spirits attending the witches. *Harpier* is derived from *harpy*, a birdlike monster of classical mythology.

4 **Swelt'red . . . got:** sweated out poison while sleeping.

5 **fenny snake:** a snake from the fens, or marshes.

6 **fork:** forked tongue.
7 **blindworm:** small, harmless, limbless lizard, once believed to be poisonous.
8 **howlet:** small owl.

9 **maw and gulf:** stomach and gullet.
10 **ravined:** ravenous.

11 **Ditch-delivered:** born in a ditch.
12 **slab:** sticky.
13 **chaudron** [shō′drən]: entrails.

ALL. Double, double, toil and trouble;
    Fire burn and caldron bubble.

35 **SECOND WITCH.** Cool it with a baboon's blood,
    Then the charm is firm and good.

[HECATE, *goddess of witches, enters and addresses the other*
THREE WITCHES.]

HECATE. O, well done! I commend your pains;
    And everyone shall share i' th' gains:
    And now about the caldron sing,
40   Like elves and fairies in a ring,
    Enchanting all that you put in.

[*Music and a song are heard offstage.* HECATE *leaves.*]

SECOND WITCH. By the pricking of my thumbs,
    Something wicked this way comes:
      Open, locks,
45   Whoever knocks!

[MACBETH *enters.*]

MACBETH. How now, you secret, black, and midnight hags!
    What is 't you do?

ALL.   A deed without a name.

MACBETH. I conjure you, by that which you profess,[14]
    Howe'er you come to know it, answer me:
50   Though you untie the winds and let them fight
    Against the churches; though the yesty[15] waves
    Confound[16] and swallow navigation up;
    Though bladed corn be lodged[17] and trees blown down;
    Though castles topple on their warders' heads;
55   Though palaces and pyramids do slope[18]
    Their heads to their foundations; though the treasure
    Of nature's germens[19] tumble all together,
    Even till destruction sicken, answer me
    To what I ask you.[20]

FIRST WITCH.   Speak.

SECOND WITCH.   Demand.

THIRD WITCH.   We'll answer.

60 **FIRST WITCH.** Say, if th' hadst rather hear it from our mouths,
    Or from our masters?

MACBETH.   Call 'em, let me see 'em.

FIRST WITCH. Pour in sow's blood, that hath eaten

14 **that . . . profess:** witchcraft.

15 **yesty:** foamy.

16 **Confound:** destroy.

17 **lodged:** beaten down.

18 **slope:** bend.

19 **germens:** seeds of all life.

20 **Though you untie . . . I ask
you:** Macbeth must know the truth,
whatever the cost.

Her nine farrow;[21] grease that's sweaten
From the murderer's gibbet[22] throw
Into the flame.

65 **ALL.**   Come, high or low,
Thyself and office[23] deftly show!

[*The* THREE APPARITIONS, *or ghosts—an Armored Head, a
Bloody Child, and a Child Crowned—that appear in turn
here are symbolic of the stages of* MACBETH'S *downfall.
Their significance is unknown to* MACBETH *at this time.
Thunder is heard as the* FIRST APPARITION, *the armored head
of a warrior, appears. This head symbolizes* MACBETH'S *future battle with* MACDUFF.]

MACBETH. Tell me, thou unknown power—

FIRST WITCH.   He knows thy thought:
Hear his speech, but say thou nought.

FIRST APPARITION. Macbeth! Macbeth! Macbeth! Beware
    Macduff!
70 Beware the Thane of Fife. Dismiss me: enough.

[*The* FIRST APPARITION *disappears.*]

MACBETH. Whate'er thou art, for thy good caution thanks:
Thou has harped[24] my fear aright. But one word more—

FIRST WITCH. He will not be commanded. Here's another,
More potent than the first.

[*More thunder as the* SECOND APPARITION, *a Bloody Child,
appears. The Bloody Child symbolizes* MACDUFF *at birth.*]

75 **SECOND APPARITION.** Macbeth! Macbeth! Macbeth!

MACBETH. Had I three ears, I'd hear thee.

SECOND APPARITION. Be bloody, bold, and resolute! Laugh to
    scorn
The pow'r of man, for none of woman born
Shall harm Macbeth.

[*The* SECOND APPARITION *disappears.*]

80 **MACBETH.** Then live, Macduff: what need I fear of thee?
But yet I'll make assurance double sure,
And take a bond of fate.[25] Thou shalt not live;
That I may tell pale-hearted fear it lies,
And sleep in spite of thunder.

[*Thunder sounds as the* THIRD APPARITION, *a Crowned Child
with a tree in his hand, appears. This child symbolizes*
MALCOLM, KING DUNCAN'S *elder son.*]

21 **farrow:** young pigs.
22 **gibbet** [jib'it]: gallows.

23 **office:** your function.

24 **harped:** guessed.

25 **take . . . fate:** get a guarantee
from fate that he will be safe.

                                  What is this,
85   That rises like the issue of a king,
      And wears upon his baby-brow the round
      And top of sovereignty?[26]

      ALL.   Listen, but speak not to 't.

      THIRD APPARITION. Be lion-mettled, proud, and take no care
      Who chafes, who frets, or where conspirers are:
90   Macbeth shall never vanquished be until
      Great Birnam Wood to high Dunsinane Hill
      Shall come against him.[27]

      [The THIRD APPARITION disappears.]

      MACBETH.   That will never be.
      Who can impress[28] the forest, bid the tree
      Unfix his earth-bound root? Sweet bodements,[29] good!
95   Rebellious dead, rise never, till the Wood
      Of Birnam rise, and our high-placed Macbeth
      Shall live the lease of nature, pay his breath
      To time and mortal custom.[30] Yet my heart
      Throbs to know one thing. Tell me, if your art
100   Can tell so much: shall Banquo's issue ever
      Reign in this kingdom?

      ALL.   Seek to know no more.

      MACBETH. I will be satisfied. Deny me this,
      And an eternal curse fall on you! Let me know
      Why sinks that caldron? And what noise is this?

      [Oboes are heard.]

105   FIRST WITCH. Show!

      SECOND WITCH. Show!

      THIRD WITCH. Show!

      ALL. Show his eyes, and grieve his heart;
      Come like shadows, so depart!

      [A pantomime passes across the stage. In the show are the
      apparitions of eight kings, representing the eight Stuart
      kings of Scotland. The eighth king represents James I of
      England, also known as King James VI of Scotland. He
      was a descendant of BANQUO and reigned at the time
      MACBETH was written. The last king has a mirror in his
      hand so that MACBETH can look into the future. BANQUO'S
      GHOST appears at the end of the procession.]

110   MACBETH. Thou art too like the spirit of Banquo. Down!
      Thy crown does sear mine eyelids. And thy hair,

26 **top of sovereignty:** crown.

27 **Macbeth . . . him:** Macbeth will never be conquered unless the forest of Great Birnam marches twelve miles to his castle on Dunsinane Hill.

28 **impress:** force into service.
29 **bodements:** prophecies.

30 **live . . . custom:** live and die a natural death.

Thou other gold-bound brow, is like the first.
A third is like the former. Filthy hags!
Why do you show me this? A fourth! Start, eyes!
115 What, will the line stretch out to th' crack of doom?
Another yet! A seventh! I'll see no more.
And yet the eighth appears, who bears a glass
Which shows me many more; and some I see
That twofold balls and treble scepters[31] carry:
120 Horrible sight! Now I see 'tis true;
For the blood-boltered[32] Banquo smiles upon me,
And points at them for his.

[*The* APPARITIONS *in the pantomime vanish.*]

What, is this so?

FIRST WITCH. Ay, sir, all this is so. But why
Stands Macbeth thus amazedly?[33]
125 Come, sisters, cheer we up his sprites,[34]
And show the best of our delights:
I'll charm the air to give a sound,
While you perform your antic round,[35]
That this great king may kindly say
130 Our duties did his welcome pay.

[*Music plays as the* WITCHES *dance and vanish.*]

MACBETH. Where are they? Gone? Let this pernicious hour
Stand aye accursed in the calendar![36]
Come in, without there!

[LENNOX *enters.*]

LENNOX.   What's your Grace's will?

MACBETH. Saw you the weird sisters?

LENNOX.   No, my lord.

MACBETH. Came they not by you?

135 LENNOX.   No indeed, my lord.

MACBETH. Infected be the air whereon they ride,
And damned all those that trust them! I did hear
The galloping of horse. Who was 't came by?

LENNOX. 'Tis two or three, my lord, that bring you word
Macduff is fled to England.

140 MACBETH.   Fled to England?

LENNOX. Ay, my good lord.

MACBETH. [*Aside.*] Time, thou anticipat'st[37] my dread exploits.

The flighty purpose never is o'ertook
Unless the deed go with it.[38] From this moment
145 The very firstlings of my heart[39] shall be
The firstlings of my hand. And even now,
To crown my thoughts with acts, be it thought and done:
The castle of Macduff I will surprise;
Seize upon Fife; give to th' edge o' th' sword
150 His wife, his babes, and all unfortunate souls
That trace[40] him in his line. No boasting like a fool;
This deed I'll do before this purpose cool:
But no more sights!—Where are these gentlemen?
Come, bring me where they are.

[MACBETH *leaves with* LENNOX.]

38 **The flighty . . . it:** The fleeting plan is never fulfilled unless it is carried out at once.
39 **firstlings . . . heart:** first thoughts and impulses.
40 **trace:** succeed.

Scene ii. MACDUFF'S *castle at Fife.*

[*In Fife, on the southeast coast of Scotland,* LADY MACDUFF, *her son, and* ROSS *enter a room in* MACDUFF'S *castle.* LADY MACDUFF *is upset and angry with her husband for leaving Scotland.*]

LADY MACDUFF. What had he done, to make him fly the land?

ROSS. You must have patience, madam.

LADY MACDUFF.   He had none:
His flight was madness. When our actions do not,
Our fears do make us traitors.[1]

ROSS.   You know not
5   Whether it was his wisdom or his fear.

LADY MACDUFF. Wisdom! To leave his wife, to leave his babes,
His mansion and his titles,[2] in a place
From whence himself does fly? He loves us not;
He wants the natural touch:[3] for the poor wren,
10   The most diminutive of birds, will fight,
Her young ones in her nest, against the owl.
All is the fear and nothing is the love;
As little is the wisdom, where the flight
So runs against all reason.

ROSS.   My dearest coz,[4]
15   I pray you, school[5] yourself. But, for your husband,
He is noble, wise, judicious, and best knows
The fits o' th' season.[6] I dare not speak much further:
But cruel are the times, when we are traitors
And do not know ourselves;[7] when we hold rumor
20   From what we fear,[8] yet know not what we fear,
But float upon a wild and violent sea

1 **When . . . traitors:** Although we may not be traitors, displaying our fears gives us the appearance of guilt.

2 **his titles:** all he is entitled to, his possessions.

3 **wants . . . touch:** lacks the feeling of natural affection.

4 **coz** [kuz]: an affectionate shortening of *cousin.* (Macduff and Ross are cousins.)
5 **school:** control.
6 **fits . . . season:** violent disorders of the time.
7 **we . . . ourselves:** we are treated as traitors but do not know of any treason.
8 **hold . . . fear:** interpret rumors based on our fears.

Each way and move. I take my leave of you.
Shall not be long but I'll be here again.
Things at the worst will cease, or else climb upward
25 To what they were before. [*He addresses* MACDUFF'*s son.*]
My pretty cousin,
Blessing upon you!

LADY MACDUFF. Fathered he is, and yet he's fatherless.

ROSS. I am so much a fool, should I stay longer,
It would be my disgrace and your discomfort.[9]
I take my leave at once.

[ROSS *leaves.*]

30 **LADY MACDUFF.**   Sirrah, your father's dead:
And what will you do now? How will you live?

SON. As birds do, mother.

LADY MACDUFF.   What, with worms and flies?

SON. With what I get, I mean; and so do they.

LADY MACDUFF. Poor bird! thou'dst never fear the net nor
lime,[10]
35 The pitfall nor the gin.[11]

SON. Why should I, mother? Poor birds they are not set for.
My father is not dead, for all your saying.

LADY MACDUFF. Yes, he is dead: how wilt thou do for a
father?

SON. Nay, how will you do for a husband?

40 **LADY MACDUFF.** Why, I can buy me twenty at any market.

SON. Then you'll buy 'em to sell[12] again.

LADY MACDUFF. Thou speak'st with all thy wit, and yet, i'
faith,
With wit enough for thee.[13]

SON. Was my father a traitor, mother?

45 **LADY MACDUFF.** Ay, that he was.

SON. What is a traitor?

LADY MACDUFF. Why, one that swears and lies.[14]

SON. And be all traitors that do so?

LADY MACDUFF. Every one that does so is a traitor, and must
be hanged.

50 **SON.** And must they all be hanged that swear and lie?

9 **It . . . discomfort:** I would disgrace myself and embarrass you by weeping.

10 **lime:** birdlime, a sticky substance smeared on branches to catch birds.
11 **pitfall . . . gin:** traps or snares.

12 **sell:** betray.

13 **for thee:** for a child.

14 **swears and lies:** takes an oath and breaks it.

LADY MACDUFF. Every one.

SON. Who must hang them?

LADY MACDUFF. Why, the honest men.

SON. Then the liars and swearers are fools; for there are liars
55 and swearers enow[15] to beat the honest men and hang up
them.

LADY MACDUFF. Now, God help thee, poor monkey! But how
wilt thou do for a father?

SON. If he were dead, you'd weep for him. If you would not,
60 it were a good sign that I should quickly have a new
father.

LADY MACDUFF. Poor prattler, how thou talk'st!

[*A* MESSENGER *comes in.*]

MESSENGER. Bless you, fair dame! I am not to you known,
Though in your state of honor I am perfect.[16]
65 I doubt[17] some danger does approach you nearly:
If you will take a homely[18] man's advice,
Be not found here; hence, with your little ones.
To fright you thus, methinks I am too savage;
To do worse to you were fell[19] cruelty,
70 Which is too nigh your person. Heaven preserve you!
I dare abide no longer.

[*The* MESSENGER *leaves quickly.*]

LADY MACDUFF.   Whither should I fly?
I have done no harm. But I remember now
I am in this earthly world, where to do harm
Is often laudable, to do good sometime
75 Accounted dangerous folly. Why then, alas,
Do I put up that womanly defense,
To say I have done no harm?—What are these faces?

[*The* MURDERERS *hired by* MACBETH *enter.*]

MURDERER. Where is your husband?

LADY MACDUFF. I hope, in no place so unsanctified
Where such as thou mayst find him.

80 **MURDERER.**   He's a traitor.

SON. Thou li'st, thou shag-eared[20] villain!

MURDERER.   What, you egg!

[*The* MURDERER *stabs the child.*]

---

15 **enow:** enough.

16 **in . . . perfect:** I know of your honorable rank.
17 **I doubt:** I fear.
18 **homely:** simple.

19 **fell:** fierce.

20 **shag-eared:** with shaggy hair about his ears.

Young fry of treachery![21]

SON.   He has killed me, mother:
Run away, I pray you!

[*The* BOY *dies as* LADY MACDUFF *runs off crying, "Murder!"*
The MURDERERS *pursue her.*]

Scene iii. *The palace of the King of England.*

[MACDUFF *has come to England in an attempt to ally himself*
with MALCOLM, KING DUNCAN'*s elder son and rightful heir to*
the Scottish crown. He meets MALCOLM *in front of the palace*
of Edward the Confessor, the devoutly religious King of Eng-
land.]

MALCOLM. Let us seek out some desolate shade, and there
Weep our sad bosoms empty.

MACDUFF.   Let us rather
Hold fast the mortal[1] sword, and like good men
Bestride our down-fall'n birthdom.[2] Each new morn
5   New widows howl, new orphans cry, new sorrows
Strike heaven on the face, that it resounds
As if it felt with Scotland and yelled out
Like syllable of dolor.[3]

MALCOLM.   What I believe, I'll wail;
What know, believe; and what I can redress,
10   As I shall find the time to friend,[4] I will.
What you have spoke, it may be so perchance.
This tyrant, whose sole[5] name blisters our tongues,
Was once thought honest:[6] you have loved him well;
He hath not touched you yet. I am young; but something
15   You may deserve of him through me;[7] and wisdom[8]
To offer up a weak, poor, innocent lamb
T' appease an angry god.

MACDUFF. I am not treacherous.

MALCOLM.   But Macbeth is.
A good and virtuous nature may recoil
20   In an imperial charge.[9] But I shall crave your pardon;
That which you are, my thoughts cannot transpose:[10]
Angels are bright still, though the brightest[11] fell:
Though all things foul would wear the brows of grace,
Yet grace must still look so.[12]

MACDUFF.   I have lost my hopes.[13]

21 **Young . . . treachery:** child
spawned by a traitor.

1 **mortal:** deadly.

2 **Bestride . . . birthdom:** stand
over, protect, our native land, which
has been beaten down.

3 **Like . . . dolor:** a similar cry.

4 **to friend:** friendly.

5 **sole:** very.

6 **honest:** good.

7 **something . . . me:** you may
benefit by betraying me to Macbeth.
8 **and wisdom:** and it is wise.

9 **recoil . . . charge:** reverse itself
by royal command.
10 **transpose:** change; my
suspicions alone cannot make you a
traitor.
11 **the brightest:** Lucifer.
12 **Though . . . so:** Even if all foul
things looked gracious, grace would
not change its appearance.
13 **my hopes:** my hopes of saving
Scotland from Macbeth.

MALCOLM. Perchance even there where I did find my
25   doubts.[14]
         Why in that rawness[15] left you wife and child,
         Those precious motives, those strong knots of love,
         Without leave-taking? I pray you,
         Let not my jealousies[16] be your dishonors,
30   But mine own safeties.[17] You may be rightly just
         Whatever I shall think.

MACDUFF.   Bleed, bleed, poor country:
         Great tyranny, lay thou thy basis sure,
         For goodness dare not check thee: wear thou thy wrongs;
         The title is affeered.[18] Fare thee well, lord:
35   I would not be the villain that thou think'st
         For the whole space that's in the tyrant's grasp
         And the rich East to boot.

MALCOLM.   Be not offended:
         I speak not as in absolute fear of you.
         I think our country sinks beneath the yoke;
40   It weeps, it bleeds, and each new day a gash
         Is added to her wounds. I think withal
         There would be hands uplifted in my right;[19]
         And here from gracious England[20] have I offer
         Of goodly thousands: but, for all this,
45   When I shall tread upon the tyrant's head,
         Or wear it on my sword, yet my poor country
         Shall have more vices than it had before,
         More suffer, and more sundry ways than ever,
         By him that shall succeed.

MACDUFF.   What should he be?[21]

50   **MALCOLM.** It is myself I mean, in whom I know
         All the particulars of vice so grafted[22]
         That, when they shall be opened,[23] black Macbeth
         Will seem as pure as snow, and the poor state
         Esteem him as a lamb, being compared
55   With my confineless harms.[24]

55   **MACDUFF.**   Not in the legions
         Of horrid hell can come a devil more damned
         In evils to top Macbeth.

MALCOLM.   I grant him bloody,
         Luxurious,[25] avaricious, false, deceitful,
         Sudden, malicious, smacking of every sin
60   That has a name: but there's no bottom, none,
         In my voluptuousness: your wives, your daughters,
         Your matrons and your maids, could not fill up

---

14 **Perchance . . . doubts:** Malcolm is suspicious of Macduff's desertion of his wife and children.
15 **rawness:** unprotected condition.

16 **jealousies:** suspicions.
17 **safeties:** protections.

18 **affeered:** confirmed by law.

19 **in my right:** on behalf of my claim.
20 **England:** the King of England, Edward the Confessor.

21 **What . . . be:** Who could be worse than Macbeth?

22 **grafted:** implanted.
23 **opened:** in bloom.

24 **confineless harms:** boundless evils.

25 **Luxurious:** lecherous.

The cistern of my lust, and my desire
All continent impediments[26] would o'erbear,
65 That did oppose my will. Better Macbeth
Than such an one to reign.

    MACDUFF.   Boundless intemperance
In nature[27] is a tyranny; it hath been
Th' untimely emptying of the happy throne,
And fall of many kings. But fear not yet
70 To take upon you what is yours: you may
Convey[28] your pleasures in a spacious plenty,
And yet seem cold, the time you may so hoodwink.
We have willing dames enough. There cannot be
That vulture in you, to devour so many
75 As will to greatness dedicate themselves,
Finding it so inclined.

    MALCOLM.   With this there grows
In my most ill-composed affection[29] such
A stanchless avarice[30] that, were I King,
I should cut off the nobles for their lands,
80 Desire his[31] jewels and this other's house:
And my more-having would be as a sauce
To make me hunger more, that I should forge
Quarrels unjust against the good and loyal,
Destroying them for wealth.

    MACDUFF.   This avarice
85 Sticks deeper, grows with more pernicious root
Than summer-seeming[32] lust, and it hath been
The sword of our slain kings.[33] Yet do not fear.
Scotland hath foisons[34] to fill up your will
Of your mere own.[35] All these are portable,[36]
90 With other graces weighed.[37]

    MALCOLM. But I have none: the king-becoming graces,
As justice, verity, temp'rance, stableness,
Bounty, perseverance, mercy, lowliness,
Devotion, patience, courage, fortitude,
95 I have no relish of them, but abound
In the division of each several crime,[38]
Acting it many ways. Nay, had I pow'r, I should
Pour the sweet milk of concord into hell,
Uproar the universal peace, confound[39]
All unity on earth.

100 **MACDUFF.**   O Scotland, Scotland!

    MALCOLM. If such a one be fit to govern, speak:
I am as I have spoken.

26 **continent impediments:** restraints.

27 **nature:** man's nature.

28 **Convey:** secretly manage.

29 **affection:** personality.

30 **stanchless avarice:** never-ending, insatiable greed.

31 **his:** that man's.

32 **summer-seeming:** summerlike.
33 **The . . . kings:** The sword that killed our kings.
34 **foisons** [foi'zənz]: plenty, abundance.
35 **mere own:** own property.
36 **portable:** bearable.
37 **weighed:** counterbalanced.

38 **division . . . crime:** variations of each kind of crime.

39 **confound:** destroy.

MACDUFF.   Fit to govern!
No, not to live. O nation miserable!
With an untitled[40] tyrant bloody-sceptered,
105   When shalt thou see thy wholesome days again,
Since that the truest issue of thy throne[41]
By his own interdiction[42] stands accursed,
And does blaspheme his breed?[43] Thy royal father
Was a most sainted king: the queen that bore thee,
110   Oft'ner upon her knees than on her feet,
Died every day she lived.[44] Fare thee well!
These evils thou repeat'st upon thyself
Hath banished me from Scotland. O my breast,
Thy hope ends here!

MALCOLM.   Macduff, this noble passion,
115   Child of integrity, hath from my soul
Wiped the black scruples, reconciled my thoughts
To thy good truth and honor. Devilish Macbeth
By many of these trains[45] hath sought to win me
Into his power; and modest wisdom[46] plucks me
120   From over-credulous haste: but God above
Deal between thee and me! For even now
I put myself to thy direction, and
Unspeak mine own detraction;[47] here abjure
The taints and blames I laid upon myself,
125   For[48] strangers to my nature. I am yet
Unknown to woman, never was forsworn,[49]
Scarcely have coveted what was mine own,
At no time broke my faith, would not betray
The devil to his fellow, and delight
130   No less in truth than life. My first false speaking
Was this upon myself. What I am truly,
Is thine and my poor country's to command:
Whither indeed, before thy here-approach,
Old Siward, with ten thousand warlike men,
135   Already at a point,[50] was setting forth.
Now we'll together, and the chance of goodness
Be like our warranted quarrel![51] Why are you silent?

MACDUFF. Such welcome and unwelcome things at once
'Tis hard to reconcile.

[*An* ENGLISH DOCTOR *enters.*]

MALCOLM. Well, more anon. Comes the King forth, I pray
140   you?

DOCTOR. Ay, sir. There are a crew of wretched souls
That stay his cure:[52] their malady convinces

40 **untitled:** having no right to the throne.

41 **truest . . . throne:** child of the true king.
42 **interdiction:** exclusion.
43 **blaspheme . . . breed:** slander his ancestry.

44 **Died . . . lived:** lived every day always prepared for death.

45 **trains:** enticements.
46 **modest wisdom:** prudence.

47 **detraction:** slander.

48 **For:** as.
49 **was forsworn:** broke my oath.

50 **Old Siward . . . at a point:** Old Siward was the general of the English forces, and his troops were prepared.
51 **the chance . . . quarrel:** may our chance of success be as good as our cause is just.

52 **stay his cure:** wait for him to heal them. It was believed that King Edward could heal by touch—a power James I felt he had inherited.

The great assay of art;[53] but at his touch,
Such sanctity hath heaven given his hand,
They presently amend.[54]

145 **MALCOLM.**   I thank you, doctor.

[*The* DOCTOR *leaves.*]

MACDUFF. What's the disease he means?

MALCOLM.   'Tis called the evil:[55]
A most miraculous work in this good King,
Which often since my here-remain in England
I have seen him do. How he solicits heaven,
150 Himself best knows: but strangely visited people,
All swoll'n and ulcerous, pitiful to the eye,
The mere[56] despair of surgery, he cures,
Hanging a golden stamp[57] about their necks,
Put on with holy prayers: and 'tis spoken,
155 To the succeeding royalty he leaves
The healing benediction. With this strange virtue
He hath a heavenly gift of prophecy,
And sundry blessings hang about his throne
That speak him full of grace.

[ROSS *enters.*]

MACDUFF.   See, who comes here?

160 **MALCOLM.** My countryman; but yet I know him not.

MACDUFF. My ever gentle[58] cousin, welcome hither.

MALCOLM. I know him now: good God, betimes[59] remove
The means that makes us strangers!

ROSS.   Sir, amen.

MACDUFF. Stands Scotland where it did?

ROSS.   Alas, poor country!
165 Almost afraid to know itself! It cannot
Be called our mother but our grave, where nothing[60]
But who knows nothing is once[61] seen to smile;
Where sighs and groans, and shrieks that rent the air,
Are made, not marked; where violent sorrow seems
170 A modern ecstasy.[62] The dead man's knell
Is there scarce asked for who, and good men's lives
Expire before the flowers in their caps,
Dying or ere[63] they sicken.

MACDUFF.   O, relation
Too nice,[64] and yet too true!

53 **convinces . . . art:** defies the best efforts of medical science.

54 **presently amend:** recover at once.

55 **the evil:** scrofula [skrof'yə lə], a skin disease called "the King's evil" because it was believed that the King's touch would cure it.

56 **mere:** utter.

57 **stamp:** coin.

58 **gentle:** noble.

59 **betimes:** quickly.

60 **nothing:** no one.

61 **once:** at any time.

62 **modern ecstasy:** common emotion.

63 **ere:** before.

64 **nice:** exact.

MALCOLM.   What's the newest grief?

175 ROSS. That of an hour's age doth hiss the speaker;[65]
Each minute teems[66] a new one.

MACDUFF.   How does my wife?

ROSS. Why, well.

MACDUFF.   And all my children?

ROSS.   Well too.

MACDUFF. The tyrant has not battered at their peace?

ROSS. No; they were well at peace when I did leave 'em.

180 MACDUFF. Be not a niggard of your speech: how goes 't?

ROSS. When I came hither to transport the tidings,
Which I have heavily borne, there ran a rumor
Of many worthy fellows that were out;[67]
Which was to my belief witnessed the rather,[68]
185 For that I saw the tyrant's power[69] afoot.
Now is the time of help. Your eye in Scotland
Would create soldiers, make our women fight,
To doff[70] their dire distresses.

MALCOLM.   Be 't their comfort
We are coming thither. Gracious England[71] hath
190 Lent us good Siward and ten thousand men;
An older and a better soldier none
That Christendom gives out.

ROSS.   Would I could answer
This comfort with the like! But I have words
That would be howled out in the desert air,
Where hearing should not latch[72] them.

195 MACDUFF.   What concern they?
The general cause or is it a fee-grief[73]
Due to some single breast?

ROSS.   No mind that's honest
But in it shares some woe, though the main part
Pertains to you alone.

MACDUFF.   If it be mine,
200 Keep it not from me, quickly let me have it.

ROSS. Let not your ears despise my tongue for ever,
Which shall possess them with the heaviest sound
That ever yet they heard.

MACDUFF.   Humh! I guess at it.

65 **That . . . speaker:** There are so many new griefs that hour-old news is hissed because it is out of date.
66 **teems:** gives birth to.

67 **out:** in open rebellion.
68 **witnessed the rather:** confirmed.
69 **power:** army.

70 **doff:** put off.

71 **Gracious England:** the King of England.

72 **latch:** catch.

73 **fee-grief:** a personal grief.

ROSS. Your castle is surprised; your wife and babes
205   Savagely slaughtered. To relate the manner,
     Were, on the quarry[74] of these murdered deer,
     To add the death of you.

MALCOLM.   Merciful heaven!
     What, man! Ne'er pull your hat upon your brows;
     Give sorrow words. The grief that does not speak
210   Whispers the o'er-fraught[75] heart, and bids it break.

MACDUFF. My children too?

ROSS.   Wife, children, servants, all
     That could be found.

MACDUFF.   And I must be from thence!
     My wife killed too?

ROSS.   I have said.

MALCOLM.   Be comforted.
     Let's make us med'cines of our great revenge,
215   To cure this deadly grief.

MACDUFF. He[76] has no children. All my pretty ones?
     Did you say all? O hell-kite![77] All?
     What, all my pretty chickens and their dam[78]
     At one fell swoop?

MALCOLM. Dispute it[79] like a man.

220 **MACDUFF.**   I shall do so;
     But I must also feel it as a man.
     I cannot but remember such things were,
     That were most precious to me. Did heaven look on,
     And would not take their part? Sinful Macduff,
225   They were all struck for thee! Naught[80] that I am,
     Not for their own demerits but for mine
     Fell slaughter on their souls. Heaven rest them now!

MALCOLM. Be this the whetstone of your sword. Let grief
     Convert to anger; blunt not the heart, enrage it.

230 **MACDUFF.** O, I could play the woman with mine eyes,
     And braggart with my tongue! But, gentle heavens,
     Cut short all intermission; front to front[81]
     Bring thou this fiend of Scotland and myself;
     Within my sword's length set him. If he 'scape,
     Heaven forgive him too!

235 **MALCOLM.**   This time goes manly.
     Come, go we to the King. Our power is ready;

74 **quarry:** heap of game slain in a hunt.

75 **o'er-fraught:** overburdened.

76 **He:** may refer to Malcolm or Macbeth.
77 **hell-kite:** bird of prey.
78 **dam:** mother.

79 **Dispute it:** resist your grief.

80 **Naught:** wicked.

81 **front to front:** face to face.

Our lack is nothing but our leave.[82] Macbeth
Is ripe for shaking, and the pow'rs above
Put on their instruments.[83] Receive what cheer you may.
240   The night is long that never finds the day.

[*They all leave.*]

82 **Our . . . leave:** We have everything except permission to go.

83 **Put . . . instruments:** urge us onward as their agents.

STUDY QUESTIONS

Recalling

1. In Act IV, Scene i, what does Macbeth learn from each of the three apparitions? What additional question does he ask the witches, and by what means do they answer him?
2. At the end of Scene i, what does Macbeth vow to do to Macduff's family?
3. At the beginning of Scene iii, how does Malcolm test Macduff's loyalty? How does Macduff finally convince Malcolm that he is not on Macbeth's side?
4. What awful news does Ross bring Macduff? At the end of Scene iii, what action do Malcolm and Macduff plan?

Interpreting

5. What does Macbeth's final speech in Scene i reveal about his state of mind?

6. Describe the characters of Lady Macduff and her son, and explain your reaction to them. How does their fate color your opinion of Macbeth?
7. How do you react to the portion of Scene iii where Macduff is told his family's fate? What do you learn about Macduff's character from this scene?
8. Assess the state of Scotland under Macbeth's rule. Who supports Macbeth at this point in the play?
9. How does Scene iii advance the action of the play?

Extending

10. If Macbeth were to seek your advice about how he should react to the witches' latest prophecies, how would you respond to him? What would you advise him to do?

ACT V

Scene i. MACBETH's *castle at Dunsinane.*

[*It is late at night in* MACBETH's *castle at Dunsinane. A* GEN-
TLEWOMAN *who serves* LADY MACBETH *enters with a* SCOTTISH
PHYSICIAN. *They have come to observe* LADY MACBETH, *who has
recently begun to sleepwalk.*]

DOCTOR. I have two nights watched with you, but can
perceive no truth in your report. When was it she last
walked?

GENTLEWOMAN. Since his Majesty went into the field,[1] I have
5   seen her rise from her bed, throw her nightgown upon
her, unlock her closet,[2] take forth paper, fold it, write
upon 't, read it, afterwards seal it, and again return to
bed; yet all this while in a most fast sleep.

DOCTOR. A great perturbation in nature,[3] to receive at once
10   the benefit of sleep and do the effects of watching![4] In
this slumb'ry agitation, besides her walking and other
actual performances, what, at any time, have you heard
her say?

GENTLEWOMAN. That, sir, which I will not report after her.

15 **DOCTOR.** You may to me, and 'tis most meet[5] you should.

GENTLEWOMAN. Neither to you nor anyone, having no witness
to confirm my speech.

[LADY MACBETH *enters, carrying a candlestick.*]

Lo you, here she comes! This is her very guise,[6] and,
upon my life, fast asleep! Observe her; stand close.[7]

20 **DOCTOR.** How came she by that light?

GENTLEWOMAN. Why, it stood by her. She has light by her
continually. 'Tis her command.

[LADY MACBETH *moves across the stage, unaware that others
are watching her.*]

DOCTOR. You see, her eyes are open.

GENTLEWOMAN. Ay, but their sense[8] are shut.

25 **DOCTOR.** What is it she does now? Look, how she rubs her
hands.

GENTLEWOMAN. It is an accustomed action with her, to seem
thus washing her hands: I have known her continue in
this a quarter of an hour.

1 **into the field:** joined the army on
the battlefield to repress rebellious
subjects.

2 **closet:** a chest or box.

3 **perturbation in nature:** disorder of
the body and mind.

4 **effects of watching:** actions of
one awake.

5 **meet:** suitable.

6 **guise:** custom.

7 **close:** hidden.

8 **their sense:** power of sight.

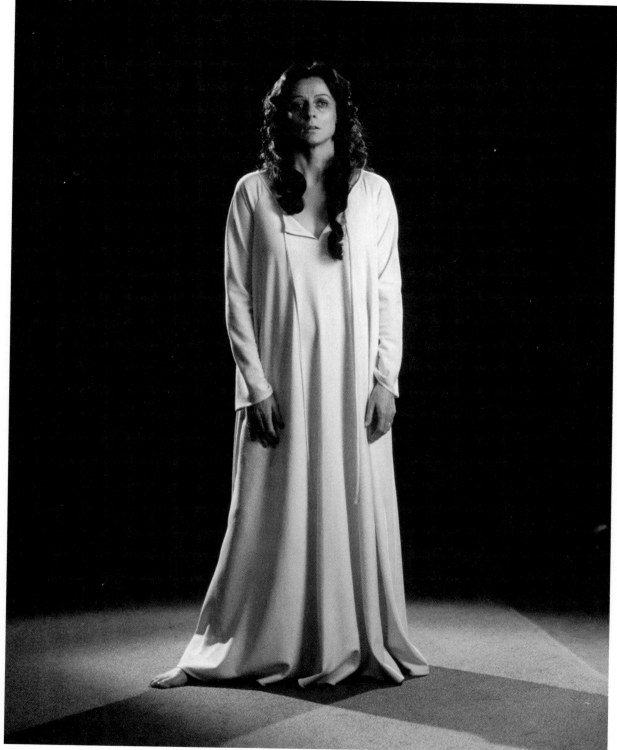

30 **LADY MACBETH.** Yet here's a spot.

DOCTOR. Hark! she speaks. I will set down what comes from her, to satisfy[9] my remembrance the more strongly.

LADY MACBETH. [*She sets down the candlestick and rubs her hands as if she were washing them.*] Out, damned spot!
35   Out, I say! One: two: why, then 'tis time to do 't.[10] Hell is murky. Fie, my lord, fie! A soldier, and afeard? What need we fear who knows it, when none can call our pow'r to accompt?[11] Yet who would have thought the old man to have had so much blood in him?

DOCTOR. Do you mark that?

40 **LADY MACBETH.** The Thane of Fife had a wife. Where is she now? What, will these hands ne'er be clean? No more o' that, my lord, no more o' that! You mar all with this starting.

DOCTOR. Go to,[12] go to! You have known what you should not.

45 **GENTLEWOMAN.** She has spoke what she should not, I am sure of that. Heaven knows what she has known.

LADY MACBETH. Here's the smell of the blood still. All the perfumes of Arabia will not sweeten this little hand. Oh, oh, oh!

50 **DOCTOR.** What a sigh is there! The heart is sorely charged.[13]

GENTLEWOMAN. I would not have such a heart in my bosom for the dignity[14] of the whole body.

DOCTOR. Well, well, well—

GENTLEWOMAN. Pray God it be, sir.

55 **DOCTOR.** This disease is beyond my practice. Yet I have known those which have walked in their sleep who have died holily in their beds.

LADY MACBETH. Wash your hands; put on your nightgown; look not so pale! I tell you yet again, Banquo's buried. He
60   cannot come out on 's[15] grave.

DOCTOR. Even so?

LADY MACBETH. To bed, to bed! There's knocking at the gate. Come, come, come, come, give me your hand! What's done cannot be undone. To bed, to bed, to bed!

[LADY MACBETH *leaves.*]

65 **DOCTOR.** Will she go now to bed?

GENTLEWOMAN. Directly.

DOCTOR. Foul whisp'rings[16] are abroad. Unnatural deeds
    Do breed unnatural troubles. Infected minds
    To their deaf pillows will discharge their secrets.
70   More needs she the divine than the physician.
    God, God forgive us all! Look after her;
    Remove from her the means of all annoyance,[17]
    And still[18] keep eyes upon her. So good night.
    My mind she has mated[19] and amazed my sight:
    I think, but dare not speak.

75 GENTLEWOMAN.   Good night, good doctor.

    [*They leave.*]

Scene ii. *Near Dunsinane.*

[*In the countryside near Dunsinane soldiers enter with the
Scottish noblemen* MENTEITH, CAITHNESS, ANGUS, *and* LENNOX.
*The soldiers are carrying drums and flags. They are all on
the way to join forces with an approaching English army to
rebel against Macbeth.*]

MENTEITH. The English pow'r[1] is near, led on by Malcolm,
    His uncle Siward and the good Macduff.
    Revenges burn in them; for their dear causes
    Would to the bleeding and the grim alarm
    Excite the mortified man.[2]

5 ANGUS.   Near Birnam Wood
    Shall we well[3] meet them; that way are they coming.

CAITHNESS. Who knows if Donalbain be with his brother?

LENNOX. For certain, sir, he is not. I have a file[4]
    Of all the gentry: there is Siward's son,
10 And many unrough[5] youths that even now
    Protest[6] their first of manhood.

MENTEITH.   What does the tyrant?

CAITHNESS. Great Dunsinane he strongly fortifies.
    Some say he's mad; others, that lesser hate him,
    Do call it valiant fury: but, for certain,
15 He cannot buckle his distempered cause
    Within the belt of rule.[7]

ANGUS.   Now does he feel
    His secret murders sticking on his hands;
    Now minutely revolts upbraid his faith-breach.[8]

16 **Foul whisp'rings:** evil rumors.

17 **annoyance:** injury.
18 **still:** always.
19 **mated:** bewildered.

1 **pow'r:** army.

2 **alarm . . . man:** would call to
arms even the dead.

3 **well:** probably.

4 **file:** list.

5 **unrough:** beardless.
6 **Protest:** assert.

7 **Within . . . rule:** under self-
control.

8 **minutely . . . faith-breach:** Every
minute revolts reproach his disloyalty.

Those he commands move only in command,
20 Nothing in love. Now does he feel his title
Hang loose about him, like a giant's robe
Upon a dwarfish thief.

MENTEITH.   Who then shall blame
His pestered⁹ senses to recoil and start,
When all that is within him does condemn
Itself for being there?

25 CAITHNESS.   Well, march we on,
To give obedience where 'tis truly owed.
Meet we the med'cine of the sickly weal,¹⁰
And with him pour we, in our country's purge,
Each drop of us.¹¹

LENNOX.   Or so much as it needs
30 To dew the sovereign flower and drown the weeds.¹²
Make we our march towards Birnam.

[*They march off.*]

9 **pestered:** tormented.

10 **the med'cine . . . weal:** Malcolm and his supporters will heal the sickly community.
11 **pour . . . us:** spill our blood to cleanse our country.

12 **To . . . weeds:** to water the royal flower (Malcolm) and drown the evil (Macbeth).

Scene iii. The castle at Dunsinane.

[MACBETH, *the* DOCTOR, *and attendants enter a room in Dunsinane Castle.* MACBETH *has heard reports of the approaching English and rebel Scottish forces, but he disregards them. He feels secure in his knowledge of the* WITCHES' *predictions: that no one born of a woman will be able to harm him and that he will be unconquered until Birnam Wood marches twelve miles to his castle on Dunsinane Hill.*]

MACBETH. Bring me no more reports; let them fly all!¹
Till Birnam Wood remove to Dunsinane
I cannot taint² with fear. What's the boy Malcolm?
Was he not born of woman? The spirits that know
5 All mortal consequences³ have pronounced me thus:
"Fear not, Macbeth; no man that's born of woman
Shall e'er have power upon thee." Then fly, false thanes,
And mingle with the English epicures.⁴
The mind I sway⁵ by and the heart I bear
10 Shall never sag with doubt nor shake with fear.

[*A* SERVANT *enters.*]

The devil damn thee black, thou cream-faced loon!⁶
Where got'st thou that goose look?

SERVANT. There is ten thousand—

MACBETH.   Geese, villain?

1 **let . . . all:** let the noblemen who are deserting us go.

2 **taint:** be infected.

3 **mortal consequences:** the events of human fate.

4 **epicures** [ep′i kyoorz′]: gluttons. The Scots, who ate plain food, believed that the English dined on rich food.
5 **sway:** move.

6 **loon:** rogue, worthless rascal.

SERVANT.   Soldiers, sir.

MACBETH. Go prick thy face and over-red thy fear,
15   Thou lily-livered boy. What soldiers, patch?[7]
      Death of thy soul! Those linen[8] cheeks of thine
      Are counselors to fear.[9] What soldiers, whey-face?

SERVANT. The English force, so please you.

MACBETH. Take thy face hence.

      [*The* SERVANT *leaves, and* MACBETH *calls for* SEYTON, *his
      trusted officer.*]

                              Seyton!—I am sick at heart,
20   When I behold—Seyton, I say!—This push[10]
      Will cheer me ever, or disseat[11] me now.
      I have lived long enough. My way of life
      Is fall'n into the sear,[12] the yellow leaf,
      And that which should accompany old age,
25   As honor, love, obedience, troops of friends,
      I must not look to have; but, in their stead,
      Curses not loud but deep, mouth-honor,[13] breath,
      Which the poor heart would fain deny, and dare not.
      Seyton!

      [SEYTON *enters.*]

SEYTON. What's your gracious pleasure?

30 MACBETH.   What news more?

SEYTON. All is confirmed, my lord, which was reported.

MACBETH. I'll fight, till from my bones my flesh be hacked.
      Give me my armor.

SEYTON.   'Tis not needed yet.

MACBETH. I'll put it on.
35   Send out moe[14] horses, skirr[15] the country round.
      Hang those that talk of fear. Give me mine armor.
      How does your patient, doctor?

DOCTOR.   Not so sick, my lord,
      As she is troubled with thick-coming fancies
      That keep her from her rest.

MACBETH.   Cure her of that.
40   Canst thou not minister to a mind diseased,
      Pluck from the memory a rooted sorrow,
      Raze out[16] the written troubles of the brain,
      And with some sweet oblivious antidote
      Cleanse the stuffed bosom of that perilous stuff
      Which weighs upon the heart?

7 **patch:** fool.

8 **linen:** pale as linen.

9 **Are . . . fear:** prompt others to fear.

10 **push:** effort in battle.

11 **disseat:** unthrone.

12 **the sear:** a withered state.

13 **mouth-honor:** honor from the lips, not from the heart.

14 **moe:** more.
15 **skirr:** scour.

16 **Raze out:** erase.

45 **DOCTOR.**   Therein the patient
    Must minister to himself.

    MACBETH. Throw physic[17] to the dogs, I'll none of it.
    Come, put mine armor on. Give me my staff.
    Seyton, send out—Doctor, the thanes fly from me—
50 Come, sir, dispatch. If thou couldst, doctor, cast
    The water[18] of my land, find her disease
    And purge it to a sound and pristine health,
    I would applaud thee to the very echo,
    That should applaud again—Pull 't off,[19] I say—
55 What rhubarb, senna, or what purgative drug,
    Would scour these English hence? Hear'st thou of them?

    DOCTOR. Ay, my good lord; your royal preparation
    Makes us hear something.

    MACBETH.   Bring it[20] after me.
    I will not be afraid of death and bane[21]
60 Till Birnam Forest come to Dunsinane.

    DOCTOR. [*Aside.*] Were I from Dunsinane away and clear,
    Profit again should hardly draw me here.

    [*They leave.*]

17 **physic:** medicine.

18 **cast the water:** diagnose the illness.

19 **Pull 't off:** remove the piece of armor.

20 **it:** his armor.
21 **bane:** destruction.

Scene iv. Near Birnam Wood.

[*In the countryside near Birnam Wood, not far from Dunsinane, the English and the rebel Scottish troops have joined forces. A group of soldiers and noblemen enter marching. Among them are a drummer, flagbearer,* MALCOLM, MACDUFF, MENTEITH, CAITHNESS, ANGUS, *and* SIWARD, *the general sent by the King of England, and his son,* YOUNG SIWARD.]

    MALCOLM. Cousins, I hope the days are near at hand
    That chambers will be safe.[1]

    MENTEITH.   We doubt it nothing.

    SIWARD. What wood is this before us?

    MENTEITH.   The Wood of Birnam.

    MALCOLM. Let every soldier hew him down a bough
5   And bear 't before him. Thereby shall we shadow[2]
    The numbers of our host, and make discovery[3]
    Err in report of us.

    SOLDIERS.   It shall be done.

    SIWARD. We learn no other but the confident tyrant
    Keeps still in Dunsinane, and will endure
    Our setting down[4] before 't.

1 **That chambers . . . safe:** when we can sleep in our beds without fear of being murdered.

2 **shadow:** conceal.

3 **discovery:** these who see us.

4 **setting down:** laying siege to it.

10   **MALCOLM.**   'Tis his main hope,
      For where there is advantage to be given
      Both more and less have given him the revolt,[5]
      And none serve with him but constrainèd things
      Whose hearts are absent too.

      MACDUFF.   Let our just censures
15   Attend the true event,[6] and put we on
      Industrious soldiership.

      SIWARD.   The time approaches,
      That will with due decision make us know
      What we shall say we have and what we owe.[7]
      Thoughts speculative their unsure hopes relate,
20   But certain issue strokes must arbitrate:[8]
      Towards which advance the war.[9]

      [*They march off.*]

5 more . . . revolt: People of high and low rank have turned against him.

6 our . . . event: Let our true judgment wait until the battle is over.

7 owe: own.

8 strokes must arbitrate: battle must decide.
9 war: army.

Scene v. The castle at Dunsinane.

[*Inside Dunsinane Castle,* MACBETH, SEYTON, *and other soldiers, including a drummer and flagbearer, prepare for battle.*]

      MACBETH. Hang out our banners on the outward walls.
      The cry is still "They come!" Our castle's strength
      Will laugh a siege to scorn. Here let them lie
      Till famine and the ague[1] eat them up.
5   Were they not forced[2] with those that should be ours,
      We might have met them dareful,[3] beard to beard,
      And beat them backward home.

      [*A cry is heard within the castle.*]

                        What is that noise?

      SEYTON. It is the cry of women, my good lord.

      [SEYTON *leaves.*]

      MACBETH. I have almost forgot the taste of fears:
10   The time has been, my senses would have cooled
      To hear a night-shriek, and my fell[4] of hair
      Would at a dismal treatise[5] rouse and stir
      As life were in 't. I have supped full with horrors.
      Direness, familiar to my slaughterous thoughts,
      Cannot once start[6] me.

      [SEYTON *returns, and as* MACBETH *learns of his wife's death, he reveals his attitude toward life and time.*]

15   Wherefore was that cry?

1 ague: fever.
2 forced: reinforced.
3 dareful: boldly.

4 fell: scalp.
5 dismal treatise: ominous story.

6 start: startle.

SEYTON. The Queen, my lord, is dead.

MACBETH. She should have died hereafter;[7]
   There would have been a time for such a word.[8]
   Tomorrow, and tomorrow, and tomorrow
20 Creeps in this petty pace from day to day,
   To the last syllable of recorded time;
   And all our yesterdays have lighted fools
   The way to dusty death. Out, out, brief candle!
   Life's but a walking shadow, a poor player
25 That struts and frets his hour upon the stage
   And then is heard no more. It is a tale
   Told by an idiot, full of sound and fury
   Signifying nothing.

   [*A messenger comes in.*]

   Thou com'st to use thy tongue; thy story quickly!

30 **MESSENGER.** Gracious my lord,
   I should report that which I say I saw,
   But know not how to do 't.

MACBETH.   Well, say, sir.

MESSENGER. As I did stand my watch upon the hill,
   I looked toward Birnam, and anon, methought,
   The wood began to move.

35 **MACBETH.**   Liar and slave!

MESSENGER. Let me endure your wrath, if 't be not so.
   Within this three mile may you see it coming;
   I say a moving grove.

MACBETH.   If thou speak'st false,
   Upon the next tree shalt thou hang alive,
40 Till famine cling[9] thee. If thy speech be sooth,[10]
   I care not if thou dost for me as much.
   I pull in resolution, and begin
   To doubt th' equivocation of the fiend[11]
   That lies like truth: "Fear not, till Birnam Wood
45 Do come to Dunsinane!" And now a wood
   Comes toward Dunsinane. Arm, arm, and out!
   If this which he avouches[12] does appear,
   There is nor flying hence nor tarrying here.
   I 'gin to be aweary of the sun,
50 And wish th' estate o' th' world were now undone.
   Ring the alarum bell! Blow wind, come wrack!
   At least we'll die with harness[13] on our back.

   [*They all leave.*]

7 **She . . . hereafter:** It would have been better if she had died at some other time.
8 **word:** message ("The queen is dead").

9 **cling:** wither.
10 **sooth:** truth.

11 **equivocation** [i kwiv′ə kā′shən] **. . . fiend:** double talk of the weird sisters.

12 **avouches:** affirms, asserts.

13 **harness:** armor.

Scene vi. Near the castle at Dunsinane.

[MALCOLM, SIWARD, MACDUFF, *and their soldiers, hidden by the tree boughs they are carrying, advance toward Dunsinane Castle.*]

MALCOLM. Now near enough. Your leavy[1] screens throw
    down,
    And show like those you are. You, worthy uncle,[2]
    Shall, with my cousin, your right noble son,
    Lead our first battle.[3] Worthy Macduff and we
5   Shall take upon 's what else remains to do,
    According to our order.[4]

SIWARD.   Fare you well.
    Do we but find the tyrant's power[5] tonight,
    Let us be beaten, if we cannot fight.

MACDUFF. Make all our trumpets speak; give them all breath,
10   Those clamorous harbingers[6] of blood and death.

[*Blaring trumpets and the sounds of battle are heard as they leave.*]

1 **leavy:** leafy.

2 **uncle:** Siward, general of the English forces.

3 **battle:** battalion.

4 **order:** plan.

5 **power:** forces.

6 **harbingers:** messengers.

Scene vii. Near the castle at Dunsinane.

[*On another part of the battlefield outside the castle,* MACBETH *enters.*]

MACBETH. They have tied me to a stake; I cannot fly,
    But bearlike I must fight the course.[1] What's he
    That was not born of woman? Such a one
    Am I to fear, or none.

[YOUNG SIWARD *enters and challenges* MACBETH.]

YOUNG SIWARD. What is thy name?

5 MACBETH.   Thou'lt be afraid to hear it.

YOUNG SIWARD. No; though thou call'st thyself a hotter name
    Than any is in hell.

MACBETH.   My name's Macbeth.

YOUNG SIWARD. The devil himself could not pronounce a title
    More hateful to mine ear.

MACBETH.   No, nor more fearful.

10 YOUNG SIWARD. Thou liest, abhorrèd tyrant; with my sword
    I'll prove the lie thou speak'st.

1 **bearlike . . . course:** Like a bear tied to a stake, I must fight until the end. In Elizabethan sport a bear was chained to a stake and attacked by dogs.

[*They fight, and* YOUNG SIWARD *is slain.*]

MACBETH.   Thou wast born of woman.
But swords I smile at, weapons laugh to scorn,
Brandished by man that's of a woman born.

[MACBETH *leaves as the sounds of battle mount.* MACDUFF *enters.*]

MACDUFF. That way the noise is. Tyrant, show thy face!
15   If thou be'st slain and with no stroke of mine,
My wife and children's ghosts will haunt me still.
I cannot strike at wretched kerns,[2] whose arms
Are hired to bear their staves.[3] Either thou, Macbeth,
Or else my sword, with an unbattered edge,
20   I sheathe again undeeded.[4] There thou shouldst be;
By this great clatter, one of greatest note
Seems bruited.[5] Let me find him, Fortune!
And more I beg not.

[*More battle sounds are heard as* MACDUFF *leaves.* MALCOLM *and* OLD SIWARD *enter.*]

SIWARD. This way, my lord. The castle's gently rend'red:[6]
25   The tyrant's people on both sides do fight;
The noble thanes do bravely in the war;
The day almost itself professes yours,
And little is to do.

MALCOLM.   We have met with foes
That strike beside us.[7]

SIWARD.   Enter, sir, the castle.

[*They leave as the sounds of battle continue.*]

2 **kerns:** hired Irish soldiers.

3 **staves:** spears.

4 **undeeded:** unused.

5 **bruited:** proclaimed, reported.

6 **gently rend'red:** easily surrendered.

7 **strike . . . us:** deliberately miss us.

Scene viii. Near the castle at Dunsinane.

[MACBETH *enters in another part of the battlefield, still ready to fight to the end despite overwhelming opposition.*]

MACBETH. Why should I play the Roman fool, and die
On mine own sword?[1] Whiles I see lives,[2] the gashes
Do better upon them.

[MACDUFF *enters.*]

MACDUFF.   Turn, hell-hound, turn!

MACBETH. Of all men else I have avoided thee.
5   But get thee back! My soul is too much charged
With blood of thine already.

1 **play . . . sword:** die like Brutus or Cassius, who killed themselves with their own swords rather than face defeat.
2 **Whiles . . . lives:** so long as I see living men.

MACDUFF. I have no words:
My voice is in my sword, thou bloodier villain
Than terms can give thee out!³

[*They fight.*]

MACBETH. Thou losest labor:
As easy mayst thou the intrenchant air
10 With thy keen sword impress as make me bleed:⁴

3 **Than . . . out:** than words can describe you.

4 **as easy . . . me bleed:** You will have no more success in making me bleed than you would in making the air bleed.

Macbeth Act V, Scene viii **221**

Let fall thy blade on vulnerable crests;
I bear a charmèd life, which must not yield
To one of woman born.

MACDUFF.   Despair thy charm,
And let the angel[5] whom thou still hast served
15 Tell thee, Macduff was from his mother's womb
Untimely ripped.[6]

MACBETH. Accursèd be that tongue that tells me so,
For it hath cowed my better part of man![7]
And be these juggling fiends no more believed,
20 That palter[8] with us in a double sense;
That keep the word of promise to our ear,
And break it to our hope. I'll not fight with thee.

MACDUFF. Then yield thee, coward,
And live to be the show and gaze o' th' time:[9]
25 We'll have thee, as our rarer monsters are,
Painted upon a pole,[10] and underwrit,
"Here may you see the tyrant."

MACBETH.   I will not yield,
To kiss the ground before young Malcolm's feet,
And to be baited with the rabble's curse.
30 Though Birnam Wood be come to Dunsinane,
And thou opposed, being of no woman born,
Yet I will try the last.[11] Before my body
I throw my warlike shield. Lay on, Macduff;
And damned be him that first cries "Hold, enough!"

*[They leave, fighting. More trumpet blasts and battle cries
are heard. They reenter fighting, and* MACBETH *is slain.*
MACDUFF *removes* MACBETH's *body. After he leaves,* MALCOLM,
OLD SIWARD, ROSS, *various thanes and soldiers, including a
drummer and flagbearer, enter.]*

35 **MALCOLM.** I would the friends we miss were safe arrived.

SIWARD. Some must go off;[12] and yet, by these I see,
So great a day as this is cheaply bought.

MALCOLM. Macduff is missing, and your noble son.

ROSS. Your son, my lord, has paid a soldier's debt:
40 He only lived but till he was a man;
The which no sooner had his prowess confirmed
In the unshrinking station[13] where he fought,
But like a man he died.

SIWARD.   Then he is dead?

5 **angel:** fallen angel, fiend.

6 **Macduff . . . ripped:** Macduff's mother died before giving birth to him; therefore he was not "of woman born."
7 **better . . . man:** courage.

8 **palter:** deal deceitfully.

9 **o' th' time:** spectacle of the age.

10 **We'll . . . pole:** Like a freak (monster) in a sideshow, we will paint your face on a post and place it outside a showman's booth.

11 **I . . . last:** I will fight to the end.

12 **go off:** die (in battle).

13 **unshrinking station:** place where he stood firm.

ROSS. Ay, and brought off the field. Your cause of sorrow
45 Must not be measured by his worth, for then
It hath no end.

SIWARD.   Had he his hurts before?

ROSS. Ay, on the front.

SIWARD.   Why then, God's soldier be he!
Had I as many sons as I have hairs,
I would not wish them to a fairer death:
And so his knell is knolled.

50 **MALCOLM.**   He's worth more sorrow,
And that I'll spend for him.

SIWARD.   He's worth no more:
They say he parted well and paid his score:
And so God be with him! Here comes newer comfort.

[MACDUFF *enters with* MACBETH's *head.*]

MACDUFF. Hail, King! for so thou art: behold, where stands
55 Th' usurper's cursèd head. The time is free.[14]
I see thee compassed with thy kingdom's pearl,[15]
That speak my salutation in their minds,
Whose voices I desire aloud with mine:
Hail, King of Scotland!

ALL.   Hail, King of Scotland!

[*There is a trumpet flourish.*]

60 **MALCOLM.** We shall not spend a large expense of time
Before we reckon with your several loves,[16]
And make us even with you.[17] My thanes and kinsmen,
Henceforth be earls, the first that ever Scotland
In such an honor named. What's more to do,
65 Which would be planted newly with the time[18]—
As calling home our exiled friends abroad
That fled the snares of watchful tyranny,
Producing forth the cruel ministers
Of this dead butcher and his fiendlike queen,
70 Who, as 'tis thought, by self and violent hands
Took off her life—this, and what needful else
That calls upon us, by the grace of Grace[19]
We will perform in measure, time, and place:[20]
So thanks to all at once and to each one,
75 Whom we invite to see us crowned at Scone.

[*They all leave to a flourish of trumpets.*]

14 **The . . . free:** Our country is free.

15 **compassed . . . pearl:** surrounded by the noblest in the kingdom.

16 **reckon . . . loves:** reward each of you for your loyalty.

17 **make . . . you:** pay what we owe you.

18 **What's . . . time:** What remains to be done at the beginning of this new era.

19 **Grace:** God.

20 **in . . . place:** with decorum at the appropriate time and place.

STUDY QUESTIONS

Recalling

1. At the beginning of Act V, Scene i, why are the doctor and gentlewoman observing Lady Macbeth?
2. As she is sleepwalking in Scene i, what prior incidents does Lady Macbeth refer to? List four or five such incidents. Whom is Lady Macbeth talking about when she says, "The Thane of Fife had a wife. Where is she now?"
3. In Scene ii what do Caithness and Angus say Macbeth is doing to prepare for the upcoming war? How do they describe Macbeth's state of mind?
4. What prophecy from Act IV, Scene i, is Malcolm fulfilling in Act V, Scene iv, when he gives his men orders as they reach the wood of Birnam?
5. What does Macbeth learn has happened to his wife in Scene v? Where is Macbeth going at the end of Scene v?
6. Which of the witches' prophecies does Macduff fulfill in Scene viii? What is Macbeth's first reaction to Macduff's statement? Does he change his mind?
7. Who finally kills Macbeth? Who becomes the King of Scotland?

Interpreting

8. Compare Lady Macbeth's behavior in Act V, Scene i, with her actions in Act II, Scene iii. How has she changed, and to what do you attribute the changes? What is different about her relationship with Macbeth?
9. In Scene iii where is Macbeth? What does he say and do that corresponds to the description of him given by Caithness and Angus in Scene ii?
10. In Scene v, lines 17–28, how does Macbeth express his attitude toward life after he learns of his wife's fate?
11. How is Macbeth's behavior in Scene viii reminiscent of accounts of him given in Act I, Scene ii?

Extending

12. How do you think Scotland will fare under Malcolm's rule? Base your answer on his final speech. Does he share any of the characteristics of the play's other kings, Duncan and Macbeth?

VIEWPOINT

For three and a half centuries critics have tried to explain Shakespeare's universal popularity. To Samuel Johnson, whose own writings appear on page 354, Shakespeare is

> the poet that holds up to his readers a faithful mirror of manners and of life. His characters are not modified by the customs of particular places, unpracticed by the rest of the world; . . . they are the genuine progeny [children] of common humanity, such as the world will always supply. . . .

■ Do you agree or disagree with Johnson's observations? Choose examples of Macbeth's, Lady Macbeth's, and Banquo's behavior to support your answer.

LITERARY FOCUS

The Total Effect

Before putting on a play, a director must have a clear idea of how the various elements will work together to make the performance a success. For instance, in *Macbeth* a director would want to emphasize plot, character, setting and atmosphere, irony, and theme in an effort to convey to the audience the total effect of the play.

Thinking About Plot

The **plot** of a literary work is a sequence of related incidents that revolve around a **conflict,** or struggle. The conflict may be **internal** (within the character) or **external** (between the character and another person, society, fate, or environment). A playwright generally presents the essential information about the characters and their lives in the first act. This background information is called **exposition.** As the play proceeds, **rising action** builds the conflict to a **climax,** a decisive turning point and a moment of great tension. In a tragedy the climax is usually in the middle of the play, when something that will lead to the downfall of the tragic hero takes place. Following the crisis, the **falling action** depicts the disastrous reversal of the tragic hero's fortunes and leads to the **resolution,** when the conflict ends and the outcome of the play is made known.

1. Give examples of internal and external conflict from Act I.
2. Make a list of important background information given in Act I. What happens at the end

of Act I that begins the rising action of the play?

3. Identify the rising action in Acts II and III.
4. Where in Act III do you think the climax—the moment of greatest intensity—occurs?
5. What falling action in Acts IV and V signals the downfall of Macbeth?
6. What is the resolution of the play?

Thinking About Character

We learn about a character in a play by seeing how the character looks and acts. Through speeches the character reveals what he or she thinks and feels. The speeches of the others let us know how they regard the character. Some characters remain static, or unchanged, throughout the course of the story or drama. These characters, who are generally minor, are called **flat characters.** Others, dynamic, or **round characters,** are a mix of many changing qualities that grow and develop as the story unfolds.

1. Which characters in Macbeth would you consider to be flat? Give several examples of static behavior in support of your decisions.
2. How does Shakespeare use soliloquies and asides to reveal character? Give examples from the speeches of two or three characters.
3. Analyze the personality of one of the leading characters in *Macbeth.* How is the character's personality revealed? Cite examples of the reactions of others and the character's own actions and conversations.

Thinking About Setting and Atmosphere

The **setting,** or locale, is the place and time in which the action of a literary work occurs. Descriptions of the setting often enhance the overall mood or **atmosphere.**

1. What mood does the setting of Act I, Scene i, create? What impressions of the play to come does the setting inspire?
2. What is the significance of darkness and light in *Macbeth*? How does it contribute to the overall atmosphere of the play?

Thinking About Irony

Irony involves a contrast between appearance and reality. In **verbal** irony there is a contrast between what is stated and what is actually meant— when a person says one thing but means the opposite. **Dramatic** irony occurs when the audience or reader knows something a character does not

and therefore understands the speech or action more fully than the character does.

1. Find an example of verbal irony in the conversation between Banquo and Macbeth at the beginning of Act III, Scene i.
2. Find an example of dramatic irony in the beginning of Act I, Scene vi.
3. What is ironical about Macbeth's entrance in Act I, Scene iv?

Thinking About Theme

All the preceding elements work together to point to the play's **themes,** or general statements about life.

1. Explain how *Macbeth* is a story of one man's attempts to control the future.
2. Explain the importance of the witches and their prophecies. To what extent do they control Macbeth's destiny? To what extent does he govern his own free will?
3. Discuss the impact of Macbeth's actions on nature. Why do storms occur? Why is time upset? Why is Macbeth himself unable to sleep "naturally" during the course of the play?

COMPOSITION

Writing About the Total Effect
Describe the total effect of *Macbeth.* That is, what was the impact of the play on you after you finished reading it? Support your statement by explaining how Shakespeare uses the following literary elements to achieve this effect: plot, character, setting and atmosphere, imagery, irony, and theme. *For help with this assignment, refer to Lesson 8 in the Writing About Literature Handbook at the back of this book.*

Writing a Speech
Imagine that Malcolm has asked you to give a speech for him at his coronation at Scone. Scots are coming from great distances to see the new king. They are weary of the turmoil of Macbeth's reign, and they are looking for assurances from Malcolm that his rule will restore peace. Malcolm is your friend, and you have been with him ever since his father, Duncan, was killed. In your speech, explain why you think he will be an effective king. Support your opinions with examples of his behavior and actions that you have recently observed.

Thomas Campion *1567–1620*

One of the most famous of the Elizabethan songwriters, Thomas Campion wrote almost all of his verse to be set to music. Much of that poetry is in the form of airs, or brief songs, for which he often wrote the music himself. Campion was the son of a London law clerk and a lady whose family was prominent at court. Orphaned at an early age, he attended Cambridge University and for a time studied law before deciding on a medical career. After serving briefly with the earl of Essex, one of Elizabeth's favorite courtiers, in a military campaign to assist the Protestants in France, Campion returned to England and set up his medical practice. He worked as a London physician until the time of his death.

Campion's first airs appeared anonymously at the back of a 1591 edition of Sir Philip Sidney's *Astrophel and Stella;* Campion then collaborated with Philip Rosseter on *A Book of Airs* (1601), to which each writer contributed about half the songs. Campion's first solo collection was *Two Books of Airs,* published about a decade later; other solo collections followed. Campion also wrote masques, musical dramatic entertainments popular at court, and he produced an early work of literary criticism, *Observations in the Art of English Poesy* (1602).

Campion's lyrics are noted for their seemingly simple sweetness that masks a polished craftsmanship and for their quiet but insightful observations about love and friendship. The following lyric, "When to Her Lute Corinna Sings," is a famous example.

■ If Campion were writing this song today, whom might he ask to sing it?

Thomas Campion

When to Her Lute Corinna Sings

When to her lute Corinna sings,
Her voice revives the leaden strings,
And doth in highest notes appear,
As any challenged echo clear;
5 But when she doth of mourning speak,
Even with her sighs the strings do break.

And as her lute doth live or die,
Led by her passion, so must I:
For when of pleasure she doth sing,
10 My thoughts enjoy a sudden spring;
But if she doth of sorrow speak,
Even from my heart the strings do break.

Detail, *The Lute Player*, Orazio Gentileschi, c. 1610.

STUDY QUESTIONS

Recalling

1. According to the first stanza, what does Corinna's voice revive? What happens when she sings of mourning?
2. In addition to affecting her lute, what do Corinna's different moods dictate?

Interpreting

3. What sort of mood is being described in the first four lines? What details in the poem helped you determine the mood?
4. Given the effects on the speaker described in the second stanza, what is probably the speaker's relationship with Corinna?

Extending

5. What kinds of music do you find most expressive of human emotions? Who are some of your favorite composers or performers of these kinds of music?

VIEWPOINT

In introducing one of his books of airs, Thomas Campion himself stated:

Short airs, if they be skillfully framed and naturally expressed, are like quick and good epigrams [short, witty verses] in poetry, many of them showing as much artifice, and breeding as great difficulty, as a larger poem.

■ In what ways is "When to Her Lute" both "skillfully framed" and "naturally expressed"? What are some popular twentieth-century songs that you feel display the same combination of "artifice" and simplicity?

Sir Francis Bacon   *1561–1626*

As a young man Francis Bacon wrote, "I have taken all knowledge to be my province." His accomplishments would seem to support this extraordinary claim: *The Advancement of Learning* sets down nothing less than the progress of human knowledge up to his own time; his *Essays and Counsels* were a landmark in English prose composition; and his ideas about the importance of observation and experiment (empiricism) form the basis of the modern scientific method.

Bacon was born in London, the son of a government minister in Queen Elizabeth's court. After attending Trinity College, Cambridge, and training as a lawyer, he held a series of government posts and was knighted in 1603. A supporter of King James I, he rose to the position of Lord Chancellor of England, the highest honor in the legal profession. In 1621 he was convicted of taking bribes by James's enemies and was forced to retire from public life. Thereafter he pursued his interests in science and philosophy. Scientists today owe their reliance on the inductive method of reasoning to Bacon. That is, he promoted the idea that generalizations should be made only after careful consideration of facts. As obvious as this idea is to us, it was revolutionary during Bacon's lifetime, when scholars still preferred deductive reasoning—moving from generalizations to specifics instead of vice versa. In addition, Bacon introduced the concept of hypotheses to scientists, arguing that scientists needed to make initial assumptions before beginning their experiments. Bacon even died in the service of science: He developed bronchitis after collecting snow to study refrigeration of a chicken.

Of all Bacon's writings the most popular remain his *Essays and Counsels,* which he began publishing in 1597. The **essay,** a brief prose composition exploring a single subject, was a development of the Renaissance, and Bacon was the first English writer to make use of this new literary form and shape it to his own taste. Unlike the warm, personal essays of Bacon's European contemporaries, the Baconian essay is objective, compact, and logical.

Bacon packs his essays full of meaning and omits specific examples or illustrations to make the general comments clearer. Nevertheless, their author's shrewd judgments about human nature make them worth the effort required to read them, for much of what Bacon writes about his own age applies equally well to ours.

■ As you read "Of Ambition," think about how it could relate to Shakespeare's character Macbeth and to other people, past or present, real or fictional.

Detail, *Portrait of a Young Man,* Agnolo Bronzino, c. 1550.

Sir Francis Bacon

Of Ambition

Ambition is like choler; which is a humor[1] that maketh men active, earnest, full of alacrity, and stirring, if it be not stopped. But if it be stopped, and cannot have his way, it becometh adust,[2] and thereby malign and venomous. So ambitious men, if they find the way open for their rising, and still get forward, they are rather busy than dangerous; but if they be checked in their desires, they become secretly discontent, and look upon men and matters with an evil eye, and are best pleased when things go backward; which is the worst property in a servant of a prince or state. Therefore, it is good for princes, if they use ambitious men, to handle it so as they be still progressive and not retrograde:[3] which because it cannot be without inconvenience, it is good not to use such natures at all. For if they rise not with their service, they will take order[4] to make their service fall with them.

But since we have said it were good not to use men of ambitious natures, except it be upon necessity, it is fit we speak in what cases they are of necessity. Good commanders in the wars must be taken, be they never so ambitious:[5] for the use of their service dispenseth with the rest; and to take a soldier without ambition is to pull off his spurs. There is also great use of ambitious men in being screens to princes in matters of danger and envy: for no

1. **humor:** Elizabethans believed that the body contained four humors, or fluids, that combined in different ways from individual to individual to determine temperament. The fluids were blood, phlegm, black bile (melancholy), and red bile (*choler,* or irritability; hot temperedness).
2. **adust:** overheated, scorched.

3. **still . . . retrograde:** always moving forward rather than backward.
4. **take order:** proceed.
5. **be . . . ambitious:** no matter how ambitious they are.

man will take that part, except he be like a seeled[6] dove, that mounts and mounts because he cannot see about him. There is use also of ambitious men in pulling down the greatness of any subject that overtops: as Tiberius used Macro in the pulling down of Sejanus.[7]

Since therefore they must be used in such cases, there resteth[8] to speak how they are to be bridled, that they may be less dangerous. There is less danger of them if they be of mean[9] birth than if they be noble; and if they be rather harsh of nature than gracious and popular; and if they be rather new raised[10] than grown cunning and fortified in their greatness. It is counted by some a weakness in princes to have favorites; but it is of all others the best remedy against ambitious great ones. For when the way of pleasuring and displeasuring lieth by the favorite, it is impossible any other should be overgreat. Another means to curb them is to balance them by others as proud as they. But then there must be some middle counselors to keep things steady; for without that ballast the ship will roll too much. At the least, a prince may animate and inure[11] some meaner persons to be, as it were, scourges[12] to ambitious men.

As for the having of them obnoxious[13] to ruin, if they be of fearful natures, it may do well; but if they be stout and daring, it may precipitate their designs and prove dangerous. As for the pulling of them down, if the affairs require it, and that[14] it may not be done with safety suddenly, the only way is the interchange continually of favors and disgraces;[15] whereby they may not know what to expect, and be, as it were, in a wood.[16] Of ambitions, it is less harmful, the ambition to prevail in great things than that other, to appear in everything; for that breeds confusion and mars business. But yet it is less danger to have an ambitious man stirring in business than great in dependences.[17]

He that seeketh to be eminent amongst able men hath a great task; but that is ever good for the public. But he that plots to be the only figure amongst ciphers[18] is the decay of a whole age. Honor[19] hath three things in it: the vantage ground to do good; the approach to kings and principal persons; and the raising of a man's own fortunes. He that hath the best of these intentions, when he aspireth, is an honest man; and that prince that can discern of these intentions in another that aspireth is a wise prince. Generally, let princes and states choose such ministers as are more sensible of duty than of rising; and such as love business rather upon conscience than upon bravery:[20] and let them discern[21] a busy nature from a willing mind.

---

6. **seeled:** with eyelids sewn together. Falcons were seeled in order to train them to fly in high circles to hunt before returning to their trainers.

7. **Tiberius** [tī bēr′ē əs] . . . **Sejanus** [sa jā′nəs]: For many years Sejanus was chief aide and confidant to the Roman emperor Tiberius. The emperor grew suspicious of him and had him put to death in A.D. 31.

8. **resteth:** remains.

9. **mean:** lowly, humble.

10. **new raised:** recently elevated to greatness.

11. **inure:** accustom.

12. **scourges:** whips (to keep them on good behavior).

13. **obnoxious:** liable.

14. **that:** presuming.

15. **disgraces:** dismissals from (royal) favor.

16. **in a wood:** that is, lost in the woods; confused.

17. **stirring . . . dependences:** working to advance himself rather than waiting and expecting advancement automatically.

18. **ciphers:** people of no importance; nonentities.

19. **Honor:** exalted rank or position.

20. **bravery:** ostentation, show.

21. **discern:** distinguish.

STUDY QUESTIONS

Recalling

1. What does the first paragraph advise princes to do about using ambitious men?
2. According to the second paragraph, in what three specific cases must princes use ambitious men? In such cases, what characteristics itemized in paragraph 3 will make the men less dangerous?
3. What are the three advantages of a position of honor, according to the last paragraph? How does Bacon define an honest man?
4. Generally, what kind of ministers should princes and states choose, according to the last paragraph?

Interpreting

5. According to Bacon, in what or whom are ambitious people interested? In what or whom should a good public servant be interested?
6. Describe the kind of writer that Bacon seems to be. For example, is he perceptive? Is he naive? Support your answers with details from the essay.

Extending

7. How, according to Bacon's essay, might Duncan have dealt with the threat of Macbeth's ambition?

VOCABULARY STUDY

Synonyms

A **synonym** is a word that has the same or nearly the same meaning as another word. *Begin* and *start* are synonyms. The words in capitals are from "Of Ambition." Choose the word that is *nearest* the meaning of the word in capitals, *as the word is used in the selection.* Write the number of each item and the letter of your choice on a separate sheet.

1. ALACRITY: (a) eagerness (b) agitation (c) firmness (d) cleverness
2. VENOMOUS: (a) dishonest (b) malicious (c) mischievous (d) contagious
3. BRIDLED: (a) saddled (b) restrained (c) tamed (d) angered
4. BALLAST: (a) sails (b) steering device (c) captain (d) stabilizer
5. ANIMATE: (a) proclaim (b) harden (c) inspire (d) dehumanize
6. PRECIPITATE: (a) indicate (b) hasten (c) condense (d) foreshadow
7. MARS: (a) impairs (b) disfigures (c) battles (d) ends
8. EMINENT: (a) haughty (b) competent (c) lowly (d) prominent

COMPOSITION

Writing About Nonfiction

Explain the purpose of Bacon's essay "Of Ambition." First discuss the various techniques that Bacon uses, such as facts, examples, and opinion. Be sure to cite examples of each technique from the selection. Then tell how these techniques help Bacon accomplish the purpose you have identified. *For help with this assignment, refer to Lesson 4 in the Writing About Literature Handbook at the back of this book.*

Writing an Essay

Try writing a brief composition using Bacon's essay as a model. Choose a topic, and jot down your thoughts about it. (Among the topics Bacon himself wrote about are truth, envy, travel, friendship, riches, studies, and beauty.) Concentrate on a few general observations regarding the topic: (1) how it affects people, (2) when it is necessary, (3) how to use it. Avoid emotional language and personal anecdotes. Polish your prose into three coherent paragraphs that express your thoughts as clearly and logically as possible.

The King James Bible

What has been called "the noblest monument of English prose" appeared in 1611, during Shakespeare's lifetime. It was the result of seven years of labor by a group of notable scholars and clergymen under orders of King James I. Many other translations of the Bible are in existence, but the King James Bible, as it came to be called, was the first English-language translation to receive widespread, lasting acceptance among English-speaking people.

Bible means "books." The Christian Bible consists of the books of the Old Testament, originally in Hebrew, and the New Testament, originally in Greek. Before the Protestant Reformation the Bible was ordinarily read in Latin, though an early English translation of the complete Holy Scriptures was made by the Wycliffites, or Lollards, unsuccessful religious reformers of Chaucer's day. With the Reformation came many translations into the **vernacular**, the language of the people.

William Tyndale's 1525 translation of the New Testament was the first English translation to be printed, but Tyndale's work on the Old Testament ended abruptly with his execution in 1535 during the religious turmoil of the period. Other English translations appeared soon after, notably the Great Bible of Miles Coverdale; the Geneva Bible, translated by English Calvinists living in Switzerland; and the Rheims Bible, translated by English Catholics living in France. However, it was to Tyndale's masterful prose that the King James translators turned when they began their efforts in 1604.

The resulting King James, or Authorized, Version of the Holy Bible was for centuries not only the most widely read English Bible, but the most widely read English book. Thus it exerted an enormous stabilizing influence on the English language, which had been changing steadily since the Norman Conquest.

The King James Bible is written chiefly in prose, but some portions use **free verse**, poetry without a regular rhythm, or meter, but poetry nevertheless. This is true of the Book of Psalms, perhaps the most frequently read book of the Old Testament. The **psalms**, or songs of praise, are most commonly attributed to David, king of Israel in 1000 B.C. On the following pages are two of the best-known psalms, preceded by a portion of what is probably the Bible's most famous book, the Book of Genesis, which tells of the Creation and the Garden of Eden. Genesis, the first book of the Old Testament, is part of the Pentateuch, the five opening books of the Bible attributed to the great prophet Moses.

Detail from *The Creation of the Animals,* Raphael, sixteenth century.

The King James Bible

from **Genesis**

Chapter 2

In the day that the Lord God made the earth and the heavens,

And every plant of the field before it was in the earth, and every herb of the field before it grew: for the Lord God had not caused it to rain upon the earth, and there was not a man to till the ground.

But there went up a mist from the earth, and watered the whole face of the ground.

And the Lord God formed man of the dust of the ground, and breathed into his nostrils the breath of life; and man became a living soul.

And the Lord God planted a garden eastward in Eden; and there he put the man whom he had formed.

And out of the ground made the Lord God to grow every tree that is pleasant to the sight, and good for food; the tree of life also in the midst of the garden, and the tree of knowledge of good and evil. . . .

And the Lord God took the man, and put him into the garden of Eden, to dress it and to keep it.

And the Lord God commanded the man, saying, Of every tree of the garden thou mayest freely eat:

But of the tree of the knowledge of good and evil thou shalt not eat of it: for in the day that thou eatest thereof thou shalt surely die.

And the Lord God said, It is not good that the man should be alone, I will make him an help meet for him.

And out of the ground the Lord God formed every beast of the field, and every fowl of the air; and brought them unto Adam to see what he would call them: and whatsoever Adam called every living creature that was the name thereof.

And Adam gave names to all cattle, and to the fowl of the air, and to every beast of the field; but for Adam there was not found an help meet for him.

And the Lord God caused a deep sleep to fall upon Adam, and he slept: and he took one of his ribs, and closed up the flesh instead thereof;

And the rib, which the Lord God had taken from man, made he a woman, and brought her unto the man.

And Adam said, This is now bone of my bones, and flesh of my flesh: she shall be called Woman, because she was taken out of Man.

Therefore shall a man leave his father and his mother, and shall cleave unto his wife: and they shall be one flesh.

And they were both naked, the man and his wife, and were not ashamed.

Chapter 3

Now the serpent was more subtle than any beast of the field which the Lord God had made. And he said unto the woman, Yea, hath God said, Ye shall not eat of every tree of the garden?

And the woman said unto the serpent, We may eat of the fruit of the trees of the garden:

But of the fruit of the tree which is in the midst of the garden, God hath said, Ye shall not eat of it, neither shall ye touch it, lest ye die.

And the serpent said unto the woman, Ye shall not surely die:

For God doth know that in the day ye eat thereof, then your eyes shall be opened, and ye shall be as gods, knowing good and evil.

And when the woman saw that the tree was good for food, and that it was pleasant to the eyes, and a tree to be desired to make one wise, she took of the fruit thereof, and did eat, and gave also unto her husband with her; and he did eat.

And the eyes of them both were opened, and they knew that they were naked; and they sewed fig leaves together, and made themselves aprons.

And they heard the voice of the Lord God walking in the garden in the cool of the day: and Adam and his wife hid themselves from the presence of the Lord God amongst the trees of the garden.

And the Lord God called unto Adam, and said unto him, Where art thou?

And he said, I heard thy voice in the garden, and I was afraid, because I was naked; and I hid myself.

And he said, Who told thee that thou wast naked? Hast thou eaten of the tree, whereof I commanded thee that thou shouldest not eat?

And the man said, The woman whom thou gavest to be with me, she gave me of the tree, and I did eat.

And the Lord God said unto the woman, What is this that thou hast done? And the woman said, The serpent beguiled me, and I did eat.

And the Lord God said unto the serpent, Because thou hast done this, thou art cursed above all cattle, and above every beast of the field; upon thy belly shalt thou go, and dust shalt thou eat all the days of thy life:

And I will put enmity between thee and the woman, and between thy seed and her seed; it shall bruise thy head, and thou shalt bruise his heel.

Unto the woman he said, I will greatly multiply thy sorrow, and thy conception; in sorrow thou shalt bring forth children; and thy desire shalt be to thy husband, and he shall rule over thee.

And unto Adam he said, Because thou hast hearkened unto the voice of thy wife, and hast eaten of the tree of which I commanded thee, saying, Thou shalt not eat of it: cursed is the ground for thy sake; in sorrow shalt thou eat of it all the days of thy life;

Thorns also and thistles shall it bring forth to thee; and thou shalt eat the herb of the field;

In the sweat of thy face shalt thou eat bread, till thou return unto the ground; for out of it wast thou taken: for dust thou art, and unto dust shalt thou return.

And Adam called his wife's name Eve; because she was the mother of all living.

Unto Adam also, and to his wife, did the Lord God make coats of skins, and clothed them.

And the Lord God said, Behold, the man is become as one of us, to know good and evil: and now, lest he put forth his hand, and take also of the tree of life, and eat, and live for ever:

Therefore the Lord God sent him forth from the garden of Eden to till the ground from whence he was taken.

So he drove out the man; and he placed at the east of the garden of Eden, Cherubims, and a flaming sword which turned every way, to keep the way of the tree of life.

Psalm 8

O Lord our Lord,
How excellent is thy name in all the earth!
Who hast set thy glory above the heavens.
Out of the mouths of babes and sucklings hast thou ordained
    strength because of thine enemies,
5 That thou mightest still the enemy and the avenger.
When I consider thy heavens, the work of thy fingers,
The moon and the stars, which thou hast ordained;
What is man, that thou art mindful of him?
And the son of man, that thou visitest him?
10 For thou hast made him a little lower than the angels,
And hast crowned him with glory and honor.
Thou madest him to have dominion over the works of thy hands;
Thou hast put all things under his feet:
All sheep and oxen,
15 Yea, and the beasts of the field;
The fowl of the air, and the fish of the sea,
And whatsoever passeth through the paths of the seas.
O Lord our Lord,
How excellent is thy name in all the earth!

Psalm 23

The Lord is my shepherd; I shall not want.[1]
He maketh me to lie down in green pastures: he leadeth me be-
    side the still waters.
He restoreth my soul:[2] he leadeth me in the paths of righteous-
    ness for his name's sake.
Yea, though I walk through the valley of the shadow of death,
    I will fear no evil: for thou art with me; thy rod and thy staff
    they comfort me.
5 Thou preparest a table before me in the presence of mine
    enemies: thou anointest my head with oil; my cup runneth over.
Surely goodness and mercy shall follow me all the days of my
    life: and I will dwell in the house of the Lord forever.[3]

---

1. **want:** be in need.
2. **soul:** here, vitality.

3. **dwell . . . forever:** worship in the temple
as long as I live.

ACTIVE READING

Sound in Drama

We think of drama as literature; yet it is important to remember when we read a play that the author wrote it to be staged and performed. Reading a play is a very different experience from that of actually seeing and hearing it in performance. Nevertheless, if we read carefully and *imaginatively,* we will find that the experience can be just as rewarding.

We can make a play come to life for us in several ways. First, we must place ourselves in the theater; we must imagine ourselves among the real theater audience for which the play was created. Further, as we read, we should carefully note and imaginatively *respond to* the stage directions, which will evoke in our mind's eye the particulars of the setting; the lighting of each scene; and the costumes, physical appearance, and gestures of the performers.

Stage directions can help us to summon up another vital dimension of the play in performance: its *sound.* Just as you should try to picture the particular actor, so you must try to "hear" the music, the natural sounds, and even the inflections of voice that the playwright has imagined.

Consider, for example, the opening stage direction of *Macbeth.* We are somewhere in the midst of Scotland:

In the midst of a great storm of thunder and lightning, THREE WITCHES *appear in a deserted, outdoor place.*

We are given at the outset not only a stunning visual image but also a component of sound that sets a tone and a mood for the entire play. While three witches confer, a violent storm rages and swirls. The violence of the setting foreshadows and symbolizes the turbulence—psychological and emotional as well as physical—that courses through much of the play. The sound of the storm also evokes a sense of elemental terror: The characters in this play will encounter and contend with mysterious and awesome forces. We should "hear" this storm not only at the beginning but *throughout* the opening scene. By truly hearing the storm, we hear a good deal more that may enlighten us about the play as a whole.

Vocal inflections are another important sound element that we must listen for as we read a play. Often these variations in the tone or pitch of a character's voice are not indicated in stage directions. Nevertheless, we can hear them if we keep the character and the situation in mind—and our ears open.

Thus, in Act I, Scene vii, Macbeth has second thoughts about murdering Duncan. Lady Macbeth urges him on, however, scolding him for his sudden meekness. Angry and defiant, knowing that his decision might go either way—but sensing that he will decide against his better self—Macbeth responds. He is terrified at the thought of murder; yet he understands at the same time that he cannot resist the idea. If we read these lines sensitively, we can hear the fear and frustration engendered by this awful conflict:

[*with clenched teeth, almost hissing*] Prithee, PEACE!
[*boldly*] I dare do ALL that may become a MAN;
[*subsiding to a frightened whisper*] Who dares do MORE is none.

Hearing these inflections as we read, we gain a clearer impression of Macbeth's psychological state at this moment. It is a critical moment: Macbeth must decide whether or not to murder his king, and the *way* he speaks is at least as revealing as what he says. By paying attention to vocal inflections—and to the whole dimension of sound in the drama—we give ourselves a richer and more illuminating experience in reading.

REVIEW:
THE ENGLISH VOICE

Love and Poetry

The Elizabethan love lyrics are one of the glories of literature. Within the strict conventions of their time, these sonnets and songs succeed time after time in giving love a voice. Descending from the courtly love tradition of the Middle Ages, in which a man worshiped a highborn lady from afar, Elizabethan lyrics brilliantly blend passion and elegance, body and mind. They escape the negative effects of artificiality, though they abound with cleverness and wit. They escape because the Elizabethans knew perfectly well that such "love" was a convention, an accepted poetic device. These poems triumph because they accept artifice and step beyond it: They unite the timeless power of love and the life-giving power of poetry itself.

Wyatt
Drownèd is reason that should
me consort,
And I remain despairing of the
port.

Sidney
"Fool," said my Muse to me,
"look in thy heart, and write!"

Spenser
But that which fairest is, but few
behold,

Her mind, adorned with virtues
manifold.

". . . Where whenas death shall
all the world subdue,
Our love shall live, and later life
renew."

Marlowe
Come live with me and be my
love,
And we will all the pleasures
prove

Shakespeare
So long as men can breathe or
eyes can see,
So long lives this, and this gives
life to thee.

Love alters not with his brief
hours and weeks,
But bears it out even to the edge
of doom.

Campion
And as her lute doth live or die,
Led by her passion, so must I:

In Elizabethan lyrics love is celebrated in all its aspects. We still marvel at the ability of many of the poems to evoke a love that is both real and ideal, earthly and heavenly. The conventions of the time—and faith in the power of poetry—enabled Elizabethan poets to sing of love as both a mortal delight and an immortal possibility.

Key to Illustrations on Pages 106–107.

1. Portrait of Sir Francis Bacon, Paul van Somer (c. 1576–1621).

2. Detail, engraving of Macbeth and Banquo meeting the Three Witches, from Raphael Holinshed's *Chronicles,* 1577.

3. *A Young Man,* miniature by Nicholas Hilliard (1537–1619).

4. Detail, design for a tapestry depicting the defeat of the Spanish Armada.

5. Costume from the time of James I.

6. Portrait of Sir Philip Sidney (1554–1586), artist unknown.

7. Detail, title page to *The Mariners Mirrour,* an Elizabethan book.

8. Coat of arms of Elizabeth I.

9. Monument to William Shakespeare, erected in 1740 in Westminster Abbey, London.

10. Detail, *The Tower of London,* etching by Wenceslaus Hollar (1607–1677).

Key to Illustrations appears on page 307.

THE SEVENTEENTH CENTURY

1625–1700

Political and Religious Upheaval

In England the seventeenth century was a time of political and religious turmoil punctuated with violence that surprised and shocked England's neighbors on the Continent. The disputes in part resulted from the struggle for power between Parliament, which wanted more authority, and the throne, which held the theory that kings ruled by a "divine right" bestowed by God, not by the consent of Parliament.

Parliamentary power versus a self-righteous monarchy was not the only cause of dissension in this period, however. Religion was also an important factor. The ruler of England was also the head of the Church of England, or Anglican Church, which Henry VIII had established in 1534.

Charles I, who came to the throne in 1625, proved to be politically stubborn and untrustworthy. He continued to alienate Parliament, many of whose members were Puritans, fervent Protestant critics of both the Roman Catholic Church and the Church of England. These Puritans disliked Charles's insistence on the divine right of kings, his continuation of restrictions on Puritan preaching, and his several attempts to do without Parliament altogether. In 1642

Replica of Isaac Newton's reflecting telescope, 1671.

civil war broke out between the royalists—the king and his supporters—and the supporters of Parliament. Most landed aristocrats supported the royalist cause. They were noted for their long hair and their gallant and witty manner and were often called Cavaliers. The plainly dressed Parliamentary forces were recognized by their closely cropped hair and grim determination. Owing to their appearance, they were called Roundheads.

Oliver Cromwell—a Puritan member of Parliament and a military genius as well as a religious fanatic—brought victory to the Parliamentary forces and temporarily ended the monarchy in 1649. The Parliamentarians attempted to make the end of the monarchy permanent: After having ruled for almost a quarter of a century, Charles I was beheaded.

The stern Puritans frowned on all forms of frivolity, including the theater and even the lovely lyrics of the court poets. Yet despite their solemn and often gloomy attitudes, the Puritans became extremely powerful, chiefly because Cromwell proved a strong and efficient leader. (It was twenty-nine years earlier that a group of Puritans, the Pilgrims, left England for the New World in search of religious freedom. Now, however, Puritans in England wielded power enough to have the king deposed and Cromwell installed at the head of the government.) However, Cromwell

was a dictator. In an effort to control the nation's morals, he enacted laws that invaded and severely restricted personal liberties. Theaters were shut down; Catholics and Anglicans were denied freedom of worship; and massacres were conducted against Irish forces that challenged Puritan rule.

Oliver Cromwell—England's first nonroyal ruler—headed England as Lord Protector of the Commonwealth for nine violent years until his death in 1658. When his son Richard attempted to fill his shoes, he failed. By 1660 the English people had had their fill of Puritanism and were happy to restore the monarchy to a Stuart king. At the invitation of Parliament, the eldest son of Charles I returned to London from his exile in France and Holland and assumed the throne as Charles II. His return in 1660 is called the **Restoration,** and the term is also used to describe the entire last four decades of the century.

Equally important during the Restoration was the scientific

and philosophical growth to which Englishmen were contributing. London at this time was the center of new theories in both science and philosophy, and Charles II had a serious interest in the progress of science. In 1660 the Royal Society of London was established to promote scientific research, and in 1662 it was officially chartered by Charles II. Of the many scientific contributions, perhaps the most outstanding were those of the great English mathematician and astronomer Sir Isaac Newton, who formulated, among a great many other things, the law of gravity.

Charles II's reign was followed by the brief, unhappy reign of his brother James II, who came to the throne in 1685. James's Roman Catholicism and his stiff-headedness did not ingratiate him with the English people. In the so-called Glorious Revolution of 1688—a revolution without violence or bloodshed—Parliament invited James's Protestant daughter Mary and her Dutch husband and cousin, William of Orange, to accept the British crown. James II fled to permanent exile in France. In 1689 a Bill of Rights that limited a monarch's powers was enacted. No longer would an absolute monarch reign above the law. Now the propertied classes would rule through a Parliament elected by them. Thus, during the reign of William and Mary, Parliamentary government was firmly established in England. The cen-

Costumes of the midseventeenth century.

tury closed near the end of their reign.

Life in Seventeenth-Century England

Any statement about the quality of seventeenth-century English life depends on which part of the century is under discussion. In the early years of the century, most things were very much as they had been in Queen Elizabeth's day. The years during the Cromwellian revolution and Protectorate were a time darkened by fear, violence, and soul searching. The years following the Restoration were merry, although they were marred by a major plague and a severe fire in the nation's capital.

When the first Stuart king, James I, came down from Scotland to ascend the English throne in 1603, he observed great houses and large estates along the way and expressed surprise at the richness of the country he was to govern. Toward the end of the century, the nation's wealth might better have been judged by observing London's increased commercial activity and size. By 1700 the greater metropolitan area of London included over 600,000 inhabitants, 200,000 of whom lived within the city proper. Furthermore, Bristol and Norwich were now cities of about 30,000 people. Still, other English cities were very small, usually with populations under 10,000.

In 1665 the Great Plague swept through London, leaving over 68,000 dead. After the city was devastated by the Great Fire in 1666, the famous architect Christopher Wren oversaw its rebuilding. According to one record, the fire consumed 13,200 houses, 400 streets, and almost 90 of London's 101 churches. Directed by Wren, the rebuilding of 51 churches was completed by 1700.

The English textile industry was growing throughout the century, but it was still a "cottage industry," carried on chiefly in the homes of the poor—and, to a surprising extent, by children. Young children spent their days darning woolen socks, and the profits from their labors would make some London or Bristol merchant rich. These were the children of the poor, of course, but all children in those days were kept well occupied in one way or another, and children of the well-to-do spent their time studying. It was not too unusual for a child of five to be able to write and translate both Latin and Greek (a fact that may explain the preponderance of young, well-educated playwrights and poets in that day).

At least children were not in the coal mines as they would be later, although in the seventeenth century coal was beginning to be an important English commodity. It was shipped from the town of Newcastle, for example, to London and even abroad. *Shipped* is exactly the word, for it was transported by ships traveling down the eastern coast of England and up the Thames River to London docks. Transporting goods of any kind in any substantial quantity over land for long distances was seldom thought of, for most roads were rutty, boggy, or concealed in whirls of dust, and bridges were so poorly built that they were a danger to life and limb.

A traveler along the English roads during the late seventeenth century might, nevertheless, come across the beginnings of overland travel—perhaps a market-bound "long-wagon," pulled by as many as eight huge dray horses, or a pack-horse train not unlike those used in the American West. After 1637, at least on the best roads, a traveler on foot might have to step aside for a public mail coach carrying paying passengers as well as the mail. Later in the century mail service was improved with the introduction of the "penny post" and hourly pickups of mail in London during daytime hours.

Detail, *Nell Gwyn,* from the studio of Sir Peter Lely, c. 1675.

Poetry in Seventeenth-Century England

As in the Elizabethan era, poetry again dominates the literature of the seventeenth century. John Donne and Ben Jonson, who began their careers in Elizabethan times, were the most important poets of the early seventeenth century—or **Jacobean** era, as the reign of James I is sometimes called. Donne wrote what has become known as **metaphysical poetry,** rugged in rhythm and personal in tone, but highly philosophical in its ideas and filled with unusual, intellectually demanding metaphors. Jonson introduced **neoclassicism,** a revival of the formal, polished poetic forms of ancient Greece and especially ancient Rome. In contrast to Donne, he employed careful, musical meters but wrote with images that were more typically "poetic" and put forth ideas that were easier to grasp.

Both poets exerted an enormous influence on the younger poets of the **Caroline** period, the reign of Charles I. George Herbert, known for his religious verse, was clearly in the metaphysical school; Robert Herrick, famed for short, musical lyrics, was foremost of the so-called **Sons of Ben.** Yet Donne's and Jonson's influence was not always mutually exclusive; many younger poets—Sir John Suckling, for example, and Andrew Marvell—often employed the farfetched metaphors and witty paradoxes associated with Donne in poems whose pol-

ished, musical style shows the influence of Jonson.

Herrick and Suckling were prominent **Cavalier poets,** midseventeenth-century poets who took the side of the royalists in the civil war. Other poets of the time, such as Andrew Marvell and John Milton, were members of the Puritan camp. Milton, the greatest poet of the century, remained outside either Donne's or Jonson's influence and instead developed his own remarkable style. His epic *Paradise Lost,* a work of over ten thousand lines, takes its place in Western literature alongside Homer's *Iliad* (page 805) and *Odyssey,* Virgil's *Aeneid* (page 864), and Dante's *Divine Comedy* (page 884) and in English literature alongside *Beowulf* (page 9) and Edmund Spenser's *Faerie Queene* (page 120).

During the Restoration the most influential poet was John Dryden, who was Charles II's poet laureate. Dryden wrote commemorative odes and biting verse satire; he also perfected

Ben Jonson's neoclassicism and helped make it the chief literary movement of the century to come.

Drama in Seventeenth-Century England

We left drama in the last unit at its height—in the hands of Shakespeare, Marlowe, and others, with acting companies formed and playhouses built and filled with appreciative audiences. As the seventeenth century progresses into the reign of Charles I, the new plays are neither bone-shaking tragedies, like those of Shakespeare and Marlowe, nor the traditional, rather simple-minded comedies that grew out of medieval morality plays and Roman comedies. Rather, early seventeenth-century theater saw satiric comedies by Ben Jonson, tragicomedies, and a kind of melodrama. As the terms *satiric comedy, tragicomedy,* and *comedy of manners* suggest, comedy was becoming more sophisticated, less dependent upon stock situations—like mistaken identity—and on pratfalls and other sight gags. The manners of the English upper class became the source of situations and of humor. Also, the introduction of a new element, called wit, reflected the influence—to some degree, at least—of the masterfully inventive, witty French playwright Molière (see page 904).

At the beginning of the civil war in 1642, the Puritans, who regarded drama as frivolous,

Izaak Walton, whose classic *The Compleat Angler* has taught many the joys of fishing.

made theater illegal in England. Plays were still produced, of course, in private houses and even in playhouses until the hoofbeats of mounted law enforcers signaled the evening raid.

If the theater lost its momentum in the years of Cromwell's Commonwealth, it sprang to life joyfully when, in 1660, young King Charles II restored the easygoing, theater-loving monarchy. Women actresses, like the famous Nell Gwyn, began to play female roles. The drama that came to life in the last half of the seventeenth century has been called, aptly enough, Restoration comedy. To be sure, a few tragicomedies from the past were popular on the newly lighted stages. However, during the later seventeenth century French-influenced playwrights created more sophisticated plays, still based on the manners of upper-class society but sharpened with wit and satire.

Prose in Seventeenth-Century England

Generally speaking, the prose of the seventeenth century was not used for imaginative literature. When John Milton wrote his great narrative *Paradise Lost,* he turned, as his predecessors had, to poetry. With one interesting exception, the prose works that we are concerned with in seventeenth-century literature are works of nonfiction— essays and histories, works about religion and science, and works reflecting a new interest in what was going on, in London as well as in a country trout stream. Toward the end of the century, major works of literary criticism began to appear, and criticism became a kind of literature in itself.

The fiction exception mentioned above is John Bunyan's *Pilgrim's Progress,* an allegory about a hero named Christian, who, carrying Sin on his shoulders and a Bible in one hand, with the help of another character called Helpful, overcomes obstacles such as Vanity on his journey, or pilgrimage, to heaven. *The Pilgrim's Progress* was written to provide uplifting entertainment for the poor. No other book in the seventeenth century reached a greater number of people.

The bulk of seventeenth-century prose—nonfiction— developed because of several influences, not the least of which was the continuing marvel of Caxton's printing press. Some writers created prose for the growing bureaucracy that demanded a large body of legal and governmental writings. Some writers produced prose in response to the spirit of scientific inquiry that was sweeping England. Some relied on prose to persuade wide audiences to adopt certain religious and political convictions. And yet other writers turned to prose for their own eccentric reasons: Robert Burton wrote a brilliant, gloomy, undefinable work called *The Anatomy of Melancholy.* Izaak Walton wrote a fascinating manual on fishing (and many an angler since has been playfully called an Izaak Walton). Samuel Pepys kept a private, coded diary that was deciphered over a century later and is today considered the finest diary in English.

Donne, Milton, and Dryden all produced important prose works: Donne, a series of religious meditations; Milton, a number of Puritan political tracts; and Dryden, the first major works of literary criticism in English. Throughout the century there was a movement toward a simpler, more straightforward prose style. The Puritans encouraged simple language just as they encouraged simple dress; after the Restoration the Royal Society declared that its members should use a plainer, more efficient prose. The development of more modern-sounding prose reminds us that the seventeenth century was in all ways a period of continuing exploration and experimentation—in politics, in religion, in science, and in language.

TIME LINE

1625 James I dies; Charles I becomes king

1628 William Harvey publishes treatise on the circulation of blood

1633 John Donne, *Poems*
George Herbert, *The Temple*

1635 Public mail service set up

1637 Public mail coaches carry passengers

Ben Jonson dies

John Donne

1630 America: John Winthrop, Puritan leader, founds Boston

1637 Japan: European contacts prohibited

Europe: Ferdinand III becomes Holy Roman Emperor

1638 America: Harvard, first college, established

1640 Holland: Rembrandt Van Rijn, *Self-Portrait*

Public Mail Coach

1642 Outbreak of civil war

All theaters closed by order of the Puritans

1644 John Milton, *Areopagitica*, on freedom of the press

1646 Sir John Suckling, *Fragmenta Aurea*

1648 Robert Herrick, *Hesperides*

1649 Charles I beheaded; Oliver Cromwell becomes Lord Protector of England

Richard Lovelace, "To Lucasta"

Oliver Cromwell

John Milton

Harvard

1642 America: Education becomes compulsory in Massachusetts

1644 China: Ming dynasty ends; Manchu dynasty begins

1650 Tea first drunk in England

1651 Thomas Hobbes, *Leviathan*, political philosophy in support of monarchy

1653 Izaak Walton, *The Compleat Angler*

1650 America: Anne Bradstreet, *The Tenth Muse Lately Sprung up in America*

1651 Africa: Dutch settle at Cape of Good Hope

Molière

Coronation of Charles II

Great Fire of London 1666

John Dryden

1655 Cromwell dissolves Parliament, prohibits Anglican services

1657 Drinking chocolate introduced in London

Marvell becomes Milton's assistant

1658 Oliver Cromwell dies; his son Richard succeeds him

1660 End of the Protectorate; Charles II restored to throne

The Royal Society of London established to promote scientific research
Samuel Pepys begins his diary (to 1669)

1661 Coronation of Charles II

1665 Isaac Newton experiments on gravitation

Great Plague kills over 68,000 in London

1666 Great Fire of London

1667 John Milton, *Paradise Lost*

1668 John Dryden, *Essay of Dramatic Poesy*

1674 John Bunyan, *The Pilgrim's Progress*

1685 Charles II dies; James II succeeds his brother

1687 John Dryden, "A Song for Saint Cecilia's Day"

1688 Glorious Revolution: Overthrow of James II, and accession of William and Mary

1689 Bill of Rights ensures freedoms for Parliament

1690 John Locke, *Essay Concerning Human Understanding*, influential work describing human mental processes

1654 France: Coronation of Louis XIV at Rheims

1657 France: First stockings and fountain pens manufactured

1659 France: Molière, "The Flying Doctor"

1660 Denmark: Danish crown becomes hereditary

1664 America: English capture New Amsterdam from the Dutch

1665 America: First theatrical performance takes place in Virginia

1666 Italy: Antonio Stradivari labels his first violin

1675 Japan: Bashō publishes poetry

1685 China: All ports opened to foreign trade

1690 America: *New England Primer*, a textbook for colonial youth

John Donne   *1572–1631*

Along with Ben Jonson (see page 261), John Donne was the most influential poet of the first half of the seventeenth century. With the Restoration, Donne's style of poetry fell from critical favor, and only in our own century was his reputation reestablished.

The same swings of fortune that have marked his reputation since his death also seem to have marked Donne's life. Donne first won attention in Elizabethan London as Jack Donne, author of witty, often irreverent love poems. Those love poems matured when he married Anne More, the niece of his employer. Far from advancing Donne's interests, the marriage angered Anne's influential family, lost Donne his job, and consigned the couple to years of poverty. Probably for political reasons, Donne, a Roman Catholic by birth, converted to the Church of England when he was nineteen. With time, however, he became profoundly religious and, following the death of his wife in 1617, turned increasingly to the writing of religious verse and prose sermons and meditations. By the time of his own death, Donne was the Dean of St. Paul's Cathedral, one of the highest offices in the Church of England, and he had acquired a reputation as the greatest preacher of his day.

Though Donne began writing in the Elizabethan era, his poetry is not written in typical Elizabethan style. Instead of using predictable, flowing meters and harmonious images drawn from nature, Donne often employs irregular rhythms and startles us with unusual images and metaphors. His tone is less formal and his word choice simpler than most Elizabethans', yet his verse also makes far greater demands on our intellect, forcing us to follow an elaborate metaphor or a witty argument or a complex philosophical speculation. The eighteenth-century writer Samuel Johnson, who was highly critical of the "unnatural" images and rhythms of Donne's verse, gave it the name **metaphysical poetry**, a term that has since been used by Donne's admirers as well as his detractors. Though originally *metaphysical* simply meant "philosophical" or "intellectual," the word is now more broadly applied to any English poetry of the early or middle seventeenth century that, in one way or another, shows Donne's influence.

The conversational tone, the rugged rhythms, and the images drawn from nontraditional sources all give Donne's poetry a distinctly modern flavor. Because it displays a clever intellect and is often philosophical, many earlier critics mistakenly assumed that Donne's poetry lacks feeling. Twentieth-century readers rarely make that mistake.

■ In what ways do the following selections suggest that human beings are forever connected and never really alone?

Introducing *A Valediction:* Forbidding Mourning

The poem that appears on the following page is one of Donne's most celebrated verses, and the simile at the end of the poem is one of the most famous in all of English poetry. In order to begin to understand this poem, however, it helps to know a bit about the circumstances under which Donne wrote it; to learn something about how he, as a man in the early 1600s, viewed the universe; and to review beforehand the elaborate simile of the last three stanzas.

Donne was addressing his wife in this poem, according to Izaak Walton (1593–1683), the English writer who was Donne's biographer. Donne was about to leave his wife to go to France. Already he himself was feeling forebodings at the separation, and indeed his misgivings were confirmed later when his wife gave birth to a stillborn child during his absence abroad. Nevertheless, he was determined to still his and his wife's tears upon parting by writing this **valediction**, or statement made as a farewell.

Donne gleaned his images for lines 5–16 of this poem from what he and others in the seventeenth century thought about the universe. During this period in England and on the Continent, people believed that the earth was the center of the universe. Around the earth in concentric spheres were situated the other heavenly bodies. God and the angels were in control of the entire system. People generally believed that all existence below the sphere of the moon—including existence on the earth—was inferior. Only in the heavenly spheres beyond the moon was there a perfect existence.

At the end of the poem (lines 25–36), Donne introduces and develops a simile involving a compass, the instrument used for drawing arcs or circles. Also called a pair of compasses, this instrument consists of two pointed legs connected at one end by a pivot. To draw the arc or circle, one of the legs is kept in a stationary, upright position while the other swings around in a circular motion.

John Donne

A Valediction: Forbidding Mourning

As virtuous men pass mildly away,
    And whisper to their souls to go,
Whilst some of their sad friends do say
    The breath goes now, and some say, No;

5 So let us melt,[1] and make no noise,
    No tear-floods, nor sigh-tempests move,
'Twere profanation[2] of our joys
    To tell the laity[3] our love.

Moving of th' earth brings harms and fears,
10   Men reckon what it did and meant;
But trepidation of the spheres,
    Though greater far, is innocent.[4]

Dull sublunary[5] lovers' love
    (Whose soul is sense)[6] cannot admit
15 Absence, because it doth remove
    Those things which elemented it.[7]

But we by a love so much refined
    That our selves know not what it is,
Inter-assurèd[8] of the mind,
20   Care less, eyes, lips, and hands to miss.

Our two souls therefore, which are one,
    Though I must go, endure not yet
A breach, but an expansion,
    Like gold to airy thinness beat.[9]

25 If they be two, they are two so
    As stiff twin compasses[10] are two;
Thy soul, the fixed foot, makes no show
    To move, but doth, if th' other do.

And though it in the center sit,
30   Yet when the other far doth roam,
It leans and hearkens after it,
    And grows erect, as it comes home.

Such wilt thou be to me, who must
    Like th' other foot, obliquely run;
35 Thy firmness makes my circle just,[11]
    And makes me end where I begun.

---

1. **melt:** part, change state. This line may also refer to the quietness with which pure gold melts.
2. **profanation:** debasement; violation.
3. **laity:** laymen; nonclergy. Here, the speaker is implying he and his beloved are like priest and priestess as opposed to the laity.
4. **Moving . . . innocent:** Earthquakes are harmful and dangerous, whereas the much greater movements of the celestial spheres are harmless.
5. **sublunary** [sub lōō′nər ē]: under the moon, or earthly. Everything under the moon's sphere, including the earth, was considered subject to change; all beyond that sphere was permanent and perfect.
6. **Whose . . . sense:** whose essence is the senses, not the mind.
7. **which elemented it:** which constituted its essential nature.

8. **Inter-assurèd:** mutually assured.
9. **Like . . . beat:** Gold leaf is made by beating gold into tissue-thin pieces. Baser metals would break up under the beating. "Airy" in this line refers to the buoyancy of gold leaf.
10. **twin compasses:** the two legs of a geometrical compass.
11. **just:** true, accurate.

STUDY QUESTIONS

Recalling

1. According to lines 1–4, how do virtuous men die, and, in contrast, how do observers of dying men sometimes react?
2. What kind of behavior mentioned in lines 1–4 does the speaker in lines 5–6 recommend he and his beloved follow? What, according to lines 7–8, would happen if the lovers cried out and told everyone of their love?
3. What is the difference between earthquakes and "trepidation of the spheres," as stated in lines 9–12?
4. When sublunary lovers are absent from each other, what does the absence cause to be removed, according to lines 13–16? What attitude toward absence do such lovers feel?
5. In contrast to the sublunary lovers of lines 13–16, what kind of love does the speaker claim he and his beloved share (lines 17–20)? Consequently, what happens to their souls upon parting, according to lines 21–24?
6. Paraphrase the last three stanzas of the poem, explaining what happens to the two feet of a compass as one moves away and then returns.

Interpreting

7. What effect is achieved by the speaker's associating himself and his beloved with the spheres (line 11)?
8. What, if anything, is startling about the speaker's comparing himself and his beloved to the two feet of a compass? Why? What is appropriate about the image?
9. Why should the parting of the lovers not be a cause for mourning? What is true love, according to this poem? How persuasive is the speaker?

Extending

10. How would you describe this poem to someone? What would you say about its complexity? Does its complexity add to or detract from its impact on you?

VIEWPOINT

According to one critic, Donne's love poetry *speaks* to the beloved rather than *sings* to her. It even argues with her; and in doing so,

> the poet's passionate argument does not allow for those stately, self-contained lines whose perfection redeems many a lifeless sonnet. There is hardly a line in Donne's poem which makes sense by itself. . . . The unit is not the line . . . and not even the stanza but the entire poem in its serpentine swerving from one excitement to another.

—Mario Praz

■ Examine Donne's "Valediction." Does Praz's insight on the poem's structure seem to be accurate? Support your answer with specifics.

LITERARY FOCUS

Conceit

A **conceit** (from the Italian *concetto,* meaning "concept") is an elaborate metaphor or simile that makes a comparison between two significantly different things. The comparison may seem far-fetched at first but, when examined, gains clarity and persuasion. The conceit not only brings together two entirely different images or ideas but then develops the comparison in detail, so as to highlight the similarities.

Donne and the other so-called metaphysical poets used conceits frequently. Of all the conceits they devised, none is more famous than the example developed through the final three stanzas of "A Valediction: Forbidding Mourning." As we have seen, there the souls of the two lovers are compared to the two legs of a geometrical compass—a startling image at first but one that becomes clearer the more we think about it.

Thinking About Conceit

■ Another unusual simile in the sixth stanza—extravagant enough to be considered a conceit—compares the parting of lovers with a process of working gold. Explain and justify the conceit.

Donne's *Holy Sonnets,* nineteen in all, were written soon after his wife Anne had died. In them Donne presents his profound thoughts on religious faith and immortality. The three sonnets that follow are probably the most famous in the series.

John Donne

Holy Sonnet 4

At the round earth's imagined corners, blow
Your trumpets, angels;[1] and arise, arise
From death, you numberless infinities
Of souls, and to your scattered bodies go;
5 All whom the flood did, and fire shall, o'erthrow,
All whom war, dearth, age, agues,[2] tyrannies,
Despair, law, chance hath slain, and you whose eyes
Shall behold God, and never taste death's woe.[3]
But let them sleep, Lord, and me mourn a space;
10 For if above all these my sins abound,
'Tis late to ask abundance of Thy grace.
When we are there. Here on this lowly ground,
Teach me how to repent; for that's as good
As if Thou hadst sealed my pardon with Thy blood.

---

1. **round earth's . . . angels:** In Revelation (Apocalypse), the New Testament book that describes Judgment Day, chapter 7 speaks of four angels with trumpets, who stand at the four corners of the earth and control the winds.

2. **agues:** fevers.

3. **you whose eyes . . . woe:** you who will be alive at the time of Judgment Day.

Holy Sonnet 10

Death, be not proud, though some have callèd thee
Mighty and dreadful, for thou art not so;
For those whom you think'st thou dost overthrow
Die not, poor Death, nor yet canst thou kill me.
5 From rest and sleep, which but thy pictures[1] be,
Much pleasure, then from thee much more must flow,
And soonest our best men with thee do go,
Rest of their bones and souls' delivery.[2]
Thou art slave to fate, chance, kings, and desperate men,
10 And dost with poison, war, and sickness dwell,
And poppy,[3] or charms can make us sleep as well,
And better than thy stroke; why swell'st[4] thou then?
One short sleep past, we wake eternally,
And Death shall be no more; Death, thou shalt die.

---

1. **pictures:** images.
2. **And . . . delivery:** Our best men die willingly, in order to rest their bones and free their souls. (Compare the opening of "A Valediction.")
3. **poppy:** opium.
4. **swell'st:** swell with pride.

Detail of a stained-glass dove, French, sixteenth century.

John Donne

Holy Sonnet 14

Batter my heart, three-personed God,[1] for You
As yet but knock, breathe, shine, and seek to mend.
That I may rise and stand, overthrow me and bend
Your force to break, blow, burn, and make me new.
5 I, like an usurped town to another due,[2]
Labor to admit You, but O, to no end!
Reason, Your viceroy[3] in me, me should defend
But is captived, and proves weak or untrue.
Yet dearly I love You and would be lovèd fain,[4]
10 But am betrothed unto Your enemy.
Divorce me, untie, or break that knot again,
Take me to You, imprison me, for I,
Except You enthrall me,[5] never shall be free,
Nor ever chaste except You ravish me.

---

1. **three-personed God:** the Trinity, or union of three divine forms (the Father, the Son, and the Holy Ghost) in one God-head.
2. **to another due:** holding allegiance to another.
3. **viceroy:** deputy.
4. **fain:** gladly; readily.
5. **Except You enthrall me:** unless you enslave me.

By 1623 Donne was a distinguished minister in the Church of England. In that year he fell seriously ill. He recovered, and the illness provoked a group of private prose meditations, or thoughts, on his mortality. One of the most famous, Meditation XVII, draws its central image from the custom of sounding the village bell to signal that someone was about to die. Others in the village, hearing the death knell, would offer prayers for the dying person's soul. The following selection is an excerpt from Meditation XVII.

from **Meditation XVII**

Nunc lento sonitu dicunt, Morieris
Now this bell, tolling softly for another,
       says to me, Thou must die

Perchance he for whom this bell tolls may be so ill as that he knows not it tolls for him; and perchance I may think myself so much better than I am, as that they who are about me and see my state, may have caused it to toll for me, and I know not that. . . .

All mankind is of one author, and is one volume. When one man dies, one chapter is not torn out of the book, but translated into a better language, and every chapter must be so translated. God employs several translators. Some pieces are translated by age, some by sickness, some by war, some by justice. But God's hand is in every translation; and his hand shall bind up all our scattered leaves again for that library where every book shall lie open to one another. As therefore the bell that rings to a sermon calls not upon the preacher only, but upon the congregation to come, so this bell calls us all; but how much more me, who am brought so near the door by this sickness. . . .

The bell doth toll for him that thinks it doth; and though it intermit[1] again, yet from that minute that that occasion wrought[2] upon him, he is united to God. Who casts not up his eye to the sun when it rises? But who takes off his eye from a comet when that breaks out? Who bends not his ear to any bell which upon any occasion rings? But who can remove it from that bell which is passing a piece of himself out of this world?

No man is an island, entire of itself; every man is a piece of the continent, a part of the main.[3] If a clod be washed away by the sea, Europe is the less, as well as if a promontory were, as well as if a manor of thy friend's or of thine own were. Any man's death diminishes me, because I am involved in mankind, and therefore never send to know for whom the bell tolls; it tolls for thee.

---

1. **intermit:** stop for a time.
2. **wrought:** made an impression.
3. **main:** mainland.

STUDY QUESTIONS

Holy Sonnet 4

Recalling

1. According to the first eight lines, what happens at the "round earth's imagined corners"? Who arises and goes to their "scattered bodies"?
2. In the last six lines, what does the speaker first ask of the Lord? For what does he say it is late? What does he then ask the Lord to do "Here on this lowly ground"?

Interpreting

3. What event described in the Bible do the first eight lines also describe?
4. Explain in your own words what the speaker, in the last six lines, realizes it is too late to do. When is it too late? When and where must it be accomplished?

Extending

5. What Renaissance discovery does the phrase "round earth's imagined corners" reflect?

Holy Sonnet 10

Recalling

1. According to the first four lines, what should Death not be? Why not?
2. According to the speaker, what two experiences are the "pictures" of Death? What do these experiences give people?
3. To what four things does the speaker say Death is actually a slave? With what does he say Death dwells?
4. According to lines 13–14, when will Death die?

Interpreting

5. To what event, described in the Bible, is the speaker referring in the last two lines? What does he mean when he says that "Death shall be no more" at this time?
6. What standard portrait of death is negated in this poem? What does the poem achieve by personifying death—that is, by giving it human characteristics?

Extending

7. What are some of the emotions that death prompts in different people?

Holy Sonnet 14

Recalling

1. Identify seven specific things the speaker asks God to do in the first four lines.

2. To what does the speaker compare himself in lines 5–6? According to lines 9–10, for what reason is the speaker unable to be loved by God?
3. According to the last lines, what is the only way that the speaker will be free?

Interpreting

4. Explain in your own words the conceit, or elaborate comparison, presented in lines 5–14. Be sure to explain to whom or what the speaker is comparing (a) himself, (b) God, and (c) God's "enemy."
5. To whom is the speaker referring when he speaks of God's "enemy" (line 10)? To what age-old battle does the battle for the "usurped town" refer?
6. For what is the speaker basically asking in this poem? What do the images and word choice help convey about the feelings behind that request?

Extending

7. In what way do Donne's sonnets conform to standard sonnet patterns established in the Elizabethan era? In what ways are Donne's sonnets different from Elizabethan sonnets?

from *Meditation XVII*

Recalling

1. To what is humanity compared at the start of the second paragraph? According to that paragraph, what happens when one man dies?
2. According to the last paragraph, of what is every person a part? When the death bell tolls for any person, for whom does it toll?

Interpreting

3. Who is the author of the "volume" of all humankind? What does Donne mean by "one [man's] chapter"? To what is he referring when he says that the chapter is "translated into a better language"?
4. What does "No man is an island" literally mean? Given the ideas expressed in the second paragraph, why does Donne conclude that no man is an island?

Extending

5. In what ways have events and changes in our own century made the statement "No man is an island" even truer today than it was in Donne's time?

From the Restoration until the end of the last century, Donne's poetry was criticized because it did not conform to the harmonious metrical patterns admired in those eras. Samuel Taylor Coleridge was one of a handful of nineteenth-century critics to recognize that

to read Dryden, Pope [and other great poets since the Restoration], you need only count syllables; but to read Donne, you must measure time, and discover the time of each word by the sense of passion.

■ Think about the "passion" behind the words in the first eight lines of Holy Sonnet 4 or the first four lines of Holy Sonnet 14. Then read these lines aloud, assigning to different words the lengths of time you think appropriate. (Be sure to consider the punctuation, which will provide clues to timing.) Do the irregular rhythms enhance the power of the poems? Why or why not?

LITERARY FOCUS

Paradox

Perhaps more than any other poet, Donne is famous for his thought-provoking paradoxes. A **paradox** is a statement or a situation that at first seems impossible or self-contradictory but that actually may be true, either in fact or in a figurative sense. An example occurs in lines 12–13 of Holy Sonnet 14. At first it seems contradictory for the speaker to say he will never be free unless God enslaves him; however, after giving the statement some thought, we understand the idea behind it: The speaker means that he will never achieve salvation, or freedom from his sins, unless he becomes totally submissive to God's will.

Like the conceit, the paradox became a typical device of metaphysical poetry. A number of Donne's imitators used paradoxes simply to display their witty intellect, but in Donne's verse the paradox is often central to a poem's meaning.

Thinking About Paradox
■ Why are the last four words in Holy Sonnet 10 a paradox? Is the paradox central to the poem's meaning? If so, explain why.

COMPOSITION

Writing About a Quotation
■ Donne's statement "No man is an island, entire of itself" is very famous. Discuss its significance in Meditation XVII. First explain what Donne means by the statement. Then demonstrate how that particular statement is the essence of the entire piece. That is, show how other statements by Donne lead to the conclusion that "No man is an island." *For help with this assignment, refer to Lesson 5 in the Writing About Literature Handbook at the back of this book.*

Writing a Letter
■ Write a letter to John Donne responding to his statement "No man is an island, entire of itself." Begin by telling him whether you agree or disagree with his view. Then defend your position by citing instances from current events or your own experience.

George Herbert   *1593–1633*

Unlike John Donne, who rose from relative obscurity to become one of England's highest-ranking Anglican clergymen, George Herbert was born into one of England's most eminent families and deliberately sought obscurity. Herbert's brother was Lord Herbert of Cherbury, a well-known scholar and diplomat; his cousins included the powerful earls of Pembroke. Educated at Cambridge University, Herbert seemed headed for a career of public prominence when instead he took holy orders and chose to spend his life as the parson of a humble country parish.

Herbert's decision was based on deep religious conviction, a conviction that he also expressed in his poetry. Almost all of his poems are **devotional verse**—that is, lyric poetry devoted to religion. His chief work is *The Temple,* a collection of 160 religious poems that he wrote over the years but made no attempt to publish until just before he died. He also composed verse in Latin and a prose work about his life as a country parson.

Herbert was strongly influenced by John Donne, a close friend of Herbert's mother. Though his poetry lacks the sophistication and passion of Donne's religious verse, it instead shows a quiet devotion. Like Donne and the other metaphysical poets, Herbert often used conceit and paradox; in addition, he enjoyed experimenting with the format of his verse. For example, he wrote a number of acrostic poems, in which the first letters of each line spell out a message; he also wrote poetry whose shape reflects its content. Such a poem is "Easter Wings," whose two stanzas are shaped to resemble the wings of the title. When the poem was first printed, the stanzas were placed on their sides so that their wing shapes were even more apparent.

■ The invention of the printing press encouraged sixteenth- and seventeenth-century poets to experiment with the shape of their poems. What inventions have prompted twentieth-century poets to experiment with their creations?

George Herbert

Easter Wings

Lord, who createdst man in wealth and store,[1]
  Though foolishly he lost the same,
    Decaying more and more,
      Till he became
5   Most poor:
      With thee
    O let me rise
  As larks, harmoniously,
And sing this day thy victories:
10 Then shall the fall further the flight in me.

My tender age in sorrow did begin:
  And still with sicknesses and shame
    Thou didst so punish sin,
      That I became
15   Most thin.
      With thee
    Let me combine,
  And feel this day thy victory:
For, if I imp[2] my wing on thine,
20 Affliction shall advance the flight in me.

---

1. **store:** abundance; plenty.
2. **imp:** graft; implant. When a hunting falcon's wing was damaged, feathers were grafted onto it to help the bird fly.

STUDY QUESTIONS

Recalling

1. Whom does the poem address?
2. According to the first stanza, what happened to man after the Creation? What does the speaker hope to do?
3. According to the second stanza, what caused the speaker to become "most thin"? With whom does he wish to "combine"?

Interpreting

4. To what biblical event does line 2 refer? In what way is that event related to the sin that afflicts the speaker in the second stanza?
5. To what day does "this day" (line 9) refer? Where in the poem do you learn what "this day" is?
6. For what is the speaker basically asking in this poem?
7. In what way are wing-shaped stanzas appropriate to the poem's content?

Andrew Marvell   *1621–1678*

Though Andrew Marvell created some of seventeenth-century England's finest poetry, in his own day he was known first and foremost as a public servant. After graduating from Cambridge and spending several years on the Continent, Marvell took a post as tutor to a daughter of a general of the Parliamentary army. It was in this position, in the early 1650s, that Marvell wrote most of the lyric poetry for which he is now famous. In 1657 he was appointed assistant to the great writer John Milton, then serving as a high official in Oliver Cromwell's Puritan government. After the Restoration, when Milton's life was in danger, he was saved (to write his greatest poetry) by the intervention of Marvell, now a member of Parliament from his home town of Hull. Unlike some others who had supported the Puritan cause, Marvell managed to survive the Restoration and went on to serve in Parliament until his death in 1678. Only in 1681 was his earlier lyric poetry published, and only gradually did it attract the attention and high regard that it now enjoys.

Marvell's poetry ingeniously presents serious, sometimes harsh and satiric, sentiments behind graceful, often witty façades. His polished lines with their even rhythms show the influence of Ben Jonson and of such great Elizabethan poets as Christopher Marlowe and Sir Walter Raleigh, yet his poetry is also metaphysical in the depth of its concerns and in its brilliant use of paradox, conceit, and logical argument. "To His Coy Mistress," one of the most famous poems in the English language, is highly illustrative of Marvell's eclectic style.

■ How would you persuade someone to do something he or she seems disinclined to do? Would you use a logical argument? Would you exaggerate your claims?

Andrew Marvell

To His Coy Mistress[1]

Had we but world enough, and time,
This coyness, lady, were no crime.
We would sit down, and think which way
To walk, and pass our long love's day.
5 Thou by the Indian Ganges'[2] side
Shouldst rubies find; I by the tide
Of Humber[3] would complain. I would
Love you ten years before the Flood,
And you should, if you please, refuse
10 Till the conversion of the Jews.[4]
My vegetable love should grow
Vaster than empires and more slow;
An hundred years should go to praise
Thine eyes, and on thy forehead gaze;
15 Two hundred to adore each breast,
But thirty thousand to the rest;
An age at least to every part,
And the last age should show your heart.
For, lady, you deserve this state,[5]
20 Nor would I love at lower rate.
　　But at my back I always hear
Time's wingèd chariot hurrying near;
And yonder all before us lie
Deserts of vast eternity.
25 Thy beauty shall no more be found;
Nor, in thy marble vault, shall sound
My echoing song; then worms shall try
That long-preserved virginity,
And your quaint honor turn to dust,
30 And into ashes all my lust:
The grave's a fine and private place,
But none, I think, do there embrace.
　　Now therefore, while the youthful hue
Sits on thy skin like morning dew,

35 And while thy willing soul transpires[6]
At every pore with instant fires,
Now let us sport us while we may,
And now, like amorous birds of prey,
Rather at once our time devour
40 Than languish in his slow-chapped power.[7]
Let us roll all our strength and all
Our sweetness up into one ball,
And tear our pleasures with rough strife
Thorough[8] the iron gates of life:
45 Thus, though we cannot make our sun
Stand still, yet we will make him run.

---

6. **transpires:** breathes out; exudes.
7. **slow-chapped power:** slow-jawed power; power
that devours slowly.
8. **Thorough:** through.

---

1. **Mistress:** sweetheart.
2. **Indian Ganges':** referring to the Ganges, a river in
India.
3. **Humber:** a river that flows through Hull, Marvell's
home town.
4. **the conversion of the Jews:** Judgment Day. According
to Christian tradition, the Jews will convert to Christianity
on Judgment Day.
5. **this state:** this stateliness; this dignified pace.

STUDY QUESTIONS

Recalling

1. According to lines 1–20, what would not be a "crime" if the speaker and his beloved had "world enough, and time"? In what manner would the speaker's "vegetable love" grow?
2. According to lines 21–32, what does the speaker "always hear"? Where does the speaker think none embrace?
3. According to lines 33–46, when should the speaker and his beloved "sport us while we may," or enjoy themselves? Rather than languishing in time's "slow-chapped power," what should they do?

Interpreting

4. What does the speaker mean in describing the love he would like to offer as "vegetable love" (line 11)? In contrast, what sort of behavior is he recommending in lines 41–42?
5. What do lines 21–32 suggest is the relationship between time and beauty? Between time and passion? What does the phrase "slow-chapped power" (line 40) add to this view of time's actions?
6. What might the speaker literally mean in lines 45–46?
7. Does the central message of the poem apply to love only, or to life in general? What is that message?

Extending

8. Do you agree with the central message of the poem? Why or why not?

LITERARY FOCUS

Logical Argument

The intellectual sophistication of "metaphysical" poetry is reflected not only by thought-provoking conceits and paradoxes but by logical, clever arguments. "To His Coy Mistress" presents one of the most famous of those arguments, and it does so with almost mathematical logic. The poem consists of three verse-paragraphs (each beginning with an indented line) that divide the argument into three steps. The first verse paragraph opens with a supposition and from it offers a possible outcome:

If we had *x* [supposition], we would do *y* [outcome].

The second verse paragraph refutes the supposition:

But we have the reverse of *x*.

The third verse paragraph then draws a logical conclusion:

Therefore, we must do the reverse of *y*.

Thinking About Logical Argument

1. Summarize the poem by filling in the *x*'s and *y*'s in the argument outlined above.
2. Using the same basic logic, write an argument on an entirely different topic.

COMPARING WRITERS

1. In addition to presenting a logical argument, what does Marvell's poem have in common with the poetry of John Donne (pages 246–252)? In what ways is it different?
2. What is similar about the speaker, his purpose, and his audience in "To His Coy Mistress" and the speaker, purpose, and audience in Marlowe's "Passionate Shepherd" (page 129)? In what way is the view of time in Marvell's poem similar to the view presented in Raleigh's "Nymph's Reply" (page 130)?

Ben Jonson *1572–1637*

Reared to the bricklayer's trade and without the benefit of a formal university education, Ben Jonson, by force of will, made himself a great scholar of the classics and consequently affected English literature for nearly two hundred years. He was an active and hot-tempered man—a soldier, a duelist, and a brawler—who mellowed only in middle age.

Jonson's major contribution to English poetry was to turn it away from Petrarch's Italian models and instead adapt the poetic forms that had been used by the classic writers of ancient times. Whether writing terse satire or lyrical songs, Jonson was influenced by Roman poets who had composed centuries before in Latin. As a result, Jonson wrote disciplined English, introducing specific and strong language, great order and balance, plainness and restraint. He was the forerunner of English **neoclassicism**, a revival of the style and attitude of classical literature.

As Donne had his imitators—poets of the metaphysical school, who wrote in his manner—so Ben Jonson inspired a host of imitators and followers, collectively known as the **Tribe of Ben** or **Sons of Ben**. He was particularly admired by the Cavalier poets, younger writers who supported the royalist cause in the civil war with the Puritans. Indeed, the influence of Ben Jonson was felt during the entire century—through example, through critical pronouncements, and through the memory of the poet's formidable personality. It was felt most strongly at the century's end in the work of John Dryden, who passed on Jonson's return to classicism as the dominant literary movement of the eighteenth century.

Jonson was also an excellent playwright. His first dramatic success, *Every Man in His Humor,* was performed by Shakespeare's acting company in 1598. From 1605 on, Jonson produced dramatic spectacles in the court of King James I, who in 1616 made Jonson the poet laureate (the official poet of the nation). However, Jonson's once vast reputation as a dramatist suffered by constant comparison with his peerless contemporary, for what writer could stand to be compared continually with Shakespeare? During Shakespeare's lifetime Jonson resented such persistent comparisons, and even spoke slightingly of his competitor. Yet after the greater playwright's death in 1616, when friends were assembling Shakespeare's plays for publication, they turned to the rival dramatist Ben Jonson to write the dedication. What he wrote appeared in the opening pages of the collected plays in 1623. It is a tribute by one playwright to another and is as eloquent and generous as it is fair-minded.

■ What are some of the specific things you would mention about Shakespeare if you were writing a tribute to him?

Ben Jonson

To the Memory of My Beloved Master, William Shakespeare

To draw no envy, Shakespeare, on thy name,
Am I thus ample¹ to thy book and fame;
While I confess thy writings to be such
As neither man, nor muse, can praise too much.
5 'Tis true, and all men's suffrage.² But these ways
Were not the paths I meant unto thy praise;
For silliest³ ignorance on these may light,
Which, when it sounds at best, but echoes right;
Or blind affection, which doth ne'er advance
10 The truth, but gropes, and urgeth all by chance;
Or crafty malice might pretend this praise,
And think to ruin, where it seemed to raise. . . .
But thou art proof against them, and, indeed,
Above the ill fortune of them, or the need.
15 I therefore will begin. Soul of the age!
The applause, delight, the wonder of our stage!
My Shakespeare, rise! I will not lodge thee by
Chaucer, or Spenser, or bid Beaumont⁴ lie
A little further, to make thee a room;
20 Thou art a monument without a tomb,
And art alive still while thy book doth live
And we have wits to read and praise to give.
That I not mix thee so, my brain excuses,
I mean with great, but disproportioned⁵ Muses;
25 For if I thought my judgment were of years,
I should commit thee surely with thy peers,
And tell how far thou didst our Lyly outshine,
Or sporting Kyd, or Marlowe's⁶ mighty line.
And though thou hadst small⁷ Latin and less Greek
30 From thence to honor thee, I would not seek
For names; but call forth thundering Aeschylus,

---

1. **ample:** liberal, unstinted in praise.
2. **suffrage:** agreement.
3. **silliest:** simplest.
4. **Beaumont:** Francis Beaumont (1584–1616), playwright who was a contemporary of Shakespeare. Chaucer, Spenser, and Beaumont were buried in Westminster Abbey in London; Shakespeare was buried in Stratford.
5. **disproportioned:** not comparable.
6. **Lyly . . . Kyd . . . Marlowe:** English playwrights, contemporaries of Shakespeare.
7. **small:** a limited knowledge of.

Euripides, and Sophocles[8] to us;
Pacuvius, Accius,[9] him of Cordova[10] dead,
To life again, to hear thy buskin[11] tread,
35 And shake a stage; or, when thy socks[12] were on,
Leave thee alone for the comparison
Of all that insolent Greece or haughty Rome
Sent forth, or since did from their ashes come.
Triumph, my Britain, thou hast one to show
40 To whom all scenes[13] of Europe homage owe.
He was not of an age, but for all time!
And all the Muses still were in their prime,
When, like Apollo,[14] he came forth to warm
Our ears, or like a Mercury[15] to charm!
45 Nature herself was proud of his designs
And joyed to wear the dressing of his lines!
Which were so richly spun, and woven so fit,[16]
As,[17] since, she will vouchsafe no other wit.
The merry Greek, tart Aristophanes,
50 Neat Terence, witty Plautus,[18] now not please,
But antiquated and deserted lie,
As they were not of Nature's family.
Yet must I not give Nature all; thy art,
My gentle Shakespeare, must enjoy a part.
55 For though the poet's matter nature be,
His art doth give the fashion; and, that he
Who casts[19] to write a living line, must sweat
(Such as thine are) and strike the second heat
Upon the Muses' anvil; turn the same
60 (And himself with it) that he thinks to frame,
Or, for the laurel,[20] he may gain a scorn;
For a good poet's made, as well as born.
And such wert thou! Look how the father's face
Lives in his issue; even so the race
65 Of Shakespeare's mind and manners brightly shines

---

8. **Aeschylus** [es′kə ləs], **Euripides** [yoo rip′ə dēz′], **and**
Sophocles [sof′ə klēz′]: classical Greek tragic dramatists.
9. **Pacuvius** [pə koo′vē əs], **Accius** [ak′ē əs]: Roman tragic playwrights.
10. **him of Cordova** [kôr dō′və]: Seneca, Roman dramatist born in Cordova, Spain.
11. **buskin:** high boot, worn by tragic actors.
12. **socks:** worn by comic actors.
13. **scenes:** stages.
14. **Apollo:** in classical mythology the god of music and poetry;
also, god of the sun.
15. **Mercury:** Roman messenger of the gods, and god of cleverness.
16. **fit:** appropriately.
17. **As:** that.
18. **Aristophanes,** [ar′is tof′ə nēz′] . . . **Terence,** [ter′əns]. . . . **Plautus** [plô′təs]:
classical comic playwrights, the first Greek, the other two Roman.
19. **casts:** sets out.
20. **laurel:** fame or distinction.

In his well turnèd, and true filèd[21] lines;
In each of which he seems to shake a lance,[22]
As brandished at the eyes of ignorance.
Sweet Swan of Avon![23] what a sight it were

70 To see thee in our waters yet appear,
And make those flights upon the banks of Thames,
That so did take Eliza, and our James![24]
But stay, I see thee in the hemisphere
Advanced, and made a constellation there!

75 Shine forth, thou Star of poets, and with rage[25]
Or influence, chide or cheer the drooping stage,
Which, since thy flight from hence, hath mourned like night,
And despairs day, but for thy volume's light.[26]

---

21. **true filèd:** accurately refined; polished.
22. **shake a lance:** pun on the name *Shake-speare.*
23. **Avon:** Shakespeare was born and died in Stratford, on the Avon River.
24. **Eliza . . . James:** Queen Elizabeth and King James I, before
whom Shakespeare's plays were performed.
25. **rage:** rapture, poetic imagination.
26. **thy volume's light:** that is, this present (1623) publication of your plays.

STUDY QUESTIONS

Recalling

1. What does Jonson say in lines 1–12 are the wrong motivations for praising Shakespeare?
2. What does Jonson say in lines 17–22 about a burial place for Shakespeare?
3. How does Shakespeare compare to his contemporary playwrights, according to lines 27–28?
4. Whom does Jonson call forth in lines 30–34 to appreciate Shakespeare's tragedies? What does Jonson say in lines 35–38 about comparing Shakespeare's comedies to others'?
5. According to lines 53–62, what are the two influences that account for Shakespeare's great achievement?
6. What does Jonson wish for in lines 69–72? How has the "drooping stage" reacted since Shakespeare's death? According to the end of the poem, what will help remedy this situation?

Interpreting

7. According to Jonson, why was Shakespeare "not of an age, but for all time"?

8. What can we learn from this poem about Jonson's intellect? His attitude toward literature as a profession? His attitude toward Shakespeare's accomplishments? Cite specific examples.

Extending

9. Several of Shakespeare's sonnets (see pages 133–137) proclaim that the beloved is immortalized by poetry. How does Ben Jonson reinforce the idea of art as a route to eternity in his poem?

VIEWPOINT

The literary critic Edmund Wilson says of Ben Jonson:

The one thing he really loved was literature, and, having served it as well as he could, no touchiness of personal pride could keep him from honoring one who had been fitted to serve it better. . . .

■ Examine lines 45–48. For what specific poetic talent does Jonson praise Shakespeare most?

Ben Jonson

On My First Son[1]

Farewell, thou child of my right hand,[2] and joy;
   My sin was too much hope of thee, loved boy,
Seven years thou wert lent to me, and I thee pay,
   Exacted by thy fate, on the just[3] day.
5 O, could I lose all father[4] now! For why
   Will man lament the state he should envy?
To have so soon 'scaped world's and flesh's rage,
   And, if no other misery, yet age!
Rest in soft peace, and, asked, say, "Here doth lie
10   Ben Jonson his[5] best piece of poetry";
For whose sake, henceforth, all his vows be such
   As what he loves may never like too much.

---

1. Ben Jonson's first son was born in 1596 and died in 1603 of the plague.
2. **child of my right hand:** the literal translation of the Hebrew name Benjamin, which was the son's name.
3. **just:** exact.
4. **lose all father:** lose all feeling or hopes of being a father.
5. **Ben Jonson his:** Ben Jonson's. The use of a pronoun instead of the possessive was common in Jonson's day.

STUDY QUESTIONS

Recalling
1. What does the speaker say his sin was? What price does he say fate exacted for the sin?
2. What specific question does the speaker ask? What does he say his son has escaped?
3. What does the speaker vow in the last lines?

Interpreting
4. Restate the question in lines 5–6.
5. What does the speaker mean when he calls his son his "best piece of poetry"? Why might he make the vow he makes in line 12?

LITERARY FOCUS

Tone
Just as a person speaks in a certain tone of voice that reveals his or her attitude, written literature also has a **tone** that reflects the writer's attitude toward his or her subject or audience. The tone may be formal, casual, angry, thoughtful, puzzled, or sarcastic, among other things. It may be uniform throughout a work or may vary. Many elements affect the tone of a poem: word choice, punctuation, line length, imagery, figurative language, rhythm, and rhyme. For example, an *O* at the beginning of a line can signal strong emotion; a question can make the tone seem puzzled or thoughtful; a plodding rhythm can help express exhaustion or despair.

Thinking About Tone
1. Identify the chief tone in Jonson's poem.
2. What elements help indicate the tone of the first sentence in line 5? How is it different from the tone elsewhere in the poem?

The delicacy and polish of Jonson's verse are exemplified most clearly in the following lines, which have served as the lyrics of an abidingly popular song.

Ben Jonson

Song: To Celia

Drink to me only with thine eyes,
    And I will pledge[1] with mine;
Or leave a kiss but in the cup,
    And I'll not look for wine.
5 The thirst that from the soul doth rise
    Doth ask a drink divine;
But might I of Jove's[2] nectar[3] sup,
    I would not change for thine.

I sent thee late[4] a rosy wreath,
10   Not so much honoring thee
As giving it a hope, that there
    It could not withered be.
But thou thereon didst only breathe,
    And sent'st it back to me;
15 Since when it grows, and smells, I swear,
    Not of itself, but thee.

---

1. **pledge:** drink a toast.
2. **Jove's:** Jupiter's; referring to the Roman ruler of the gods.
3. **nectar:** the drink of the gods.
4. **late:** recently.

STUDY QUESTIONS

Recalling
1. What signs is the speaker looking for in lines 1–4?
2. What would the speaker prefer over Jove's divine nectar?
3. According to lines 10–13, why did the speaker send a wreath of roses to his beloved? What did she do with it?

Interpreting
4. With what qualities does the speaker endow his beloved?
5. What proof does the poem offer that the speaker will be persistent in his love?

Robert Herrick   *1591–1674*

Though Robert Herrick was not quite the aristocrat we picture a Cavalier poet to be, his poetry is perhaps the finest example of the kind of lyrics for which the Cavalier poets are known—playful, delicate, witty verses. As a young man Herrick spent a number of years in London as one of the Tribe of Ben; later he accepted a church appointment as a rural rector in southwest England. In his new surroundings the transplanted Londoner was at first miserable, but gradually he learned to love country life, and many of his finest poems speak of nature and of simple country pleasures. During the Puritan years the Royalist Herrick lost his position and decided to return to London to publish his verse. He was deeply disappointed to discover that he had outlived most of his old London friends— and there was no one he missed more than Ben Jonson.

Jonson's verse and classical interests were vital in forming Herrick's poetic tastes. His poems, like many of Jonson's, are modest in scope, crystal clear, but rich and polished.

■ What different views of time are held by young people and by older people? In what ways do the old react to the loss of dear friends and other ravages of time?

Robert Herrick

To the Virgins, to Make Much of Time

Gather ye rosebuds while ye may,
  Old time is still a-flying;
And this same flower that smiles today,
  Tomorrow will be dying.

5 The glorious lamp of heaven, the sun,
  The higher he's a-getting,
The sooner will his race be run,
  And nearer he's to setting.

That age is best which is the first,
10   When youth and blood are warmer;
But being spent, the worse, and worst
  Times still succeed the former.

Then be not coy, but use your time,
  And, while ye may, go marry;
15 For, having lost but once your prime,
  You may forever tarry.

Robert Herrick

An Ode for Him

Ah, Ben!
Say how or when
Shall we, thy guests,
Meet at those lyric feasts
5   Made at the Sun,
The Dog, the Triple Tun,[1]
Where we such clusters[2] had
As made us nobly wild, not mad;
And yet each verse of thine
10 Outdid the meat, outdid the frolic wine.

My Ben!
Or[3] come again,
Or send to us
Thy wit's great overplus;
15   But teach us yet
Wisely to husband[4] it,
Lest we that talent spend,
And having once brought to an end
That precious stock, the store
20 Of such a wit the world should have no more.

---

1. **Sun . . . Dog . . . Triple Tun:** London taverns in which Jonson and his followers gathered.
2. **clusters:** clusters of grapes; that is, wine.
3. **Or:** either.
4. **husband:** conserve.

To the Virgins, to Make Much of Time

Recalling

1. According to the first stanza, when should the young maidens gather their rosebuds? What is "a-flying"? What will happen to the flower that "smiles today"?

2. According to the third stanza, which age is best? What happens when that age is "spent"?

3. In the last stanza, what does the speaker tell the maidens to do? What does he say may happen once they pass their prime?

Interpreting

4. What view of time is presented in this poem? What does the sun (stanza 2) symbolize, or represent?

5. Does "gather ye rosebuds while ye may" (stanza 1) simply mean "while ye may, go marry" (stanza 4)? If not, what is its more general message?

Extending

6. Herrick himself never married. What does this biographical detail suggest about the feelings that prompted this poem?

An Ode for Him

Recalling

1. What adjective describes the feasts attended by Jonson and his circle? What "outdid" the meat and wine at those feasts?

2. What "overplus," or surplus item, is Jonson asked to bestow if he cannot "come again"? According to the last lines, why must this item be husbanded by others?

Interpreting

3. With what tone or attitude does the speaker recall his meetings with Jonson? What is his attitude toward Jonson himself?

4. What contrast regarding Jonson's wit and the wit of others does the second stanza imply? What criticism of other writers' poetry is implied in lines 15–16?

LITERARY FOCUS

The Carpe-Diem Theme

In Latin **carpe diem** [kär'pe dē'em] means "Seize the day"; the phrase was first made famous by the ancient Roman poet Horace. Today the phrase is used to describe the many works of literature in which the theme says, "Make the most of life's opportunities while you can." The carpe-diem theme was especially popular in English literature of the sixteenth and seventeenth centuries. Herrick's "To the Virgins, to Make Much of Time" is one of its best-known expressions; Andrew Marvell's "To His Coy Mistress" (page 259) is another.

Thinking About the Carpe-Diem Theme

1. What one line in Herrick's poem most strongly expresses the carpe-diem theme in figurative terms?

2. What is similar about the situations used to express the theme in Herrick's poem and in Marvell's "To His Coy Mistress"?

COMPOSITION

Writing a Comparison/Contrast

■ Write an essay in which you compare and contrast Herrick's "To the Virgins" with Andrew Marvell's "To His Coy Mistress" (page 259). In your essay discuss specific literary elements such as theme, tone, diction (word choice), imagery, symbolism, speaker, and audience. Conclude by stating which poem you think more effective, and why. *For help with this assignment, refer to Lesson 2 in the Writing About Literature Handbook at the back of this book.*

Writing a Tribute

■ Write a speech or a poem that pays tribute to an author whose works you particularly admire. In your tribute, make specific references to the writer's accomplishments, as Herrick does in "An Ode for Him" and as Jonson does in "To the Memory of My Beloved Master, William Shakespeare" (page 262).

Sir John Suckling   *1609–1642*

The literary remains of Sir John Suckling only begin to capture the wit and sophistication for which he was famous in his lifetime. A leading figure in the court of Charles I, the aristocratic Suckling was said to be able to compose a clever poem at the drop of a hat, and tales of his gallantry were legion. Following the Puritan takeover, Suckling was forced into exile and died in abject poverty in Paris.

Suckling's verse, like that of the other Cavalier poets, shows the strong influence of Ben Jonson in its simple, polished diction and careful meters. Suckling was also familiar with Donne and is "metaphysical" in his brilliant use of conceit and paradox. The two poems here display the ironical wit that was Suckling's own special trademark.

■ How do people in love usually behave? For how long would you say "true love" should last?

Sir John Suckling

Song: Why So Pale and Wan?

Why so pale and wan, fond lover?
    Prithee,[1] why so pale?
Will, when looking well can't move her,
    Looking ill prevail?
5   Prithee, why so pale?

Why so dull and mute, young sinner?
    Prithee, why so mute?
Will, when speaking well can't win her,
    Saying nothing do 't?
10   Prithee, why so mute?

Quit, quit for shame! This will not move,
    This cannot take her.
If of herself she will not love,
    Nothing can make her:
15   The devil take her!

---

1. **Prithee:** I pray thee; please.

The Constant Lover

Out upon it! I have loved
  Three whole days together,
And am like to love three more,
  If it prove fair weather.

5 Time shall molt away his wings
  Ere he shall discover
In the whole wide world again
  Such a constant lover.

But the spite on 't is, no praise
10   Is due at all to me:
Love with me had made no stays,
  Had it any been but she.

Had it any been but she,
  And that very face,
15 There had been at least ere this
  A dozen dozen in her place.

STUDY QUESTIONS

Why So Pale and Wan?

Recalling

1. According to the speaker, why is the lover's sickly appearance unreasonable? Why is the lover's silence unreasonable?
2. Restate in your own words the speaker's advice in the last three lines.

Interpreting

3. What sort of advice, in general, does the speaker offer the lover?
4. In offering this advice, what does the speaker reveal about his own attitude toward love and toward life in general?

Extending

5. How is the attitude toward love expressed in Suckling's poems different from the attitude you have encountered in most love poetry of the Elizabethan era?

The Constant Lover

Recalling

1. For how long has the speaker been in love thus far? For how much longer will he be in love "if it prove fair weather"?
2. What does the speaker call himself in stanza 2?
3. According to the last two stanzas, why does the speaker feel he deserves no praise? What would have happened "had it any been but she"?

Interpreting

4. What sort of lover is the speaker in reality? Identify three phrases that help reveal the kind of lover he really is.
5. How would you describe the poem's tone, or attitude toward its subject?

Richard Lovelace   *1618–1658*

Richard Lovelace was the perfect model of a seventeenth-century court favorite. On a visit to Oxford University in 1636, the king and queen of England were so favorably impressed by the student Lovelace that they arranged for a degree to be awarded to him on the spot. Later Lovelace became a leading figure among the Cavalier poets—polished, gallant, and worldly supporters of King Charles I. Like the others, he remained loyal to the king throughout the turbulent civil war period. That support led to the poet's imprisonment by the Puritan government and his death in poverty at the early age of thirty-nine.

Lovelace's best poetry shows the influence of Ben Jonson. It is graceful and witty and, in true Cavalier fashion, often addresses the themes of love, war, and loyalty to the king.

▇ How does a soldier feel when he or she goes off to war and leaves loved ones behind? How might the memory of loved ones help in a time of crisis?

Richard Lovelace

To Lucasta, Going to the Wars

Tell me not, sweet, I am unkind,
   That from the nunnery[1]
Of thy chaste breast and quiet mind
   To war and arms I fly.

5 True, a new mistress now I chase,
   The first foe in the field;
And with a stronger faith embrace
   A sword, a horse, a shield.

Yet this inconstancy[2] is such
10   As you too shall adore;
I could not love thee, dear, so much,
   Loved I not honor more.

---

1. **nunnery:** convent; cloister.
2. **inconstancy:** fickleness.

To Althea, from Prison

When Love with unconfinèd wings
   Hovers within my gates,
And my divine Althea brings
   To whisper at the grates;
5 When I lie tangled in her hair
   And fettered[1] to her eye,
The gods[2] that wanton[3] in the air
   Know no such liberty.

When flowing cups run swiftly round,
10   With no allaying Thames,[4]
Our careless heads with roses bound,
   Our hearts with loyal flames;
When thirsty grief in wine we steep,
   When healths[5] and draughts[6] go free,
15 Fishes that tipple in the deep
   Know no such liberty.

When, like committed linnets,[7] I
   With shriller throat shall sing
The sweetness, mercy, majesty,
20   And glories of my King;
When I shall voice aloud how good
   He is, how great should be,
Enlargèd[8] winds that curl the flood
   Know no such liberty.

25 Stone walls do not a prison make,
   Nor iron bars a cage:
Minds innocent and quiet take
   That for an hermitage.[9]
If I have freedom in my love,
30   And in my soul am free,
Angels alone, that soar above,
   Enjoy such liberty.

---

1. **fettered:** bound.
2. **gods:** In some versions of the poem, the word is *birds* instead of *gods.*
3. **wanton:** sport; play.
4. **cups . . . Thames** [temz]: wine with no diluting water. (The Thames is a river.)
5. **healths:** toasts.
6. **draughts** [drafts]: drinks.

7. **committed linnets:** caged songbirds.
8. **Enlargèd:** released, as from imprisonment.
9. **hermitage:** secluded dwelling place; private retreat.

STUDY QUESTIONS

To Lucasta, Going to the Wars

Recalling

1. After deserting Lucasta, what new "mistress" does the speaker pursue?
2. What things does the speaker embrace now that he has left Lucasta?
3. Who or what does the speaker love more than Lucasta?

Interpreting

4. What contrasts does the speaker cite between the two "mistresses"?
5. What is the meaning of the last two lines of the poem? Why will Lucasta adore the speaker's inconstancy?

To Althea, from Prison

Recalling

1. Where is the speaker?
2. With what three occasions does he associate liberty?
3. Identify the images of freedom that appear at the end of each of the four stanzas.
4. What does the prison offer the speaker, according to the last stanza? What conditions may enable him to enjoy the kind of liberty that angels have?

Interpreting

5. What is ironical about the words "tangled" and "fettered" in lines 5 and 6?
6. In what way is the speaker really free despite his imprisonment?

Richard Lovelace **273**

John Milton   *1608–1674*

As Chaucer towers over the literary world of medieval England, and as Shakespeare is the supreme writer of the Elizabethan Age, so John Milton is the outstanding English poet of the seventeenth century.

At an early age this citizen of London realized his purpose: "By labor and intent study (which I take to be my portion in this life) joined with the strong propensity of nature, I might perhaps leave something so written to aftertimes as they should not willingly let it die." Milton's labor and study extended from his years as a student at St. Paul's School in London, through university years at Cambridge, through five years of reading day and night in English, Latin, Greek, Hebrew, French, and Italian, and on through two more years of travel abroad that ended in 1639, when he was over thirty. Already that long period of study had combined with the "strong propensity of nature"—his poetic gifts and inclinations—to produce distinguished poetry, including *Lycidas,* the finest elegy in English, written upon the death of a close friend.

Despite this extensive preparation, Milton's poetic performance was interrupted by the outbreak of civil war in England. As a staunch supporter of the Parliamentary cause against the Royalists, the poet devoted twenty years out of the prime of his life, from 1640 to 1660, to defending the Puritan Commonwealth against its enemies and detractors. During that long interlude he wrote primarily prose pamphlets on matters relating to the new government. Indeed, as Latin Secretary in Cromwell's government, he labored so diligently in preparing state documents that his eyesight began to fail him. By 1652 he was blind.

When the royalists managed finally, in 1660, to triumph over Cromwell's followers and restore the monarchy, the poet found himself also in figurative darkness, with all that he had worked for repudiated by the English people. For a while his very life was in danger, but through the help of men like Andrew Marvell (page 258) his life was spared.

Milton then moved to a village west of London, where he began his masterpiece, conceiving and memorizing portions of it at night, and dictating what he had created to secretaries in the morning. In that way he wrote *Paradise Lost,* a work of over ten thousand lines, the greatest epic in our language.

■ How does a student feel when, after extensive years of study, he or she is unable to begin practicing his or her chosen life's work? Why might blindness be especially difficult for a writer?

John Milton

How Soon Hath Time

How soon hath Time, the subtle thief of youth,
   Stolen on his wing my three-and twentieth year!
   My hasting days fly on with full career,[1]
   But my late spring no bud or blossom shew'th.[2]
5 Perhaps my semblance[3] might deceive[4] the truth
   That I to manhood am arrived so near;
   And inward ripeness doth much less appear,
   That some more timely-happy spirits endu'th.[5]
   Yet, be it less or more, or soon or slow,
10   It shall be still[6] in strictest measure even[7]
   To that same lot,[8] however mean or high,
Toward which Time leads me, and the will of Heaven.
   All is, if I have grace to use it so,
   As ever in my great Task-Master's eye.

---

1. **career:** speed.
2. **shew'th:** shows.
3. **semblance:** appearance.
4. **deceive:** prove false.
5. **endu'th:** endows.
6. **still:** always.
7. **even:** equal or adequate.
8. **lot:** fate.

STUDY QUESTIONS

Recalling

1. How does Milton refer to time in the first line of the poem?
2. According to line 4, what has the poet's "late spring" not yet shown?
3. According to lines 10–12, in what does the poet place his faith?

Interpreting

4. What is appropriate about the personification of time in lines 1–2?
5. What do the "bud" and "blossom" of line 4 represent? How does Milton extend the plant imagery in line 7?
6. In line 13, "All" may refer to time or to talent. What is the meaning of lines 13–14 in each case?

In this sonnet, also referred to as "On His Blindness," Milton uses **allusions**, or references to other works the reader is supposed to know. He refers to the Parable of the Talents from Matthew 25 : 14–30, where a servant is scolded by his master for hiding his one talent—fifteen years' wages—instead of using it for profit. Thus Milton gives *talent* a double meaning in the sonnet.

John Milton

When I Consider How My Light Is Spent

When I consider how my light is spent
    Ere[1] half my days in this dark world and wide,
    And that one talent which is death to hide
    Lodged with me useless, though my soul more bent
5 To serve there with my Maker, and present
    My true account, lest He returning chide,
    "Doth God exact day-labor, light denied?"
    I fondly[2] ask. But Patience, to prevent
That murmur, soon replies, "God doth not need
10   Either man's work or His own gifts. Who best
    Bear His mild yoke, they serve Him best. His state
Is kingly: thousands[3] at His bidding speed,
    And post[4] o'er land and ocean without rest;
    They also serve who only stand and wait."

1. **Ere:** before.
2. **fondly:** foolishly.

3. **thousands:** that is, of angels.
4. **post:** hasten.

STUDY QUESTIONS

Recalling
1. What is the speaker lamenting in lines 1–2?
2. What happens if the talent is hidden, according to line 3? What does the speaker want to do with the talent?
3. What does the speaker ask in line 7?
4. What does Patience say God asks for?

Interpreting
5. What two meanings does *talent* have?
6. What is the speaker's mood in lines 1–8?
7. What are the two kinds of activity pictured in lines 9–14? In what category does the speaker place himself?
8. Does the speaker find consolation? Explain.

Extending
9. Are the themes of Milton's sonnets alike?

Introducing **Paradise Lost**

Paradise Lost is an epic divided into twelve books, or chapters. An **epic** is a long narrative poem that records, in grave and stately language, heroic exploits and majestic events. Before Milton, the chief epics in English literature were the Anglo-Saxon *Beowulf* (page 9), virtually unknown in Milton's day, and Spenser's *Faerie Queene* (page 120), which Milton did know and admire, although *Paradise Lost* soon eclipsed *The Faerie Queene* in literary prominence.

Steeped in both classical and biblical scholarship, Milton set out to write a Christian epic as spacious and universal as Homer's *Iliad* (page 805) and *Odyssey* and Virgil's *Aeneid* (page 864), the great epics of ancient Greece and Rome. Milton selected as his subject the fall of man—that is, the biblical story in which Satan tempts Adam and Eve to commit the original sin (eating the forbidden fruit) and thereby fall from God's grace, after which they are exiled from Paradise, or the Garden of Eden (see page 233). In working with this subject matter, Milton wanted to "justify the ways of God to men." He also hoped to achieve "things unattempted yet in prose or rhyme."

In light of this second aim, Milton created for *Paradise Lost* his own poetic style, different from either Donne's or Jonson's. For one thing, he writes formally, distancing himself from his subject matter; for another, he writes in blank verse, which until Milton's attempt was not often used for writing other than drama. In addition, while Milton does use metaphors and sometimes extends them over many lines, he does not employ ingenious conceits and other "metaphysical" devices serving to display a witty intellect. Though he draws relentlessly on the classics and the Bible, his scholarship has no hint of boastfulness, for Milton the Puritan believed that to serve God, the poet—especially the poet writing on so lofty a topic as the fall of man—must suppress his ego wherever possible. Nevertheless, in spite of its scholarly, formal style, *Paradise Lost* has always enjoyed great reader appeal, in part because its masterful lines so eloquently express profound universal truths, in part because its heroes and villains—and especially its chief villain, Satan—have such vivid personalities of their own.

Book I opens, as classical epics do, with an **invocation**, or call to a Muse to inspire the poet at the outset of his ambitious task. It then recounts how the rebellious angel Lucifer, now renamed Satan ("the Adversary"), awakens to find himself banished to Hell, from where he and his followers plot revenge on God.

John Milton

from **Paradise Lost**

from **Book I**

Of man's first disobedience, and the fruit
Of that forbidden tree whose mortal taste
Brought death into the world, and all our woe,
With loss of Eden, till one greater Man[1]

5 Restore us, and regain the blissful seat,
Sing, Heavenly Muse, that on the secret top
Of Oreb, or of Sinai, didst inspire
That shepherd[2] who first taught the chosen seed
In the beginning how the Heavens and Earth

10 Rose out of Chaos;[3] or, if Sion[4] hill
Delight thee more, and Siloa's brook[5] that flowed
Fast[6] by the oracle of God, I thence
Invoke thy aid to my adventurous song,
That with no middle flight intends to soar

15 Above the Aonian mount,[7] while it pursues
Things unattempted yet in prose or rhyme.
And chiefly thou, O Spirit,[8] that dost prefer
Before all temples the upright heart and pure,
Instruct me, for thou know'st; thou from the first

20 Wast present, and with mighty wings outspread
Dovelike sat'st brooding[9] on the vast abyss
And mad'st it pregnant: what in me is dark,
Illumine; what is low, raise and support;
That, to the highth of this great argument,[10]

25 I may assert[11] Eternal Providence,
And justify the ways of God to men.
   Say first, for Heaven hides nothing from thy view,
Nor the deep tract of Hell, say first what cause
Moved our grand[12] parents in that happy state,

30 Favored of Heaven so highly, to fall off
From their Creator, and transgress his will
For one restraint,[13] lords of the world besides.
Who first seduced them to that foul revolt?
The infernal Serpent; he it was whose guile,

35 Stirred up with envy and revenge, deceived
The mother of mankind, what time[14] his pride
Had cast him out from Heaven, with all his host
Of rebel angels, by whose aid, aspiring
To set himself in glory above his peers,

40 He trusted to have equaled the Most High,
If he opposed, and, with ambitious aim
Against the throne and monarchy of God,

1 **greater Man:** Christ.

2 **secret top . . . shepherd:** mysterious top of Oreb, or Mount Sinai, on which the shepherd Moses received the law of God.
3 **first taught . . . Chaos:** first taught the Jews of the Creation. Moses is traditionally regarded as the divinely inspired author of the first five books of the Bible, including Genesis, which tells of the Creation.
4 **Sion** [sī'ən]: hill in Jerusalem on which stood the Temple ("the oracle of God").
5 **Siloa's** [si lō'əz] **brook:** stream near Jerusalem.
6 **Fast:** close.
7 **Aonian** [ā ō'nē ən] **mount:** Mount Helicon, home of the Muses of Greek mythology.
8 **Spirit:** Holy Spirit.

9 **brooding:** that is, as a bird on a nest.

10 **highth . . . argument:** height of this great theme.
11 **assert:** defend; champion.

12 **grand:** first.

13 **one restraint:** that is, the prohibition from eating fruit of the tree of knowledge.

14 **what time:** when.

Expulsion from the Garden of Eden, Thomas Cole, c. 1827.

Raised impious war in Heaven and battle proud,
With vain attempt. Him the Almighty Power
45 Hurled headlong flaming from the ethereal sky,
With hideous ruin and combustion, down
To bottomless perdition, there to dwell
In adamantine[15] chains and penal fire,
Who durst defy the Omnipotent to arms.
50   Nine times the space that measures day and night
To mortal men, he with his horrid crew
Lay vanquished, rolling in the fiery gulf,
Confounded though immortal. But his doom
Reserved him to more wrath; for now the thought
55 Both of lost happiness and lasting pain
Torments him: round he throws his baleful eyes,
That witnessed[16] huge affliction and dismay,
Mixed with obdúrate pride and steadfast hate.
At once, as far as angels' ken,[17] he views
60 The dismal situation waste and wild:
A dungeon horrible, on all sides round,
As one great furnace flamed; yet from those flames
No light, but rather darkness visible
Served only to discover sights of woe,
65 Regions of sorrow, doleful shades, where peace
And rest can never dwell, hope never comes
That comes to all; but torture without end
Still urges,[18] and a fiery deluge, fed
With ever-burning sulfur unconsumed.
70 Such place Eternal Justice had prepared
For those rebellious; here their prison ordained
In utter darkness, and their portion set,
As far removed from God and light of Heaven
As from the center thrice to the utmost pole.[19]
75 O how unlike the place from whence they fell!
There the companions of his fall, o'erwhelmed
With floods and whirlwinds of tempestuous fire,
He soon discerns; and, weltering by his side,
One next himself in power, and next in crime,
80 Long after known in Palestine, and named
Beelzebub.[20] To whom the Archenemy,
And thence in Heaven called Satan, with bold words
Breaking the horrid silence, thus began:
   "If thou beest he—but O, how fallen! how changed
85 From him—who in the happy realms of light,
Clothed with transcendent brightness, didst outshine
Myriads, though bright—if he whom mutual league,
United thoughts and counsels, equal hope
And hazard in the glorious enterprise,

15 **adamantine:** hard as diamonds.

16 **witnessed:** showed.

17 **ken:** sight.

18 **Still urges:** always presses.

19 **center . . . pole:** three times the distance from the earth's center to the outermost point of the universe.

20 **Beelzebub** [bē el′zə bub]: Though the name is often used to mean Satan himself, Milton uses it for another fallen angel, Satan's second in command.

90 Joined with me once, now misery hath joined
    In equal ruin: into what pit thou seest
    From what highth fallen! so much the stronger proved
    He with his thunder; and till then who knew
    The force of those dire arms? Yet not for those,
95 Nor what the potent Victor in his rage
    Can else inflict, do I repent or change,
    Though changed in outward luster; that fixed mind,
    And high disdain from sense of injured merit,
    That with the Mightiest raised me to contend,
100 And to the fierce contention brought along
    Innumerable force of spirits armed
    That durst dislike his reign, and, me preferring,
    His utmost power with adverse power opposed
    In dubious battle on the plains of Heaven,
105 And shook his throne. What though the field be lost?
    All is not lost; the unconquerable will,
    And study of revenge, immortal hate,
    And courage never to submit or yield:
    And what is else not to be overcome?
110 That glory never shall his wrath or might
    Extort from me. To bow and sue for grace
    With suppliant knee, and deify his power
    Who, from the terror of this arm, so late
    Doubted[21] his empire—that were low indeed;

21 **Doubted:** feared for.

115 That were an ignominy and shame beneath
    This downfall; since, by fate, the strength of gods,
    And this empyreal[22] substance, cannot fail;
    Since, through experience of this great event,
    In arms not worse, in foresight much advanced,

22 **empyreal:** heavenly; therefore, nonmaterial and indestructible.

120 We may with more successful hope resolve
    To wage by force or guile eternal war,
    Irreconcilable, to our grand Foe,
    Who now triumphs, and in the excess of joy
    Sole reigning holds the tyranny of Heaven."

125   So spake the apostate[23] Angel, though in pain,
    Vaunting[24] aloud but racked with deep despair;
    And him thus answered soon his bold compeer:[25]
        "O Prince, O Chief of many thronèd Powers,
    That led the embattled Seraphim[26] to war

23 **apostate:** renegade.
24 **Vaunting:** boasting.
25 **compeer:** companion; peer.

26 **Seraphim:** the highest-ranking angels.

130 Under thy conduct, and, in dreadful deeds
    Fearless, endangered Heaven's perpetual King;
    And put to proof his high supremacy,
    Whether upheld by strength, or chance, or fate;
    Too well I see and rue the dire event,
135 That with sad overthrow and foul defeat
    Hath lost us Heaven, and all this mighty host

In horrible destruction laid thus low,
As far as gods and heavenly essences
Can perish: for the mind and spirit remains
140 Invincible, and vigor soon returns,
Though all our glory extinct, and happy state
Here swallowed up in endless misery.
But what if he our Conqueror (whom I now
Of force believe almighty, since no less
145 Than such could have o'erpowered such force as ours)
Have left us this our spirit and strength entire,
Strongly to suffer and support our pains,
That we may so suffice his vengeful ire,
Or do him mightier service as his thralls[27]   27 **thralls:** slaves.
150 By right of war, whate'er his business be,
Here in the heart of Hell to work in fire,
Or do his errands in the gloomy deep?
What can it then avail, though yet we feel
Strength undiminished, or eternal being
155 To undergo eternal punishment?"
        Whereto with speedy words the Archfiend replied:
"Fallen Cherub,[28] to be weak is miserable,   28 **Cherub:** angel.
Doing or suffering;[29] but of this be sure,   29 **Doing or suffering:** active or passive.
To do aught good never will be our task,
160 But ever to do ill our sole delight,
As being the contrary to his high will
Whom we resist. If then his providence
Out of our evil seek to bring forth good,
Our labor must be to pervert that end,
165 And out of good still[30] to find means of evil;   30 **still:** always.
Which ofttimes may succeed so as perhaps
Shall grieve him, if I fail not,[31] and disturb   31 **if I fail not:** if I am not mistaken.
His inmost counsels from their destined aim.
But see! The angry Victor hath recalled
170 His ministers of vengeance and pursuit
Back to the gates of Heaven: the sulfurous hail,
Shot after us in storm, o'erblown hath laid
The fiery surge that from the precipice
Of Heaven received us falling; and the thunder,
175 Winged with red lightning and impetuous rage,
Perhaps hath spent his shafts, and ceases now
To bellow through the vast and boundless deep.
Let us not slip[32] the occasion, whether scorn   32 **slip:** lose.
Or satiate[33] fury yield it from our Foe.   33 **satiate:** satisfied.
180 Seest thou yon dreary plain, forlorn and wild,
The seat of desolation, void of light,
Save what the glimmering of these livid flames
Casts pale and dreadful? Thither let us tend

From off the tossing of these fiery waves;
185 There rest, if any rest can harbor there;
And, reassembling our afflicted powers,[34]
Consult how we may henceforth most offend
Our Enemy, our own loss how repair,
How overcome this dire calamity,
190 What reinforcement we may gain from hope;
If not, what resolution from despair."
  Thus Satan, talking to his nearest mate,
With head uplift above the wave and eyes
That sparkling blazed, his other parts besides
195 Prone on the flood, extended long and large,
Lay floating many a rood,[35] in bulk as huge
As whom the fables name of monstrous size,
Titanian, or Earthborn, that warred on Jove,
Briareos or Typhon,[36] whom the den
200 By ancient Tarsus held, or that sea beast
Leviathan,[37] which God of all his works
Created hugest that swim the ocean stream:
Him, haply slumbering on the Norway foam,
The pilot of some small night-foundered skiff,
205 Deeming some island oft, as seamen tell,
With fixèd anchor in his scaly rind,
Moors by his side under the lee, while night
Invests the sea, and wishèd morn delays.
So stretched out huge in length the Archfiend lay,
210 Chained on the burning lake; nor ever thence
Had risen or heaved his head, but that the will
And high permission of all-ruling Heaven
Left him at large to his own dark designs,
That with reiterated crimes he might
215 Heap on himself damnation, while he sought
Evil to others; and enraged might see
How all his malice served but to bring forth
Infinite goodness, grace, and mercy, shown
On man by him seduced, but on himself
220 Treble confusion, wrath, and vengeance poured.
  Forthwith upright he rears from off the pool
His mighty stature; on each hand the flames
Driven backward slope their pointing spires, and, rolled
In billows, leave in the midst a horrid vale.
225 Then with expanded wings he steers his flight
Aloft, incumbent[38] on the dusky air
That felt unusual weight; till on dry land
He lights—if it were land that ever burned
With solid, as the lake with liquid, fire;
230 And such appeared in hue as when the force

34 **afflicted powers:** stricken forces; overthrown armies.

35 **rood:** measure equaling about a quarter of an acre.

36 **fables . . . Typhon:** In Greek mythology, Zeus (the Roman Jove or Jupiter) successfully battled the Titans with the help of the earthborn Giant Briareos; Typhon of Tarsus was a monstrous serpent who attacked Zeus.
37 **Leviathan** [lə vī′ə thən]: biblical sea monster.

38 **incumbent:** lying.

Of subterranean wind transports a hill
Torn from Pelorus,[39] or the shattered side
Of thundering Etna,[40] whose combustible
And fueled entrails, thence conceiving fire,
235 Sublimed[41] with mineral fury, aid the winds,
And leave a singèd bottom all involved[42]
With stench and smoke. Such resting found the sole
Of unblest feet. Him followed his next mate,
Both glorifying to have scaped the Stygian[43] flood
240 As gods, and by their own recovered strength,
Not by the sufferance of supernal[44] power.
  "Is this the region, this the soil, the clime,"
Said then the lost Archangel, "this the seat
That we must change for Heaven, this mournful gloom
245 For that celestial light? Be it so, since he
Who now is sovereign can dispose and bid
What shall be right: farthest from him is best,
Whom reason hath equaled, force hath made supreme
Above his equals. Farewell, happy fields
250 Where joy forever dwells! Hail, horrors! hail,
Infernal world! and thou, profoundest Hell,
Receive thy new possessor: one who brings
A mind not to be changed by place or time.
The mind is its own place, and in itself
255 Can make a Heaven of Hell, a Hell of Heaven.
What matter where, if I be still the same,
And what I should be, all but less than He
Whom thunder hath made greater? Here at least
We shall be free; the Almighty hath not built
260 Here for his envy, will not drive us hence:
Here we may reign secure; and, in my choice,
To reign is worth ambition, though in Hell:
Better to reign in Hell than serve in Heaven."

39 **Pelorus** [pə lôr′əs]: cape in Sicily.
40 **Etna:** volcano on Sicily.

41 **Sublimed:** vaporized.
42 **involved:** enveloped.

43 **Stygian:** hellish. *Stygian* is the adjective form of *Styx,* the name of the river that, in Greek mythology, flows through the Underworld.
44 **supernal:** heavenly.

STUDY QUESTIONS

Recalling

1. According to the invocation (lines 1–26), what subject does Milton want to portray? What adjective does he first use to describe his Muse? What kinds of things does he want his "adventurous song" to pursue? What does he wish to "assert" and "justify"?

2. For what reason have the angels been cast from Heaven? According to Satan's first speech to Beelzebub (lines 84–124), what would be "an ignominy and shame beneath this downfall"? What may the two "with more successful hope" resolve?

3. In his second speech to Beelzebub (lines 156–191), what does Satan say is "miserable"? What does he say will be the chief task of the fallen angels?

4. According to lines 209–220, by whose permission does Satan actually make all movement?

5. In his final speech (lines 242–263), what sort of mind does Satan say he has? What does he say his mind can do? What does he feel is better than serving in Heaven?

Interpreting

6. By calling on a Muse, what does Milton imply about his poetic talent?

7. Identify at least three human flaws that Satan displays.

8. What does Satan's statement in lines 254–255 suggest about reality? Why is this a blasphemous idea?

9. What past experience makes Hell especially unpleasant for Satan and his followers? What desire might nevertheless prompt Satan to draw the conclusion in line 263? Why is Satan's assumption that he will rule in Hell an example of dramatic irony?

Extending

10. In what ways does Satan resemble the hero of a tragedy—such as Shakespeare's *Macbeth,* for example?

VIEWPOINT

In his book on *Major British Writers,* critic Douglas Bush reminds us that

in writing an epic, above all an epic on such a theme as his, Milton naturally wished to raise the reader's mind above mundane affairs, to create a world and an atmosphere befitting his divine and superhuman characters. . . . Milton's elevation of style has the effect of keeping action and scene and characters at a requisite aesthetic distance; everything must have recognizable reality, but not too much.

■ What is "recognizable reality" in Milton's description of Hell? What in the description places Hell beyond our grasp? In what other descriptions in this section does Milton provide "recognizable reality, but not too much"?

LITERARY FOCUS

Style

Through his or her choice and arrangement of words, an author achieves a **style** that distinguishes the author's way of writing from the writing of others. Elements of style include subject and tone, structure, diction, and use of poetic devices.

Subject and tone. In writing *Paradise Lost,* Milton chooses a **subject** in keeping with his devout Puritan beliefs and his scholarly background. His subject is the fall of man; his plot, characters, settings, and themes are drawn from the Bible and are grave and consequential. Milton's **tone,** or attitude toward his subject and audience, is a serious and formal one, appropriate for his grave and lofty subject matter.

Structure. Milton abandons prose for what he called "English heroic verse without rhyme, as that of Homer in Greek and Virgil in Latin" and what we call **blank verse,** or unrhymed lines of iambic pentameter. Not only does blank verse help him imitate the sweeping effect of Homer's and Virgil's classical epics, but it also contributes to his serious tone. Shorter, rhymed lines, because they tend to establish a singsong effect, would have been less suitable.

Sentence length also adds to the sweeping grandeur of the poem. Milton does not squeeze his sentences into one or two lines; instead, he creates extravagant sentences that continue over many lines of verse.

Diction. Milton's **diction,** or word choice, is also elevated. Everyday language would be inappropriate, for it would fatally diminish the epic majesty of the poem. Milton makes use of an extensive vocabulary; in addition, he ensures that his *characters'* diction is suitable to their superhuman status.

Use of poetic devices. Probably the two poetic devices most characteristic of Milton's style are imagery and allusion. Milton's **imagery,** or use of sensory language, is vividly effective in his description of Hell in lines 50–74, for example, and in his description of Satan in lines 192–210. Even more overwhelming is his use of **allusions**—short references to people, places, and events outside the work. Almost all of Milton's allusions are to people, places, and events in classical literature or the Bible. Allusions to these great works stress his serious purpose and help give his poetry a spaciousness and universality that extend it beyond its immediate context.

Thinking About Style

1. To show that the poem uses iambic pentameter, copy two lines and mark the stressed (′) and unstressed (˘) syllables. How many sentences do the poem's first sixteen lines contain?
2. Illustrate examples of Milton's extensive vocabulary by listing three synonyms that he uses for "heavenly."
3. Identify three specific images that Milton uses in describing Hell in lines 50–74.
4. Explain how the allusions in lines 6–10 help to elevate Milton's invocation.

VOCABULARY

Antonyms

Antonyms are words that have opposite or nearly opposite meanings. *Start* and *end* are antonyms. The words in capitals are from *Paradise Lost.* Choose the word that is *most nearly the opposite* of each word in capitals, *as the word is used in the selection.* Write the number of each item and the letter of your choice on a separate sheet.

1. ABYSS: (a) enthusiasm (b) pinnacle (c) chaos (d) monk
2. INFERNAL: (a) celestial (b) diabolical (c) fiery (d) monotonous
3. IMPIOUS: (a) elfin (b) wicked (c) holy (d) intentional
4. OBDURATE: (a) flexible (b) endless (c) cantankerous (d) clever
5. IGNOMINY: (a) misfortune (b) wisdom (c) disgrace (d) esteem

COMPOSITION

Writing About Theme

▧ Write an essay that shows how Milton illuminates the theme, or main idea, of this section of *Paradise Lost.* Begin with a sentence or paragraph that expresses the theme; then explain how Milton develops the theme through plot, characterization, setting, tone, and irony. *For help with this assignment, refer to Lesson 6 in the Writing About Literature Handbook at the back of this book.*

Expanding on a Quotation

▧ Select a quotation from *Paradise Lost,* and show how it might *figuratively* apply to a situation outside the poem. For example, you might write about a real or fictional person who can figuratively "make a Heaven of Hell, a Hell of Heaven" or a person who believes it is "better to reign in Hell than serve in Heaven." Your application might take the form of a character description or a short-short story.

John Bunyan   *1628–1688*

The son of a poor tinsmith, John Bunyan received little education other than a firm grounding in the Bible, yet he wrote the only major work of prose fiction that seventeenth-century England produced. After experiencing a religious conversion, Bunyan joined one of the new Puritan groups, the Baptists, who had recently separated from Puritan Congregationalists. Discovering his natural facility with words, he soon became a preacher, only to be twice arrested after the Restoration for preaching without a license. It was during his second term of imprisonment that he began *The Pilgrim's Progress.*

The Pilgrim's Progress is a religious **allegory**—that is, a work in which characters, settings, and events are all symbols aimed at teaching a moral lesson. One of its most famous incidents tells of Faithful and Christian, two pilgrims bound for the Celestial City, who are forced to pass through a town called Vanity that is holding its town fair.

What are some of the ways in which people display their vanity?

John Bunyan

from **The Pilgrim's Progress**

Christian and Faithful at Vanity Fair

Then I saw in my dream that when they[1] were got out of the wilderness, they presently saw a town before them, and the name of that town is Vanity; and at the town there is a fair kept, called Vanity Fair: it is kept all the year long; it beareth the name of Vanity Fair because the town where it is kept is lighter than vanity; and also because all that is there sold, or that cometh thither, is vanity. As is the saying of the wise, "All that cometh is vanity."

This fair is no new-erected business, but a thing of ancient standing; I will show you the original of it.

Almost five thousand years agone, there were pilgrims walking to the Celestial City, as these two honest persons are; and Beelzebub, Apollyon, and Legion,[2] with their companions, perceiving by the path that the pilgrims made, that their way to the city lay through this town of Vanity, they contrived here to set up a fair; a fair wherein should be sold all sorts of vanity, and that it should last all the year long: therefore at this fair are all such merchandise sold, as houses, lands, trades, places, honors, preferments, titles, countries. . . .

After further description of Vanity Fair and its history, Bunyan returns to the plight of his present-day pilgrims, Christian and Faithful.

Now these pilgrims, as I said, must needs go through this fair. Well, so they did: but, behold,

---

1. **they:** Christian and Faithful.

2. **Beelzebub, Apollyon, and Legion:** devils; evil spirits.

even as they entered into the fair, all the people in the fair were moved, and the town itself as it were in a hubbub about them; and that for several reasons, for—

First, the pilgrims were clothed with such kind of raiment as was diverse from the raiment of any that traded in that fair. The people, therefore, of the fair, made a great gazing upon them: some said they were fools, some they were bedlams,[3] and some they are outlandish[4] men.

Secondly, and as they wondered at their apparel, so they did likewise at their speech; for few could understand what they said; they naturally spoke the language of Canaan,[5] but they that kept the fair were the men of this world; so that, from one end of the fair to the other, they seemed barbarians[6] each to the other.

Thirdly, but that which did not a little amuse the merchandisers was that these pilgrims set very light by[7] all their wares; they cared not so much as to look upon them; and if they called upon them[8] to buy, they would put their fingers in their ears, and cry, "Turn away mine eyes from beholding vanity," and look upward, signifying that their trade and traffic was in heaven.

One chanced mockingly, beholding the carriage[9] of the men, to say unto them, "What will ye buy?" But they, looking gravely upon him, answered, "We buy the truth." At that there was an occasion taken to despise the men the more; some mocking, some taunting, some speaking reproachfully, and some calling upon others to smite them. At last things came to a hubbub and great stir in the fair, insomuch that all order was confounded. Now was word presently brought to the great one of the fair, who quickly came down, and deputed some of his most trusty friends to take these men into examination, about whom the fair was almost overturned. So the men were brought to examination; and they that sat upon them asked them whence they came, whither they went, and what they did there, in such an unusual garb? The men told them that they were pilgrims and strangers in the world, and that they were going to their own country, which was the heavenly Jerusalem; and that they had given no occasion to the men of the town, nor yet to the merchandisers, thus to abuse them, and to let[10] them in their journey, except it was for that, when one asked them what they would buy, they said they would buy the truth. But they that were appointed to examine them did not believe them to be any other than bedlams and mad, or else such as came to put all things into a confusion in the fair. Therefore they took them and beat them, and besmeared them with dirt, and then put them into the cage, that they might be made a spectacle to all the men of the fair.

There, therefore, they lay for some time, and were made the objects of any man's sport, or malice, or revenge, the great one of the fair laughing still at all that befell them. But the men being patient, and not rendering railing[11] for railing, but contrariwise, blessing, and giving good words for bad, and kindness for injuries done, some men in the fair that were more observing and less prejudiced than the rest began to check and blame the baser sort for their continual abuses done by them to the men; they,[12] therefore, in angry manner, let fly at them again, counting them as bad as the men in the cage, and telling them that they seemed confederates, and should be made partakers of their misfortunes. The other replied that for aught they could see, the men were quiet, and sober, and intended nobody any harm; and that there were many that traded in their fair that were more worthy to be put into the cage, yea, and pillory[13] too, than were the men they had abused. Thus, after di-

---

3. **bedlams:** madmen.
4. **outlandish:** foreign.
5. **language of Canaan:** Hebrew, the language of God's chosen people. After the Exodus from Egypt, the Jews returned to the Promised Land, then called Canaan.
6. **barbarians:** those who speak a foreign language; therefore, foreigners.
7. **set very light by:** had little regard for.
8. **they called upon them:** that is, the merchandisers called upon the pilgrims.
9. **carriage:** behavior.

10. **let:** hinder.
11. **railing:** bitter speech; strong criticism.
12. **they:** that is, the baser ones.
13. **pillory:** instrument for public punishment consisting of a wooden board with holes in which to lock the offender's head and hands.

verse words had passed on both sides, the men behaving themselves all the while very wisely and soberly before them, they fell to some blows among themselves, and did harm one to another. Then were these two poor men brought before their examiners again, and there charged as being guilty of the late hubbub that had been in the fair. So they beat them pitifully, and hanged irons upon them, and led them in chains up and down the fair, for an example and a terror to others, lest any should speak in their behalf or join themselves unto them. But Christian and Faithful behaved themselves yet more wisely, and received the ignominy and shame that was cast upon them with so much meekness and patience that it won to their side, though but few in comparison of the rest, several of the men in the fair. This put the other party yet into greater rage, insomuch that they concluded[14] the death of these two men. Wherefore they threatened that neither cage nor irons should serve their turn, but that they should die for the abuse they had done, and for deluding the men of the fair.

Then were they remanded to the cage again, until further order should be taken with them. So they put them in, and made their feet fast in the stocks. . . .[15]

Then a convenient time being appointed, they brought them forth to their trial, in order to their condemnation. When the time was come, they were brought before their enemies and arraigned. The Judge's name was Lord Hate-good. Their indictment was one and the same in substance, though somewhat varying in form; the contents whereof were this—

"That they were enemies to and disturbers of their trade; that they had made commotions and divisions in the town, and had won a party to their own most dangerous opinions, in contempt of the law of their prince." . . .

Faithful is brought to trial separately from Christian. During the trial, witnesses such as Envy and Superstition accuse Faithful, but he responds to their attacks with quotations from the Bible.

Then went the jury out, whose names were Mr. Blind-man, Mr. No-good, Mr. Malice, Mr. Love-lust, Mr. Live-loose, Mr. Heady, Mr. High-mind, Mr. Enmity, Mr. Liar, Mr. Cruelty, Mr. Hate-light, and Mr. Implacable—who every one gave in his private verdict against him among themselves, and afterward unanimously concluded to bring him in guilty before the Judge. And first, among themselves, Mr. Blind-man, the foreman, said, "I see clearly that this man is a heretic." Then said Mr. No-good, "Away with such a fellow from the earth." "Ay," said Mr. Malice, "for I hate the very looks of him." Then said Mr. Love-lust, "I could never endure him." "Nor I," said Mr. Live-loose, "for he would always be condemning my way." "Hang him, hang him," said Mr. Heady. "A sorry scrub,"[16] said Mr. High-mind. "My heart riseth against him," said Mr. Enmity. "He is a rogue," said Mr. Liar. "Hanging is too good for him," said Mr. Cruelty. "Let us despatch him out of the way," said Mr. Hate-light. Then said Mr. Implacable, "Might I have all the world given me, I could not be reconciled to him; therefore, let us forthwith bring him in guilty of death." And so they did; therefore he was presently condemned to be had from the place where he was, to the place from whence he came, and there to be put to the most cruel death that could be invented.

They, therefore, brought him out, to do with him according to their law; and first they scourged him, then they buffeted[17] him, then they lanced his flesh with knives; after that, they stoned him with stones, then pricked him with their swords; and, last of all, they burned him to ashes at the stake. Thus came Faithful to his end.

Now I saw that there stood behind the multitude a chariot and a couple of horses,[18] waiting for Faithful, who (so soon as his adversaries had despatched him) was taken up into it, and straightway was carried up through the clouds,

14. **concluded:** decided upon.
15. **stocks:** instrument of punishment consisting of a heavy wooden frame with holes in which to lock the offender's legs.

16. **scrub:** insignificant person.
17. **scourged . . . buffeted:** whipped and punched.
18. **chariot . . . horses:** an allusion to the biblical story of Elijah, who ascended to heaven in a chariot of fire (II Kings 2:11).

with sound of trumpet, the nearest way to the celestial gate.

But as for Christian, he had some respite, and was remanded back to prison. So he there remained for a space; but He that overrules all things, having the power of their rage in his own hand, so wrought it about,[19] that Christian for that time escaped them, and went his way.

19. **wrought it about:** worked it; shaped events.

STUDY QUESTIONS

Recalling

1. When does the town of Vanity hold its fair? Who first set up the fair?
2. What is the actual destination of the pilgrims compelled to walk through the fair? For what three reasons do the citizens of Vanity immediately recognize that Faithful and Christian are foreigners?
3. Throughout the humiliation and violence to which they are subjected, how do Faithful and Christian behave? What causes the citizens of Vanity to begin fighting among themselves? Who is blamed for the fighting?
4. At Faithful's trial, what is the judge's name? Identify the names of four of the twelve jurors. After they find Faithful guilty, to what do they sentence him?
5. According to the narrator, what is waiting for Faithful after the sentence is carried out? To what gate will it take Faithful?

Interpreting

6. Explain the double meaning of *vanity* in the opening paragraph and throughout the selection.
7. Identify two aspects of the material world that the selection criticizes. What, in general, does the selection suggest about the material world?
8. What does the Celestial City symbolize, or represent? Based on Faithful's experiences, what central message about faith does the selection convey?

LITERARY FOCUS

Allegory

An **allegory** is a narrative or dramatic work in which almost all the characters, settings, and events are symbols representing abstract ideas and in which the overall purpose is to teach a moral lesson. Allegories may take the form of prose fiction, like *The Pilgrim's Progress;* they may be narrative poetry, like *The Faerie Queene* (page 120); or they may be dramas, like the morality plays of the Middle Ages. In simpler allegories, the characters and settings are often given names that clarify the abstract qualities they represent. For example, in *The Pilgrim's Progress,* the character who represents faith is simply named Faithful, and the town that represents vanity is called Vanity.

Thinking About Allegory

■ Identify at least four more characters and one more setting used as symbols in this selection from *The Pilgrim's Progress.* What moral lesson does the selection teach?

VOCABULARY

Words from British History

The word *bedlam,* used in Bunyan's selection, has an interesting origin. Originally, *Bethlehem* was the name of a London insane asylum. Londoners slurred the word in pronouncing it— *Bet'lem* or *bedlam*—and began using it to mean any insane asylum or its patients. Over the centuries the word came to mean what it means today, "any place or scene of great confusion."

Each of the following words or expressions has its origin in a historical person, place, or event in the British Isles. Use a dictionary to find the meaning and origin of each word.

1. badminton
2. derrick
3. canter
4. cardigan
5. in the clink

John Dryden *1631–1700*

John Dryden was the outstanding English poet from the Restoration in 1660 to the end of the century. He was born to a Puritan family in London and was graduated from Cambridge University in 1654. His earliest successful poem, *Heroic Stanzas,* extolled the virtues of Oliver Cromwell, the leader of the movement to rid England of a monarchy. Yet with Cromwell's death and the return of the monarchy, Dryden (like many others in search of order) immediately gave his allegiance to Charles II, the new Stuart king. That allegiance to Charles and later to his Catholic brother James II never faltered, even after the Stuarts had been driven into exile in 1688 and Dryden himself had been deprived of the title poet laureate that they had bestowed on him twenty years earlier.

Dryden wrote verse in several forms: odes, verse dramas, biting satires, and translations of classical authors. Unlike many of his predecessors, Dryden wrote in celebration of noteworthy occasions more often than in response to more personal experiences. Among Dryden's most important legacies to the poets of the next century was his mastery of the **heroic couplet**, paired lines of rhyming iambic pentameter. Another major contribution is Dryden's dignified, unaffected, and always musical language. Both of these poetic elements, along with Dryden's interest in the classics, reflect the influence of Ben Jonson. By fostering Jonson's literary ideas and perfecting his classically inspired forms, Dryden initiated the great age of English neoclassicism, the revival of the styles and attitudes of classical literature, which would remain the dominant literary movement throughout the eighteenth century.

Dryden wrote notable prose as well, including literary criticism of Shakespeare, Chaucer, and others that is as sound in judgment now as when he conceived it. In fact, he is sometimes considered the father of English criticism. His prose is among the first prose that strikes us as modern: It is written in a manner that resembles speech.

Dryden wrote "A Song for St. Cecilia's Day," which begins on the following page, in memory of a Roman woman and Christian martyr who has traditionally been regarded as the patron saint of music and the inventor of the organ. He composed the poem in the form of an ode for a celebration in her memory on November 22, 1687.

Originally a Greek choral song in honor of gods and goddesses, the **ode** as developed by Dryden is a lyric poem of irregular line lengths and stanzas, addressing a serious subject, and written in a dignified style. In 1739 the composer George Frederick Handel composed a score to accompany this ode.

■ For whom would you write an ode?

In this selection, as in one selection in each unit, you will find notes in the right-hand margin that highlight parts of the selection. These notes point out important ideas of the literary period and draw your attention to literary elements and techniques covered in the Literary Focuses. Page numbers in the notes refer you to more extensive discussions of these important ideas and elements.

John Dryden

A Song for St. Cecilia's Day

1

From harmony, from heavenly harmony
    This universal frame[1] began;
  When Nature underneath a heap
    Of jarring atoms[2] lay,
5   And could not heave her head,
The tuneful voice was heard from high,
    "Arise, ye more than dead."
Then cold and hot and moist and dry[3]
    In order to their stations leap,
10   And music's power obey.
From harmony, from heavenly harmony
    This universal frame began:
    From harmony to harmony
Through all the compass of the notes it ran,
15 The diapason[4] closing full in man.

Imagery (p. 177): Dryden enhances his meaning by appealing to the sense of sound.

2

What passion cannot music raise and quell?
    When Jubal struck the corded shell,
  His listening brethren stood around,
    And, wondering, on their faces fell
20   To worship that celestial sound:

Allusion (p. 286): The poet assumes readers are familiar with Jubal, the biblical father of music (Genesis 4:21), whose harp is here described as made from tortoise shell ("corded shell").

1. **universal frame:** the structure of the universe.
2. **jarring atoms:** chaos preceding the arrangement of the universe.
3. **cold . . . dry:** describes earth, fire, water, and air, of which it was thought everything was composed.
4. **diapason** [dī′ə pā′zən]: range of tones of a musical scale; also complete harmony. Dryden is also thinking of the Chain of Being, a view that ordered creation from inanimate nature up through humankind.

Less than a god they thought there could not dwell
  Within the hollow of that shell,
  That spoke so sweetly and so well.
What passion cannot music raise and quell?

3

25   The trumpet's loud clangor
        Excites us to arms
      With shrill notes of anger
        And mortal[5] alarms.
      The double, double, double beat
30   Of the thund'ring drum
        Cries, "Hark, the foes come;
Charge, charge, 'tis too late to retreat."

4

      The soft complaining flute
In dying notes discovers[6]
35   The woes of hopeless lovers,
Whose dirge is whispered by the warbling lute.

Tone (p. 656): The overall tone
is one of celebration, but it
changes somewhat as each
different musical instrument is
described.

5

      Sharp violins proclaim
Their jealous pangs and desperation,
Fury, frantic indignation,
40 Depth of pains and height of passion,
      For the fair, disdainful dame.

6

      But Oh! What art can teach,
      What human voice can reach,
      The sacred organ's praise?
45   Notes inspiring holy love,
Notes that wing their heavenly ways
      To mend the choirs above.

Seventeenth-century idea:
Religion was an overriding
concern (p. 239).

Allusion (p. 286): Here Dryden
alludes to the musician who, in
Greek mythology, enchanted
trees and stones and tamed wild
beasts with his music.

7

Orpheus could lead the savage race,
And trees unrooted left their place,
50   Sequacious of[7] the lyre;
But bright Cecilia raised the wonder higher;
When to her organ vocal breath was given,
An angel heard and straight appeared,
      Mistaking earth for heaven.

---

5. **mortal:** preceding or accompanying death.
6. **discovers:** reveals.
7. **Sequacious of:** following.

Grand Chorus

55 As from the power of sacred lays[8]
    The spheres began to move,
    And sung the great Creator's praise
      To all the blest above;
    So when the last and dreadful hour
60 This crumbling pageant[9] shall devour,
    The trumpet[10] shall be heard on high,
    The dead shall live, the living die,
    And music shall untune the sky.

Seventeenth-century idea: It was believed that heavenly bodies were set in transparent, spherical shells revolving around the earth, put in motion by angelic songs (p. 247).

Paradox (p. 255): The last two lines make statements that at first seem impossible, until we understand the truth behind them.

---

8. **lays:** songs.
9. **pageant:** universe and the spectacle it represents.
10. **trumpet:** the last trumpet, which announces the biblical Judgment Day, or end of the universe (I Corinthians 15:52).

STUDY QUESTIONS

Recalling

1. From what, according to the first stanza, did the universe begin?
2. According to lines 21–23, why did the listeners worship the sound of Jubal's instrument?
3. What musical instruments are referred to in the poem?
4. According to lines 52–54, why did an angel pay a visit to earth?
5. With what sound will the world end, according to the Grand Chorus?

Interpreting

6. Based on an understanding of the Chain of Being (see footnote 4), what is the relationship between notes of a musical scale and all natural things? What does man represent in line 15?
7. What passions are stirred by different instruments in stanzas 3–6? What relationship exists in each of the stanzas between the sound of the words and the instrument that is being described?
8. Of all the musical instruments mentioned throughout the poem, which receives the highest praise? Why?

9. Explain the two paradoxes in the last two lines of the Grand Chorus.

Extending

10. On what occasions in our daily lives does music reflect or heighten our emotions?

COMPOSITION

Writing About a Quotation

▧ Show how Dryden centers his poem around the line "What passion cannot music raise and quell?" Demonstrate how each of stanzas 3–7 expands on that line. Conclude by explaining how the Grand Chorus relates to that line. *For help with this assignment, refer to Lesson 5 in the Writing About Literature Handbook at the back of this book.*

Writing a Description

▧ Read stanzas 3–6 aloud to appreciate the effect of sound on meaning. Think of two contrasting situations—such as climbing up a steep mountain through brush and coasting down a slide into a pool. Describe the two experiences, choosing language with sounds that help convey the difficulty of one situation and the ease of the other.

Dryden was a master of **satire**, literature that exposes to ridicule the vices and follies of people or societies. His verse satire *MacFlecknoe*, whose famous opening appears below, was a response to the criticism of playwright Thomas Shadwell (1642?–1692), who had challenged Dryden's position as the heir to Ben Jonson by claiming to display more of Jonson's wit and impeccable style than Dryden did. *MacFlecknoe* suggests that Shadwell is not Jonson's heir but rather the successor of a recently deceased, notoriously incompetent Irish writer named Richard Flecknoe. (In Irish, *Mac* means "son of.")

John Dryden

from **MacFlecknoe**

All human things are subject to decay,
And, when fate summons, monarchs must obey.
This Flecknoe found, who, like Augustus,[1] young
Was called to empire and had governed long:
5 In prose and verse was owned, without dispute,
Through all the realms of Nonsense, absolute.
This agèd prince, now flourishing in peace,
And blest with issue of a large increase,[2]
Worn out with business, did at length debate
10 To settle the succession of the state;
And, pond'ring which of all his sons was fit
To reign, and wage immortal war with wit,
Cried, " 'Tis resolved; for nature pleads that he
Should only rule who most resembles me:
15 Sh—— alone my perfect image bears,
Mature in dullness from his tender years;

Sh—— alone of all my sons is he
Who stands confirmed in full stupidity.
The rest to some faint meaning make pretense,
20 But Sh—— never deviates into sense.
Some beams of wit on other souls may fall,
Strike through, and make a lucid interval;
But Sh——'s genuine night admits no ray,
His rising fogs prevail upon the day:
25 Besides, his goodly fabric[3] fills the eye,
And seems designed for thoughtless majesty:
Thoughtless as monarch oaks that shade the plain
And, spread in solemn state, supinely reign.
Heywood and Shirley[4] were but types of thee,
30 Thou last great prophet of tautology:[5]
Even I, a dunce of more renown than they,
Was sent before but to prepare thy way.

---

1. **Augustus:** first emperor of Rome. Augustus became emperor in 27 B.C., when he was thirty-two, and ruled for forty-five years.
2. **issue . . . increase:** a large number of offspring.

3. **fabric:** framework; body.
4. **Heywood . . . Shirley:** Thomas Heywood (1575?–1641) and James Shirley (1596–1666), dramatists who by Dryden's day were considered only minor talents.
5. **tautology:** needless repetition, in different language, of the same idea; for example, "false lie."

Dryden's *Essay of Dramatic Poesy* is among the first important works of literary criticism in English. Though Dryden called it an essay, the work takes the form of a dialogue between characters who are actually Dryden and his literary friends: Neander is Dryden himself; Eugenius is the poet Charles Sackville, later Earl of Dorset; Lisideius is Sir Charles Sedley, another Restoration poet; and Crites is Sir Robert Howard, Dryden's brother-in-law and a playwright. In the following famous passage, "Neander" expresses his opinion of Shakespeare, Jonson, and other dramatists.

John Dryden

from An Essay of Dramatic Poesy

As Neander was beginning to examine *The Silent Woman*,[1] Eugenius, earnestly regarded him. "I beseech you, Neander," said he, "gratify the company, and me in particular, so far as, before you speak of the play, to give us a character of the author; and tell us frankly your opinion, whether you do not think all writers, both French and English, ought to give place to him."

"I fear," replied Neander, "that in obeying your commands I shall draw some envy[2] on myself. Besides, in performing them, it will be first necessary to speak somewhat of Shakespeare and Fletcher,[3] his rivals in poesy; and one of them, in my opinion, at least his equal, perhaps his superior.

"To begin, then, with Shakespeare. He was the man who, of all modern and perhaps ancient poets, had the largest and most comprehensive soul. All the images of nature were still[4] present to him, and he drew them, not laboriously, but luckily; when he describes anything, you more than see it, you feel it too. Those who accuse him to have wanted[5] learning give him the greater commendation: he was naturally learned; he needed not the spectacles of books to read nature; he looked inwards, and found her there. I cannot say he is everywhere alike; were he so, I should do him injury to compare him with the greatest of mankind. He is many times flat, insipid; his comic wit degenerating into clenches,[6] his serious swelling into bombast. But he is always great when some great occasion is presented to him; no man can say he ever had a fit subject for his wit[7] and did not then raise himself as high above the rest of poets *quantum lenta solent inter virburna cupressi.*[8] The consideration of this made Mr. Hales of Eton[9] say that there was no subject of which any poet ever writ but he would produce it much better done in Shakespeare; and however others are now generally preferred before him, yet the age wherein he lived, which had contemporaries with him

---

1. *The Silent Woman:* satirical comedy by Ben Jonson, originally called *Epicoene; or, The Silent Woman* (1609).
2. **envy:** spite; resentment.
3. **Fletcher:** John Fletcher (1579–1625), who usually wrote his plays in collaboration with Francis Beaumont (1584–1616).
4. **still:** always; constantly.

5. **wanted:** lacked; required.
6. **clenches:** puns.
7. **wit:** intellectual powers; imagination.
8. *quantum . . . cupressi:* Latin for "as cypresses customarily rise above more yielding shrubs," a quotation from the *Eclogues* of Roman poet Virgil.
9. **Mr. Hales of Eton:** John Hales (1584–1656), scholar who taught at Oxford University and the Eton Public School and was much admired by Ben Jonson and Sir John Suckling.

Fletcher and Jonson, never equaled them to him in their esteem; and in the last king's[10] court, when Ben's reputation was at highest, Sir John Suckling, and with him the greater part of the courtiers, set our Shakespeare far above him.

"Beaumont and Fletcher, of whom I am next to speak, had, with the advantage of Shakespeare's wit, which was their precedent, great natural gifts, improved by study. . . . Their plots were generally more regular than Shakespeare's, especially those which were made before Beaumont's death; and they understood and imitated the conversation of gentlemen much better, whose wild debaucheries and quickness of wit in repartees no poet before them could paint as they have done. Humor, which Ben Jonson derived from particular persons, they made it not their business to describe; they represented all the passions very lively, but above all, love. I am apt to believe the English language in them arrived to its highest perfection; what words have since been taken in are rather superfluous than ornamental. Their plays are now the most pleasant and frequent entertainments of the stage, two of theirs being acted through the year for one of Shakespeare's or Jonson's. The reason is because there is a certain gaiety in their comedies and pathos in their more serious plays which suits generally with all men's humors. Shakespeare's language is likewise a little obsolete, and Ben Jonson's wit comes short of theirs.

"As for Jonson, to whose character I am now arrived, if we look upon him while he was himself (for his last plays were but his dotage), I think him the most learned and judicious writer which any theater ever had. He was a most severe judge of himself, as well as others. One cannot say he wanted wit, but rather that he was frugal of it. In his works you find little to retrench or alter. Wit and language and humor also in some measure we had before him, but something of art was wanting to the drama till he came. He managed his strength to more advantage than any who preceded him. You seldom find him making[11] love in any of his scenes, or endeavoring to move the passions; his genius was too sullen and saturnine to do it gracefully, especially when he knew he came after those who had performed both to such a height. Humor was his proper sphere; and in that he delighted most to represent mechanic people.[12] He was deeply conversant in the ancients, both Greek and Latin, and he borrowed boldly from them; there is scarce a poet or historian among the Roman authors of those times whom he has not translated in *Sejanus* and *Catiline*.[13] But he has done his robberies so openly that one may see he fears not to be taxed by any law. He invades authors like a monarch; and what would be theft in other poets is only victory in him. With the spoils of these writers he so represents old Rome to us, in its rites, ceremonies, and customs, that if one of their poets had written either of his tragedies, we had seen[14] less of it than in him. If there was any fault in his language, 'twas that he weaved it too closely and laboriously, in his comedies especially. Perhaps, too, he did a little too much Romanize our tongue, leaving the words which he translated almost as much Latin as he found them; wherein, though he learnedly followed their language, he did not enough comply with the idiom of ours. If I would compare him with Shakespeare, I must acknowledge him the more correct poet, but Shakespeare the greater wit. Shakespeare was the Homer, or father, of our dramatic poets; Jonson was the Virgil,[15] the pattern of elaborate writing. I admire him, but I love Shakespeare. To conclude of him: as he has given us the most correct plays, so, in the precepts which he has laid down in his *Discoveries*,[16] we have as many and profitable rules for perfecting the stage, as any wherewith the French can furnish us. . . ."

---

10. **last king's:** Charles I's.

11. **making:** depicting; creating.

12. **mechanic people:** people who work with their hands; artisans.

13. ***Sejanus* and *Catiline*:** tragedies by Jonson.

14. **had seen:** would have seen.

15. **Homer . . . Virgil:** Homer's *Iliad* and *Odyssey,* the first important epics in Western literature, were composed in the oral tradition; Virgil's *Aeneid,* composed centuries later, was a *written* epic displaying a more sophisticated craft.

16. ***Discoveries:*** Jonson's miscellaneous notes and other prose, collected as *Timber; or, Discoveries Made upon Men and Matter* (1640).

STUDY QUESTIONS

MacFlecknoe

Recalling

1. Through what realms is the aged Flecknoe "without dispute" the absolute ruler?
2. Which of his sons does Flecknoe decide should succeed him? List four reasons he gives for choosing this son.
3. In the last four lines, how does Flecknoe describe himself and his role?

Interpreting

4. In Dryden's opinion, what sort of writer is Flecknoe? What sort of writer is Sh——?
5. What sort of poem do the opening lines seem to be introducing? How does use of such an opening help create humor? What allusion adds to the humor? Why?
6. What does "last great prophet" suggest about a writer's importance? Why does linking this phrase with "tautology" create a humorous contrast? Find two more phrases that create similar humorous contrasts.
7. Dryden presents the poem in heroic couplets, rhymed pairs of lines using the iambic pentameter associated with heroic, or epic, poetry. What is their effect in this poem? Why would blank verse not be as effective?

Extending

8. Who is Sh——? Do you think Dryden's use of the long dash instead of the writer's full name fooled many of Dryden's contemporaries? If not, why do you think Dryden used it?

An Essay

Recalling

1. What does Eugenius suggest that Neander's opinion of Ben Jonson might be? With what statement in the second paragraph does Neander refute Eugenius' assumption?
2. According to Neander, what did Shakespeare, "of all modern and perhaps ancient poets," have? In what way was Shakespeare "learned"?
3. What is Neander's explanation for the then-current popularity of Beaumont's and Fletcher's plays over Shakespeare's and Jonson's?
4. What does Neander say was "wanting to the drama" before Jonson's arrival? In what does he say Jonson was "deeply conversant"?
5. In distinguishing between Shakespeare and Jonson, what comparison does Neander make to Homer and Virgil? After making that comparison, what does Neander say are his own feelings toward Shakespeare and Jonson?

Interpreting

6. What chief distinction between Shakespeare and Jonson does "Neander," or Dryden, make? Which of the two writers does Dryden like better, and why?
7. What does the opinion of "Mr. Hales of Eton" (paragraph 3) suggest about Shakespeare's scope? Why do you think Dryden cites this opinion and Sir John Suckling's?
8. What does the selection reveal about Dryden's literary tastes in general?

Samuel Pepys   *1633–1703*

In a century known for remarkable offerings in poetry, Samuel Pepys is one of the most important contributors of prose. The fifth child of a well-to-do tailor, Samuel Pepys (pronounced "Peeps") was born in London and studied on scholarships at Cambridge University. Having no independent means, he initially relied on the patronage of his wealthy and influential relatives, the Montagus, especially Edward Montagu, first Earl of Sandwich. With their assistance, he was appointed to his first position in the navy office in 1660.

Through hard work and loyalty, Pepys received additional appointments and rose quickly in the navy office. In 1672 he was appointed Secretary of the Admiralty, or navy department, and under his watchful direction the British navy regained its efficiency and reputation as a major power on the seas. However, his successful public career came to an end with the Glorious Revolution of 1688, and Pepys spent his remaining years in leisurely retirement.

More impressive even than the contributions he made to England in his role as a high public official is the extraordinary private legacy that Pepys left to future generations. On New Year's Day 1660, the then twenty-seven-year-old Pepys began in shorthand a diary that he would keep faithfully for the next nine years, until his failing eyesight forced him to stop. Consisting of six volumes, the diary was not completely deciphered and published until 1825. It is now considered the most famous and valuable diary in English.

Pepys's diary is an endlessly fascinating document, partly because its author was such an important official in the British Admiralty and thus had access to the king and to many other significant Englishmen of the period. In part, the six volumes of diary manuscript are riveting because Pepys was such an enthusiastic and curious individual, full of vitality, willing to see everything and go everywhere, and able to report his experiences and observations fully and honestly. The diary also holds our attention because in the period and place he wrote of there was so much to see: the pageantry of King Charles's ascent to the throne, a horrible plague that ran through London, and the Great Fire of 1666 that destroyed a third of the city, to mention just some of the drama. Finally, the diary reveals the domestic and personal details of one man's life. In fact, no other source gives so vivid a sense of what being alive in London would have been like in the second half of the seventeenth century. Two excerpts from the diary begin on the following page.

▪ What sort of historical information would you put in a diary? What sort of information would you leave out?

Samuel Pepys

from **The Diary**

The Coronation of Charles II

April 23, 1661.   Coronation Day. About four I rose and got to the Abbey, where I followed Sir J. Denham,[1] the Surveyor, with some company that he was leading in. And with much ado, by the favor of Mr. Cooper, his man, did get up into a great scaffold across the north end of the Abbey, where with a great deal of patience I sat from past four till eleven before the King came in. And a great pleasure it was to see the Abbey raised in the middle, all covered with red, and a throne (that is a chair) and footstool on the top of it; and all the officers of all kinds, so much as the very fiddlers, in red vests.

At last comes in the Dean and Prebends[2] of Westminster, with the Bishops (many of them in cloth-of-gold copes),[3] and after them the Nobility, all in their Parliament robes, which was a most magnificent sight. Then the Duke, and the King with a scepter (carried by my Lord Sandwich) and sword and mond[4] before him, and the crown too. The King in his robes, bare-headed, which was very fine. And after all had placed themselves, there was a sermon and the service; and then in the Choir at the high altar, the King passed through all the ceremonies of the Coronation, which to my great grief I and most in the Abbey could not see. The crown being put upon his head, a great shout began, and he came forth to the throne; and there passed more ceremonies: as taking the oath, and having things read to him by the Bishop; and his Lords (who put on their caps as soon as the King put on his crown) and bishops came and kneeled before him. And

three times the King at Arms[5] went to the three open places on the scaffold and proclaimed that if anyone could show any reason why Charles Stuart should not be King of England, that now he should come and speak. And a General Pardon also was read by the Lord Chancellor, and medals flung up and down by my Lord Cornwallis, of silver, but I could not come by any. But so great a noise that I could make but little of the music; and indeed, it was lost to everybody.

I went out a little while before the King had done all his ceremonies, and went round the Abbey to Westminster Hall, all the way within rails, and ten thousand people, with the ground covered with blue cloth; and scaffolds all the way. Into the Hall I got, where it was very fine with hangings and scaffolds one upon another full of brave[6] ladies; and my wife in one little one, on the right hand. Here I stayed walking up and down, and at last, upon one of the side stalls, I stood and saw the King come in with all the persons (but the soldiers) that were yesterday in the cavalcade; and a most pleasant sight it was to see them in their several robes. And the King came in with his crown on, and his scepter in his hand, under a canopy borne up by six silver staves, carried by Barons of the Cinque Ports,[7] and little bells at every end.

And after a long time, he got up to the farther end, and all set themselves down at their several tables; and that was also a brave sight; and the King's first course carried up by the Knights of the Bath. And many fine ceremonies there was of the herald's leading up people before him, and bowing; and my Lord of Albe-

---

1. **Sir J. Denham:** Sir John Denham (1615–1669), English poet and architect.
2. **Prebends** [preb′əndz]: high church officials.
3. **copes:** mantles or capes.
4. **mond:** ceremonial orb or ball of gold or other precious material, representing the globe of the earth.

5. **King at Arms:** chief herald.
6. **brave:** finely dressed.
7. **Cinque** [singk] **Ports:** five English Channel ports.

marle's going to the kitchen and eat[8] a bit of the first dish that was to go to the King's table. But, above all, was these three Lords, Northumberland, and Suffolk, and the Duke of Ormond, coming before the courses on horseback, and staying so all dinnertime, and at last to bring up [Dymock] the King's champion,[9] all in armor on horseback, with his spear and target carried before him. And a herald proclaims, "That if any dare deny Charles Stuart to be lawful King of England, here was a champion that would fight with him"; and with these words, the champion flings down his gauntlet, and all this he do three times in his going up toward the King's table. At last when he is come, the King drinks to him and then sends him the cup, which is of gold, and he drinks it off and then rides back again with the cup in his hand. I went from table to table to see the bishops and all others at their dinner, and was infinitely pleased with it. And at the Lords' table, I met with William Howe, and he spoke to my Lord[10] for me, and he did give me four rabbits and a pullet, and so I got it and Mr. Creed and I got Mr. Michell to give us some bread, and so we at a stall eat it, as everybody else did what they could get. I took a great deal of pleasure to go up and down, and look upon the ladies, and to hear the music of all sorts, but above all, the twenty-four violins.

The London Fire

September 2, 1666. (Lord's Day.) Some of our maids sitting up late last night to get things ready against our feast today, Jane called us up about three in the morning, to tell us of a great fire they saw in the city. So I rose and slipped on my nightgown, and went to her window, and thought it to be on the back side of Mark Lane at the farthest; but, being unused to such fires as followed, I thought it far enough off; and so went to bed again and to sleep. About seven rose again to dress myself, and there looked out at the window, and saw the fire not so much as it was and farther off. So to my closet to set things to rights after yesterday's cleaning.

By and by Jane comes and tells me that she hears that above 300 houses have been burned down tonight by the fire we saw, and that it is now burning down all Fish Street, by London Bridge. So I made myself ready presently, and walked to the Tower,[1] and there got up upon one of the high places, Sir J. Robinson's little son going up with me; and there I did see the houses at the end of the bridge all on fire, and an infinite great fire on this and the other side the end of the bridge; which, among other people, did trouble me for poor little Michell and our Sarah on the bridge.[2] So down, with my heart full of trouble, to the Lieutenant of the Tower, who tells me that it began this morning in the King's baker's house in Pudding Lane, and that it hath burned St. Magnus Church and most part of Fish Street already. So I down to the waterside, and there got a boat and through bridge,[3] and there saw a lamentable fire. Poor Michell's house, as far as the Old Swan, already burned that way, and the fire running farther, that in a very little time it got as far as the Steel Yard, while I was there. Everybody endeavoring to remove their goods, and flinging into the river or bringing them into lighters[4] that lay off; poor people staying in their houses as long as till the very fire touched them, and then running into boats, or clambering from one pair of stairs by the waterside to another. And among other things, the poor pigeons, I perceive, were loath to leave their houses, but hovered about the windows and balconies till they were, some of them

---

8. **eat** [et]: past tense.
9. **King's champion:** a ceremonial office at the coronation; the office had been held by the Dymock family since the coronation of Richard II in 1377.
10. **my Lord:** Pepys's lifelong patron, the Earl of Sandwich.

---

1. **Tower:** the Tower of London.
2. **on the bridge:** London Bridge, the only bridge over the Thames River at that time; its sides were lined with shops and houses.
3. **through bridge:** under the arches.
4. **lighters:** barges.

burned, their wings, and fell down. Having stayed, and in an hour's time seen the fire rage every way, and nobody, to my sight, endeavoring to quench it, but to remove their goods, and leave all to the fire, and having seen it get as far as the Steel Yard, and the wind mighty high and driving it into the City;[5] and everything, after so long a drought, proving combustible, even the very stones of churches. I to Whitehall, and there up to the King's closet[6] in the Chapel, where people come about me, and I did give them an account dismayed them all, and word was carried in to the King. So I was called for and did tell the King and Duke of York[7] what I saw, and that unless his Majesty did command houses to be pulled down nothing could stop the fire. They seemed much troubled, and the King commanded me to go to my Lord Mayor from him and command him to spare no houses, but to pull down before the fire every way. The Duke of York bid me tell him that if he would have any more soldiers he shall; and so did my Lord Arlington afterward, as a great secret. Here meeting with Captain Cocke, I in his coach, which he lent me, and Creed with me to Paul,[8] and there walked along Watling Street, as well as I could, every creature coming away laden with goods to save, and here and there sick people carried away in beds. Extraordinary good goods carried in carts and on backs. At last met my Lord Mayor in Canning Street, like a man spent, with a handkerchief about his neck. To the King's message he cried, like a fainting woman, "Lord! what can I do? I am spent: people will not obey me. I have been pulling down houses; but the fire overtakes us faster than we can do it." That he needed no more soldiers and that, for himself, he must go and refresh himself, having been up all night.

So he left me, and I him, and walked home, seeing people all almost distracted, and no manner of means used to quench the fire. The houses, too, so very thick thereabouts and full of matter for burning, as pitch and tar, in Thames Street; and warehouses of oil, and wines, and brandy, and other things. Here I saw Mr. Issake Houblon, the handsome man, prettily dressed and dirty, at his door at Dowgate, receiving some of his brothers' things, whose houses were on fire; and, as he says, have been removed twice already; and he doubts (as it soon proved) that they must be in a little time removed from his house also which was a sad consideration. And to see the churches all filling with goods by people who themselves should have been quietly there at this time.

By this time it was about twelve o'clock; and so home. Soon as dined, away, and walked through the city, the streets full of nothing but people and horses and carts laden with goods, ready to run over one another, and removing goods from one burned house to another. They now removing out of Canning Street (which received goods in the morning) into Lombard Street, and farther; and among others I now saw my little goldsmith, Stokes, receiving some friend's goods, whose house itself was burned the day after. We parted at Paul's; he home, and I to Paul's Wharf, where I had appointed a boat to attend me, and took in Mr. Carcasse and his brother, whom I met in the street, and carried them below and above bridge, to and again to see the fire, which was now got farther, both below and above, and no likelihood of stopping it. Met with the King and Duke of York in their barge, and with them to Queenhithe, and there called Sir Richard Browne to them. Their order was only to pull down houses apace,[9] and so below bridge at the waterside; but little was or could be done, the fire coming upon them so fast. Good hopes there was of stopping it at the Three Cranes above, and at Buttolph's Wharf below bridge, if

---

5. **City:** the commercial center of London, the part that lay within what had been the medieval city walls.
6. **closet:** room for private devotion.
7. **Duke of York:** King Charles' brother, later James II.
8. **Paul:** St. Paul's Cathedral. The original St. Paul's was destroyed in the fire.

---

9. **apace:** swiftly.

Detail, *The Great Fire of London,* Dutch School, c. 1666.

care be used; but the wind carries it into the City, so as we know not by the waterside what it do there. River full of lighters and boats taking in goods, and good goods swimming in the water, and only I observed that hardly one lighter or boat in three that had the goods of a house in, but there was a pair of virginals[10] in it.

_____

10. **pair of virginals:** type of harpsichord.

Having seen as much as I could now, I away to Whitehall by appointment and there walked to St. James's Park, and there met my wife and Creed and walked to my boat; and there upon the water again, and to the fire up and down, it still increasing, and the wind great. So near the fire as we could for smoke; and all over the Thames, with one's face in the wind, you were almost burned with a shower of firedrops. This is very true; so as houses were burned by these drops and flakes of fire, three or four, nay, five or six houses, one from another. When we could endure no more upon the water, we to a little alehouse on the Bankside, over against the Three Cranes, and there stayed till it was dark almost, and saw the fire grow; and, as it grew darker, appeared more and more, and in corners and upon steeples, and between churches and houses, as far as we could see up the hill of the City, in a most horrid malicious bloody flame not like the fine flame of an ordinary fire. Barbary and her husband away before us. We stayed till, it being darkish, we saw the fire as only one entire arch of fire from this to the other side of the bridge and in a bow up the hill for an arch of above a mile long: it made me weep to see it. The churches, houses, and all on fire and flaming at once; and a horrid noise the flames made, and the crackling of houses at their ruin.

So home with a sad heart, and there find everybody discoursing and lamenting the fire; and poor Tom Hater come with some few of his goods saved out of his house, which is burned upon Fish Street Hill. I invited him to lie at my house, and did receive his goods, but was deceived in his lying there, the news coming every moment of the growth of the fire; so as we were forced to begin to pack up our own goods and prepare for their removal; and did by moonshine (it being brave dry, and moonshine, and warm weather) carry much of my goods into the garden, and Mr. Hater and I did remove my money and iron chests into my cellar, as thinking that the safest place. And got my bags of gold into my office, ready to carry away, and my chief papers of accounts also there, and my tallies into a box by themselves. So great was our fear, as Sir W. Batten hath carts come out of the country to fetch away his goods this night. We did put Mr. Hater, poor man, to bed a little; but he got but very little rest, so much noise being in my house, taking down of goods.

3rd. About four o'clock in the morning, my Lady Batten sent me a cart to carry away all my money, and plate, and best things, to Sir W. Rider's at Bednall Green. Which I did, riding myself in my nightgown in the cart; and, Lord! to see how the streets and the highways are crowded with people running and riding, and getting of carts at any rate to fetch away things. I find Sir W. Rider tired with being called up all night, and receiving things from several friends. His house full of goods, and much of Sir W. Batten's and Sir W. Pen's. I am eased at my heart to have my treasure so well secured. Then home, with much ado to find a way, nor any sleep all this night to me nor my poor wife.

STUDY QUESTIONS

Recalling
1. How does the crowd react when the crown is placed upon the king's head? What further ceremonies occur in the Abbey after the king is crowned?
2. On what day and hour does news of the Great Fire of London first reach Pepys? Who is the first to tell him of it? What had been planned in the Pepys household for that day?
3. Why does Pepys, along with his wife and Creed, find it difficult to remain on the river?
4. When the Pepys household is forced to begin packing up its own goods, why does the diarist take his money and iron chests into his cellar? How does Pepys ultimately carry his money and valuables away from his house?

Interpreting
5. In what mood does the diarist witness the coronation proceedings? How much can you infer from his behavior at the coronation? Does he like crowds, music, and pretty women?
6. What evidence from the diary entry on the London fire would lead you to conclude that Pepys is civic-minded?

Extending

7. The crowning of an English monarch partakes of a long tradition. What aspects of the banquet ceremony seem particularly medieval, out of the mythical court of Malory's King Arthur?

VIEWPOINT

It has been said that Pepys's diary

is so intimate that we feel closer to Pepys than we do to almost any [other] man who has ever written.

—A. C. Baugh

■ Do you agree or disagree with that assessment? What would cause you to identify with a writer?

LITERARY FOCUS

Diaries and Journals

Diaries are personal, day-by-day accounts of impressions and events kept by an individual. Most diaries are private and if published at all are generally not published until after the death of the author. While **journals** also chronicle daily thoughts and events, they are usually less intimate than diaries.

Diaries bring us directly into contact with another person going about his daily business. Pepys's diary is full of the kind of details that would never find their way into an epic poem or a tragic drama: for example, his delight in purchasing a new knife, his irritation at a household servant, his jealousies, and his domestic triumphs and disappointments. These are not the stuff of heroic literature, but they agree with the scale on which most of us lead our lives.

Thinking About Diaries and Journals

■ From the excerpts reprinted here from Pepys's diary, find at least two other reactions or incidents that are appropriate to a diary but not to an epic.

VOCABULARY

Word Origins

Excerpts from Pepys's diary allow us a first-hand view of the English spoken and written by ordinary Englishmen in the seventeenth century. Many of the common nouns that Pepys uses have been in the English language since Old English days. They have developed from Anglo-Saxon or Germanic origins. Many other common nouns in the Pepys excerpts have other histories, however. As explained on page 97, French has had a large impact on the English vocabulary. So, too, have other Latin-based languages such as Italian. Using a good dictionary, look up each of the following words from Pepys's diary, and indicate whether the word came into English from French or from Italian.

1. coronation	6. balconies
2. cavalcade	7. herald
3. scepter	8. scaffolds
4. gauntlet	9. champion
5. violins	10. treasure

COMPOSITION

Citing Evidence and Documenting

■ Write an essay arguing, first, that Pepys was an efficient, businesslike man and, then, that he was a fun-loving, lively man. In order to defend your two portraits of Pepys, cite phrases and sentences from the diary entries. *For help with citing evidence and documenting your sources, see Lesson 3 in the Writing About Literature Handbook at the back of this book.*

Writing a Diary Entry

■ In the form of a diary entry, describe an unusual event that your personal observation enables you to write about confidently. Include specific details to let your reader experience the event fully.

COMPARING WRITERS

■ Reconsider all the works you have read by seventeenth-century writers in this unit. What generalization can you make about their diction, or word choice? How does the diction of the four prose works (by Donne, Bunyan, Dryden, and Pepys) compare? How is the language of Donne's and Jonson's poetry similar, and how is it different? Which poem of the era displays the most elevated diction? Why is its diction appropriate for its subject?

ACTIVE READING

Sound in Poetry

The sound of a poem contributes greatly to the effect that it has on us as readers. Ideally, we should read a poem aloud to appreciate fully its impact.

Poets seek to create an overall pattern or quality of sound that is *appropriate to* the particular mood and meaning of a poem. In order to accomplish this goal, poets manipulate and experiment with the *form* of poetry—for instance, with the various techniques of rhythm, rhyme, alliteration, assonance, consonance, and so on. In all great poems and in any poem that we would call successful, the poet has managed to discover not only the proper words and the proper structure but also exactly the right *sound* needed to convey the sense.

The nineteenth-century English poet Gerard Manley Hopkins (page 538) underscored the importance of sound in poetry when he defined poetry as "speech framed . . . to be heard for its own sake and interest even over and above its interest of meaning." This is perhaps an exaggeration. We should not consider the sound of a poem— no matter how lovely or thrilling it is—to be *more* important than its meaning. We should not even regard the two elements as separable. In any good poem sound and meaning are intertwined and interdependent: Each supports and in turn relies upon the other. If when reading a poem we discount or devalue either element, then we diminish the poem as a whole—and, hence, our *experience* of it. Nevertheless, Hopkins' statement shows just how crucial the component of sound was to *him*.

Poets attempt, then, to produce a special fabric of sound through which meaning can be communicated more directly and forcefully. Consider, for example, Dryden's "Song for St. Cecilia's Day," in which he marvels at the power of music to move us in countless ways. He examines the different effects of musical instruments:

The double, double, double beat
  Of the thund'ring drum . . .
  The soft complaining flute
  In dying notes discovers
  The woes of hopeless lovers.

To emphasize the rousing, rhythmic, pounding qualities of the drum, the poet twice repeats the word *double*. He mainly uses heavy, percussive consonant sounds: "*Th*e," "*dou*-*ble*," "*beat*," "*thund*'ring," "*d*rum." Moreover, the very words *drum* and *beat* sound their meanings; they are, in short, *onomatopoetic* words. One result of these choices is that when we read these lines, we hear the strong, steady beat of a drum. In contrast, Dryden uses quieter, softer consonants and combinations of letters to evoke the gentle, wistful, and sometimes mournful sound of the flute. Notice, for instance, the repetition of light, breathy *f* sounds and delicate *l* sounds: "so*f*t," "comp*l*aining," "*f*lute," "hope*l*ess," "*l*overs." Notice, too, the repetition of *o* sounds: "The w*o*es *o*f h*o*peless l*o*vers." We hear the lonely, plaintive flute in the distance somewhere and, perhaps, even feel some of the sadness it expresses.

When sound and sense are merged, as they are in Dryden's poem, the impact can be emotional as well as intellectual. The poem can reach us and move us with surprising immediacy— much like music can.

REVIEW:
THE ENGLISH VOICE

A Sense of Place

A keen awareness of place has always marked the finest writers. Certainly the *Beowulf* poet, Chaucer, and Shakespeare possessed to a high degree this sense of their surroundings, their environment, the physical reality of their worlds. In the same way, the sense of place gave solidity to seventeenth-century writing.

Journeys and geography took on a new interest after the discoveries made by Elizabethan explorers. This was the century of sailing to America; establishing settlements; trading with India, China, Japan, and Africa. In literature, no matter how metaphysical or unearthly the vision, the concrete sense of place brought it home.

Donne
No man is an island, entire of itself; every man is a piece of the continent, a part of the main.

Marvell
Thou by the Indian Ganges'
  side
Shouldst rubies find; I by the
  tide
Of Humber would complain.

Jonson
But stay, I see thee in the hemi-sphere
Advanced, and made a constellation there!

Shine forth, thou Star of poets.

Milton
"Is this the region, this the soil, the clime,"
Said then the lost Archangel, "this the seat
That we must change for Heaven?"...

Bunyan
And the name of that town is Vanity; and at the town there is a fair kept, called Vanity Fair... because the town where it is kept is lighter than vanity.

Pepys
It is now burning down all Fish Street.... So I... walked to the Tower, and... did see the houses at the end of the bridge all on fire.... It begun this morning in the King's baker's house in Pudding Lane.... It hath burned St. Magnus Church.

Geography, history, metaphysics, and poetry unite in these voices. Donne saw a human "continent." Jonson transformed a poet into a guiding star. Pepys made a city seem as wide as a world. Milton described the unknown and unknowable; Bunyan, perhaps the all too familiar.

Key to Illustrations on Pages 238–239

1. Detail, *The Great Fire of London*, engraving by Wenceslaus Hollar, (1607–1677).
2. Portrait of Ben Jonson (1572–1637), Isaac Oliver.
3. Portrait of John Donne (1572–1631), after Isaac Oliver.
4. Detail, nineteenth-century engraving of Sir Isaac Newton dispersing sunlight through a prism.
5. Seventeenth-century penny-post envelope.
6. Detail, *Charles II of England in the Bay of Dordrecht During His Journey from Mordyk to Delft in 1660*, Willem II van de Velde (1633–1707).
7. Detail, map of London showing London Bridge, 1650.
8. Detail from a seventeenth-century engraving of St. Paul's Cathedral.
9. Portrait of John Milton (1608–1674), artist unknown.

Key to Illustrations appears on page 385.

THE EIGHTEENTH CENTURY

1700–1798

Political and Economic Developments

As the bells of London rang in the year 1700, William III sat alone on the throne. His wife Mary had died six years before. Two years later William himself died and was succeeded by Mary's sister Anne.

The Glorious Revolution that brought William and Mary to England in 1688 had put limitations on the monarchy that would lead, over the centuries, to real democracy. Yet the legitimacy of their rule was not agreed upon by all. Irish Catholics rallied behind the deposed James II; after their rebellion was crushed, penal laws robbed them of political and religious freedom for over a century. Many Scots, too, were Jacobites—supporters of James II and his son James Stuart. However, with the Act of Union of 1707, England and Scotland were politically joined as Great Britain, and in 1745 the last Jacobite rebellion in Scotland was quelled.

Louis XIV, king of France, had also backed James II, but the battle for supremacy between England and France went beyond the matter of the monarchy. As it had been in the struggle with Spain in the time of Elizabeth I, the question was really who would lead Europe as a commercial and colonial power. Thus, throughout the eighteenth century, periodic wars with France disturbed the English peace.

Spinning machine invented by Sir Thomas Arkwright (1732–1792).

During Queen Anne's reign, Parliament—composed of the House of Lords and the House of Commons—found itself dominated by two rival political parties. These parties—the Whigs and the Tories—went on to form the fundamental opposition within the Parliament for the rest of the century. The Tories included most of the British nobility, represented in the House of Lords, and the lesser landowners, known as the "squirearchy" or landed gentry. They sought to advance agricultural interests and preferred an end to the continuing conflicts with France. The Whigs were chiefly from the growing merchant class and represented urban, commercial interests. They sought to promote war with France, which they hoped would lead to British dominance in trade.

Queen Anne favored the Tories. However, Anne outlived all her children, and when she became ill in 1713, many Tories threw support to the Catholic James Stuart, hoping he would convert to the Church of England. He would not, and since by law the crown could not go to a Catholic, it went to the next Protestant in line, a distant relative, the Elector of Hanover, Germany, who in 1714 came to Britain's throne as George I. This marks the beginning of Georgian England, for the first four kings of the new House of Hanover were all named George.

George I spoke no English and was easily guided by politicians in Parliament. He favored the Whigs, since the Tories at first had not supported him. During his reign the Whig-dominated House of Commons—to which members were elected—grew in importance, while the hereditary House of Lords lost some of its superior status. The new power of the House of Commons was another milestone on the road to democracy, although only a small percentage of the population was allowed to vote.

Beginning in the reign of George I, the king's cabinet of ministers, or advisers, were chosen from Parliament. The greatest or "prime" minister of the time was Robert Walpole, a clever Whig who made himself indispensable to the newcomer from Hanover and his successor, George II. During one of the many wars with France—called the Seven Years' War (1756–1763) in Europe and the French and Indian War in America—another Whig leader took center stage. His name was William Pitt. More than any other politician, Pitt saw the need for naval supremacy if Britain were to end commercial competition from France once and for all. His plans were thwarted in 1760 when George II died and was succeeded by his grandson, George III.

Unlike George I and George II, George III believed that the king should play an active role in politics. The costly Seven Years' War had grown unpopular among the Tory squirearchy, with whom the new king was in sympathy. In 1761 George forced Pitt to resign, and two years later an inconclusive peace treaty with the French was signed.

At about this time Britain was undergoing something that would have overwhelming effects on the future of the world. We now call it the Industrial Revolution, but it was not a revolution in the sense of something that happened suddenly. Rather, it was a gradual process of change from "cottage industries," where workers produced goods in their homes, to factory manufacturing, in which goods were produced in far greater quantities and in far less time with the help of newly invented machinery.

The Industrial Revolution, even in its infancy, made factory owners very influential. It became their policy to keep industry from spreading to the colonies. The colonies, they felt, should not be allowed to rival

Detail, *Covent Garden Market,* John Collet, c. 1760.

Britain as producers of finished goods, but should be kept subordinate as suppliers of raw materials and markets for British goods. This policy infuriated many colonists in America. Nor were they pleased when, after the Seven Years' War, their mother country attempted to refill her emptied coffers with a number of irregular taxes. In a series of disastrous decisions, King George III and the now-Tory government pushed the colonists into rebellion, and George III earned for himself the name of tyrant in most American history books.

Naturally, France came to the aid of the Americans. Help also came from the Whig party, which grew critical of Tory policies in America. The American Revolution, as a result, divided British public opinion. Furthermore, poor communications between Britain and the American colonies made it difficult for Britain to conduct the war. After their defeat at Yorktown, the British were forced to sign a treaty setting an amazing precedent: In 1783, Britain recognized America as an independent nation.

Beginning in 1783 a son of William Pitt, also named William, rose on the political scene. Unlike his father, he was able to work with the king, and he soon became the leader of a restructured Tory party. Pitt came to power hoping to solve domestic problems neglected during the almost constant warfare of preceding decades. When in 1789 the French Revolution broke out, assisting the French monarchy was the last thing in Pitt's mind. Ironically, it was the French revolutionaries who declared war on England, putting an end to Pitt's peacetime plans and eventually sweeping Britain into war against the French dictator Napoleon. That conflict, however, was resolved in the nineteenth century.

Life in the Eighteenth Century

The eighteenth century has been called the **Age of Reason,** for it was a time when prevailing philosophy argued that almost anything could be achieved through the calm workings of the human mind. It has been called the **Age of Classicism,** for it saw in all the arts a fascination with ancient Greece and Rome. It has been called the **Age of Elegance,** for it displayed among the upper classes an elegant style of life, a style that ended when the effects of the Industrial Revolution became pronounced and the French Revolution destroyed the belief in an orderly hierarchy in society.

If we look at the hierarchy of eighteenth-century English society, we find first the nobility, then the landed gentry, then the merchants and professionals like doctors and lawyers, and finally the bulk of the population—the poor. For the small group who were not poor, life was very pleasant. The center of social activity was London, to which the nobility and all political families flocked during the social season, the spring session of Parliament. The chief resort was the city of Bath, an architectural gem built over mineral waters thought to be healthful.

The City of London bustled with commerce. In the coffee and chocolate houses, Tories and Whigs argued politics, exchanged gossip, and perused the latest journals.

Whatever the state of Anglo-French relations, British dress was decidedly influenced by fashions in France. Men wore colorful knee breeches and equally colorful coats, vests, and stockings; women wore lavish costumes and laced themselves into corsets so tight that breathing was difficult. Both sexes wore wigs or powdered their hair until a 1790s hair powder tax led to "natural" hairdos.

The arts in this Age of Elegance lack the simplicity of, for example, Elizabethan music. The

Commode made by Thomas Chippendale, 1771–1773.

music of George Frederick Handel dominated the first half of the century, for the German-born composer enjoyed the patronage of the Hanover kings. In architecture we see the Classical influence in the magnificent homes designed by the Adam brothers, with their columns, porticoes, and tall, wide windows that—for the first time in those centuries without electricity—let in the sunlight. Elegant, too, are the grounds of Georgian estates, with landscapes by Lancelot "Capability" Brown, and the interiors of Georgian homes, with their Chippendale, Hepplewhite, and Sheraton furniture and family portraits by Joshua Reynolds and Thomas Gainsborough. Another eighteenth-century painter, William Hogarth, is more famous for satirical sketches of upper-class absurdity and lower-class poverty.

Scientific and technological advances went hand-in-hand with the Industrial Revolution. Especially important were James Watt's steam engine (1769), which provided an efficient means of harnessing power, and James Hargreaves' spinning jenny (1770), which revolutionized the textile industry. The mid-century development of vaccinations helped end the epidemics of earlier centuries, though practices such as bloodletting to reduce fevers still caused many untimely deaths. Coach accidents were also a common cause of death, for with the new prosperity more people traveled, and though roadside inns grew more splendid, the roads themselves remained muddy and dangerous.

Nevertheless, beginning in about 1760 England experienced a population boom, due in part to the new vaccinations and in part to farming improvements that increased England's food supply. This population explosion in turn swelled the ranks of the new labor force that would be an important factor in the century to come.

Literature in the Eighteenth Century

Eighteenth-century literature reflects the ideas and interests of the Age of Reason, the Age of Classicism, the Age of Elegance. Works show a sense of order and moderation; writers display their "wit," or cleverness, but usually not their heart and soul. Prose arguments are calm and logical; poems are carefully structured and often make classical allusions. Many writers satirize "elegant" society or politics, but even when their humor grows bitter, they never abandon the detached, urbane tone of the eighteenth-century wit.

Eighteenth-century England is often called the **Augustan Age,** a reference to the prosperous Rome of Emperor Augustus, when commerce and great literature also thrived. Augustan literature is sometimes divided into two periods, each named for its most influential man of letters—the **Age of Pope** and, after 1750, the **Age of Johnson.**

Alexander Pope was the leading literary figure of Queen Anne's day, the greatest of the so-called Queen Anne Wits. In the work of Pope and his colleagues, the idea of an orderly, hierarchic society modeled on that of "the ancients" is most pronounced. Pope portrays this **Classical**—or **neoclassical**—thinking in long poems such as *Essay on Man,* while in *The Rape of the Lock* he mocks the foibles of "elegant" society.

Pope's fellow Tory Jonathan Swift wrote satire with a sharper edge. In *Gulliver's Travels* he lampoons the events of the day; but this imaginative and biting satire is delightful even to readers today who know nothing of the politics of the age. Swift is also famous for satiric poems and essays.

Samuel Johnson was the great man of letters of midcentury Georgian England. He is noted not only for what he wrote—the first great English *Dictionary,*

Detail, *A Scene from the Beggar's Opera,*
William Hogarth, 1728.

among other things—but for what he believed and said. His witty ideas and conversation are captured by his friend James Boswell in *The Life of Samuel Johnson,* the first modern biography in English.

In addition to Pope and Swift, talented Augustan poets include Matthew Prior, John Gay, Oliver Goldsmith, and William Cowper. Cowper is noted for religious verse with traces of the strong emotion that marks the late eighteenth-century reaction to Classicism known as **Romanticism,** which is described in the next unit. Even more important poets who marked the transition to Romanticism are Thomas Gray, Robert Burns, and William Blake.

Drama in the Eighteenth Century

Most eighteenth-century drama continues the traditions of Restoration playwrights, although tragedies were not as fine as in the preceding century. **Sentimental tragedies** were popular with the growing audience from the merchant class, and the interest in classical literature prompted many **classical tragedies** modeled on those of ancient Rome.

The Augustan comedies are far more memorable than Augustan tragedies. They include John Gay's *Beggar's Opera,* a play with ballads; Oliver Goldsmith's *She Stoops to Conquer;* and Richard Brinsley Sheridan's *Ri-*

vals and *School for Scandal,* satires that gave the stage such famous characters as Mrs. Malaprop.

Prose and the Novel in the Eighteenth Century

The greatest achievements of Augustan literature were not in poetry or drama, however, but in prose. The age gave us not only Johnson's *Dictionary* and Boswell's biography but England's first major literary magazines, *The Tatler* and *The Spectator.* These journals, produced by Joseph Addison and Richard Steele, contain serious essays like those of Francis Bacon and less formal essays known for their satiric humor.

Literary letters flourish in the hands of Lord Chesterfield, while in the area of literary criticism, the outstanding figures are Pope and Johnson. Notable contributions in history, politics, and philosophy include the writings of David Hume; Edward

Gibbon's *Decline and Fall of the Roman Empire* (1776–1788); Adam Smith's *Wealth of Nations* (1776); and Edmund Burke's *Reflections on the Revolution in France* (1790).

However, no prose achievement can outshine the tremendous strides made in the long fictional prose work known as the **novel.** Daniel Defoe's *Robinson Crusoe* (1719), the tale of a traveler shipwrecked on a tropical island, we can number among the best eighteenth-century novels Henry Fielding's *Tom Jones* (1749), Laurence Sterne's *Tristram Shandy* (1759–1767), and Oliver Goldsmith's *Vicar of Wakefield* (1766). Popular types of eighteenth-century novels include the **picaresque novel,** a series of loosely strung episodes about an adventurer or a lovable rogue, best represented by the works of Tobias Smollett; the **novel of sentiment,** a moral tale of romance and tears, such as Samuel Richardson's *Clarissa* (1747–1748); the **gothic novel,** pioneered in English by Horace Walpole and best illustrated by Anne Radcliffe's *Mysteries of Udolpho* (1794); and the **novel of manners,** witty society tales such as those by Fanny Burney and Maria Edgeworth. The modern novel as we know it began to take shape in the eighteenth century; in the nineteenth and twentieth centuries it would evolve into one of the crowning glories of English literature.

TIME LINE

St. Paul's London

1702 William III dies; Queen Anne's reign begins

1707 Union of England and Scotland as Great Britain

1709 Addison and Steele, *The Tatler*

1710 Christopher Wren completes St. Paul's Cathedral

1712 Alexander Pope, *The Rape of the Lock*

1714 George I begins reign

1719 Daniel Defoe, *Robinson Crusoe*

1720 Wallpaper becomes fashionable

1721 Sir Robert Walpole becomes Prime Minister

1726 Jonathan Swift, *Gulliver's Travels*

1727 George II becomes king

1732 Covent Garden Opera House opens

1741 Handel composes *Messiah*

1749 Henry Fielding, *Tom Jones*

1751 Thomas Gray, "Elegy Written in a Country Churchyard"

1752 David Hume, *Political Discourses*

1755 Samuel Johnson, *Dictionary of the English Language*

1701 Japan: Hakuseki writes history of feudal lords

1703 Russia: Peter the Great lays foundations of St. Petersburg

1709 Italy: Invention of pianoforte

1712 India: War of Succession

1714 Holland: Fahrenheit devises mercury thermometer

1721 Germany: Bach completes *Brandenburg Concertos*

1727 Brazil: Coffee first planted

1733 America: Benjamin Franklin, *Poor Richard's Almanack*

1741 Germany: First translation of Shakespeare published

1742 Sweden: Celsius devises the centigrade thermometer

1749 Portugal: Sign language for deaf invented

Jonathan Swift

Dr. Johnson's Dictionary

Samuel Johnson

1756 The Seven Years' War begins

1760 George III begins reign

Josiah Wedgwood founds his pottery works

1765 Parliament passes the Stamp Act

1769 Painter Joshua Reynolds knighted

James Watt patents steam engine

1772 Thomas Chippendale produces furniture

1774 Lord Chesterfield, *Letters to His Son*

1775 Richard Sheridan, *The Rivals*

1783 William Pitt made Prime Minister by George III

1786 Robert Burns, *Poems Chiefly in the Scottish Dialect*

1789 William Blake, *Songs of Innocence*

1791 James Boswell, *The Life of Samuel Johnson*

Thomas Paine, *The Rights of Man*

1794 Mrs. Ann Radcliffe, *The Mysteries of Udolpho*

William Blake, *Songs of Experience*

George III

Watts steam engine

Chippendale furniture

Songs of Innocence by William Blake

Rosetta Stone

1756 France: Sèvres porcelain factory founded

1759 France: Voltaire writes *Candide*

1762 France: Rousseau writes *The Social Contract*

1765 Europe: Potato becomes popular food

1769 France: Shakespeare's *Hamlet* produced

1773 America: Boston Tea Party

1774 Austria: F. A. Mesmer develops hypnosis

1775 America: Revolutionary War begins

1783 America: Treaty of Paris ends the Revolutionary War

1786 Austria: Mozart composes *The Marriage of Figaro*

1789 France: French Revolution begins as mob storms the Bastille

1799 Egypt: Rosetta Stone found

Daniel Defoe   *1660?–1731*

Daniel Defoe is often called the father of the English novel. Not only did he produce *Robinson Crusoe,* which many regard as the first "true" English novel, but he went on to create a string of successful novels, something no writer before him had ever done.

Born Daniel Foe, Defoe may have changed his name to seem more aristocratic (in French names, a *de* signals nobility), or he may have changed it as part of his work as a government spy. Because of those spying activities, much of Defoe's early life is shrouded in mystery. We do know that he was raised a Puritan, though apparently not a devout one, and that his father was a London butcher. Defoe began his literary career with a series of highly satirical poems and pamphlets that more than once placed him in political hot water, despite his work as a government agent. Defoe also worked as a journalist, a background that would prove extremely valuable to his later fiction writing.

In 1719 Defoe published *Robinson Crusoe,* the tale of a fictional sailor shipwrecked on a tropical island. Its success led Defoe to write other book-length prose fictions—or **novels,** as such works were beginning to be called—among them *Moll Flanders* (1722) and *A Journal of the Plague Year* (1722). Most of Defoe's novels are narrated by the title character and claim to be autobiographies. *A Journal of the Plague Year* varies the format slightly by claiming to be a **journal,** a person's day-to-day account of a period in his or her life.

Defoe was inspired to write about the plague in 1721, when Britain braced itself for an epidemic following reports of plague on the Continent. The outbreak never occurred, but for a time interest in the Great Plague of 1665 was renewed. Defoe's *Journal* recounts the experiences of a fictional Londoner, known only as H. F., during 1665, the "plague year." Defoe himself was only five at the time of the tragedy, but he carefully researched his facts by conducting interviews with older survivors. The result is a startlingly realistic historical novel in which all of Defoe's journalistic skills are vividly displayed. The following extract touches on one of Defoe's chief purposes in writing the *Journal*—to examine the reactions of human beings in a time of great stress and devastation.

■ If you were to write a journal, what great historic event would you choose to document?

An English woodcut of the Great Plague of 1665, seventeenth century.

Daniel Defoe

from **A Journal of the Plague Year**

As I went along Houndsditch[1] one morning about eight o'clock there was a great noise. It is true, indeed, there was not much crowd, because people were not very free to gather together, or to stay long together when they were there; nor did I stay long there. But the outcry was loud enough to prompt my curiosity, and I called to one that looked out of a window, and asked what was the matter.

A watchman, it seems, had been employed to keep his post at the door of a house which was infected, or said to be infected, and was shut up. He had been there all night for two nights together, as he told his story, and the day watchman had been there one day, and was now come to relieve him. All this while no noise had been heard in the house, no light had been seen; they called for nothing, sent him on no errands, which used to be the chief business of the watchmen; neither had they given him any disturbance, as he said, from the Monday afternoon, when he heard great crying and screaming in the house, which, as he supposed, was occasioned by some of the family dying just at that time. It seems, the

---

1. **Houndsditch:** London street on the site of an old moat. The narrator lives nearby, in a part of the city that was the hardest hit by the plague.

An English woodcut showing Londoners fleeing to the countryside to escape the Plague, seventeenth century.

night before, the dead cart, as it was called, had been stopped there, and a servant maid had been brought down to the door dead, and the buriers or bearers, as they were called, put her into the cart, wrapped only in a green rug, and carried her away.

The watchman had knocked at the door, it seems, when he heard that noise and crying, as above, and nobody answered a great while; but at last one looked out and said with an angry, quick tone, and yet a kind of crying voice, or a voice of one that was crying, "What d'ye want, that ye make such a knocking?" He answered, "I am the watchman! How do you do? What is the matter?" The person answered, "What is that to you? Stop the dead cart." This, it seems, was about one o'clock. Soon after, as the fellow said, he stopped the dead cart, and then knocked again, but nobody answered. He continued knocking, and the bellman called out several times, "Bring out your dead"; but nobody answered, till the man that drove the cart, being called to other houses, would stay no longer, and drove away.

The watchman knew not what to make of all this, so he let them alone till the morning man or day watchman, as they called him, came to relieve him. Giving him an account of the particulars, they knocked at the door a great while, but nobody answered; and they observed that the window or casement at which the person had looked out who had answered before continued open, being up two pairs of stairs.

Upon this the two men, to satisfy their curiosity, got a long ladder, and one of them went up to the window and looked into the room, where he saw a woman lying dead upon the floor in a dismal manner. . . . But though he called aloud, and putting in his long staff, knocked hard on the floor, yet nobody stirred or answered; neither could he hear any noise in the house.

He came down again upon this, and acquainted his fellow, who went up also; and finding it just so, they resolved to acquaint either the Lord Mayor or some other magistrate[2] of it, but did not offer to go in at the window. The magistrate, it seems, upon the information of the two men, ordered the house to be broken open, a constable[3] and other persons being appointed to

2. **Lord Mayor . . . magistrate:** the mayor of London or some other local official.
3. **constable:** in Defoe's day, a member of the local militia in charge of policing riots, epidemics, and violent crimes. London's civilian police force was not established until the nineteenth century.

be present, that nothing might be plundered; and accordingly it was so done, when nobody was found in the house but that young woman, who having been infected and past recovery, the rest had left her to die by herself, and were every one gone, having found some way to delude the watchman, and to get open the door, or get out at some back door, or over the tops of the houses, so that he knew nothing of it; and as to those cries and shrieks which he heard, it was supposed they were the passionate cries of the family at the bitter parting, which, to be sure, it was to them all, this being the sister to the mistress of the family. The man of the house, his wife, several children, and servants, being all gone and fled, whether sick or sound, that I could never learn; nor, indeed, did I make much inquiry after it.

Many such escapes were made out of infected houses, as particularly when the watchman was sent on some errand; for it was his business to go on any errand that the family sent him on; that is to say, for necessaries, such as food and physic;[4] to fetch physicians, if they would come, or surgeons, or nurses, or to order the dead cart, and the like; but with this condition, too, that when he went he was to lock up the outer door of the house and take the key away with him. To evade this, and cheat the watchmen, people got two or three keys made to their locks, or they found ways to unscrew the locks such as were screwed on, and so take off the lock, being in the inside of the house, and while they sent away the watchman to the market, to the bake-house, or for one trifle or another, open the door and go out as often as they pleased. But this being found out, the officers afterward had orders to padlock up the doors on the outside, and place bolts on them as they thought fit.

At another house, as I was informed, in the street next within Aldgate,[5] a whole family was shut up and locked in because the maidservant was taken sick. The master of the house had complained by his friends to the next alderman[6] and to the Lord Mayor, and had consented to have the maid carried to the pesthouse,[7] but was refused; so the door was marked with a red cross, a padlock on the outside, as above, and a watchman set to keep the door, according to public order.

After the master of the house found there was no remedy, but that he, his wife, and his children were to be locked up with this poor distempered[8] servant, he called to the watchman, and told him he must go then and fetch a nurse for them to attend this poor girl, for that it would be certain death to them all to oblige them to nurse her; and told him plainly that if he would not do this, the maid must perish either of the distemper or be starved for want of food, for he was resolved none of his family should go near her; and she lay in the garret four stories high, where she could not cry out, or call to anybody for help.

The watchman consented to that, and went and fetched a nurse, as he was appointed, and brought her to them the same evening. During this interval the master of the house took his opportunity to break a large hole through his shop into a bulk or stall, where formerly a cobbler[9] had sat, before or under his shop window; but the tenant, as may be supposed at such a dismal time as that, was dead or removed, and so he had the key in his own keeping. Having made his way into this stall, which he could not have done if the man had been at the door, the noise he was obliged to make being such as would have alarmed the watchman; I say, having made his way into this stall, he sat still till the watchman returned with the nurse, and all the next day also. But the night following, having contrived to send the watchman on another trifling errand, which, as I take it, was to an apothecary's[10] for a plaster[11] for the maid, which he was to stay for the making up, or some other such errand that might secure his staying some time; in that time he conveyed himself and all his family out of the house, and left the nurse and the watchman to bury the poor wench—that is, throw her into the cart—and take care of the house.

I could give a great many such stories as these, diverting enough, which in the long course of that dismal year I met with—that is, heard of—and which are very certain to be true, or very near the truth; that is to say, true in the general: for no man could at such a time learn all the particulars.

---

4. **physic:** medicine.
5. **Aldgate:** London neighborhood named for a nearby gate in the city walls. The City of London, the square mile around St. Paul's Cathedral, was once surrounded by walls.
6. **alderman:** high-ranking member of the town council.
7. **pesthouse:** hospital in which people with contagious diseases were isolated.
8. **distempered:** diseased.

9. **cobbler:** shoe repairer.
10. **apothecary's:** druggist's.
11. **plaster:** pasty medicinal ointment, used here to soothe the swollen and broken skin characteristic of bubonic plague.

STUDY QUESTIONS

Recalling

1. According to the narrator, by what means are deceased plague victims removed from their homes? To what buildings are infected people sometimes taken?
2. For what purpose are watchmen employed at infected or possibly infected homes? Why are they sometimes sent on false errands?
3. In both the Houndsditch and Aldgate incidents, what do the survivors manage to do? Whom do they leave behind?

Interpreting

4. What adjective would you use to describe the behavior of the family in the Aldgate home toward the infected maidservant? Is the behavior of the survivors in the Houndsditch home precisely the same? Explain your answer.
5. Based on the selection's details, describe the reactions of London citizens, in general, to the Great Plague. What seems to motivate their actions? How would you describe the response of local government?

Extending

6. How do you think people in your town or city would behave if a great plague struck today? What institutions do we now have to deal with such crises?

LITERARY FOCUS

The Early English Novel

The novel, as its name implies, is a relatively recent literary development. It arose from the prose romances of the Middle Ages—works like Thomas Malory's *Morte D'Arthur* (page 99), which recount legends rooted in history. During the Renaissance, writers like Spain's Miguel de Cervantes (see page 894) branched away from legend and began creating prose fiction from their own imaginations. Thus was born the **novel**, loosely defined as a book-length or longer work of prose fiction. Many scholars elaborate on that definition, how-ever; the *Oxford English Dictionary* defines a novel as a "fictitious prose narrative of considerable length, in which characters and actions representative of real life are portrayed in a plot of more or less complexity." Given the latter definition, there is much dispute over the identity of the first "true" English novel.

In the Elizabethan Age a number of English writers produced book-length prose fictions: Sir Philip Sidney (page 117) wrote *Arcadia* (1590), a prose romance, for example, and Thomas Deloney wrote three books about fictional English tradesmen. Some scholars call these works novels; others claim that these books, because their plots and characterization are sketchy, are merely *forerunners* of the novel. Similarly, the seventeenth century produced a significant English prose fiction, John Bunyan's *Pilgrim's Progress* (page 287). Nevertheless, because its plot lacks complexity and its chief purpose is religious instruction rather than the depiction of real-life situations, *The Pilgrim's Progress* is also usually identified as a forerunner of the novel.

This brings us to what most critics regard as the first "true" English novel, Daniel Defoe's *Robinson Crusoe* (1719). Taking advantage of public interest in the New World, Defoe created a fictional account of a sailor shipwrecked on an island off Venezuela. The book clearly tries to reproduce real life—Defoe even claimed that Crusoe's story was autobiography, for under the title he added "Written by Himself." Even more important are the real-life conflicts around which the plot revolves: the struggle between Crusoe and society that leads to his becoming a sailor and the battle between Crusoe and nature as he seeks to survive on the island. Such real-life conflicts would become standard in English novels for centuries to come.

Thinking About the Early English Novel

■ Identify four details that make *A Journal of the Plague Year* seem to be a real-life account. Around what conflicts with nature and society does the selection revolve?

Jonathan Swift   *1667–1745*

Jonathan Swift is generally thought to be the greatest prose writer of the eighteenth century. He was a man whom many considered a misanthrope (one who hates humankind) because his writings were deeply critical of humanity. It was, however, his deep love for humanity that caused him to criticize it, and his great dream was to cure the ills of his age through humor.

Swift was born of English parents in Ireland and was educated at Trinity College, Dublin. In 1689, with hopes of beginning a political career, he traveled to England to become private secretary to Sir William Temple, a wealthy aristocrat, essayist, and former ambassador to Holland. Swift hoped that Temple, a trusted friend of King William, would return to political life. However, Temple was content to be an occasional adviser to the king, and a few years later a disappointed Swift returned to Ireland to become a minister. After a short, unhappy time in a country parish, Swift returned to Temple's employment and served as his secretary until Temple's death in 1699.

It was in Temple's house that Swift began to write. He first composed awkward odes in the classical style of the ancient Greek poet Pindar, but he soon realized that he had a gift for humorous prose on religious and political themes. By 1697 he had written *A Tale of a Tub,* a comic piece that ridiculed the extravagances of religion, literature, and academia. It was published in 1704 together with *The Battle of the Books,* a mock debate between ancient and modern authors. *A Tale of a Tub* established Swift's position as a great wit and genius of the age, and he began a short collaboration with Joseph Addison and Richard Steele (page 332) on their popular journal *The Tatler.*

After Temple's death, Swift returned to Ireland to be a pastor in a small Protestant parish. In 1710 he became a powerful advocate of the new Tory government, and in 1713, in recognition of his skillful articles and pamphlets in defense of Tory policies, Queen Anne appointed Swift dean of St. Patrick's Cathedral in Dublin. For the more than thirty years until his death, Swift served as dean of St. Patrick's and as champion of the Irish cause. He wrote many pamphlets to protest the suffering of the Irish under their British rulers, and he taught the Irish the power of the boycott when he encouraged them to refuse to accept English goods that competed with their own industries. In his later years Swift underwent a mental decline to which he finally succumbed in 1745. His friends stayed loyal to him, and the Irish people continue to this day to celebrate him as a hero. The generosity of spirit, deep learning, and harsh but humane humor that informed his writing were a great gift to the literary tradition.

Gulliver's Travels (1726) is Swift's greatest achievement. He fashions his observations of the ways of men and women, kings and queens, courts and ministers, into a **parody**, or humorous imitation, of a travel book, one of the most popular kinds of literature in the early eighteenth century. In *Gulliver's Travels* Swift used the form to expose the inadequacies of British politics and society. Captain Gulliver is a ship's surgeon who is washed up on a number of imaginary shores. In each country he makes observations about society in general, and the perspective he gains leaves him sadly disillusioned. He finally returns to England with a painful recognition of his own country's flaws.

Gulliver's first voyage takes him to the island of Lilliput [lil′ ə put′], inhabited by people who are only six inches tall. The Lilliputians [lil′ ə pū′shənz] find Gulliver asleep, shipwrecked and exhausted by his long swim to shore, and they immobilize him by fastening him to the earth with threads and tiny stakes.

■ If you were to parody certain aspects of twentieth-century life, what would they be?

Jonathan Swift

Gulliver's Travels

from **A Voyage to Lilliput**

When I awaked, it was just daylight. I attempted to rise, but was not able to stir: for as I happened to lie on my back, I found my arms and legs were strongly fastened on each side to the ground; and my hair, which was long and thick, tied down in the same manner. I likewise felt several slender ligatures across my body, from my armpits to my thighs. I could only look upwards; the sun began to grow hot, and the light offended my eyes. I heard a confused noise about me, but in the posture I lay, could see nothing except the sky.

In a little time I felt something alive moving on my left leg, which advancing gently forward over my breast, came almost up to my n; when bending my eyes downwards as much as I could, I perceived it to be a human creature not six inches high, with a bow and arrow in his hands, and a quiver at his back. In the meantime, I felt at least forty more of the same kind (as I conjectured) following the first. . . .

I a little loosened the strings that tied down my hair on the left side; so that I was just able to turn my head about two inches. But the creatures ran off a second time, before I could seize them; whereupon there was a great shout in a very shrill accent; and after it ceased, I heard one of them cry aloud, *Tolgo Phonac;* when in an instant I felt above a hundred arrows discharged on my left hand, which

Engraving from an early edition of *Gulliver's Travels*.

pricked me like so many needles; and besides, they shot another flight into the air, as we do bombs in Europe. . . .

I had reason to believe I might be a match for the greatest armies they could bring against me, if they were all of the same size with him that I saw. But fortune disposed otherwise of me. When the people observed I was quiet, they discharged no more arrows; but, by the noise increasing, I knew their numbers were greater; and about four yards from me, over against my right ear, I heard a knocking for above an hour, like people at work; when turning my head that way, as well as the pegs and strings would permit me, I saw a stage erected about a foot and a half from the ground, capable of holding four of the inhabitants, with two or three ladders to mount it: from whence one of them, who seemed to be a person of quality,[1]

made me a long speech, whereof I understood not one syllable. . . .

He appeared to be of a middle age, and taller than any of the other three who attended him; whereof one was a page,[2] who held up his train,[3] and seemed to be somewhat longer than my middle finger; the other two stood one on each side to support him. He acted every part of an orator; and I could observe many periods of threatenings, and others of promises, pity, and kindness.

I answered in a few words, but in the most submissive manner, lifting up my left hand and both my eyes to the sun, as calling him for a witness; and being almost famished with hunger, having not eaten a morsel for some hours before I left the ship, I found the demands of nature so strong upon me that I could not for-

1. **person of quality:** nobleman.

2. **page:** court servant.
3. **train:** long part of his robe that would otherwise trail on the ground.

bear showing my impatience (perhaps against the strict rules of decency) by putting my finger frequently on my mouth, to signify that I wanted food. The *Hurgo* (for so they call a great lord, as I afterwards learned) understood me very well. He descended from the stage, and commanded that several ladders should be applied to my sides, on which above a hundred of the inhabitants mounted, and walked towards my mouth, laden with baskets full of meat, which had been provided and sent thither by the King's orders upon the first intelligence he received of me. I observed there was the flesh of several animals, but could not distinguish them by the taste. There were shoulders, legs, and loins shaped like those of mutton, and very well dressed, but smaller than the wings of a lark. I eat them by two or three at a mouthful; and took three loaves at a time, about the bigness of musket bullets. They supplied me as fast as they could, showing a thousand marks of wonder and astonishment at my bulk and appetite. . . .

I took up the two officers in my hands, put them first into my coat pockets, and then into every other pocket about me, except my two fobs,[4] and another secret pocket which I had no mind should be searched, wherein I had some little necessaries of no consequence to any but myself. In one of my fobs there was a silver watch, and in the other a small quantity of gold in a purse. These gentlemen, having pen, ink, and paper about them, made an exact inventory of every thing they saw; and when they had done, desired I would set them down, that they might deliver it to the Emperor. This inventory I afterwards translated into English, and is word for word as follows.

Imprimis.[5] In the right coat pocket of the *Great Man-Mountain* (for so I interpret the words *Quinbus Flestrin*) after the strictest search, we found only one great piece of coarse cloth, large enough to be a footcloth[6]

for your Majesty's chief room of state. In the left pocket, we saw a huge silver chest, with a cover of the same metal, which we, the searchers, were not able to lift. We desired it should be opened; and one of us stepping into it, found himself up to the mid-leg in a sort of dust, some part whereof flying up to our faces set us both a-sneezing for several times together. In his right waistcoat[7] pocket, we found a prodigious bundle of white thin substances, folded one over another, about the bigness of three men, tied with a strong cable, and marked with black figures, which we humbly conceive to be writings, every letter almost half as large as the palm of our hands. In the left, there was a sort of engine,[8] from the back of which were extended twenty long poles, resembling the pallisado's[9] before your Majesty's court, wherewith we conjecture the Man-Mountain combs his head, for we did not always trouble him with questions, because we found it a great difficulty to make him understand us. In the large pocket on the right side of his middle cover (so I translate the word *ranfu-lo,* by which they meant my breeches), we saw a hollow pillar of iron, about the length of a man, fastened to a strong piece of timber, larger than the pillar; and upon one side of the pillar were huge pieces of iron sticking out, cut into strange figures, which we know not what to make of. In the left pocket, another engine of the same kind. In the smaller pocket on the right side were several round flat pieces of white and red metal, of different bulk: some of the white, which seemed to be silver, were so large and heavy that my comrade and I could hardly lift them. In the left pocket were two black pillars irregularly shaped: we could not, without difficulty, reach the top of them as we stood at the bottom of his pocket. One of them was covered, and seemed all of a piece; but at the upper end of the other, there appeared a white round substance, about twice the bigness of our heads.

---

4. **fobs:** small pockets for watches.
5. *Imprimis* [im pri′mis]: in the first place.
6. **footcloth:** rug.

7. **waistcoat** [wes′kət]: vest.
8. **engine:** device.
9. **pallisado's** [pal′ə sā′dōz]: fence poles.

Within each of these was enclosed a prodigious plate of steel, which, by our orders, we obliged him to show us, because we apprehended they might be dangerous engines. He took them out of their cases, and told us that in his own country his practice was to shave his beard with one of these and to cut his meat with the other. There were two pockets which we could not enter: these he called his fobs; they were two large slits cut into the top of his middle cover, but squeezed close by the pressure of his belly. Out of the right fob hung a great silver chain, with a wonderful kind of engine at the bottom. We directed him to draw out whatever was at the end of that chain, which appeared to be a globe, half silver, and half of some transparent metal; for on the transparent side we saw certain strange figures circularly drawn, and thought we could touch them, until we found our fingers stopped with that lucid substance. He put this engine to our ears, which made an incessant noise like that of a water mill. And we conjecture it is either some unknown animal, or the god that he worships; but we are more inclined to the latter opinion, because he assured us (if we understood him right, for he expressed himself very imperfectly) that he seldom did any thing without consulting it. He called it his oracle,[10] and said it pointed out the time for every action of his life. From the left fob he took out a net almost large enough for a fisherman, but contrived to open and shut like a purse, and served him for the same use: we found therein several massy pieces of yellow metal, which if they be of real gold, must be of immense value.

Having thus, in obedience to your Majesty's commands, diligently searched all his pockets, we observed a girdle[11] about his waist made of the hide of some prodigious animal, from which, on the left side, hung a sword of the length of five men and on the right, a bag or pouch divided into two cells, each cell capable of holding three of your Majesty's subjects. In one of these cells were several globes or balls of a most ponderous metal, about the bigness of our heads, and required a strong hand to lift them: the other cell contained a heap of certain black grains, but of no great bulk or weight, for we could hold about fifty of them in the palms of our hands.

This is an exact inventory of what we found about the body of the Man-Mountain, who used us with great civility and due respect to your Majesty's commission. Signed and sealed on the fourth day of the eighty-ninth moon of your Majesty's auspicious reign. . . .

I had sent so many memorials and petitions for my liberty that his Majesty at length mentioned the matter first in the cabinet, and then in a full council. . . .

Because the reader may perhaps be curious to have some idea of the style and manner of expression peculiar to that people, as well as to know the articles upon which I recovered my liberty, I have made a translation of the whole instrument, word for word, as near as I was able, which I here offer to the public.

GOLBASTO MOMAREN EVLAME GURDILO SHEFIN MULLY ULLY GUE, most mighty Emperor of Lilliput, delight and terror of the universe, whose dominions extend five thousand *blustrugs* (about twelve miles in circumference), to the extremities of the globe; monarch of all monarchs, taller than the sons of men; whose feet press down to the center, and whose head strikes against the sun; at whose nod the princes of the earth shake their knees; pleasant as the spring, comfortable as the summer, fruitful as autumn, dreadful as winter. His most sublime Majesty proposeth to the Man-Mountain, lately arrived at our celestial dominions, the following articles, which by a solemn oath he shall be obliged to perform.

First, The Man-Mountain shall not depart from our dominions, without our license under our great seal.

Secondly, He shall not presume to come into our metropolis, without our express order; at which time, the inhabitants shall have two

---

10. **oracle:** prophet; infallible guide.
11. **girdle:** belt.

hours warning, to keep within their doors.

Thirdly, The said Man-Mountain shall confine his walks to our principal high roads; and not offer to walk or lie down in a meadow, or field of corn.

Fourthly, As he walks the said roads, he shall take the utmost care not to trample upon the bodies of any of our loving subjects, their horses, or carriages; nor take any of our said subjects into his hands, without their own consent.

Fifthly, If an express require extraordinary dispatch, the Man-Mountain shall be obliged to carry in his pocket the messenger and horse, a six days journey once in every moon, and return the said messenger back (if so required) safe to our Imperial Presence.

Sixthly, He shall be our ally against our enemies in the island of *Blefuscu,* and do his utmost to destroy their fleet, which is now preparing to invade us.

Seventhly, That the said Man-Mountain shall, at his times of leisure, be aiding and assisting to our workmen, in helping to raise certain great stones, towards covering the wall of the principal park and other our royal buildings.

Eighthly, That the said Man-Mountain shall, in two moons time, deliver in an exact survey of the circumference of our dominions, by a computation of his own paces round the coast.

Lastly, That upon his solemn oath to observe all the above articles, the said Man-Mountain shall have a daily allowance of meat and drink, sufficient for the support of 1728 of our subjects, with free access to our Royal Person, and other marks of our favor. Given at our Palace at Belfaborac the twelfth day of the ninety-first moon of our reign.

I swore and subscribed to these articles with great cheerfulness and content, although some of them were not so honorable as I could have wished. . . .

Gulliver's second voyage takes him to the island of Brobdingnag [brob'ding nag'], somewhere in the Pacific Ocean in the vicinity of Alaska. In this adventure the tables are turned, for the Brobdingnagians [brob'ding nag'e ənz] are twelve times as tall as Gulliver. Eventually Gulliver finds himself in the court of the king and queen of Brobdingnag, learning the ways of another strange and remote society.

from A Voyage to Brobdingnag

Every Wednesday (which, as I have before observed, was their Sabbath), the King and Queen, with the royal issue of both sexes, dine together in the apartment of his Majesty; to whom I was now become a favorite; and at these times my little chair and table were placed at his left hand before one of the saltcellars. This prince took a pleasure in conversing with me, inquiring into the manners, religion, laws, government, and learning of Europe, wherein I gave him the best account I was able. His apprehension was so clear, and his judgment so exact, that he made very wise reflections and observations upon all I said. But, I confess, that after I had been a little too copious in talking of my own beloved country; of our trade, and wars by sea and land, of our schisms in religion, and parties in the state; the prejudices of his education prevailed so far, that he could not forbear taking me up in his right hand, and stroking me gently with the other; after a hearty fit of laughing, asked me whether I were a Whig or a Tory.[12] Then turning to his first minister, who waited behind him with a white staff, near as tall as the mainmast of the *Royal Sovereign,* he observed how contemptible a thing was human grandeur, which could be mimicked by such diminutive insects as I. "And yet," said he, "I dare engage, those creatures have their titles and distinctions of honor; they contrive little nests and burrows, that they call houses and cities; they make a figure in dress and equipage;[13] they

---

12. **Whig . . . Tory:** the two principal British political parties.
13. **equipage** [ek'wə pij]: horses and carriages.

love, they fight, they dispute, they cheat, they betray." And thus he continued on, while my color came and went several times, with indignation to hear our noble country, the mistress of arts and arms, the scourge of France, the arbitress of Europe, the seat of virtue, piety, honor and truth, the pride and envy of the world, so contemptuously treated. . . .

I one day took the freedom to tell his Majesty that the contempt he discovered towards Europe, and the rest of the world, did not seem answerable to those excellent qualities of mind that he was master of, that reason did not extend itself with the bulk of the body. On the contrary, we observed in our country that the tallest persons were usually least provided with it. That among other animals, bees and ants had the reputation of more industry, art, and sagacity than many of the larger kinds. And that, as inconsiderable as he took me to be, I hoped I might live to do his Majesty some signal service. The King heard me with attention, and began to conceive a much better opinion of me than he had ever before. He desired I would give him as exact an account of the government of England as I possibly could, because, as fond as princes commonly are of their own customs (for so he conjectured of other monarchs by my former discourses), he should be glad to hear of any thing that might deserve imitation.

Imagine with thy self, courteous reader, how often I then wished for the tongue of Demosthenes or Cicero,[14] that might have enabled me to celebrate the praise of my own dear native country in a style equal to its merits and felicity. . . .

This conversation was not ended under five audiences, each of several hours, and the King heard the whole with great attention, frequently taking notes of what I spoke, as well as memorandums of what questions he intended to ask me.

When I had put an end to these long discourses, his Majesty in a sixth audience, consulting his notes, proposed many doubts, queries, and objections, upon every article. He asked what methods were used to cultivate the minds and bodies of our young nobility, and in what kind of business they commonly spent the first and teachable part of their lives. What course was taken to supply that assembly, when any noble family became extinct. What qualifications were necessary in those who are to be created new lords:[15] whether the humor of the prince, a sum of money to a court lady or a prime minister, or a design of strengthening a party opposite to the public interest ever happened to be motives in those advancements. What share of knowledge these lords had in the laws of their country, and how they came by it, so as to enable them to decide the properties of their fellow subjects in the last resort. Whether they were always so free from avarice, partialities, or want that a bribe, or some other sinister view, could have no place among them. Whether those holy lords I spoke of were constantly promoted to that rank upon account of their knowledge in religious matters, and the sanctity of their lives; had never been compliers with the times, while they were common priests; or slavish chaplains to some nobleman, whose opinions they continued servilely to follow after they were admitted into that assembly.

He then desired to know what arts were practiced in electing those whom I called commoners.[16] Whether a stranger with a strong purse[17] might not influence the vulgar voters to choose him before their own landlords or the most considerable gentleman in the neighborhood. How it came to pass that people were so violently bent upon getting into this assembly, which I allowed to be a great trouble and expense, often to the ruin of their fam-

---

14. **Demosthenes** [də mos′thə nēz′] . . . **Cicero** [sis′ə ro′]: ancient Greek orator (384?–322 B.C.) and Roman orator (106–43 B.C.), respectively.

15. **lords:** English nobles and high-ranking clergy who comprised the upper branch of Parliament, the House of Lords.
16. **commoners:** elected representatives who comprise the lower branch of Parliament.
17. **a strong purse:** much money.

ilies, without any salary or pension: because this appeared such an exalted strain of virtue and public spirit that his Majesty seemed to doubt it might possibly not be always sincere. And he desired to know whether such zealous gentlemen could have any views of refunding themselves for the charges and trouble they were at, by sacrificing the public good to the designs of a weak and vicious prince, in conjunction with a corrupted ministry. He multiplied his questions, and sifted me thoroughly upon every part of this head; proposing numberless inquiries and objections, which I think it not prudent or convenient to repeat.

Upon what I said in relation to our courts of justice, his Majesty desired to be satisfied in several points. And this I was the better able to do, having been formerly almost ruined by a long suit in chancery,[18] which was decreed for me with costs. He asked what time was usually spent in determining between right and wrong; and what degree of expense. Whether advocates and orators had liberty to plead in causes manifestly known to be unjust, vexatious, or oppressive. Whether party in religion or politics were observed to be of any weight in the scale of justice. Whether those pleading orators were persons educated in the general knowledge of equity; or only in provincial, national, and other local customs. Whether they or their judges had any part in penning those laws, which they assumed the liberty of interpreting and glossing[19] upon at their pleasure. Whether they had ever at different times pleaded for and against the same cause, and cited precedents to prove contrary opinions. Whether they were a rich or a poor corporation. Whether they received any pecuniary reward for pleading or delivering their opinions. And particularly whether they were ever admitted as members in the lower senate.[20]

He fell next upon the management of our

treasury, and said he thought my memory had failed me, because I computed our taxes at about five or six million a year; and when I came to mention the issues, he found they sometimes amounted to more than double; for, the notes he had taken were very particular in this point; because he hoped, as he told me, that the knowledge of our conduct might be useful to him; and he could not be deceived in his calculations. But, if what I told him were true, he was still at a loss how a kingdom could run out of its estate like a private person. He asked me who were our creditors and where we found money to pay them. He wondered to hear me talk of such chargeable and extensive wars; that, certainly we must be a quarrelsome people, or live among very bad neighbors; and that our generals must needs be richer than our kings. He asked what business we had out of our own islands, unless upon the score of trade or treaty, or to defend the coasts with our fleet. Above all, he was amazed to hear me talk of a mercenary standing army in the midst of peace, and among a free people. He said if we were governed by our own consent in the persons of our representatives, he could not imagine of whom we were afraid, or against whom we were to fight, and would hear my opinion, whether a private man's house might not better be defended by himself, his children, and family than by half a dozen rascals picked up at a venture in the streets, for small wages, who might get a hundred times more by cutting their throats.

He laughed at my odd kind of arithmetic (as he was pleased to call it) in reckoning the numbers of our people by a computation drawn from the several sects among us in religion and politics. He said he knew no reason why those who entertain opinions prejudicial to the public should be obliged to change or should not be obliged to conceal them. And, as it was tyranny in any government to require the first, so it was weakness not to enforce the second; for, a man may be allowed to keep poisons in his closet, but not to vend them about as cordials.

He observed that among the diversions of

---

18. **chancery:** British court that handles equity and common-law cases. Gulliver won his suit but lost all his money in paying the lawyers.
19. **glossing:** commenting.
20. **senate:** here, of the Houses of Parliament: referring to the House of Commons.

our nobility and gentry[21] I had mentioned gaming.[22] He desired to know at what age this entertainment was usually taken up, and when it was laid down. How much of their time it employed; whether it ever went so high as to affect their fortunes. Whether mean vicious people, by their dexterity in that art, might not arrive at great riches, and sometimes keep our very nobles in dependence, as well as habituate them to vile companions; wholly take them from the improvement of their minds, and force them by the losses they received, to learn and practice that infamous dexterity upon others.

He was perfectly astonished with the historical account I gave him of our affairs during the last century, protesting it was only a heap of conspiracies, rebellions, murders, massacres, revolutions, banishments, the very worst effects that avarice, faction, hypocrisy, perfidiousness, cruelty, rage, madness, hatred, envy, lust, malice, and ambition could produce.

His Majesty in another audience was at the pains to recapitulate the sum of all I had spoken; compared the questions he made with the answers I had given; then taking me into his hands, and stroking me gently, delivered himself in these words, which I shall never forget, nor the manner he spoke them in. My little friend *Grildrig,* you have made a most admirable panegyric[23] upon your country. You have clearly proved that ignorance, idleness, and vice are the proper ingredients for qualifying a legislator. That laws are best explained, interpreted, and applied by those whose interest and abilities lie in perverting, confounding, and eluding them. I observe among you some lines of an institution, which in its original might have been tolerable; but these half erased, and the rest wholly blurred and blotted by corruptions. It doth not appear from all you have said how any one perfection is required towards the procurement of any one station among you; much less that men are ennobled on account of their virtue, that priests are advanced for their piety or learning, soldiers for their conduct or valor, judges for their integrity, senators for the love of their country, or counselors for their wisdom. As for yourself (continued the King) who have spent the greatest part of your life in traveling, I am well disposed to hope you may hitherto have escaped many vices of your country. But, by what I have gathered from your own relation, and the answers I have with much pains wringed and extorted from you, I cannot but conclude the bulk of your natives to be the most pernicious race of little odious vermin that nature ever suffered to crawl upon the surface of the earth. . . .

Nothing but an extreme love of truth could have hindered me from concealing this part of my story. It was in vain to discover my resentments, which were always turned into ridicule; and I was forced to rest with patience, while my noble and most beloved country was so injuriously treated. I am heartily sorry as any of my readers can possibly be that such an occasion was given; but this prince happened to be so curious and inquisitive upon every particular that it could not consist either with gratitude or good manners to refuse giving him what satisfaction I was able. Yet thus much I may be allowed to say in my own vindication that I artfully eluded many of his questions and gave to every point a more favorable turn by many degrees than the strictness of truth would allow. For I have always born that laudable partiality to my own country, which Dionysius Halicarnassensis[24] with so much justice recommends to an historian. I would hide the frailties and deformities of my political mother, and place her virtues and beauties in the most advantageous light. This was my sincere endeavor in those many discourses I had with that mighty monarch, although it unfortunately failed of success.

---

21. **gentry:** landowners ranking just below the nobility.
22. **gaming:** gambling.
23. **panegyric** [pan′ə jir′ik]: speech of praise.

24. **Dionysius** [dī′ə nish′əs] **Halicarnassensis** [hal′ə kär na sen′sis]: Greek writer who lived in Rome and tried to persuade the conquered Greeks to submit to the Romans. Swift is being ironic.

STUDY QUESTIONS

Recalling

1. Why do the Lilliputians stop attacking Gulliver?
2. What does Gulliver convince the Lilliputians that he needs? How does he make his wishes clear?
3. What two things do the Lilliputians think Gulliver's watch might be? Why do they think it might be the latter?
4. Name four services that the "Man-Mountain" agrees to provide for the Lilliputians in exchange for his liberty.
5. Why does the king of Brobdingnag ask Gulliver to give an exact account of the government of England? What does Gulliver say the king did as he listened to the account?
6. List five topics that the king questions in the sixth audience with Gulliver.
7. In the second-to-last paragraph, what conclusion does the king draw about the rest of Gulliver's race?

Interpreting

8. What aspects of human nature does Swift seem to be satirizing through Gulliver's huge size in Lilliput? Why is this contrast effective?
9. Reread the final paragraph of "A Voyage to Brobdingnag." How does Gulliver's statement that he gave "every point a more favorable turn by many degrees" affect your opinion of the king and of Gulliver?

Extending

10. Do you think Swift's technique of ridicule is more or less effective than simple, direct criticism? Why?

VIEWPOINT

The late renowned scholar Samuel Holt Monk reminds us that Gulliver

is *not* Jonathan Swift. . . . He is a fully rendered, objective, dramatic character.

Monk goes on to suggest not only that Swift's and Gulliver's perspectives are different but that Swift created a character who is far from the perfect hero.

■ In what ways is Gulliver a dramatic fictional character? In what ways is he a less than perfect hero?

LITERARY FOCUS

Satire

A **satire** exposes the vices and follies of individuals or societies in such a way that they appear ridiculous. Satire ranges from gentle mockery to violent condemnation. It may take any literary shape—poetry, drama, novel, or essay. Whatever the form, the satirist's intent is always to set a moral standard for society and, through the use of humor and wit, to inspire readers to see a particular point of view. As Swift wrote of himself, "His satire points at no defect, / But what all mortals may correct."

Thinking About Satire

■ What are some elements of society that Swift exposes as ridiculous in *Gulliver's Travels*? Is the satire "gentle" or "violent"?

VOCABULARY

Synonyms

A **synonym** is a word that has the same or nearly the same meaning as another word. For example, *love* and *adore* are synonyms. The words in capital letters come from *Gulliver's Travels*. Choose the word that is *nearest* the meaning of the word in capitals, *as the word is used in the selection*.

1. PRODIGIOUS: (a) expensive (b) enormous (c) glorious (d) profound
2. CONJECTURE: (a) guess (b) scribble (c) explore (d) devise
3. CONTRIVE: (a) decorate (b) conceal (c) explore (d) devise
4. SAGACITY: (a) cleverness (b) wisdom (c) talent (d) power
5. FELICITY: (a) pride (b) wealth (c) happiness (d) consistency
6. SANCTITY: (a) sanity (b) cleanliness (c) poverty (d) holiness
7. VEXATIOUS: (a) annoying (b) delirious (c) detrimental (d) lethal
8. PERFIDIOUSNESS: (a) discomfort (b) treachery (c) persuasiveness (d) evil
9. PERNICIOUS: (a) destructive (b) tasteless (c) ill-mannered (d) stingy
10. ODIOUS: (a) condescending (b) loathsome (c) ugly (d) putrid

Joseph Addison 1672–1719
Richard Steele 1672–1729

Joseph Addison.

One of the most famous literary collaborations of all time was that of Joseph Addison and Richard Steele. Their friendship began when they were classmates at the Charterhouse School in London, and it continued through their years at Oxford University. After receiving their degrees, the two went their separate ways for a time. Steele headed straight for London, where he captured much notoriety for his charm and gallantry. He was an officer in the army; the editor of the *London Gazette,* an official newspaper of the Whig party; a member of Parliament; and a theater manager. Addison became known as an excellent Latin scholar, and his long poem *The Campaign* (1704) won him considerable fame. From 1704 to 1710, he served in a variety of government positions.

The two men had very different personalities. Addison was a man of vast learning, serious, prudent, and, although charming with his close friends, reserved in public. His writing is considered to have the better style of the pair. Steele, on the other hand, was buoyant and witty, playful, energetic, and a bit irresponsible; his writing is more creative and inventive than Addison's. The two balanced each other and worked well together, for they shared the same values. Their mutual goal was to improve the manners, morals, and minds of their readers. In 1709 Steele began to publish *The Tatler,* a periodical focusing on news, poetry, learning, philosophy, and general London gossip, and he asked his friend Joseph Addison to contribute notes and articles. Through their short essays the two attempted to reform the manners of the age, refine its tastes, and provide topics of discussion at the popular coffee houses of London. *The Tatler* was discontinued in 1711 for political reasons, but Addison and Steele quickly started a new journal, *The Spectator,* which was issued daily except Sundays from 1711 to 1712.

Richard Steele.

The Spectator was to be nonpolitical and was to "bring philosophy out of the closets and libraries, schools and colleges, to dwell in the clubs and assemblies, at tea-tables and in coffee-houses." The essays that Addison and Steele wrote were of two types: serious essays on such well-known topics as marriage, education, and friendship; and "occasional essays" that, according to Addison, dealt with "the folly, extravagance, and caprice of the present age." Their venture was highly successful.

Despite their success, Addison and Steele again went their separate ways in 1712. The two quarreled over a political matter in 1717, and Addison died in 1719. Nonetheless, their friendship resulted in a great achievement, the creation of the periodical essay.

■ Have you ever taken part in a successful collaboration? What made this project-oriented partnership a productive endeavor?

Steele's vibrant personality made him uniquely suited for involvement in the theater. His gifts to the London stage, as playwright, critic, and theater manager, were rewarded as Steele quickly became a favorite among the best London actors of his day. His devotion to the stage, however, was not simply that of a playful and affectionate man; it also involved a more serious approach that is often reflected in his writing. Steele was one of the foremost practitioners of "sensibility," a literary manner that reveals a sympathetic heart and a quickness to respond to the joys and sorrows of others. Although it is most often used in comedy, Steele maintains the values of sensibility in his more serious philosophical essays. The following essay from *The Tatler* discusses the death of Thomas Betterton, the famous Shakespearean actor of the early eighteenth century.

Richard Steele

from **The Tatler**

The Funeral of Thomas Betterton

Having received notice that the famous actor Mr. Betterton was to be interred this evening in the cloisters[1] near Westminster Abbey,[2] I was resolved to walk thither, and see the last office done to a man whom I had always very much admired, and from whose action I had received more strong impressions of what is great and noble in human nature than from the arguments of the most solid philosophers, or the descriptions of the most charming poets I had ever read. As the rude and untaught multitude are no way wrought upon more effectually than by seeing public punishments and executions, so men of letters and education feel their humanity most forcibly exercised when they attend the obsequies of men who had arrived at any perfection in liberal accomplishments. Theatrical action is to be esteemed as such, except it be objected that we cannot call that an art which cannot be attained by art. Voice, stature, motion, and other gifts must be very bountifully bestowed by nature, or labor and industry will but push the unhappy endeavorer, in that way, the further off his wishes.

Such an actor as Mr. Betterton ought to be recorded with the same respect as Roscius[3] among the Romans. The greatest orator[4] has thought fit to quote his judgment, and celebrate his life. Roscius was the example to all that would form themselves into proper and winning behavior. His action was so well adapted to the sentiments he expressed that the youth of Rome thought they wanted only to be virtuous to be as graceful in their appearance as Roscius. The imagination took a

1. **cloisters:** covered walk.
2. **Westminster Abbey:** great Gothic cathedral in London where many distinguished citizens are buried.

3. **Roscius** [rō′shəs]: greatest Roman actor of his day (126–62 B.C.).
4. **greatest orator:** Cicero, sometimes called Tully (106–43 B.C.), Roman speaker and writer.

lovely impression of what was great and good; and they who never thought of setting up for the art of imitation became themselves imitable characters.

There is no human invention so aptly calculated for the forming of a free-born people as that of a theater. Tully reports that the celebrated player of whom I am speaking used frequently to say, "The perfection of an actor is only to become what he is doing." Young men, who are too unattentive to receive lectures, are irresistibly taken with performances. Hence it is that I extremely lament the little relish the gentry of this nation have at present for the just and noble representations in some of our tragedies. The operas, which are of late introduced, can leave no trace behind them that can be of service beyond the present moment. To sing and to dance are accomplishments very few have any thoughts of practicing; but to speak justly, and move gracefully, is what every man thinks he does perform, or wishes he did.

I have hardly a notion that any performer of antiquity could surpass the action of Mr. Betterton in any of the occasions in which he has appeared on our stage. The wonderful agony which he appeared in, when he examined the circumstance of the handkerchief in *Othello*;[5] the mixture of love that intruded upon his mind upon the innocent answers Desdemona makes, betrayed in his gesture such a variety and vicissitude of passions as would admonish a man to be afraid of his own heart, and perfectly convince him that it is to stab it, to admit that worst of daggers, jealousy. Whoever reads in his closet this admirable scene will find that he cannot, except he has as warm an imagination as Shakespeare himself, find any but dry, incoherent, and broken sentences; but a reader that has seen Betterton act it observes there could not be a word added;

that longer speeches had been unnatural, nay impossible, in Othello's circumstances. The charming passage in the same tragedy, where he tells the manner of winning the affection of his mistress, was urged with so moving and graceful an energy that while I walked in the cloisters, I thought of him with the same concern as if I waited for the remains of a person who had in real life done all that I had seen him represent. The gloom of the place, and faint lights before the ceremony appeared, contributed to the melancholy disposition I was in; and I began to be extremely afflicted that Brutus and Cassius[6] had any difference; that Hotspur's[7] gallantry was so unfortunate; and that the mirth and good humor of Falstaff[8] could not exempt him from the grave. Nay, this occasion in me, who look upon the distinctions amongst men to be merely scenical, raised reflections upon the emptiness of all human perfection and greatness in general; and I could not but regret that the sacred heads which lie buried in the neighborhood of this little portion of earth in which my poor old friend is deposited are returned to dust as well as he, and that there is no difference in the grave between the imaginary and the real monarch. This made me say of human life itself with *Macbeth*:

Tomorrow, tomorrow, and tomorrow,
Creeps in a stealing pace from day to day,
To the last moment of recorded time!
And all our yesterdays have lighted fools
To their eternal night! Out, out short candle
Life's but a walking shadow, a poor player
That struts and frets his hour upon the stage,
And then is heard no more.[9]

---

5. **handkerchief in *Othello*:** Shakespeare's Othello demanded to see the handkerchief he had given to his wife, Desdemona, believing she had given it to another man and was thus unfaithful to him.

6. **Brutus . . . Cassius:** In Shakespeare's *Julius Caesar,* the co-conspirators quarrel after Caesar's death.
7. **Hotspur:** Sir Henry Percy in Shakespeare's *Henry IV* insisted on facing young Prince Hal alone in battle and died in the combat.
8. **Falstaff:** Sir John Falstaff, the lovable old coward in Shakespeare's *Henry IV* and *Henry V.*
9. **Tomorrow . . . heard no more:** Steele quotes, not completely accurately, from an early and somewhat different edition of *Macbeth.*

The famous eighteenth-century critic Samuel Johnson (page 353) recommended that "whoever wishes to attain an English style, familiar but not coarse, and elegant but not ostentatious, must give his days and nights to the volumes of Addison." Addison perfected his famous style in the person of the Spectator, a fictional character whose observations of London life were recorded in *The Spectator*. He is learned, thoughtful, and serious yet has a good sense of humor. In their journal *The Spectator*, Addison and Steele printed many letters in response to the Spectator's essays, some of which were real, but most of which were invented by Addison himself. By printing these fictional letters, Addison could create a dialogue between the Spectator and his supposed readers. The following letter from Ralph Crotchet gives an excellent example of Addison's ironic yet acute observations of London life and the character of his fellow human beings.

Model for Active Reading

In this selection, as in one selection in each unit, you will find notes in the right-hand margin that highlight parts of the selection. Those notes point out important ideas of the literary period and draw your attention to literary elements and techniques covered in the Literary Focuses. Page numbers in the notes will refer you to more extensive discussions of these important ideas and elements.

Joseph Addison

from **The Spectator**

The Cries of London

There is nothing which more astonishes a foreigner, and frights a country squire,[1] than the cries of London. My good friend Sir Roger often declares that he cannot get them out of his head, or go to sleep for them, the first week that he is in town. On the contrary, Will Honeycomb[2] calls them the *ramage de la ville*,[3] and prefers them to the sounds of larks and nightingales, with all the music of the fields and woods. I have lately received a letter from some very odd fellow upon this subject, which I shall leave with my reader, without saying anything further of it.

Informal essay (p. 339): The personal nature and rambling structure of an informal essay allow its author to introduce fictional characters and even a letter in its midst.

---

1. **country squire:** gentleman landowner in the country.
2. **Sir Roger . . . Will Honeycomb:** fictional friends of the Spectator.
3. *ramage de la ville* [rä mäzh′də lä vēl′]: French for "chirping of the town."

Sir,—

I am a man of all business, and would willingly turn my head to anything for an honest livelihood. I have invented several projects for raising many millions of money without burthening[4] the subject, but I cannot get the Parliament to listen to me, who look upon me, forsooth, as a crack and a projector;[5] so that despairing to enrich either myself or my country by this public spiritedness, I would make some proposals to you relating to a design which I have very much at heart, and which may procure me a handsome subsistence, if you will be pleased to recommend it to the cities of London and Westminster.[6]

The post I would aim at is to be Comptroller General of the London Cries, which are at present under no manner of rules or discipline. I think I am pretty well qualified for this place, as being a man of very strong lungs, of great insight into all the branches of our British trades and manufactures, and of a competent skill in music.

The cries of London may be divided into vocal and instrumental. As for the latter, they are at present under a very great disorder. A freeman[7] of London has the privilege of disturbing a whole street for an hour together, with the twanking of a brass kettle or a frying pan. The watchman's thump at midnight startles us in our beds, as much as the breaking in of a thief. The sowgelder's[8] horn has indeed something musical in it, but this is seldom heard within the liberties. I would therefore propose, that no instrument of this nature should be made use of, which I have not tuned and licensed, after having carefully examined in what manner it may affect the ears of her Majesty's liege subjects.

Vocal cries are of a much larger extent, and, indeed, so full of incongruities and barbarisms, that we appear a distracted city to foreigners, who do not comprehend the meaning of such enormous outcries. Milk is generally sold in a note above *ela*,[9] and in sounds so exceeding shrill, that it often sets our teeth on edge. The chimney sweeper is confined to no certain pitch; he sometimes utters himself in the deepest bass, and sometimes in the sharpest treble, sometimes in the highest, and sometimes in the lowest note of the gamut.[10] The same observation might be made on the retailers of small coal, not to mention broken glasses or brick dust. In these, therefore, and the like cases, it should be my care to sweeten and mellow the voices of these itinerant tradesmen, before they make

Eighteenth-century idea: Classifying things into categories is common in Neoclassical literature (p. 312), for the practice follows the scientific method of Aristotle, the Greek philosopher. Here, of course, the categories are not very philosophical or scientific.

Eighteenth-century idea: The urbane eighteenth-century writer displays his wit, or cleverness (p. 312).

---

4. **burthening:** burdening.
5. **projector:** one who invents outrageous business schemes.
6. **Westminster:** a borough of London.
7. **freeman:** merchant.
8. **sowgelder:** one who neuters pigs.
9. ***ela*** [ē′lä′]: a very high note in the musical register.
10. **gamut:** the whole series of notes used by musicians.

Cries of London, "Green-Vegetable Seller" (left) and "Shrimp Girl" (right), P. Sandby (1725–1809).

their appearance in our streets, as also to accommodate their cries to their respective wares; and to take care in particular that those may not make the most noise who have the least to sell, which is very observable in the venders of card matches, to whom I cannot but apply that old proverb of "Much cry, but little wool."

Some of these last mentioned musicians are so very loud in the sale of these trifling manufactures, that an honest splenetic[11] gentleman of my acquaintance bargained with one of them never to come into the street where he lived. But what was the effect of this contract? Why, the whole tribe of card matchmakers which frequent that quarter passed by his door the very next day, in hopes of being bought off after the same manner.

It is another great imperfection in our London cries, that there is no just time nor measure observed in them. Our news should, indeed, be published in a very quick time, because it is a commodity that will not keep cold. It should not, however, be cried with the same precipitation as fire: yet this is generally the case. A bloody battle alarms the town from one end to another in an instant. Every motion of the French is published in so great a hurry, that one would think the enemy were at our gates.[12] This likewise I would take upon me to regulate in such a manner, that there should be some distinction made between the spreading of a victory, a march, or an encampment, a Dutch, a Portugal, or a Spanish mail.[13] Nor must I omit, under this head, those excessive alarms with which several boisterous rustics infest our streets in turnip season; and which are more inexcusable, because these are wares which are in no danger of cooling upon their hands.

There are others who affect a very slow time, and are, in my opinion, much more tunable than the former; the cooper,[14] in particular, swells his last note in a hollow voice, that is not without its harmony; nor can I forbear being inspired with a most agreeable melancholy, when I hear that sad and solemn air with which the

> **Verbal irony** (p. 225): The contrast between what is stated ("musicians") and what is meant (quite the reverse) is an example of verbal irony, a common tool of the eighteenth-century wit.

---

11. **splenetic:** afflicted with low spirits.
12. **Every motion . . . gates:** England and France had been at war, although peace negotiations were in progress.
13. **Dutch . . . mail:** Mail coaches brought letters and news from abroad.
14. **cooper:** one who makes wooden containers, barrels.

public are very often asked if they have any chairs to mend. Your own memory may suggest to you many other lamentable ditties of the same nature, in which the music is wonderfully languishing and melodious.

I am always pleased with that particular time of the year which is proper for the pickling of dill and cucumbers; but, alas, this cry, like the song of the nightingale, is not heard above two months. It would therefore be worthwhile to consider whether the same air might not in some cases be adapted to other words.

It might likewise deserve our most serious consideration, how far, in a well-regulated city, those humorists are to be tolerated, who, not contented with the traditional cries of their forefathers, have invented particular songs and tunes of their own; such as was, not many years since, the pastry man, commonly known by the name of the colly-molly-puff; and such as is at this day the vender of powder and washballs,[15] who, if I am rightly informed, goes under the name of Powder Watt.

I must not here omit one particular absurdity which runs through this whole vociferous generation, and which renders their cries very often not only incommodious, but altogether useless to the public; I mean that idle accomplishment, which they all of them aim at, of crying so as not to be understood. Whether or no they have learned this from several of our affected singers, I will not take upon me to say; but most certain it is, that people know the wares they deal in rather by their tunes than by their words; insomuch, that I have sometimes seen a country boy run out to buy apples of a bellows-mender, and gingerbread from a grinder of knives and scissors. Nay, so strangely infatuated are some very eminent artists of this particular grace in a cry, that none but their acquaintance are able to guess at their profession; for who else can know that "Work if I had it" should be the signification of a corn-cutter?

Forasmuch therefore, as persons of this rank are seldom men of genius or capacity, I think it would be very proper, that some man of good sense and sound judgment should preside over these public cries, who should permit none to lift up their voices in our streets, that have not tunable throats, and are not only able to overcome the noise of the crowd, and the rattling of coaches, but also to vend their respective merchandises in apt phrases, and in the most distinct and agreeable sounds. I do therefore humbly recommend myself as a person rightly qualified for this post; and if I meet with fitting encouragement, shall communicate some other projects which I have by me, that may no less conduce to the emolument of the public.

I am, Sir, etc.

Ralph Crotchet

Satire (p. 331): The entire essay ridicules the abundance of cries on London's streets, though the satire here is mild rather than bitter.

Parody (p. 323): In this humorous imitation of a letter, a typical eighteenth-century letter closing is employed.

---

15. **powder and washballs:** talcum powder and soap.

STUDY QUESTIONS

The Funeral of Thomas Betterton

Recalling

1. At the beginning of his essay, what does Steele say he has learned from Betterton's acting?
2. In the third paragraph how does Steele say the theater helps to form "a free-born people"? What advantages do the theater's tragedies have over the opera's?

Interpreting

3. Express in your own words Steele's final reflections on Betterton's death at the end of the last paragraph.
4. Why is the quotation from *Macbeth* an appropriate ending for this essay?

Extending

5. Do you agree with Steele's observations about the influence of actors on the general public? Why or why not?

The Cries of London

Recalling

1. According to the first paragraph of Addison's essay, what is the subject of Crotchet's letter?
2. What post does Crotchet propose for himself? What are his three qualifications for this post?
3. In the fourth and fifth paragraphs what duties does he propose for himself with regard to "instrumental cries" and "vocal cries," respectively?
4. List four of Crotchet's complaints about the cries of London.
5. At the end of his letter, what does Crotchet say he will do if he is considered rightly qualified for the post?

Interpreting

6. How would you characterize the tone of Crotchet's letter?
7. How do you think the Spectator views Crotchet's proposals? What evidence do you find in the selection to support this opinion?
8. What is *your* opinion of Crotchet?

Extending

9. In what ways do modern city street sounds differ from those of eighteenth-century London?

LITERARY FOCUS

The Essay

An **essay** is generally a short prose composition that discusses a single subject. First used by the French writer Michel de Montaigne, the word comes from the French *essai,* meaning "attempt," and is an apt description of the loose and highly personal thoughts Montaigne recorded. Francis Bacon (page 228) wrote more structured, philosophical discourses. He was the first Englishman to introduce the term *essay* and the first English essayist.

The difference between Montaigne's and Bacon's essays reveals the range and flexibility of the form and points to a standard distinction often made between essay styles. Bacon's type of essay, the **formal essay,** often argues a single point of view in an impersonal, structured, and logical way and usually uses highly serious language. Montaigne's type of essay, the **informal essay,** is more free-form and rambling and is usually highly personal. An informal essay sometimes employs character and description and often uses a fluid, colloquial, and even humorous language.

Thinking About the Essay

■ What qualities make Steele's essay "The Funeral of Thomas Betterton" formal or informal? Support your answer with specific examples from the essay.

COMPOSITION

Writing About Nonfiction

■ In a brief composition on either "The Funeral of Sir Thomas Betterton" or "The Cries of London," state the author's purpose in writing. Then cite with examples the particular techniques that the author uses, such as facts, statistics, examples, and opinion, to accomplish the purpose of the essay. *For help with this assignment, refer to Lesson 4 in the Writing About Literature Handbook at the back of this book.*

Writing an Informal Essay

■ Write either a brief descriptive essay (like Addison's) or a brief meditative essay (like Steele's) in which you try to convey the feeling of a place or person. The essay should be free form, in fluid or even humorous language.

Alexander Pope   *1688–1744*

In an age of satire, Alexander Pope was the greatest verse satirist. His achievements are especially notable in light of the hardships he had to overcome. Born a Catholic, he was therefore barred from attending a university or receiving a government post, the source of income on which many writers of the day depended. In addition he had contracted tuberculosis of the spine in childhood and was permanently crippled, never growing beyond four feet six inches tall and suffering from severe pain throughout his life.

Pope recognized his own limitations, and from an early age he labored to overcome them. He began by giving himself the strict classical education that most other young men received at school, and at the age of twenty-one he published a group of pastoral, or nature, poems. Almost immediately he was hailed as a literary prodigy and brought into a tight London literary circle that included Swift, Addison, Steele, and the poets John Gay and John Arbuthnot. His *Essay on Criticism* (1711) impressed Londoners with its evidence of learning and good judgment, and by the age of twenty-five Pope was acknowledged England's greatest living poet. By 1718 he was the first English author to support himself solely by his writings.

Pope's poems rapidly developed from the gentle lyrics of his earlier years into biting satires of English society and politics. Like his friend Jonathan Swift, he saw the age as one badly in need of the correction that satire could offer. Unfortunately, his satires gained him many enemies, who brutally attacked not only his poetry but also his religion and his physical deformities. When he was not busy writing poems and cultivating the magnificent garden at his estate at Twickenham [twit'nam], he was busy defending himself from his enemies, who had labeled him "the wicked wasp of Twickenham," a title that unfairly portrays him as a mean-spirited man who lashed out at all around him. Fortunately, the loyalty of his friends attests to the fact that he was gentler and more generous than his critics liked to portray.

Pope believed that moral and artistic correctness went hand-in-hand and that one could best practice this correctness by following the models of the ancient Greek and Roman authors. He felt that many of the ills of society could be cured by looking back to classical civilization. All of his poetry reflects these neoclassical values, whether it be the informative *Essay on Criticism; The Dunciad,* his sparkling satire of literary pretension; or the philosophical *Essay on Man.* It is not Pope's philosophy, however, but the brilliance of his poetic art that qualifies him as one of the greatest poets in the English language. The compression of his language, its clarity, glitter, exactness, and beauty—lyrical by turns, satiric by turns—all these qualities unite to form verses that only a master craftsman could create.

Pope's *Rape of the Lock,* one of his greatest comic poems, was based on an actual event. A wealthy baron named Lord Petre had cut a lock of hair from the beautiful Arabella Fermor's head and refused to give it back. A great scandal ensued. At the urging of his friend John Caryll, to whom he addresses the poem, Pope created a miniature masterpiece of satire out of the event.

Although Pope was certainly mocking the extravagance of the drawing room society that is his subject, his careful observation of the details of that society shows that he also had an appreciation of its beauties. Belinda, the heroine of the poem, is a fully developed character, and her world, despite its frivolity, is a complete one.

Pope wrote two versions of *The Rape of the Lock.* In 1712 he published a two-canto version, a tremendously popular poem that Joseph Addison considered to be perfect. In 1713 Pope began a second, expanded version of five cantos, which included supernatural characters and an elaborate card game. The original two-canto version Addison so admired is presented here.

■ What are the dangers of being overly concerned with the trends and fashions of the day?

Alexander Pope

The Rape of the Lock

Canto I

What dire offense from amorous causes springs,
What mighty quarrels rise from trivial things,
I sing—This verse to C—l,[1] Muse![2] is due;
This, even Belinda may vouchsafe to view:
5 Slight is the subject, but not so the praise,
If she inspire, and he approve my lays.
  Say what strange motive, goddess! could compel
A well-bred lord t'assault a gentle belle?[3]
Oh say what stranger cause, yet unexplored,
10 Could make a gentle belle reject a lord?
And dwells such rage in softest bosoms then?
And lodge such daring souls in little men?
  Sol[4] through white curtains did his beams display,

---

1. **C——l:** Pope's friend, John Caryll, who suggested the subject of the poem.
2. **Muse:** the poet's inspiring goddess.
3. **belle:** young lady, in this case Belinda, the heroine of the poem.
4. **Sol:** the sun.

And oped those eyes which brighter shine than they;
15 Shock[5] just had given himself the rousing shake,
And nymphs prepared their chocolate[6] to take;
Thrice the wrought slipper knocked against the ground,[7]
And striking watches the tenth hour resound.
Belinda rose, and 'midst attending dames
20 Launched on the bosom of the silver Thames:[8]
A train of well dressed youths around her shone,
And every eye was fixed on her alone;
Her lively looks a sprightly mind disclose,
Quick as her eyes, and as unfixed as those:
25 Favors to none, to all she smiles extends;
Oft she rejects, but never once offends.
Bright as the sun her eyes the gazers strike,
And, like the sun, they shine on all alike.
Yet graceful ease, and sweetness void of pride,
30 Might hide her faults, if belles had faults to hide:
If to her share some female errors fall,
Look on her face, and you'll forgive them all.
   This nymph, to the destruction of mankind,
Nourished two locks, which graceful hung behind
35 In equal curls, and well conspired to deck
With shining ringlets her smooth ivory neck.
Love in these labyrinths his slaves detains,
And mighty hearts are held in slender chains.
With hairy sprindges[9] we the birds betray,
40 Slight lines of hair surprise the finny prey,[10]
Fair tresses man's imperial race ensnare,
And beauty draws us with a single hair.
   Th' adventrous Baron the bright locks admired,
He saw, he wished, and to the prize aspired:
45 Resolved to win, he meditates the way,
By force to ravish, or by fraud betray;
For when success a lover's toil attends,
Few ask, if fraud or force attained his ends.
   For this, ere Phoebus[11] rose, he had implored
50 Propitious heaven, and every power adored,
But chiefly Love—to Love an altar built,

The lovely, lively Belinda awakes and then takes a boat trip on the Thames River (lines 19–20).

Belinda has two curls resting on her neck (lines 33–35).

The Baron admires them and resolves to obtain them (lines 43–45).

---

5. **Shock:** one of Belinda's dogs.
6. **chocolate:** hot cocoa, a morning beverage.
7. **Thrice . . . ground:** Belinda is banging her slipper on the ground to call her maid.
8. **Thames:** the river that passes through London.
9. **sprindges** [sprinʹjəz]: traps containing nooses. Pope is detailing the uses of hair for entrapment.
10. **finny prey:** fish, which are caught with hairlike fishline.
11. **Phoebus** [fēʹbəs]: the sun; Phoebus Apollo was god of the sun.

Of twelve vast French romances, neatly gilt.
There lay the sword-knot[12] Sylvia's hands had sown,
With Flavia's[13] busk[14] that oft had rapped his own:
55 A fan, a garter, half a pair of gloves;
And all the trophies of his former loves.
With tender billet-doux[15] he lights the pyre,
And breaths three amorous sighs to raise the fire.
Then prostrate falls, and begs with ardent eyes
60 Soon to obtain, and long possess the prize:
The powers gave ear, and granted half his prayer,
The rest, the winds dispersed in empty air.

   Close by those meads[16] for ever crowned with flowers,
Where Thames with pride surveys his rising towers,
65 There stands a structure of majestic frame,[17]
Which from the neighboring Hampton takes its name.
Here Britain's statesmen oft the fall foredoom
Of foreign tyrants, and of nymphs at home;
Here thou, great Anna![18] whom three realms obey,
70 Dost sometimes counsel take—and sometimes tea.
   Hither our nymphs and heroes did resort,
To taste awhile the pleasures of a court;
In various talk the cheerful hours they passed,
Of, who was bitt, or who capotted[19] last:
75 This speaks the glory of the British Queen,
And that describes a charming Indian screen;
A third interprets motions, looks, and eyes;
At every word a reputation dies.
Snuff, or the fan, supply each pause of chat,
80 With singing, laughing, ogling, and all that.
   Now, when declining from the noon of day,
The sun obliquely shoots his burning ray;
When hungry judges soon the sentence sign,
And wretches hang that jury men may dine;
85 When merchants from th' Exchange[20] return in peace,
And the long labors of the toilette[21] cease—

The fashionable people—including Belinda and the Baron— gather at Hampton Court to take tea (lines 63–72).

---

12. **sword-knot:** ribbon tied to the hilt of a sword.
13. **Sylvia's . . . Flavia's:** referring to young ladies who had flirted with the Baron in the past.
14. **busk:** a strip used to support a corset.
15. **billet-doux** [bil′ē doo′]: love letter.
16. **meads:** wet, grassy lands.
17. **structure . . . frame:** Hampton Court, the royal palace.
18. **Anna:** Queen Anne, who ruled Great Britain and Ireland, and claimed to rule France: thus, "whom three Realms obey."
19. **bitt . . . capotted:** card-playing terms for "cheated" and "scored all the tricks," respectively.
20. **Exchange:** the place where merchants traded their goods.
21. **toilette** [twä let′]: the process of washing and grooming oneself.

The board's with cups and spoons, alternate, crowned;[22]
The berries crackle, and the mill turns round;
On shining altars of Japan they raise
90 The silver lamp, and fiery spirits blaze;
From silver spouts the grateful liquors glide,
And China's earth receives the smoking tide;
At once they gratify their smell and taste,
While frequent cups prolong the rich repast.
95 Coffee (which makes the politician wise,
And see through all things with his half-shut eyes),
Sent up in vapors to the Baron's brain
New stratagems, the radiant lock to gain.
Ah cease rash youth! desist ere 'tis too late,
100 Fear the just gods, and think of Scylla's fate![23]
Changed to a bird, and sent to flit in air,
She dearly pays for Nisus' injured hair!
      But when to mischief mortals bend their mind,
How soon fit instruments of ill they find?
105 Just then, Clarissa[24] drew with tempting grace
A two-edged weapon from her shining case;
So ladies in romance assist their knight,
Present the spear, and arm him for the fight.
He takes the gift with reverence, and extends
110 The little engine[25] on his fingers' ends,
This just behind Belinda's neck he spread,
As o'er the fragrant steams she bends her head:
He first expands the glittering forfex[26] wide
T'inclose the lock; then joins it, to divide;
115 One fatal stroke the sacred hair does sever
From the fair head, forever, and forever!
      The living fires come flashing from her eyes,
And screams of horror rend th' affrighted skies.
Not louder shrieks by dames to Heaven are cast,
120 When husbands die, or lap dogs breath their last,
Or when rich china vessels fallen from high,
In glittering dust and painted fragments lie!
      Let wreaths of triumph[27] now my temples twine
(The victor cried), the glorious prize is mine!

The Baron snips off one of Belinda's curls—the rape of the lock (lines 109–116).

As Belinda laments, the victorious Baron rejoices (lines 117–124).

---

22. **board's . . . crowned:** tray on which coffee will be served. Lines 87–94 describe the preparation and serving of coffee. The beans ("berries") crackle when they are roasted and then are ground in the mill. The "altars of Japan" are lacquered tables. Coffee ("the smoking tide") is poured into Chinese porcelain cups ("China's earth").
23. **Scylla's** [sil′əz] **fate:** Scylla plucked out one of her father Nisus' hairs, on which the safety of the kingdom depended. As punishment, she was turned into a bird.
24. **Clarissa:** a young lady who disapproves of Belinda's vanity.
25. **engine:** device.
26. **forfex:** scissors.
27. **wreaths of triumph:** Ancient Greek victors wore wreaths on their heads.

A portrait by Thomas Gainsborough, 1775.

125　While fish in streams, or birds delight in air,
　　　Or in a coach and six[28] the British fair,
　　　As long as *Atalantis*[29] shall be read,
　　　Or the small pillow grace a lady's bed,
　　　While visits[30] shall be paid on solemn days,
130　When numerous wax-lights in bright order blaze,
　　　While nymphs take treats, or assignations give,
　　　So long my honor, name and praise shall live!
　　　　What time would spare, from steel receives its date,
　　　And monuments, like men, submit to fate!
135　Steel did the labor of the gods destroy,
　　　And strike to dust th'aspiring towers of Troy;[31]
　　　Steel could the works of mortal pride confound,
　　　And hew triumphal arches to the ground.
　　　What wonder then, fair nymph! thy hairs should feel
140　The conquering force of unresisted steel?

---

28. **coach and six:** a prestigious carriage with six horses.
29. ***Atalantis:*** a popular gossipy romance in which real society people were thinly disguised as fictional characters.
30. **visits:** The regular evening visit was a serious ritual for the society lady, who was accompanied by servants carrying candles ("wax-lights").
31. **And strike . . . Troy:** According to legend, the swords of the Ancient Greeks conquered Troy.

Canto II

But anxious cares the pensive nymph oppressed,
And secret passions labored in her breast.
Not youthful kings in battle seized alive,
Not scornful virgins who their charms survive,
5 Not ardent lover robbed of all his bliss,
Not ancient lady when refused a kiss,
Not tyrants fierce that unrepenting die,
Not Cynthia[32] when her manteau's[33] pinned awry,
E'er felt such rage, resentment, and despair,
10 As thou, sad virgin! for thy ravished hair.
    While her racked soul repose and peace requires,
The fierce Thalestris[34] fans the rising fires.
O wretched maid (she spreads her hands, and cried,
And Hampton's echoes, wretched maid! replied)
15 Was it for this you took such constant care,
Combs, bodkins, leads, pomatums,[35] to prepare?
For this your locks in paper durance[36] bound,
For this with torturing irons wreathed around?
Oh had the youth but been content to seize
20 Hairs less in sight—or any hairs but these!
Gods! shall the ravisher display this hair,
While the fops envy, and the ladies stare!
Honor forbid! at whose unrivaled shrine
Ease, pleasure, virtue, all, our sex resign.
25 Methinks already I your tears survey,
Already hear the horrid things they say,
Already see you a degraded toast,[37]
And all your honor in a whisper lost!
How shall I, then, your helpless fame defend?
30 'Twill then be infamy to seem your friend!
And shall this prize, th' inestimable prize,
Exposed through crystal to the gazing eyes,
And heightened by the diamond's circling rays,
On that rapacious hand forever blaze?
35 Sooner shall grass in Hyde Park Circus[38] grow,
And wits take lodgings in the sound of Bow;[39]
Sooner let earth, air, sea, to chaos fall,
Men, monkeys, lap dogs, parrots, perish all!

Belinda and her friends are furious that the Baron has cut the lock (line 20).

The Baron intends to encase Belinda's lock in a ring and wear it (lines 31–34).

---

32. **Cynthia:** any young lady.
33. **manteau** [man tō']: a loose cloak worn by women.
34. **Thalestris:** [thə les'tris]: Belinda's friend, named for the Queen of the Amazons, a nation of women warriors.
35. **bodkins . . . pomatums:** beauty aids and concoctions.
36. **durance:** forced confinement.
37. **toast:** a woman whom men praise and make toasts to.
38. **Hyde Park Circus:** a crowded circular drive.
39. **Bow:** a mercantile area where no fashionable wit would live.

She said; then raging to Sir Plume[40] repairs,
40 And bids her beau demand the precious hairs:
(Sir Plume, of amber snuffbox justly vain,
And the nice conduct of a clouded cane[41])
With earnest eyes, and round unthinking face,
He first the snuffbox opened, then the case,
45 And thus broke out—"My Lord, why, what the devil?
"Z—ds! d—the lock! 'fore Gad, you must be civil!
"Plague on't! 'tis past a jest—nay prithee, pox![42]
"Give her the hair"—he spoke, and rapped his box.
"It grieves me much" (replied the peer again)
50 "Who speaks so well should ever speak in vain.
But by this lock, this sacred lock I swear,
(Which never more shall join its parted hair,
Which never more its honors shall renew,
Clipped from the lovely head where once it grew)
55 That while my nostrils draw the vital air,
This hand, which won it, shall forever wear."
He spoke, and speaking in proud triumph spread
The long-contended honors of her head.
But see! the nymph in sorrow's pomp appears,
60 Her eyes half languishing, half drowned in tears;
Now livid pale her cheeks, now glowing red;
On her heaved bosom hung her drooping head,
Which, with a sigh, she raised; and thus she said,
"For ever cursed be this detested day,
65 Which snatched my best, my favorite curl away!
Happy! ah ten times happy, had I been,
If Hampton Court these eyes had never seen!
Yet am not I the first mistaken maid,
By love of courts to numerous ills betrayed.
70 Oh had I rather unadmired remained
In some lone isle, or distant northern land;
Where the gilt chariot never marked the way,
Where none learn ombre,[43] none e'er taste bohea![44]
There kept my charms concealed from mortal eye,
75 Like roses that in deserts bloom and die.
What moved my mind with youthful lords to roam?
O had I stayed, and said my prayers at home!
'Twas this, the morning omens did fortell;
Thrice from my trembling hand the patchbox[45] fell;

Despite Sir Plume's entreaties, the Baron swears he will always wear the ring (lines 39–56).

In a soliloquy Belinda mourns her fate and the fate of her curl. She wishes she had heeded the morning's omens (her silent parrot and unkind dog), and she finds no comfort in the lock that remains because she fears its fate will be the same as that of the one already lost (lines 63–89).

---

40. **Sir Plume:** Thalestris' "beau."
41. **amber . . . cane:** Most fashionable men took snuff and carried canes. Sir Plume's accessories are particularly fine.
42. **Z——ds . . . pox:** common oaths.
43. **ombre** [om'bər]: a fashionable card game.
44. **bohea** [bō hē']: a popular kind of tea.
45. **patchbox:** box in which Belinda keeps her patches, or small pieces of black silk used to cover facial blemishes.

80   The tottering china shook without a wind,
    Nay, Poll[46] sat mute, and Shock was most unkind!
    See the poor remnants of this slighted hair!
    My hands shall rend what even thy own did spare.
    This, in two sable ringlets taught to break,
85   Once gave new beauties to the snowy neck.
    The sister lock now sits uncouth, alone,
    And in its fellow's fate foresees its own;
    Uncurled it hangs! the fatal shears demands;
    And tempts once more thy sacrilegious hands."
90   She said: the pitying audience melt in tears,
    But Fate and Jove[47] had stopped the Baron's ears.
    In vain Thalestris with reproach assails,
    For who can move when fair Belinda fails?
    Not half so fixed the Trojan could remain,
95   While Anna begged and Dido[48] raged in vain.
    To arms, to arms! the bold Thalestris cries,
    And swift as lightning to the combat flies.
    All side in parties, and begin th' attack;
    Fans clap, silks rustle, and tough whalebones[49] crack;
100   Heroes' and heroines' shouts confusedly rise,
    And base, and treble voices strike the skies.
    No common weapons in their hands are found,
    Like gods they fight, nor dread a mortal wound.
     So when bold Homer makes the gods engage,[50]
105   And heavenly breasts with human passions rage;
    'Gainst Pallas, Mars, Latona, Hermes[51] arms;
    And all Olympus[52] rings with loud alarms.
    Jove's thunder roars, heaven trembles all around;
    Blue Neptune[53] storms, the bellowing deeps resound;
110   Earth shakes her nodding towers, the ground gives way,
    And the pale ghosts start at the flash of day!
     While through the press enraged Thalestris flies,
    And scatters deaths around from both her eyes,
    A beau and Witling perished in the throng,
115   One died in metaphor, and one in song.
    O cruel nymph! a living death I bear,
    Cried Dapperwit, and sunk beside his chair.

Belinda's friends help her try to convince the Baron to return the lock (lines 90–111).

The battle rages between the wits—the Baron's forces—and the hairs—Belinda's forces (lines 112–129).

---

46. **Poll:** parrot.
47. **Jove:** God.
48. **Trojan . . . Dido:** In Virgil's *Aeneid,* the Trojan Aeneas was unmoved by Dido's great passion for him and the pleas of Dido's sister Anna on her behalf.
49. **whalebones:** Whalebones were used for support in corsets.
50. **Homer . . . engage:** In Homer's *Iliad* the gods are involved in the battle.
51. **Pallas . . . Hermes:** gods involved in the Trojan War, according to Homer's *Iliad.*
52. **Olympus:** mountain home of the Greek gods.
53. **Neptune:** god of the sea.

A mournful glance Sir Fopling[54] upwards cast,
Those eyes are made so killing—was his last:
120 Thus on Meander's[55] flowery margin lies
Th' expiring swan, and as he sings he dies.

As bold Sir Plume had drawn Clarissa down,
Chloë stepped in, and killed him with a frown;
She smiled to see the doughty hero slain,
125 But at her smile, the beau revived again.

Now Jove suspends his golden scales in air,
Weighs the men's wits against the lady's hair;
The doubtful beam long nods from side to side;
At length the wits mount up, the hairs subside.

130 See fierce Belinda on the Baron flies,
With more than usual lightning in her eyes;
Nor feared the chief th' unequal fight to try,
Who sought no more than on his foe to die.
But this bold lord, with manly strength endued,
135 She with one finger and a thumb subdued:
Just where the breath of life his nostrils drew,
A charge of snuff the wily virgin threw;
Sudden, with starting tears each eye o'erflows,
And the high dome re-echoes to his nose.

140 "Now meet thy fate," th'incensed virago[56] cried,
And drew a deadly bodkin[57] from her side.
"Boast not my fall," he said, "insulting foe!
Thou by some other shalt be laid as low.
Nor think, to die dejects my lofty mind;
145 All that I dread, is leaving you behind!
Rather than so, ah let me still survive,
And still burn on, in Cupid's flames, alive."

"Restore the lock!" she cries; and all around
"Restore the lock!" the vaulted roofs rebound.
150 Not fierce Othello in so loud a strain
Roared for the handkerchief that caused his pain.[58]
But see! how oft ambitious aims are crossed,
And chiefs contend 'till all the prize is lost!
The lock, obtained with guilt, and kept with pain,
155 In every place is sought, but sought in vain:
With such a prize no mortal must be blessed,
So Heaven decrees! with Heaven who can contest?

Belinda throws snuff at the Baron, and he sneezes (lines 130–139).

The lock cannot be found, and there is speculation about what happened to it (lines 153–167).

---

54. **Witling . . . Dapperwit . . . Fopling:** conventional names in
Restoration comedy for silly, vain men.
55. **Meander:** river that passed through Troy.
56. **virago** [vi rä′go]: female warrior, in this case Belinda.
57. **bodkin:** dagger.
58. **Othello . . . pain:** Shakespeare's Othello demands to see the
handkerchief he had given his wife, believing her to have given it to
another man and thus to be unfaithful to him.

Some thought it mounted to the lunar sphere,
Since all that man ever lost, is treasured there.
160 There Hero's wits are kept in pondrous vases,
And beau's in snuffboxes and tweezer cases.[59]
There broken vows, and deathbed alms are found,
And lovers' hearts with ends of riband[60] bound;
The courtier's promises, and sick man's prayers,
165 The smiles of harlots, and the tears of heirs,
Cages for gnats, and chains to yoke a flea;
Dried butterflies, and tomes of casuistry.
But trust the Muse—she saw it upward rise,
Though marked by none but quick poetic eyes:
170 (Thus Rome's great founder to the heavens withdrew,[61]
To Proculus[62] alone confessed in view.)
A sudden star, it shot through liquid air,
And drew behind a radiant trail of hair.
Not Berenice's[63] locks first rose so bright,
175 The skies bespangling with disheveled light.
This, the beau monde[64] shall from the mall[65] survey,
As through the moonlight shade they nightly stray,
And hail with music its propitious ray.
This Partridge[66] soon shall view in cloudless skies,
180 When next he looks through Galileo's[67] eyes;
And hence th' egregious wizard shall foredoom
The fate of Louis, and the fall of Rome.
Then cease, bright nymph! to mourn the ravished hair
Which adds new glory to the shining sphere!
185 Not all the tresses that fair head can boast
Shall draw such envy as the lock you lost.
For, after all the murders of your eye,
When, after millions slain, your self shall die;
When those fair suns shall set, as set they must,
190 And all those tresses shall be laid in dust;
This lock, the Muse shall consecrate to fame,
And midst the stars inscribe Belinda's name!

The star will be an eternal tribute to Belinda (lines 188–191).

---

59. **tweezer cases:** elaborate cases with grooming aids.
60. **riband** [rib′ənd]: decorative ribbon.
61. **Rome's . . . withdrew:** Rome's founder, according to legend, is Romulus, who was snatched up into heaven.
62. **Proculus:** a Roman who claimed to have seen Romulus being taken up to heaven.
63. **Berenice's:** referring to the Queen of Ancient Cyrene and Egypt (c. 273–221 B.C.), whose husband named a comet after her, "Berenice's Hair."
64. **beau monde** [bō mond′]: fashionable world.
65. **mall:** fashionable place for walking.
66. **Partridge:** the astrologer John Partridge (1644–1715), who every year mistakenly predicted the downfall of the King of France ("Louis") and of the Pope ("Rome").
67. **Galileo:** Galileo Galilei (1564–1642), the great Italian astronomer who vastly improved the newly invented telescope.

STUDY QUESTIONS

Recalling

1. From what do mighty quarrels often rise, according to line 2 of Canto I?
2. According to line 20, where is Belinda at the opening of Canto I?
3. In lines 63–70 of Canto I, where is she and what is she doing when the baron cuts her hair? Who aids the baron in his quest?
4. According to lines 136–137 of Canto II, what does Belinda throw at the baron? What happens to the lock in the end, according to lines 172–178? What does the Muse do with the lock and with Belinda's name?

Interpreting

5. Reread lines 23–32 and lines 49–62 in Canto I. From the details Pope presents, describe the characters of Belinda and the Baron.
6. In Canto I, lines 103–122, how does Pope use tone and diction to satirize the rape of the lock?
7. In Canto II, lines 185–192, compare Belinda's fate to the fate of her lock. Does Pope offer adequate consolation for her loss?

VIEWPOINT

Critic Cleanth Brooks does not believe that Pope is simply satirizing Belinda. He argues

that Belinda's dressing table does glow with a special radiance and charm, and that Pope, though amused by the vanity which it represents, is at the same time thoroughly alive to a beauty which it actually possesses.

■ Do you agree that Pope both appreciates Belinda's beauty and satirizes it? Point to specific passages to explain your answer.

LITERARY FOCUS

The Mock-Epic

The **mock-epic** is exactly what the word implies: an imitation epic, or long narrative poem, that makes fun of a society that cannot live up to the standards of the classical heroic epic. The mock-heroic style makes a trivial subject appear ridiculous by using elevated language to describe a mundane event. The mock-epic uses epic conventions to imitate in a comic way the characters, events, and linguistic structures that had become traditional in such classical epics as Homer's *Iliad* and Virgil's *Aeneid* (see pages 805 and 864). Some of the most important **epic conventions** are a hero whose bravery allows him to overcome great trials, a major battle scene, a discussion of the hero's weapon, gods who participate in or direct the action, and epic similes in which the things compared are each elaborately and lengthily described.

Thinking About the Mock-Epic

1. What in *The Rape of the Lock* corresponds to the epic hero, battle scene, and description of the weapon, which were conventional in classical epics?
2. Find one example of a mock-epic simile.
3. Find one specific example of lines in which Pope uses elevated language to describe something trivial. Explain how the language makes the thing described appear ridiculous.

COMPOSITION

Writing About Irony

■ Throughout *The Rape of the Lock* Pope juxtaposes (places side by side) for ironic effect both grand and ridiculous ideas, events, and images. Write a brief essay in which you first describe and explain these ironic juxtapositions. Then discuss the way in which they relate to the larger purpose of the poem. You might want to look especially at some of the following lines: Canto I, lines 69–70, 75–76, 77–78, 85–86, 107–110, 121–124, 136–140; Canto II, lines 3–8, 35–38, 160–167.

Writing a Mock-Heroic Description

■ Think of a trivial quarrel, and write a brief prose description of it using the most inflated language you can. Try to include a battle scene and an epic hero.

COMPARING WRITERS

■ Compare and contrast the satire in *Gulliver's Travels* and *The Rape of the Lock*. In discussing the techniques of satire that Swift and Pope use, consider their tone, word choice, and treatment of plot, setting, character, and theme.

Much of Pope's genius lay in his use of the **heroic couplet** (two rhymed lines in iambic pentameter) that was the basis of his poetry. Where in other poets the form, with its regular rhythms and insistent rhymes, seems heavy and labored, in Pope it seems light and effortless. The compact way in which he phrased old ideas into **epigrams** (brief philosophical sayings) makes him one of the most frequently quoted poets today.

Alexander Pope

Epigrams

T'is education forms the common mind:
Just as the twig is bent the tree's inclined.
    —Moral Essays, Epistle IV, lines 247–248

A little learning is a dangerous thing;
Drink deep, or taste not the Pierian spring.[1]
    —Essay on Criticism, Part II, lines 15–16

To err is human, to forgive divine.
    —Ibid., line 325

True wit is Nature to advantage dressed,
What oft was thought, but ne'er so well
    expressed.
    —Ibid., lines 97–98

Be not the first by whom the new are tried,
Nor yet the last to lay the old aside.
    —Ibid., lines 135–136

For fools rush in where angels fear to tread.
    —Ibid., Part III, line 66

Hope springs eternal in the human breast:
Man never is, but always to be blessed.
    —Essay on Man, Epistle I, lines 95–96

Know then thyself, presume not God to scan;
The proper study of mankind is man.
    —Ibid., Epistle II, lines 1–2

---

1. **Pierian** [pī ēr′ē ən] **spring:** a spring in Macedonia, supposedly sacred to the Muses and an inspiration to poets and artists.

STUDY QUESTIONS

Recalling
1. What is Pope's definition of "true wit"?
2. What, according to Pope, should people know? What does Pope believe people should study?

Interpreting
3. What does Pope's definition of true wit suggest about originality?
4. Find at least two epigrams in which Pope recommends moderation and carefulness. Explain his recommendations.
5. Which of the epigrams are heroic couplets?

Samuel Johnson *1709–1784*

The second half of the eighteenth century, the period between Pope (page 340) and Wordsworth (page 394), is often called the **Age of Johnson**. It was so named after Samuel Johnson—critic, poet, playwright, lexicographer, essayist, and biographer—the period's most learned, versatile, and influential literary figure. He was renowned as a superb conversationalist and respected as a moralist with a special insight into human experience. Johnson may not have been the greatest writer of his time, but his conservative values and his deep sensibility reflected the age and had a profound impact on it.

Johnson was born in the northern cathedral town of Litchfield, where his father ran a small bookstore. The family was poor, and his father's lack of money forced Johnson to leave Oxford University without taking a degree. Success for Johnson, as for Pope, came only with hardship, and for most of his life Johnson struggled against poverty. After he left Oxford, he supported himself and his new wife with a number of teaching and journalism jobs, none of which was a financial success and none of which could satisfy his literary ambitions. By the 1740s, however, he began to produce works of considerable importance, including the essays for his popular periodicals, *The Rambler* and *The Idler,* which critics praised as equal if not superior to Addison and Steele's *Spectator.* With the publication of the great *Dictionary of the English Language* (1775), his reputation was secure. *Lives of the Poets* (1779–1781), ten volumes of critical biographies written in his later years, had a deep influence on the critics that followed him.

In all his writings Dr. Johnson (so-called because of the honorary degrees bestowed upon him by Oxford University and the University of Dublin) held to a few general principles: A writer must both please and instruct; he must not offend against morality or religion; he must neither copy others nor attempt anything so original as to be odd. Even those who do not agree with these principles must admit to the wit and grace with which Johnson elaborated them.

In 1746 Johnson published the *Plan* of his *Dictionary,* dedicating it to Lord Chesterfield, at that time an important secretary of state. Although Chesterfield showed some initial interest and made several suggestions, he offered no patronage, or monetary assistance, and Johnson was forced to proceed without Chesterfield's help. After the *Dictionary* was completed, Chesterfield published two articles praising it (perhaps hoping that Johnson would, even after Chesterfield's neglect, dedicate the work to him). Johnson responded with a letter, which appears on the following page.

■ If you were a writer, what might be the pros and cons of having a patron support you and your work?

Samuel Johnson

Letter to Lord Chesterfield

To the Right Honorable the Earl of Chesterfield

February 7, 1755

My Lord:

I have been lately informed by the proprietor of the *World*[1] that two papers in which my *Dictionary* is recommended to the public were written by your Lordship. To be so distinguished is an honor which, being very little accustomed to favors from the great, I know not well how to receive, or in what terms to acknowledge.

When upon some slight encouragement I first visited your Lordship, I was overpowered like the rest of mankind by the enchantment of your address,[2] and I could not forbear to wish that I might boast myself *"le vainqueur du vainqueur de la terre"*;[3] that I might obtain that regard for which I saw the world contending; but I found my attendance so little encouraged that neither pride nor modesty would suffer me to continue it. When I had once addressed your Lordship in public, I had exhausted all the art of pleasing which a retired and uncourtly scholar can possess. I had done all that I could; and no man is well pleased to have his all neglected, be it ever so little.

Seven years, my Lord, have now passed since I waited in your outward rooms or was repulsed from your door, during which time I have been pushing on my work through difficulties of which it is useless to complain, and have brought it at last to the verge of publication without one act of assistance, one word of encouragement, or one smile of favor. Such treatment I did not expect, for I never had a patron before.

The shepherd in Virgil grew at last acquainted with Love, and found him a native of the rocks.[4]

Is not a patron, my Lord, one who looks with unconcern on a man struggling for life in the water and, when he has reached ground, encumbers him with help? The notice which you have been pleased to take of my labors, had it been early, had been kind; but it has been delayed till I am indifferent and cannot enjoy it; till I am solitary and cannot impart it; till I am known and do not want it. I hope it is no very cynical asperity not to confess obligations where no benefit has been received, or to be unwilling that the public should consider me as owing that to a patron which Providence has enabled me to do for myself.

Having carried on my work thus far with so little obligation to any favorer of learning, I shall not be disappointed though I should conclude it, if less be possible, with less; for I have been long wakened from that dream of hope in which I once boasted myself with so much exultation, my Lord,

> your Lordship's most humble,
> most obedient servant,
> Sam: Johnson

---

1. *World:* newspaper in which Lord Chesterfield had praised Johnson.
2. **address:** conversation.
3. *le vainqueur . . . terre* [lə van kər′ dyōō van kər′ də lä ter′]: French for "the conqueror of the conqueror of the earth."

4. **The shepherd . . . rocks:** In a work by the Roman poet Virgil (70–19 B.C.) a shepherd complains that love was born among jagged rocks.

Johnson's great *Dictionary of the English Language,* published in 1755, was a truly exceptional accomplishment for one individual. To complete a similar French dictionary, over forty members of the French Academy had labored for over forty years. Yet Johnson, working alone in impoverished circumstances and frequently plagued by illness, produced in only seven years a dictionary that none had matched and that none would match for many years to come. It seemed a miracle, and Johnson was justly proud.

In his Preface to the *Dictionary,* Johnson talks about his reasons for undertaking the project and his feelings on its completion. The definitions reprinted here show both the straightforwardness of most of the definitions and the author's occasional turns into wit and satire.

Samuel Johnson

from The Preface to A Dictionary of the English Language

In hope of giving longevity to that which its own nature forbids to be immortal, I have devoted this book, the labor of years, to the honor of my country that we may no longer yield the palm of philology without a contest to the nations of the continent. The chief glory of every people arises from its authors. Whether I shall add anything by my own writings to the reputation of English literature must be left to time. Much of my life has been lost under the pressures of disease; much has been trifled away; and much has always been spent in provision for the day that was passing over me; but I shall not think my employment useless or ignoble, if by my assistance foreign nations and distant ages gain access to the propagators of knowledge and understand the teachers of truth; if my labors afford light to the repositories of science and add celebrity to Bacon, to Hooker, to Milton, and to Boyle.[1]

When I am animated by this wish, I look with pleasure on my book, however defective, and deliver it to the world with the spirit of a man that has endeavored well. That it will immediately become popular I have not promised to myself. A few wild blunders and risible absurdities, from which no work of such multiplicity was ever free, may for a time furnish folly with laughter and harden ignorance into contempt; but useful diligence will at last prevail, and there never can be wanting some who distinguish desert; who will consider that no

---

1. **Bacon . . . Boyle:** writers whom Johnson quotes throughout the *Dictionary.*

dictionary of a living tongue ever can be perfect, since while it is hastening to publication, some words are budding and some falling away; that a whole life cannot be spent upon syntax and etymology, and that even a whole life would not be sufficient; that he whose design includes whatever language can express must often speak of what he does not understand; that a writer will sometimes be hurried by eagerness to the end and sometimes faint with weariness under a task which Scaliger[2] compares to the labors of the anvil and the mine; that what is obvious is not always known and what is known is not always present; that sudden fits of inadvertency will surprise vigilance, slight avocations will seduce attention, and casual eclipses of the mind will darken learning; and that the writer shall often in vain trace his memory at the moment of need for that which yesterday he knew with intuitive readiness and which will come uncalled into his thoughts tomorrow.

In this work, when it shall be found that much is omitted, let it not be forgotten that much likewise is performed; and though no book was ever spared out of tenderness to the author and the world is little solicitous to know whence proceeded the faults of that which it condemns, yet it may gratify curiosity to inform it that the English Dictionary was written with little assistance of the learned and without any patronage of the great; not in the soft obscurities of retirement or under the shelter of academic bowers, but amidst inconvenience and distraction, in sickness and in sorrow. It may repress the triumph of malignant criticism to observe that if our language is not here fully displayed, I have only failed in an attempt which no human powers have hitherto completed. If the lexicons of ancient tongues, now immutably fixed and comprised in a few volumes, be yet, after the toil of successive ages, inadequate and delusive; if the aggregated knowledge and co-operating diligence of the Italian academicians did not secure them from the censure of Beni;[3] if the embodied critics of France, when fifty years had been spent upon their work, were obliged to change its economy[4] and give their second edition another form, I may surely be contented without the praise of perfection, which, if I could obtain in this gloom of solitude, what would it avail me? I have protracted my work till most of those whom I wished to please have sunk into the grave and success and miscarriage are empty sounds. I therefore dismiss it with frigid tranquillity, having little to fear or hope from censure or from praise.

2. **Scaliger:** J. J. Scaliger (1540–1609) suggested that criminals be sentenced to writing dictionaries.

3. **Beni:** Paola Beni severely criticized the Italian Academy's dictionary.
4. **economy:** organization.

from **A Dictionary of the English Language**

anthology *n.*   A collection of flowers.

club *n.*   An assembly of good fellows, meeting under certain conditions.
> What right has any man to meet in factious *clubs* to vilify the government?
> Dryden, *Medal, Dedication.*

imagination *n.*   **1.** Fancy; the power of forming ideal pictures; the power of representing things absent to one's self or others.   **2.** Conception; image in the mind; idea.   **3.** Contrivance; scheme.

kind *adj.*   Benevolent; filled with general good-will.
> By the *kind* gods, 'tis most ignobly done
> To pluck me by the beard.
> Shakespeare, *King Lear.*

lexicographer *n.*   A writer of dictionaries; a harmless drudge that busies himself in tracing the original, and detailing the signification of words.

man *n.*   **1.** Human being.
> The king is but a *man* as I am; the violet smells to him as it doth to me; the element shows to him as it doth to me, all his senses have but human conditions.
> Shakespeare.

2. Not a woman.   **3.** Not a boy.   **4.** A word of familiarity bordering on contempt.   **5.** Not a beast.

nature *n.*   **1.** An imaginary being supposed to preside over the material and animal world.   **2.** The constitution of an animated body.
> We're not ourselves.
> When *nature,* being oppressed, commands the mind
> To suffer with the body.
> Shakespeare, *King Lear.*

3. Disposition of mind; temper.   **4.** The regular course of things.   **5.** Natural affection, or reverence; native sensations.   **6.** Sort; species.   **7.** Physics; the science which teaches the qualities of things.

oats *n.*   A grain, which in England is generally given to horses, but in Scotland supports the people.[1]

pastern[2] *n.*   The knee of a horse.
> I will not change my horse with any that treads on four *pasterns.*
> Shakespeare, *Henry V.*

patron *n.*   One who countenances, supports, or protects. Commonly a wretch who supports with insolence, and is paid with flattery.

pension *n.*   An allowance made to anyone without an equivalent. In England it is generally understood to mean pay given to a state hireling for treason to his country.

peppermint *n.*   Mint eminently hot.

slothful *adj.*   Idle; lazy; sluggish; inactive; indolent; dull of motion.
> The desire of the *slothful* killeth him; for his hands refuse to labor. Proverbs, *xxi: 25.*

smoke *n.*   The visible effluvium,[3] or sooty exhalation from anything burning.

sneeze *n.*   Emission of wind audibly by the nose.

wit *n.*   **1.** The powers of the mind; the mental faculties; the intellects. This is the original signification.   **2.** Imagination; quickness of fancy.   **3.** Sentiments produced by quickness of fancy.   **4.** A man of fancy.   **5.** A man of genius.   **6.** Sense and judgment.   **7.** In the plural. Sound mind; intellect not crazed.   **8.** Contrivance; strategem; power of expedients.

yawn *v.*   **1.** To gape; to oscitate; to have the mouth opened involuntarily by fumes, as in sleepiness.

youth *n.*   The part of life succeeding to childhood and adolescence; the time from fourteen to twenty-eight.

---

2. **pastern:** actually part of a horse's foot. When an acquaintance asked Johnson why he had defined it as a knee, instead of making an elaborate defense, he answered, "Ignorance, Madam, pure ignorance."
3. **effluvium:** disagreeable vapor.

---

1. **in Scotland . . . people:** Johnson's disdain for the Scottish was well known.

STUDY QUESTIONS

Letter to Lord Chesterfield

Recalling

1. According to paragraphs 1 and 2, why is Johnson writing this letter?
2. Why did Johnson first visit Lord Chesterfield? Summarize his impression of Chesterfield and treatment by him.
3. How many years passed between that first meeting and Johnson's writing of this letter? What did Johnson do in the interim?
4. What is Johnson's definition of a patron, according to paragraph 5?

Interpreting

5. In what specific ways does Johnson's definition of a patron relate to his situation with Lord Chesterfield?
6. In your own words explain how Johnson feels about the notice Lord Chesterfield has taken of his work.
7. What appears to be the real purpose of Johnson's letter?

from Preface; from Dictionary

Recalling

1. According to paragraph 1, why has Johnson written the Dictionary?
2. Give four reasons why no dictionary can ever be perfect.
3. According to the last paragraph, under what conditions was the Dictionary written?

Interpreting

4. What argument against the Dictionary does Johnson anticipate and address in the Preface? Is his justification convincing? Why or why not?
5. What does Johnson's definition of lexicographer suggest about his presentation of himself? Compare the tone of this definition with the tone in the Preface.
6. Which definitions seem especially sarcastic or satiric? Explain.

Extending

7. Look up in a modern dictionary two of the words Johnson defines. How do the modern definitions differ from Johnson's? What do the differences suggest about the changes in the meaning of the word?

VOCABULARY

Antonyms

Antonyms are words that have opposite or nearly opposite meanings. For example, *bright* and *dim* are antonyms. The words in capital letters are from "Letter to Lord Chesterfield" and the Preface to *A Dictionary of the English Language*. Choose the word that is *most nearly the opposite* of each word in capitals, *as the word is used in the selection.*

1. ENCUMBERS: (a) burdens (b) surrounds (c) relieves (d) lavishes
2. ASPERITY: (a) courtesy (b) compliment (c) hope (d) bitterness
3. RISIBLE: (a) ridiculous (b) invisible (c) serious (d) hostile
4. INADVERTENCY: (a) caution (b) error (c) singlemindedness (d) flawlessness
5. VIGILANCE: (a) precision (b) violence (c) carelessness (d) humility

COMPOSITION

Developing a Thesis Statement

▨ Develop a thesis statement about Samuel Johnson's "Letter to Lord Chesterfield," and in a brief essay defend your thesis with examples from the letter. To develop your statement, you may wish to consider Johnson's use of events, point of view, or tone. *For help with this assignment, refer to Lesson 1 in the Writing About Literature Handbook at the back of this book.*

Writing Definitions

▨ Write four definitions in the style of Samuel Johnson. You may define any words of your own choosing, but some possibilities are *friendship, education, politics.* Illustrate your definitions with brief quotations from literature.

COMPARING WRITERS

▨ Show how the writings of Addison and Steele and Johnson are typical of the eighteenth century. Discuss four characteristics of the period, and cite quotations and specific details in support of each from the works you have read.

James Boswell   *1740–1795*

The modern art of biography would not be what it is today were it not for James Boswell, author of *The Life of Samuel Johnson* (1791). For many years Boswell was known only as Johnson's biographer. Now he is known to be a fascinating literary personality in his own right—due to the unexpected discovery from the 1920s through 1940s of an abundance of his personal papers.

Boswell was a gentleman in the full eighteenth-century meaning of the word. He came from a wealthy and ancient Scottish family and was heir to a large estate, circumstances that helped him gain entry into the upper circles of London society. In addition, he was charming, personable, an excellent listener, and somehow able to make people feel they could share their deepest secrets with him. Yet these qualities alone did not make him a natural biographer; Boswell also had a lifelong habit of keeping a diary and observing and remembering an event or conversation until he had time to write it down. He developed an outstanding memory for detail and a style of writing that could capture and interpret in a few sentences the character of an individual.

Boswell's first important literary work, *An Account of Corsica,* was published in 1768. As part of a tour of Europe, he had visited the island. His journal documents his experiences and includes an account of his visit to the Corsican patriot General Pascal Paoli.

Boswell's natural habitat, however, was intellectual and socially vigorous London. Although he spent some time in Scotland establishing a successful law practice and raising a family, he could not stay away from London for long. Because of his social status and personal charm, he was able to mingle with such men as the painter Sir Joshua Reynolds, the playwright and novelist Oliver Goldsmith, and of course the great sage, scholar, and critic Dr. Johnson.

In 1763, when he was twenty-two, Boswell met the fifty-three-year-old Johnson. The two were friends until Johnson's death in 1784, and Boswell devoted close to thirty years to collecting information for his monumental biography of over 500,000 words. He scrutinized Johnson's every move and questioned him on any topic, even asking him, "What would you do, sir, if you were locked up in a tower with a baby?" In 1773 the two traveled to the Scottish Highlands and the Hebrides Islands. Boswell described the trip in his *Journal of a Tour to the Hebrides,* which he published a year after Johnson's death. Eight years later he published his *Life of Johnson.* Thanks to Boswell's vast descriptive and interpretive skill, the account of their friendship allows us a glimpse into two great eighteenth-century minds.

■ If you were to write a biography of a person, famous or unknown, about whom would you write? Why?

Detail, *Dr. Johnson in Anteroom of Lord Chesterfield, Waiting for an Audience,* E. M. Ward, 1748.

James Boswell

from **The Life of Samuel Johnson**

To write the life of him who excelled all mankind in writing the lives of others,[1] and who, whether we consider his extraordinary endowments, or his various works, has been equalled by few in any age, is an arduous and may be reckoned in me a presumptuous task.

Had Dr. Johnson written his own life, in conformity with the opinion which he has given that every man's life may be best written by himself; had he employed in the preservation of his own history that clearness of narration and elegance of language in which he has embalmed so many eminent persons, the world would probably have had the most perfect example of biography that was ever exhibited. But although he at different times, in a desultory manner, committed to writing many

particulars of the progress of his mind and fortunes, he never had persevering diligence enough to form them into a regular composition. Of these memorials a few have been preserved; but the greater part was consigned by him to the flames, a few days before his death.

As I had the honor and happiness of enjoying his friendship for upwards of twenty years; as I had the scheme of writing his life constantly in view; as he was well apprised of this circumstance, and from time to time obligingly satisfied my inquiries, by communicating to me the incidents of his early years; as I acquired a facility in recollecting, and was very assiduous in recording, his conversation, of which the extraordinary vigor and vivacity constituted one of the first features of his character; and as I have spared no pains in obtaining materials concerning him, from every quarter where I could discover that they were to be found, and

---

1. **writing . . . others:** Johnson wrote a series of biographical essays entitled *The Lives of the Poets.*

have been favored with the most liberal communications by his friends; I flatter myself that few biographers have entered upon such a work as this, with more advantages, independent of literary abilities, in which I am not vain enough to compare myself with some great names who have gone before me in this kind of writing.

Had his other friends been as diligent and ardent as I was, he might have been almost entirely preserved. As it is, I will venture to say that he will be seen in this work more completely than any man who has ever yet lived.

What I consider as the peculiar value of the following work is the quantity that it contains of Johnson's conversation, which is universally acknowledged to have been eminently instructive and entertaining, and of which the specimens that I have given upon a former occasion have been received with so much approbation that I have good grounds for supposing that the world will not be indifferent to more ample communications of a similar nature.

Of one thing I am certain, that considering how highly the small portion which we have of the table talk and other anecdotes of our celebrated writers is valued, and how earnestly it is regretted that we have not more, I am justified in preserving rather too many of Johnson's sayings, than too few; especially as from the diversity of dispositions it cannot be known with certainty beforehand, whether what may seem trifling to some, and perhaps to the collector himself, may not be most agreeable to many; and the greater number that an author can please in any degree, the more pleasure does there arise to a benevolent mind.

1763. This is to me a memorable year; for in it I had the happiness to obtain the acquaintance of that extraordinary man whose memoirs I am now writing; an acquaintance which I shall ever esteem as one of the most fortunate circumstances in my life. Though then but two-and-twenty, I had for several years read his works with delight and instruction, and had the highest reverence for their author, which had grown up in my fancy into a kind of mysterious veneration, by figuring to myself a state of solemn elevated abstraction, in which I supposed him to live in the immense metropolis of London. Mr. Gentleman,[2] a native of Ireland, who passed some years in Scotland as a player, and as an instructor in the English language, a man whose talents and worth were depressed by misfortunes, had given me a representation of the figure and manner of Dictionary Johnson as he was then generally called; and during my first visit to London, which was for three months in 1760, Mr. Derrick[3] the poet, who was Gentleman's friend and countryman, flattered me with hopes that he would introduce me to Johnson, an honor of which I was very ambitious. But he never found an opportunity; which made me doubt that he had promised to do what was not in his power; till Johnson some years afterwards told me, "Derrick, Sir, might very well have introduced you. I had a kindness for Derrick, and am sorry he is dead."

In the summer of 1761 Mr. Thomas Sheridan was at Edinburgh, and delivered lectures upon the English Language and Public Speaking to large and respectable audiences. I was often in his company, and heard him frequently expatiate upon Johnson's extraordinary knowledge, talents, and virtues, repeat his pointed sayings, describe his particularities, and boast of his being his guest sometimes till two or three in the morning. At his house I hoped to have many opportunities of seeing the sage, as Mr. Sheridan obligingly assured me I should not be disappointed. . . .

Mr. Thomas Davies[4] the actor, who then kept a bookseller's shop in Russel Street, Covent Garden,[5] told me that Johnson was very much his friend, and came frequently to his house, where he more than once invited me to meet him: but by some unlucky accident or other he was prevented from coming to us.

2. **Mr. Gentleman:** Francis Gentleman (1728–1784), actor and dramatist.
3. **Mr. Derrick:** Samuel Derrick (1724–1769), author.
4. **Mr. Thomas Davies:** actor, bookseller, and author (1712–1785).
5. **Covent Garden:** area of London with many booksellers.

At last, on Monday the 16th of May, when I was sitting in Mr. Davies's back parlor, after having drunk tea with him and Mrs. Davies, Johnson unexpectedly came into the shop; and Mr. Davies having perceived him through the glass door in the room in which we were sitting, advancing towards us—he announced his awful approach to me, somewhat in the manner of an actor in the part of Horatio, when he addresses Hamlet on the appearance of his father's ghost,[6] "Look, my Lord, it comes." I found that I had a very perfect idea of Johnson's figure, from the portrait of him painted by Sir Joshua Reynolds[7] soon after he had published his Dictionary, in the attitude of sitting in his easy chair in deep meditation; which was the first picture his friend did for him, which Sir Joshua very kindly presented to me, and from which an engraving has been made for this work. Mr. Davies mentioned my name, and respectfully introduced me to him. I was much agitated; and recollecting his prejudice against the Scotch, of which I had heard much, I said to Davies, "Don't tell where I come from."

"From Scotland," cried Davies, roguishly. "Mr. Johnson (said I), I do indeed come from Scotland, but I cannot help it."

I am willing to flatter myself that I meant this as light pleasantry to soothe and conciliate him, and not as an humiliating abasement at the expense of my country. But however that might be, this speech was somewhat unlucky; for with that quickness of wit for which he was so remarkable, he seized the expression "come from Scotland," which I used in the sense of being of that country; and, as if I had said that I had come away from it, or left it, retorted, "That, Sir, I find, is what a very great many of your countrymen cannot help."

This stroke stunned me a good deal; and when we had sat down, I felt myself not a little embarrassed, and apprehensive of what might come next. He then addressed himself to Davies: "What do you think of Garrick?[8] He has re-fused me an order for the play for Miss Williams,[9] because he knows the house will be full, and that an order would be worth three shillings."

Eager to take any opening to get into conversation with him, I ventured to say, "O, Sir, I cannot think Mr. Garrick would grudge such a trifle to you."

"Sir (said he, with a stern look), I have known David Garrick longer than you have done: and I know no right you have to talk to me on the subject."

Perhaps I deserved this check; for it was rather presumptuous in me, an entire stranger, to express any doubt of the justice of his animadversion[10] upon his old acquaintance and pupil. I now felt myself much mortified, and began to think, that the hope which I had long indulged of obtaining his acquaintance was blasted. And, in truth, had not my ardor been uncommonly strong, and my resolution uncommonly persevering, so rough a reception might have deterred me forever from making any further attempts. Fortunately, however, I remained upon the field not wholly discomfited; and was soon rewarded by hearing some of his conversation, of which I preserved the following short minute, without marking the questions and observations by which it was produced.

Speaking of one who with more than ordinary boldness attacked public measures and the royal family, he said, "I think he is safe from the law, but he is an abusive scoundrel; and instead of applying to my Lord Chief Justice to punish him, I would send half a dozen footmen and have him well ducked."[11] . . .

I was highly pleased with the extraordinary vigor of his conversation, and regretted that I was drawn away from it by an engagement at another place. I had, for a part of the evening, been left alone with him, and had ventured to

---

6. **Horatio . . . ghost:** Shakespeare's Hamlet is told of his father's ghost by his friend Horatio.
7. **Sir Joshua Reynolds:** great portrait painter.
8. **Garrick:** the great actor David Garrick (1717–1779).
9. **Miss Williams:** Garrick gave a benefit performance for his impoverished friend, the blind poet Anna Williams (1706–1783), also a friend of Johnson's.
10. **animadversion** [an'ə mad'vur'zhən]: unfavorable comments.
11. **ducked:** thrown into a body of water.

make an observation now and then, which he received very civilly; so that I was satisfied that though there was a roughness in his manner, there was no ill nature in his disposition. Davies followed me to the door, and when I complained to him a little of the hard blows which the great man had given me, he kindly took upon him to console me by saying, "Don't be uneasy. I can see he likes you very well."

A few days afterwards I called on Davies, and asked him if he thought I might take the liberty of waiting on Mr. Johnson at his chambers in the Temple. He said I certainly might, and that Mr. Johnson would take it as a compliment. So on Tuesday the 24th of May, after having been enlivened by the witty sallies of Messieurs Thornton, Wilkes, Churchill, and Lloyd,[12] with whom I had passed the morning, I boldly repaired to Johnson. His chambers were on the first floor of No. 1, Inner Temple Lane, and I entered them with an impression given me by the Reverend Dr. Blair,[13] of Edinburgh, who had been introduced to him not long before, and described his having "found the Giant in his den," an expression which, when I came to be pretty well acquainted with Johnson, I repeated to him, and he was diverted at this picturesque account of himself. Dr. Blair had been presented to him by Dr. James Fordyce.[14] At this time the controversy concerning the pieces published by Mr. James Macpherson,[15] as translations of Ossian, was at its height. Johnson had all along denied their authenticity; and, what was still more provoking to their admirers, maintained that they had no merit. The subject having been introduced by Dr. Fordyce, Dr. Blair, relying on the internal evidence of their antiquity, asked Dr. John-

son whether he thought any man of a modern age could have written such poems. Johnson replied, "Yes, Sir, many men, many women, and many children." . . .

He received me very courteously: but, it must be confessed, that his apartment, and furniture, and morning dress, were sufficiently uncouth. His brown suit of clothes looked very rusty: he had on a little old shriveled unpowdered wig, which was too small for his head; his shirtneck and knees of his breeches were loose; his black worsted stockings ill drawn up; and he had a pair of unbuckled shoes by way of slippers. But all these slovenly particularities were forgotten the moment that he began to talk. Some gentlemen, whom I do not recollect, were sitting with him; and when they went away, I also rose; but he said to me, "Nay, don't go."

"Sir (said I), I am afraid that I intrude upon you. It is benevolent to allow me to sit and hear you."

He seemed pleased with this compliment, which I sincerely paid him, and answered, "Sir, I am obliged to any man who visits me."

I have preserved the following short minute of what passed this day. . . .

Talking of Garrick, he said, "He is the first man in the world for sprightly conversation."

When I rose a second time, he again pressed me to stay, which I did.

He told me that he generally went abroad at four in the afternoon, and seldom came home till two in the morning. I took the liberty to ask if he did not think it wrong to live thus, and not make more use of his great talents. He owned it was a bad habit.

Before we parted, he was so good as to promise to favor me with his company one evening at my lodgings: and, as I took my leave, shook me cordially by the hand. It was almost needless to add that I felt no little elation at having now so happily established an acquaintance of which I had been so long ambitious.

My readers will, I trust, excuse me for being thus minutely circumstantial, when it is considered that the acquaintance of Dr. John-

12. **Thornton . . . Lloyd:** Bonnell Thornton, journalist; Charles Churchill, satirist; Robert Lloyd, poet and essayist; John Wilkes, political radical.
13. **Reverend Dr. Blair:** Hugh Blair (1718–1800), Professor at the University of Edinburgh.
14. **Dr. James Fordyce:** a preacher in Scotland (1720–1796).
15. **Mr. James Macpherson:** Macpherson (1736–1796) had published a group of poems which he claimed were translations of a Gaelic epic, "Ossian." The work was probably partly authentic and partly of Macpherson's own composition.

son was to me a most valuable acquisition, and laid the foundation of whatever instruction and entertainment they may receive from my collections concerning the great subject of the work which they are now perusing. . . .

On Friday, March 31, I supped with him and some friends at a tavern. One of the company attempted, with too much forwardness, to rally him on his late appearance at the theater; but had reason to repent of his temerity.

"Why, Sir, did you go to Mrs. Abington's[16] benefit? Did you see?"

JOHNSON. "No, Sir."

"Did you hear?"

JOHNSON. "No, Sir."

"Why, then, Sir, did you go?"

JOHNSON. "Because, Sir, she is a favorite of the public; and when the public cares the thousandth part for you that it does for her, I will go to your benefit too."

Next morning I won a small bet from Lady Diana Beauclerk,[17] by asking him as to one of his particularities, which her Ladyship laid I durst not do. It seems he had been frequently observed at the club to put into his pocket the Seville oranges, after he had squeezed the juice of them into the drink which he made for himself. Beauclerk and Garrick talked of it to me, and seemed to think that he had a strange unwillingness to be discovered. We could not divine what he did with them; and this was the bold question to be put. I saw on his table the spoils of the preceding night, some fresh peels nicely scraped and cut into pieces.

"O, Sir (said I), I now partly see what you do with the squeezed oranges which you put into your pocket at the Club."

JOHNSON. "I have a great love for them."

BOSWELL. "And pray, Sir, what do you do with them? You scrape them it seems, very neatly, and what next?"

JOHNSON. "Let them dry, Sir."

BOSWELL. "And what next?"

JOHNSON. "Nay, Sir, you shall know their fate no further."

BOSWELL. "Then the world must be left in the dark. It must be said (assuming a mock solemnity), he scraped them and let them dry, but what he did with them next, he never could be prevailed upon to tell."

JOHNSON. "Nay. Sir, you should say it more emphatically:—he could not be prevailed upon, even by his dearest friends, to tell. . . ."

Talking of biography, I said, in writing a life, a man's peculiarities should be mentioned, because they mark his character.

JOHNSON. "Sir, there is no doubt as to peculiarities: the question is, whether a man's vices should be mentioned. . . ."

When Lord Hailes and he sat one morning calmly conversing in my house at Edinburgh, I well remember that Dr. Johnson maintained that, "If a man is to write a panegyric,[18] he may keep vices out of sight; but if he professes to write a life, he must represent it really as it was. . . ."

He sometimes could not bear being teased with questions. I was once present when a gentleman asked so many, as, "What did you do, Sir?" "What did you say, Sir?" that he at last grew enraged, and said, "I will not be put to the *question*. Don't you consider, Sir, that these are not the manners of a gentleman? I will not be baited with *what* and *why*; what is this? what is that? why is a cow's tail long? why is a fox's tail bushy?"

The gentleman, who was a good deal out of countenance, said, "Why, Sir, you are so good, that I venture to trouble you."

JOHNSON. "Sir, my being so *good* is no reason why you should be so *ill*. . . ."

The gentleman who had dined with us at Dr. Percy's[19] came in. Johnson attacked the Americans with intemperate vehemence of abuse. I said something in their favor; and added, that I was always sorry, when he talked on that subject. This, it seems, exasperated

16. **Mrs. Abington's:** referring to Frances Abington (1737–1815), actress.
17. **Lady Diana Beauclerk:** amateur artist (1734–1808).
18. **panegyric:** poem or other work of praise.
19. **Dr. Percy's:** referring to Thomas Percy (1729–1811), editor.

him; though he said nothing at the time. The cloud was charged with sulfurous vapor, which was afterwards to burst in thunder. We talked of a gentleman who was running out his fortune in London; and I said, "We must get him out of it. All his friends must quarrel with him, and that will soon drive him away."

JOHNSON. "Nay, Sir, we'll send *you* to him. If your company does not drive a man out of his house, nothing will."

This was a horrible shock, for which there was no visible cause. I afterwards asked him why he had said so harsh a thing.

JOHNSON. "Because, Sir, you made me angry about the Americans."

BOSWELL. "But why did you not take your revenge directly?"

JOHNSON (smiling). "Because, Sir, I had nothing ready. A man cannot strike till he has his weapons."

This was a candid and pleasant confession.

STUDY QUESTIONS

Recalling

1. Name three advantages that Boswell cites as qualifications for being Johnson's biographer.
2. What peculiar value does Boswell feel his biography has? What justifies Boswell in "preserving rather too many of Johnson's sayings, than too few"?
3. Briefly summarize the circumstances of Boswell's first encounter with Johnson.
4. What compliment does Johnson pay Boswell at the end of the anecdote about the Seville oranges?

Interpreting

5. Describe and explain one instance of Johnson's wit.
6. On the whole, how does Johnson regard Boswell? Are his emotions consistent or do they vary? Refer to specific conversations in the selection.

LITERARY FOCUS

Biography and Autobiography

A **biography** is an account of a person's life and character. As the form has developed, biographies have become more personal, conveying more of the subject's day-to-day life, ideas, and relationship to society. The modern biography often has a psychological orientation and attempts to describe the subconscious motivations of its subject.

When Dr. Johnson suggested that each person's life is best related by that individual, he was recommending **autobiography,** a person's narrative of his or her own life. Autobiographies are not always the most accurate accounts; a person may forget events or wish to hide certain facts. They can, however, offer intricate insights into a person's self-concept.

Thinking About Biography and Autobiography

1. Do you agree that a biographer should be absolutely truthful? Why or why not?
2. How would you describe Boswell's attitude toward Johnson? Do you think he presents Johnson with an unbiased point of view?
3. In what ways might *The Life of Johnson* have been different had it been an autobiography?

COMPOSITION

Citing Evidence

Write a brief essay in which you describe Johnson. Begin with a physical description, then discuss his character traits, and then his beliefs. Be sure to cite as evidence for your points specific details from Boswell's work. *For help with this assignment, refer to Lesson 3 in the Writing About Literature Handbook at the back of this book.*

Writing a Biographical Sketch

Write a brief biographical sketch, using specific situations to portray the character of a person. Use some of Boswell's techniques, such as including dialogue, using detail to describe surroundings, and recording your own reactions.

Thomas Gray   *1716–1771*

Although Thomas Gray wrote few poems during his lifetime, his place in eighteenth-century literature is distinctive and assured primarily because of one poem, "Elegy Written in a Country Churchyard." Gray is also an important transitional figure between the neoclassical writers of the seventeenth and eighteenth centuries (who applied the literary standards and forms of ancient Greece and Rome to their writing) and the Romantic poets of the early nineteenth century. While Gray used many neoclassical techniques—personified concepts such as Fame and Fate, elevated poetic language, and classical forms—his love of nature and belief in the common man anticipated important ideals of the Romantic poets.

Gray was, before anything else, a scholar. He studied Greek and Latin intensively and eventually became a professor at Cambridge University. However, like some other professors of his day, he never gave a single lecture. Rather than teaching, he spent his time advising students and exploring the libraries, where his studies led him to discover the beauties of English and Scottish ballads and Welsh and Norse literature that would later become important to the Romantics.

Gray was not eager to have his poetry published. In 1748 a friend sponsored the anonymous publication of Gray's first three poems. In 1751 Gray allowed his "Elegy Written in a Country Churchyard" to be printed only because he had heard that an imperfect version was about to be published without his consent. Because he felt that a gentleman should not accept payment for writing poetry, he let his publisher keep all the profits. In 1757 he was offered the position of poet laureate (poet to the royal family), an honor he declined. He published several more volumes of poetry before his death in 1771. Gray's poetic output was small because he composed each poem with painstaking care, phrasing and rephrasing until he felt that each was perfect.

Gray's "Elegy Written in a Country Churchyard," begun after the death of his close friend Richard West, took Gray nine years to complete. Today it is one of the world's most famous and beloved poems. Even Samuel Johnson, who in general did not admire Gray's work, wrote, "The Churchyard abounds with images which find a mirror in every mind, and with sentiments to which every bosom returns an echo."

■ Which would you prefer—a simple life in one location or a sophisticated life with many homes and lots of travel? What are the advantages and disadvantages of each life style?

Thomas Gray

Elegy Written in a Country Churchyard

The curfew tolls the knell of parting day,
  The lowing herd wind slowly o'er the lea,[1]
The plowman homeward plods his weary way,
  And leaves the world to darkness and to me.

5 Now fades the glimmering landscape on the sight,
  And all the air a solemn stillness holds,
Save where the beetle wheels his droning flight,
  And drowsy tinklings lull the distant folds;

Save that from yonder ivy-mantled tower
10 The moping owl does to the moon complain
Of such, as wandering near her secret bower,
  Molest her ancient solitary reign.

Beneath those rugged elms, that yew-tree's shade,
  Where heaves the turf in many a moldering heap,
15 Each in his narrow cell forever laid,
  The rude[2] forefathers of the hamlet sleep.

The breezy call of incense-breathing Morn,
  The swallow twittering from the straw-built shed,
The cock's shrill clarion, or the echoing horn,[3]
20 No more shall rouse them from their lowly bed.

For them no more the blazing hearth shall burn,
  Or busy housewife ply her evening care;
No children run to lisp their sire's return,
  Or climb his knees the envied kiss to share.

25 Oft did the harvest to their sickle yield,
  Their furrow oft the stubborn glebe[4] has broke;
How jocund did they drive their team afield!
  How bowed the woods beneath their sturdy stroke!

Let not Ambition mock their useful toil,
30 Their homely joys, and destiny obscure;

---

1. **lea:** meadow.
2. **rude:** uneducated.
3. **horn:** hunter's horn.
4. **glebe:** soil.

Nor Grandeur hear, with a disdainful smile,
    The short and simple annals of the poor.

The boast of heraldry,[5] the pomp of power,
    And all that beauty, all that wealth e'er gave,
35 Awaits alike the inevitable hour.
    The paths of glory lead but to the grave.

Nor you, ye proud, impute to these the fault,
    If Memory o'er their tomb no trophies[6] raise,
Where through the long-drawn aisle and fretted vault[7]
40   The pealing anthem swells the note of praise.

Can storied urn[8] or animated[9] bust
    Back to its mansion call the fleeting breath?
Can Honor's voice provoke[10] the silent dust,
    Or Flattery soothe the dull cold ear of Death?

45 Perhaps in this neglected spot is laid
    Some heart once pregnant with celestial fire;
Hands that the rod of empire might have swayed,
    Or waked to ecstasy the living lyre.

But Knowledge to their eyes her ample page
50   Rich with the spoils of time did ne'er unroll;
Chill Penury repressed their noble rage,
    And froze the genial current of the soul.

Full many a gem of purest ray serene,
    The dark unfathomed caves of ocean bear:
55 Full many a flower is born to blush unseen,
    And waste its sweetness on the desert air.

Some village Hampden,[11] that with dauntless breast
    The little tyrant of his fields withstood;

---

    5. **heraldry:** coat of arms; noble birth.
    6. **trophies:** pictures or figures symbolizing the
achievements of the dead person.
    7. **fretted vault:** church ceiling decorated with
a pattern of intersecting straight lines.
    8. **storied urn:** funeral urn bearing a story of
the deceased in pictures.
    9. **animated:** lifelike.
    10. **provoke:** move to life.
    11. **Hampden:** John Hampden (1594–1643), a
heroic statesman who fought against unfair
taxation.

Some mute inglorious Milton[12] here may rest,
60   Some Cromwell[13] guiltless of his country's blood.

The applause of listening senates to command,
    The threats of pain and ruin to despise,
To scatter plenty o'er a smiling land,
    And read their history in a nation's eyes,

65 Their lot forbade: nor circumscribed alone
    Their growing virtues, but their crimes confined;
Forbade to wade through slaughter to a throne,
    And shut the gates of mercy on mankind,

The struggling pangs of conscious truth to hide,
70   To quench the blushes of ingenuous shame,
Or heap the shrine of Luxury and Pride
    With incense kindled at the Muse's flame.

Far from the madding[14] crowd's ignoble strife,
    Their sober wishes never learned to stray;
75 Along the cool sequestered vale of life
    They kept the noiseless tenor of their way.

Yet ev'n these bones from insult to protect
    Some frail memorial still erected nigh,
With uncouth[15] rhymes and shapeless sculpture decked,
80   Implores the passing tribute of a sigh.

Their name, their years, spelt by the unlettered Muse,
    The place of fame and elegy supply:
And many a holy text around she strews,
    That teach the rustic moralist to die.

85 For who to dumb Forgetfulness a prey,
    This pleasing anxious being e'er resigned,
Left the warm precincts of the cheerful day,
    Nor cast one longing, lingering look behind?

On some fond breast the parting soul relies,
90   Some pious drops the closing eye requires;

---

12. **Milton:** John Milton (1608–1674), one of the
greatest English poets.
13. **Cromwell:** Oliver Cromwell (1599–1658),
great English statesman and general who was
nonetheless responsible for much bloodshed.
14. **madding:** frenzied.
15. **uncouth:** innocently artless.

Ev'n from the tomb the voice of Nature cries,
    Ev'n in our ashes live their wonted fires.

For thee,[16] who mindful of the unhonored dead
    Dost in these lines their artless tale relate;
95 If chance, by lonely contemplation led,
    Some kindred spirit shall inquire thy fate,

Haply[17] some hoary-headed[18] swain may say,
    "Oft have we seen him at the peep of dawn
Brushing with hasty steps the dews away
100   To meet the sun upon the upland lawn.

"There at the foot of yonder nodding beech
    That wreathes its old fantastic roots so high,
His listless length at noontide would he stretch,
    And pore upon the brook that babbles by.

105 "Hard by yon wood, now smiling as in scorn,
    Muttering his wayward fancies he would rove,
Now drooping, woeful wan, like one forlorn,
    Or crazed with care, or crossed in hopeless love.

"One morn I missed him on the customed hill,
110   Along the heath, and near his favorite tree;
Another came; nor yet beside the rill,
    Nor up the lawn, nor at the wood was he;

"The next with dirges due in sad array
    Slow through the churchway path we saw him borne.
115 Approach and read (for thou canst read) the lay,
    Graved on the stone beneath yon aged thorn."[19]

The Epitaph[20]

Here rests his head upon the lap of Earth
    A youth to Fortune and to Fame unknown.
Fair Science frowned not on his humble birth,
120   *And Melancholy marked him for her own.*

---

16. **thee:** Gray is addressing himself.
17. **Haply:** perhaps.
18. **hoary-headed:** white-haired.
19. **thorn:** hawthorn tree.
20. **Epitaph:** an inscription on a tombstone; a brief poem composed in memory of someone who has died.

Large was his bounty, and his soul sincere,
  Heaven did a recompense as largely send:
He gave to Misery all he had, a tear,
  He gained from Heaven ('twas all he wished) a friend.

125 *No farther seek his merits to disclose,*
  Or draw his frailties from their dread abode
  (There they alike in trembling hope repose),
  The bosom of his Father and his God.

STUDY QUESTIONS

Recalling

1. According to lines 13–16, what lies beneath the rugged elms and the yew-tree's shade?
2. Name five of the "homely joys" from lines 17–30 that will no longer be experienced.
3. In lines 33–36 what do heraldry, power, beauty, and wealth all await? What path will they all follow?
4. In lines 45–48 and lines 57–60 what does Gray speculate that some of the country people might have had the potential to become? In lines 73–76 what does he say the country people did?
5. To whom is Gray referring in lines 93–116? What observations does the swain make in lines 97–116?

Interpreting

6. What kind of person is described in the epitaph? What does this person have in common with the other kinds of people mentioned in the elegy?
7. What kinds of life does Gray refer to in the elegy? How do they differ? Which does Gray seem to prefer?
8. What truths common to all humankind do you think Gray is expressing?

Extending

9. In what ways are Gray's statements about human nature still valid in today's world?

LITERARY FOCUS

The Elegy

Although the **elegy** has a long tradition dating from Latin and Greek literature, it was only in the sixteenth century that it gained its modern definition: a serious poem lamenting a death or another great loss. The elegy is a poem of mourning, but the poet often finds consolation in contemplation of a common human truth. For example, the Anglo-Saxon lyric "The Seafarer" laments the miseries of the speaker's seafaring way of life.

Thinking About the Elegy

■ What does Gray's "Elegy" mourn? Is it just the death of one individual or does it go beyond? Cite evidence from the poem.

VOCABULARY

Expressive Verbs and Adjectives

■ In "Elegy Written in a Country Churchyard" Thomas Gray uses a rich variety of strong, expressive verbs and adjectives. Select five verbs and five adjectives from the following list of words from Gray's poem, and write five sentences of your own, using a different combination of verb and adjective for each one.

Verbs	Adjectives
plods	glimmering
wheels	droning
lull	moldering
heaves	breezy
rouse	jocund
ply	fleeting
drive	serene
impute	dauntless
implores	sequestered
strews	artless

Robert Burns   *1759–1796*

Robert Burns, still celebrated as a Scottish national hero, wrote simple lyrics that continue to capture the imagination of readers around the world. Although dignified literary circles immediately recognized Burns's genius, his poetic voice was that of the Scottish peasant. Even when he was fully accepted by Edinburgh high society, he never lost his connection to the land and to the simple people who inspired his poetry.

Burns, the son of a poor farmer, spent his childhood reading not only the great body of English literature but also all the traditional Scottish poets. Although he liked to portray himself as an artist whose work was the spontaneous overflow of natural feeling, he was actually quite well educated by the time he began to write, and his work reflects his wide reading. Songs that seem naive are actually elaborately crafted lyrics based on a long Scottish tradition. Poems that appear to be simple commentaries on day-to-day life are in reality subtle satires in the best neoclassical tradition. Burns was not altogether unaware of the conflict between his image as poet of the common people and the reality of his acceptance by high society. Although he spent much time in Edinburgh after the brilliant success of his first volume of poems, he soon realized that once the novelty of being the "peasant-poet" wore off, the upper classes with whom he mingled might lose interest. In 1788 he returned to farming and became a devoted father and family man, but he continued to write and edit several collections of Scottish songs.

Burns wrote many poems in standard English, but his best work is in Scottish dialect that, if difficult to understand today, nonetheless evokes the true spirit of the Scottish peasant. There is a heartiness to his language, a generosity that is underscored by a tenderness for both the natural and the human worlds. Burns was a great believer in the values of the American and French revolutions: democracy, equality, and justice. These values infuse both his long lyrics and his more than three hundred songs. The songs, on which his reputation rests, celebrate the joy of being human, of loving, working, laughing with friends, or standing up for one's country. On the basis of his songs, which talk of common people in common language, Burns is often called a pre-Romantic, a precursor to Wordsworth (page 394).

Sadly enough, Burns's devotion to his country and to the peasant life was the cause of his early death. He had developed a heart disease from overly strenuous work on his father's farm as a boy, and he finally succumbed to it at the age of thirty-seven. But Burns the poet lives on in spirit when every year on New Year's Eve people join hands and sing his beautiful song "Auld Lang Syne."

■ Which of Burns's values does "Auld Lang Syne" suggest to you?

Robert Burns

A Man's a Man for A' That

Is there, for honest poverty,
  That hangs his head, and a' that?
The coward slave, we pass him by,
  We dare be poor for a' that!
5   For a' that, and a' that,
      Our toils obscure, and a' that;
  The rank is but the guinea's stamp,[1]
  The man's the gowd[2] for a' that.

What tho' on hamely fare we dine,
10 Wear hodden-gray,[3] and a' that;
Gie fools their silks, and knaves their wine,
  A man's a man for a' that:
    For a' that, and a' that,
      Their tinsel show, and a' that;
15 The honest man, though e'er sae poor,
    Is king o' men for a' that.

Ye see yon birkie,[4] ca'd a lord,
  Wha struts, and stares, and a' that;
Though hundreds worship at his word,

20 He's but a coof[5] for a' that:
    For a' that, and a' that,
      His riband, star, and a' that
  The man of independent mind,
    He looks and laughs at a' that.

25 A prince can mak a belted knight,
  A marquis, duke, and a' that;
But an honest man's aboon[6] his might,
  Guid faith he mauna fa'[7] that!
    For a' that, and a' that,
30   Their dignities, and a' that,
  The pith o' sense, and pride o' worth,
  Are higher rank than a' that.

Then let us pray that come it may,
  As come it will for a' that,
35 That sense and worth, o'er a' the earth,
  May bear the gree,[8] an' a' that.
    For a' that, and a' that,
     It's coming yet, for a' that,
  That man to man, the warld o'er
40   Shall brothers be for a' that.

---

1. **guinea's stamp:** picture stamped superficially on a coin to show its value.
2. **gowd:** gold.
3. **hodden-gray:** the coarse gray cloth of the poor.
4. **birkie:** young man.

5. **coof:** fool.
6. **aboon:** above.
7. **mauna fa':** must not get.
8. **bear the gree:** get the reward.

STUDY QUESTIONS

Recalling

1. In stanza 2 who does Burns say is the king?
2. How does the independent man respond to the lord who struts, according to stanza 3?
3. Name three qualities that place the honest man above the marquis and duke, according to stanza 4.
4. In the last stanza for what does Burns pray? What does he say is yet to come?

Interpreting

5. Which characteristics does Burns suggest belong only to the rich? Only to the poor?
6. Which does Burns seem to favor, the rich or the poor? Support your answer.
7. Explain the views of brotherhood that Burns expresses in the poem.

Extending

8. Do you think Burns's views of the rich in any way contradict his idea of brotherhood?

Robert Burns

To a Mouse

*On Turning Her up in Her Nest with
the Plow, November, 1785*

Wee, sleekit, cow'rin, tim'rous beastie,
O, what a panic's in thy breastie!
Thou need na start awa sae hasty
    Wi' bickering brattle![1]
5 I wad be laith[2] to rin an' chase thee
    Wi' murd'ring pattle![3]

I'm truly sorry man's dominion
Has broken Nature's social union,
An' justifies that ill opinion
10   Which makes thee startle
At me, thy poor, earth-born companion,
    An' fellow-mortal!

I doubt na, whiles,[4] but thou may thieve;
What then? poor beastie, thou maun[5] live!
15 A daimen-icker in a thrave[6]
    'S a sma' request:
I'll get a blessin wi' the lave,[7]
    An' never miss 't!

Thy wee-bit housie, too, in ruin!
20 Its silly wa's the win's are strewin'!
An' naething, now, to big[8] a new ane,
    O' foggage[9] green!

An' bleak December's winds ensuin',
    Baith snell[10] an' keen!

25 Thou saw the fields laid bare and waste,
An' weary winter comin' fast,
An' cozie here, beneath the blast,
    Thou thought to dwell,
Till crash! the cruel coulter[11] passed
30   Out-through thy cell.

That wee-bit heap o' leaves an' stibble
Hast cost thee mony a weary nibble!
Now thou's turned out, for a' thy trouble,
    But[12] house or hald,[13]
35 To thole[14] the winter's sleety dribble,
    An' cranreuch[15] cauld!

But Mousie, thou art no thy lane,[16]
In proving foresight may be vain:
The best-laid schemes o' mice an' men
40   Gang aft a-gley,[17]
An' lea'e us nought but grief an' pain,
    For promised joy.

Still thou art blest, compared wi' me!
The present only toucheth thee:
45 But och! I backward cast my e'e
    On prospects drear!
An' forward though I canna see,
    I guess an' fear!

---

1. **Wi' . . . brattle:** in sudden flight.
2. **wad be laith:** would be loath.
3. **pattle:** paddle used to clean a plow.
4. **whiles:** sometimes.
5. **maun:** must.
6. **daimen . . . thrave:** an occasional ear of grain from a shock.
7. **lave:** rest.
8. **big:** build.
9. **foggage:** rough grass.

10. **snell:** sharp.
11. **coulter:** cutter on a plow.
12. **But:** without.
13. **hald:** home.
14. **thole:** withstand.
15. **cranreuch:** frost.
16. **no thy lane:** not alone.
17. **Gang . . . a-gley:** go often awry.

John Anderson My Jo

John Anderson my jo,[1] John,
    When we were first acquent,
Your locks were like the raven,
    Your bonie[2] brow was brent;[3]
5 But now your brow is beld,[4] John,
    Your locks are like the snow;
But blessings on your frosty pow,[5]
    John Anderson my Jo.

John Anderson my jo, John,
10   We clamb[6] the hill thegither;
And mony[7] a canty[8] day, John,
    We've had wi' ane anither:
Now we maun[9] totter down, John,
    And hand in hand we'll go,
15 And sleep thegither at the foot,
    John Anderson, my Jo.

---

1. **jo:** joy (friendly address).
2. **bonie:** beautiful.
3. **brent:** unwrinkled.
4. **beld:** bald.
5. **pow:** head.

6. **clamb:** climbed.
7. **mony:** many.
8. **canty:** cheerful, merry.
9. **maun:** must.

STUDY QUESTIONS

To a Mouse

Recalling

1. According to stanza 2, what has man's domin-ion broken? Who are fellow-mortals?
2. What has happened to the mouse's house, ac-cording to stanza 4?
3. According to stanza 7, what often happens to the "best-laid schemes"? What are we left with in the end?
4. Why is the mouse blessed compared with Burns, according to the last stanza?

Interpreting

5. What is Burns's view of the mouse's misfor-tune? What does this view suggest about his attitude toward nature?
6. What do Burns's comments about the mouse's plight reveal about his own personality?

John Anderson My Jo

Recalling

1. Describe John Anderson as he is depicted in stanza 1. Describe him as depicted in stanza 2.
2. According to stanza 2, what did John Ander-son and the speaker do together?

Interpreting

3. What is the main difference in John Anderson from stanza 1 to stanza 2?
4. What might the hill and the foot of the hill each represent?
5. What does the poem suggest about Burns's at-titude toward old age?

Extending

6. Why do you think Burns's poems appealed so much to Scottish peasants?

William Blake   *1757–1827*

Poet, artist, and mystic—William Blake was not content with the prevailing neoclassical values of his day. His interest in the supernatural and his imaginative experimentation classify him, like Robert Burns, as a pre-Romantic. Yet Blake was not part of any artistic movement, and he followed no style but his own.

Blake grew up in London, surrounded by the grit and poverty of the new industrial age. As a child he received virtually no education, but he did briefly attend drawing school and, at fourteen, was apprenticed to an engraver. Over the next years he found time to read widely and began writing his own poetry. In 1778, when he had completed his apprenticeship, he became a professional engraver and, for the next twenty years, earned a living by supplying booksellers and publishers with copperplate engravings. In 1789 he published a volume of lyric poems called *Songs of Innocence; Songs of Experience,* a companion volume, followed in 1794. The books were illustrated, engraved, and printed on copperplates by a new process Blake had devised.

Blake's engravings and paintings are an important part of his artistic expression, for the verbal and visual work together to evoke one unified impression. Blake himself manufactured all his poems that appeared during his lifetime. In the last twenty years of his life, his genius as an artist, especially evident in his illustrations of Chaucer's Canterbury pilgrims, Dante's *Divine Comedy,* and the Book of Job, overshadowed his work as a poet.

Throughout his life Blake was influenced by his childhood fascination with the Bible and by the ideas of the German mystic Jacob Boehme. As he grew older, Blake became more and more caught up in his mystical faith and his visions of a heavenly world. His most heavily symbolic works, including *The Marriage of Heaven and Hell* (1790), *The Gates of Paradise* (1793), and *Jerusalem* (1804), reflect his ever-deepening reflections about God and man.

As some of his titles suggest, part of Blake's mystical vision is to view the universe in contrasts—a marriage of heaven and hell, a place of innocence and experience. The poems in *Songs of Innocence* examine good, passivity, and reason; those in the companion volume *Songs of Experience* look at evil, violence, and unreasonable emotion. Many of the poems in one volume have their contrasting parallel in the other. The following pages present three pairs of parallel poems from the two volumes and conclude with two additional poems from *Songs of Experience.*

■ If you could meet William Blake, what would you ask him about his poetry? His beliefs? His life?

William Blake

Introduction to Songs of Innocence

Piping down the valleys wild,
Piping songs of pleasant glee,
On a cloud I saw a child,
And he laughing said to me:

5 "Pipe a song about a Lamb!"
So I piped with merry cheer.
"Piper, pipe that song again";
So I piped; he wept to hear.

"Drop thy pipe, thy happy pipe;
10 Sing thy songs of happy cheer."
So I sung the same again,
While he wept with joy to hear.

"Piper, sit thee down and write
In a book, that all may read."
15 So he vanish'd from my sight,
And I plucked a hollow reed,

And I made a rural pen,
And I stained the water clear,
And I wrote my happy songs
20 Every child may joy to hear.

Introduction to Songs of Experience

Hear the voice of the Bard!
Who Present, Past and Future sees;
Whose ears have heard
The Holy Word
5 That walked among the ancient trees,

Calling the lapsed Soul
And weeping in the evening dew:
That might control
The starry pole,[1]
10 And fallen, fallen light renew!

"O Earth, O Earth, return!
Arise from out the dewy grass;
Night is worn,
And the morn
15 Rises from the slumberous mass.

"Turn away no more;
Why wilt thou turn away?
The starry floor,
The watery shore,
20 Is given thee till the break of day."

---

1. **pole:** here, expanse of sky; heavens. (*Pole* can refer to either end of the heavenly, as well as earthly, sphere.)

The title page from *Songs of Innocence*, a volume of poetry written, illustrated, and printed by William Blake.

William Blake

Infant Joy

"I have no name:
I am but two days old."
What shall I call thee?
"I happy am,
5 Joy is my name."
Sweet joy befall thee!

Pretty joy!
Sweet joy but two days old,
Sweet joy I call thee:
10 Thou dost smile,
I sing the while,
Sweet joy befall thee!

Infant Sorrow

My mother groaned! my father wept.
Into the dangerous world I leapt:
Helpless, naked, piping loud:
Like a fiend hid in a cloud.

5 Struggling in my father's hands,
Striving against my swaddling bands,[1]
Bound and weary I thought best
To sulk upon my mother's breast.

---

1. **swaddling bands:** narrow bands of cloth tightly wrapped around infants to prevent them from injuring themselves. The centuries-old practice, which actually did more harm than good, was beginning to be criticized in Blake's day.

The Lamb

Little Lamb, who made thee?
  Dost thou know who made thee?
Gave thee life and bid thee feed,
By the stream and o'er the mead;[1]
5 Gave thee clothing of delight,
Softest clothing woolly bright;
Gave thee such a tender voice,
Making all the vales rejoice!
  Little Lamb who made thee?
10   Dost thou know who made thee?

  Little Lamb I'll tell thee,
  Little Lamb I'll tell thee!
He is callèd by thy name,
For he calls himself a Lamb,
15 He is meek and he is mild,
He became a little child:
I a child and thou a lamb,
We are callèd by his name.
  Little Lamb God bless thee.
20   Little Lamb God bless thee.

---

1. **mead:** wet, grassy land.

The Tiger

Tiger! Tiger! burning bright
In the forests of the night,
What immortal hand or eye
Could frame thy fearful symmetry?

5 In what distant deeps or skies
Burnt the fire of thine eyes?
On what wings dare he aspire?
What the hand, dare seize the fire?

And what shoulder and what art,
10 Could twist the sinews of thy heart?
And when thy heart began to beat,
What dread hand? and what dread feet?

What the hammer? what the chain?
In what furnace was thy brain?
15 What the anvil? what dread grasp
Dare its deadly terrors clasp?

When the stars threw down their spears,
And water'd heaven with their tears,
Did he smile his work to see?
20 Did he who made the Lamb make thee?

Tiger! tiger! burning bright
In the forests of the night,
What immortal hand or eye
Dare frame thy fearful symmetry?

"Infant Joy" from *Songs of Innocence.*

"The Tiger" from *Songs of Experience,* a volume of poetry written, illustrated, and printed by William Blake.

William Blake

A Poison Tree

I was angry with my friend:
I told my wrath, my wrath did end.
I was angry with my foe:
I told it not, my wrath did grow.

5 And I watered it in fears,
Night and morning with my tears;
And I sunnèd it with smiles,
And with soft deceitful wiles.

And it grew both day and night,
10 Till it bore an apple bright.
And my foe beheld it shine,
And he knew that it was mine,

And into my garden stole,
When the night had veiled the pole;[1]
15 In the morning glad I see
My foe outstretched beneath the tree.

---

1. **pole:** sky; heavens.

The Sick Rose

O Rose, thou art sick.
The invisible worm
That flies in the night
In the howling storm

5 Has found out thy bed
Of crimson joy,
And his dark secret love
Does thy life destroy.

"A Poison Tree" from _Songs of Experience._

STUDY QUESTIONS

Introduction to Songs of Innocence

Recalling

1. What is the speaker piping as he pipes "down the valleys wild"?
2. What does the child request in stanza 2? In stanza 4? According to stanza 5, why does the speaker write his "happy songs"?

Interpreting

3. What sort of poems, for what sort of audience, does this introduction suggest *Songs of Innocence* will contain? What does "rural pen" imply about the poems?
4. How do sound and rhythm enhance the poem's mood? Why is the diction suitable?

Introduction to Songs of Experience

Recalling

1. What does the Bard see in stanza 1? Whom does he call in stanza 2? What does he do "in the evening dew"?
2. What commands does the speaker make in stanza 3? In stanza 4?

Interpreting

3. What sort of poems does this introduction suggest *Songs of Experience* will contain? What does line 6 suggest about the audience?
4. How do sound and rhythm enhance this poem's mood?

Infant Joy

Recalling

1. How old is the child?
2. What does the child say its name is?

Interpreting

3. How many people are speaking? How might they be related? What lines does each speak?
4. Is the child actually named Joy? If not, what does line 9 mean?

Infant Sorrow

Recalling

1. According to stanza 1, what did the mother do? The father? Into what sort of world has the speaker "leapt"?
2. What is the speaker "striving against"?

Interpreting

3. What is the speaker's attitude toward life? Cite details to support your answer.
4. What contrasting views of the world do "Infant Joy" and "Infant Sorrow" present? How do the parents' attitudes toward the two infants differ? What social problem may have caused the parents' attitude here?

The Lamb

Recalling

1. What does the speaker ask the lamb in stanza 1? What three things does he say the lamb was given?
2. According to stanza 2, what does the maker call himself? What did he become? Who is the speaker in the poem?

Interpreting

3. Who is the maker? How do you know?
4. What qualities does the lamb represent?
5. What does line 18 imply about the speaker?

The Tiger

Recalling

1. What question does the speaker ask in stanza 1? In stanza 6?
2. According to stanzas 2 and 3, what is in the tiger's eyes? What is its heart like?
3. What four possible means or tools for making the tiger are mentioned in stanza 4?

Interpreting

4. What qualities does the tiger represent?
5. What central metaphor does stanza 4 use? Why is it appropriate?
6. What more general question is the speaker really asking in line 20?

A Poison Tree

Recalling

1. What action ended the speaker's anger with his friend? Why did the anger with his foe not end, according to stanza 1? What did that anger eventually bear?
2. What did the foe do one night? What did the speaker see the next morning?

Interpreting

3. What apparently happened to the foe?
4. To what two things mentioned in the poem does the title refer? What allusions do the title and line 10 make?

5. What does stanza 1 imply about human nature?
6. What central message about anger does the poem convey?

The Sick Rose

Recalling
1. According to stanza 1, what has the worm caused the rose to be?
2. What has the worm "found out"? What specific aspect of the worm destroys the rose?

Interpreting
3. What does "howling storm" suggest about the worm? In contrast, what does "crimson joy" suggest about the rose?
4. On a figurative level, what might this poem be describing? Why is the worm "invisible"?

Extending
5. In which of Blake's poems do you find him at his most mystical? Why?

VIEWPOINT

The critic Robert F. Gleckner observes that in Blake's poems the speaker

> is unobtrusive [does not call attention to itself], but many times a faithful interpretation of the poem depends upon a correct determination of the speaker and perspective.

■ What different identities do the speakers have in the Blake poems you have read? Choose three poems, and show how an understanding of each poem depends upon a correct determination of the speaker.

LITERARY FOCUS

Symbolism

A **symbol** is a person, place, object, or experience that exists on both a literal and a figurative level. For example, in "The Tiger," the tiger is literally the animal but figuratively represents something abstract. Symbols are often more complex than other figures of speech because they can have a wide range of interpretations. The tiger does not necessarily represent only one abstract quality—evil, for instance—but also represents a range of related qualities—violence, cruelty, and the like.

Part of our understanding of what a symbol represents comes from our knowledge of what the symbol literally is like. For example, a tiger literally *is* a ferocious beast, dangerous to humans. However, a tiger is also a graceful creature, and many other things besides. Another writer might use the tiger as a symbol of grace and beauty; a third, as a symbol of freedom. Thus, in interpreting a symbol's figurative meaning, we must pay careful attention to its context, or surroundings. In the context of "The Tiger," the tiger clearly represents something dangerous and evil, for it has a "fearful symmetry," comes from "the forests of the night," has a twisted heart, and so on.

The use of symbols in a literary work is called **symbolism.**

Thinking About Symbolism

■ Consider what a worm and a rose literally are like. Then examine "The Sick Rose," the context in which they appear. What range of related qualities might they each represent?

Meter and Scansion

In poetry, **meter** refers to a regular, predictable pattern of stressed and unstressed syllables. Almost all English poetry written before the twentieth century uses meter.

The basic unit of meter is the **foot,** which usually contains one stressed syllable (marked ´) and one or two unstressed syllables (marked ˘). In identifying meter, we identify the predominant *kind* of foot and the *number* of feet that each line of verse contains.

The predominant kind of foot will be one of the following:

iamb: 1 unstressed + 1 stressed syllable
trochee: 1 stressed + 1 unstressed syllable
anapest: 2 unstressed + 1 stressed syllable
dactyl: 1 stressed + 2 unstressed syllables

There are two other kinds of feet, but neither can be the predominant foot in a line:

spondee: 2 stressed syllables
pyrrhic: 2 unstressed syllables

The number of feet in a line will usually be one of the following:

monometer = 1 foot   **dimeter** = 2 feet

trimeter = 3 feet   **hexameter** = 6 feet
tetrameter = 4 feet   **heptameter** = 7 feet
pentameter = 5 feet   **octameter** = 8 feet

The predominant kind of foot is combined with the number of feet in the line to give us the line's meter. For example, the meter of this line from Byron's "Destruction of Sennacherib" is *anapestic tetrameter*—it has four anapests:

The Assýr / ian came dówn / like a wólf /

on the fóld.

The meter of this line from Tennyson's "Charge of the Light Brigade" is *dactylic dimeter*—it has two dactyls:

Cánnon to / ríght of thĕm.

In marking a poem to determine meter—a process called **scansion,** or **scanning** the poem— always examine more than one line. If the poem is divided into stanzas, scan an entire stanza, since the metric pattern may be stanza-based, not line-based. For example, most folk ballads present four-line stanzas in which lines of iambic tetrameter alternate with lines of iambic trimeter. If you looked only at one line, you would not get the complete picture.

Few poems maintain a perfect meter in every line. In this line from Jonson's "Song: To Celia," for example, the meter is clearly *iambic tetrameter*—the predominant foot is the iamb, and there are four feet—but a trochee replaces an iamb in the first foot:

Drínk to / me ón / ly wíth / thine éyes.

Scanning poems using trochaic or dactylic meters can also be complicated by seemingly incomplete feet at the ends of lines. Consider this stanza from Blake's "The Tiger":

Tíger! / tíger! / búrning / bright˘

Ín the / fórests / óf the / night,˘

Whát im / mórtal / hánd or / eye

Cóuld / fráme thy / féarful / sýmme / try?˘

The final trochee in each line is not really incomplete: In lines 1, 2, and 4, a pause completes it; in line 3, where there is no pause, the final trochee is actually completed at the start of the next line (*Could*). Of course, if we looked only at line 4, we might think the line is iambic; however, when we examine the stanza as a whole, we recognize that the predominant foot is the trochee and the meter is *trochaic tetrameter*.

Thinking About Meter and Scansion

■ Copy and scan the last stanza of "Infant Sorrow." What is the predominant foot? What substitute foot is used in the first foot of line 6? How does Blake complete the final foot in lines 5, 6, and 8? In line 7? Based on your answers, identify the meter.

COMPARING WRITERS

■ Of the three transitional poets—Gray, Burns, and Blake—who do you feel is closest to eighteenth-century neoclassicism? Who do you feel is furthest from it? Cite details from the writers' works to support your opinions.

ACTIVE READING

Implication and Inference

When we read, as when we listen, we can deepen our appreciation of what is being said by looking for implications and making inferences. Be careful not to confuse these two terms: Remember that the writer or speaker *implies* and the reader or listener *infers*. Drawing the proper inference, understanding the writer's implication, is illuminating and often pleasurable and is an important part of what makes literature an experience of *discovery*.

In general, we can say that more intelligence, more precision, more subtlety, more grace—in short, more artistry—are needed to imply a thought or an idea than to stand up, open wide one's mouth, and bellow it forth. A simple line drawing by a skillful artist can catch a person's essence as well as or better than a copiously detailed painting. A gesture or a look can speak volumes. An implication can tell more than a bald statement and can tell it more directly and more powerfully.

Why is an implication more *powerful?* Rather than being told an idea, we discover it for ourselves. Arriving at a conclusion on our own, we understand it better and remember it longer. Because the idea has in a sense come to us from "within" (we have *inferred* it), its impact is immeasurably greater.

Look, for example, at Samuel Johnson's "Letter to Lord Chesterfield." Despite its brevity, this document expresses a great deal. It is a remarkable instance of the *penetrating* power of implication. The author begins respectfully enough and harmlessly, but the second sentence already indicates that the letter will be no mere note of complacent thanks:

. . . To be so distinguished is an honor which, being very little accustomed to favors from the great, I know not well how to receive, or in what terms to acknowledge.

Johnson acknowledges that he has been honored, but at the same time he observes that such "favors from the great" have been few—so few, indeed, that he has no idea even how to react. He *implies* that the matter extends far beyond gratefulness for this particular favor. Lord Chesterfield is in for something more.

With extraordinary conciseness, Johnson demonstrates the essential falseness of the patronage system. After all, Johnson explains that he has the arduous task of compiling the *Dictionary* without the least assistance from Chesterfield, who now wants to consider himself Johnson's patron. Chesterfield has not given "one act of assistance, one word of encouragement, or one smile of favor."

Johnson seems to say, "So *this* is what patrons do—nothing! So *this* is what patronage is all about: *Now* I know!"

To reinforce these sentiments, he then alludes to Virgil's eighth *Eclogue:*

The shepherd in Virgil grew at last acquainted with Love, and found him a native of the rocks.

The shepherd bitterly laments that love must have been born among barren rocks. By way of analogy, Johnson implies that at last he has learned the true meaning of patronage, and it proves most cold and hard, dry and unyielding.

Samuel Johnson showed great skill in writing a letter bristling with implications. A careful reader must use skills to untangle, or infer, Johnson's meaning and tone.

REVIEW: THE ENGLISH VOICE

A Human Perspective

The eighteenth century—the age of reason, neoclassicism, order, and elegance—was a time particularly conscious of perspective. In literary and cultural terms perspective is a sense of proportion, of the relationship of one thing to another, of one person or class or idea or attitude to another. It was a sense of perspective that gave rise to a century of reasoned essays, objective criticism, and elegant satire.

The eighteenth century demanded not only a balanced perspective but a human one. People were the gauge of what was important or what was trivial, of what was possible and what was not.

Swift

He observed how contemptible a thing was human grandeur, which could be mimicked by such diminutive insects as I.

Steele

The imagination took a lovely impression of what was great and good; and they who never thought of setting up for the art of imitation became themselves imitable characters.

Addison

It should be my care . . . in particular that those may not make the most noise who have the least to sell.

Pope

Know then thyself, presume not God to scan;
The proper study of mankind is man.

Johnson

In this work, when it shall be found that much is omitted, let it not be forgotten that much likewise is performed.

Gray

The paths of glory lead but to the grave.

Burns

The best-laid schemes o' mice an' men
Gang aft a-gley.

Addison and Steele put English society into perspective for their readers. Swift and Pope did more: They put the whole human race into perspective. In the preface to his *Dictionary*, Johnson used the model of a great literary endeavor to put all of human endeavor into perspective. Gray and Burns used nature to achieve the same vision: a human perspective, neither too high nor too low, neither too large nor too small, but balanced, ordered, reasoned.

Key to Illustrations on Pages 308–309

1. Portrait of Robert Burns, Nasmyth Alexander (1758–1840).
2. Detail, *Cries of London,* "*Mop Sellers,*" an eighteenth-century watercolor, Paul Sandby (1725–1809).
3. Detail, portrait, Thomas Gainsborough, 1775.
4. Detail, *Coffee House,* eighteenth-century, artist unknown.
5. Portrait of Jonathan Swift, Charles Gervas.
6. Detail, engraving depicting London and London Bridge from the Surrey side of the Thames, 1707.
7. *Dr. Johnson,* Sir Joshua Reynolds (1723–1792).
8. Pulteney Bridge, Bath, England.
9. Poem from *Songs of Experience,* written, illustrated, and printed by William Blake, 1794.

385

Key to Illustrations appears on page 483.

THE ROMANTIC AGE

1798–1837

The intellectuals who lived from 1798 to about 1837 knew there was something unique and dramatic about their times, even if no one officially named the period the Romantic Age until much later in the 1800s. Said one of them, the great essayist William Hazlitt, "There was a mighty ferment in the heads of statesmen and poets, kings and people. . . . It was a time of promise, a renewal of the world—and of letters." During this period much of Europe, including England—and eventually America—experienced a monumental upheaval in political, economic, social, and philosophical systems. Revolutionary attitudes crashed across the Old World, and out of the new energy came a new literature.

The Political Background

During the early 1800s the French situation dominated England's foreign policy. The French Revolution had begun in 1789 as a protest against royal despotism, an assertion of the equality of people. In its early phases the French Revolution had seemed to offer great hope for common people. At the outbreak of the French Revolution, most enlightened people in Great Britain had felt sympathy for the democratic ideals of the revolutionaries in France. Yet once the revolutionary government in France had achieved power, it resorted to brutality. The violence—notably, the massacres of imprisoned nobility; the execution of King Louis XVI and his wife, Marie Antoinette; and the guillotining of thousands during the Reign of Terror (1793–1794) under Robespierre—made continued English sentiment in favor of the French Revolution difficult, if not completely impossible.

Furthermore, in 1793 revolutionary France declared war on England. From that point until 1815, with no more than a brief respite, England and France were engaged in the Napoleonic Wars. Napoleon Bonaparte—a brilliant young Corsican, one of the most successful military strategists the world has ever known, and originally a champion of the French Revolution—gained control of France and became emperor in 1804.

The British fought Napoleon on land and sea. Admiral Horatio Nelson became a British national hero by completely annihilating French naval power at the Battle of Trafalgar (1805) off the coast of Spain. Napoleon remained victorious on land until another British hero, the Duke of Wellington, beat Napoleon's armies in Spain and then, in the fatal blow, at the Battle of Waterloo, in 1815. Subsequently, the peace conference, the Congress of Vienna, restored the absolute monarchies to France and to other European nations whose

royalty Napoleon had overthrown in his attempt to dominate Europe. With the return of France to its prerevolutionary condition, the hopes of democratic idealists were crushed.

During this time of conflict with France, England had severe domestic political problems as well. To begin with, England's Hanoverian king, George III, was on the throne (from 1760 to 1820), but in 1811 he was declared permanently and incurably insane. His son George, the Prince of Wales, was made regent, or stand-in ruler, until the father's death in 1820. Then he was crowned George IV and began a ten-year reign. He became a fiercely intolerant foe of the liberal minority.

Domestic repression against political reformers and agitators grew severe as the Napoleonic Wars with France continued. Measures were enacted to restrict freedoms of assembly, of speech, and of the press.

After Napoleon's defeat, dissent and agitation for reform

continued, but during the years 1815 to 1820, the conservative Tory party exhibited an unyieldingly repressive attitude toward the call for reform from England's liberals. Workers had no legal recourse, for labor unions were illegal, nor did workers have a vote, and the government maintained a policy of *laissez faire,* or noninterference.

In 1830 George IV died and was succeeded by his more liberal brother William IV. During William's reign the growing need for parliamentary reform was finally addressed when Parliament passed the historic First Reform Bill of 1832. This bill extended the right to vote—not to the working class but at least to much of the newly well-to-do middle class. In 1800 less than 5 percent of adult males in England had the right to vote for Parliament. Finally, in 1832, more Englishmen for the first time gained the right to elect their leaders.

Life in England During the Romantic Age

The Industrial Revolution had begun in the 1760s, and certainly by the end of the Romantic Age its effects had produced drastic social and economic changes. New machines and power tools replaced hand tools, transforming an agricultural nation into an urbanized, industrialized one. In rural England home industry was destroyed, agricultural laborers were paid

The Factory Children from *The Costume of Yorkshire*, George Walker, 1814.

less than subsistence wages, and land fell into fewer, more powerful hands. In the cities a large new working class developed. Most of these people were poor factory workers who faced a life of drudgery, squalor, long hours, harsh treatment, and bad health. Children suffered exploitation because they were a cheap source of labor, easy to discipline and easy to recruit.

For the rich, the Regency (1811–1820) was a time of extravagance and lavish social display. In fashion, men's styles were influenced by the tastes of George "Beau" Brummel, who introduced the practices of stiffening cravats and wearing dark clothing instead of the formerly colorful knee breeches, vests, and coats. Women abandoned tight bodices and stiff corsets in favor of high-waisted, flowing gowns such as those worn by Napoleon's empress Josephine. Beginning in the 1790s, hairpowder and wigs were largely discarded. Men and women wore their hair in classical curls —as can be seen in portraits of Lord Byron.

However, it would be a mistake to assume that all Englishmen of comfortable means were oblivious to the plight of the poor. Among liberal intellectuals, like the poet Lord Byron and the social philosopher William Godwin, and among reform-minded members of the Church of England, there was a growing humanitarian feeling. Slave trade in the British colo-

nies was made illegal in 1807, and slavery itself was abolished throughout Britain's overseas colonies in 1833. On the whole, though, the rich were largely indifferent to the deprivation and suffering of the poor.

Scientific achievements in the areas of geology, chemistry, physics, and astronomy flourished during the Romantic Age. The drop in the country's death rate was attributable to some limited advances in medicine including the reduction of smallpox, the increase of hospitals, and better medical treatment in childbirth. However, the general state of medicine was still poor, and people did not clearly understand the relationship between dirt and disease.

In sum, the Romantic Age in England saw excruciating living conditions as well as the possibility for relief and improvement. The strength of the common working people and the promise of freedom from oppression were keenly felt by the Romantic poets.

Poetry and Essays in the Romantic Age

The literary movement called Romanticism represented a renewal of the emphasis on human emotions, which had existed before the 1700s and that had never totally died out. While Romanticism in the 1800s signaled a new mood, the world had witnessed earlier cultural movements that also merit the name *Romanticism*. Specifically, the ancient Greek epics (see pages 805 and 864) can be called Romantic, as can much literature of the Medieval Period (page 45) and of the Renaissance, or Elizabethan Age (page 107). All these writings— and the writings of the English Romantic Age under study here—emphasize human adventure, passion, delight, love of splendor, of extravagance, and of the supernatural. The Romantic tradition in all these periods can be viewed in contrast to another main literary tradition—Classicism or neoclassicism. The pendulum of literary taste seems to swing between the two traditions.

Examine the following lists, which contrast elements, outlooks, and concerns associated with the neoclassicism of the 1700s and the Romanticism of the early 1800s. Keep in mind also that although earlier literary periods can indeed be seen as typically Romantic, the period discussed here (1798–1837) is considered *the* Romantic Age.

Detail, *Lake Windermere*, William Linton (1791–1876).

Neoclassical	Romantic
tradition	experiment
society	individual
urban	rural
artificial	nature loving
intellect, reason	imagination, emotion
public, objective	private, subjective
clear, logical scientific	mysterious, supernatural
aristocratic	common
cultivated	primitive
conformist	independent
constraint	spontaneity
formal diction	natural diction

Three notable poets of the 1700s—Thomas Gray, William Blake, and Robert Burns—were in many respects as "romantic" as any poets of the Romantic Age, but the work of these three was isolated. Why did English literature change its views and philosophies, its aims and subject matter, so decisively at just the turn of the century?

Certainly, the historical issues and developments of the time played a major role in provoking and shaping the new literary movement of Romanticism: One critic has said, "The French Revolution and Napoleon made a clean sweep; after them it was no longer possible to think, act, or write as if the old forms still had life." Also, the Industrial Revolution, its urban-ization of English life, and its abuses against the working class called for a change in literary concerns and style. The Romantic poets in England also owed much to the Swiss-born French philosopher, Jean Jacques Rousseau (1712–1778). In his philosophies Rousseau rebelled against the cold logic of the 1700s and championed freedom and experimentation. He believed that man was most perfect in a state of nature, free from artificial societal restraints.

The Romantic Age in English literature begins in 1798 with the publication of *Lyrical Ballads,* the product of a great creative collaboration between the poets William Wordsworth and Samuel Taylor Coleridge. This volume revolutionized poetry—both in its theory and its subject matter.

In the Preface accompanying the second edition of *Lyrical Ballads,* Wordsworth enunciated his aims, among which was his belief that poetry should reflect spontaneity and emotion rather than the more sedate, or-dered tones of the previous generation. Wordsworth also stressed a desire to depict commonplace situations involving common people living in natural settings. Coleridge chose to concentrate his efforts on the supernatural. But both poets intended that their work—whether a treatment of the ordinary or of the mysterious—would stimulate an awareness of the workings of the human mind and personality. With respect to poetic form, they advocated using natural, ordinary speech over the formal, stylized diction of the 1700s.

Perhaps it is in their view of nature and natural phenomena and in their treatment of the supernatural and mysterious that the Romantics differed most profoundly from the neoclassicists. Partly as a reaction against the urbanizing, dehumanizing effects of the Industrial Revolution, the Romantic poets regarded nature in a fresh light and abandoned the well-tended gardens of the 1700s for the wilderness.

Though Romanticism shared with neoclassicism an interest in the past, Romanticism emphasized Ancient Greece over Ancient Rome. Furthermore, the Romantic concern with the past encompassed a renewed interest in the Middle Ages. Finally, the Romantics paid greater attention to the works of Shakespeare, Spenser, and Milton than had literary critics of the neoclassical era.

The essence of the English

Mary Shelley (1797–1851), Richard Rothwell, 1841.

Romantic Age is contained in the works of five poets—Wordsworth and Coleridge constituting the so-called first generation of Romantic poets, and Percy Bysshe Shelley, Lord Byron, and John Keats composing the second generation. These poets also wrote essays and letters explaining their ideas about poetry. In addition, Charles Lamb, William Hazlitt, and Thomas de Quincey wrote personal and subjective essays on a wide range of subjects.

Drama in the Romantic Age

Drama did not flourish during the Romantic Age. Only two theaters—Drury Lane and Covent Garden—were licensed to produce spoken drama. Audiences at both theaters were usually boisterous and unrefined. Thus, the main type of drama produced was simplistic, extreme melodrama in which all the poor are good and all the rich are evil.

Still, some of the leading Romantic poets wrote so-called **closet drama,** poetic drama written to be read rather than produced. Among the better-known plays of this type are Shelley's tragedy *The Cenci,* Byron's *Manfred,* and Coleridge's *Remorse.*

The Novel in the Romantic Age

The **gothic novel** became increasingly popular during the Romantic Age. This kind of novel often involved the supernatural and was set against foreboding backgrounds such as haunted castles and gloomy ruins. Perhaps the most famous gothic novel published during this time was *Frankenstein,* written by Mary Shelley, the wife of the Romantic poet Percy Bysshe Shelley. *Frankenstein* goes beyond the gothic interest in the supernatural to explore the nature of evil and the possible consequences of mechanization in the new industrial age.

Two of the most popular and respected novelists in English literature wrote during the Romantic Age. One, Sir Walter Scott, wrote novels of adventure and helped establish the historical novel as an enduring form. Scott was immensely popular during his lifetime. Reflecting the Romantic interest in the past, he set many of his novels in England and Scotland of old. For example, Scott wrote about thirteenth-century England in *Ivanhoe,* a complex romance. Like the French philosopher Rousseau, Scott believed there was more to life than reason alone and incorporated his fascination with the marvelous and uncommon into his work. In this and in his love of nature and of a legendary past, Scott was a true product of the Romantic Age.

The other major novelist writing during the Romantic Age was Jane Austen. Austen's novels were drastically different from Scott's. Though she wrote during the height of this period, she remained remarkably unaffected by Romantic literary influences. Her plots concerned domestic situations, with sensitivity and manners dominant. Her most famous novel, *Pride and Prejudice,* is about a genteel eighteenth-century family in an English country town. Realistic in tone, graceful, and deliberately decorous in the fashion of the **novel of manners,** Austen's novels usually revolve around the business of finding appropriate husbands for marriageable daughters. Much of the plot unfolds through brilliant conversations, as in the dialogue of a play. This dialogue reveals character and directs plot in a stylish, "modern" way. Austen had a keen ear for conversation and a wit tuned to satire. She was truly more representative of the neoclassical tradition of eighteenth-century literature than of the Romantic Period. Although she received little public recognition during her lifetime, Austen is now one of the best-loved English novelists and one who—in her use of dialogue—helped to develop the modern novel.

TIME LINE

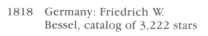

1798   William Wordsworth and
Samuel Coleridge, *Lyrical
Ballads*

                                        1800   America: Washington, D.C.,
becomes the new capital

1801   Act of Union of Great Britain
and Ireland

                                          1804   France: Napoleon crowns
himself emperor

1805   Battle of Trafalgar; Admiral
Nelson defeats Napoleon

1807   First gaslights on London
streets

      Charles and Mary Lamb, *Tales
from Shakespeare*

                                          1808   Austria: German composer
Ludwig van Beethoven,
Symphony No. 5

1811   Regency period begins

1812   New Drury Lane Theatre
erected in London

                                          1812   America: War declared on
Great Britain

                                                Germany: The Brothers
Grimm, *Fairy Tales*

1813   Jane Austen, *Pride and
Prejudice*

                                          1813   Mexico: Independence is
declared

1814   First practical steam
locomotive constructed

                                          1814   America: British forces burn
Washington, D.C.

1815   Duke of Wellington leads final
defeat of Napoleon at
Waterloo

                                          1815   Austria: Congress of Vienna

                                                France: Bourbons restored to
throne

1816   Samuel Taylor Coleridge,
"Kubla Khan"

1817   William Hazlitt, *The
Characters of Shakespeare's
Plays*

1818   George Gordon, Lord Byron,
begins *Don Juan*

                                          1818   Germany: Friedrich W.
Bessel, catalog of 3,222 stars

      Mary Wollstonecraft Shelley,
*Frankenstein, or The Modern
Prometheus*

	BRITISH EVENTS		**WORLD EVENTS**
1820	John Keats, "Ode to a Nightingale"	1820	Greece: Discovery of *Venus de Milo,* classical statue carved about 150 B.C.
	Sir Walter Scott, *Ivanhoe*		America: Missouri Compromise
	Percy Bysshe Shelley, *Prometheus Unbound*		
	Charles Lamb begins *Essays of Elia*		
	George III dies; George IV becomes king		
1825	Workers are allowed to form labor unions	1825	Russia: Bolshoi Ballet established in Moscow
1826	First railroad tunnel built for Liverpool–Manchester Railway	1826	America: James Fenimore Cooper, *The Last of the Mohicans*
	Royal Zoological Society is founded	1828	America: First passenger and freight railroad constructed
			America: Noah Webster, *American Dictionary of the English Language*
1829	Metropolitan police force established in London by Sir Robert Peel	1829	Austria: Frédéric Chopin's debut in Vienna
1830	William IV ascends the throne	1831	Germany: Johann Wolfgang von Goethe completes *Faust*
1832	Britain occupies the Falkland Islands	1832	America: First horse-drawn trolleys in New York
1834	Two-wheeled, one-horse hansom cabs introduced	1834	America: Cyrus McCormick patents reaper
			France: Louis Braille perfects system of characters enabling the blind to read
1835	W. H. Fox Talbot takes the earliest negative photograph	1835	Denmark: Hans Christian Andersen, *Fairy Tales*
			America: Phineas T. Barnum holds his first exhibition
		1836	America: Davy Crockett killed at the Alamo
1837	Victoria ascends the throne		
	First railway telegraph installed in London		

JOHN KEATS

PERCY BYSSHE SHELLEY

English Literature: The Romantic Age **393**

William Wordsworth   *1770–1850*

William Wordsworth in collaboration with his friend and colleague Samuel Taylor Coleridge (page 407) was the first poet to announce the literary ideals of the English Romantic Age. Wordsworth was born in England's Lake District, a land of breathtaking scenery, and the most beautiful region in the entire country. His mother died when he was eight, and he, along with his three brothers, was sent to study at the excellent grammar school at Hawkshead, also in the Lake District. There he grew up, free to wander through the countryside, hiking and skating. As we shall see, these early opportunities to commune with nature would have a profound effect on much of Wordsworth's poetry. He received a fine education, both at the grammar school and at Cambridge University, from which he was graduated in 1791.

While in France during 1791 and 1792, he became an ardent supporter of the French Revolution, which he (and many other liberal Englishmen) enthusiastically interpreted as championing the cause of human liberty. During this time he also fell passionately in love with a French girl, Annette Vallon. Though he wished to remain in France because of the revolution and because of his love for Annette, lack of money forced his departure for England. The outbreak of war between England and France in 1793 prevented Wordsworth's immediate return to France, and his conscience plagued him, his loyalties divided between the two countries. Then he grew ever more disillusioned with the course of the French Revolution as events there became increasingly violent and the revolution departed drastically from the original democratic ideals he had so admired. Guilt over his inability to marry Annette, unhappiness at not finding suitable employment, and the growing certainty that the French Revolution was not the example for humankind that he had once thought it could be brought Wordsworth to the brink of mental collapse. He fell into a period of deep depression.

In 1795, almost three years after returning from a second visit to France, he came into enough money to move into a small cottage with his sister, Dorothy, who was his close friend and confidant. Soon afterward, he met Coleridge, and this meeting resulted in what is certainly the most significant friendship in all of English literature. With the companionship and support of Dorothy and Coleridge, who deeply admired Wordsworth's poetry and convinced him of its worth, Wordsworth recovered from the despair that had engulfed him for several years.

"All good poetry is the spontaneous overflow of powerful feelings." This remark occurs in the course of Wordsworth's Preface to *Lyrical Ballads* of 1800. Spontaneity, excess, power, and emotion:

Those are the traits of Romanticism, subscribed to by Wordsworth in that slim volume of poems entitled *Lyrical Ballads,* first published in 1798, written jointly by him and Coleridge. That book is the cornerstone of English Romanticism. Late in the eighteenth century other poets—Gray and Burns and Blake—had reacted against the strict demands of neoclassicism. Yet none rebelled as consciously, as consistently, and as influentially as did Wordsworth, working closely with his friend Coleridge. Wordsworth's Preface, written for the second edition of *Lyrical Ballads* in 1800, explains the principles underlying his and Coleridge's new approach to poetry and may thus serve as the formal announcement of a new literary age.

Dryden, Pope, and Johnson—giants of neoclassicism—had seen poetry as an aristocratic pursuit, calculated rather than spontaneous, more a matter of wit than power, an endeavor more of the mind than the heart. Through poetry, aristocrats spoke to aristocrats. To Wordsworth, however, and to Coleridge, poetry was more properly regarded as people speaking to people—and not in heroic couplets but in whatever form might be suitable to a particular occasion. Wordsworth, in particular, called for the use of natural, commonplace diction in literary works.

Unlike the neoclassicists, Wordsworth was convinced of the importance of subjectivity in poetry. He believed that poetry "takes its origin from emotion recollected in tranquillity." In other words, true poetry, conceived in spontaneous emotion, takes on meaning and shape as the poet contemplates the subject. Thus poetry reflects the poet's subjective reactions and reasoned reflections. Nor should poets choose for their subjects lords and ladies, with all their courtly affectations. Instead, they should write, so Wordsworth felt, of "humble and rustic" people, whose feelings were genuine and unspoiled, living out their lives close to nature. Clearly nature, which had been a major element of the poet's youth, had a substantial influence on Wordsworth's poetic inspiration. The response of the individual human mind to the simple, universal truths and beauty revealed in nature fascinated Wordsworth. He focused on the natural and ordinary in an attempt to explore the relationship between nature and our inner life.

Wordsworth spent most of his long life back in the beautiful Lake District with his wife, Mary (who had been a childhood friend), and his beloved sister, Dorothy. Although he continued to compose poetry into old age, his greatest poems had been written by then, most of them done in a single remarkable decade—between 1797 and 1807—while he and Coleridge were consciously altering the direction of English literature.

In which period would you have felt more comfortable—the neoclassical, with its emphasis on intellect, logic, and restraint, or the Romantic, with its stress on emotion, spontaneity, and experiment?

"One afternoon in 1801," Wordsworth recalled, "my sister read to me the sonnets of Milton. I had long been well acquainted with them, but I was particularly struck on that occasion with the dignified simplicity and majestic harmony that runs through most of them. . . ." The experience was so inspiring that the poet proceeded to write three sonnets of his own that same day. In the course of his lifetime, Wordsworth went on to write more than 130 sonnets—including some of the very best in the language. He returned the sonnet form to the prestigious position from which it had fallen during the eighteenth century. Wordsworth wrote the greatest of his sonnets by 1807, when he published his collected *Poems in Two Volumes.*

William Wordsworth

The World Is Too Much with Us

The world is too much with us; late and soon,
Getting and spending, we lay waste our powers;
Little we see in Nature that is ours;
We have given our hearts away, a sordid boon![1]
5 This sea that bares her bosom to the moon,
The winds that will be howling at all hours,
And are up-gathered now like sleeping flowers,
For this, for everything, we are out of tune;
It moves us not.—Great God! I'd rather be
10 A Pagan suckled in a creed outworn;
So might I, standing on this pleasant lea,[2]
Have glimpses that would make me less forlorn;
Have sight of Proteus[3] rising from the sea;
Or hear old Triton[4] blow his wreathèd horn.

---

1. **boon:** gift, favor.
2. **lea** [lē]: meadow.
3. **Proteus** [prō′tē əs]: in classical mythology, a sea god who could assume various forms.
4. **Triton** [trīt′ən]: in classical mythology, a figure who was half man and half fish and blew upon a conch-shell horn.

London, 1802

Milton! thou shouldst be living at this hour:
England hath need of thee: she is a fen[1]
Of stagnant waters: altar, sword, and pen,
Fireside, the heroic wealth of hall and bower,
5 Have forfeited their ancient English dower[2]
Of inward happiness. We are selfish men;
Oh! raise us up, return to us again;
And give us manners, virtue, freedom, power.
Thy soul was like a Star, and dwelt apart;
10 Thou hadst a voice whose sound was like the sea:
Pure as the naked heavens, majestic, free,
So didst thou travel on life's common way,
In cheerful godliness; and yet thy heart
The lowliest duties on herself did lay.

---

1. **fen:** swamp, bog.
2. **dower:** gift, endowment.

It Is a Beauteous Evening, Calm and Free

It is a beauteous evening, calm and free,
The holy time is quiet as a Nun
Breathless with adoration; the broad sun
Is sinking down in its tranquility;
5 The gentleness of heaven broods o'er the Sea:
Listen! the mighty Being is awake,
And doth with his eternal motion make
A sound like thunder—everlastingly.
Dear Child! dear Girl! that walkest with me here,
10 If thou appear untouched by solemn thought,
Thy nature is not therefore less divine:
Thou liest in Abraham's bosom[1] all the year,
And worship'st at the Temple's inner shrine,
God being with thee when we know it not.

---

1. **Abraham's bosom:** heaven (Luke 16:22).

William Wordsworth

Composed upon Westminster Bridge, September 3, 1802

Earth has not anything to show more fair:
Dull would he be of soul who could pass by
A sight so touching in its majesty;
This City now doth, like a garment, wear
5 The beauty of the morning; silent, bare,
Ships, towers, domes, theaters, and temples lie
Open unto the fields, and to the sky;
All bright and glittering in the smokeless air.
Never did sun more beautifully steep[1]
10 In his first splendor, valley, rock, or hill;
Ne'er saw I, never felt, a calm so deep!
The river glideth at his own sweet will:
Dear God! the very houses seem asleep;
And all that mighty heart is lying still!

---

1. **steep:** saturate.

The Houses of Parliament, Winslow Homer, 1881.

STUDY QUESTIONS

The World Is Too Much with Us

Recalling

1. What do we do that causes us to "lay waste our powers" (line 2)?
2. According to lines 5–7, with what, specifically, are we "out of tune"?
3. Beginning in the middle of line 9 (in the sestet of the sonnet), what kind of life and what kinds of sights would make the speaker "less forlorn"?

Interpreting

4. What aspect of the world "is too much with us," according to this poem? In general terms, what does the speaker suggest we turn to instead?
5. In the context of the poem, what do Proteus and Triton represent? How might an older, pagan creed enable the speaker to have a greater feeling of identity with nature?
6. What emotion can you attribute to this poem's speaker? Explain your reasoning.

Extending

7. Explain why this poem remains relevant.

London, 1802

Recalling

1. Why should Milton, the seventeenth-century poet, be living during Wordsworth's day, according to line 2?
2. According to lines 5–6, what have the English forfeited?
3. What Miltonic characteristics, listed in line 8, are longed for by the poet (recently returned from France and struck by "the vanity and parade" of England)?

Interpreting

4. What is conveyed about English society of the time by the image of England as "a fen/Of stagnant waters"?
5. What do altar, sword, pen, and fireside stand for?

6. Based on the second part of the sonnet (lines 9–14), what do you think Wordsworth most admires about Milton?

Extending

7. Compare the pictures of London in "Composed upon Westminster Bridge" and in "London, 1802." How can the pictures be so different?

It Is a Beauteous Evening, Calm and Free

Recalling

1. What adjectives and nouns in lines 1–5 describe the mood of the evening?
2. What does the speaker hear in lines 6–8?
3. With whom does the speaker walk, and how does that person appear?

Interpreting

4. How does Wordsworth give nature a spiritual significance in the sonnet's first eight lines?
5. What contrast exists between the sonnet's first eight lines and its last six?
6. What is the speaker's feeling about childhood, implicit in the final four lines of this sonnet?

Composed upon Westminster Bridge

Recalling

1. What two statements of praise for London does the speaker offer in lines 1–3?
2. At what time of day is London being described in this poem, which Wordsworth later said was "composed on the roof of a coach, on my way to France"? What specific elements of the London landscape does the speaker applaud in lines 5–8?
3. According to line 11, what is the dominant atmosphere of London at this time?

Interpreting

4. What is the city being likened to in lines 4–5? What is the city being compared to in lines 9–10? Explain the personification in lines 12–14.
5. What is surprising about the picture of the city in this poem? Consider in your answer the contrast between "touching" and "majesty" (line 3).

This is one of five poems on a similar subject, written during the winter of 1798–1799 while Wordsworth was in Germany with his sister, Dorothy, and his friend Coleridge, who was studying German philosophy at the University of Göttingen. They are known as the Lucy poems—the name mentioned in three of them.

William Wordsworth

A Slumber Did My Spirit Seal

A slumber did my spirit seal;
   I had no human fears:
She seemed a thing that could not feel
   The touch of earthly years.

5 No motion has she now, no force;
   She neither hears nor sees;
Rolled round in earth's diurnal[1] course,
   With rocks, and stones, and trees.

---

1. **diurnal** [dī urn′əl]: daily.

Detail, *Near Dunkeld,* John Samuel Raven (1829–1877).

"No poem of mine," writes Wordsworth, "was composed under circumstances more pleasant for me to remember than this." He had brought his sister to visit a beautiful rural landscape—complete with an abbey, or church building—just over the Welsh border. Five years earlier, in 1793, the poet had passed through the same region alone. Now, under these pleasant circumstances, he began composing verses in his head, completing a poem in the course of this second walking tour. "Not a line of it was altered, and not any part of it written down till I reached Bristol."

Lines Composed a Few Miles Above Tintern Abbey

Five years have passed; five summers, with the length
Of five long winters! and again I hear
These waters, rolling from their mountain springs
With a soft inland murmur. Once again
5 Do I behold these steep and lofty cliffs,
That on a wild secluded scene impress
Thoughts of more deep seclusion; and connect
The landscape with the quiet of the sky.
The day is come when I again repose
10 Here, under this dark sycamore, and view
These plots of cottage ground, these orchard tufts,
Which at this season, with their unripe fruits,
Are clad in one green hue, and lose themselves
'Mid groves and copses.[1] Once again I see
15 These hedgerows, hardly hedgerows, little lines
Of sportive wood run wild; these pastoral farms,
Green to the very door; and wreaths of smoke
Sent up, in silence, from among the trees!
With some uncertain notice, as might seem
20 Of vagrant dwellers in the houseless woods,
Or of some Hermit's cave, where by his fire
The Hermit sits alone.
                              These beauteous forms,
Through a long absence, have not been to me

---

1. **copses** [kops'əz]: grove of small trees or bushes.

As is a landscape to a blind man's eye;
25 But oft, in lonely rooms, and 'mid the din
Of towns and cities, I have owed to them,
In hours of weariness, sensations sweet,
Felt in the blood, and felt along the heart;
And passing even into my purer mind,
30 With tranquil restoration—feelings too
Of unremembered pleasure; such, perhaps,
As have no slight or trivial influence
On that best portion of a good man's life,
His little, nameless, unremembered acts
35 Of kindness and of love. Nor less, I trust,
To them I may have owed another gift,
Of aspect more sublime; that blessed mood,
In which the burthen[2] of the mystery,
In which the heavy and the weary weight
40 Of all this unintelligible world,
Is lightened—that serene and blessed mood,
In which the affections gently lead us on—
Until, the breath of this corporeal frame[3]
And even the motion of our human blood
45 Almost suspended, we are laid asleep
In body, and become a living soul;
While with an eye made quiet by the power
Of harmony, and the deep power of joy,
We see into the life of things.
                                      If this
50 Be but a vain belief, yet, oh! how oft—
In darkness and amid the many shapes
Of joyless daylight; when the fretful stir
Unprofitable, and the fever of the world,
Have hung upon the beatings of my heart—
55 How oft, in spirit, have I turned to thee,
O sylvan[4] Wye![5] thou wanderer through the woods,
How often has my spirit turned to thee!

    And now, with gleams of half-extinguished thought
With many recognitions dim and faint,
60 And somewhat of a sad perplexity,
The picture of the mind revives again;
While here I stand, not only with the sense
Of present pleasure, but with pleasing thoughts
That in this moment there is life and food

---

2. **burthen:** burden.
3. **corporeal** [kôr pôr′ē əl] **frame:** physical body.
4. **sylvan** [sil′vən]: wooded.
5. **Wye** [wī]: river that runs near Tintern Abbey.

Detail, *Tintern Abbey*, Henry Harris
(c. 1805–1865).

65 For future years. And so I dare to hope,
Though changed, no doubt, from what I was when first
I came among these hills; when like a roe[6]
I bounded o'er the mountains, by the sides
Of the deep rivers, and the lonely streams,
70 Wherever nature led—more like a man
Flying from something that he dreads than one
Who sought the thing he loved. For nature then
(The coarser pleasures of my boyish days,
And their glad animal movements all gone by)
75 To me was all in all.—I cannot paint
What then I was. The sounding cataract[7]
Haunted me like a passion; the tall rock,
The mountain, and the deep and gloomy wood,
Their colors and their forms, were then to me
80 An appetite; a feeling and a love,
That had no need of a remoter charm,
By thought supplied, nor any interest
Unborrowed from the eye.—That time is past,
And all its aching joys are now no more,
85 And all its dizzy raptures. Nor for this
Faint[8] I, nor mourn nor murmur; other gifts
Have followed; for such loss, I would believe,
Abundant recompense. For I have learned
To look on nature, not as in the hour
90 Of thoughtless youth; but hearing oftentimes
The still, sad music of humanity,
Nor harsh nor grating, though of ample power
To chasten and subdue. And I have felt
A presence that disturbs me with the joy
95 Of elevated thoughts; a sense sublime
Of something far more deeply interfused,
Whose dwelling is the light of setting suns,
And the round ocean and the living air,
And the blue sky, and in the mind of man:
100 A motion and a spirit, that impels
All thinking things, all objects of all thought,
And rolls through all things. Therefore am I still
A lover of the meadows and the woods,
And mountains; and of all that we behold
105 From this green earth; of all the mighty world
Of eye, and ear—both what they half create,
And what perceive; well pleased to recognize
In nature and the language of the sense

---

6. **roe:** kind of deer.
7. **cataract:** waterfall.
8. **Faint:** lose heart or courage; become depressed.

William Wordsworth **403**

The anchor of my purest thoughts, the nurse,
110 The guide, the guardian of my heart, and soul
Of all my moral being.
                              Nor perchance,
If I were not thus taught, should I the more
Suffer[9] my genial[10] spirits to decay:
For thou art with me here upon the banks
115 Of this fair river; thou my dearest Friend,[11]
My dear, dear Friend; and in thy voice I catch
The language of my former heart, and read
My former pleasures in the shooting lights
Of thy wild eyes. Oh! yet a little while
120 May I behold in thee what I was once,
My dear, dear Sister! and this prayer I make,
Knowing that Nature never did betray
The heart that loved her; 'tis her privilege,
Through all the years of this our life, to lead
125 From joy to joy: for she can so inform[12]
The mind that is within us, so impress
With quietness and beauty, and so feed
With lofty thoughts, that neither evil tongues,
Rash judgments, nor the sneers of selfish men,
130 Nor greetings where no kindness is, nor all
The dreary intercourse of daily life,
Shall e'er prevail against us, or disturb
Our cheerful faith, that all which we behold
Is full of blessings. Therefore let the moon
135 Shine on thee in thy solitary walk;
And let the misty mountain winds be free
To blow against thee: and, in after years,
When these wild ecstasies shall be matured
Into a sober pleasure; when thy mind
140 Shall be a mansion for all lovely forms,
Thy memory be as a dwelling place
For all sweet sounds and harmonies; oh! then,
If solitude, or fear, or pain, or grief
Should be thy portion, with what healing thoughts
145 Of tender joy wilt thou remember me,
And these my exhortations! Nor, perchance—
If I should be where I no more can hear
Thy voice, nor catch from thy wild eyes these gleams
Of past existence—wilt thou then forget

---

9. **Suffer:** allow.
10. **genial:** relating to "genius" (natural disposition or powers).
11. **Friend:** Dorothy Wordsworth, the poet's sister.
12. **inform:** inspire.

150 That on the banks of this delightful stream
We stood together; and that I, so long
A worshiper of Nature, hither came
Unwearied in that service: rather say
With warmer love—oh! with far deeper zeal
155 Of holier love. Nor wilt thou then forget
That after many wanderings, many years
Of absence, these steep woods and lofty cliffs,
And this green pastoral landscape, were to me
More dear, both for themselves and for thy sake!

STUDY QUESTIONS

A Slumber Did My Spirit Seal

Recalling

1. Into what state did the speaker's spirit seal him? While in that state, why, according to lines 3 and 4, did the speaker have no earthly fears?
2. In the second stanza what has happened to the "she" of the poem?

Interpreting

3. What does the speaker learn by the second stanza?
4. Is the language of the poem complex or simple? What is the effect of such diction in this context?

Lines Composed a Few Miles Above Tintern Abbey

Recalling

1. What is impressed "on a wild secluded scene" (line 6), and what does the speaker notice now that five years have passed?
2. In lines 25–26 where does the speaker say he spent the five years? According to lines 26–41, in what two ways has this scene of nature influenced the speaker during the five years since he first viewed it?
3. What thoughts, described in lines 63–65, does the poet experience in addition to his "sense of present pleasure" while standing at the Wye river?
4. According to line 75, what role did nature play for the speaker in his adolescence? In place of his earlier view of nature, what does the speaker now see in nature (lines 93–111)?
5. What does the speaker wish for his sister in lines 116–120? In lines 134–146?
6. Why does the speaker consider nature dear to him, according to the last line?

Interpreting

7. In what terms would you describe the opening scene of the poem? What effect is suggested by the speaker's "repose" (line 9)? Based on lines 12–13, in what season would you say the speaker is revisiting the Wye valley?
8. How does the speaker convey the impression that he first hears and then sees the scene described in lines 2–5?
9. What do you suppose is that "something" the speaker refers to in line 96 when looking on nature?
10. In the context of the poem, what is the meaning of "Nature never did betray/The heart that loved her" (lines 122–123)?

Extending

11. Can you think of temporary enthusiasms—fads or interests—that, unlike Nature, might "betray" their adherents because of their impermanence or lack of real value?

VIEWPOINT

Matthew Arnold (page 535) wrote of Wordsworth's poetry:

The cause of its greatness is simple, and may be told quite simply. Wordsworth's poetry is great because of the extraordinary power with which Wordsworth feels the joy offered to us in nature, the joy offered to us in the simple primary affections and duties; and because of the extraordinary powers with which, in case after case, he shows us this joy, and renders it so as to make us share it.

■ Which of Wordsworth's poems presented here best convey that sense of joy? What specific phrases impart joy so vividly that we are led to share it?

LITERARY FOCUS

Structure

Structure refers to the units of thought that make up a literary work—the building blocks by means of which the work is put together in an organized and meaningful fashion. Thus, structure involves far more than the poem's verse form and arrangement: It is the sequence of thoughts and images that work together to impart the meaning of the poem. Perceiving the structure, or organizing principle, of a literary work helps us to understand it better—all the more so when the work is long and complex.

The structure of "A Slumber Did My Spirit Seal" (page 400) is as simple as the poem itself, and this simplicity contributes enormously to the power of the poem. In that poem the structure coincides with the stanzas: two units of thought, one in the past ("did," "had," "seemed") and one in the present ("now" and the present tense). All of stanza 1 refers to what "She" was; all of stanza 2 refers to what "She" is now.

"Tintern Abbey" is made more accessible if we follow the larger units of thought by means of which the poem moves forward. Wordsworth believed that poetry "takes its origin from emotion recollected in tranquillity." Two emotional responses to a particular scene are reported in "Tintern Abbey," and these responses serve as the poem's organizing principle.

Clearly the first twenty-two lines of the poem are grouped around a single idea, or purpose: to describe a natural scene. The end of that description is signaled by the gathering together of the various details in the summarizing phrase "These

beauteous forms" (line 22). What follows, for a number of lines, concerns the recollection of this same scene during the past five years: where that recollection has taken place and what its effect has been. Then Wordsworth presents a related thought, which, paraphrased, suggests, "Whether the memory of this beautiful landscape has been all I think it has or not, it is true that I have thought about it often." "And now . . . " (line 58) signals the commencement of yet another unit of thought—back to the present.

We must be alert to language that signals such thought shifts in a work. "Therefore" is one such word (lines 102, 134), drawing a conclusion from what has gone before. "Nor" (lines 111 and 146) is another. By becoming more sensitive to larger blocks of meaning—to the structure of a poem or story—we are better able to understand details within and related to those meanings.

Thinking About Structure

1. Line 111 introduces to the poem a new element that continues through to its conclusion. What is that new element?
2. That unit of thought from line 111 to the end of the poem might be subdivided at line 134. How do the two parts of the larger unit relate to each other? How do they differ?

COMPOSITION

Writing About Literature and Its Period

■ Write a brief essay that begins with this statement: "'Lines Composed a Few Miles Above Tintern Abbey' typifies Romantic poetry." Identify at least three aspects of the poem that mark it as Romantic, perhaps dealing with each aspect in a paragraph of its own. Support each point with quotations and specific details from the poem. *For help with this assignment, refer to Lesson 10 in the Writing About Literature Handbook at the back of this book.*

Describing a Scene

■ Think of a scene that awakens a strong emotion: of delighted awe, as in "Tintern Abbey," or of fright or exhilaration or disgust. In a paragraph or two describe the scene by choosing details that awaken the appropriate emotion in your reader, without mentioning specifically what that emotion is. You may begin with details of sound and work up to details of sight.

Samuel Taylor Coleridge
1772–1834

Samuel Taylor Coleridge is the other great figure besides Wordsworth in what is known as the first generation of Romantics. These two poets (distinguished from the so-called second generation: Byron, Shelley, and Keats) were close friends and collaborators, though their personal lives were in marked contrast and their literary accomplishments explored quite different areas of human experience.

Coleridge was born in England's Devonshire countryside. His father was a clergyman, and when he died, Samuel, then nine years old, was sent to school in London. While he was still quite young, tales such as *Robinson Crusoe* and the *Arabian Nights* enthralled Coleridge, and from an early age he enjoyed the worlds of fantasy and the exotic. At school he was an outstandingly brilliant student and, in 1791, went on to study at Cambridge University. There, however, he became increasingly unhappy and disillusioned with university life. In 1793 he left school to enlist in the army under the alias Silas Tomkyn Comberbacke, a pseudonym whose first initials were the same as his real ones. It was immediately apparent that Coleridge was completely and hopelessly unfit for army service, and, through the intervention of his brothers, he was discharged. Though he returned to Cambridge, he left the university in 1794 without obtaining a degree.

As a young man Coleridge was quite an idealist—in particular about the French Revolution. Only later, as the course of the revolution changed undeniably, did his idealism give way to disillusionment and disappointment.

In 1795 Coleridge met Wordsworth for the first time. The meeting proved momentous, and Wordsworth and his sister, Dorothy, soon moved to Somerset to be near Coleridge, who lived in the neighborhood with his wife, Sara. The two poets spent endless hours in each other's company and began their famous poetic collaboration. For Coleridge this period—leading up to their publication of *Lyrical Ballads* in 1798—was the happiest and most fulfilling of his life.

While Wordsworth's life was in its broadest outlines serene, Coleridge's was tormented, in part because early in life he developed rheumatism. Opium was then a standard medical treatment for such a painful malady, and in the course of persistent attacks, Coleridge became dependent on the drug. "Yet to my fellow men," he wrote, "I may say that I was seduced into the *accursed* Habit ignorantly."

Despite a life filled with illness and depression, Coleridge did a prodigious amount of work. He was the greatest literary critic of his age and one of the two or three greatest critics in the history of English literature; no one has more acute things to say on Shakespeare than does Coleridge. According to the testimony of many who heard him, he was also the finest conversationalist since Samuel Johnson. He was a noted lecturer, an influential philosopher, a theologian, and a journalist as well. The collected work of this towering figure (who faulted himself for not doing more) fills twenty volumes and seven notebooks. Included in that work are several poems supreme of their kind in the whole range of English literature.

The direction in which Coleridge's imagination led him resulted in a kind of Romantic poetry with notable differences from Wordsworth's. Wordsworth wrote poetry that strove "to give the charm of novelty to things of every day." Coleridge, on the other hand, directed his attention to "persons and characters supernatural, or at least romantic," but in a way that made them credible, that gave them "a semblance of truth sufficient to procure for these shadows of imagination that willing suspension of disbelief . . . which constitutes poetic faith." One poet dealt with the familiar; the other, with the strange and unfamiliar. Yet both exulted in expressing the sense of wonder that delights Romantics, whether found far off or close at hand.

■ Has artistic imagination ever transported you out of a bored state into a state of aliveness and joy? When? How?

Introducing Kubla Khan

Coleridge apparently had two explanations for the composition of this poem. On the one hand, he testifies that he devised this fragment under the influence of a painkiller (opium), prescribed for him "in consequence of a slight indisposition." According to this account, he had been reading about Kubla Khan [ko͞o′blə kän]—the thirteenth-century founder of the Mongol dynasty in China—in a travel book when, due to the drug's influence, he fell asleep. Upon waking from a three-hour dream, he found himself possessed of some two to three hundred lines of vivid poetry, which he began immediately to set down—only to be interrupted by "a person on business from Porlock," a nearby town. By the time the visitor had left, he had forgotten the rest of the poem. According to the other, more likely account of Coleridge's composition of "Kubla Khan," the poem was conceived during a daydream and did not come to him as a finished product after a dream. Regardless of which account of Coleridge's inspiration is accurate, the poem is a haunting elaboration of the passage Coleridge had been reading from *Purchas His Pilgrimage* (1613): "Here the Khan Kubla commanded a palace to be built, and a stately garden there-unto. And thus ten miles of fertile ground were enclosed with a wall."

Samuel Taylor Coleridge

Kubla Khan

In Xanadu[1] did Kubla Khan
A stately pleasure dome decree:[2]
Where Alph,[3] the sacred river, ran
Through caverns measureless to man
5   Down to a sunless sea.
So twice five miles of fertile ground
With walls and towers were girdled round:
And there were gardens bright with sinuous rills,[4]
Where blossomed many an incense-bearing tree;
10 And here were forests ancient as the hills,
Enfolding sunny spots of greenery.

But oh! that deep romantic[5] chasm which slanted
Down the green hill athwart[6] a cedarn[7] cover!
A savage place! as holy and enchanted
15 As e'er beneath a waning moon was haunted
By woman wailing for her demon lover!
And from this chasm, with ceaseless turmoil seething,
As if this earth in fast thick pants were breathing,
A mighty fountain momently[8] was forced:
20 Amid whose swift half-intermitted burst
Huge fragments vaulted like rebounding hail,
Or chaffy grain beneath the thresher's flail:
And 'mid these dancing rocks at once and ever
It flung up momently the sacred river.
25 Five miles meandering with a mazy motion
Through wood and dale the sacred river ran,
Then reached the caverns measureless to man,
And sank in tumult to a lifeless ocean:
And 'mid this tumult Kubla heard from far
30 Ancestral voices prophesying war!
    The shadow of the dome of pleasure
    Floated midway on the waves;

---

1. **Xanadu** [zan′ə doo′]: an indefinite region in Asia and Europe.
2. **decree:** order to be built.
3. **Alph:** probably the Greek river, Alpheus, or a reference to the classical Greek river god of that name.
4. **rills:** small streams, brooks.
5. **romantic:** having imaginative appeal.
6. **athwart:** across.
7. **cedarn:** made of cedar.
8. **momently:** from moment to moment.

Where was heard the mingled measure
From the fountain and the caves.
35 It was a miracle of rare device,[9]
A sunny pleasure dome with caves of ice!

A damsel with a dulcimer[10]
In a vision once I saw:
It was an Abyssinian[11] maid,
40 And on her dulcimer she played,
Singing of Mount Abora.[12]
Could I revive within me
Her symphony and song,
To such a deep delight 'twould win me,
45 That with music loud and long,
I would build that dome in air,
That sunny dome! those caves of ice!
And all who heard should see them there,
And all should cry, Beware! Beware!
50 His flashing eyes, his floating hair!
Weave a circle round him thrice,
And close your eyes with holy dread,
For he on honeydew hath fed,
And drunk the milk of Paradise.

---

9. **device:** design.
10. **dulcimer** [dul′sə mər]: stringed musical instrument
played by striking the strings with light hammers.
11. **Abyssinian** [ab′ə sin′ē ən]: from Ethiopia in Africa.
12. **Mount Abora:** probably Mount Amara in Abyssinia.

STUDY QUESTIONS

Recalling
1. What are the distinctive details of the pleasure dome in Xanadu, as described in the first eleven lines?
2. What images in the second stanza then emphasize that the world outside the dome is "A savage place" (line 14)?
3. What do the "Ancestral voices" (in line 30) predict?
4. What vision is introduced at line 37? What aspect of the vision does the speaker long to recover? What does he want to build?

Interpreting
5. To which different senses does the poem's opening description appeal?
6. What or whom do you suppose the damsel of the vision represents to the speaker?

Extending
7. "Kubla Khan" presents an exotic world—one that is strange and distant. How does the exotic continue to have an appeal? What current books or movies focus on mysterious, alien, or magical settings, characters, or situations?

Initially Wordsworth collaborated with Coleridge on the composition of "The Rime of the Ancient Mariner." Before dropping out of the joint venture, Wordsworth suggested several memorable details, including the shooting of the albatross and the ship's navigation by dead men. "The Rime" is an account of a sea voyage to distant places, with crime, death, and inhuman suffering as parts of the ghastly adventure. Some years after completing the poem, Coleridge himself wrote prose explanations for the margins to help the reader follow the movement of the narrative.

Samuel Taylor Coleridge

The Rime of the Ancient Mariner

ARGUMENT

How a Ship having passed the Line was driven by storms to the cold Country towards the South Pole, and how from thence she made her course to the tropical Latitude of the Great Pacific Ocean, and of the strange things that befell: and in what manner the Ancyent Marinere came back to his own Country.

PART I

It is an ancient Mariner,
And he stoppeth one of three.
—"By thy long gray beard and glittering eye,
Now wherefore stopp'st thou me?

An ancient Mariner meeteth three Gallants bidden to a wedding feast, and detaineth one.

5 "The Bridegroom's doors are opened wide,
And I am next of kin,
The guests are met, the feast is set:
May'st hear the merry din."

He holds him with his skinny hand;
10 "There was a ship," quoth he.
"Hold off! unhand me, graybeard loon!"
Eftsoons[1] his hand dropped he.

He holds him with his glittering eye—
The Wedding Guest stood still,
15 And listens like a three years' child:
The Mariner hath his will.

The Wedding Guest is spellbound by the eye of the old seafaring man and constrained to hear his tale.

---

1. **Eftsoons:** at once.

The Wedding Guest sat on a stone:
He cannot choose but hear;
And thus spake on that ancient man,
20 The bright-eyed Mariner.

"The ship was cheered, the harbor cleared,
Merrily did we drop
Below the kirk,[2] below the hill,
Below the lighthouse top.

25 "The Sun came up upon the left,
Out of the sea came he!
And he shone bright, and on the right
Went down into the sea.

*The Mariner tells how
the ship sailed
southward with a good
wind and fair weather,
till it reached the Line.[3]*

"Higher and higher every day,
30 Till over the mast at noon[4]—"
The Wedding Guest here beat his breast,
For he heard the loud bassoon.

The bride hath paced into the hall,
Red as a rose is she;
35 Nodding their heads before her goes
The merry minstrelsy.

*The Wedding Guest
heareth the bridal music;
but the Mariner
continueth his tale.*

The Wedding Guest he beat his breast,
Yet he cannot choose but hear;
And thus spake on that ancient man,
40 The bright-eyed Mariner.

"And now the Storm-blast came, and he
Was tyrannous and strong;
He struck with his o'ertaking wings,
And chased us south along.

*The ship driven by a
storm toward the South
Pole.*

45 "With sloping masts and dipping prow,
As who pursued with yell and blow
Still treads the shadow of his foe,
And forward bends his head,
The ship drove fast, loud roared the blast,
50 And southward aye[5] we fled.

"And now there came both mist and snow,
And it grew wondrous cold:
And ice, mast-high, came floating by,
As green as emerald.

---

2. **kirk:** Scottish for "church."
3. **Line:** equator.
4. **over . . . noon:** Sun's position indicates that ship has reached equator.
5. **aye:** ever.

55 "And through the drifts the snowy clifts
    Did send a dismal sheen:
    Nor shapes of men nor beasts we ken[6]—
    The ice was all between.

The land of ice, and of fearful sounds, where no living thing was to be seen.

    "The ice was here, the ice was there,
60 The ice was all around:
    It cracked and growled, and roared and howled,
    Like noises in a swound![7]

    "At length did cross an Albatross,
    Thorough[8] the fog it came;
65 As if it had been a Christian soul,
    We hailed it in God's name.

Till a great sea bird, called the Albatross, came through the snow-fog, and was received with great joy and hospitality.

    "It ate the food it ne'er had eat,[9]
    And round and round it flew.
    The ice did split with a thunder-fit;
70 The helmsman steered us through!

    "And a good south wind sprung up behind;
    The Albatross did follow,
    And every day, for food or play,
    Came to the mariners' hollo!

And lo! the Albatross proveth a bird of good omen, and followeth the ship as it returned northward through fog and floating ice.

75 "In mist or cloud, on mast or shroud,[10]
    It perched for vespers[11] nine;
    Whiles all the night, through fog-smoke white,
    Glimmered the white Moon-shine."

    "God save thee, ancient Mariner!
80 From the fiends, that plague thee thus!—
    Why look'st thou so?"[12]—"With my crossbow
    I shot the Albatross!"

The ancient Mariner inhospitably killeth the pious bird of good omen.

PART II

    "The Sun now rose upon the right:[13]
    Out of the sea came he,
85 Still hid in mist, and on the left
    Went down into the sea.

———————

   6. **ken:** Scottish for "saw"; "knew."
   7. **swound:** fainting fit, swoon.
   8. **Thorough:** through.
   9. **eat** [et]: old form of past participle of eat.
  10. **shroud:** rope supporting the mast.
  11. **vespers:** evenings.
  12. **"God . . . so?":** spoken by the Wedding Guest.
  13. **The Sun . . . right:** The sun's position indicates that ship is traveling north.

"And the good south wind still blew behind,
But no sweet bird did follow,
Nor any day for food or play
90 Came to the mariners' hollo!

"And I had done a hellish thing,
And it would work 'em woe:
For all averred, I had killed the bird
That made the breeze to blow.
95 Ah, wretch! said they, the bird to slay,
That made the breeze to blow!

"Nor dim nor red, like God's own head,
The glorious Sun uprist:[14]
Then all averred, I had killed the bird
100 That brought the fog and mist.
'Twas right, said they, such birds to slay,
That bring the fog and mist.

"The fair breeze blew, the white foam flew,
The furrow[15] followed free;
105 We were the first that ever burst
Into that silent sea.

"Down dropped the breeze, the sails dropped down,
'Twas sad as sad could be;
And we did speak only to break
110 The silence of the sea!

"All in a hot and copper sky,
The bloody Sun, at noon,
Right up above the mast did stand,
No bigger than the Moon.

115 "Day after day, day after day,
We stuck, nor breath nor motion;
As idle as a painted ship
Upon a painted ocean.

"Water, water, everywhere,
120 And all the boards did shrink;
Water, water, everywhere,
Nor any drop to drink.

*His shipmates cry out
against the ancient
Mariner for killing the
bird of good luck.*

*But when the fog cleared
off they justify the same,
and thus make
themselves accomplices
in the crime.*

*The fair breeze
continues; the ship
enters the Pacific Ocean,
and sails northward,
even till it reaches the
Line.*

*The ship hath been
suddenly becalmed.*

*And the Albatross begins
to be avenged.*

---

14. **uprist:** uprose.
15. **furrow:** ship's wake.

Engraving by Gustave Doré (1832–1883).

"The very deep did rot: O Christ!
That ever this should be!
125 Yea, slimy things did crawl with legs
Upon the slimy sea.

"About, about, in reel and rout[16]
The death-fires[17] danced at night;
The water, like a witch's oils,
130 Burned green, and blue and white.

"And some in dreams assurèd were
Of the Spirit that plagued us so;
Nine fathom[18] deep he had followed us
From the land of mist and snow.

A Spirit had followed them; one of the invisible inhabitants of this planet, neither departed souls nor angels. They are very numerous, and there is no climate or element without one or more.

135 "And every tongue, through utter drought,
Was withered at the root;
We could not speak, no more than if
We had been choked with soot.

"Ah! well-a-day! what evil looks
140 Had I from old and young!
Instead of the cross, the Albatross
About my neck was hung.

The shipmates, in their sore distress, would fain throw the whole guilt on the ancient Mariner: in sign whereof they hang the dead sea bird round his neck.

PART III

"There passed a weary time. Each throat
Was parched, and glazed each eye.
145 A weary time! a weary time!
How glazed each weary eye,
When looking westward, I beheld
A something in the sky.

The ancient Mariner beholdeth a sign in the element afar off.

"At first it seemed a little speck,
150 And then it seemed a mist;
It moved and moved, and took at last
A certain shape, I wist.[19]

"A speck, a mist, a shape, I wist!
And still it neared and neared:
155 As if it dodged a water sprite,
It plunged and tacked and veered.

---

16. **rout:** disorderly crowd.
17. **death-fires:** St. Elmo's fire, an electrical effect lighting masts
of ships; believed by seamen to be a portent of disaster.
18. **fathom:** unit of measure equal to six feet.
19. **wist:** knew.

"With throats unslaked, with black lips baked,
We could nor laugh nor wail;
Through utter drought all dumb we stood!
160 I bit my arm, I sucked the blood,
And cried, A sail! a sail!

At its nearer approach, it seemeth him to be a ship; and at a dear ransom he freeth his speech from the bonds of thirst.

"With throats unslaked, with black lips baked,
Agape they heard me call:
Gramercy![20] they for joy did grin,
165 And all at once their breath drew in,
As they were drinking all.

A flash of joy;

"See! see! (I cried) she tacks no more!
Hither to work us weal;[21]
Without a breeze, without a tide,
170 She steadies with upright keel!

And horror follows. For can it be a ship that comes onward without wind or tide?

"The western wave was all aflame,
The day was well nigh done!
Almost upon the western wave
Rested the broad bright Sun;
175 When that strange shape drove suddenly
Betwixt us and the Sun.

"And straight the Sun was flecked with bars,
(Heaven's Mother send us grace!)
As if through a dungeon grate he peered
180 With broad and burning face.

It seemeth him but the skeleton of a ship.

"Alas! (thought I, and my heart beat loud)
How fast she nears and nears!
Are those *her* sails that glance in the Sun,
Like restless gossameres?[22]

185 "Are those her ribs through which the Sun
Did peer, as through a grate?
And is that Woman all her crew?
Is that a Death? and are there two?
Is Death that woman's mate?

And its ribs are seen as bars on the face of the setting Sun. The Specter-Woman and her Death mate, and no other on board the skeleton ship.

190 "*Her* lips were red, *her* looks were free,
Her locks were yellow as gold:
Her skin was as white as leprosy,
The Nightmare Life-in-Death was she,
Who thicks man's blood with cold.

Like vessel, like crew!

---

20. **Gramercy** [grə mur′sē]: great thanks.
21. **work us weal:** do us good, benefit us.
22. **gossameres:** spiderwebs.

195 "The naked hulk alongside came,
And the twain were casting dice;
'The game is done! I've won! I've won!'
Quoth she, and whistles thrice.

Death and Life-in-Death have diced for the ship's crew, and she (the latter) winneth the ancient Mariner.

"The Sun's rim dips; the stars rush out:
200 At one stride comes the dark;
With far-heard whisper, o'er the sea,
Off shot the specter bark.

No twilight, within the courts of the Sun.

"We listened and looked sideways up!
Fear at my heart, as at a cup,
205 My lifeblood seemed to sip!
The stars were dim, and thick the night,
The steersman's face by his lamp gleamed white;
From the sails the dew did drip—
Till clomb²³ above the eastern bar
210 The hornèd²⁴ Moon, with one bright star
With the nether²⁵ tip.

At the rising of the Moon,

"One after one, by the star-dogged Moon,²⁶
Too quick for groan or sigh,
Each turned his face with a ghastly pang,
215 And cursed me with his eye.

One after another,

"Four times fifty living men,
(And I heard nor sigh nor groan)
With heavy thump, a lifeless lump,
They dropped down one by one.

His shipmates drop down dead.

220 "The souls did from their bodies fly—
They fled to bliss or woe!
And every soul, it passed me by
Like the whizz of my crossbow!"

But Life-in-Death begins her work on the ancient Mariner.

PART IV
"I fear thee, ancient Mariner!
225 I fear thy skinny hand!
And thou art long, and lank, and brown,
As is the ribbed sea-sand.

The Wedding Guest feareth that a Spirit is talking to him;

"I fear thee and thy glittering eye,
And thy skinny hand, so brown."—

---

23. **clomb:** climbed.
24. **hornèd:** crescent.
25. **nether:** lower.
26. **star-dogged Moon:** sign of impending evil.

230 "Fear not, fear not, thou Wedding Guest!
This body dropped not down.

"Alone, alone, all, all alone,
Alone on a wide wide sea!
And never a saint took pity on
235 My soul in agony.

"The many men, so beautiful!
And they all dead did lie:
And a thousand thousand slimy things
Lived on; and so did I.

240 "I looked upon the rotting sea,
And drew my eyes away;
I looked upon the rotting deck,
And there the dead men lay.

"I looked to heaven, and tried to pray;
245 But or^{27} ever a prayer had gushed,
A wicked whisper came, and made
My heart as dry as dust.

"I closed my lids, and kept them close,
And the balls like pulses beat;
250 For the sky and sea, and the sea and the sky
Lay like a load on my weary eye,
And the dead were at my feet.

"The cold sweat melted from their limbs,
Nor rot nor reek did they:
255 The look with which they looked on me
Had never passed away.

"An orphan's curse would drag to hell
A spirit from on high;
But oh! more horrible than that
260 Is a curse in a dead man's eye!
Seven days, seven nights, I saw that curse,
And yet I could not die.

"The moving Moon went up the sky,
And nowhere did abide:
265 Softly she was going up,
And a star or two beside—

But the ancient Mariner assureth him of his bodily life, and proceedeth to relate his horrible penance.

He despiseth the creatures of the calm.

And envieth that they should live, and so many lie dead.

But the curse liveth for him in the eye of the dead men.

In his loneliness and fixedness he yearneth towards the journeying Moon, and the stars that still move onward; and everywhere the blue sky belongs to them, and is their appointed rest, and their native country and their own natural homes, which they enter unannounced, as lords that are certainly expected, and yet there is a silent joy at their arrival.

---

27. **or:** before.

"Her beams bemocked the sultry main,
Like April hoar-frost spread;
But where the ship's huge shadow lay,
270 The charmèd water burned alway
A still and awful red.

"Beyond the shadow of the ship,
I watched the water snakes:
They moved in tracks of shining white,
275 And when they reared, the elfish light
Fell off in hoary flakes.

By the light of the Moon he beholdeth God's creatures of the great calm.

"Within the shadow of the ship
I watched their rich attire:
Blue, glossy green, and velvet black,
280 They coiled and swam; and every track
Was a flash of golden fire.

"O happy living things! no tongue
Their beauty might declare:
A spring of love gushed from my heart,
285 And I blessed them unaware;
Sure my kind saint took pity on me,
And I blessed them unaware.

Their beauty and their happiness.

He blesseth them in his heart.

"The selfsame moment I could pray;
And from my neck so free
290 The Albatross fell off, and sank
Like lead into the sea."

The spell begins to break.

PART V

"Oh sleep! it is a gentle thing,
Beloved from pole to pole!
To Mary Queen the praise be given!
295 She sent the gentle sleep from Heaven,
That slid into my soul.

"The silly[28] buckets on the deck,
That had so long remained,
I dreamed that they were filled with dew;
300 And when I awoke it rained.

By grace of the holy Mother, the ancient Mariner is refreshed with rain.

"My lips were wet, my throat was cold,
My garments all were dank;

─────────
28. **silly:** plain, simple.

Sure I had drunken in my dreams,
And still my body drank.

305 "I moved, and could not feel my limbs:
I was so light—almost
I thought that I had died in sleep,
And was a blessed ghost.

"And soon I heard a roaring wind:
310 It did not come anear;
But with its sound it shook the sails,
That were so thin and sere.

"The upper air burst into life!
And a hundred fire-flags[29] sheen,[30]
315 To and fro they were hurried about!
And to and fro, and in and out,
The wan stars danced between.

"And the coming wind did roar more loud,
And the sails did sigh like sedge;[31]
320 And the rain poured down from one black cloud;
The Moon was at its edge.

"The thick black cloud was cleft, and still
The Moon was at its side:
Like waters shot from some high crag,
325 The lightning fell with never a jag,
A river steep and wide.

"The loud wind never reached the ship,
Yet now the ship moved on!
Beneath the lightning and the Moon
330 The dead men gave a groan.

"They groaned, they stirred, they all uprose,
Nor spake, nor moved their eyes;
It had been strange, even in a dream,
To have seen those dead men rise.

335 "The helmsman steered, the ship moved on;
Yet never a breeze up-blew;
The mariners all 'gan work the ropes,

---

29. **fire-flags:** the aurora australis, or southern lights.
30. **sheen:** shone.
31. **sedge:** marsh grass.
32. **inspired:** filled with a spirit.

Where they were wont[33] to do;
They raised their limbs like lifeless tools—
340 We were a ghastly crew.

"The body of my brother's son
Stood by me, knee to knee:
The body and I pulled at one rope,
But he said nought to me."

345 "I fear thee, ancient Mariner!"
"Be calm, thou Wedding Guest!
'Twas not those souls that fled in pain,
Which to their corses[34] came again,
But a troop of spirits blessed:

But not by the souls of the men, nor by demons of earth or middle air, but by a blessed troop of angelic spirits, sent down by the invocation of the guardian saint.

350 "For when it dawned—they dropped their arms,
And clustered round the mast;
Sweet sounds rose slowly through their mouths,
And from their bodies passed.

"Around, around, flew each sweet sound,
355 Then darted to the Sun;
Slowly the sounds came back again,
Now mixed, now one by one.

"Sometimes a-dropping from the sky
I heard the skylark sing;
360 Sometimes all little birds that are,
How they seemed to fill the sea and air
With their sweet jargoning![35]

"And now 'twas like all instruments,
Now like a lonely flute;
365 And now it is an angel's song,
That makes the heavens be mute.

"It ceased; yet still the sails made on
A pleasant noise till noon,
A noise like of a hidden brook
370 In the leafy month of June,
That to the sleeping woods all night
Singeth a quiet tune.

---

33. **wont:** accustomed.
34. **corses:** corpses.
35. **jargoning:** warbling.

"Till noon we quietly sailed on,
Yet never a breeze did breathe:
375 Slowly and smoothly went the ship,
Moved onward from beneath.

"Under the keel nine fathom deep,
From the land of mist and snow,
The Spirit slid: and it was he
380 That made the ship to go.
The sails at noon left off their tune,
And the ship stood still also.

"The Sun, right up above the mast,
Had fixed her to the ocean:
385 But in a minute she 'gan stir,
With a short uneasy motion—
Backwards and forwards half her length
With a short uneasy motion.

"Then like a pawing horse let go,
390 She made a sudden bound:
It flung the blood into my head,
And I fell down in a swound.

"How long in that same fit I lay,
I have not[36] to declare;
395 But ere my living life returned,
I heard, and in my soul discerned,
Two voices in the air.

"'Is it he?' quoth one, 'Is this the man?
By him who died on cross,
400 With his cruel bow he laid full low
The harmless Albatross.

"'The Spirit who bideth by himself
In the land of mist and snow,
He loved the bird that loved the man
405 Who shot him with his bow.'

"The other was a softer voice,
As soft as honeydew:
Quoth he, 'The man hath penance done,
And penance more will do.' "

The lonesome Spirit from the South Pole carries on the ship as far as the Line, in obedience to the angelic troop, but still requireth vengeance.

The Polar Spirit's fellow demons, the invisible inhabitants of the element, take part in his wrong; and two of them relate, one to the other, that penance long and heavy for the ancient Mariner hath been accorded to the Polar Spirit, who returneth southward.

---

36. **have not:** have not the ability or knowledge.

PART VI

FIRST VOICE

410 "'But tell me, tell me! speak again,
Thy soft response renewing—
What makes that ship drive on so fast?
What is the ocean doing?'

SECOND VOICE

"'Still as a slave before his lord,
415 The ocean hath no blast;
His great bright eye most silently
Up to the Moon is cast—

"'If he may know which way to go;
For she guides him smooth or grim.
420 See, brother, see! how graciously
She looketh down on him.'

FIRST VOICE

"'But why drives on that ship so fast,
Without or wave or wind?'

SECOND VOICE

"'The air is cut away before,
425 And closes from behind.'

"'Fly, brother, fly! more high, more high!
Or we shall be belated:[37]
For slow and slow that ship will go,
When the Mariner's trance is abated.'

430 "I woke, and we were sailing on
As in a gentle weather:
'Twas night, calm night, the moon was high;
The dead men stood together.

"All stood together on the deck,
435 For a charnel-dungeon[38] fitter:
All fixed on me their stony eyes,
That in the Moon did glitter.

"The pang, the curse, with which they died,
Had never passed away:

The Mariner hath been cast into a trance; for the angelic power causeth the vessel to drive northward faster than human life could endure.

The supernatural motion is retarded; the Mariner awakes, and his penance begins anew.

---

37. **belated:** made late.
38. **charnel-dungeon:** vault to hold bones of the dead.

440 I could not draw my eyes from theirs,
Nor turn them up to pray.

"And now this spell was snapped: once more
I viewed the ocean green,
And looked far forth, yet little saw
445 Of what had else been seen—

"Like one, that on a lonesome road
Doth walk in fear and dread,
And having once turned round walks on,
And turns no more his head;
450 Because he knows, a frightful fiend
Doth close behind him tread.

"But soon there breathed a wind on me,
Nor sound nor motion made:
Its path was not upon the sea,
455 In ripple or in shade.

"It raised my hair, it fanned my cheek
Like a meadow-gale of spring—
It mingled strangely with my fears,
Yet it felt like a welcoming.

460 "Swiftly, swiftly flew the ship,
Yet she sailed softly too:
Sweetly, sweetly blew the breeze—
On me alone it blew.

"Oh! dream of joy! is this indeed
465 The lighthouse top I see?
Is this the hill? is this the kirk?
Is this mine own countree?

"We drifted o'er the harbor bar,
And I with sobs did pray—
470 O let me be awake, my God!
Or let me sleep alway.

"The harbor bay was clear as glass,
So smoothly it was strewn!⁴⁰
And on the bay the moonlight lay,
475 And the shadow of the Moon.

"The rock shone bright, the kirk no less,
That stands above the rock:

The curse is finally expiated.[39]

And the ancient Mariner beholdeth his native country.

---

39. **expiated:** paid for, made amends for.
40. **strewn:** spread.

The moonlight steeped in silentness
The steady weathercock.

480 "And the bay was white with silent light
Till, rising from the same,
Full many shapes, that shadows were,
In crimson colors came.

The angelic spirits leave the dead bodies,

"A little distance from the prow
485 Those crimson shadows were:
I turned my eyes upon the deck—
Oh, Christ! what saw I there!

"Each corse lay flat, lifeless and flat,
And, by the holy rood!⁴¹
490 A man all light, a seraph⁴² man,
On every corse there stood.

And appear in their own forms of light.

"This seraph band, each waved his hand:
It was a heavenly sight!
They stood as signals to the land,
495 Each one a lovely light;

"This seraph band, each waved his hand,
No voice did they impart—
No voice; but oh! the silence sank
Like music on my heart.

500 "But soon I heard the dash of oars,
I heard the Pilot's cheer;
My head was turned perforce⁴³ away,
And I saw a boat appear.

"The Pilot and the Pilot's boy,
505 I heard them coming fast:
Dear Lord in Heaven! it was a joy
The dead men could not blast.

"I saw a third—I heard his voice:
It is the Hermit good!
510 He singeth loud his godly hymns
That he makes in the wood.
He'll shrieve⁴⁴ my soul, he'll wash away
The Albatross's blood."

---

41. **rood:** cross.
42. **seraph:** highest in the rank of angels.
43. **perforce:** of necessity.
44. **shrieve** [shrēv]: hear confession, grant forgiveness, impose penance.

PART VII

"This Hermit good lives in that wood

515 Which slopes down to the sea.
How loudly his sweet voice he rears!
He loves to talk with mariners
That come from a far countree.

The Hermit of the wood.

"He kneels at morn, and noon, and eve—
520 He hath a cushion plump:
It is the moss that wholly hides
The rotted old oak stump.

"The skiff boat neared: I heard them talk,
'Why, this is strange, I trow!'[45]
525 Where are those lights so many and fair,
That signal made but now?'

"'Strange, by my faith!' the Hermit said—
'And they answered not our cheer!
The planks looked warped! and see those sails,
530 How thin they are and sere!
I never saw aught like to them,
Unless perchance it were

*Approacheth the ship
with wonder.*

"'Brown skeletons of leaves that lag
My forest-brook along;
535 When the ivy tod[46] is heavy with snow,
And the owlet whoops to the wolf below,
That eats the she-wolf's young.'

"'Dear Lord! it hath a fiendish look,'
(The Pilot made reply)
540 'I am a-feared'—'Push on, push on!'
Said the Hermit cheerily.

"The boat came closer to the ship,
But I nor spake nor stirred;
The boat came close beneath the ship,
545 And straight[47] a sound was heard.

"Under the water it rumbled on,
Still louder and more dread:
It reached the ship, it split the bay;
The ship went down like lead.

*The ship suddenly
sinketh.*

---

45. **trow:** believe.
46. **ivy tod:** ivy bush.
47. **straight:** straightaway, immediately.

550 "Stunned by that loud and dreadful sound,
Which sky and ocean smote,
Like one that hath been seven days drowned
My body lay afloat;
But swift as dreams, myself I found
555 Within the Pilot's boat.

The ancient Mariner is saved in the Pilot's boat.

"Upon the whirl, where sank the ship,
The boat spun round and round;
And all was still, save that the hill
Was telling of the sound.

560 "I moved my lips—the Pilot shrieked
And fell down in a fit;
The holy Hermit raised his eyes,
And prayed where he did sit.

"I took the oars: the Pilot's boy,
565 Who now doth crazy go,
Laughed loud and long, and all the while
His eyes went to and fro.
'Ha! ha!' quoth he, 'full plain I see,
The Devil knows how to row.'

570 "And now, all in my own countree,
I stood on the firm land!
The Hermit stepped forth from the boat,
And scarcely he could stand.

"'O shrieve me, shrieve me, holy man!'
575 The Hermit crossed his brow.[48]
'Say quick,' quoth he, 'I bid thee say—
What manner of man art thou?'

The ancient Mariner earnestly entreateth the Hermit to shrieve him; and the penance of life falls on him.

"Forthwith this frame of mine was wrenched
With a woeful agony,
580 Which forced me to begin my tale;
And then it left me free.

"Since then, at an uncertain hour,
That agony returns;
And till my ghastly tale is told,
585 This heart within me burns.

And ever and anon throughout his future life an agony constraineth him to travel from land to land,

"I pass, like night, from land to land;
I have strange power of speech;
That moment that his face I see,

---

48. **crossed his brow:** made the sign of the cross on his forehead.

I know the man that must hear me:
590 To him my tale I teach.

"What loud uproar bursts from that door!
The wedding guests are there:
But in the garden-bower the bride
And bridemaids singing are:
595 And hark the little vesper bell,
Which biddeth me to prayer!

"O Wedding Guest! this soul hath been
Alone on a wide, wide sea:
So lonely 'twas, that God himself
600 Scarce seemèd there to be.

"Oh sweeter than the marriage feast,
'Tis sweeter far to me,
To walk together to the kirk
With a goodly company!—

605 "To walk together to the kirk,
And all together pray,
While each to his great Father bends,
Old men, and babes, and loving friends,
And youths and maidens gay!

610 "Farewell, farewell! but this I tell
To thee, thou Wedding Guest!
He prayeth well, who loveth well
Both man and bird and beast.

And to teach by his own example love and reverence to all things that God made and loveth.

"He prayeth best, who loveth best
615 All things both great and small;
For the dear God who loveth us,
He made and loveth all."

The Mariner, whose eye is bright,
Whose beard with age is hoar,
620 Is gone: and now the Wedding Guest
Turned from the bridegroom's door.

He went like one that hath been stunned,
And is of sense forlorn:[49]
A sadder and a wiser man,
625 He rose the morrow morn.

---

49. **forlorn:** bereft, stripped of.

STUDY QUESTIONS

Recalling

1. In Part I what happens to the wedding guest? Summarize the voyage as described by the ancient Mariner in Part I, noting his admission in lines 81–82.
2. In the beginning of Part II, explain the immediate consequence of the crime, and then tell what happens to the ship in the loneliness of the Pacific. How do the ancient Mariner's fellow crewmen single him out for punishment?
3. Who are the two people aboard the strange vessel in Part III, and what are they doing? What is the outcome of their activity?
4. In Part IV what happens when the Mariner prays?
5. What reasons are given at lines 402–405 for the actions of the lonesome Polar Spirit? What is the Mariner's fate, according to lines 408–409?
6. By what miraculous means, detailed in Part VI, does the Mariner's ship return home? What does the Mariner hope for in lines 512–513?
7. According to lines 582–590, what has been the fate of the Mariner since returning to shore? What, according to lines 612–617, is the moral of the Mariner's story?

Interpreting

8. What do you think is meant by the term "Life-in-Death," introduced in Part III when Death wins all the crew except for one? How does the phrase "Life-in-Death" describe the Mariner's life subsequently?
9. Identify at least three vivid details and images that help Coleridge succeed in making the reader willingly "suspend disbelief" and accept the possibility of the story.
10. How do we know that the Mariner's penance is for his act of contempt against a living creature? How is this illustrated throughout the poem?

Extending

11. Coleridge here is imitating the ballad form that "Sir Patrick Spens" (page 53) exemplifies. What similarities—in stanza form, in diction, in subject matter, and in style—do you see between the two? Why is ballad form appropriate for Coleridge's poem?

VIEWPOINT

Robert Penn Warren has explained "The Rime of the Ancient Mariner" is in part a statement about sin, punishment, repentance, and redemption:

> The Mariner shoots the bird; suffers various pains, the greatest of which is loneliness and spiritual anguish; upon recognizing the beauty of the foul sea snakes experiences a gush of love for them and is able to pray; is returned miraculously to his home port, where he discovers the joy of human communion in God, and utters the moral, "He prayeth best, who loveth best. . . ."

■ To what evidence can you point that supports Warren's assertion concerning the Mariner's greatest pain? What relation do you see between the sea snakes and the albatross? How does the Mariner bear his burden of repentance?

LITERARY FOCUS

Sound in Poetry

To be appreciated fully, a poem should be read aloud, for its very sound contributes to its effectiveness and brings pleasure. Much of that pleasure comes from repetition of sound.

Rhyme is the repetition of the final stressed vowel sound and any succeeding sounds in a word: *decree/sea, ran/man, seething/breathing.* So-called **masculine rhyme** involves the rhyming of only stressed syllables: *decree/sea, ran/man;* **feminine** rhyme involves unstressed syllables as well: *seething/breathing, pleasure/measure.* In **near rhyme** (also called **off rhyme** and **slant rhyme**) the rhyme is imperfect: *Khan/man, enchanted/haunted.* When rhyme occurs at the ends of lines, we have **end rhyme,** as when *Khan, ran,* and *man* rhyme in lines 1, 3, and 4 of "Kubla Khan." When rhyme occurs within a line, we have **internal rhyme,** as when *met* and *set* rhyme in line 7 of "The Ancient Mariner."

In addition to rhyme, there are other agreeable repetitions in poetry. Repetition of nearby consonant sounds is called **alliteration:** *Kubla Khan, measureless to man.* Repetition of nearby vowel sounds is called **assonance:** *twice five miles.* (The term *assonance* also refers to near rhymes in which the similarity is in the vowel sound: *time/mine.* The term **consonance** is used for near rhymes in which the similarity is in the consonant sound: *forced/burst.*)

A final important sound effect in poetry is **onomatopoeia,** which refers to a word whose sound suggests its meaning. *Buzz* and *hum* are obvious examples of words with sounds that suggest their meaning. In addition, sometimes a whole line of poetry may be onomatopoeic:

Five miles meandering with a mazy motion

The very sound of the line imitates what is being described, a river flowing leisurely in the woods.

Thinking About Sound in Poetry

1. Find at least two other examples of internal rhyme in "The Rime of the Ancient Mariner."
2. What examples of alliteration do you find in lines 6 and 7 of "Kubla Khan"?
3. What examples of assonance do you find in lines 17 and 20 of "Kubla Khan"?
4. Find an example of onomatopoeia in lines 59–62 of "The Rime of the Ancient Mariner."

VOCABULARY

Archaic Words

Coleridge used words that were already out of date by the late eighteenth century, when he wrote "The Rime of the Ancient Mariner." We use the term **archaic** to describe words that are old-fashioned or that belong to an earlier period. For example, Coleridge used *Eftsoons* (line 12), *swound* (line 62), and *rood* (line 489). In particular, he used old past-tense forms of verbs.

1. Find the archaic past-tense verb in each of the following lines, and explain its meaning: line 19, line 98, line 152, line 209.
2. Suggest why Coleridge chose to use archaic words. What effect do they create?

COMPOSITION

Writing About a Symbol

Discuss the symbolism of the Albatross in "The Rime of the Ancient Mariner." Begin by report-ing what the bird first represents (lines 63–78). Then describe what its murder causes and the possible meaning of hanging the dead bird around the Mariner's neck. Conclude by ex-plaining when and why the Albatross fell from the Mariner, and then briefly give the meaning of the expression *an albatross around one's neck. For help with this assignment, refer to Lesson 5 in the Writing About Literature Hand-book at the back of this book.*

Describing a Journey

Consider the progress of the ship's journey in "The Rime of the Ancient Mariner." Describe the journey accurately in two or three para-graphs that cite relevant lines from the poem. In writing your paragraphs consider the follow-ing questions: How accurate is the description of the voyage? To begin with, why does the Mariner mention kirk, hill, and lighthouse top in that order in lines 23–24? Compare the order with that in the stanza beginning at line 464. What language in line 466 indicates that the ship is sailing from Scotland? In what direction is the ship going when the sun comes up upon the left (line 25)? Where is it when the sun is directly over the mast at noon (line 30?) What other lines in the poem help you to follow the progress of the ship?

COMPARING WRITERS

1. It has been said that although Coleridge's sub-ject matter is so different from Wordsworth's the two poets create similar effects; that is, they both convey the Romantic spirit of won-der. What spirit, or sense, of wonder can you find in "The Rime of the Ancient Mariner"? In the poems included here by Wordsworth?
2. While acknowledging that Wordsworth and Coleridge created worlds of wonder, comment on the realism in the poems by both these writers. Find examples of each poet's realism of detail as he develops a picture or a mood.
3. Find examples of Wordsworth's turning to na-ture as a source of inspiration and assurance. Based on "Kubla Khan," when or how does nature offer comfort to Coleridge?

George Gordon, Lord Byron
1788–1824

Though his poetry is now regarded as the least representative of the Romantic movement with which he is identified, the image that his contemporaries had of George Gordon, Lord Byron was of the arch-Romantic, extraordinary in almost every way. Byron was uncommonly handsome; Coleridge said he had scarcely ever seen "so beautiful a countenance." However, Byron had a handicap—a club foot—that both physically and psychologically distressed him all his life. To compensate for this impairment he became an outstanding athlete: a masterful swimmer, horseman, boxer, cricket player, and fencer.

A descendant of two aristocratic but flamboyant and violent families, Byron unexpectedly inherited his title at the age of ten when his great-uncle, known as the Wicked Lord, died. Thereupon he was sent to Harrow, a famous private school. Later, as a student at Cambridge University, he was known for his lavish and fashionable life style and flamboyant behavior; he even kept a tame bear as a pet. After graduating from Cambridge, he embarked upon an adventurous journey, traveling on horseback across Portugal and Spain and on to distant lands that few Englishmen had visited, including such unfamiliar places as Asia Minor and mountainous Albania. Returning, he effortlessly wrote a poem in Spenserian stanzas, *Childe Harold's Pilgrimage*—a travelogue, narrated by an eloquent but emotional fictitious tourist—that made him the toast of London society. In his own words, "I awoke one morning and found myself famous." That was when he was twenty-four. In addition, Byron the poet was also a champion of liberal political causes, and, as a member of the House of Lords, he became an active spokesman for the extreme liberal faction of the Whig party. In this capacity he bravely defended the rebelling Nottingham weavers whose jobs had been threatened by new textile machines.

Soon, however, his fame had turned to notoriety, as the dashing young poet became the center of scandals, including an early and much publicized separation from his very proper young wife. In 1816, when he was twenty-eight, Byron went into self-imposed exile, never to return to England. The rest of his brief life was lived on the Continent, mostly in Italy. During his travels he befriended the poet Percy Bysshe Shelley (page 441), with whom he developed a productive intellectual relationship. Always an outspoken defender of personal and political freedom, Byron died shortly after his thirty-sixth birthday, having exhausted his energies training Greek troops fighting for independence from Turkey.

His life is assuredly a romantic one: His scandalous behavior, idealism, attractiveness, defiance of conventionality, and superlative gifts all contribute to our notion of Byron as the quintessential

Romantic. Yet in literary terms he now seems the least Romantic of the five great poets who best exemplify that movement of the early nineteenth century. Byron's love poems, like "She Walks in Beauty," are graceful, musical compliments reminiscent of the love poems of Ben Jonson (page 261), the father of neoclassicism, and those of the Cavalier poets influenced by Jonson, such as Richard Lovelace (page 272). *Don Juan,* among Byron's greatest literary achievements, seems more in the spirit of the mock-epics of Alexander Pope (page 340) and John Dryden (page 291), two neoclassical poets whom Byron himself acknowledged as his masters. In short, Byron—that arch-Romantic in life—in literature is deeply indebted to neoclassicism for much of his most impressive poetry.

Why then is Byron considered a Romantic poet? The answer to this question lies in his chief contribution to his age, namely the creation of the so-called **Byronic hero,** a character who embodied the yearnings of all Romantics. Readers knew enough about Byron's life—the scandals associated with his name, his passionate nature, his fierce hatred of oppression, and his self-imposed exile from England—to assume that the unconventional, brooding heroes he created in poems like *Childe Harold's Pilgrimage* and *The Corsair* were all self-portraits. In most ways they were not, for Byron was usually a witty, gregarious, generous, and loyal man of the world. Nonetheless, that hardly mattered; what mattered was the extraordinary influence the Byronic hero had on the poet's contemporaries and on successive generations of English and American writers. The mysterious Mr. Rochester, with whom the heroine falls in love in Charlotte Brontë's *Jane Eyre* (page 516), is modeled on the Byronic hero; so too is the self-destructive Heathcliff of *Wuthering Heights,* a novel by Charlotte's sister Emily Brontë (page 522).

What, or who, is a Byronic hero? In the poet's own words, he is one in whom there is mixed much to love and to hate, one whose "silences formed a theme for other's prate," or chatter. The Byronic hero is an aloof wanderer, a moody, smoldering individual, isolated from the common run of humanity. An outsider, silent, passionate, gloomy, and mysterious, he seemed to be something new in literature. Actually, Byron did not invent this character; in many ways he is a descendant of Milton's Satan in *Paradise Lost* (page 277). Yet is was Byron who ineradicably impressed the character on the world's imagination: the restless, doom-driven, alien spirit, harboring some nameless, mysterious guilt from the past as he moves with quiet scorn and defiant individualism through the present.

■ Do you think that a Byronic hero ever finds peace of mind? Why or why not?

This poem, written for music, was inspired by the sight of the poet's cousin by marriage, the beautiful Lady Wilmot Horton, who appeared at a party dressed in a black mourning gown scattered with spangles, or bits of sparkling material.

George Gordon, Lord Byron

She Walks in Beauty

1

She walks in beauty, like the night
  Of cloudless climes and starry skies;
And all that's best of dark and bright
  Meet in her aspect and her eyes:
5 Thus mellowed to that tender light
  Which heaven to gaudy day denies.

2

One shade the more, one ray the less,
  Had half impaired the nameless grace
Which waves in every raven tress,
10   Or softly lightens o'er her face;
Where thoughts serenely sweet express
  How pure, how dear their dwelling place.

3

And on that cheek, and o'er that brow,
  So soft, so calm, yet eloquent,
15 The smiles that win, the tints that glow,
  But tell of days in goodness spent,
A mind at peace with all below,
  A heart whose love is innocent!

Stanzas Written on the Road Between Florence and Pisa

Oh, talk not to me of a name great in story—
The days of our youth are the days of our glory;
And the myrtle[1] and ivy[2] of sweet two-and-twenty
Are worth all your laurels,[3] though ever so plenty.

5 What are garlands and crowns to the brow that is wrinkled?
'Tis but as a dead-flower with May-dew besprinkled:
Then away with all such from the head that is hoary!
What care I for the wreaths that can *only* give glory!

Oh Fame!—if I e'er took delight in thy praises,
10 'Twas less for the sake of thy high-sounding phrases,
Than to see the bright eyes of the dear one discover,
She thought that I was not unworthy to love her.

There chiefly I sought thee, *there* only I found thee;
Her glance was the best of the rays that surround thee;
15 When it sparkled o'er aught that was bright in my story,
I knew it was love, and I felt it was glory.

---

1. **myrtle:** a plant sacred to Venus, goddess of love in classical mythology.
2. **ivy:** a plant sacred to Bacchus, god of wine in classical mythology.
3. **laurels:** foliage of the laurel tree, an emblem of honor or distinction.

STUDY QUESTIONS

She Walks in Beauty

Recalling

1. How clearly does the poem picture its subject? What do her eyes look like? What color is her hair? What expression does she wear?

Interpreting

2. To what in the poem's opening lines does the black gown worn by the beautiful woman correspond? To what do the spangles scattered on her dress correspond?
3. Why is day described as "gaudy"?
4. How are the woman's mind and heart reflected in her appearance?

Stanzas Written on the Road Between Florence and Pisa

Recalling

1. In the first stanza with what does the speaker equate glory?
2. According to lines 5–9, what can give someone glory?
3. In the last stanza what does the speaker consider to be glory and to be worth more than fame?

Interpreting

4. What is the only delight that fame has provided the speaker?

George Gordon, Lord Byron   **435**

Childe Harold's Pilgrimage first made famous the unconventional, brooding, Romantic figure who would come to be called the **Byronic hero.** Divided into four cantos published over a six-year period (1812–1818), the long poem recounts the wanderings of a young man whom Byron calls Childe Harold. (In medieval times a *childe* was a candidate for knighthood.) Sick of society and of revelry, Harold embarks on a series of journeys across Europe, only to encounter more disillusionment in the wake of the Napoleonic Wars. Here a slightly older Harold resumes his tortured travels.

George Gordon, Lord Byron

from **Childe Harold's Pilgrimage**

from **Canto III**

XI

But who can view the ripened rose, nor[1] seek
To wear it? Who can curiously behold
The smoothness and the sheen of beauty's cheek,
Nor feel the heart can never all grow old?
5 Who can contemplate Fame through clouds unfold
The star which rises o'er her steep, nor climb?
Harold, once more within the vortex,[2] rolled
On with the giddy circle, chasing Time,
Yet with a nobler aim than in his youth's fond[3] prime.

XII

10 But soon he knew himself the most unfit
Of men to herd with Man, with whom he held
Little in common; untaught to submit
His thoughts to others, though his soul was quelled
In youth by his own thoughts; still uncompelled,
15 He would not yield dominion of his mind
To spirits against whom his own rebelled;
Proud though in desolation; which could find
A life within itself, to breathe without mankind.

---

1. **nor:** and not.
2. **vortex:** whirlpool.
3. **fond:** foolish.

XIII

Where rose the mountains, there to him were friends;
20 Where rolled the ocean, thereon was his home;
Where a blue sky, and glowing clime, extends,
He had the passion and the power to roam;
The desert, forest, cavern, breaker's foam,
Were unto him companionship; they spake
25 A mutual language, clearer than the tome[4]
Of his land's tongue, which he would oft forsake
For Nature's pages glassed[5] by sunbeams on the lake.

XIV

Like the Chaldean,[6] he could watch the stars,
Till he had peopled them with beings bright
30 As their own beams; and earth, and earth-born jars,[7]
And human frailties, were forgotten quite:
Could he have kept his spirit to that flight
He had been[8] happy; but this clay will sink
Its spark immortal, envying it the light
35 To which it mounts, as if to break the link
That keeps us from yon heaven which woos us to its brink.

XV

But in man's dwellings he became a thing
Restless and worn, and stern and wearisome,
Drooped as a wild-born falcon with clipped wing,
40 To whom the boundless air alone were home:
Then came his fit[9] again, which to overcome,
As eagerly the barred-up bird will beat
His breast and beak against his wiry dome
Till the blood tinge his plumage, so the heat
45 Of his impeded soul would through his bosom eat.

XVI

Self-exiled Harold wanders forth again,
With nought of hope left, but with less of gloom;
The very knowledge that he lived in vain,
That all was over on this side the tomb,

---

4. **tome:** book.

5. **glassed:** made glasslike.

6. **Chaldean** [kal dē′ən]: The Chaldeans, an ancient tribe of Asia Minor, were noted astronomers.

7. **jars:** discordancies; clashes; conflicts.

8. **had been:** would have been.

9. **fit:** mood.

50   Had made Despair a smilingness assume,
    Which, though 'twere wild—as on the plundered wreck
    When mariners would madly meet their doom
    With drafts intemperate on the sinking deck—
    Did yet inspire a cheer, which he forbore to check.[10]

---

10. **forbore to check:** did not try to control.

STUDY QUESTIONS

Recalling

1. According to stanza XI, what is Harold "once more within"? What is he chasing?
2. According to stanza XII, in what is Harold "untaught"?
3. For what does Harold often forsake "his land's tongue"? What happens to "this clay" (stanza XIV) to spoil his joy?
4. To what is Harold in "man's dwellings" compared in stanza XV?
5. What makes Harold's despair assume a "smilingness" (stanza XVI)? To what sort of mariner is he compared?

Interpreting

6. What is Harold's relationship to society? In what way is nature beneficial to him?
7. Explain in your own words the cause of Harold's unhappiness (stanza XIV) and his "smilingness" (stanza XVI).

LITERARY FOCUS

Stanza Form

A **stanza** in poetry is a recurrent group of a definite number of lines, usually bound together by a rhyme scheme. Among the most common stanza forms are the **couplet,** or two-line stanza; the **triplet,** or three-line stanza; the **quatrain,** or four-line stanza; the **sestet,** or six-line stanza; and the **octave,** or eight-line stanza.

More specific names are given to widely used stanza forms that employ specific rhyme schemes and meters. (For more on meter, see page 382). For example, rhymed couplets in iambic pentameter are called **heroic couplets;** quatrains of iambic pentameter rhymed *abab* are called **heroic stanzas,** or sometimes **elegiac stanzas** after Gray's famous elegy (page 367).

Triplets that employ rhyme are often called **tercets.** Sometimes, all three lines of a triplet rhyme with one another. Sometimes, the first and third lines rhyme while the middle line rhymes with the first and third lines of the next triplet, to form the rhyme scheme *aba bcb cdc* and so on. This form, first popularized in Italy, is called **terza rima;** Shelley uses it in "Ode to the West Wind" (page 445).

Two longer stanza forms are noteworthy because of their recurrent use in English poetry. **Ottava rima,** another Italian form, has eight-line iambic pentameter stanzas rhymed *abababcc;* Byron uses it in *Don Juan* (page 439). The **Spenserian stanza,** introduced in *The Faerie Queene* (page 121), uses nine-line stanzas rhymed *ababbcbcc,* in which the first eight lines are iambic pentameter and the last line (called an *alexandrine*) is iambic hexameter.

Thinking About Stanza Forms

▇ Show that *Childe Harold's Pilgrimage* is written in Spenserian stanzas by copying two stanzas, scanning them, and using letters to indicate the rhyme schemes.

The achievement of Byron's that has best stood the test of time is the long, unfinished mock-epic *Don Juan*. The work, considered Byron's masterpiece, is written in **ottava rima**, a stanzaic form consisting of eight iambic pentameter lines, rhyming *abababcc*. The English poet thoroughly mastered this Italian form in the nearly two thousand stanzas that make up *Don Juan*.

Based loosely on the character of a legendary fourteenth-century Spaniard, Byron's Juan (pronounced jōō′ən) wanders from Spain to Greece, Russia, and England. The true delight of the work lies less in the story itself than in the speaker's commentary, as often off the subject as on. Here, for example, are five stanzas in which the speaker abandons the hero to talk about himself.

Self-Portrait from **Don Juan**

But now at thirty years my hair is gray
    (I wonder what it will be like at forty?
I thought of a peruke[1] the other day)—
    My heart is not much greener; and, in short, I
5 Have squandered my whole summer while 'twas May,
    And feel no more the spirit to retort; I
Have spent my life, both interest and principal,
And deem not, what I deemed, my soul invincible.

No more—no more—Oh! never more on me
10   The freshness of the heart can fall like dew,
Which out of all the lovely things we see
    Extracts emotions beautiful and new;
Hived in our bosoms like the bag o' the bee:
    Think'st thou the honey with those objects grew?
15 Alas! 'twas not in them, but in thy power
To double even the sweetness of a flower.

No more—no more—Oh! never more, my heart,
    Canst thou be my sole world, my universe!
Once all in all, but now a thing apart,
20   Thou canst not be my blessing or my curse:
The illusion's gone for ever, and thou art
    Insensible, I trust, but none the worse,
And in thy stead I've got a deal of judgment,
Though heaven knows how it ever found a lodgment.[2]

---

1. **peruke** [pə rōōk′]: wig.
2. **lodgment:** dwelling place.

25 My days of love are over; me no more
    The charms of maid, wife, and still less of widow,
Can make the fool of which they made before—
    In short, I must not lead the life I did do;
The credulous hope of mutual minds is o'er,
30   The copious use of claret is forbid too,
So for a good old-gentlemanly vice,
I think I must take up with avarice. . . .
    Ambition was my idol, which was broken
    Before the shrines of Sorrow, and of Pleasure;
35 And the two last have left me many a token
    O'er which reflection may be made at leisure;
Now, like Friar Bacon's brazen head,[3] I've spoken,
    "Time is, Time was, Time's past:"—a chymic[4] treasure
Is glittering youth, which I have spent betimes[5]—
40 My heart in passion, and my head on rhymes.

----

3. **Friar . . . head:** The reference is to a play in which the medieval
philosopher Roger Bacon is represented as having fashioned of brass a
head that could speak.
4. **chymic** [kim′ik]: alchemic; of counterfeit gold.
5. **betimes:** early.

STUDY QUESTIONS

Recalling

1. Why does the speaker think of getting a wig?
2. What power is attributed to the heart in lines 15–16? In stanza 3 what has come to take the place of the illusions once fostered in the speaker's heart but now gone forever?
3. What, according to the fourth stanza, must the "aging" speaker give up? Which "good old-gentlemanly vice" does he plan to take up?
4. According to the last lines of this excerpt, on what was the speaker's heart fixed before his youth had been consumed?

Interpreting

5. What do you imagine the speaker's mood is in this self-portrait? Discuss the content and tone, considering the rhymes and their effect.

Extending

6. What aspects of *Don Juan* remind you of Dryden's poetry (page 291) and Pope's (page 340)?

VIEWPOINT

Leslie A. Marchand, one of Byron's contemporary biographers, points out:

Byron was frequently plagued by the character he had created for himself in *Childe Harold*. That poem had made him famous and had fixed upon him indelibly the reputation of the unsocial and melancholy wanderer. . . . It is a curious phenomenon that Byron's European reputation through the nineteenth century rested chiefly upon the popular distillation of the . . . unhappy Childe and very little upon the cynical realism and exuberant satire of *Don Juan*.

■ What examples of "cynical realism" and "exuberant satire" does this selection from *Don Juan* contain? Do you think it just a "curious phenomenon" that Byron was more strongly associated with the Childe Harold character, or might there have been other reasons for the stronger impression that *Childe Harold's Pilgrimage* left on readers? Cite evidence to support your opinion.

Percy Bysshe Shelley *1792–1822*

His belief in human perfectability, his conviction that beauty and love could guide life's meaning, and his radical but perceptive social and political philosophies distinguish Percy Bysshe Shelley as the greatest idealist among the Romantic poets. Although his ancestors were wealthy and conventional members of the Sussex aristocracy, Shelley proved to be a nonconformist throughout his life. As a young student at Sion House Academy and then at the famous private school of Eton, he developed attractions to science and especially to gothic romances that were to influence his adult preoccupations and writing. While attending Eton Shelley began to read radical literature and decided to devote his life to opposing hypocrisy and injustice. Shortly after entering Oxford University he was expelled for refusing to deny authorship of a pamphlet entitled "The Necessity of Atheism." His expulsion created a breach with his father that was never mended.

Shelley then went to London, where his sisters were in school. There he met young Harriet Westbrooke, a classmate of his sisters, whom he soon married in order to rescue her from what he regarded as her father's tyranny. In keeping with Shelley's interest in humanitarian causes, they spent their honeymoon in Ireland, participating in the movement for the reform of government and Catholic emancipation. Returning to London, Shelley met the radical philosopher William Godwin, whose theories had already influenced him as a student. Having drifted apart from Harriet, Shelley fell in love with the philosopher's daughter, Mary Wollstonecraft Godwin, who was to be his second wife. (Mary Godwin, while still in her teens, wrote the novel *Frankenstein,* a work that proved more popular during the poet's lifetime than anything he himself had written.)

Shelley's was in many ways an unhappy life. His health was poor, and, in spite of his sensitive and inquisitive nature, his motives were often misunderstood. He himself acknowledged that his good impulses often backfired on him and were "the source of all sorts of mischief." He was regarded by most of his contemporaries—those who did not know him personally—as scarcely less than a monster. It was known that his controversial views had led to his expulsion from Oxford, that his father had disinherited him, that his first wife had apparently committed suicide in despair, and that the courts had taken custody of his children from that marriage.

As a result of his strong commitment to unconventional social views, Shelley was considered a revolutionary and was treated like a pariah. In 1818 he, like his fellow poet Byron, exiled himself from England in disgust. Before he was thirty, he was drowned in a boating accident during a violent storm off the coast of Italy, and his body was found washed ashore with a volume of Keats and another of Sophocles in his pockets. He was cremated on the beach; Byron, who had been on the sailing expedition, attended the funeral. Shelley's ashes were buried in the Protestant cemetery in Rome. At his death Shelley's volumes of poetry remained for the most part unsold, his public undiscovered.

Despite financial difficulties and personal worries of his own, Shelley had always been singularly generous to others. After Shelley's death the poet Lord Byron wrote to his London publisher, "You were all brutally mistaken about Shelley." In Switzerland and Italy Byron had come to know the younger poet well. He was, so the lord insisted, "the best and least selfish man I ever knew. I never knew one who was not a beast in comparison."

Now Shelley—who had almost no audience when he died—is justly regarded as one of the greatest of the English Romantics, a fierce idealist whose verses illustrate his hope for the future and his devotion to human betterment. William Wordsworth believed that "Shelley is one of the best *artists* of us all: I mean in workmanship of style." Furthermore, Shelley wrote an impressive amount of poetry, and in an outstanding number of forms. *Adonais,* an elegy on the death of John Keats, is one of his finest works, and *Prometheus Unbound,* a dramatic poem in the manner of Greek tragedy, is another masterpiece. He also wrote sonnets, satires, odes, allegories, hymns, a splendid play in the Elizabethan manner—and, in prose, marvelous travel letters and a wonderful though uncompleted piece of literary criticism ("A Defense of Poetry"). At his death he was in the midst of a poem, *The Triumph of Life,* that might well have developed into the greatest work in a charged and compressed career.

Ozymandias [ōz i man′dē əs] was the Greek name for Ramses II, the pharaoh who ruled Egypt during the thirteenth century B.C. During his rule Ramses II conducted an extensive building program and was responsible for the largest statue in Egypt, which bore the inscription: "I am Ozymandias, king of kings; if anyone wishes to know what I am and where I lie, let him surpass me in some of my exploits."

Ramses II was also known as the pharaoh who oppressed the Israelites. Shelley—always an ardent challenger of oppression—depicts the ironical outcome of the pharaoh's legacy in this sonnet, a favorite poetic form of the Romantics.

■ Shelley sometimes directly addresses inanimate objects in the following selections. Do you ever talk to "things"? Why do you think you do this?

Percy Bysshe Shelley

Ozymandias

I met a traveler from an antique land
Who said: Two vast and trunkless legs of stone
Stand in the desert . . . Near them, on the sand,
Half sunk, a shattered visage lies, whose frown,
5 And wrinkled lip, and sneer of cold command,
Tell that its sculptor well those passions read
Which yet survive, stamped on these lifeless things,
The hand that mocked them,[1] and the heart[2] that fed:
And on the pedestal these words appear:
10 "My name is Ozymandias, king of kings:
Look on my works, ye Mighty, and despair!"
Nothing beside remains. Round the decay
Of that colossal wreck, boundless and bare
The lone and level sands stretch far away.

---

1. **The hand . . . them:** the sculptor's hand that
"mocked" (imitated and ridiculed) the ruler's passions.
2. **heart:** the king's heart; "hand" and "heart" are both
direct objects of "survive" (line 7).

Painting by Elihu Vedder (1836–1923).

To ——

Music, when soft voices die,
Vibrates in the memory—
Odors, when sweet violets sicken,
Live within the sense they quicken.
5 Rose leaves, when the rose is dead,
Are heaped for the belovèd's[1] bed;
And so thy thoughts,[2] when thou art gone,
Love itself shall slumber on.

---

1. **the belovèd's:** the rose's.
2. **thy thoughts:** thoughts of thee.

A Dirge

Rough wind, that moanest loud
    Grief too sad for song;
Wild wind, when sullen cloud
    Knells all the night long;
5 Sad storm, whose tears are vain,
Bare woods, whose branches strain,
Deep caves and dreary main[1]—
    Wail, for the world's wrong!

---

1. **main:** the open sea.

STUDY QUESTIONS

Ozymandias

Recalling

1. What has happened to the statue, according to lines 3–4?
2. Which facial expressions recording Ozymandias' passions still survive, according to lines 4–5?
3. What words appear on the pedestal of the statue? What else, besides the statue, remains of Ozymandias' vast achievements, his "works"?

Interpreting

4. Based on how the sculptor captured Ozymandias, what were the pharaoh's passions, or emotions? In what sense do those emotions survive?
5. What might Ozymandias have wanted onlookers to despair of? At the time of the traveler's report, what should the mighty despair of, given the condition of the statue and its surroundings? Explain the poem's irony.

Extending

6. What effect does Shelley achieve by putting the poem in the words of "a traveler from an antique land"?

To ——

Recalling

1. What three images of loveliness that can disappear are mentioned in lines 1–6? What happens after each kind of loveliness sickens or dies?
2. In line 7 what is the fourth image of loveliness?

Interpreting

3. In what way do the first six lines help explain the meaning and tone of the last two lines?

A Dirge

Recalling

1. What natural elements are represented as wailing forth the dirge (a funeral song, a song of mourning)?
2. For what are they mourning?

Interpreting

3. Based on what you know about history and Shelley, what do you understand by the phrase "the world's wrong" (line 8)? Give examples to explain your answer.
4. Why would a Romantic poet expect nature to mourn the world's wrong?

This poem was written in a forest near Florence, Italy, "on a day," says Shelley, "when that tempestuous wind, whose temperature is at once mild and animating [invigorating], was collecting the vapors which pour down the autumnal rains."

Ode to the West Wind

1

O wild West Wind, thou breath of Autumn's being,
Thou, from whose unseen presence the leaves dead
Are driven, like ghosts from an enchanter fleeing,

Yellow, and black, and pale, and hectic[1] red,
5 Pestilence-stricken multitudes: O thou,
Who chariotest to their dark wintry bed

The wingèd seeds, where they lie cold and low,
Each like a corpse within its grave, until
Thine azure sister of the Spring[2] shall blow

10 Her clarion[3] o'er the dreaming earth, and fill
(Driving sweet buds like flocks to feed in air)
With living hues and odors plain and hill:

Wild Spirit, which art moving everywhere;
Destroyer and preserver; hear, oh, hear!

2

15 Thou on whose stream, mid the steep sky's commotion,
Loose clouds like earth's decaying leaves are shed,
Shook from the tangled boughs of Heaven and Ocean,[4]

---

1. **hectic:** relating to the reddening of the face caused by hectic fever, which accompanies wasting diseases.
2. **sister . . . Spring:** the wind that will accompany spring.
3. **clarion:** sound of a trumpet.
4. **tangled . . . Ocean:** a metaphorical representation of the manner in which clouds are formed by a suspension of water ("Ocean") in air ("Heaven").

Angels[5] of rain and lightning: there are spread
On the blue surface of thine aëry surge,
20 Like the bright hair uplifted from the head

Of some fierce Maenad,[6] even from the dim verge
Of the horizon to the zenith's height,
The locks of the approaching storm. Thou dirge

Of the dying year, to which this closing night
25 Will be the dome of a vast sepulcher,
Vaulted with all thy congregated might

Of vapors, from whose solid atmosphere
Black rain, and fire, and hail will burst: oh, hear!

3

Thou who didst waken from his summer dreams
30 The blue Mediterranean, where he lay,
Lulled by the coil of his crystàlline streams,

Beside a pumice[7] isle in Baiae's bay,[8]
And saw in sleep old palaces and towers
Quivering within the wave's intenser day,

35 All overgrown with azure moss and flowers
So sweet, the sense faints picturing them! Thou
For whose path the Atlantic's level powers

Cleave themselves into chasms, while far below
The sea-blooms and the oozy woods which wear
40 The sapless foliage of the ocean, know

---

5. **Angels:** messengers.
6. **Maenad** [mē′nad]: a female worshiper of Bacchus, classical mythological god of wine and revelry.
7. **pumice** [pum′is]: volcanic rock.
8. **Baiae's** [bā′yēz] **bay:** an ancient resort in Italy.

Thy voice, and suddenly grow gray with fear,
And tremble and despoil themselves: oh, hear!

4

If I were a dead leaf thou mightest bear,
If I were a swift cloud to fly with thee;
45 A wave to pant beneath thy power, and share

The impulse of thy strength, only less free
Than thou, O uncontrollable! If even
I were as in my boyhood, and could be

The comrade of thy wanderings over Heaven,
50 As then, when to outstrip thy skyey speed
Scarce seemed a vision; I would ne'er have striven

As thus with thee in prayer in my sore need.
Oh, lift me as a wave, a leaf, a cloud!
I fall upon the thorns of life! I bleed!

55 A heavy weight of hours has chained and bowed
One too like thee: tameless, and swift, and proud.

5

Make me thy lyre,[9] even as the forest is:
What if my leaves are falling like its own!
The tumult of thy mighty harmonies

60 Will take from both a deep, autumnal tone,
Sweet though in sadness. Be thou, Spirit fierce,
My spirit! Be thou me, impetuous one!

Drive my dead thoughts over the universe
Like withered leaves to quicken a new birth!
65 And, by the incantation of this verse,

Scatter, as from an unextinguished hearth
Ashes and sparks, my words among mankind!
Be through my lips to unawakened earth

The trumpet of a prophecy! O Wind,
70 If Winter comes, can Spring be far behind?

---

9. **lyre:** refers to the aeolian [ē ō′lē ən] harp, a stringed instrument
that produces musical sounds when the wind passes over it.

Recalling

1. From line 1 on, whom or what is being addressed in this poem? What does the speaker ask of the addressee at the very end of stanzas 1, 2, and 3?
2. On what natural object does the wind's power show itself in stanza 1? In stanza 2? In stanza 3? Find these objects again in stanza 4, which serves as a summary of stanzas 1–3.
3. What is the speaker's present situation, as revealed in lines 54 and 55–56?
4. What does the speaker ask for in line 57? What does he ask the wind to do with his thoughts and words (lines 63–67)?

Interpreting

5. Why, at the end of stanza 1, is the west wind referred to as "Destroyer and preserver"? That is, what does winter, which the west wind brings, destroy? What does it preserve? What is the poet's final vision of winter in line 70?
6. How does the speaker in stanza 4 compare himself to the wind in terms of power and freedom? What might be the literal meaning of the "thorns of life" (line 54)?
7. By stanza 5 how has the speaker's attitude progressed? In your own words explain what the speaker hopes to accomplish.
8. In what way are nature and imagination related, according to this poem? Consider what this poem says about the effect that each can have. By examining word choice, rhythms, and the rhyme scheme, consider also how imagination captures nature in this very poem. (Each section has four stanzas of **terza rima,** interlocking three-line groups rhymed *aba bcb cdc ded,* and concludes with a couplet rhymed *ee.*)

LITERARY FOCUS

Personification and Apostrophe

The more our emotions are involved, the more likely we are to use **figurative language,** writing that contains one or more figures of speech such as metaphor, personification, and apostrophe.

Metaphor, we recall, involves an implied comparison between two dissimilar things. Shelley's words at line 67 of "Ode to the West Wind" are metaphorically compared to ashes and sparks. **Personification** is a specific kind of metaphor, in which an inanimate object, an animal, or an abstraction is compared to a person and endowed with human characteristics. In lines 29–31, the Mediterranean Sea is compared to a person—a "he" who wakens "from his summer dreams." This picture stirs our emotions more than a sea that remained simply a body of water.

When a personification is addressed directly, the result is called **apostrophe.** Thus, Shelley apostrophizes the west wind throughout the poem, addressing it from first to last as though it could hear and respond, being the "Wild Spirit" that it is. Similarly, the same poet apostrophizes natural objects or phenomena in "A Dirge."

Apostrophe may also involve directly addressing an absent person as though he or she were present. Wordsworth apostrophizes the dead poet Milton when he invokes that poet's aid by writing "Milton! thou shouldst be living at this hour" (page 397). The effect of this kind of apostrophe is still the same: By speaking directly and emotionally, the poet heightens the reader's involvement.

Thinking About Personification and Apostrophe

1. How is love personified in Shelley's "To ___"?
2. How is "heart" personified in "Ozymandias"?
3. What is apostrophized in Byron's "Stanzas Written on the Road Between Florence and Pisa" (page 435)?

COMPOSITION

Analyzing the Structure of a Poem

■ "Ode to the West Wind" is a highly structured poem. In an essay discuss the structure of the poem in ways that will enlarge your reader's appreciation of Shelley's achievement. Begin by explaining how the first three stanzas resemble each other. Be sure to discuss what single idea holds those stanzas together. Then show how stanzas 4 and 5 differ from the first three and how they move the poem forward.

Writing a Personification

■ In a prose paragraph or two personify one element of nature. You may choose as your subject the ocean, the sun, a brook, a simple tree, or any other element of nature you think will lend itself well to personification. Describe the object by showing it sounding, moving, and otherwise appearing human.

John Keats   *1795–1821*

All three of the great "second generation" of Romantic poets died young. Byron (page 432) died at the age of thirty-six, Shelley (page 441) died when he was twenty-nine. But John Keats was only twenty-five when he died. Moreover, he had not been precocious; his earliest poems, written in his late teens, are conventional and unpromising, and, in fact, most of Keats's great work was done in a single year, 1819, when he was twenty-three. Thereafter, the debilitating effects of tuberculosis made writing impossible. Yet already, in that short time, the young man had composed poetry that places him among the five or six greatest English poets—work far superior to anything Chaucer or Shakespeare or Milton had done at a comparable age.

Keats's ancestry and background would have seemed hardly conducive to forming a poet. Byron was an aristocrat, educated at the best schools. Shelley, too, was born into an old, aristocratic family, which assured him leisure to pursue the life of the mind. Keats's father, however, was a hostler, grooming horses at a London livery stable. The elder Keats died from a fall from a horse when his son John was eight; Keats's mother, the daughter of the stable's proprietor and also of modest origins, died when he was fourteen. As a boy Keats was sent to a nearby private school where the headmaster's son, who was one of his teachers, encouraged his literary interests. After the death of Keats's mother, however, the young man's guardian took him out of school. There was to be no Cambridge or Oxford in the life of this orphan but rather an apprenticeship to a surgeon and apothecary, or druggist, at a time when medicine enjoyed none of the prestige as a profession that it does now.

Nonetheless, Keats the humble medical student was soon to meet various literary personalities in London. Leigh Hunt—an editor who was a political radical and a friend of Shelley and Byron—was among them. Hunt encouraged the young man in the writing that he had already begun, and Keats soon abandoned medicine in favor of poetry. As noted, those early efforts at verse were not impressive. Keats had not even started to write until he was eighteen. Suddenly, at twenty-one, he produced his first great poem (and one of the greatest sonnets in the language): "On First Looking into Chapman's Homer."

From that time on, Keats consciously and triumphantly fashioned himself into a major poet, growing almost month by month in ability. His letters reveal that growth less as a miracle than as something worked for, something brought about. The result was that in the space of nine months in 1819, from January through September, he was able to produce a dazzling succession of outstanding poems: *The*

Eve of St. Agnes, "La Belle Dame sans Merci," six superlative odes, and more astonishing sonnets. Then, soon after this period of intense creative activity, illness made the poet set down his pen.

During the fall of 1818, Keats had fallen deeply in love with Fanny Brawne, an attractive and lively girl who was devoted to the poet. Although they became engaged, Keats's extreme commitment to his poetry, his lack of money, and, especially, his increasingly poor health made it impossible for them to marry. His mother and youngest brother had died of tuberculosis. Keats himself contracted the disease—a terrifying and dreadful nineteenth-century malady. Friends took him to Italy, in hopes that the warmer climate would prolong his life, but his condition was hopeless. He died in Rome early in 1821 and was buried there, in the same cemetery where Shelley's remains would be placed the following year.

Keats's poetry is distinctive for its unusual physical concreteness and its rich appeal to all of the senses. While many Romantic poets—including Wordsworth and Shelley—describe objects, Keats actually *presents* them. In this way he is able to stimulate the reader's senses as though the object were actually present. Furthermore, Keats believed that the poet should subordinate his own identity in order to enable the poem's subject to emerge fully. His ability to capture his subject's unique characteristics often allows the reader to experience a feeling of direct identification and participation. Finally, though Keats is known as a sensuous poet, his greatness also lies in the fact that he was an outstanding philosophical poet whose works portray experience as a complexity of unavoidable, inherent contradictions and opposites.

The first two Keats poems presented are sonnets and provide us with an opportunity to examine Keats's use of both the Petrarchan (Italian) and Shakespearean (English) sonnet forms. Keats composed "On First Looking into Chapman's Homer" after his friend and former schoolteacher, Charles Cowden Clarke, introduced him to a translation of the Greek poet Homer. The translation was by George Chapman, an Elizabethan poet. The two friends read the translation together through the night. Keats returned home at dawn, and Clarke received this sonnet with the morning mail.

▰ Have you ever encountered a work of art from a former time and been temporarily transported back to that time? When? What was the work of art?

John Keats

On First Looking into Chapman's Homer

Much have I traveled in the realms of gold,
   And many goodly states and kingdoms seen;
   Round many western islands have I been
Which bards[1] in fealty[2] to Apollo[3] hold.
5 Oft of one wide expanse had I been told
   That deep-browed Homer ruled as his demesne;[4]
   Yet did I never breathe its pure serene[5]
Till I heard Chapman speak out loud and bold:
Then felt I like some watcher of the skies
10   When a new planet swims into his ken;[6]
Or like stout Cortez[7] when with eagle eyes
   He stared at the Pacific—and all his men
Looked at each other with a wild surmise—
   Silent, upon a peak in Darien.[8]

---

1. **bards:** poets.
2. **fealty** [fē′əl tē]: loyalty owed by a feudal tenant to his lord.
3. **Apollo:** in classical mythology, the god of poetry and music.
4. **demesne** [di mān′]: realm, domain; feudal possession.
5. **serene:** clear, calm air.
6. **ken:** view.
7. **Cortez** [kôr tez′]: Hernando Cortez (1485–1547), Spanish conquistador of Mexico, whom Keats erroneously credits with the discovery of the Pacific Ocean, which was discovered by Balboa in 1513.
8. **Darien** [där′ē en′]: the Isthmus of Panama.

STUDY QUESTIONS

Recalling

1. What was the "one wide expanse," described in lines 5–7, that the speaker had not explored in his reading? By what means, according to line 8, was he admitted into that literary region?
2. According to lines 9–14, what events did the speaker's experience resemble?

Interpreting

3. What, literally, are "the realms of gold" referred to in the first line of this poem?
4. What do the Pacific, the planet, and Homer's poetry have in common with respect to the effects on their beholders?
5. What is appropriate about Keats's choice of metaphors for this sonnet? In answering, comment on the division of thought between the octave (lines 1–8) and the sestet (lines 9–14).

Extending

6. What is your reaction to learning of Keats's celebrated mistake in line 11?

Tears, Idle Tears

Tears, idle[1] tears, I know not what they mean,
Tears from the depth of some divine despair
Rise in the heart, and gather to the eyes,
In looking on the happy autumn-fields,
5 And thinking of the days that are no more.

Fresh as the first beam glittering on a sail,
That brings our friends up from the underworld,
Sad as the last which reddens over one
That sinks with all we love below the verge;[2]
10 So sad, so fresh, the days that are no more.

Ah, sad and strange as in dark summer dawns
The earliest pipe of half-awakened birds
To dying ears, when unto dying eyes
The casement[3] slowly grows a glimmering square;
15 So sad, so strange, the days that are no more.

Dear as remembered kisses after death,
And sweet as those by hopeless fancy feigned[4]
On lips that are for others; deep as love,
Deep as first love, and wild with all regret;
20 O Death in Life, the days that are no more!

---

1. **idle:** useless, pointless.
2. **verge:** edge or rim; here, the horizon.
3. **casement:** type of window.
4. **feigned:** imagined.

Like Milton's *Lycidas* and Shelley's *Adonais,* Tennyson's *In Memoriam A. H. H.* commemorates the death of a gifted young man at the threshold of his life. *In Memoriam* differs from the earlier elegies in that it is not a single poem written in a short period of time but rather a series of 131 lyrics written over a period of seventeen years to express the poet's reaction to Arthur Hallam's death. Together the lyrics form a spiritual autobiography tracing Tennyson's shifting emotions as the years pass. The poet moves from desolation, despair, and grief to reconciliation and hope. The lyric that follows, also known as "Ring Out, Wild Bells," occurs late in the sequence. It is a response on New Year's Eve to the end of yet another year.

Alfred, Lord Tennyson

from In Memoriam A. H. H.

Ring out, wild bells, to the wild sky,
  The flying cloud, the frosty light:
  The year is dying in the night;
Ring out, wild bells, and let him die.

5 Ring out the old, ring in the new,
  Ring, happy bells, across the snow:
  The year is going, let him go;
Ring out the false, ring in the true.

Ring out the grief that saps the mind,
10   For those that here we see no more;
  Ring out the feud of rich and poor,
Ring in redress to all mankind.

Ring out a slowly dying cause,
  And ancient forms of party strife;
15   Ring in the nobler modes of life,
With sweeter manners, purer laws.

Ring out the want, the care, the sin,
  The faithless coldness of the times;
  Ring out, ring out my mournful rhymes,
20 But ring the fuller minstrel in.

Ring out false pride in place and blood,
  The civic slander and the spite;
  Ring in the love of truth and right,
Ring in the common love of good.

25 Ring out old shapes of foul disease;
  Ring out the narrowing lust of gold;
  Ring out the thousand wars of old,
Ring in the thousand years of peace.

Ring in the valiant man and free,
30   The larger heart, the kindlier hand;
  Ring out the darkness of the land,
Ring in the Christ that is to be.[1]

---

1. **the Christ . . . be:** reference to the New Testament account in the Book of Revelations of the second coming of Christ.

At eighty-one Tennyson wrote the following poem, and just a few days before his death he asked that it be placed at the end of every edition of his work.

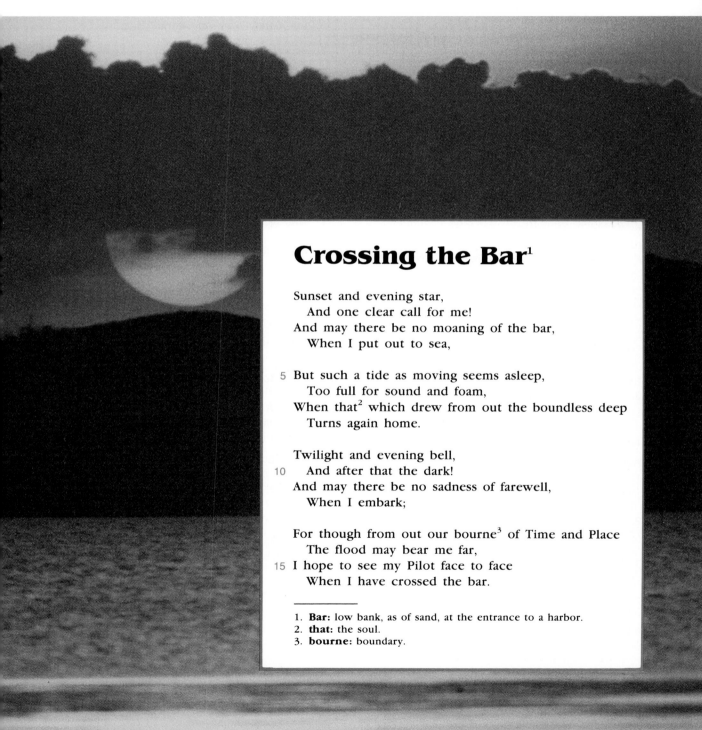

Crossing the Bar[1]

Sunset and evening star,
    And one clear call for me!
And may there be no moaning of the bar,
    When I put out to sea,

5 But such a tide as moving seems asleep,
    Too full for sound and foam,
When that[2] which drew from out the boundless deep
    Turns again home.

Twilight and evening bell,
10   And after that the dark!
And may there be no sadness of farewell,
    When I embark;

For though from out our bourne[3] of Time and Place
    The flood may bear me far,
15 I hope to see my Pilot face to face
    When I have crossed the bar.

———————

1. **Bar:** low bank, as of sand, at the entrance to a harbor.
2. **that:** the soul.
3. **bourne:** boundary.

STUDY QUESTIONS

Ulysses

Recalling

1. What is Ulysses' present situation as he describes it in lines 1–5? What past experiences does he recall in lines 7–17?
2. What does Ulysses say in lines 22–24 about making an end? What does his "gray spirit" (line 30) yearn to do?
3. To whom is Ulysses leaving the scepter and the isle? In lines 35–38 what two things does he say his successor will do for those he rules? In lines 39–43 how does Ulysses further describe his successor?
4. Whom is Ulysses addressing? In lines 51–53 what does he say may yet be done?
5. In lines 57–61, what does he ask his friends to seek with him? According to lines 65–70, what qualities do Ulysses and his friends still possess, despite the passage of time?

Interpreting

6. Contrast Ulysses' present life with his earlier days. What is his attitude toward each part of his life?
7. Describe Ulysses' personality from his comments about his present and past as well as his hopes for the future. What view of life does he advocate? What is he actually seeking in leaving Ithaca?

Extending

8. Why might people feel as Ulysses does? What human need does Ulysses' speech express?

The Splendor Falls on Castle Walls

Recalling

1. What setting is described in the first stanza? What visual details make up this setting? What does the bugle set flying?
2. In the second stanza what blows from "cliff and scar"? What words in lines 7–10 describe these sounds?
3. In lines 13–14 where do the echoes die? What other echoes are mentioned in lines 15–16? Where do they roll, and for how long will they grow?

Interpreting

4. What do you think Tennyson means by "Elfland" in line 10?

5. What is meant by "our echoes" in line 15? In what ways are these echoes different from the "wild echoes" made by the horns of Elfland?

Extending

6. What "splendor" might have been fading from the world that Tennyson knew? Has it faded completely from *our* world? Explain.

Tears, Idle Tears

Recalling

1. According to the first stanza, from what do the tears rise? When do they rise?
2. Where do the friends mentioned in line 7 come from? Where do they go?
3. In lines 10 and 15, what various qualities does the speaker ascribe to "the days that are no more"? With what does the last line associate these days?

Interpreting

4. Why is the speaker weeping, and why are the tears "idle"?
5. What view of memory does the poem express? Do you agree with this view?

Extending

6. Why do you think pleasant sights often make people sad?

from In Memoriam A. H. H.

Recalling

1. What does the speaker say about the old year in lines 3–4?
2. Make a list of things the speaker wants the wild bells to ring out.
3. What things does he want the bells to ring in?

Interpreting

4. Which of these wishes pertains only to the speaker? To whom or what do the others apply?
5. What overall hope do the wishes express?

Extending

6. Which of the poem's hopes can be applied to the world today?

Crossing the Bar

Recalling

1. What requests does the speaker make in lines 3–4 and 11–12? According to line 8, where is the tide going?

2. What does the speaker hope to see when he has crossed the bar, according to line 15?

Interpreting

3. What does Tennyson actually mean by "crossing the bar"?
4. In what way does the poem express a consolation to those the speaker leaves behind?
5. What can you infer about Tennyson's attitude toward death from this poem?

LITERARY FOCUS

Rhythm and Meter

In poetry **rhythm** refers to the alternation between stressed and unstressed syllables in the lines of verse. **Meter,** more fully discussed on page 382, is a type of rhythm in which the alternation between stressed and unstressed syllables is predictable and regular. In reading a poem that has meter, we need to pay attention to the pattern of stresses. However, we should not allow that pattern to take over the poem and turn it into singsong. Rather, we also need to pay attention to the meaning and sound of individual words and to punctuation, occasionally changing the regularity of the meter when the content seems to demand it. For example, the meter of *In Memoriam A. H. H.* is *iambic tetrameter* (see page 382): The predominant foot is the iamb, and there are four feet in each line. However, meaning, sound, and punctuation suggest that the opening lines should be read as follows (the double slash shows a longer pause):

Ring out, / wild bells, // to the / wild sky, //

The fly / ing cloud, // the frost / y light;/

The year / is dy / ing in / the night; //

Ring out, / wild bells, // and let / him die. //

Thinking About Rhythm and Meter

■ Read "Ulysses" aloud, and describe the pattern of stressed and unstressed syllables in each line. What meter does the poem use? Give three or four examples of points at which a sensitive reader might alter that meter.

VOCABULARY

Analogies

An **analogy** is a comparison. Analogy items appear on vocabulary tests as double comparisons between two pairs of words. You may be given the first pair of words and asked to find or complete a second pair that have the same relationship to each other as the first pair. For example, you would complete the analogy TOP : BOTTOM : : _____ : _____ with the pair HIGH : LOW, since both pairs of words are antonyms, or opposites. In other cases, the paired words may be related as synonyms, as different grammatical forms of the same word, as a part and a whole, or as different degrees of the same quality.

The first capitalized word in each of the following items comes from one of the poems by Tennyson. Choose the letter of the pair of words that best completes the analogy.

1. STRIFE : CONFLICT : :
   - (a) home : residence
   - (b) song : dance
   - (c) love : hate
   - (d) light : dark
2. BARREN : BARRENNESS : :
   - (a) night : fortnight
   - (b) hungry : hunger
   - (c) bold : bolt
   - (d) red : blue
3. UNBURNISHED : FILTHY : :
   - (a) amusing : hilarious
   - (b) bright : shiny
   - (c) quiet : noisy
   - (d) read : write
4. SLANDER : PRAISE : :
   - (a) street : road
   - (b) ugliness : beauty
   - (c) snow : rain
   - (d) shout : yell
5. VESSEL : DECK : :
   - (a) boat : ship
   - (b) house : floor
   - (c) wave : storm
   - (d) land : sky

COMPOSITION

Writing About a Symbol

■ Discuss Tennyson's use of the tide as a symbol in "Crossing the Bar." First explain the symbolic meaning of the tide in line 5. Then discuss its significance for the poem as a whole. Be sure to explain how the symbol of the tide is related to the other images in the poem and its overall theme. *For help with this assignment, refer to Lesson 5 in the Writing About Literature Handbook at the back of this book.*

Creating a Symbol

■ Write a poem about an object that could represent a particular time or part of your life—for example, your years in high school. Describe the object clearly in your poem, and show why it has a larger meaning for you.

Alfred, Lord Tennyson **501**

Robert Browning   *1812–1889*

Robert Browning is one of the two great pillars on which Victorian poetry rests, the other being Alfred, Lord Tennyson. These two towering figures could not have been more different, both as men and as poets. Tennyson was introverted, withdrawn, and often melancholy; Browning was open, social, and generally optimistic. Tennyson's poetry is melodic and beautifully polished; Browning's is intentionally harsh and "unpoetic," echoing the language of lively conversation. Tennyson's work sounds the true Victorian note of noble sentiment, deep melancholy, and almost mystical exaltation. In contrast, Browning strikes twentieth-century readers as the more modern writer, not only because of his colloquial and quirky diction, but also because of his interest in human psychology and his use of sensational subject matter.

Browning was raised in a household of modest but genteel means on the outskirts of London. His father, a bank official, pursued scholarship as a hobby, collecting a library of six thousand books. Educated at home, young Browning developed unusually broad knowledge in the classics, painting, poetry, and the theater.

After writing lyrical verse that imitated Byron and Shelley, Browning began to find his own poetic voice with the dramatic, psychological *Paracelsus* (1835). After making an unsuccessful foray into drama in *Strafford* (1837) and spending two years in Italy, Browning wrote his long, difficult *Sordello* (1840), a poem that English readers found obscure and that made its author unpopular. Browning followed this work with a series of poems and dramas entitled *Bells and Pomegranates,* published from 1841 to 1846. This series includes the play *Pippa Passes* (1841) and other dramatic works, but it is most notable for a series of short dramatic monologues in which interesting, complex characters reveal themselves in informal and seemingly offhand remarks. Browning found in this combination of poetry, drama, and colloquial language a new and congenial style for himself.

When he was still largely unknown, Browning came across a volume of poetry by the popular Elizabeth Barrett, a semi-invalid who was six years older than he. He fell in love with the poems and then with the poet herself. Despite her father's strenuous disapproval, the two poets eloped in 1846. Their happy life together in Italy revived Mrs. Browning. She remained much more famous than her husband, who was chiefly known as Mrs. Browning's devoted partner in an idyllically romantic marriage.

After his wife's death in 1861, Browning returned to England with their son. It was only then, in his fifties, that Browning established his own reputation as a poet with additional collections of dramatic monologues such as *Dramatis Personae* (1866). His masterpiece in this vein is *The Ring and the Book* (1869), a novel-length series of dramatic monologues presenting a dozen different views of a murder that actually took place in seventeenth-century Italy.

Although delayed, Browning's eventual fame was bountiful. He nearly became the beloved Tennyson's equal among Victorian readers; later, Browning's feeling for the unruliness of life and human psychology and his experimentation with discordant, prosaic diction would make him seem a modern poet before his time.

Pippa, the young girl who speaks in this poem, works exhausting hours in the silk mills and endures the full range of hardships associated with industrial life. Yet her optimism eventually triumphs. This poem contains the most famous lines written by Browning, and yet they are not typical of his poetry.

Browning frequently writes about people and what makes them happy. Who are some happy people that you know? What makes them happy?

Robert Browning

from **Pippa Passes**

The year's at the spring
And day's at the morn;
Morning's at seven;
The hillside's dew-pearled;

5 The lark's on the wing;
The snail's on the thorn;
God's in his heaven—
All's right with the world!

STUDY QUESTIONS

Recalling

1. During what time of year and day does the poem take place?
2. What other details of the setting does Pippa mention? What opinion does she express in lines 7–8?

Interpreting

3. What qualities or attributes of the world does Pippa stress in her song?
4. What does she leave out and why? Why do you suppose Pippa's song does not reflect the difficult conditions of her own life?

Extending

5. Do people in real life ever feel as Pippa does?

The Brownings spent their married life happily in Italy, where the warm climate eased Mrs. Browning's health. However, in the springtime especially, moments of homesickness would visit them.

Robert Browning

Home-Thoughts, from Abroad

1

Oh, to be in England
Now that April's there,
And whoever wakes in England
Sees, some morning, unaware,
5 That the lowest boughs and the brushwood sheaf
Round the elm-tree bole[1] are in tiny leaf,
While the chaffinch sings on the orchard bough
In England—now!

2

And after April, when May follows,
10 And the whitethroat builds, and all the swallows!
Hark, where my blossomed peartree in the hedge
Leans to the field and scatters on the clover
Blossoms and dewdrops—at the bent spray's edge—
That's the wise thrush; he sings each song twice over,
15 Lest you should think he never could recapture
The first fine careless rapture!
And though the fields look rough with hoary dew,
All will be gay when noontide wakes anew
The buttercups, the little children's dower[2]
20 —Far brighter than this gaudy melon-flower![3]

---

1. **bole:** tree trunk.
2. **dower:** endowment, gift.
3. **melon-flower:** large, trumpet-shaped yellow bloom from a melon plant (such as a cantaloupe or pumpkin). Browning contrasts this flower, which is native to a warm climate, with the smaller buttercups seen in early spring in England.

The time is the sixteenth century. The place is a castle in Ferrara, a province in northern Italy. The duke who owns the castle is negotiating with an emissary from a count over his possible betrothal to the count's daughter. The two men pause before the painting of a beautiful young woman, the duke's first wife.

My Last Duchess

Ferrara

That's my last Duchess painted on the wall,
Looking as if she were alive. I call
That piece a wonder, now: Frà Pandolf's[1] hands
Worked busily a day, and there she stands.
5 Will't please you sit and look at her? I said
"Frà Pandolf" by design,[2] for never read
Strangers like you that pictured countenance,
The depth and passion of its earnest glance,
But to myself they turned (since none puts by
10 The curtain I have drawn for you, but I)
And seemed as they would ask me, if they durst,[3]
How such a glance came there; so, not the first
Are you to turn and ask thus. Sir, 'twas not
Her husband's presence only, called that spot
15 Of joy into the Duchess' cheek: perhaps
Frà Pandolf chanced to say, "Her mantle laps
Over my lady's wrist too much," or "Paint
Must never hope to reproduce the faint
Half-flush that dies along her throat": such stuff
20 Was courtesy, she thought, and cause enough
For calling up that spot of joy. She had
A heart—how shall I say?—too soon made glad,
Too easily impressed; she liked whate'er
She looked on, and her looks went everywhere.
25 Sir, 'twas all one! My favor at her breast,
The dropping of the daylight in the West,

---

1. **Frà Pandolf's:** Brother Pandolf's; refers to the work
of a fictitious painter who is also a friar.
2. **by design:** intentionally.
3. **durst:** dared.

The bough of cherries some officious fool
Broke in the orchard for her, the white mule
She rode with round the terrace—all and each
30 Would draw from her alike the approving speech,
Or blush, at least. She thanked men—good! but thanked
Somehow—I know not how—as if she ranked
My gift of a nine-hundred-years-old name
With anybody's gift. Who'd stoop to blame
35 This sort of trifling? Even had you skill
In speech—(which I have not)—to make your will
Quite clear to such an one, and say, "Just this
Or that in you disgusts me; here you miss,
Or there exceed the mark"—and if she let
40 Herself be lessoned so, nor plainly set
Her wits to yours, forsooth,[4] and made excuse,
—E'en then would be some stooping; and I choose
Never to stoop. Oh sir, she smiled, no doubt,
Whene'er I passed her; but who passed without
45 Much the same smile? This grew; I gave commands;
Then all smiles stopped together. There she stands
As if alive. Will't please you rise? We'll meet
The company below, then. I repeat,
The Count your master's known munificence[5]
50 Is ample warrant that no just pretense[6]
Of mine for dowry[7] will be disallowed;
Though his fair daughter's self, as I avowed
At starting, is my object. Nay, we'll go
Together down, sir! Notice Neptune,[8] though,
55 Taming a sea horse, thought a rarity,
Which Claus of Innsbruck[9] cast in bronze for me!

---

4. **forsooth:** in truth.
5. **munificence:** generosity.
6. **just pretense:** legitimate claim.
7. **dowry:** financial settlement given to the groom by the bride's father.
8. **Neptune:** in classical mythology, the god of the sea.
9. **Claus of Innsbruck:** fictitious sculptor from Innsbruck, Austria.

STUDY QUESTIONS

Home-Thoughts, from Abroad

Recalling

1. During what season does the poem take place? Where does the speaker want to be?
2. According to lines 3–6, what might someone in the speaker's homeland notice when he wakes one morning? What might he hear in line 7?
3. What does the speaker's peartree do, according to the second stanza?
4. What two flowers does the speaker compare in lines 19–20? What words does he apply to each?

Interpreting

5. Where is the speaker? How do you know?
6. What picture of his present surroundings does the image in line 20 create? What contrast between his homeland and present surroundings does the speaker suggest?

My Last Duchess

Recalling

1. How does the duke describe his wife in lines 22–23? Name four of the things that all drew "approving speech" from her. What "gift" did he give his wife, and how did she rank this gift?
2. How does the duke explain why he never told his wife about his feelings? What did he do instead, and what happened (line 46)?
3. To what does the duke call the emissary's attention as they go downstairs?

Interpreting

4. What are the duke's feelings about his late wife? How do you know? Do you think they are justified?
5. Contrast the personality of the duke with that of his first wife.
6. What do you think really happened to the duke's first wife?
7. In what way might the duke's reference in the last three lines to the sea horse be related to his account of his marriage?

Extending

8. What report do you think the emissary should make to the count about the proposed marriage of his daughter to the duke?

LITERARY FOCUS

Dramatic Monologue

A **dramatic monologue** is a poem that resembles a speech from a play; spoken by someone who differs markedly from the poet, the dramatic monologue consists entirely of the words that this person utters on a single occasion, usually to a silent listener. A dramatic monologue usually presents the speaker at a crucial point in his or her life, often a moment of conflict. Unlike a play, the dramatic monologue does not directly portray the action that leads up to the character's speech. However, through the speaker's words, we come to understand the situation that prompts the speech and, more important, the speaker's own personality. In most dramatic monologues the speaker reveals more than he or she realizes.

A number of Victorian poets experimented with dramatic monologues. For example, Tennyson's "Ulysses" presents a complex speaker who defines his attitude toward life as he speaks. However, no poet used the form of the dramatic monologue as often or as successfully as Robert Browning. The dramatic monologue allowed Browning to explore human psychology without commenting directly on it. Browning's dramatic monologues move from one emotion to another and seem improvised from moment to moment, like everyday speech; they often manage to capture the changing, quicksilver quality of life itself.

Thinking About Dramatic Monologues

1. What personality traits does the duke reveal in his monologue? What traits does he reveal without fully realizing that he is doing so? Explain, using specific lines from the poem.
2. In "My Last Duchess" find three examples of contractions, interrupted sentences, parenthetical expressions, or other aspects of a conversational style.
3. What different emotions does the duke convey during the monologue? When do you think he is most intense, and why?

COMPOSITION

Writing a Comparison/Contrast

Compare and contrast Browning's "My Last Duchess" with Tennyson's "Ulysses." First point out the traits that these two dramatic monologues have in common. Then explain the ways in which they differ, both in the personalities of the speakers and the ways in which these personalities are revealed. End by indicating which poem you prefer and the reasons for your preference. *For help with this assignment, refer to Lesson 2 in the Writing About Literature Handbook at the back of this book.*

Writing a Dramatic Monologue

Invent a character quite unlike yourself, and write a dramatic monologue for this character. Before writing, decide on the situation in which the character is speaking and the person whom he or she is addressing. Try to make the character's words both natural and revealing. Your monologue may be in prose or poetry.

Elizabeth Barrett Browning
1806–1861

When she met Robert Browning in 1845, Elizabeth Barrett had already established her name as a poet with four highly popular volumes of poetry. Her work was characterized by enthusiasm, directness, and a warmly felt sense of social responsibility. Yet the author of what were often passionate poems lived a fragile and sheltered life, having suffered a series of illnesses in her adolescence. The favorite daughter of a possessive and tyrannical father, she was enduring the life of an invalid and recluse when Robert Browning read her poems and fell in love with her.

To Elizabeth Barrett's father, Browning looked like a failure. Despite this strong opposition Browning persisted, and the couple managed to elope to Italy. There, for several years, Elizabeth Barrett Browning wrote a series of sonnets expressing her love for her husband. She published them in 1850 under the title *Sonnets from the Portuguese,* to make them appear to be translated from Portuguese, thereby disguising their deeply personal nature.

■ For what do you want to be loved? What qualities endear another person to you?

Elizabeth Barrett Browning

If Thou Must Love Me

If thou must love me, let it be for naught
Except for love's sake only. Do not say
"I love her for her smile—her look—her way
Of speaking gently—for a trick of thought
5 That falls in well with mine, and certes¹ brought
A sense of pleasant ease on such a day"—
For these things in themselves, Beloved, may
Be changed, or change for thee—and love, so wrought,²
May be unwrought so. Neither love me for
10 Thine own dear pity's wiping my cheeks dry—
A creature might forget to weep, who bore
Thy comfort long, and lose thy love thereby!
But love me for love's sake, that evermore
Thou mayst love on, through love's eternity.

---

1. **certes** [sur′tēz]: certainly, truly.
2. **wrought**: fashioned.

How Do I Love Thee?

How do I love thee? Let me count the ways.
I love thee to the depth and breadth and height
My soul can reach, when feeling out of sight
For the ends of Being and ideal Grace.
5 I love thee to the level of everyday's
Most quiet need, by sun and candle light.
I love thee freely, as men strive for Right;
I love thee purely, as they turn from Praise.
I love thee with the passion put to use
10 In my old griefs, and with my childhood's faith.
I love thee with a love I seemed to lose
With my lost saints—I love thee with the breath,
Smiles, tears, of all my life!—and, if God choose,
I shall but love thee better after death.

STUDY QUESTIONS

If Thou Must Love Me

Recalling

1. Why does the speaker want to be loved?
2. According to lines 2–6, for what four things does the speaker not want her beloved to love her? What reasons does she give?
3. What additional reasons for loving her does she mention? Why does she reject these?
4. For how long does she hope to be loved?

Interpreting

5. What kind of love does the speaker not want? From what is she trying to protect her love?
6. What kind of love does the speaker want?

How Do I Love Thee?

Recalling

1. How many different ways does the speaker love her beloved, according to this poem?
2. To what depth, breadth, and height does the speaker love her beloved? To what level?
3. With what sort of faith does she love him?
4. What will she do "if God choose"?

Interpreting

5. In what sense is the type of love mentioned in lines 2–4 different from that mentioned in lines 5–6? Explain how these types of love show the range of the speaker's feeling.
6. What feeling is the speaker describing when she refers to "a love I seemed to lose/With my lost saints"? What is she saying that her beloved means to her?

Extending

7. This sonnet is probably the most-quoted love poem in the English language. What qualities, both in its content and its style, make "How Do I Love Thee?" memorable?

COMPARING WRITERS

1. Compare the use of rhyme, rhythm, and other sound devices in poems by two or more of the Victorian poets presented here. What effects does each poet produce through the use of these devices? Which poem is more striking in its use of sound, and why?
2. Compare the speakers in poems by two or more of these writers. Do you identify the speaker with the poet, or is the speaker someone clearly different from the poet? How do you know? In each case briefly describe the speaker, and identify the emotions he or she expresses in the poem.

Charles Dickens   *1812–1870*

Charles Dickens was the most popular British author of the Victorian Age, and more than a hundred years after his death, his work is still popular both in print and in dramatic and musical versions. The magic that millions still find in Dickens' novels can be traced, at least in part, to the eccentric, colorful array of characters that he created: the gullible Pickwick of *The Pickwick Papers* (1836–1837), the villainous Fagin of *Oliver Twist* (1837–1839), the pathetic Little Nell of *The Old Curiosity Shop* (1840–1841), the miserly Scrooge of *A Christmas Carol* (1843), the shiftless Micawber of *David Copperfield* (1849–1850), the honorable Sydney Carton of *A Tale of Two Cities* (1859), the bitter Miss Havisham of *Great Expectations* (1860–1861).

Like most Realist authors, Dickens based his characters on his own experience. In fact, many people believe that his father was the model for Micawber and that his mother inspired Mrs. Nickleby in *Nicholas Nickleby* (1838–1839). Dickens was born in Portsmouth in southern England, the second of eight children. His father was a clerk who worked for the navy. The family repeatedly moved in order to escape creditors. When his father was finally sent to a debtors' prison, Charles, then twelve, began working in a warehouse pasting labels on pots of shoe.blacking. After a sudden inheritance improved the family's fortunes, Charles found work as a lawyer's clerk and then as a reporter. His literary career began with the success of *Sketches by Boz,* a collection of vignettes about life in the city that he wrote for a London newspaper. *Boz* led to *The Pickwick Papers,* his first novel.

While Dickens has entertained millions with his novels, he also intended them as a means of social reform. Human welfare could not keep pace with the technological advances of his time, and Dickens did much to expose evil byproducts of industrialization: child labor, debtors' prisons, ruinous financial speculation, inhuman legal procedures, and mismanagement of schools, orphanages, prisons, and hospitals.

Dickens' novels add up to a vast panorama of human nature and of Victorian life. The following selection from *Oliver Twist* introduces Oliver, an orphan who must depend on the mercies of public support. When he turns nine, Oliver becomes too old for the orphanage. He is brought by Mr. Bumble, a parish official, to a workhouse, a kind of prison where the poor must work for a meager upkeep. When we meet him, Oliver has been given a slice of bread so that he will not look hungry when he appears before the parish board of directors to be introduced to his new home.

■ Dickens was aware of many of the social problems of his day and wrote to call attention to them. If you were Dickens, what social problems would you want to call attention to today?

Charles Dickens

from **Oliver Twist**

Oliver had not been within the walls of the workhouse a quarter of an hour, and had scarcely completed the demolition of a second slice of bread, when Mr. Bumble, who had handed him over to the care of an old woman, returned; and, telling him it was a board night, informed him that the board had said he was to appear before it forthwith.

Not having a very clearly defined notion of what a live board was, Oliver was rather astounded by this intelligence, and was not quite certain whether he ought to laugh or cry. He had no time to think about the matter, however; for Mr. Bumble gave him a tap on the head with his cane, to wake him up, and another on the back to make him lively, and bidding him follow, conducted him into a large whitewashed room, where eight or ten fat gentlemen were sitting round a table. At the top of the table, seated in an armchair rather higher than the rest, was a particularly fat gentleman, with a very round, red face.

"Bow to the board," said Bumble. Oliver brushed away two or three tears that were lingering in his eyes; and seeing no board but the table, fortunately bowed to that.

"What's your name, boy?" said the gentleman in the high chair.

Oliver was frightened at the sight of so many gentlemen, which made him tremble; and the beadle[1] gave him another tap behind, which made him cry. These two causes made him answer in a very low and hesitating voice; whereupon a gentleman in a white waistcoat[2] said he was a fool. Which was a capital way of raising his spirits, and putting him quite at his ease.

"Boy," said the gentleman in the high chair, "listen to me. You know you're an orphan, I suppose?"

"What's that, sir?" inquired poor Oliver.

"The boy *is* a fool—I thought he was," said the gentleman in the white waistcoat.

"Hush!" said the gentleman who had spoken first. "You know you've got no father or mother, and that you were brought up by the parish, don't you?"

"Yes sir," replied Oliver, weeping bitterly.

"What are you crying for?" inquired the gentleman in the white waistcoat. And to be sure it was very extraordinary. What *could* the boy be crying for?

"I hope you say your prayers every night," said another gentleman in a gruff voice; "and pray for the people who feed you, and take care of you—like a Christian."

"Yes, sir," stammered the boy. The gentleman who spoke last was unconsciously right. It would have been *very* like a Christian, and a marvelously good Christian too, if Oliver had prayed for the people who fed and took care of *him.* But he hadn't, because nobody had taught him.

"Well! You have come here to be educated, and taught a useful trade," said the red-faced gentleman in the high chair.

"So you'll begin to pick oakum[3] tomorrow morning at six o'clock," added the surly one in the white waistcoat.

For the combination of both these blessings in the one simple process of picking oakum, Oliver bowed low, by the direction of the beadle, and was hurried away to a large ward: where, on a rough hard bed, he sobbed himself to sleep. What a noble illustration of the tender laws of England! They let the paupers go to sleep!

Poor Oliver! He little thought, as he lay sleeping in happy unconsciousness of all around him, that the board had that very day arrived at a decision which would exercise the

---

1. **beadle:** minor officer of a parish, or church district.
2. **waistcoat** [wes′kət]: vest.

3. **pick oakum:** tear apart old rope for the stringy fiber that was used in sealing the seams of boats.

most material influence over all his future fortunes. But they had. And this was it:

The members of this board were very sage, deep, philosophical men; and when they came to turn their attention to the workhouse, they found out at once, what ordinary folks would never have discovered—the poor people like it! It was a regular place of public entertainment for the poorer classes; a tavern where there was nothing to pay; a public breakfast, dinner, tea, and supper all the year round; a brick and mortar elysium, where it was all play and no work. "Oho!" said the board, looking very knowing; "we are the fellows to set this to rights; we'll stop it all, in no time." So, they established the rule, that all poor people should have the alternative (for they would compel nobody, not they) of being starved by a gradual process in the house, or by a quick one out of it. With this view, they contracted with the waterworks to lay on an unlimited supply of water; and with a corn factor to supply periodically small quantities of oatmeal; and issued three meals of thin gruel a day, with an onion twice a week, and half a roll on Sundays. They made a great many other wise and humane regulations, having reference to the ladies, which it is not necessary to repeat; kindly undertook to divorce poor married people, in consequence of the great expense of a suit in Doctors' Commons; and, instead of compelling a man to support his family, as they had theretofore done, took his family away from him, and made him a bachelor! There is no saying how many applicants for relief, under these last two heads, might have started up in all classes of society, if it had not been coupled with the workhouse; but the board were long-headed men, and had provided for this difficulty. The relief was inseparable from the workhouse and the gruel; and that frightened people.

For the first six months after Oliver Twist was removed, the system was in full operation. It was rather expensive at first, in consequence of the increase in the undertaker's bill, and the necessity of taking in the clothes of all the paupers, which fluttered loosely on their wasted, shrunken forms, after a week or two's gruel.

But the number of workhouse inmates got thin as well as the paupers; and the board were in ecstasies.

The room in which the boys were fed was a large stone hall, with a copper[4] at one end: out of which the master, dressed in an apron for the purpose, and assisted by one or two women, ladled the gruel at mealtimes. Of this festive composition, each boy had one porringer,[5] and no more—except on occasions of great public rejoicing, when he had two ounces and a quarter of bread besides. The bowls never wanted washing. The boys polished them with their spoons till they shone again; and when they had performed this operation (which never took very long, the spoons being nearly as large as the bowls), they would sit staring at the copper, with such eager eyes, as if they could have devoured the very bricks of which it was composed; employing themselves, meanwhile, in sucking their fingers most assiduously, with the view of catching up any stray splashes of gruel that might have been cast thereon. Boys have generally excellent appetites. Oliver Twist and his companions suffered the tortures of slow starvation for three months: at last they got so voracious and wild with hunger that one boy, who was tall for his age, and hadn't been used to that sort of thing (for his father had kept a small cook's shop), hinted darkly to his companions, that unless he had another basin of gruel *per diem,* he was afraid he might some night happen to eat the boy who slept next him, who happened to be a weakly youth of tender age. He had a wild, hungry eye; and they implicitly believed him. A council was held, lots were cast who should walk up to the master after supper that evening and ask for more; and it fell to Oliver Twist.

The evening arrived; the boys took their places. The master, in his cook's uniform, stationed himself at the copper; his pauper assistants ranged themselves behind him; the gruel

---

4. **copper:** large container, originally but not necessarily made of copper.
5. **porringer** [pôr′ in jər]: small, shallow bowl.

was served out; and a long grace was said over the short commons.[6] The gruel disappeared; the boys whispered each other, and winked at Oliver, while his next neighbors nudged him. Child as he was, he was desperate with hunger, and reckless with misery. He rose from the table; and advancing to the master, basin and spoon in hand, said, somewhat alarmed at his own temerity:

"Please, sir, I want some more."

The master was a fat, healthy man; but he turned very pale. He gazed in stupefied astonishment on the small rebel for some seconds; and then clung for support to the copper. The assistants were paralyzed with wonder; the boys with fear.

"What!" said the master at length, in a faint voice.

"Please, sir," replied Oliver, "I want some more."

The master aimed a blow at Oliver's head with the ladle, pinioned him in his arms, and shrieked aloud for the beadle.

The board were sitting in solemn conclave,[7] when Mr. Bumble rushed into the room in great excitement, and addressing the gentleman in the high chair, said:

"Mr. Limbkins, I beg your pardon, sir! Oliver Twist has asked for more!"

There was a general start. Horror was depicted on every countenance.

"For *more!*" said Mr. Limbkins. "Compose yourself, Bumble, and answer me distinctly. Do I understand that he asked for more, after he had eaten the supper allotted by the dietary?"[8]

"He did, sir," replied Bumble.

"That boy will be hung," said the gentleman in the white waistcoat. "I know that boy will be hung."

Nobody controverted the prophetic gentleman's opinion. An animated discussion took place. Oliver was ordered into instant confinement; and a bill was next morning pasted on the outside of the gate, offering a reward of

five pounds to anybody who would take Oliver Twist off the hands of the parish. In other words, five pounds and Oliver Twist were offered to any man or woman who wanted an apprentice,[9] to any trade, business, or calling.

"I never was more convinced of anything in my life," said the gentleman in the white waistcoat, as he knocked at the gate and read the bill next morning: "I never was more convinced of anything in my life, than I am that that boy will come to be hung."

---

6. **commons:** ration or allowance of food.
7. **conclave:** private meeting.
8. **dietary** [dī′ə ter′ē]: daily ration or allowance of food.

9. **apprentice** [ə pren′tis]: trainee who works in return for instruction in a trade.

STUDY QUESTIONS

Recalling

1. Describe the gentlemen of the board. Relate the circumstances that lead the gentlemen of the board to think Oliver a fool.
2. What is the weekly menu at the workhouse? Give two new workhouse regulations, and describe the results.
3. Briefly outline the events that lead to the prediction that Oliver will be hung some day.
4. What is the message on the bill that is pasted on the workhouse gate?

Interpreting

5. Compare the physical description of the board with the physical description of the boys. What does the comparison imply?
6. What is the official attitude toward the poor? What does the board think of its own efforts on behalf of the poor?
7. Explain what is implied by the prediction that Oliver will be hung and by the bill that is posted on the gate.

Extending

8. What insights into human nature do you find in the behavior of Oliver and of the board?

VIEWPOINT

One critic explained Dickens' style of characterization as an ability to view all people as children see adults. To children adults are

> odd, arbitrary, incomprehensible, sometimes absurdly comic, sometimes terrifying, sometimes both at once. Scarcely ever are they ordinary.

—W. Allen, *The English Novel*

■ Which adjectives in the quotation apply to the adults in the excerpt? Why? Why is a child's view of adults important to this scene?

LITERARY FOCUS

Elements of the Novel

The **novel,** loosely defined as a long work of narrative prose fiction (see page 321), came of age in England with such early contributions as Daniel Defoe's *Robinson Crusoe* (1719), Samuel Richardson's *Pamela* (1740), and Henry Fielding's *Tom Jones* (1749). The nineteenth century, however, saw the novel really blossom as a literary genre and as a form of entertainment for the new middle class, and the works of Charles Dickens exemplify that success.

Because of its length, the novel usually has a complicated plot. **Plot** is the sequence of events in a narrative, each event causing or leading to the next. A novel usually has several subplots in addition to its central plot. A **subplot** is a less important plot that is somehow related to the main action of the narrative. A novel also has many characters, major and minor, and often has a variety of settings. **Setting** is the time and place of a narrative, and a novel can take place in a number of locations and over a long period of time. Because a novel may contain many subplots, characters, and settings, it can also have more than one **theme,** or general statement about life.

Many Victorian novels were written in installments for magazines; as a result, they are often very long. They present a detailed, richly populated world that offers the reader a high level of involvement and an impressive record of British life and thought in the 1800s.

Thinking About Elements of the Novel

■ What theme is implied by the excerpt from *Oliver Twist*? Explain how plot, character, and setting suggest the theme.

COMPOSITION

Writing About Literature and Its Period

■ Write an essay to demonstrate how Dickens, as represented by the excerpt from *Oliver Twist,* exemplifies his era in the ideas he explores and the literary techniques he uses. First identify the period. Then state several characteristics of the time; include popular literary techniques as well as prevalent ideas and achievements. For each characteristic of the period, give examples from the excerpt from *Oliver Twist. For help with this assignment, refer to Lesson 10 in the Writing About Literature Handbook at the back of this book.*

Continuing the Story

■ The excerpt from *Oliver Twist* comes very early in the novel. Imagine your own continuation of the novel, and write a short excerpt that would come near the end. Try to relate your excerpt to details in the portion you have read. Use details in your excerpt that imply events in Oliver's life up to that point.

Charlotte Brontë   *1816–1855*

The daughter of an Irish-born Protestant clergyman, Charlotte Brontë grew up in the tiny village of Haworth on the edge of the bleak Yorkshire moors. Tragedy came early in her life when her mother died in 1821; not long afterward Charlotte's two older sisters, Maria and Elizabeth, succumbed to tuberculosis and typhus, both brought on by their stay at a poorly run girls' boarding school that would later become the model of Charlotte's Lowood School in *Jane Eyre*. In the gloomy Haworth Parsonage behind the church where their father worked, the four remaining Brontë children offset their unhappy, isolated lives by spinning tales of imaginary worlds and exotic characters. From this childhood play came a wealth of later creativity: Charlotte, Anne, and Emily (see page 522) all won distinction as writers; their brother Branwell became a painter. Nevertheless, their lives were tragically foreshortened by the family curse, tuberculosis: Branwell died of it in September of 1848; Emily, just a few months later; and Anne succumbed the following year. Charlotte, the only one of the six Brontë children to reach the age of thirty, died of tuberculosis in March of 1855, less than a year after her marriage. She was not yet thirty-nine years old.

Despite her brief life and the specter of death that haunted her family, Charlotte was able to produce a number of poems and novels, including one work for which she will always be remembered, the novel *Jane Eyre*. Charlotte published *Jane Eyre* in 1847 under the pen name Currer Bell, but the book was an instant success that soon drew its author from anonymity. Not only could Charlotte now publish other novels, including some that had been rejected before, but she became the subject of one of the Victorian era's most famous biographies, *The Life of Charlotte Brontë* by Elizabeth Gaskell.

An absorbing tale, *Jane Eyre* blends Realism and Romanticism in recounting, with the detail typical of Victorian fiction, the life of its title character from childhood on. Like Dickens' Oliver Twist, Jane Eyre first faces life as a penniless young orphan. Following the death of her uncle, she is treated miserably in her uncle's home. Her cousins Eliza, Georgiana, and John taunt her poverty and bully her unmercifully; her aunt, Mrs. Reed, treats her unjustly, often punishing Jane for fights and other mischief initiated by the Reed children.

▮ Has anyone ever put words in your mouth? How did you react? What was the person's response to your reaction?

Charlotte Brontë

from **Jane Eyre**

It was the fifteenth of January, about nine o'clock in the morning. Bessie was gone down to breakfast; my cousins had not yet been summoned to their mama; Eliza was putting on her bonnet and warm garden coat to go and feed her poultry, an occupation of which she was fond, and not less so of selling the eggs to the housekeeper and hoarding up the money she thus obtained. She had a turn for traffic, and a marked propensity for saving, shown not only in the vending of eggs and chickens but also in driving hard bargains with the gardener about flower roots, seeds, and slips of plants, that functionary having orders from Mrs. Reed to buy from this young lady all the products of her parterre[1] she wished to sell; and Eliza would have sold the hair off her head if she could have made a handsome profit thereby. As to her money, she first secreted it in odd corners, wrapped in a rag or an old curl paper;[2] but some of these hoards having been discovered by the housemaid, Eliza, fearful of one day losing her valued treasure, consented to entrust it to her mother, at a usurious rate of interest—fifty or sixty percent, which interest she exacted every quarter, keeping her accounts in a little book with anxious accuracy.

Georgiana sat on a high stool, dressing her hair at the glass, and interweaving her curls with artificial flowers and faded feathers, of which she had found a store in a drawer in the attic. I was making my bed, having received strict orders from Bessie to get it arranged before she returned (for Bessie now frequently employed me as a sort of under-nurserymaid,[3] to tidy the room, dust the chairs, etc.). Having spread the quilt and folded my nightdress, I went to the windowseat to put in order some picture books and doll's-house furniture scattered there; an abrupt command from Georgiana to let her playthings alone (for the tiny chairs and mirrors, the fairy plates and cups were her property) stopped my proceedings, and then, for lack of other occupation, I fell to breathing on the frostflowers with which the window was fretted, and thus clearing a space in the glass through which I might look out on the grounds, where all was still and petrified under the influence of a hard frost.

From this window were visible the porter's[4] lodge and the carriage road, and just as I had dissolved so much of the silver-white foliage veiling the panes as left room to look out, I saw the gates thrown open and a carriage roll through. I watched it ascending the drive with indifference; carriages often came to Gateshead, but none ever brought visitors in whom I was interested. It stopped in front of the house, the doorbell rang loudly, the newcomer was admitted. All this being nothing to me, my vacant attention soon found livelier attraction in the spectacle of a little hungry robin, which came and chirruped on the twigs of the leafless cherry tree nailed against the wall near the casement. The remains of my breakfast of bread and milk stood on the table, and having crumbled a morsel of roll, I was tugging at the sash to put out the crumb on the windowsill when Bessie came running upstairs into the nursery.

"Miss Jane, take off your pinafore;[5] what are you doing there? Have you washed your hands and face this morning?" I gave another tug before I answered, for I wanted the bird to be secure of its bread; the sash yielded, I scattered the crumbs, some on the stone sill, some on the cherry-tree bough, then, closing the window, I replied:

---

1. **parterre:** garden in which the flower beds are arranged to form a pattern.
2. **curl paper:** small piece of paper used for curling hair.
3. **under-nurserymaid:** The nursery is the part of the house in which children sleep, play, and study.

4. **porter's:** gatekeeper's.
5. **pinafore:** sleeveless housedress worn over a dress.

"No, Bessie; I have only just finished dusting."

"Troublesome, careless child! And what are you doing now? You look quite red, as if you had been about some mischief; what were you opening the window for?"

I was spared the trouble of answering, for Bessie seemed in too great a hurry to listen to explanations; she hauled me to the washstand, inflicted a merciless but happily brief scrub on my face and hands with soap, water, and a coarse towel; disciplined my head with a bristly brush, denuded me of my pinafore, and then hurrying me to the top of the stairs, bid me go down directly, as I was wanted in the breakfast room.

I would have asked who wanted me; I would have demanded if Mrs. Reed was there, but Bessie was already gone, and had closed the nursery door upon me. I slowly descended. For nearly three months, I had never been called to Mrs. Reed's presence; restricted so long to the nursery, the breakfast, dining, and drawing rooms were become for me awful regions, on which it dismayed me to intrude.

I now stood in the empty hall; before me was the breakfast-room door, and I stopped, intimidated and trembling. What a miserable little poltroon[6] had fear, engendered of unjust punishment, made of me in those days! I feared to return to the nursery, and feared to go forward to the parlor; ten minutes I stood in agitated hesitation. The vehement ringing of the breakfast-room bell decided me; I *must* enter.

"Who could want me?" I asked inwardly, as with both hands I turned the stiff door handle which, for a second or two, resisted my efforts. "What should I see beside Aunt Reed in the apartment? A man or a woman?" The handle turned, the door unclosed, and passing through and curtseying low, I looked up at—a black pillar!—such, at least, appeared to me, at first sight, the straight, narrow, sable-clad shape standing erect on the rug; The grim face at the top was like a carved mask, placed above the shaft by way of capital.

---

6. **poltroon:** complete coward.

Mrs. Reed occupied her usual seat by the fireside; she made a signal to me to approach; I did so, and she introduced me to the stony stranger with the words: "This is the little girl respecting whom I applied to you."

He, for it was a man, turned his head slowly toward where I stood, and having examined me with the two of two inquisitive-looking gray eyes which twinkled under a pair of bushy brows, said solemnly, and in a bass voice: "Her size is small; what is her age?"

"Ten years."

"So much?" was the doubtful answer; and he prolonged his scrutiny for some minutes. Presently he addressed me:

"Your name, little girl?"

"Jane Eyre, sir."

In uttering these words, I looked up: he seemed to me a tall gentleman, but then I was very little; his features were large, and they and all the lines of his frame were equally harsh and prim.

"Well, Jane Eyre, and are you a good child?"

Impossible to reply to this in the affirmative; my little world held a contrary opinion. I was silent. Mrs. Reed answered for me by an expressive shake of the head, adding soon, "Perhaps the less said on that subject the better, Mr. Brocklehurst."

"Sorry indeed to hear it! She and I must have some talk," and bending from the perpendicular, he installed his person in the armchair, opposite Mrs. Reed's. "Come here," he said.

I stepped across the rug; he placed me square and straight before him. What a face he had, now that it was almost on a level with mine! what a great nose! and what a mouth! and what large prominent teeth!

"No sight so sad as that of a naughty child," he began, "especially a naughty little girl. Do you know where the wicked go after death?"

"They go to hell," was my ready and orthodox answer.

"And what is hell? Can you tell me that?"

"A pit full of fire."

"And should you like to fall into that pit, and to be burning there forever?"

"No, sir."

"What must you do to avoid it?"

I deliberated a moment; my answer, when it did come, was objectionable: "I must keep in good health, and not die."

"How can you keep in good health? Children younger than you die daily. I buried a little child of five years old only a day or two since—a good little child, whose soul is now in heaven. It is to be feared the same could not be said of you, were you to be called hence."

Not being in a condition to remove his doubts, I only cast my eyes down on the two large feet planted on the rug, and sighed, wishing myself far enough away.

"I hope that sigh is from the heart, and that you repent of ever having been the occasion of discomfort to your excellent benefactress."

"Benefactress! benefactress!" said I, inwardly. "They all call Mrs. Reed my benefactress; if so, a benefactress is a disagreeable thing."

"Do you say your prayers night and morning?" continued my interrogator.

"Yes, sir."

"Do you read your Bible?"

"Sometimes."

"With pleasure? Are you fond of it?"

"I like Revelations, and the book of Daniel, and Genesis and Samuel, and a little bit of Exodus, and some parts of Kings and Chronicles, and Job and Jonah."

"And the Psalms? I hope you like them?"

"No, sir."

"No? Oh, shocking! I have a little boy, younger than you, who knows six Psalms by heart; and when you ask him which he would rather have, a gingerbread nut[7] to eat or a verse of a Psalm to learn, he says: 'Oh! the verse of a Psalm! Angels sing Psalms'; says he, 'I wish to be a little angel here below'; he then gets two nuts in recompense for his infant piety."

"Psalms are not interesting," I remarked.

"That proves you have a wicked heart; and you must pray to God to change it, to give you a new and clean one, to take away your heart of stone and give you a heart of flesh."

I was about to propound a question, touching the manner in which that operation of changing my heart was to be performed, when Mrs. Reed interposed, telling me to sit down; she then proceeded to carry on the conversation herself.

"Mr. Brocklehurst, I believe I intimated in the letter which I wrote to you three weeks ago that this little girl has not quite the character and disposition I could wish; should you admit her into Lowood school, I should be glad if the superintendent and teachers were requested to keep a strict eye on her, and above all, to guard against her worst fault, a tendency to deceit. I mention this fact in your hearing, Jane, that you may not attempt to impose on Mr. Brocklehurst."

Well might I dread, well might I dislike Mrs. Reed, for it was her nature to wound me cruelly; never was I happy in her presence: however carefully I obeyed, however strenuously I strove to please her, my efforts were still repulsed and repaid by such sentences as the above. Now, uttered before a stranger, the accusation cut me to the heart: I dimly perceived that she was already obliterating hope from the new phase of existence which she destined me to enter; I felt, though I could not have expressed the feeling, that she was sowing aversion and unkindness along my future path; I saw myself transformed under Mr. Brocklehurst's eye into an artful, obnoxious child, and what could I do to remedy the injury?

"Nothing, indeed!" thought I, as I struggled to repress a sob, and hastily wiped away some tears, the impotent evidences of my anguish.

"Deceit is, indeed, a sad fault in a child," said Mr. Brocklehurst; "it is akin to falsehood, and all liars will have their portion in the lake burning with fire and brimstone; she shall, however, be watched, Mrs. Reed; I will speak to Miss Temple and the teachers."

"I should wish her to be brought up in a manner suiting her prospects," continued my benefactress; "to be made useful, to be kept humble; as for the vacations, she will, with your permission, spend them always at Lowood."

---

7. **gingerbread nut:** fruit of the doum, or gingerbread, tree, so named because the fruit tastes like gingerbread.

"Your decisions are perfectly judicious, madam," returned Mr. Brocklehurst. "Humility is a Christian grace, and one peculiarly appropriate to the pupils of Lowood; I, therefore, direct that especial care shall be bestowed on its cultivation among them. I have studied how best to mortify in them the worldly sentiment of pride; and, only the other day, I had a pleasing proof of my success. My second daughter, Augusta, went with her mama to visit the school, and on her return she exclaimed: 'Oh, dear papa, how quiet and plain all the girls at Lowood look; with their hair combed behind their ears, and their long pinafores, and those little holland[8] pockets outside their frocks—they are almost like poor people's children! And,' said she, 'they looked at my dress and mama's as if they had never seen a silk gown before.'"

"This is the state of things I quite approve," returned Mrs. Reed. "Had I sought all England over, I could scarcely have found a system more exactly fitting a child like Jane Eyre. Consistency, my dear Mr. Brocklehurst; I advocate consistency in all things."

"Consistency, madam, is the first of Christian duties, and it has been observed in every arrangement connected with the establishment of Lowood: plain fare, simple attire, unsophisticated accommodations, hardy and active habits; such is the order of the day in the house and its inhabitants."

"Quite right, sir. I may then depend upon this child being received as a pupil at Lowood, and there being trained in conformity to her position and prospects?"

"Madam, you may; she shall be placed in that nursery of chosen plants—and I trust she will show herself grateful for the inestimable privilege of her election."

"I will send her, then, as soon as possible, Mr. Brocklehurst; for, I assure you, I feel anxious to be relieved of a responsibility that was becoming too irksome."

"No doubt, no doubt, madam, and now I wish you good morning. I shall return to Brocklehurst Hall in the course of a week or two; my good friend, the archdeacon,[9] will not permit me to leave him sooner. I shall send Miss Temple notice that she is to expect a new girl, so that there will be no difficulty about receiving her. Good-bye."

"Good-bye, Mr. Brocklehurst; remember me to Mrs. and Miss Brocklehurst, and to Augusta and Theodore, and Master Broughton Brocklehurst."

"I will, madam. Little girl, here is a book entitled the 'Child's Guide'; read it with prayer, especially that part containing 'an account of the awfully sudden death of Martha G——, a naughty child addicted to falsehood and deceit.'"

With these words Mr. Brocklehurst put into my hand a thin pamphlet sewed in a cover, and having rung for his carriage, he departed.

Mrs. Reed and I were left alone. Some minutes passed in silence; she was sewing, I was watching her. Mrs. Reed might be at that time some six- or seven-and-thirty; she was a woman of robust frame, square shouldered and strong limbed, not tall, and, though stout, not obese; she had a somewhat large face, the underjaw being much developed and very solid; her brow was low, her chin large and prominent, mouth and nose sufficiently regular; under her light eyebrows glimmered an eye devoid of ruth;[10] her skin was dark and opaque, her hair nearly flaxen; her constitution was sound as a bell—illness never came near her; she was an exact, clever manager; her household and tenantry[11] were thoroughly under her control; her children, only, at times defied her authority, and laughed it to scorn; she dressed well, and had a presence and port[12] calculated to set off handsome attire.

Sitting on a low stool, a few yards from her armchair, I examined her figure; I perused her features. In my hand I held the tract, containing

---

8. **holland:** a type of linen or heavy cotton first made in Holland.

9. **archdeacon:** in the Church of England, church official ranking just below a bishop and assisting the bishop in his duties.

10. **ruth:** compassion; pity.

11. **tenantry:** tenant farmers on her estate.

12. **port:** way of carrying oneself.

the sudden death of the Liar, to which narrative my attention had been pointed as to an appropriate warning. What had just passed; what Mrs. Reed had said concerning me to Mr. Brocklehurst; the whole tenor of their conversation, was recent, raw, and stinging in my mind; I had felt every word as acutely as I had heard it plainly, and a passion of resentment fomented now within me.

Mrs. Reed looked up from her work; her eye settled on mine, her fingers at the same time suspended their nimble movements.

"Go out of the room; return to the nursery," was her mandate. My look or something else must have struck her as offensive, for she spoke with extreme though suppressed irritation. I got up; I went to the door; I came back again; I walked to the window, across the room, then close up to her.

Speak I must; I had been trodden on severely, and *must* turn, but how? What strength had I to dart retaliation at my antagonist? I gathered my energies and launched them in this blunt sentence:

"I am not deceitful: if I were, I should say I loved *you,* but I declare I do not love you; I dislike you the worst of anybody in the world except John Reed; and this book about the liar you may give to your girl, Georgiana, for it is she who tells lies, and not I."

Mrs. Reed's hands still lay on her work inactive; her eye of ice continued to dwell freezingly on mine.

"What more have you to say?" she asked, rather in the tone in which a person might address an opponent of adult age than such as is ordinarily used to a child.

That eye of hers, that voice stirred every antipathy I had. Shaking from head to foot, thrilled with ungovernable excitement, I continued:

"I am glad you are no relation[13] of mine; I will never call you aunt again as long as I live. I will never come to see you when I am grown up; and if anyone asks me how I liked you, and how you treated me, I will say the very thought of you makes me sick and that you treated me with miserable cruelty."

"How dare you affirm that, Jane Eyre?"

"How dare I, Mrs. Reed? How dare I? Because it is the *truth.* You think I have no feelings, and that I can do without one bit of love or kindness; but I cannot live so, and you have no pity. I shall remember how you thrust me back—roughly and violently thrust me back—into the red room,[14] and locked me up there, to my dying day; though I was in agony, though I cried out, while suffocating with distress, 'Have mercy! Have mercy, Aunt Reed!' And that punishment you made me suffer because your wicked boy struck me—knocked me down for nothing. I will tell anybody who asks me questions this exact tale. People think you a good woman, but you are bad; hard-hearted. *You* are deceitful!"

Ere I had finished this reply, my soul began to expand, to exult, with the strangest sense of freedom, of triumph, I ever felt. It seemed as if an invisible bond had burst, and that I had struggled out into unhoped-for liberty. Not without cause was this sentiment: Mrs. Reed looked frightened; her work had slipped from her knee; she was lifting up her hands, rocking herself to and fro, and even twisting her face as if she would cry.

"Jane, you are under a mistake; what is the matter with you? Why do you tremble so violently? Would you like to drink some water?"

"No, Mrs. Reed."

"Is there anything else you wish for, Jane? I assure you, I desire to be your friend."

"Not you. You told Mr. Brocklehurst I had a bad character, a deceitful disposition; and I'll let everybody at Lowood know what you are, and what you have done."

"Jane, you don't understand these things; children must be corrected for their faults."

"Deceit is not my fault!" I cried out in a savage, high voice.

"But you are passionate, Jane, that you must allow; and now return to the nursery—there's a dear—and lie down a little."

---

13. **relation:** here, blood relation. Mrs. Reed is Jane's aunt by marriage.

14. **red room:** room with red furnishings. When Jane was younger, Mrs. Reed unjustly punished her by locking her in the room in which Jane's uncle had died.

"I am not your dear; I cannot lie down; send me to school soon, Mrs. Reed, for I hate to live here."

"I will indeed send her to school soon," murmured Mrs. Reed, sotto voce;[15] and gathering up her work, she abruptly quitted the apartment.

I was left there alone—winner of the field. It was the hardest battle I had fought, and the first victory I had gained. I stood awhile on the rug, where Mr. Brocklehurst had stood, and I enjoyed my conqueror's solitude. First, I smiled to myself and felt elated; but this fierce pleasure subsided in me as fast as did the accelerated throb of my pulses. A child cannot quarrel with its elders, as I had done, cannot give its furious feelings uncontrolled play, as I had given mine, without experiencing afterward the pang of remorse and the chill of reaction. A ridge of lighted heath,[16] alive, glancing, devouring, would have been a meet[17] emblem of my mind when I accused and menaced Mrs. Reed; the same ridge, black and blasted after the flames are dead, would have represented as meetly my subsequent condition, when half an hour's silence and reflection had shown me the madness of my conduct, and the dreariness of my hated and hating position.

---

15. **sotto voce:** in an undertone. The expression, from Italian, literally means "under the voice."

16. **lighted heath:** moorland that has caught fire.
17. **meet:** suitable; appropriate.

STUDY QUESTIONS

Recalling

1. With what duties is Jane often employed in the nursery? For what reason is she summoned to meet the visitor?
2. As what sort of child has Mrs. Reed described Jane to Mr. Brocklehurst? What effect does Jane fear this description will have on her future?
3. In what manner does Mrs. Reed say she wishes Jane to be brought up? What are her plans for Jane's vacations?
4. According to Mr. Brocklehurst, how did his daughter Augusta describe the girls at Lowood? What did the girls look at "as if they had never seen" them before?
5. Summarize Jane's behavior after the departure of the visitor. What changing feelings does Jane experience in the last paragraph?

Interpreting

6. Contrast Jane's treatment in the Reed household with the treatment of Eliza and Georgiana. Is Mrs. Reed poor? What does your answer stress about her treatment of Jane?
7. What ironic contrasts do the details about Augusta Brocklehurst's visit to Lowood reveal about Lowood and the Brocklehursts? What sort of person is Mr. Brocklehurst?
8. Briefly describe Jane's character as revealed in the selection. What differences do you perceive between young Jane and the older woman who narrates the story?

COMPARING WRITERS

Compare the two selections you have read from the Victorian novels *Jane Eyre* and *Oliver Twist*. What is similar about the title characters' situations in life? About their personalities and responses to events? What do the situations in which the two main characters find themselves reveal about Victorian life and about Victorian novelists' attempts to achieve social awareness and effect social change?

Emily Brontë   *1818–1855*

Despite her tragically brief life, Emily Jane Brontë, like her sisters Charlotte (see page 515) and Anne, made a lasting mark in English literature. The most poetic of the three writing sisters and probably the shyest, Emily was also the most strongly affected by the childhood tales of imaginary lands that the Brontë children invented. In fact, almost all of Emily's poetry is set in a mythical kingdom called Gondal that she and her sister Anne created, although the sequence of the poems and their relationship to Gondal's cast of characters is still the subject of scholarly research.

Some of Emily's verse was published in 1846 in *Poems by Currer, Ellis, and Acton Bell,* the pen names of Charlotte, Emily, and Anne Brontë. Emily also used the pen name Ellis Bell in publishing her only novel, *Wuthering Heights* (1847), a poetic tale of passion and tragedy on the Yorkshire moors. Though today regarded as a classic, *Wuthering Heights* was not as well received as Charlotte's *Jane Eyre* (1847), no doubt because it was more lavishly Romantic and less clearly structured than Charlotte's great novel or the other Victorian novels popular at the time. Emily's poetry, too, though instantly recognized by Charlotte as the finest of the three sisters' poetic efforts, took some years to gain critical acclaim. Those few poems that first grew popular—inspirational poems like "No Coward Soul Is Mine"—are not really typical of the moody lyrics and mystical Gondolian narratives that comprise most of Emily's verse. "Hope" is more representative.

■ Emily Dickinson said that hope is a thing with feathers. Do you think that Emily Brontë would agree?

Emily Brontë

Hope

Hope was but a timid friend;
She sat without[1] the grated den,
Watching how my fate would tend,
Even as selfish-hearted men.

5 She was cruel in her fear;
Through the bars, one dreary day,
I looked out to see her there,
And she turned her face away!

Like a false guard, false watch keeping,
10 Still, in strife, she whispered peace;
She would sing while I was weeping;
If I listened, she would cease.

False she was, and unrelenting;
When my last joys strewed the ground,
15 Even Sorrow saw, repenting,
Those sad relics scattered round;

Hope—whose whisper would have given
Balm to all my frenzied pain—
Stretched her wings and soared to heaven;
20 Went—and ne'er returned again!

---

1. **without:** outside.

STUDY QUESTIONS

Recalling

1. According to stanza 1, what kind of friend was Hope? Outside what did she sit?
2. According to stanza 2, what cruel thing did Hope do "one dreary day"?
3. When did Hope sing (stanza 3)? What happened when the speaker listened?
4. According to the last two stanzas, who repented upon seeing the speaker's last joys strewn on the ground? What did Hope do?

Interpreting

5. Explain in your own words the kind of person to which Hope is compared in this poem. To what is Hope compared in line 19? In addition to hope, what other emotion does the poem personify?
6. To what is the speaker comparing herself in lines 2 and 6?
7. What emotional situation does this poem figuratively describe? Into what state has the speaker's emotional situation deteriorated by the poem's end?

Extending

8. To what would you compare hope if you were writing figuratively about it? To what would you compare sorrow?

Dante Gabriel Rossetti.

Christina Rossetti,
as photographed by Lewis Carroll.

Dante Gabriel Rossetti   *1828–1882*
Christina Rossetti   *1830–1894*

Equally famous as a painter and a writer, Dante Gabriel Rossetti had his literary path marked out for him when his parents named him for the great Italian poet Dante Alighieri. Born in London, Dante Gabriel was the son of Gabriele Rossetti, an Italian poet and liberal forced into exile for political reasons, and Frances Mary Polidori Rossetti, sister of the same Dr. Polidori who had accompanied Lord Byron to Switzerland and participated in the famous horror-story competition described by Mary Shelley in her introduction to *Frankenstein* (page 478). Educated at King's College in London, where his father taught Italian, Rossetti also studied under various noted painters of the day. In 1848 he joined with artists William Holman Hunt and John Everett Millais to form the **Pre-Raphaelite Brotherhood,** a neo-Romantic society whose stated aim was to return the arts to the simplicity and unstudied passion that they felt was exhibited in Italian art before the advent of Renaissance painter Raphael. The principles of this movement are evident not only in Rossetti's paintings but in his poetry, most of which first appeared in *The Germ,* the periodical put out by the Pre-Raphaelites. Though it took time for the Pre-Raphaelites to gain acceptance, they were championed by the great Victorian art critic John Ruskin and by decorative artist William Morris, who became Rossetti's close friends. Most of Rossetti's paintings were eventually displayed in London's prestigious Royal Academy; his *Ballads and Sonnets* were collected a year before he died.

Though less influenced by Pre-Raphaelite principles than her brother Dante Gabriel, Christina Rossetti did serve as an artist's model for her brother and his painter friends. The youngest of the four Rossetti children, Christina grew interested in writing at an early age and brought out her first volume of verse when she was only seventeen. However, it was not until 1862 that she published *Goblin Market and Other Poems,* the collection that made her famous. A devout Anglican, Christina twice refused marriage proposals because of religious differences and the poor health that plagued her adult life. Among her later religious works is an unusual diary called *Time Flies* (1885), written in prose and verse. Nevertheless, it is for the well-crafted earlier love poems of *Goblin Market* that Christina Rossetti is today best remembered.

■ Most people do not find noon a silent time. If you wanted to spend a quiet noon, where would you go? Why would you want to spend a silent noon?

Detail from *The Blessed Damozel*, 1878, Dante Gabriel Rossetti. Fogg Art Museum, Cambridge, Massachusetts.

Dante Gabriel Rossetti

Silent Noon

Your hands lie open in the long fresh grass,
The finger points look through like rosy blooms:
Your eyes smile peace. The pasture gleams and glooms
’Neath billowing skies that scatter and amass.
5 All round our nest, far as the eye can pass,
Are golden kingcup[1] fields with silver edge
Where the cow parsley skirts the hawthorn hedge.
’Tis visible silence, still as the hourglass.
Deep in the sun-searched growths the dragonfly
10 Hangs like a blue thread loosened from the sky:
So this winged hour is dropped to us from above.
Oh! clasp we to our hearts, for deathless dower,[2]
This close-companioned inarticulate hour
When twofold silence was the song of love.

---

1. **kingcup:** buttercup.   2. **dower:** gift; inheritance.

Detail, *Early Lovers*, Frederick Smallfield, nineteenth century.

Christina Rossetti

Sonnet

Remember me when I am gone away,
Gone far away into the silent land;
When you can no more hold me by the hand,
Nor I half turn to go yet turning stay.
5 Remember me when no more day by day
You tell me of our future that you planned:
Only remember me; you understand
It will be late to counsel then or pray.
Yet if you should forget me for a while
10 And afterward remember, do not grieve:
For if the darkness and corruption leave
A vestige of the thoughts that once I had,
Better by far you should forget and smile
Than that you should remember and be sad.

STUDY QUESTIONS

Silent Noon

Recalling

1. Summarize the setting (time and place) of the poem.
2. According to the opening octave, what do the beloved's eyes "smile"? What sort of silence surrounds the lovers' nest?
3. According to the closing sestet, from where is the lovers' "winged" hour dropped? What two other adjectives are used to describe the hour? What sort of song is the "twofold silence"?

Interpreting

4. What mood or atmosphere does this sonnet capture? Identify five images or figures of speech that help it capture this mood or atmosphere.
5. Explain the paradox, or seeming contradiction, in the final line.
6. How is the phrase "visible silence" (line 8) related to the whole idea of the poem?

Extending

7. Examine the explanation of the Pre-Raphaelite Brotherhood given in the biography of Dante Gabriel Rossetti on page 524. In what ways does this poem follow Pre-Raphaelite principles? What does the poem's view of nature share with the view of Romantic Age poets like William Wordsworth?

Sonnet

Recalling

1. According to the opening octave, when should the person addressed in this sonnet remember the speaker? Into what land will the speaker have gone? Of what will the person addressed no longer tell the speaker?

2. In the closing sestet, about what does the speaker say not to grieve? What advice does she give in the last two lines?

Interpreting

3. What is the relationship between the speaker and the person addressed? Considering lines 5–6, what different views do the speaker and the person addressed seem to have of that relationship?
4. What might "the silent land" (line 2) be?

Extending

5. In your opinion, is the advice in the closing lines of the poem good advice in most situations? Why or why not?

COMPOSITION

Writing About Poetry

▪ Choose either of the sonnets by the Rossettis, and write a brief essay in which you show how the poem's various elements help contribute to the emotion that the poem expresses or the mood that it creates. Among the elements you might consider are the poem's speaker, sound, structure, imagery, figurative language, and diction (word choice). *For help with this assignment, refer to Lesson 7 in the Writing About Literature Handbook at the back of this book.*

Writing a Description

▪ Write your own description of a silent moment, as Dante Gabriel Rossetti does in "Silent Noon." The silence you describe may be the result of love, shock, grief, or another emotion, or it may simply be the silence of a place that is ordinarily quiet. Use vivid images and figures of speech, as Rossetti does, to capture the silence.

Lewis Carroll   *1832–1898*

Throughout his lifetime Oxford mathematics professor Charles Lutwidge Dodgson persisted in denying that he had written anything but those mathematical studies published under his own name. Actually, however, he had created, under the pen name Lewis Carroll, two of the world's most enduring children's classics, works that appeal to children and adults alike.

The son of a church rector, Dodgson attended the Rugby School and then went on to Oxford University, where he studied mathematics and became a life fellow at his college, Christ Church. An able mathematician, Dodgson was not a particularly inspiring lecturer, for he was generally ill at ease among adults. He blossomed, however, in the company of children and could apparently delight them for hours with the stories he invented. One day, on a boat trip up the River Isis, he told an especially entertaining story to the three young daughters of the college dean—Alice, Lorina, and Edith Liddell. The girls begged him to write the tale down, and he did so, presenting the manuscript, which he called *Alice's Adventures Underground,* to young Alice Liddell as a Christmas present. Colleagues who saw the work were so delighted with it that they persuaded Dodgson to have it published. Under the pen name Lewis Carroll, he published an expanded version of the manuscript, retitled *Alice's Adventures in Wonderland,* in 1865. The book, charmingly illustrated by artist John Tenniel, was an instant success. In 1872 Lewis Carroll published an equally popular sequel, *Through the Looking Glass and What Alice Found There.*

Though the identity of Lewis Carroll was widely known, the modest mathematics teacher preferred to deny authorship of the books that had made Carroll's name famous. Even after he became acquainted with such literary luminaries as Alfred, Lord Tennyson, and the Rossettis, Dodgson still felt happiest in children's company. As an amateur photographer, he became noted for his pictures of children; as an ordained deacon in the Anglican Church, he sometimes preached to all-children congregations. In addition, Lewis Carroll produced other works of children's literature, but only the long poem *The Hunting of the Snark* (1876) achieved the enduring success of the *Alice* books.

Alice's adventures begin when she falls down a rabbit hole that leads to a strange new world. In this "wonderland" she encounters many odd characters, few of them more famous than the mad Hatter, the sleepy Dormouse, and the March Hare, guests at a very unusual tea party.

■ What typical American custom might Lewis Carroll portray in an unusual way?

Lewis Carroll

from **Alice's Adventures in Wonderland**

A Mad Tea Party

There was a table set out under a tree in front of the house, and the March Hare and the Hatter were having tea at it; a Dormouse was sitting between them, fast asleep, and the other two were using it as a cushion, resting their elbows on it, and talking over its head. "Very uncomfortable for the Dormouse," thought Alice; "only, as it's asleep, I suppose it doesn't mind."

The table was a large one, but the three were all crowded together at one corner of it. "No room! No room!" they cried out, when they saw Alice coming. "There's *plenty* of room!" said Alice indignantly, and she sat down in a large armchair at one end of the table.

"Have some wine," the March Hare said in an encouraging tone.

Alice looked all round the table, but there was nothing on it but tea. "I don't see any wine," she remarked.

"There isn't any," said the March Hare.

"Then it wasn't very civil of you to offer it," said Alice angrily.

"It wasn't very civil of you to sit down without being invited," said the March Hare.

"I didn't know it was *your* table," said Alice; "it's laid for a great many more than three."

"Your hair wants cutting," said the Hatter. He had been looking at Alice for some time with great curiosity, and this was his first speech.

"You should learn not to make personal remarks," Alice said with some severity; "it's very rude."

The Hatter opened his eyes very wide on hearing this; but all he *said* was, "Why is a raven like a writing desk?"

"Come, we shall have some fun now!" thought Alice. "I'm glad they've begun asking riddles. I believe I can guess that," she added aloud.

"Do you mean that you think you can find out the answer to it?" said the March Hare.

"Exactly so," said Alice.

"Then you should say what you mean," the March Hare went on.

"I do," Alice hastily replied; "at least—at least, I mean what I say—that's the same thing, you know."

"Not the same thing a bit!" said the Hatter. "Why, you might just as well say that 'I see what I eat' is the same thing as 'I eat what I see'!"

"You might just as well say," added the March Hare, "that 'I like what I get' is the same thing as 'I get what I like'!"

"You might just as well say," added the Dormouse, who seemed to be talking in his sleep, "that 'I breathe when I sleep' is the same thing as 'I sleep when I breathe'!"

"It *is* the same thing with you," said the Hatter, and here the conversation dropped, and the party sat silent for a minute, while Alice thought over all she could remember about ravens and writing desks, which wasn't much.

The Hatter was the first to break the silence. "What day of the month is it?" he said, turning to Alice. He had taken his watch out of his pocket, and was looking at it uneasily, shaking it every now and then, and holding it to his ear.

Alice considered a little, and said, "The fourth."

"Two days wrong!" sighed the Hatter. "I told you butter wouldn't suit the works!" he added, looking angrily at the March Hare.

"It was the *best* butter," the March Hare meekly replied.

"Yes, but some crumbs must have got in as well," the Hatter grumbled; "you shouldn't have put it in with the breadknife."

The March Hare took the watch and looked at it gloomily; then he dipped it into his cup of tea, and looked at it again; but he could think of nothing better to say than his first remark, "It was the *best* butter, you know."

Alice had been looking over his shoulder with some curiosity. "What a funny watch!" she remarked. "It tells the day of the month, and doesn't tell what o'clock it is!"

"Why should it?" muttered the Hatter. "Does *your* watch tell you what year it is?"

"Of course not," Alice replied very readily; "but that's because it stays the same year for such a long time together."

"Which is just the case with *mine*," said the Hatter.

Alice felt dreadfully puzzled. The Hatter's remark seemed to her to have no sort of meaning in it, and yet it was certainly English. "I don't quite understand you," she said, as politely as she could.

"The Dormouse is asleep again," said the Hatter, and he poured a little hot tea onto its nose.

The Dormouse shook its head impatiently, and said, without opening its eyes, "Of course, of course; just what I was going to remark myself."

"Have you guessed the riddle yet?" the Hatter said, turning to Alice again.

"No, I give it up," Alice replied; "what's the answer?"

"I haven't the slightest idea," said the Hatter.

"Nor I," said the March Hare.

Alice sighed wearily. "I think you might do something better with the time," she said, "than wasting it in asking riddles that have no answers."

"If you knew Time as well as I do," said the Hatter, "you wouldn't talk about wasting *it*. It's *him*."

"I don't know what you mean," said Alice.

"Of course you don't!" the Hatter said, tossing his head contemptuously. "I dare say you never even spoke to Time!"

"Perhaps not," Alice cautiously replied; "but I know I have to beat time when I learn music."

"Ah! That accounts for it," said the Hatter. "He won't stand beating. Now, if you only kept on good terms with him, he'd do almost anything you liked with the clock. For instance, suppose it were nine o'clock in the morning, just time to begin lessons: you'd only have to whisper a hint to Time, and round goes the clock in a twinkling! Half-past one, time for dinner!"

("I only wish it was," the March Hare said to itself in a whisper.)

"That would be grand, certainly," said Alice thoughtfully; "but then—I shouldn't be hungry for it, you know."

"Not at first, perhaps," said the Hatter; "but you could keep it to half past one as long as you like."

"Is that the way *you* manage?" Alice asked.

The Hatter shook his head mournfully. "Not I!" he replied. "We quarrelled last March—just before *he* went mad, you know"—(pointing with his teaspoon at the March Hare)—"it was at the great concert given by the Queen of Hearts, and I had to sing:

"Twinkle, twinkle, little bat!
How I wonder what you're at!

You know the song, perhaps?"

"I've heard something like it," said Alice.

"It goes on, you know," the Hatter continued, "in this way:

"Up above the world you fly,
Like a tea tray in the sky.
Twinkle, twinkle—"

Here the Dormouse shook itself, and began singing in its sleep, *"Twinkle, twinkle, twinkle, twinkle—"* and went on so long that they had to pinch it to make it stop.

"Well, I'd hardly finished the first verse," said the Hatter, "when the Queen bawled out, 'He's murdering the time! Off with his head!'"

"How dreadfully savage!" exclaimed Alice.

"And ever since that," the Hatter went on, in a mournful tone, "he won't do a thing I ask! It's always six o'clock now."

A Mad Tea Party, engraving after the design by Sir John Tenniel
for the first edition of *Alice's Adventures in Wonderland,* 1865.

A bright idea came into Alice's head. "Is that the reason so many tea things are put out here?" she asked.

"Yes, that's it," said the Hatter with a sigh; "it's always tea time, and we've no time to wash the things between whiles."

"Then you keep moving round, I suppose?" said Alice.

"Exactly so," said the Hatter, "as the things get used up."

"But when you come to the beginning again?" Alice ventured to ask.

"Suppose we change the subject," the March Hare interrupted, yawning. "I'm getting tired of this. I vote the young lady tells us a story."

"I'm afraid I don't know one," said Alice, rather alarmed at the proposal.

"Then the Dormouse shall!" they both cried. "Wake up, Dormouse!" And they pinched it on both sides at once.

The Dormouse slowly opened his eyes. "I wasn't asleep," he said in a hoarse, feeble voice; "I heard every word you fellows were saying."

"Tell us a story!" said the March Hare.

"Yes, please do!" pleaded Alice.

"And be quick about it," added the Hatter, "or you'll be asleep again before it's done."

"Once upon a time there were three little sisters," the Dormouse began, in a great hurry; "and their names were Elsie, Lacie, and Tillie; and they lived at the bottom of a well—"

"What did they live on?" said Alice, who always took a great interest in questions of eating and drinking.

"They lived on treacle,"[1] said the Dormouse, after thinking a minute or two.

"They couldn't have done that, you know," Alice gently remarked; "they'd have been ill."

"So they were," said the Dormouse; "*very* ill."

Alice tried a little to fancy to herself what such an extraordinary way of living would be like, but it puzzled her too much, so she went on: "But why did they live at the bottom of a well?"

"Take some more tea," the March Hare said to Alice, very earnestly.

"I've had nothing yet," Alice replied, in an offended tone, "so I can't take more."

"You mean you can't take *less*," said the Hatter; "it's very easy to take *more* than nothing."

"Nobody asked *your* opinion," said Alice.

"Who's making personal remarks now?" the Hatter asked triumphantly.

Alice did not quite know what to say to this; so she helped herself to some tea and bread and butter, and then turned to the Dormouse, and repeated her question, "Why did they live at the bottom of a well?"

The Dormouse again took a minute or two to think about it, and then said, "It was a treacle well."

"There's no such thing!" Alice was beginning very angrily, but the Hatter and the March Hare went "Sh! sh!" and the Dormouse sulkily remarked, "If you can't be civil, you'd better finish the story for yourself."

"No, please go on!" Alice said very humbly, "I won't interrupt you again. I dare say there may be *one*."

"One, indeed!" said the Dormouse indignantly. However, he consented to go on. "And so these three little sisters—they were learning to draw, you know—"

"What did they draw?" said Alice, quite forgetting her promise.

"Treacle," said the Dormouse, without considering at all this time.

"I want a clean cup," interrupted the Hatter. "Let's all move one place on."

He moved on as he spoke, and the Dormouse followed him; the March Hare moved into the Dormouse's place, and Alice rather unwillingly took the place of the March Hare. The Hatter was the only one who got any advantage from the change; and Alice was a good deal worse off than before, as the March Hare had just upset the milk jug into his plate.

Alice did not wish to offend the Dormouse again, so she began very cautiously: "But I don't understand. Where did they draw the treacle from?"

"You can draw water out of a water well," said the Hatter; "so I should think you could draw treacle out of a treacle well—eh, stupid?"

---

1. **treacle:** molasses.

"But they were *in* the well," Alice said to the Dormouse, not choosing to notice this last remark.

"Of course they were," said the Dormouse; "well in."

This answer so confused poor Alice that she let the Dormouse go on for some time without interrupting it.

"They were learning to draw," the Dormouse went on, yawning and rubbing its eyes, for it was getting very sleepy; "and they drew all manner of things—everything that begins with an M—"

"Why with an M?" said Alice.

"Why not?" said the March Hare.

Alice was silent.

The Dormouse had closed its eyes by this time, and was going off into a doze; but, on being pinched by the Hatter, it woke up again with a little shriek, and went on: "That begins with an M, such as mouse traps, and the moon, and memory, and muchness—you know you say things as 'much of a muchness'[2]—did you ever see such a thing as a drawing of a muchness?"

"Really, now you ask me," said Alice, very much confused, "I don't think—"

"Then you shouldn't talk," said the Hatter.

This piece of rudeness was more than Alice could bear; she got up in great disgust, and walked off. The Dormouse fell asleep instantly, and neither of the others took the least notice of her going, though she looked back once or twice, half hoping that they would call after her; the last time she saw them, they were trying to put the Dormouse into the teapot.

"At any rate, I'll never go *there* again!" said Alice, as she picked her way through the wood. "It's the stupidest tea party I ever was at in all my life!"

---

2. **'much of a muchness'**: chiefly British expression for "all of a sameness; much alike."

The Dormouse in the teapot from the Lewis Carroll window at the Daresbury Church.

STUDY QUESTIONS

Recalling

1. With what remark do the March Hare, the Hatter, and the Dormouse greet Alice when she comes across their tea party? What is Alice's reaction to this remark?
2. What is unusual about the Hatter's watch? About the riddle he asks? About the song he sang at the Queen of Hearts' concert?
3. Of what did the Queen accuse the Hatter when he sang the song? According to the Hatter, what has happened since then to explain the perpetual tea party? What explains the large size of the table?
4. Why does the Dormouse grow indignant with Alice when he tells his story? Why must he be pinched during his story?
5. What does Alice conclude about the tea party in the final paragraph?

Interpreting

6. In what ways does Alice differ from the sentimentally portrayed children often encountered in fairy tales and other children's stories?
7. A pun is a humorous play on word meanings; for example, "The octopus came into battle *well-armed.*" Identify three puns in the selection. In addition to puns, what are some other examples of language play that the selection includes?
8. How does this incident treat the typically British custom of taking tea? Why would Carroll's treatment be both appealing to and suitable for children?

Extending

9. Why do you think *Alice's Adventures in Wonderland* appeals to older readers as well as to children? Which details or passages did you find especially humorous or imaginative?

VIEWPOINT

In an introduction to *Alice's Adventures in Wonderland,* literary critic Robin Denniston once pointed out:

> "The genius of Lewis Carroll," it has been written, "lay in applying skill in logic to topsy-turveydom with an inventiveness which has never been surpassed. . . ." Logic is vital to nonsense—to Lewis Carroll's nonsense anyhow, [and] Carroll's nonsense has . . . a lighthearted assumption of normality which provides a large part of the magic.

▧ Cite two specific instances from the selection in which Alice applies logic to nonsense. Where else is logic employed? Do you agree that a "lighthearted assumption of normality" provides a large part of the "magic"? Why or why not?

COMPOSITION

Analyzing Humor

▧ Write an essay in which you discuss the different means by which Carroll achieves humor in this selection. Consider the overall setting, the characters and their actions, and any exaggeration or mild satire that Carroll uses in portraying these elements. Also examine Carroll's use of logic, puns, parody, and otherwise witty or clever dialogue.

Writing a Children's Story

▧ Write your own brief nonsense story that you think will appeal to both adults and children. Like Carroll, provide an imaginative setting and characters, and try to include humor based on puns, parody, exaggeration, and other devices.

Matthew Arnold   *1822–1888*

The nineteenth century brought enormous changes to England. In the midst of whatever had been gained by these changes, many wrote of what had been lost. No one expressed this sense of loss more eloquently than Matthew Arnold.

Arnold grew up as the son of the most renowned educator in early Victorian England, the headmaster of the famous Rugby School. However, to his somber father's dismay, the young Arnold turned himself into a flamboyant dandy, dressing in eccentric clothes and cultivating bright, witty speech. Then in his mid-twenties Arnold surprised his family and friends by publishing a volume of melancholy and profoundly serious verse, *The Strayed Reveller, and Other Poems* (1849). This work and its successor, *Empedocles on Etna, and Other Poems* (1852), both reflect Arnold's lifelong love of classical Greek culture. Arnold produced only a few more volumes of poetry, but the work is of so high a quality that he is regarded as the greatest Victorian poet after Tennyson and Browning.

Marrying in 1851, and unable to support a family by writing poetry, Arnold took a job as an inspector of elementary schools. For thirty-five years he traveled over England's wretched roads and stayed at dreary inns in order to inspect the dismal schools of the period. The labor was exhausting, but Arnold performed it with skill and good cheer. He also wrote extensive and valuable reports about European education in his capacity as foreign assistant commissioner on education.

Arnold became known first as a poet, but he achieved equal success with his prose works. Besides being an expert in the field of education, Arnold wrote brilliant criticism of literature and of all other aspects of culture. His masterful works in this vein include *Essays in Criticism* (1865–1881), *On Translating Homer* (1861), *Culture and Anarchy* (1869), and *Literature and Dogma* (1873).

Arnold's prose, especially that written late in his life, tends to reassure readers by looking toward the noblest aspects of experience and underlining the purposefulness of human endeavor. In his poetry, however, Arnold often addresses the deep sense of loss and futility felt by many over the economic and social changes that swept across nineteenth-century England. Of all his poems, "Dover Beach" is the most famous. Dover is on Britain's southeast coast, on a narrow strait of water that separates England from France, only twenty miles away. Lights on the French coast can be seen from the beach, which stretches beneath the famous white cliffs—huge chalk peaks that line the English shore.

■ Sitting on the rocky beach at Dover you see either the steep chalk cliffs or the rough, gray English Channel. Imagine you are on this beach, and describe your reaction to it.

Matthew Arnold

Dover Beach

The sea is calm tonight.
The tide is full, the moon lies fair
Upon the straits[1]—on the French coast the
   light
Gleams and is gone; the cliffs of England
   stand,
5 Glimmering and vast, out in the tranquil bay.
Come to the window, sweet is the night air!
Only, from the long line of spray
Where the sea meets the moon-blanched
   land,
Listen! you hear the grating roar
10 Of pebbles which the waves draw back, and
   fling,
At their return, up the high strand,[2]
Begin, and cease, and then again begin,
With tremulous cadence slow, and bring
The eternal note of sadness in.

15 Sophocles[3] long ago
Heard it on the Aegean,[4] and it brought
Into his mind the turbid ebb and flow
Of human misery; we

Find also in the sound a thought,
20 Hearing it by his distant northern sea.

The Sea of Faith
Was once, too, at the full, and round earth's
   shore
Lay like the folds of a bright girdle[5] furled.
But now I only hear
25 Its melancholy, long, withdrawing roar,
Retreating, to the breath
Of the night wind, down the vast edges
   drear
And naked shingles[6] of the world.

Ah, love, let us be true
30 To one another! for the world, which seems
To lie before us like a land of dreams,
So various, so beautiful, so new,
Hath really neither joy, nor love, nor light,
Nor certitude, nor peace, nor help for pain;
35 And we are here as on a darkling[7] plain
Swept with confused alarms of struggle and
   flight,
Where ignorant armies clash by night.

---

1. **straits:** Strait of Dover, between England and France.
2. **strand:** shore.
3. **Sophocles** [sof′ə klēz]: Sophocles (496?–406 B.C.) was a Greek tragic dramatist, the author of *Oedipus Rex* and *Antigone*.
4. **Aegean** [i jē′ən]: arm of the Mediterranean Sea between Greece and Turkey.

5. **girdle:** garment such as a belt or sash, worn about the waist; anything that encircles or confines.
6. **shingles:** beach gravel composed of water-worn stones or pebbles.
7. **darkling:** lying in darkness.

STUDY QUESTIONS

Recalling

1. What does the speaker see from the window in lines 1–6? What does he hear in lines 9–14? In line 14 what does the sea bring in?
2. According to the second stanza, what did this sound bring to Sophocles' mind?
3. What, according to the speaker, was once "at the full"? How has it changed, according to lines 24–28?
4. In lines 29–30 what plea does the speaker address to his listener? How does he describe the world in lines 30–34? In the poem's last three lines, to what does he compare the world in which he and his listener live?

Interpreting

5. Describe the mood of the opening lines of the poem. Where and why does the mood shift?
6. In what way has the world not changed since the time of Sophocles, according to Arnold?
7. What does Arnold mean by the "Sea of Faith"? Why does he say it was once full but is now withdrawing?
8. According to the last stanza of the poem, how does this withdrawal affect human affairs? What does Arnold suggest is the only refuge from this state of things?

Extending

9. Do you think the view of human life presented in "Dover Beach" is applicable to today's world? Why or why not?

VIEWPOINT

The American critic Lionel Trilling saw Arnold as the Victorian most ahead of his time:

Perhaps more than any other man of his time and nation he perceived the changes that were taking place in the conditions of life and in the minds of men to bring into being the world we now know. In certain respects he was, of all the intellectual figures of his period, the most modern.

■ To what changes "in the conditions of life and in the minds of men" was Arnold responding in "Dover Beach"? Referring to specific lines, describe the attitude of the poem toward these changes. Does "Dover Beach" seem more in tune with the modern world than the other Victorian poems you have read so far? Why or why not?

COMPOSITION

Writing About Poetry

■ Discuss the meaning of "Dover Beach," and show how Arnold uses the techniques of poetry to express this meaning. Begin by stating the theme of the poem in one sentence. Then show how Arnold illuminates this theme through his speaker and use of sound, tone, imagery, and figurative language. *For help with this assignment, refer to Lesson 7 in the Writing About Literature Handbook at the back of this book.*

Writing About a Scene

■ Write a poem that describes a particular scene in details and language that evoke a definite mood. You may want to describe a serene lake or an unruly street scene, but be sure that you use concrete images that allow your reader to see and hear what you are describing and to feel the mood that you want to convey.

Gerard Manley Hopkins   *1844–1889*

Through much of his brief life, Gerard Manley Hopkins was a Jesuit priest. Brought up an Anglican, he was influenced by the religious reformer John Henry Newman and converted to Roman Catholicism while studying at Oxford University. A devout and scholarly man, Hopkins worked briefly among the poor in the slums of Liverpool but fled from the dirt and the vice that he saw there. He was then given a church in Oxford and eventually became a professor of Greek at the University of Dublin. Hopkins had no interest in worldly fame and was uneasy about reconciling his poetry with his priestly duties. In fact, his poems were not published until 1918, long after his death.

Hopkins wrote much of his poetry while studying for the priesthood. The subject of his poems is usually religious; their musical patterns are often elaborate. Had the poems appeared during Hopkins' own lifetime, they may not have been accepted because the verse is worlds away from the work of most Victorians. The twentieth century, however, responded with enthusiasm to what sounded amazingly modern both in diction and in melody.

■ If you had a special talent, would you share it with others, or would you shun worldly fame?

Gerard Manley Hopkins

Pied[1] Beauty

Glory be to God for dappled things—
    For skies of couple-color as a brinded[2] cow;
      For rose-moles all in stipple[3] upon trout that swim;
Fresh-firecoal chestnut-falls;[4] finches' wings;
5   Landscape plotted and pieced—fold, fallow, and plow;
      And áll trádes, their gear and tackle and trim.

All things counter,[5] original, spare, strange;
    Whatever is fickle, freckled (who knows how?)
      With swift, slow; sweet, sour; adazzle, dim;
10 He fathers-forth whose beauty is past change:
      Praise him.

---

1. **Pied:** spotted.
2. **brinded:** streaked.
3. **in stipple:** dotted with tiny spots.
4. **Fresh-firecoal chestnut-falls:** roasted chestnuts.
5. **counter:** contrary, contrasting.

God's Grandeur

The world is charged with the grandeur of God.
　It will flame out, like shining from shook foil;[1]
　It gathers to a greatness, like the ooze of oil
Crushed.[2] Why do men then now not reck his rod?[3]
5 Generations have trod, have trod, have trod;
　And all is seared with trade; bleared, smeared with toil;
　And wears man's smudge and shares man's smell: the soil
Is bare now, nor can foot feel, being shod.

And for all this, nature is never spent;
10 　There lives the dearest freshness deep down things;
And though the last lights off the black West went,
　Oh, morning, at the brown brink eastward, springs—
Because the Holy Ghost over the bent
　World broods[4] with warm breast and with ah! bright wings.

---

1. **foil:** gold leaf, which is gold hammered into a thin sheet, or tinsel.
2. **Crushed:** squeezed from olives.
3. **reck his rod:** heed his power.
4. **broods:** hovers protectively like a bird on eggs.

Spring and Fall

To a Young Child

Márgarét, are you gríeving
Over Goldengrove unleaving?[1]
Leáves, líke the things of man, you
With your fresh thoughts care for, can you?
5 Ah! ás the heart grows older
It will come to such sights colder
By and by, nor spare a sigh
Though worlds of wanwood[2] leafmeal[3] lie;
And yet you will weep and know why.
10 Now no matter, child, the name:
Sórrow's spríngs áre the same,
Nor mouth had, no nor mind, expressed
What heart heard of, ghost[4] guessed:
It ís the blight man was born for,
15 It is Margaret you mourn for.

---

1. **unleaving:** losing its leaves.
2. **wanwood** [won′wood]: pale wood.
3. **leafmeal:** crushed decomposed leaves.
4. **ghost:** spirit.

STUDY QUESTIONS

Pied Beauty

Recalling
1. Name four dappled things for which the speaker gives glory to God in the first stanza.
2. List at least five adjectives that are used to describe creation in the second stanza.
3. What advice does the speaker give to the reader in the second stanza?

Interpreting
4. Why do you think Hopkins uses pied, or spotted, things as proof of the greatness of creation?
5. Explain your interpretation of line 10. What contrast is implied in the phrase "past change"?

God's Grandeur

Recalling
1. Based on the first three lines, name three qualities of God's grandeur.
2. According to lines 4–8, in what ways has humanity changed the world?
3. Give two examples that the speaker uses to show that "nature is never spent." What reason does the speaker give for this?

Interpreting
4. Find three examples of alliteration in the poem. Find two examples of internal rhyme.
5. What is the rhyme scheme of the poem? Give two examples of how the rhyme affects line breaks in the poem.
6. According to the poem, what is nature's relationship with God? With humanity?

Spring and Fall

Recalling
1. At the beginning of the poem, what emotion does Margaret feel? Why?
2. In what way does the heart change as it gets older?
3. According to the last three lines, what has the heart heard of and the ghost, or Margaret's soul, guessed?

Interpreting
4. What do the following word coinages suggest to you: Goldengrove, unleaving, and leafmeal?

5. Explain the comparison that the poem makes between the seasons of the year and a human life.
6. According to line 11, all sorrow comes from the same source. Explain how the poem's final two lines suggest the nature of that source.

LITERARY FOCUS

Sprung Rhythm
The sound of a poem by Gerard Manley Hopkins is unique because of a technique for which the poet created the term *sprung rhythm*. **Sprung rhythm** is a kind of meter in which each foot contains one stressed syllable, usually the first, and any number of unstressed syllables. Hopkins believed this to be the rhythm of natural speech. Study the following lines:

Már ga / rét are / yóu / gríev ing

Notice that the number of unstressed syllables may vary from foot to foot. Also, in sprung rhythm two accented syllables may occur together, as in the fifth and sixth syllables of the example.

Thinking About Sprung Rhythm
■ Scan the first stanza of "Pied Beauty." Mark each accented syllable, and divide each line into feet. Choose one line, and count the unaccented syllables in each foot on that line.

VOCABULARY

Antonyms
Antonyms are words that have opposite or nearly opposite meanings. *Long* and *short* are antonyms. The words in capitals are from Hopkins' poems. Choose the word that is *most nearly the opposite* of each word in capitals, *as the word is used in the selections.*

1. SEARED: (a) moist (b) withered (c) visible (d) consumed
2. BLEARED: (a) exhausted (b) blind (c) illusory (d) lucid
3. DAPPLED: (a) juicy (b) handsome (c) uniform (d) spotted
4. FICKLE: (a) courteous (b) loyal (c) obedient (d) cooperative
5. BLIGHT: (a) destiny (b) well-being (c) truth (d) disease

Thomas Hardy   *1840–1928*

Thomas Hardy was born in Dorsetshire in southwestern England. He was educated locally and was apprenticed to an ecclesiastical architect. For much of his early life, Hardy wavered between careers in architecture and in literature, winning prizes in architecture and design while also composing poems, essays, and short stories. The success of his writing caused him finally to abandon architecture in his early thirties.

Hardy's home and the surrounding districts played an important role in his literary career. The region is agricultural, and across its rugged surface stand monuments of the past: Saxon and Roman ruins and the great boulders of Stonehenge, which extend back into prehistory. Before the Norman invasion of 1066, the area had been the Anglo-Saxon kingdom of Wessex. Hardy revived the name to describe the setting for a long string of novels, among them *Far from the Madding Crowd* (1874), his first popular success; *The Return of the Native* (1878); *The Mayor of Casterbridge* (1886); and *Tess of the D'Urbervilles* (1891). The novels all set a harsh vision of life against the bleakly beautiful landscape that Hardy knew well. His characters are subject to a blind fate that, like the landscape, is indifferent to human pain and suffering. This view of nature as an implacable force is the cornerstone of **Naturalism,** an offshoot of Realism to which Hardy was among the first English writers to subscribe.

The failure of Hardy's most pessimistic—and possibly his greatest—novel, *Jude the Obscure* (1895), angered him and contributed to his decision to abandon the form of the novel. Hardy felt that he had expressed his philosophy of life as well as he could within a novel, and after 1896 he turned to verse exclusively.

Hardy wrote *The Dynasts* (1903–1908), a patriotic verse play about the Napoleonic Wars. He then turned his attention to lyric poems that combine strict form and musical patterns with everyday, nonpoetic language. This poetry represents a second literary career for Hardy, already ranked among the greatest Victorian novelists. This last of the great Victorians, as Hardy has been called, died in 1928. His ashes are buried in Westminster Abbey, but, because of his lasting relationship with his home district, his heart is buried in Wessex.

◼ If you were a writer, in what ways would your surroundings influence your writing?

Thomas Hardy

A Thunderstorm in Town

(A Reminiscence: 1893)

She wore a new "terra-cotta"[1] dress,
And we stayed, because of the pelting storm,
Within the hansom's[2] dry recess,
Though the horse had stopped; yea, motionless
5   We sat on, snug and warm.

Then the downpour ceased, to my sharp sad pain,
And the glass that had screened our forms before
Flew up, and out she sprang to her door:
I should have kissed her if the rain
10   Had lasted a minute more.

---

1. **"terra-cotta":** rust-colored.
2. **hansom:** horse-drawn carriage.

Rainy Day, Boston 1885, Childe Hassam.

The Man He Killed

"Had he and I but met
  By some old ancient inn,
We should have sat us down to wet
  Right many a nipperkin![1]

5 "But ranged as infantry,
  And staring face to face,
I shot at him as he at me,
  And killed him in his place.

"I shot him dead because—
10 Because he was my foe,

Just so—my foe of course he was;
  That's clear enough; although

"He thought he'd 'list,[2] perhaps,
  Off-hand like—just as I—
15 Was out of work—had sold his traps—
  No other reason why.

"Yes; quaint and curious war is!
  You shoot a fellow down
You'd treat if met where any bar is,
20 Or help to half-a-crown."[3]

---

1. **nipperkin:** small glass for ale, beer, or wine.

2. **'list:** enlist (in the military).
3. **half-a-crown:** coin.

STUDY QUESTIONS

A Thunderstorm in Town

Recalling

1. Describe what happens in the first eight lines of the poem.
2. According to the last two lines, what might the speaker have done? What prevented him?

Interpreting

3. What words in the first stanza describe the mood inside the cab?
4. Explain why the speaker feels pain over the end of the storm.
5. Does fate play a role in the poem, or is the speaker responsible for his unhappiness?

The Man He Killed

Recalling

1. According to the first stanza, what would have happened if the two men had met in an inn?

2. Based on the second stanza, describe the circumstances under which the two men actually meet.
3. In the third stanza what reason does the speaker give for shooting?
4. In what ways does the speaker compare tne dead man to himself in the fourth stanza?

Interpreting

5. Explain the irony of line 17 and of the poem in general.
6. Hardy's novels deal pessimistically with the power of fate. In what sense is "The Man He Killed" similarly pessimistic?

Extending

7. Why do you think Hardy chose the title he did instead of something like "The Victor"? What details in the poem would be left out if the poem's attitude toward war were more positive?

In this selection, as in one selection in each unit, you will find notes in the right-hand margin that highlight parts of the selection. These notes point out important ideas of the literary period and draw your attention to literary elements and techniques covered in the Literary Focuses. Page numbers in the notes will refer you to more extensive discussions of these important ideas and elements.

Thomas Hardy

The Darkling[1] Thrush

I leant upon a coppice gate[2]
  When Frost was specter-gray,
And Winter's dregs made desolate
  The weakening eye of day.
5 The tangled bine[3] stems scored the sky
  Like strings of broken lyres,
And all mankind that haunted nigh
  Had sought their household fires.

The land's sharp features seemed to be
10   The Century's corpse[4] outleant,[5]
His crypt the cloudy canopy,
  The wind his death lament.
The ancient pulse of germ[6] and birth
  Was shrunken hard and dry,
15 And every spirit upon earth
  Seemed fervorless as I.

At once a voice arose among
  The bleak twigs overhead
In a full-hearted evensong
20   Of joy illimited;

Rhythm (p. 501): Lines of four beats alternate with lines of three beats. Each three-beat line achieves a note of finality in keeping with the gloomy mood of the poem.

Victorian idea: End-of-century pessimism was a reaction to the optimism that preceded it (p. 487).

---

1. **Darkling:** in the dark.
2. **coppice** [kopʹis] **gate:** gate leading to a coppice, which is a thicket, or small wood.
3. **bine:** a twining stem.
4. **Century's corpse:** The poem was written on December 31, 1900, the last of the nineteenth century.
5. **outleant:** outstretched.
6. **germ:** seed or bud.

An aged thrush, frail, gaunt, and small,
   In blast-beruffled plume,
Had chosen thus to fling his soul
   Upon the growing gloom.

25 So little cause for carolings
   Of such ecstatic sound
Was written on terrestrial things
   Afar or nigh around,
That I could think there trembled through
30   His happy good-night air
Some blessed Hope, whereof he knew
   And I was unaware.

> **Realism** (p. 487): The thrush is described realistically, rather than with the idealism of the Romantic poet.

> **Rhyme** (p. 430): The end rhymes alternate to form a pattern that is followed throughout the poem.

STUDY QUESTIONS

Recalling

1. What words or phrases in the first stanza tell us the season of the year and the time of day?
2. To what does the speaker compare the land, the sky, and the wind in the second stanza?
3. Describe the sound that the speaker hears in the third stanza and its source.
4. According to the fourth stanza, what does the speaker think as a result of the sound?

Interpreting

5. Explain how imagery and diction create a grim mood in the first stanza.
6. Why is death an appropriate image in the second stanza?
7. Why is it more effective for the thrush to be old and frail than young and strong?

LITERARY FOCUS

Naturalism

Throughout the Victorian Age we see the growing influence of **Realism,** the new literary movement that stressed the importance of writing realistically about everyday people and events from ordinary life. **Naturalism** was an outgrowth of Realism strongly influenced by new theories in science and economics. To Naturalist writers, a realistic picture of the world was a very harsh one.

Nature was shown in the cold light of science as a force completely indifferent to the human misery it often caused; society, too, was portrayed as an overwhelming force indifferent to individual human suffering. Naturalist writers often depicted characters in conflict with nature's harshest manifestations—floods, blizzards, and the like—or working-class heroes involved in social struggles that they did not understand and would inevitably lose. Clearly, the Naturalist view of nature was totally different from the Romantic view; yet Naturalists did share with the Romantics a certain idealism, for in brutally exposing society's ills, their aim was often social reform.

The ideas of Naturalism were first set down by the French writer Emile Zola (1840–1902). Thomas Hardy was among the first English writers to embrace those ideas, and to them he added a pessimistic fatalism of his own. Though Hardy's naturalism is most clearly exhibited in his fiction—which usually pits its main characters in a grim conflict with nature, society, and fate—it is also evident in much of his poetry.

Thinking About Naturalism

■ Explain how "The Man He Killed" and "The Darkling Thrush" show the influence of Naturalism. Does "A Thunderstorm in Town" also show that influence? Why or why not?

Oscar Wilde   *1854–1900*

In his short life Oscar Wilde managed to win both widespread acclaim and strong public disapproval. The son of a prominent Irish surgeon, Wilde studied classics at Dublin's Trinity College and at Oxford, where he won the coveted Newdigate Prize for poetry. His academic success should have earned him a teaching fellowship, but he had adopted such extravagant behavior that he offended university officials. Having no real income, he relied on his charm and witty conversation to conquer society—and conquer he did, becoming one of London's most sought-after dinner guests. At the same time he established a reputation for literary criticism and won fame with his poetic horror tale, *The Picture of Dorian Gray* (1891). Wilde's greatest success, however, was achieved on the stage, with such witty comedies as *Lady Windermere's Fan* (1892) and *The Importance of Being Earnest* (1895).

As a critic, Wilde drew attention to the French Symbolist poets, whose work then influenced his own. The **Symbolist** movement was a reaction to Realism that, like Romanticism, saw the communication of emotion as poetry's chief aim but, unlike earlier Romanticism, insisted that emotion must be implied—through the use of symbols, vivid imagery, and musical language—rather than stated directly. Many Symbolists also proclaimed that art was superior to nature, and this became a guiding principle of Wilde's literary criticism, which made famous the cry of "art for art's sake." In the following lines Wilde expresses his critical views.

■ What does "art for art's sake" mean to you?

Oscar Wilde

from The Preface to The Picture of Dorian Gray

The artist is the creator of beautiful things.
To reveal art and conceal the artist is art's aim.
The critic is he who can translate into another
     manner or a new material his impression of
     beautiful things.
The highest, as the lowest, form of criticism is a
     mode of autobiography.
Those who find ugly meanings in beautiful things
     are corrupt without being charming. This is a
     fault.
Those who find beautiful meanings in beautiful

things are the cultivated. For these there is
     hope.
They are the elect to whom beautiful things
     mean only Beauty. . . .
Books are well written, or badly written. That is
     all.
The nineteenth-century dislike of Realism is the
     rage of Caliban[1] seeing his own face in a glass.

---

1. **Caliban:** the primitive savage in Shakespeare's *Tempest.*

The nineteenth-century dislike of Romanticism is the rage of Caliban not seeing his own face in a glass. . . .

No artist desires to prove anything. Even things that are true can be proved. . . .

No artist is ever morbid. The artist can express everything.

Thought and language are to the artist instruments of an art.

From the point of view of form, the type[2] of all the arts is the art of the musician. From the point of view of feeling, the actor's craft is the type.

All art is at once surface and symbol.

Those who go beneath the surface do so at their peril.

Those who read the symbol do so at their peril.

It is the spectator, and not life, that art really mirrors.

Diversity of opinion about a work of art shows that the work is new, complex, and vital.

When critics disagree, the artist is in accord with himself.

We can forgive a man for making a useful thing as long as he does not admire it. The only excuse for making a useless thing is that one admires it intensely.

All art is quite useless.

---

2. **type:** archetype; perfect example; model.

STUDY QUESTIONS

Recalling

1. According to the opening lines, what is the artist? Who are "the elect"?
2. According to Wilde, what can a book be? What does art mirror and not mirror? What does "diversity of opinion about a work" show?
3. What two generalizations does Wilde make about "no artist"? About "all art"?

Interpreting

4. In saying that art is beautiful, what does Wilde mean by "beautiful"?

5. Explain the two remarks involving Caliban. What later statement attacks Realism? What does that statement suggest about the artist's role in society?
6. What effect does Wilde feel art should have on its audience? For the sake of what person or thing does he feel art exists?

Extending

7. Wilde and those sharing his views of art were often called Decadents. Do you find the term appropriate? Why or why not?

Rudyard Kipling   *1865–1936*

Born in Bombay, India, Rudyard Kipling was the first major English writer to deal almost exclusively with the colonial experience. Although he was educated in England, Kipling early in life grew to love the varied cultures and atmosphere of the Indian subcontinent. At seventeen he returned to India as a newspaper editor, and it was in the English-language newspapers of India that Kipling first found a ready means for publishing his short stories.

Kipling's skillfulness as a short story writer soon proved profitable. Two volumes of stories about Indian life—*Plain Tales from the Hills* and *Soldiers Three*—were published in 1888, and by 1889 Kipling had become internationally famous. At the same time he was producing some of his best poetry, including *Departmental Ditties* (1886) and *Barrack-Room Ballads* (1892), collections of musical verse that blended Romantic adventure with Realistic detail in depicting the life of soldiers on the Indian frontier.

Kipling continued to live abroad, dwelling for several years in the United States after his marriage to an American woman. There he wrote *The Jungle Book* (1894), a collection of charming animal tales for children. Around the turn of the century, after traveling to various outposts of the British Empire, he became enamored of the idea of imperial England, and for the rest of his life he was a loud and vociferous proponent of British imperialism. He continued to produce works set in India, including *Kim* (1901), a novel about the adventures of a young boy. In 1907 his work was recognized with the award of the Nobel Prize for Literature.

In Kipling's later years his work, with its overtones of an increasingly unpopular imperialism, drew attacks from literary critics and readers alike. Kipling himself became cynical and bitter, an attitude heightened by the death of his only son in World War I. Today Kipling is still criticized, but even those who condemn his political attitudes have come to recognize the respect he showed for native cultures and the careful, loving attention he gave to detailing Indian life. Though Kipling's dated imperialism sometimes clouds our vision of him, his vivid depiction of foreign climes and his tremendous sense of adventure continue to delight readers. "The Ballad of East and West," one of Kipling's most famous poems, is a good illustration of his concerns. After reading the poem silently, you may want to increase your pleasure by reading it aloud.

■ Kipling lived in and wrote about India. This poem begins with the phrase "East is East, and West is West." To what East and West does he refer? What differences does he imply?

Rudyard Kipling

The Ballad of East and West

Oh, East is East, and West is West, and never the twain shall meet,
Till Earth and Sky stand presently at God's great Judgment Seat;
But there is neither East nor West, Border, nor Breed, nor Birth,
When two strong men stand face to face, though they come from the
    ends of the earth!

5 Kamal is out with twenty men to raise the Borderside,
And he has lifted[1] the Colonel's mare that is the Colonel's pride:
He has lifted her out of the stable door between the dawn and the day,
And turned the calkins[2] upon her feet, and ridden her far away.
Then up and spoke the Colonel's son that led a troop of the Guides:[3]
10 "Is there never a man of all my men can say where Kamal hides?"

Then up and spoke Mohammed Khan, the son of the Ressaldar:[4]
"If ye know the track of the morning mist, ye know where his pickets[5]
    are.
At dusk he harries the Abazai[6]—at dawn he is into Bonair,
But he must go by Fort Bukloh to his own place to fare.
15 So if ye gallop to Fort Bukloh as fast as a bird can fly,
By the favor of God ye may cut him off ere he win to the Tongue of
    Jagai.[7]
But if he be past the Tongue of Jagai, right swiftly turn ye then,
For the length and breadth of that grisly plain is sown with Kamal's
    men.
There is rock to the left, and rock to the right, and low lean thorn
    between,
20 And ye may hear a breech-bolt snick[8] where never a man is seen."

The Colonel's son has taken a horse, and a raw, rough dun[9] was he.
With the mouth of a bell and the heart of Hell and the head of the
    gallows tree.
The Colonel's son to the Fort has won, they bid him to stay to eat—
Who rides at the tail of a Border thief, he sits not long at his meat.
25 He's up and away from Fort Bukloh as fast as he can fly,

---

1. **lifted:** stolen.
2. **calkins:** metal pieces that prevent horseshoes from slipping.
3. **Guides:** army scouts who rode on horseback.
4. **Ressaldar:** commander of the native cavalry serving with Britain's Indian army.
5. **pickets:** sentries.
6. **Abazai:** an Afghan tribe.
7. **Tongue of Jagai:** mountain pass in what is now northern Pakistan.
8. **breech-bolt snick:** click made when the cartridge is inserted into a gun to prepare for firing.
9. **dun:** brownish-gray horse.

Till he was aware of his father's mare in the gut of the Tongue of Jagai,
Till he was aware of his father's mare with Kamal upon her back,
And when he could spy the white of her eye, he made the pistol crack.
He has fired once, he has fired twice, but the whistling ball went wide.
30 "Ye shoot like a soldier," Kamal said. "Show now if ye can ride!"

It's up and over the Tongue of Jagai, as blown dust devils[10] go;
The dun he fled like a stag of ten, but the mare like a barren doe.
The dun he leaned against the bit and slugged his head above,
But the red mare played with the snaffle[11] bars, as a maiden plays with
    a glove.
35 There was rock to the left, and rock to the right, and low lean thorn
        between,
And thrice he heard a breech-bolt snick, though never a man was seen.
They have ridden the low moon out of the sky, their hoofs drum up
        the dawn;
The dun he went like a wounded bull, but the mare like a new-roused
        fawn.

The dun he fell at a watercourse—in a woeful heap fell he,
40 And Kamal has turned the red mare back, and pulled the rider free.
He has knocked the pistol out of his hand—small room was there to
        strive,
"'Twas only by favor of mine," quoth he, "ye rode so long alive:
There was not a rock for twenty mile, there was not a clump of tree,
But covered a man of my own men with his rifle cocked on his knee.
45 If I had raised my bridle hand, as I have held it low,
The little jackals[12] that flee so fast were feasting all in a row;
If I had bowed my head on my breast, as I have held it high,
The kite[13] that whistles above us now were gorged till she could not
        fly."

Lightly answered the Colonel's son, "Do good to bird and beast,
50 But count who come for the broken meats before thou makest a feast.
If there should follow a thousand swords to carry my bones away,
Belike[14] the price of a jackal's meal were more than a thief could pay.
They will feed their horse on the standing crop, their men on the
        garnered[15] grain;
The thatch of the byres[16] will serve their fires when all the cattle are
        slain.

---

10. **dust devils:** small whirlwinds that raise columns of dust.
11. **snaffle:** type of bit, the metal mouthpiece of a horse's bridle.
12. **jackals:** wild Asian dogs that live as scavengers, eating the flesh of dead bodies.
13. **kite:** scavenger bird similar to a hawk.
14. **Belike:** quite likely; probably.
15. **garnered:** stored.
16. **thatch of the byres:** straw roofing material of the cow barns.

55 But if thou thinkest the price be fair—thy brethren wait to sup;
The hound is kin to the jackal spawn—howl, dog, and call them up!
And if thou thinkest the price be high, in steer and gear and stack,
Give me my father's mare again, and I'll fight my own way back!"

Kamal has gripped him by the hand and set him upon his feet.
60 "No talk shall be of dogs," said he, "when wolf and gray wolf meet.
May I eat dirt if thou hast hurt of me in deed or breath.
What dam of lances[17] brought thee forth to jest at the dawn with
Death?"
Lightly answered the Colonel's son, "I hold by the blood of my clan.
Take up the mare for my father's gift—by God, she has carried a man!"
65 The red mare ran to the Colonel's son and nuzzled against his breast.
"We be two strong men," said Kamal then, "but she loveth the
younger best.
So she shall go with a lifter's dower:[18] my turquoise-studded rein,
My broidered saddle and saddlecloth, and silver stirrups twain."
The Colonel's son a pistol drew and held it muzzle-end;
70 "Ye have taken the one from a foe," said he. "Will ye take the mate
from a friend?"
"A gift for a gift," said Kamal straight, "a limb for the risk of a limb.
Thy father has sent his son to me; I'll send my son to him!"
With that he whistled his only son, that dropped from a mountain
crest—

17. **dam of lances:** mother of soldiers.
18. **lifter's dower:** thief's gift.

He trod the ling[19] like a buck in spring, and he looked like a lance in rest.

75 "Now here is thy master," Kamal said, "who leads a troop of the Guides,

And thou must ride at his left side as shield on shoulder rides.

Till Death or I cut loose the tie, at camp and board and bed,

Thy life is his—thy fate it is to guard him with thy head.

So thou must eat the White Queen's[20] meat, and all her foes are thine,

80 And thou must harry thy father's hold[21] for the peace of the Border line,

And thou must make a trooper tough and hack thy way to power—

Belike they will raise thee to Ressaldar when I am hanged in Peshawur."[22]

They have looked each other between the eyes, and there they found no fault;

They have taken the Oath of the Brother-in-Blood on leavened bread and salt;

85 They have taken the Oath of Brother-in-Blood on fire and fresh-cut sod,

On the hilt and the haft of the Khyber knife,[23] and the Wondrous Names of God.

The Colonel's son he rides the mare and Kamal's boy the dun,

And two have come back to Fort Bukloh, where there went forth but one.

And when they drew to the Quarter-Guard,[24] full twenty swords flew clear—

90 There was not a man but carried his feud with the blood of the mountaineer.

"Ha' done![25] Ha' done!" said the Colonel's son. "Put up the steel at your sides!

Last night ye had struck at a Border thief—tonight 'tis a man of the Guides!"

Oh, East is East, and West is West, and never the twain shall meet,

Till Earth and Sky stand presently at God's great Judgment Seat;

95 *But there is neither East nor West, Border, nor Breed, nor Birth,*

When two strong men stand face to face, though they come from the ends of the earth!

---

19. **ling:** heather.

20. **White Queen's:** Queen Victoria's.

21. **harry . . . hold:** participate in raids against Kamal's strongholds.

22. **Peshawur:** city in what is now Pakistan.

23. **Khyber knife:** curved short sword.

24. **Quarter Guard:** soldiers who remain on guard duty while their battalions are encamped.

25. **Ha' done!:** Have done! Stop!

STUDY QUESTIONS

Recalling

1. According to the opening lines, when shall East and West meet? When is there neither East nor West?
2. What has Kamal stolen? How many men does the Colonel's son take with him in pursuit?
3. After the Colonel's son finds Kamal, to what sort of race does Kamal challenge him? Why does Kamal win?
4. After the race, what does Kamal say would have happened "if I had raised my bridle hand"? Summarize the Colonel's son's response. What does Kamal ask him about a "dam of lances"?
5. What gift does the Colonel's son try to give Kamal? What "gifts" do they eventually exchange? What oath do they take?
6. What will Kamal's son become?

Interpreting

7. To what do East and West in the opening and closing lines refer? Restate lines 3–4 in your own words. When we first read line 4, to what sort of meeting does it seem to refer? By the time we read line 96, into what has that meeting blossomed?
8. Why do Kamal and the Colonel's son admire each other?

9. Examine the meter of lines 21–38. What is the effect of the frequent substitution of anapests for iambs?

Extending

10. In what ways is this poem characteristic of ballads (page 55)? How does its structure differ from that of most ballads?

LITERARY FOCUS

Narrative Poetry

Both the epic and the ballad are types of **narrative poetry,** verse that tells a story. Like a prose story or a novel, a narrative poem has a *plot* that involves *characters* in a particular *setting,* and these elements work together to communicate a *theme,* or main idea. Though a narrative poem often includes dialogue, it also includes lines spoken directly to us by the **narrator,** or storyteller, who may or may not be a character in the plot.

Thinking About Narrative Poetry

1. Summarize the plot of "The Ballad of East and West," identify the main characters and overall setting, and show how these elements work together to communicate a theme.
2. Is the narrator a character in the plot? Does he state the theme? If so, where?

A. E. Housman *1859–1936*

Alfred Edward Housman was born a little north of Hardy country in the far west of England. He spent his youth in and around Shropshire, an agricultural region like Hardy's Wessex. As a gifted young man Housman was enrolled at Oxford University, where he was expected to excel. Four years later, however, he astounded his friends by failing his final examinations. As a result, Housman took a job in the patent office in London to support himself while continuing his classical studies independently.

Housman's private pursuit of knowledge was so successful that, on the basis of articles he published in scholarly journals, he was eventually awarded a professorship at the University of London. In 1911 he was appointed professor of Latin at Cambridge University, a prestigious position that he held for a quarter of a century until his death. During his long lifetime he became known as one of the greatest classical scholars of his age.

Housman's output as a poet is small; he wrote little more than a hundred poems. In 1896 he published *A Shropshire Lad,* a slim volume of verse that made him famous. Twenty-six years passed before his next slim volume, *Last Poems,* appeared. Because of the reputation of the first book, *Last Poems* was an instant success. A third book, *More Poems,* was compiled by his brother and published after Housman's death.

Housman's poems are mournful and pessimistic statements about the transient nature of love and youth, about nature's savage beauty, and about human vanity. Many are written in the voice of a country boy stranded in London. The language is direct; the rhythm is pronounced. Housman traced his inspiration to Scottish folk ballads and the songs of Shakespeare. His poems resemble those earlier works in their simplicity, their clarity, and their haunting power, a power that comes from the poet's ability to say a great deal in a small space and to imply even more.

Is Housman's subject of the transient nature of love and youth relevant today? Why or why not? Give examples of modern writing or music to support your decision.

La Primavera (Spring), Jean François Millet (1814–1875).

A. E. Housman

Loveliest of Trees

Loveliest of trees, the cherry now
Is hung with bloom along the bough,
And stands about the woodland ride
Wearing white for Eastertide.

5   Now, of my threescore years and ten,[1]
Twenty will not come again,
And take from seventy springs a score,
It only leaves me fifty more.

And since to look at things in bloom
10 Fifty springs are little room,
About the woodlands I will go
To see the cherry hung with snow.

------

1. **threescore . . . ten:** seventy years, the human life span according to the Bible.

When I Was One-and-Twenty

When I was one-and-twenty
I heard a wise man say,
"Give crowns and pounds and guineas[1]
But not your heart, away;
5 Give pearls away and rubies
But keep your fancy free."[2]
But I was one-and-twenty—
No use to talk to me.

When I was one-and-twenty
10 I heard him say again,
"The heart out of the bosom
Was never given in vain;
'Tis paid with sighs a plenty
And sold for endless rue."[3]
15 And I am two-and-twenty,
And oh, 'tis true, 'tis true.

------

1. **crowns . . . guineas:** denominations of money.
2. **keep . . . free:** stay free of the power of love.
3. **rue:** sorrow, remorse.

A. E. Housman

To an Athlete Dying Young

The time you won your town the race
We chaired you through the market place;
Man and boy stood cheering by,
And home we brought you shoulder-high.

5 Today, the road all runners come,
Shoulder-high we bring you home,
And set you at your threshold down,
Townsman of a stiller town.

Smart lad, to slip betimes[1] away
10 From fields where glory does not stay
And early though the laurel[2] grows
It withers quicker than the rose.

Eyes the shady night has shut
Cannot see the record cut,
15 And silence sounds no worse than cheers
After earth has stopped the ears:
Now you will not swell the rout[3]
Of lads that wore their honors out,
Runners whom renown outran
20 And the name died before the man.

So set, before its echoes fade,
The fleet foot on the sill of shade,
And hold to the low lintel[4] up
The still-defended challenge cup.

25 And round that early-laureled head
Will flock to gaze the strengthless dead,
And find unwithered on its curls
The garland briefer than a girl's.

---

1. **betimes:** early.
2. **laurel:** symbol of victory or distinction.
3. **rout:** crowd.
4. **lintel:** horizontal piece over a door or window.

STUDY QUESTIONS

Loveliest of Trees

Recalling
1. Based on the first stanza, describe the loveliest tree. At what time of year is this poem set?
2. How old is the speaker of the poem? In the last stanza what does the speaker say that he or she will do?

Interpreting
3. According to lines 5–10, what is the speaker's attitude about his or her age?
4. Do you think the snow in the last two lines is meant to be literal? Why or why not?

When I Was One-and-Twenty

Recalling
1. According to the first stanza, what should a person not give away? What should be given away instead? What is the speaker's reaction to this advice?
2. According to the second stanza, what is the price that is paid for one's heart? What is the speaker's reaction to the advice in the second stanza?

Interpreting
3. Explain the effect of the repetition in the poem's last line.
4. What happens in the speaker's life in the time between the two stanzas? Explain how we know this from the poem.
5. In what ways would the impact of the poem be different if the speaker were much older in the second stanza?

Extending
6. Explain what the poem implies about the relationship between the old and the young.

To an Athlete Dying Young

Recalling
1. At what sport did the athlete excel? Describe the scene that is detailed in the first stanza.
2. What is the second occasion on which the athlete is carried shoulder-high? What words or phrases are used in the second stanza to describe death?
3. What is likely to happen to "glory" in the third

stanza, "the record" in the fourth stanza, "honors" and "the name" in the fifth stanza?

4. According to the third stanza, what happens to the laurel? Describe the garland in the last stanza.

Interpreting

5. Explain why the speaker says that the athlete is smart to die young.

Extending

6. What does the poem imply about problems that most successful athletes must face?

LITERARY FOCUS

Lyric Poetry

Poetry is traditionally classified into one of three types. **Narrative poetry** tells a story; Kipling's "Ballad of East and West" is an example. **Dramatic poetry** reveals character through monologue and dialogue; Robert Browning's "My Last Duchess" is an example. **Lyric poetry** expresses personal thoughts and feelings; Tennyson's "Tears, Idle Tears" is an example. The elements of each type may be blended; for instance, "The Ballad of East and West" does express personal thoughts about East-West relations, and it does reveal character through dialogue. However, as its *chief purpose* is to tell a story, it is considered a narrative poem.

A lyric poem may describe an object, a person, or an event, but the central concern of the poem is the emotion that is awakened by the subject of the description. Therefore, we read lyric poetry to consider a poet's ideas and to share the feelings that are associated with them. The emotions that are expressed may remind us of our own emotional experiences, or they may cause us to imagine how we would respond to circumstances like those in the poem.

Lyric poetry is usually brief and can take many shapes. For example, the ode and the sonnet are two types of lyric. Most lyric poetry is very musical. The name itself comes from *lyre*, the guitarlike instrument that was originally used to accompany the recitation of such poetry. We still use the word *lyric* to refer to the words of songs, and most songs are expressions of emotion.

Thinking About Lyric Poetry

Choose one of Housman's poems, and explain why it is considered a lyric poem: "Loveliest of Trees," "When I Was One-And-Twenty," or "To an Athlete Dying Young." First explain the basic situation behind the poem. Then tell what thoughts this situation arouses in the speaker. Finally explain what emotions are associated with these thoughts.

COMPOSITION

Applying a Statement About Literature

One concern of Housman's poetry is that so much in life is transient and does not last. Choose one of the poems by Housman that are presented here, and explain how this statement applies to the poem. First explain the statement in your own words. Then demonstrate how the statement fits the poem. Give examples from the poem to support your opinion. *For help with this assignment, refer to Lesson 9 in the Writing About Literature Handbook at the back of this book.*

Conveying an Emotional Response

In "Loveliest of Trees" Housman says that fifty years is hardly enough time to appreciate the beauty of a cherry orchard. Choose a natural phenomenon that you think deserves similar enthusiasm, and describe it in poetry or in prose. Use details that are vivid enough to convey your own emotional response.

COMPARING WRITERS

1. Explain how two of these narrative works display elements of both Realism and Romanticism: the selection from *Oliver Twist,* the selection from *Jane Eyre,* the selection from *Alice in Wonderland,* "The Ballad of East and West." Which lyric or dramatic poems in this unit also show the influence of both literary movements? From two of those poems, supply examples of each movement's influence.

2. What view of life do "My Last Duchess," "Dover Beach," and "The Darkling Thrush" share? Though Hardy is most closely associated with Naturalism, do you detect Naturalist ideas in "Dover Beach"? Explain your answer by citing examples from the poem.

3. Both the Pre-Raphaelite Brotherhood and the Symbolist movement were resurgences of Romanticism. What Romantic ideas or attitudes are displayed in the selections by Dante Gabriel Rossetti and Oscar Wilde? In what way are the two writers' attitudes toward nature different? Which attitude is more Romantic?

ACTIVE READING

Active, Imaginative Reading

A fabulous wealth of literature is available to us as a rich source of pleasure and knowledge, for literature opens up an infinite variety of *experience*. To make the most of the experience, however, we must in turn open ourselves up: That is, we must read actively and *imaginatively.*

Active, imaginative reading means several things. It means reading alertly and inquisitively. If something confuses us or strikes us as obscure, we should not pass by it but should question it, think it through, turn it over in our minds until we can make sense of it. We should drop all preconceptions and familiar ways of seeing and feeling. We must read with open minds and hearts, for to resist automatically what seems strange is to cheat ourselves of much knowledge and pleasure. We must accept—at least for a while—what the author gives us and try to understand it on its own terms.

Truly imaginative reading also means giving ourselves up to the language of a work, to its particular rhythm and sound. We must read carefully and very slowly at first, until we can naturally "feel" the flow of the words and allow it to carry us out of ourselves and into the world of the characters and the vision of the writer.

For example, we might read Tennyson's poem "Ulysses" (page 494) from a distance, saying to ourselves, "This is just a poem after all; this is just someone's idea of what Ulysses might have felt when he grew old." We would understand the poem this way and perhaps even come to admire it, but we probably would not truly *feel* the sentiments it expresses. On the other hand, we might read the poem from "the inside." We might, first of all, remember what we know about Ulysses—his story, his character, his time. Then we might try to enter fully and deeply into his thoughts and feelings. We might try to submerge ourselves in his situation: Here is a great and accomplished man and a tireless spirit. Although old and weary, he still yearns "to strive, to seek, to find, and not to yield." Also, if we read with an awareness of the somber, stately rhythm of the language, we will appreciate the poem on an even profounder level. We will realize the hero's pride and dignity and expansiveness of vision, and we will comprehend the true majesty of his feelings.

We must use our imaginations in a somewhat different way when we read Hopkins' poem "God's Grandeur" (page 539). Here it is less a matter of entering into a character's consciousness and mood than of reacting as openly as we can to the emotions and inspirations of the poet. We must try to see what the poet sees, think what he thinks, feel what he feels. We must, like the poet, lose ourselves momentarily in nature. If we can, then we will have a truer idea of what the poet means by God's "grandeur." We will have a clearer sense of what he means by "the dearest freshness deep down things." We will ourselves recognize the exquisite joy that impels the poet to utter that surprising and wonderfully expressive "ah!" that interrupts the final ecstatic line.

By observing more closely, we not only see more but also understand more thoroughly. By attempting to know all that a character knows, we obtain more profound insight into that character's mind and heart and being. Through closer involvement *inside* a work, we derive greater pleasure and, moreover, give ourselves a richer, more poignant, more meaningful experience.

REVIEW: THE ENGLISH VOICE

Losses

Victorian literature describes an era of empire, progress, self-assurance, and optimism. Yet close readings of Victorian poetry and prose reveal something more: an undercurrent of regret, a tone of nostalgia, a haunting sense of loss.

Tennyson

Though much is taken, much
*   abides; and though*
We are not now that strength
*   which in old days*
Moved earth and heaven, that
*   which we are, we are—*

Deep as first love, and wild
*   with all regret;*
O Death in Life, the days that
*   are no more!*

Ring out the grief that saps the
*   mind,*
For those that here we see no
*   more.*

Robert Browning

Oh, to be in England
Now that April's there.

Elizabeth Barrett Browning

I love thee with the passion put
*   to use*
In my old griefs, and with my
*   childhood's faith.*
I love thee with a love I seemed
*   to lose*
With my lost saints.

Arnold

Ah, love, let us be true
To one another! for the world,
*   which seems*
To lie before us like a land of
*   dreams,*
So various, so beautiful, so
*   new,*
Hath really neither joy, nor
*   love, nor light,*
Nor certitude, nor peace, nor
*   help for pain.*

Hopkins

It is the blight man was born
*   for,*
It is Margaret you mourn for.

Hardy

I should have kissed her if the
*   rain*
*   Had lasted a minute more.*

Housman

Now, of my threescore years
*   and ten,*
Twenty will not come again,
And take from seventy springs
*   a score,*
It only leaves me fifty more.

The death of loved ones, the passing of time, emptiness of spirit, even homesickness—these too are Victorian subjects. Beneath Victorian assertions of life, love, and moral fervor flow currents of unease.

Key to Illustrations on Pages 484–485

1. Elizabeth Barrett Browning (1806–1861), engraving.

2. Photograph of heavy traffic on London Bridge, late nineteenth century.

3. Detail, *The Opening of the First Victorian Parliament under Responsible Government*, sketch by William Strutt, 1856.

4. Alfred, Lord Tennyson, lithograph, c. 1885.

5. Detail, portrait of Queen Victoria, Prince Albert, and their children, from Queen Victoria's Jubilee brochure, 1897.

6. Florence Nightingale in hospital at Scutari in Crimea.

7. Detail, *The Bayswater Omnibus*, George W. Joy, 1895.

8. Detail, *Industry of the Tyne*, Bell Scott.

9. Detail, *The Quadrant, Regent Street*, print by E. Walker, 1852.

10. Detail, pen and ink drawing by R. W. Boss showing Dickens in his study at Gad's Hill.

Key to Illustrations appears on page 777.

THE TWENTIETH CENTURY

1900–Present

Challenge and Change

During the nineteenth century Britons proudly believed that the sun never set on the British Empire. The twentieth century, however, brought enormous changes to England, a nation that had always taken pride in its stability and its solid traditions. Both internally and externally, England found it had to achieve a new identity.

Queen Victoria, the very symbol of empire for more than sixty years, died in 1901. As the twentieth century progressed, that empire gradually became the British Commonwealth, a federation of independent nations united under the merely symbolic power of the British crown. The national wealth and international influence that had been a way of life during the days of empire were quickly becoming things of the past. In addition, the relationships among the long-established classes of English society began to break down as the power of the common people increased.

While its empire was shrinking, Britain—now officially known as the United Kingdom of Great Britain and Northern Ireland—made great changes affecting the everyday life of English men, women, and children. In 1928 universal suffrage was finally achieved, more than seven hundred years after the Magna Carta. Labor unions were formed to protect industrial workers and miners. After

Victoria Station, R. Jack, 1916. The painting depicts English soldiers waiting to leave for France during World War I.

World War II the government assumed responsibility for public housing, pensions, unemployment, and the nation's railroads and mines, and a national health program made medical care available to everyone.

Queen Victoria had symbolized nineteenth-century England—a strict moral code, prosperity, contentment, and an unquestioning attitude toward authority. The Edwardian era, however—the reign of Edward VII (1901–1910) and the remaining four years before World War I—saw those characteristics begin to break down, especially with widespread questioning of authority in politics, social matters, religion, and art. Later, through the reigns of George V and George VI and into the time of Elizabeth II, who assumed the throne in 1952, the British Commonwealth began to acquire an image different from that of the empire under authoritarian Victoria. The image is not that of the king but the commoner, not the queen but the prime minister, not the royalist but the rebel. Of course, Britain still reveres its royal family. However, the modern British identity seems to have been shaped more by people who wore no crowns—people like Prime Minister Winston Churchill and opponents of the empire like Indian leader Mohandas ("Mahatma") Gandhi and Irish nationalist Charles Stewart Parnell.

The "troubles" in Ireland are themselves a large part of Britain's image in the modern world. In 1920 six predominantly Protestant counties in the north of Ireland became a separate entity known as Northern Ireland. Two years later the rest of Ireland broke with Great Britain to form the Irish Free State. Anxiety and violence accompanied Irish nationalism and independence and continue to do so even in our own decade.

The greatest changes, however, in Britain's identity resulted from the two world wars that scar our century. Their cost in life and property contributed greatly to the decline of British power and resources, forced a redefinition of the British world view, and brought forth a great outpouring of literature.

The Great War

Britain was largely unprepared when World War I began in 1914. This was the first war to involve modern weapons—tanks, planes, and poison gas. In four years of combat, most of it endured in trenches across the face of Europe, one million Britons were killed.

The Great War, as it was called, had an effect on British and European attitudes that was unparalleled. It is important to remember that the people who fought in World War I were Victorians: They had grown up with a set of ideals and attitudes that were about to be shattered by the gruesome reality of modern warfare. One English officer, typical of the gentlemen who went to Europe to fight, gave four soccer balls to his men and offered a reward to the one who would kick the ball through the German lines during an attack. The officer and many of his men were killed, never surviving to feel the skepticism and bitterness that marked the postwar generation.

Those who fought never forgot what it was like to live in the trenches. It seemed to many as if the whole world had simply become a place made of mud. Poets Siegfried Sassoon and Rupert Brooke, among others, recorded the agony and courage of those who lost their lives and those who, though still alive, had lost their spirit.

Contemporary Britain

The twenties in England saw the same disillusion and breakdown of values that afflicted America

Winston S. Churchill (1874–1965).

after the war. Political commitment and a spirit of reform set in with the thirties, but this new spirit bowed before the onslaught of Adolf Hitler. Winston Churchill, a courageous and inspiring prime minister, led Britain through the dark days of World War II. From 1939 to 1945, England desperately needed that inspiration, for the Battle of Britain was fought not only by soldiers but by the British people at home. German aircraft tried to bomb England to its knees. Children were evacuated from cities; all Britons grew familiar with food shortages, air raids, and underground shelters. A fire-tested Britain emerged into the postwar world.

After the war the Labor Party created programs to meet Britain's enormous economic problems, aware that the sun was indeed setting on the empire. More British colonies achieved home rule, including India and Palestine. In 1957 Prime Minister Anthony Eden was forced to resign when his military effort to keep the Suez Canal open met with international protest. The Irish troubles continued to be one of the greatest causes of British anxiety. In 1982, however, Prime Minister Margaret Thatcher prevented Argentina from annexing one of the remnants of the empire, the Falkland Islands.

Britain helped to create the modern world, and the modern world has created a new Britain. The national identity is still a

subject of controversy among British writers. There is no doubt, however, of the quantity and quality of literature that Britain has produced in our time.

Twentieth-Century British Literature

Modern Britain continues to produce literature worthy of the nation that bred Shakespeare. During the Edwardian Age there came on the literary scene a new attitude often called modernism. **Modernism** is not one movement but an umbrella term for a variety of movements that all had in common a desire to break with the past, to change the very structure of literature and all the arts. Writers and other artists were creating a new way of seeing the world, of listening to it, and of expressing feelings about it. Spurred by the shock of World War I, modernism reached its peak from 1914 to 1930, but it redefined and redirected modern literature for the rest of the

century.

Modernist poets broke out of established meters and experimented with free verse, an approach that stressed matching rhythm to meaning. New developments in psychology were also incorporated into literature, especially the stream-of-consciousness technique, which changed the very structure of fiction. Writers and other artists now stressed the importance of showing emotion rather than stating it directly. Their new approaches forced readers to participate and draw conclusions for themselves.

The subject matter of literature changed too. With the shocks of the wars, technological advances, and greater social freedom, writers realized that they could and should write about *anything*. No subject was too dignified or undignified, too familiar or remote, to appear in a modern poem or novel.

Modern Poetry

No poet better demonstrates the range of modern poetic possibilities than the Irishman William Butler Yeats. Yeats also provides a bridge from the Victorian Age into the twentieth century. His early Romantic work, produced before the century turned, gradually became more realistic and direct, personal yet politically committed, and finally mystical and visionary. Yeats remains, in the opinion of many readers, the finest poet of our time.

T. S. Eliot, an American expatriate, responded to the horror of World War I and the confusion of modern life with *The Waste Land* (1922). *The Waste Land* is a fragmented poem of disillusion and the difficulty of human communication in the modern world. With its portrayal of "hollow" people, its unconnected images, and its use of myths of the past to describe the present, it is perhaps the single most influential poem of the century.

W. H. Auden, Stephen Spender, and Louis MacNeice—important poets of the 1930s—suggested that the world could be improved. A liberal spirit of reform moves through their work. The Welshman Dylan Thomas, on the other hand, did not burden his poems with social or political ideas. His affirmation of life and his overpowering love of language make his poems sing with a musical quality surpassed only by William Butler Yeats.

After decades of innovation, poets since World War II have been free to develop in many different directions. The tradition of British poetry offers today's poets a wealth of sources to learn from or to react against. As a result, contemporary poetry ranges from Thom Gunn's use of nonpoetic language and subject matter to Ted Hughes's fascination with animals, from Charles Tomlinson's abstract images to Geoffrey Hill's new uses of myths.

Scene from a recent Abbey Theatre (Dublin) production of a Sean O'Casey play.

Modern Drama

Drama in modern Britain thrives. Several major playwrights and theatrical movements, many accomplished actors, and innovative directors have established Britain's theaters as models for the world.

William Butler Yeats started the trend to poetic drama with plays based on Irish folklore, including *On Baile's Strand* (1904). Yeats helped found the Irish National Theatre, a company that produced two remarkable playwrights and plays that are inescapably Irish in mood and content, mixing cynical comedy with stark realism. John Millington Synge's masterpiece is *The Playboy of the Western World* (1907), and Sean O'Casey is best known for *Juno and the Paycock* (1925) and *The Plough and the Stars* (1926).

Another Irish-born playwright left Ireland when he was twenty to become an Englishman and an entire theatrical

movement in himself—George Bernard Shaw. Shaw had a satiric wit and an almost puritanical concern for setting things right. He applied his satirical approach to such contemporary and eternal themes as war, religion, and women's rights. *Pygmalion* is one of Shaw's most popular plays, a box-office success as well as a biting satire on male-female relationships and British class distinctions.

British dramatists of the twentieth century cover a broad spectrum of styles. Some followed traditions of the past, producing the "well-made play," with its carefully developed plot, characters, and setting. J. M. Barrie, for example, created such plays as *The Admirable Crichton* (1902) and *Peter Pan* (1904).

The well-made plot is less important than mood and character in the plays of T. S. Eliot and Harold Pinter. Eliot wrote several verse plays, including *Murder in the Cathedral* (1935), and several philosophical "comedies," including *The Cocktail Party* (1950). Harold Pinter's dramas, like *The Birthday Party* (1958), seem realistic but all have a sinister undercurrent beneath his characters' seemingly ordinary conversation. No playwright has been more experimental than Samuel Beckett, whose most famous play is *Waiting for Godot* (1952). Combinations of philosophy and comedy, reason and

Illustration from an early edition of Joseph Conrad's *Lord Jim*.

absurdity, Beckett's plays continue to be controversial and influential.

Modern Prose

The Victorian tradition of great novel writing has continued into the twentieth century. During the Edwardian Age, Realism and Naturalism flourished in British novels, and modernism began to have its effect on novel form.

Virginia Woolf said, "On or about December 1910 human nature changed." Woolf knew perfectly well that it was not human nature that had changed but the ways human beings perceived one another. She reflected this enormous change in her elegant, intellectual, and introspective novels. Her use of stream of consciousness, lyric imagery, and sophisticated wit made modern masterpieces of *Mrs. Dalloway* (1922) and *To the Lighthouse* (1927).

Polish-born Joseph Conrad, for whom English was a second language, wrote lush and vivid adventures like *Lord Jim* (1900) that explored such themes as honor, fate, identity, and disillusion. The novels of D. H. Lawrence offered new definitions of human relationships and intense psychological insight into the working classes.

Woolf, Conrad, and Lawrence explored new territory for fiction. In this respect, however, no writer can match Irish novelist James Joyce. Joyce took the stream-of-consciousness technique to its limits in *Ulysses* (1922), creating a book that is simultaneously realistic, symbolic, poetic, didactic, comic, ironic, and mythic. In 1939 he published *Finnegans Wake,* a book that takes language itself to its limits. After Joyce every writer of fiction in our time has had to think differently about the nature of the novel.

These novelists and others—among them E. M. Forster, John Galsworthy, Aldous Huxley, Ford Madox Ford, George Orwell, Evelyn Waugh, Graham Greene, Doris Lessing, and V. S. Naipaul—also produced short stories. The short story is a recent development in fiction, although its roots go back to Chaucer. The genre came late to Britain, which saw its first successful short story writers—Rudyard Kipling and Sir Arthur Conan Doyle, for example—near the end of the Victorian Age. In this century, however, Britain's best novelists have also written superb short stories. In fact, some authors—like Katherine Mansfield, Saki (H. H. Munro), Frank O'Connor, Sean O'Faolain, and Nadine Gordimer—established their literary reputations largely through short stories.

In the space age, with all its advances in technology, the world seems to be a smaller place. Nevertheless, literature remains a major source of understanding and entertainment, just as it was in the times of Chaucer, Shakespeare, and Keats. Throughout this worldwide community, the global village, people continue to look to British literature for a glorious tradition that is still growing and seeking new directions.

TIME LINE

Year	Event
1901	Victoria dies; Edward VII becomes king
1902	Joseph Conrad, *Heart of Darkness*
1905	First motor buses in London
1910	Edward VII dies; George V becomes king
	D. H. Lawrence, "Goose Fair"
1911	Rupert Brooke, *Poems*
1912	George Bernard Shaw, *Pygmalion*
1913	Suffragette demonstrations in London
1914	World War I begins
1917	Siegfried Sassoon, *Counter-Attack and Other Poems*
	W. B. Yeats, "The Wild Swans at Coole"
1918	Women over thirty are allowed to vote
1919	Lady Astor first woman elected to Parliament
1920	Parliament passes Government of Ireland Act
1922	Katherine Mansfield, *The Garden Party and Other Stories*
	James Joyce, *Ulysses*
1925	T. S. Eliot, "The Hollow Men"
1929	Virginia Woolf, *A Room of One's Own*
1936	King Edward VIII abdicates; succeeded by George VI
1939	James Joyce, *Finnegans Wake*

Year	Event
1901	China: Boxer uprising ends
1902	South Africa: Boer War ends
	Egypt: Aswan Dam opens
1909	India: Tagore, *Gitanjali*
1910	France: Marie Curie, *Treatise on Radiography*
1911	China: Manchu Dynasty falls; republic proclaimed
1913	Africa: Albert Schweitzer opens hospital in French Equatorial Africa
1914	Panama Canal opens
1917	Russia: Revolution forces the czar from power
	Austria: Sigmund Freud, *Introduction to Psychoanalysis*
1918	Italy: Luigi Pirandello, *Six Characters in Search of an Author*
1920	Belgium: First postwar Olympic games held
1922	India: Gandhi sentenced to prison for civil disobedience
	France: James Joyce publishes *Ulysses*
1925	Germany: Franz Kafka, *The Trial*
1929	Worldwide economic crisis after New York stock market crashes
1936	Spain: Civil War begins
1939	World War II begins when Germany invades Poland

KING EDWARD VII

T. S. ELIOT

VIRGINIA WOOLF

JAMES JOYCE

WAR ENDS

DYLAN THOMAS

British Events	World Events
1940 Winston Churchill becomes prime minister	1940 France: German army enters Paris
W. H. Auden, "Musée des Beaux Arts"	European composers move to America: Stravinsky, Bartók, Hindemith, and Weill
1945 George Orwell, *Animal Farm*	1945 Japan: U.S. drops atomic bombs
Dylan Thomas, "Fern Hill"	Japanese surrender ends World War II
1948 Wartime bread rationing ends	1946 France: Peace conference held in Paris
1952 George VI dies; Elizabeth II becomes queen	1948 Israel becomes a nation
1957 Samuel Beckett, *Endgame*	1958 European Common Market created
1958 First parking meters in London	1959 U.S.S.R.: Rocket launched with monkeys aboard
1959 Robert Graves, *Collected Poems*	1960 Argentina: Jorge Luis Borges, *El hacedor* (*Dreamtigers*)
Geoffrey Hill, *For the Unfallen*	1961 Germany: Berlin Wall is built
V. S. Naipaul, *Miguel Street*	
1961 Louis MacNeice, *Eighty-five Poems*	
Sean O'Faolain, *I Remember, I Remember*	
1962 Doris Lessing, *The Golden Notebook*	
1965 Westminster Abbey is nine hundred years old	1965 In separate voyages American and Soviet astronauts walk in space
1966 Graham Greene, *The Comedians*	1968 Columbia: Gabriel García Márquez, *A Hundred Years of Solitude*
1967 Elizabeth II takes part in Canadian centennial	
1972 Forty-seven-day coal strike cripples Britain	1972 Philippines: Discovery of the Tasaday, a Stone Age tribe that lives in caves
1973 Great Britain joins the Common Market	1973 World energy crisis caused by oil shortages and embargo
1979 Margaret Thatcher first woman to become prime minister	1975 Mexico: International Women's Year World Conference
1984 Ted Hughes becomes poet laureate	
1987 Computers introduced on London Stock Exchange	1982 Germany: Heinrich Böll, *Safety Net*

DRAMA

George Bernard Shaw   *1856–1950*

George Bernard Shaw is now considered the greatest modern British playwright, yet he did not begin to write drama until he was middle-aged. He made up for lost time with an amazing output of forty-seven plays during a creative life that spanned the Victorian and modern eras. Irish by birth, Shaw came to England at the age of twenty and lived in and near London throughout the rest of his life. After writing several unsuccessful novels, the young Shaw turned to reviewing in order to earn a living. From his mother, an aspiring singer, he had learned much about music, and he combined this knowledge with excellent taste and a sparkling prose style to become the most influential music critic of his day.

Shaw's lively intelligence did not confine itself to art, fiction, and music. At an early age he became committed to the cause of social reform. He joined the Fabian movement, a type of socialism founded in England in the 1880s to reform the social, economic, and political systems gradually through peaceful, democratic measures. Although he was shy by nature, Shaw turned himself into an outstanding public speaker. He continued to participate actively in politics the rest of his life. However, he found a particularly satisfying forum for his ideas in reviewing drama and, eventually, in writing plays of his own.

In the 1890s Shaw became recognized as London's wittiest and most stimulating drama critic. He took drama very seriously; in particular, he idolized the Norwegian dramatist Henrik Ibsen, whose unsparing critique of middle-class life revealed to Shaw the potential impact of drama upon society. After writing his influential essay "The Quintessence of Ibsenism" (1891), Shaw began to try his own hand at writing plays. The result, *Widowers' Houses* (produced in 1892), proved to be the first of many plays to come in the years ahead.

At first Shaw's plays were too controversial for English theatergoers, who were accustomed to light or sentimental entertainments but not to provocative examinations of moral and social issues. However, Shaw continued to write and publish his plays, usually accompanying them with lengthy and argumentative prefaces that expressed his ideas on a wide range of subjects. Eventually he established himself as the leading British playwright of the modern period with such works as *Arms and the Man* (1894), *Candida* (1895), *Caesar and Cleopatra* (1898), *Man and Superman* (1903), *Major Barbara* (1907), *Pygmalion* (1912), *Heartbreak House* (1917), and *Saint Joan* (1923). For those achievements the playwright was awarded the Nobel Prize for Literature in 1925.

Introducing **Pygmalion**

Pygmalion [pig māl′yən], written in 1912 and first produced in England in 1914, remains one of Shaw's most popular works. Not only is the play constantly revived, but it was the basis of the acclaimed musical *My Fair Lady.* The title *Pygmalion* refers to a mythological king of Cyprus who carved a statue of a woman so beautiful that he fell in love with her. Aphrodite, goddess of love, answered the lovesick prayers by bringing his statue, Galatea, to life. Shaw's play concerns a professor of phonetics (the study of the sounds of speech) who attempts to remold a flower seller from the London slums into a refined lady by teaching her how to speak proper English.

Pygmalion gave Shaw a platform for many of his concerns. He was passionately interested in the English language and the varieties of ways in which people spoke (and misspoke) it. Shaw longed to simplify and reform English; he once pointed out that the rules of spelling in English are so inconsistent and confusing that the word *fish* could conceivably be spelled "ghoti" if the speller used the sound of *gh* in *enough,* the sound of *o* in *women,* and the sound of *ti* in the suffix *-tion.* The text of *Pygmalion* reflects some of his efforts at simplifying English usage—principally his omission of apostrophes in contractions such as *Ive* and *dont. Pygmalion* also allowed Shaw to present ideas about other topics that concerned him—such matters as social equality, male and female roles, and the relationship between what people seem to be and what they really are. Like his other successful plays, *Pygmalion* wins us over with its charm and then startles us out of our preconceptions with its keen intelligence.

Key Ideas in *Pygmalion*

As you read *Pygmalion,* look for references to each of the following. If you keep track of what Shaw says about these topics, you will begin to grasp the play's most important themes.

* Social equality
* The rights and social position of women
* Relationships between men and women
* Appearance and reality
* Language and individual identity

■ Suppose that a promoter offered to make you a rock star and, with your permission and hard work, did. Would your life suddenly become perfect? What problems might you have?

PREFACE TO PYGMALION

A Professor of Phonetics

The English have no respect for their language, and will not teach their children to speak it. They cannot spell it because they have nothing to spell it with but an old foreign alphabet of which only the consonants—and not all of them—have any agreed speech value. Consequently no man can teach himself what it should sound like from reading it; and it is impossible for an Englishman to open his mouth without making some other Englishman despise him. Most European languages are now accessible in black and white to foreigners: English and French are not thus accessible even to Englishmen and Frenchmen. The reformer we need most today is an energetic phonetic enthusiast: that is why I have made such a one the hero of a popular play.

There have been heroes of that kind crying in the wilderness for many years past. When I became interested in the subject towards the end of the eighteen-seventies, the illustrious Alexander Melville Bell, the inventor of Visible Speech, had emigrated to Canada, where his son invented the telephone; but Alexander J. Ellis[1] was still a London Patriarch, with an impressive head always covered by a velvet skull cap, for which he would apologize to public meetings in a very courtly manner. He and Tito Pagliardini,[2] another phonetic veteran, were men whom it was impossible to dislike. Henry Sweet,[3] then a young man, lacked their sweetness of character: he was about as conciliatory to conventional mortals as Ibsen[4] or Samuel Butler.[5] His great ability as a phonetician (he was, I think, the best of them all at his job) would have entitled him to high official recognition, and perhaps enabled him to popularize his subject, but for his Satanic contempt for all academic dignitaries and persons in general who thought more of Greek than of phonetics. Once, in the days when the Imperial Institute rose in South Kensington, and Joseph Chamberlain[6] was booming the Empire, I induced the editor of a leading monthly review to commission an article from Sweet on the imperial importance of his subject. When it arrived, it contained nothing but a savagely derisive attack on a professor of language and literature

1. **Alexander J. Ellis** (1814–1890): English philologist and mathematician.

2. **Tito Pagliardini** [tē′tō pal yär dē′nē]
3. **Henry Sweet** (1845–1912): English grammarian and philologist.
4. **Ibsen:** Henrik Ibsen (1828–1906), Norwegian playwright, admired by Shaw for his portrayals of society.
5. **Samuel Butler** (1835–1902): English novelist.
6. **Joseph Chamberlain** (1836–1914): British statesman, known as the greatest orator of his time.

whose chair Sweet regarded as proper to a phonetic expert only. The article, being libellous, had to be returned as impossible; and I had to renounce my dream of dragging its author into the limelight. When I met him afterwards, for the first time for many years, I found to my astonishment that he, who had been a quite tolerably presentable young man, had actually managed by sheer scorn to alter his personal appearance until he had become a sort of walking repudiation of Oxford and all its traditions. It must have been largely in his own despite that he was squeezed into something called a Readership[7] of phonetics there. The future of phonetics rests probably with his pupils, who all swore by him; but nothing could bring the man himself into any sort of compliance with the university to which he nevertheless clung by divine right in an intensely Oxonian[8] way. I daresay his papers, if he has left any, include some satires that may be published without too destructive results fifty years hence. He was, I believe, not in the least an ill-natured man: very much the opposite, I should say; but he would not suffer fools gladly; and to him all scholars who were not rabid phoneticians were fools.

Those who knew him will recognize in my third act the allusion to the Current Shorthand in which he used to write postcards. It may be acquired from a four and sixpenny manual published by the Clarendon Press. The postcards which Mrs Higgins describes are such as I have received from Sweet. I would decipher a sound which a cockney would represent by *zerr,* and a Frenchman by *seu,* and then write demanding with some heat what on earth it meant. Sweet, with boundless contempt for my stupidity, would reply that it not only meant but obviously was the word Result, as no other word containing that sound, and capable of making sense with the context, existed in any language spoken on earth. That less expert mortals should require fuller indications was beyond Sweet's patience. Therefore, though the whole point of his Current Shorthand is that it can express every sound in the language perfectly, vowels as well as consonants, and that your hand has to make no stroke except the easy and current ones with which you write m, n, and u, l, p, and q, scribbling them at whatever angle comes easiest to you, his unfortunate determination to make this remarkable and quite legible script serve also as a shorthand reduced it in his own practice to the most inscrutable of cryptograms.[9] His true objective was the provision of a full, accurate, legible script for our language; but he was led past that by his contempt for the popular Pitman system of shorthand, which he called the Pitfall system. The triumph of Pitman was a triumph of business organization: there was a weekly paper to persuade you to learn Pitman: there were cheap textbooks and exercise books and transcripts of speeches for you to copy, and schools where experienced teachers coached you up to the necessary proficiency. Sweet could not organize his market in that fashion. He might as well have been the Sybil[10] who tore up the leaves of prophecy that nobody would attend to. The four and sixpenny manual, mostly in his lithographed handwriting, that was never vulgarly advertized, may perhaps some day be taken up by a syndicate and pushed upon the public as The Times pushed the Encyclopaedia Britannica; but until then it will certainly not prevail against Pitman. I have bought three copies of it during my lifetime; and I am informed by the publishers that its cloistered existence is still a steady and healthy one. I actually learned the system two several times; and yet the shorthand in which I am writing these lines is Pitman's. And the reason is, that my secretary cannot transcribe Sweet, having been perforce taught in the schools of Pitman. In America I could use the commercially organized Gregg shorthand, which has taken a hint from Sweet by making its letters writable (current, Sweet would have called them) instead of having to be geometrically

---

7. **Readership:** type of teaching position.
8. **Oxonian:** pertaining to Oxford University.

9. **cryptograms:** words written in code.
10. **Sybil:** prophetess in Greek and Roman mythology.

drawn like Pitman's; but all these systems, including Sweet's, are spoilt by making them available for verbatim reporting, in which complete and exact spelling and word division are impossible. A complete and exact phonetic script is neither practicable nor necessary for ordinary use; but if we enlarge our alphabet to the Russian size, and make our spelling as phonetic as Spanish, the advance will be prodigious.

Pygmalion Higgins is not a portrait of Sweet, to whom the adventure of Eliza Doolittle would have been impossible; still, as will be seen, there are touches of Sweet in the play. With Higgins's physique and temperament Sweet might have set the Thames on fire. As it was, he impressed himself professionally on Europe to an extent that made his comparative personal obscurity, and the failure of Oxford to do justice to his eminence, a puzzle to foreign specialists in his subject. I do not blame Oxford, because I think Oxford is quite right in demanding a certain social amenity from its nurslings (heavens knows it is not exorbitant in its requirement!); for although I well know how hard it is for a man of genius with a seriously underrated subject to maintain serene and kindly relations with the men who underrate it, and who keep all the best places for less important subjects which they profess without originality and sometimes without much capacity for them, still, if he overwhelms them with wrath and disdain, he cannot expect them to heap honors on him.

Of the later generations of phoneticians I know little. Among them towered Robert Bridges, to whom perhaps Higgins may owe his Miltonic sympathies, though here again I must disclaim all portraiture. But if the play makes the public aware that there are such people as phoneticians, and that they are among the most important people in England at present, it will serve its turn.

I wish to boast that Pygmalion has been an extremely successful play, both on stage and screen, all over Europe and North America as well as at home. It is so intensely and deliberately didactic, and its subject is esteemed so dry, that I delight in throwing it at the heads of the wiseacres[11] who repeat the parrot cry that art should never be didactic. It goes to prove my contention that great art can never be anything else.

Finally, and for the encouragement of people troubled with accents that cut them off from all high employment, I may add that the change wrought by Professor Higgins in the flower-girl is neither impossible nor uncommon. The modern concierge's[12] daughter who fulfills her ambition by playing the Queen of Spain in Ruy Blas[13] at the Théâtre Français is only one of many thousands of men and women who have sloughed off their native dialects and acquired a new tongue. Our West End shop assistants and domestic servants are bilingual. But the thing has to be done scientifically, or the last state of the aspirant may be worse than the first. An honest slum dialect is more tolerable than the attempts of phonetically untaught persons to imitate the plutocracy.[14] Ambitious flower-girls who read this play must not imagine that they can pass themselves off as fine ladies by untutored imitation. They must learn their alphabet over again, and different, from a phonetic expert. Imitation will only make them ridiculous.

NOTE FOR TECHNICIANS. A complete representation of the play as printed in this edition is technically possible only on the cinema screen or on stages furnished with exceptionally elaborate machinery. For ordinary theatrical use the scenes separated by rows of asterisks are to be omitted.

In the dialogue an e upside down indicates the indefinite vowel, sometimes called obscure or neutral, for which, though it is one of the commonest sounds in English speech, our wretched alphabet has no letter.

---

11. **wiseacres:** smart alecks.
12. **concierge's:** A concierge [kon′ sē urzh′] is the caretaker of a building.
13. **Ruy Blas** [roo ē′ blas′]: poetic drama by French writer Victor Hugo (1802–1885).
14. **plutocracy:** the wealthy.

Eliza Doolittle.　　　Alfred Doolittle.　　　Henry Higgins.

George Bernard Shaw

Pygmalion

CHARACTERS

HENRY HIGGINS	MRS EYNSFORD HILL	TAXIMEN
COLONEL PICKERING	MISS EYNSFORD HILL	COUNT NEPOMMUCK
FREDDY EYNSFORD HILL	CONSTABLES	HOST
ALFRED DOOLITTLE	MRS HIGGINS	HOSTESS
BYSTANDERS	MRS PEARCE	FOOTMEN
ELIZA DOOLITTLE	PARLORMAID	

ACT ONE

London at 11.15 P.M. *Torrents of heavy summer rain. Cab whistles blowing frantically in all directions. Pedestrians running for shelter into the portico of St Paul's church (not Wren's cathedral but Inigo Jones's church in Covent Garden vegetable market), among them a lady and her daughter in evening dress. All are peering out gloomily at the rain, except one man with his back turned to the rest, wholly preoccupied with a notebook in which he is writing.*

The church clock strikes the first quarter.[1]

THE DAUGHTER [*in the space between the central pillars, close to the one on her left*] I'm getting chilled to the bone. What can Freddy be doing all this time? He's been gone twenty minutes.

THE MOTHER [*on her daughter's right*] Not so long. But he ought to have got us a cab by this.

A BYSTANDER [*on the lady's right*] He wont get no cab not until half-past eleven, missus, when they come back after dropping their theatre fares.

THE MOTHER. But we must have a cab. We cant stand here until half-past eleven. It's too bad.

---

1. **first quarter:** fifteen minutes after the hour.

THE BYSTANDER. Well, it ain't my fault, missus.

THE DAUGHTER. If Freddy had a bit of gumption, he would have got one at the theatre door.

THE MOTHER. What could he have done, poor boy?

THE DAUGHTER. Other people got cabs. Why couldnt he?

FREDDY *rushes in out of the rain from the Southampton Street side, and comes between them closing a dripping umbrella. He is a young man of twenty, in evening dress, very wet round the ankles.*

THE DAUGHTER. Well, havnt you got a cab?

FREDDY. Theres not one to be had for love or money.

THE MOTHER. Oh, Freddy, there must be one. You cant have tried.

THE DAUGHTER. It's too tiresome. Do you expect us to go and get one ourselves?

FREDDY. I tell you theyre all engaged. The rain was so sudden: nobody was prepared; and everybody had to take a cab. Ive been to Charing Cross one way and nearly to Ludgate Circus the other; and they were all engaged.

THE MOTHER. Did you try Trafalgar Square?

FREDDY. There wasnt one at Trafalgar Square.

THE DAUGHTER. Did you try?

FREDDY. I tried as far as Charing Cross Station. Did you expect me to walk to Hammersmith?

THE DAUGHTER. You havnt tried at all.

THE MOTHER. You really are very helpless, Freddy. Go again; and dont come back until you have found a cab.

FREDDY. I shall simply get soaked for nothing.

THE DAUGHTER. And what about us? Are we to stay here all night in this draught,[2] with next to nothing on? You selfish pig—

FREDDY. Oh, very well: I'll go, I'll go. [*He opens*

___

2. **draught** [draft]: draft.

his umbrella and dashes off Strandwards, but comes into collision with a flower girl who is hurrying in for shelter, knocking her basket out of her hands. A blinding flash of lightning, followed instantly by a rattling peal of thunder, orchestrates the incident].

THE FLOWER GIRL. Nah then, Freddy: look wh' y' gowin, deah.[3]

FREDDY. Sorry [*he rushes off*].

THE FLOWER GIRL [*picking up her scattered flowers and replacing them in the basket*] Theres menners f' yer! Tə-oo banches o voylets trod into the mad.[4] [*She sits down on the plinth*[5] *of the column sorting her flowers, on the lady's right. She is not at all a romantic figure. She is perhaps eighteen, perhaps twenty, hardly older. She wears a little sailor hat of black straw that has long been exposed to the dust and soot of London and has seldom if ever been brushed. Her hair needs washing rather badly: its mousy color can hardly be natural. She wears a shoddy black coat that reaches nearly to her knees and is shaped to her waist. She has a brown skirt with a coarse apron. Her boots are much the worse for wear. She is no doubt as clean as she can afford to be; but compared to the ladies she is very dirty. Her features are no worse then theirs; but their condition leaves something to be desired; and she needs the services of a dentist*].

THE MOTHER. How do you know that my son's name is Freddy, pray?

THE FLOWER GIRL. Ow, eez yə-ooa san, is e? Wal, fewd dan y' də-ooty bawmz a mather should, eed now bettern to spawl a pore gel's flahrzn than ran awy athaht pyin. Will ye-oo py me f'them?[6] [*Here, with apologies, this desperate*

___

3. **Nah . . . deah:** "Now then, Freddy: look where you're going, dear."
4. **Theres . . . mad:** "There's manners for you! Two bunches of violets trod into the mud."
5. **plinth:** block at the bottom of a column.
6. **Ow . . . them?** "Oh, he's your son, is he? Well, if you'd done your duty by him as a mother should, he'd know better than to spoil a poor girl's flowers and then run away without paying. Will you pay me for them?"

attempt to represent her dialect without a phonetic alphabet must be abandoned as un-intelligible outside London].

THE DAUGHTER. Do nothing of the sort, mother. The idea!

THE MOTHER. Please allow me, Clara. Have you any pennies?

THE DAUGHTER. No. Ive nothing smaller than sixpence.

THE FLOWER GIRL [*hopefully*] I can give you change for a tanner,[7] kind lady.

THE MOTHER [*to* CLARA] Give it to me. [CLARA *parts reluctantly*]. Now. [*to the* GIRL] This is for your flowers.

THE FLOWER GIRL. Thank you kindly, lady.

THE DAUGHTER. Make her give you the change. These things are only a penny a bunch.

THE MOTHER. Do hold your tongue, Clara. [*To the* GIRL] You can keep the change.

THE FLOWER GIRL. Oh, thank you, lady.

THE MOTHER. Now tell me how you know that young gentleman's name.

THE FLOWER GIRL. I didnt.

THE MOTHER. I heard you call him by it. Dont try to deceive me.

THE FLOWER GIRL [*protesting*] Who's trying to deceive you? I called him Freddy or Charlie same as you might yourself if you was talking to a stranger and wished to be pleasant.

THE DAUGHTER. Sixpence thrown away! Really, mamma, you might have spared Freddy that. [*She retreats in disgust behind the pillar*].

An elderly gentleman of the amiable military type rushes into the shelter, and closes a dripping umbrella. He is in the same plight as FREDDY, *very wet above the ankles. He is in evening dress, with a light over-coat. He takes the place left vacant by the* DAUGHTER.

THE GENTLEMAN. Phew!

THE MOTHER [*to the* GENTLEMAN] Oh, sir, is there any sign of its stopping?

THE GENTLEMAN. I'm afraid not. It started worse than ever about two minutes ago [*he goes to the plinth beside the* FLOWER GIRL; *puts up his foot on it; and stoops to turn down his trouser ends*].

THE MOTHER. Oh dear! [*She retires sadly and joins her daughter*].

THE FLOWER GIRL [*taking advantage of the military gentleman's proximity to establish friendly relations with him*] If it's worse, it's a sign it's nearly over. So cheer up, Captain; and buy a flower off a poor girl.

THE GENTLEMAN. I'm sorry. I havnt any change.

THE FLOWER GIRL. I can give you change, Captain.

THE GENTLEMAN. For a sovereign?[8] Ive nothing less.

THE FLOWER GIRL. Garn! Oh do buy a flower off me, Captain. I can change half-a-crown. Take this for tuppence.

THE GENTLEMAN. Now dont be troublesome: theres a good girl. [*Trying his pockets*] I really havnt any change—Stop: heres three hapence, if thats any use to you [*he retreats to the other pillar*].

THE FLOWER GIRL [*disappointed, but thinking three half-pence better than nothing*] Thank you, sir.

THE BYSTANDER [*to the* GIRL] You be careful: give him a flower for it. Theres a bloke[9] here behind taking down every blessed word youre saying. [*All turn to the man who is taking notes*].

---

7. **tanner:** slang for *sixpence*.

8. **sovereign:** English coin, as are *half-a-crown* and *tuppence* (two pence) in the lines that follow.
9. **bloke:** slang for man or fellow.

THE FLOWER GIRL [*springing up terrified*] I aint done nothing wrong by speaking to the gentleman. Ive a right to sell flowers if I keep off the kerb. [*Hysterically*] I'm a respectable girl: so help me, I never spoke to him except to ask him to buy a flower off me.

> *General hubbub, mostly sympathetic to the* FLOWER GIRL, *but deprecating her excessive sensibility. Cries of* Dont start hollerin. Who's hurting you? Nobody's going to touch you. Whats the good of fussing? Steady on. Easy, easy, etc., *come from the elderly staid spectators, who pat her comfortingly. Less patient ones bid her shut her head, or ask her roughly what is wrong with her. A remoter group, not knowing what the matter is, crowd in and increase the noise with question and answer:* Whats the row?[10] What-she do? Where is he? A tec[11] taking her down. What! him? Yes: him over there: Took money off the gentleman, etc.

THE FLOWER GIRL [*breaking through them to the* GENTLEMAN, *crying wildly*] Oh, sir, dont let him charge me. You dunno what it means to me. Theyll take away my character and drive me on the streets for speaking to gentlemen. They—

THE NOTE TAKER [*coming forward on her right, the rest crowding after him*] There! there! there! there! who's hurting you, you silly girl? What do you take me for?

THE BYSTANDER. It's aw rawt: e's a genleman: look at his bə-oots.[12] [*Explaining to the* NOTE TAKER] She thought you was a copper's nark, sir.

THE NOTE TAKER [*with quick interest*] Whats a copper's nark?

THE BYSTANDER [*inapt at definition*] It's a— well, it's a copper's nark, as you might say. What else would you call it? A sort of informer.

THE FLOWER GIRL [*still hysterical*] I take my Bible oath I never said a word—

THE NOTE TAKER [*overbearing but good-humored*] Oh, shut up, shut up. Do I look like a policeman?

THE FLOWER GIRL [*far from reassured*] Then what did you take down my words for? How do I know whether you took me down right? You just shew[13] me what youve wrote about me. [*The* NOTE TAKER *opens his book and holds it steadily under her nose, though the pressure of the mob trying to read it over his shoulders would upset a weaker man*]. Whats that? That aint proper writing. I cant read that.

THE NOTE TAKER. I can. [*Reads, reproducing her pronunciation exactly*] "Cheer ap, Keptin; n' baw ya flahr orf a pore gel."[14]

THE FLOWER GIRL [*much distressed*] It's because I called him Captain. I meant no harm. [*To the* GENTLEMAN] Oh, sir, dont let him lay a charge agen me for a word like that. You—

THE GENTLEMAN. Charge! I make no charge. [*To the* NOTE TAKER] Really, sir, if you are a detective, you need not begin protecting me against molestation by young women until I ask you. Anybody could see that the girl meant no harm.

THE BYSTANDERS GENERALLY [*demonstrating against police espionage*] Course they could. What business is it of yours? You mind your own affairs. He wants promotion, he does. Taking down people's words! Girl never said a word to him. What harm if she did? Nice thing a girl cant shelter from the rain without being insulted, etc., etc., etc. [*She is conducted by the more sympathetic demonstrators back to her plinth, where she resumes her seat and struggles with her emotion*].

THE BYSTANDER. He aint a tec. He's a blooming

---

10. **row** [rou]: trouble, disturbance.
11. **tec:** slang abbreviation for detective.
12. **It's . . . bə-oots:** "It's all right; he's a gentleman: look at his boots."

13. **shew** [shō]: archaic spelling of *show*.
14. **Cheer . . . gel:** "Cheer up, Captain; and buy a flower off a poor girl."

busybody: thats what he is, I tell you, look at his bə-oots.

THE NOTE TAKER [*turning on him genially*] And how are all your people down at Selsey?

THE BYSTANDER [*suspiciously*] Who told you my people come from Selsey?

THE NOTE TAKER. Never you mind. They did. [*To the* GIRL] How do you come to be up so far east? You were born in Lisson Grove.

THE FLOWER GIRL [*appalled*] Oh, what harm is there in my leaving Lisson Grove? It wasnt fit for a pig to live in; and I had to pay four-and-six[15] a week. [*In tears*] Oh, boo-hoo-oo—

THE NOTE TAKER. Live where you like; but stop that noise.

THE GENTLEMAN [*to the* GIRL] Come, come! he cant touch you: you have a right to live where you please.

A SARCASTIC BYSTANDER [*thrusting himself between the* NOTE TAKER *and the* GENTLEMAN] Park Lane, for instance. I'd like to go into the Housing Question with you, I would.

THE FLOWER GIRL [*subsiding into a brooding melancholy over her basket, and talking very low-spiritedly to herself*] I'm a good girl, I am.

THE SARCASTIC BYSTANDER [*not attending to her*] Do you know where *I* come from?

THE NOTE TAKER [*promptly*] Hoxton.

Titterings. Popular interest in the NOTE TAK-ER'S *performance increases.*

THE SARCASTIC ONE [*amazed*] Well, who said I didnt? Bly me! you know everything, you do.

THE FLOWER GIRL [*still nursing her sense of injury*] Aint no call to meddle with me, he aint.

THE BYSTANDER [*to her*] Of course he aint. Dont you stand it from him. [*To the* NOTE TAKER] See here: what call have you to know about people what never offered to meddle with you?

THE FLOWER GIRL. Let him say what he likes. I dont want to have no truck with him.

THE BYSTANDER. You take us for dirt under your feet, dont you? Catch you taking liberties with a gentleman!

THE SARCASTIC BYSTANDER. Yes: tell him where he come from if you want to go fortune-telling.

THE NOTE TAKER. Cheltenham, Harrow, Cambridge, and India.

THE GENTLEMAN. Quite right.

Great laughter. Reaction in the NOTE TAKER'S *favor. Exclamations of* He knows all about it. Told him proper. Hear him tell the toff[16] where he come from? *etc.*

THE GENTLEMAN. May I ask, sir, do you do this for your living at a music hall?

THE NOTE TAKER. I've thought of that. Perhaps I shall some day.

The rain has stopped; and the persons on the outside of the crowd begin to drop off.

THE FLOWER GIRL [*resenting the reaction*] He's no gentleman, he aint, to interfere with a poor girl.

THE DAUGHTER [*out of patience, pushing her way rudely to the front and displacing the* GENTLEMAN, *who politely retires to the other side of the pillar*] What on earth is Freddy doing? I shall get pneumownia if I stay in this draught any longer.

THE NOTE TAKER [*to himself, hastily making a note of her pronunciation of "monia"*] Earls-court.

THE DAUGHTER [*violently*] Will you please keep your impertinent remarks to yourself.

THE NOTE TAKER. Did I say that out loud? I didnt mean to. I beg your pardon. Your mother's Epsom, unmistakeably.

THE MOTHER [*advancing between the* DAUGHTER

---

15. **four-and-six:** four shillings six pence, then $1.50.

16. **toff:** slang for fashionable gentleman.

and the NOTE TAKER] How very curious! I was brought up in Largelady Park, near Epsom.

THE NOTE TAKER [*uproariously amused*] Ha! ha! What a devil of a name! Excuse me. [*To the* DAUGHTER] You want a cab, do you?

THE DAUGHTER. Dont dare speak to me.

THE MOTHER. Oh please, please, Clara. [*Her daughter repudiates her with an angry shrug and retires haughtily*] We should be so grateful to you, sir, if you found us a cab. [*The* NOTE TAKER *produces a whistle*] Oh, thank you. [*She joins her daughter*].

The NOTE TAKER *blows a piercing blast.*

THE SARCASTIC BYSTANDER. There! I knowed he was a plainclothes copper.

THE BYSTANDER. That aint a police whistle: thats a sporting whistle.

THE FLOWER GIRL [*still preoccupied with her wounded feelings*] He's no right to take away my character.[17] My character is the same to me as any lady's.

THE NOTE TAKER. I dont know whether youve noticed it; but the rain stopped about two minutes ago.

THE BYSTANDER. So it has. Why didnt you say so before? and us losing our time listening to your silliness! [*He walks off towards the Strand*].

THE SARCASTIC BYSTANDER. I can tell where you come from. You come from Anwell. Go back there.

THE NOTE TAKER [*helpfully*] Hanwell.

THE SARCASTIC BYSTANDER [*affecting great distinction of speech*] Thenk you, teacher. Haw haw! So long [*he touches his hat with mock respect and strolls off*].

THE FLOWER GIRL. Frightening people like that! How would he like it himself?

THE MOTHER. It's quite fine now, Clara. We can walk to a motor bus. Come. [*She gathers her skirts above her ankles and hurries off towards the Strand*].

THE DAUGHTER. But the cab—[*her mother is out of hearing*]. Oh, how tiresome! [*She follows angrily*].

All the rest have gone except the NOTE TAKER, *the* GENTLEMAN, *and the* FLOWER GIRL, *who sits arranging her basket, and still pitying herself in murmurs.*

THE FLOWER GIRL. Poor girl! Hard enough for her to live without being worried and chivied.[18]

THE GENTLEMAN [*returning to his former place on the* NOTE TAKER*'s left*] How do you do it, if I may ask?

THE NOTE TAKER. Simply phonetics. The science of speech. Thats my profession: also my hobby. Happy is the man who can make a living by his hobby! You can spot an Irishman or a Yorkshireman by his brogue. *I* can place any man within six miles. I can place him within two miles in London. Sometimes within two streets.

THE FLOWER GIRL. Ought to be ashamed of himself, unmanly coward.

THE GENTLEMAN. But is there a living in that?

THE NOTE TAKER. Oh yes. Quite a fat one. This is an age of upstarts. Men begin in Kentish Town with £80 a year, and end in Park Lane with a hundred thousand. They want to drop Kentish Town; but they give themselves away every time they open their mouths. Now I can teach them—

THE FLOWER GIRL. Let him mind his own business and leave a poor girl—

THE NOTE TAKER [*Explosively*] Woman: cease this detestable boohooing instantly; or else seek the shelter of some other place of worship.

---

17. **character:** reputation.

18. **worried and chivied:** worried and tormented.

THE FLOWER GIRL [*with feeble defiance*] Ive a right to be here if I like, same as you.

THE NOTE TAKER. A woman who utters such depressing and disgusting sounds has no right to be anywhere—no right to live. Remember that you are a human being with a soul and the divine gift of articulate speech: that your native language is the language of Shakespear and Milton and The Bible; and dont sit there crooning like a bilious pigeon.

THE FLOWER GIRL [*quite overwhelmed, looking up at him in mingled wonder and deprecation without daring to raise her head*] Ah-ah-ah-ow-ow-ow-oo!

THE NOTE TAKER [*whipping out his book*] Heavens! what a sound! [*He writes; then holds out the book and reads, reproducing her vowels exactly*] Ah-ah-ah-ow-ow-ow-oo!

THE FLOWER GIRL [*tickled by the performance, and laughing in spite of herself*] Garn![19]

THE NOTE TAKER. You see this creature with her kerbstone English: the English that will keep

_____

19. **Garn!**: "Go on!"

her in the gutter to the end of her days. Well, sir, in three months I could pass that girl off as a duchess at an ambassador's garden party. I could even get her a place as lady's maid or shop assistant, which requires better English.

THE FLOWER GIRL. What's that you say?

THE NOTE TAKER. Yes, you squashed cabbage leaf, you disgrace to the noble architecture of these columns, you incarnate insult to the English language: I could pass you off as the Queen of Sheba. [*To the* GENTLEMAN] Can you believe that?

THE GENTLEMAN. Of course I can. I am myself a student of Indian dialects; and—

THE NOTE TAKER [*eagerly*] Are you? Do you know Colonel Pickering, the author of Spoken Sanscrit?

THE GENTLEMAN. I am Colonel Pickering. Who are you?

THE NOTE TAKER. Henry Higgins, author of Higgins's Universal Alphabet.

PICKERING [*with enthusiasm*] I came from India to meet you.

HIGGINS. I was going to India to meet you.

PICKERING. Where do you live?

HIGGINS. 27A Wimpole Street. Come and see me tomorrow.

PICKERING. I'm at the Carlton. Come with me now and lets have a jaw[20] over some supper.

HIGGINS. Right you are.

THE FLOWER GIRL [to PICKERING, *as he passes her*] Buy a flower, kind gentleman. I'm short for my lodging.

PICKERING. I really havnt any change. I'm sorry [*he goes away*].

HIGGINS [*shocked at the* GIRL's *mendacity*[21]] Liar. You said you could change half-a-crown.

THE FLOWER GIRL [*rising in desperation*] You ought to be stuffed with nails, you ought. [*Flinging the basket at his feet*] Take the whole blooming basket for sixpence.

The church clock strikes the second quarter.

HIGGINS [*hearing in it the voice of God, rebuking him for his Pharisaic*[22] *want of charity to the poor girl*] A reminder. [*He raises his hat solemnly; then throws a handful of money into the basket and follows* PICKERING].

THE FLOWER GIRL [*picking up a half-crown*] Ah-ow-ooh! [*Picking up a couple of florins*] Aaah-ow-ooh! [*Picking up several coins*] Aaaaah-ow-ooh! [*Picking up a half-sovereign*] Aaaaaaaaaaaah-ow-ooh!!!

FREDDY [*springing out of a taxicab*] Got one at last. Hallo! [*To the* GIRL] Where are the two ladies that were here?

THE FLOWER GIRL. They walked to the bus when the rain stopped.

---

20. **jaw:** slang for *chat.*
21. **mendacity:** lying.
22. **Pharisaic** [far′ə sā′ik]: alluding to the Pharisees, a group among the ancient Jews known for their strictness.

FREDDY. And left me with a cab on my hands! Damnation!

THE FLOWER GIRL [*with grandeur*] Never mind, young man. I'm going home in a taxi. [*She sails off to the cab. The driver puts his hand behind him and holds the door firmly shut against her. Quite understanding his mistrust, she shews him her handful of money*]. A taxi fare aint no object to me, Charlie. [*He grins and opens the door*]. Here. What about the basket?

THE TAXIMAN. Give it here. Tuppence extra.

LIZA. No: I dont want nobody to see it. [*She crushes it into the cab and gets in, continuing the conversation through the window*] Goodbye, Freddy.

FREDDY [*dazedly raising his hat*] Goodbye.

TAXIMAN. Where to?

LIZA. Bucknam Pellis [Buckingham Palace].

TAXIMAN. What d'ye mean—Bucknam Pellis?

LIZA. Dont you know where it is? In the Green Park, where the King lives. Goodbye, Freddy. Dont let me keep you standing there. Goodbye.

FREDDY. Goodbye. [*He goes*].

TAXIMAN. Here? Whats this about Bucknam Pellis? What business have you at Bucknam Pellis?

LIZA. Of course I havnt none. But I wasnt going to let him know that. You drive me home.

TAXIMAN. And wheres home?

LIZA. Angel Court, Drury Lane, next Meiklejohn's oil shop.

TAXIMAN. That sounds more like it, Judy. [*He drives off*].

* * * * * *

Let us follow the taxi to the entrance to Angel Court, a narrow little archway between two shops, one of them Meiklejohn's oil shop. When it stops there, Eliza gets out, dragging her basket with her.

LIZA. How much?

TAXIMAN [*indicating the taximeter*] Cant you read? A shilling.

LIZA. A shilling for two minutes!!

TAXIMAN. Two minutes or ten: it's all the same.

LIZA. Well, I dont call it right.

TAXIMAN. Ever been in a taxi before?

LIZA [*with dignity*] Hundreds and thousands of times, young man.

TAXIMAN [*laughing at her*] Good for you, Judy. Keep the shilling, darling, with best love from all at home. Good luck! [*He drives off*].

LIZA [*humiliated*] Impidence!

She picks up the basket and trudges up the alley with it to her lodging: a small room with very old wall paper hanging loose in the damp places. A broken pane in the window is mended with paper. A portrait of a popular actor and a fashion plate of ladies' dresses, all wildly beyond poor ELIZA'S *means, both torn from newspapers, are pinned up on the wall. A birdcage hangs in the window; but its tenant died long ago: it remains as a memorial only.*

These are the only visible luxuries: the rest is the irreducible minimum of poverty's needs: a wretched bed heaped with all sorts of coverings that have any warmth in them, a draped packing case with a basin and jug on it and a little looking glass over it, a chair and table, the refuse of some suburban kitchen, and an American alarum clock on the shelf above the unused fireplace: the whole lighted with a gas lamp with a penny in the slot meter. Rent: four shillings a week.

Here Eliza, chronically weary, but too excited to go to bed, sits, counting her new riches and dreaming and planning what to do with them, until the gas goes out, when she enjoys for the first time the sensation of being able to put in another penny without grudging it. This prodigal[23] mood does not extinguish her gnawing sense of the need for economy sufficiently to prevent her from calculating that she can dream and plan in bed more cheaply and warmly than sitting up without a fire. So she takes off her shawl and skirt and adds them to the miscellaneous bedclothes. Then she kicks off her shoes and gets into bed without any further change.

---

23. **prodigal:** extravagant, spendthrift.

STUDY QUESTIONS

Recalling
1. What is Higgins writing down when he first appears? What is Liza's reaction to his activities?
2. Why is the crowd suspicious of Higgins at first? What skill does he demonstrate to win them over? How does he make his living?
3. Why is Higgins offended by Liza? What does he say will keep her in the gutter all her life? What boasts does he make about her?
4. Describe Liza's mood when she goes to bed.

Interpreting
5. Explain how Liza's speech and behavior show that she comes from a different class from the mother and daughter she meets in the beginning of Act I.
6. What are your impressions of Liza and of Higgins in Act I? What seems most important to each? How does each treat other people? In what other ways are they different?
7. What effect does Shaw create by using labels rather than names for the characters through most of Act I?

Extending
8. Why do you think people often base their impressions of others on the way they speak? Why might it be difficult to change one's accent?

ACT TWO

Next day at 11 A.M. HIGGINS's *laboratory in Wimpole Street. It is a room on the first floor, looking on the street, and was meant for the drawing room. The double doors are in the middle of the back wall; and persons entering find in the corner to their right two tall file cabinets at right angles to one another against the walls. In this corner stands a flat writing-table, on which are a phonograph, a laryngoscope,[1] a row of tiny organ pipes with a bellows, a set of lamp chimneys for singing flames with burners attached to a gas plug in the wall by an indiarubber tube, several tuning-forks of different sizes, a life-size image of half a human head, shewing in section the vocal organs, and a box containing a supply of wax cylinders for the phonograph.*

Further down the room, on the same side, is a fireplace, with a comfortable leather-covered easy-chair at the side of the hearth nearest the door, and a coal-scuttle. There is a clock on the mantlepiece. Between the fireplace and the phonograph table is a stand for newspapers.

On the other side of the central door, to the left of the visitor, is a cabinet of shallow drawers. On it is a telephone and the telephone directory. The corner beyond, and most of the side wall, is occupied by a grand piano, with the keyboard at the end furthest from the door, and a bench for the players extending the full length of the keyboard. On the piano is a dessert dish heaped with fruit and sweets, mostly chocolates.

The middle of the room is clear. Besides the easy-chair, the piano bench, and two chairs at the phonograph table, there is one stray chair. It stands near the fireplace. On the walls, engravings: mostly Piranesis[2] and mezzotint[3] portraits. No paintings.

PICKERING *is seated at the table, putting down some cards and a tuning-fork which he has been using.* HIGGINS *is standing up near him, closing two or three file drawers which are hanging out. He appears in the morning light as a robust, vital, appetizing sort of man of forty or thereabouts, dressed in a professional-looking black frock-coat with a white linen collar and black silk tie. He is of energetic, scientific type, heartily, even violently interested in everything that can be studied as a scientific subject, and careless about himself and other people, including their feelings. He is, in fact, but for his years and size, rather like a very impetuous baby "taking notice" eagerly and loudly, and requiring almost as much watching to keep him out of unintended mischief. His manner varies from genial bullying when he is in a good humor to stormy petulance when anything goes wrong; but he is so entirely frank and void of malice that he remains likeable even in his least reasonable moments.*

HIGGINS [*as he shuts the last drawer*] Well, I think thats the whole show.

PICKERING. It's really amazing. I havnt taken half of it in, you know.

HIGGINS. Would you like to go over any of it again?

PICKERING [*rising and coming to the fireplace, where he plants himself with his back to the fire*] No, thank you: not now. I'm quite done up for this morning.

HIGGINS [*following him, and standing beside him on his left*] Tired of listening to sounds?

PICKERING. Yes. It's a fearful strain. I rather fancied myself because I can pronounce twenty-four distinct vowel sounds; but your hundred

---

1. **laryngoscope** [lə rin′ gə skōp]: instrument for examining the throat.
2. **Piranesis** [pēr′ ə nā′zēz]: works of the Italian artist Giambattista Piranesi (1720–1778).

3. **mezzotint** [met′sō tint]: engraving made from a metal plate, producing an effect of light and shade.

and thirty beat me. I cant hear a bit of difference between most of them.

HIGGINS [chuckling, and going over to the piano to eat sweets] Oh, that comes with practice. You hear no difference at first; but you keep on listening, and presently you find theyre all as different as A from B. [MRS PEARCE looks in: she is HIGGINS's housekeeper]. Whats the matter?

MRS PEARCE [hesitating, evidently perplexed] A young woman asks to see you, sir.

HIGGINS. A young woman! What does she want?

MRS PEARCE. Well, sir, she says youll be glad to see her when you know what she's come about. She's quite a common girl, sir. Very common indeed. I should have sent her away, only I thought perhaps you wanted her to talk into your machines. I hope Ive not done wrong; but really you see such queer people sometimes—youll excuse me, I'm sure, sir—

HIGGINS. Oh, thats all right, Mrs Pearce. Has she an interesting accent?

MRS PEARCE. Oh, something dreadful, sir, really. I dont know how you can take an interest in it.

HIGGINS [to PICKERING] Lets have her up. Shew her up, Mrs Pearce [he rushes across to his working table and picks out a cylinder to use on the phonograph].

MRS PEARCE [only half resigned to it] Very well, sir. It's for you to say. [She goes downstairs].

HIGGINS. This is rather a bit of luck. I'll shew you how I make records. We'll set her talking; and I'll take it down first in Bell's Visible Speech; then in broad Romic; and then we'll get her on the phonograph so that you can turn her on as often as you like with the written transcript before you.

MRS PEARCE [returning] This is the young woman, sir.

The FLOWER GIRL enters in state. She has a hat with three ostrich feathers, orange, sky-blue, and red. She has a nearly clean apron, and the shoddy coat has been tidied a little. The pathos of this deplorable figure, with its innocent vanity and consequential air, touches PICKERING, who has already straightened himself in the presence of MRS PEARCE. But as to HIGGINS, the only distinction he makes between men and women is that when he is neither bullying nor exclaiming to the heavens against some feather-weight cross,[4] he coaxes women as a child coaxes its nurse when it wants to get anything out of her.

HIGGINS [brusquely, recognizing her with unconcealed disappointment, and at once, babylike, making an intolerable grievance of it] Why, this is the girl I jotted down last night. She's no use: Ive got all the records I want of the Lisson Grove lingo; and I'm not going to waste another cylinder on it. [To the GIRL] Be off with you: I dont want you.

THE FLOWER GIRL. Dont you be so saucy. You aint heard what I come for yet. [To MRS PEARCE, who is waiting at the door for further instructions] Did you tell him I come in a taxi?

MRS PEARCE. Nonsense, girl! What do you think a gentleman like Mr Higgins cares what you came in?

THE FLOWER GIRL. Oh, we are proud! He aint above giving lessons, not him: I heard him say so. Well, I aint come here to ask for any compliment; and if my money's not good enough I can go elsewhere.

HIGGINS. Good enough for what?

THE FLOWER GIRL. Good enough for yə-oo. Now you know, dont you? I'm come to have lessons, I am. And to pay for em tə-oo: make no mistake.

HIGGINS [stupent[5]] Well!!! [Recovering his breath with a gasp] What do you expect me to say to you?

_____

4. **feather-weight cross:** a very minor burden to bear.
5. **stupent:** amazed.

THE FLOWER GIRL. Well, if you was a gentleman, you might ask me to sit down, I think. Dont I tell you I'm bringing you business?

HIGGINS. Pickering: shall we ask this baggage to sit down, or shall we throw her out of the window?

THE FLOWER GIRL [running away in terror to the piano, where she turns at bay] Ah-ah-oh-ow-ow-ow-oo! [Wounded and whimpering] I wont be called a baggage when Ive offered to pay like any lady.

Motionless, the two men stare at her from the other side of the room, amazed.

PICKERING [gently] But what is it you want?

THE FLOWER GIRL. I want to be a lady in a flower shop stead of sellin at the corner of Tottenham Court Road. But they wont take me unless I can talk more genteel. He said he could teach me. Well, here I am ready to pay him—not asking any favor—and he treats me zif[6] I was dirt.

MRS PEARCE. How can you be such a foolish ignorant girl as to think you could afford to pay Mr Higgins?

THE FLOWER GIRL. Why shouldnt I? I know what lessons cost as well as you do; and I'm ready to pay.

HIGGINS. How much?

THE FLOWER GIRL [coming back to him, triumphant] Now youre talking! I thought youd come off it when you saw a chance of getting back a bit of what you chucked at me last night. [Confidentially] Youd had a drop in,[7] hadnt you?

HIGGINS [peremptorily] Sit down.

THE FLOWER GIRL. Oh, if youre going to make a compliment of it—

HIGGINS [thundering at her] Sit down.

MRS PEARCE [severely] Sit down, girl. Do as youre told.

THE FLOWER GIRL. Ah-ah-ah-ow-ow-oo! [She stands, half rebellious, half bewildered].

PICKERING [very courteous] Wont you sit down? [He places the stray chair near the hearthrug between himself and HIGGINS].

LIZA [coyly] Dont mind if I do. [She sits down. PICKERING returns to the hearthrug].

HIGGINS. Whats your name?

THE FLOWER GIRL. Liza Doolittle.

HIGGINS [declaiming gravely]
Eliza, Elizabeth, Betsy and Bess,
They went to the woods to get a bird's nes':

PICKERING. They found a nest with four eggs in it:

HIGGINS. They took one apiece, and left three in it.

They laugh heartily at their own fun.

LIZA. Oh, dont be silly.

MRS PEARCE [placing herself behind ELIZA's chair] You mustnt speak to the gentleman like that.

LIZA. Well, why wont he speak sensible to me?

HIGGINS. Come back to business. How much do you propose to pay me for the lessons?

LIZA. Oh, I know whats right. A lady friend of mine gets French lessons for eighteenpence an hour from a real French gentleman. Well, you wouldnt have the face to ask me the same for teaching me my own language as you would for French; so I wont give more than a shilling.[8] Take it or leave it.

HIGGINS [walking up and down the room, rattling his keys and his cash in his pockets] You know, Pickering, if you consider a shilling, not as a simple shilling, but as a percentage of this

---

6. **zif:** "as if."
7. **had a drop in:** been drinking.

8. **a shilling:** equivalent to about thirty cents.

girl's income, it works out as fully equivalent to sixty or seventy guineas[9] from a millionaire.

PICKERING. How so?

HIGGINS. Figure it out. A millionaire has about £150 a day. She earns about half-a-crown.

LIZA [*haughtily*] Who told you I only—

HIGGINS [*continuing*] She offers me two-fifths of her day's income for a lesson. Two-fifths of a millionaire's income for a day would be somewhere about £60. It's handsome. By George, it's enormous! it's the biggest offer I ever had.

LIZA [*rising, terrified*] Sixty pounds! What are you talking? I never offered you sixty pounds. Where would I get—

HIGGINS. Hold your tongue.

LIZA [*weeping*] But I aint got sixty pounds. Oh—

MRS PEARCE. Dont cry, you silly girl. Sit down. Nobody is going to touch your money.

HIGGINS. Somebody is going to touch you, with a broomstick, if you dont stop snivelling. Sit down.

LIZA [*obeying slowly*] Ah-ah-ah-ow-oo-o! One would think you was my father.

HIGGINS. If I decide to teach you, I'll be worse than two fathers to you. Here [*he offers her his silk handkerchief*]!

LIZA. Whats this for?

HIGGINS. To wipe your eyes. To wipe any part of your face that feels moist. Remember: thats your handkerchief; and thats your sleeve. Dont mistake the one for the other if you wish to become a lady in a shop.

LIZA, *utterly bewildered, stares helplessly at him.*

MRS PEARCE. It's no use talking to her like that, Mr Higgins: she doesnt understand you. Besides, youre quite wrong: she doesnt do it that way at all [*she takes the handkerchief*].

LIZA [*snatching it*] Here! You give me that handkerchief. He gev it to me, not to you.

PICKERING [*laughing*] He did. I think it must be regarded as her property, Mrs Pearce.

MRS PEARCE [*resigning herself*] Serve you right, Mr Higgins.

PICKERING. Higgins: I'm interested. What about the ambassador's garden party? I'll say youre the greatest teacher alive if you make that good. I'll bet you all the expenses of the experiment you cant do it. And I'll pay for the lessons.

LIZA. Oh, you are real good. Thank you, Captain.

HIGGINS [*tempted, looking at her*] It's almost irresistible. She's so deliciously low—so horribly dirty—

LIZA [*protesting extremely*] Ah-ah-ah-ah-ow-ow-oo-oo!!! I aint dirty: I washed my face and hands afore I come, I did.

PICKERING. Youre certainly not going to turn her head with flattery, Higgins.

MRS PEARCE [*uneasy*] Oh, dont say that, sir: theres more ways than one of turning a girl's head; and nobody can do it better than Mr Higgins, though he may not always mean it. I do hope, sir, you wont encourage him to do anything foolish.

HIGGINS [*becoming excited as the idea grows on him*] What is life but a series of inspired follies? The difficulty is to find them to do. Never lose a chance: it doesnt come every day. I shall make a duchess of this draggletailed guttersnipe.

LIZA [*strongly deprecating this view of her*] Ah-ah-ah-ow-ow-oo!

HIGGINS [*carried away*] Yes: in six months—in three if she has a good ear and a quick tongue—I'll take her anywhere and pass her off as anything. We'll start today: now! this

---

9. **sixty . . . guineas:** equivalent to about $250.

moment! Take her away and clean her, Mrs Pearce. Monkey Brand,[10] if it wont come off any other way. Is there a good fire in the kitchen?

MRS PEARCE [*protesting*] Yes; but—

HIGGINS [*storming on*] Take all her clothes off and burn them. Ring up Whitely or somebody for new ones. Wrap her up in brown paper til they come.

LIZA. Youre no gentleman, youre not, to talk of such things. I'm a good girl, I am; and I know what the like of you are, I do.

HIGGINS. We want none of your Lisson Grove prudery here, young woman. Youve got to learn to behave like a duchess. Take her away, Mrs Pearce. If she gives you any trouble, wallop her.

LIZA [*springing up and running between* PICKERING *and* MRS PEARCE *for protection*] No! I'll call the police, I will.

MRS PEARCE. But Ive no place to put her.

HIGGINS. Put her in the dustbin.[11]

LIZA. Ah-ah-ah-ow-ow-oo!

PICKERING. Oh come, Higgins! be reasonable.

MRS PEARCE [*resolutely*] You must be reasonable, Mr Higgins: really you must. You cant walk over everybody like this.

HIGGINS, *thus scolded, subsides. The hurricane is succeeded by a zephyr of amiable surprise.*

HIGGINS [*with professional exquisiteness of modulation*] I walk over everybody! My dear Mrs Pearce, my dear Pickering, I never had the slightest intention of walking over anyone. All I propose is that we should be kind to this poor girl. We must help her to prepare and fit herself for her new station in life. If I did not express myself clearly it was because I did not wish to hurt her delicacy, or yours.

---

10. **Monkey Brand:** harsh cleaning agent.
11. **dustbin:** garbage can.

LIZA, *reassured, steals back to her chair.*

MRS PEARCE [*to* PICKERING] Well, did you ever hear anything like that, sir?

PICKERING [*laughing heartily*] Never, Mrs Pearce: never.

HIGGINS [*patiently*] Whats the matter?

MRS PEARCE. Well, the matter is, sir, that you cant take a girl up like that as if you were picking up a pebble on the beach.

HIGGINS. Why not?

MRS PEARCE. Why not! But you dont know anything about her. What about her parents? She may be married.

LIZA. Garn!

HIGGINS. There! As the girl very properly says, Garn! Married indeed! Dont you know that a woman of that class looks a worn out drudge of fifty a year after she's married?

LIZA. Whood marry me?

HIGGINS [*suddenly resorting to the most thrillingly beautiful low tones in his best elocutionary style*] By George, Eliza, the streets will be strewn with the bodies of men shooting themselves for your sake before Ive done with you.

MRS PEARCE. Nonsense, sir. You mustnt talk like that to her.

LIZA [*rising and squaring herself determinedly*] I'm going away. He's off his chump, he is. I dont want no balmies teaching me.

HIGGINS [*wounded in his tenderest point by her insensibility to his elocution*] Oh, indeed! I'm mad, am I? Very well, Mrs Pearce: you neednt order the new clothes for her. Throw her out.

LIZA [*whimpering*] Nah-ow. You got no right to touch me.

MRS PEARCE. You see now what comes of being saucy. [*Indicating the door*] This way, please.

LIZA [*almost in tears*] I didnt want no clothes.

I wouldnt have taken them [*she throws away the handkerchief*]. I can buy my own clothes.

HIGGINS [*deftly retrieving the handkerchief and intercepting her on her reluctant way to the door*] Youre an ungrateful wicked girl. This is my return for offering to take you out of the gutter and dress you beautifully and make a lady of you.

MRS PEARCE. Stop, Mr Higgins. I wont allow it. It's you that are wicked. Go home to your parents, girl; and tell them to take better care of you.

LIZA. I aint got no parents. They told me I was big enough to earn my own living and turned me out.

MRS PEARCE. Wheres your mother?

LIZA. I aint got no mother. Her that turned me out was my sixth stepmother. But I done without them. And I'm a good girl, I am.

HIGGINS. Very well, then, what on earth is all this fuss about? The girl doesnt belong to anybody—is no use to anybody but me. [*He goes to* MRS PEARCE *and begins coaxing*]. You can adopt her, Mrs Pearce: I'm sure a daughter would be a great amusement to you. Now dont make any more fuss. Take her downstairs; and—

MRS PEARCE. But whats to become of her? Is she to be paid anything? Do be sensible, sir.

HIGGINS. Oh, pay her whatever is necessary: put it down in the housekeeping book. [*Impatiently*] What on earth will she want with money? She'll have her food and her clothes. She'll only drink if you give her money.

LIZA [*turning on him*] Oh you are a brute. It's a lie: nobody ever saw the sign of liquor on me. [*To* PICKERING] Oh, sir: youre a gentleman: dont let him speak to me like that.

PICKERING [*in good-humored remonstrance*] Does it occur to you, Higgins, that the girl has some feelings?

HIGGINS [*looking critically at her*] Oh no, I dont think so. Not any feelings that we need bother about. [*Cheerily*] Have you, Eliza?

LIZA. I got my feelings same as anyone else.

HIGGINS [*to* PICKERING, *reflectively*] You see the difficulty?

PICKERING. Eh? What difficulty?

HIGGINS. To get her to talk grammar. The mere pronunciation is easy enough.

LIZA. I dont want to talk grammar. I want to talk like a lady in a flower-shop.

MRS PEARCE. Will you please keep to the point, Mr Higgins. I want to know on what terms the girl is to be here. Is she to have any wages? And what is to become of her when youve finished your teaching? You must look ahead a little.

HIGGINS [*impatiently*] Whats to become of her if I leave her in the gutter? Tell me that, Mrs Pearce.

MRS PEARCE. Thats her own business, not yours, Mr Higgins.

HIGGINS. Well, when Ive done with her, we can throw her back into the gutter; and then it will be her own business again; so thats all right.

LIZA. Oh, youve no feeling heart in you: you dont care for nothing but yourself. [*She rises and takes the floor resolutely*]. Here! Ive had enough of this. I'm going [*making for the door*]. You ought to be ashamed of yourself, you ought.

HIGGINS [*snatching a chocolate cream from the piano, his eyes suddenly beginning to twinkle with mischief*] Have some chocolates, Eliza.

LIZA [*halting, tempted*] How do I know what might be in them? Ive heard of girls being drugged by the like of you.

HIGGINS *whips out his penknife; cuts a chocolate in two; puts one half into his mouth and bolts it; and offers her the other half.*

HIGGINS. Pledge of good faith, Eliza. I eat one half: you eat the other. [LIZA *opens her mouth to retort: he pops the half chocolate into it*]. You shall have boxes of them, barrels of them, every day. You shall live on them. Eh?

LIZA [*who has disposed of the chocolate after being nearly choked by it*] I wouldnt have ate it, only I'm too ladylike to take it out of my mouth.

HIGGINS. Listen, Eliza. I think you said you came in a taxi.

LIZA. Well, what if I did? Ive as good a right to take a taxi as anyone else.

HIGGINS. You have, Eliza; and in future you shall have as many taxis as you want. You shall go up and down and round the town in a taxi every day. Think of that, Eliza.

MRS PEARCE. Mr Higgins: youre tempting the girl. It's not right. She should think of the future.

HIGGINS. At her age! Nonsense! Time enough to think of the future when you havnt any future to think of. No, Eliza: do as this lady does: think of other people's futures; but never think of your own. Think of chocolates, and taxis, and gold, and diamonds.

LIZA. No: I dont want no gold and no diamonds. I'm a good girl, I am. [*She sits down again, with an attempt at dignity*].

HIGGINS. You shall remain so, Eliza, under the care of Mrs Pearce. And you shall marry an officer in the Guards, with a beautiful moustache: the son of a marquis, who will disinherit him for marrying you, but will relent when he sees your beauty and goodness—

PICKERING. Excuse me, Higgins; but I really must interfere. Mrs Pearce is quite right. If this girl is to put herself in your hands for six months for an experiment in teaching, she must understand thoroughly what she's doing.

HIGGINS. How can she? She's incapable of understanding anything. Besides, do any of us understand what we are doing? If we did, would we ever do it?

PICKERING. Very clever, Higgins; but not to the present point. [*To* ELIZA] Miss Doolittle—

LIZA [*overwhelmed*] Ah-ah-ow-oo!

HIGGINS. There! Thats all youll get out of Eliza. Ah-ah-ow-oo! No use explaining. As a military man you ought to know that. Give her her orders: thats enough for her. Eliza: you are to live here for the next six months, learning how to speak beautifully, like a lady in a florist's shop. If youre good and do whatever youre told, you shall sleep in a proper bedroom, and have lots to eat, and money to buy chocolates and take rides in taxis. If youre naughty and idle you will sleep in the back kitchen among the black beetles, and be walloped by Mrs Pearce with a broomstick. At the end of six months you shall go to Buckingham Palace in a carriage, beautifully dressed. If the King finds out youre not a lady, you will be taken by the police to the Tower of London, where your head will be cut off as a warning to other presumptuous flower girls. If you are not found out, you shall have a present of seven-and-six-pence to start life with as a lady in a shop. If you refuse this offer you will be a most ungrateful wicked girl; and the angels will weep for you. [*To* PICKERING] Now are you satisfied, Pickering? [*To* MRS PEARCE] Can I put it more plainly and fairly, Mrs Pearce?

MRS PEARCE [*patiently*] I think youd better let me speak to the girl properly in private. I dont know that I can take charge of her or consent to the arrangement at all. Of course I know you dont mean her any harm; but when you get what you call interested in people's accents, you never think or care what may happen to them or you. Come with me, Eliza.

HIGGINS. Thats all right. Thank you, Mrs Pearce. Bundle her off to the bath-room.

LIZA [*rising reluctantly and suspiciously*] Youre a great bully, you are. I wont stay here if I dont like. I wont let nobody wallop me. I never asked to go to Bucknam Palace, I didnt. I was never in trouble with the police, not me. I'm a good girl—

MRS PEARCE. Dont answer back, girl. You dont understand the gentleman. Come with me. [*She leads the way to the door, and holds it open for* ELIZA].

LIZA [*as she goes out*] Well, what I say is right. I wont go near the King, not if I'm going to have my head cut off. If I'd known what I was letting myself in for, I wouldnt have come here. I always been a good girl; and I never offered to say a word to him; and I dont owe him nothing; and I dont care; and I wont be put upon; and I have my feelings the same as anyone else—

MRS PEARCE *shuts the door; and* ELIZA's *plaints are no longer audible.*

    *   *   *   *   *   *

Eliza is taken upstairs to the third floor greatly to her surprise; for she expected to be taken down to the scullery.[12] There Mrs Pearce opens a door and takes her into a spare bedroom.

12. **scullery:** workroom adjoining a kitchen, used for cleaning utensils and other rough kitchen work.

MRS PEARCE. I will have to put you here. This will be your bedroom.

LIZA. O-h, I couldnt sleep here, missus. It's too good for the likes of me. I should be afraid to touch anything. I aint a duchess yet, you know.

MRS PEARCE. You have got to make yourself as clean as the room: then you wont be afraid of it. And you must call me Mrs Pearce, not missus. [*She throws open the door of the dressing-room, now modernized as a bathroom*].

LIZA. Gawd! whats this? Is this where you wash clothes? Funny sort of copper[13] I call it.

MRS PEARCE. It is not a copper. This is where we wash ourselves, Eliza, and where I am going to wash you.

LIZA. You expect me to get into that and wet myself all over! Not me. I should catch my death. I knew a woman did it every Saturday night; and she died of it.

13. **copper:** large tub for washing clothes.

MRS PEARCE. Mr Higgins has the gentlemen's bathroom downstairs; and he has a bath every morning, in cold water.

LIZA. Ugh! He's made of iron, that man.

MRS PEARCE. If you are to sit with him and the Colonel and be taught you will have to do the same. They wont like the smell of you if you dont. But you can have the water as hot as you like. There are two taps: hot and cold.

LIZA [weeping] I couldnt. I dursnt. Its not natural: it would kill me. Ive never had a bath in my life: not what youd call a proper one.

MRS PEARCE. Well, dont you want to be clean and sweet and decent, like a lady? You know you cant be a nice girl inside if youre a dirty slut outside.

LIZA. Boohoo!!!!

MRS PEARCE. Now stop crying and go back into your room and take off all your clothes. Then wrap yourself in this [Taking down a gown from its peg and handing it to her] and come back to me. I will get the bath ready.

LIZA [all tears] I cant. I wont. I'm not used to it. Ive never took off all my clothes before. It's not right: it's not decent.

MRS PEARCE. Nonsense, child. Dont you take off all your clothes every night when you go to bed?

LIZA [amazed] No. Why should I? I should catch my death. Of course I take off my skirt.

MRS PEARCE. Do you mean that you sleep in the underclothes you wear in the daytime?

LIZA. What else have I to sleep in?

MRS PEARCE. You will never do that again as long as you live here. I will get you a proper nightdress.

LIZA. Do you mean change into cold things and lie awake shivering half the night? You want to kill me, you do.

MRS PEARCE. I want to change you from a frowzy slut to a clean respectable girl fit to sit with the gentlemen in the study. Are you going to trust me and do what I tell you or be thrown out and sent back to your flower basket?

LIZA. But you dont know what the cold is to me. You dont know how I dread it.

MRS PEARCE. Your bed won't be cold here: I will put a hot water bottle in it. [Pushing her into the bedroom] Off with you and undress.

LIZA. Oh, if only I'd known what a dreadful thing it is to be clean I'd never have come. I didnt know when I was well off. I— [MRS PEARCE pushes her through the door, but leaves it partly open lest her prisoner should take to flight].

MRS PEARCE puts on a pair of white rubber sleeves, and fills the bath, mixing hot and cold, and testing the result with the bath thermometer. She perfumes it with a handful of bath salts and adds a palmful of mustard. She then takes a formidable looking long handled scrubbing brush and soaps it profusely with a ball of scented soap.

ELIZA comes back with nothing on but the bath gown huddled tightly round her, a piteous spectacle of abject terror.

MRS PEARCE. Now come along. Take that thing off.

LIZA. Oh I couldnt, Mrs Pearce: I reely couldnt. I never done such a thing.

MRS PEARCE. Nonsense. Here: step in and tell me whether it's hot enough for you.

LIZA. Ah-oo! Ah-oo! It's too hot.

MRS PEARCE [deftly snatching the gown away and throwing ELIZA down on her back]. It wont hurt you. [She sets to work with the scrubbing brush].

ELIZA's screams are heartrending.

* * * * * *

Meanwhile the Colonel has been having it out with Higgins about Eliza. Pickering has come from the hearth to the chair and seated himself astride of it with his arms on the back to cross-examine him.

PICKERING. Excuse the straight question, Higgins. Are you a man of good character where women are concerned?

HIGGINS [*moodily*] Have you ever met a man of good character where women are concerned?

PICKERING. Yes: very frequently.

HIGGINS [*dogmatically, lifting himself on his hands to the level of the piano, and sitting on it with a bounce*] Well, I havnt. I find that the moment I let a woman make friends with me, she becomes jealous, exacting, suspicious, and a damned nuisance. I find that the moment I let myself make friends with a woman, I become selfish and tyrannical. Women upset everything. When you let them into your life, you find that the woman is driving at one thing and youre driving at another.

PICKERING. At what, for example?

HIGGINS [*coming off the piano restlessly*] Oh, Lord knows! I suppose the woman wants to live her own life; and the man wants to live his; and each tries to drag the other on to the wrong track. One wants to go north and the other south; and the result is that both have to go east, though they both hate the east wind. [*He sits down on the bench at the keyboard*]. So here I am, a confirmed old bachelor, and likely to remain so.

PICKERING [*rising and standing over him gravely*] Come, Higgins! You know what I mean. If I'm to be in this business I shall feel responsible for that girl. I hope it's understood that no advantage is to be taken of her position.

HIGGINS. What! That thing! Sacred, I assure you. [*Rising to explain*] You see, she'll be a pupil; and teaching would be impossible unless pupils were sacred. Ive taught scores of American millionairesses how to speak English: the best looking women in the world. I'm seasoned.

They might as well be blocks of wood. I might as well be a block of wood. It's—

MRS PEARCE *opens the door. She has* ELIZA's *hat in her hand.* PICKERING *retires to the easy-chair at the hearth and sits down.*

HIGGINS [*eagerly*] Well, Mrs Pearce: is it all right?

MRS PEARCE [*at the door*] I just wish to trouble you with a word, if I may, Mr Higgins.

HIGGINS. Yes, certainly. Come in. [*She comes forward*]. Dont burn that, Mrs Pearce. I'll keep it as a curiosity. [*He takes the hat*].

MRS PEARCE. Handle it carefully, sir, please. I had to promise her not to burn it; but I had better put it in the oven for a while.

HIGGINS [*putting it down hastily on the piano*] Oh! thank you. Well, what have you to say to me?

PICKERING. Am I in the way?

MRS PEARCE. Not in the least, sir. Mr Higgins: will you please be very particular what you say before the girl?

HIGGINS [*sternly*] Of course. I'm always particular about what I say. Why do you say this to me?

MRS PEARCE [*unmoved*] No, sir: youre not at all particular when youve mislaid anything or when you get a little impatient. Now it doesnt matter before me: I'm used to it. But you really must not swear before the girl.

HIGGINS [*indignantly*] I swear! [*Most emphatically*] I never swear. I detest the habit. What the devil do you mean?

MRS PEARCE [*stolidly*] Thats what I mean, sir. You swear a great deal too much. I dont mind your damning and blasting, and what the devil and where the devil and who the devil—

HIGGINS. Mrs Pearce: this language from your lips! Really!

MRS PEARCE [*not to be put off*]—but there is a

certain word[14] I must ask you not to use. The girl used it herself when she began to enjoy the bath. It begins with the same letter as bath. She knows no better: she learnt it at her mother's knee. But she must not hear it from your lips.

HIGGINS [*loftily*] I cannot charge myself with having ever uttered it, Mrs Pearce. [*She looks at him steadfastly. He adds, hiding an uneasy conscience with a judicial air*] Except perhaps in a moment of extreme and justifiable excitement.

MRS PEARCE. Only this morning, sir, you applied it to your boots, to the butter, and to the brown bread.

HIGGINS. Oh, that! Mere alliteration, Mrs Pearce, natural to a poet.

MRS PEARCE. Well, sir, whatever you choose to call it, I beg you not to let the girl hear you repeat it.

HIGGINS. Oh, very well, very well. Is that all?

MRS PEARCE. No, sir. We shall have to be very particular with this girl as to personal cleanliness.

HIGGINS. Certainly. Quite right. Most important.

MRS PEARCE. I mean not to be slovenly about her dress or untidy in leaving things about.

HIGGINS [*going to her solemnly*] Just so. I intended to call your attention to that. [*He passes on to* PICKERING, *who is enjoying the conversation immensely*]. It is these little things that matter, Pickering. Take care of the pence and the pounds will take care of themselves is as true of personal habits as of money. [*He comes to anchor on the hearthrug, with the air of a man in an unassailable position*].

MRS PEARCE. Yes, sir. Then might I ask you not to come down to breakfast in your dressing-gown, or at any rate not to use it as a napkin

to the extent you do, sir. And if you would be so good as not to eat everything off the same plate, and to remember not to put the porridge saucepan out of your hand on the clean tablecloth, it would be a better example to the girl. You know you nearly choked yourself with a fishbone in a jam only last week.

HIGGINS [*routed from the hearthrug and drifting back to the piano*] I may do these things sometimes in absence of mind; but surely I dont do them habitually. [*Angrily*] By the way: my dressing-gown smells most damnably of benzine.

MRS PEARCE. No doubt it does, Mr Higgins. But if you will wipe your fingers—

HIGGINS [*yelling*] Oh very well, very well: I'll wipe them in my hair in future.

MRS PEARCE. I hope youre not offended, Mr Higgins.

HIGGINS [*shocked at finding himself thought capable of an unamiable sentiment*] Not at all, not at all. Youre quite right, Mrs Pearce: I shall be particularly careful before the girl. Is that all?

MRS PEARCE. No, sir. Might she use some of those Japanese dresses you brought from abroad? I really cant put her back into her old things.

HIGGINS. Certainly. Anything you like. Is that all?

MRS PEARCE. Thank you, sir. Thats all. [*She goes out*].

HIGGINS. You know, Pickering, that woman has the most extraordinary ideas about me. Here I am, a shy, diffident sort of man. Ive never been able to feel really grown-up and tremendous, like other chaps. And yet she's firmly persuaded that I'm an arbitrary overbearing bossing kind of person. I cant account for it.

MRS PEARCE *returns.*

MRS PEARCE. If you please, sir, the trouble's be-

---

14. **certain word:** The word is *bloody,* in England much stronger profanity early in the century than it is now.

ginning already. Theres a dustman[15] downstairs, Alfred Doolittle, wants to see you. He says you have his daughter here.

PICKERING [*rising*] Phew! I say!

HIGGINS [*promptly*] Send the blackguard[16] up.

MRS PEARCE. Oh, very well, sir. [*She goes out*].

PICKERING. He may not be a blackguard, Higgins.

HIGGINS. Nonsense. Of course he's a blackguard.

PICKERING. Whether he is or not, I'm afraid we shall have some trouble with him.

HIGGINS [*confidently*] Oh no: I think not. If theres any trouble he shall have it with me, not I with him. And we are sure to get something interesting out of him.

PICKERING. About the girl?

HIGGINS. No. I mean his dialect.

PICKERING. Oh!

MRS PEARCE [*at the door*] Doolittle, sir. [*She admits* DOOLITTLE *and retires*].

ALFRED *is an elderly but vigorous dustman, clad in the costume of his profession, including a hat with a back brim covering his neck and shoulders. He has well marked and rather interesting features, and seems equally free from fear and conscience. He has a remarkably expressive voice, the result of a habit of giving vent to his feelings without reserve. His present pose is that of wounded honor and stern resolution.*

DOOLITTLE [*at the door, uncertain which of the two gentlemen is his man*] Professor Iggins?

HIGGINS. Here. Good morning. Sit down.

DOOLITTLE. Morning, Governor. [*He sits down magisterially*]. I come about a very serious matter, Governor.

---

15. **dustman:** garbage collector.
16. **blackguard** [blag′ərd]: rascal, scoundrel.

HIGGINS [*to* PICKERING] Brought up in Hounslow. Mother Welsh, I should think. [DOOLITTLE *opens his mouth, amazed.* HIGGINS *continues*] What do you want, Doolittle?

DOOLITTLE [*menacingly*] I want my daughter: thats what I want. See?

HIGGINS. Of course you do. Youre her father, arnt you? You dont suppose anyone else wants her, do you? I'm glad to see you have some spark of family feeling left. She's upstairs. Take her away at once.

DOOLITTLE [*rising, fearfully taken aback*] What!

HIGGINS. Take her away. Do you suppose I'm going to keep your daughter for you?

DOOLITTLE [*remonstrating*] Now, now, look here, Governor. Is this reasonable? Is it fairity to take advantage of a man like this? The girl belongs to me. You got her. Where do I come in? [*He sits down again*].

HIGGINS. Your daughter had the audacity to come to my house and ask me to teach her how to speak properly so that she could get a place in a flower-shop. This gentleman and my housekeeper have been here all the time. [*Bullying him*] How dare you come here and attempt to blackmail me? You sent her here on purpose.

DOOLITTLE [*protesting*] No, Governor.

HIGGINS. You must have. How else could you possibly know that she is here?

DOOLITTLE. Don't take a man up like that, Governor.

HIGGINS. The police shall take you up. This is a plant—a plot to extort money by threats. I shall telephone for the police [*he goes resolutely to the telephone and opens the directory*]

DOOLITTLE. Have I asked you for a brass farthing? I leave it to the gentleman here: have I said a word about money?

HIGGINS [throwing the book aside and marching down on DOOLITTLE with a poser] What else did you come for?

DOOLITTLE [sweetly] Well, what would a man come for? Be human, Governor.

HIGGINS [disarmed] Alfred: did you put her up to it?

DOOLITTLE. So help me, Governor. I never did. I take my Bible oath I aint seen the girl these two months past.

HIGGINS. Then how did you know she was here?

DOOLITTLE ["most musical, most melancholy"] I'll tell you, Governor, if youll only let me get a word in. I'm willing to tell you. I'm wanting to tell you. I'm waiting to tell you.

HIGGINS. Pickering: this chap has a certain natural gift of rhetoric. Observe the rhythm of his native woodnotes wild. "I'm willing to tell you: I'm wanting to tell you: I'm waiting to tell you." Sentimental rhetoric! thats the Welsh strain in him. It also accounts for his mendacity and dishonesty.

PICKERING. Oh, please, Higgins: I'm west country myself. [To DOOLITTLE] How did you know the girl was here if you didnt send her?

DOOLITTLE. It was like this, Governor. The girl took a boy in the taxi to give him a jaunt. Son of her landlady, he is. He hung about on the chance of her giving him another ride home. Well, she sent him back for her luggage when she heard you was willing for her to stop here. I met the boy at the corner of Long Acre and Endell Street.

HIGGINS. Public house. Yes?

DOOLITTLE. The poor man's club, Governor: why shouldnt I?

PICKERING. Do let him tell his story, Higgins.

DOOLITTLE. He told me what was up. And I ask you, what was my feelings and my duty as a father? I says to the boy, "You bring me the luggage," I says—

PICKERING. Why didnt you go for it yourself?

DOOLITTLE. Landlady wouldnt have trusted me with it, Governor. She's that kind of woman: you know. I had to give the boy a penny afore he trusted me with it, the little swine. I brought it to her just to oblige you like, and make myself agreeable. Thats all.

HIGGINS. How much luggage?

DOOLITTLE. Musical instrument, Governor. A few pictures, a trifle of jewelry, and a birdcage. She said she didnt want no clothes. What was I to think from that, Governor? I ask you as a parent what was I to think?

HIGGINS. So you came to rescue her from worse than death, eh?

DOOLITTLE [appreciatively: relieved at being so well understood] Just so, Governor. That's right.

PICKERING. But why did you bring her luggage if you intended to take her away?

DOOLITTLE. Have I said a word about taking her away? Have I now?

HIGGINS [determinedly] Youre going to take her away, double quick. [He crosses to the hearth and rings the bell].

DOOLITTLE [rising] No, Governor. Dont say that. I'm not the man to stand in my girl's light. Heres a career opening for her, as you might say; and—

MRS PEARCE opens the door and awaits orders.

HIGGINS. Mrs Pearce: this is Eliza's father. He has come to take her away. Give her to him. [He goes back to the piano, with an air of washing his hands of the whole affair].

DOOLITTLE. No. This is a misunderstanding. Listen here—

MRS PEARCE. He cant take her away. Mr. Higgins: how can he? You told me to burn her clothes.

DOOLITTLE. Thats right. I cant carry the girl

through the streets like a blooming monkey, can I? I put it to you.

HIGGINS. You have put it to me that you want your daughter. If she has no clothes go out and buy her some.

DOOLITTLE [desperate] Wheres the clothes she come in? Did I burn them or did your missus here?

MRS PEARCE. I am the housekeeper, if you please. I have sent for some clothes for your girl. When they come you can take her away. You can wait in the kitchen. This way, please.

> DOOLITTLE, much troubled, accompanies her to the door; then hesitates; finally turns confidentially to HIGGINS.

DOOLITTLE. Listen here, Governor. You and me is men of the world, aint we?

HIGGINS. Oh! Men of the world, are we? Youd better go, Mrs Pearce.

MRS PEARCE. I think so, indeed, sir. [She goes, with dignity].

PICKERING. The floor is yours, Mr Doolittle.

DOOLITTLE [to PICKERING] I thank you, Governor. [To HIGGINS, who takes refuge on the piano bench, a little overwhelmed by the proximity of his visitor; for DOOLITTLE has a professional flavour of dust about him]. Well, the truth is, Ive taken a sort of fancy to you, Governor; and if you want the girl, I'm not so set on having her back home again but what I might be open to an arrangement. Regarded in the light of a young woman, she's a fine handsome girl. As a daughter she's not worth her keep; and so I tell you straight. All I ask is my rights as a father; and youre the last man alive to expect me to let her go for nothing; for I can see youre one of the straight sort, Governor. Well, whats a five-pound note to you? and whats Eliza to me? [He turns to his chair and sits down judicially].

PICKERING. I think you ought to know, Doolittle, that Mr Higgins's intentions are entirely honorable.

DOOLITTLE. Course they are, Governor. If I thought they wasnt, I'd ask fifty.

HIGGINS [revolted] Do you mean to say that you would sell your daughter for £50?

DOOLITTLE. Not in a general way I would; but to oblige a gentleman like you I'd do a good deal, I do assure you.

PICKERING. Have you no morals, man?

DOOLITTLE [unabashed] Cant afford them, Governor. Neither could you if you was as poor as me. Not that I mean any harm, you know. But if Liza is going to have a bit out of this, why not me too?

HIGGINS [troubled] I dont know what to do, Pickering. There can be no question that as a matter of morals it's a positive crime to give this chap a farthing. And yet I feel a sort of rough justice in his claim.

DOOLITTLE. Thats it, Governor. Thats all I say. A father's heart, as it were.

PICKERING. Well, I know the feeling; but really it seems hardly right—

DOOLITTLE. Dont say that, Governor. Dont look at it that way. What am I, Governors both? I ask you, what am I? I'm one of the undeserving poor: thats what I am. Think of what that means to a man. It means that he's up agen middle class morality all the time. If theres anything going, and I put in for a bit of it, it's always the same story: "Youre undeserving; so you cant have it." But my needs is as great as the most deserving widows' that ever got money out of six different charities in one week for the death of the same husband. I dont need less than a deserving man: I need more. I dont eat less hearty than him; and I drink a lot more. I want a bit of amusement, cause I'm a thinking man. I want cheerfulness and a song and a band when I feel low. Well, they charge me just the same for everything as they charge the deserving. What is middle class morality? Just an excuse for never giving me anything. Therefore, I ask you, as two gentlemen, not to play that game on me. I'm playing straight with you. I aint pretending to be deserving. I'm undeserving; and I mean to go on being undeserving. I like it; and thats the truth. Will you take advantage of a man's nature to do him out of the price of his own daughter what he's brought up and fed and clothed by the sweat of his brow until she's growed big enough to be interesting to you two gentlemen? Is five pounds unreasonable? I put it to you; and I leave it to you.

HIGGINS [*rising, and going over to* PICKERING] Pickering: if we were to take this man in hand for three months, he could choose between a seat in the Cabinet and a popular pulpit in Wales.

PICKERING. What do you say to that, Doolittle?

DOOLITTLE. Not me, Governor, thank you kindly. Ive heard all the preachers and all the prime ministers—for I'm a thinking man and game for politics or religion or social reform same as all the other amusements—and I tell you it's a dog's life any way you look at it. Undeserving poverty is my line. Taking one station in society with another, it's—it's—well, it's the only one that has any ginger in it, to my taste.

HIGGINS. I suppose we must give him a fiver.

PICKERING. He'll make a bad use of it, I'm afraid.

DOOLITTLE. Not me, Governor, so help me I wont. Dont you be afraid that I'll save it and spare it and live idle on it. There wont be a penny of it left by Monday: I'll have to go to work same as if I'd never had it. It wont pauperize me, you bet. Just one good spree for myself and the missus, giving pleasure to ourselves and employment to others, and satisfaction to you to think it's not been throwed away. You couldnt spend it better.

HIGGINS [*taking out his pocket book and coming between* DOOLITTLE *and the piano*] This is irresistible. Lets give him ten. [*He offers two notes to the* DUSTMAN].

DOOLITTLE. No, Governor. She wouldnt have the heart to spend ten; and perhaps I shouldnt neither. Ten pounds is a lot of money: it makes a man feel prudent like; and then goodbye to happiness. You give me what I ask you, Governor: not a penny more, and not a penny less.

PICKERING. Why dont you marry that missus of yours? I rather draw the line at encouraging that sort of immorality.

DOOLITTLE. Tell her so, Governor: tell her so. I'm willing. It's me that suffers by it. Ive no hold on her. I got to be agreeable to her. I got to give her presents. I got to buy her clothes something sinful. I'm a slave to that woman, Governor, just because I'm not her lawful husband. And she knows it too. Catch her marrying me! Take my advice, Governor: marry Eliza while she's young and dont know no better. If you dont youll be sorry for it after. If you do, she'll be sorry for it after; but better her than you, because youre a man, and she's only a woman and dont know how to be happy anyhow.

HIGGINS. Pickering: if we listen to this man another minute, we shall have no convictions left. [*To* DOOLITTLE] Five pounds I think you said.

DOOLITTLE. Thank you kindly, Governor.

HIGGINS. Youre sure you wont take ten?

DOOLITTLE. Not now. Another time, Governor.

HIGGINS [*handing him a five-pound note*] Here you are.

DOOLITTLE. Thank you, Governor. Good morning. [*He hurries to the door, anxious to get away with his booty. When he opens it he is confronted with a dainty and exquisitely clean young* JAPANESE LADY *in a simple blue cotton kimono printed cunningly with small white jasmine blossoms.* MRS PEARCE *is with her. He gets out of her way deferentially and apologizes*]. Beg pardon, miss.

THE JAPANESE LADY. Garn! Dont you know your own daughter?

DOOLITTLE	[*exclaiming*	Bly me! it's Eliza!
HIGGINS	*simul-*	Whats that? This!
PICKERING	*taneously*]	By Jove!

LIZA. Dont I look silly?

HIGGINS. Silly?

MRS PEARCE [*at the door*] Now, Mr Higgins, please dont say anything to make the girl conceited about herself.

HIGGINS [*conscientiously*] Oh! Quite right, Mrs Pearce. [*To* ELIZA] Yes: damned silly.

MRS PEARCE. Please, sir.

HIGGINS [*correcting himself*] I mean extremely silly.

LIZA. I should look all right with my hat on. [*She takes up her hat; puts it on; and walks across the room to the fireplace with a fashionable air*].

HIGGINS. A new fashion, by George! And it ought to look horrible!

DOOLITTLE [*with fatherly pride*] Well, I never thought she'd clean up as good looking as that, Governor. She's a credit to me, aint she?

LIZA. I tell you, it's easy to clean up here. Hot and cold water on tap, just as much as you like, there is. Woolly towels, there is; and a towel horse[17] so hot, it burns your fingers. Soft brushes to scrub yourself, and a wooden bowl of soap smelling like primroses. Now I know why ladies is so clean. Washing's a treat for them. Wish they could see what it is for the like of me!

HIGGINS. I'm glad the bathroom met with your approval.

LIZA. It didnt: not all of it; and I dont care who hears me say it. Mrs Pearce knows.

HIGGINS. What was wrong, Mrs Pearce?

MRS PEARCE [*blandly*] Oh, nothing, sir. It doesnt matter.

LIZA. I had a good mind to break it. I didnt know which way to look. But I hung a towel over it, I did.

---

17. **towel horse:** towel rack; this one is heated to dry the towels.

HIGGINS. Over what?

MRS PEARCE. Over the looking-glass, sir.

HIGGINS. Doolittle: you have brought your daughter up too strictly.

DOOLITTLE. Me! I never brought her up at all, except to give her a lick of a strap now and again. Dont put it on me, Governor. She aint accustomed to it, you see: thats all. But she'll soon pick up your free-and-easy ways.

LIZA. I'm a good girl, I am; and I wont pick up no free-and-easy ways.

HIGGINS. Eliza: if you say again that youre a good girl, your father shall take you home.

LIZA. Not him. You dont know my father. All he come here for was to touch you for some money to get drunk on.

DOOLITTLE. Well, what else would I want money for? To put into the plate in church, I suppose. [*She puts out her tongue at him. He is so incensed by this that* PICKERING *presently finds it necessary to step between them*]. Dont you give me none of your lip; and dont let me hear you giving this gentleman any of it neither, or youll hear from me about it. See?

HIGGINS. Have you any further advice to give her before you go, Doolittle? Your blessing, for instance.

DOOLITTLE. No, Governor: I aint such a mug as to put up my children to all I know myself. Hard enough to hold them in without that. If you want Eliza's mind improved, Governor, you do it yourself with a strap. So long, gentlemen. [*He turns to go*].

HIGGINS [*impressively*] Stop. Youll come regularly to see your daughter. It's your duty, you know. My brother is a clergyman; and he could help you in your talks with her.

DOOLITTLE [*evasively*] Certainly, I'll come, Governor. Not just this week, because I have a job at a distance. But later on you may depend on me. Afternoon, gentlemen. Afternoon, maam. [*He touches his hat to* MRS PEARCE, *who disdains the salutation and goes out. He winks at* HIGGINS, *thinking him probably a fellow-sufferer from* MRS PEARCE*'s difficult disposition, and follows her*].

LIZA. Don't you believe the old liar. He'd as soon you set a bulldog on him as a clergyman. You wont see him again in a hurry.

HIGGINS. I dont want to, Eliza. Do you?

LIZA. Not me. I dont want never to see him again, I dont. He's a disgrace to me, he is, collecting dust,[18] instead of working at his trade.

PICKERING. What is his trade, Eliza?

LIZA. Talking money out of other people's pockets into his own. His proper trade's a navvy;[19] and he works at it sometimes too—for exercise—and earns good money at it. Aint you going to call me Miss Doolittle any more?

PICKERING. I beg your pardon, Miss Doolittle. It was a slip of the tongue.

LIZA. Oh, I dont mind; only it sounded so genteel. I should just like to take a taxi to the corner of Tottenham Court Road and get out there and tell it to wait for me, just to put the girls in their place a bit. I wouldnt speak to them, you know.

PICKERING. Better wait til we get you something really fashionable.

HIGGINS. Besides, you shouldnt cut your old friends now that you have risen in the world. Thats what we call snobbery.

LIZA. You dont call the like of them my friends now, I should hope. Theyve took it out of me often enough with their ridicule when they had the chance; and now I mean to get a bit of my own back. But if I'm to have fashionable clothes, I'll wait. I should like to have some. Mrs Pearce says youre going to give me some to wear in bed at night different to what I wear in the daytime; but it do seem a waste of money when you could get something to shew.

_____
18. **collecting dust:** picking up garbage.
19. **navvy** [nav′ē]: unskilled laborer, ditchdigger.

Besides, I never could fancy changing into cold things on a winter night.

MRS PEARCE [*coming back*] Now, Eliza. The new things have come for you to try on.

LIZA. Ah-ow-oo-ooh! [*She rushes out*].

MRS PEARCE [*following her*] Oh, dont rush about like that, girl. [*She shuts the door behind her*].

HIGGINS. Pickering: we have taken on a stiff job.

PICKERING [*with conviction*] Higgins: we have.

* * * * * *

There seems to be some curiosity as to what Higgins's lessons to Eliza were like. Well, here is a sample: the first one.

Picture Eliza, in her new clothes, and feeling her inside put out of step by a lunch, dinner, and breakfast of a kind to which it is unaccustomed, seated with Higgins and the Colonel in the study, feeling like a hospital out-patient at a first encounter with the doctors.

Higgins, constitutionally unable to sit still, discomposes her still more by striding restlessly about. But for the reassuring presence and quietude of her friend the Colonel she would run for her life, even back to Drury Lane.

HIGGINS. Say your alphabet.

LIZA. I know my alphabet. Do you think I know nothing? I dont need to be taught like a child.

HIGGINS [*thundering*] Say your alphabet.

PICKERING. Say it, Miss Doolittle. You will understand presently. Do what he tells you; and let him teach you in his own way.

LIZA. Oh well, if you put it like that—Ahyee, bəyee, cəyee, dəyee—

HIGGINS [*with the roar of a wounded lion*] Stop. Listen to this, Pickering. This is what we pay for as elementary education. This unfortunate animal has been locked up for nine years in school at our expense to teach her to speak and read the language of Shakespear and Milton. And the result is Ahyee, Bə-yee, Cə-yee, Dəyee. [*To* ELIZA] Say A, B, C, D.

LIZA [*almost in tears*] But I'm sayin it. Ahyee, Bəyee, Cəyee—

HIGGINS. Stop. Say a cup of tea.

LIZA. A cappətə-ee.

HIGGINS. Put your tongue forward until it squeezes against the top of your lower teeth. Now say cup.

LIZA. C-c-c—I cant. C-Cup.

PICKERING. Good. Splendid, Miss Doolittle.

HIGGINS. By Jupiter, she's done it the first shot. Pickering: we shall make a duchess of her. [*To* ELIZA] Now do you think you could possibly say tea? Not tə-yee, mind: if you ever say bə-yee cə-yee də-yee again you shall be dragged round the room three times by the hair of your head. [*Fortissimo*] T, T, T, T.

LIZA [*weeping*] I cant hear no difference cep that it sounds more genteel-like when you say it.

HIGGINS. Well, if you can hear the difference, what the devil are you crying for? Pickering: give her a chocolate.

PICKERING. No, no. Never mind crying a little, Miss Doolittle: you are doing very well; and the lessons wont hurt. I promise you I wont let him drag you round the room by your hair.

HIGGINS. Be off with you to Mrs Pearce and tell her about it. Think about it. Try to do it by yourself: and keep your tongue well forward in your mouth instead of trying to roll it up and swallow it. Another lesson at half-past four this afternoon. Away with you.

ELIZA, *still sobbing, rushes from the room.*

And that is the sort of ordeal Eliza has to go through for months before we meet her again on her first appearance in London society of the professional class.

STUDY QUESTIONS

Recalling

1. What proposition does Liza offer Higgins when she first comes to his study? Why is he impressed?
2. What bet does Colonel Pickering offer Higgins? Summarize the plan that results from this bet.
3. What new experiences is Liza exposed to at Higgins' house? Describe her reactions to these experiences.
4. What various concerns about the experiment with Liza are expressed by Mrs. Pearce and Colonel Pickering? What answers does Higgins give them?
5. Why does Doolittle visit Higgins? Why does he not recognize Liza at first?

Interpreting

6. In what ways must Liza change if Higgins is to pass her off as a lady?

7. Describe Higgins' attitude toward Liza, and contrast it with Colonel Pickering's treatment of her. What does this contrast reveal about the two men?
8. What qualities does Liza reveal by coming to Higgins for lessons? What qualities does she show in her various responses to Higgins and to Pickering? What traits in her character indicate that she is not just an ordinary flower girl?
9. What does Doolittle mean by calling himself a member of the "undeserving poor" and by his complaints about "middle class morality"? What serious point does Shaw make in Doolittle's statement that he cannot afford to have morals?

Extending

10. Is proper speech still as important as it seems to Liza in *Pygmalion*? Why or why not?

ACT THREE

It is MRS HIGGINS's *at-home day.*[1] *Nobody has yet arrived. Her drawing room, in a flat on Chelsea Embankment, has three windows looking on the river; and the ceiling is not so lofty as it would be in an older house of the same pretension. The windows are open, giving access to a balcony with flowers in pots. If you stand with your face to the windows, you have the fireplace on your left and the door in the right-hand wall close to the corner nearest the windows.*

MRS HIGGINS *was brought up on Morris and Burne Jones;*[2] *and her room, which is very unlike her son's room in Wimpole Street, is not crowded with furniture and little tables and nicknacks. In the middle of the room there is a big ottoman; and this, with the carpet, the Morris wall-papers, and the Morris chintz window curtains and brocade covers of the ottoman and its cushions, supply all the ornament, and are much too handsome to be hidden by odds and ends of useless things. A few good oil-paintings from the exhibitions in the Grosvenor Gallery thirty years ago (the Burne Jones, not the Whistler*[3] *side of them) are on the walls. The only landscape is a Cecil Lawson*[4] *on the scale of a Rubens.*[5] *There is a portrait of* MRS HIGGINS *as she was when she defied the fashion in her youth in one of the beautiful Rossettian*[6] *costumes which, when caricatured by people who did not understand, led to the absurdities of popular estheticism in the eighteen-seventies.*

In the corner diagonally opposite the door MRS HIGGINS, *now over sixty and long past taking the trouble to dress out of the fashion sits writing at an elegantly simple writing-table with a bell button within reach of her hand. There is a Chippendale chair further back in the room between her and the window nearest her side. At the other side of the room, further forward, is an Elizabethan chair roughly carved in the taste of Inigo Jones.*[7] *On the same side a piano in a decorated case. The corner between the fireplace and the window is occupied by a divan cushioned in Morris chintz.*

It is between four and five in the afternoon.

The door is opened violently; and HIGGINS *enters with his hat on.*

MRS HIGGINS [*dismayed*] Henry! [*Scolding him*] What are you doing here today? It is my at-home day; you promised not to come. [*As he bends to kiss her, she takes his hat off, and presents it to him*].

HIGGINS. Oh bother! [*He throws the hat down on the table*].

MRS HIGGINS. Go home at once.

HIGGINS [*kissing her*] I know, mother. I came on purpose.

MRS HIGGINS. But you mustnt. I'm serious, Henry. You offend all my friends: they stop coming whenever they meet you.

HIGGINS. Nonsense! I know I have no small talk; but people dont mind. [*He sits on the settee*].

MRS HIGGINS. Oh! dont they? Small talk indeed! What about your large talk? Really, dear, you mustnt stay.

HIGGINS. I must. Ive a job for you. A phonetic job.

---

1. **at-home day:** specified day of the week when a lady regularly receives visitors, who need no invitation.
2. **Morris, Burne Jones:** William Morris (1834–1896) and Sir Edward Coley Burne Jones (1833–1898), Victorian artists who influenced interior decoration in ways of which Shaw approved.
3. **Whistler:** James Abbott McNeill Whistler (1834–1903), popular American painter who lived in England.
4. **Cecil Lawson:** Cecil Gordon Lawson (1851–1882), English landscape painter.
5. **Rubens:** Flemish painter Peter Paul Rubens (1577–1640), famous for his monumental paintings.
6. **Rossettian:** referring to the stylized work of Dante Gabriel Rossetti (1828–1882), painter and poet.

7. **Inigo Jones** (1573–1652): English architect and stage designer.

MRS HIGGINS. No use, dear. I'm sorry; but I cant get round your vowels; and though I like to get pretty postcards in your patent shorthand, I always have to read the copies in ordinary writing you so thoughtfully send me.

HIGGINS. Well, this isnt a phonetic job.

MRS HIGGINS. You said it was.

HIGGINS. Not your part of it. Ive picked up a girl.

MRS HIGGINS. Does that mean that some girl has picked you up?

HIGGINS. Not at all. I dont mean a love affair.

MRS HIGGINS. What a pity!

HIGGINS. Why?

MRS HIGGINS. Well, you never fall in love with anyone under forty-five. When will you discover that there are some rather nice-looking young women about?

HIGGINS. Oh, I cant be bothered with young women. My idea of a lovable woman is somebody as like you as possible. I shall never get into the way of seriously liking young women: some habits lie too deep to be changed. [*Rising abruptly and walking about, jingling his money and his keys in his trouser pockets*] Besides, theyre all idiots.

MRS HIGGINS. Do you know what you would do if you really loved me, Henry?

HIGGINS. Oh bother! What? Marry, I suppose.

MRS HIGGINS. No. Stop fidgeting and take your hands out of your pockets. [*With a gesture of despair, he obeys and sits down again*]. Thats a good boy. Now tell me about the girl.

HIGGINS. She's coming to see you.

MRS HIGGINS. I dont remember asking her.

HIGGINS. You didnt. *I* asked her. If youd known her you wouldnt have asked her.

MRS HIGGINS. Indeed! Why?

HIGGINS. Well, it's like this. She's a common flower girl. I picked her off the kerbstone.

MRS HIGGINS. And invited her to my at-home!

HIGGINS [*rising and coming to her to coax her*] Oh, thatll be all right. Ive taught her to speak properly; and she has strict orders as to her behavior. She's to keep to two subjects: the weather and everybody's health—Fine day and How do you do, you know—and not to let herself go on things in general. That will be safe.

MRS HIGGINS. Safe! To talk about our health! about our insides! perhaps about our outsides! How could you be so silly, Henry?

HIGGINS [*impatiently*] Well, she must talk about something. [*He controls himself and sits down again*]. Oh, she'll be all right: dont you fuss. Pickering is in it with me. Ive a sort of bet on that I'll pass her off as a duchess in six months. I started on her some months ago; and she's getting on like a house on fire. I shall win my bet. She has a quick ear; and she's easier to teach than my middle-class pupils because she's had to learn a complete new language. She talks English almost as you talk French.

MRS HIGGINS. Thats satisfactory, at all events.

HIGGINS. Well, it is and it isnt.

MRS HIGGINS. What does that mean?

HIGGINS. You see, Ive got her pronunciation all right; but you have to consider not only how a girl pronounces, but what she pronounces; and thats where—

They are interrupted by the PARLORMAID, *announcing guests.*

THE PARLORMAID. Mrs and Miss Eynsford Hill. [*She withdraws*].

HIGGINS. Oh Lord! [*He rises; snatches his hat from the table; and makes for the door; but before he reaches it his mother introduces him*].

MRS *and* MISS EYNSFORD HILL *are the mother and daughter who sheltered from the rain in Covent Garden. The mother is well bred, quiet, and has the habitual anxiety of straitened means. The daughter has acquired a gay air of being very much at home in society: the bravado of genteel poverty.*

MRS EYNSFORD HILL [*to* MRS HIGGINS] How do you do? [*They shake hands*].

MISS EYNSFORD HILL. How d'you do? [*She shakes*].

MRS HIGGINS [*introducing*] My son Henry.

MRS EYNSFORD HILL. Your celebrated son! I have so longed to meet you, Professor Higgins.

HIGGINS [*glumly, making no movement in her direction*] Delighted. [*He backs against the piano and bows brusquely*].

MISS EYNSFORD HILL [*going to him with confident familiarity*] How do you do?

HIGGINS [*staring at her*] Ive seen you before somewhere. I havnt the ghost of a notion where; but Ive heard your voice. [*Drearily*] It doesnt matter. Youd better sit down.

MRS HIGGINS. I'm sorry to say that my celebrated son has no manners. You mustnt mind him.

MISS EYNSFORD HILL [*gaily*] I dont. [*She sits in the Elizabethan chair*].

MRS EYNSFORD HILL [*a little bewildered*] Not at all. [*She sits on the ottoman between her daughter and* MRS HIGGINS, *who has turned her chair away from the writing-table*].

HIGGINS. Oh, have I been rude? I didnt mean to be.

He goes to the central window, through which, with his back to the company, he contemplates the river and the flowers in Battersea Park on the opposite bank as if they were a frozen desert.
  The PARLORMAID *returns, ushering in* Pickering.

THE PARLORMAID. Colonel Pickering. [*She withdraws*].

PICKERING. How do you do, Mrs Higgins?

MRS HIGGINS. So glad youve come. Do you know Mrs Eynsford Hill—Miss Eynsford Hill? [*Exchange of bows. The* COLONEL *brings the Chippendale chair a little forward between* MRS HILL *and* MRS HIGGINS, *and sits down*].

PICKERING. Has Henry told you what weve come for?

HIGGINS [*over his shoulder*] We were interrupted: damn it!

MRS HIGGINS. Oh, Henry, Henry, really!

MRS EYNSFORD HILL [*half rising*] Are we in the way?

MRS HIGGINS [*rising and making her sit down again*] No, no. You couldnt have come more fortunately: we want you to meet a friend of ours.

HIGGINS [*turning hopefully*] Yes, by George! We want two or three people. You'll do as well as anybody else.

The PARLORMAID *returns, ushering* FREDDY.

THE PARLORMAID. Mr Eynsford Hill.

HIGGINS [*almost audibly, past endurance*] God of Heaven! another of them.

FREDDY [*shaking hands with* MRS HIGGINS] Ahdedo?[8]

MRS HIGGINS. Very good of you to come. [*Introducing*] Colonel Pickering.

FREDDY [*bowing*] Ahdedo?

MRS HIGGINS. I dont think you know my son, Professor Higgins.

FREDDY [*going to* HIGGINS] Ahdedo?

HIGGINS [*looking at him much as if he were a pickpocket*] I'll take my oath Ive met you before somewhere. Where was it?

FREDDY. I dont think so.

HIGGINS [*resignedly*] It dont matter, anyhow. Sit down.

---

8. **Ahdedo:** "How do you do?"

He shakes FREDDY's *hand, and almost slings him on to the ottoman with his face to the window; then comes round to the other side of it.*

HIGGINS. Well, here we are, anyhow! [*He sits down on the ottoman next* MRS EYNSFORD HILL, *on her left*] And now, what the devil are we going to talk about until Eliza comes?

MRS HIGGINS. Henry: you are the life and soul of the Royal Society's soirées;[9] but really youre rather trying on more commonplace occasions.

HIGGINS. Am I? Very sorry. [*Beaming suddenly*] I suppose I am, you know. [*Uproariously*] Ha, ha!

MISS EYNSFORD HILL [*who considers* HIGGINS *quite eligible matrimonially*] I sympathize. I havnt any small talk. If people would only be frank and say what they really think!

HIGGINS [*relapsing into gloom*] Lord forbid!

MRS EYNSFORD HILL [*taking up her daughter's cue*] But why?

HIGGINS. What they think they ought to think is bad enough, Lord knows; but what they really think would break up the whole show. Do you suppose it would be really agreeable if I were to come out now with what *I* really think?

MISS EYNSFORD HILL [*gaily*] Is it so very cynical?

HIGGINS. Cynical! Who the dickens said it was cynical? I mean it wouldnt be decent.

MRS EYNSFORD HILL [*seriously*] Oh! I'm sure you dont mean that, Mr Higgins.

HIGGINS. You see, we're all savages, more or less. We're supposed to be civilized and cultured—to know all about poetry and philosophy and art and science, and so on; but how many of us know even the meanings of these names? [*To* MISS HILL] What do you know of poetry? [*To* MRS HILL] What do you know of science? [*Indicating* FREDDY] What does he know

of art or science or anything else? What the devil do you imagine I know of philosophy?

MRS HIGGINS [*warningly*] Or of manners, Henry?

THE PARLORMAID [*opening the door*] Miss Doolittle. [*She withdraws*].

HIGGINS [*rising hastily and running to* MRS HIGGINS] Here she is, mother. [*He stands on tiptoe and makes signs over his mother's head to* ELIZA *to indicate to her which lady is her hostess*].

ELIZA, *who is exquisitely dressed, produces an impression of such remarkable distinction and beauty as she enters that they all rise, quite fluttered. Guided by* HIGGINS's *signals, she comes to* MRS HIGGINS *with studied grace.*

LIZA [*speaking with pedantic correctness of pronunciation and great beauty of tone*] How do you do, Mrs Higgins? [*She gasps slightly in making sure of the H in Higgins, but is quite successful*]. Mr Higgins told me I might come.

MRS HIGGINS [*cordially*] Quite right: I'm very glad indeed to see you.

PICKERING. How do you do, Miss Doolittle?

LIZA [*shaking hands with him*] Colonel Pickering, is it not?

MRS EYNSFORD HILL. I feel sure we have met before, Miss Doolittle. I remember your eyes.

LIZA. How do you do? [*She sits down on the ottoman gracefully in the place just left vacant by* HIGGINS].

MRS EYNSFORD HILL [*introducing*] My daughter Clara.

LIZA. How do you do?

CLARA [*impulsively*] How do you do? [*She sits down on the ottoman beside* ELIZA, *devouring her with her eyes*].

FREDDY [*coming to their side of the ottoman*] Ive certainly had the pleasure.

---

9. **soirées:** social gatherings held in the evening.

MRS EYNSFORD HILL [*introducing*] My son Freddy.

LIZA. How do you do?

FREDDY *bows and sits down in the Elizabethan chair, infatuated.*

HIGGINS [*suddenly*] By George, yes: it all comes back to me! [*They stare at him*]. Covent Garden! [*Lamentably*] What a damned thing!

MRS HIGGINS. Henry, please! [*He is about to sit on the edge of the table*] Dont sit on my writing-table: youll break it.

HIGGINS [*sulkily*] Sorry.

He goes to the divan, stumbling into the fender[10] *and over the fire-irons on his way; extricating himself with muttered imprecations; and finishing his disastrous journey by throwing himself so impatiently on the divan that he almost breaks it.* MRS HIGGINS *looks at him, but controls herself and says nothing.*

A long and painful pause ensues.

MRS HIGGINS [*at last, conversationally*] Will it rain, do you think?

LIZA. The shallow depression in the west of these islands is likely to move slowly in an easterly direction. There are no indications of any great change in the barometrical situation.

FREDDY. Ha! ha! how awfully funny!

LIZA. What is wrong with that, young man? I bet I got it right.

FREDDY. Killing!

MRS EYNSFORD HILL. I'm sure I hope it wont turn cold. Theres so much influenza about. It runs right through our whole family regularly every spring.

LIZA [*darkly*] My aunt died of influenza: so they said.

MRS EYNSFORD HILL [*clicks her tongue sympathetically*]!!!

---

10. **fender:** metal guard before a fireplace.

LIZA [*in the same tragic tone*] But it's my belief they done the old woman in.

MRS HIGGINS [*puzzled*] Done her in?

LIZA. Y-e-e-e-es, Lord love you! Why should she die of influenza? She come through diphtheria right enough the year before. I saw her with my own eyes. Fairly blue with it, she was. They all thought she was dead; but my father he kept ladling gin down her throat til she came to so sudden that she bit the bowl off the spoon.

MRS EYNSFORD HILL [*startled*] Dear me!

LIZA [*piling up the indictment*] What call would a woman with that strength in her have to die of influenza? What become of her new straw hat that should have come to me? Somebody pinched it; and what I say is, them as pinched it done her in.

MRS EYNSFORD HILL. What does doing her in mean?

HIGGINS [*hastily*] Oh, thats the new small talk. To do a person in means to kill them.

MRS EYNSFORD HILL [*to* ELIZA, *horrified*] You surely dont believe that your aunt was killed?

LIZA. Do I not! Them she lived with would have killed her for a hat-pin, let alone a hat.

MRS EYNSFORD HILL. But it cant have been right for your father to pour spirits down her throat like that. It might have killed her.

LIZA. Not her. Gin was mother's milk to her. Besides, he'd poured so much down his own throat that he knew the good of it.

MRS EYNSFORD HILL. Do you mean that he drank?

LIZA. Drank! My word! Something chronic.

MRS EYNSFORD HILL. How dreadful for you!

LIZA. Not a bit. It never did him no harm what I could see. But then he did not keep it up regular. [*Cheerfully*] On the burst, as you might say, from time to time. And always more agreeable when he had a drop in. When he was out of work, my mother used to give him fourpence and tell him to go out and not come back until he'd drunk himself cheerful and loving-like. Theres lots of women has to make their husbands drunk to make them fit to live with. [*Now quite at her ease*] You see, it's like this. If a man has a bit of conscience, it always takes him when he's sober; and then it makes him low-spirited. A drop of booze just takes that off and makes him happy. [*To* FREDDY, *who is in convulsions of suppressed laughter*] Here! what are you sniggering at?

FREDDY. The new small talk. You do it so awfully well.

LIZA. If I was doing it proper, what was you laughing at? [*To* HIGGINS] Have I said anything I oughtnt?

MRS HIGGINS [*interposing*] Not at all, Miss Doolittle.

LIZA. Well, thats a mercy, anyhow. [*Expansively*] What I always say is—

HIGGINS [*rising and looking at his watch*] Ahem!

LIZA [*looking round at him; taking the hint; and rising*] Well: I must go. [*They all rise.* FREDDY *goes to the door*]. So pleased to have met you. Goodbye. [*She shakes hands with* MRS HIGGINS].

MRS HIGGINS. Goodbye.

LIZA. Goodbye, Colonel Pickering.

PICKERING. Goodbye, Miss Doolittle. [*They shake hands*].

LIZA [*nodding to the others*] Goodbye, all.

FREDDY [*opening the door for her*] Are you walking across the Park, Miss Doolittle? If so—

LIZA [*with perfectly elegant diction*] Walk! Not bloody likely. [*Sensation*]. I am going in a taxi. [*She goes out*].

PICKERING *gasps and sits down.* FREDDY *goes out on the balcony to catch another glimpse of* ELIZA.

MRS EYNSFORD HILL [*suffering from shock*] Well, I really cant get used to the new ways.

CLARA [*throwing herself discontentedly into the Elizabethan chair*] Oh, it's all right, mamma, quite right. People will think we never go anywhere or see anybody if you are so old-fashioned.

MRS EYNSFORD HILL. I daresay I am very old-fashioned; but I do hope you wont begin using that expression, Clara. I have got accustomed to hear you talking about men as rotters, and calling everything filthy and beastly; though I do think it horrible and unladylike. But this last is really too much. Dont you think so, Colonel Pickering?

PICKERING. Dont ask me. Ive been away in India for several years; and manners have changed so much that I sometimes dont know whether I'm at a respectable dinnertable or in a ship's forecastle.

CLARA. It's all a matter of habit. Theres no right or wrong in it. Nobody means anything by it. And it's so quaint, and gives such a smart emphasis to things that are not in themselves very witty. I find the new small talk delightful and quite innocent.

MRS EYNSFORD HILL [*rising*] Well, after that, I think it's time for us to go.

PICKERING *and* HIGGINS *rise.*

CLARA [*rising*] Oh yes: we have three at-homes to go to still. Goodbye, Mrs Higgins. Goodbye, Colonel Pickering. Goodbye, Professor Higgins.

HIGGINS [*coming grimly at her from the divan, and accompanying her to the door*] Goodbye. Be sure you try on that small talk at the three at-homes. Dont be nervous about it. Pitch it in strong.

CLARA [*all smiles*] I will. Goodbye. Such nonsense, all this early Victorian prudery!

HIGGINS [*tempting her*] Such damned nonsense!

CLARA. Such bloody nonsense!

MRS EYNSFORD HILL [*convulsively*] Clara!

CLARA. Ha! ha! [*She goes out radiant, conscious of being thoroughly up to date, and is heard descending the stairs in a stream of silvery laughter*].

FREDDY [*to the heavens at large*] Well, I ask you— [*He gives it up, and comes to* MRS HIGGINS]. Goodbye.

MRS HIGGINS [*shaking hands*] Goodbye. Would you like to meet Miss Doolittle again?

FREDDY [*eagerly*] Yes, I should, most awfully.

MRS HIGGINS. Well, you know my days.[11]

FREDDY. Yes. Thanks awfully. Goodbye. [*He goes out*].

MRS EYNSFORD HILL. Goodbye, Mr Higgins.

HIGGINS. Goodbye. Goodbye.

MRS EYNSFORD HILL [*to* PICKERING] It's no use. I shall never be able to bring myself to use that word.

PICKERING. Dont. It's not compulsory, you know. Youll get on quite well without it.

MRS EYNSFORD HILL. Only, Clara is so down on me if I am not positively reeking with the latest slang. Goodbye.

PICKERING. Goodbye [*They shake hands*].

MRS EYNSFORD HILL [*to* MRS HIGGINS] You mustnt mind Clara. [PICKERING, *catching from her lowered tone that this is not meant for him to hear, discreetly joins* HIGGINS *at the window*]. We're so poor! and she gets so few parties, poor child! She doesnt quite know. [MRS HIGGINS, *seeing that her eyes are moist, takes her hand sympathetically and goes with her to the door*]. But the boy is nice. Dont you think so?

MRS HIGGINS. Oh, quite nice. I shall always be delighted to see him.

MRS EYNSFORD HILL. Thank you, dear. Goodbye. [*She goes out*].

HIGGINS [*eagerly*] Well? Is Eliza presentable [*he swoops on his mother and drags her to the ottoman, where she sits down in* ELIZA*'s place with her son on her left*]?

PICKERING *returns to his chair on her right.*

MRS HIGGINS. You silly boy, of course she's not presentable. She's a triumph of your art and of her dressmaker's; but if you suppose for a moment that she doesnt give herself away in every sentence she utters, you must be perfectly cracked about her.

PICKERING. But dont you think something might be done? I mean something to eliminate the sanguinary[12] element from her conversation.

MRS HIGGINS. Not as long as she is in Henry's hands.

HIGGINS [*aggrieved*] Do you mean that my language is improper?

MRS HIGGINS. No, dearest: it would be quite proper—say on a canal barge; but it would not be proper for her at a garden party.

HIGGINS [*deeply injured*] Well I must say—

PICKERING [*interrupting him*] Come, Higgins: you must learn to know yourself. I havnt heard such language as yours since we used to review the volunteers in Hyde Park twenty years ago.

HIGGINS [*sulkily*] Oh, well, if you say so, I suppose I dont always talk like a bishop.

MRS HIGGINS [*quieting* HENRY *with a touch*] Colonel Pickering: will you tell me what is the exact state of things in Wimpole Street?

PICKERING [*cheerfully: as if this completely changed the subject*] Well, I have come to live there with Henry. We work together at my Indian Dialects; and we think it more convenient—

---

11. **my days:** the days on which she receives visitors.

12. **sanguinary:** bloody. Pickering is alluding to Eliza's use of the slang term *bloody*.

MRS HIGGINS. Quite so. I know all about that: it's an excellent arrangement. But where does this girl live?

HIGGINS. With us, of course. Where should she live?

MRS HIGGINS. But on what terms? Is she a servant? If not, what is she?

PICKERING [slowly] I think I know what you mean, Mrs Higgins.

HIGGINS. Well, dash me if *I* do! Ive had to work at the girl every day for months to get her to her present pitch. Besides, she's useful. She knows where my things are, and remembers my appointments and so forth.

MRS HIGGINS. How does your housekeeper get on with her?

HIGGINS. Mrs Pearce? Oh, she's jolly glad to get so much taken off her hands; for before Eliza came, she used to have to find things and remind me of my appointments. But she's got some silly bee in her bonnet about Eliza. She keeps saying "You dont think, sir": doesnt she, Pick?

PICKERING. Yes: thats the formula. "You dont think, sir." Thats the end of every conversation about Eliza.

HIGGINS. As if I ever stop thinking about the girl and her confounded vowels and consonants. I'm worn out, thinking about her, and watching her lips and her teeth and her tongue, not to mention her soul, which is the quaintest of the lot.

MRS HIGGINS. You certainly are a pretty pair of babies, playing with your live doll.

HIGGINS. Playing! The hardest job I ever tackled: make no mistake about that, mother. But you have no idea how frightfully interesting it is to take a human being and change her into a quite different human being by creating a new speech for her. It's filling up the deepest gulf that separates class from class and soul from soul.

PICKERING [drawing his chair closer to MRS HIGGINS and bending over to her eagerly] Yes: it's enormously interesting. I assure you, Mrs Higgins, we take Eliza very seriously. Every week—every day almost—there is some new change. [Closer again] We keep records of every stage—dozens of gramophone disks and photographs—

HIGGINS [assailing her at the other ear] Yes, by George: it's the most absorbing experiment I ever tackled. She regularly fills our lives up: doesnt she, Pick?

PICKERING. We're always talking Eliza.

HIGGINS. Teaching Eliza.

PICKERING. Dressing Eliza.

MRS HIGGINS. What!

HIGGINS. Inventing new Elizas.

HIGGINS. PICKERING.	[speaking together]	You know, she has the most extraordinary quickness of ear: I assure you, my dear Mrs Higgins, that girl
HIGGINS. PICKERING.		just like a parrot. Ive tried her with every is a genius. She can play the piano quite beautifully.
HIGGINS. PICKERING.		possible sort of sound that a human being can make— We have taken her to classical concerts and to music
HIGGINS. PICKERING.		Continental dialects, African dialects, Hottentot halls; and it's all the same to her: she plays everything

HIGGINS. clicks, things it took
me years to get hold
of; and

PICKERING. she hears right off
when she comes
home, whether it's

HIGGINS. [*speaking together*] she picks them up
like a shot, right
away, as if she had

PICKERING. Beethoven and
Brahms or Lehar and
Lionel Monckton;

HIGGINS. been at it all her life.

PICKERING. though six months
ago, she'd never as
much as touched a
piano—

MRS HIGGINS [*putting her fingers in her ears, as they are by this time shouting one another down with an intolerable noise*] Sh-sh-sh—sh! [*They stop*].

PICKERING. I beg your pardon. [*He draws his chair back apologetically*].

HIGGINS. Sorry. When Pickering starts shouting nobody can get a word in edgeways.

MRS HIGGINS. Be quiet, Henry. Colonel Pickering: dont you realize that when Eliza walked in Wimpole Street, something walked in with her?

PICKERING. Her father did. But Henry soon got rid of him.

MRS HIGGINS. It would have been more to the point if her mother had. But as her mother didnt something else did.

PICKERING. But what?

MRS HIGGINS [*unconsciously dating herself by the word*] A problem.

PICKERING. Oh, I see. The problem of how to pass her off as a lady.

HIGGINS. I'll solve that problem. Ive half solved it already.

MRS HIGGINS. No, you two infinitely stupid male creatures: the problem of what is to be done with her afterwards.

HIGGINS. I dont see anything in that. She can go her own way, with all the advantages I have given her.

MRS HIGGINS. The advantages of that poor woman who was here just now! The manners and habits that disqualify a fine lady from earning her own living without giving her a fine lady's income! Is that what you mean?

PICKERING [*indulgently, being rather bored*] Oh, that will be all right, Mrs Higgins. [*He rises to go*].

HIGGINS [*rising also*] We'll find her some light employment.

PICKERING. She's happy enough. Dont you worry about her. Goodbye. [*He shakes hands as if he were consoling a frightened child, and makes for the door*].

HIGGINS. Anyhow, theres no good bothering now. The thing's done. Goodbye, mother. [*He kisses her, and follows* PICKERING].

PICKERING [*turning for a final consolation*] There are plenty of openings. We'll do whats right. Goodbye.

HIGGINS [*to* PICKERING *as they go out together*] Lets take her to the Shakespear exhibition at Earls Court.

PICKERING. Yes: lets. Her remarks will be delicious.

HIGGINS. She'll mimic all the people for us when we get home.

PICKERING. Ripping.[13] [*Both are heard laughing as they go downstairs*].

MRS HIGGINS [*rises with an impatient bounce, and returns to her work at the writing-table. She sweeps a litter of disarranged papers out of the way; snatches a sheet of paper from her*

---

13. **Ripping:** "Splendid!"

stationery case; and tries resolutely to write. At the third time she gives it up; flings down her pen; grips the table angrily and exclaims] Oh, men! men!! men!!!

*   *   *   *   *   *

Clearly Eliza will not pass as a duchess yet; and Higgins's bet remains unwon. But the six months are not yet exhausted and just in time Eliza does actually pass as a princess. For a glimpse of how she did it imagine an Embassy in London one summer evening after dark. The hall door has an awning and a carpet across the sidewalk to the kerb, because a grand reception is in progress. A small crowd is lined up to see the guests arrive.

A Rolls-Royce car drives up. Pickering in evening dress, with medals and orders, alights, and hands out Eliza, in opera cloak, evening dress, diamonds, fan, flowers and all accessories. Higgins follows. The car drives off; and the three go up the steps and into the house, the door opening for them as they approach.

Inside the house they find themselves in a spacious hall from which the grand staircase rises. On the left are the arrangements for the gentlemen's cloaks. The male guests are depositing their hats and wraps there.

On the right is a door leading to the ladies' cloakroom. Ladies are going in cloaked and coming out in splendor. Pickering whispers to Eliza and points out the ladies' room. She goes into it. Higgins and Pickering take off their overcoats and take tickets for them from the attendant.

One of the guests, occupied in the same way, has his back turned. Having taken his ticket, he turns round and reveals himself as an important looking young man with an astonishingly hairy face. He has an enormous moustache, flowing out into luxuriant whiskers. Waves of hair cluster on his brow. His hair is cropped closely at the back, and glows with oil. Otherwise he is very smart. He wears several worthless orders. He is ev-

idently a foreigner, guessable as a whiskered Pandour[14] from Hungary; but in spite of the ferocity of his moustache he is amiable and genially voluble.

Recognizing Higgins, he flings his arms wide apart and approaches him enthusiastically.

WHISKERS. Maestro, maestro [*he embraces* HIGGINS *and kisses him on both cheeks*]. You remember me?

HIGGINS. No I dont. Who the devil are you?

WHISKERS. I am your pupil: your first pupil, your best and greatest pupil. I am little Nepommuck, the marvellous boy. I have made your name famous throughout Europe. You teach me phonetic. You cannot forget ME.

HIGGINS. Why dont you shave?

NEPOMMUCK. I have not your imposing appearance, your chin, your brow. Nobody notice me when I shave. Now I am famous: they call me Hairy Faced Dick.

HIGGINS. And what are you doing here among all these swells?

NEPOMMUCK. I am interpreter. I speak 32 languages. I am indispensable at these international parties. You are great cockney specialist: you place a man anywhere in London the moment he open his mouth. I place any man in Europe.

A FOOTMAN *hurries down the grand staircase and comes to* NEPOMMUCK.

FOOTMAN. You are wanted upstairs. Her Excellency cannot understand the Greek gentleman.

NEPOMMUCK. Thank you, yes, immediately.

The FOOTMAN *goes and is lost in the crowd.*

NEPOMMUCK [*to* HIGGINS] This Greek diplomatist pretends he cannot speak nor understand English. He cannot deceive me. He is the

---

14. **Pandour:** bodyguard or servant of a Hungarian nobleman.

son of a Clerkenwell watchmaker. He speaks English so villainously that he dare not utter a word of it without betraying his origin. I help him to pretend; but I make him pay through the nose. I make them all pay. Ha ha! [*He hurries upstairs*].

PICKERING. Is this fellow really an expert? Can he find out Eliza and blackmail her?

HIGGINS. We shall see. If he finds her out I lose my bet.

ELIZA *comes from the cloakroom and joins them.*

PICKERING. Well, Eliza, now for it. Are you ready?

LIZA. Are you nervous, Colonel?

PICKERING. Frightfully. I feel exactly as I felt before my first battle. It's the first time that frightens.

LIZA. It is not the first time for me, Colonel. I have done this fifty times—hundreds of times—in my little piggery in Angel Court in my day-dreams. I am in a dream now. Promise me not to let Professor Higgins wake me; for if he does I shall forget everything and talk as I used to in Drury Lane.

PICKERING. Not a word, Higgins. [*To* ELIZA] Now, ready?

LIZA. Ready.

PICKERING. Go.

They mount the stairs, HIGGINS *last.* PICKERING *whispers to the* FOOTMAN *on the first landing.*

FIRST LANDING FOOTMAN. Miss Doolittle, Colonel Pickering, Professor Higgins.

SECOND LANDING FOOTMAN. Miss Doolittle, Colonel Pickering, Professor Higgins.

At the top of the staircase the AMBASSADOR *and his* WIFE, *with* NEPOMMUCK *at her elbow, are receiving.*

HOSTESS [*taking* Eliza's *hand*] How d'ye do?

HOST [*same play*] How d'ye do? How d'ye do, Pickering?

LIZA [*with a beautiful gravity that awes her hostess*] How do you do? [*She passes on to the drawingroom*].

HOSTESS. Is that your adopted daughter, Colonel Pickering? She will make a sensation.

PICKERING. Most kind of you to invite her for me. [*He passes on*].

HOSTESS [*to* NEPOMMUCK] Find out all about her.

NEPOMMUCK [*bowing*] Excellency—[*he goes into the crowd*].

HOST. How d'ye do, Higgins? You have a rival here tonight. He introduced himself as your pupil. Is he any good?

HIGGINS. He can learn a language in a fortnight—knows dozens of them. A sure mark of a fool. As a phonetician, no good whatever.

HOSTESS. How d'ye do, Professor?

HIGGINS. How do you do? Fearful bore for you this sort of thing. Forgive my part in it. [*He passes on*].

In the drawing room and its suite of salons the reception is in full swing. Eliza passes through. She is so intent on her ordeal that she walks like a somnambulist[15] in a desert instead of a débutante in a fashionable crowd. They stop talking to look at her, admiring her dress, her jewels, and her strangely attractive self. Some of the younger ones at the back stand on their chairs to see.

The Host and Hostess come in from the staircase and mingle with their guests. Higgins, gloomy and contemptuous of the whole business, comes into the group where they are chatting.

HOSTESS. Ah, here is Professor Higgins: he will tell us. Tell us all about the wonderful young lady, Professor.

---

15. **somnambulist:** sleepwalker.

HIGGINS [*almost morosely*] What wonderful young lady?

HOSTESS. You know very well. They tell me there has been nothing like her in London since people stood on their chairs to look at Mrs Langtry.[16]

NEPOMMUCK *joins the group, full of news.*

HOSTESS. Ah, here you are at last, Nepommuck. Have you found out all about the Doolittle lady?

NEPOMMUCK. I have found out all about her. She is a fraud.

HOSTESS. A fraud! Oh no.

NEPOMMUCK. YES, yes. She cannot deceive me. Her name cannot be Doolittle.

HIGGINS. Why?

NEPOMMUCK. Because Doolittle is an English name. And she is not English.

HOSTESS. Oh, nonsense! She speaks English perfectly.

NEPOMMUCK. Too perfectly. Can you shew me any English woman who speaks English as it should be spoken? Only foreigners who have been taught to speak it speak it well.

HOSTESS. Certainly she terrified me by the way she said How d'ye do. I had a schoolmistress who talked like that; and I was mortally afraid of her. But if she is not English what is she?

NEPOMMUCK. Hungarian.

ALL THE REST. Hungarian!

NEPOMMUCK. Hungarian. And of royal blood. I am Hungarian. My blood is royal.

HIGGINS. Did you speak to her in Hungarian?

NEPOMMUCK. I did. She was very clever. She said "Please speak to me in English: I do not understand French." French! She pretends not to know the difference between Hungarian and French. Impossible: she knows both.

HIGGINS. And the blood royal? How did you find that out?

NEPOMMUCK. Instinct, maestro, instinct. Only the Magyar races can produce that air of the divine right, those resolute eyes. She is a princess.

HOST. What do you say, Professor?

HIGGINS. I say an ordinary London girl out of

---

16. **Mrs. Langtry:** Lily Langtry (1852–1929), celebrated English actress and beauty.

the gutter and taught to speak by an expert. I place her in Drury Lane.

NEPOMMUCK. Ha ha ha! Oh, maestro, maestro, you are mad on the subject of cockney dialects. The London gutter is the whole world for you.

HIGGINS [*to the* HOSTESS] What does your Excellency say?

HOSTESS. Oh, of course I agree with Nepommuck. She must be a princess at least.

HOST. Not necessarily legitimate, of course. Morganatic[17] perhaps. But that is undoubtedly her class.

HIGGINS. I stick to my opinion.

---

17. **Morganatic** [môr'gə nat'ik]: referring to a marriage between royalty and a commoner. Although such a marriage is valid, the children do not inherit titles.

HOSTESS. Oh, you are incorrigible.

The group breaks up, leaving HIGGINS *isolated.* PICKERING *joins him.*

PICKERING. Where is Eliza? We must keep an eye on her.

ELIZA *joins them.*

LIZA. I dont think I can bear much more. The people all stare so at me. An old lady has just told me that I speak exactly like Queen Victoria. I am sorry if I have lost your bet. I have done my best; but nothing can make me the same as these people.

PICKERING. You have not lost it, my dear. You have won it ten times over.

HIGGINS. Let us get out of this. I have had enough of chattering to these fools.

PICKERING. Eliza is tired; and I am hungry. Let us clear out and have supper somewhere.

STUDY QUESTIONS

Recalling
1. What does Liza discuss at Mrs. Higgins' gathering? How does Higgins explain her to the guests, and how do they react to her?
2. According to Mrs. Higgins, what "problem" walked in the door with Liza? What answer do Higgins and Pickering give Mrs. Higgins?
3. Whom do Higgins and Liza meet at the ambassador's party? What conclusion regarding Liza does this person draw and why?
4. How is Pickering's bet with Higgins resolved?

Interpreting
5. At Mrs. Higgins' gathering, in what way does Liza "give herself away in every sentence"? Why do you think the Eynsford Hills accept Higgins' explanation of Liza's conversation?
6. Contrast Mrs. Higgins with her son. Why do his and Pickering's attitude toward Liza prompt Mrs. Higgins' outburst on page 609?
7. Describe the change in Liza from her tea in Mrs. Higgins' parlor to the embassy ball.

LITERARY FOCUS

Dramatic Conventions
Dramatic conventions are practices that we accept on stage but that differ from real-life behavior. In Shakespeare's plays, for instance, we accept the conventions of blank verse, soliloquies, and asides.

One very important function of dramatic conventions is to portray shifts in time. The passage of days, months, even years is presented on stage through such conventions as breaks in the action, variations in the set, and, most important, changes in the characters. Similarly, dramatic action operates within the convention that time on stage is often *telescoped,* or speeded up—Liza's bath takes much less time than an actual bath would. Such dramatic conventions help to bridge the gap between stage life and real life.

Thinking About Dramatic Conventions
◼ In what ways is the passage of time signaled from Act Two to Act Three of *Pygmalion* and from the first to the second part of Act Three?

ACT FOUR

The Wimpole Street laboratory. Midnight. Nobody in the room. The clock on the mantelpiece strikes twelve. The fire is not alight: it is a summer night.

Presently HIGGINS *and* PICKERING *are heard on the stairs.*

HIGGINS [*calling down to* PICKERING] I say, Pick: lock up, will you? I shant be going out again.

PICKERING. Right. Can Mrs Pearce go to bed? We dont want anything more, do we?

HIGGINS. Lord, no!

ELIZA *opens the door and is seen on the lighted landing in all the finery in which she has just won* HIGGINS's *bet for him. She comes to the hearth, and switches on the electric lights there. She is tired: her pallor contrasts strongly with her dark eyes and hair; and her expression is almost tragic. She takes off her cloak; puts her fan and gloves on the piano; and sits down on the bench, brooding and silent.* HIGGINS, *in evening dress, with overcoat and hat, comes in, carrying a smoking jacket which he has picked up downstairs. He takes off the hat and overcoat; throws them carelessly on the newspaper stand; disposes of his coat in the same way; puts on the smoking jacket; and throws himself wearily into the easy-chair at the hearth.* PICKERING, *similarly attired, comes in. He also takes off his hat and overcoat, and is about to throw them on* HIGGINS's *when he hesitates.*

PICKERING. I say: Mrs Pearce will row if we leave these things lying about in the drawing room.

HIGGINS. Oh, chuck them over the bannisters into the hall. She'll find them there in the morning and put them away all right. She'll think we were drunk.

PICKERING. We are, slightly. Are there any letters?

HIGGINS. I didnt look. [PICKERING *takes the overcoats and hats and goes downstairs.* HIGGINS *begins half singing half yawning an air from* La Fanciulla del Golden West.[1] *Suddenly he stops and exclaims*] I wonder where the devil my slippers are!

ELIZA *looks at him darkly; then rises suddenly and leaves the room.*

HIGGINS *yawns again, and resumes his song.*

PICKERING *returns, with the contents of the letter-box in his hand.*

PICKERING. Only circulars, and this coroneted billet-doux[2] for you. [*He throws the circulars into the fender, and posts himself on the hearthrug, with his back to the grate*].

HIGGINS [*glancing at the billet-doux*] Moneylender. [*He throws the letter after the circulars*].

ELIZA *returns with a pair of large down-at-heel slippers. She places them on the carpet before* HIGGINS, *and sits as before without a word.*

HIGGINS [*yawning again*] Oh Lord! What an evening! What a crew! What a silly tomfoolery! [*He raises his shoe to unlace it, and catches sight of the slippers. He stops unlacing and looks at them as if they had appeared there of their own accord*]. Oh! theyre there, are they?

PICKERING [*stretching himself*]. Well, I feel a bit tired. It's been a long day. The garden party, a dinner party, and the reception! Rather too much of a good thing. But youve won your bet, Higgins. Eliza did the trick, and something to spare, eh?

HIGGINS [*fervently*] Thank God it's over!

ELIZA *flinches violently; but they take no no-*

---

1. **La Fanciulla** [la fan choo′la] **del Golden West:** *The Girl of the Golden West,* opera by Italian composer Giacomo Puccini (1858–1924).
2. **coroneted billet-doux** [bil′ā doo′]: love letter decorated with a small crown.

tice of her; and she recovers herself and sits stonily as before.

PICKERING. Were you nervous at the garden party? *I* was. Eliza didnt seem a bit nervous.

HIGGINS. Oh, she wasnt nervous. I knew she'd be all right. No: it's the strain of putting the job through all these months that has told on me. It was interesting enough at first, while we were at the phonetics; but after that I got deadly sick of it. If I hadnt backed myself to do it I should have chucked the whole thing up two months ago. It was a silly notion: the whole thing has been a bore.

PICKERING. Oh come! the garden party was frightfully exciting. My heart began beating like anything.

HIGGINS. Yes, for the first three minutes. But when I saw we were going to win hands down, I felt like a bear in a cage, hanging about doing nothing. The dinner was worse: sitting gorging there for over an hour, with nobody but a damned fool of a fashionable woman to talk to! I tell you, Pickering, never again for me. No more artificial duchesses. The whole thing has been simple purgatory.

PICKERING. Youve never been broken in properly to the social routine. [*Strolling over to the piano*] I rather enjoy dipping into it occasionally myself: it makes me feel young again. Anyhow, it was a great success: an immense success. I was quite frightened once or twice because Eliza was doing it so well. You see, lots of the real people cant do it at all: theyre such fools that they think style comes by nature to people in their position; and so they never learn. Theres always something professional about doing a thing superlatively well.

HIGGINS. Yes: thats what drives me mad: the silly people dont know their own silly business. [*Rising*] However, it's over and done with; and now I can go to bed at last without dreading tomorrow.

ELIZA's *beauty becomes murderous.*

PICKERING. I think I shall turn in too. Still, it's been a great occasion: a triumph for you. Goodnight. [*He goes*].

HIGGINS [*following him*] Goodnight. [*Over his shoulder, at the door*] Put out the lights, Eliza; and tell Mrs Pearce not to make coffee for me in the morning: I'll take tea. [*He goes out*].

ELIZA *tries to control herself and feel indifferent as she rises and walks across to the hearth to switch off the lights. By the time she gets there she is on the point of screaming. She sits down in* HIGGINS's *chair and holds on hard to the arms. Finally she gives way and flings herself furiously on the floor, raging.*

HIGGINS [*in despairing wrath outside*] What the devil have I done with my slippers? [*He appears at the door*].

LIZA [*snatching up the slippers, and hurling them at him one after the other with all her force*] There are your slippers. And there. Take your slippers; and may you never have a day's luck with them!

HIGGINS [*astounded*] What on earth—! [*He comes to her*]. Whats the matter? Get up. [*He pulls her up*] Anything wrong?

LIZA [*breathless*] Nothing wrong—with you. Ive won your bet for you, havnt I? Thats enough for you. *I* dont matter, I suppose.

HIGGINS. You won my bet! You! Presumptuous insect! *I* won it. What did you throw those slippers at me for?

LIZA. Because I wanted to smash your face. I'd like to kill you, you selfish brute. Why didnt you leave me where you picked me out of—in the gutter? You thank God it's all over, and that now you can throw me back again there, do you? [*She crisps her fingers[3] frantically*].

HIGGINS [*looking at her in cool wonder*] The creature is nervous, after all.

---

3. **crisps her fingers:** clenches them into fists.

LIZA [*gives a suffocated scream of fury, and instinctively darts her nails at his face*]!!

HIGGINS [*catching her wrists*] Ah! would you? Claws in, you cat. How dare you shew your temper to me? Sit down and be quiet. [*He throws her roughly into the easy-chair*].

LIZA [*crushed by superior strength and weight*] Whats to become of me? Whats to become of me?

HIGGINS. How the devil do I know whats to become of you? What does it matter what becomes of you?

LIZA. You dont care. I know you dont care. You wouldnt care if I was dead. I'm nothing to you—not so much as them slippers.

HIGGINS [*thundering*] Those slippers.

LIZA [*with bitter submission*] Those slippers. I didnt think it made any difference now.

A pause. ELIZA *hopeless and crushed.* HIGGINS *a little uneasy.*

HIGGINS [*in his loftiest manner*] Why have you begun going on like this? May I ask whether you complain of your treatment here?

LIZA. No.

HIGGINS. Has anybody behaved badly to you? Colonel Pickering? Mrs Pearce? Any of the servants?

LIZA. No.

HIGGINS. I presume you dont pretend that *I* have treated you badly?

LIZA. No.

HIGGINS. I am glad to hear it. [*He moderates his tone*]. Perhaps youre tired after the strain of the day. Will you have a glass of champagne? [*He moves towards the door*].

LIZA. No. [*Recollecting her manners*] Thank you.

HIGGINS [*good-humored again*] This has been coming on you for some days. I suppose it was natural for you to be anxious about the garden party. But thats all over now. [*He pats her kindly on the shoulder. She writhes*]. Theres nothing more to worry about.

LIZA. No. Nothing more for you to worry about. [*She suddenly rises and gets away from him by going to the piano bench, where she sits and hides her face*]. Oh God! I wish I was dead.

HIGGINS [*staring after her in sincere surprise*] Why? In heaven's name, why? [*Reasonably, going to her*] Listen to me, Eliza. All this irritation is purely subjective.

LIZA. I dont understand. I'm too ignorant.

HIGGINS. It's only imagination. Low spirits and nothing else. Nobody's hurting you. Nothing's wrong. You go to bed like a good girl and sleep it off. Have a little cry and say your prayers: that will make you comfortable.

LIZA. I heard your prayers. "Thank God it's all over!"

HIGGINS [*impatiently*] Well, dont you thank God it's all over? Now you are free and can do what you like.

LIZA [*pulling herself together in desperation*] What am I fit for? What have you left me fit for? Where am I to go? What am I to do? Whats to become of me?

HIGGINS [*enlightened, but not at all impressed*] Oh, thats whats worrying you, is it? [*He thrusts his hands into his pockets, and walks about in his usual manner, rattling the contents of his pockets, as if condescending to a trivial subject out of pure kindness*]. I shouldnt bother about it if I were you. I should imagine you wont have much difficulty in settling yourself somewhere or other, though I hadnt quite realized that you were going away. [*She looks quickly at him: he does not look at her, but examines the dessert stand on the piano and decides that he will eat an apple*]. You might marry, you know. [*He bites a large piece out of the apple and munches it noisily*]. You see,

Eliza, all men are not confirmed old bachelors like me and the Colonel. Most men are the marrying sort (poor devils!); and youre not bad-looking: it's quite a pleasure to look at you sometimes—not now, of course, because youre crying and looking as ugly as the very devil; but when youre all right and quite yourself, youre what I should call attractive. That is, to the people in the marrying line, you understand. You go to bed and have a good nice rest; and then get up and look at yourself in the glass; and you wont feel so cheap.

ELIZA *again looks at him, speechless, and does not stir.*

The look is quite lost on him: he eats his apple with a dreamy expression of happiness, as it is quite a good one.

HIGGINS [*a genial afterthought occurring to him*] I daresay my mother could find some chap or other who would do very well.

LIZA. We were above that at the corner of Tottenham Court Road.

HIGGINS [*waking up*] What do you mean?

LIZA. I sold flowers. I didnt sell myself. Now youve made a lady of me I'm not fit to sell anything else. I wish youd left me where you found me.

HIGGINS [*slinging the core of the apple decisively into the grate*] Tosh, Eliza. Dont you insult human relations by dragging all this cant[4] about buying and selling into it. You neednt marry the fellow if you dont like him.

LIZA. What else am I to do?

HIGGINS. Oh, lots of things. What about your old idea of a florist's shop? Pickering could set you up in one: he has lots of money. [*Chuckling*] He'll have to pay for all those togs you have been wearing today; and that, with the hire of the jewellery, will make a big hole in

two hundred pounds. Why, six months ago you would have thought it the millennium to have a flower shop of your own. Come! youll be all right. I must clear off to bed: I'm devilish sleepy. By the way, I came down for something: I forgot what it was.

LIZA. Your slippers.

HIGGINS. Oh yes, of course. You shied them at me. [*He picks them up, and is going out when she rises and speaks to him*].

LIZA. Before you go, sir—

HIGGINS [*dropping the slippers in his surprise at her calling him Sir*] Eh?

LIZA. Do my clothes belong to me or to Colonel Pickering?

HIGGINS [*coming back into the room as if her question were the very climax of unreason*] What the devil use would they be to Pickering?

LIZA. He might want them for the next girl you pick up to experiment on.

HIGGINS [*shocked and hurt*] Is that the way you feel towards us?

LIZA. I dont want to hear anything more about that. All I want to know is whether anything belongs to me. My own clothes were burnt.

HIGGINS. But what does it matter? Why need you start bothering about that in the middle of the night?

LIZA. I want to know what I may take away with me. I dont want to be accused of stealing.

HIGGINS [*now deeply wounded*] Stealing! You shouldnt have said that, Eliza. That shews a want of feeling.

LIZA. I'm sorry. I'm only a common ignorant girl; and in my station I have to be careful. There cant be any feelings between the like of you and the like of me. Please will you tell me what belongs to me and what doesnt?

HIGGINS [*very sulky*] You may take the whole damned houseful if you like. Except the jewels.

---

4. cant: hollow words and borrowed phrases, repeated without thought.

Theyre hired.[5] Will that satisfy you? [*He turns on his heel and is about to go in extreme dudgeon[6]*].

LIZA [*drinking in his emotion like nectar,[7] and nagging him to provoke a further supply*] Stop, please. [*She takes off her jewels*]. Will you take these to your room and keep them safe? I dont want to run the risk of their being missing.

HIGGINS [*furious*] Hand them over. [*She puts them into his hands*]. If these belonged to me instead of to the jeweller, I'd ram them down your ungrateful throat. [*He perfunctorily thrusts them into his pockets, unconsciously decorating himself with the protruding ends of the chains*].

LIZA [*taking a ring off*]. This ring isnt the jeweller's: it's the one you bought me in Brighton. I dont want it now. [HIGGINS *dashes the ring violently into the fireplace, and turns on her so threateningly that she crouches over the piano with her hands over her face, and exclaims*] Dont you hit me.

HIGGINS. Hit you! You infamous creature, how dare you accuse me of such a thing? It is you who have hit me. You have wounded me to the heart.

LIZA [*thrilling with hidden joy*] I'm glad. Ive got a little of my own back, anyhow.

HIGGINS [*with dignity, in his finest professional style*] You have caused me to lose my temper: a thing that has hardly ever happened to me before. I prefer to say nothing more tonight. I am going to bed.

LIZA [*pertly*] Youd better leave a note for Mrs Pearce about the coffee; for she wont be told by me.

HIGGINS [*formally*] Damn Mrs Pearce; and damn the coffee; and damn you; and [*wildly*] damn my own folly in having lavished my hard-

---

5. **hired:** rented.
6. **dudgeon:** anger.
7. **nectar:** in mythology, the drink of the gods.

earned knowledge and the treasure of my regard and intimacy on a heartless guttersnipe. [*He goes out with impressive decorum, and spoils it by slamming the door savagely*].

ELIZA *goes down on her knees on the hearthrug to look for the ring. When she finds it she considers for a moment what to do with it. Finally she flings it down on the dessert stand and goes upstairs in a tearing rage.*

* * * * * *

The furniture of Eliza's room has been increased by a big wardrobe and a sumptuous dressing-table. She comes in and switches on the electric light. She goes to the wardrobe; opens it; and pulls out a walking dress, a hat, and a pair of shoes, which she throws on the bed. She takes off her evening dress and shoes; then takes a padded hanger from the wardrobe; adjusts it carefully in the evening dress; and hangs it in the wardrobe, which she shuts with a slam. She puts on her walking shoes, her walking dress, and hat. She takes her wrist watch from the dressing-table and fastens it on. She pulls on her gloves; takes her vanity bag; and looks into it to see that her purse is there before hanging it on her wrist. She makes for the door. Every movement expresses her furious resolution.

She takes a last look at herself in the glass.

She suddenly puts out her tongue at herself; then leaves the room, switching off the electric light at the door.

Meanwhile, in the street outside, Freddy Eynsford Hill, lovelorn, is gazing up at the second floor, in which one of the windows is still lighted.

The light goes out.

FREDDY. Goodnight, darling, darling, darling.

ELIZA *comes out, giving the door a considerable bang behind her.*

LIZA. Whatever are you doing here?

FREDDY. Nothing. I spend most of my nights here. It's the only place where I'm happy. Dont laugh at me, Miss Doolittle.

LIZA. Dont you call me Miss Doolittle, do you hear? Liza's good enough for me. [*She breaks down and grabs him by the shoulders*] Freddy: you dont think I'm a heartless guttersnipe, do you?

FREDDY. Oh no, no, darling: how can you imagine such a thing? You are the loveliest, dearest—

He loses all self-control and smothers her with kisses. She, hungry for comfort, responds. They stand there in one another's arms.

An elderly police constable arrives.

CONSTABLE [*scandalized*] Now then! Now then!! Now then!!!

They release one another hastily.

FREDDY. Sorry, constable. Weve only just become engaged.

They run away.

The constable shakes his head, reflecting on his own courtship and on the vanity of human hopes. He moves off in the opposite direction with slow professional steps.

The flight of the lovers takes them to Cavendish Square. There they halt to consider their next move.

LIZA [*out of breath*] He didnt half give me a fright, that copper. But you answered him proper.

FREDDY. I hope I havnt taken you out of your way. Where were you going?

LIZA. To the river.

FREDDY. What for?

LIZA. To make a hole in it.

FREDDY [*horrified*] Eliza, darling. What do you mean? What's the matter?

LIZA. Never mind. It doesnt matter now. There's nobody in the world now but you and me, is there?

FREDDY. Not a soul.

They indulge in another embrace, and are

*again surprised by a much younger con-
stable.*

SECOND CONSTABLE. Now then, you two! What's
this? Where do you think you are? Move along
here, double quick.

FREDDY. As you say, sir, double quick.

They run away again, and are in Hanover
Square before they stop for another conference.

FREDDY. I had no idea the police were so dev-
ilishly prudish.

LIZA. It's their business to hunt girls off the
streets.

FREDDY. We must go somewhere. We cant wander about the streets all night.

LIZA. Cant we? I think it'd be lovely to wander
about for ever.

FREDDY. Oh, darling.

*They embrace again, oblivious of the ar-
rival of a crawling taxi. It stops.*

TAXIMAN. Can I drive you and the lady anywhere, sir?

They start asunder.

LIZA. Oh, Freddy, a taxi. The very thing.

FREDDY. But, damn it, I've no money.

LIZA. I have plenty. The Colonel thinks you
should never go out without ten pounds in
your pocket. Listen. We'll drive about all night;
and in the morning I'll call on old Mrs Higgins
and ask her what I ought to do. I'll tell you all
about it in the cab. And the police wont touch
us there.

FREDDY. Righto! Ripping. [*To the* TAXIMAN]
Wimbledon Common. [*They drive off*].

STUDY QUESTIONS

Recalling

1. What do Higgins and Pickering talk about
   when they return to Wimpole Street? What
   does Higgins say when Pickering congratu-
   lates him? How does Liza react to Higgins?
2. Describe Liza's behavior to Higgins after Pickering leaves. How does she reply to his comment that she can do anything she likes now?
3. What various futures does Higgins outline for
   Liza? How does she answer his suggestion
   that his mother might find her a husband?
4. What does Freddy tell Liza when she meets
   him? What do they do?

Interpreting

5. Describe Liza's feelings after the party. Why
   might she feel as she does?
6. What does Higgins reveal about his personality
   in his treatment of Liza after the party? Why
   do you think he is wounded by Liza's behavior?
7. What new sides do Liza and Higgins both reveal in their argument?

Extending

8. What are the risks of changing a human being
   "into quite a different human being"? Under
   what circumstances might such an undertaking
   be justified?

ACT FIVE

MRS HIGGINS's *drawing room. She is at her writing-table as before. The* PARLORMAID *comes in.*

THE PARLORMAID [*at the door*] Mr Henry, maam, is downstairs with Colonel Pickering.

MRS HIGGINS. Well, shew them up.

THE PARLORMAID. Theyre using the telephone, maam. Telephoning to the police, I think.

MRS HIGGINS. What!

THE PARLORMAID [*coming further in and lowering her voice*] Mr Henry is in a state, maam. I thought I'd better tell you.

MRS HIGGINS. If you had told me that Mr Henry was not in a state it would have been more surprising. Tell them to come up when theyve finished with the police. I suppose he's lost something.

THE PARLORMAID. Yes, maam [*going*].

MRS HIGGINS. Go upstairs and tell Miss Doolittle that Mr Henry and the Colonel are here. Ask her not to come down til I send for her.

THE PARLORMAID. Yes, maam.

HIGGINS *bursts in. He is, as the* PARLORMAID *has said, in a state.*

HIGGINS. Look here, mother: heres a confounded thing!

MRS HIGGINS. Yes, dear. Good morning. [*He checks his impatience and kisses her, whilst the* PARLORMAID *goes out*]. What is it?

HIGGINS. Eliza's bolted.[1]

MRS HIGGINS [*calmly continuing her writing*] You must have frightened her.

HIGGINS. Frightened her! nonsense! She was left last night, as usual, to turn out the lights and all that; and instead of going to bed she changed her clothes and went right off: her

_____
1. **bolted:** run away.

bed wasnt slept in. She came in a cab for her things before seven this morning; and that fool Mrs Pearce let her have them without telling me a word about it. What am I to do?

MRS HIGGINS. Do without, I'm afraid, Henry. The girl has a perfect right to leave if she chooses.

HIGGINS [*wandering distractedly across the room*] But I cant find anything. I dont know what appointments Ive got. I'm—[PICKERING *comes in.* MRS HIGGINS *puts down her pen and turns away from the writing-table*].

PICKERING [*shaking hands*] Good morning, Mrs Higgins. Has Henry told you? [*He sits down on the ottoman*].

HIGGINS. What does that ass of an inspector say? Have you offered a reward?

MRS HIGGINS [*rising in indignant amazement*] You dont mean to say you have set the police after Eliza.

HIGGINS. Of course. What are the police for? What else could we do? [*He sits in the Elizabethan chair*].

PICKERING. The inspector made a lot of difficulties. I really think he suspected us of some improper purpose.

MRS HIGGINS. Well, of course he did. What right have you to go to the police and give the girl's name as if she were a thief, or a lost umbrella, or something? Really! [*She sits down again, deeply vexed*].

HIGGINS. But we want to find her.

PICKERING. We cant let her go like this, you know, Mrs Higgins. What were we to do?

MRS HIGGINS. You have no more sense, either of you, than two children. Why—

The PARLORMAID *comes in and breaks off the conversation.*

THE PARLORMAID. Mr Henry: a gentleman wants

to see you very particular. He's been sent on from Wimpole Street.

HIGGINS. Oh, bother! I cant see anyone now. Who is it?

THE PARLORMAID. A Mr Doolittle, sir.

PICKERING. Doolittle! Do you mean the dustman?

THE PARLORMAID. Dustman! Oh no, sir: a gentleman.

HIGGINS [springing up excitedly] By George, Pick, it's some relative of hers that she's gone to. Somebody we know nothing about. [To the PARLORMAID] Send him up, quick.

THE PARLORMAID. Yes, sir. [She goes].

HIGGINS [eagerly, going to his mother] Genteel relatives! now we shall hear something. [He sits down in the Chippendale chair].

MRS HIGGINS. Do you know any of her people?

PICKERING. Only her father: the fellow we told you about.

THE PARLORMAID [announcing] Mr Doolittle. [She withdraws].

DOOLITTLE enters. He is resplendently dressed as for a fashionable wedding, and might, in fact, be the bridegroom. A flower in his buttonhole, a dazzling silk hat, and patent leather shoes complete the effect. He is too concerned with the business he has come on to notice MRS HIGGINS. He walks straight to HIGGINS, and accosts him with vehement reproach.

DOOLITTLE [indicating his own person] See here! Do you see this? You done this.

HIGGINS. Done what, man?

DOOLITTLE. This, I tell you. Look at it. Look at this hat. Look at this coat.

PICKERING. Has Eliza been buying you clothes?

DOOLITTLE. Eliza! not she. Why would she buy me clothes?

MRS HIGGINS. Good morning, Mr Doolittle. Wont you sit down?

DOOLITTLE [taken aback as he becomes conscious that he has forgotten his hostess] Asking your pardon, maam. [He approaches her and shakes her proffered hand]. Thank you. [He sits down on the ottoman, on PICKERING's right]. I am that full of what has happened to me that I cant think of anything else.

HIGGINS. What the dickens has happened to you?

DOOLITTLE. I shouldnt mind if it had only happened to me: anything might happen to anybody and nobody to blame but Providence, as you might say. But this is something that you done to me: yes, you, Enry Iggins.

HIGGINS. Have you found Eliza?

DOOLITTLE. Have you lost her?

HIGGINS. Yes.

DOOLITTLE. You have all the luck, you have. I aint found her; but she'll find me quick enough now after what you done to me.

MRS HIGGINS. But what has my son done to you, Mr Doolittle?

DOOLITTLE. Done to me! Ruined me. Destroyed my happiness. Tied me up and delivered me into the hands of middle class morality.

HIGGINS [rising intolerantly and standing over DOOLITTLE] Youre raving. Youre drunk. Youre mad. I gave you five pounds. After that I had two conversations with you, at half-a-crown an hour. Ive never seen you since.

DOOLITTLE. Oh! Drunk am I? Mad am I? Tell me this. Did you or did you not write a letter to an old blighter in America that was giving five millions to found Moral Reform Societies all over the world, and that wanted you to invent a universal language for him?

HIGGINS. What! Ezra D. Wannafeller! He's dead. [He sits down again carelessly].

DOOLITTLE. Yes: he's dead; and I'm done for. Now did you or did you not write a letter to him to say that the most original moralist at present in England, to the best of your knowledge, was Alfred Doolittle, a common dustman?

HIGGINS. Oh, after your first visit I remember making some silly joke of the kind.

DOOLITTLE. Ah! You may well call it a silly joke. It put the lid on me right enough. Just give him the chance he wanted to shew that Americans is not like us: that they reckonize and respect merit in every class of life, however humble. Them words is in his blooming will, in which, Henry Higgins, thanks to your silly joking, he leaves me a share in his Pre-digested Cheese Trust worth three thousand a year on condition that I lecture for his Wannafeller Moral Reform World League as often as they ask me up to six times a year.

HIGGINS. The devil he does! Whew! [*Brightening suddenly*] What a lark!

PICKERING. A safe thing for you, Doolittle. They wont ask you twice.

DOOLITTLE. It aint the lecturing I mind. I'll lecture them blue in the face, I will, and not turn a hair. It's making a gentleman of me that I object to. Who asked him to make a gentleman of me? I was happy. I was free. I touched pretty nigh everybody for money when I wanted it, same as I touched you, Enry Iggins. Now I am worrited; tied neck and heels; and everybody touches me for money. It's a fine thing for you, says my solicitor.[2] Is it? says I. You mean it's a good thing for you, I says. When I was a poor man and had a solicitor once when they found a pram[3] in the dust cart, he got me off, and got shut of me and got me shut of him as quick as he could. Same with the doctors: used to shove me out of the hospital before I could hardly stand on my legs, and nothing to pay. Now they finds out that I'm not a healthy man and cant live unless they looks after me twice a day. In the house I'm not let do a hand's turn for myself: somebody else must do it and touch me for it. A year ago I hadnt a relative in the world except two or three that wouldnt speak to me. Now Ive fifty, and not a decent week's wages among the lot of them. I have to live for others and not for myself: that middle class morality. You talk of losing Eliza. Dont you be anxious: I bet she's on my doorstep by this: she that could support herself easy by selling flowers if I wasnt respectable. And the next one to touch me will be you, Enry Iggins. I'll have to learn to speak middle class language from you, instead of speaking proper English. Thats where youll come in; and I daresay thats what you done it for.

MRS HIGGINS. But, my dear Mr Doolittle, you need not suffer all this if you are really in earnest. Nobody can force you to accept this bequest. You can repudiate it. Isnt that so, Colonel Pickering?

PICKERING. I believe so.

DOOLITTLE [*softening his manner in deference to her sex*] Thats the tragedy of it, maam. It's easy to say chuck it; but I havnt the nerve. Which of us has? We're all intimidated. Intimidated, maam: thats what we are. What is there for me if I chuck it but the workhouse in my old age? I have to dye my hair already to keep my job as a dustman. If I was one of the deserving poor, and had put by a bit, I could chuck it; but then why should I, acause the deserving poor might as well be millionaires for all the happiness they ever has. They dont know what happiness is. But I, as one of the undeserving poor, have nothing between me and the pauper's uniform but this here blasted three thousand a year that shoves me into the middle class. (Excuse the expression, maam; youd use it yourself if you had my provocation.) Theyve got you every way you turn: it's a choice between the Skilly of the workhouse and the Char Bydis[4] of the middle class; and I

---

2. **solicitor:** type of lawyer.
3. **pram:** baby carriage.

4. **Skilly, Char Bydis:** alluding to Scylla [sil′ə] and Charybdis [kə rib′ dis], a treacherous rock and whirlpool on either side of the narrow passage between Italy and Sicily. Represented by the Greeks as two monsters, Scylla and Charybdis have come to stand for any two dangers neither of which can be avoided without risking the other.

havnt the nerve for the workhouse. Intimidated: thats what I am. Broke. Bought up. Happier men than me will call for my dust, and touch me for their tip; and I'll look on helpless, and envy them. And thats what your son has brought me to. [*He is overcome by emotion*].

MRS HIGGINS. Well, I'm very glad youre not going to do anything foolish, Mr Doolittle. For this solves the problem of Eliza's future. You can provide for her now.

DOOLITTLE [*with melancholy resignation*] Yes, maam: I'm expected to provide for everyone now, out of three thousand a year.

HIGGINS [*jumping up*] Nonsense! he cant provide for her. He shant provide for her. She doesnt belong to him. I paid him five pounds for her. Doolittle: either youre an honest man or a rogue.

DOOLITTLE [*tolerantly*] A little of both, Henry, like the rest of us: a little of both.

HIGGINS. Well, you took that money for the girl; and you have no right to take her as well.

MRS HIGGINS. Henry: dont be absurd. If you want to know where Eliza is, she is upstairs.

HIGGINS [*amazed*] Upstairs!!! Then I shall jolly soon fetch her downstairs. [*He makes resolutely for the door*].

MRS HIGGINS [*rising and following him*] Be quiet, Henry. Sit down.

HIGGINS. I—

MRS HIGGINS. Sit down, dear; and listen to me.

HIGGINS. Oh very well, very well, very well. [*He throws himself ungraciously on the ottoman, with his face towards the windows*]. But I think you might have told us this half an hour ago.

MRS HIGGINS. Eliza came to me this morning. She told me of the brutal way you two treated her.

HIGGINS [*bounding up again*] What!

PICKERING [*rising also*] My dear Mrs Higgins, she's been telling you stories. We didnt treat her brutally. We hardly said a word to her; and we parted on particularly good terms. [*Turning on* HIGGINS] Higgins: did you bully her after I went to bed?

HIGGINS. Just the other way about. She threw my slippers in my face. She behaved in the most outrageous way. I never gave her the slightest provocation. The slippers came bang into my face the moment I entered the room— before I had uttered a word. And used perfectly awful language.

PICKERING [*astonished*] But why? What did we do to her?

MRS HIGGINS. I think I know pretty well what you did. The girl is naturally rather affectionate, I think. Isnt she, Mr Doolittle?

DOOLITTLE. Very tender-hearted, maam. Takes after me.

MRS HIGGINS. Just so. She had become attached to you both. She worked very hard for you, Henry. I dont think you quite realize what anything in the nature of brain work means to a girl of her class. Well, it seems that when the great day of trial came, and she did this wonderful thing for you without making a single mistake, you two sat there and never said a word to her, but talked together of how glad you were that it was all over and how you had been bored with the whole thing. And then you were surprised because she threw your slippers at you! *I* should have thrown the fire-irons at you.

HIGGINS. We said nothing except that we were tired and wanted to go to bed. Did we, Pick?

PICKERING [*shrugging his shoulders*] That was all.

MRS HIGGINS [*ironically*] Quite sure?

PICKERING. Absolutely. Really, that was all.

MRS HIGGINS. You didnt thank her, or pet her, or admire her, or tell her how splendid she'd been.

HIGGINS [impatiently] But she knew all about that. We didnt make speeches to her, if thats what you mean.

PICKERING [conscience stricken] Perhaps we were a little inconsiderate. Is she very angry?

MRS HIGGINS [returning to her place at the writing-table] Well, I'm afraid she wont go back to Wimpole Street, especially now that Mr Doolittle is able to keep up the position you have thrust on her; but she says she is quite willing to meet you on friendly terms and to let bygones be bygones.

HIGGINS [furious] Is she, by George? Ho!

MRS HIGGINS. If you promise to behave yourself, Henry, I'll ask her to come down. If not, go home; for you have taken up quite enough of my time.

HIGGINS. Oh, all right. Very well. Pick: you behave yourself. Let us put on our best Sunday manners for this creature that we picked out of the mud. [He flings himself sulkily into the Elizabethan chair].

DOOLITTLE [remonstrating] Now, now, Enry Iggins! Have some consideration for my feelings as a middle class man.

MRS HIGGINS. Remember your promise, Henry. [She presses the bell-button on the writing-table]. Mr Doolittle: will you be so good as to step out on the balcony for a moment. I dont want Eliza to have the shock of your news until she has made it up with these two gentlemen. Would you mind?

DOOLITTLE. As you wish, lady. Anything to help Henry to keep her off my hands. [He disappears through the window].

The PARLORMAID answers the bell. PICKERING sits down in DOOLITTLE's place.

MRS HIGGINS. Ask Miss Doolittle to come down, please.

THE PARLORMAID. Yes, maam. [She goes out].

MRS HIGGINS. Now, Henry: be good.

HIGGINS. I am behaving myself perfectly.

PICKERING. He is doing his best, Mrs Higgins.

A pause. HIGGINS throws back his head; stretches out his legs; and begins to whistle.

MRS HIGGINS. Henry, dearest, you dont look at all nice in that attitude.

HIGGINS [pulling himself together] I was not trying to look nice, mother.

MRS HIGGINS. It doesnt matter, dear. I only wanted to make you speak.

HIGGINS. Why?

MRS HIGGINS. Because you cant speak and whistle at the same time.

HIGGINS groans. Another very trying pause.

HIGGINS [springing up, out of patience] Where the devil is that girl? Are we to wait here all day?

ELIZA enters, sunny, self-possessed, and giving a staggeringly convincing exhibition of ease of manner. She carries a little work-basket, and is very much at home. PICKERING is too much taken aback to rise.

LIZA. How do you do, Professor Higgins? Are you quite well?

HIGGINS [choking] Am I— [He can say no more].

LIZA. But of course you are: you are never ill. So glad to see you again, Colonel Pickering. [He rises hastily; and they shake hands]. Quite chilly this morning, isnt it? [She sits down on his left. He sits beside her].

HIGGINS. Dont you dare try this game on me. I taught it to you; and it doesnt take me in. Get up and come home; and dont be a fool.

ELIZA takes a piece of needlework from her basket, and begins to stitch at it, without taking the least notice of this outburst.

MRS HIGGINS. Very nicely put, indeed, Henry. No woman could resist such an invitation.

HIGGINS. You let her alone, mother. Let her speak for herself. You will jolly soon see whether she has an idea that I havnt put into her head or a word that I havnt put into her mouth. I tell you I have created this thing out of the squashed cabbage leaves of Covent Garden; and now she pretends to play the fine lady with me.

MRS HIGGINS [*placidly*] Yes, dear; but youll sit down, wont you?

HIGGINS *sits down again, savagely.*

LIZA [*to* PICKERING, *taking no apparent notice of* HIGGINS, *and working away deftly*] Will you drop me altogether now that the experiment is over, Colonel Pickering?

PICKERING. Oh dont. You mustnt think of it as an experiment. It shocks me, somehow.

LIZA. Oh, I'm only a squashed cabbage leaf—

PICKERING [*impulsively*] No.

LIZA [*continuing quietly*]—but I owe so much to you that I should be very unhappy if you forgot me.

PICKERING. It's very kind of you to say so, Miss Doolittle.

LIZA. It's not because you paid for my dresses. I know you are generous to everybody with money. But it was from you that I learnt really nice manners; and that is what makes one a lady, isnt it? You see it was so very difficult for me with the example of Professor Higgins always before me. I was brought up to be just like him, unable to control myself, and using bad language on the slightest provocation. And I should never have known that ladies and gentlemen didnt behave like that if you hadnt been there.

HIGGINS. Well!!

PICKERING. Oh, thats only his way, you know. He doesnt mean it.

LIZA. Oh, *I* didnt mean it either, when I was a flower girl. It was only my way. But you see I did it; and thats what makes the difference after all.

PICKERING. No doubt. Still, he taught you to speak; and I couldnt have done that, you know.

LIZA [*trivially*] Of course: that is his profession.

HIGGINS. Damnation!

LIZA [*continuing*] It was just like learning to dance in the fashionable way: there was nothing more than that in it. But do you know what began my real education?

PICKERING. What?

LIZA [*stopping her work for a moment*] Your calling me Miss Doolittle that day when I first came to Wimpole Street. That was the beginning of self-respect for me. [*She resumes her stitching*] And there were a hundred little things you never noticed, because they came naturally to you. Things about standing up and taking off your hat and opening doors—

PICKERING. Oh, that was nothing.

LIZA. Yes: things that shewed you thought and felt about me as if I were something better than a scullery-maid; though of course I know you would have been just the same to a scullery-maid if she had been let into the drawing room. You never took off your boots in the dining room when I was there.

PICKERING. You mustnt mind that. Higgins takes off his boots all over the place.

LIZA. I know. I am not blaming him. It is his way, isnt it? But it made such a difference to me that you didnt do it. You see, really and truly, apart from the things anyone can pick up (the dressing and the proper way of speaking, and so on), the difference between a lady and a flower girl is not how she behaves, but how she's treated. I shall always be a flower girl to Professor Higgins, because he always treats me as a flower girl, and always will; but I know I can be a lady to you, because you always treat me as a lady, and always will.

MRS HIGGINS. Please dont grind your teeth, Henry.

PICKERING. Well, this is really very nice of you, Miss Doolittle.

LIZA. I should like you to call me Eliza, now, if you would.

PICKERING. Thank you. Eliza, of course.

LIZA. And I should like Professor Higgins to call me Miss Doolittle.

HIGGINS. I'll see you damned first.

MRS HIGGINS. Henry! Henry!

PICKERING [laughing] Why dont you slang back at him? Dont stand it. It would do him a lot of good.

LIZA. I cant. I could have done it once; but now I cant go back to it. You told me, you know, that when a child is brought to a foreign country, it picks up the language in a few weeks, and forgets its own. Well, I am a child in your country. I have forgotten my own language, and can speak nothing but yours. Thats the real break-off with the corner of Tottenham Court Road. Leaving Wimpole Street finishes it.

PICKERING [much alarmed] Oh! but youre coming back to Wimpole Street, arnt you? Youll forgive Higgins?

HIGGINS [rising] Forgive! Will she, by George! Let her go. Let her find out how she can get on without us. She will relapse into the gutter in three weeks without me at her elbow.

DOOLITTLE appears at the centre window. With a look of dignified reproach at HIGGINS, he comes slowly and silently to his daughter, who, with her back to the window, is unconscious of his approach.

PICKERING. He's incorrigible, Eliza. You wont relapse, will you?

LIZA. No: not now. Never again. I have learnt my lesson. I dont believe I could utter one of the old sounds if I tried. [DOOLITTLE touches her on the left shoulder. She drops her work, losing her self-possession utterly at the spectacle of her father's splendor] A-a-a-a-ah-ow-ooh!

HIGGINS [with a crow of triumph] Aha! Just so. A-a-a-a-ahowooh! A-a-a-a-ahowooh! A-a-a-a-ahowooh! Victory! Victory! [He throws himself on the divan, folding his arms, and spraddling arrogantly].

DOOLITTLE. Can you blame the girl? Dont look at me like that, Eliza. It aint my fault. Ive come into some money.

LIZA. You must have touched a millionaire this time, dad.

DOOLITTLE. I have. But I'm dressed something special today. I'm going to St George's, Hanover Square. Your stepmother is going to marry me.

LIZA [angrily] Youre going to let yourself down to marry that low common woman!

PICKERING [quietly] He ought to, Eliza. [To DOOLITTLE] Why has she changed her mind?

DOOLITTLE [sadly] Intimidated, Governor. Intimidated. Middle class morality claims its victim. Wont you put on your hat, Liza, and come and see me turned off?

LIZA. If the Colonel says I must, I—I'll [almost sobbing] I'll demean myself. And get insulted for my pains, like enough.

DOOLITTLE. Dont be afraid: she never comes to words with anyone now, poor woman! respectability has broke all the spirit out of her.

PICKERING [squeezing ELIZA's elbow gently] Be kind to them, Eliza. Make the best of it.

LIZA [forcing a little smile for him through her vexation] Oh well, just to shew theres no ill feeling. I'll be back in a moment. [She goes out].

DOOLITTLE [sitting down beside PICKERING] I feel uncommon nervous about the ceremony, Colonel. I wish youd come and see me through it.

PICKERING. But youve been through it before, man. You were married to Eliza's mother.

DOOLITTLE. Who told you that, Colonel?

PICKERING. Well, nobody told me. But I concluded—naturally—

DOOLITTLE. No: that aint the natural way, Colonel: it's only the middle class way. My way was always the undeserving way. But dont say nothing to Eliza. She dont know: I always had a delicacy about telling her.

PICKERING. Quite right. We'll leave it so, if you dont mind.

DOOLITTLE. And youll come to the church, Colonel, and put me through straight?

PICKERING. With pleasure. As far as a bachelor can.

MRS HIGGINS. May I come, Mr Doolittle? I should be very sorry to miss your wedding.

DOOLITTLE. I should indeed be honored by your condescension, maam; and my poor old woman would take it as a tremenjous compliment. She's been very low, thinking of the happy days that are no more.

MRS HIGGINS [rising] I'll order the carriage and get ready. [The men rise, except HIGGINS]. I shant be more than fifteen minutes. [As she goes to the door ELIZA comes in, hatted and buttoning her gloves]. I'm going to the church to see your father married, Eliza. You had better come in the brougham[5] with me. Colonel Pickering can go on with the bridegroom.

MRS HIGGINS goes out. ELIZA comes to the middle of the room between the centre window and the ottoman. PICKERING joins her.

DOOLITTLE. Bridegroom. What a word! It makes a man realize his position, somehow. [He takes up his hat and goes towards the door].

PICKERING. Before I go, Eliza, do forgive Higgins and come back to us.

_____
5. brougham [broom]: a kind of carriage.

LIZA. I dont think dad would allow me. Would you, dad?

DOOLITTLE [sad but magnanimous] They played you off very cunning, Eliza, them two sportsmen. If it had been only one of them, you could have nailed him. But you see, there was two; and one of them chaperoned the other, as you might say. [To PICKERING] It was artful of you, Colonel; but I bear no malice: I should have done the same myself. I been the victim of one woman after another all my life, and I dont grudge you two getting the better of Liza. I shant interfere. It's time for us to go, Colonel. So long, Henry. See you in St George's, Eliza. [He goes out].

PICKERING [coaxing] Do stay with us, Eliza. [He follows DOOLITTLE].

ELIZA goes out on the balcony to avoid being alone with HIGGINS. He rises and joins her there. She immediately comes back into the room and makes for the door; but he goes along the balcony and gets his back to the door before she reaches it.

HIGGINS. Well, Eliza, youve had a bit of your own back, as you call it. Have you had enough? and are you going to be reasonable? Or do you want any more?

LIZA. You want me back only to pick up your slippers and put up with your tempers and fetch and carry for you.

HIGGINS. I havnt said I wanted you back at all.

LIZA. Oh, indeed. Then what are we talking about?

HIGGINS. About you, not about me. If you come back I shall treat you just as I have always treated you. I cant change my nature; and I dont intend to change my manners. My manners are exactly the same as Colonel Pickering's.

LIZA. Thats not true. He treats a flower girl as if she was a duchess.

HIGGINS. And I treat a duchess as if she was a flower girl.

LIZA. I see [*She turns away composedly, and sits on the ottoman, facing the window*]. The same to everybody.

HIGGINS. Just so.

LIZA. Like father.

HIGGINS [*grinning, a little taken down*] Without accepting the comparison at all points, Eliza, it's quite true that your father is not a snob, and that he will be quite at home in any station of life to which his eccentric destiny may call him. [*Seriously*] The great secret, Eliza, is not having bad manners or good manners or any other particular sort of manners, but having the same manner for all human souls: in short, behaving as if you were in Heaven, where there are no third-class carriages, and one soul is as good as another.

LIZA. Amen. You are a born preacher.

HIGGINS [*irritated*] The question is not whether I treat you rudely, but whether you ever heard me treat anyone else better.

LIZA [*with sudden sincerity*] I dont care how you treat me. I dont mind your swearing at me. I shouldnt mind a black eye: Ive had one before this. But [*standing up and facing him*] I wont be passed over.

HIGGINS. Then get out of my way; for I wont stop for you. You talk about me as if I were a motor bus.

LIZA. So you are a motor bus: all bounce and go, and no consideration for anyone. But I can do without you: dont think I cant.

HIGGINS. I know you can. I told you you could.

LIZA [*wounded, getting away from him to the other side of the ottoman with her face to the hearth*] I know you did, you brute. You wanted to get rid of me.

HIGGINS. Liar.

LIZA. Thank you. [*She sits down with dignity*]

HIGGINS. You never asked yourself, I suppose, whether *I* could do without you.

LIZA [*earnestly*] Dont you try to get round me. Youll have to do without me.

HIGGINS [*arrogant*] I can do without anybody. I have my own soul: my own spark of divine fire. But [*with sudden humility*] I shall miss you, Eliza. [*He sits down near her on the ottoman*] I have learnt something from your idiotic notions: I confess that humbly and gratefully. And I have grown accustomed to your voice and appearance. I like them, rather.

LIZA. Well, you have both of them on your gramophone and in your book of photographs. When you feel lonely without me, you can turn the machine on. It's got no feelings to hurt.

HIGGINS. I cant turn your soul on. Leave me those feelings; and you can take away the voice and the face. They are not you.

LIZA. Oh, you are a devil. You can twist the heart in a girl as easy as some could twist her arms to hurt her. Mrs Pearce warned me. Time and again she has wanted to leave you; and you always got round her at the last minute. And you dont care a bit for her. And you dont care a bit for me.

HIGGINS. I care for life, for humanity; and you are a part of it that has come my way and been built into my house. What more can you or anyone ask?

LIZA. I wont care for anybody that doesnt care for me.

HIGGINS. Commercial principles, Eliza. Like [*reproducing her Covent Garden pronunciation with professional exactness*] s'yollin voylets [selling violets], isnt it?

LIZA. Dont sneer at me. It's mean to sneer at me.

HIGGINS. I have never sneered in my life. Sneering doesnt become either the human face or the human soul. I am expressing my righteous contempt for Commercialism. I dont and wont trade in affection. You call me a brute because you couldnt buy a claim on me by fetching my slippers and finding my spectacles. You were a fool: I think a woman fetching a man's slippers is a disgusting sight: did I ever fetch your slippers? I think a good deal more of you for throwing them in my face. No use slaving for me and then saying you want to be cared for: who cares for a slave? If you come back, come back for the sake of good fellowship; for youll get nothing else. Youve had a thousand times as much out of me as I have out of you; and if you dare to set up your little dog's tricks of fetching and carrying slippers against my creation of a Duchess Eliza, I'll slam the door in your silly face.

LIZA. What did you do it for if you didnt care for me?

HIGGINS [*heartily*] Why, because it was my job.

LIZA. You never thought of the trouble it would make for me.

HIGGINS. Would the world ever have been made if its maker had been afraid of making trouble? Making life means making trouble. Theres only one way of escaping trouble; and thats killing things. Cowards, you notice, are always shrieking to have troublesome people killed.

LIZA. I'm no preacher: I dont notice things like that. I notice that you dont notice me.

HIGGINS [*jumping up and walking about intolerantly*] Eliza: youre an idiot. I waste the treasures of my Miltonic mind by spreading them before you. Once for all, understand that I go my way and do my work without caring twopence what happens to either of us. I am not intimidated, like your father and your stepmother. So you can come back or go to the devil: which you please.

LIZA. What am I to come back for?

HIGGINS [*bouncing up on his knees on the ottoman and leaning over it to her*] For the fun of it. Thats why I took you on.

LIZA [*with averted face*] And you may throw me out tomorrow if I dont do everything you want me to?

HIGGINS. Yes; and you may walk out tomorrow if I dont do everything you want me to.

LIZA. And live with my stepmother?

HIGGINS. Yes, or sell flowers.

LIZA. Oh, if I only could go back to my flower basket! I should be independent of both you and father and all the world! Why did you take my independence from me? Why did I give it up? I'm a slave now, for all my fine clothes.

HIGGINS. Not a bit. I'll adopt you as my daughter and settle money on you if you like. Or would you rather marry Pickering?

LIZA [*looking fiercely round at him*] I wouldnt marry you if you asked me; and youre nearer my age than what he is.

HIGGINS [*gently*] Than he is: not "than what he is."

LIZA [*losing her temper and rising*] I'll talk as I like. Youre not my teacher now.

HIGGINS [*reflectively*] I dont suppose Pickering would, though. He's as confirmed an old bachelor as I am.

LIZA. Thats not what I want; and dont you think it. I've always had chaps enough wanting me that way. Freddy Hill writes to me twice and three times a day, sheets and sheets.

HIGGINS [*disagreeably surprised*] Damn his impudence! [*He recoils and finds himself sitting on his heels*].

LIZA. He has a right to if he likes, poor lad. And he does love me.

HIGGINS [*getting off the ottoman*] You have no right to encourage him.

LIZA. Every girl has a right to be loved.

HIGGINS. What! By fools like that?

LIZA. Freddy's not a fool. And if he's weak and poor and wants me, may be he'd make me happier than my betters that bully me and dont want me.

HIGGINS. Can he make anything of you? Thats the point.

LIZA. Perhaps I could make something of him. But I never thought of us making anything of one another; and you never think of anything else. I only want to be natural.

HIGGINS. In short, you want me to be as infatuated about you as Freddy? Is that it?

LIZA. No I dont. Thats not the sort of feeling I want from you. And dont you be too sure of yourself or of me. I could have been a bad girl if I'd liked. Ive seen more of some things than you, for all your learning. Girls like me can drag gentlemen down to make love to them easy enough. And they wish each other dead the next minute.

HIGGINS. Of course they do. Then what in thunder are we quarrelling about?

LIZA [*much troubled*] I want a little kindness. I know I'm a common ignorant girl, and you a book-learned gentleman; but I'm not dirt under your feet. What I done (*correcting herself*) what I did was not for the dresses and the taxis: I did it because we were pleasant together and I come—came—to care for you; not to want you to make love to me, and not forgetting the difference between us, but more friendly like.

HIGGINS. Well, of course. Thats just how I feel. And how Pickering feels. Eliza: youre a fool.

LIZA. Thats not a proper answer to give me [*she sinks on the chair at the writing-table in tears*].

HIGGINS. It's all youll get until you stop being a common idiot. If youre going to be a lady, youll have to give up feeling neglected if the men you know dont spend half their time snivelling over you and the other half giving you black eyes. If you cant stand the coldness of my sort of life, and the strain of it, go back to the gutter. Work til youre more a brute than a human being; and then cuddle and squabble and drink til you fall asleep. Oh, it's a fine life, the life of the gutter. It's real: it's warm: it's violent: you can feel it through the thickest skin: you can taste it and smell it without any training or any work. Not like Science and Literature and Classical Music and Philosophy and Art. You find me cold, unfeeling, selfish, dont you? Very well: be off with you to the sort of people you like. Marry some sentimental hog or other with lots of money, and a thick pair of lips to kiss you with and a thick pair of boots to kick you with. If you cant appreciate what youve got, youd better get what you can appreciate.

LIZA [*desperate*] Oh, you are a cruel tyrant. I cant talk to you: you turn everything against me: I'm always in the wrong. But you know very well all the time that youre nothing but a bully. You know I cant go back to the gutter, as you call it, and that I have no real friends in the world but you and the Colonel. You know well I couldnt bear to live with a low common man after you two; and it's wicked and cruel of you to insult me by pretending I could. You think I must go back to Wimpole Street because I have nowhere else to go but father's. But dont you be too sure that you have me under your feet to be trampled on and talked down. I'll marry Freddy, I will, as soon as I'm able to support him.

HIGGINS [*thunderstruck*] Freddy!!! that young fool! That poor devil who couldnt get a job as an errand boy even if he had the guts to try for it! Woman: do you not understand that I have made you a consort for a king?

LIZA. Freddy loves me: that makes him king enough for me. I dont want him to work: he wasnt brought up to it as I was. I'll go and be a teacher.

HIGGINS. Whatll you teach, in heaven's name?

LIZA. What you taught me. I'll teach phonetics.

HIGGINS. Ha! ha! ha!

LIZA. I'll offer myself as an assistant to that hairyfaced Hungarian.

HIGGINS [*rising in a fury*] What! That impostor! that humbug! that toadying ignoramus! Teach him my methods! my discoveries! You take one step in his direction and I'll wring your neck. [*He lays hands on her*]. Do you hear?

LIZA [*defiantly non-resistant*] Wring away. What do I care? I knew youd strike me some day. [*He lets her go, stamping with rage at having forgotten himself, and recoils so hastily that he stumbles back into his seat on the ottoman*]. Aha! Now I know how to deal with you. What a fool I was not to think of it before! You cant take away the knowledge you gave me. You said I had a finer ear than you. And I can be civil and kind to people, which is more than you can. Aha! [*Purposely dropping her aitches to annoy him*] Thats done you, Enry Iggins, it az. Now I dont care that [*snapping her fingers*] for your bullying and your big talk. I'll advertize it in the papers that your duchess is only a flower girl that you taught, and that she'll teach anybody to be a duchess just the same in six months for a thousand guineas. Oh, when I think of myself crawling under your feet and being trampled on and called names, when all the time I had only to lift up my finger to be as good as you, I could just kick myself.

HIGGINS [*wondering at her*] You damned impudent slut, you! But it's better than snivelling; better than fetching slippers and finding spectacles, isnt it? [*Rising*] By George, Eliza. I said I'd make a woman of you; and I have. I like you like this.

LIZA. Yes: you turn round and make up to me now that I'm not afraid of you, and can do without you.

HIGGINS. Of course I do, you little fool. Five minutes ago you were like a millstone round my neck. Now youre a tower of strength: a consort battleship. You and I and Pickering will be three old bachelors instead of only two men and a silly girl.

MRS HIGGINS *returns dressed for the wedding.* ELIZA *instantly becomes cool and elegant.*

MRS HIGGINS. The carriage is waiting, Eliza. Are you ready?

LIZA. Quite. Is the Professor coming?

MRS HIGGINS. Certainly not. He cant behave himself in church. He makes remarks out loud all the time on the clergyman's pronunciation.

LIZA. Then I shall not see you again, Professor. Goodbye. [*She goes to the door*].

MRS HIGGINS [*coming to* HIGGINS] Goodbye, dear.

HIGGINS. Goodbye, mother. [*He is about to kiss her, when he recollects something*]. Oh, by the way, Eliza, order a ham and a Stilton cheese, will you? And buy me a pair of reindeer gloves, number eights, and a tie to match that new suit of mine. You can choose the color. [*His cheerful, careless, vigorous voice shews that he is incorrigible*].

LIZA [*disdainfully*] Number eights are too small for you if you want them lined with lamb's wool. You have three new ties that you have forgotten in the drawer of your washstand. Colonel Pickering prefers double Gloucester to Stilton; and you dont notice the difference. I telephoned Mrs Pearce this morning not to forget the ham. What you are to do without me I cannot imagine. [*She sweeps out*].

MRS HIGGINS. I'm afraid youve spoilt that girl, Henry. I should be uneasy about you and her if she were less fond of Colonel Pickering.

HIGGINS. Pickering! Nonsense; she's going to marry Freddy. Ha ha! Freddy! Freddy!! Ha ha ha ha!!!!! [*He roars with laughter as the play ends*].

EPILOGUE

The rest of the story need not be shewn in action, and indeed, would hardly need telling if our imaginations were not so enfeebled by their lazy dependence on the ready-mades and reach-me-downs of the ragshop in which Romance keeps its stock of "happy endings" to misfit all stories. Now, the history of Eliza Doolittle, though called a romance because the transfiguration it records seems exceedingly improbable, is common enough. Such transfigurations have been achieved by hundreds of resolutely ambitious young women since Nell Gwynne[1] set them the example by playing queens and fascinating kings in the theatre in which she began by selling oranges. Nevertheless, people in all directions have assumed, for no other reason than that she became the heroine of a romance, that she must have married the hero of it. This is unbearable, not only because her little drama, if acted on such a thoughtless assumption, must be spoiled, but because the true sequel is patent to anyone with a sense of human nature in general, and of feminine instinct in particular.

Eliza, in telling Higgins she would not marry him if he asked her, was not coquetting:[2] she was announcing a well-considered decision. When a bachelor interests, and dominates, and teaches, and becomes important to a spinster, as Higgins with Eliza, she always, if she has character enough to be capable of it, considers very seriously indeed whether she will play for becoming that bachelor's wife, especially if he is so little interested in marriage that a determined and devoted woman might capture him if she set herself resolutely to do it. Her decision will depend a good deal on whether she is really free to choose; and that, again, will depend on her age and income. If she is at the end of her youth, and has no security for her livelihood, she will marry him because she must marry anybody who will provide for her. But at Eliza's age a good-looking girl does not feel that pressure: she feels free to pick and choose. She is therefore guided by her instinct in the matter. Eliza's instinct tells her not to marry Higgins. It does not tell her to give him up. It is not in the slightest doubt as to his remaining one of the strongest personal interests in her life. It would be very sorely strained if there was another woman likely to supplant her with him. But as she feels sure of him on that last point, she has no doubt at all as to her course, and would not have any, even if the difference of twenty years in age, which seems so great to youth, did not exist between them.

As our own instincts are not appealed to by her conclusion, let us see whether we cannot discover some reason in it. When Higgins excused his indifference to young women on the ground that they had an irresistible rival in his mother, he gave the clue to his inveterate old-bachelordom. The case is uncommon only to the extent that remarkable mothers are uncommon. If an imaginative boy has a sufficiently rich mother who has intelligence, personal grace, dignity of character without harshness, and a cultivated sense of the best art of her time to enable her to make her house beautiful, she sets a standard for him against which very few women can struggle, besides effecting for him a disengagement of his affections, his sense of beauty, and his idealism from his specifically sexual impulses. This makes him a standing puzzle to the huge number of uncultivated people who have been brought up in tasteless homes by commonplace or disagreeable parents, and to whom, consequently, literature, painting, sculpture, music, and affectionate personal relations come as modes of sex if they come at all. The word passion means nothing else to them; and that Higgins could have a passion for phonetics and idealize his mother instead of Eliza, would seem to them absurd and unnatural. Nevertheless, when

---

1. **Nell Gwynne** (1650–1687): actress and favorite of Charles II. From being a peddler of oranges, she rose to the heights of late seventeenth-century English society.
2. **coquetting:** being flirtatiously coy.

we look round and see that hardly anyone is too ugly or disagreeable to find a wife or a husband if he or she wants one, whilst many old maids and bachelors are above the average in quality and culture, we cannot help suspecting that the disentanglement of sex from the associations with which it is so commonly confused, a disentanglement which persons of genius achieve by sheer intellectual analysis, is sometimes produced or aided by parental fascination.

Now, though Eliza was incapable of thus explaining to herself Higgins's formidable powers of resistance to the charm that prostrated Freddy at the first glance, she was instinctively aware that she could never obtain a complete grip of him, or come between him and his mother (the first necessity of the married woman). To put it shortly, she knew that for some mysterious reason he had not the makings of a married man in him, according to her conception of a husband as one to whom she would be his nearest and fondest and warmest interest. Even had there been no mother-rival, she would still have refused to accept an interest in herself that was secondary to philosophic interests. Had Mrs Higgins died, there would still have been Milton and the Universal Alphabet. Landor's[3] remark that to those who have the greatest power of loving, love is a secondary affair, would not have recommended Landor to Eliza. Put that along with her resentment of Higgins's domineering superiority, and her mistrust of his coaxing cleverness in getting round her and evading her wrath when he had gone too far with his impetuous bullying, and you will see that Eliza's instinct had good grounds for warning her not to marry her Pygmalion.

And now, whom did Eliza marry? For if Higgins was a predestinate old bachelor, she was most certainly not a predestinate old maid. Well, that can be told very shortly to those who have not guessed it from the indications she has herself given them.

Almost immediately after Eliza is stung into proclaiming her considered determination not to marry Higgins, she mentions the fact that young Mr Frederick Eynsford Hill is pouring out his love for her daily through the post. Now Freddy is young, practically twenty years younger than Higgins: he is a gentleman (or, as Eliza would qualify him, a toff), and speaks like one. He is nicely dressed, is treated by the Colonel as an equal, loves her unaffectedly, and is not her master, nor ever likely to dominate her in spite of his advantage of social standing. Eliza has no use for the foolish romantic tradition that all women love to be mastered, if not actually bullied and beaten. "When you go to women" says Nietzsche[4] "take your whip with you." Sensible despots have never confined that precaution to women: they have taken their whips with them when they have dealt with men, and been slavishly idealized by the men over whom they have flourished the whip much more than by women. No doubt there are slavish women as well as slavish men; and women, like men, admire those that are stronger than themselves. But to admire a strong person and to live under that strong person's thumb are two different things. The weak may not be admired and hero-worshipped; but they are by no means disliked or shunned; and they never seem to have the least difficulty in marrying people who are too good for them. They may fail in emergencies; but life is not one long emergency: it is mostly a string of situations for which no exceptional strength is needed, and with which even rather weak people can cope if they have a stronger partner to help them out. Accordingly, it is a truth everywhere in evidence that strong people, masculine or feminine, not only do not marry stronger people, but do not shew any preference for them in selecting their friends. When a lion meets another with a louder roar "the first lion thinks the last a bore." The man or

---

3. **Landor's:** referring to English writer Walter Savage Landor (1775–1864).

4. **Nietzsche** [nē′chə]: Friedrich Wilhelm Nietzsche (1844–1900), influential German philosopher.

woman who feels strong enough for two, seeks for every other quality in a partner than strength.

The converse is also true. Weak people want to marry strong people who do not frighten them too much; and this often leads them to make the mistake we describe metaphorically as "biting off more than they can chew." They want too much for too little; and when the bargain is unreasonable beyond all bearing, the union becomes impossible: it ends in the weaker party being either discarded or borne as a cross, which is worse. People who are not only weak, but silly or obtuse as well, are often in these difficulties.

This being the state of human affairs, what is Eliza fairly sure to do when she is placed between Freddy and Higgins? Will she look forward to a lifetime of fetching Higgins's slippers or to a lifetime of Freddy fetching hers? There can be no doubt about the answer. Unless Freddy is biologically repulsive to her, and Higgins biologically attractive to a degree that overwhelms all her other instincts, she will, if she marries either of them, marry Freddy.

And that is just what Eliza did.

Complications ensued; but they were economic, not romantic. Freddy had no money and no occupation. His mother's jointure,[5] a last relic of the opulence of Largelady Park, had enabled her to struggle along in Earlscourt with an air of gentility, but not to procure any serious secondary education for her children, much less give the boy a profession. A clerkship at thirty shillings a week was beneath Freddy's dignity, and extremely distasteful to him besides. His prospects consisted of a hope that if he kept up appearances somebody would do something for him. The something appeared vaguely to his imagination as a private secretaryship or a sinecure[6] of some sort. To his mother it perhaps appeared as a marriage to some lady of means who could not resist her boy's niceness. Fancy her feelings when he married a flower girl who had become disclassed under extraordinary circumstances which were now notorious!

It is true that Eliza's situation did not seem wholly ineligible. Her father, though formerly a dustman, and now fantastically disclassed, had become extremely popular in the smartest society by a social talent which triumphed over every prejudice and every disadvantage. Rejected by the middle class, which he loathed, he had shot up at once into the highest circles by his wit, his dustmanship (which he carried like a banner), and his Nietzschean transcendence of good and evil. At intimate ducal dinners he sat on the right hand of the Duchess; and in country houses he smoked in the pantry and was made much of by the butler when he was not feeding in the dining room and being consulted by cabinet ministers. But he found it almost as hard to do all this on [three] thousand a year as Mrs Eynsford Hill to live in Earlscourt on an income so pitiably smaller that I have not the heart to disclose its exact figure. He absolutely refused to add the last straw to his burden by contributing to Eliza's support.

Thus Freddy and Eliza, now Mr and Mrs Eynsford Hill, would have spent a penniless honeymoon but for a wedding present of £500 from the Colonel to Eliza. It lasted a long time because Freddy did not know how to spend money, never having had any to spend, and Eliza, socially trained by a pair of old bachelors, wore her clothes as long as they held together and looked pretty, without the least regard to their being many months out of fashion. Still, £500 will not last two young people for ever; and they both knew, and Eliza felt as well, that they must shift for themselves in the end. She could quarter herself on Wimpole Street because it had come to be her home; but she was quite aware that she ought not to quarter Freddy there, and that it would not be good for his character if she did.

Not that the Wimpole Street bachelors objected. When she consulted them, Higgins de-

---

5. **jointure:** widow's inheritance, payable only during her lifetime; surviving children do not benefit.
6. **sinecure** [sin′ə kyoor′]: salaried position requiring little or no work.

clined to be bothered about her housing problem when that solution was so simple. Eliza's desire to have Freddy in the house with her seemed of no more importance than if she had wanted an extra piece of bedroom furniture. Pleas as to Freddy's character, and the moral obligation on him to earn his own living, were lost on Higgins. He denied that Freddy had any character, and declared that if he tried to do any useful work some competent person would have the trouble of undoing it: a procedure involving a net loss to the community, and great unhappiness to Freddy himself, who was obviously intended by Nature for such light work as amusing Eliza, which, Higgins declared, was a much more useful and honorable occupation than working in the city. When Eliza referred again to her project of teaching phonetics, Higgins abated not a jot of his violent opposition to it. He said she was not within ten years of being qualified to meddle with his pet subject; and as it was evident that the Colonel agreed with him, she felt she could not go against them in this grave matter, and that she had no right, without Higgins's consent, to exploit the knowledge he had given her; for his knowledge seemed to her as much his private property as his watch: Eliza was no communist. Besides, she was superstitiously devoted to them both, more entirely and frankly after her marriage than before it.

It was the Colonel who finally solved the problem, which had cost him much perplexed cogitation. He one day asked Eliza, rather shyly, whether she had quite given up her notion of keeping a flower shop. She replied that she had thought of it, but had put it out of her head, because the Colonel had said, that day at Mrs Higgins's, that it would never do. The Colonel confessed that when he said that, he had not quite recovered from the dazzling impression of the day before. They broke the matter to Higgins that evening. The sole comment vouchsafed by him very nearly led to a serious quarrel with Eliza. It was to the effect that she would have in Freddy an ideal errand boy.

Freddy himself was next sounded on the subject. He said he had been thinking of a shop himself; though it had presented itself to his pennilessness as a small place in which Eliza should sell tobacco at one counter whilst he sold newspapers at the opposite one. But he agreed that it would be extraordinarily jolly to go early every morning with Eliza to Covent Garden and buy flowers on the scene of their first meeting: a sentiment which earned him many kisses from his wife. He added that he had always been afraid to propose anything of the sort, because Clara would make an awful row about a step that must damage her matrimonial chances, and his mother could not be expected to like it after clinging for so many years to that step of the social ladder on which retail trade is impossible.

This difficulty was removed by an event highly unexpected by Freddy's mother. Clara, in the course of her incursions into those artistic circles which were the highest within her reach, discovered that her conversational qualifications were expected to include a grounding in the novels of Mr H. G. Wells.[7] She borrowed them in various directions so energetically that she swallowed them all within two months. The result was a conversion of a kind quite common today. A modern Acts of the Apostles would fill fifty whole Bibles if anyone were capable of writing it.

Poor Clara, who appeared to Higgins and his mother as a disagreeable and ridiculous person, and to her own mother as in some inexplicable way a social failure, had never seen herself in either light; for, though to some extent ridiculed and mimicked in West Kensington like everybody else there, she was accepted as a rational and normal—or shall we say inevitable?—sort of human being. At worst they called her The Pusher; but to them no more than to herself had it ever occurred that she was pushing the air, and pushing it in a wrong direction. Still, she was not happy. She

---

7. **H. G. Wells:** Herbert George Wells (1866–1946), English novelist, historian, and social reformer.

was growing desperate. Her one asset, the fact that her mother was what the Epsom greengrocer called a carriage lady, had no exchange value, apparently. It had prevented her from getting educated, because the only education she could have afforded was education with the Earlscourt greengrocer's daughter. It had led her to seek the society of her mother's class; and that class simply would not have her, because she was much poorer than the greengrocer, and, far from being able to afford a maid, could not afford even a housemaid, and had to scrape along at home with an illiberally treated general servant. Under such circumstances nothing could give her an air of being a genuine product of Largelady Park. And yet its tradition made her regard a marriage with anyone within her reach as an unbearable humiliation. Commercial people and professional people in a small way were odious to her. She ran after painters and novelists; but she did not charm them; and her bold attempts to pick up and practise artistic and literary talk irritated them. She was, in short, an utter failure, an ignorant, incompetent, pretentious, unwelcome, penniless, useless little snob; and though she did not admit these disqualifications (for nobody ever faces unpleasant truths of this kind until the possibility of a way out dawns on them) she felt their effects too keenly to be satisfied with her position.

Clara had a startling eyeopener when, on being suddenly awakened to enthusiasm by a girl of her own age who dazzled her and produced in her a gushing desire to take her for a model, and gain her friendship, she discovered that this exquisite apparition had graduated from the gutter in a few months time. It shook her so violently, that when Mr H. G. Wells lifted her on the point of his puissant[8] pen, and placed her at the angle of view from which the life she was leading and the society to which she clung appeared in its true relation to real human needs and worthy social structure, he effected a conversion and a conviction of sin

comparable to the most sensational feats of General Booth[9] or Gypsy Smith. Clara's snobbery went bang. Life suddenly began to move with her. Without knowing how or why, she began to make friends and enemies. Some of the acquaintances to whom she had been a tedious or indifferent or ridiculous affliction, dropped her: others became cordial. To her amazement she found that some "quite nice" people were saturated with Wells, and that this accessibility to ideas was the secret of their niceness. People she had thought deeply religious, and had tried to conciliate on that tack with disastrous results, suddenly took an interest in her, and revealed a hostility to conventional religion which she had never conceived possible except among the most desperate characters. They made her read Galsworthy; and Galsworthy exposed the vanity of Largelady Park and finished her. It exasperated her to think that the dungeon in which she had languished for so many unhappy years had been unlocked all the time, and that the impulses she had so carefully struggled with and stifled for the sake of keeping well with society, were precisely those by which alone she could have come into any sort of sincere human contact. In the radiance of these discoveries, and the tumult of their reaction, she made a fool of herself as freely and conspicuously as when she so rashly adopted Eliza's expletive in Mrs Higgins's drawing room; for the new-born Wellsian had to find her bearings almost as ridiculously as a baby; but nobody hates a baby for its ineptitudes, or thinks the worse of it for trying to eat the matches; and Clara lost no friends by her follies. They laughed at her to her face this time; and she had to defend herself and fight it out as best she could.

When Freddy paid a visit to Earlscourt (which he never did when he could possibly help it) to make the desolating announcement that he and his Eliza were thinking of black-

---

8. **puissant** [pwis'ənt]: powerful.

9. **General Booth:** William Booth (1829–1912), founder of the Salvation Army.

ening the Largelady scutcheon[10] by opening a shop, he found the little household already convulsed by a prior announcement from Clara that she also was going to work in an old furniture shop in Dover Street, which had been started by a fellow Wellsian. This appointment Clara owed, after all, to her old social accomplishment of Push. She had made up her mind that, cost what it might, she would see Mr Wells in the flesh; and she had achieved her end at a garden party. She had better luck than so rash an enterprise deserved. Mr Wells came up to her expectations. Age had not withered him, nor could custom stale his infinite variety in half an hour. His pleasant neatness and compactness, his small hands and feet, his teeming ready brain, his unaffected accessibility, and a certain fine apprehensiveness which stamped him as susceptible from his topmost hair to his tipmost toe, proved irresistible. Clara talked of nothing else for weeks and weeks afterwards. And as she happened to talk to the lady of the furniture shop, and that lady also desired above all things to know Mr Wells and sell pretty things to him, she offered Clara a job on the chance of achieving that end through her.

And so it came about that Eliza's luck held, and the expected opposition to the flower shop melted away. The shop is in the arcade of a railway station not very far from the Victoria and Albert Museum; and if you live in that neighborhood you may go there any day and buy a buttonhole from Eliza.

Now here is a last opportunity for romance. Would you not like to be assured that the shop was an immense success, thanks to Eliza's charms and her early business experience in Covent Garden? Alas! the truth is the truth: the shop did not pay for a long time, simply because Eliza and her Freddy did not know how to keep it. True, Eliza had not to begin at the very beginning: she knew the names and prices of the cheaper flowers; and her elation was unbounded when she found that Freddy, like all youths educated at cheap, pretentious, and thoroughly inefficient schools, knew a little Latin. It was very little, but enough to make him appear to her a Porson or Bentley,[11] and to put him at his ease with botanical nomenclature. Unfortunately he knew nothing else; and Eliza, though she could count money up to eighteen shillings or so, and had acquired a certain familiarity with the language of Milton from her struggles to qualify herself for winning Higgins's bet, could not write out a bill without utterly disgracing the establishment. Freddy's power of stating in Latin that Balbus built a wall and that Gaul was divided into three parts[12] did not carry with it the slightest knowledge of accounts or business: Colonel Pickering had to explain to him what a cheque book and a bank account meant. And the pair were by no means easily teachable. Freddy backed up Eliza in her obstinate refusal to believe that they could save money by engaging a bookkeeper with some knowledge of the business. How, they argued, could you possibly save money by going to extra expense when you already could not make both ends meet? But the Colonel, after making the ends meet over and over again, at last gently insisted; and Eliza, humbled to the dust by having to beg from him so often, and stung by the uproarious derision of Higgins, to whom the notion of Freddy succeeding at anything was a joke that never palled, grasped the fact that business, like phonetics, has to be learned.

On the piteous spectacle of the pair spending their evenings in shorthand schools and polytechnic classes, learning bookkeeping and typewriting with incipient junior clerks, male and female, from the elementary schools, let me not dwell. There were even classes at the London School of Economics, and a humble personal appeal to the director of that institution to recommend a course bearing on the

---

10. **scutcheon** [skuch′ən]: coat of arms.

11. **Porson, Bentley:** celebrated Latin scholars.
12. **Balbus . . . parts:** alluding to elementary Latin exercises. Caesar's *Gallic Wars* begins with the latter statement.

flower business. He, being a humorist, explained to them the method of the celebrated Dickensian essay on Chinese Metaphysics by the gentleman who read an article on China and an article on Metaphysics and combined the information. He suggested that they should combine the London School with Kew Gardens. Eliza, to whom the procedure of the Dickensian gentleman seemed perfectly correct (as in fact it was) and not in the least funny (which was only her ignorance), took the advice with entire gravity. But the effort that cost her the deepest humiliation was a request to Higgins, whose pet artistic fancy, next to Milton's verse, was calligraphy and who himself wrote a most beautiful Italian hand, that he would teach her to write. He declared that she was congenitally incapable of forming a single letter worthy of the least of Milton's words; but she persisted; and again he suddenly threw himself into the task of teaching her with a combination of stormy intensity, concentrated patience, and occasional bursts of interesting disquisition on the beauty and nobility, the august mission and destiny, of human handwriting. Eliza ended by acquiring an extremely uncommercial script which was a positive extension of her personal beauty, and spending three times as much on stationery as anyone else because certain qualities and shapes on paper became indispensable to her. She could not even address an envelope in the usual way because it made the margins all wrong.

Their commercial schooldays were a period of disgrace and despair for the young couple. They seemed to be learning nothing about flower shops. At last they gave it up as hopeless, and shook the dust of the shorthand schools, and the polytechnics, and the London School of Economics from their feet for ever. Besides, the business was in some mysterious way beginning to take care of itself. They had somehow forgotten their objections to employing other people. They came to the conclusion that their own way was the best, and that they had really a remarkable talent for business. The Colonel, who had been compelled for some years to keep a sufficient sum on current account at his bankers to make up their deficits, found that the provision was unnecessary: the young people were prospering. It is true that there was not quite fair play between them and their competitors in trade. Their week-ends in the country cost them nothing, and saved them the price of their Sunday dinners; for the motor car was the Colonel's; and he and Higgins paid the hotel bills. Mr F. Hill, florist and greengrocer (they soon discovered that there was money in asparagus; and asparagus led to other vegetables), had an air which stamped the business as classy; and in private life he was still Frederick Eynsford Hill, Esquire. Not that there was any swank[13] about him: nobody but Eliza knew that he had been christened Frederick Chaloner. Eliza herself swanked like anything.

That is all. That is how it has turned out. It is astonishing how much Eliza still manages to meddle in the housekeeping at Wimpole Street in spite of the shop and her own family. And it is notable that though she never nags her husband, and frankly loves the Colonel as if she were his favorite daughter, she has never got out of the habit of nagging Higgins that was established on the fatal night when she won his bet for him. She snaps his head off on the faintest provocation, or on none. He no longer dares to tease her by assuming an abysmal inferiority of Freddy's mind to his own. He storms and bullies and derides; but she stands up to him so ruthlessly that the Colonel has to ask her from time to time to be kinder to Higgins; and it is the only request of his that brings a mulish expression into her face. Nothing but some emergency or calamity great enough to break down all likes and dislikes, and throw them both back on their common humanity—and may they be spared any such trial!—will ever alter this. She knows that Higgins does not need her, just as her father did not need her. The very scrupulousness with

---

13. **swank:** ostentatious swagger.

which he told her that day that he had become used to having her there, and dependent on her for all sorts of little services, and that he should miss her if she went away (it would never have occurred to Freddy or the Colonel to say anything of the sort) deepens her inner certainty that she is "no more to him than them slippers"; yet she has a sense, too, that his indifference is deeper than the infatuation of commoner souls. She is immensely interested in him. She has even secret mischievous moments in which she wishes she could get him alone, on a desert island, away from all ties and with nobody else in the world to consider, and just drag him off his pedestal and see him making love like any common man. We all have private imaginations of that sort. But when it comes to business, to the life that she really leads as distinguished from the life of dreams and fancies, she likes Freddy and she likes the Colonel; and she does not like Higgins and Mr Doolittle. Galatea never does quite like Pygmalion: his relation to her is too godlike to be altogether agreeable.

STUDY QUESTIONS

Recalling
1. Explain the reasons for Doolittle's changed appearance. How does he feel about his new life in comparison to his old life? Why?
2. For what does Liza express gratitude to Pickering? What does she say is the real difference between a lady and a flower girl?
3. What does Higgins tell Liza is "the great secret" about handling other people?
4. What sort of feeling does Liza deny that she wants from Higgins? What does she want?
5. What two things does Liza say she will do with her life? How does Higgins react to her?

Interpreting
6. Why would Doolittle's money become a burden to him? What relationship does Shaw present among social position, wealth, morality, and happiness through the character of Doolittle?
7. What has Liza gained as a result of Higgins' experiment? What has she lost?
8. Why do you think Higgins refuses to let Liza go?
9. What does Liza want that Higgins is unwilling to give? In one sentence state the position of each in their final debate. With whom do you agree?

Extending
10. Were you satisfied with Shaw's account of Liza's future in the Epilogue? Why or why not?

VIEWPOINT

Critic I. Wardle argues that Shaw's most important theme is the liberation of the human mind:

> Whenever [Shaw's plays] record a victory, it is the victory of *Pygmalion*—the release of a free, autonomous creature from the petrified forest of unexamined values and social conditioning.
> —"The Plays," in *The Genius of Shaw*

■ From what "unexamined values and social conditioning" does Shaw seek to free people in *Pygmalion*? Do you agree that Liza is more free at the end of the play than at the beginning? Why or why not?

LITERARY FOCUS

The Total Effect
In staging a play like *Pygmalion*, a director should pay attention to the individual elements of plot, character, setting, tone, symbol, and theme and should keep in mind the total effect that these elements will produce on an audience when they come together in a performance.

Thinking About Plot
1. What are the major conflicts in *Pygmalion*? Keep in mind conflicts that occur within characters, between characters, and between characters and external forces such as the social system. How are these various conflicts resolved?

Thinking About Character

2. Describe the various changes that occur in Liza over the course of the play. Higgins says that he created the Liza we see at the end of the play. To what extent is this true?
3. Name several of Higgins' most outstanding shortcomings. What appealing qualities does he also reveal?

Thinking About Setting

4. Most of the play takes place in pleasant rooms of upper-class society. In what ways do these rooms contrast with the rainy street scene and Liza's lodgings of Act I?
5. Describe the social setting of the play, particularly the contrast between the upper and lower classes.

Thinking About Tone

6. The tone of *Pygmalion* mixes the serious and the comic. Choose one purely comic moment, and explain why it is funny. Find one moment when Shaw is absolutely earnest. What point is being made?

Thinking About Symbol

7. Keeping in mind who Pygmalion was in Greek legend, explain the symbolic implications of the title *Pygmalion.*

Thinking About Theme

8. According to *Pygmalion,* what is the relationship between language and class? Between the way a person speaks and his identity?
9. What various views concerning women's social position are presented in *Pygmalion?*
10. Why would aspects of appearance such as clothes, manners, and speech have such a profound effect on someone's life? What does *Pygmalion* suggest about the relationship between appearance and reality?

VOCABULARY

Dialect

In Act I of *Pygmalion,* Henry Higgins demonstrates his ability to identify a person's background purely on the basis of dialect. A **dialect** is a type of speech that differs from the standard form of a language; the difference occurs mostly in pronunciation but also in vocabulary and grammar. Speakers of English in the United States use many different regional dialects, some of the most recognizable being those heard in New England, New York City, and the South.

In Britain people also speak in many different dialects, some of which differ so much from the English we know that we would probably not be able to understand them. In the first two acts of *Pygmalion,* Liza Doolittle speaks a dialect known as **cockney,** which is common among people of the lower class who live in London's East End. Shaw attempts to reproduce the exact sound of this dialect in Liza's first three speeches in the play and again in Act II in her attempt to say the alphabet in Higgins' study. Besides affecting her pronunciation, Liza's cockney dialect includes numerous lapses from standard grammar (such as using present tense for past tense) and special vocabulary words—such as "garn," which actually means "go on," and might be translated into the common American expression "You've got to be kidding."

■ Look at Liza's first three speeches in Act I, and list all the differences you can find between her pronunciation and grammar and standard English.

COMPOSITION

Writing About the Total Effect

■ Explain the total effect that you think makes *Pygmalion* popular on stage as well as on film and television and in its musical version. First describe the impact that the play had on you. Then explain how Shaw uses the following elements to achieve this effect: (a) plot, (b) character, (c) setting, (d) theme, and (e) tone. *For help with this assignment, refer to Lesson 8 in the Writing About Literature Handbook at the back of this book.*

Writing About a Play's Ending

■ In the Epilogue to *Pygmalion,* Shaw explains why Liza cannot marry Higgins. On the other hand, the film and musical versions of *Pygmalion* both end with Liza's return to Higgins. Indicate which ending you find the more logical and satisfying outcome to the play. Then use evidence from the play such as the characters' behavior and statements to support your choice of ending.

POETRY

William Butler Yeats   1865–1939

William Butler Yeats is considered by many to be the greatest poet writing in English in this century. The son of a painter, Yeats was born in Sandymount, Ireland, and attended school in Dublin. He loved to read and daydream, especially during his summers at his grandparents' home in the wild country of County Sligo on Ireland's northwest coast.

Yeats studied painting but soon abandoned his studies to become a professional writer. His interest in Irish culture led him to collect and publish Irish legends and write poems and plays based on Irish myths. As a result of this work, Yeats soon became a central figure in the Irish Renaissance, a turn-of-the-century movement to revive an Irish national language and celebrate Celtic traditions. In 1889 Yeats published his first volume of poems. Later, with his friend Lady Augusta Gregory, he founded the Irish National Theatre Society, and he began to write plays based on Irish legends.

However, Yeats's interest in Ireland was not merely literary and linguistic. Inspired by the beautiful Maud Gonne, a leader of the Irish National Movement, which sought to free Ireland from British rule, Yeats developed an interest in Irish politics. Gonne was his Joan of Arc, his Helen of Troy, and he courted her unsuccessfully for over thirteen years. After her marriage to another Irish political leader, Yeats finally admitted defeat in love and turned his full attention to his work. He himself eventually married years later.

During the 1920s Yeats gained even more prominence in both political and literary circles. He became a senator in the Irish Free State in 1922 and received the Nobel Prize for Literature in 1923. In 1925 Yeats published his major philosophical and historical prose work, *A Vision*.

Yeats began his poetic career as a Romantic and finished it as a poet of the modern world. His early work was strongly influenced by Blake and Shelley, the Pre-Raphaelites (see page 487), and Irish mythology. These early poems were often simple, musical, romantic, and dreamlike. In the middle of his career, his poetry became less dreamlike and more direct and realistic; his imagery became more economical and his tone more conversational. In the last stages of his poetic career, his interest in a universal system of historical cycles dominated his work. Although some of his later works are obscure and complex, the best of these poems touch universal concerns and demonstrate a brilliant balance between emotion and intellect.

■ What Romantic themes might you find in Yeats's poems?

"Down by the Salley Gardens" is a good example of Yeats's early poetry. Like the other poems he wrote early in his career, it is simply structured, Romantic, musical, and based on traditional Irish lore. By his own account, the poem is an expansion of "three lines imperfectly remembered" from an Irish folk song that he once heard an old peasant woman sing in Sligo.

William Butler Yeats

Down by the Salley Gardens[1]

Down by the salley gardens my love and I did meet;
She passed the salley gardens with little snow-white feet.
She bid me take love easy, as the leaves grow on the tree;
But I, being young and foolish, with her would not agree.

5 In a field by the river my love and I did stand,
And on my leaning shoulder she laid her snow-white hand.
She bid me take life easy, as the grass grows on the weirs;[2]
But I was young and foolish, and now am full of tears.

---

1. **Salley Gardens:** willow gardens. *Salley* is a variant of *sallow,* which means "willow."
2. **weirs** [wērz]: earth piled in river or stream beds to back up or change the course of the water.

STUDY QUESTIONS

Recalling
1. In line 3 what does the speaker's love advise him to do? What is his response?
2. What suggestion does his love make in line 7?
3. How does he describe himself in each stanza?

Interpreting
4. Find four specific changes from the first to the second stanza. How and why does the speaker's emotional state change?

5. In the long run, does his sweetheart's advice prove to be correct or incorrect? How do you know?
6. Where in the poem does Yeats use repetition and parallelism? Explain how these techniques add to the poem's meaning and emotional impact.

Extending
7. Why do you think advice often seems more sensible in retrospect than at the time it is offered?

It is believed that Yeats wrote this poem for Major Robert Gregory, the son of his friend Lady Augusta Gregory. Major Gregory, an artist and aviator, was killed in action over Italy during World War I while flying for England's Royal Flying Corps.

An Irish Airman Foresees His Death

I know that I shall meet my fate
Somewhere among the clouds above;
Those that I fight I do not hate,
Those that I guard I do not love;[1]
5 My country is Kiltartan[2] Cross,
My countrymen Kiltartan's poor,
No likely end could bring them loss
Or leave them happier than before

Nor law, nor duty bade me fight,
10 Nor public men, nor cheering crowds,
A lonely impulse of delight
Drove to this tumult in the clouds;
I balanced all, brought all to mind,
The years to come seemed waste of breath,
15 A waste of breath the years behind
In balance with this life, this death.

---

1. **Those . . . love:** Many Irish volunteered to fight on the side of the English in World War I in spite of Ireland's technical neutrality and ongoing struggle for independence from England.
2. **Kiltartan:** village near the estate of the Gregory family.

STUDY QUESTIONS

Recalling

1. Who is the speaker of the poem? How does he feel about the people he fights for and against?
2. In contrast, who are *his* people? What effect does he think his fate will have on them?
3. According to the second stanza, what things did not motivate the speaker to fight? What drove him "to this tumult in the clouds"?
4. With what phrase does the speaker characterize both past and future? In the last line what does he balance against the past and future?

Interpreting

5. What is the speaker's attitude toward the war and toward his own survival? How do you know?
6. Why would *delight* be an unusual word for someone in the speaker's circumstances to use? What does it reveal about the speaker?
7. What do the words *this life, this death* mean? Why might "this life, this death" be more valuable to him than the rest of his life?

Extending

8. Why do you think people in grave danger are often calm in their acceptance of death?

William Butler Yeats

The Lake Isle of Innisfree

I will arise and go now, and go to Innisfree,
And a small cabin build there, of clay and wattles[1] made:
Nine bean-rows will I have there, a hive for the honeybee,
And live alone in the bee-loud glade.

5 And I shall have some peace there, for peace comes dropping
     slow,
Dropping from the veils of the morning to where the cricket
     sings;
There midnight's all a glimmer, and noon a purple glow,
And evening full of the linnet's[2] wings.

I will arise and go now, for always night and day
10 I hear lake water lapping with low sounds by the shore;
While I stand on the roadway, or on the pavements gray,
I hear it in the deep heart's core.

---

1. **wattles:** networks of woven twigs used for walls, roofs, and crude huts.
2. **linnet's:** referring to a European singing bird.

The Wild Swans at Coole

The trees are in their autumn beauty,
The woodland paths are dry,
Under the October twilight the water
Mirrors a still sky;
5 Upon the brimming water among the stones
Are nine and fifty swans.

The nineteenth autumn has come upon me
Since I first made my count;
I saw, before I had well finished,
10 All suddenly mount
And scatter wheeling in great broken rings
Upon their clamorous wings.

I have looked upon those brilliant creatures,
And now my heart is sore.
15 All's changed since I, hearing at twilight,
The first time on this shore,
The bell beat of their wings above my head,
Trod with a lighter tread.

Unwearied still, lover by lover,
20 They paddle in the cold
Companionable streams or climb the air;
Their hearts have not grown old;
Passion or conquest, wander where they will,
Attend upon them still.

25 But now they drift on the still water,
Mysterious, beautiful;
Among what rushes will they build,
By what lake's edge or pool
Delight men's eyes when I awake some day
30 To find they have flown away?

STUDY QUESTIONS

The Lake Isle of Innisfree

Recalling

1. According to the first stanza, where does the speaker intend to go, what will he do there, and how will he live?
2. From the second stanza list three physical characteristics of the place to which the speaker wants to go.
3. Where is the speaker now, according to line 11?
4. What does the speaker hear, and how does he hear this sound, according to the third stanza?

Interpreting

5. Contrast the speaker's present location with the place that beckons him. What is the emotional effect of this contrast?
6. Describe the speaker's current emotional state. Is he contented or frustrated? Is this mood momentary or ongoing? How do you know?
7. Instead of actually going to Innisfree, what is the speaker doing in the poem? How does hearing something "in the deep heart's core" differ from hearing it with one's ears?
8. Explain how Yeats uses sound images to heighten the emotional effect of the poem.

The Wild Swans at Coole

Recalling

1. For how many years has the speaker been observing the swans? What did they do the first year that the speaker counted them? What are they doing now?
2. According to line 14, how does the speaker feel now? According to line 18, how did he react the first time he heard the "bell beat" of the swans' wings?
3. According to stanza 4, in what ways have the swans remained the same?
4. What does the speaker anticipate that he will find when he awakes "some day"?

Interpreting

5. Point out the various contrasts the speaker might be drawing in the fourth stanza between the swans and himself.
6. Why might the passage of time change the speaker's response to the swans?

7. What do you think the swans symbolize to the speaker?

Extending

8. In what ways can seeing a beautiful scene in nature be a painful experience?

VIEWPOINT

"The Lake Isle of Innisfree" was influenced by Yeats's reading of *Walden*, a book in which the nineteenth-century American writer Henry David Thoreau describes his retreat from the city into a simple cabin by a forest pond. Yeats wrote his poem after the sight of a small fountain in a shop window in London brought the sound of Sligo's lake water lapping back into his consciousness. However, the poem is more than an exercise in escapism, as critic Thomas L. Byrd, Jr., notes:

> In the first place, the poem is grounded in reality. Innisfree is as real as Walden Pond. . . . If Innisfree represents escape, it is the escape of the seeking hermit.
> —*The Early Poetry of W. B. Yeats*

■ What specific concrete details help to ground "The Lake Isle of Innisfree" in reality? What is the poem's speaker escaping, and what is he seeking?

COMPOSITION

Writing About Form in Poetry

■ In a paragraph or two, describe the effect of Yeats's use of different line lengths in "The Lake Isle of Innisfree." Begin by describing the various patterns of line length in the poem—in particular, Yeats's combination of longer and shorter lines. Then analyze the visual, rhythmic, and other effects of these different line lengths. End by explaining how these different line lengths add to the poem's overall meaning and emotional impact.

Imitating a Poet's Style

■ Write a poem of at least two stanzas that expresses a longing for a particular place. Try to imitate several aspects of Yeats's style in "The Lake Isle of Innisfree." Begin with the words "I will arise and go now, and go to _____." Use vivid, specific images of sight and sound to describe and contrast your special place with your present location.

"The Second Coming" is based on Yeats's special theory of history. According to his theory, cycles of history and nature occur every two thousand years. During this time one civilization grows, improves, decays, and dissolves, and then a new civilization takes its place. The title of the poem refers to the New Testament prediction of the return of Jesus Christ to the earth at the end of the world.

William Butler Yeats

The Second Coming

Turning and turning in the widening gyre[1]
The falcon cannot hear the falconer;
Things fall apart; the center cannot hold;
Mere anarchy is loosed upon the world,
5 The blood-dimmed tide is loosed, and everywhere
The ceremony of innocence is drowned;
The best lack all conviction, while the worst
Are full of passionate intensity.

Surely some revelation[2] is at hand;
10 Surely the Second Coming is at hand.
The Second Coming! Hardly are those words out
When a vast image out of *Spiritus Mundi*[3]
Troubles my sight: somewhere in sands of the desert
A shape with lion body and the head of a man,[4]
15 A gaze blank and pitiless as the sun,
Is moving its slow thighs, while all about it
Reel shadows of the indignant desert birds.
The darkness drops again; but now I know
That twenty centuries[5] of stony sleep
20 Were vexed to nightmare by a rocking cradle,
And what rough beast, its hour come round at last,
Slouches toward Bethlehem to be born?

---

1. **gyre** [jīr]: circular or spiral form or motion, which Yeats uses as the symbol for the winding up and winding down of cycles of history.
2. **revelation:** disclosure; in Christian teaching, God's unfolding of His will to the human race.
3. ***Spiritus Mundi*** [spir′i təs mo͞on′dē]: world soul or spirit that, according to Yeats's theories, acts as a universal memory for all people.
4. **A shape . . . man:** the sphinx.
5. **twenty centuries:** Yeats's cycles each lasted two thousand years.

Byzantium was the name of the eastern Roman Empire and also designated the Greek Christian civilization. During Europe's Dark Ages its capital, Constantinople, now Istanbul, was a great artistic center, containing several magnificent churches decorated with mosaics of holy men portrayed in the stylized, two-dimensional manner that typified Byzantine art. Yeats wrote several poems about Byzantium, which he regarded as a kind of holy city of the imagination, a place where the spiritual and the artistic came together.

William Butler Yeats

Sailing to Byzantium

1

That is no country[1] for old men. The young
In one another's arms, birds in the trees
—Those dying generations—at their song,
The salmon falls, the mackerel-crowded seas,
5 Fish, flesh, or fowl, commend all summer long
Whatever is begotten, born, and dies.
Caught in that sensual music all neglect
Monuments of unaging intellect.

2

An aged man is but a paltry thing,
10 A tattered coat upon a stick, unless
Soul clap its hands and sing, and louder sing
For every tatter in its mortal dress,
Nor is there singing school but studying
Monuments of its own magnificence;
15 And therefore I have sailed the seas and come
To the holy city of Byzantium.

---

1. **That . . . country:** the sensual world where time passes and death is certain to occur.

3

O sages standing in God's holy fire
As in the gold mosaic of a wall,[2]
Come from the holy fire, perne in a gyre,[3]
20 And be the singing masters of my soul.
Consume my heart away; sick with desire
And fastened to a dying animal
It knows not what it is; and gather me
Into the artifice of eternity.

4

25 Once out of nature I shall never take
My bodily form from any natural thing,
But such a form as Grecian goldsmiths make
Of hammered gold and gold enameling
To keep a drowsy Emperor awake;
30 Or set upon a golden bough to sing[4]
To lords and ladies of Byzantium
Of what is past, or passing, or to come.

---

2. **sages . . . wall:** wise old men (sages) depicted on the mosaic walls of Byzantine churches.
3. **perne in a gyre:** descend or spin with a whirling, spiral motion.
4. **To keep . . . sing:** Byzantine Emperor Theophilus is said to have ordered his artisans to make him a gold and silver tree in which mechanical birds perched and sang.

STUDY QUESTIONS

The Second Coming

Recalling

1. Describe the behavior of the falcon in lines 1–2.
2. What two things are loosed upon the world, and what is drowned?
3. What contrast do lines 7–8 draw between "the best" and "the worst"?
4. Describe the creature that the speaker envisions crawling through the desert.
5. Where is the "rough beast" going, and why is it going there?

Interpreting

6. What picture of human affairs is created in stanza 1?

7. Explain what seems to be happening in stanza 2, and describe the speaker's attitude toward this event. Use examples from the poem.
8. This poem was written in 1919, shortly after the end of World War I, which had devastated much of Europe. What relationship can you see between war and the events of this poem?

Sailing to Byzantium

Recalling

1. What do the inhabitants of the country described in stanza 1 "commend"? What do they "neglect"?
2. In what terms does the speaker describe old age in lines 9–10?
3. List three requests that the speaker addresses to the sages, or wise men, in the third stanza.

4. Describe the bodily form that the speaker wants to assume when he is "out of nature," and list two of the things the speaker says he would do.

Interpreting

5. In the country described in stanza 1, what aspect of life seems most important?
6. In what ways does Byzantium differ from the first country? Why might the speaker prefer Byzantium?
7. Explain how the golden bird described in stanza 4 differs from the birds mentioned in stanza 1. Why might the speaker choose the form of the golden bird over that of "any natural thing"?
8. What is the speaker's attitude toward aging and death? What does the poem say about the relationship between body and soul? Nature and art?

LITERARY FOCUS

Yeats and Symbolism

A **symbol** is a figure of speech in which a person, object, or situation represents something in addition to its literal meaning. A symbol usually creates a correspondence between something concrete and something abstract: For example, a growing plant might symbolize life itself.

The **Symbolist** movement in literature was begun in France around 1885 by a group of poets that included Baudelaire [bōd'əl ār'], Rimbaud [ram bō'], and Mallarmé [ma lär mā']. The poems of the French Symbolists are richly musical and include vivid symbols whose larger meanings are suggested rather than directly stated. The Symbolist movement, popularized in Britain by Oscar Wilde (see page 546), had a profound effect on Yeats and a group of younger British and American poets, including T. S. Eliot.

Yeats was especially aware of the power of symbols because of his interest in visionary and mystical experiences. From the writings of mystics, Yeats borrowed the idea that all human beings share in one great reservoir of experience and emotion, a reservoir that can be tapped through the use of symbols. Yeats repeatedly used in his poems certain symbols, such as the sun, moon, bird, rose, and tower, because he be-

lieved that these symbols had the power to evoke common human feelings and experiences.

Thinking About Yeats and Symbolism

■ Choose a symbol in "Sailing to Byzantium," and explain what it represents. What qualities in the symbol suggest its larger meaning?

VOCABULARY

Synonyms

A **synonym** is a word that has the same or nearly the same meaning as another word. *Walk* and *stroll* are synonyms. The words in capitals are from Yeats's poems. Choose the word that is *nearest* the meaning of the word in capitals, *as the word is used in the selection.*

1. TUMULT: (a) somersault (b) tranquillity (c) sandwich (d) uproar
2. BRIMMING: (a) full (b) wide (c) overflowing (d) stupendous
3. CLAMOROUS: (a) noisy (b) grateful (c) loving (d) ingenious
4. REVELATION: (a) recognition (b) disclosure (c) homecoming (d) alteration
5. ANARCHY: (a) chaos (b) ignorance (c) brutality (d) injustice

COMPOSITION

Writing a Comparison/Contrast

■ Compare and contrast Yeats's "Second Coming" and "Sailing to Byzantium." Begin by pointing out the similarities between the content and literary techniques of the two poems. Then note the differences between them. In particular, compare and contrast Yeats's use of symbols to express his ideas in the two poems. *For help with this assignment, refer to Lesson 2 in the Writing About Literature Handbook at the back of this book.*

Writing a Poem About a Transformation

■ Write a brief poem expressing a wish to be transformed into someone or something else. Your poem should use precise images to describe the person or creature you would like to become. You should also make clear the reasons that you desire such a transformation.

T. S. Eliot   *1888–1965*

Thomas Stearns Eliot was one of the most influential writers of his time and a pioneer among the modernist poets whose view of life was radically altered by World War I. Recognizing that the war had undermined many people's faith in the systems that had once ordered human existence, Eliot sought to make sense of modern life. He was determined, as he put it, "to see both beauty and ugliness, to see the boredom, the horror and the glory."

Eliot was born in St. Louis, Missouri, where his grandfather had founded Washington University. His family was strict, religious, and literary. Shy and frail as a boy, Eliot studied literature and philosophy at Harvard University, wrote for college magazines, and took boxing lessons at night. After receiving his master's degree in 1910, he studied at Oxford and at the Sorbonne in Paris. He moved permanently to England in 1915 and became a British subject seven years later. Still, he remained American in many ways. He sometimes signed his name Thomas (Missouri) Eliot, and he loved American folk songs, comic strips, and the movies of the Marx Brothers. Marrying in 1915, Eliot eventually became a successful partner in a publishing firm.

T. S. Eliot's early poems capture the alienation and spiritual bankruptcy felt by many writers of his time. He returned frequently to these matters in his first volume of poetry, *Prufrock and Other Observations* (1917), as well as in his subsequent works, *The Waste Land* (1922) and "The Hollow Men" (1925). After these works, however, Eliot's poetry began to show the stirrings of religious faith. "Ash Wednesday" (1930), written after his conversion to the Church of England, protrays his climb from despair to hope and from disillusionment to belief. In his masterpiece, the *Four Quartets* (1943), he affirms his belief in spiritual values in the midst of war.

In 1948 Eliot was awarded the Nobel Prize for Literature, becoming the first American-born poet to be so honored. However, Eliot found success with other forms of writing besides poetry. He published influential literary criticism, and, like Yeats, wrote poetic dramas. Among his best-known plays are *Murder in the Cathedral* (1935), *The Family Reunion* (1939), and *The Cocktail Party* (1950).

Eliot's poems are known for their concrete images, irregular rhythms, shifting moods, and "patchwork" presentation of religious, historical, mythological, and literary references. His poetry also mixes elevated language with slang and colloquial expressions. Like other modernists, Eliot believed that poetry should not state emotions directly; rather, the poet should select images that trigger these emotions in the reader.

■ Eliot's use of repetition of words, phrases, ideas, and images helps his readers understand his poems. Why is repetition a useful device for writer and reader?

In "Preludes" a speaker offers what seem to be random observations on his surroundings. A prelude is any performance or act that leads up to a main event; in particular, a musical prelude is a short piece based on a repeated phrase.

T. S. Eliot

Preludes

1

The winter evening settles down
With smell of steaks[1] in passageways.
Six o'clock.
The burned-out ends of smoky days.
5 And now a gusty shower wraps
The grimy scraps
Of withered leaves about your feet
And newspapers from vacant lots;
The showers beat
10 On broken blinds and chimney pots,
And at the corner of the street
A lonely cab horse steams and stamps.
And then the lighting of the lamps.

2

The morning comes to consciousness
15 Of faint stale smells of beer
From the sawdust-trampled street
With all its muddy feet that press
To early coffee stands.
With the other masquerades
20 That time resumes,
One thinks of all the hands
That are raising dingy shades
In a thousand furnished rooms.

3

You tossed a blanket from the bed,
25 You lay upon your back, and waited;
You dozed, and watched the night revealing
The thousand sordid images

Of which your soul was constituted;
They flickered against the ceiling.
30 And when all the world came back
And the light crept up between the shutters
And you heard the sparrows in the gutters,
You had such a vision of the street
As the street hardly understands;
35 Sitting along the bed's edge, where
You curled the papers from your hair,
Or clasped the yellow soles of feet
In the palms of both soiled hands.

4

His soul stretched tight across the skies
40 That fade behind a city block,
Or trampled by insistent feet
At four and five and six o'clock;
And short square fingers stuffing pipes,
And evening newspapers, and eyes
45 Assured of certain certainties,
The conscience of a blackened street
Impatient to assume the world.

I am moved by fancies that are curled
Around these images, and cling:
50 The notion of some infinitely gentle
Infinitely suffering thing.

Wipe your hand across your mouth,
    and laugh;
The worlds revolve like ancient women
Gathering fuel in vacant lots.

---

1. **steaks:** When this poem was composed, steak was a common meal of the lower classes.

"The Hollow Men" is one of Eliot's most dramatic and powerful poems. It is an example of his "patchwork" style of writing, which juxtaposes various literary, mythological, religious, historical, and cultural references as well as different styles of speech. In "The Hollow Men" Eliot joins to his own poetic voice the echoes of other voices—literary works, prayers, even nursery rhymes—to create a uniquely modern lament for his own time.

The Hollow Men

Mistab Kurtz[1]—*he dead.*

A penny for the Old Guy[2]

1

We are the hollow men
We are the stuffed men
Leaning together
Headpiece filled with straw. Alas!
5 Our dried voices, when
We whisper together
Are quiet and meaningless
As wind in dry grass
Or rats' feet over broken glass
10 In our dry cellar

Shape without form, shade without color,
Paralyzed force, gesture without motion;

Those who have crossed
With direct eyes, to death's other Kingdom[3]
15 Remember us—if at all—not as lost
Violent souls, but only
As the hollow men
The stuffed men.

2

Eyes I dare not meet in dreams
20 In death's dream kingdom
These do not appear:
There, the eyes are
Sunlight on a broken column
There, is a tree swinging
25 And voices are
In the wind's singing
More distant and more solemn
Than a fading star.

1. *Mistab Kurtz:* character in Joseph Conrad's short novel *Heart of Darkness.* Kurtz sets out to civilize the natives in Africa and instead becomes one of them and dies in the jungle. He is described as being "hollow to the core."

2. *A penny . . . Old Guy:* traditional expression used by English children on Guy Fawkes Day, November 5. Guy Fawkes (1570–1606) tried and failed to blow up the Houses of Parliament and was subsequently hanged. On Guy Fawkes Day children burn straw dummies representing him.

3. **Those . . . Kingdom:** the virtuous who have gone to Heaven, according to Dante's *Paradiso.* The *Paradiso,* which is the final section of the *Divine Comedy,* describes the soul's union with God in Heaven (page 883).

Let me be no nearer
30 In death's dream kingdom
Let me also wear
Such deliberate disguises
Rat's coat, crowskin, crossed staves[4]
In a field
35 Behaving as the wind behaves
No nearer—

Not that final meeting
In the twilight kingdom

3

This is the dead land
40 This is the cactus land
Here the stone images
Are raised, here they receive
The supplication[5] of a dead man's hand
Under the twinkle of a fading star.

45 Is it like this
In death's other kingdom
Waking alone
At the hour when we are
Trembling with tenderness
50 Lips that would kiss
Form prayers to broken stone.

4

The eyes are not here
There are no eyes here
In this valley of dying stars
55 In this hollow valley
This broken jaw of our lost kingdoms

In this last of meeting places
We grope together
And avoid speech
60 Gathered on this beach of the tumid river[6]

Sightless, unless
The eyes reappear
As the perpetual star
Multifoliate rose[7]
65 Of death's twilight kingdom
The hope only
Of empty men.

5

Here we go round the prickly pear[8]
Prickly pear prickly pear
70 *Here we go round the prickly pear*
At five o'clock in the morning.

Between the idea
And the reality
Between the motion
75 And the act[9]
Falls the Shadow
       For Thine is the Kingdom[10]

Between the conception
And the creation
80 Between the emotion
And the response
Falls the Shadow
       Life is very long[11]

Between the desire
85 And the spasm
Between the potency[12]
And the existence

---

4. **staves:** wood strips, rods, or staffs. Crossed staves suggest scarecrows.
5. **supplication:** a humble prayer or plea.
6. **tumid river:** swollen river; in Dante's *Inferno,* the condemned must cross the River Acheron in order to pass from the world of the living into Hell.

7. **star . . . rose:** The star and the rose are traditional symbols for Christ and the Virgin Mary. Dante described Paradise as a "multifoliate rose"—a rose with many leaves.
8. **Here . . . pear:** version of a well-known nursery rhyme; prickly pear is a desert cactus.
9. **Between . . . act:** reference to *Julius Caesar,* Act II, Scene i, 63–65: "Between the acting of a dreadful thing/And the first motion, all the interim is/Like a phantasma or a hideous dream."
10. **For . . . Kingdom:** These words come from the ending of the Lord's Prayer.
11. **Life . . . long:** quotation from another Joseph Conrad novel, *An Outcast of the Islands;* these words are spoken to a character who, like Kurtz, is "hollow."
12. **potency:** power; in this case, to procreate.

Between the essence
And the descent
90 Falls the Shadow
                    For Thine is the Kingdom

For Thine is
Life is
For Thine is the

95 *This is the way the world ends*
This is the way the world ends
This is the way the world ends
Not with a bang but a whimper.

STUDY QUESTIONS

Preludes

Recalling

1. List five specific images of evening and morning presented in sections 1 and 2.
2. In section 3 what does the person described by the speaker see? What does night reveal to this person, according to lines 26–28?
3. In section 4 what does the speaker find moving? To what does the speaker compare the revolving worlds?

Interpreting

4. What is the mood of "Preludes"? Choose four images, one in each section, and explain how each of them conveys this mood.
5. Is the laughter referred to in line 52 good or bad? How do you know? Describe the vision of the universe that the poem ends with.
6. What images in the poem might be particularly associated with twentieth-century existence? Point out the aspects of modern life that Eliot emphasizes most. Summarize the view of modern life that the poem expresses.

Extending

7. Do you think this poem paints an accurate picture of modern life? If not, what alternative images would you offer?

The Hollow Men

Recalling

1. What words and phrases do the hollow men use to describe their heads and voices in part 1?
2. List four images of "death's dream kingdom" in part 2. What disguise does the hollow man want to wear in this place?
3. What adjectives describe the land of the hollow men in part 3?
4. What four lines are repeated throughout part 5? How does the world end, according to line 95?

Interpreting

5. Describe the life of the hollow men. What do they seem to lack?
6. Lines 13–14 refer to those who have had faith, led good lives, and gone to Paradise. In what ways are the hollow men different from these people?
7. What do you think Eliot means by the Shadow? What effect does the Shadow seem to have on human action, according to the hollow men?
8. Explain how the repetitions in part 5 add to the power of the poem. Is it fitting that the world of the hollow men ends as it does? Why or why not?

9. Why do you think Eliot portrays modern people as hollow men? What qualities in modern life does Eliot lament in this poem?

Extending

10. Do you think the poem is equally applicable to our own time as it was to the period after World War I? Why or why not?

LITERARY FOCUS

Free Verse

Free verse is poetry with no fixed rhythm, or meter. Though it was used before the twentieth century—in the biblical Psalms (page 235), for example, and by Matthew Arnold (page 536)—not until the modernist era did poets like T. S. Eliot establish its widespread use in English-language poetry. However, as Eliot himself pointed out, free verse is in some ways "a contradiction in terms." No poet is "free" to write down anything at all, break it into lines, and call it "verse," or poetry. Poetry requires far more care in word choice and word placement; in fact, because poets using free verse are not limited by metric patterns, they have many more choices about where to break lines and must take time to find the word placement that will achieve just the right effect. In addition, there must be some reason for using free verse, some overall relationship between form and meaning. Many modernists chose free verse to stress that they were breaking the pattern of past traditions; in the aftermath of World War I, others used it to help capture the formlessness that they perceived in modern life.

Thinking About Free Verse

■ In what way is the use of free verse in "The Hollow Men" related to the poem's overall meaning? Examine the word placement in part 3. Why has Eliot broken the lines where he has?

Allusion

An **allusion** is a short reference in a work to something outside the work, usually to another piece of literature or to a well-known person, place, or event from history, religion, or mythology. T. S. Eliot relies heavily on allusions from many different sources, often patching together such diverse materials as the Bible, works of literature, myths, and even nursery rhymes and popular jingles. By referring to many different historical periods, types of works, styles of speech, and even languages, Eliot creates a complex and varying tone in his own works. In addition, his allusions often create a picture of modern life as a kind of grab bag full of broken fragments of the past, with no wholeness or order of its own.

Thinking About Allusion

1. What lines in "The Hollow Men" contain allusions? From what kinds of sources (biblical, historical, literary, and so on) are they drawn?
2. What is the effect of the allusions in part 5 of "The Hollow Men"?

COMPOSITION

Writing About Tone

■ The tone of a work is the attitude its author expresses toward his or her subject. In a brief essay analyze the tone of "Preludes." First identify the emotion or emotions the poem conveys, explaining how Eliot's choices of words and images create this tone. Then point out any changes in the tone, and explain how these changes reveal the poem's meaning.

Writing a Collage Poem

■ Write a free-verse poem that is a stream of related images. These images do not need to be connected into a single story or scene. However, they should be vivid and concrete, as Eliot's are in "Preludes," and they should eventually add up to a dominant impression, conveying a definite emotion of some kind.

COMPARING WRITERS

1. What symbols do Yeats and Eliot use in their poetry to represent modern life? What overall view of modern life does each poet express?
2. Yeats and Eliot both attempted to show the relationship between their time and universal human problems. Compare each poet's use of symbolism, allusion, and other techniques to add a universal dimension to his poetry.

Siegfried Sassoon   *1886–1967*

Siegfried Sassoon is chiefly known as one of the poets who voiced their generation's anger over the futility and suffering of World War I. Born to a wealthy and prominent family, Sassoon spent his youth living the life of an English country gentleman. After leaving school he moved to London, where he published several slim volumes of verse celebrating the beauties of nature and English country life. At this stage his work was typical of the **Georgian poets,** whose pastoral, patriotic poems were published between 1911 and 1922, during the early part of the reign of King George V.

However, Sassoon's poetry changed drastically after he entered the British Army to fight in World War I. His battle experiences made him bitter and angry about the horrors of war. After the war ended, Sassoon worked as the literary editor of a newspaper and continued to write poetry. In addition to poetry, Sassoon wrote stories and novels, and his later works include memoirs, satire, meditations, and love lyrics. His *Collected Poems* was finally published in 1947.

Sassoon's poem "Everyone Sang" does not directly describe the fighting and suffering on the western front, but it does concern World War I. Sassoon wrote the poem in response to the welcome news of the armistice on November 11, 1918, when people all over the world rejoiced that the "war to end all wars" was finally over.

■ What contrasting emotions might someone feel at the end of a long ordeal?

Siegfried Sassoon

Everyone Sang

Everyone suddenly burst out singing;
And I was filled with such delight
As prisoned birds must find in freedom,
Winging wildly across the white
5 Orchards and dark green fields;
     on—on—and out of sight.

Everyone's voice was suddenly lifted;
And beauty came like the setting sun:
My heart was shaken with tears; and horror
Drifted away . . . O, but Everyone
10 Was a bird; and the song was wordless;
     the singing will never be done.

Rupert Brooke   *1887–1915*

Rupert Brooke was handsome, charming, intelligent, privileged, and beloved—a "golden young Apollo," as one of his friends described him. Because of his early, tragic death in World War I, he has remained that golden young poet forever, and it is partly because of his early death that his reputation as a poet survives.

Brooke began to write for pleasure at an early age and won a prize for his verse while still in school. Popular and energetic, he played football and cricket and edited the school magazine. His early published poems are associated with **Georgian poetry**: traditional verse that sings of country life and patriotic ideals—a kind of poetry in keeping with Brooke's happy, sheltered youth.

In his mid-twenties Brooke left his native England to travel extensively in Europe, America, and the South Seas. It was in Tahiti in 1913 that he wrote some of his most famous poems.

He returned to England and enlisted in the wartime navy. During the last year of his life, he wrote his series of war sonnets, which are traditional, formal, and patriotic in tone. "The Soldier" is the most famous of these poems. Unlike so many of his contemporaries, Brooke never wrote angry or bitter descriptions of battle, possibly because he spent so little time in the trenches. He died on his way to battle: While traveling to Turkey, he was stricken with blood poisoning and died on a Greek island. Ironically, his death brought him almost immediate fame as both a poet and a symbol of innocent youth struck down by war.

■ Brooke's "Soldier" is idealistic. What are the positive and negative aspects of being idealistic about war and death?

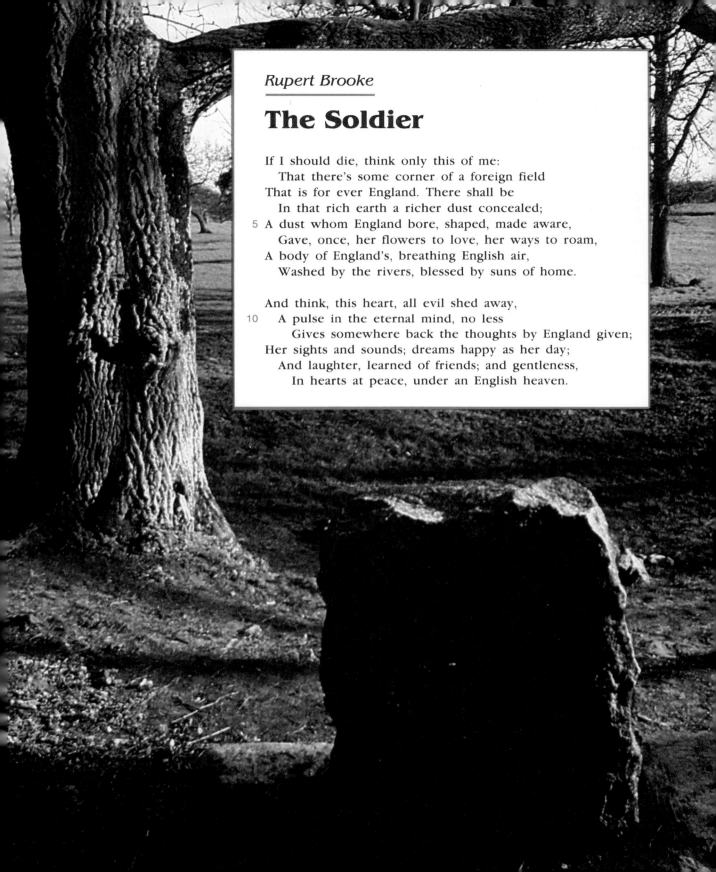

Rupert Brooke

The Soldier

If I should die, think only this of me:
    That there's some corner of a foreign field
That is for ever England. There shall be
    In that rich earth a richer dust concealed;
5 A dust whom England bore, shaped, made aware,
    Gave, once, her flowers to love, her ways to roam,
A body of England's, breathing English air,
    Washed by the rivers, blessed by suns of home.

And think, this heart, all evil shed away,
10   A pulse in the eternal mind, no less
      Gives somewhere back the thoughts by England given;
Her sights and sounds; dreams happy as her day;
    And laughter, learned of friends; and gentleness,
      In hearts at peace, under an English heaven.

Stephen Spender   *born 1909*

For over fifty years Stephen Spender has remained a prominent voice among British authors. The son of a journalist and Oxford lecturer, he showed an early interest in literature. The year before he entered Oxford he began his own printing press, printing up a volume of his own poems along with a batch of chemical labels. While still in college, he published a second volume of poems and became associated with a small circle of poets led by W. H. Auden.

The publication in 1933 of his *Poems* firmly established Spender's place among a circle of poets that included Auden, Louis MacNeice, and Cecil Day Lewis. These poets had all been deeply affected by World War I. They blamed the decline of Britain in the 1920s and 1930s on the loss of faith in humanity and the social order as a result of the war. The work of these poets reflected the economic and political turbulence of the 1930s: the worldwide Depression, the rise of fascism and Nazism, and the Spanish civil war. However, unlike modernist writers of the 1920s, they did not condemn modern society or regard social injustice as evidence of civilization's collapse. Instead they chose positive protest, political involvement, and artistic expression as healthy ways of confronting an ailing world. Their poetry, which examines and attempts to correct grave social, political, and economic problems of their time, illustrates what is sometimes called **literature of conscience**.

Spender has had a varied career. He has taught at several British and American universities and edited the artistic magazines *Encounter* and *Horizon*. He has remained active in literary circles, writing criticism, short stories, and a novel in addition to poetry. Among his recent work is *The Thirties and After: Poetry, Politics, People, 1933–1970* (1979).

Spender's poetry is somewhat more romantic and direct in its tone than that of the other poets in his circle. His work is less satiric and more lyrical than Auden's, more personal than MacNeice's. In addition, Spender did more than the others to turn the machine and the technological society it eventually produced into legitimate subjects for poetry. "I Think Continually of the Truly Great," however, draws much of its impact from Spender's intensely lyrical use of nature images.

■ Beowulf fought monsters and dragons to gain lasting fame. Must a person win wars to be considered great?

Stephen Spender

I Think Continually of Those Who Were Truly Great

I think continually of those who were truly great.
Who, from the womb, remembered the soul's history
Through corridors of light where the hours are suns,
Endless and singing. Whose lovely ambition
5 Was that their lips, still touched with fire,
Should tell of the Spirit, clothed from head to foot in song.
And who hoarded from the Spring branches
The desires falling across their bodies like blossoms.

What is precious, is never to forget
10 The essential delight of the blood drawn from ageless springs
Breaking through rocks in worlds before our earth.
Never to deny its pleasure in the simple morning light
Nor its grave evening demand for love.
Never to allow gradually the traffic to smother
15 With noise and fog, the flowering of the Spirit.

Near the snow, near the sun, in the highest fields,
See how these names are feted[1] by the waving grass
And by the streamers of white cloud
And whispers of wind in the listening sky.
20 The names of those who in their lives fought for life,
Who wore at their hearts the fire's center.
Born of the sun, they traveled a short while toward the sun
And left the vivid air signed with their honor.

---

1. **feted** [fāt′əd]: honored or commemorated with a fete, or celebration.

STUDY QUESTIONS

Everyone Sang (Sassoon)

Recalling

1. What does the speaker feel when everyone bursts out singing? To what does he compare this feeling?
2. In the second stanza what happens to the speaker's heart? What "Drifted away"?
3. How long will the singing last, according to line 10?

Interpreting

4. Why is everyone singing? Explain why the simile in the first stanza is appropriate to the situation in the poem.
5. In the second stanza why might beauty come like the "setting" rather than rising sun?
6. What different emotions does the speaker express from the beginning to the end of the poem? What causes his emotions to change?

Extending

7. Why might we be powerfully moved when a large group of people suddenly respond in unison to something? Can you think of instances when such a response is exhilarating? When it is frightening?

The Soldier (Brooke)

Recalling

1. What does the speaker want people to think of him if he should die?
2. According to lines 5–8, what did England do for the speaker?
3. What will his heart become? What sorts of thoughts will his heart give back?

Interpreting

4. What is the speaker's attitude toward England? What words and images in the poem convey this emotion?
5. What is the speaker's attitude toward death? In what sense can life win out over death?
6. In what ways is "The Soldier" more than simply an English soldier's poem about his homeland? What might be its more universal theme and appeal?

Extending

7. How would you define the word *patriot*? What different meanings might the word have for different people?

I Think Continually . . . (Spender)

Recalling

1. What is the ambition of the "truly great"?
2. According to the second stanza, what things should not be forgotten? What should not be denied? What should not be allowed to happen?
3. According to lines 22–23, of what were the truly great born, and what did they do?
4. Point out five nature images in lines 8–19.

Interpreting

5. Describe the personal qualities of the "truly great." What does Spender mean when he says that great people "fought for life"?
6. Why do you think Spender describes these special people with terms like *Spirit, fire,* and *the sun*?
7. Why might Spender turn to nature for imagery to salute great human beings?

COMPOSITION (Brooke)

Writing About a Quotation

■ Discuss the meaning of the lines "That there's some corner of a foreign field / That is for ever England." First explain the specific meaning of these lines at the point at which they occur in "The Soldier." Then explain the significance of the lines in relation to the overall meaning of the poem. *For help with this assignment, refer to Lesson 5 in the Writing About Literature Handbook at the back of this book.*

Writing a Poem About a Person

■ In a short poem list and describe those characteristic articles that you might place in a time capsule to represent yourself or some famous person for all time.

COMPARING WRITERS

1. What similarities in outlook can you find in the poems of Sassoon, Brooke, and Spender? Are their poems positive, neutral, or negative in their descriptions of human life?
2. All three poets use nature imagery in describing human affairs and problems. In at least two of these poems, relate the feelings evoked by these images of nature. What differences can you detect in each poet's view of nature?

Louis MacNeice   *1907–1963*

Louis MacNeice was a member of the group of British poets that included Stephen Spender, W. H. Auden, and Cecil Day Lewis. Like these other writers, he too produced literature aimed at correcting the grave social, economic, and political problems that afflicted Europe in the 1930s. However, he has come to be regarded as one of the most original and least typical writers in this group.

The son of a Protestant bishop, MacNeice was born and reared in Belfast, Ireland. After graduating from Oxford, he taught at several universities, combining his teaching career with a heavy writing schedule. From serious poetry he branched out into writing light verse, criticism, poetic drama, and travel literature. MacNeice and his friend and fellow poet W. H. Auden collaborated in recording their observations and feelings during a trip to Iceland in *Letters from Iceland* (1937), a mixture of poetry and prose.

During the 1940s MacNeice worked for the British Broadcasting Corporation as a producer and feature writer, changing jobs in 1950 to direct the British Institute in Athens. He also continued to teach from time to time, always leaving time for his two greatest passions— writing and tennis.

Although MacNeice's early association with Auden, Spender, and other poets of the 1930s is important, his work deviated from theirs in some significant ways. While the others believed that poetry truly could change the world, MacNeice was more cautious about poetry's impact on society. He saw the poet not as an engineer of social change but rather as an entertainer, a commentator, a broadcaster of the truth, whose message was made up of both fact and emotion. His poetry was less political and more literary than that of his associates, and his style was often colloquial, or drawn from everyday speech.

During World War II MacNeice's poetry darkened and became more introspective and philosophical than his earlier work. However, his later poems regained the lyricism for which he is now known, a lyricism demonstrated in "The Park."

■ Which poets you have studied would agree with MacNeice that poets are entertainers and broadcasters? Why do you think so?

Louis MacNeice

The Park

Through a glass greenly[1] men as trees walking[2]
Led by their dogs, trees as torrents
Loosed by the thaw, tulips as shriekmarks
(Yelps of delight), lovers as coracles[3]
5 Riding the rapids: Spring as a spring
Releasing the jack-in-a-box of a fanfare.

Urban enclave[4] of lawns and water,
Lacquered ducks and young men sculling,[5]
Children who never had seen the country
10 Believing it this while those who had once
Known real country ignore the void
Their present imposes, their past exposes.

South and east lie the yellowed terraces
Grandiose, jerrybuilt,[6] ghosts of gracious
15 Living, and north those different terraces
Where great white bears with extensile[7]
    necks,
Convicted sentries, lope their beat,
No rest for their paws till the day they die.

Fossils of flesh, fossils of stucco:
20 Between them the carefully labeled flower
    beds
And the litter baskets, but also between
    them
Through a grille gaily men as music
Forcing the spring to loose the lid,
To break the bars, to find the world.

---

1. **Through . . . greenly:** a playful version of the
Biblical quotation "We see through a glass, darkly" (I
Corinthians, 13 : 12).
2. **men . . . walking:** a reference to the New
Testament episode in which Jesus cured a blind man,
who then said that he saw "men as trees walking."
3. **coracles** [kôr′ə kəlz]: small boats made with wicker
frames covered with hides.
4. **enclave:** self-contained unit within a foreign
community.
5. **sculling:** rowing with large oars.
6. **jerrybuilt:** cheaply or hastily made.
7. **extensile:** able to be extended or stretched.

Robert Graves   *1895–1985*

Robert Graves was one of the most prolific writers in the twentieth century. He is famous as a scholar and novelist as well as a poet, and his varied literary output of over one hundred books includes biographical and autobiographical works, translations, works of literary criticism, and studies of such subjects as anthropology and psychology.

Graves was born in Wimbledon, England; his father was a poet with a passion for Irish folklore. In 1914 Graves left school to enlist in the Royal Welsh Fusiliers, serving alongside Siegfried Sassoon. Badly wounded early in the war, Graves began writing poetry during his recovery. In 1916 his first two volumes of poetry, *Over the Brazier* and *Goliath and David,* established his reputation as an antiwar poet. After the war Graves married, resumed his education at Oxford, and later pursued his interests in writing, scholarship, and teaching. Although he taught at Oxford for many years, he did not always live in England. As a young man, he taught in Cairo, Egypt, and in more recent years he made his home in Majorca [mə yôr′kə], an island off the coast of Spain.

Graves's work is a mixture of the traditional and the modern, of traditional forms and modern sensibilities. Even his historical novels, which are based on ancient history and myth and include the popular works *I, Claudius* and *Claudius, the God,* use the idiom of the twentieth century. Graves's earliest poetry reflects the traditional style of the Georgian poets. As he developed as a poet, his subject matter shifted first to philosophy and later to personal and romantic relationships. Regardless of period, however, all of his best poems combine irony and sensitivity with a smoothly lyrical style. As he says of his own poetic standards, "My minimum requirement of a poem is that it should make prose sense as well as poetic sense," a rule that he obeys in "Song: Sullen Moods."

■ Songs and sullen moods hardly seem to go together. Why not? Can you think of situations when they might?

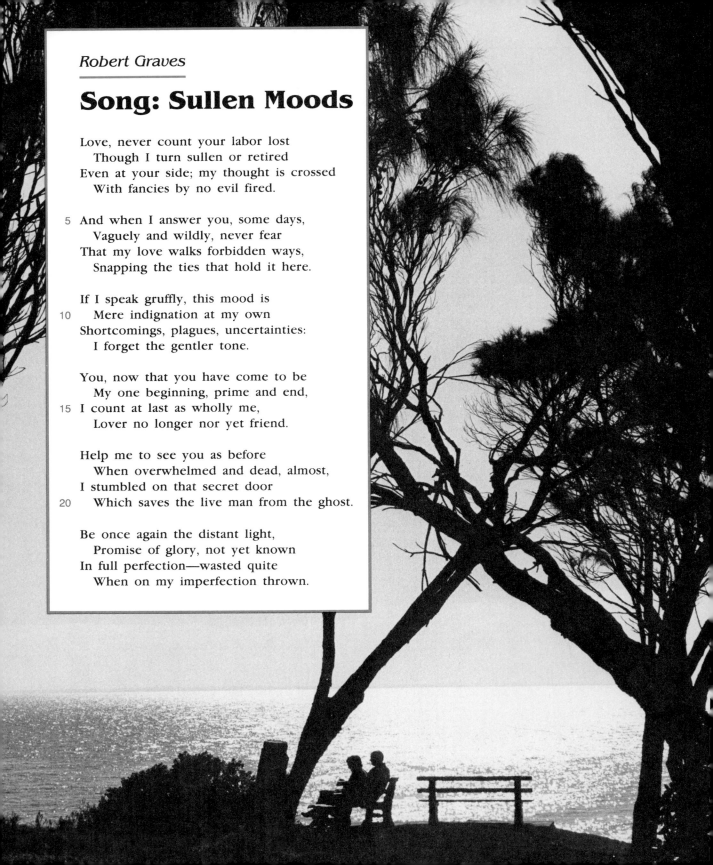

Robert Graves

Song: Sullen Moods

Love, never count your labor lost
    Though I turn sullen or retired
Even at your side; my thought is crossed
    With fancies by no evil fired.

5 And when I answer you, some days,
    Vaguely and wildly, never fear
That my love walks forbidden ways,
    Snapping the ties that hold it here.

If I speak gruffly, this mood is
10   Mere indignation at my own
Shortcomings, plagues, uncertainties:
    I forget the gentler tone.

You, now that you have come to be
    My one beginning, prime and end,
15 I count at last as wholly me,
    Lover no longer nor yet friend.

Help me to see you as before
    When overwhelmed and dead, almost,
I stumbled on that secret door
20   Which saves the live man from the ghost.

Be once again the distant light,
    Promise of glory, not yet known
In full perfection—wasted quite
    When on my imperfection thrown.

STUDY QUESTIONS

The Park (MacNeice)

Recalling

1. In the first stanza to what does MacNeice compare the men walking in the park? List three other comparisons that MacNeice makes in this stanza.
2. What term in line 7 describes the park? What do the children in lines 9–10 believe the park to be? What must be ignored by the people mentioned in lines 10–12?
3. For what three reasons are the men in the park "forcing the spring," according to lines 23–24?

Interpreting

4. What conflict is expressed in the image of "Lacquered ducks" in line 8? What might this image have in common with the images of the bears in the zoo and the "carefully labeled flower beds" in line 20?
5. What do you think MacNeice means by the word *void* in line 11? Is the park part of the void or a refuge from it? Defend your answer.
6. To what is the park superior? To what is it inferior? By the end of the poem, does the park seem more a positive place or a negative place? Why?
7. What is MacNeice saying about the relationship between the works of human beings and the works of nature?

Extending

8. What needs does a park satisfy for people who live in a city? How important do you think such needs are to the quality of human life?

Song: Sullen Moods (Graves)

Recalling

1. In line 7 what does the speaker say his love should never fear? What explanation does the speaker give in the third stanza for his own gruffness?
2. In the fourth stanza what does the speaker say

his love has now come to be?
3. In the last stanza what does the speaker ask his love to become again?

Interpreting

4. Restate in your own words the various requests, stated or implied, that the speaker makes of his love in the first three stanzas. What do these requests show about the speaker's attitude toward his love and toward himself?
5. What view of love does the fourth stanza suggest?
6. In what ways is the speaker's former feeling for his love different from his present feeling? Why do you think he now wants to see his love as he saw her before?

Extending

7. Why do you think people often take those they love for granted?

COMPOSITION (MacNeice)

Writing About a Symbol

Discuss MacNeice's use of the bears as a symbol in "The Park." Begin by explaining the symbolic meaning of the bears when they first appear in the third stanza. Then discuss the significance of the bears to the poem as a whole, showing how MacNeice uses the bears to help reveal the theme of "The Park." *For help with this assignment, refer to Lesson 5 in the Writing About Literature Handbook at the back of this book.*

Writing with Imagery

Write either a pair of stanzas or a pair of paragraphs in which you use contrasting images. Your first stanza or paragraph should use imagery from nature to describe an industrial or mechanical object or scene (for example, a lawn mower, an assembly line, a traffic jam). Your second stanza or paragraph should use technological imagery to describe an animal, a plant, or a scene from the natural world.

W. H. Auden   *1907–1973*

After Yeats and Eliot, Wystan Hugh Auden is the most influential British poet in the modern period. Auden spent the first thirty-two years of his life in England and most of the remainder in the United States. Like T. S. Eliot, whose life followed the opposite pattern, Auden is often regarded as both a British and an American writer.

The young Auden had no particular literary ambitions; his father was a respected physician, his mother a nurse, and Auden himself originally planned to become a mining engineer. Auden studied at Oxford University, where he became the leader of the group that included Stephen Spender, Louis MacNeice, and Cecil Day Lewis. He shared their disenchantment with the modern world as well as their determination to provide political and poetic alternatives to its ills. In 1928 Spender published twenty-six of Auden's poems, and in that same year Auden went to Germany to study politics and psychology.

During the 1930s Auden was something of a romantic radical who delighted in shocking both readers and friends with his language and opinions; by his own admission he loved to show off. However, his life and his work became more subdued after 1940. In 1937 he married the daughter of German novelist Thomas Mann so that she could leave Nazi Germany. In that same year Auden also set off to aid the Loyalists in the Spanish civil war. On returning to England, he received the King's Poetry Medal. Perhaps the greatest change in Auden's work came from his return to the practice of Christianity.

In 1939 Auden moved to the United States, giving frequent lectures at American universities. Seven years after his arrival in America, he became a U.S. citizen, and the following year he won the Pulitzer Prize. In addition to poetry, Auden wrote drama, criticism, blues music, musical librettos, and nonsense verse. Among his best-known works are *On This Island* (1937), *For the Time Being* (1944), and *The Age of Anxiety* (1947).

Auden's work shows the influence of Eliot, Yeats, German poetry, and German cabaret lyrics, which lent a dark wit and potential violence to his poetry. As his friend Stephen Spender once said, Auden's poetry has a "vitality, an explosive violence that leaves his contemporaries dazed." Still, above the impulse to shock, Auden's work preserves a strict morality, a vision of humanity's responsibility to create a more humane world.

W. B. Yeats died in January 1939. Nine months later World War II erupted in Europe. Soon after, Auden wrote this tribute, reflecting also on the state of the world Yeats had left behind.

■ Auden was concerned that people seem to have lost the will to feel strong emotion. How can you account for this loss? What in modern life contributes to the loss?

W. H. Auden

In Memory of W. B. Yeats

1

He disappeared in the dead of winter:
The brooks were frozen, the airports almost deserted,
And snow disfigured the public statues;
The mercury sank in the mouth of the dying day.
5 O all the instruments agree
The day of his death was a dark cold day.

Far from his illness
The wolves ran on through the evergreen forests,
The peasant river was untempted by the fashionable quays;[1]
10 By mourning tongues
The death of the poet was kept from his poems.

But for him it was his last afternoon as himself,
An afternoon of nurses and rumors;
The provinces of his body revolted,
15 The squares of his mind were empty,
Silence invaded the suburbs,
The current of his feeling failed: he became his admirers.

Now he is scattered among a hundred cities
And wholly given over to unfamiliar affections;
20 To find his happiness in another kind of wood
And be punished under a foreign code of conscience.
The words of a dead man
Are modified in the guts of the living.

But in the importance and noise of tomorrow
25 When the brokers are roaring like beasts on the floor of the
      Bourse,[2]
And the poor have the sufferings to which they are fairly
      accustomed,
And each in the cell of himself is almost convinced of his freedom;
A few thousand will think of this day
As one thinks of a day when one did something slightly unusual.
30 O all the instruments agree
The day of his death was a dark cold day.

---

1. **quays** [kēz]: loading docks or banks beside a waterway.
2. **Bourse** [bŏŏrs]: the Paris Stock Exchange.

2

You were silly like us: your gift survived
    it all;
The parish of rich women, physical decay,
Yourself; mad Ireland hurt you into
    poetry.
35 Now Ireland has her madness and her
    weather still,
For poetry makes nothing happen:
    it survives
In the valley of its saying where
    executives
Would never want to tamper; it flows
    south
From ranches of isolation and the busy
    griefs,
40 Raw towns that we believe and die in;
    it survives,
A way of happening, a mouth.

3

Earth, receive an honored guest;
William Yeats is laid to rest:
Let the Irish vessel lie
45 Emptied of its poetry.

Time that is intolerant
Of the brave and innocent,
And indifferent in a week
To a beautiful physique,

50 Worships language and forgives
Everyone by whom it lives;
Pardons cowardice, conceit,
Lays its honors at their feet.

55 Time that with this strange excuse
Pardoned Kipling and his views,[3]
And will pardon Paul Claudel,[4]
Pardons him for writing well.

In the nightmare of the dark
60 All the dogs of Europe bark,
And the living nations wait,
Each sequestered[5] in its hate;

Intellectual disgrace
Stares from every human face,
And the seas of pity lie
65 Locked and frozen in each eye.

Follow, poet, follow right
To the bottom of the night,
With your unconstraining voice
Still persuade us to rejoice;

70 With the farming of a verse
Make a vineyard of the curse,
Sing of human unsuccess
In a rapture of distress;

In the deserts of the heart
75 Let the healing fountain start,
In the prison of his days
Teach the free man how to praise.

---

3. **Kipling . . . views:** English writer Rudyard
Kipling (1865–1936) was criticized for supporting
imperialism.
4. **pardon Paul Claudel** [klō del']: French poet,
dramatist, and statesman Paul Claudel (1868–1955)
was attacked for his antidemocratic views, which
Yeats to some extent shared.
5. **sequestered:** set apart. Lines 60–61 refer to
World War II, then in progress.

STUDY QUESTIONS

Recalling

1. What happens to the words of the dead, according to lines 22–23?
2. What of Yeats survived, according to line 32? What various things did it survive?
3. What three things does time care nothing about? What does time worship, and whom does it forgive?
4. List the six requests that Auden makes of the dead Yeats in the last three stanzas.

Interpreting

5. What, according to this poem, are the various differences between Yeats's life and his poetry? Between any poet's life and his or her poetry?
6. When Auden says in line 36 that "poetry makes nothing happen," what things is he actually talking about? What *can* poetry do, according to this poem?
7. Explain how Auden's references to world affairs are related to his views on poetry.

Extending

8. What do you think is the value of poetry? Can poetry make the world better in any way?

LITERARY FOCUS

Paradox

A **paradox** is a statement or situation that at first seems impossible or self-contradictory but may be true in fact or in a figurative sense. For example, Wordsworth's metaphor "the child is father to the man" is a paradox that expresses a figurative truth about the relationship between a child's imagination and that of the adult he becomes. The word *paradox* comes from a Greek expression meaning "contrary to popular opinion or expectation."

As a literary device, paradox can serve many functions. It can attract attention to a difficult idea and persuade readers to accept it. Paradox can also dramatize the fact that experience is full of apparent contradictions.

Sometimes paradox is one literary technique among many used in a poem; at other times, however, paradox can be the basis for an entire poem. The seventeenth-century poet John Donne, for example, is famous for his frequent and extended use of paradox. Modern poets—Auden among them—also find paradox a particularly apt way of expressing the contradictions of their own time.

Thinking About Paradox

1. Point out the paradoxes in the lines "Sing of human unsuccess / In a rapture of distress." What truth might lie behind those apparent contradictions? Find two other seeming contradictions in the last twelve lines of the poem, and explain them as well.
2. Would you have preferred these lines if they had been more straightforward and less paradoxical? Why or why not?

COMPOSITION

Writing About Sound in a Poem

Write an essay about the effect of sound in Auden's "In Memory of W. B. Yeats." Using examples, describe the change in the poem's rhythm and rhyme that occurs in section 3. Then explain how this change affects the emotional impact of the poem.

Writing a Poem of Tribute

Write a short poem in which you pay tribute to someone whom you admire. Be sure to include that person's character traits as well as his or her achievements and effect on you.

In "Musée des Beaux Arts" Auden uses the work of the great painters—the "Old Masters"—as a backdrop for comments about human nature. In particular, he refers to "The Fall of Icarus," a work by the sixteenth-century Flemish painter Pieter Brueghel [broo′gəl]. Icarus is a figure from Greek mythology who tried to fly but fell to his death when his man-made wings melted in the sun.

W. H. Auden

Musée des Beaux Arts

About suffering they were never wrong,
The Old Masters: how well they understood
Its human position; how it takes place
While someone else is eating or opening a window or just
    walking dully along;
5 How, when the aged are reverently, passionately waiting
For the miraculous birth, there always must be
Children who did not specially want it to happen, skating
On a pond at the edge of the wood:
They never forgot
10 That even the dreadful martyrdom must run its course
Anyhow in a corner, some untidy spot
Where the dogs go on with their doggy life and the torturer's
    horse
Scratches its innocent behind on a tree.

In Brueghel's *Icarus,* for instance: how everything turns away
15 Quite leisurely from the disaster; the ploughman may
Have heard the splash, the forsaken cry,
But for him it was not an important failure; the sun shone
As it had to on the white legs disappearing into the green
Water; and the expensive delicate ship that must have seen
20 Something amazing, a boy falling out of the sky,
Had somewhere to get to and sailed calmly on.

Opposite page: The Fall of Icarus, Pieter
Brueghel the Elder, sixteenth century.

STUDY QUESTIONS

Recalling

1. What, according to lines 3–4, did the Old Masters understand about suffering?
2. What disaster occurs in the second stanza?
3. How does "everything" react to this disaster? Give two of the examples of such behavior listed in that stanza.

Interpreting

4. What is the place of suffering, miraculous birth, and martyrdom within human affairs?
5. What contrast can you see between expressions like "doggy life" and "forsaken cry"? Relate this contrast in Auden's diction to the two views of life he presents in this poem.
6. Does Auden sympathize with or condemn the behavior he describes? How do you know?

Extending

7. Explain why people often react as they do in this poem. Do you think these reactions show human nature in a positive or negative light?

VIEWPOINT

The speaker of a "typical" Auden poem often views human experience with an overseeing eye. According to critic Richard Hoggart, the best picture of Auden's writing would portray

> a landscape and a wanderer. . . . The Wanderer . . . is physically isolated and surveys from a great height the interesting but muddled life of those below; he can see a possible order in the muddle which they do not see, and he would like to help it emerge. He is detached and slightly clinical. He is compassionate but also rather coldly reformative.
>
> —Auden, A Collection of Critical Essays

In what ways does the speaker in "Musée des Beaux Arts" seem isolated high above those he describes? What overall order does he see in these events? At what points in the poem does the speaker seem compassionate? Clinical?

Dylan Thomas   *1914–1953*

Dylan Thomas' ardent romanticism and passion for language have made him one of the most popular poets in the twentieth century. Thomas was born in South Wales, where he was formally educated only through grammar school. He knew as a young boy that he wanted to be a writer, and he vigorously read and wrote throughout his youth. By the age of twenty, he had published his first volume of poetry, *Eighteen Poems,* for which he received instant critical acclaim. After serving as an antiaircraft gunner during World War II, Thomas became a commentator on poetry for the British Broadcasting Corporation.

In 1949 he began visiting the United States for poetry-reading tours; he quickly became a celebrity on American college campuses, developing a reputation as one of the best performers of poetry in modern times. Between these visits Thomas would return to his wife and children in the Welsh village of Laugharne, where his personal life was always stormy. While on tour in New York, he died suddenly of pneumonia.

Not long before his death, Thomas' *Collected Poems* was published, along with his now-famous radio play, *Under Milk Wood.* Besides these works Thomas wrote essays, reminiscences, short stories, scripts for documentary films, and one novel. Still, Dylan Thomas remains best known for his radiant poetry. Thomas saw himself as a modern-day descendant of the English Romantic poets. His writing was not intellectual and restrained like that of Eliot; unlike Auden, Spender, and their colleagues, he had little interest in righting social wrongs. Instead, Thomas was fascinated with the inner workings of the mind and enchanted with the potency of language.

At first glance, many of Thomas' poems seem to be disorderly, overwhelming outpourings of language. However, although the sheer sound of words does sometimes overpower sense in his early poetry, Thomas' mature poems are neither dizzy with sound nor chaotic. Influenced by the oral tradition of the ancient Welsh bards, Thomas wrote unconventional and intensely musical poems, but his work was highly disciplined and was often based on elaborate patterns. As Thomas himself once said, " . . . a poem of mine is, or should be, a watertight section of the stream that is flowing all ways, all warring images within it should be reconciled for that small stop of time."

Thomas' Welsh childhood provides material for much of his poetry. Other major themes in his work include wartime London, religion, his own emotional life, and the relationship of life to death.

■ What advice would you give to someone who might not have much longer to live?

Dylan Thomas

Do Not Go Gentle into That Good Night

Do not go gentle into that good night,
Old age should burn and rave at close of day;
Rage, rage against the dying of the light.

Though wise men at their end know dark is right,
5 Because their words had forked no lightning they
Do not go gentle into that good night.

Good men, the last wave by, crying how bright
Their frail deeds might have danced in a green bay,
Rage, rage against the dying of the light.

10 Wild men who caught and sang the sun in flight,
And learn, too late, they grieved it on its way,
Do not go gentle into that good night.

Grave men, near death, who see with blinding sight
Blind eyes could blaze like meteors and be gay,
15 Rage, rage against the dying of the light.

And you, my father, there on the sad height,
Curse, bless, me now with your fierce tears, I pray.
Do not go gentle into that good night.
Rage, rage against the dying of the light.

STUDY QUESTIONS

Recalling

1. What does the speaker tell the person he is addressing not to do? What does he want that person to do instead?
2. What do wise men know? What do they do in spite of this knowledge, and why?
3. Whom is the speaker addressing? Where is this person, according to line 16?

Interpreting

4. How would you interpret the words *good night* and *the dying of the light*? What might dark and light symbolize in the poem?
5. For what reasons might the different men mentioned in the poem refuse to "go gentle"?
6. What is actually happening to the person whom the speaker addresses? How does the speaker feel about it, and how do you know?
7. Describe the emotional impact of the poem and the view of life and death it expresses.

LITERARY FOCUS

Villanelle

The **villanelle** is a poetic form that consists of nineteen lines divided into five three-line stanzas called **tercets** and a final four-line stanza called a **quatrain**. All of the lines in the villanelle use only two end rhymes, with the rhyme scheme following the pattern: *aba aba aba aba aba abaa.* In addition, almost half of the poem is made up of repeated lines: Line 1 is repeated in lines 6, 12, and 18, while line 3 is repeated in lines 9, 15, and 19.

This careful and intricate arrangement of lines is meant to appear simple and spontaneous. Based on an Italian word, *villanello,* which means "rural" or "rustic," the villanelle was invented by French poets as a pastoral poem with a light, lyric tone. Poets in the nineteenth and twentieth centuries took up this form and removed the original restrictions on its subject matter and tone. Today villanelles are written on many different subjects in a wide variety of tones. "Do Not Go Gentle into That Good Night" is perhaps the most famous modern example of the form.

Thinking About the Villanelle

1. Does Thomas' poem exactly follow the formal requirements of the villanelle with respect to number of lines, repetition, stanza form, and rhyme scheme? In what ways is it different from the original villanelles?
2. Explain how the repeated lines add to the meaning and emotional impact of this poem.

COMPARING WRITERS

1. Referring to at least one of the poems by W. H. Auden and by Dylan Thomas that you have read, compare the attitudes of these poets toward suffering and death. Which seems more accepting of suffering and mortality?
2. Which poet, Auden or Thomas, touches you more? Explain.

"Fern Hill," Dylan Thomas' famous poem about childhood, first appeared in 1945 and is considered one of his best works. Written during a highly creative, productive year of his life, it captures an "Eden-like memory" for all time. The poem is also a fine example of Thomas' characteristic uses of original images, rich symbols, and dazzling language.

Dylan Thomas

Fern Hill

Now as I was young and easy under the apple boughs
About the lilting house and happy as the grass was green,
   The night above the dingle[1] starry,
    Time let me hail and climb
5   Golden in the heydays[2] of his eyes,
And honored among wagons I was prince of the apple towns
And once below a time I lordly had the trees and leaves
     Trail with daisies and barley
   Down the rivers of the windfall light.

10   And as I was green and carefree, famous among the barns
About the happy yard and singing as the farm was home,
   In the sun that is young once only,
    Time let me play and be
   Golden in the mercy of his means,
15 And green and golden I was huntsman and herdsman, the calves
Sang to my horn, the foxes on the hills barked clear and cold,
    And the sabbath rang slowly
   In the pebbles of the holy streams.

All the sun long it was running, it was lovely, the hay
20 Fields high as the house, the tunes from the chimneys, it was air
    And playing, lovely and watery
     And fire green as grass.
    And nightly under the simple stars
As I rode to sleep the owls were bearing the farm away,

---

1. **dingle:** small, wooded valley nestled between steep hills.
2. **heydays:** periods of one's greatest vitality.

25 All the moon long I heard, blessed among stables, the nightjars[3]
     Flying with the ricks,[4] and the horses
        Flashing into the dark.

And then to awake, and the farm, like a wanderer white
With the dew, come back, the cock on his shoulder: it was all
30   Shining, it was Adam and maiden,
       The sky gathered again
      And the sun grew round that very day.
So it must have been after the birth of the simple light
In the first, spinning place, the spellbound horses walking warm
35   Out of the whinnying green stable
      On to the fields of praise.

And honored among foxes and pheasants by the gay house
Under the new made clouds and happy as the heart was long,
     In the sun born over and over,
40   I ran my heedless ways,
     My wishes raced through the house high hay
And nothing I cared, at my sky blue trades, that time allows
In all his tuneful turning so few and such morning songs
     Before the children green and golden
45   Follow him out of grace,

Nothing I cared, in the lamb white days, that time would
        take me
Up to the swallow thronged loft by the shadow of my hand,
     In the moon that is always rising,
      Nor that riding to sleep
50   I should hear him fly with the high fields
And wake to the farm forever fled from the childless land.
Oh as I was young and easy in the mercy of his means,
     Time held me green and dying
     Though I sang in my chains like the sea.

---

3. **nightjars:** grayish-brown birds that sing at night.
4. **ricks:** stacks of hay in the open air.

STUDY QUESTIONS

Recalling

1. According to lines 10–11, what is the setting of the poem? List five details of the setting mentioned in the poem.
2. In the first two stanzas what four things does time let the speaker do? List five words that the speaker uses to describe himself in these stanzas.
3. In the fifth stanza what does the speaker say he cared nothing about? What words does the speaker use to describe himself in stanza 6 as time held him?

Interpreting

4. What mood predominates for most of the poem? Point out four or five images, and explain how they help to create this mood.
5. In what way does the mood of the poem shift, and what causes this shift?
6. Why do you think Thomas refers so often to the colors green and gold? What do these colors seem to symbolize in the poem? What combination of ideas does he suggest at the end, when he says he was "green and dying"?
7. Of what are children not aware, according to the poem? What does the poem seem to be saying about childhood? About time?

Extending

8. Why do you think time seems to move differently for children and for adults?

LITERARY FOCUS

Diction

Diction is another term for word choice. Good writers choose their words carefully and precisely so that these words express exactly what the writer intends. In choosing their words writers are mindful of three things in particular: the word's **denotation,** or dictionary definition, its various **connotations,** or suggested meanings and associations, and its *sound.* When choosing among several words with similar denotations, a writer can usually sense which word sounds best and brings the most appropriate associations into a given text.

Styles change in diction, and what sounds appropriate to the writers of one century might sound barbaric or pompous to the writers of another time. If Dr. Samuel Johnson (page 353) were to visit us, he might be offended by our casual way of speaking and writing. We, in turn, might find his diction rather stiff and unnatural.

Individual writers can often be recognized by their word choices from one work to the next. Some may characteristically prefer plain words of one syllable, while others prefer to spangle their writing with more colorful or unusual words. Some may like to jar their readers with odd combinations of words, while others write in a seamlessly graceful style. Dylan Thomas is one writer whose diction is as characteristic and recognizable as his signature. For example, in "Fern Hill" notice his playful phrase "once below a time" and his adverb "lordly" (line 7).

Thinking About Diction

1. Find other illustrations of Thomas' use of unusual or playful diction in "Fern Hill," and explain the effect of these word choices.
2. Based on your reading of "Fern Hill," make up a list of qualities you would expect to see in the diction of a Dylan Thomas poem. Give examples from "Fern Hill."

COMPOSITION

Writing About Poetry

Explain the meaning of "Fern Hill," and show how Thomas uses poetic techniques to illuminate this meaning. In particular, explain how Thomas uses speaker, sound, imagery, and figurative language to present his visions of childhood and time. Point out the various changes in these elements throughout the poem, and relate these changes to the poem's meaning. *For help with this assignment, see Lesson 7 in the Writing About Literature Handbook at the back of this book.*

Writing a Poem About Childhood

Write a lyrical, colorful, image-packed poem depicting a childhood scene as Thomas has done in "Fern Hill." Your choice of details should convey emotion about the subject.

Charles Tomlinson   *born 1927*

According to English critic Donald Davie, Charles Tomlinson is the "most original and accomplished of all our postwar poets." However, Tomlinson has also been criticized for leaving the human element out of his work. Born at Staffordshire in England, Tomlinson graduated from Cambridge and took a secretarial job in northern Italy. He now teaches at the University of Bristol and has been a visiting professor at several American universities. He also translates French, Italian, and German poetry.

In "Suggestions for the Improvement of a Sunset" Tomlinson characteristically focuses on the natural, rather than the human, world. Nevertheless, he claims that even in those poems that do not contain humans, his "theme is relationship."

■ If you were asked to improve the nighttime sky, what suggestions would you make?

Charles Tomlinson

Suggestions for the Improvement of a Sunset

Darkening the edges of the land,
Imperceptibly it must drain out colors
Drawing all light into its center.

Six points of vantage[1] provide us with six sunsets.

5 The sea partakes of the sky. It is less
Itself than the least pool which, if threatened,
Prizes lucidity.

The pond is lime green, an enemy
Of gold, bearing no change but shadow.

10 Seen from above, the house would resemble
A violin, abandoned, and lost in its own darkness;

Diminished, through the wrong end of a glass,
A dice ambushed by lowering greens;

Accorded its true proportions,
15 The stone would give back the light
Which, all day, it has absorbed.

The afterglow, broken by leaves and windows,
Confirms green's triumph[2] against yellow.

---

1. **points of vantage:** positions from which something is viewed.
2. **afterglow . . . green's triumph:** In the last instant of
sunset a green flash appears at the rim of the sinking sun.

Thom Gunn *born 1929*

Thomson William Gunn is associated with "The Movement" of the 1950s, which consisted of a group of poets who met at Oxford University and who wrote poems about ordinary life in a deliberately conversational style. Born in England, Gunn has spent much of his time in the United States. He has studied at both Cambridge and Stanford universities and taught at the University of California at Berkeley from 1957 to 1966. As he does in "Taylor Street," Gunn writes poems that anchor ideas in concrete physical details.

■ If a stranger watched your street from morning to night for one day, what would he see? What wouldn't he see? Could he describe your street accurately?

Thom Gunn

Taylor Street

The small porch of imitation
marble is never sunny, but
outside the front door he
sits on his kitchen chair facing
5 the street. In the bent yellowish
face, from under the brim
of a floppy brown hat,
his small eyes watch what
he is not living. But he
10 lives what he can:
watches without a smile, with
a certain strain, the warmth
of his big crumpled
body anxiously cupped
15 by himself in himself, as
he leans over himself not
over the cold railing, unmoving but carefully getting
a little strength from the sight of the
20 passers-by. He has it
all planned: he will live
here morning by morning.

STUDY QUESTIONS

Suggestions for . . . (Tomlinson)

Recalling

1. Of the six "points of vantage" that the speaker presents, list the two described in lines 5–9.
2. From what "point of vantage" would the house resemble a violin? From what "point of vantage" would it resemble dice?
3. List the two "points of vantage" described in the final two stanzas.
4. What does the "afterglow" confirm?

Interpreting

5. In your own words, describe each of the six sunsets portrayed in the poem.
6. What various spatial relationships does the speaker experiment with? What color relationships does the poem establish?
7. What tone does the title lend the poem? Is it possible to improve a sunset? What do the speaker's six vantage points actually do?

Extending

8. Suggest five more ways of "improving" a sunset.

Taylor Street (Gunn)

Recalling

1. Where is the subject of the poem sitting? Point out three of the physical details Gunn uses to describe this man.
2. What, according to lines 8–9, does he watch? How does he watch it, according to lines 11–18?
3. What does he get from the passers-by? What is his plan for living his life?

Interpreting

4. In your own words, describe the life of the man in the poem. What is his attitude toward life?
5. What is the speaker's attitude toward the man? Does the speaker admire him, pity him, ridicule him? How do you know?
6. What is the significance of the fact that the title of the poem does not mention the man on whom the poem focuses?
7. In what sense might the meaning of the poem extend beyond this one man?

Extending

8. Why do you think inactive people often like to watch busy city streets?

LITERARY FOCUS

Elements of Style in Modern Poetry

Modern poetry is as complex and diverse as the world that has given rise to it. Unlike earlier poets, modern poets recognize no limits on content, writing about any subject, no matter how seemingly unworthy.

Modern poetry draws on all types and levels of language. Rather than being confined to traditional poetic diction, much modern poetry actually uses "antipoetic" diction: jarring combinations of apparently incompatible words. Furthermore, modern poetry often replaces strict meter, rhyme, and traditional poetic form with the freer rhythms of ordinary "unpoetic" speech. As a result, the line between poetry and prose has become difficult to draw, and word placement, line length, and other visual effects have become especially important in modern poetry. When modern poets do use traditional poetic forms such as couplets, quatrains, ballads, and sonnets, they usually ring unexpected, experimental twists on these old forms. In short, modern poets have changed poetry so that it can speak of and to their time.

Thinking About Modern Poetry

■ Using specific examples, discuss the ways in which "Taylor Street" represents the tendencies of modern poetry. Consider in particular the poet's subject matter, diction, imagery, figurative language, form, and organization.

COMPOSITION (Tomlinson)

Writing About Literature and Its Period

■ Write an essay showing how "Suggestions for the Improvement of a Sunset" exemplifies the poetry of the modern period. Begin by listing the most important characteristics of modern poetry. Then give examples of these characteristics in the poem. *For help with this assignment, see Lesson 10 in the Writing About Literature Handbook at the back of this book.*

Writing a Series of Related Poems

■ Write three or four poems, of no more than five lines each, presenting different views of the same subject. For example, you may vary your spatial perspective, or you may want to describe the same thing at different times or from the point of view of different speakers.

© Rollie McKenna

Ted Hughes   *born 1930*

Ted Hughes is known chiefly for his unflinching portrayal of the violence and fierce beauty of the natural world. He spent his childhood roaming the farms and moors of his native Yorkshire and showed a passion for capturing and studying animals. From the time he began to write poetry at fifteen, this fascination with the animal world has found its way into his work.

After serving in the Royal Air Force as a mechanic, Hughes attended Cambridge University, where he learned all of the works in Yeats's *Collected Poems* by heart. His first volume of poetry, *Hawk in the Rain* (1957), brought him instant acclaim—a rare occurrence that permitted him to devote the bulk of his time to teaching and writing. During the late 1950s Hughes spent several years in the United States with his first wife, the American poet Sylvia Plath (who died in 1963), but since that time he has resided in England. In 1984 he was named Britain's poet laureate.

Hughes admits that one of the early influences on his writing was Dylan Thomas. Although Hughes's poetry tends to be more compact than Thomas', both poets use urgent rhythms, record a wild inner music, and return again and again to the theme of death in life. Throughout his poetry Hughes portrays nature as a violent, vivid, gripping force. He often focuses on the similarities and differences between predatory animals and human beings, sympathizing more often with the former than the latter. His creatures are powerful, watchful, and spontaneous, and their behavior often carries messages about human nature. However, Hughes's messages are seldom moralistic, predictable, or reassuring, as can be seen in "Hawk Roosting," one of his most characteristic poems.

■ Why might a poet assume the identity of an animal?

Ted Hughes

Hawk Roosting

I sit in the top of the wood, my eyes closed.
Inaction, no falsifying dream
Between my hooked head and hooked feet:
Or in sleep rehearse perfect kills and eat.

5 The convenience of the high trees!
The air's buoyancy and the sun's ray
Are of advantage to me;
And the earth's face upward for my inspection.

My feet are locked upon the rough bark.
10 It took the whole of Creation
To produce my foot, my each feather:
Now I hold Creation in my foot

Or fly up, and revolve it all slowly—
I kill where I please because it is all mine.
15 There is no sophistry[1] in my body:
My manners are tearing off heads—

The allotment of death.
For the one path of my flight is direct
Through the bones of the living.
20 No arguments assert my right:

The sun is behind me.
Nothing has changed since I began.
My eye has permitted no change.
I am going to keep things like this.

---

1. **sophistry:** false but clever and believable reasoning or argument.

STUDY QUESTIONS

Recalling

1. Where does the speaker sit? What does he rehearse in his sleep?
2. What does he say he holds in his foot? Of what do his manners consist?
3. Why has nothing changed, according to the speaker? What does he plan to do?

Interpreting

4. Who is the speaker? What traits make him seem human? Inhuman?
5. Describe the speaker's image of himself and of the world. How valid do you find his view of life?
6. What do you think the speaker means by "no falsifying dream"? What does he mean by lines 18–19?
7. Describe the emotional effect of the poem—is it amusing, frightening, moving, or something else altogether? Explain how Hughes creates that effect.

8. What does the poet's view of nature seem to be? Do you think the poem also portrays an aspect of _human_ nature? Explain.

COMPOSITION

Writing About Poetry

■ Discuss the meaning of "Hawk Roosting," and explain how Hughes's poetic techniques develop this meaning. In particular, explain how his choice of speaker, diction, tone, and imagery reveal the meaning of the poem. _For help with this assignment, refer to Lesson 7 in the Writing About Literature Handbook at the back of this book._

Writing from Another Point of View

■ Write a poem from the point of view of an animal, as Hughes does in "Hawk Roosting." Your animal speaker should describe the way in which it looks at the world and then explain its motivation for some act. As Hughes does, use concrete, gripping, and precise images.

Geoffrey Hill   *born 1932*

Geoffrey Hill's impersonal, historical, and extremely formal poetry departs sharply from the work of his contemporaries. Born in Worcestershire, England, he was educated at Oxford University. Since his graduation he has served as professor of English and senior lecturer at the University of Leeds in northern England.

Hill's style is highly controlled and often adheres to strict patterns of meter and rhyme. His subject matter is often significant—death, love, suffering, war, God—and his tone is intensely serious. Because his lines and poems are short, Hill has been called "a poet of pain and economy."

In "Merlin" Hill demonstrates his taste for history, legend, and serious subject matter. Using Arthurian legend as his backdrop, he writes from the point of view of Merlin, the famous sorcerer who was well acquainted with both past and future.

■ What other literary characters in this book might Hill consider fitting subjects for a poem?

Geoffrey Hill

Merlin

I will consider the outnumbering dead:
For they are the husks of what was rich seed.
Now, should they come together to be fed,
They would outstrip the locusts' covering tide.

5 Arthur, Elaine, Mordred;[1] they are all gone
Among the raftered galleries of bone.
By the long barrows of Logres[2] they are made one,
And over their city stands the pinnacled corn.

---

1. **Arthur, Elaine, Mordred:** references to the legend of King Arthur. According to some versions of this legend, Elaine was an innocent young woman who died for her love of Arthur's chief knight, Sir Lancelot, and Mordred was Arthur's evil nephew who ultimately destroyed the order of the Round Table and killed Arthur in battle.
2. **Logres:** that part of Britain now known as England.

Seamus Heaney   *born 1939*

Seamus [shā′məs] Heaney was born in County Derry, Ireland, and his Irish heritage has remained at the center of his writing. The eldest of nine children, Heaney grew up on his father's farm. He became aware at a very early age of the difficult and violent history of his homeland. Educated at Queens University in Belfast, he worked first as a secondary school teacher; later he taught at Queens University and the University of California at Berkeley, as well as at other universities in Ireland and America.

Beginning with his first volume of poems, *Death of a Naturalist* (1966), Heaney has written about both modern and ancient Ireland. His work depicts the people, landscape, crafts, politics, history, and myths of his native land, particularly the bitter conflicts between Ireland and England over the independence and unification of the divided Irish state. In addition, Heaney's fascination with archaic lore extends beyond Irish forebears to Danes, Normans, and Vikings.

Heaney's work is known for its phrasing, which is fresh and striking, and for its vivid imagery, which is often tactile, energetic, and violent. His sense of history is personal as well as political and mythic. In "Follower" he reveals in intimate and clear-eyed detail his need to acknowledge both the gifts and the burdens of the past.

■ "What goes around comes around" is a popular saying. What exactly does it mean? Does Heaney's poem illustrate the epigram?

Seamus Heaney

Follower

My father worked with a horse plough,
His shoulders globed like a full sail strung
Between the shafts and the furrow.
The horses strained at his clicking tongue.

5 An expert. He would set the wing
And fit the bright steel-pointed sock.
The sod rolled over without breaking.
At the headrig, with a single pluck

Of reins, the sweating team turned round
10 And back into the land. His eye
Narrowed and angled at the ground,
Mapping the furrow exactly.

I stumbled in his hobnailed[1] wake,
Fell sometimes on the polished sod;
15 Sometimes he rode me on his back
Dipping and rising to his plod.

I wanted to grow up and plough,
To close one eye, stiffen my arm.
All I ever did was follow
20 In his broad shadow round the farm.

I was a nuisance, tripping, falling,
Yapping always. But today
It is my father who keeps stumbling
Behind me, and will not go away.

---

1. **hobnailed:** marked by the short, hard-headed nails used as studs in shoes.

STUDY QUESTIONS

Merlin (Hill)

Recalling

1. Whom does the speaker say he will consider? What would happen if these people should "come together"?
2. What people does he mention in stanza 2? Where does he say they are?
3. What now stands over their city?

Interpreting

4. Whom do the dead outnumber? How can the numerous dead be "made one"?
5. What might the figures of Arthur, Elaine, and Mordred symbolize? In what figurative sense were they once "rich seed"? What might be absent from a land and time from which these figures are "all gone"?
6. What might Merlin himself symbolize?
7. What view of life, death, and time does the poem express?

Extending

8. In what senses is this a modern poem? In what ways does it differ from modern poetry?

Follower (Heaney)

Recalling

1. From the first three stanzas, list four details of the father's activities.
2. What did the speaker want to do when he grew up? What did he do while his father worked?
3. What does the speaker say about his father today?

Interpreting

4. Prove that the speaker admires his father's activities in stanzas 1–3. In what senses is his father "expert"?
5. Since the poem is autobiographical, the speaker became a poet, not a farmer like his father. Do you think the speaker has any regrets about his decision not to work the land? How can you tell?

6. What do you think the last sentence of the poem means? What might the "stumbling" father who "will not go away" symbolize?

Extending

7. In what way can the past be both a gift and a burden?

COMPOSITION (Hill)

Writing About a Symbol

■ Briefly discuss the harvest as a symbol in "Merlin." First point out the specific images and stages of the harvest presented in the poem. Then indicate the symbolic meaning of the harvest in the poem, and explain how this symbol is related to the theme of the poem as a whole. *For help with this assignment, see Lesson 5 in the Writing About Literature Handbook at the back of this book.*

Writing as a Historical Character

■ Choose a figure from legend or history (for example, King Arthur, Paul Bunyan, Cleopatra), and write a short poem from that character's point of view, describing his or her views of life and the world. Be sure to choose language and ideas appropriate to your speaker.

COMPARING WRITERS

1. Compare at least two of the following contemporary poets: Gunn, Hughes, Heaney, Tomlinson, and Hill. What similarities in content and style can you find among them, particularly in their portrayal of the workings of the mind? What major differences can you find?
2. Consider all of the following twentieth-century British poets that you have studied: Yeats, Eliot, Sassoon, Brooke, Spender, MacNeice, Graves, Auden, Thomas, Gunn, Hughes, Heaney, Tomlinson, and Hill. Based on your knowledge of these poets, if you had to provide a character sketch of a "typical" twentieth-century poet, what characteristics would you include?

PROSE

Joseph Conrad   *1857–1924*

When Joseph Conrad first arrived in England at the age of twenty, he spoke virtually no English. Yet he wrote his first novel, *Almayer's Folly* (1895), in English and continued to use his adopted language to create a string of great novels, including *Lord Jim* (1900), *Nostromo* (1904), and *Victory* (1915). Conrad was born Josef Teodor Conrad Nalecz Korzeniowski in Russian-occupied Poland. His father was exiled to northern Russia because of activities on behalf of Polish independence, and both his parents died before he was ten. He left Poland at sixteen and, inspired by books about the sea, became an apprentice seaman first for France and then for England. He sailed to Asia, South America, and Africa, locales that would later become settings for his fiction. In 1886 he became a British subject and a ship's captain. After publishing his first book, he married, left the sea, and devoted himself to his family and his literary career.

Conrad wrote fiction about the sea and the "mysterious corners" of the world that had captivated his youth. His stories and novels convey the glamour and terror of the nomadic life of a nineteenth-century seaman. Yet they are much more than adventure stories. Dark seas, winding inlets, and dense jungles serve as backdrop and symbol for Conrad's real concerns—the contrast between individuality and human communication, between illusion and reality. Life at sea provides a model for Conrad's ideal of human interdependence; exotic ports-of-call represent the dark, unknown areas of human experience where characters wrestle with moral choices that will shape their lives. Conrad experimented with unusual, sometimes multiple, points of view to demonstrate the complexity of experience and the difficulty of human communication. His first-person storytellers are often intermediate narrators, characters who are not directly involved in the action and, therefore, can provide both firsthand information and objective detachment. At his dramatic climaxes characters and readers alike arrive at what Conrad called a "moral discovery [that] should be the object of every tale."

The sea, the jungle, and the moral tug-of-war that they represent are all present in "The Lagoon." As with all of Conrad's best work, this story requires that the reader patiently follow the seemingly pointless turns and the seemingly unrelated events that are the scattered clues to Conrad's vision of reality. Gradually patience is rewarded as the various pieces fall into a pattern and the reader is faced with a moment of discovery.

■ The word lagoon has definite connotations. What mental picture do you have of a lagoon?

Joseph Conrad

The Lagoon

The white man, leaning with both arms over the roof of the little house in the stern of the boat, said to the steersman—

"We will pass the night in Arsat's clearing. It is late."

The Malay[1] only grunted, and went on looking fixedly at the river. The white man rested his chin on his crossed arms and gazed at the wake of the boat. At the end of the straight avenue of forests cut by the intense glitter of the river, the sun appeared unclouded and dazzling, poised low over the water that shone smoothly like a band of metal. The forests, somber and dull, stood motionless and silent on each side of the broad stream. At the foot of big, towering trees, trunkless nipa palms rose from the mud of the bank, in bunches of leaves enormous and heavy, that hung unstirring over the brown swirl of eddies. In the stillness of the air every tree, every leaf, every bough, every tendril of creeper and every petal of minute blossoms seemed to have been bewitched into an immobility perfect and final. Nothing moved on the river but the eight paddles that rose flashing regularly, dipped together with a single splash; while the steersman swept right and left with a periodic and sudden flourish of his blade describing a glinting semicircle above his head. The churned-up water frothed alongside with a confused murmur. And the white man's canoe, advancing upstream in the short-lived disturbance of its own making, seemed to enter the portals of a land from which the very memory of motion had forever departed.

The white man, turning his back upon the setting sun, looked along the empty and broad expanse of the sea-reach.[2] For the last three miles of its course the wandering, hesitating river, as if enticed irresistibly by the freedom of an open horizon, flows straight into the sea, flows straight to the east—to the east that harbors both light and darkness. Astern of the boat the repeated call of some bird, a cry discordant and feeble, skipped along over the smooth water and lost itself, before it could reach the other shore, in the breathless silence of the world.

The steersman dug his paddle into the stream, and held hard with stiffened arms, his body thrown forward. The water gurgled aloud; and suddenly the long straight reach seemed to pivot on its center, the forests swung in a semicircle, and the slanting beams of sunset touched the broadside of the canoe with a fiery glow, throwing the slender and distorted shadows of its crew upon the streaked glitter of the river. The white man turned to look ahead. The course of the boat had been altered at right angles to the stream, and the carved dragon-head of its prow was pointing now at a gap in the fringing bushes of the bank. It glided through, brushing the overhanging twigs, and disappeared from the river like some slim and amphibious creature leaving the water for its lair in the forests.

The narrow creek was like a ditch: tortuous, fabulously deep; filled with gloom under the thin strip of pure and shining blue of the heaven. Immense trees soared up, invisible behind the festooned draperies of creepers. Here and there, near the glistening blackness of the water, a twisted root of some tall tree showed amongst the tracery of small ferns, black and dull, writhing and motionless, like an arrested snake. The short words of the paddlers reverberated loudly between the thick and somber walls of vegetation. Darkness oozed out from between the trees, through the tangled maze of the creepers, from behind the great fantastic and unstirring leaves; the darkness, mysterious

---

1. **Malay** [mā′lā]: inhabitant of the Malay peninsula in Southeast Asia.
2. **sea-reach**: straight course of a river when it approaches the sea.

and invincible; the darkness scented and poisonous of impenetrable forests.

The men poled in the shoaling[3] water. The creek broadened, opening out into a wide sweep of a stagnant lagoon. The forests receded from the marshy bank, leaving a level strip of bright green, reedy grass to frame the reflected blueness of the sky. A fleecy pink cloud drifted high above, trailing the delicate coloring of its image under the floating leaves and the silvery blossoms of the lotus. A little house, perched on high piles, appeared black in the distance. Near it, two tall nibong palms, that seemed to have come out of the forests in the background, leaned slightly over the ragged roof, with a suggestion of sad tenderness and care in the droop of their leafy and soaring heads.

The steersman, pointing with his paddle, said, "Arsat is there. I see his canoe fast between the piles."

The polers ran along the sides of the boat glancing over their shoulders at the end of the day's journey. They would have preferred to spend the night somewhere else than on this lagoon of weird aspect and ghostly reputation. Moreover, they disliked Arsat, first as a stranger, and also because he who repairs a ruined house, and dwells in it, proclaims that he is not afraid to live amongst the spirits that haunt the places abandoned by mankind. Such a man can disturb the course of fate by glances or words; while his familiar ghosts are not easy to propitiate by casual wayfarers upon whom they long to wreak the malice of their human master. White men care not for such things, being unbelievers and in league with the Father of Evil, who leads them unharmed through the invisible dangers of this world. To the warnings of the righteous they oppose an offensive pretense of disbelief. What is there to be done?

So they thought, throwing their weight on the end of their long poles. The big canoe glided on swiftly, noiselessly, and smoothly, toward Arsat's clearing, till, in a great rattling of poles thrown down, and the loud murmurs of "Allah[4] be praised!" it came with a gentle knock against the crooked piles below the house.

The boatmen with uplifted faces shouted discordantly, "Arsat! O Arsat!" Nobody came. The white man began to climb the rude ladder giving access to the bamboo platform before the house. The juragan[5] of the boat said sulkily, "We will cook in the sampan, and sleep on the water."

"Pass my blankets and the basket," said the white man, curtly.

He knelt on the edge of the platform to receive the bundle. Then the boat shoved off, and the white man, standing up, confronted Arsat, who had come out through the low door of his hut. He was a man young, powerful, with broad chest and muscular arms. He had nothing on but his sarong.[6] His head was bare. His big, soft eyes stared eagerly at the white man, but his voice and demeanor were composed as he asked, without any words of greeting—

"Have you medicine, Tuan?"[7]

"No," said the visitor in a startled tone. "No. Why? Is there sickness in the house?"

"Enter and see," replied Arsat, in the same calm manner, and turning short round, passed again through the small doorway. The white man, dropping his bundles, followed.

In the dim light of the dwelling he made out on a couch of bamboos a woman stretched on her back under a broad sheet of red cotton cloth. She lay still, as if dead; but her big eyes, wide open, glittered in the gloom, staring upward at the slender rafters, motionless and unseeing. She was in a high fever, and evidently

3. **shoaling** [shō′ling]: shallow water difficult to navigate.

4. **Allah** [al′ə]: name for God in the Moslem religion.
5. **juragan** [jōō ä′gän]: master of a sampan [sam′pan′], or flat-bottomed boat with a cabin made of mats.
6. **sarong** [sə rông′]: brightly colored cloth worn as a skirt.
7. **Tuan** [twän]: Malayan for "sir," usually applied to Europeans.

unconscious. Her cheeks were sunk slightly, her lips were partly open, and on the young face there was the ominous and fixed expression—the absorbed, contemplating expression of the unconscious who are going to die. The two men stood looking down at her in silence.

"Has she been long ill?" asked the traveler.

"I have not slept for five nights," answered the Malay, in a deliberate tone. "At first she heard voices calling her from the water and struggled against me who held her. But since the sun of today rose she hears nothing—she hears not me. She sees nothing. She sees not me—me!"

He remained silent for a minute, then asked softly—

"Tuan, will she die?"

"I fear so," said the white man, sorrowfully. He had known Arsat years ago, in a far country in times of trouble and danger, when no friendship is to be despised. And since his Malay friend had come unexpectedly to dwell in the hut on the lagoon with a strange woman, he had slept many times there, in his journeys up and down the river. He liked the man who knew how to keep faith in council and how to fight without fear by the side of his white friend. He liked him—not so much perhaps as a man likes his favorite dog—but still he liked him well enough to help and ask no questions, to think sometimes vaguely and hazily in the midst of his own pursuits, about the lonely man and the long-haired woman with audacious face and triumphant eyes, who lived together hidden by the forests—alone and feared.

The white man came out of the hut in time to see the enormous conflagration of sunset put out by the swift and stealthy shadows that, rising like a black and impalpable vapor above the tree tops, spread over the heaven, extinguishing the crimson glow of floating clouds and the red brilliance of departing daylight. In a few moments all the stars came out above the intense blackness of the earth and the great lagoon gleaming suddenly with reflected lights resembled an oval patch of night sky flung down into the hopeless and abysmal night of the wilderness. The white man had some supper out of the basket, then collecting a few sticks that lay about the platform, made up a small fire, not for warmth, but for the sake of the smoke, which would keep off the mosquitoes. He wrapped himself in the blankets and sat with his back against the reed wall of the house, smoking thoughtfully.

Arsat came through the doorway with noiseless steps and squatted down by the fire. The white man moved his outstretched legs a little.

"She breathes," said Arsat in a low voice, anticipating the expected question. "She breathes and burns as if with a great fire. She speaks not; she hears not—and burns!"

He paused for a moment, then asked in a quiet, incurious tone—

"Tuan . . . will she die?"

The white man moved his shoulders uneasily and muttered in a hesitating manner—

"If such is her fate."

"No, Tuan," said Arsat, calmly. "If such is my fate. I hear, I see, I wait. I remember . . . Tuan, do you remember the old days? Do you remember my brother?"

"Yes," said the white man. The Malay rose suddenly and went in. The other, sitting still outside, could hear the voice in the hut. Arsat said: "Hear me! Speak!" His words were succeeded by a complete silence. "O Diamelen!" he cried, suddenly. After that cry there was a deep sigh. Arsat came out and sank down again in his old place.

They sat in silence before the fire. There was no sound within the house, there was no sound near them; but far away on the lagoon they could hear the voices of the boatmen ringing fitful and distinct on the calm water. The fire in the bows of the sampan shone faintly in the distance with a hazy red glow. Then it died out. The voices ceased. The land and the water slept invisible, unstirring and mute. It was as though there had been nothing left in the world but the glitter of stars streaming, ceaseless and vain, through the black stillness of the night.

The white man gazed straight before him into the darkness with wide-open eyes. The fear and fascination, the inspiration and the wonder of death—of death near, unavoidable, and unseen, soothed the unrest of his race and stirred the most indistinct, the most intimate of his thoughts. The ever-ready suspicion of evil, the gnawing suspicion that lurks in our hearts, flowed out into the stillness round him—into the stillness profound and dumb, and made it appear untrustworthy and infamous, like the placid and impenetrable mask of an unjustifiable violence. In that fleeting and powerful disturbance of his being the earth enfolded in the starlight peace became a shadowy country of inhuman strife, a battlefield of phantoms terrible and charming, august or ignoble, struggling ardently for the possession of our helpless hearts. An unquiet and mysterious country of inextinguishable desires and fears.

A plaintive murmur rose in the night; a murmur saddening and startling, as if the great solitudes of surrounding woods had tried to whisper into his ear the wisdom of their immense and lofty indifference. Sounds hesitating and vague floated in the air round him, shaped themselves slowly into words; and at last flowed on gently in a murmuring stream of soft and monotonous sentences. He stirred like a man waking up and changed his position slightly. Arsat, motionless and shadowy, sitting with bowed head under the stars, was speaking in a low and dreamy tone—

". . . for where can we lay down the heaviness of our trouble but in a friend's heart? A man must speak of war and of love. You, Tuan, know what war is, and you have seen me in time of danger seek death as other men seek life! A writing may be lost; a lie may be written; but what the eye has seen is truth and remains in the mind!"

"I remember," said the white man, quietly. Arsat went on with mournful composure—

"Therefore I shall speak to you of love. Speak in the night. Speak before both night and love are gone—and the eye of day looks upon my sorrow and my shame; upon my blackened face; upon my burned-up heart."

A sigh, short and faint, marked an almost imperceptible pause, and then his words flowed on, without a stir, without a gesture.

"After the time of trouble and war was over and you went away from my country in the pursuit of your desires, which we, men of the islands, cannot understand, I and my brother became again, as we had been before, the sword bearers of the Ruler. You know we were men of family, belonging to a ruling race, and more fit than any to carry on our right shoulder the emblem of power. And in the time of prosperity Si Dendring showed us favor, as we, in time of sorrow, had showed to him the faithfulness of our courage. It was a time of peace. A time of deer hunts and cock fights; of idle talks and foolish squabbles between men whose bellies are full and weapons are rusty.

But the sower watched the young rice shoots grow up without fear, and the traders came and went, departed lean and returned fat into the river of peace. They brought news, too. Brought lies and truth mixed together, so that no man knew when to rejoice and when to be sorry. We heard from them about you also. They had seen you here and had seen you there. And I was glad to hear, for I remembered the stirring times, and I always remembered you, Tuan, till the time came when my eyes could see nothing in the past, because they had looked upon the one who is dying there—in the house."

He stopped to exclaim in an intense whisper, "O Mara bahia![8] O Calamity!" then went on speaking a little louder:

"There's no worse enemy and no better friend than a brother, Tuan, for one brother knows another, and in perfect knowledge is strength for good or evil. I loved my brother. I went to him and told him that I could see nothing but one face, hear nothing but one voice. He told me: 'Open your heart so that she can see what is in it—and wait. Patience is wisdom. Inchi Midah may die or our Ruler may throw off his fear of a woman!' . . . I waited! . . . You remember the lady with the veiled face, Tuan, and the fear of our Ruler before her cunning and temper. And if she wanted her servant, what could I do? But I fed the hunger of my heart on short glances and stealthy words. I loitered on the path to the bath houses in the daytime, and when the sun had fallen behind the forest I crept along the jasmine hedges of the women's courtyard. Unseeing, we spoke to one another through the scent of flowers, through the veil of leaves, through the blades of long grass that stood still before our lips; so great was our prudence, so faint was the murmur of our great longing. The time passed swiftly . . . and there were whispers amongst women—and our enemies watched—my brother was gloomy, and I began to think of killing and of a fierce death. . . . We are of a people who take what they want—

like you whites. There is a time when a man should forget loyalty and respect. Might and authority are given to rulers, but to all men is given love and strength and courage. My brother said, 'You shall take her from their midst. We are two who are like one.' And I answered, 'Let it be soon, for I find no warmth in sunlight that does not shine upon her.' Our time came when the Ruler and all the great people went to the mouth of the river to fish by torchlight. There were hundreds of boats, and on the white sand, between the water and the forests, dwellings of leaves were built for the households of the Rajahs.[9] The smoke of cooking fires was like a blue mist of the evening, and many voices rang in it joyfully. While they were making the boats ready to beat up the fish, my brother came to me and said, 'Tonight!' I looked to my weapons, and when the time came our canoe took its place in the circle of boats carrying the torches. The lights blazed on the water, but behind the boats there was darkness. When the shouting began and the excitement made them like mad we dropped out. The water swallowed our fire, and we floated back to the shore that was dark with only here and there the glimmer of embers. We could hear the talk of slave girls amongst the sheds. Then we found a place deserted and silent. We waited there. She came. She came running along the shore, rapid and leaving no trace, like a leaf driven by the wind into the sea. My brother said gloomily, 'Go and take her; carry her into our boat.' I lifted her in my arms. She panted. Her heart was beating against my breast. I said, 'I take you from those people. You came to the cry of my heart, but my arms take you into my boat against the will of the great!' 'It is right,' said my brother. 'We are men who take what we want and can hold it against many. We should have taken her in daylight.' I said, 'Let us be off'; for since she was in my boat I began to think of our Ruler's many men. 'Yes. Let us be off,' said my brother. 'We are cast out and this boat is our country now—and the sea is our refuge.' He lingered

---

8. **O Mara bahia!** [ō′mä′rä bä hī′ä]

9. **Rajahs** [rä′jəz]: Malayan chiefs.

with his foot on the shore, and I entreated him to hasten, for I remembered the strokes of her heart against my breast and thought that two men cannot withstand a hundred. We left, paddling downstream close to the bank; and as we passed by the creek where they were fishing, the great shouting had ceased, but the murmur of voices was loud like the humming of insects flying at noonday. The boats floated, clustered together, in the red light of torches, under a black roof of smoke; and men talked of their sport. Men that boasted, and praised, and jeered—men that would have been our friends in the morning, but on that night were already our enemies. We paddled swiftly past. We had no more friends in the country of our birth. She sat in the middle of the canoe with covered face; silent as she is now; unseeing as she is now—and I had no regret at what I was leaving because I could hear her breathing close to me—as I can hear her now."

He paused, listened with his ear turned to the doorway, then shook his head and went on:

"My brother wanted to shout the cry of challenge—one cry only—to let the people know we were freeborn robbers who trusted our arms and the great sea. And again I begged him in the name of our love to be silent. Could I not hear her breathing close to me? I knew the pursuit would come quick enough. My brother loved me. He dipped his paddle without a splash. He only said, 'There is half a man in you now—the other half is in that woman. I can wait. When you are a whole man again, you will come back with me here to shout defiance. We are sons of the same mother.' I made no answer. All my strength and all my spirit were in my hands that held the paddle—for I longed to be with her in a safe place beyond the reach of men's anger and of women's spite. My love was so great that I thought it could guide me to a country where death was unknown, if I could only escape from Inchi Midah's fury and from our Ruler's sword. We paddled with haste, breathing through our teeth. The blades bit deep into the smooth water. We passed out of the river; we flew in clear channels amongst the shallows. We skirted the black coast; we skirted the sand beaches where the sea speaks in whispers to the land; and the gleam of white sand flashed back past our boat, so swiftly she ran upon the water. We spoke not. Only once I said, 'Sleep, Diamelen, for soon you may want all your strength.' I heard the sweetness of her voice, but I never turned my head. The sun rose and still we went on. Water fell from my face like rain from a cloud. We flew in the light and heat. I never looked back, but I knew that my brother's eyes, behind me, were looking steadily ahead, for the boat went as straight as a bushman's dart, when it leaves the end of the sumpitan. There was no better paddler, no better steersman than my brother. Many times, together, we had won races in that canoe. But we never had put out our strength as we did then—then, when for the last time we paddled together! There was no braver or stronger man in our country than my brother. I could not spare the strength to turn my head and look at him, but every moment I heard the hiss of his breath getting louder behind me. Still he did not speak. The sun was high. The heat clung to my back like a flame of fire. My ribs were ready to burst, but I could no longer get enough air into my chest. And then I felt I must cry out with my last breath, 'Let us rest!' . . . 'Good!' he answered; and his voice was firm. He was strong. He was brave. He knew not fear and no fatigue . . . My brother!"

A murmur powerful and gentle, a murmur vast and faint; the murmur of trembling leaves, of stirring boughs, ran through the tangled depths of the forests, ran over the starry smoothness of the lagoon, and the water between the piles lapped the slimy timber once with a sudden splash. A breath of warm air touched the two men's faces and passed on with a mournful sound—a breath loud and short like an uneasy sigh of the dreaming earth.

Arsat went on in an even, low voice.

"We ran our canoe on the white beach of a little bay close to a long tongue of land that seemed to bar our road; a long wooded cape going far into the sea. My brother knew that place. Beyond the cape a river has its entrance, and through the jungle of that land there is a narrow path. We made a fire and cooked rice. Then we lay down to sleep on the soft sand in the shade of our canoe, while she watched. No sooner had I closed my eyes than I heard her cry of alarm. We leaped up. The sun was half-way down the sky already, and coming in sight in the opening of the bay we saw a prau[10] manned by many paddlers. We knew it at once; it was one of our Rajah's praus. They were watching the shore, and saw us. They beat the gong, and turned the head of the prau into the bay. I felt my heart become weak within my breast. Diamelen sat on the sand and covered her face. There was no escape by sea. My brother laughed. He had the gun you had given him, Tuan, before you went away, but there was only a handful of powder. He spoke to me quickly: 'Run with her along the path. I shall keep them back, for they have no firearms, and landing in the face of a man with a gun is certain death for some. Run with her. On the other side of that wood there is a fisherman's house—and a canoe. When I have fired all the shots I will follow. I am a great runner, and before they can come up we shall be gone. I will hold out as long as I can, for she is but a woman—that can neither run nor fight, but she has your heart in her weak hands.' He dropped behind the canoe. The prau was coming. She and I ran, and as we rushed along the path I heard shots. My brother fired—once—twice—and the booming of the gong ceased. There was silence behind us. That neck of land is narrow. Before I heard my brother fire the third shot I saw the shelving shore, and I saw the water again; the mouth of a broad river. We crossed a grassy glade. We ran down to the water. I saw a low hut above the black mud, and a small canoe hauled up. I heard another shot behind me. I thought, 'That is his last charge.' We rushed down to the canoe; a man came running from the hut, but I leaped on him, and we rolled together in the mud. Then I got up, and he lay still at my feet. I don't

know whether I had killed him or not. I and Diamelen pushed the canoe afloat. I heard yells behind me, and I saw my brother run across the glade. Many men were bounding after him, I took her in my arms and threw her into the boat, then leaped in myself. When I looked back I saw that my brother had fallen. He fell and was up again, but the men were closing round him. He shouted, 'I am coming!' The men were close to him. I looked. Many men. Then I looked at her. Tuan, I pushed the canoe! I pushed it into deep water. She was kneeling forward looking at me, and I said, 'Take your paddle,' while I struck the water with mine. Tuan, I heard him cry. I heard him cry my name twice; and I heard voices shouting, 'Kill! Strike!' I never turned back. I heard him calling my name again with a great shriek, as when life is going out together with the voice—and I never turned my head. My own name! . . . My brother! Three times he called—but I was not afraid of life. Was she not there in that canoe? And could I not with her find a country where death is forgotten—where death is unknown!"

The white man sat up. Arsat rose and stood, an indistinct and silent figure above the dying embers of the fire. Over the lagoon a mist drifting and low had crept, erasing slowly the glittering images of the stars. And now a great expanse of white vapor covered the land: it flowed cold and gray in the darkness, eddied in noiseless whirls round the tree trunks and about the platform of the house, which seemed to float upon a restless and impalpable illusion of a sea. Only far away the tops of the trees stood outlined on the twinkle of heaven, like a somber and forbidding shore—a coast deceptive, pitiless and black.

Arsat's voice vibrated loudly in the profound peace.

"I had her there! I had her! To get her I would have faced all mankind. But I had her—and—"

His words went out ringing into the empty distances. He paused, and seemed to listen to them dying away very far—beyond help and

---

10. **prau** [prou]: fast Malayan boat with a large sail.

beyond recall. Then he said quietly—

"Tuan, I loved my brother."

A breath of wind made him shiver. High above his head, high above the silent sea of mist the drooping leaves of the palms rattled together with a mournful and expiring sound. The white man stretched his legs. His chin rested on his chest, and he murmured sadly without lifting his head—

"We all love our brothers."

Arsat burst out with an intense whispering violence—

"What did I care who died? I wanted peace in my own heart."

He seemed to hear a stir in the house—listened—then stepped in noiselessly. The white man stood up. A breeze was coming in fitful puffs. The stars shone paler as if they had retreated into the frozen depths of immense space. After a chill gust of wind there were a few seconds of perfect calm and absolute silence. Then from behind the black and wavy line of the forests a column of golden light shot up into the heavens and spread over the semicircle of the eastern horizon. The sun had risen. The mist lifted, broke into drifting patches, vanished into thin flying wreaths; and the unveiled lagoon lay, polished and black, in the heavy shadows at the foot of the wall of trees. A white eagle rose over it with a slanting and ponderous flight, reached the clear sunshine and appeared dazzlingly brilliant for a moment, then soaring higher, became a dark and motionless speck before it vanished into the blue as if it had left the earth forever. The white man, standing gazing upward before the doorway, heard in the hut a confused and broken murmur of distracted words ending with a loud groan. Suddenly Arsat stumbled out with outstretched hands, shivered, and stood still for some time with fixed eyes. Then he said—

"She burns no more."

Before his face the sun showed its edge above the tree tops rising steadily. The breeze freshened; a great brilliance burst upon the lagoon, sparkled on the rippling water. The forests came out of the clear shadows of the morning, became distinct, as if they had rushed nearer—to stop short in a great stir of leaves, of nodding boughs, of swaying branches. In the merciless sunshine the whisper of unconscious life grew louder, speaking in an incomprehensible voice round the dumb darkness of that human sorrow. Arsat's eyes wandered slowly, then stared at the rising sun.

"I can see nothing," he said half aloud to himself.

"There is nothing," said the white man, moving to the edge of the platform and waving his hand to his boat. A shout came faintly over the lagoon and the sampan began to glide toward the abode of the friend of ghosts.

"If you want to come with me, I will wait all the morning," said the white man, looking away upon the water.

"No, Tuan," said Arsat, softly. "I shall not eat or sleep in this house, but I must first see my road. Now I can see nothing—see nothing! There is no light and no peace in the world; but there is death—death for many. We are sons of the same mother—and I left him in the midst of enemies; but I am going back now."

He drew a long breath and went on in a dreamy tone:

"In a little while I shall see clear enough to strike—to strike. But she has died, and . . . now . . . darkness."

He flung his arms wide open, let them fall along his body, then stood still with unmoved face and stony eyes, staring at the sun. The white man got down into his canoe. The polers ran smartly along the sides of the boat, looking over their shoulders at the beginning of a weary journey. High in the stern, his head muffled up in white rags, the juragan sat moody, letting his paddle trail in the water. The white man, leaning with both arms over the grass roof of the little cabin, looked back at the shining ripple of the boat's wake. Before the sampan passed out of the lagoon into the creek he lifted his eyes. Arsat had not moved. He stood lonely in the searching sunshine; and he looked beyond the great light of a cloudless day into the darkness of a world of illusions.

STUDY QUESTIONS

Recalling

1. Find details of the openness and brightness of the river and of the narrowness and darkness of the creek and lagoon. What does the story's last sentence say about light and dark?
2. Why do the polers dislike Arsat? Why does the white man like him?
3. Why did Arsat not court and marry the woman in the standard way? What finally happens to the woman?
4. Briefly explain how Arsat and his brother take the woman away. Tell what happens to Arsat's brother.
5. At the end of the story, what does Arsat intend to do?

Interpreting

6. What illusions about love and death did Arsat once hold? In what ways are his illusions related to the story's contrast between light and dark?
7. In what ways is Arsat an outcast? Why has the lagoon been a fitting place for him to live?
8. Explain Arsat's decision to leave the lagoon. What do you think he is looking for?

Extending

9. Use "The Lagoon" as an example, and explain why people—even those who consider themselves loners—must relate to a larger community.

LITERARY FOCUS

The Short Story

The major elements of the short story are plot, characterization, setting, point of view, and theme. When analyzing a story, we can examine each element separately, but in a good story these elements interact to form one total effect, the impact on the reader.

Plot is the sequence of events in a story, each event causing or leading to the next. A **conflict,** or struggle between opposing forces, is at the center of every plot.

Characterization is the personality of a character in a story and the method by which the author reveals that personality. Characters are influenced by events of the plot and can affect events also.

Setting is the place and time in which a story happens. Setting can contribute to plot and to our understanding of characters.

Point of view is the relationship of the storyteller to the story. An author's choice of narrator can sometimes reveal his or her opinion of events and characters in a story.

Theme is a story's main idea. A theme usually extends beyond the confines of a story to form a general statement about life. A story's theme is usually implied through the title, through the outcome of the plot, through changes in character or setting, or through the author's choice of point of view. A theme should be stated as a sentence.

Thinking About the Short Story

1. Identify a conflict that Arsat faces in "The Lagoon." Explain the effect of the conflict on his personality.
2. Explain how the setting of "The Lagoon" adds to the plot and to the personalities of the characters.
3. "The Lagoon" has two different narrators. Identify them. In what sense does the story's point of view demonstrate Arsat's alienation?
4. What do you think is Conrad's attitude about the individual's responsibility to the community? What is the theme of "The Lagoon"?

COMPOSITION

Developing a Thesis Statement

◾ Develop a thesis statement about "The Lagoon," and in a brief essay defend your thesis with examples from the story. To develop your statement, you may wish to consider one of the following elements of the story: (a) the use of figurative language, (b) the internal lives of characters, or (c) the setting. *For help with this assignment, refer to Lesson 1 in the Writing About Literature Handbook at the back of this book.*

Writing a Letter

◾ Imagine that you are the white man of Conrad's story. Write a letter about Arsat to a friend. First explain what you know of Arsat. Then describe your feelings both while Arsat was telling his story and later after you had time to think about the experience. Conclude your letter by telling what you think finally happened to Arsat.

John Galsworthy   *1867–1933*

John Galsworthy is best known for his realistic depictions of contemporary upper-class British society. His characters are born to privilege; his settings include elegant drawing rooms and manicured gardens. Galsworthy himself was a member of the wealthy and intellectual class he wrote about.

Born in Surrey in southern England, Galsworthy attended New College, Oxford. He trained as a lawyer but never practiced. Instead, he traveled throughout the world, and at thirty he began to write. The novel that established his reputation was *The Man of Property* (1906). This was the first in a series of novels later brought together as *The Forsyte Saga,* a study of several generations in one wealthy family. These novels were so popular that when the hero, Soames Forsyte, died in one novel, his death was announced in the *London Times.* In 1929 Galsworthy was awarded the British Order of Merit, and in 1932 he received the Nobel Prize for Literature.

"The Japanese Quince" is representative Galsworthy. In one brief, seemingly plotless incident, the author provides a rich insight into an individual and, perhaps, into an entire social class.

■ Perhaps you do not know everyone in your English class. If you found yourself in a classroom with a classmate you did not know, would you initiate a conversation? Why?

John Galsworthy

The Japanese Quince

As Mr. Nilson, well known in the City,[1] opened the window of his dressing room on Campden Hill, he experienced a peculiar sweetish sensation in the back of his throat, and a feeling of emptiness just under his fifth rib. Hooking the window back, he noticed that a little tree in the Square Gardens had come out in blossom, and that the thermometer stood at sixty. "Perfect morning," he thought; "spring at last!"

Resuming some meditations on the price of Tintos, he took up an ivory-backed handglass and scrutinized his face. His firm, well-colored cheeks, with their neat brown moustaches, and his round, well-opened, clear gray eyes, wore a reassuring appearance of good health. Putting on his black frock coat, he went downstairs.

In the dining room his morning paper was laid out on the sideboard. Mr. Nilson had scarcely taken it in his hand when he again became aware of that queer feeling. Somewhat concerned, he went to the French window and descended the scrolled iron steps into the fresh air. A cuckoo clock struck eight.

"Half an hour to breakfast," he thought; "I'll take a turn in the Gardens."

He had them to himself, and proceeded to pace the circular path with his morning paper clasped behind him. He had scarcely made two revolutions, however, when it was borne in on him that, instead of going away in the fresh air, the feeling had increased. He drew several

---

1. **the City:** financial district of London.

deep breaths, having heard deep breathing recommended by his wife's doctor; but they aug-
mented rather than diminished the sensation—
as of some sweetish liquor in course within
him, together with a faint aching just above his
heart. Running over what he had eaten the
night before, he could recollect no unusual
dish, and it occurred to him that it might possibly be some smell affecting him. But he could
detect nothing except a faint sweet lemony
scent, rather agreeable than otherwise, which
evidently emanated from the bushes budding in
the sunshine. He was on the point of resuming
his promenade, when a blackbird close by
burst into song, and, looking up, Mr. Nilson
saw at a distance of perhaps five yards a little
tree, in the heart of whose branches the bird
was perched. He stood staring curiously at this
tree, recognizing it for that which he had noticed from his window. It was covered with
young blossoms, pink and white, and little
bright green leaves both round and spiky; and
on all this blossom and these leaves the sunlight glistened. Mr. Nilson smiled; the little tree
was so alive and pretty! And instead of passing
on, he stayed there smiling at the tree.

"Morning like this!" he thought; "and here
I am the only person in the Square who has
the—to come out and—!" But he had no
sooner conceived this thought than he saw
quite near him a man with his hands behind
him, who was also staring up and smiling at
the little tree. Rather taken aback, Mr. Nilson
ceased to smile, and looked furtively at the
stranger. It was his next-door neighbor, Mr.
Tandram, well known in the City, who had occupied the adjoining house for some five years.
Mr. Nilson perceived at once the awkwardness
of his position, for, being married, they had not
yet had occasion to speak to one another.
Doubtful as to his proper conduct, he decided
at last to murmur: "Fine morning!" and was
passing on, when Mr. Tandram answered:
"Beautiful, for the time of year!" Detecting a
slight nervousness in his neighbor's voice, Mr.
Nilson was emboldened to regard him openly.
He was of about Mr. Nilson's own height, with

firm, well-colored cheeks, neat brown moustaches, and round, well-opened, clear gray
eyes; and he was wearing a black frock coat.
Mr. Nilson noticed that he had his morning paper clasped behind him as he looked up at the
little tree. And, visited somehow by the feeling
that he had been caught out, he said abruptly:
"Er—can you give me the name of that
tree?"

Mr. Tandram answered:

"I was about to ask you that," and stepped
toward it. Mr. Nilson also approached the tree.

"Sure to have its name on, I should think,"
he said.

Mr. Tandram was the first to see the little
label, close to where the blackbird had been
sitting. He read it out.

"Japanese quince!"

"Ah!" said Mr. Nilson, "thought so. Early
flowerers."

"Very," assented Mr. Tandram, and added:
"Quite a feelin' in the air today."

Mr. Nilson nodded.

"It was a blackbird singin'," he said.

"Blackbirds," answered Mr. Tandram. "I prefer them to thrushes myself; more body in the
note." And he looked at Mr. Nilson in an almost friendly way.

"Quite," murmured Mr. Nilson. "These ex-
otics, they don't bear fruit. Pretty blossom!"
and he again glanced up at the blossom, thinking: "Nice fellow, this, I rather like him."

Mr. Tandram also gazed at the blossom. And
the little tree, as if appreciating their attention,
quivered and glowed. From a distance the
blackbird gave a loud, clear call. Mr. Nilson
dropped his eyes. It struck him suddenly that
Mr. Tandram looked a little foolish; and, as if
he had seen himself, he said: "I must be going
in. Good morning!"

A shade passed over Mr. Tandram's face, as
if he, too, had suddenly noticed something
about Mr. Nilson.

"Good morning," he replied, and clasping
their journals to their backs they separated.

Mr. Nilson retraced his steps toward his
garden window, walking slowly so as to avoid

arriving at the same time as his neighbor. Having seen Mr. Tandram mount his scrolled iron steps, he ascended his own in turn. On the top step he paused.

With the slanting spring sunlight darting and quivering into it, the Japanese quince seemed more living than a tree. The blackbird had returned to it, and was chanting out his heart.

Mr. Nilson sighed; again he felt that queer sensation, that choky feeling in his throat.

The sound of a cough or sigh attracted his attention. There, in the shadow of his French window, stood Mr. Tandram, also looking forth across the Gardens at the little quince tree.

Unaccountably upset, Mr. Nilson turned abruptly into the house, and opened his morning paper.

STUDY QUESTIONS

Recalling

1. Describe the unusual sensation that Mr. Nilson feels in the morning.
2. Describe the appearance of Mr. Nilson and of Mr. Tandram.
3. What circumstances lead to the conversation between the two men?
4. Describe the manner in which Mr. Nilson walks home from the garden.

Interpreting

5. What do you think is the explanation for Mr. Nilson's unusual sensation?
6. In what ways are Mr. Nilson and Mr. Tandram alike? Why is the similarity significant?
7. Explain why Mr. Nilson becomes "unaccountably upset." What does the story imply about his way of life?
8. Explain the symbolism of the quince and of the names *Nilson* and *Tandram*.

Extending

9. What do you think Mr. Nilson will do during the rest of his day? Do you think he will think of the Japanese quince again? Why or why not?

LITERARY FOCUS

Conflict

A **conflict,** or a struggle between opposing forces, exists at the center of every plot and is a frame on which the plot is structured. Conflicts can be internal or external. An **internal conflict** occurs within a character who, for example, struggles to accept reality or to understand a new idea. Because modern fiction often deals with emotional and psychological states, the internal conflict is common in modern stories. An **external conflict** is a struggle between two characters or between a character and nature, society, or fate. Because the opponents are more readily identifiable, an external conflict is usually more obvious than an internal conflict.

Thinking About Conflict

1. What forces within Mr. Nilson are in conflict?
2. Is the conflict in "The Japanese Quince" resolved? Explain your opinion.

COMPOSITION

Writing a Comparison/Contrast

Compare and contrast Conrad's "Lagoon" and Galsworthy's "Japanese Quince." To do this, point out similarities and differences in content and literary technique. You may wish to consider the following elements of the stories: (a) the relationships between major characters and their communities, (b) the internal lives of characters, and (c) the settings. *For help with this assignment, refer to Lesson 2 in the Writing About Literature Handbook at the back of this book.*

Writing a Character Sketch

Galsworthy tells us a great deal about Mr. Nilson with just a few carefully chosen details. Write a brief sketch of a person who is walking alone through a park. Describe your character's appearance and manner. Include just enough details to suggest the character's personality, career, and daily life.

E. M. Forster   *1879–1970*

In his writing Edward Morgan Forster attacked Victorian hypocrisy and attempted to break the British of their prejudices. Forster became associated with the **Bloomsbury Group**, writers and other artists who often gathered in the Bloomsbury section of London and who shared a love of the arts and a contempt for things Victorian. Forster established his reputation with five novels, including *A Room with a View* (1908), and *A Passage to India* (1924).

"The Beauty of Life" is an early essay that, among other things, examines Walt Whitman, the nineteenth-century American poet whose optimism and vigorous life style Forster much admired.

■ What do you think contributes to the beauty of life?

E. M. Forster

The Beauty of Life

The subject of this article—a magnificent subject—was suggested by the editor.[1] "Would it not be possible," he wrote, "to illustrate the beauty and the wonder of life, to show that they are always manifest wheresoever and howsoever life and force are manifested?" But unfortunately it is a subject that could only be treated by a poet—by a poet who was at the same time a man of action; whose enthusiasm had stood the test of hard facts; whose vision of things as they ought to be had been confirmed and strengthened by his experience of things as they are—by such a poet as Walt Whitman.[2]

> *I believe a leaf of grass is no less than the journey-work of the stars,*
> *And the pismire[3] is equally perfect, and a grain of sand, and the egg of the wren,*
> *And the tree toad is a chef-d'oeuvre[4] for the highest,*

> *And the running blackberry would adorn the parlors of heaven.*

Whitman knew what life was. He was not praising its beauty from an armchair. He had been through all that makes it hideous to most men—poverty, the battlefield, the hospitals—and yet could believe that life, whether as a whole or in detail, was perfect, that beauty is manifest wherever life is manifested. He could glorify the absurd and the repulsive; he could catalog the parts of a machine from sheer joy that a machine has so many parts; he could sing not only of farming and fishing, but also of "leather-dressing, coach-making, boiler-making, rope-twisting, distilling, sign-painting, lime-burning, cotton-picking, electro-plating, electro-typing, stereo-typing";[5] one of the lines in one of his poems runs thus! He went the "whole hog," in fact, and he ought to be writing this article.

But most of us have to be content with a less vigorous attitude. We may follow the whole-

---

1. **editor:** the editor of *The Working Men's College Journal,* in which this article first appeared.
2. **Walt Whitman:** American poet (1819–1892); author of *Leaves of Grass.*
3. **pismire:** ant.
4. **chef-d'oeuvre** [she dōō′vrə]: French for "finest work; crowning achievement."

5. **electro-plating . . . stereo-typing:** Electroplating is the process of covering a metal surface with another metal in order to protect or enhance the surface; it is also called stereotyping. Electrotyping is a printing method in which electroplating is employed on letter molds.

hogger at moments, and no doubt it is our fault and not his when we don't follow him; but we cannot follow him always. We may agree that the egg of the wren is perfect, that the running blackberry would adorn the parlors of heaven; but what about the pismire and the tree toad? Do they seem equally perfect? Farming is wonderful because it probes the mystery of the earth; fishing, because it probes the sea. But what about "electro-plating, electro-typing, stereo-typing"? To most of us life seems partly beautiful, partly ugly; partly wonderful, partly dull; there is sunshine in it, but there are also clouds, and we cannot always see that the clouds have silver linings. What are we to do? How is the average man to make the best of what he does see? For it is no good him pretending to see what he doesn't.

One might define the average educated man as optimist by instinct, pessimist by conviction. Few of us are thorough optimists; we have seen too much misery to declare glibly that all is for the best in the best of all possible worlds.[6] Nations arming to the teeth; the growing cleavage between rich and poor; these symptoms, after nineteen hundred years of Christianity, are not calculated to comfort an intelligent person. But we are not thorough pessimists either. We are absolutely certain, though we cannot prove it, that life is beautiful. Fine weather—to take what may seem a small example; fine weather during the whole of a day; the whole city cheered by blue sky and sunshine. What a marvelous blessing that is! The thorough pessimist may reply that city weather is more often wet, and that a fine day is only a scrap in the midst of squalor. Possibly. But it is a scrap that glows like a jewel. If we hope for a great deal of beauty in life, we may be disappointed; nature has not cut her stuff thus; she cannot be bothered about us to this extent. But we may hope for *intensity* of beauty; that is absolutely certain, and never, since the beginning of time, has a man gone through life without moments of overwhelming joy. Perhaps,

Mr. X., you will contradict this. But can you contradict it from your own experience? Can you sincerely say, "Never since I was born have I had one moment of overwhelming joy"? Don't reply, "I've been happy, but think of poor Mr. Y." It's no answer; for if Mr. Y. is questioned, he too will assuredly reply, "I've been happy," perhaps adding, "but think of poor Mr. X."

Here then is what one may call the irreducible minimum, the inalienable dowry of humanity: Beauty in scraps. It may seem a little thing after the comprehensive ecstasies of Whitman, but it is certain; it is for all men in all times, and we couldn't avoid it even if we wanted to. The beauty of the fine day amid dingy weather; the beauty of the unselfish action amid selfishness: the beauty of friendship amid indifference: we cannot go through life without experiencing these things, they are as certain as the air in the lungs. Some people have luck, and get more happiness than others, but every one gets something. And therefore, however pessimistic we are in our convictions, however sure we are that civilization is going to the dogs on account of those abominable—(here insert the name of the political party that you most dislike)—we yet remain optimists by instinct; we personally have had glorious times, and may have them again.

That is the position, as it appears to the average modern man. To him life is not all gold, as Whitman would have it; it is not even strung on a golden thread, as the great Victorian poets would have it, but it is pure gold in parts—it contains scraps of inexpressible beauty. And it is in his power to make a great deal of the scraps. He can, in the first place, practice cheerfulness. He can dwell on the wonderful moments of his existence, rather than on the dull hours that too often separate those moments. He can realize that quality is more precious than quantity. He can—to put it in plain English—stop grumbling. Grumbling is the very devil. It pretends that the whole of life is dull, and that the wonderful moments are not worth considering. Dante,[7] a

6. **all . . . worlds:** paraphrase of a famous line from *Candide*, a satirical novel by the French philosopher Voltaire (1694–1778). Voltaire actually used the line—and wrote the novel—to mock the optimism of other philosophers of his day.

7. **Dante . . . Hell:** Italian poet Dante Alighieri (1265–1321) describes the souls consigned to Hell in *The Inferno*, the first part of his epic *The Divine Comedy*.

man of the soundest sense, puts grumblers deep into Hell. They lie at the bottom of a dirty pond, and their words bubble to the surface saying, "Once we were sullen in the sweet sunlit air. Now we are sullen in the mud." Of course grumbling springs from a very real outside evil—from all the undoubted sorrow that there is in the world, and that no optimism can explain away. But it always flows far from its source. It pretends that the whole world is sorrow, a view that is as false as it is depressing; and if we sometimes resent the shallow optimist, who calls "peace" where there is no peace, we may equally resent the shallow grumbler, who complains of war before war is declared, and who is either regretting the disasters of the past or expecting disaster in the future. To such a man, life can have no beauty. He can never open his eyes and look at the present, which may be full of sweet air and sunlight. If it is night, he cannot remember that the sun set yesterday and may rise tomorrow. He goes through existence pretending that he is at the bottom of a mud pond, as indeed he is, but it is a pond of his own digging. One must distinguish between such a man and the pessimist. The pessimist denies that life as a whole is beautiful, but he never denies the existence of beauty. Great men have been pessimists: Lucretius, Michelangelo, Cromwell, Thomas Hardy.[8] But the grumbler denies everything, and no grumbler ever became a great man; he would not think it worthwhile.

If cheerfulness is one great help toward seeing the beauty in life, courage is certainly another. The average man needs to be just a little braver. He loses so much happiness through what might be termed "minor cowardices." Why are we so afraid of doing the "wrong thing," of wearing the "wrong clothes," of knowing the "wrong people," of pronouncing the names of artists or musicians wrongly? What in the name

of Beauty does it matter? Why don't we trust ourselves more and the conventions less? If we first of all dress ourselves appropriately and fashionably, and then fill our minds with fashionable thoughts, and then go out in search of Romance with a fashionable and appropriate friend, is it likely that we shall find Romance? Is it likely that Life will give herself away to us, unless we also give ourselves away? There are occasions when one must be conventional—one's bread and butter often depends upon it; but there are occasions when one need not be, and on those occasions life opens her wonder-house. That is why one's happiest moments usually come on holidays. It is not that the surroundings are different. It is that we are different. We have not to pretend that we are valuable members of society—that if it wasn't for us, electro-plating, electro-typing, stereo-typing, and the rest would come to an end. We have not to impress people by our ability or taste. We have merely to be ourselves, and like what we like. A little courage does the trick. The world is touched at once with a magical glow; the sea, the sky, the mountains, our fellow creatures, are all transfigured, and we return to work with unforgettable memories.

To sum up. A few great men—mostly poets—have found life absolutely beautiful, in all its aspects. Other great men have found it threaded, as it were, on a beautiful chain. But the average man finds that it is beautiful in parts only, and it is his attitude that is touched upon in this article. No definition of the Beauty of Life is offered, because it is "this to me and that to thee." Some people find it reflected in pictures and poems; others, going to life direct, find it in human intercourse or in scenery; while a few have even found it in the higher truths of mathematics. But everyone, except the grumbler and perhaps the coward, finds it somewhere; and if the article contains anything, it contains a few tips which may make beauty easier to find. Be cheerful. Be courageous. Don't bother too much about "developing the aesthetic sense," as books term it, for if the heart and the brain are kept clean, the aesthetic sense will develop of itself. In your spare time, never study a subject that bores you,

---

8. **Lucretius . . . Hardy:** Titus Lucretius Carus (96?–55 B.C.), Roman philosopher and poet; Michelangelo Buonarroti (1475–1564), Italian painter, sculptor, and architect; Oliver Cromwell (1599–1658), Puritan who headed England's government from 1653 to 1658; and Thomas Hardy (1840–1928), English novelist and poet.

however important other people tell you it is; but choose out of the subjects that don't bore you, the subject that seems to you most important, and study that. You may say, "Oh, yes, it's jolly easy to preach like this." But it's also jolly easy to practice. The above precepts contain nothing heroical, nothing that need disturb our daily existence or diminish our salaries. They aren't difficult, they are just a few tips that may help us to see the wonders, physical and spiritual, by which we are surrounded. Modern civilization does not lead us away from Romance, but it does try to lead us past it, and we have to keep awake. We must insist on going to look round the corner now and then, even if other people think us a little queer, for as likely as not something beautiful lies round the corner. And if we insist, we may have a reward that is even greater than we expected, and see for a moment with the eyes of a poet—may see the universe, not merely beautiful in scraps, but beautiful everywhere and for ever.

> *The sun and stars that float in the open air,*
> *The apple-shaped earth and we upon it,*
>   *surely the drift of them is something*
>   *grand.*
> *I do not know what it is except that it is*
>   *grand, and that it is happiness.*

One final tip; read Walt Whitman. He is the true optimist—not the professional optimist who shuts his eyes and shirks, and whose palliatives do more harm than good, but one who has seen and suffered much and yet rejoices. He is not a philosopher or a theologian; he cannot answer the ultimate question, and tell us what life is. But he is absolutely certain that it is grand, that it is happiness, and that "wherever life and force are manifested, beauty is manifested."

STUDY QUESTIONS

Recalling

1. According to paragraph 2, what had Whitman "been through"? What could he believe? In contrast, what does Forster say life seems like to most of us (paragraph 3)?
2. How does Forster "define" the average educated man in paragraph 4? What contrast does Forster make between a "grumbler" and a pessimist in paragraph 6?
3. According to paragraph 7, what two qualities are each a "great help towards seeing the beauty in life"? What should we not fear being, at least on occasion? What reward may we have if we "look round the corner now and then" (paragraph 8)?

Interpreting

4. What does Forster mean, in general, by "the beauty of life"?
5. What does Forster basically admire about Whitman? What sort of behavior does he suggest can help us to be more like Whitman?

COMPOSITION

Writing About Nonfiction

■ Write an essay examining Forster's purpose in writing "The Beauty of Life" and the techniques he uses to achieve it. Begin by stating his purpose. Then discuss each general point he makes, and show how he supports that point by using figurative language, examples, quotations, or other details. *For help with this assignment, refer to Lesson 4 in the Writing About Literature Handbook at the back of this book.*

Writing an Essay of Ideas

■ What is your prescription for appreciating "The Beauty of Life"? Explain your ideas in an essay that uses examples, quotations, and figurative language to support your points.

James Joyce   *1882–1941*

By experimenting with language, plot, and characterization, James Joyce earned a place as one of the most influential writers of the modern period. Joyce was concerned with inner reality, the psychological reactions people have to their surroundings. Many "events" in his fiction take place in his characters' minds. Certainly Joyce's characters move and act in the world, but the author directs our attention inside, to the mind and its response to external happenings.

Joyce was born into a large family in Dublin, Ireland, and attended school and college there. A fine student, he was an avid reader of classical and modern literature, and he mastered a number of languages, including Latin. Feeling stifled by his surroundings, Joyce left his homeland permanently and spent most of his time in Trieste, Paris, Zurich, and Rome. For a time he supported himself by teaching languages.

Much of Joyce's fiction is autobiographical. *Dubliners* (1914) is a collection of stories dealing with the life and the character of Dublin, the city he called "the center of paralysis." In fact, Joyce set all of his work in Dublin and uses the city as a microcosm, or miniature model, of the world. *A Portrait of the Artist as a Young Man* (1916) is based on Joyce's life up to 1902. It is a moving account of an adolescent's struggle for maturity and independence as well as a statement on the meaning of art. *Ulysses* (1922) is the story of a day in the lives of three Dubliners, including Stephen Dedalus, the hero of *Portrait*. The novel makes frequent allusions to Homer's *Odyssey* and observes parallels between the ancient and modern worlds. The cyclical nature of history is explored again in *Finnegans Wake*, in which one Dublin family represents humanity throughout history.

The psychological aspect of Joyce's work and his experiments with literary form often challenge his readers. For this reason and because of his frankness, Joyce had great difficulty getting his work published. *Dubliners* was rejected by twenty-two publishers before being printed; *Ulysses* was banned for many years in England and America. As a result, Joyce did not make money from his writing. He died penniless in Switzerland after fleeing German-occupied France during World War II.

"Araby" is a typical story from *Dubliners* in which much of the plot takes place within the mind of the main character. Like most of Joyce's best fiction, the story has for a climax a stunning realization that changes a character's way of looking at life.

■ Have you ever looked forward to and made big plans for a trip or party that did not meet your expectations? How did you feel? What do you remember about the event?

James Joyce

Araby

North Richmond Street, being blind,[1] was a quiet street except at the hour when the Christian Brothers' School set the boys free. An uninhabited house of two stories stood at the blind end, detached from its neighbors in a square ground. The other houses of the street, conscious of decent lives within them, gazed at one another with brown imperturbable faces.

The former tenant of our house, a priest, had died in the back drawing room. Air, musty from having been long enclosed, hung in all the rooms, and the waste room behind the kitchen was littered with old useless papers. Among these I found a few paper-covered books, the pages of which were curled and damp: *The Abbot,* by Walter Scott, *The Devout Communicant* and *The Memoirs of Vidocq.*[2] I liked the last best because its leaves were yellow. The wild garden behind the house contained a central apple tree and a few straggling bushes under one of which I found the late

---

1. **blind:** dead end.

2. ***The Abbot . . . Vidocq*** [vē dôk′]: historical tale, a manual of religious instruction, and the recollections of a French adventurer, respectively.

tenant's rusty bicycle pump. He had been a very charitable priest; in his will he had left all his money to institutions and the furniture of his house to his sister.

When the short days of winter came dusk fell before we had well eaten our dinners. When we met in the street the houses had grown somber. The space of sky above us was the color of ever-changing violet and toward it the lamps of the street lifted their feeble lanterns. The cold air stung us and we played till our bodies glowed. Our shouts echoed in the silent street. The career of our play brought us through the dark muddy lanes behind the houses where we ran the gantlet of the rough tribes from the cottages, to the back doors of the dark dripping gardens where odors arose from the ashpits, to the dark odorous stables where a coachman smoothed and combed the horse or shook music from the buckled harness. When we returned to the street, light from the kitchen windows had filled the areas. If my uncle was seen turning the corner we hid in the shadow until we had seen him safely housed. Or if Mangan's sister came out on the doorstep to call her brother in to his tea we watched her from our shadow peer up and down the street. We waited to see whether she would remain or go in and, if she remained, we left our shadow and walked up to Mangan's steps resignedly. She was waiting for us, her figure defined by the light from the half-opened door. Her brother always teased her before he obeyed and I stood by the railings looking at her. Her dress swung as she moved her body and the soft rope of her hair tossed from side to side.

Every morning I lay on the floor in the front parlor watching her door. The blind was pulled down to within an inch of the sash so that I could not be seen. When she came out on the doorstep my heart leaped. I ran to the hall, seized my books and followed her. I kept her brown figure always in my eye and, when we came near the point at which our ways diverged, I quickened my pace and passed her. This happened morning after morning. I had never spoken to her, except for a few casual words, and yet her name was like a summons to all my foolish blood.

Her image accompanied me even in places the most hostile to romance. On Saturday evenings when my aunt went marketing I had to go to carry some of the parcels. We walked through the flaring streets, jostled by drunken men and bargaining women, amid the curses of laborers, the shrill litanies of shopboys who stood on guard by the barrels of pigs' cheeks, the nasal chanting of street singers, who sang a *come-all-you* about O'Donovan Rossa,[3] or a ballad about the troubles in our native land. These noises converged in a single sensation of life for me: I imagined that I bore my chalice safely through a throng of foes. Her name sprang to my lips at moments in strange prayers and praises which I myself did not understand. My eyes were often full of tears (I could not tell why) and at times a flood from my heart seemed to pour itself out into my bosom. I thought little of the future. I did not know whether I would ever speak to her or not or, if I spoke to her, how I could tell her of my confused adoration. But my body was like a harp and her words and gestures were like fingers running upon the wires.

One evening I went into the back drawing room in which the priest had died. It was a dark rainy evening and there was no sound in the house. Through one of the broken panes I heard the rain impinge upon the earth, the fine incessant needles of water playing in the sodden beds. Some distant lamp or lighted window gleamed below me. I was thankful that I could see so little. All my senses seemed to desire to veil themselves and, feeling that I was about to slip from them, I pressed the palms of my hands together until they trembled, murmuring: *"O love! O love!"* many times.

At last she spoke to me. When she addressed the first words to me I was so confused that I did not know what to answer. She asked me was I going to *Araby.* I forget

---

3. *come-all-you* . . . **Rossa:** ballad about an Irish hero.

whether I answered yes or no. It would be a splendid bazaar, she said; she would love to go.

"And why can't you?" I asked.

While she spoke she turned a silver bracelet round and round her wrist. She could not go, she said, because there would be a retreat[4] that week in her convent.[5] Her brother and two other boys were fighting for their caps and I was alone at the railings. She held one of the spikes, bowing her head toward me. The light from the lamp opposite our door caught the white curve of her neck, lit up her hair that rested there and, falling, lit up the hand upon the railing. It fell over one side of her dress and caught the white border of a petticoat, just visible as she stood at ease.

"It's well for you," she said.

"If I go," I said, "I will bring you something."

What innumerable follies laid waste my waking and sleeping thoughts after that evening! I wished to annihilate the tedious intervening days. I chafed against the work of school. At night in my bedroom and by day in the classroom her image came between me and the page I strove to read. The syllables of the word *Araby* were called to me through the silence in which my soul luxuriated and cast an Eastern enchantment over me. I asked for leave to go to the bazaar on Saturday night. My aunt was surprised and hoped it was not some Freemason[6] affair. I answered few questions in class. I watched my master's face pass from amiability to sternness; he hoped I was not beginning to idle. I could not call my wandering thoughts together. I had hardly any patience with the serious work of life which, now that it stood between me and my desire, seemed to me child's play, ugly monotonous child's play.

On Saturday morning I reminded my uncle that I wished to go to the bazaar in the eve-

ning. He was fussing at the hallstand, looking for the hat brush, and answered me curtly:

"Yes, boy, I know."

As he was in the hall I could not go into the front parlor and lie at the window. I left the house in bad humor and walked slowly toward the school. The air was pitilessly raw and already my heart misgave me.

When I came home to dinner my uncle had not yet been home. Still it was early. I sat staring at the clock for some time and, when its ticking began to irritate me, I left the room. I mounted the staircase and gained the upper part of the house. The high cold empty gloomy rooms liberated me and I went from room to room singing. From the front window I saw my companions playing below in the street. Their cries reached me weakened and indistinct and, leaning my forehead against the cool glass, I looked over at the dark house where she lived. I may have stood there for an hour, seeing nothing but the brown-clad figure cast by my imagination, touched discreetly by the lamplight at the curved neck, at the hand upon the railings and at the border below the dress.

When I came downstairs again I found Mrs. Mercer sitting at the fire. She was an old garrulous woman, a pawnbroker's widow, who collected used stamps for some pious purpose. I had to endure the gossip of the tea table. The meal was prolonged beyond an hour and still my uncle did not come. Mrs. Mercer stood up to go: she was sorry she couldn't wait any longer, but it was after eight o'clock and she did not like to be out late, as the night air was bad for her. When she had gone I began to walk up and down the room, clenching my fists. My aunt said:

"I'm afraid you may put off your bazaar for this night of Our Lord."

At nine o'clock I heard my uncle's latchkey in the hall door. I heard him talking to himself and heard the hallstand rocking when it had received the weight of his overcoat. I could interpret these signs. When he was midway through his dinner I asked him to give me the money to go to the bazaar. He had forgotten.

---

4. **retreat:** seclusion of a group for prayer, meditation, and religious study.
5. **convent:** school run by an order of nuns.
6. **Freemason:** international secret service society, also called the Free and Accepted Masons.

"The people are in bed and after their first sleep now," he said.

I did not smile. My aunt said to him energetically:

"Can't you give him the money and let him go? You've kept him late enough as it is."

My uncle said he was very sorry he had forgotten. He said he believed in the old saying: *All work and no play makes Jack a dull boy.* He asked me where I was going and, when I had told him a second time he asked me did I know *The Arab's Farewell to His Steed.*[7] When I left the kitchen he was about to recite the opening lines of the piece to my aunt.

I held a florin[8] tightly in my hand as I strode down Buckingham Street toward the station. The sight of the streets thronged with buyers and glaring with gas recalled to me the purpose of my journey. I took my seat in a third-class carriage of a deserted train. After an intolerable delay the train moved out of the station slowly. It crept onward among ruinous houses and over the twinkling river. At Westland Row Station a crowd of people pressed to the carriage doors; but the porters moved them back, saying that it was a special train for the bazaar. I remained alone in the bare carriage. In a few minutes the train drew up beside an improvised wooden platform. I passed out onto the road and saw by the lighted dial of a clock that it was ten minutes to ten. In front of me was a large building which displayed the magical name.

I could not find any sixpenny entrance and, fearing that the bazaar would be closed, I passed in quickly through a turnstile, handing a shilling to a weary-looking man. I found myself in a big hall girdled at half its height by a gallery. Nearly all the stalls were closed and the greater part of the hall was in darkness. I recognized a silence like that which pervades a church after a service. I walked into the center of the bazaar timidly. A few people were gathered about the stalls which were still open. Before a curtain, over which the words *Café Chantant*[9] were written in colored lamps, two men were counting money on a salver.[10] I listened to the fall of the coins.

Remembering with difficulty why I had come I went over to one of the stalls and examined porcelain vases and flowered tea sets. At the door of the stall a young lady was talking and laughing with two young gentlemen. I remarked their English accents and listened vaguely to their conversation.

"O, I never said such a thing!"

"O, but you did!"

"O, but I didn't!"

"Didn't she say that?"

"Yes. I heard her."

"O, there's a . . . fib!"

Observing me the young lady came over and asked me did I wish to buy anything. The tone of her voice was not encouraging; she seemed to have spoken to me out of a sense of duty. I looked humbly at the great jars that stood like Eastern guards at either side of the dark entrance to the stall and murmured:

"No, thank you."

The young lady changed the position of one of the vases and went back to the two young men. They began to talk of the same subject. Once or twice the young lady glanced at me over her shoulder.

I lingered before her stall, though I knew my stay was useless, to make my interest in her wares seem the more real. Then I turned away slowly and walked down the middle of the bazaar. I allowed the two pennies to fall against the sixpence in my pocket. I heard a voice call from one end of the gallery that the light was out. The upper part of the hall was now completely dark.

Gazing up into the darkness I saw myself as a creature driven and derided by vanity; and my eyes burned with anguish and anger.

---

7. *The Arab's . . . Steed:* popular nineteenth-century poem.
8. **florin:** a former two-shilling coin. At the time of the story one shilling was worth approximately twenty-five American cents.

9. *Café Chantant:* café with musical entertainment.
10. **salver** [sal′vər]: tray, usually used for serving food.

STUDY QUESTIONS

Recalling

1. At what times of day does the boy usually see Mangan's sister? When does he think of her?
2. What promise does the boy make to the girl?
3. Why is the boy late for the bazaar? Describe the bazaar.
4. How does the boy feel at the end of the story?

Interpreting

5. Contrast the boy's expectations of the bazaar with his usual surroundings.
6. Explain how the boy reveals to the reader his infatuation with the girl. Give two examples of his inexperience with girls.
7. Why does the bazaar become a negative experience for the boy? What do you think the experience teaches him about dreams as opposed to reality?

VIEWPOINT

The famous literary critic Edmund Wilson compared what happens in Joyce's fiction to what goes on in the mind just before sleep:

> Images or words in the conscious mind take on an ominous significance . . . incidents swell with meaning. . . .
>
> —*Axel's Castle*

Find at least two significant images in "Araby." Explain how the incident at the bazaar swells with meaning.

LITERARY FOCUS

Plot

Plot is the sequence of events in a story, each event causing or leading to the next. The author of a story arranges and orders events of a plot to capture, hold, and heighten our interest as the story progresses. To accomplish this involvement, the development of a plot generally includes the following points: The **exposition,** usually at the beginning of the story, introduces characters, settings, and situations that are important to the story. The **narrative hook** is the point at which the conflict begins. The **rising action** adds complications to the conflict and increases our interest. The **climax** is the point of our highest interest and emotional involvement in

the story, the point at which we know how the conflict will be resolved. The **falling action** shows the result of the climax and ends with the **resolution,** or denouement, the final outcome.

Because modern fiction often experiments with plot, many modern stories have unusual plot structures: The information usually presented in the exposition may be gradually revealed throughout the story instead. A story may end at the climax, leaving the reader at the peak of emotional involvement. Another story may not have a dramatic climax, and the reader may be free to form a personal interpretation of the outcome. James Joyce created his own innovation for the climax of a story. His stories often end with an **epiphany,** a sudden realization—by the reader as well as a character—of the true nature of a person, place, object, or situation.

Thinking About Plot

1. List the points in the plot of "Araby" that are the story's exposition, narrative hook, rising action, climax, and, if any, falling action and resolution.
2. Is the climax of "Araby" an epiphany? Why?

COMPOSITION

Citing Evidence

A good short story is particular and universal. That is, a good story is specific in its plot, characters, and setting but has concerns that are common to all people. Cite evidence from the story to show that "Araby" is particular and universal. To do this, cite examples from the story—verbatim and in paraphrase—to show that the story has a specific plot, characters, and setting. Then, still citing evidence from the story, explain how the story represents an experience that is common to most people. *For help with this assignment, refer to Lesson 3 in the Writing About Literature Handbook at the back of this book.*

Writing a Journal Entry

Imagine that you are the boy in "Araby" twenty years later, and write a journal entry about your memories of the events in the story. In writing your entry, consider the following questions: Does the adult remember the events with joy or sadness? Did these events have a lasting effect on the boy? What became of the boy's infatuation with Mangan's sister?

Katherine Mansfield   *1888–1923*

In a relatively short career Katherine Mansfield exerted a major influence on the modern short story. Mansfield was born in New Zealand and spent most of her childhood there, but she attended Queens College in London. By the age of nineteen, she had published a few short vignettes and was determined to achieve fame as a writer. Back in New Zealand after college, she felt that her homeland restricted her, and she returned to London in 1908. Mansfield wrote short stories, poetry, literary criticism, and a journal. Ironically the stories inspired by her early life in New Zealand brought her first success. Always plagued by poor health, she died of tuberculosis at the age of thirty-five.

Mansfield's *Journal* (1927) affords an insight into her personality and explains her literary goals and methods, but she is best known for her short stories. The stories—collected in volumes such as *In a German Pension* (1911) and *The Garden Party* (1922)—reflect the complexity and confusion of the modern age. Mansfield writes about ordinary events, quiet moments that gradually reveal their significance.

"The Singing Lesson" illustrates Mansfield's talent for characterization. By eavesdropping on the thoughts racing through Miss Meadows' mind, the reader forms a finely etched portrait of a complicated woman.

■ Should you let someone else's mood affect you? How can you prevent its affecting you?

Katherine Mansfield

The Singing Lesson

With despair—cold, sharp despair—buried deep in her heart like a wicked knife, Miss Meadows, in cap and gown and carrying a little baton, trod the cold corridors that led to the music hall. Girls of all ages, rosy from the air, and bubbling over with that gleeful excitement that comes from running to school on a fine autumn morning, hurried, skipped, fluttered by; from the hollow classrooms came a quick drumming of voices; a bell rang; a voice like a bird cried, "Muriel." And then there came from the staircase a tremendous knock-knock-knocking. Someone had dropped her dumbbells.

The Science Mistress stopped Miss Meadows.

"Good mor-ning," she cried, in her sweet, affected drawl. "Isn't it cold? It might be winter."

Miss Meadows, hugging the knife, stared in hatred at the Science Mistress. Everything about her was sweet, pale, like honey. You would not have been surprised to see a bee caught in the tangles of that yellow hair.

"It is rather sharp," said Miss Meadows, grimly.

The other smiled her sugary smile.

"You look fro-zen," said she. Her blue eyes opened wide; there came a mocking light in them. (Had she noticed anything?)

"Oh, not quite as bad as that," said Miss Meadows, and she gave the Science Mistress, in exchange for her smile, a quick grimace and passed on. . . .

Forms[1] Four, Five, and Six were assembled in the music hall. The noise was deafening. On the platform, by the piano, stood Mary Beazley, Miss Meadows' favorite, who played accompaniments. She was turning the music stool. When she saw Miss Meadows she gave a loud, warning "Sh-sh! girls!" and Miss Meadows, her hands thrust in her sleeves, the baton under her arm, strode down the center aisle, mounted the steps, turned sharply, seized the brass music stand, planted it in front of her, and gave two sharp taps with her baton for silence.

"Silence, please! Immediately!" and, looking at nobody, her glance swept over that sea of colored flannel blouses, with bobbing pink faces and hands, quivering butterfly hair bows, and music books outspread. She knew perfectly well what they were thinking. "Meady is in a wax."[2] Well, let them think it! Her eyelids quivered; she tossed her head, defying them. What could the thoughts of those creatures matter to someone who stood there bleeding to death, pierced to the heart, to the heart, by such a letter—

. . . "I feel more and more strongly that our marriage would be a mistake. Not that I do not love you. I love you as much as it is possible for me to love any woman, but, truth to tell, I have come to the conclusion that I am not a marrying man, and the idea of settling down fills me with nothing but—" and the word "disgust" was scratched out lightly and "regret" written over the top.

Basil! Miss Meadows stalked over to the piano. And Mary Beazley, who was waiting for this moment, bent forward; her curls fell over her cheeks while she breathed, "Good morning, Miss Meadows," and she motioned toward rather than handed to her mistress a beautiful yellow chrysanthemum. This little ritual of the flower had been gone through for ages and ages, quite a term and a half. It was as much part of the lesson as opening the piano. But this morning, instead of taking it up, instead of tucking it into her belt while she leaned over Mary and said, "Thank you, Mary. How very nice! Turn to page thirty-two," what was Mary's horror when Miss Meadows totally ignored the chrysanthemum, made no reply to her greeting, but said in a voice of ice, "Page fourteen, please, and mark the accents well."

Staggering moment! Mary blushed until the tears stood in her eyes, but Miss Meadows was gone back to the music stand; her voice rang through the music hall.

"Page fourteen. We will begin with page fourteen. 'A Lament.'[3] Now, girls, you ought to know it by this time. We shall take it all together; not in parts, all together. And without expression. Sing it, though, quite simply, beating time with the left hand."

She raised the baton; she tapped the music stand twice. Down came Mary on the opening chord; down came all those left hands, beating the air, and in chimed those young, mournful voices:—

Fast! Ah, too Fast Fade the Ro-o-ses of Pleasure;
 Soon Autumn yields unto Wi-i-nter Drear.
Fleetly! Ah, Fleetly Mu-u-sic's Gay Measure
 Passes away from the Listening Ear.

Good Heavens, what could be more tragic than that lament! Every note was a sigh, a sob, a groan of awful mournfulness. Miss Meadows lifted her arms in the wide gown and began conducting with both hands. ". . . I feel more and more strongly that our marriage would be a mistake. . . ." she beat. And the voices cried: *Fleetly! Ah, Fleetly.* What could have possessed him to write such a letter! What could have

---

1. **Forms:** grades in British schools.
2. **in a wax:** in a rage; angry.

3. **'A Lament':** song expressing sorrow or grief.

led up to it! It came out of nothing. His last letter had been all about a fumed-oak bookcase he had bought for "our" books, and a "natty little hall stand" he had seen, "a very neat affair with a carved owl on a bracket, holding three hat brushes in its claws." How she had smiled at that! So like a man to think one needed three hat brushes! *From the Listening Ear,* sang the voices.

"Once again," said Miss Meadows. "But this time in parts. Still without expression." *Fast! Ah, too Fast.* With the gloom of the contraltos[4] added, one could scarcely help shuddering. *Fade the Roses of Pleasure.* Last time he had come to see her, Basil had worn a rose in his buttonhole. How handsome he had looked in that bright blue suit, with that dark red rose! And he knew it, too. He couldn't help knowing it. First he stroked his hair, then his moustache; his teeth gleamed when he smiled.

"The headmaster's wife keeps on asking me to dinner. It's a perfect nuisance. I never get an evening to myself in that place."

"But can't you refuse?"

"Oh, well, it doesn't do for a man in my position to be unpopular."

Music's Gay Measure, wailed the voices. The willow trees, outside the high, narrow windows, waved in the wind. They had lost half their leaves. The tiny ones that clung wriggled like fishes caught on a line. ". . . I am not a marrying man. . . ." The voices were silent; the piano waited.

"Quite good," said Miss Meadows, but still in such a strange, stony tone that the younger girls began to feel positively frightened. "But now that we know it, we shall take it with expression. As much expression as you can put into it. Think of the words, girls. Use your imaginations. *Fast! Ah, too Fast,"* cried Miss Meadows. "That ought to break out—a loud, strong *forte*[5]—a lament. And then in the second line, *Winter Drear,* make that *Drear* sound as if a cold wind were blowing through it. *Dreear!"* said she so awfully that Mary Beazley, on the music stool, wriggled her spine. "The third line should be one crescendo.[6] *Fleetly! Ah, Fleetly Music's Gay Measure.* Breaking on the first word of the last line, *Passes.* And then on the word, *Away,* you must begin to die . . . to fade . . . until *The Listening Ear* is nothing more than a faint whisper. . . . You can slow down as much as you like almost on the last line. Now, please."

Again the two light taps; she lifted her arms again. *Fast! Ah, too Fast.* ". . . and the idea of settling down fills me with nothing but disgust—" Disgust was what he had written. That was as good as to say their engagement was definitely broken off. Broken off! Their engagement! People had been surprised enough that she had got engaged. The Science Mistress would not believe it at first. But nobody had been as surprised as she. She was thirty. Basil was twenty-five. It had been a miracle, simply a miracle, to hear him say, as they walked home from church that very dark night, "You know, somehow or other, I've got fond of you." And he had taken hold of the end of her ostrich feather boa. *Passes away from the Listening Ear.*

"Repeat! Repeat!" said Miss Meadows. "More expression, girls! Once more!"

---

4. **contraltos** [kən tral′tōz]: singers with the lowest female singing voice.

5. *forte* [fôr′tā]: increase in volume.
6. **crescendo** [kri shen′dō]: increase in volume.

Fast! Ah, too Fast. The older girls were crimson; some of the younger ones began to cry. Big spots of rain blew against the windows, and one could hear the willows whispering, ". . . not that I do not love you. . . ."

"But, my darling, if you love me," thought Miss Meadows, "I don't mind how much it is. Love me as little as you like." But she knew he didn't love her. Not to have cared enough to scratch out that word "disgust," so that she couldn't read it! *Soon Autumn yields unto Winter Drear.* She would have to leave the school, too. She could never face the Science Mistress or the girls after it got known. She would have to disappear somewhere. *Passes away.* The voices began to die, to fade, to whisper . . . to vanish. . . .

Suddenly the door opened. A little girl in blue walked fussily up the aisle, hanging her head, biting her lips, and twisting the silver bangle on her red little wrist. She came up the steps and stood before Miss Meadows.

"Well, Monica, what is it?"

"Oh, if you please, Miss Meadows," said the little girl, gasping, "Miss Wyatt wants to see you in the mistress's room."

"Very well," said Miss Meadows. And she called to the girls, "I shall put you on your honor to talk quietly while I am away." But they were too subdued to do anything else. Most of them were blowing their noses.

The corridors were silent and cold; they echoed to Miss Meadows' steps. The head mistress sat at her desk. For a moment she did not look up. She was as usual disentangling her eyeglasses, which had got caught in her lace tie. "Sit down, Miss Meadows," she said very kindly. And then she picked up a pink envelope from the blotting pad. "I sent for you just now because this telegram has come for you."

"A telegram for me, Miss Wyatt?"

Basil! He had committed suicide, decided Miss Meadows. Her hand flew out, but Miss Wyatt held the telegram back a moment. "I hope it's not bad news," she said, so more than kindly. And Miss Meadows tore it open.

"Pay no attention to letter, must have been mad, bought hat stand today—Basil," she read.

She couldn't take her eyes off the telegram.

"I do hope it's nothing very serious," said Miss Wyatt, leaning forward.

"Oh, no, thank you, Miss Wyatt," blushed Miss Meadows. "It's nothing bad at all. It's"—and she gave an apologetic little laugh—"it's from my *fiancé* saying that . . . saying that—" There was a pause. "I *see,*" said Miss Wyatt. And another pause. Then—"You've fifteen minutes more of your class, Miss Meadows, haven't you?"

"Yes, Miss Wyatt." She got up. She half ran toward the door.

"Oh, just one minute, Miss Meadows," said Miss Wyatt. "I must say I don't approve of my teachers having telegrams sent to them in school hours, unless in case of very bad news, such as death," explained Miss Wyatt, "or a very serious accident, or something to that effect. Good news, Miss Meadows, will always keep, you know."

On the wings of hope, of love, of joy, Miss Meadows sped back to the music hall, up the aisle, up the steps, over to the piano.

"Page thirty-two, Mary," she said, "page thirty-two," and, picking up the yellow chrysanthemum, she held it to her lips to hide her smile. Then she turned to the girls, rapped with her baton: "Page thirty-two, girls. Page thirty-two."

We come here To-day with Flowers o'erladen,
With Baskets of Fruit and Ribbons to boot,
To-oo Congratulate. . . .

"Stop! Stop!" cried Miss Meadows. "This is awful. This is dreadful." And she beamed at her girls. "What's the matter with you all? Think, girls, think of what you're singing. Use your imaginations. *With Flowers o'erladen. Baskets of Fruit and Ribbons to boot.* And *Congratulate.*" Miss Meadows broke off. "Don't look so doleful, girls. It ought to sound warm, joyful, eager. *Congratulate.* Once more. Quickly. All together. Now then!"

And this time Miss Meadows' voice sounded over all the other voices—full, deep, glowing with expression.

STUDY QUESTIONS

Recalling

1. At the beginning of the story, what is Miss Meadows' mood? To what object is her mood compared?
2. Explain the contents of the letter that Miss Meadows thinks about during her lesson.
3. In what way does Miss Meadows cause Mary Beazley "horror"?
4. Describe the incident that interrupts the singing lesson.
5. What fault does Miss Meadows find with the class when she returns?

Interpreting

6. Describe Miss Meadows' manner in class before and after the interruption. Use details from the story to show which type of behavior is more typical for Miss Meadows.
7. Relate Miss Meadows' treatment of other people and the songs she chooses to her emotional states.
8. Describe Basil's personality, and explain his relationship with Miss Meadows.

Extending

9. Do you think that Miss Meadows should be as happy as she is about Basil's telegram?

LITERARY FOCUS

Point of View

Point of view is the relationship of the **narrator,** or storyteller, to the story. The author's choice of narrator influences the information and the emotional involvement that the story provides.

A story told in the **first-person point of view** is narrated by a character in the story. A first-person narrator relates personal experience, using the pronoun *I*. Because we are reading a personal account, we sympathize with the narrator and become emotionally involved in the story. The first-person narrator, however, may tell only one side of a story and may actually deceive the reader either deliberately or because he or she does not know the truth.

A story told in the **limited third-person point of view** is narrated by the author but from the limited viewpoint of only one character. The narrator is detached from the action and uses the pronoun *he* or *she*. Because we read the thoughts of only one character, we sympathize with him or her. The character, however, may not completely understand a situation, and therefore we too are denied full information.

A story told in the **omniscient point of view** is narrated by the author who reveals the thoughts and feelings of *all* the characters. An omniscient narrator uses the third person—*he* or *she*—and stands completely outside the story. Because the narrator is detached, he or she can always be trusted.

Thinking About Point of View

1. What is the point of view of "The Singing Lesson"? Explain your answer.
2. Explain how the point of view of "The Singing Lesson" keeps complete information from the reader but still inspires sympathy for Miss Meadows.

D. H. Lawrence   *1885–1930*

D. H. Lawrence helped to define modern literature with his carefully constructed, highly original, and socially conscious novels and short stories. David Herbert Lawrence was born in a small coal mining town in Nottinghamshire, England. Lawrence left school at an early age, held a number of jobs, and then completed his education. His life was marred by poor health, and he traveled extensively—to Italy, Australia, and Mexico—to improve his condition. Besides fiction, Lawrence wrote poetry and travel books; he was also a talented painter. He died of tuberculosis in southern France.

A recurring concern in Lawrence's fiction is the effect of the Industrial Revolution. Lawrence felt that the scientific-industrial age both separated people from their own feelings and estranged them from nature. In his stories and especially in novels like *Sons and Lovers* (1913), *The Rainbow* (1915), and *Women in Love* (1921), he wrote of the need for harmony with nature and for integration of the individual's body and spirit.

"Goose Fair" demonstrates Lawrence's concern with the influence of industrialization. He exemplifies the differences between classes by contrasting two young women of very dissimilar backgrounds. In just a few pages the story parades before the reader a wide array of characters who embody the struggles that filled Lawrence's work and changed England.

■ What are two or three ways in which industrialization might alienate people from nature and from each other?

D. H. Lawrence

Goose Fair

1

Through the gloom of evening, and the flare of torches of the night before the fair, through the still fogs of the succeeding dawn came paddling the weary geese, lifting their poor feet that had been dipped in tar for shoes, and trailing them along the cobblestones into the town. Last of all, in the afternoon, a country girl drove in her dozen birds, disconsolate because she was so late. She was a heavily built girl, fair, with regular features, and yet unprepossessing. She needed chiseling down, her contours were brutal. Perhaps it was weariness that hung her eyelids a little lower than was

pleasant. When she spoke to her clumsily lagging birds it was in a snarling nasal tone. One of the silly things sat down in the gutter and refused to move. It looked very ridiculous, but also rather pitiful, squat there with its head up, refusing to be urged on by the ungentle toe of the girl. The latter swore heavily, then picked up the great complaining bird, and fronting her road stubbornly, drove on the lamentable eleven.

No one had noticed her. This afternoon the women were not sitting chatting on their doorsteps, seaming up the cotton hose, or swiftly

D. H. Lawrence   **717**

passing through their fingers the piled white lace; and in the high dark house the song of the hosiery frames was hushed: "Shackety-boom, Shackety-shackety-boom, Z—zzz!" As she dragged up Hollow Stone, people returning from the fair chaffed her and asked her what o'clock it was. She did not reply, her look was sullen. The Lace Market was quiet as the Sabbath: even the great brass plates on the doors were dull with neglect. There seemed an afternoon atmosphere of raw discontent. The girl stopped a moment before the dismal prospect of one of the great warehouses that had been gutted with fire. She looked at the lean, threatening walls and watched her white flock waddling in reckless misery below, and she would have laughed out loud had the wall fallen flat upon them and relieved her of them. But the wall did not fall, so she crossed the road, and walking on the safe side, hurried after her charge. Her look was even more sullen. She remembered the state of trade—Trade, the invidious[1] enemy; Trade, which thrust out its hand and shut the factory doors, and pulled the stockingers[2] off their seats, and left the web half-finished on the frame; Trade, which mysteriously choked up the sources of the rivulets of wealth, and blacker and more secret than a pestilence, starved the town. Through this morose atmosphere of bad trade, in the afternoon of the first day of the fair, the girl strode down to the Poultry with eleven sound geese and one lame one to sell.

The Frenchmen were at the bottom of it! So everybody said, though nobody quite knew how. At any rate, they had gone to war with the Prussians and got beaten, and trade was ruined in Nottingham!

A little fog rose up, and the twilight gathered around. Then they flared abroad their torches in the fair, insulting the night. The girl still sat in the Poultry, and her weary geese unsold on the stones, illuminated by the hissing lamp of a man who sold rabbits and pigeons and such-like assorted livestock.

---

1. **invidious** [in vid′ē əs]: offensively unfair.
2. **stockingers:** hosiery knitters or weavers.

2

In another part of the town, near Sneinton Church, another girl came to the door to look at the night. She was tall and slender, dressed with the severe accuracy which marks the girl of superior culture. Her hair was arranged with simplicity about the long, pale, cleanly cut face. She leaned forward very slightly to glance down the street, listening. She very carefully preserved the appearance of having come quite casually to the door, yet she lingered and lingered and stood very still to listen when she heard a footstep, but when it proved to be only a common man, she drew herself up proudly and looked with a small smile over his head. He hesitated to glance into the open hall, lighted so spaciously with a scarlet-shaded lamp, and at the slim girl in brown silk lifted up before the light. But she, she looked over his head. He passed on.

Presently she started and hung in suspense. Somebody was crossing the road. She ran down the steps in a pretty welcome, not effuse,[3] saying in quick but accurately articulated words: "Will! I began to think you'd gone to the fair. I came out to listen to it. I felt almost sure you'd gone. You're coming in, aren't you?" She waited a moment anxiously. "We expect you to dinner, you know," she added wistfully.

The man, who had a short face and spoke with his lip curling up on one side, in a drawling speech with ironically exaggerated intonation, replied after a short hesitation:

"I'm awfully sorry, I am, straight,[4] Lois. It's a shame. I've got to go round to the biz. Man proposes—the devil disposes." He turned aside with irony in the darkness.

"But surely, Will!" remonstrated the girl, keenly disappointed.

"Fact, Lois!—I feel wild about it myself. But I've got to go down to the works. They may be getting a bit warm down there, you know"—he jerked his head in the direction of the fair. "If the Lambs get frisky!—they're a bit off about the work, and they'd just be in their

---

3. **effuse** [i fūz′]: poured out freely.
4. **straight:** honestly.

element if they could set a lighted match to something——"

"Will, you don't think——!" exclaimed the girl, laying her hand on his arm in the true fashion of romance, and looking up at him earnestly.

"Dad's not sure," he replied, looking down at her with gravity. They remained in this attitude for a moment, then he said:

"I might stop a bit. It's all right for an hour, I should think."

She looked at him earnestly, then said in tones of deep disappointment and of fortitude: "No, Will, you must go. You'd better go——"

"It's a shame!" he murmured, standing a moment at a loose end. Then, glancing down the street to see he was alone, he put his arm round her waist and said in a difficult voice: "How goes it?"

She let him keep her for a moment, then he kissed her as if afraid of what he was doing. They were both uncomfortable.

"Well——!" he said at length.

"Good night!" she said, setting him free to go.

He hung a moment near her, as if ashamed. Then "Good night," he answered, and he broke away. She listened to his footsteps in the night, before composing herself to turn indoors.

"Helloa!" said her father, glancing over his paper as she entered the diningroom. "What's up, then?"

"Oh, nothing," she replied, in her calm tones. "Will won't be here to dinner tonight."

"What, gone to the fair?"

"No."

"Oh! What's got him then?"

Lois looked at her father, and answered:

"He's gone down to the factory. They are afraid of the hands."

Her father looked at her closely.

"Oh, aye!" he answered, undecided, and they sat down to dinner.

3

Lois retired very early. She had a fire in her bedroom. She drew the curtains and stood holding aside a heavy fold, looking out at the night. She could see only the nothingness of the fog; not even the glare of the fair was evident, though the noise clamored small in the distance. In front of everything she could see her own faint image. She crossed to the dressing table, and there leaned her face to the mirror, and looked at herself. She looked a long time, then she rose, changed her dress for a dressing jacket, and took up *Sesame and Lilies*.[5]

Late in the night she was roused from sleep by a bustle in the house. She sat up and heard a hurrying to and fro and the sound of anxious voices. She put on her dressing gown and went out to her mother's room. Seeing her mother at the head of the stairs, she said in her quick clean voice:

"Mother, what is it?"

"Oh, child, don't ask me! Go to bed, dear, do! I shall surely be worried out of my life."

"Mother, what is it?" Lois was sharp and emphatic.

"I hope your father won't go. Now I do hope your father won't go. He's got a cold as it is."

"Mother, tell me what it is?" Lois took her mother's arm.

"It's Selby's. I should have thought you would have heard the fire engine, and Jack isn't in yet. I hope we're safe!" Lois returned to her bedroom and dressed. She coiled her plaited[6] hair, and having put on a cloak, left the house.

She hurried along under the fog-dripping trees toward the meaner part of the town. When she got near, she saw a glare in the fog, and closed her lips tight. She hastened on till she was in the crowd. With peaked, noble face she watched the fire. Then she looked a little wildly over the fire-reddened faces in the crowd, and catching sight of her father, hurried to him.

"Oh, Dadda—is he safe? Is Will safe——?"

"Safe, aye, why not? You've no business

---

5. **Sesame and Lilies:** book by English writer John Ruskin (1819–1900).
6. **plaited** [plā′tid]: braided.

here. Here, here's Sampson, he'll take you home. I've enough to bother me; there's my own place to watch. Go home now, I can't do with you here."

"Have you seen Will?" she asked.

"Go home—Sampson, just take Miss Lois home—now!"

"You don't really know where he is—father?"

"Go home now—I don't want you here——" her father ordered peremptorily.

The tears sprang to Lois' eyes. She looked at the fire and the tears were quickly dried by fear. The flames roared and struggled upward. The great wonder of the fire made her forget even her indignation at her father's light treatment of herself and of her lover. There was a crashing and bursting of timber, as the first floor fell in a mass into the blazing gulf, splashing the fire in all directions, to the terror of the crowd. She saw the steel of the machines growing white-hot and twisting like flaming letters. Piece after piece of the flooring gave way, and the machines dropped in red ruin as the wooden framework burned out. The air became unbreathable; the fog was swallowed up; sparks went rushing up as if they would burn the dark heavens; sometimes cards of lace went whirling into the gulf of the sky, waving with wings of fire. It was dangerous to stand near this great cup of roaring destruction.

Sampson, the gray old manager of Buxton

and Co.'s, led her away as soon as she would turn her face to listen to him. He was a stout, irritable man. He elbowed his way roughly through the crowd, and Lois followed him, her head high, her lips closed. He led her for some distance without speaking, then at last, unable to contain his garrulous irritability, he broke out:

"What do they expect? What can they expect? They can't expect to stand a bad time. They spring up like mushrooms as big as a house side, but there's no stability in 'em. I remember William Selby when he'd run on my errands. Yes, there's some as can make much out of little, and .there's some as can make much out of nothing, but they find it won't last. William Selby's sprung up in a day, and he'll vanish in a night. You can't trust to luck alone. Maybe he thinks it's a lucky thing this fire has come when things are looking black. But you can't get out of it as easy as that. There's been a few too many of 'em. No, indeed, a fire's the last thing I should hope to come to—the very last!"

Lois hurried and hurried, so that she brought the old manager panting in distress up the steps of her home. She could not bear to hear him talking so. They could get no one to open the door for some time. When at last Lois ran upstairs, she found her mother dressed, but all unbuttoned again, lying back in the chair in her daughter's room, suffering from palpitation of the heart, with *Sesame and Lilies* crushed beneath her. Lois administered brandy, and her decisive words and movements helped largely to bring the good lady to a state of recovery sufficient to allow of her returning to her own bedroom.

Then Lois locked the door. She glanced at her fire-darkened face, and taking the flattened Ruskin out of the chair, sat down and wept. After a while she calmed herself, rose and sponged her face. Then once more on that fatal night she prepared for rest. Instead, however, of retiring, she pulled a silk quilt from her disordered bed and, wrapping it round her, sat miserably to think. It was two o'clock in the morning.

4

The fire was sunk to cold ashes in the grate, and the gray morning was creeping through the half-opened curtains like a thing ashamed, when Lois awoke. It was painful to move her head: her neck was cramped. The girl awoke in full recollection. She sighed, roused herself and pulled the quilt closer about her. For a little while she sat and mused. A pale, tragic resignation fixed her face like a mask. She remembered her father's irritable answer to her question concerning her lover's safety—"Safe, aye—why not?" She knew that he suspected the factory of having been purposely set on fire. But then, he had never liked Will. And yet—and yet—Lois' heart was heavy as lead. She felt her lover was guilty. And she felt she must hide her secret of his last communication to her. She saw herself being cross-examined—"When did you last see this man?" But she would hide what he had said about watching at the works. How dreary it was—and how dreadful. Her life was ruined now, and nothing mattered any more. She must only behave with dignity, and submit to her own obliteration. For even if Will were never accused, she knew in her heart he was guilty. She knew it was over between them.

It was dawn among the yellow fog outside, and Lois, as she moved mechanically about her toilet,[7] vaguely felt that all her days would arrive slowly struggling through a bleak fog. She felt an intense longing at this uncanny hour to slough the body's trammeled weariness and to issue at once into the new bright warmth of the far Dawn where a lover waited transfigured; is it so easy and pleasant in imagination to step out of the chill gray dampness of another terrestrial daybreak, straight into the sunshine of the eternal morning? And who can escape his hour? So Lois performed the meaningless routine of her toilet, which at last she made meaningful when she took her black dress, and fastened a black jet brooch at her throat.

---

7. **toilet** [toi′lit]: act of dressing and grooming oneself.

Then she went downstairs and found her father eating a mutton chop. She quickly approached and kissed him on the forehead. Then she retreated to the other end of the table. Her father looked tired, even haggard.

"You are early," he said, after a while. Lois did not reply. Her father continued to eat for a few moments, then he said:

"Have a chop—here's one! Ring for a hot plate. Eh, what? Why not?"

Lois was insulted, but she gave no sign. She sat down and took a cup of coffee, making no pretense to eat. Her father was absorbed, and had forgotten her.

"Our Jack's not come home yet," he said at last.

Lois stirred faintly. "Hasn't he?" she said.

"No." There was silence for a time. Lois was frightened. Had something happened also to her brother? This fear was closer and more irksome.

"Selby's was cleaned out, gutted. We had a near shave of it——"

"You have no loss, Dadda?"

"Nothing to mention." After another silence, her father said:

"I'd rather be myself than William Selby. Of course it may merely be bad luck—you don't know. But whatever it was, I wouldn't like to add one to the list of fires just now. Selby was at the 'George' when it broke out—I don't know where the lad was——!"

"Father," broke in Lois, "why do you talk like that? Why do you talk as if Will had done it?" She ended suddenly. Her father looked at her pale, mute face.

"I don't talk as if Will had done it," he said. "I don't even think it."

Feeling she was going to cry, Lois rose and left the room. Her father sighed, and leaning his elbows on his knees, whistled faintly into the fire. He was not thinking about her.

Lois went down to the kitchen and asked Lucy, the parlor maid, to go out with her. She somehow shrank from going alone, lest people should stare at her overmuch: and she felt an overpowering impulse to go to the scene of the tragedy, to judge for herself.

The churches were chiming half-past eight when the young lady and the maid set off down the street. Nearer the fair, swarthy, thin-legged men were pushing barrels of water toward the market place, and the gypsy women, with hard brows, and dressed in tight velvet bodices, hurried along the pavement with jugs of milk, and great brass water ewers and loaves and breakfast parcels. People were just getting up, and in the poorer streets was a continual splash of tea leaves, flung out on to the cobblestones. A teapot came crashing down from an upper story just behind Lois, and she, starting round and looking up, thought that the trembling, drink-bleared man at the upper window, who was stupidly staring after his pot, had had designs on her life; and she went on her way shuddering at the grim tragedy of life.

In the dull October morning the ruined factory was black and ghastly. The window frames were all jagged, and the walls stood gaunt. Inside was a tangle of twisted debris, the iron, in parts red with bright rust, looking still hot; the charred wood was black and satiny; from disheveled heaps, sodden with water, a faint smoke rose dimly. Lois stood and looked. If he had done that! He might even be dead there, burned to ash and lost forever. It was almost soothing to feel so. He would be safe in the eternity which now she must hope in.

At her side the pretty, sympathetic maid chatted plaintively. Suddenly, from one of her lapses into silences, she exclaimed:

"Why if there isn't Mr. Jack!"

Lois turned suddenly and saw her brother and her lover approaching her. Both looked soiled, untidy and wan. Will had a black eye, some ten hours old, well colored. Lois turned very pale as they approached. They were looking gloomily at the factory, and for a moment did not notice the girls.

"I'll be jiggered if there ain't our Lois!" exclaimed Jack, the reprobate,[8] swearing under his breath.

---

8. **reprobate** [rep′rə bāt′]: unprincipled person.

"Oh, God!" exclaimed the other in disgust.

"Jack, where have you been?" said Lois sharply, in keen pain, not looking at her lover. Her sharp tone of suffering drove her lover to defend himself with an affectation of comic recklessness.

"In quod,"[9] replied her brother, smiling sickly.

"Jack!" cried his sister very sharply.

"Fact."

Will Selby shuffled on his feet and smiled, trying to turn away his face so that she should not see his black eye. She glanced at him. He felt her boundless anger and contempt, and with great courage he looked straight at her, smiling ironically. Unfortunately his smile would not go over his swollen eye, which remained grave and lurid.

"So I look pretty?" he inquired with a hateful twist of his lip.

"Very!" she replied.

"I thought I did," he replied. And he turned to look at his father's ruined works, and he felt miserable and stubborn. The girl standing there so clean and out of it all! Oh, God, he felt sick. He turned to go home.

The three went together, Lois silent in anger and resentment. Her brother was tired and overstrung, but not suppressed. He chattered on, blindly.

"It was a lark we had! We met Bob Osborne and Freddy Mansell coming down Poultry. There was a girl with some geese. She looked a tanger sitting there, all like statues, her and the geese. It was Will who began it. He offered her threepence and asked her to begin the show. She called him a—she called him something, and then somebody poked an old gander to stir him up, and somebody squirted him in the eye. He upped and squawked and started off with his neck out. Laugh! We nearly killed ourselves, keeping back those old birds with squirts and teasers. Oh, Lum! Those old geese, oh, scrimmy, they didn't know where to turn, they fairly went off their dots, coming at us right an' left, and such a row—it was fun, you never knew? Then the girl she got up and knocked somebody over the jaw, and we were right in for it. Well, in the end, Billy here got hold of her round the waist——"

"Oh, dry it up!" exclaimed Will bitterly.

Jack looked at him, laughed mirthlessly, and continued: "An' we said we'd buy her birds. So we got hold of one goose apiece—an' they took some holding. I can tell you—and off we set round the fair, Billy leading with the girl. The bloomin' geese squawked an' pecked. Laugh—I thought I should a' died. Well, then we wanted the girl to have her birds back—and then she fired up. She got some other chaps on her side, and there was a proper old row. The girl went tooth and nail for Will there—she was dead set against him. She gave him a black eye, by gum, and we went at it, I can tell you. It was a free fight, a beauty, an' we got run in. I don't know what became of the girl."

Lois surveyed the two men. There was no glimmer of a smile on her face, though the maid behind her was sniggering. Will was very bitter. He glanced at his sweetheart and at the ruined factory.

"How's dad taken it?" he asked, in a biting, almost humble tone.

"I don't know," she replied coldly. "Father's in an awful way. I believe everybody thinks you set the place on fire."

Lois drew herself up. She had delivered her blow. She drew herself up in cold condemnation and for a moment enjoyed her complete revenge. He was despicable, abject in his disheveled, disfigured, unwashed condition.

"Aye, well, they made a mistake for once," he replied, with a curl of the lip.

Curiously enough, they walked side by side as if they belonged to each other. She was his conscience-keeper. She was far from forgiving him, but she was still farther from letting him go. And he walked at her side like a boy who has to be punished before he can be exonerated. He submitted. But there was a genuine bitter contempt in the curl of his lip.

---

9. **quod** [kwäd]: British slang for "prison."

STUDY QUESTIONS

Recalling

1. Describe the country girl and Lois. What is each doing when she first appears?
2. According to the narrator, what is "the state of trade" at the time of the story?
3. What reason does Will give Lois for not joining her for dinner?
4. What news does Lois learn late at night from her mother? In what way does Lois think Will is involved in this event?
5. Briefly outline the pranks that cause Jack and Will to be arrested.

Interpreting

6. What connection does the story imply between trade, agriculture, and manufacturing?
7. In what ways does the story show an antagonism between classes? Between people and nature?
8. Describe the relationship between Lois and Will. In what ways does Lois show that she does not understand her own feelings for Will?
9. Why do you think Lawrence titled the story "Goose Fair"?

Extending

10. Who do you think started the fire? Why does Lawrence not tell us who started it?

LITERARY FOCUS

Characterization

Characterization is the personality of a character in a short story; it is also the method by which the author reveals that personality. Characters can be many-sided and changing, as surprising as real people, or they can be simple and one dimensional. They must, however, seem true to life and act in believable ways. To make characters credible, the author must supply **motivation,** stated or implied reasons for their behavior.

Characterization can be direct or indirect. With **direct characterization** the author directly states facts about a character's personality; with **indi-** rect characterization the author reveals a character's personality indirectly through the character's physical appearance, words, thoughts, and actions or through what other characters say about that character. In addition, the author may present a **flat character**—one with only one personality trait—or a **round,** or **complex, character**—one with many different, even contradictory, traits. A character can also be dynamic or static. **Dynamic characters** change in the course of a story because of the influence of events or other people. **Static characters** remain primarily the same throughout a story.

Thinking About Characterization

1. What motivation does the story imply for Jack and Will in their argument with the country girl?
2. What personality traits of the country girl do we learn through direct characterization? Through indirect characterization?
3. Explain how Lois is a realistic character, both round and dynamic.

COMPOSITION

Writing About a Symbol

◼ Many objects, characters, and actions in Lawrence's fiction are symbolic. Write a brief essay about one symbol in "Goose Fair." First identify the symbol, and explain its meaning. Then discuss the significance of the symbol in the story as a whole, explaining how it relates to the theme of the story. *For help with this assignment, refer to Lesson 5 in the Writing About Literature Handbook at the back of this book.*

Writing a Sequel to the Story

◼ Write a short continuation of "Goose Fair" in which Lois and the country girl meet. Write in omniscient point of view (page 716), and include narration, description, and dialogue. Be sure to explain the circumstances of their meeting and to demonstrate the fact that they come from very different backgrounds.

Virginia Woolf   *1882–1941*

In her critical essays Virginia Woolf set standards for modern fiction, and she met those standards in a string of finely detailed, introspective novels and stories. Woolf grew up in a home where famous intellectuals and artists were frequent guests. Her father, Sir Leslie Stephen, was the first editor of the *Dictionary of National Biography,* and he introduced his children to great minds and great books. As an adult Woolf founded the Hogarth Press with her husband, Leonard Woolf, who was also a writer. They published much of their own work and became the center of the **Bloomsbury Group**, a circle of famous artists, writers, and philosophers that was named for a London neighborhood where they congregated.

Woolf began her writing career as a literary critic. She used her reviews and essays to promote her strong opinions about what fiction should be. For example, she thought that writers could get close to real life only by basing their work in their own feelings. In 1915 she began to put her theories into practice in her first novel, *The Voyage Out.* She continued to refine her style in eight other novels—among them *Mrs. Dalloway* (1925) and *To the Lighthouse* (1927)—and four collections of short stories.

Woolf's work was a deliberate attempt to break the conventions of fiction. She saw life not as a series of carefully arranged bright lights but as "a luminous halo, a semi-transparent envelope surrounding us from the beginning of consciousness to the end." In other words, life is not a neatly arranged series of major events but a process we live every day. To be faithful to this idea, her fiction avoids plot as we know it and instead swirls through the consciousness of characters, revealing the essence of their lives. With James Joyce, Woolf was among the first to use this stream-of-consciousness technique. Her stories are quiet episodes seen through the minds of the characters. The intention was to "examine for a moment an ordinary mind on an ordinary day," to uncover people as they really are. By pouring out one thought after another in a steady stream, characters reveal who they are and what they feel. Mabel Waring is such a character, and in "The New Dress" she reveals herself to us through a constant stream of memories, thoughts, and observations.

■ Have you ever gone to a party in the wrong kind of clothes? How did you feel? What did you say? Did anyone at the party notice your clothes?

Virginia Woolf

The New Dress

Mabel had her first serious suspicion that something was wrong as she took her cloak off and Mrs. Barnet, while handing her the mirror and touching the brushes and thus drawing her attention, perhaps rather markedly, to all the appliances for tidying and improving hair, complexion, clothes, which existed on the dressing table, confirmed the suspicion—that it was not right, not quite right, which growing stronger as she went upstairs and springing at her with conviction as she greeted Clarissa Dalloway, she went straight to the far end of the room, to a shaded corner where a looking glass hung and looked. No! It was not *right*. And at once the misery which she always tried to hide, the profound dissatisfaction—the sense she had had, ever since she was a child, of being inferior to other people—set upon her, relentlessly, remorselessly, with an intensity which she could not beat off, as she would when she woke at night at home, by reading Borrow[1] or Scott;[2] for oh these men, oh these women, all were thinking—"What's Mabel wearing? What a fright she looks! What a hideous new dress!"—their eyelids flickering as they came up and then their lids shutting rather tight. It was her own appalling inadequacy; her cowardice; her mean, water-sprinkled blood that depressed her. And at once the whole of the room where, for ever so many hours, she had planned with the little dressmaker how it was to go, seemed sordid, repulsive; and her own drawing room so shabby, and herself, going out, puffed up with vanity as she touched the letters on the hall table and said, "How dull!" to show off— all this now seemed unutterably silly, paltry, and provincial. All this had been absolutely de-stroyed, shown up, exploded, the moment she came into Mrs. Dalloway's drawing room.

What she had thought that evening when, sitting over the teacups, Mrs. Dalloway's invitation came, was that, of course, she could not be fashionable. It was absurd to pretend it even—fashion meant cut, meant style, meant thirty guineas at least—but why not be original? Why not be herself, anyhow? And, getting up, she had taken that old fashion book of her mother's, a Paris fashion book of the time of the Empire, and had thought how much prettier, more dignified, and more womanly they were then, and so set herself—oh, it was foolish—trying to be like them, pluming herself in fact, upon being modest and old-fashioned and very charming, giving herself up, no doubt about it, to an orgy of self-love, which deserved to be chastised, and so rigged herself out like this.

But she dared not look in the glass. She could not face the whole horror—the pale yellow, idiotically old-fashioned silk dress with its long skirt and its high sleeves and its waist and all the things that looked so charming in the fashion book, but not on her, not among all these ordinary people. She felt like a dressmaker's dummy standing there, for young people to stick pins into.

"But, my dear, it's perfectly charming!" Rose Shaw said, looking her up and down with that little satirical pucker of the lips which she expected—Rose herself being dressed in the height of the fashion, precisely like everybody else, always.

We are all like flies trying to crawl over the edge of the saucer, Mabel thought, and repeated the phrase as if she were crossing herself, as if she were trying to find some spell to annul this pain, to make this agony endurable. Tags of Shakespeare, lines from books she had read ages ago, suddenly came to her when she

---

1. **Borrow:** George Borrow (1803–1881), English traveler and novelist.
2. **Scott:** Sir Walter Scott (1771–1832), Scottish poet, novelist, journalist.

was in agony, and she repeated them over and over again. "Flies trying to crawl," she repeated. If she could say that over often enough and make herself see the flies, she would become numb, chill, frozen, dumb. Now she could see flies crawling slowly out of a saucer of milk with their wings stuck together; and she strained and strained (standing in front of the looking glass, listening to Rose Shaw) to make herself see Rose Shaw and all the other people there as flies, trying to hoist themselves out of something, or into something, meager, insignificant, toiling flies. But she could not see them like that, not other people. She saw herself like that—she was a fly, but the others were dragonflies, butterflies, beautiful insects, dancing, fluttering, skimming, while she alone dragged herself up out of the saucer. (Envy and spite, the most detestable of the vices, were her chief faults.)

"I feel like some dowdy, decrepit, horribly dingy old fly," she said, making Robert Haydon stop just to hear her say that, just to reassure herself by furbishing up a poor weak-kneed phrase and so showing how detached she was, how witty, that she did not feel in the least out of anything. And, of course, Robert Haydon answered something quite polite, quite insincere, which she saw through instantly, and said to herself, directly he went (again from some book), "Lies, lies, lies!" For a party makes things either much more real, or much less real, she thought; she saw in a flash to the bottom of Robert Haydon's heart; she saw through everything. She saw the truth. *This* was true, this drawing room, this self, and the other false. Miss Milan's little workroom was really terribly hot, stuffy, sordid. It smelled of clothes and cabbage cooking; and yet, when Miss Milan put the glass in her hand, and she looked at herself with the dress on, finished, an extraordinary bliss shot through her heart. Suffused with light, she sprang into existence. Rid of cares and wrinkles, what she had dreamed of herself was there—a beautiful woman. Just for a second (she had not dared look longer, Miss Milan wanted to know about the length of the skirt), there looked at her, framed in the scrolloping mahogany, a gray-white, mysteriously smiling, charming girl, the core of herself, the soul of herself; and it was not vanity only, not only self-love that made her think it good, tender, and true. Miss Milan said that the skirt could not well be longer; if anything the skirt, said Miss Milan, puckering her forehead, considering with all her wits about her, must be shorter; and she felt, suddenly, honestly, full of love for Miss Milan, much, much fonder of Miss Milan than of anyone in the whole world, and

Detail, *The Masquerade Dress,* Robert Henri, 1911.

could have cried for pity that she should be crawling on the floor with her mouth full of pins, and her face red and her eyes bulging—that one human being should be doing this for another, and she saw them all as human beings merely, and herself going off to her party, and Miss Milan pulling the cover over the canary's cage, or letting him pick a hempseed from between her lips, and the thought of it, of this side of human nature and its patience and its endurance and its being content with such miserable, scanty, sordid little pleasures filled her eyes with tears.

And now the whole thing had vanished. The dress, the room, the love, the pity, the scrolloping looking glass, and the canary's cage—all had vanished, and here she was in a corner of Mrs. Dalloway's drawing room, suffering tortures, woken wide awake to reality.

But it was all so paltry, weak-blooded, and petty-minded to care so much at her age with two children, to be still so utterly dependent on people's opinions and not have principles or convictions, not to be able to say as other people did, "There's Shakespeare! There's death! We're all weevils in a captain's biscuit"—or whatever it was that people did say.

She faced herself straight in the glass; she pecked at her left shoulder; she issued out into the room, as if spears were thrown at her yellow dress from all sides. But instead of looking fierce or tragic, as Rose Shaw would have done—Rose would have looked like Boadicea[3] —she looked foolish and self-conscious, and simpered like a schoolgirl and slouched across the room, positively slinking, as if she were a beaten mongrel, and looked at a picture, an engraving. As if one went to a party to look at a picture! Everybody knew why she did it—it was from shame, from humiliation.

"Now the fly's in the saucer," she said to herself, "right in the middle, and can't get out,

and the milk," she thought, rigidly staring at the picture, "is sticking its wings together."

"It's so old-fashioned," she said to Charles Burt, making him stop (which by itself he hated) on his way to talk to someone else.

She meant, or she tried to make herself think that she meant, that it was the picture and not her dress that was old-fashioned. And one word of praise, one word of affection from Charles would have made all the difference to her at the moment. If he had only said, "Mabel, you're looking charming tonight!" it would have changed her life. But then she ought to have been truthful and direct. Charles said nothing of the kind, of course. He was malice itself. He always saw through one, especially if one were feeling particularly mean, paltry, or feeble-minded.

"Mabel's got a new dress!" he said, and the poor fly was absolutely shoved into the middle of the saucer. Really, he would like her to drown, she believed. He had no heart, no fundamental kindness, only a veneer of friendliness. Miss Milan was much more real, much kinder. If only one could feel that and stick to it always. "Why," she asked herself—replying to Charles much too pertly, letting him see that she was out of temper, or "ruffled" as he called it ("Rather ruffled?" he said and went on to laugh at her with some woman over there)—"Why," she asked herself, "can't I feel one thing always, feel quite sure that Miss Milan is right, and Charles wrong and stick to it, feel sure about the canary and pity and love and not be whipped all round in a second by coming into a room full of people?" It was her odious, weak, vacillating character again, always giving at the critical moment and not being seriously interested in conchology, etymology, botany, archaeology, cutting up potatoes and watching them fructify[4] like Mary Dennis, like Violet Searle.

Then Mrs. Holman, seeing her standing there, bore down upon her. Of course a thing

---

3. **Boadicea** [bō ad′ə sē′ə]: queen in ancient Britain who led a revolt against the Romans, was defeated, and poisoned herself in A.D. 62.

4. **fructify**: bear fruit.

like a dress was beneath Mrs. Holman's notice, with her family always tumbling downstairs or having the scarlet fever. Could Mabel tell her if Elmthorpe was ever let for August and September? Oh, it was a conversation that bored her unutterably!—it made her furious to be treated like a house agent or a messenger boy, to be made use of. Not to have value, that was it, she thought, trying to grasp something hard, something real, while she tried to answer sensibly about the bathroom and the south aspect and the hot water to the top of the house; and all the time she could see little bits of her yellow dress in the round looking glass which made them all the size of boot buttons or tadpoles; and it was amazing to think how much humiliation and agony and self-loathing and effort and passionate ups and downs of feeling were contained in a thing the size of a threepenny bit. And what was still odder, this thing, this Mabel Waring, was separate, quite disconnected; and though Mrs. Holman (the black button) was leaning forward and telling her how her eldest boy had strained his heart running, she could see her, too, quite detached in the looking glass, and it was impossible that the black dot, leaning forward, gesticulating, should make the yellow dot, sitting solitary, self-centered, feel what the black dot was feeling, yet they pretended.

"So impossible to keep boys quiet"—that was the kind of thing one said.

And Mrs. Holman, who could never get enough sympathy and snatched what little there was greedily, as if it were her right (but she deserved much more for there was her little girl who had come down this morning with a swollen kneejoint), took this miserable offering and looked at it suspiciously, grudgingly, as if it were a halfpenny when it ought to have been a pound and put it away in her purse, must put up with it, mean and miserly though it was, times being hard, so very hard; and on she went, creaking, injured Mrs. Holman, about the girl with the swollen joints. Ah, it was tragic, this greed, this clamor of human beings, like a row of cormorants,[5] barking and flapping their wings for sympathy—it was tragic, could one have felt it and not merely pretended to feel it!

But in her yellow dress tonight she could not wring out one drop more; she wanted it all, all for herself. She knew (she kept on looking into the glass, dipping into that dreadfully showing up blue pool) that she was condemned, despised, left like this in a backwater, because of her being like this a feeble, vacillating creature; and it seemed to her that the yellow dress was a penance which she had deserved, and if she had been dressed like Rose Shaw, in lovely, clinging green with a ruffle of swansdown, she would have deserved that; and she thought that there was no escape for her—none whatever. But it was not her fault altogether, after all. It was being one of a family of ten; never having money enough, always skimping and paring; and her mother carrying great cans, and the linoleum worn on the stair edges, and one sordid little domestic tragedy after another—nothing catastrophic, the sheep farm failing, but not utterly; her eldest brother marrying beneath him but not very much—there was no romance, nothing extreme about them all. They petered out respectably in seaside resorts; every watering place had one of her aunts even now asleep in some lodging with the front windows not quite facing the sea. That was so like them—they had to squint at things always. And she had done the same—she was just like her aunts. For all her dreams of living in India, married to some hero like Sir Henry Lawrence,[6] some empire builder (still the sight of a native in a turban filled her with romance), she had failed utterly. She had married Hubert, with his safe, permanent underling's job in the Law Courts, and they managed tolerably in a smallish house without proper

---

5. **cormorants:** large swimming and diving birds with webbed feet and voracious appetites. Greedy people are sometimes referred to as cormorants.
6. **Sir Henry Lawrence:** (1806–1857), English general and administrator in India.

maids and hash when she was alone or just bread and butter, but now and then—Mrs. Holman was off, thinking her the most dried up, unsympathetic twig she had ever met, absurdly dressed, too, and would tell everyone about Mabel's fantastic appearance—now and then, thought Mabel Waring, left alone on the blue sofa, punching the cushion in order to look occupied, for she would not join Charles Burt and Rose Shaw, chattering like magpies and perhaps laughing at her by the fireplace—now and then, there did come to her delicious moments, reading the other night in bed, for instance, or down by the sea on the sand in the sun at Easter—let her recall it—a great tuft of pale sand grass standing all twisted like a shock of spears against the sky, which was blue like a smooth china egg, so firm, so hard, and then the melody of the waves—"Hush, hush," they said, and the children's shouts paddling—yes, it was a divine moment, and there she lay, she felt, in the hand of the Goddess who was the world; rather a hard-hearted, but very beautiful Goddess, a little lamb laid on the altar (one did think these silly things, and it didn't matter so long as one never said them). And also with Hubert sometimes she had quite unexpectedly—carving the mutton for Sunday lunch, for no reason, opening a letter, coming into a room—divine moments, when she said to herself (for she would never say this to anybody else), "This is it. This has happened. This is it!" And the other way about it was equally surprising—that is, when everything was arranged—music, weather, holidays, every reason for happiness was there—then nothing happened at all. One wasn't happy. It was flat, just flat, that was all.

Her wretched self again, no doubt! She had always been a fretful, weak, unsatisfactory mother, a wobbly wife, lolling about in a kind of twilight existence with nothing very clear or very bold, or more one thing than another, like all her brothers and sisters, except perhaps Herbert—they were all the same poor water-veined creatures who did nothing. Then in the midst of this creeping, crawling life, suddenly she was on the crest of a wave. That wretched fly—where had she read the story that kept coming into her mind about the fly and the saucer?—struggled out. Yes, she had those moments. But now that she was forty, they might come more and more seldom. By degrees she would cease to struggle any more. But that was deplorable! That was not to be endured! That made her feel ashamed of herself!

She would go to the London Library tomorrow. She would find some wonderful, helpful, astonishing book, quite by chance, a book by a clergyman, by an American no one had ever heard of; or she would walk down the Strand and drop, accidentally, into a hall where a miner was telling about the life in the pit, and suddenly she would become a new person. She would be absolutely transformed. She would wear a uniform; she would be called Sister Somebody; she would never give a thought to clothes again. And forever after she would be perfectly clear about Charles Burt and Miss Milan and this room and that room; and it would be always, day after day, as if she were lying in the sun or carving the mutton. It would be it!

So she got up from the blue sofa, and the yellow button in the looking glass got up too, and she waved her hand to Charles and Rose to show them she did not depend on them one scrap, and the yellow button moved out of the looking glass, and all the spears were gathered into her breast as she walked toward Mrs. Dalloway and said, "Good night."

"But it's too early to go," said Mrs. Dalloway, who was always so charming.

"I'm afraid I must," said Mabel Waring. "But," she added in her weak, wobbly voice which only sounded ridiculous when she tried to strengthen it, "I have enjoyed myself enormously."

"I have enjoyed myself," she said to Mr. Dalloway, whom she met on the stairs.

"Lies, lies, lies!" she said to herself, going downstairs, and "Right in the saucer!" she said to herself as she thanked Mrs. Barnet for helping her and wrapped herself round and round and round in the Chinese cloak she had worn these twenty years.

STUDY QUESTIONS

Recalling

1. How long has Mabel had feelings of inferiority? What brings out these feelings at the party?
2. Find at least three flaws that Mabel sees in her own personality.
3. Briefly outline Mabel's family background and marriage.
4. Give at least three examples of what Mabel considers happy moments from her everyday life.

Interpreting

5. What do we learn about Mabel from her reasons for choosing the new dress?
6. What kinds of activity and people does Mabel most and least enjoy? Explain how her preferences relate to her upbringing.
7. Explain how Mabel's plan to become a new person reveals a cause of her unhappiness.
8. In what ways does her sense of inferiority become a barrier between Mabel and other people?

Extending

9. In what ways can self-criticism be helpful? In what ways can it be harmful?

LITERARY FOCUS

Stream of Consciousness

Stream of consciousness is a term originated by American psychologist William James to describe human thought as a continuous flow of observation and reflection. Our minds jump without apparent logic and without rest from one thought to another. In literature **stream of consciousness** is a method of writing that imitates human thought with a continuous and formless flow of ideas, feelings, observations, and memories. Unlike stories with conventional plots, stream-of-consciousness stories may change topic suddenly and illogically in order to imitate the way the mind suddenly shifts from one thought to another. The author seldom speaks directly to the reader but allows characters to reveal themselves through their thoughts. Stream of consciousness can be written in first or third person. The technique was pioneered by James Joyce in his first novel, *A Portrait of the Artist as a Young Man.*

Thinking About Stream of Consciousness

1. In what sense is "The New Dress" a stream-of-consciousness story?
2. Find at least two examples of sudden shifts in the narrative that imitate the way that the mind jumps from one thought to another.

COMPOSITION

Writing About Character

Because "The New Dress" is a stream-of-consciousness story, we learn about Mabel indirectly from her own thoughts and actions. Describe your impressions of Mabel's personality, and explain how the story gave you the impressions. To do this, identify at least four personality traits; be sure that at least two traits are positive traits that Mabel herself may not be aware of. For each trait explain what specific thoughts or actions in the story revealed the trait to you.

Writing with Stream-of-Consciousness Technique

Write a short sketch of a person whose problem is the opposite of Mabel's, a superiority complex. Use the stream-of-consciousness technique, and be sure that everything in your sketch is in the form of your character's thoughts. First record your character's impressions of a setting in which other people are present. Then give the character's impressions of other people and of himself or herself.

COMPARING WRITERS

Choose two or more of the following stories: "The Lagoon," "The Japanese Quince," "Araby," "The Singing Lesson," " Goose Fair," and "The New Dress." Compare the ways in which the stories delve into the minds of their characters. To what extent is external reality pictured in each story? How deeply does each story delve into a character's thoughts? How much sympathy is created for the character by revealing that character's thoughts?

George Orwell   *1903–1950*

George Orwell wrote fiction and nonfiction that was inspired by a strong social conscience. He was born Eric Blair in Bengal, India. His father was a minor customs official who sacrificed to send his son to preparatory schools in England. Eric felt inferior among his wealthier schoolmates, and human relationships were always difficult for him. The class distinctions that he learned at school also made him sympathetic to the working class and to victims of injustice. Such attitudes later influenced some of his most successful writing, which includes novels, essays, and autobiographical nonfiction.

Instead of going to college, Orwell joined the Indian Imperial Police in Burma in southeast Asia. He worked there five years and developed a permanent distaste for imperialism, or the maintenance of a colonial empire such as the colonies Britain had in Asia. This experience also provided the material for *Burmese Days* (1934), his first novel. After returning to Europe, Orwell held a number of menial jobs that kept him on the edge of poverty. From this experience he wrote *Down and Out in Paris and London* (1933). In 1936 he was wounded while fighting for the Loyalists (those fighting against military dictatorship) in the Spanish civil war. He recorded his observations of the war and his disillusionment with the infighting of the Loyalists in *Homage to Catalonia* (1938).

Orwell was inspired by his experiences in Spain and by World War II to write the novels for which he is best known. *Animal Farm* (1945) is a fable and a satire on dictatorships. *Nineteen Eight-Four* (1949) is Orwell's prophetic warning about the spread of totalitarianism. Both novels demonstrate his chief concern as a writer: to alert humanity to the evils of political tyranny.

"Shooting an Elephant," though it reads much like a short story, is actually a nonfiction piece, a personal essay recounting one of Orwell's experiences as a member of the Indian Imperial Police in Burma. It is one of Orwell's most famous shorter works, a strong attack on the effects of imperialism on both the colonizers and the colonized.

■ Have you ever had to do something you did not want to do because it was your job or because someone expected you to do it? How did you feel?

George Orwell

Shooting an Elephant

In Moulmein,[1] in Lower Burma, I was hated by large numbers of people—the only time in my life that I have been important enough for this to happen to me. I was subdivisional police officer of the town, and in an aimless, petty kind of way anti-European feeling was very bitter. No one had the guts to raise a riot, but if a European woman went through the bazaars alone somebody would probably spit betel juice[2] over her dress. As a police officer I was an obvious target and was baited whenever it seemed safe to do so. When a nimble Burman tripped me up on the football field and the referee (another Burman) looked the other way, the crowd yelled with hideous laughter. This happened more than once. In the end the sneering yellow faces of young men that met me everywhere, the insults hooted after me when I was at a safe distance, got badly on my nerves. The young Buddhist priests were the worst of all. There were several thousands of them in the town and none of them seemed to have anything to do except stand on street corners and jeer at Europeans.

All this was perplexing and upsetting. For at that time I had already made up my mind that imperialism was an evil thing and the sooner I chucked up my job and got out of it the better. Theoretically—and secretly, of course—I was all for the Burmese and all against their oppressors, the British. As for the job I was doing, I hated it more bitterly than I can perhaps make clear. In a job like that you see the dirty work of Empire at close quarters. The wretched prisoners huddling in the stinking cages of the lockups, the gray, cowed faces of the long-term convicts, the scarred buttocks of the men who had been flogged with bamboos—all these oppressed me with an intolerable sense of guilt. But I could get

nothing into perspective. I was young and ill-educated and I had had to think out my problems in the utter silence that is imposed on every Englishman in the East. I did not even know that the British Empire is dying, still less did I know that it is a great deal better than the younger empires that are going to supplant it. All I knew was that I was stuck between my hatred of the empire I served and my rage against the evil-spirited little beasts who tried to make my job impossible. With one part of my mind I thought of the British Raj[3] as an unbreakable tyranny, as something clamped down, in *saecula saeculorum,*[4] upon the will of prostrate peoples; with another part I thought that the greatest joy in the world would be to drive a bayonet into a Buddhist priest's guts. Feelings like these are the normal byproducts of imperialism; ask any Anglo-Indian official, if you can catch him off duty.

One day something happened which in a roundabout way was enlightening. It was a tiny incident in itself, but it gave me a better glimpse than I had had before of the real nature of imperialism—the real motives for which despotic governments act. Early one morning the sub-inspector at a police station the other end of town rang me up on the phone and said that an elephant was ravaging the bazaar. Would I please come and do something about it? I did not know what I could do, but I wanted to see what was happening and I got on to a pony and started out. I took my rifle, an old .44 Winchester and much too small to kill an elephant, but I thought the noise might be useful *in terrorem.*[5] Various Burmans stopped me on the way and told me about the elephant's doings. It was not, of course, a wild elephant, but a tame one which had gone

---

1. **Moulmein** [mo͞ol mān′]
2. **betel** [bēt′əl] **juice:** mixture of leaves, lime, and the juice of betel-palm nuts; commonly chewed in Asia and the South Pacific.

3. **Raj** [räj]: government or rule, especially in India or elsewhere in Asia.
4. *in saecula saeculorum* [in sē′ko͞o lə sē′ko͞o lôr′əm]: Latin for "forever and ever."
5. *in terrorem:* Latin for "for terror."

"must."[6] It had been chained up, as tame elephants always are when their attack of "must" is due, but on the previous night it had broken its chain and escaped. Its mahout,[7] the only person who could manage it when it was in that state, had set out in pursuit, but had taken the wrong direction and was now twelve hours' journey away, and in the morning the elephant had suddenly reappeared in the town. The Burmese population had no weapons and were quite helpless against it. It had already destroyed somebody's bamboo hut, killed a cow and raised some fruit stalls and devoured the stock; also it had met the municipal rubbish van and, when the driver jumped out and took to his heels, had turned the van over and inflicted violence upon it.

The Burmese subinspector and some Indian constables[8] were waiting for me in the quarter where the elephant had been seen. It was a very poor quarter, a labyrinth of squalid bamboo huts, thatched with palm-leaf, winding all over a steep hillside. I remember that it was a cloudy, stuffy morning at the beginning of the rains. We began questioning the people as to where the elephant had gone and, as usual, failed to get any definite information. That is invariably the case in the East; a story always sounds clear enough at a distance, but the nearer you get to the scene of events the vaguer it becomes. Some of the people said that the elephant had gone in one direction, some said that he had gone in another, some professed not even to have heard of any elephant. I had almost made up my mind that the whole story was a pack of lies, when we heard yells a little distance away. There was a loud, scandalized cry of "Go away, child! Go away this instant!" and an old woman with a switch[9] in her hand came around the corner of a hut, violently shooing away a crowd of naked children. Some more women followed, clicking their tongues and exclaiming; evidently there was something that the children ought not to have seen. I

rounded the hut and saw a man's dead body sprawling in the mud. He was an Indian, a black Dravidian coolie,[10] almost naked, and he could not have been dead many minutes. The people said that the elephant had come suddenly upon him round the corner of the hut, caught him with its trunk, put its foot on his back and ground him into the earth. This was the rainy season and the ground was soft, and his face had scored a trench a foot deep and a couple of yards long. He was lying on his belly with arms crucified and head sharply twisted to one side. His face was coated with mud, the eyes wide open, the teeth bared and grinning with an expression of unendurable agony. (Never tell me, by the way, that the dead look peaceful. Most of the corpses I have seen looked devilish.) The friction of the great beast's foot had stripped the skin from his back as neatly as one skins a rabbit. As soon as I saw the dead man I sent an orderly[11] to a friend's house nearby to borrow an elephant rifle. I had already sent back the pony, not wanting it to go mad with fright and throw me if it smelt the elephant.

The orderly came back in a few minutes with a rifle and five cartridges, and meanwhile some Burmans had arrived and told us that the elephant was in the paddy fields below, only a few hundred yards away. As I started forward practically the whole population of the quarter flocked out of the houses and followed me. They had seen the rifle and were all shouting excitedly that I was going to shoot the elephant. They had not shown much interest in the elephant when he was merely ravaging their homes, but it was different now that he was going to be shot. It was a bit of fun to them, as it would be to an English crowd; besides they wanted the meat. It made me vaguely uneasy. I had no intention of shooting the elephant—I had merely sent for the rifle to defend myself if necessary—and it is always unnerving to have a crowd following you. I marched down the hill, looking and feeling a fool, with the rifle over my shoulder and an ever-

---

6. **gone "must"**: gone into a dangerous frenzy that periodically attacks some animals.
7. **mahout** [mə hoōt']: elephant keeper.
8. **constables**: police officers.
9. **switch**: twig or stick used for whipping.

10. **Dravidian coolie**: menial worker belonging to a race of people from southern India and Sri Lanka.
11. **orderly**: military aid.

growing army of people jostling at my heels. At the bottom, when you got away from the huts, there was a metaled[12] road and beyond that a miry waste of paddy fields a thousand yards across, not yet ploughed but soggy from the first rains and dotted with coarse grass. The elephant was standing eight yards from the road, his left side toward us. He took not the slightest notice of the crowd's approach. He was tearing up bunches of grass, beating them against his knees to clean them and stuffing them into his mouth.

I had halted on the road. As soon as I saw the elephant I knew with perfect certainty that I ought not to shoot him. It is a serious matter to shoot a working elephant—it is comparable to destroying a huge and costly piece of machinery—and obviously one ought not to do it if it can possibly be avoided. And at that distance, peacefully eating, the elephant looked no more dangerous than a cow. I thought then and I think now that his attack of "must" was already passing off; in which case he would merely wander harmlessly about until the mahout came back and caught him. Moreover, I did not in the least want to shoot him. I decided that I would watch him for a little while to make sure that he did not turn savage again, and then go home.

But at that moment I glanced round at the crowd that had followed me. It was an immense crowd, two thousand at the least and growing every minute. It blocked the road for a long distance on either side. I looked at the sea of yellow faces above the garish clothes—faces all happy and excited over this bit of fun, all certain that the elephant was going to be shot. They were watching me as they would watch a conjurer about to perform a trick. They did not like me, but with the magical rifle in my hands I was momentarily worth watching. And suddenly I realized that I should have to shoot the elephant after all. The people expected it of me and I had to do it; I could feel their two thousand wills pressing me forward, irresistibly. And it was at this moment, as I stood there with the rifle in my hands, that I first grasped the hollowness, the fu-

tility of the white man's dominion in the East. Here was I, the white man with his gun, standing in front of the unarmed native crowd—seemingly the leading actor of the piece; but in reality I was only an absurd puppet pushed to and fro by the will of those yellow faces behind. I perceived in this moment that when the white man turns tyrant it is his own freedom that he destroys. He becomes a sort of hollow, posing dummy, the conventionalized figure of a sahib.[13] For it is the condition of his rule that he shall spend his life in trying to impress the "natives," and so in every crisis he has got to do what the "natives" expect of him. He wears a mask, and his face grows to fit it. I had got to shoot the elephant. I had committed myself to doing it when I sent for the rifle. A sahib has got to act like a sahib; he has got to appear resolute, to know his own mind and do definite things. To come all that way, rifle in hand, with two thousand people marching at my heels, and then to trail feebly away, having done nothing—no, that was impossible. The crowd would laugh at me. And my whole life, every white man's life in the East, was one long struggle not to be laughed at.

But I did not want to shoot the elephant. I watched him beating his bunch of grass against his knees, with that preoccupied grandmotherly air that elephants have. It seemed to me that it would be murder to shoot him. At that age I was not squeamish about killing animals, but I had never shot an elephant and never wanted to. (Somehow it always seems worse to kill a *large* animal.) Besides, there was the beast's owner to be considered. Alive, the elephant was worth at least a hundred pounds; dead, he would only be worth the value of his tusks, five pounds, possibly. But I had got to act quickly. I turned to some experienced-looking Burmans who had been there when we arrived, and asked them how the elephant had been behaving. They all said the same thing: he took no notice of you if you left him alone, but he might charge if you went too close to him.

---

12. **metaled:** paved.

13. **sahib** [sä′(h)ib, sä′(h)ēb]: title used by natives of India to address a European gentleman.

It was perfectly clear to me what I ought to do. I ought to walk up to within, say, twenty-five yards of the elephant and test his behavior. If he charged, I could shoot; if he took no notice of me, it would be safe to leave him until the mahout came back. But also I knew that I was going to do no such thing. I was a poor shot with a rifle, and the ground was soft mud into which one would sink at every step. If the elephant charged and I missed him, I should have about as much chance as a toad under a steamroller. But even then I was not thinking particularly of my own skin, only of the watchful yellow faces behind. For at that moment, with the crowd watching me, I was not afraid in the ordinary sense, as I would have been if I had been alone. A white man mustn't be frightened in front of "natives"; and so, in general, he isn't frightened. The sole thought in my mind was that if anything went wrong those two thousand Burmans would see me pursued, caught, trampled on and reduced to a grinning corpse like that Indian up the hill. And if that happened it was quite probable that some of them would laugh. That would never do. There was only one alternative. I shoved the cartridges into the magazine and lay down on the road to get a better aim.

The crowd grew very still, and a deep, low, happy sigh, as of people who see the theater curtain go up at last, breathed from innumerable throats. They were going to have their bit of fun after all. The rifle was a beautiful German thing with cross-hair sights. I did not then know that in shooting an elephant one would shoot to cut an imaginary bar running from earhole to earhole. I ought, therefore, as the elephant was sideways on, to have aimed straight at his earhole; actually I aimed several inches in front of this, thinking the brain would be further forward.

When I pulled the trigger I did not hear the bang or feel the kick—one never does when a shot goes home—but I heard the devilish roar of glee that went up from the crowd. In that instant, in too short a time, one would have thought, even for the bullet to get there, a mysterious, terrible change had come over the elephant. He neither stirred nor fell, but every line of his body had altered. He looked suddenly stricken, shrunken, immensely old, as though the frightful impact of the bullet had paralyzed him without knocking him down. At last, after what seemed a long time—it might have been five seconds, I dare say—he sagged flabbily to his knees. His mouth slobbered. An enormous senility seemed to have settled upon him. One could have imagined him thousands of years old. I fired again into the same spot. At the second shot he did not collapse but climbed with desperate slowness to his feet and stood weakly upright, with legs sagging and head drooping. I fired a third time. That was the shot that did for him. You could see the agony of it jolt his whole body and knock the last remnant of strength from his legs. But in falling he seemed for a moment to rise, for as his hind legs collapsed beneath him he seemed to tower upward like a huge rock toppling, his trunk reaching skyward like a tree. He trumpeted, for the first and only time. And then down he came, his belly toward me, with a crash that seemed to shake the ground even where I lay.

I got up. The Burmans were already racing past me across the mud. It was obvious that the elephant would never rise again, but he was not dead. He was breathing very rhythmically with long rattling gasps, his great mound of a side painfully rising and falling. His mouth was wide open—I could see far down into caverns of pale pink throat. I waited a long time for him to die, but his breathing did not weaken. Finally I fired my two remaining shots into the spot where I thought his heart must be. The thick blood welled out of him like red velvet, but still he did not die. His body did not even jerk when the shots hit him, the tortured breathing continued without a pause. He was dying, very slowly and in great agony, but in some world remote from me where not even a bullet could damage him further. I felt that I had got to put an end to that dreadful noise. It seemed dreadful to see the great beast lying there, powerless to move and yet powerless to die, and not even to be able to finish him. I sent back for my small rifle and poured shot after shot into his heart and down his throat. They seemed to make no impression. The tortured gasps continued as steadily as the ticking of a clock.

In the end I could not stand it any longer and went away. I heard later that it took him half an hour to die. Burmans were bringing dahs[14] and baskets even before I left, and I was told they had stripped his body almost to the bones by the afternoon.

Afterward, of course, there were endless discussions about the shooting of the elephant. The owner was furious, but he was only an Indian and could do nothing. Besides, legally I had done the right thing, for a mad elephant has to be killed, like a mad dog, if its owner fails to control it.

Among the Europeans opinion was divided. The older men said I was right, the younger men said it was a damn shame to shoot an elephant for killing a coolie, because an elephant was worth more than any damn Coringhee[15] coolie. And afterward I was very glad that the coolie had been killed; it put me legally in the right and it gave me a sufficient pretext for shooting the elephant. I often wondered whether any of the others grasped that I had done it solely to avoid looking a fool.

---

14. **dahs:** large knives.

15. **Coringhee** [kôr ing´ē]: port in southeastern India.

STUDY QUESTIONS

Recalling

1. According to the first three paragraphs, what attitude did "large numbers of people" have toward Orwell when he worked as a police officer in Burma? What was his own attitude toward his job and toward imperialism? In what way was the "tiny incident" involving the elephant "enlightening"?

2. What caused the tame elephant to behave so wildly? What was its worst offense?

3. For what reasons did Orwell not wish to shoot the elephant? For what chief reason did he shoot it? Why was he "very glad" that the coolie had been killed?

Interpreting

4. What does Orwell's behavior in this incident suggest were the effects of colonialism on those colonizers who had a conscience? What type of colonizer does Orwell criticize in reporting the remarks of the "younger Europeans" in the last paragraph?

5. Based on the behavior of most of the natives, what does the incident suggest were the effects of colonialism on the colonized?

6. What might the elephant symbolize? On this symbolic level, what would its slow death represent? What would Orwell's killing it for fear of going too close symbolize?

Extending

7. Describe some situations in which contemporary individuals must go against the dictates of their conscience.

VOCABULARY

Words from Asian Languages

British colonization of Asia brought many new words to English. For example, *shampoo* and *pajamas* come from Hindi, one of India's most widely spoken languages, as do *coolie* and *sahib*, both used by Orwell in his essay. The following English words were all borrowed from the languages of India or the Orient. Look up each word in a dictionary, list its meaning and origin, and then use the word in a sentence.

1. dinghy
2. gung-ho
3. jackal
4. sarong
5. typhoon

Frank O'Connor   *1903–1966*

Frank O'Connor, the pen name of Michael O'Donovan, was born in Cork, Ireland, and spent his early years in abject poverty. He received little formal education but read widely and began writing as a boy. For his activities in the Irish Republican Army, O'Connor served a one-year prison term. After his release he found employment as a librarian, first in Cork and later in Dublin, a job that allowed him to continue his self-education and writing. His first volume of short stories, *Guests of the Nation* (1931), received much critical acclaim and allowed him to become a director of Dublin's famous Abbey Theatre, for which he collaborated on several plays. Nevertheless, his strength remained his short stories, which sold well in both Ireland and America.

O'Connor's stories have been called quintessentially Irish and have been especially praised for their lyrical language; in fact, O'Connor himself once said that storytelling is "the nearest thing one can get to the quality of a pure lyric poem."

■ Have you ever considered writing a letter to yourself to be opened in twenty years? What might you include in such a letter?

Frank O'Connor

Masculine Protest

For months things had been getting worse between Mother and me. At the time I was twelve, and we were living in Boharna, a small town twenty miles from the city[1]—Father, Mother, Martha, and I. Father worked in the County Council and we didn't see much of him. I suppose that threw me more on Mother, but I could be perfectly happy sitting with her all day if only she let me. She didn't, though. She was always inventing excuses to get rid of me, even giving me money to go to the pictures, which she knew Father didn't like because I wasn't very bright at school and he thought the pictures were bad for me.

I blamed a lot of it on Martha at first. Martha was sly, and she was always trying to get inside me with Mother. She was always saving, whereas I always found money burned a hole in my pocket, and it was only to spite her that I kept a savings bank[2] at all. As well as that, she told Mother about all the scrapes I got into. They weren't what you'd really call scrapes. It was just that we had a gang in our neighborhood, which was the classy one of the town, and we were always having battles with the slummy kids from the other side of town who wanted to play in our neighborhood. I was the Chief Gang Leader, and it was my job to keep them from expanding beyond their own frontiers.

Martha let on not to understand why I should be Chief Gang Leader. She let on not to know why we didn't want the slum kids overrunning

---

1. **the city:** Cork, Ireland.

2. **savings bank:** here, savings account.

our locality. Though she knew better than to tell Mother when I made Viking raids on the housekeeping money, she was always at me in a low, bloodcurdling voice, following me round like a witch. "You'll be caught yet, Denis Halligan. You'll be caught. The police will be after you. You took three shillings[3] out of Mummy's purse. God sees you!" Sometimes she drove me so wild that I went mad and twisted her arm or pulled her hair, and she went off screeching, and I got a licking.

I had managed to kid myself into the belief that one day Mother would understand; one day she would wake up and see that the affection of Dad and Martha was insincere; that the two of them had long ago ganged up against her, and that I, the black sheep, was the one who really loved her.

This revelation was due to take place in rather unusual circumstances. We were all to be stranded in some dangerous desert, and Mother, with her ankle broken, would tell us to leave her to her fate, the way they did in storybooks. Dad and Martha, of course, would leave her, with only a pretense of concern, but I, in my casual way, would simply fold my hands about my knees and ask listlessly: "What use is life to me without you?" Nothing more; I was against any false drama, any raising of the voice. I had never been one for high-flown expressions like Martha: just the lift of the shoulder, the way I pulled a grass-blade to chew (it needn't be a desert), and Mother would realize at last that though I wasn't demonstrative—just a plain, rough, willing chap—I really had a heart of gold.

The trouble about Mother was that she had a genius for subjecting hearts of gold to intolerable strain. It wasn't that she was actively unkind, for she thought far too much of the impression she wanted to make to be anything like that. It was just that she didn't care a damn. She was al-

ways away from home. She visited friends in Galway, Dublin, Birr, and Athlone,[4] and all we ever got to see of her was the flurry between one foray and the next, while she was packing and unpacking.

Things came to a head when she told me she wouldn't be at home for my birthday. At the same time, always conscientious, she had arranged a very nice treat for Martha and me. But the treat wasn't the same thing that I had been planning, when I proposed to bring a couple of fellows along and show Mother off to them, and I began to bawl. The trouble was that the moment I did, I seemed to have no reasons on my side. It was always like that with Mother; she invariably had all the reasons on her side, and made you feel contrary and a pig, but that was worse instead of better. You felt then that she was taking advantage of you. I sobbed and stamped and asked why she hadn't done that to Martha and why she was doing it to me. She looked at me coldly and said I was a pretty picture and that I had no manliness. Of course, I saw she was in the right about that too, and that there was no excuse for a fellow of my age complaining against not being treated like his younger sister, and that only made me madder still.

"Go on!" I screamed. "Who's trying to stop you? All you want is people to admire you."

I knew when I had said it that it was awful, and expected her to give me a clout, but she only drew herself up, looking twice as dignified and beautiful.

"That is a contemptible remark, Denis," she said in a biting tone. "It's one I wouldn't have expected even from you."

The way she said it made me feel like the scum of the earth. And then she went off for the evening in a car with the Clarkes, leaving Martha and me alone. Martha looked at me, half in pity, half in amusement. She was never really disappointed in Mother, because she expected less of her. Martha was born sly.

---

3. **shillings:** silver coins, each worth one twentieth of a pound; replaced by the five-pence piece in 1971. (Ireland uses the same currency system as Britain, although the Irish pound is today evaluated separately on the world market.)

---

4. **Galway . . . Athlone:** Irish cities.

"What did I tell you?" she said, though she hadn't told me anything.

"Go on!" I said in a thick voice. "You sucker!" Then I went upstairs and bawled and used all the dirty words I knew. I knew now it was all over between Mother and me; that no circumstances would ever occur which would show how much I loved her, because after what had happened I could not live in the same house with her again. For quite a while I thought about suicide, but I put that on one side, because the only way I could contemplate committing suicide was by shooting, and my air pistol was not strong enough for that. I took out my post-office book.[5] I had four pounds fifteen[6] in the bank. As I've said, it was purely out of spite against Martha, but that made no difference now. It was enough to keep me for a month or so till I found some corner where people wanted me; a plain rough-spoken chap who only needed a little affection. I was afraid of nothing in the way of work. I was strong and energetic. At the worst, I could always make for Dublin, where my grandfather and

Auntie May lived. I knew they would be glad to help me, because they thought that Dad had married the wrong woman and never pretended to like Mother. When Mother had told me this I was furious, but now I saw that they were probably cleverer than I was. It would give me great satisfaction to reach their door and tell Auntie May in my plain straightforward way: "You were right and I was wrong." For the last time I looked round my bedroom and burst into fresh tears. There is something heartrending about leaving for the last time a place where you have spent so much of your life. Then, trying to steady myself, I grabbed a little holy picture from the mantelpiece and a favorite storybook from the bookshelf and ran downstairs. Martha heard me taking out my bike and came to see. It had a dynamo lamp[7] and a three-speed gear; a smashing bike!

"Where are you off to?" she asked.

"Never mind!" I said as I cycled off.

I had no particular feelings about seeing Martha for the last time.

Then I had my first shock, because as I cycled into Main Street I saw that all the shops were

---

5. **post-office book:** bank book. Post offices in Britain and Ireland often include savings-bank facilities.
6. **four pounds fifteen:** four pounds, fifteen shillings.

7. **dynamo lamp:** electric headlight whose battery is recharged by pedaling.

shuttered for the weekly half-holiday[8] and I knew the Post Office would be shut too and I could not draw out my savings. It was the first time I felt what people so often feel in afterlife, that Fate has made a plaything of you. Why should I have had my final quarrel with Mother on the one day in the week when I could not get away from her? If that wasn't Fate, what was? And I knew my own weakness of character better than anyone. I knew that if I put it off until next day, the sight of Mother would be sufficient to set me servilely seeking for pardon. Even setting off across Ireland without a penny would be better than that.

Then I had what I thought was an inspiration. The city was only twenty miles away, and the General Post Office was bound to be open. I had calculated my time to and from school at twelve miles an hour; even allowing for the distance, it wouldn't take me more than two hours. As well as that, I had been to the city for the Christmas shopping, so I knew the look of it. I could get my money and stay in a hotel or have tea and then set off for Dublin. I liked that idea. Cycling all the way up through Ireland in the dark, through sleeping towns and villages; seeing the dawn break over Dublin as I cycled down the slopes of the Dublin mountains; arriving at Auntie May's door in the Shelbourne Road when she was lighting the fire—that would be smashing. I could imagine how she would greet me—"Child of grace, where did you come from?" "Ah, just cycled." My natural modesty always came out in those daydreams of mind, for I never, under any circumstances, made a fuss. Absolutely smashing!

All the same, it was no joke, a trip like that. I cycled slowly and undecidedly out the familiar main road where we walked on Sunday, past the little suburban houses. It was queer how hard it was to break away from places and people and things you knew. I thought of letting it go and of

doing the best I could to patch it up with Mother. I thought of the gang and at that a real lump rose in my throat. Tomorrow night, when my absence was noticed, there would be a new Chief Gang Leader; somebody like Eddie Humphreys who would be so prim and cautious that he would be afraid to engage the enemy which threatened us on every side. In that moment of weakness I nearly turned back. At the same moment it brought me renewed decision, for I knew that I had not been chosen Chief Gang Leader because I was a little sissy like Eddie Humphreys but because I was afraid of nothing.

At one moment my feet had nearly stopped pedaling; at the next I was pedaling for all I was worth. It was as sudden as that, like the moment when you find yourself out of your depth and two inclinations struggle in you—to swim like hell back to the shallows or strike out boldly for the other side. Up to that I had thought mainly of what was behind me; now I thought only of what was ahead of me, and it was frightening enough. I was aware of great distances, of big cloud masses on the horizon, of the fragility of my tires compared with the rough surface of the road, and I thought only of the two-hour journey ahead of me. The romantic picture of myself cycling across Ireland in the dark disappeared. I should be quite content to get the first stage over me.

For the last ten miles I wasn't even tempted to look at the scenery. I was doubled over the handlebars. Things just happened; the road bent away under me; wide green rivers rose up and slipped away again under me, castles soared from the roadside with great arches blocked out in masses of shadow.

Then at last the little rocky fields closed behind me like a book, and the blessed electric-light poles escorted me up the last hill, and I floated proudly down between comfortable villas with long gardens till I reached the bridge. The city was stretched out on the other side of the river, shining in the evening light, and my heart rose at the thought that I had at least shown Mother whether or not I had manliness. I dismounted from my bicycle and pushed it along

8. **weekly half-holiday:** Local stores and businesses in Britain and Ireland often close for an afternoon on one weekday each week.

the Main Street, looking at the shops. They were far more interesting than the shops at home, and the people looked better too.

I found the Post Office in a side street and went up to the counter with my savings-bank book.

"I want to draw out my money," I said.

The clerk looked at the clock.

"You can't do that, sonny," he said. "The savings-bank counter is shut."

"When will it open again?" I asked.

"Not till tomorrow. Any time after nine."

"But can't I get it now?"

"No. The clerk is gone home now."

I slouched out of the Post Office with despair in my heart. I took my bicycle and pushed it wearily back to the Main Street. The crowds were still going by, but now it looked long and wide and lonesome, for I had no money and I didn't know a soul. Without a meal and a rest, I could not even set out for Dublin, if I had the heart, which I knew I hadn't. Nor could I even return home, for it was already late and I was dropping with weariness. One side of the Main Street was in shadow; the shadow seemed to spread with extraordinary rapidity, and you felt that the city was being quenched as with snuffers.[9]

It was only then that I thought of Father. It was funny that I had not thought of him before, even when thinking of Grandfather and Auntie May. I had thought of these as allies against Mother, but I hadn't even considered him as an ally. Now as I thought of him, everything about him seemed different. It wasn't only the hunger and panic. It was something new for me. It was almost love. With fresh energy I pushed my bicycle back to the Post Office, left it outside the door where I could see it, and went up to the clerk I had already spoken to.

"Could I make a telephone call?" I asked.

"You could to be sure," he said. "Have you the money?"

"No, sir."

"Well, you can't make a call without the money. Where is it to?"

"Boharna," I said.

At once his face took on a severe expression.

"That's one and threepence," he said.

"And I can't ring unless I have the money?"

"Begor,[10] you can't. I couldn't ring myself without that."

I went out and took my bicycle again. This time I could see no way out. I dawdled along the street, leaving my bicycle by the curb and gazing in shop windows. In one I found a mirror in which I could see myself full-length. I looked old and heartbroken. It was just like a picture of a child without a home, and I blinked away my tears.

Then, as I approached a public house,[11] I saw a barman in shirtsleeves standing by the door. I remembered that I had seen him already on my way down and that he had looked at me. He nodded and smiled and I stopped. I was glad of anyone making a friendly gesture in that strange place.

"Are you waiting for someone?" he asked.

"No," I said. "I wanted to make a phone call."

"You're not from these parts?"

"No," I said. "I'm from Boharna."

"Are you, begor?" he said. "Was it on the bus you came?"

"No," I replied modestly. "I biked it."

"Biked it?"

"Yes."

"That's a hell of a distance," he said.

"It is long," I agreed.

"What did you come all that way for?" he asked in surprise.

"Ah, I was running away from home," I said despondently.

"You were what?" he asked in astonishment. "You're not serious."

"But I am," I said, very close to tears. "I did my best, but then I couldn't stick it any longer

---

9. **snuffers:** device used for extinguishing burning candles.

10. **Begor:** common Irish exclamation, originally meaning "by God!"; also *begorra.*

11. **public house:** tavern; often shortened to *pub.*

and I cleared out." I turned my head away because this time I was really crying.

"Oh, begor, I know what 'tis like," he said in a friendlier tone. "I did it myself."

"Did you?" I asked eagerly, forgetting my grief. This, I felt, was the very man I wanted to meet.

"Ah, indeed I did. I did it three times what's more. By that time they were getting fed up with me. Anyway, they say practice makes perfect. Tell me, is it your old fellow?"

"No," I said with a sigh. "My mother."

"Ah, do you tell me so? That's worse again. 'Tis bad enough to have the old man at you, but 'tis the devil entirely when the mother is against you. What are you going to do now?"

"I don't know," I said. "I wanted to get to Dublin, but the savings bank is shut, and all my money is in it."

"That's tough luck. Sure, you can't get anywhere without money. I'm afraid you'll have to go back and put up with it for another while."

"But I can't," I said. "'Tis twenty miles."

"'Tis all of that, begor. You couldn't go on the bus?"

"I can't. I haven't the money. That's what I asked them in the Post Office, to let me ring up Daddy, but they wouldn't."

"Where's your daddy?" he asked, and when I told him: "Ah, we'll try and get him for you anyway. Come on in."

There was a phone in the corner, and he rang up and asked for Daddy. Then he gave me a big smile and handed me the receiver. I heard Daddy's voice and I nearly wept with delight.

"Hullo, son," he said in astonishment. "Where on earth are you?"

"In the city, Daddy," I said modestly—even then I couldn't bring myself to make a lot of it, the way another fellow would.

"The city?" he repeated incredulously. "What took you there?"

"I ran away from home, Dad," I said, trying to make it sound as casual as possible.

"Oh!" he exclaimed and there was a moment's pause. I was afraid he was going to get angry, but his tone remained the same. "Had a row?"[12]

"Yes, Dad."

"And how did you get there?"

"On the bike."

"All the way? But you must be dead."

"Just a bit tired," I said modestly.

"Tell me, did you even get a meal?"

"No, Dad. The savings bank was shut."

"Ah, blazes!" he said softly. "Of course, it's the half-day. And what are you going to do now?"

"I don't know, Dad. I thought you might tell me."

"Well, what about coming home?" he said, beginning to laugh.

"I don't mind, Dad. Whatever you say."

"Hold on now till I see what the buses are like. . . . Hullo! You can get one in forty minutes' time—seven ten. Tell the conductor I'll be meeting you and I'll pay your fare. Will that be all right?"

"That's grand, Dad," I said, feeling that the world was almost right again.

When I finished, the barman was waiting for me with his coat on. He had got another man to look after the bar for him.

"Now, you'd better come and have a cup of tea with me before your bus goes," he said. "The old bike will be safe outside."

He took me to a café, and I ate cake after cake and drank tea and he told me about how he'd run away himself. You could see he was a real hard case, worse even than I was. The first time, he'd pinched a bicycle and cycled all the way to Dublin, sleeping in barns and deserted cottages. The police had brought him home and his father had belted hell out of him. They caught him again the second time, but the third time he'd joined the army and not returned home for years.

He put me and my bicycle on the bus and paid my fare. He made me promise to tell Dad that he'd done it and that Dad owed me the money. He said in this world you had to stand up for your rights. He was a rough chap, but you

---

12. **row** [rou]: quarrel; squabble.

could see he had a good heart. It struck me that maybe only rough chaps had hearts as good as that.

Dad was waiting for me at the bus stop, and he looked at me and laughed.

"Well, the gouger!"[13] he said. "Who ever would think that the son of a good-living, upright man like me would turn into a common tramp."

All the same I could see he was pleased, and as he pushed my bike down the street he made me tell him all about my experiences. He laughed over the barman and promised to give me the fare. Then, seeing him so friendly, I asked the question that had been on my mind the whole way back on the bus.

"Mummy back yet, Dad?"

"No, son," he said. "Not yet. She probably won't be in till late."

What I was really asking him, of course, was "Does she know?" and now I was torn by the desire to ask him not to tell her, but it choked me. It would have seemed too much like trying to gang up against her. But he seemed to know what I was thinking, for he added with a sort of careful casualness that he had sent Martha to the pictures. I guessed that that was to get her out of the way so that she couldn't bring the story to Mother, and when we had supper together and washed up afterwards, I knew I was right.

Mother came in before we went to bed, and Father talked to her just as though nothing had happened. He was a little bit more forthcoming than usual, but that was the only indication he gave, and I was fascinated, watching him create an understanding between us. It was an understanding in more ways than one, because it dawned on me gradually that, like myself and the barman, Dad too had once run away from home, and for some reason—perhaps because the bank was shut or because he was hungry, tired, and lonely—he had come back. People mostly came back, but their protest remained to distinguish them from all the others who had never run away. It was the real sign of their manhood.

I never ran away after that. I never felt I needed to.

---

13. **gouger:** swindler.

STUDY QUESTIONS

Recalling

1. According to the opening paragraphs, what has been happening "for months"? In what ways does Martha annoy Denis? In his daydreams, whose affections does Denis hope to win?
2. What prompts Denis to run away? Where does he plan to go? Why must he go to Cork?
3. What disappointment awaits Denis in Cork? What generous act does the barman perform? What does he say he did three times?
4. With what attitude does Denis' father greet him when he gets off the bus? Does his father tell his mother about his running off?
5. According to the final paragraphs, what has been created between Denis and his father? What dawns on Denis? What does Denis never need to do again?

Interpreting

6. With what two people does Denis develop bonds in this story? Why does Denis feel as he does in the last paragraph?
7. In what way is the title appropriate to the story's events and resolution?

VIEWPOINT

In introducing O'Connor's *Collected Stories,* critic Richard Ellman notes that the stories

pass into our experience like incidents we have ourselves known or almost known. . . . They sum up a provincial culture in terms that are less provincial but never cosmopolitan. Detachment from his own country was not one of Frank O'Connor's aims.

■ What details of "Masculine Protest" help capture the local color of Ireland? What details touch on universal experiences that seem like "incidents we have ourselves known"?

Graham Greene *born 1904*

Among the finest writers of postwar Britain, Graham Greene has produced a string of popular spy thrillers, which he calls his "entertainments," as well as more serious works of literature. The grandnephew of Victorian writer Robert Louis Stevenson, Greene grew up in Hertfordshire, north of London, where his father was the headmaster of the exclusive Berkhamsted School. The young Greene came to detest the brutalities of boarding-school life, and at sixteen he rebelliously ran away. For six months he was placed in the care of a London psychoanalyst who also happened to be a writer. Later Greene would call these months the happiest time of his life. Not only had he escaped the hated Berkhamsted School, but, encouraged by the sympathetic doctor, Greene discovered writing for himself.

Greene attended Oxford University and, upon graduation in 1925, published a volume of poetry. For the next few years he worked as a journalist, eventually finding himself on the staff of one of Britain's best newspapers, the *London Times*. With the publication of *The Man Within* (1929), Greene established himself as a novelist; not long afterward came two major early novels, *Brighton Rock* (1938) and *The Power and the Glory* (1940).

In common with many other English authors, Greene served in British Intelligence during World War II. His experiences helped him in the writing of his spy novels, many of which were turned into popular films. A convert to Roman Catholicism, Greene often treats moral and religious themes in his more serious fiction; in fact, poet and critic Louise Bogan once pointed out that even Greene's spy novels have "a close parallel in the religious dramas of salvation and redemption." A worldwide traveler, Greene is also noted for his realistic depiction of cold war and Third World politics in novels like *The Heart of the Matter* (1948), *The Quiet American* (1956), and *The Comedians* (1966). In addition, he has produced such humorous satires as *Our Man in Havana* (1958), a parody of his own spy thrillers.

Novels are not the only literary form that Greene has mastered: He has also written plays, screenplays, a collection of essays called *The Lost Childhood* (1951), an autobiography (1971), and a number of volumes of superb short stories that deal with a broad range of topics and concerns. Many of Greene's stories are darkly realistic; others, lightly satirical. "A Shocking Accident" draws on Greene's early school experiences and reflects his more satirical side.

■ Has a shocking situation ever caused you to laugh? What about that situation was comical?

A Shocking Accident

1

Jerome was called into his housemaster's[1] room in the break between the second and the third class on a Thursday morning. He had no fear of trouble, for he was a warden—the name that the proprietor and headmaster of a rather expensive preparatory school had chosen to give to approved, reliable boys in the lower forms[2] (from a warden one became a guardian and finally before leaving, it was hoped for Marlborough or Rugby,[3] a crusader). The housemaster, Mr. Wordsworth, sat behind his desk with an appearance of perplexity and apprehension. Jerome had the odd impression when he entered that he was a cause of fear.

"Sit down, Jerome," Mr. Wordsworth said. "All going well with the trigonometry?"

"Yes, sir."

"I've had a telephone call, Jerome. From your aunt. I'm afraid I have bad news for you."

"Yes, sir?"

"Your father has had an accident."

"Oh."

Mr. Wordsworth looked at him with some surprise. "A serious accident."

"Yes, sir?"

Jerome worshiped his father: the verb is exact. As man re-creates God, so Jerome re-created his father—from a restless widowed author into a mysterious adventurer who traveled in far places—Nice, Beirut, Majorca, even the Canaries.[4] The time had arrived about his eighth birthday when Jerome believed that his father either "ran guns" or was a member of the British Secret Service. Now it occurred to him that his father might have been wounded in "a hail of machine-gun bullets."

Mr. Wordsworth played with the ruler on his desk. He seemed at a loss how to continue. He said, "You know your father was in Naples?"

"Yes, sir."

"Your aunt heard from the hospital today."

"Oh."

Mr. Wordsworth said with desperation, "It was a street accident."

"Yes, sir?" It seemed quite likely to Jerome that they would call it a street accident. The police of course had fired first; his father would not take human life except as a last resort.

"I'm afraid your father was very seriously hurt indeed."

"Oh."

"In fact, Jerome, he died yesterday. Quite without pain."

"Did they shoot him through the heart?"

"I beg your pardon. What did you say, Jerome?"

"Did they shoot him through the heart?"

"Nobody shot him, Jerome. A pig fell on him." An inexplicable convulsion took place in the nerves of Mr. Wordsworth's face; it really looked for a moment as though he were going to laugh. He closed his eyes, composed his features and said rapidly as though it were necessary to expel the story as quickly as possible, "Your father was walking along a street in Naples when a pig fell on him. A shocking accident. Apparently in the poorer quarters of Naples they keep pigs on their balconies. This one was on the fifth floor. It had grown too fat. The balcony broke. The pig fell on your father."

Mr. Wordsworth left his desk rapidly and went to the window, turning his back on Jerome. He shook a little with emotion.

Jerome said, "What happened to the pig?"

---

1. **housemaster's:** referring to the adult in charge of a school dormitory.
2. **forms:** grades.
3. **Marlborough or Rugby:** prestigious English public schools. (In England, "public schools" are expensive private schools; the term "public" merely dates back to a time when these schools were the first schools opened outside the home.)
4. **Nice . . . Canaries:** fashionable upper-class seaside resorts.

2

This was not callousness on the part of Jerome, as it was interpreted by Mr. Wordsworth to his colleagues (he even discussed with them whether, perhaps, Jerome was yet fitted to be a warden). Jerome was only attempting to visualize the strange scene to get the details right. Nor was Jerome a boy who cried; he was a boy who brooded, and it never occurred to him at his preparatory school that the circumstances of his father's death were comic—they were still part of the mystery of life. It was later, in his first term at his public school, when he told the story to his best friend, that he began to realize how it affected others. Naturally after that disclosure he was known, rather unreasonably, as Pig.

Unfortunately his aunt had no sense of humor. There was an enlarged snapshot of his father on the piano; a large sad man in an unsuitable dark suit posed in Capri[5] with an umbrella (to guard him against sunstroke), the Faraglione rocks[6] forming the background. By the age of sixteen Jerome was well aware that the portrait looked more like the author of *Sunshine and Shade* and *Rambles in the Balearics* than an agent of the Secret Service. All the same he loved the memory of his father; he still possessed an album filled with picture postcards (the stamps had been soaked off long ago for his other collection), and it pained him when his aunt embarked with strangers on the story of his father's death.

"A shocking accident," she would begin, and the stranger would compose his or her features into the correct shape for interest and commiseration. Both reactions, of course, were false, but it was terrible for Jerome to see how suddenly, midway in her rambling discourse, the interest would become genuine. "I can't think how such things can be allowed in a civilized country," his aunt would say. "I suppose one has to regard Italy as civilized. One is prepared for all kinds of things abroad, of course, and my brother was a great traveler. He always carried a water filter with him. It was far less expensive, you know, than buying all those bottles of mineral water. My brother always said that his filter paid for his dinner wine. You can see from that what a careful man he was, but who could possibly have expected when he was walking along the Via Dottore Manuele Panucci on his way to the Hydrographic Museum[7] that a pig would fall on him?" That was the moment when the interest became genuine.

Jerome's father had not been a very distinguished writer, but the time always seems to come, after an author's death, when somebody thinks it worth his while to write a letter to the *Times Literary Supplement* announcing the preparation of a biography and asking to see any letters or documents or receive any anecdotes from friends of the dead man. Most of the biographies, of course, never appear—one wonders whether the whole thing may not be an obscure form of blackmail and whether many a potential writer of a biography or thesis finds the means in this way to finish his education at Kansas or Nottingham.[8] Jerome, however, as a chartered accountant,[9] lived far from the literary world. He did not realize how small the menace really was, or that the danger period for someone of his father's obscurity had long passed. Sometimes he rehearsed the method of recounting his father's death so as to reduce the comic element to its smallest dimensions—it would be of no use to refuse information, for in that case the biographer would undoubtedly visit his aunt, who was living to a great old age with no sign of flagging.

It seemed to Jerome that there were two possible methods—the first led gently up to the accident, so that by the time it was described the listener was so well prepared that the death came really as an anticlimax. The chief danger of laughter in such a story was always surprise.

---

5. **Capri** [ka prē′]: picturesque Italian island in the Bay of Naples.
6. **Faraglione** [fa ral yō′nä] **rocks:** rock islets worn into fantastic shapes by the waves.

7. **Hydrographic Museum:** aquatic museum; aquarium.
8. **Kansas or Nottingham:** the University of Kansas or the University of Nottingham, England. Greene is merely choosing what he believes to be lesser-known universities in America and Britain.
9. **chartered accountant:** the British equivalent of a certified public accountant.

When he rehearsed this method Jerome began boringly enough.

"You know Naples and those high tenement buildings? Somebody once told me that the Neapolitan[10] always feels at home in New York just as the man from Turin feels at home in London because the river runs in much the same way in both cities. Where was I? Oh, yes, Naples, of course. You'd be surprised in the poorer quarters what things they keep on the balconies of those sky-scraping tenements—not washing, you know, or bedding, but things like livestock, chickens or even pigs. Of course the pigs get no exercise whatever and fatten all the quicker." He could imagine how his hearer's eyes would have glazed by this time. "I've no idea, have you, how heavy a pig can be, but these old buildings are all badly in need of repair. A balcony on the fifth floor gave way under one of those pigs. It struck the third floor balcony on its way down and sort of ricocheted into the street. My father was on the way to the Hydrographic Museum when the pig hit him. Coming from that height and that angle, it broke his neck." This was really a masterly attempt to make an intrinsically interesting subject boring.

The other method Jerome rehearsed had the virtue of brevity.

"My father was killed by a pig."

"Really? In India?"

"No, in Italy."

"How interesting. I never realized there was pig-sticking[11] in Italy. Was your father keen on polo?"

In course of time, neither too early nor too late, rather as though, in his capacity as a chartered accountant, Jerome had studied the statistics and taken the average, he became engaged to be married: to a pleasant fresh-faced girl of twenty-five whose father was a doctor in Pinner.[12] Her name was Sally, her favorite author was still Hugh Walpole,[13] and she had adored

babies ever since she had been given a doll at the age of five which moved its eyes and made water. Their relationship was contented rather than exciting, as became the love affair of a chartered accountant; it would never have done if it had interfered with the figures.

One thought worried Jerome, however. Now that within a year he might himself become a father, his love for the dead man increased; he realized what affection had gone into the picture postcards. He felt a longing to protect his memory, and uncertain whether this quiet love of his would survive if Sally were so insensitive as to laugh when she heard the story of his father's death. Inevitably she would hear it when Jerome brought her to dinner with his aunt. Several times he tried to tell her himself, as she was naturally anxious to know all she could that concerned him.

"You were very small when your father died?"

"Just nine."

"Poor little boy," she said.

"I was at school. They broke the news to me."

"Did you take it very hard?"

"I can't remember."

"You never told me how it happened."

"It was very sudden. A street accident."

"You'll never drive fast, will you, Jemmy?" (She had begun to call him "Jemmy.") It was too late then to try the second method—the one he thought of as the pig-sticking one.

They were going to marry quietly in a registry office and have their honeymoon at Torquay.[14] He avoided taking her to see his aunt until a week before the wedding, but then the night came, and he could not have told himself whether his apprehension was more for his father's memory or the security of his own love.

The moment came all too soon. "Is that Jemmy's father?" Sally asked, picking up the portrait of the man with the umbrella.

"Yes, dear. How did you guess?"

"He has Jemmy's eyes and brow, hasn't he?"

"Has Jerome lent you his books?"

---

10. **Neapolitan:** person from Naples.
11. **pig-sticking:** sport, popular in India, in which wild boars are hunted with spears.
12. **Pinner:** typical middle-class suburb of London.
13. **Hugh Walpole:** pleasant but conventional English novelist (1884–1941) popular with middle-class readers.

14. **Torquay** [tôr kē´]: English seaside resort popular with middle-class vacationers and honeymooners.

"No."

"I will give you a set for your wedding. He wrote so tenderly about his travels. My own favorite is *Nooks and Crannies.* He would have had a great future. It made that shocking accident all the worse."

"Yes?"

Jerome longed to leave the room and not see that loved face crinkle with irresistible amusement.

"I had so many letters from his readers after the pig fell on him." She had never been so abrupt before.

And then the miracle happened. Sally did not laugh. Sally sat with open eyes of horror while his aunt told her the story, and at the end, "How

horrible," Sally said. "It makes you think, doesn't it? Happening like that. Out of a clear sky."

Jerome's heart sang with joy. It was as though she had appeased his fear forever. In the taxi going home he kissed her with more passion than he had ever shown and she returned it. There were babies in her pale blue pupils, babies that rolled their eyes and made water.

"A week today," Jerome said, and she squeezed his hand. "Penny for your thoughts, my darling."

"I was wondering," Sally said, "what happened to the poor pig?"

"They almost certainly had it for dinner," Jerome said happily and kissed the dear child again.

STUDY QUESTIONS

Recalling

1. According to part 1, from what into what has Jerome re-created his father?
2. What accident does the housemaster report? What final question does Jerome ask him?
3. According to part 2, what never occurred to Jerome until he reached public school? Until that time, of what were the circumstances of his father's death a part? What nickname did Jerome get in public school?
4. What career does Jerome choose? What background details are supplied about Sally, the girl to whom he becomes engaged?
5. What final question does Sally ask when she learns of Jerome's father's accident? What is Jerome's response?

Interpreting

6. Despite Jerome's boyhood imaginings, what was his father really like?
7. Why must Jerome later adopt different ways of describing his father's death? In what chief way do these conversations differ from his initial reaction to the death?
8. What sort of person is Sally? How do story events prove that Jerome was right in choosing to marry her?
9. Identify two aspects of British society that the story criticizes or satirizes. What is the author's tone or attitude in describing Jerome?

Extending

10. What ingredients do you think are necessary for a good marriage?

Samuel Beckett   *born 1906*

Some twentieth-century writers focus on the minds of their characters to find the essence of reality and truth. Samuel Beckett differs from them because he denies the existence of absolute, universal reality. According to Beckett, the only thing that humankind can be sure of is that it exists. His work is free of abstractions like truth and beauty, goodness and evil. Beckett aims to communicate an experience instead of a message. His readers try to feel that experience, not find meaning in it.

The lack of meaning in his work stems from Beckett's belief that life itself has no meaning that we can discover with any certainty. To him life consists of intellectual games that we create to pass the time. The games, the way we pass the time, are the essence of life for Beckett, and they make up the action in his plays, novels, stories, and film scripts.

Samuel Beckett was born in Dublin, Ireland, and attended Trinity College there. He taught literature at colleges in Ireland and France, settling for a time in Paris, where he was a friend of James Joyce. Beckett often helped Joyce, who was nearly blind, by taking dictation and copying out portions of Joyce's books. During World War II Beckett worked for a time with the French resistance to German occupation. He also served with the Irish Red Cross.

After the war Beckett wrote his most famous play, *Waiting for Godot* (1953). The play is a cornerstone of what is called **theater of the absurd**, a kind of drama that illustrates life's supposed futility with formless, plotless plays. The first line of *Godot* is "Nothing to be done," and nothing happens in the play. Two people await the arrival of someone who never appears. To Beckett this pointless waiting is an experience that captures life's essence.

"Still" is a short prose work describing a concrete experience. Read it carefully in order to live the experience that Beckett is communicating. Then decide for yourself whether the author is also implying a message.

■ Everyone has an interior monologue that is constant. Try for a minute or two to transcribe what is going on in your head and what your hands and feet and eyes are doing.

Samuel Beckett

Still

Bright at last close of a dark day the sun shines out at last and goes down. Sitting quite still at valley window normally turn head now and see it the sun low in the southwest sinking. Even get up certain moods and go stand by western window quite still watching it sink and then the afterglow. Always quite still some reason some time past this hour at open window facing south in small upright wicker chair with armrests. Eyes stare out unseeing till first movement some time past close though unseeing still while still light. Quite still again then all quite quiet apparently till eyes open again while still light though less. Normally turn head now ninety degrees to watch sun which if already gone then fading afterglow. Even get up certain moods and go stand by western window till quite dark and even some evenings some reason long after. Eyes then open again while still light and close again in what if not quite a single movement almost. Quite still again then at open window facing south over the valley in this wicker chair though actually close inspection not still at all but trembling all over. Close inspection namely detail by detail all over to add up finally to this whole not still at all but trembling all over. But casually in this failing light impression dead still even the hands clearly trembling and the breast faint rise and fall. Legs side by side broken right angles at the knees as in that old statue some old god twanged at sunrise and again at sunset. Trunk likewise dead plumb right up to top of skull seen from behind including nape clear of chairback. Arms likewise broken right angles at the elbows forearms along armrests just right length forearms and rests for hands clenched lightly to rest on ends. So quite still again then all quite quiet apparently eyes closed which to anticipate when they open again if they do in time then dark or some degree of starlight or moonlight or both. Normally watch night fall however long from this narrow chair or standing by western window quite still either case. Quite still namely staring at some one thing alone such as tree or bush a detail alone if near if far the whole if far enough till it goes. Or by eastern window certain moods staring at some point on the hillside such as that beech in whose shade once quite still till it goes. Chair some reason always same place same position facing south as though clamped down whereas in reality no lighter no more movable imaginable. Or anywhere any ope staring out at nothing just failing light quite still till quite dark though of course no such thing just less light still when less did not seem possible. Quite still then all this time eyes open when discovered then closed then opened and closed again no other movement any kind though of course not still at all when suddenly or so it looks this movement impossible to follow let alone describe. The right hand slowly opening leaves the armrest taking with it the whole forearm complete with elbow and slowly rises opening further as it goes and turning a little deasil[1] till midway to the head it hesitates and hangs half open trembling in mid air. Hangs there as if half inclined to return that is sink back slowly closing as it goes and turning the other way till as and where it began clenched lightly on end of rest. Here because of what comes now not midway to the head but almost there before it hesitates and hangs there trembling as if half inclined etc. Half no but on the verge when in its turn the head moves from its place forward and down among the ready fingers where no sooner received and held it weighs on down till elbow meeting armrest brings this last movement to an end and all still once more. Here back a little way to that suspense before head to rescue as if hand's

---

1. **deasil** [dē′zəl]: clockwise.

need the greater and on down in what if not quite a single movement almost till elbow against rest. All quite still again then head in hand namely thumb on outer edge of right socket index ditto left and middle on left cheekbone plus as the hours pass lesser contacts each more or less now more now less with the faint stirrings of the various parts as night wears on. As if even in the dark eyes closed not enough and perhaps even more than ever necessary against that no such thing the further shelter of the hand. Leave it so all quite still or try listening to the sounds all quite still head in hand listening for a sound.

STUDY QUESTIONS

Recalling

1. In a few words describe the scene that the watcher is looking at.
2. From what two vantage points does the watcher observe this scene?
3. Find at least four descriptive details that are added to the basic scene as the selection continues.
4. Find at least three details that describe the watcher's movements as the selection continues.

Interpreting

5. Explain two different meanings of the word *still* that the selection implies.
6. What is "trembling all over"? Why?
7. "Close inspection namely detail by detail all over to add up finally to this whole. . . ." In what sense does this quotation from "Still" apply to the entire selection?
8. What quality of human experience does Beckett illustrate by gradually adding details to one basic scene?
9. Do you think "Still" has a message, or is it simply the description of an experience? Explain your opinion.

Extending

10. In what sense does "Still" represent typical human behavior?

LITERARY FOCUS

Elements of Style in Modern Prose

Style is made up of an author's choice and arrangement of words to convey both an idea and the author's individuality. Elements of style include subject, diction, and structure.

Subject is the topic of a literary work, the experience or idea being written about. Modern authors have responded to the rapid expansion of human knowledge by exploring new topics for literature, for example, the effects of technology on life or the working of the human mind.

Diction is the author's use of appropriate words to convey a particular meaning. The choice of words should suit the situation and subject being written about and should also reflect the author's personality. Modern authors have experimented with diction to create startling effects. They may use technical scientific language; they may sacrifice meaning and use words purely for their sound.

Structure is the framework or general plan of a piece of literature. The structure of an essay is its outline, or the scheme of its thesis statement and topic sentences. The structure of a short story is its plot and the arrangement of events in the plot. An example of a modern innovation in structure is the stream-of-consciousness story, which dispenses with plot and imitates the continuous flow of human thought.

Thinking About Elements of Style

1. What subject is Beckett writing about in "Still"? What does his choice of subject reveal about Beckett?
2. In what sense does Beckett's diction—the use of simple vocabulary and repetition—fit his subject?
3. Describe the structure of "Still." In what way does the structure of the selection match its subject?

Sean O'Faolain *born 1900*

Sean O'Faolain [shôn′ ō fā′lin] is an Irish author whose homeland supplies themes, settings, and characters for his short stories and novels. He has also written travel books, biographies, critical studies, and an autobiography. Born John Whelan in Cork, Ireland, he changed his name to its Gaelic variant when he was sixteen. He was educated in Ireland and at Harvard University. After fighting in the Irish Revolution (1918–1921), O'Faolain lectured at colleges in the United States and in England. He discovered what would become the subject of his fiction while attending a play in his home town: "Here was a most moving play about Irish peasants, shopkeeping and farming folk, men and women who could have been anyone of my uncles and aunts down the country. It brought me strange and wonderful news—that writers could also write books and plays about the common everyday reality of Irish life."

"The Sugawn Chair," a small cameo of Irish life, is about the kind of people O'Faolain knows best. He portrays them honestly but with warmth and compassion, and the mood established early in the story casts a glow throughout.

■ When you are an adult, what are some of the sights, sounds, events you will want to talk about?

Sean O'Faolain

The Sugawn Chair

Every autumn I am reminded of an abandoned sugawn chair that languished for years, without a seat, in the attic of my old home. It is associated in my mind with an enormous sack which the carter used to dump with a thud on the kitchen floor around every October. I was a small kid then, and it was as high as myself. This sack had come "up from the country," a sort of diplomatic messenger from the fields to the city. It smelled of dust and hay and apples, for the top half of it always bulged with potatoes, and, under a layer of hay, the bottom half bulged with apples. Its arrival always gave my mother great joy and a little sorrow, because it came from the farm where she had been born. Immediately she saw it she glowed with pride in having a "back," as she called it—meaning something behind her more solid and permanent than city streets,

though she was also saddened by the memories that choked her with this smell of hay and potatoes from the home farm, and apples from the little orchard near the farmhouse. My father, who had also been born on a farm, also took great pleasure in these country fruits, and as the two of them stood over the sack, in the kitchen, in the middle of the humming city, everything that their youth had meant to them used to make them smile and laugh and use words that they had never used during the rest of the year, and which I thought magical: words like *late sowing, clover crop, inch field, marl bottom, headlands, tubers,* and the names of potatoes, British Queens or Arran Banners, that sounded to me like the names of regiments. For those moments my father and mother became a young, courting couple again. As they stood over that sack, as you might say warming their hands to it, they were intensely happy, close to each other, in love again. To me they were two very old people. Counting back now, I reckon that they were about forty-two or forty-three.

One autumn evening after the sack arrived, my father went up to the attic and brought down the old sugawn chair. I suppose he had had it sent up from his home farm. It was the only thing of its kind in our house, which they had filled—in the usual peasants' idea of what constitutes elegance—with plush chairs, gold-framed pictures of Stags at Bay, and exotic tropical birds, pelmets[1] on the mantelpieces, Delft shepherdesses, Chinese mandarins[2] with nodding heads, brass bedsteads with mighty knobs and mother-of-pearl escutcheons[3] set with bits of mirror, vast mahogany chiffoniers,[4] and so on. But the plush-bottomed chairs, with their turned legs and their stiff backs, were for show, not for comfort, whereas in the old country sugawn chair my da could tilt and squeak and rock to his behind's content.

It had been in the place for years, rockety, bockety, chipped and well polished, and known simply as "your father's chair," until the night when, as he was reading the *Evening Echo* with his legs up on the kitchen range, there was a sudden rending noise, and down he went through the seat of it. There he was then, bending over, with the chair stuck on to him, and my mother and myself in the splits of laughter, pulling it from him while he cursed like a trooper. This was the wreck that he now suddenly brought down from the dusty attic.

The next day, he brought in a great sack of straw from the Cornmarket, a half-gallon of porter[5] and two old buddies from the street— an ex-soldier known to the kids around as "Tear-'em-and-ate-'em" and a little dwarf of a man who guarded the stage door at the Opera House when he was not behind the sacristan[6] at the chapel. I was enchanted when I heard what they were going to do. They were going to make ropes of straw—a miracle I had never heard of—and reseat the chair. Bursting with pride in my da, I ran out and brought in my best pal, and the two of us sat quiet as cats on the kitchen table, watching the three men filling the place with dust, straw, and loud arguments as they began to twist the ropes for the bottom of the chair.

More strange words began to float in the air with the dust: *scallops,*[7] *flat tops, bulrushes, cipeens,*[8] *fields in great heart . . .* And when the three sat down for a swig of porter, and looked at the old polished skeletons in the middle of the floor, they began to rub the inside of their thighs and say how there was no life at all like the country life, and my mother poured out more porter for them, and laughed happily when my da began to talk about horses, and harrows,[9] and a day after the plough, and how, for *that* much, he'd throw up this blooming city life altogether and settle down on a bit of a farm for the heel of his days.

This was a game of which he, she and I never got tired, a fairy tale that was so alluring it did not matter that they had not enough money to buy a window box, let alone a farm of land.

"Do you remember that little place," she would say, "that was going last year down at Nantenan?"[10]

When she said that, I could see the little reedy fields of Limerick that I knew from hol-

---

1. **pelmets** [pel′məts]: horizontal moldings.
2. **Delft . . . mandarins:** small sculptured figurines.
3. **escutcheons** [es kuch′ənz]: shield shapes displaying a coat of arms.
4. **chiffoniers** [shif′ə nērz′]: large, heavy chests of drawers.
5. **porter:** bitter, heavy beer.

6. **sacristan** [sak′ris tən]: official in charge of the sacristy, the room in a church were ceremonial robes and sacred objects are kept.
7. *scallops* [skôl′əps]: long wooden rods from salley trees, used in making thatched roofs and baskets.
8. *cipeens* [kip′ēnz]: small twigs often used for starting fires.
9. **harrows:** implements used to break up and level plowed land.
10. **Nantenan** [nan′ti nən]: town in County Limerick in southwestern Ireland.

idays with my uncle, and the crumbling stone walls of old demesnes[11] with the moss and saffron lichen on them, and the willow sighing softly by the Deel,[12] and I could smell the wet turf rising in the damp air, and, above all, the tall wildflowers of the mallow, at first cabbage-leaved, then pink and coarse, then gossamery, then breaking into cakes that I used to eat—a rank weed that is the mark of ruin in so many Irish villages, and whose profusion and color is for me the sublime emblem of Limerick's loneliness, loveliness and decay.

"Ah!" my da would roar. "You and your blooming old Limerick! That bog of a place! Oh, but why didn't I grab that little farm I was looking at two years ago there below Emo!"[13]

"Oho, ho, ho!" she would scoff. "The Queen's! The Lousy Queen's! I'd live like a tiger and die like a Turk for Limerick. For one patch of good old Limerick. Oh, Limerick, my love, and it isn't alike! Where would you get spuds and apples the like of them in the length and breadth of the Queen's County?"

And she grabbed a fist of hay from the bag and buried her face in it, and the tears began to stream down her face, and me and my pal screaming with laughter at her, and the sacristan lauding Tipperary,[14] and the voices rose as Tear-'em-and-ate-'em brought up the River Barrow[15] and the fields of Carlow, until my da jumped up with:

"Come on, lads, the day is dyin' and acres wide before us!"

For all that, the straw rope was slow in emerging. Their arguments about it got louder and their voices sharper. At first all their worry had been whether the kitchen was long enough for the rope; but so far, only a few, brief

---

11. **demesnes** [di mānz′]: large estates or land holdings that were usually enclosed by walls.
12. **Deel:** river in County Limerick.
13. **Emo:** town in County Laois [lēsh], once known as Queen's County, southwest of Dublin.
14. **Tipperary:** inland county in the south having the richest agricultural region in Ireland.
15. **River Barrow:** river flowing through County Carlow, southwest of Dublin.

---

worms of straw lay on the red tiles. The sacristan said: "That bloody straw is too moist." When he was a boy in Tipp he never seen straw the like o' that. Tear-'em-and-ate-'em said that straw was old straw. When he was a lad in Carlow they never used old straw. Never! Under no possible circumstances! My dad said: "What's wrong with that straw is it's too bloomin' short!" And they began to kick the bits with their toes, and grimace at the heap on the floor, and pick up bits and fray them apart and throw them aside until the whole floor was like a stable. At last they put on their coats, and gave the straw a final few kicks, and my pal jumped down and said he was going back to his handball and, in my heart, I knew that they were three imposters.

The kitchen was tidy that evening when I came back with the *Evening Echo.* My da was standing by the sack of potatoes. He had a spud in his fist, rubbing off the dust of its clay with his thumb. When he saw me he tossed it back in the sack, took the paper, took one of the plush-bottom chairs and sat on it with a little grimace. I did not say anything, but young as I was, I could see that he was not reading what he was looking at. Who knows what he was seeing at that moment.

For years the anatomy of the chair stood in one of the empty attics. It was there for many years after my father died. When my mother died and I had to sell out the few bits of junk that still remained from their lives, the dealer would not bother to take the useless frame, so that when, for the last time, I walked about the echoing house, I found it standing alone in the middle of the bare attic. As I looked at it I smelled apples, and the musk of Limerick's dust, and the turf-tang[16] from its cottages, and the mallows among the limestone ruins, and I saw my mother and my father again as they were that morning—standing over the autumn sack, their arms about one another, laughing foolishly, and madly in love again.

---

16. **turf-tang:** the smell of burning peat.

STUDY QUESTIONS

Recalling

1. What association does the sugawn chair hold for the narrator?
2. Where is the chair kept? Where does the narrator suppose the chair came from? Why is it no longer used?
3. What do the father and his friends plan to do with the chair? What is the narrator's original opinion of this plan?
4. What do the father and his friends actually do instead? What is the narrator's opinion of them?
5. What finally happens to the chair?

Interpreting

6. Explain the effect of the sack on the mother and father. Why did it have this effect?
7. Explain the symbolism of the chair and of the father's inability to repair it.

Extending

8. At the end of the story, what do you think the narrator did with the chair? Why?

LITERARY FOCUS

Atmosphere

Atmosphere is the mood of a story. It is created through (1) the story's **setting,** or time and place, and (2) the author's **tone,** or attitude toward the subject of the story. The result is a frame of mind in which the story places the reader. The setting is usually described in the story's exposition and establishes the mood. For example, the description of a vast deserted tropical beach may set a mood of mystery or isolation. Atmosphere is reinforced by tone, through which the author reveals an attitude toward the events and characters of a story through the choice of particular words and details. The tone of a story—which may be comic, tragic, nostalgic, eerie, and so on—will help to create its overall mood.

Thinking About Atmosphere

1. Explain why setting—the story's actual setting and the farm setting that we never see—is important to the impact of "The Sugawn Chair." What atmosphere is established by the difference between the two settings?
2. What is the author's tone in the story? Give at least three examples of words or details that convey the tone. Explain how this tone contributes to the atmosphere of the story.

COMPOSITION

Writing About Theme

■ Write a brief essay about the theme of "The Sugawn Chair." First identify the theme of the story. Then show how O'Faolain illuminates this theme through the following elements of the story: (a) plot, (b) characterization, (c) setting, (d) point of view, (e) tone, and (f) symbolism. *For help with this assignment, refer to Lesson 6 in the Writing About Literature Handbook at the back of this book.*

Writing a Journal Entry

■ Write a fictional journal entry in which you describe an object that awakens associations for you, as the sack or the sugawn chair does for the narrator of the story. First describe an ordinary object. Then narrate an event or describe a setting associated with the object.

Doris Lessing   *born 1919*

Doris Lessing's varied career has encompassed realistic novels, psychological novels, and science fiction. Unsatisfied with the lack of humanity in the fiction writers of the 1950s, Lessing turned for inspiration to older novels such as Tolstoy's *War and Peace* and Stendhal's *Red and the Black*. "I was looking," she wrote, "for the warmth, the compassion, the humanity, the love of people which illuminates the literature of the nineteenth century and which makes all these old novels a statement of faith in man himself."

Lessing was born in Iran of British parents. When she was five, the family moved to Rhodesia in southern Africa. She grew up in a sparsely populated district, and being alone much of the time, she read a great deal. Lessing moved to England in 1949. A year later she published her first novel, *The Grass Is Singing*, a story that takes place in Rhodesia.

In her early work Lessing chose a direct, traditional style of narrative. Her subjects were her African experiences and various social issues, especially the problems of women in modern society. With *The Golden Notebook* (1962) she began to experiment with the psychological novel, a form she continued in *Briefing for a Descent into Hell* (1971). Over a period of years, Lessing also produced *Children of Violence,* a multivolume work about the harsh realities and the effects of war.

"I hold the view," Lessing has said, "that the realist novel, the realist story, is the highest form of prose writing." "A Mild Attack of Locusts" illustrates Lessing's realism. The story interweaves a deep knowledge of the Rhodesian farmlands with a sensitive portrayal of complex human beings.

Model for Active Reading

In this selection you will find notes in the right-hand margin that highlight parts of the selection. These notes point out important ideas of the literary period and draw your attention to literary elements and techniques covered in the Literary Focuses. Page numbers in the notes refer you to more extensive discussions of these important ideas and elements.

■ Do you think an attack of locusts can ever be considered "mild"? What might Lessing imply by her use of this word?

Doris Lessing

A Mild Attack of Locusts

The rains that year were good; they were coming nicely just as the crops needed them—or so Margaret gathered when the men said they were not too bad. She never had an opinion of her own on matters like the weather, because even to know about what seems a simple thing like the weather needs experience. Which Margaret had not got. The men were Richard, her husband, and old Stephen, Richard's father, a farmer from way back; and these two might argue for hours whether the rains were ruinous or just ordinarily exasperating. Margaret had been on the farm three years. She still did not understand how they did not go bankrupt altogether, when the men never had a good word for the weather, or the soil, or the government. But she was getting to learn the language. Farmers' language. And they neither went bankrupt nor got very rich. They jogged along doing comfortably.

Their crop was maize.[1] Their farm was three thousand acres on the ridges that rise up toward the Zambesi escarpment[2]—high, dry, wind-swept country, cold and dusty in winter, but now, in the wet season, steamy with the heat rising in wet soft waves off miles of green foliage. Beautiful it was, with the sky blue and brilliant halls of air, and the bright green folds and hollows of country beneath, and the mountains lying sharp and bare twenty miles off across the rivers. The sky made her eyes ache; she was not used to it. One does not look so much at the sky in the city she came from. So that evening when Richard said: "The government is sending out warnings that locusts are expected, coming down from the breeding grounds up North," her instinct was to look about her at the trees. Insects—swarms of them—horrible! But Richard and the old man had raised their eyes and were looking up over the mountain. "We haven't had locusts in seven years," they said. "They go in cycles, locusts do." And then: "There goes our crop for this season!"

But they went on with the work of the farm just as usual until one day they were coming up the road to the homestead for the midday break, when old Stephen stopped, raised his finger and pointed: "Look, look, there they are!"

Out ran Margaret to join them, looking at the hills. Out came the servants from the kitchen. They all stood and gazed. Over the rocky levels of the mountain was a streak of rust-colored air. Locusts. There they came.

At once Richard shouted at the cookboy. Old Stephen yelled at

Exposition (p. 711): The first two paragraphs provide background information, introduce the characters, and establish the **limited third-person point of view** (p. 716).

Modern idea: The story deals with the colonial experience, of increasing interest as the Commonwealth began to acquire a new image in the twentieth century (p. 562).

Setting (p. 698): The story is set on a farm in Africa. The steamy, beautiful landscape also supplies an **atmosphere** (p. 756).

Narrative hook (p. 711): The conflict begins when the threat of locusts is introduced.

1. **maize** [māz]: corn.
2. **Zambesi** [zam bē′zē] **escarpment**: steep cliffs along the Zambesi River in southern Africa.

the houseboy. The cookboy ran to beat the old plowshare hanging from a tree branch, which was used to summon the laborers at moments of crisis. The houseboy ran off to the store to collect tin cans, any old bit of metal. The farm was ringing with the clamor of the gong; and they could see the laborers come pouring out of the compound, pointing at the hills and shouting excitedly. Soon they had all come up to the house, and Richard and old Stephen were giving them orders—Hurry, hurry, hurry.

And off they ran again, the two white men with them, and in a few minutes Margaret could see the smoke of fires rising from all around the farmlands. Piles of wood and grass had been prepared there. There were seven patches of bared soil, yellow and oxblood color and pink, where the new mealies were just showing, making a film of bright green; and around each drifted up thick clouds of smoke. They were throwing wet leaves onto the fires now, to make it acrid and black. Margaret was watching the hills. Now there was a long, low cloud advancing, rust-color still, swelling forward and out as she looked. The telephone was ringing. Neighbors—quick, quick, there come the locusts. Old Smith had had his crop eaten to the ground. Quick, get your fires started. For of course, while every farmer hoped the locusts would overlook his farm and go on to the next, it was only fair to warn each other; one must play fair. Everywhere, fifty miles over the countryside, the smoke was rising from myriads[3] of fires. Margaret answered the telephone calls, and between calls she stood watching the locusts. The air was darkening. A strange darkness, for the sun was blazing—it was like the darkness of a veldt[4] fire, when the air gets thick with smoke. The sunlight comes down distorted, a thick, hot orange. Oppressive it was, too, with the heaviness of a storm. The locusts were coming fast. Now half the sky was darkened. Behind the reddish veils in front, which were the advance guards of the swarm, the main swarm showed in dense black cloud, reaching almost to the sun itself.

Margaret was wondering what she could do to help. She did not know. Then up came old Stephen from the lands. "We're finished, Margaret, finished! Those beggars can eat every leaf and blade off the farm in half an hour! And it is only early afternoon—if we can make enough smoke, make enough noise till the sun goes down, they'll settle somewhere else perhaps. . . ." And then: "Get the kettle going. It's thirsty work, this."

So Margaret went to the kitchen, and stoked up the fire, and boiled the water. Now, on the tin roof of the kitchen she could hear the thuds and bangs of falling locusts, or a scratching slither as one skidded down. Here were the first of them. From down on the lands came the beating and banging and clanging of a hundred

Conflict (p. 701): The story's **external conflict** pits the farmers against nature—the locusts.

Style (p. 752): Vivid word choice allows us to picture the locust attack.

---

3. **myriads** [mir′ē ədz]: countless numbers.
4. **veldt** [velt]: region of rolling grassland in southern Africa.

gasoline cans and bits of metal. Stephen impatiently waited while one gasoline can was filled with tea, hot, sweet and orange-colored, and the other with water. In the meantime, he told Margaret about how twenty years back he was eaten out, made bankrupt, by the locust armies. And then, still talking, he hoisted up the gasoline cans, one in each hand, by the wood pieces set cornerwise across each, and jogged off down to the road to the thirsty laborers. By now the locusts were falling like hail onto the roof of the kitchen. It sounded like a heavy storm. Margaret looked out and saw the air dark with a crisscross of the insects, and she set her teeth and ran out into it—what the men could do, she could. Overhead the air was thick, locusts everywhere. The locusts were flopping against her, and she brushed them off, heavy red-brown creatures, looking at her with their beady old-men's eyes while they clung with hard, serrated legs. She held her breath with disgust and ran through into the house. There it was even more like being in a heavy storm. The iron roof was reverberating, and the clamor of iron from the lands was like thunder. Looking out, all the trees were queer and still, clotted with insects, their boughs weighed to the ground. The earth seemed to be moving, locusts crawling everywhere, she could not see the lands at all, so thick was the swarm. Toward the mountains it was like looking into driving rain—even as she watched, the sun was blotted out with a fresh onrush of them. It was a half-night, a perverted blackness. Then came a sharp crack from the bush—a branch had snapped off. Then another. A tree down the slope leaned over and settled heavily to the ground. Through the hail of insects a man came running. More tea, more water was needed. She supplied them. She kept the fires stoked and filled cans with liquid, and then it was four in the afternoon, and the locusts had been pouring across overhead for a couple of hours. Up came old Stephen again, crunching locusts underfoot with every step, locusts clinging all over him; he was cursing and swearing, banging with his old hat at the air. At the doorway he stopped briefly, hastily pulling at the clinging insects and throwing them off, then he plunged into the locust-free living room.

"All the crops finished. Nothing left," he said.

But the gongs were still beating, the men still shouting, and Margaret asked: "Why do you go on with it, then?"

"The main swarm isn't settling. They are heavy with eggs. They are looking for a place to settle and lay. If we can stop the main body settling on our farm, that's everything. If they get a chance to lay their eggs, we are going to have everything eaten flat with hoppers[5] later on." He picked a stray locust off his shirt and split it down with his thumbnail—it was clotted inside with eggs. "Imagine that multiplied by millions. You ever seen a hopper swarm on the march? Well, you're lucky."

Internal conflict (p. 701): Margaret struggles to overcome her revulsion of the locusts in order to help.

Rising action (p. 711): The locust attack and the human reactions carry the story toward its **climax.** The possibility that the locusts will lay eggs adds a complication to the plot.

---

5. **hoppers:** slang for baby locusts.

Margaret thought an adult swarm was bad enough. Outside now the light on the earth was a pale, thin yellow, clotted with moving shadows; the clouds of moving insects thickened and lightened like driving rain. Old Stephen said, "They've got the wind behind them, that's something."

"Is it very bad?" asked Margaret fearfully, and the old man said emphatically: "We're finished. This swarm may pass over, but once they've started, they'll be coming down from the North now one after another. And then there are the hoppers—it might go on for two or three years."

Margaret sat down helplessly, and thought: Well, if it's the end, it's the end. What now? We'll all three have to go back to town. . . . But at this, she took a quick look at Stephen, the old man who had farmed forty years in this country, been bankrupt twice, and she knew nothing would make him go and become a clerk in the city. Yet her heart ached for him, he looked so tired, the worry lines deep from nose to mouth. Poor old man. . . . He had lifted up a locust that had got itself somehow into his pocket, holding it in the air by one leg. "You've got the strength of a steel spring in those legs of yours," he was telling the locust, good-humoredly. Then, although he had been fighting locusts, squashing locusts, yelling at locusts, sweeping them in great mounds into the fires to burn for the last three hours, nevertheless he took this one to the door and carefully threw it out to join its fellows, as if he would rather not harm a hair of its head. This comforted Margaret; all at once she felt irrationally cheered. She remembered it was not the first time in the last three years the man had announced their final and irremediable ruin.

"Get me a drink, lass," he then said, and she set the bottle of whisky by him.

In the meantime, out in the pelting storm of insects, her husband was banging the gong, feeding the fires with leaves, the insects clinging to him all over—she shuddered. "How can you bear to let them touch you?" she asked. He looked at her, disapproving. She felt suitably humble—just as she had when he had first taken a good look at her city self, hair waved and golden, nails red and pointed. Now she was a proper farmer's wife, in sensible shoes and a solid skirt. She might even get to letting locusts settle on her— in time.

Having tossed back a whisky or two, old Stephen went back into the battle, wading now through glistening brown waves of locusts.

Five o'clock. The sun would set in an hour. Then the swarm would settle. It was as thick overhead as ever. The trees were ragged mounds of glistening brown.

Margaret began to cry. It was all so hopeless—if it wasn't a bad season, it was locusts; if it wasn't locusts, it was army worm[6] or

Characterization (p. 724): We are told **directly** of Margaret's helplessness, but we see Stephen **indirectly** through his actions and through Margaret's impressions.

Theme (p. 698): Lessing uses Stephen's ability to recover from hardship as an example of the power of the human spirit.

Modern idea: Despair is a frequent reaction to problems in modern life (p. 563).

6. **army worm:** larvae of certain moths that destroy crops.

veldt fires. Always something. The rustling of the locust armies was like a big forest in the storm; their settling on the roof was like the beating of the rain; the gound was invisible in a sleek, brown, surging tide—it was like being drowned in locusts, submerged by the loathsome brown flood. It seemed as if the roof might sink in under the weight of them, as if the door might give in under their pressure and these rooms fill with them—and it was getting so dark . . . she looked up. The air was thinner; gaps of blue showed in the dark, moving clouds. The blue spaces were cold and thin—the sun must be setting. Through the fog of insects she saw figures approaching. First old Stephen, marching bravely along, then her husband, drawn and haggard with weariness. Behind them the servants. All were crawling all over with insects. The sound of the gongs had stopped. She could hear nothing but the ceaseless rustle of a myriad wings.

The two men slapped off the insects and came in.

"Well," said Richard, kissing her on the cheek, "the main swarm has gone over."

"For heaven's sake," said Margaret angrily, still half crying, "what's here is bad enough, isn't it?" For although the evening air was no longer black and thick, but a clear blue, with a pattern of insects whizzing this way and that across it, everything else—trees, buildings, bushes, earth—was gone under the moving brown masses.

"If it doesn't rain in the night and keep them here—if it doesn't rain and weight them down with water, they'll be off in the morning at sunrise."

"We're bound to have some hoppers. But not the main swarm—that's something."

Margaret roused herself, wiped her eyes, pretended she had not been crying, and fetched them some supper, for the servants were too exhausted to move. She sent them down to the compound to rest.

She served the supper and sat listening. There is not one maize plant left, she heard. Not one. The men would get the planters out the moment the locusts had gone. They must start all over again.

But what's the use of that, Margaret wondered, if the whole farm was going to be crawling with hoppers? But she listened while they discussed the new government pamphlet that said how to defeat the hoppers. You must have men out all the time, moving over the farm to watch for movement in the grass. When you find a patch of hoppers, small lively black things, like crickets, then you dig trenches around the patch or spray them with poison from pumps supplied by the government. The government wanted them to cooperate in a world plan for eliminating this plague forever. You should attack locusts at the source. Hoppers, in short. The men were talking as if they were planning a war, and Margaret listened, amazed.

Round character (p. 724): We see Margaret's hopelessness, anger, courage, and kindness.

In the night it was quiet; no sign of the settled armies outside, except sometimes a branch snapped, or a tree could be heard crashing down.

Margaret slept badly in the bed beside Richard, who was sleeping like the dead, exhausted with the afternoon's fight. In the morning she woke to yellow sunshine lying across the bed—clear sunshine, with an occasional blotch of shadow moving over it. She went to the window. Old Stephen was ahead of her. There he stood outside, gazing down over the bush. And she gazed, astounded—and entranced, much against her will. For it looked as if every tree, every bush, all the earth, were lit with pale flames. The locusts were fanning their wings to free them of the night dews. There was a shimmer of red-tinged gold light everywhere.

She went out to join the old man, stepping carefully among the insects. They stood and watched. Overhead the sky was blue, blue and clear.

"Pretty," said old Stephen, with satisfaction.

Well, thought Margaret, we may be ruined, we may be bankrupt, but not everyone has seen an army of locusts fanning their wings at dawn.

Over the slopes, in the distance, a faint red smear showed in the sky, thickened and spread. "There they go," said old Stephen. "There goes the main army, off south."

And now from the trees, from the earth all round them, the locusts were taking wing. They were like small aircraft, maneuvering for the takeoff, trying their wings to see if they were dry enough. Off they went. A reddish-brown steam was rising off the miles of bush, off the lands, the earth. Again the sunlight darkened.

And as the clotted branches lifted, the weight on them lightening, there was nothing but the black spines of branches, trees. No green left, nothing. All morning they watched, the three of them, as the brown crust thinned and broke and dissolved, flying up to mass with the main army, now a brownish-red smear in the southern sky. The lands which had been filmed with green, the new tender mealie plants, were stark and bare. All the trees stripped. A devastated landscape. No green, no green anywhere.

By midday the reddish cloud had gone. Only an occasional locust flopped down. On the ground were the corpses and the wounded. The African laborers were sweeping these up with branches and collecting them in tins.

"Ever eaten sun-dried locust?" asked old Stephen. "That time twenty years ago, when I went broke, I lived on mealie meal and dried locusts for three months. They aren't bad at all—rather like smoked fish, if you come to think of it."

But Margaret preferred not even to think of it.

After the midday meal the men went off to the lands. Everything was to be replanted. With a bit of luck another swarm would not come traveling down just this way. But they hoped it would

Paradox (p. 671): The beauty of the locusts contrasts with the destruction they cause. Such paradoxes are common in modern literature.

Climax (p. 711): The locusts fly away, and the tension reaches a peak. The climax is followed by the **falling action**.

Modern idea: The description of the dead locusts uses images of war. Such imagery is common in modern literature (p. 563).

rain very soon, to spring some new grass, because the cattle would die otherwise—there was not a blade of grass left on the farm. As for Margaret, she was trying to get used to the idea of three or four years of locusts. Locusts were going to be like bad weather, from now on, always imminent. She felt like a survivor after war— if this devastated and mangled countryside was not ruin, well, what then was ruin?

But the men ate their supper with good appetites.

"It could have been worse," was what they said. "It could be much worse."

Resolution (p. 711): The falling action ends. The ending is typically modern because the problem is not completely solved.

STUDY QUESTIONS

Recalling

1. How long has Margaret lived on the farm? Give two examples of her lack of experience.
2. Name three actions the farmers take to ward off the locusts.
3. Explain why the farmers want to keep the locusts from settling.
4. What do the locusts actually do to the farm?
5. What plans do the farmers make? In what way do they assess the attack of locusts?

Interpreting

6. The events of the story are narrated through the consciousness of Margaret, a novice on the farm. What effect does this point of view have on the impact of the story?
7. Find examples of Stephen's pessimism and of his optimism. Explain the contradiction.

LITERARY FOCUS

Theme

Theme is a story's main idea, a general statement about life. A theme goes beyond the specific details of a story to some universal meaning. For example, although Joyce's "Araby" is about a particular young Irishman at a bazaar in Dublin, the theme of the story should be applicable to the life of anyone, anywhere. In addition, a theme is always expressed as a sentence. For example, the theme of "Araby" may be stated as "Unrealistic expectations lead to disappointment."

A theme can be directly **stated** or **implied**, and all the elements of a story point in some way

to the theme. The title may imply an opinion of what happens in the story. The outcome of the plot may suggest a lesson about life. Characterization may reveal the author's ideas about people in general, and setting may suggest an attitude about the world. Point of view may tell us how the author wants us to react to the story. Symbols represent abstract ideas and, therefore, direct us to the author's concerns.

Thinking About Theme

■ State the theme of "A Mild Attack of Locusts." Explain how this theme develops out of the story and how it is universally applicable.

VOCABULARY

Antonyms

Antonyms are words that have opposite or nearly opposite meanings. *Quiet* and *loud* are antonyms. The words in capitals are from "A Mild Attack of Locusts." Choose the word that is *most nearly the opposite* of each word in capitals, *as the word is used in the selection.*

1. RUINOUS: (a) optimistic (b) constructive
   (c) calamitous (d) disastrous
2. EXASPERATING: (a) tiresome (b) hopeful
   (c) pleasing (d) necessary
3. ACRID: (a) mild (b) bitter
   (c) brilliant (d) melodious
4. SERRATED: (a) jagged (b) fashionable
   (c) smooth (d) peculiar
5. REVERBERATING: (a) musical (b) anxious
   (c) still (d) quaking

Nadine Gordimer   *born 1923*

Nadine Gordimer has written novels and short stories, and her work has appeared regularly in periodicals such as the *New Yorker* and the *Atlantic*. Born in Springs, near Johannesburg, South Africa, she was educated there at private schools and—for one year—at the University of Witwatersrand. She has lectured extensively and was a visiting professor to the United States.

Gordimer's fiction reflects the concern with racial problems that has dominated life in South Africa in this century. Her themes include the political and social consequences of apartheid, South Africa's policy of strict racial segregation. The stories, however, are more than sociological journalism. While they grow out of the South African scene, they have universal application and appeal.

The settings of Nadine Gordimer's fiction range from sophisticated South African suburbs to huts with thatched roofs and mud floors. She is equally adept at writing about society matrons, native peddlers, and professional hunters. The stories focus on the observed moment, the brief but revealing incident.

"The Train from Rhodesia" is a sad but beautiful story demonstrating Gordimer's ability to arrest the reader's attention with a telling moment of reality.

▇ A wise person said that receiving gifts is more difficult than giving them. Do you agree? Be able to defend your answer.

Nadine Gordimer

The Train from Rhodesia

The train came out of the red horizon and bore down toward them over the single straight track.

The stationmaster came out of his little brick station with its pointed chalet roof, feeling the creases in his serge uniform in his legs as well. A stir of preparedness rippled through the squatting native vendors waiting in the dust; the face of a carved wooden animal, eternally surprised, stuck out of a sack. The stationmaster's barefoot children wandered over. From the gray mud huts with the untidy heads that stood within a decorated mud wall, chickens, and dogs with their skin stretched like parchment over their bones, followed the piccanins[1] down to the track. The flushed and perspiring west cast a reflection, faint, without heat, upon the station, upon the tin shed marked "Goods," upon the walled kraal,[2] upon the gray tin house of the stationmaster and upon the sand, that lapped all around, from sky

---

1. **piccanins:** native children.
2. **kraal** [kräl]: in southern Africa, a fenced enclosure for livestock; corral.

to sky, cast little rhythmical cups of shadow, so that the sand became the sea, and closed over the children's black feet softly and without imprint.

The stationmaster's wife sat behind the mesh of her veranda. Above her head the hunk of a sheep's carcass moved slightly, dangling in a current of air.

They waited.

The train called out, along the sky; but there was no answer; and the cry hung on: I'm coming . . . I'm coming . . .

The engine flared out now, big, whisking a dwindling body behind it; the track flared out to let it in.

Creaking, jerking, jostling, gasping, the train filled the station.

Here, let me see that one—the young woman curved her body further out of the corridor window. Missus? smiled the old boy, looking at the creatures he held in his hand. From a piece of string on his gray finger hung a tiny woven basket; he lifted it, questioning. No, no, she urged, leaning down toward him, across the height of the train, toward the man in the piece of old rug; that one, that one, her hand commanded. It was a lion, carved out of soft dry wood that looked like spongecake; heraldic, black and white, with impressionistic detail burnt in. The old man held it up to her still smiling, not from the heart, but at the cus-

tomer. Between its Vandyke teeth, in the mouth opened in an endless roar too terrible to be heard, it had a black tongue. Look, said the young husband, if you don't mind! And round the neck of the thing, a piece of fur (rat? rabbit? meerkat?); a real mane, majestic, telling you somehow that the artist had delight in the lion.

All up and down the length of the train in the dust the artists sprang, walking bent, like performing animals, the better to exhibit the fantasy held toward the faces on the train. Buck, startled and stiff, staring with round black and white eyes. More lions, standing erect, grappling with strange, thin, elongated warriors who clutched spears and showed no fear in their slits of eyes. How much, they asked from the train, how much?

Give me penny, said the little ones with nothing to sell. The dogs went and sat, quite still, under the dining car, where the train breathed out the smell of meat cooking with onion.

A man passed beneath the arch of reaching arms meeting gray-black and white in the exchange of money for the staring wooden eyes, the stiff wooden legs sticking up in the air; went along under the voices and the bargaining, interrogating the wheels. Past the dogs; glancing up at the dining car where he could stare at the faces, behind glass, drinking beer, two by two, on either side of a uniform railway vase with its pale dead flower. Right to the end, to the guard's van, where the stationmaster's children had just collected their mother's two loaves of bread; to the engine itself, where the stationmaster and the driver stood talking against the steaming complaint of the resting beast.

The man called out to them, something loud and joking. They turned to laugh, in a twirl of steam. The two children careered over the sand, clutching the bread, and burst through the iron gate and up the path through the garden in which nothing grew.

Passengers drew themselves in at the corridor windows and turned into compartments to fetch money, to call someone to look. Those sitting inside looked up: suddenly different, caged faces, boxed in, cut off, after the contact of outside. There was an orange a piccanin would like. . . . What about that chocolate? It wasn't very nice. . . .

A young girl had collected a handful of the hard kind, that no one liked, out of the chocolate box, and was throwing them to the dogs, over at the dining car. But the hens darted in, and swallowed the chocolates, incredibly quick and accurate, before they had even dropped in the dust, and the dogs, a little bewildered, looked up with their brown eyes, not expecting anything.

—No, leave it, said the girl, don't take it. . . .

Too expensive, too much, she shook her head and raised her voice to the old boy, giving up the lion. He held it up where she had handed it to him. No, she said, shaking her head. Three-and-six?[3] insisted her husband, loudly. Yes baas! laughed the boy. *Three-and-six?*—the young man was incredulous. Oh leave it—she said. The young man stopped. Don't you want it? he said, keeping his face closed to the boy. No, never mind, she said, leave it. The old native kept his head on one side, looking at them sideways, holding the lion. Three-and-six, he murmured, as old people repeat things to themselves.

The young woman drew her head in. She went into the coupé[4] and sat down. Out of the window, on the other side, there was nothing; sand and bush; a thorn tree. Back through the open doorway, past the figure of her husband in the corridor, there was the station, the voices, wooden animals waving, running feet. Her eye followed the funny little valance of scrolled wood that outlined the chalet roof of the station; she thought of the lion and smiled. That bit of fur round the neck. But the wooden buck, the hippos, the elephants, the baskets that already bulked out of their brown paper under the seat and on the luggage rack! How will they look at home? Where will you put them? What will they mean away from the places you found them? Away from the unreality of the last few weeks? The man outside. But he is not part of the unreality; he is for good now. Odd . . . somewhere there was an idea that he, that living with him, was part of the holiday, the strange places.

Outside, a bell rang. The stationmaster was leaning against the end of the train, green flag rolled in readiness. A few men who had got down to stretch their legs sprang onto the train, clinging to the observation platforms, or perhaps merely standing on the iron step, holding the rail; but on the train, safe from the one

---

3. **Three-and-six:** three shillings and a sixpence, the equivalent of approximately thirty-four American cents when the story takes place.
4. **coupé** [ko͞o pā′]: in British trains, a half-compartment at the end of a passenger car with only one row of seats.

dusty platform, the one tin house, the empty sand.

There was a grunt. The train jerked. Through the glass the beer drinkers looked out, as if they could not see beyond it. Behind the flyscreen, the stationmaster's wife sat facing back at them beneath the darkening hunk of meat.

There was a shout. The flag drooped out. Joints not yet coordinated, the segmented body of the train heaved and bumped back against itself. It began to move; slowly the scrolled chalet moved past it, the yells of the natives, running alongside, jetted up into the air, fell back at different levels. Staring wooden faces waved drunkenly, there, then gone, questioning for the last time at the windows. Here, one-and-six baas!—As one automatically opens a hand to catch a thrown ball, a man fumbled wildly down his pocket, brought up the shilling and sixpence and threw them out; the old native, gasping, his skinny toes splaying the sand, flung the lion.

The piccanins were waving, the dogs stood, tails uncertain, watching the train go: past the mud huts, where a woman turned to look, up from the smoke of the fire, her hand pausing on her hip.

The stationmaster went slowly in under the chalet.

The old native stood, breath blowing out the skin between his ribs, feet tense, balanced in the sand, smiling and shaking his head. In his opened palm, held in the attitude of receiving, was the retrieved shilling and sixpence.

The blind end of the train was being pulled helplessly out of the station.

The young man swung in from the corridor, breathless. He was shaking his head with laughter and triumph. Here! he said. And waggled the lion at her. One-and-six!

What? she said.

He laughed. I was arguing with him for fun, bargaining—when the train had pulled out already, he came tearing after. . . . One-and-six baas! So there's your lion.

She was holding it away from her, the head with the open jaws, the pointed teeth, the black tongue, the wonderful ruff of fur facing her. She was looking at it with an expression of not seeing, of seeing something different. Her face was drawn up, wryly, like the face of a discomforted child. Her mouth lifted nervously at the corner. Very slowly, cautious, she lifted her finger and touched the mane, where it was joined to the wood.

But how could you, she said. He was shocked by the dismay of her face.

Good heavens, he said, what's the matter?

If you wanted the thing, she said, her voice rising and breaking with the shrill impotence of anger, why didn't you buy it in the first place? If you wanted it, why didn't you pay for it? Why didn't you take it decently, when he offered it? Why did you have to wait for him to run after the train with it, and give him one-and-six? One-and-six!

She was pushing it at him, trying to force him to take it. He stood astonished, his hands hanging at his sides.

But you wanted it! You liked it so much?

—It's a beautiful piece of work, she said fiercely, as if to protect it from him.

You liked it so much! You said yourself it was too expensive—

Oh *you*—she said, hopeless and furious. *You*. . . . She threw the lion onto the seat.

He stood looking at her.

She sat down again in the corner and, her face slumped in her hand, stared out of the window. Everything was turning round inside her. One-and-six. One-and-six. One-and-six for the wood and the carving and the sinews of the legs and the switch of the tail. The mouth open like that and the teeth. The black tongue, rolling, like a wave. The mane round the neck. To give one-and-six for that. The heat of shame mounted through her legs and body and sounded in her ears like the sound of sand pouring. Pouring, pouring. She sat there, sick. A weariness, a tastelessness, the discovery of a void made her hands slacken their grip, atrophy emptily, as if the hour was not worth their grasp. She was feeling like this again. She had thought it was something to do with single-ness, with being alone and belonging too much to oneself.

She sat there not wanting to move or speak, or to look at anything, even; so that the mood should be associated with nothing, no object, word or sight that might recur and so recall the feeling again. . . . Smuts[5] blew in grittily,

---

5. **smuts:** black grimy particles; soot.

settled on her hands. Her back remained at ex-actly the same angle, turned against the young man sitting with his hands drooping between his sprawled legs, and the lion, fallen on its side in the corner.

The train had cast the station like a skin. It called out to the sky, I'm coming, I'm coming; and again, there was no answer.

STUDY QUESTIONS

Recalling
1. Describe the station and the people there at the beginning of the story.
2. Give three examples of the activity that begins when the train arrives at the station.
3. What are the woman's thoughts about the souvenirs of her "holiday" and about her husband?
4. Explain the steps that lead to the purchase of the carved lion. Describe the woman's reaction to the purchase.

Interpreting
5. What does the arrival of the train mean to the people at the station?
6. What does the incident with the lion tell us about the relationship between the woman and her husband?
7. In what sense does the station symbolize the woman's psychological condition?

Extending
8. Use the story as an example to explain the differ-ence between being alone and being lonely.

COMPOSITION

Writing About Significant Details
■ Explain the use of significant detail in "The Train from Rhodesia." First choose at least two details from the story. Then explain the inferences that can be made from each detail. Finally explain how the use of such details adds to the richness of the story. Although you may use any details from the story you wish, you may want to consider one or more of the following: (a) the woman's thoughts about her souvenirs and what they say about her personality, (b) the description of the station and what it symbolizes, and (c) the description of the lion and why the author itemizes its features.

Writing a Friendly Letter
■ Imagine that you are traveling by train through an empty landscape like the one depicted in the story. Write a letter to a friend describing the land through which you are traveling and the feelings that the landscape inspires in you.

V. S. Naipaul   *born 1932*

V. S. Naipaul was born on the island of Trinidad in the West Indies, to which his family had originally immigrated from India. Growing up in Trinidad's large ethnic Indian community, he became steeped in both Asian and West Indian cultures. He attended Oxford University as a scholarship student and after graduation settled permanently in England, where his novel *The Mystic Masseur* (1957) and short story collection *Miguel Street* (1959) quickly impressed critics with their ironic yet compassionate depiction of West Indian life. Other novels followed, including the highly acclaimed *A House for Mr. Biswas* (1961), *In a Free State* (1971), and *A Bend in the River* (1979). Naipaul's interest in his ethnic background spurred many trips to India and resulted in two nonfiction works about Indian life, *An Area of Darkness* (1965) and *India: A Wounded Civilization* (1977). Naipaul has also published other nonfiction books and contributes both fiction and nonfiction to English journals.

"B. Wordsworth" is a moving account of an impoverished Trinidadian poet and his effects on a young boy. Like most of the stories from *Miguel Street,* it is at once setting-specific and universal.

■ What is the significance of the name "Wordsworth" for a fictional poet?

V. S. Naipaul

B. Wordsworth

Three beggars called punctually every day at the hospitable houses in Miguel Street. At about ten an Indian came in his dhoti[1] and white jacket, and we poured a tin of rice into the sack he carried on his back. At twelve an old woman smoking a clay pipe came and she got a cent. At two a blind man led by a boy called for his penny.

Sometimes we had a rogue.[2] One day a man called and said he was hungry. We gave him a meal. He asked for a cigarette and wouldn't go until we had lit it for him. That man never came again.

The strangest caller came one afternoon at about four o'clock. I had come back from school and was in my home-clothes. The man said to me, "Sonny, may I come inside your yard?"

He was a small man and he was tidily dressed. He wore a hat, a white shirt and black trousers.

I asked, "What you want?"

He said, "I want to watch your bees."

We had four small gru-gru palm trees,[3] and they were full of uninvited bees.

I ran up the steps and shouted, "Ma, it have a man outside here. He say he want to watch the bees."

My mother came out, looked at the man and asked in an unfriendly way, "What you want?"

The man said, "I want to watch your bees."

---

1. **dhoti** [dō′tē]: loincloth worn by Hindu men.
2. **rogue:** here, a wandering beggar; a tramp.

3. **gru-gru palm trees:** spiny-trunked West Indian palm trees with edible nuts.

His English was so good, it didn't sound natural, and I could see my mother was worried.

She said to me, "Stay here and watch him while he watch the bees."

The man said, "Thank you, Madam. You have done a good deed today."

He spoke very slowly and very correctly, as though every word was costing him money.

We watched the bees, this man and I, for about an hour, squatting near the palm trees.

The man said, "I like watching bees. Sonny, do you like watching bees?"

I said, "I ain't have the time."

He shook his head sadly. He said, "That's what I do, I just watch. I can watch ants for days. Have you ever watched ants? And scorpions, and centipedes, and *congorees*—have you watched those?"

I shook my head.

I said, "What you does do, mister?"

He got up and said, "I am a poet."

I said, "A good poet?"

He said, "The greatest in the world."

"What your name, mister?"

"B. Wordsworth."

"B for Bill?"

"Black. Black Wordsworth. White Wordsworth[4] was my brother. We share one heart. I can watch a small flower like the morning glory and cry."

I said, "Why you does cry?"

"Why, boy? Why? You will know when you grow up. You're a poet, too, you know. And when you're a poet you can cry for everything."

I couldn't laugh.

He said, "You like your mother?"

"When she not beating me."

He pulled out a printed sheet from his hip pocket and said, "On this paper is the greatest poem about mothers and I'm going to sell it to you at a bargain price. For four cents."

I went inside and I said, "Ma, you want to buy a poetry for four cents?"

My mother said, "Tell that blasted man to haul his tail away from my yard, you hear."

I said to B. Wordsworth, "My mother say she ain't have four cents."

B. Wordsworth said, "It is the poet's tragedy."

And he put the paper back in his pocket. He didn't seem to mind.

I said, "Is a funny way to go round selling poetry like that. Only calypsonians[5] do that sort of thing. A lot of people does buy?"

He said, "No one has yet bought a single copy."

"But why you does keep on going round, then?"

He said, "In this way I watch many things, and I always hope to meet poets."

I said, "You really think I is a poet?"

"You're as good as me," he said.

And when B. Wordsworth left, I prayed I would see him again.

About a week later, coming back from school one afternoon, I met him at the corner of Miguel Street.

He said, "I have been waiting for you for a long time."

I said, "You sell any poetry yet?"

He shook his head.

He said, "In my yard I have the best mango tree in Port-of-Spain.[6] And now the mangoes are ripe and red and very sweet and juicy. I have waited here for you to tell you this and to invite you to come and eat some of my mangoes."

He lived in Alberto Street in a one-roomed hut placed right in the center of the lot. The yard seemed all green. There was the big mango tree. There was a coconut tree and there was a plum tree. The place looked wild, as though it wasn't in the city at all. You couldn't see all the big concrete houses in the street.

He was right. The mangoes were sweet and juicy. I ate about six, and the yellow mango juice

4. **White Wordsworth:** William Wordsworth (1770–1850), British Romantic poet.

5. **calypsonians:** performers of calypso songs, ballads native to Trinidad. Calypso songs are usually humorous or satirical and are accompanied by syncopated music.

6. **Port-of-Spain:** the capital of Trinidad and one of the chief ports in the West Indies.

ran down my arms to my elbows and down my mouth to my chin and my shirt was stained.

My mother said when I got home, "Where you was? You think you is a man now and could go all over the place? Go cut a whip[7] for me."

She beat me rather badly, and I ran out of the house swearing that I would never come back. I went to B. Wordsworth's house. I was so angry, my nose was bleeding.

B. Wordsworth said, "Stop crying, and we will go for a walk."

I stopped crying, but I was breathing short. We went for a walk. We walked down St. Clair Avenue to the Savannah and we walked to the racecourse.

B. Wordsworth said, "Now, let us lie on the grass and look up at the sky, and I want you to think how far those stars are from us."

I did as he told me, and I saw what he meant. I felt like nothing, and at the same time I had never felt so big and great in all my life. I forgot all my anger and all my tears and all the blows.

When I said I was better, he began telling me the names of the stars, and I particularly remembered the constellation of Orion the Hunter, though I don't really know why. I can spot Orion even today, but I have forgotten the rest.

Then a light was flashed into our faces, and we saw a policeman. We got up from the grass.

The policeman said, "What you doing here?"

B. Wordsworth said, "I have been asking myself the same question for forty years."

We became friends, B. Wordsworth and I. He told me, "You must never tell anybody about me and about the mango tree and the coconut tree and the plum tree. You must keep that a secret. If you tell anybody, I will know, because I am a poet."

I gave him my word and I kept it.

I liked his little room. It had no more furniture than George's front room, but it looked cleaner and healthier. But it also looked lonely.

One day I asked him, "Mister Wordsworth, why you does keep all this bush in your yard? Ain't it does make the place damp?"

He said, "Listen, and I will tell you a story.

---

7. **cut a whip:** that is, cut a branch to use as a whip.

Once upon a time a boy and girl met each other and they fell in love. They loved each other so much they got married. They were both poets. He loved words. She loved grass and flowers and trees. They lived happily in a single room, and then one day, the girl poet said to the boy poet, 'We are going to have another poet in the family.' But this poet was never born, because the girl died, and the young poet died with her, inside her. And the girl's husband was very sad, and he said he would never touch a thing in the girl's garden. And so the garden remained, and grew high and wild."

I looked at B. Wordsworth, and as he told me this lovely story, he seemed to grow older. I understood his story.

We went for long walks together. We went to the Botanical Gardens and the Rock Gardens. We climbed Chancellor Hill in the late afternoon and watched the darkness fall on Port-of-Spain, and watched the lights go on in the city and on the ships in the harbor.

He did everything as though he were doing it for the first time in his life. He did everything as though he were doing some church rite.

He would say to me, "Now, how about having some ice cream?"

And when I said yes, he would grow very serious and say, "Now, which café shall we patronize?" As though it were a very important thing. He would think for some time about it, and finally say, "I think I will go and negotiate the purchase with that shop."

The world became a most exciting place.

One day, when I was in his yard, he said to me, "I have a great secret which I am now going to tell you."

I said, "It really secret?"

"At the moment, yes."

I looked at him, and he looked at me. He said, "This is just between you and me, remember. I am writing a poem."

"Oh." I was disappointed.

He said, "But this is a different sort of poem. This is the greatest poem in the world."

I whistled.

He said, "I have been working on it for more

than five years now. I will finish it in about twenty-two years from now, that is, if I keep on writing at the present rate."

"You does write a lot, then?"

He said, "Not any more. I just write one line a month. But I make sure it is a good line."

I asked, "What was last month's good line?"

He looked up at the sky, and said, *The past is deep.*"

I said, "It is a beautiful line."

B. Wordsworth said, "I hope to distill the experiences of a whole month into that single line of poetry. So, in twenty-two years, I shall have written a poem that will sing to all humanity."

I was filled with wonder.

Our walks continued. We walked along the sea wall at Docksite one day, and I said, "Mr. Wordsworth, if I drop this pin in the water, you think it will float?"

He said, "This is a strange world. Drop your pin, and let us see what will happen."

The pin sank.

I said, "How is the poem this month?"

But he never told me any other line. He merely said, "Oh, it comes, you know. It comes."

Or we would sit on the sea wall and watch the liners come into the harbor.

But of the greatest poem in the world I heard no more.

I felt he was growing older.

"How you does live, Mr. Wordsworth?" I asked him one day.

He said, "You mean how I get money?"

When I nodded, he laughed in a crooked way.

He said, "I sing calypsos in the calypso season."

"And that last you the rest of the year?"

"It is enough."

"But you will be the richest man in the world when you write the greatest poem?"

He didn't reply.

One day when I went to see him in his little house, I found him lying on his little bed. He looked so old and so weak, that I found myself wanting to cry.

He said, "The poem is not going well."

He wasn't looking at me. He was looking through the window at the coconut tree, and he was speaking as though I wasn't there. He said, "When I was twenty I felt the power within myself." Then, almost in front of my eyes, I could see his face growing older and more tired. He said, "But that—that was a long time ago."

And then—I felt it so keenly, it was as though I had been slapped by my mother. I could see it clearly on his face. It was there for everyone to see. Death on the shrinking face.

He looked at me, and saw my tears and sat up.

He said, "Come." I went and sat on his knees.

He looked into my eyes, and he said, "Oh, you can see it, too. I always knew you had the poet's eye."

He didn't even look sad, and that made me burst out crying loudly.

He pulled me to his thin chest, and said, "Do you want me to tell you a funny story?" and he smiled encouragingly at me.

But I couldn't reply.

He said, "When I have finished this story, I want you to promise that you will go away and never come back to see me. Do you promise?"

I nodded.

He said, "Good. Well, listen. That story I told you about the boy poet and the girl poet, do you remember that? That wasn't true. It was something I just made up. All this talk about poetry and the greatest poem in the world, that wasn't true, either. Isn't that the funniest thing you have heard?"

But his voice broke.

I left the house, and ran home crying, like a poet, for everything I saw.

I walked along Alberto Street a year later, but I could find no sign of the poet's house. It hadn't vanished, just like that. It had been pulled down, and a big, two-storied building had taken its place. The mango tree and the plum tree and the coconut tree had all been cut down, and there was brick and concrete everywhere.

It was just as though B. Wordsworth had never existed.

STUDY QUESTIONS

Recalling

1. In the opening section, what does the tidily dressed caller want to watch? What explanation does he give for calling himself B. Wordsworth? What does he say the narrator, like himself, is?
2. Summarize the story B. Wordsworth tells to explain the overgrown shrubbery in his yard.
3. What do B. Wordsworth and the narrator usually do together in Port-of-Spain? According to the end of the second section, what does the world become for the narrator?
4. How often does B. Wordsworth add to "the greatest poem in the world"? What was the most recent line?
5. When he is dying, what does B. Wordsworth make the narrator promise? What does he confess was not true? How does the narrator run home?
6. What has happened to B. Wordsworth's house a year later?

Interpreting

7. To what love do the bees and ants, the yard plants, and the allusion to "White Wordsworth" all point? What else does B. Wordsworth teach the narrator to love?
8. What might the destruction of B. Wordsworth's house represent? For what things does the story suggest poets cry?

Extending

9. What is your own definition of a poet? Can a person be a poet and write nothing down? Explain.

COMPARING WRITERS

1. Twentieth-century fiction often concentrates on the psychological conditions of characters. Because such topics are abstract, authors sometimes use concrete objects to symbolize characters' mental states. Compare two or more of the following stories: "Still," "A Mild Attack of Locusts," "The Sugawn Chair," "The Train from Rhodesia," and "B. Wordsworth." For each story explain how a concrete object or scene helps us understand the mental state of a character.
2. Many of the contemporary British stories presented here explore childhood and adolescence. Select two such stories from this unit. Explain the specific change or realization that takes place in each story's young character, and also compare and contrast the overall view of childhood and adolescence that the stories present.
3. Much contemporary British literature deals with the colonial and postcolonial experience. Choose two or more of the following selections: "Shooting an Elephant," "A Mild Attack of Locusts," "The Train from Rhodesia," "B. Wordsworth." Compare and contrast the views each selection presents of British colonialism and its effects on native cultures.

ACTIVE READING

Sound in Prose

Earlier in this book we looked at how poets try to create patterns of sound in poetry. We saw that these patterns are built up not only through word choice but also through rhythm, rhyme, alliteration, and other techniques of sound. We saw that in poetry sound can help to evoke moods and emotions and express meanings.

In prose we cannot always point so readily to this kind of use of sound. Yet all good writers are sensitive to the effects of particular rhythms and special combinations of sounds. For example, the novelist James Joyce was acutely aware of the special effects of sound in prose. Consider the following passage from his story "Araby" (page 707), in which he describes the lively activity of children outdoors just before dark:

When the short days of winter came dusk fell before we had well eaten our dinners. When we met in the street the houses had grown somber. The space of sky above us was the color of ever-changing violet and toward it the lamps of the street lifted their feeble lanterns. The cold air stung us and we played till our bodies glowed. Our shouts echoed in the silent street. The career of our play brought us through the dark muddy lanes behind the houses where we ran the gantlet of the rough tribes from the cottages, to the back doors of the dark dripping gardens where odors arose from the ashpits, to the dark odorous stables where a coachman smoothed and combed the horse or shook music from the buckled harness.

Joyce gives us the scene and the actions. Moreover, he calls up a rich, lovely combination of impressions and moods: the children's excitement, the darkening light, the sharp cold, the hushed quiet in the streets, the sense of bustling play, the momentum of spontaneous motion. How does Joyce achieve these marvelous effects? One answer lies in his selection of wonderful details and images; a second answer lies in the very rhythm and sound of the prose.

Thus, to convey some of the children's excitement and hurry, Joyce writes with monosyllabic words primarily—for instance, "*When the short days of* winter *came dusk fell* before *we had well* eaten *our* dinners." To quicken the pace, he omits all internal punctuation, so that the first half of the passage must be read almost without pause. Also, by including a variety of soft consonant and vowel sounds, he gives the passage the quality of an eager, rapid whisper: "*When the sh*ort days *of w*inter came dusk *fell.* . . ."

In the second through fifth sentences, Joyce even captures something of what we feel when nightfall approaches, with its greater stillness and deeper darkness and silence. He now uses longer, more resonant, more somber vowel sounds: ". . . the h*o*uses had gr*ow*n somber . . . the c*o*lor of ever-changing vi*o*let . . . *our* bodies gl*ow*ed. . . . *Our* sh*ou*ts ech*o*ed. . . ."

Then, to suggest the feeling of rushing, cascading physical movement, Joyce lets the last sentence of the passage run on and on—in contrast to the preceding sentences. He adds punctuation and clause upon clause, so as to carry us along *rhythmically,* as well as through images. Thus, we "see" and "feel" the children's escapades through "the dark muddy lanes" to "the dark dripping gardens" to "the dark odorous stables."

Try to imagine this extraordinary passage without these nuances of sound and rhythm. We would have the scene and the actions, and the story would proceed. However, the whole imaginative texture—what is unstated yet touches our senses, our emotions, and perhaps even our memories—would be lost.

REVIEW: THE ENGLISH VOICE

The Artist's View

The writers of the past, on the rare occasions when they paid any attention to their own roles, identified themselves as chroniclers or singers, entertainers or sonneteers, lexicographers or moralists, rhapsodists or seers. The modern writer, on the other hand, emphasizes that he or she is, above all, an *artist*.

Usually in celebration, though sometimes in self-defense, the voice of the modern artist insists: I am a maker, a creator, an artificer. I wield imagination as my weapon, my shield, my tool for reshaping reality.

Shaw

Yes, you squashed cabbage leaf, you disgrace to the noble architecture of these columns, you incarnate insult to the English language: I could pass you off as the Queen of Sheba.

Yeats

*. . . Gather me
Into the artifice of eternity.*

Eliot

*I am moved by fancies that are curled
Around these images. . . .*

Auden

*Follow, poet, follow right
To the bottom of the night,*

*With your unconstraining voice
Still persuade us to rejoice.*

Hughes

*I sit in the top of the wood, my eyes closed. . . .
Now I hold Creation in my foot.*

Forster

A few great men—mostly poets—have found life absolutely beautiful, in all its aspects.

Joyce

Her name sprang to my lips at moments in strange prayers and praises which I myself did not understand.

Woolf

But why not be original? Why not be herself, anyhow?

Naipaul

"I hope to distill the experiences of a whole month into that single line of poetry. So, in twenty-two years, I shall have written a poem that will sing to all humanity."

The modern artist never tires of celebrating creation, imagination, originality. The lesson of this celebration is clear: Reality is what the artists in all of us make of it.

Key to Illustrations on Pages 560–561.

1. Wedding of Prince Charles and Lady Diana Spencer, St. Paul's Cathedral, London, July 29, 1981.
2. Virginia Woolf (1882–1941).
3. Detail, *Still Life with Spots*, Ben Nicholson (1884–1980).
4. The Houses of Parliament and Westminster Bridge, London.
5. William Butler Yeats (1865–1939).
6. *Working Model for Standing Figure: Knife Edge*, Henry Moore, bronze, 1961.
7. Joseph Conrad (1857–1924).
8. Detail, French cartoon depicting a suffragette rally in London, 1908.
9. Scene from 1938 film version of George Bernard Shaw's *Pygmalion*.

Key to Illustrations appears on page 961.

MASTERPIECES OF WORLD LITERATURE

On the upcoming pages is a sampling of great works in world literature, literature originally written in a language other than English. From the *Gilgamesh* epic of ancient Mesopotamia to a short story by the contemporary Colombian writer Gabriel García Márquez, the selections cover a range of human achievement that spans roughly four thousand years. In choosing the selections, the focus has been on the old and the new. Among the "old" are some of the formative works in literary history, works like Homer's *Iliad* and Dante's *Divine Comedy* that influenced the directions future literature would take. Among the "new" are works by some of this century's most outstanding authors—like Franz Kafka, whose imaginative fiction has added the term *Kafkaesque* to the dictionary, and Jorge Luis Borges, one of the world's most influential men of letters since World War II. However, whether the works are thousands of years old or written in our own lifetime, they all speak in the timeless, universal voice that is the hallmark of great literature.

Classics from the Past

Gilgamesh, which opens the upcoming section, is the world's oldest known epic, perhaps the world's oldest written

An Iranian terra-cotta jar decorated with an ibex, c. 3500 B.C.

poem. Its hero was king of the Sumerian city of Uruk, in southern Mesopotamia, in about 2700 B.C. Mesopotamia, which means "the land between the rivers," was an ancient region between the Tigris and Euphrates rivers in what today is Iraq. It has been called the cradle of civilization, for it was here that humanity established its first known cities, its first known codes of law, and—what is most important from the viewpoint of literary history—its first known writing. Because the *Gilgamesh* epic was written down, it could be unearthed by archaeologists and pieced together by scholars centuries later. Remarkably, their efforts revealed a literary masterpiece that, for all its antiquity, speaks powerfully to readers of today.

Traveling north and west from Mesopotamia, through Asia Minor (present-day Asian Turkey) and across the Aegean Sea, one comes to the continent of Europe and the land of Greece, the birthplace of western civilization. Here the groundwork was laid for the political, philosophical, and artistic achievements of western Europe and, eventually, America. Greek literature is often divided into three periods, the epic age, the lyric age, and the dramatic age—all represented on the upcoming pages. The epic age was the age of Homer, the blind poet who, according to tradition, composed the two great epics on which all Greek

literature is founded, the *Iliad* and the *Odyssey*. Homer lived around 850 B.C., and his *Iliad* recounts the story of the Trojan War, in which the Greeks fought the city of Troy, in Asia Minor, about three hundred and fifty years before Homer's time. The epic blends heroic adventure with thought-provoking human relationships and is a rich source from which subsequent writers have drawn again and again.

About two hundred years after Homer lived, Greece became noted for its lyric poetry. Representing this lyric age is the vivid verse of Sappho, one of the world's first women writers. From the dramatic age, or fifth century B.C.—the era when the city-state of Athens flourished and the ideas of democracy were born—comes the *Antigone* of Sophocles, who along with his contemporaries Aeschylus and Euripides gave the world its first great tragedies. *Antigone* focuses on a princess who must choose between her duty to the state and the dic-

tates of her own conscience, a conflict that still arises time and again in the modern world.

Greek civilization had an enormous impact on that of ancient Rome, which grew from an insignificant city on the Italian peninsula into the capital of a vast empire. By the era of the Emperor Augustus, who ruled from 27 B.C. to A.D. 14, Rome had become the center of the western—and much of the eastern—world. It was also producing its greatest literature—works like Virgil's *Aeneid* and Ovid's *Metamorphoses,* both represented on the pages ahead.

Unlike Homer's *Iliad,* which was composed in the oral tradition, Virgil's *Aeneid* was a consciously literary work. Nevertheless, it did draw on Homer's masterpiece, telling the story of the legendary Trojan warrior Aeneas, who fled Troy after its fall and, after wandering through North Africa and on into Italy, supposedly founded the city of Rome. More sophisticated than Homer's epics, the *Aeneid* is regarded as the greatest poem written in Latin, the language of ancient Rome.

Another landmark of Latin literature was the *Metamorphoses,* a verse retelling of Greek and Roman myths. The masterwork of the poet Ovid, the *Metamorphoses* in some ways qualifies as one of the world's first storybooks; it is also among our most important sources of information about classical mythology.

Detail from an illuminated medieval manuscript depicting the siege of Jerusalem during the Crusades.

Rome officially fell in A.D. 476, and the subsequent chaos in western Europe resulted in what is often called the Dark Ages. Elsewhere, however, civilizations flourished. The Byzantine, or Eastern Roman, Empire, headquartered in Byzantium (present-day Istanbul, Turkey), reached the height of its glory under Justinian I, who ruled from A.D. 527 to 565. In the same century book printing was developed in China; and in about A.D. 613, in what today is Saudi Arabia, the great prophet Mohammed began the teachings that would result in the establishment of the Moslem faith in the Arab world. By the end of the eighth century, the Arab Empire was experiencing its golden age. The Moslem religion continued to spread— among the Moors of North Africa, for example, who gained a foothold in western Europe with their control of Spain, and among the peoples of Turkey and Persia (present-day Iran). Both Spain and Persia became important centers of Moslem learning, and it was in Persia, some time in the eleventh century, that one of the Moslem world's greatest poets was born. Known as Omar Khayyám, he was in his own time famous chiefly as an astronomer and a mathematician. However, an English version of his magnificent *rubáiyát,* or quatrains, was created centuries later by Victorian poet Edward FitzGerald, and now *The Rubáiyát of Omar*

Khayyám enjoys an international reputation.

Throughout this glorious era in the Moslem world, western Europe produced little written literature in any language other than Latin. Latin was the language of Church scholarship, and works written in the **vernacular,** or languages spoken by the people (French, Italian, and so on), were generally viewed with little respect. The man who did more than any other writer to raise the prestige of the vernacular was the brilliant Italian poet Dante, author of *The Divine Comedy.* This Italian masterpiece, an allegoric epic about a journey to hell, purgatory, and heaven, is widely regarded as the finest literary work of Europe's Middle Ages.

Dante lived around the turn of the fourteenth century, when Italy was already beginning to experience the revival of learning that would swell into the **Renaissance,** or "rebirth" of western civilization. From the time of the Crusades (1096–

1291), western Europe's unsuccessful attempt to wrest the holy city of Jerusalem from Moslem hands, new ideas had been sweeping in from the East. In 1271 Marco Polo visited the opulent court of Kublai Khan in China, and he returned to Italy with reports of marvelous inventions and riches beyond any European's dreams. The Italian Renaissance is usually dated from about 1325; and over the next three centuries its influence spread north and west. In 1453 a German named Johann Gutenberg built Europe's first printing press, a landmark event in European literary history. In 1492 the Spanish, united under Ferdinand and Isabella, succeeded in driving out the Moors; and in the same year Christopher Columbus, sailing for Spain and searching for the Orient, instead landed in the New World. Spain emerged as the most powerful of Europe's new colonial powers; and Spanish literature, at the beginning of the seventeenth century, produced the world's first great masterpiece in a new literary genre that would revolutionize reading tastes: the novel. This great Spanish classic was Miguel de Cervantes' *Don Quixote,* the sometimes touching, sometimes hilarious story of an idealist in a practical world. *Don Quixote* is still widely viewed as one of the finest novels of all time.

The same century that produced Spain's literary giant, Cervantes, also produced another

Detail from a Chinese hanging scroll depicting the woods and valleys of Mount Yu, 1372.

grand master on the other side of the world: Bashō, the father of Japanese haiku poetry. Also writing in the late seventeenth century was Molière, whose satirical comedies were the crowning glory of the classical age of French drama.

Molière enjoyed the patronage of France's powerful monarch Louis XIV, the "Sun King," who built the magnificent palace at Versailles and helped usher in the so-called Age of Elegance. The eighteenth-century French philosopher Jean-Jacques Rousseau criticized that age and in doing so became the father of Romanticism. It was a German writer, however, who first took Rousseau's ideas and turned them into poetry. His name was Johann Wolfgang von Goethe, and his masterpiece was *Faust,* a verse drama published early in the nineteenth century. Based on German legend, *Faust* tells the story of a scholar who sells his soul to the devil in return for complete knowledge. A pillar of the Romantic movement, *Faust* influenced such American writers as Washington Irving and Nathaniel Hawthorne and such English writers as Lord Byron and Mary Shelley.

Classics from the Present

In our own century the tremendous strides taken in transportation and communications have made the world seem a smaller place. Once-distant lands are now just a plane ride away, and we can pick up a phone and call just about any nation on earth. Two world wars and the threat of nuclear warfare have created a frightening new image of a humanity capable of global destruction, yet at the same time they have drawn us together, forcing us to recognize that the problems of any nation can quickly become the problems of every nation—that indeed, as John Donne once said, "No man is an island."

This "shrinking-world" phenomenon has meant that the writers of the world have themselves become a more international community. Most of the twentieth-century authors represented on the pages ahead are the product not of one nation but of many nations. The great German-language lyric poet Rainer Maria Rilke was born in then-Austrian-controlled Czechoslovakia, lived for some time in France, and died in Switzerland; the Chilean poet Gabriela Mistral spent several years in Italy, Mexico, and the United States.

Indian poet Tagore went to school in England, and when Gabriel García Márquez received the Nobel Prize, it was as a writer of both Colombia and Mexico.

The expanded artistic community has meant that the literature of one nation—or one continent—is often affected by the literature of another. The mystical philosophies of India and the creative innovation of contemporary Latin American literature have had their impact on the writers of Europe, just as European modernism has affected writers from nations as far apart as Japan and Argentina.

The first modern writer to appear in the upcoming section is India's Rabindranath Tagore, one of this century's most respected and beloved authors. Usually writing in Bengali, one of several tongues spoken in India, Tagore produced plays, novels, short stories, and essays in addition to the poetry for which he is most famous. In 1913 he became the first Asian writer to be honored with the Nobel Prize for Literature.

Italy's Luigi Pirandello is widely regarded as one of the four or five greatest dramatists of the twentieth century. He is also a master of fiction; in fact, he often based his plays on his own short stories. Like many early twentieth-century writers, Pirandello reflects new ideas in psychology and often portrays the inner workings of his characters' minds.

Detail from *Landscape, New Mexico,* Marsden Hartley, 1919–1920.

Rainer Maria Rilke was among the most original of modern poets. Many of his poems are highly personal examinations; others are what he called "object poems," aimed at capturing the changeable essence of some object or creature. Though he wrote in German, his lush imagery and careful craftsmanship have influenced poets writing in many other languages, including English.

Like Rilke, Franz Kafka was a highly innovative writer who was born in Czechoslovakia and wrote in German. Kafka's fiction is noted for strange, baffling incidents resembling those that occur in nightmares; and today bizarre, nightmarish elements of surrealism ("beyond realism") have come to be called *Kafkaesque.*

Although most famous for his novel *Doctor Zhivago,* Boris Pasternak was first and foremost a poet. He is considered one of this century's finest Russian authors; yet, ironically, most of his works were published outside his homeland. In the Soviet Union Pasternak's imaginative ideas and skeptical political views resulted in official censorship, although his work has been privately circulated to Russian readers.

One of the most significant developments in recent years has been the outpouring of major literature from Latin America. The Chilean poet Gabriela Mistral was South America's first Nobel Prize winner; she was also one of the world's first women authors to receive that prestigious award. Simplicity and freshness mark her style; among the many topics of her verse are nature, childhood, the passage of time, and the role of women.

The multitalented Jorge Luis Borges wrote poetry, essays, and short stories, and he also won distinction as a translator. In addition, Borges served as director of Argentina's National Library and taught at various universities all over the world. His broad scope and knowledge of world literature place him among the century's most eminent literary critics; and his interest in Asian customs and philosophies, especially those of the Middle East, add a fascinating dimension to much of his poetry and fiction.

The poetry of Pablo Neruda is noted for its powerful, sometimes brutal imagery in capturing the unexplored stretches of the South American landscape— the Chilean deserts, the Andean heights—which he often uses to symbolize the unexplored reaches of the human mind. In addition, Neruda's work displays strong political commitment, often championing the rights of the working class. Neruda has been a major influence on other Latin American poets, and his international reputation—like that of fellow Chilean Gabriela Mistral—was acknowledged with a Nobel Prize.

The upcoming selections conclude with a short story by Gabriel García Márquez, one of the most eminent writers of contemporary Latin American fiction. Although García Márquez has lived outside his native Colombia for many years (mostly in Mexico), he continues to set his fiction in drowsy, isolated villages that bear a strong resemblance to Aracataca, the Colombian town where he grew up. His stories and novels also make use of myth and folklore and often contain supernatural or surrealistic elements.

Only the future will reveal which of the modern authors represented on the pages ahead will enjoy the enduring fame of a Homer or a Virgil. Nevertheless, in our own time each of these authors has found an international audience, and each has influenced not merely the literature of his or her own nation but the literature of the world.

WORLD EVENTS TIME LINE

c. 3100 B.C.	Sumer: Invention of writing	
c. 3000 B.C.	Egypt: Development of papyrus	
c. 1850 B.C.	Sumer: Oldest surviving Gilgamesh poems	
c. 1193 B.C.	Asia Minor: Trojan War	
c. 1100 B.C.	Israel: King David composes Psalms	
c. 850 B.C.	Greece: Homer's *Iliad* composed	
c. 600 B.C.	Mexico: Beginnings of Mayan civilization	
c. 595 B.C.	Greece: Sappho composes lyrics	
551 B.C.	China: Birth of Confucius	
528 B.C.	India: Buddha begins teaching	
443 B.C.	Greece: Sophocles, *Antigone*	
c. 30 B.C.	Rome: Virgil begins *Aeneid*	
4 B.C.	Palestine: Birth of Jesus	
A.D. 5	Rome: Ovid, *Metamorphoses*	
381	Rome: Christianity becomes state religion	
449	Britain: Anglo-Saxon invasions	
476	Fall of western Roman Empire	
527	Byzantium: Justinian becomes emperor (to 565)	
c. 700	England: *Beowulf* composed	
c. 750	Western Europe: Beginnings of feudalism	

Gilgamesh

Marco Polo

Leonardo da Vinci

800	Peru: Incas build Macchu Picchu
1053	Europe: Roman Catholic and Eastern Orthodox churches split
1066	England: Norman Conquest
1075	Persia: Omar Khayyám writes poems
1096	Europe and Mideast: Crusades begin (to 1291)
1271	China: Marco Polo of Italy visits court of Kublai Khan
1307	Italy: Dante begins *Divine Comedy*
1325	Italy: Beginning of Renaissance
1345	Black Death kills one third of population from India to Ireland (to 1351)
1387	England: Chaucer begins *Canterbury Tales*
1428	France: Joan of Arc lifts siege of Orléans
1450	North America: Iroquois unite under Great Binding Law
1453	Germany: Gutenberg prints Bible on Europe's first printing press
1492	Columbus lands in New World
1503	Italy: Leonardo da Vinci paints *Mona Lisa*
1517	Germany: Luther posts Ninety-five Theses; Protestant Reformation begins
1519	Mexico: Cortés conquers Aztecs
1567	Brazil: Portuguese found Rio de Janiero
1590	Italy: Galileo experiments with falling objects

1605	Spain: Cervantes, *Don Quixote,* Part I
1606	England: Shakespeare, *Macbeth*
1607	North America: British establish colony at Jamestown
1609	Canada: Champlain founds Québec
1659	France: Molière, *The Flying Doctor*
1675	Japan: Bashō publishes poetry
1687	England: Isaac Newton, *Principia*
1690	India: British found Calcutta
1721	Germany: Bach composes *Brandenberg Concertos*
1760	Britain: Industrial Revolution begins
1776	America: Independence declared
1789	France: Bastille stormed; revolution begins
1798	England: Wordsworth and Coleridge, *Lyrical Ballads*
1808	Germany: Goethe, *Faust,* Part I
1815	Belgium: French emperor Napoleon defeated at Waterloo
1823	Germany: Beethoven, Symphony No. 9
1831	America: Edgar Allan Poe, *Poems*
1837	Britain: Victoria becomes queen
1848	Belgium: Marx and Engels, *Communist Manifesto*
1856	France: Flaubert, *Madame Bovary*
1859	England: Charles Darwin, *On the Origin of Species*
1861	France: Pasteur proposes theory of germs

1876	America: Alexander Graham Bell patents telephone
1889	Germany: Daimler builds first practical automobile
1900	Austria: Sigmund Freud, *Interpretation of Dreams*
1903	America: Wright brothers build first successful airplane
1905	Switzerland: Einstein proposes theory of relativity
1907	Germany: Rilke, *New Poems*
1913	India: Tagore wins Nobel Prize for Literature
1914	World War I begins (to 1918)
1917	Russian Revolution
1921	Italy: Pirandello, *Six Characters in Search of an Author*
1924	Chile: Pablo Neruda, *Twenty Poems*
1925	Austria: Franz Kafka, *The Trial* Britain: Baird transmits first television broadcasts
1939	World War II begins (to 1945)
1945	Chile's Gabriela Mistral wins Nobel Prize for Literature
1947	India and Pakistan gain independence
1949	China: People's Republic established
1957	Italy: Pasternak's *Doctor Zhivago* published
1960	Argentina: Jorge Luis Borges, *El hacedor (Dreamtigers)*
1969	America's *Apollo 11* lands on moon
1982	Colombia's Gabriel García Márquez wins Nobel Prize for Literature
1987	America: Brodsky wins Nobel Prize for Literature

Sumerian and Babylonian Poetry

The world's oldest surviving written poetry was created by the Sumerians, an ancient people who dominated the southern part of Mesopotamia (in present-day Iraq) from about 4000 to 2100 B.C. The region they dominated was then called Sumer, and the most famous of their city-states was Ur, on the Euphrates River. The Sumerians spoke a language of obscure origins, also called Sumerian, and were the first known people to devise an alphabet in order to write their language down. That alphabet consisted of wedge-shaped symbols now known as cuneiform (from *cuneus,* Latin for "wedge"), which they inscribed with a sharp instrument, called a stylus, onto clay tablets that were then hardened by baking.

Surviving Sumerian poetry includes fragments of the world's first known epics. An **epic** is a long narrative (storytelling) poem that recounts, in grave and stately language, the adventures of a hero who usually embodies his civilization's ideals. The most famous Sumerian epic hero is Gilgamesh, king of the city of Uruk.

Much of the remaining Sumerian poetry recounts myths about Sumerian gods and goddesses. The Sumerian religion was polytheistic—that is, it had many gods; yet it included a story of a great flood that in many details matches the biblical story of Noah. Sumerian religion also had a creation myth about a watery abyss where the first gods were engendered, and it spoke of a paradise called Dilmun. However, only two human beings—Ziusudra and his wife, survivors of the great flood—were ever taken by the gods to live in Dilmun. For other humans immortality in paradise was denied; instead, it was believed that people descended to a gloomy underworld after death.

Over the centuries Sumerian customs, including religious ideas and the use of cuneiform, spread to other peoples in and around Mesopotamia. Among these peoples were the Babylonians, whose chief cities were Akkad and Babylon; the Chaldeans, who lived just south of the Euphrates, near Ur; and the Assyrians, who lived north of the Tigris River and whose chief cities were Ashur and, later, Ninevah. All three of these peoples spoke dialects of Akkadian, a now extinct language of the Semitic language family (which today includes Hebrew and Arabic).

In about 2100 B.C. the Babylonians conquered the Sumerians. They dominated southern Mesopotamia until 689 B.C., and the region became known as Babylonia. The Babylonians retold Sumerian poems, including the *Gilgamesh* epic, in their Akkadian language. However, they used their own names for the Sumerian gods and other characters from Sumerian mythology—for example, Ziusudra was now called Utnapishtim. The Babylonian version of the creation myth has also been preserved.

Introducing Gilgamesh

Like the Anglo-Saxon epic *Beowulf* (page 10), the first Sumerian poems about Gilgamesh were probably composed in the oral tradition. However, with the spread of writing, the Gilgamesh poems soon came to be written down. Five Sumerian tablets containing fragments of Gilgamesh poems, dating to about 1850 B.C., still survive today, as does an Akkadian tablet from about 1800 B.C. About six hundred years later, a Babylonian poet named Sin-leqe-unnini made a complete Akkadian transcription of the epic, which in turn was copied in a text found in the library of the Assyrian king Ashurbanipal (669–630? B.C.) at Ninevah. It is this text—an Akkadian recounting that uses the Babylonian names of gods and other characters—that provides our fullest version of the epic of *Gilgamesh.*

As the world's oldest surviving epic, *Gilgamesh* is naturally of enormous importance to the study of literary history. In addition, Hittite versions of the *Gilgamesh* epic found in Asia Minor (present-day Asian Turkey) quite probably spread to Greece and influenced the epics of Homer (page 804), the first epics in western literature. However, its historical value notwithstanding, *Gilgamesh* merits attention as a great work of literature in its own right. Its adventures make for exciting storytelling, and its themes treat timeless human concerns about friendship, grief, life, death, and immortality.

Gilgamesh was probably a real king who ruled Uruk in about 2700 B.C. Renowned as a great builder, he was also said to be a wise judge, and scholars of Sumerian have variously translated his name as "hero," "old one," and "father." According to the epic, Gilgamesh is two-thirds god, one-third human. With his beloved friend Enkidu, a mortal human being, he slays two monsters—Humbaba, the keeper of the cedar forest; and the Bull of Heaven, who brought drought to the land. Unfortunately, Enkidu dies of wounds sustained in the battles. The upcoming selection from *Gilgamesh* opens just after Enkidu's death.

■ An epic hero usually embodies the ideals of his civilization. What ideals would a twentieth-century epic hero (or heroine) champion?

An Akkadian cylinder seal and the impression made by it, showing a hunter capturing a mountain goat, c. 2330–2180 B.C. Above the hunter and goat is a two-line cuneiform that identifies the owner of the seal.

from Gilgamesh

Retold by Herbert Mason

CHARACTERS

Sumerians

GILGAMESH [gil′gə mesh′]: king of Uruk [o͞o′rook]
ENKIDU: Gilgamesh's best friend, killed from wounds sustained in battle
UTNAPISHTIM: wise man of the city of Shurrupak; called Ziusudra by the Sumerians. Utnapishtim supposedly survived the great flood and was taken by the gods to live far away in paradise, earning for himself the epithet (nickname) "The Distant."
UTNAPISHTIM'S WIFE: the only other human being allowed to live in paradise
URSHANABI: Utnapishtim's boatman

Gods

SIN: god of the moon; called Nanna by the Sumerians
ANU: father of gods and god of the heavens; called An by the Sumerians
ENLIL: god of earth, wind, the air, and war; executive of Anu. By the time of the Babylonians, Enlil had become the most powerful of the gods.
ISHTAR: goddess of love, fertility, and war; called Inanna by the Sumerians
EA: god of wisdom and the arts; called Enki by the Sumerians

Monsters and Animals

SCORPION MAN AND WOMAN: husband and wife who guard the twin mountains of Mashu, from which the sun supposedly rises and descends
A SERPENT

Retold by
Herbert Mason

from **Gilgamesh**

The Quest

Gilgamesh[1] wept bitterly for his friend.
He felt himself now singled out for loss,
Apart from everyone else. The word *Enkidu*
Roamed through every thought
5 Like a hungry animal through empty lairs
In search of food. The only nourishment
He knew was grief, endless in its hidden source
Yet never ending hunger.

All that is left to one who grieves
10 Is convalescence. No change of heart or spiritual
Conversion, for the heart has changed
And the soul has been converted
To a thing that sees
How much it costs to lose a friend it loved.
15 It has grown past conversion to a world
Few enter without tasting loss,
In which one spends a long time waiting
For something to move one to proceed.
It is that inner atmosphere that has
20 An unfamiliar gravity or none at all,
Where words are flung out in the air but stay
Motionless without an answer,
Hovering about one's lips
Or arguing back to haunt
25 The memory with what one failed to say,
Until one learns acceptance of the silence
Amidst the new debris
Or turns again to grief
As the only source of privacy,
30 Alone with someone loved.
It could go on for years and years,
And has, for centuries,
For being human holds a special grief
Of privacy within the universe
35 That yearns and waits to be retouched
By someone who can take away
The memory of death.

Sumerian stone sculpture, 2750–2600 B.C.

---

1. **Gilgamesh** [gil′gə mesh′]

Gilgamesh wandered through the desert,
Alone as he had never been alone,
40 When he had craved but not known what he craved;
The dryness now was worse than the decay.
The bored know nothing of this agony,
Waiting for diversion they have never lost.
Death had taken the direction he had gained.
45 He was no more a king
But just a man who now had lost his way,
Yet had a greater passion to withdraw
Into a deeper isolation. Mad,
Perhaps insane, he tried
50 To bring Enkidu back to life
To end his bitterness,
His fear of death.
His life became a quest
To find the secret of eternal life
55 Which he might carry back to give his friend.

He had put on the skins of animals
And thrown himself in the dust, and now
He longed to hear the voice of one
Who still used words as revelations;
60 He yearned to talk to Utnapishtim,
The one who had survived the flood
And death itself, the one who knew the secret.

Before his loss, when he approached at night
The mountain passes where the lions slept,
65 He raised his eyes to Sin, the moon god, and prayed.
Now he expected help from no one.
He tried to fall asleep despite the sounds
Of movement through the trees; his chest was tight
With needless fear Enkidu would have calmed.

70 When he arrived at the mountains of Mashu,
Whose peaks reach to the shores of Heaven
And whose roots descend to Hell, he saw
The Scorpion people who guard its gate,
Whose knowledge is awesome, but whose glance is death.
75 When he saw them, his face turned ashen with dismay,
But he bowed down to them, the only way to shield himself
Against effusions of their gaze.
The Scorpion man then recognized
In Gilgamesh the flesh of gods and told his wife:
80 This one is two-thirds god, one-third man
And can survive our view, then spoke to him:

An Iranian terra-cotta jar decorated with an ibex, c. 3500 B.C.

Why have you come this route to us?
The way is arduous and long
And no one goes beyond.

85 I have come to see my father,[2]
Utnapishtim,
Who was allowed to go beyond.
I want to ask him about life and death,
To end my loss. My friend has died.
90 I want to bring him back to life.

The Scorpion interrupted him and laughed,
Being impatient with such tales and fearful of sentiment:
No one is able to explain, no one has gone
Beyond these mountains. There is only death.
95 There is no light beyond, just darkness
And cold and at daybreak a burning heat.
You will learn nothing that we do not know.
You will only come to grief.

I have been through grief! Gilgamesh screamed.
100 Even if there will be more of pain,
And heat and cold, I will go on!
Open the gate to the mountains!

All right, go! the Scorpion man said,
As if in anger with a child
105 Who had not reached the age of reason.
The gate is open! His wife added:
Be careful of the darkness. Gilgamesh saw
His going frightened them. They only seemed secure.

He entered the Road of the Sun,
110 Which was so shrouded in darkness
That he could see neither
What was ahead of him nor behind.
Thick was the darkness,
And there was no light.
115 He could see neither
What was ahead nor behind.
For days he traveled in this blindness
Without a light to guide him,
Ascending or descending,
120 He could not be sure,
Going on with only

---

2. **father:** spiritual father.

The companionship of grief
In which he felt Enkidu at his side.
He said his name: Enkidu, Enkidu,
125 To quiet his fear
Through the darkness
Where there was no light,
And where he saw neither
What was ahead nor behind

130 Until before him,
When it seemed there was no end
To loneliness,
A valley came in view
Sprinkled with precious stones
135 And fruit-filled vines.

Gazing into the valley
He felt overcome with pain
As a man
Who has been in prison
140 Feels his chains
At his release from fear.
He spoke Enkidu's name aloud
As if explaining to the valley
Why he was there, wishing his friend
145 Could see the same horizon,
Share the same delights: My friend Enkidu
Died. We hunted together. We killed Humbaba
And the Bull of Heaven. We were always
At each other's side, encouraging when one
150 Was discouraged or afraid or didn't
Understand. He was this close to me.
He held his hands together to describe
The closeness. It seemed for a moment
He could almost touch his friend,
155 Could speak to him as if he were there:
Enkidu. Enkidu. But suddenly the silence
Was deeper than before,
In a place where they had never been
Together.
160 He sat down on the ground and wept:
Enkidu. Enkidu.

As when we can recall so vividly
We almost touch,
Or think of all the gestures that we failed
165 To make.
After several minutes he stood up,

A bronze helmet decorated with gold and silver, Iranian, c. 1300 B.C.

Explaining only to himself why he
Had come—to find the secret of eternal life
To bring Enkidu back to life—
170 Recognizing now the valley was deaf
To loss known only to himself.

Gilgamesh soon comes upon Urshanabi, Utnapishtim's
boatman. Thinking that the boatman will not ferry him
to Utnapishtim, he cuts loose the boat and destroys the
Sacred Stones that the boatman had been carving on its
prow. Urshanabi, recognizing his grief, agrees to ferry
him over in a second boat that Gilgamesh fashions from
nearby trees.

Utnapishtim

Utnapishtim stood on the other shore,
His old and rugged features worn
By the seas and deserts he himself had crossed.
175 He wondered why the Sacred Stones had been destroyed,
Why the boat was only drifting,
And who the man was
Who resembled loss itself.
Before the ship had touched his shore he thought,
180 I am afraid that nothing here can help him.

The eyes of Utnapishtim seemed so full
Of hospitality
When Gilgamesh awoke
From his exhaustion.
185 As if some faces could be doorways
Into life one has an image of
But never sees. The vista was
A strange and beautiful
Release.
190 Utnapishtim was the only one whom he had met
On his journey who did not add to
His fatigue.
Gilgamesh was speaking but only to relieve
His weight of grief,
195 Not to demand an understanding:
My friend has died so many times in me,
And yet he still seems so alive,
Like a younger brother,
Then suddenly like soft tissue,
200 A dried leaf.
I was afraid.
Is there something more than death?

Some other end to friendship?
I came to you whom they call "The Distant,"
205 I crossed the mountains and the sea.
I was like a blind man, but not one
From whom someone in search can draw light.
I am so tired, so tired. I have
Killed bear, hyena, stag, ibex for food
210 And clothes. I barely crossed the sea of death.

Utnapishtim raised his hand and touched the shoulder
Of the younger man to put him at his ease.
Two things encourage me to hope, he said;
That one can come this far to bring life to a friend,
215 And that you understand how we must borrow light
From the blind. (My own right eye was damaged long ago
And my left is slowly decaying.)
Friendship is vowing toward immortality
And does not know the passing away of beauty
220 (Though take care!)
Because it aims for the spirit.
Many years ago through loss I learned
That love is wrung from our inmost heart
Until only the loved one is and we are not.
225 You have known, O Gilgamesh,
What interests me,
To drink from the Well of Immortality.
Which means to make the dead
Rise from their graves
230 And the prisoners from their cells,
The sinners from their sins.
I think love's kiss kills our heart of flesh.
It is the only way to eternal life,
Which should be unbearable if lived
235 Among the dying flowers
And the shrieking farewells
Of the overstretched arms of our spoiled hopes.

I think compassion is our God's pure act
Which burns forever,
240 And be it in Heaven or in Hell
Doesn't matter for me; because
Hell is the everlasting gift
Of His presence
To the lonely heart who is longing
245 Amid perishing phantoms and doesn't care
To find any immortality
If not in the pure loneliness of the Holy One,

This loneliness which He enjoys forever
Inside and outside of His creation.
250 It is enough for one who loves
To find his Only One singled in Himself.
And that is the cup of immortality!

Gilgamesh looked into the face of the older man
In whom he saw this loneliness.
255 He could still feel the touch of Utnapishtim's hand.

Time and space were uneventful now.
Nothing inclined him to impatience.
They talked together, walked
And sat on rocks.
260 The older man seemed pleased
To have his company,
As if an absent son or other loss
Had been slightly returned to him.
In time the younger felt
265 He knew him well enough
To say:
You sometimes seem to have a downcast look,
As if the life you have found here still
Has failed to bring you peace.
270 How did you come to find this world
And reach this life?

I did not come out of desire like you,
Said Utnapishtim; I was the choice of others.
They walked along the shore
275 And the older man told his story.

The Flood

There was a city called Shurrupak
On the bank of the Euphrates.
It was very old, and so many were the gods
Within it. They converged in their complex hearts
280 On the idea of creating a great flood.
There was Anu, their aging and weak-minded father,
The military Enlil, his adviser,
Ishtar, the sensation-craving one,
And all the rest. Ea, who was present
285 At their council, came to my house
And, frightened by the violent winds that filled the air,
Echoed all that they were planning and had said.
Man of Shurrupak, he said, tear down your house

And build a ship. Abandon your possessions
290 And the works that you find beautiful and crave,
And save your life instead. Into the ship
Bring the seed of all the living creatures.

I was overawed, perplexed,
And finally downcast. I agreed to do
295 As Ea said, but I protested: What shall I say
To the city, the people, the leaders?

Tell them, Ea said, you have learned that Enlil
The war god despises you and will not
Give you access to the city anymore.
300 Tell them for this Ea will bring the rains.

That is the way gods think, he laughed. His tone
Of savage irony frightened Gilgamesh
Yet gave him pleasure, being his friend.
They only know how to compete or echo.

305 But who am I to talk? He sighed as if
Disgusted with himself; I did as he
Commanded me to do. I spoke to them,
And some came out to help me build the ship
Of seven stories, each with nine chambers.
310 The boat was cube in shape, and sound; it held
The food and wine and precious minerals
And seed of living animals we put
In it. My family then moved inside,
And all who wanted to be with us there:
315 The game of the field, the goats of the steppe,
The craftsmen of the city came, a navigator
Came. And then Ea ordered me to close
The door. The time of the great rains had come.
O there was ample warning, yes, my friend,
320 But it was terrifying still. Buildings
Blown by the winds for miles like desert brush.
People clung to branches of trees until
Roots gave way. New possessions, now debris,
Floated on the water with their special
325 Sterile vacancy. The riverbanks failed
To hold the water back. Even the gods
Cowered like dogs at what they had done.
Ishtar cried out like a woman at the height
Of labor: O how could I have wanted
330 To do this to my people! They were *hers,*
Notice. Even her sorrow was possessive.

The metal head of a bearded man,
Iranian, 3000–2000 B.C.

Her spawn that she had killed too soon.
Old gods are terrible to look at when
They weep, all bloated like spoiled fish.
335 One wonders if they ever understand
That they have caused their grief. When the seventh day
Came, the flood subsided from its slaughter
Like hair drawn slowly back
From a tormented face.
340 I looked at the earth and all was silence.
Bodies lay like alewives, dead
And in the clay. I fell down
On the ship's deck and wept. Why? Why did they
Have to die? I couldn't understand. I asked
345 Unanswerable questions a child asks
When a parent dies—for nothing. Only slowly
Did I make myself believe—or hope—they
Might all be swept up in their fragments
Together
350 And made whole again
By some compassionate hand.
But my hand was too small
To do the gathering.
I have only known this feeling since
355 When I look out across the sea of death,
This pull inside against a littleness—myself—
Waiting for an upward gesture.

O the dove, the swallow and the raven
Found their land. The people left the ship.
360 But I for a long time could only stay inside.
I could not face the deaths I knew were there.
Then I received Enlil, for Ea had *chosen* me;
The war god touched my forehead; he blessed
My family and said:
365 Before this you were just a man, but now
You and your wife shall be like gods. You
Shall live in the distance at the rivers' mouth,
At the source. I allowed myself to be
Taken far away from all that I had seen.
370 Sometimes even in love we yearn to leave mankind.
Only the loneliness of the Only One
Who never acts like gods
Is bearable.
I am downcast because of what I've seen,
375 Not what I still have hope to yearn for.
Lost youths restored to life,
Lost children to their crying mothers,

Lost wives, lost friends, lost hopes, lost homes,
I want to bring these back to them.
380 But now there is you.
We must find something for you.
How will you find eternal life
To bring back to your friend?
He pondered busily, as if
385 It were just a matter of getting down to work
Or making plans for an excursion.
Then he relaxed, as if there were no use
In this reflection. I would grieve
At all that may befall you still,
390 If I did not know you must return
And bury your own loss and build
Your world anew with your own hands.
I envy you your freedom.

As he listened, Gilgamesh felt tiredness again
395 Come over him, the words now so discouraging,
The promise so remote, so unlike what he sought.
He looked into the old man's face, and it seemed changed,
As if this one had fought within himself a battle
He would never know, that still went on.

The Secret of Life

400 They returned to Utnapishtim's house
And to his aged wife who seemed to Gilgamesh,
In her shufflings and her faithful silence,
Like a servant only there to hold the door.
He hardly knew her as a person,
405 He had talked only to Utnapishtim,
Been only with him.
Was she all he needed as companion?

Yet when he fell asleep and Utnapishtim
Remarked to his wife with hostile irony:
410 Look at the strong man who wants life;
Sleep follows him like his shadow,
She said to her husband:
Touch him again and wake him,
So he can return in peace to his home.
415 She had learned to read her husband's moods.

Men are deceitful and incapable of peace.
I know! He said. Can't he even stay awake with me?
Sleep is like death only slothful people yearn for.

Bake loaves, he ordered her, and put them at his head,
420 One for each day he sleeps.
We'll see how long it is before he wakes.

Over her frail protest the trial was set.
After some days, Utnapishtim woke the younger man,
Who thought he had barely gone to sleep.

425 You have slept for seven days, he said.
Look at the dried-out loaves my wife has baked.
How will you bear eternal life?
It is not easy to live like gods.

What can I do to win eternal life?
430 The younger pleaded.
Wherever I go—even here—I am drawn back
To death.

Austerely Utnapishtim called out to the boatman
On the other shore and scolded him
435 For sending Gilgamesh across.
Return him to your shore, he called.
Bathe him and burn these pelts he wears,
Which can only remind him of his friend.
Let him be fresh and young again.
440 Let the band around his head be changed.
Let him return to his city untired.
His people need the sight of something new,
And the appearance of success.
His words sounded bitter.

445 I came for wisdom only, shouted Gilgamesh.

Don't hurt an old man further with your praise.
I have nothing to give you that will save.

Urshanabi crossed in his ship and obeyed.
He took the pelts from Gilgamesh,
450 And though the grieving man
Was too disheartened to protest
When they were taken from him and burned,
He cried out as if a festered wound had just
Been pierced. When it was over
455 He stood in the bow to leave
With only inner traces of his journey.
Utnapishtim contemplated him, unable to speak.
As if he were afraid of some desire to retain,

He looked down at the ground, away from Gilgamesh.

460 His wife whispered to him, saying:
He has come so far.
Have you forgotten how grief fastened onto you
And made you crave some word, some gesture, once?

Utnapishtim's face grew tight, then relaxed,
465 As when one is relieved of inner pain
By one who sees more deeply than oneself.
He looked at the younger man
Who had come into his consciousness. Youth is very
Cruel to an old face,
470 He said in a hushed voice.
It looks into its lines for wisdom
So touchingly
But there is nothing there to find.

A silver kneeling bull holding a vessel, Iranian, c. 2900 B.C.

Gilgamesh wanted to reach out to tell him
475 He was wrong, sensing suddenly the hours
One might spend alone in contemplating oldness,
As he himself had spent alone in his spoiled youth,
Seeing nothing there but time.

I know your pain too well to lie,
480 Said Utnapishtim.
I will tell you a secret I have never told.
Something to take back with you and guard.
There is a plant in the river. Its thorns
Will prick your hands as a rose thorn pricks,
485 But it will give to you new life.

He heard these words and tried to speak
But rushed instead to the old man and embraced him.
The two men held each other for a moment,
Then Utnapishtim raised his hands
490 As if to say: Enough.
And Gilgamesh looked back at him,
Then hurried off to find the plant.
He tied stones to his feet and descended
Into the river. When he saw the plant
495 Of rich rose color and ambrosial,
Shimmering in the water like a prism
Of the sunlight, he seized it, and it cut
Into his palms. He saw his blood flow in the water.

He cut the stones loose from his feet and rose

500 Up sharply to the surface and swam to shore.
He was calling out, I have it! I have it!

Urshanabi guided the ecstatic man away
To the other shore, and when they parted
Gilgamesh was alone again, but not
505 With loneliness or the memory of death.
He stopped to drink and rest beside a pool,
And soon undressed and let himself slip in
The water quietly until he was refreshed,
Leaving the plant unguarded on the ground.

510 A serpent had smelled its sweet fragrance and saw
Its chance to come from the water, and devoured
The plant, shedding its skin as slough.

When Gilgamesh rose from the pool,
His naked body glistening and refreshed,
515 The plant was gone; the discarded skin
Of a serpent was all he saw. He sat
Down on the ground, and wept.

In time he recognized this loss
As the end of his journey
520 And returned to Uruk.

Perhaps, he feared,
His people would not share
The sorrow that he knew.

He entered the city and asked a blind man
525 If he had ever heard the name Enkidu,
And the old man shrugged and shook his head,
Then turned away,
As if to say it is impossible
To keep the names of friends
530 Whom we have lost.

Gilgamesh said nothing more
To force his sorrow on another.

He looked at the walls,
Awed at the heights
535 His people had achieved
And for a moment—just a moment—
All that lay behind him
Passed from view.

STUDY QUESTIONS

The Quest

Recalling

1. How does Gilgamesh feel about Enkidu's death? What "mad, perhaps insane" idea does he have in lines 38–62?
2. To whom does Gilgamesh wish to talk? What secret does that person supposedly know?
3. According to lines 70–98, why can Gilgamesh survive the glance of the Scorpion people?
4. What is the Scorpion man's initial response when Gilgamesh asks to enter the Road of the Sun? Briefly describe the road and the place to which it leads.

Interpreting

5. What heroic qualities does Gilgamesh display in this section? In what ways is he unlike a typical hero?
6. What is paradoxical about the Road to the Sun, given its description?
7. What might be the Judeo-Christian equivalents of the Road to the Sun and the place to which it leads?

Extending

8. Compare the description of an unknown place in lines 109–129 with Milton's description of hell in *Paradise Lost* (page 277). What is similar about the two descriptions?

Utnapishtim

Recalling

1. After Gilgamesh explains his desires to Utnapishtim, what two things does Utnapishtim say encourage him to hope (lines 211–237)?
2. What is Utnapishtim's definition of friendship? What does he say is "the only way to eternal life"?

Interpreting

3. What quality of Gilgamesh's is Utnapishtim praising in line 214? To what sort of "light" might line 215 refer?
4. Explain in your own words the loneliness to which Utnapishtim refers in lines 238–252.

The Flood

Recalling

1. Which god warned Utnapishtim of the flood? What did he tell Utnapishtim to abandon?
2. Identify five people or things that accompanied Utnapishtim on the boat.
3. With what adjective does Utnapishtim describe the flood in line 320? What question did he ask after he saw the devastation?
4. After the flood, what did Enlil grant Utnapishtim and his wife?
5. After describing the flood, what question does Utnapishtim ponder? What does he conclude Gilgamesh will do (lines 390–392)? What does he say he envies?

Interpreting

6. What idea about material possessions is implied in lines 289–291?
7. What seems to be Utnapishtim's attitude toward the gods? Toward humanity? Toward immortality?

Extending

8. In what ways do Utnapishtim's experiences parallel those of Noah in the Bible?

The Secret of Life

Recalling

1. What does Gilgamesh do that angers Utnapishtim? For what reason does Utnapishtim want his boatman to burn Gilgamesh's pelts after ferrying Gilgamesh away (lines 433–444)?
2. Who prompts Utnapishtim to help Gilgamesh? About what special plant does Utnapishtim then tell Gilgamesh?
3. What eventually happens to the plant?
4. Summarize the incident with the blind man that occurs when Gilgamesh returns to Uruk. What prompts Gilgamesh to forget, for a moment, "all that lay behind him"?

Interpreting

5. What do the events involving the plant suggest about the possibilities of achieving immortality? In what way do lines 524–530 add to this idea?

6. What do lines 533–538 imply about the relationship between life and death?
7. In what ways has Gilgamesh changed since we first met him in "The Quest"?

Extending

8. Which of the ideas presented in the selection do you find most relevant today? Why?

VIEWPOINT

In his introduction to another translation of *Gilgamesh,* scholar N. K. Sanders describes the epic as

a mixture of pure adventure, of morality, and of tragedy. Through the action we are shown a very human concern with mortality, the search for knowledge, and for an escape from the common lot of man. . . . If Gilgamesh is not the first human hero, he is the first tragic hero of whom anything is known.

▨ What elements of "pure adventure" does this selection contain? What are its chief lessons in morality? In what sense is Gilgamesh a tragic hero in this selection, even though he does not lose his life or his position as king?

COMPOSITION

Writing About Theme

▨ Choose what you feel is the central theme of this selection from *Gilgamesh,* and write a brief essay about it. Begin by stating the theme.

Then show how plot events (including conflict and resolution), characterization (including dialogue), setting, and symbols all help illuminate the theme. *For help with this assignment, refer to Lesson 6 in the Writing About Literature Handbook at the back of this book.*

Writing a Research Report

▨ Write a brief factual report on an aspect of Sumerian or Babylonian civilization—for example, achievements in architecture, scientific accomplishments, development of cities, development of codes of law, or cuneiform. Research your information in at least two sources in addition to encyclopedias. Then write a factual account in your own words, and include a bibliography of your sources.

COMPARING WRITERS

1. Compare and contrast *Gilgamesh,* the world's oldest surviving epic, with *Beowulf* (page 10), Europe's oldest surviving vernacular epic. What similarities and differences are there between the attitudes toward life and death expressed in the two selections? What does each selection reveal about the civilization that produced it?
2. Compare *Gilgamesh* to Gray's "Elegy Written in a Country Churchyard" (page 367) and Tennyson's "In Memoriam A. H. H." (page 498). What similarities and differences do you find in the selections' expressions of grief and its effects? In their views of life, death, friendship, and immortality?

Homer *c. 850 B.C.*

A thousand years after the oldest surviving Gilgamesh tablets were inscribed—and at least fifteen hundred years after the first Gilgamesh poems were composed—there emerged in the European land of Greece another composer of epics. Homer, the first known poet of western literature, could neither read nor write. Singing to the accompaniment of a lyre, a small stringed instrument, he composed his poetry orally; an authoritative edition of his poems was not published until about 150 B.C., hundreds of years after his death, by scholars at the Alexandrian library in Egypt.

Little is known about Homer's life, though his authorship of the two great epic poems, the *Iliad* [il′ē əd] and the *Odyssey* [od′ə sē], is established by tradition. Some scholars believe Homer lived in a city on the eastern shore of the Aegean; others doubt he ever existed. The Greek historian Herodotus, who lived in the fifth century B.C., was one of several who wrote early biographies of Homer, but the "facts" presented in these works are largely deduced from passages in the poems credited to Homer. According to legend, Homer was a poor, old, blind poet of great wisdom, who wandered from city to city singing his verse.

By 400 B.C. Homer's epics had become classics, as well as a vital part of Greek life. They were recited as part of the great religious festivals, and Greeks revered them as a source of guidance in religious and moral matters. Every child who learned to read studied Homer, for he was regarded as a master of literature and rhetoric, too. The Greek philosophers Plato and Aristotle often referred to the epics in their own writing, and the Greek playwrights Sophocles (page 826) and Euripides based their dramas on characters and plots set down by Homer. Homer's influence gradually spread throughout the world, and he remains today one of the most widely read authors in western literature. Much of the literary heritage of the western world is rooted in his epics, and many generations of writers have been so inspired by his heroes and themes that they have created their own works around them. Among the many examples of English works directly inspired by Homer are Keats's "On First Looking into Chapman's Homer" (page 451) and Tennyson's "Ulysses" (page 494).

Introducing the **Iliad**

Four hundred years after the Trojan War, a great conflict between the Greeks and the Trojans that occurred about 1200 B.C., Homer selected material from the many tales told about its causes, battles, and heroes. Using this material, he fashioned the *Iliad* and the

Odyssey, both of which present an awesome sweep of human experience. They deal with individual thoughts and feelings, the political and military actions of two societies, and the relationship of humanity to the universe.

The name of the *Iliad* comes from the word *Ilion,* another name for the city of Troy, which was located in what is now Turkey. It was watered by the river Scamandros [skə man′drōs] and guarded by the Scaean [sē′än] gate. The *Iliad* tells the story of the Trojan War and sets the stage for the *Odyssey.* In the *Odyssey,* which takes place after the events of the *Iliad,* Homer tells of the cunning and victorious hero Odysseus' [ō dis′ē əs]* long and adventurous journey home from Troy to Greece after the Trojan War and of the resumption of his domestic and political life.

In the *Iliad* Homer tells us that the war began when Paris, a Trojan prince, abducted Helen, the queen of Sparta in Greece. For nine years the irate Greeks attacked Troy, and for nine years the Trojans successfully resisted them. As the epic begins, a plague is ravaging the Greek camp. Agamemnon [ag′ə mem′non], leader of the Greek forces, has angered the god Apollo by insulting one of Apollo's priests. Apollo had rewarded Agamemnon by giving him the priest's daughter. When the priest tried to bargain for her return, Agamemnon sent him away, and the plague began. The gods agree to end the devastation only if Agamemnon returns the prize. He obeys, but demands to be given a captive of Achilles' [ə kil′ēz], the greatest of Greek warriors, to take her place. Achilles is outraged.

While the gods watch and take sides, Achilles withdraws his powerful troops, the Myrmidons, and sulks in his camp. Without Achilles' support, the Greeks are sufficiently weakened to allow the Trojans, led by Hector, the son of King Priam [prī′əm] of Troy, to venture from the safety of their city and very nearly destroy the Greek fleet. Although Achilles cannot be persuaded to help, his friend Patroclus [pə trō′kləs] dons Achilles' armor, intending to frighten the Trojans. The Trojan Hector kills him and strips his body of the armor. Infuriated, Achilles remains idle no longer, waiting only to receive new armor from his mother, the goddess Thetis, before setting out to avenge Patroclus' death on Hector and the Trojans.

■ What do you think of Achilles' behavior? Is it suitable for a great Greek warrior?

---

*In Greek names *ch* is always pronounced like the English *k; c* and *g* are hard sounds except before *e, i, y,* and *ae,* when the *c* is pronounced *s* and the *g, j.* An *e* at the end of names is always sounded like the long *e.*

Homer

from the **Iliad**

Translated by Robert Fitzgerald

CHARACTERS

Trojans

ANDROMACHE [an drom′ə kē]: Hector's wife

HECUBA: Priam's wife

HECTOR: Priam's eldest son; leader of the Trojan warriors

PARIS: also called Alexander; Priam's son who abducted Helen, thereby causing the war

PRIAM [prī′əm]: Troy's king

ASTYANAX [as tī′ə naks′]: baby son of Hector and Andromache

Greeks

ACHAEANS [ə kē′ənz]: Greeks (the name comes from a section of northeastern Greece); also called Danaans and Argives

ACHILLES [ə kil′ēz]: leader of the Myrmidons, greatest of the Greek warriors

HELEN: Greek queen abducted by Paris

PATROCLUS [pə trō′kləs]: best friend of Achilles

Gods

APOLLO [ə pol′ō]: son of Zeus and protector of Troy, which he helped to build

ATHENA [ə thē′nə]: also called Pallas Athena; daughter of Zeus, protector of Achilles

ZEUS [zo͞os]: king of the gods

from Book 6, Hector and Andromache

Hector whirled and left his hall,
taking the same path he had come by,
along byways, walled lanes, all through the town
until he reached the Scaean Gates, whereby
5   before long he would issue on the field.
There his warmhearted lady
came to meet him, running: Andromache,
whose father, Eetion, once had ruled
the land under Mount Placus, dark with forest,
10 at Thebe under Placus—lord and king
of the Cilicians. Hector was her lord now,
head to foot in bronze; and now she joined him.
Behind her came the maid, who held the child
against her breast, a rosy baby still,
15 Hectorides,[1] the world's delight, as fresh
as a pure shining star. Scamandrius
his father named him; other men would say
Astyanax, "Lord of the Lower Town,"
as Hector singlehandedly guarded Troy.
20 How brilliantly the warrior smiled, in silence,
his eyes upon the child! Andromache
rested against him, shook away a tear,
and pressed his hand in both her own, to say:

"Oh, my wild one, your bravery will be
25 your own undoing! No pity for our child,
poor little one, or me in my sad lot—
soon to be deprived of you! soon, soon
Achaeans as one man will set upon you
and cut you down! Better for me, without you,
30 to take cold earth for mantle.[2] No more comfort,
no other warmth, after you meet your doom,
but heartbreak only. Father is dead, and Mother.
My father great Achilles killed when he
besieged and plundered Thebes, our high town,
35 citadel of Cilicians. He killed him,
but, reverent at least in this, did not
despoil him. Body, gear, and weapons forged
so handsomely, he burned, and heaped a barrow
over the ashes. Elms were planted round
40 by mountain-nymphs of him who bears the stormcloud.[3]

---

1. **Hectorides** [hek′tər ē′dez]: Greek form for the son of Hector, Astyanax.
2. **for mantle:** as a cover.
3. **him . . . stormcloud:** Zeus.

Then seven brothers that I had at home
in one day entered Death's dark place. Achilles,
prince and powerful runner, killed all seven
amid their shambling cattle and silvery sheep.
45 Mother, who had been queen of wooded Placus,
he brought with other winnings home, and freed her,
taking no end of ransom. Artemis
the Huntress[4] shot her in her father's house.
Father and mother—I have none but you,
50 nor brother, Hector; lover none but you!
Be merciful! Stay here upon the tower!
Do not bereave your child and widow me!
Draw up your troops by the wild fig tree; that way
the city lies most open, men most easily
55 could swarm the wall where it is low:
three times, at least, their best men tried it there
in company of the two called Ajax,[5] with
Idomeneus, the Atreidai, Diomedes[6]—
whether someone who had it from oracles[7]
60 had told them, or their own hearts urged them on."

Great Hector in his shimmering helmet answered:

"Lady, these many things beset my mind
no less than yours. But I should die of shame
before our Trojan men and noblewomen
65 if like a coward I avoided battle,
nor am I moved to. Long ago I learned
how to be brave, how to go forward always
and to contend for honor, Father's and mine.
Honor—for in my heart and soul I know
70 a day will come when ancient Ilion falls,
when Priam and the folk of Priam perish.
Not by the Trojans' anguish on that day
am I so overborne in mind—the pain
of Hecuba herself, or Priam king,
75 or of my brothers, many and valorous,
who will have fallen in dust before our enemies—
as by your own grief, when some armed Achaean
takes you in tears, your free life stripped away.

---

4. **Artemis** [är′tə mis] **the Huntress:** Greek goddess of hunting
and chastity.
5. **two called Ajax:** Ajax the Great and Ajax the Lesser, unrelated,
heroic Greek warriors.
6. **Idomeneus** [ī dom′ə nōos′], **the Atreidai** [a trē′i dī], **Diomedes**
[dī′ə mē′dēz]: brave hero and leader of the Cretans, the sons of Atreus
(Agamemnon and Menelaus), and a Greek warrior, respectively.
7. **oracles:** prophesying priests, believed to have been inspired by
the gods.

120 at loom and spindle, and command the maids
to busy themselves, too. As for the war,
that is for men, all who were born at Ilion,
to put their minds on—most of all for me."

He stooped now to recover his plumed helm
125 as she, his dear wife, drew away, her head
turned and her eyes upon him, brimming tears.
She made her way in haste then to the ordered
house of Hector and rejoined her maids,
moving them all to weep at sight of her.
130 In Hector's home they mourned him, living still
but not, they feared, again to leave the war
or be delivered from Achaean fury.

Neither his wife Andromache's entreaties nor his own foreboding can prevent Hector, leader of the Trojans, from confronting Achilles, the great Greek warrior. Before their battle takes place, however, Hector fights and kills Patroclus, Achilles' best friend. Achilles, in terrible rage over Patroclus' death, kills many Trojans and captures twelve Trojan youths to sacrifice at Patroclus' funeral. The gods, greatly angered by the excesses of Achilles' fury, enter the action to rebuke him. Meanwhile, all the Trojans withdraw into the walled city of Troy; only Hector remains outside, determined to confront Achilles despite his family's pleas.

from Book 22, Achilles and Hector

Hector stood firm, as huge Achilles neared.
The way a serpent, fed on poisonous herbs,
coiled at his lair upon a mountainside,
with all his length of hate awaits a man
5 and eyes him evilly: so Hector, grim
and narrow-eyed, refused to yield. He leaned
his brilliant shield against a spur of wall
and in his brave heart bitterly reflected:
"Here I am badly caught. If I take cover,
10 slipping inside the gate and wall, the first
to accuse me for it will be Polydamas,
he who told me I should lead the Trojans
back to the city on that cursed night
Achilles joined the battle. No, I would not,
15 would not, wiser though it would have been.
Now troops have perished for my foolish pride,
I am ashamed to face townsmen and women.
Someone inferior to me may say:
'He kept his pride and lost his men, this Hector!'
20 So it will go. Better, when that time comes,

that I appear as he who killed Achilles
man to man, or else that I went down
fighting him to the end before the city.
Suppose, though, that I lay my shield and helm
25 aside, and prop my spear against the wall,
and go to meet the noble Prince Achilles,
promising Helen, promising with her
all treasures that Alexander brought home
by ship to Troy—the first cause of our quarrel—
30 that he may give these things to the Atreidai?
Then I might add, apart from these, a portion
of all the secret wealth the city owns.
Yes, later I might take our counselors' oath
to hide no stores, but share and share alike
35 to halve all wealth our lovely city holds,
all that is here within the walls. Ah, no,
why even put the question to myself?
I must not go before him and receive
no quarter, no respect! Aye, then and there
40 he'll kill me, unprotected as I am,
my gear laid by, defenseless as a woman.
No chance, now, for charms from oak or stone
in parley with him—charms a girl and boy
might use when they enchant each other talking!
45 Better we duel, now at once, and see
to whom the Olympian[8] awards the glory."

These were his shifts of mood. Now close at hand
Achilles like the implacable god of war
came on with blowing crest, hefting the dreaded
50 beam of Pelian ash[9] on his right shoulder.
Bronze light played around him, like the glare
of a great fire or the great sun rising,
and Hector, as he watched, began to tremble.
Then he could hold his ground no more. He ran,
55 leaving the gate behind him, with Achilles
hard on his heels, sure of his own speed.
When that most lightning-like of birds, a hawk
bred on a mountain, swoops upon a dove,
the quarry dips in terror, but the hunter,
60 screaming, dips behind and gains upon it,
passionate for prey. Just so, Achilles
murderously cleft the air, as Hector

---

8. **the Olympian:** Zeus.
9. **beam of Pelian** [pē′lē ən] **ash:** a spear originally received by Achilles' father,
Peleus, as a wedding gift from the kind centaur Chiron [kī′ron], in whose cave
on Mount Pelion Peleus and Achilles' mother, Thetis, were married. The spear was
made of the hard wood of an ash tree from Mount Pelion.

ran with flashing knees along the wall.
They passed the lookout point, the wild fig tree—
65 with wind in all its leaves, then veered away
along the curving wagon road, and came
to where the double fountains well, the source
of eddying Scamander. One hot spring
flows out, and from the water fumes arise
70 as though from fire burning; but the other
even in summer gushes chill as hail
or snow or crystal ice frozen on water.
Near these fountains are wide washing pools
of smooth-laid stone, where Trojan wives and daughters
75 laundered their smooth linen in the days
of peace before the Achaeans came. Past these
the two men ran, pursuer and pursued,
and he who fled was noble, he behind
a greater man by far. They ran full speed,
80 and not for bull's hide or a ritual beast
or any prize that men compete for: no,
but for the life of Hector, tamer of horses.

    While Achilles pursues Hector around the walls of Troy, the
gods debate the outcome of their confrontation. Despite Hector's
lifelong respect for the gods, Zeus cannot save him from his fate.
While Athena assures Achilles of his victory, Apollo, who had pre-
viously aided Hector, abandons him. Quite alone now, Hector re-
alizes he has no choice but to stand and fight Achilles.

And when at last the two men faced each other,
Hector was the first to speak. He said:

85 "I will no longer fear you as before,
son of Peleus, though I ran from you
round Priam's town three times and could not face you.
Now my soul would have me stand and fight,
whether I kill you or am killed. So come,
90 we'll summon gods here as our witnesses,
none higher, arbiters of a pact: I swear
that, terrible as you are,
I'll not insult your corpse should Zeus allow me
victory in the end, your life as prize.
95 Once I have your gear, I'll give your body
back to Achaeans. Grant me, too, this grace."

But swift Achilles frowned at him and said:

"Hector, I'll have no talk of pacts with you,
forever unforgiven as you are.
100 As between men and lions there are none,

no concord between wolves and sheep, but all
hold one another hateful through and through,
so there can be no courtesy between us,
no sworn truce, till one of us is down
105 and glutting with his blood the war god Ares.
Summon up what skills you have. By god,
you'd better be a spearman and a fighter!
Now there is no way out. Pallas Athena
will have the upper hand of you. The weapon
110 belongs to me. You'll pay the reckoning
in full for all the pain my men have borne,
who met death by your spear."

                              He twirled and cast
his shaft with its long shadow. Splendid Hector,
keeping his eye upon the point, eluded it
115 by ducking at the instant of the cast,
so shaft and bronze shank passed him overhead
and punched into the earth. But unperceived
by Hector, Pallas Athena plucked it out
and gave it back to Achilles. Hector said:

120 "A clean miss. Godlike as you are,
you have not yet known doom for me from Zeus.
You thought you had, by heaven. Then you turned
into a word-thrower, hoping to make me lose
my fighting heart and head in fear of you.
125 You cannot plant your spear between my shoulders
while I am running. If you have the gift,
just put it through my chest as I come forward.
Now it's for you to dodge my own. Would god
you'd give the whole shaft lodging in your body!
130 War for the Trojans would be eased
if you were blotted out, bane that you are."

With this he twirled his long spearshaft and cast it,
hitting his enemy mid-shield, but off
and away the spear rebounded. Furious
135 that he had lost it, made his throw for nothing,
Hector stood bemused. He had no other.
Then he gave a great shout to Deiphobus
to ask for a long spear. But there was no one
near him, not a soul. Now in his heart
140 the Trojan realized the truth and said:

"This is the end. The gods are calling deathward.
I had thought
a good soldier, Deiphobus, was with me.

He is inside the walls. Athena tricked me.
145 Death is near, and black, not at a distance,
not to be evaded. Long ago
this hour must have been to Zeus's liking
and to the liking of his archer son.
They have been well disposed before, but now
150 the appointed time's upon me. Still, I would not
die without delivering a stroke,
or die ingloriously, but in some action
memorable to men in days to come."

With this he drew the whetted blade that hung
155 upon his left flank, ponderous and long,
collecting all his might the way an eagle
narrows himself to dive through shady cloud
and strike a lamb or cowering hare: so Hector
lanced ahead and swung his whetted blade.
160 Achilles with wild fury in his heart
pulled in upon his chest his beautiful shield—
his helmet with four burnished metal ridges
nodding above it, and the golden crest
Hephaestus[10] locked there tossing in the wind.
165 Conspicuous as the evening star that comes,
amid the first in heaven, at fall of night,
and stands most lovely in the west, so shone
in sunlight the fine-pointed spear
Achilles poised in his right hand, with deadly
170 aim at Hector, at the skin where most
it lay exposed. But nearly all was covered
by the bronze gear he took from slain Patroclus,
showing only, where his collarbones
divided neck and shoulders, the bare throat
175 where the destruction of a life is quickest.
Here, then, as the Trojan charged, Achilles
drove his point straight through the tender neck,
but did not cut the windpipe, leaving Hector
able to speak and to respond. He fell
180 aside into the dust. And Prince Achilles
now exulted:

"Hector, had you thought
that you could kill Patroclus and be safe?
Nothing to dread from me; I was not there.
All childishness. Though distant then, Patroclus'
185 comrade in arms was greater far than he—

---

10. **Hephaestus** [hi fes′təs]: Greek god of fire and divine blacksmith.

and it is I who had been left behind
that day beside the deep-sea ships who now
have made your knees give way. The dogs and kites
will rip your body. His will lie in honor
190 when the Achaeans give him funeral."

Hector, barely whispering, replied:

"I beg you by your soul and by your parents,
do not let the dogs feed on me
in your encampment by the ships. Accept
195 the bronze and gold my father will provide
as gifts, my father and her ladyship
my mother. Let them have my body back,
so that our men and women may accord me
decency of fire when I am dead."

200 Achilles the great runner scowled and said:

"Beg me no beggary by soul or parents,
whining dog! Would god my passion drove me
to slaughter you and eat you raw, you've caused
such agony to me! No man exists
205 who could defend you from the carrion pack[11]—
not if they spread for me ten times your ransom,
twenty times, and promise more as well;
aye, not if Priam, son of Dardanus,
tells them to buy you for your weight in gold!
210 You'll have no bed of death, nor will you be
laid out and mourned by her who gave you birth.
Dogs and birds will have you, every scrap."

Then at the point of death Lord Hector said:

"I see you now for what you are. No chance
215 to win you over. Iron in your breast
your heart is. Think a bit, though: this may be
a thing the gods in anger hold against you
on that day when Paris and Apollo
destroy you at the Gates, great as you are."

220 Even as he spoke, the end came, and death hid him;
spirit from body fluttered to undergloom,
bewailing fate that made him leave his youth
and manhood in the world. And as he died
Achilles spoke again. He said:

---

11. **carrion pack:** birds of prey.

225 "Die, make an end. I shall accept my own
   whenever Zeus and the other gods desire."

   At this he pulled his spearhead from the body,
   laying it aside, and stripped
   the bloodstained shield and cuirass[12] from his shoulders.
230 Other Achaeans hastened round to see
   Hector's fine body and his comely face,
   and no one came who did not stab the body.
   Glancing at one another they would say:

   "Now Hector has turned vulnerable, softer
235 than when he put the torches to the ships!"

   And he who said this would inflict a wound.
   When the great master of pursuit, Achilles,
   had the body stripped, he stood among them,
   saying swiftly:

                    "Friends, my lords and captains
240 of Argives, now that the gods at last have let me
   bring to earth this man who wrought
   havoc among us—more than all the rest—
   come, we'll offer battle around the city,
   to learn the intentions of the Trojans now.
245 Will they give up their strong point at this loss?
   Can they fight on, though Hector's dead?

                                        But wait:
   why do I ponder, why take up these questions?
   Down by the ships Patroclus' body lies
   unwept, unburied. I shall not forget him
250 while I can keep my feet among the living.
   If in the dead world they forget the dead,
   I say there, too, I shall remember him,
   my friend. Men of Achaea, lift a song!
   Down to the ships we go, and take this body,
255 our glory. We have beaten Hector down,
   to whom as to a god the Trojans prayed."

   Indeed, he had in mind for Hector's body
   outrage and shame. Behind both feet he pierced
   the tendons, heel to ankle. Rawhide cords
260 he drew through both and lashed them to his chariot,
   letting the man's head trail. Stepping aboard,
   bearing the great trophy of the arms,

---

12. **cuirass** [kwi ras´]: breastplate.

he shook the reins, and whipped the team ahead
into a willing run. A dustcloud rose
265 above the furrowing body; the dark tresses
flowed behind, and the head so princely once
lay back in dust. Zeus gave him to his enemies
to be defiled in his own fatherland. . . .

Priam, seeing his son slain, futilely begs Achilles to return Hector's body. Achilles returns to his camp to conduct funeral rites for Patroclus. Protecting Hector's body from decay and desecration, the gods send their messenger, Hermes, to lead Priam to Achilles so that Priam can retrieve the body. Achilles recognizes the will of the gods and yields the body to Priam, who carries it back to Troy for Hector's burial rites.

from Book 24, Hector's Funeral

Now, at the sight of Hector, all gave way
to loss and longing, and all crowded down
to meet the escort and body near the gates,
till no one in the town was left at home.
5 There Hector's lady and his gentle mother
tore their hair for him, flinging themselves
upon the wagon to embrace his person
while the crowd groaned. All that long day
until the sun went down they might have mourned
10 in tears before the gateway. But old Priam
spoke to them from his chariot:

              "Make way,
let the mules pass. You'll have your fill of weeping
later, when I've brought the body home."

They parted then, and made way for the wagon,
15 allowing Priam to reach the famous hall.
They laid the body of Hector in his bed,
and brought in minstrels, men to lead the dirge.
While these wailed out, the women answered, moaning.
Andromache of the ivory-white arms
20 held in her lap between her hands
the head of Hector who had killed so many.
Now she lamented:

              "You've been torn from life,
my husband, in young manhood, and you leave me
empty in our hall. The boy's a child
25 whom you and I, poor souls, conceived; I doubt
he'll come to manhood. Long before, great Troy
will go down plundered, citadel and all,

now that you are lost, who guarded it
and kept it, and preserved its wives and children.
30 They will be shipped off in the murmuring hulls
one day, and I along with all the rest.
You, my little one, either you come with me
to do some grinding labor, some base toil
for a harsh master, or an Achaean soldier
35 will grip you by the arm and hurl you down
from a tower here to a miserable death—
out of his anger for a brother, a father,
or even a son that Hector killed. Achaeans
in hundreds mouthed black dust under his blows.
40 He was no moderate man in war, your father,
and that is why they mourn him through the city.
Hector, you gave your parents grief and pain
but left me loneliest, and heartbroken.
You could not open your strong arms to me
45 from your deathbed, or say a thoughtful word,
for me to cherish all my life long
as I weep for you night and day."

Then yoking mules and oxen to their wagons
the people thronged before the city gates.
50 Nine days they labored, bringing countless loads
of firewood to the town. When Dawn that lights
the world of mortals came for the tenth day,
they carried greathearted Hector out at last,
and all in tears placed his dead body high
55 upon its pyre, then cast a torch below.
When the young Dawn with finger tips of rose
made heaven bright, the Trojan people massed
about Prince Hector's ritual fire.
All being gathered and assembled, first
60 they quenched the smoking pyre with tawny wine
wherever flames had licked their way, then friends
and brothers picked his white bones from the char
in sorrow, while the tears rolled down their cheeks.
In a golden urn they put the bones,
65 shrouding the urn with veiling of soft purple.
Then in a grave dug deep they placed it
and heaped it with great stones. The men were quick
to raise the death-mound, while in every quarter
lookouts were posted to ensure against
70 an Achaean surprise attack. When they had finished
raising the barrow, they returned to Ilion,
where all sat down to banquet in his honor
in the hall of Priam king. So they performed
the funeral rites of Hector, tamer of horses.

STUDY QUESTIONS

Hector and Andromache

Recalling

1. What reasons and advice does Andromache give to dissuade Hector from fighting?
2. What are Hector's reasons for wanting to fight?
3. Why does Hector's son cry when he sees his father? What does Hector do? What is Hector's wish for his son?
4. With what thoughts does Hector comfort his wife before he leaves?

Interpreting

5. What considerations and values are pitted against each other in this excerpt? Which set of values is finally placed above all other concerns?

Extending

6. Hector, poised between home and battleground, recognizes his responsibility to both; somehow he must justify his public actions and his private ones as well. In what cases may one's responsibility to the public good be greater than one's responsibility to home and family?

Achilles and Hector

Recalling

1. What are possible courses of action that Hector considers as Achilles approaches him? What course of action does Hector choose?
2. What comparisons does Homer use to describe Achilles in lines 48–57? How is Hector affected by Achilles' appearance?
3. What agreement does Hector attempt to make with Achilles for the burial of their bodies? What is Achilles' response?
4. Describe Hector's death.

Interpreting

5. What are the different reasons Hector and Achilles have for fighting? Which reasons seem more honorable to Homer? Why?
6. How does Homer make Hector appear vulnerable compared to Achilles?
7. What seems to be Homer's attitude toward fate? Consider especially the character of Hector.

Extending

8. Considering the respective behavior of Achilles and Hector as Hector lies dying, which of the two strikes you as a greater, more honorable man? Why? What concept of honor is implied in this excerpt?

Hector's Funeral

Recalling

1. After Hector's death, what vision of the future does Andromache imagine?
2. How long do the Trojans take to bury their dead?
3. Describe the funeral rites performed for Hector.

Interpreting

4. Hector is prepared to die fighting in order to preserve his reputation; nevertheless, he is commemorated by his people and by Homer as the man he was in peacetime: "Hector, tamer of horses." What does this representation of Hector suggest about Homer's attitude toward war and toward the concepts of honor and reputation?

Extending

5. What value can you see in the elaborate funeral rituals practiced by the Greeks and the Trojans?

VIEWPOINT

In describing the characterization of Hector in the *Iliad*, the scholar W. A. Camps writes,

What leaves us with our strongest impression about Hector is his experience, what happens to him in the story. It is a tragic experience in the classic sense of the term. . . . The pathos [the quality in something that arouses pity or sympathy] of Hector's experience is enhanced . . . by a memorable scene with his wife and baby son which fixes in our minds the cause for which he is fighting and makes us feel for him throughout the story as typically human as well as heroic.

1. In terms of what you know about Hector, how would you characterize his experience? What, in your own words, is the "pathos" of his experience?
2. In what ways is Hector both heroic and typically human?

LITERARY FOCUS

The Epithet and Homeric Simile

An **epithet** is a nickname or an adjective phrase describing a characteristic of a person or a thing. Homer's epithets are often compound, such as "rosy-fingered dawn" or "swift-footed Achilles."

Since the epic poet was constrained by the meter of his poem, it was helpful for him to be able to use an epithet plus a proper name as a building block of regular meter. When referring to a character, the poet would have at hand a stock of epithets that he knew from experience would satisfy certain metrical demands.

The **Homeric simile,** or epic simile, is longer and more elaborate than a conventional simile. It expands the comparison with a detailed and somewhat lengthy description that extends over several lines of verse. For example, at the beginning of the excerpt from Book 22, a Homeric simile describes Hector as he waits for Achilles to strike. Hector is standing firm,

> The way a serpent, fed on poisonous herbs,
> coiled at his lair upon a mountainside,
> with all his length of hate awaits a man
> and eyes him evilly.

Thinking About the Epithet and Homeric Simile

1. Find four epithets in the excerpt from Book 22. How would the meaning of the passage change if the epithets were omitted?
2. Find three Homeric similes in the excerpt from Book 22. Explain who or what is being compared, and explain what details expand the comparison into a Homeric simile.

VOCABULARY

Terms from Greek and Roman Mythology

Many English words and expressions have their origins in names or events from Greek and Roman mythology. For example, the word *cereal* comes from Ceres, the Roman goddess of agriculture. Use a dictionary to determine the meanings and origins of the following words and expressions. Then use each term in a sentence.

1. Achilles' heel
2. hector
3. martial
4. odyssey
5. titanic

Sappho   *c. 610–580 B.C.*

Sappho is considered one of the world's greatest women poets, even though only some two hundred fragments of her poems have survived. Little is known about her life: She was of noble birth, born in the late seventh century B.C., and wrote most of her poems in the early part of the sixth century. She was married and had a daughter named Cleis, and she had three brothers, to one of whom she gave some poetic advice on the topics of money and love. Sappho gathered around her a group of young women in Myteline (now part of Greece) whom she instructed in the cultural and social ways of their noble class. Together the women dedicated themselves and their poetry to Aphrodite, goddess of love, beauty, and fertility. Sappho was revered by her female followers, but her influence was far greater than her circle of students and friends. Her verse, among the world's finest lyric poetry, was widely imitated not only in ancient Greece but in ancient Rome as well.

Like later lyric poetry, Sappho's poems are personal expressions of her feelings. Brief, intense, and vivid, they reveal her private emotional life in a frank and simple manner. Her concerns were love, the joy of children, nature, and the world around her. Only one of Sappho's poems, her "Ode to Aphrodite," survives in its original, complete form. Though the majority of her poems were songs written for a single unaccompanied voice, her poems were often accompanied by both music and dance. As you encounter the following poetic fragments, try reading them aloud, listening to the natural music in the words, and visualizing the images in this long-lasting work.

■ What poem that you know and love would benefit from being accompanied by music and dance?

Sappho

Dawn

1

Tell everyone

Now, today, I shall
sing beautifully for
my friends' pleasure.

2

5 We shall enjoy it—

As for him who finds
fault, may silliness
and sorrow take him!

3

Standing by my bed

10 In gold sandals,
Dawn that very
moment awoke me.

4

I asked myself

What, Sappho, can
15 you give one who
has everything,
like Aphrodite[1]?

_____

1. **Aphrodite** [af′rə dī′tē]: Greek goddess of
love, beauty, and fertility.

Detail from a red-figured amphora, or
vase, showing a youth singing and
playing a zither, c. 490 B.C.

Day

1

At noontime

When the earth is
bright with flaming
heat falling straight down,

5 the cricket sets
up a high-pitched
singing in his wings.

2

I took my lyre and said:

Come now, my heavenly
10 tortoise shell: become
a speaking instrument.

3

Although they are

Only breath, words
which I command
15 are immortal.

4

You know the place: then

Leave Crete[1] and come to us,
waiting where the grove is
pleasantest, by precincts

20 sacred to you; incense
smokes on the altar, cold
streams murmur through the

apple branches, a young
rose thicket shades the ground,
25 and quivering leaves pour

down deep sleep; in meadows
where horses have grown sleek
among spring flowers, dill

scents the air. Queen! Cyprian[2]!
30 Fill our gold cups with love
stirred into clear nectar.

Detail, Greek kylix, or bowl, showing two girls walking, 460–450 B.C.

---

1. **Crete** [krēt]: Greek island in the Mediterranean Sea, southeast of Greece.
2. **Cyprian** [sip′rē ən]: referring to Aphrodite, who was born on the Mediterranean island of Cyprus.

Before another woman's loom in Argos
80 it may be you will pass, or at Messeis
or Hypereia fountain, carrying water,
against your will—iron constraint upon you.
And seeing you in tears, a man may say:
'There is the wife of Hector, who fought best
85 of Trojan horsemen when they fought at Troy.'
So he may say—and you will ache again
for one man who could keep you out of bondage.
Let me be hidden dark down in my grave
before I hear your cry or know you captive!"

90 As he said this, Hector held out his arms
to take his baby. But the child squirmed round
on the nurse's bosom and began to wail,
terrified by his father's great war helm—
the flashing bronze, the crest with horsehair plume
95 tossed like a living thing at every nod.
His father began laughing, and his mother
laughed as well. Then from his handsome head
Hector lifted off his helm and bent
to place it, bright with sunlight, on the ground.
100 When he had kissed his child and swung him high
to dandle him, he said this prayer:

                                     "O Zeus
and all immortals, may this child, my son,
become like me a prince among the Trojans.
Let him be strong and brave and rule in power
105 at Ilion; then someday men will say
'This fellow is far better than his father!'
seeing him home from war, and his arms
the bloodstained gear of some tall warrier slain—
making his mother proud."

                             After this prayer,
110 into his dear wife's arms he gave his baby,
whom on her fragrant breast
she held and cherished, laughing through her tears.
Hector pitied her now. Caressing her,
he said:

                     "Unquiet soul, do not be too distressed
115 by thoughts of me. You know no man dispatches me
into the undergloom against my fate;
no mortal, either, can escape his fate,
coward or brave man, once he comes to be.
Go home, attend to your own handiwork

Night

1

You are the herdsman of evening,

Hesperus,[1] you herd
homeward whatever
Dawn's light dispersed;

5 You herd sheep—herd
goats—herd children
home to their mothers.

2

Awed by her splendor,

Stars near the lovely
10 moon cover their own
bright faces when she
is roundest and lights
earth with her silver.

A red-figured amphora, or vase,
showing a youth singing and playing
a zither, c. 490 B.C.

---

1. **Hesperus** [hes′pər əs]: the evening star. In
Greek mythology Hesperus led the other stars
out into the sky.

STUDY QUESTIONS

Dawn

Recalling

1. Why does the speaker plan to sing beautifully? What will the reaction to her singing be?
2. What color are Dawn's sandals? What suddenly awoke Sappho?
3. With what question does the poet conclude?

Interpreting

4. Describe the speaker's underlying sentiments. Which lines indicate Sappho's self-confidence? Her self-doubt?
5. Reread lines 2, 11, and 12. What do these references to time add to the poem's emotional impact?
6. How does the image in line 10 relate to the poem's title? Would you describe the image as simple or elaborate? Vivid or bland? Specific or abstract?
7. What does the poem tell you about Aphrodite? What problem does she pose for the poet?

Day

Recalling

1. At what time does the poem begin? What is the earth like at this time?
2. What does Sappho entreat, or ask, her lyre to become? What adjective does she use to describe the words she commands?
3. What actions does Sappho advise Aphrodite to take?

Interpreting

4. What is Sappho's attitude toward Aphrodite? Which word in particular tells you this?
5. How would you characterize the place where Sappho resides? For what reason do you think she describes it in such detail?
6. Examine Sappho's use of sensory detail. Which adjectives do you find particularly powerful and intense? Which of her images rely on senses other than sight? To which of the four remaining senses do they appeal?

Night

Recalling

1. In Fragment 1 what does Hesperus, the evening star, bring home?
2. In Fragment 2 what do the stars do? When do they do this?

Interpreting

3. What emotional reaction do the stars have to the moon?
4. Where in the poem does Sappho employ personification? What does its use add to the emotion of the poem?
5. Which words in particular capture the moon's essence? How does the poet emphasize the intensity of the moon's brightness?
6. Does the speaker of the poem view night as a dreaded and negative phenomenon or as a comforting and positive one?

Extending

7. Based on reading Sappho's "Dawn," "Day," and "Night," how would you describe her attitude toward nature? How do you think she views her relationship to it? Is it intimate or distant? Enriching or depleting?

COMPOSITION

Analyzing the Poet's Techniques

■ Sappho's poetry is fresh, spontaneous, and exquisite. Analyze the poetic techniques she uses in any four fragments from "Dawn," "Day," or "Night." Look at her choice of vocabulary, her selection of sounds (which are different in Greek, of course, but are translated as poetically as possible), her use of adjectives and other modifiers, and her images.

Composing a Poetic Fragment

■ Compose a very short poem in the manner of Sappho's fragments. Express a sentiment in very few lines, using no more than two images.

Sophocles   *496?–406 B.C.*

The glory of ancient Greece survives in its drama as well as in its epics and lyric poetry. The fifth century B.C. was the most important period of Greek drama, when the most famous Greek dramatists—Aeschylus, Sophocles, and Euripides—were writing. Beloved and revered as a playwright in his own age, Sophocles [sof′ə klēz′] is one of the greatest tragic dramatists of all time. He lived in Athens during the most glorious period of Greek history, the Classical Period, or Golden Age, when achievements in politics, philosophy, and architecture were unparalleled. An ideal Greek citizen who participated in all forms of public life, Sophocles served as commissioner of public affairs, and in 440 B.C., when he was about fifty-five, he fought as a general in the war against the people of Samos, an island in the Aegean Sea.

However, Sophocles' lasting influence on western culture is seen in his plays, of which he is said to have written 125. Only seven have survived, and the most famous are his tragedies *Oedipus Rex, Electra,* and *Antigone* [an tig′ə nē]. More than twenty of his plays won first prize at the annual dramatic competition in Athens, and many more won second prize. Today Sophocles' plays are performed around the world, from summer festivals where they are presented in modern Greek in the ancient theater at Epidaurus, to experimental productions in English in off-Broadway playhouses.

Greek drama began in the seventh century B.C. as a part of religious rituals surrounding birth and death. Soon drama contests were held in honor of the god Dionysus, and by 534 B.C. the first contest for tragedy was held in Athens. Originally consisting of the chorus and a single actor, Greek drama gradually added more actors as the subject matter became less ritualistic. Sophocles is credited with introducing a third actor to the stage and initiating the use of painted sets.

Theatergoing for the Greeks was more than entertainment. Considered part of a citizen's education and supported by the state, Greek drama allowed mass participation in the tragedy and comedy of human experience (as many as forty thousand people attended a performance at a time). The plays, which took place during the day or for several days at a time during a festival, were presented in outdoor auditoriums. The circular orchestra where the chorus sang and danced had a background called the *skene* (from which the English word *scene* evolved).

Introducing **Antigone**

For the subject matter of his plays, Sophocles drew upon **legends,** or tales handed down for generations among the people of a certain region. The plots of *Antigone* and *Oedipus Rex* are based on the legends of the city Thebes. Sophocles knew that his audiences were familiar with these legends. For instance, those who came to see the tragedy of *Antigone* already knew that Oedipus [ed′ə pəs] was abandoned by his parents on a hillside at birth. This action was an attempt to escape the prophecy that Oedipus, as king of Thebes, would kill his father and marry his mother. After being sheltered by a shepherd and reaching maturity, Oedipus consults the oracle at Delphi [del′fī]. (The Greeks believed that the god Apollo conveyed his wisdom through the oracle, or prophet, a woman named Pythia. Cities as well as individuals sought the advice of the oracle.) When the oracle repeats the prophecy told to his parents, Oedipus attempts to prevent the tragic events by leaving the couple he believes to be his parents. Traveling to Thebes, he kills a man on the road. When he reaches the city, he is questioned by the Sphinx, a monster who sits at the gates of Thebes and kills passers-by who cannot solve her riddle. By correctly answering the riddle, Oedipus saves Thebes and marries its recently widowed queen, with whom he has two sons and two daughters. When the city is in the grip of a plague, an oracle predicts that there will be no relief until the murderer of the previous king has been revealed. At this point Oedipus learns not only that he has murdered the king but also that the king was his father. Oedipus blinds himself and leaves Thebes.

Upon Oedipus' death, his sons, Eteocles and Polyneices, agree to rule Thebes in alternate years; when Eteocles' year ends, however, he refuses to allow Polyneices to take over. Thereupon Polyneices gathers an army and attacks Thebes. In the ensuing battle the brothers kill each other. Their uncle, Creon, who succeeds them as king, buries Eteocles with full honors while proclaiming that Polyneices, as an enemy of the city, shall be denied burial.

The daughters of Oedipus, Antigone and Ismene, are therefore faced with the choice of denying a brother burial rites, thus condemning him to eternal unrest, or of disobeying the command of their uncle and king. *Antigone* opens with Antigone's decision to bury Polyneices.

Key Ideas in *Antigone*

As you read *Antigone,* look for references to each of the following ideas. You will thus grasp the play's important themes.

- The laws of the state versus the laws of tradition
- The rights and social position of women
- The consequences of uncompromising pride

▪ Can you recall some time when you were bent on a course of action and someone was determined to thwart you? How did you feel? What did you do?

Teiresias.   Ismene and Antigone.   Creon.

Sophocles

Antigone

Translated by Dudley Fitts and Robert Fitzgerald

CHARACTERS

ANTIGONE [an tig′ə nē]: daughter of Oedipus, former king of Thebes; she has vowed to give her brother Polyneices an honorable burial

ISMENE: Antigone's younger sister; she is unable to break the law in order to help Antigone bury their brother

CREON [krē′on]: the new king of Thebes, uncle of Antigone, Ismene, and Polyneices; he decrees that Polyneices' body must not be buried

EURYDICE [yoo rid′ə sē]: wife of Creon

HAIMON: son of Creon, engaged to Antigone

TEIRESIAS [tī rē′sē əs]: a blind prophet who predicts the consequences of Creon's orders

A SENTRY serving Creon

CHORUS, made up of about fifteen citizens of Thebes

GUARDS

SERVANTS

Scene. Before the palace of CREON, *king of Thebes. A central double door, and two lateral doors. A platform extends the length of the façade, and from this platform three steps lead down into the "orchestra," or chorus-ground.*

Time. Dawn of the day after the repulse of the Argive army[1] from the assault on Thebes.

Prologue

[ANTIGONE *and* ISMENE *enter from the central door of the palace.*]

ANTIGONE. Ismene, dear sister,
  You would think that we had already suffered enough
  For the curse on Oedipus:
  I cannot imagine any grief
5 That you and I have not gone through. And now—
  Have they told you of the new decree of our King Creon?

ISMENE. I have heard nothing: I know
  That two sisters lost two brothers, a double death
  In a single hour; and I know that the Argive army
10 Fled in the night; but beyond this, nothing.

ANTIGONE. I thought so. And that is why I wanted you
  To come out here with me. There is something we must do.

ISMENE. Why do you speak so strangely?

ANTIGONE. Listen, Ismene:
15 Creon buried our brother Eteocles
  With military honors, gave him a soldier's funeral,
  And it was right that he should: but Polyneices,
  Who fought as bravely and died as miserably—
  They say that Creon has sworn
20 No one shall bury him, no one mourn for him,
  But his body must lie in the fields, a sweet treasure
  For carrion birds[2] to find as they search for food.
  That is what they say, and our good Creon is coming here
  To announce it publicly: and the penalty—
  Stoning to death in the public square!
25   There it is,
  And now you can prove what you are:
  A true sister, or a traitor to your family.

ISMENE. Antigone, you are mad! What could I possibly do?

---

1. **Argive army:** soldiers from Argos who, under the leadership of Polyneices, attacked Thebes.
2. **carrion birds:** birds of prey.

ANTIGONE. You must decide whether you will help me or not.

30   **ISMENE.** I do not understand you. Help you in what?

ANTIGONE. Ismene, I am going to bury him. Will you come?

ISMENE. Bury him! You have just said the new law forbids it.

ANTIGONE. He is my brother. And he is your brother, too.

ISMENE. But think of the danger! Think what Creon will do!

35   **ANTIGONE.** Creon is not strong enough to stand in my way.

ISMENE. Ah sister!
Oedipus died, everyone hating him
For what his own search brought to light, his eyes
Ripped out by his own hand: and Iocaste died,
40   His mother and wife at once: she twisted the cords
That strangled her life; and our two brothers died,
Each killed by the other's sword. And we are left:
But oh, Antigone,
Think how much more terrible than these
45   Our own death would be if we should go against Creon
And do what he has forbidden! We are only women.
We cannot fight with men, Antigone!
The law is strong, we must give in to the law
In this thing, and in worse. I beg the dead
50   To forgive me, but I am helpless: I must yield
To those in authority. And I think it is dangerous business
To be always meddling.

ANTIGONE.   If that is what you think,
I should not want you, even if you asked to come.
You have made your choice, you can be what you want to be.
55   But I will bury him: and if I must die,
I say that this crime is holy: I shall lie down
With him in death, and I shall be as dear
To him as he to me.
                It is the dead,
Not the living, who make the longest demands:
We die forever . . .
60   You may do as you like,
Since apparently the laws of the gods mean nothing to you.

ISMENE. They mean a great deal to me: but I have no strength
To break laws that were made for the public good.

ANTIGONE. That must be your excuse, I suppose. But as for me,
I will bury the brother I love.

65   **ISMENE.**   Antigone,
I am so afraid for you!

ANTIGONE.   You need not be:
You have yourself to consider, after all.

ISMENE. But no one must hear of this, you must tell no one!
I will keep it a secret, I promise!

ANTIGONE.   Oh tell it! Tell everyone!
70 Think how they'll hate you when it all comes out
If they learn that you knew about it all the time!

ISMENE. So fiery! You should be cold with fear.

ANTIGONE. Perhaps. But I am doing only what I must.

ISMENE. But can you do it? I say that you cannot.

75 **ANTIGONE.** Very well: when my strength gives out, I shall do no more.

ISMENE. Impossible things should not be tried at all.

ANTIGONE. Go away, Ismene:
I shall be hating you soon, and the dead will, too.
For your words are hateful. Leave me my foolish plan:
80 I am not afraid of the danger: if it means death,
It will not be the worst of deaths—death without honor.

ISMENE. Go then, if you feel that you must.
You are unwise,
But a loyal friend indeed to those who love you.

[*Exit into the palace.* ANTIGONE *goes off, left. Enter the* CHORUS.]

Parados[3]

CHORUS. Now the long blade of the sun, lying   [*Strophe 1*]
Level east to west, touches with glory
Thebes of the Seven Gates. Open, unlidded
Eye of golden day! O marching light
5   Across the eddy and rush of Dirce's stream,[4]
Striking the white shields of the enemy
Thrown headlong backward from the blaze of morning!

CHORAGOS.[5] Polyneices their commander
Roused them with windy phrases,
10   He the wild eagle screaming

---

3. **Parados** [par'ə däs']: song chanted as the chorus entered the stage. Facing
one direction, the chorus chanted the **strophe** [strō'fē], and the other direction,
the **antistrophe** [an tis'trə fē].
4. **Dirce's** [dər'sēz] **stream**: Dirce, a queen of Thebes, was murdered and
thrown into the stream that thereafter bore her name.
5. **Choragos** [kôr ā'gəs]: chorus leader.

Insults above our land,
His wings their shields of snow,
His crest their marshaled helms.

CHORUS. Against our seven gates in a yawning ring   [Antistrophe 1]
15   The famished spears came onward in the night;
    But before his jaws were sated with our blood,
    Or pinefire took the garland of our towers,
    He was thrown back; and as he turned, great Thebes—
    No tender victim for his noisy power—
20   Rose like a dragon behind him, shouting war.

CHORAGOS. For God hates utterly
    The bray of bragging tongues;
    And when he beheld their smiling,
    Their swagger of golden helms,
25   The frown of his thunder blasted
    Their first man from our walls.

CHORUS. We heard his shout of triumph high in the air   [Strophe 2]
    Turn to a scream; far out in a flaming arc
    He fell with his windy torch, and the earth struck him.
30   And others storming in fury no less than his
    Found shock of death in the dusty joy of battle.

CHORAGOS. Seven captains at seven gates
    Yielded their clanging arms to the god
    That bends the battle line and breaks it.
35   These two only, brothers in blood,
    Face to face in matchless rage,
    Mirroring each the other's death,
    Clashed in long combat.

CHORUS. But now in the beautiful morning of victory   [Antistrophe 2]
40   Let Thebes of the many chariots sing for joy!
    With hearts for dancing we'll take leave of war:
    Our temples shall be sweet with hymns of praise,
    And the long night shall echo with our chorus.

Scene I

CHORAGOS. But now at last our new king is coming:
    Creon of Thebes. Menoikeus' son.
    In this auspicious dawn of his reign
    What are the new complexities
5   That shifting fate has woven for him?
    What is his counsel? Why has he summoned
    The old men to hear him?

[Enter CREON *from the palace, center. He addresses the* CHORUS *from the top step.]*

CREON. Gentlemen: I have the honor to inform you that our ship
of state, which recent storms have threatened to destroy, has
10   come safely to harbor at last, guided by the merciful wisdom of
Heaven. I have summoned you here this morning because I know
that I can depend upon you: your devotion to King Laios[6] was
absolute; you never hesitated in your duty to our late ruler Oedipus; and when Oedipus died, your loyalty was transferred to his
15   children. Unfortunately, as you know, his two sons, the princes
Eteocles and Polyneices, have killed each other in battle; and I,
as the next in blood, have succeeded to the full power of the
throne.

I am aware, of course, that no ruler can expect complete loy-
20   alty from his subjects until he has been tested in office. Nevertheless, I say to you at the very outset that I have nothing but
contempt for the kind of governor who is afraid, for whatever
reason, to follow the course that he knows is best for the state;
and as for the man who sets private friendship above the public
25   welfare—I have no use for him, either. I call God to witness that
if I saw my country headed for ruin, I should not be afraid to
speak out plainly; and I need hardly remind you that I would
never have any dealings with an enemy of the people. No one
values friendship more highly than I; but we must remember that
30   friends made at the risk of wrecking our ship are not real friends
at all.

These are my principles, at any rate, and that is why I have
made the following decisions concerning the sons of Oedipus:
Eteocles, who died as a man should die, fighting for his country,
35   is to be buried with full military honors, with all the ceremony
that is usual when the greatest heroes die; but his brother Polyneices, who broke his exile to come back with fire and sword
against his native city and the shrines of his fathers' gods, whose
one idea was to spill the blood of his blood and sell his own
40   people into slavery—Polyneices, I say, is to have no burial; no
man is to touch him or say the least prayer for him; he shall lie
on the plain, unburied; and the birds and the scavenging dogs
can do with him whatever they like.

This is my command, and you can see the wisdom behind it.
45   As long as I am king, no traitor is going to be honored with the
loyal man. But whoever shows by word and deed that he is on
the side of the state—he shall have my respect while he is living,
and my reverence when he is dead.

CHORAGOS. If that is your will, Creon son of Menoikeus,
50   You have the right to enforce it: we are yours.

---

6. **King Laios** [lā′əs]: father of Oedipus and previous king of Thebes.

CREON. That is my will. Take care that you do your part.

CHORAGOS. We are old men: let the younger ones carry it out.

CREON. I do not mean that: The sentries have been appointed.

CHORAGOS. Then what is it that you would have us do?

55 **CREON.** You will give no support to whoever breaks this law.

CHORAGOS. Only a crazy man is in love with death!

CREON. And death it is; yet money talks, and the wisest
Have sometimes been known to count a few coins too many.

[*Enter* SENTRY *from left.*]

SENTRY. I'll not say that I'm out of breath from running, King, be-
60 cause every time I stopped to think about what I have to tell
you, I felt like going back. And all the time a voice kept saying,
"You fool, don't you know you're walking straight into trouble?";
and then another voice: "Yes, but if you let somebody else get
the news to Creon first, it will be even worse than that for you!"
65 But good sense won out, at least I hope it was good sense, and
here I am with a story that makes no sense at all; but I'll tell it
anyhow, because, as they say, what's going to happen's going to
happen, and—

CREON. Come to the point. What have you to say?

70 **SENTRY.** I did not do it. I did not see who did it. You must not
punish me for what someone else has done.

CREON. A comprehensive defense! More effective, perhaps,
If I knew its purpose. Come: what is it?

SENTRY. A dreadful thing . . . I don't know how to put it—

CREON. Out with it!

75 **SENTRY.**   Well, then;
The dead man—
                    Polyneices—

[*Pause. The* SENTRY *is overcome, fumbles for words.* CREON *waits impassively.*]

                                        out there—
                                                  someone—
New dust on the slimy flesh! [*Pause. No sign from* CREON.]
Someone has given it burial that way, and
Gone—[*Long pause.* CREON *finally speaks with deadly control.*]

CREON. And the man who dared do this?

80 **SENTRY.**   I swear I
Do not know! You must believe me!

Listen:
The ground was dry, not a sign of digging, no,
Not a wheeltrack in the dust, no trace of anyone.
It was when they relieved us this morning; and one of them,
The corporal, pointed to it.

85   There it was,
The strangest—

          Look:
The body, just mounded over with light dust: you see?
Not buried really, but as if they'd covered it
Just enough for the ghost's peace. And no sign
90   Of dogs or any wild animal that had been there.

And then what a scene there was! Every man of us
Accusing the other: we all proved the other man did it,
We all had proof that we could not have done it.
We were ready to take hot iron in our hands,
95   Walk through fire, swear by all the gods,
It was not I!
I do not know who it was, but it was not I!

[CREON'*s rage has been mounting steadily, but the* SENTRY *is
too intent upon his story to notice it.*]

And then, when this came to nothing, someone said
A thing that silenced us and made us stare
100 Down at the ground: You had to be told the news,
And one of us had to do it! We threw the dice,
And the bad luck fell to me. So here I am,
No happier to be here than you are to have me:
Nobody likes the man who brings bad news.

CHORAGOS. I have been wondering, King: can it be that the gods
105   have done this?

CREON [*furiously*]. Stop!
Must you doddering wrecks
Go out of your heads entirely? "The gods!"
Intolerable!
110 The gods favor this corpse? Why? How had he served them?
Tried to loot their temples, burn their images,
Yes, and the whole state, and its laws with it!
Is it your senile opinion that the gods love to honor bad men?
A pious thought!—

                    No, from the very beginning
115 There have been those who have whispered together,
Stiff-necked anarchists, putting their heads together,
Scheming against me in alleys. These are the men,
And they have bribed my own guard to do this thing.

[*Sententiously*] Money!
120　　There's nothing in the world so demoralizing as money.
　　　Down go your cities,
　　　Homes gone, men gone, honest hearts corrupted,
　　　Crookedness of all kinds, and all for money!
　　　　　　　　　　　　　　[*To* SENTRY] But you—!
　　　I swear by God and by the throne of God,
125　　The man who has done this thing shall pay for it!
　　　Find that man, bring him to me, or your death
　　　Will be the least of your problems: I'll string you up
　　　Alive, and there will be certain ways to make you
　　　Discover your employer before you die;
　　　And the process may teach you a lesson you seem to have
130　　　missed:
　　　The dearest profit is sometimes all too dear:
　　　That depends on the source. Do you understand me?
　　　A fortune won is often misfortune.

SENTRY. King, may I speak?

CREON.　　　　　　　　　Your very voice distresses me.

135 SENTRY. Are you sure that it is my voice, and not your conscience?

CREON. By God, he wants to analyze me now!

SENTRY. It is not what I say, but what has been done, that hurts you.

CREON. You talk too much.

SENTRY.　　　　　　　　　Maybe; but I've done nothing.

CREON. Sold your soul for some silver: that's all you've done.

140 SENTRY. How dreadful it is when the right judge judges wrong!

CREON. Your figures of speech
　　　May entertain you now; but unless you bring me the man,
　　　You will get little profit from them in the end.

[*Exit* CREON *into the palace.*]

SENTRY. "Bring me the man"—!
145　　I'd like nothing better than bringing him the man!
　　　But bring him or not, you have seen the last of me here.
　　　At any rate, I am safe! [*Exit* SENTRY.]

Ode I[7]

CHORUS. Numberless are the world's wonders, but none　　　　　[*Strophe 1*]
　　　More wonderful than man; the storm-gray sea

---

7. **Ode:** song of the chorus to separate scenes.

Yields to his prows, the huge crests bear him high;
Earth, holy and inexhaustible, is graven
5 With shining furrows where his plows have gone
Year after year, the timeless labor of stallions.

The lightboned birds and beasts that cling to cover,   [*Antistrophe 1*]
The lithe fish lighting their reaches of dim water,
All are taken, tamed in the net of his mind;
10 The lion on the hill, the wild horse windy-maned,
Resign to him; and his blunt yoke has broken
The sultry shoulders of the mountain bull.

Words also, and thought as rapid as air,   [*Strophe 2*]
He fashions to his good use; statecraft is his,
15 And his the skill that deflects the arrows of snow,
The spears of winter rain: from every wind
He has made himself secure—from all but one:
In the late wind of death he cannot stand.

O clear intelligence, force beyond all measure!   [*Antistrophe 2*]
20 O fate of man, working both good and evil!
When the laws are kept, how proudly his city stands!
When the laws are broken, what of his city then?
Never may the anarchic man find rest at my hearth,
Never be it said that my thoughts are his thoughts.

Scene II

[*Reenter* SENTRY, *leading* ANTIGONE.]

CHORAGOS. What does this mean? Surely this captive woman
Is the princess, Antigone. Why should she be taken?

SENTRY. Here is the one who did it! We caught her
In the very act of burying him.—Where is Creon?

CHORAGOS. Just coming from the house.

[*Enter* CREON, *center.*]

5 CREON.   What has happened?
Why have you come back so soon?

SENTRY [*expansively*].   O King,
A man should never be too sure of anything:
I would have sworn
That you'd not see me here again; your anger
10 Frightened me so, and the things you threatened me with;
But how could I tell then
That I'd be able to solve the case so soon?

No dice-throwing this time; I was only too glad to come!

Here is this woman. She is the guilty one:

15   We found her trying to bury him.
       Take her, then; question her; judge her as you will.
       I am through with the whole thing now, and glad of it.

    CREON. But this is Antigone! Why have you brought her here?

    SENTRY. She was burying him, I tell you!

    CREON [*severely*].   Is this the truth?

20   SENTRY. I saw her with my own eyes. Can I say more?

    CREON. The details: Come, tell me quickly!

    SENTRY.   It was like this:
       After those terrible threats of yours, King,
       We went back and brushed the dust away from the body.
       The flesh was soft by now, and stinking,
25   So we sat on a hill to windward and kept guard.
       No napping this time! We kept each other awake.
       But nothing happened until the white round sun
       Whirled in the center of the round sky over us:
       Then, suddenly,
30   A storm of dust roared up from the earth, and the sky
       Went out, the plain vanished with all its trees
       In the stinging dark. We closed our eyes and endured it.

The whirlwind lasted a long time, but it passed;
And then we looked, and there was Antigone!

35   I have seen
A mother bird come back to a stripped nest, heard
Her crying bitterly a broken note or two
For the young ones stolen. Just so, when this girl
Found the bare corpse, and all her love's work wasted,

40   She wept, and cried on heaven to damn the hands
That had done this thing.

                  And then she brought more dust
And sprinkled wine three times for her brother's ghost.

We ran and took her at once. She was not afraid.
Not even when we charged her with what she had done.
She denied nothing.

45   And this was a comfort to me,
And some uneasiness: for it is a good thing
To escape from death, but it is no great pleasure
To bring death to a friend.

            Yet I always say
There is nothing so comfortable as your own safe skin!

50 CREON [*slowly, dangerously*]. And you, Antigone,
You with your head hanging—do you confess this thing?

ANTIGONE. I do. I deny nothing.

CREON [*to* SENTRY].   You may go. [*Exit* SENTRY.]
[*To* ANTIGONE] Tell me, tell me briefly:
Had you heard my proclamation touching this matter?

55 ANTIGONE. It was public. Could I help hearing it?

CREON. And yet you dared defy the law.

ANTIGONE.   I dared.
It was not God's proclamation. That final justice
That rules the world below makes no such laws.

Your edict, King, was strong,
60   But all your strength is weakness itself against
The immortal unrecorded laws of God.
They are not merely now: they were, and shall be,
Operative forever, beyond man utterly.

I knew I must die, even without your decree:
65   I am only mortal. And if I must die
Now, before it is my time to die,
Surely this is no hardship: can anyone
Living, as I live, with evil all about me,
Think death less than a friend? This death of mine
70   Is of no importance; but if I had left my brother

Lying in death unburied, I should have suffered.
Now I do not.
                                   You smile at me. Ah Creon.
Think me a fool, if you like; but it may well be
That a fool convicts me of folly.

75 CHORAGOS. Like father, like daughter: both headstrong, deaf to
          reason!
      She has never learned to yield.

      CREON.   She has much to learn.
      The inflexible heart breaks first, the toughest iron
      Cracks first, and the wildest horses bend their necks
      At the pull of the smallest curb.
                                        Pride? In a slave?
80   This girl is guilty of a double insolence,
      Breaking the given laws and boasting of it.
      Who is the man here,
      She or I, if this crime goes unpunished?
      Sister's child, or more than sister's child,
85   Or closer yet in blood—she and her sister
      Win bitter death for this!
                        [*To servants*] Go, some of you,
      Arrest Ismene. I accuse her equally.
      Bring her: You will find her sniffling in the house there.
      Her mind's a traitor: crimes kept in the dark
90   Cry for light, and the guardian brain shudders;
      But how much worse than this
      Is brazen boasting of barefaced anarchy!

      ANTIGONE. Creon, what more do you want than my death?

      CREON.   Nothing.
      That gives me everything.

      ANTIGONE.   Then I beg you: kill me.
95   This talking is a great weariness: your words
      Are distasteful to me, and I am sure that mine
      Seem so to you. And yet they should not seem so:
      I should have praise and honor for what I have done.
      All these men here would praise me
100   Were their lips not frozen shut with fear of you.
      [*Bitterly*] Ah the good fortune of kings,
      Licensed to say and do whatever they please!

      CREON. You are alone here in that opinion.

      ANTIGONE. No, they are with me. But they keep their tongues in
          leash.

105 CREON. Maybe. But you are guilty, and they are not.

ANTIGONE. There is no guilt in reverence for the dead.

CREON. But Eteocles—was he not your brother too?

ANTIGONE. My brother too.

CREON. And you insult his memory?

ANTIGONE [*softly*]. The dead man would not say that I insult it.

110 **CREON.** He would: for you honor a traitor as much as him.

ANTIGONE. His own brother, traitor or not, and equal in blood.

CREON. He made war on his country. Eteocles defended it.

ANTIGONE. Nevertheless, there are honors due all the dead.

CREON. But not the same for the wicked as for the just.

115 **ANTIGONE.** Ah Creon, Creon.
　　　Which of us can say what the gods hold wicked?

CREON. An enemy is an enemy, even dead.

ANTIGONE. It is my nature to join in love, not hate.

CREON [*finally losing patience*]. Go join them, then; if you must
　　　have your love,
120 　Find it in hell!

CHORAGOS. But see, Ismene comes:

[*Enter* ISMENE, *guarded.*]

　Those tears are sisterly, the cloud
　That shadows her eyes rains down gentle sorrow.

CREON. You too, Ismene,
125 　Snake in my ordered house, sucking my blood
　Stealthily—and all the time I never knew
　That these two sisters were aiming at my throne!
　　　　　　　　　　　　　　　　　Ismene,
　Do you confess your share in this crime, or deny it?
　Answer me.

130 **ISMENE.** Yes, if she will let me say so. I am guilty.

ANTIGONE [*coldly*]. No, Ismene. You have no right to say so.
　You would not help me, and I will not have you help me.

ISMENE. But now I know what you meant; and I am here
　To join you, to take my share of punishment.

135 **ANTIGONE.** The dead man and the gods who rule the dead
　Know whose act this was. Words are not friends.

ISMENE. Do you refuse me, Antigone? I want to die with you:

I too have a duty that I must discharge to the dead.

ANTIGONE. You shall not lessen my death by sharing it.

140 **ISMENE.** What do I care for life when you are dead?

ANTIGONE. Ask Creon. You're always hanging on his opinions.

ISMENE. You are laughing at me. Why, Antigone?

ANTIGONE. It's a joyless laughter, Ismene.

ISMENE. But can I do nothing?

ANTIGONE. Yes. Save yourself. I shall not envy you.
145 There are those who will praise you; I shall have honor, too.

ISMENE. But we are equally guilty!

ANTIGONE. No more, Ismene.
You are alive, but I belong to death.

CREON [*to the* CHORUS]. Gentlemen, I beg you to observe these girls:
One has just now lost her mind; the other,
150 It seems, has never had a mind at all.

ISMENE. Grief teaches the steadiest minds to waver, King.

CREON. Yours certainly did, when you assumed guilt with the guilty!

ISMENE. But how could I go on living without her?

CREON. You are.
She is already dead.

ISMENE. But your own son's bride!

155 **CREON.** There are places enough for him to push his plow.
I want no wicked women for my sons!

ISMENE. O dearest Haimon, how your father wrongs you!

CREON. I've had enough of your childish talk of marriage!

CHORAGOS. Do you really intend to steal this girl from your son?

CREON. No: death will do that for me.

160 **CHORAGOS.** Then she must die?

CREON [*ironically*]. You dazzle me.
—But enough of this talk!
[*To* GUARDS] You, there, take them away and guard them well:
For they are but women, and even brave men run
When they see death coming.

[ISMENE, ANTIGONE, *and* GUARDS *leave.*]

Ode II

CHORUS. Fortunate is the man who has never tasted God's   *[Strophe 1]*
     vengeance!
  Where once the anger of heaven has struck, that house is
     shaken
  Forever: damnation rises behind each child
  Like a wave cresting out of the black northeast,
5 When the long darkness under sea roars up
  And bursts drumming death upon the windwhipped sand.

  I have seen this gathering sorrow from time long past   *[Antistrophe 1]*
  Loom upon Oedipus' children: generation from generation
  Takes the compulsive rage of the enemy god.
10 So lately this last flower of Oedipus' line
  Drank the sunlight! but now a passionate word
  And a handful of dust have closed up all its beauty.

    What mortal arrogance   *[Strophe 2]*
    Transcends the wrath of Zeus?
15 Sleep cannot lull him, nor the effortless long months
  Of the timeless gods: but he is young forever,
  And his house is the shining day of high Olympos.
    All that is and shall be,
    And all the past, is his.
20 No pride on earth is free of the curse of heaven.

    The straying dreams of men   *[Antistrophe 2]*
    May bring them ghosts of joy:
  But as they drowse, the waking embers burn them;
  Or they walk with fixed eyes, as blind men walk.
25 But the ancient wisdom speaks for our own time:
    Fate works most for woe
    With folly's fairest show.
  Man's little pleasure is the spring of sorrow.

Scene III

CHORAGOS. But here is Haimon, King, the last of all your sons.
  Is it grief for Antigone that brings him here,
  And bitterness at being robbed of his bride?

[*Enter* HAIMON.]

CREON. We shall soon see, and no need of diviners.
                           —Son,
5 You have heard my final judgment on that girl:
  Have you come here hating me, or have you come
  With deference and with love, whatever I do?

HAIMON. I am your son, Father. You are my guide.
You make things clear for me, and I obey you.
10 No marriage means more to me than your continuing wisdom.

CREON. Good. That is the way to behave: subordinate
Everything else, my son, to your father's will.
This is what a man prays for, that he may get
Sons attentive and dutiful in his house,
15 Each one hating his father's enemies,
Honoring his father's friends. But if his sons
Fail him, if they turn out unprofitably,
What has he fathered but trouble for himself
And amusement for the malicious?
                                        So you are right
20 Not to lose your head over this woman.
Your pleasure with her would soon grow cold, Haimon.
Of all the people in this city, only she
Has had contempt for my law and broken it.

Do you want me to show myself weak before the people?
25 Or to break my sworn word? No, and I will not.
The woman dies.
I suppose she'll plead "family ties." Well, let her.
If I permit my own family to rebel,
How shall I earn the world's obedience?
30 Show me the man who keeps his house in hand,
He's fit for public authority.
                                        I'll have no dealings
With lawbreakers, critics of the government:
Whoever is chosen to govern should be obeyed—
Must be obeyed, in all things, great and small,
35 Just and unjust! O Haimon,
The man who knows how to obey, and that man only,
Knows how to give commands when the time comes.
You can depend on him, no matter how fast
The spears come: He's a good soldier, he'll stick it out.

40 Anarchy, anarchy! Show me a greater evil!
This is why cities tumble and the great houses rain down,
This is what scatters armies!

No, no: Good lives are made so by discipline.
We keep the laws then, and the lawmakers,
45 And no woman shall defeat us. If we must lose,
Let's lose to a man, at least! Is a woman stronger than we?

CHORAGOS. Unless time has rusted my wits,
What you say, King, is said with point and dignity.

HAIMON [*boyishly earnest*]. Father:
50 Reason is God's crowning gift to man, and you are right

To warn me against losing mine. I cannot say—
I hope that I shall never want to say!—that you
Have reasoned badly. Yet there are other men
Who can reason, too; and their opinions might be helpful.

55   You are not in a position to know everything
That people say or do, or what they feel:
Your temper terrifies them—everyone
Will tell you only what you like to hear.
But I, at any rate, can listen; and I have heard them

60   Muttering and whispering in the dark about this girl.
They say no woman has ever, so unreasonably,
Died so shameful a death for a generous act:
"She covered her brother's body. Is this indecent?
She kept him from dogs and vultures. Is this a crime?

65   Death?—She should have all the honor that we can give her!"

This is the way they talk out there in the city.

You must believe me:
Nothing is closer to me than your happiness.
What could be closer? Must not any son

70   Value his father's fortune as his father does his?
I beg you, do not be unchangeable:
Do not believe that you alone can be right.
The man who thinks that,
The man who maintains that only he has the power

75   To reason correctly, the gift to speak, the soul—
A man like that, when you know him, turns out empty.

It is not reason never to yield to reason!

In flood time you can see how some trees bend,
And because they bend, even their twigs are safe,

80   While stubborn trees are torn up, roots and all.
And the same thing happens in sailing:
Make your sheet[8] fast, never slacken—and over you go,
Head over heels and under: and there's your voyage.
Forget you are angry! Let yourself be moved!

85   I know I am young; but please let me say this:
The ideal condition
Would be, I admit, that men should be right by instinct;
But since we are all too likely to go astray,
The reasonable thing is to learn from those who can teach.

90   **CHORAGOS.** You will do well to listen to him, King,
If what he says is sensible. And you, Haimon,
Must listen to your father—both speak well.

---

8. **sheet:** rope attached to the lower corner of a sail by which the sail is moved.

CREON. You consider it right for a man of my years and experience
To go to school to a boy?

HAIMON.   It is not right
95   If I am wrong. But if I am young, and right,
What does my age matter?

CREON. You think it right to stand up for an anarchist?

HAIMON. Not at all. I pay no respect to criminals.

CREON. Then she is not a criminal?

100   HAIMON. The city would deny it, to a man.

CREON. And the city proposes to teach me how to rule?

HAIMON. Ah. Who is it that's talking like a boy now?

CREON. My voice is the one voice giving orders in this city!

HAIMON. It is no city if it takes orders from one voice.

CREON. The state is the King!

105   HAIMON.   Yes, if the state is a desert.
        [*Pause*]

CREON. This boy, it seems, has sold out to a woman.

HAIMON. If you are a woman: My concern is only for you.

CREON. So? Your "concern"! In a public brawl with your father!

HAIMON. How about you, in a public brawl with justice?

110   CREON. With justice, when all that I do is within my rights?

HAIMON. You have no right to trample on God's right.

CREON [*completely out of control*]. Fool, adolescent fool! Taken in by a woman!

HAIMON. You'll never see me taken in by anything vile.

CREON. Every word you say is for her!

HAIMON [*quietly, darkly*].   And for you.
115   And for me. And for the gods under the earth.

CREON. You'll never marry her while she lives.

HAIMON. Then she must die—But her death will cause another.

CREON. Another?
Have you lost your senses? Is this an open threat?

120   HAIMON. There is no threat in speaking to emptiness.

CREON. I swear you'll regret this superior tone of yours!
You are the empty one!

HAIMON.   If you were not my father,
I'd say you were perverse.

CREON. You girlstruck fool, don't play at words with me!

HAIMON. I am sorry. You prefer silence.

125 CREON.   Now, by God—!
I swear, by all the gods in heaven above us,
You'll watch it, I swear you shall!
                    [To the SERVANTS] Bring her out!
Bring the woman out! Let her die before his eyes!
Here, this instant, with her bridegroom beside her!

130 HAIMON. Not here, no; she will not die here, King.
And you will never see my face again.
Go on raving as long as you've a friend to endure you. [Exit
HAIMON.]

CHORAGOS. Gone, gone.
Creon, a young man in a rage is dangerous!

135 CREON. Let him do, or dream to do, more than a man can.
He shall not save these girls from death.

CHORAGOS.   These girls?
You have sentenced them both?

CREON.   No, you are right.
I will not kill the one whose hands are clean.

CHORAGOS. But Antigone?

CREON [somberly].   I will carry her far away
140 Out there in the wilderness and lock her
Living in a vault of stone. She shall have food,
As the custom is, to absolve the state of her death.
And there let her pray to the gods of hell:
They are her only gods:
145 Perhaps they will show her an escape from death,
Or she may learn,
                    though late,
That pity shown the dead is pity in vain. [Exit CREON.]

Ode III

CHORUS. Love, unconquerable   [Strophe]
Waster of rich men, keeper

Of warm lights and all-night vigil
In the soft face of a girl;
5   Sea-wanderer, forest-visitor!
Even the pure Immortals cannot escape you,
And mortal man, in his one day's dusk,
Trembles before your glory.

Surely you swerve upon ruin   [Antistrophe]
10   The just man's consenting heart,
As here you have made bright anger
Strike between father and son—
And none has conquered but love!
A girl's glance working the will of Heaven:
15   Pleasure to her alone who mocks us,
Merciless Aphrodite.[9]

Scene IV

CHORAGOS [*as* ANTIGONE *enters, guarded*]. But I can no longer
        stand in awe of this,
Nor, seeing what I see, keep back my tears.
Here is Antigone, passing to that chamber
Where all find sleep at last.

5   ANTIGONE. Look upon me, friends, and pity me
Turning back at the night's edge to say
Good-by to the sun that shines for me no longer;
Now sleepy death
Summons me down to Acheron,[10] that cold shore:
10   There is no bridesong there, nor any music.

CHORUS. Yet not unpraised, not without a kind of honor,
You walk at last into the underworld;
Untouched by sickness, broken by no sword.
What woman has ever found your way to death?

15   ANTIGONE. How often I have heard the story of Niobe,[11]
Tantalos' wretched daughter, how the stone
Clung fast about her, ivy-close: and they say
The rain falls endlessly
And sifting soft snow; her tears are never done.
20   I feel the loneliness of her death in mine.

CHORUS. But she was born of Heaven, and you
Are woman, woman-born. If her death is yours,

---

9. **Aphrodite** [af′rə dī′tē]: Greek goddess of love.
10. **Acheron** [ak′ə ron′]: in Greek mythology, one of the rivers that the soul crosses to reach Hades.
11. **Niobe** [nī′ō bē′]: Because she boasted excessively about her children, the gods punished Niobe by killing them all and by turning her into a column of stone which weeps continuously.

A mortal woman's, is this not for you
Glory in our world and in the world beyond?

25 ANTIGONE. You laugh at me. Ah, friends, friends,
Can you not wait until I am dead? O Thebes,
O men many-charioted, in love with fortune,
Dear springs of Dirce, sacred Theban grove,
Be witnesses for me, denied all pity,
30 Unjustly judged! and think a word of love
For her whose path turns
Under dark earth, where there are no more tears.

CHORUS. You have passed beyond human daring and come at last
Into a place of stone where justice sits.
35 I cannot tell
What shape of your father's guilt appears in this.

ANTIGONE. You have touched it at last: that bridal bed
Unspeakable, horror of son and mother mingling:
Their crime, infection of all our family!
40 O Oedipus, father and brother!
Your marriage strikes from the grave to murder mine.
I have been a stranger here in my own land:
All my life
The blasphemy of my birth has followed me.

45 CHORUS. Reverence is a virtue, but strength
Lives in established law: That must prevail.
You have made your choice,
Your death is the doing of your conscious hand.

ANTIGONE. Then let me go, since all your words are bitter,
50 And the very light of the sun is cold to me.
Lead me to my vigil, where I must have
Neither love nor lamentation; no song, but silence.

[CREON *interrupts impatiently.*]

CREON. If dirges and planned lamentations could put off death,
Men would be singing forever.
                    [*To the* SERVANTS] Take her, go!
55 You know your orders: take her to the vault
And leave her alone there. And if she lives or dies,
That's her affair, not ours: Our hands are clean.

ANTIGONE. O tomb, vaulted bride-bed in eternal rock,
Soon I shall be with my own again
60 Where Persephone[12] welcomes the thin ghosts underground:
And I shall see my father again, and you, Mother,
And dearest Polyneices—

---

12. **Persephone** [pər sef′ə nē]: goddess of vegetation and death; wife of Hades.

dearest indeed

To me, since it was my hand
That washed him clean and poured the ritual wine:
65 And my reward is death before my time!

And yet, as men's hearts know, I have done no wrong,
I have not sinned before God. Or if I have,
I shall know the truth in death. But if the guilt
Lies upon Creon who judged me, then, I pray,
May his punishment equal my own.

70 **CHORAGOS.**   O passionate heart.
Unyielding, tormented still by the same winds!

CREON. Her guards shall have good cause to regret their delaying.

ANTIGONE. Ah! That voice is like the voice of death!

CREON. I can give you no reason to think you are mistaken.

75 **ANTIGONE.** Thebes, and you my fathers' gods,
And rulers of Thebes, you see me now, the last
Unhappy daughter of a line of kings.
Your kings, led away to death. You will remember
What things I suffer, and at what men's hands,
80 Because I would not transgress the laws of heaven.
[*To the* GUARDS, *simply*] Come: let us wait no longer.
[*Exit* ANTIGONE, *left, guarded.*]

Ode IV

CHORUS. All Danae's[13] beauty was locked away   [*Strophe 1*]
In a brazen cell where the sunlight could not come:
A small room, still as any grave, enclosed her.
Yet she was a princess, too,
5 And Zeus in a rain of gold poured love upon her.
O child, child,
No power in wealth or war
Or tough sea-blackened ships
Can prevail against untiring destiny!

10 And Dryas' son[14] also, that furious king,   [*Antistrophe 1*]
Bore the god's prisoning anger for his pride:
Sealed up by Dionysos in deaf stone,
His madness died among echoes,
So at the last he learned what dreadful power
15 His tongue had mocked:

---

13. **Danae** [dan'ā ē']: a princess imprisoned by her father.
14. **Dryas' son:** Lycurgus, a king who, according to one legend, was imprisoned in stone by the gods for attacking Dionysos.

For he had profaned the revels.
And fired the wrath of the nine
Implacable Sisters[15] that love the sound of the flute.

[Strophe 2]

And old men tell a half-remembered tale[16]
20 Of horror done where a dark ledge splits the sea
And a double surf beats on the gray shores:
How a king's new woman, sick
With hatred for the queen he had imprisoned,
Ripped out his two sons' eyes with her bloody hands
25 While grinning Ares[17] watched the shuttle plunge
Four times: four blind wounds crying for revenge,

[Antistrophe 2]

Crying, tears and blood mingled—piteously born,
Those sons whose mother was of heavenly birth!
Her father was the god of the North Wind
30 And she was cradled by gales,
She raced with young colts on the glittering hills
And walked untrammeled in the open light;
But in her marriage deathless Fate found means
To build a tomb like yours for all her joy.

Scene V

[*Enter blind* TEIRESIAS, *led by a boy. The opening speeches of* TEIRESIAS *should be in singsong contrast to the realistic lines of* CREON.]

TEIRESIAS. This is the way the blind man comes, Princes, Princes,
  Lock-step, two heads lit by the eyes of one.

CREON. What new thing have you to tell us, old Teiresias?

TEIRESIAS. I have much to tell you: Listen to the prophet, Creon.

5 **CREON.** I am not aware that I have ever failed to listen.

TEIRESIAS. Then you have done wisely, King, and ruled well.

CREON. I admit my debt to you. But what have you to say?

TEIRESIAS. This, Creon: You stand once more on the edge of fate.

CREON. What do you mean? Your words are a kind of dread.

10 **TEIRESIAS.** Listen, Creon:
  I was sitting in my chair of augury,[18] at the place
  Where the birds gather about me. They were all a-chatter,

---

15. **nine Implacable Sisters:** the Muses, goddesses who inspire creativity in the arts and sciences.
16. **a half-remembered tale:** an ancient myth about Phineas of Thrace.
17. **Ares** [ār′ēz]: god of war and instigator of violence and suffering.
18. **augury:** practice of predicting signs and omens.

As is their habit, when suddenly I heard
A strange note in their jangling, a scream, a
15 Whirring fury: I knew that they were fighting,
Tearing each other, dying
In a whirlwind of wings clashing. And I was afraid.
I began the rites of burned-offering at the altar.
But Hephaestos[19] failed me: Instead of bright flame.
20 There was only the sputtering slime of the fat thighflesh
Melting: The entrails dissolved in gray smoke,
The bare bone burst from the welter. And no blaze!

This was a sign from heaven. My boy described it,
Seeing for me as I see for others.

25 I tell you, Creon, you yourself have brought
This new calamity upon us. Our hearths and altars
Are stained with the corruption of dogs and carrion birds
That glut themselves on the corpse of Oedipus' son.
The gods are deaf when we pray to them, their fire
30 Recoils from our offering, their birds of omen
Have no cry of comfort, for they are gorged
With the thick blood of the dead.
                                        O my son,
These are no trifles! Think: all men make mistakes,
But a good man yields when he knows his course is wrong,
35 And repairs the evil. The only crime is pride.
Give in to the dead man, then: Do not fight with a corpse—
What glory is it to kill a man who is dead?
Think, I beg you:
It is for your own good that I speak as I do.
40 You should be able to yield for your own good.

   CREON. It seems that prophets have made me their especial
        province.
   All my life long
   I have been a kind of butt for the dull arrows
   Of doddering fortunetellers!
                                        No, Teiresias:
45 If your birds—if the great eagles of God himself
   Should carry him stinking bit by bit to heaven,
   I would not yield. I am not afraid of pollution:
   No man can defile the gods.
                                        Do what you will,
   Go into business, make money, speculate
50 In India gold or that synthetic gold from Sardis,[20]
   Get rich otherwise than by my consent to bury him.
   Teiresias, it is a sorry thing when a wise man

---

19. **Hephaestos** [hi fes′təs]: god of fire and divine blacksmith.
20. **Sardis** [sär′dis]: capital of ancient Lydia in Asia Minor.

Sells his wisdom, lets out his words for hire!

TEIRESIAS. Ah Creon! Is there no man left in the world—

55 CREON. To do what—Come, let's have the aphorism!

TEIRESIAS. No man who knows that wisdom outweighs any wealth?

CREON. As surely as bribes are baser than any baseness.

TEIRESIAS. You are sick, Creon! You are deathly sick!

CREON. As you say: It is not my place to challenge a prophet.

60 TEIRESIAS. Yet you have said my prophecy is for sale.

CREON. The generation of prophets has always loved gold.

TEIRESIAS. The generation of kings has always loved brass.

CREON. You forget yourself! You are speaking to your king.

TEIRESIAS. I know it. You are a king because of me.

65 CREON. You have a certain skill; but you have sold out.

TEIRESIAS. King, you will drive me to words that—

CREON.   Say them, say them!
    Only remember: I will not pay you for them.

TEIRESIAS. No, you will find them too costly.

CREON.   No doubt. Speak:
    Whatever you say, you will not change my will.

70 TEIRESIAS. Then take this, and take it to heart!
    The time is not far off when you shall pay back
    Corpse for corpse, flesh of your own flesh.
    You have thrust the child of this world into living night,
    You have kept from the gods below the child that is theirs:
75 The one in a grave before her death, the other,
    Dead, denied the grave. This is your crime:
    And the Furies[21] and the dark gods of hell
    Are swift with terrible punishment for you.

    Do you want to buy me now, Creon?
                                          Not many days,
80 And your house will be full of men and women weeping,
    And curses will be hurled at you from far
    Cities grieving for sons unburied, left to rot
    Before the walls of Thebes.

    These are my arrows, Creon: They are all for you.

---

21. **the Furies:** three hideous, avenging spirits that pursue and punish those
who have committed crimes, particularly against kinship and society.

85 [*To* BOY] But come, child: Lead me home.
    Let him waste his fine anger upon younger men.
    Maybe he will learn at last
    To control a wiser tongue in a better head. [*Exit* TEIRESIAS.]

CHORAGOS. The old man has gone, King, but his words
90   Remain to plague us. I am old, too,
    But I cannot remember that he was ever false.

CREON. That is true . . . It troubles me.
    Oh it is hard to give in! But it is worse
    To risk everything for stubborn pride.

CHORAGOS. Creon: Take my advice.

95 CREON.   What shall I do?

CHORAGOS. Go quickly: free Antigone from her vault
    And build a tomb for the body of Polyneices.

CREON. You would have me do this?

CHORAGOS.   Creon, yes!
    And it must be done at once: God moves
100   Swiftly to cancel the folly of stubborn men.

CREON. It is hard to deny the heart! But I
    Will do it: I will not fight with destiny.

CHORAGOS. You must go yourself, you cannot leave it to others.

CREON. I will go.
          —Bring axes, servants:
105   Come with me to the tomb. I buried her, I
      Will set her free.
                Oh quickly!
      My mind misgives—
      The laws of the gods are mighty, and a man must serve them
      To the last day of his life! [*Exit* CREON.]

Paean[22]

CHORAGOS. God of many names   [*Strophe 1*]

CHORUS.   O Iacchos[23]
                                          son
      of Kadmeian Semele
                      O born of the Thunderer!
      Guardian of the West
                      Regent
      of Eleusis' plain[24]
                      O Prince of maenad Thebes[25]
5   and the Dragon Field[26] by rippling Ismenos:[27]

CHORAGOS. God of many names   [*Antistrophe 1*]

CHORUS.   the flames of torches
      flares on our hills
                  the nymphs of Iacchos
      dance at the spring of Castalia:[28]

      from the vine-close mountain
                          come ah come in ivy:
10   *Evohe evohe!*[29] sings through the streets of Thebes

CHORAGOS. God of many names   [*Strophe 2*]
CHORUS.   Iacchos of Thebes
      heavenly child
                  of Semele, bride of the Thunderer!

---

22. **Paean** [pē′ən]: hymn of praise, this one to Dionysos, at whose festival the
play was performed.
23. **Iacchos** [ī′ə kus]: the god Dionysos, son of **the Thunderer** Zeus, and
Kadmeian Semele [kad mē′ən sem′ə lē], whose father was King Kadmos,
founder of Thebes.
24. **Eleusis'** [ē loō′sis] **plain:** site of mysterious rites, over which Dionysos,
under the name Iacchos, presided.
25. **maenad** [mē′nad] **Thebes:** the city of Thebes referred to here as a
maenad, or priestess of Dionysos.
26. **Dragon Field:** field where King Kadmos was said to have planted dragon
teeth, from which grew a race of warriors.
27. **Ismenos** [is mē′nəs]: small river near Thebes.
28. **Castalia:** fountain on Mount Parnasos sacred to the Muses.
29. *Evohe evohe!* [ē vō′ē]: a cry of joy.

The shadow of plague is upon us:

come

with clement feet

oh come from Parnasos[30]

down the long slopes

15   across the lamenting water.

CHORAGOS. Io[31] Fire! Chorister of the throbbing stars!   *[Antistrophe 2]*
 O purest among the voices of the night!
 Thou son of God, blaze for us!

CHORUS. Come with choric rapture of circling Maenads
 Who cry *Io Iacche!*
20   *God of many names!*

Exodos[32]

[*Enter* MESSENGER, *left.*]

MESSENGER. Men of the line of Kadmos, you who live
 Near Amphion's[33] citadel:

       I cannot say
 Of any condition of human life "This is fixed,
 This is clearly good, or bad." Fate raises up,
5 And fate casts down the happy and unhappy alike:
 No man can foretell his fate.

        Take the case of Creon:
 Creon was happy once, as I count happiness:
 Victorious in battle, sole governor of the land,
 Fortunate father of children nobly born.
10 And now it has all gone from him! Who can say
 That a man is still alive when his life's joy fails?
 He is a walking dead man. Grant him rich.
 Let him live like a king in his great house:
 If his pleasure is gone, I would not give
15 So much as the shadow of smoke for all he owns.

CHORAGOS. Your words hint at sorrow; what is your news for us?

MESSENGER. They are dead. The living are guilty of their death.

CHORAGOS. Who is guilty? Who is dead? Speak!

MESSENGER.   Haimon.
 Haimon is dead; and the hand that killed him
 Is his own hand.

---

30. **Parnasos:** mountain sacred to Dionysos.
31. **Io!** [ī′ō]: Hail! Greetings!
32. **Exodos:** exit or final scene, opposite of the *Parados.*
33. **Amphion** [am fī′on]: ruler of ancient Thebes.

20 **CHORAGOS.** His father's? or his own?

MESSENGER. His own, driven mad by the murder his father had
   done.

CHORAGOS. Teiresias, Teiresias, how clearly you saw it all!

MESSENGER. This is my news; you must draw what conclusions you can
   from it.

CHORAGOS. But look: Eurydice, our queen:
25   Has she overheard us?

   [*Enter* EURYDICE *from the palace, center.*]

EURYDICE. I have heard something, friends:
   As I was unlocking the gate of Pallas'[34] shrine,
   For I needed her help today, I heard a voice
   Telling of some new sorrow. And I fainted
30   There at the temple with all my maidens about me.
   But speak again; whatever it is, I can bear it:
   Grief and I are no strangers.

MESSENGER.   Dearest lady,
   I will tell you plainly all that I have seen.
   I shall not try to comfort you: What is the use,
35   Since comfort could lie only in what is not true?
   The truth is always best.

                    I went with Creon
   To the outer plain where Polyneices was lying,
   No friend to pity him, his body shredded by dogs.
   We made our prayers in that place to Hecate[35]
40   And Pluto,[36] that they would be merciful. And we bathed
   The corpse with holy water, and we brought
   Fresh-broken branches to burn what was left of it,
   And upon the urn we heaped up a towering barrow
   Of the earth of his own land.

                    When we were done, we ran
45   To the vault where Antigone lay on her couch of stone.
   One of the servants had gone ahead,
   And while he was yet far off he heard a voice
   Grieving within the chamber, and he came back
   And told Creon. And as the king went closer,
50   The air was full of wailing, the words lost,
   And he begged us to make all haste. "Am I a prophet?"
   He said weeping. "And must I walk this road,
   The saddest of all that I have gone before?
   My son's voice calls me on. Oh quickly, quickly!

---

34. **Pallas:** Pallas Athena, goddess of wisdom and war.
35. **Hecate** [hek'ə tē]: goddess connected with death and the Underworld.
36. **Pluto:** god of the Underworld.

55 Look through the crevice there, and tell me
   If it is Haimon, or some deception of the gods!"

   We obeyed; and in the cavern's farthest corner
   We saw her lying:
   She had made a noose of her fine linen veil
60 And hanged herself. Haimon lay beside her,
   His arms about her waist, lamenting her,
   His love lost under ground, crying out
   That his father had stolen her away from him.

   When Creon saw him the tears rushed to his eyes
65 And he called to him: "What have you done, child? Speak to me.
   What are you thinking that makes your eyes so strange?
   O my son, my son. I come to you on my knees!"
   But Haimon spat in his face. He said not a word,
   Staring—
                      And suddenly drew his sword
70 And lunged. Creon shrank back, the blade missed; and the boy,
   Desperate against himself, drove it half its length
   Into his own side and fell. And as he died
   He gathered Antigone close in his arms again,
   Choking, his blood bright red on her white cheek.
75 And now he lies dead with the dead, and she is his
   At last, his bride in the houses of the dead.

   [*Exit* EURYDICE *into the palace.*]

   CHORAGOS. She has left us without a word. What can this mean?

   MESSENGER. It troubles me, too; yet she knows what is best,
   Her grief is too great for public lamentation,
80 And doubtless she has gone to her chamber to weep
   For her dead son, leading her maidens in his dirge.

   CHORAGOS. It may be so; but I fear this deep silence. [*Pause*]

   MESSENGER. I will see what she is doing. I will go in. [*Exit*
   MESSENGER *into the palace.*]

   [*Enter* CREON *with attendants, bearing* HAIMON's *body.*]

   CHORAGOS. But here is the king himself; oh look at him,
85 Bearing his own damnation in his arms.

   CREON. Nothing you say can touch me any more.
   My own blind heart has brought me
   From darkness to final darkness. Here you see
   The father murdering, the murdered son—
90 And all my civic wisdom!

   Haimon my son, so young, so young to die,
   I was the fool, not you; and you died for me.

CHORAGOS. That is the truth: but you were late in learning it.

CREON. This truth is hard to bear. Surely a god
95   Has crushed me beneath the hugest weight of heaven.
And driven me headlong a barbaric way
To trample out the thing I held most dear.

The pains that men will take to come to pain!

[*Enter* MESSENGER *from the palace.*]

MESSENGER. The burden you carry in your hands is heavy.
100   But it is not all: You will find more in your house.

CREON. What burden worse than this shall I find there?

MESSENGER. The queen is dead.

CREON. O port of death, deaf world,
Is there no pity for me? And you, angel of evil,
105   I was dead, and your words are death again.
Is it true, boy? Can it be true?
Is my wife dead? Has death bred death?

MESSENGER. You can see for yourself.

[*The doors are opened, and the body of* EURYDICE *is disclosed within.*]

CREON. Oh pity!
110   All true, all true, and more than I can bear!
O my wife, my son!

MESSENGER. She stood before the altar, and her heart
Welcomed the knife her own hand guided,
And a great cry burst from her lips for Megareus[37] dead,
115   And for Haimon dead, her sons; and her last breath
Was a curse for their father, the murderer of her sons.
And she fell, and the dark flowed in through her closing eyes.

CREON. O God, I am sick with fear.
Are there no swords here? Has no one a blow for me?

120 **MESSENGER.** Her curse is upon you for the deaths of both.

CREON. It is right that it should be. I alone am guilty.
I know it, and I say it. Lead me in
Quickly, friends.
I have neither life nor substance. Lead me in.

125 **CHORAGOS.** You are right, if there can be right in so much wrong.
The briefest way is best in a world of sorrow.

---

37. **Megareus** [meg′ə rōōs]: only brother of Haimon, and son of Creon and
Eurydice. He died in the battle for Thebes.

CREON. Let it come,
Let death come quickly, and be kind to me.
I would not ever see the sun again.

130 CHORAGOS. All that will come when it will; but we, meanwhile,
Have much to do. Leave the future to itself.

CREON. All my heart was in that prayer!

CHORAGOS. Then do not pray anymore: the sky is deaf.

CREON. Lead me away. I have been rash and foolish.
135 I have killed my son and my wife.
I look for comfort; my comfort lies here dead.
Whatever my hands have touched has come to nothing.
Fate has brought all my pride to a thought of dust.

[As CREON *is being led into the house, the* CHORAGOS *advances and speaks directly to the audience.*]

CHORAGOS. There is no happiness where there is no wisdom;
140 No wisdom but in submission to the gods.
Big words are always punished,
And proud men in old age learn to be wise.

STUDY QUESTIONS

Prologue Through Ode II

Recalling

1. In lines 14–25 of the Prologue, what kind of funeral does Antigone say Creon has given Eteocles? What has Creon sworn for Polyneices? What penalty must those who disobey Creon face?
2. In lines 26–31 of the Prologue, what does Antigone ask Ismene to do? In lines 36–52 what reason does Ismene give for not helping her sister?
3. In Scene I how does Creon explain his decision regarding Polyneices? What does the Sentry tell him? How does Creon react?
4. What opinion about Creon's decree do Choragos and the Chorus have in Scene I and in the Ode between Scenes I and II?
5. In Scene II, lines 56–63, what does Antigone say about Creon's decree?
6. What do we learn about Antigone's plans for marriage?

Interpreting

7. What basic conflict is represented by the debate between Antigone and Ismene in the Prologue? What would you say is Antigone's error?
8. Although convinced that he is correct, what might Creon actually be overlooking? What mistakes might he be making?

Extending

9. If you had to choose sides between Antigone and Creon now, could you? Why or why not?

Scene III Through Exodos

Recalling

1. What are Creon's arguments in his first long speech to Haimon (Scene III, lines 11–46)?
2. What two metaphors in lines 78–83 of Scene III does Haimon use to persuade Creon to be reasonable?
3. What form of punishment does Creon announce that he has planned for Antigone in Scene IV, lines 55–57?

4. In Scene V, lines 32–40, what specific advice and caution does Teiresias give Creon? What does Creon decide to do?
5. In two or three sentences describe the final outcome of the play.

Interpreting

6. What, according to the blind prophet Teiresias, is Creon's central weakness? How has this weakness affected Creon's actions and attitudes?
7. How does Creon change by the end of the play?

Extending

8. Overall, which character moves you more—Antigone or Creon? Why?

LITERARY FOCUS

Tragedy and the Tragic Hero

According to the Greek philosopher Aristotle, the function of tragedy is to arouse in the audience the emotions of fear and pity in order to produce a **catharsis,** or cleansing, of these emotions. The audience feels fear that misfortunes may befall the hero. The audience feels pity because the hero's fortunes gradually decline as a consequence of a **tragic flaw,** an error that causes the hero to commit a tragic deed and to suffer a reversal. The tragic situation in which the hero is eventually caught arises from a combination of elements in his own character and of fate, or the will of the gods. The tragic hero's courage in the face of an overpowering challenge is astonishing and praiseworthy and thus wins the sympathy of the audience.

Thinking About Tragedy and the Tragic Hero

■ Compare Antigone and Creon as classic tragic figures. What misfortunes does each suffer? What tragic flaw does each display? How does fate affect each?

VOCABULARY

Sentence Completions

Each of the following sentences contains a blank with four possible words for completing the sentence. The words are from *Antigone.* Choose the word that completes each sentence correctly and that uses the word *as the word is used in the selection.* Write the number of each item and the letter of your choice on a separate sheet.

1. Because of the extreme heat and the jagged, rocky terrain, our journey to the ancient ruins did not have a(n) _____ start.
   (a) lateral (c) headlong
   (b) guarded (d) auspicious
2. Our guide, who had grown up here, announced _____ that among the ruins the temperature was always lower.
   (a) furiously (c) sententiously
   (b) miserably (d) piteously
3. Awed by the rough, still landscape and eerie silence, we walked along quietly and _____ .
   (a) impassively (c) bitterly
   (b) expansively (d) stealthily
4. At the gate to the imposing ruins, I felt that to enter would be to _____ a timeless law.
   (a) distress (c) absolve
   (b) trample (d) transgress
5. I sensed at once that awesome festivals were once performed here for _____ gods.
   (a) implacable (c) straying
   (b) untrammeled (d) lamenting

COMPOSITION

Writing About a Quotation

■ Creon admits, "My own blind heart has brought me / From darkness to final darkness." Analyze Creon's statement. First explain in what sense he is blind. Then show the significance of Creon's statement in the play as a whole by comparing his "blindness" with the "vision" of Antigone, Haimon, and Teiresias (who is physically blind). *For help with this assignment, see Lesson 5 in the Writing About Literature Handbook at the back of this book.*

Composing a Dramatic Scene

■ Imagine a situation involving two characters who come into conflict. Both characters are unyielding. Describe a brief scene in which the two characters have a disagreement. If you like, write some dialogue for the scene and act it out with a classmate.

COMPARING WRITERS

■ Compare Homer's epic and Sophocles' drama in terms of description: For example, which work uses more description? How does its presence or absence affect the work? Are the descriptions realistic or fanciful?

Virgil *70–19 B.C.*

Rome's greatest poet, Publius Vergilius Maro (known to us as Virgil), was born near the village of Andes in northern Italy. At the age of seventeen, Virgil went to study oratory and philosophy in Rome, where he became friends with men who were to play important roles in the development of the Roman Empire. Although he himself did not participate in military or political affairs, he was throughout his life close to those in power.

Virgil lived during Rome's Golden Age, the original "Augustan Age" that the English of the eighteenth century hoped to emulate. Named for the Emperor Augustus, who ruled from 27 B.C. to A.D. 14, this was a time when Rome reached the pinnacle of its political glory. It was also an era of elegant Latin literature, produced not only by Virgil but by his friend Horace, famous for his lyrical *Odes;* by the tragedian Seneca, a philosopher and statesman as well as a great playwright; and by the poet Ovid, whose works include the brilliant retelling of Greek myths, called the *Metamorphoses* (page 875).

Virgil's first collection, ten pastoral poems called the *Eclogues,* was followed by the *Georgics,* a poetic account of the countryside and rural life that he loved. When he was forty, at the peak of his career, Virgil began work on the *Aeneid* [i nē'id], in which he sought to express Rome's greatness and destiny by glorifying its legendary origins. Nine years later, with the *Aeneid* almost completed, he contracted a fever while returning from a trip to Greece. Protesting that the poem still needed three years of revision, Virgil requested before he died that the manuscript be burned. Emperor Augustus denied the request and published the *Aeneid* posthumously.

Introducing the **Aeneid**

Unlike the *Iliad* and the *Odyssey,* which Homer composed in the tradition of oral storytelling, the *Aeneid* is a consciously literary work, written to be read as well as heard. On the other hand, the *Aeneid* resembles the *Iliad* in having a hero who fights battles and the *Odyssey* in having a hero who undertakes long journeys. Furthermore, Virgil imitated Homer's meter, use of epithets, and portrayal of the gods as manipulative.

If the *Aeneid* borrowed from Homer, it in turn had an enormous influence on almost all subsequent European epics. The Italian poet Dante not only referred to it in writing his great epic *The Divine Comedy* (page 883), but he even made Virgil a character in his own work. Britain's Edmund Spenser kept the *Aeneid* in mind when he wrote *The Faerie Queene* (page 120), and John Milton turned to it frequently in creating *Paradise Lost* (page 277). Even the anonymous author of *Beowulf,* who composed his epic in the oral tradition, was apparently familiar with Virgil's masterpiece, for *Beowulf* includes allusions to the *Aeneid* and passages that are clearly modeled on it.

The *Aeneid* fuses elements of the Homeric epics to create the story of Aeneas, the legendary Trojan prince who escapes from Troy when it is destroyed by the Greeks. Directed by the gods to found a new city that will eventually rule the world, Aeneas sets off with his aged father and young son. He eventually lands on the North African coast, where he is welcomed by the queen of Carthage, Dido, who falls in love with him as he tells her and her court about the fall of Troy. Despite his love for Dido, Aeneas continues his search and finally founds the city that will fulfill his and his people's destiny. The following excerpt tells of how the Greeks destroyed Troy and of Aeneas' departure from Troy.

▓ As modern Americans, we are too sophisticated to be taken in by Trojan Horses. Or are we?

The Trojan Horse, print after a painting by Henri Motte.

Virgil

from the **Aeneid**

Translated by C. Day Lewis

CHARACTERS

Greeks

ACHILLES: leader of the Myrmidons, greatest of the Greek warriors
ULYSSES [ū lis′ēz]: Latin name for Odysseus, Greek leader and hero of the Trojan War

Trojans

AENEAS [i nē′əs]: Trojan warrior who tells the story in first person
ANCHISES: Aeneas' father
ASCANIUS: son of Aeneas and Creusa
CASSANDRA: Trojan princess whose prophecies are not believed
CREUSA: Aeneas' wife
LAOCOON [lā ok′ō on′]: Trojan priest
PRIAM: Troy's king

Goddesses

ATHENA: Greek goddess of war and wisdom
JUNO: queen of the gods and enemy of the Trojans
MINERVA: Roman goddess of wisdom, identified with the Greek goddess Athena

from Book II

All fell silent now, and their faces were all attention
When from his place of honor Aeneas began to speak:

O queen, the griefs you bid me reopen are inexpressible—
The tale of Troy, a rich and a most tragic empire
Erased by the Greeks; most piteous events I saw with my own
5   eyes
And played no minor part in. What Myrmidon or Thessalian,[1]
What soldier of fell Ulysses[2] could talk about such events
And keep from tears? Besides, the dewy night drops fast
From heaven, and the declining stars invite to sleep.
10 But if you want so much to know what happened to us
And hear in brief a recital of Troy's last agony,
Although the memory makes me shudder, and shrink from its
     sadness,
I will attempt it.

              Broken in war and foiled by fate,
With so many years[3] already slipping away, the Greek staff
15 Constructed a horse, employing the craft of the goddess Athena[4]—
It was high as a hill, and its ribs were made from planks of
     pinewood—
To pay for their safe return to Greece, they pretended: this
     rumor
Got round. But, choosing warriors by lot, they secretly
Put them in on the blind side of the horse, until its vast
20 And cavernous belly was crammed with a party of armed men.

In sight of Troy there's an island, a well-known island, Tenedos—
Rich and powerful it was, while Priam's empire[5] stood;
Now, little but a bay, a roadstead unsafe for shipping.
Thither the Greeks sailed out, and hid on its desolate coast.
25 This was evacuation, we thought—they had sailed for Greece.
So all Troy threw off the chains of her long anguish.
We opened the gates, we enjoyed visiting the Greek camp,
Viewing the derelict positions on the abandoned beaches.
Here the Dolopes[6] camped; there, ferocious Achilles:

---

1. **Myrmidon** [mur′mə don′] **or Thessalian** [the sā′lē ən]: Greek soldiers from armies of Thessaly in northern Greece; the Myrmidons were led by the great warrior Achilles.
2. **Ulysses** [ū lis′ēz]: Latin form of Odysseus, Greek leader and hero of the Trojan War; described here as **fell**, cruel or savage.
3. **so many years:** It is the tenth and last year of the Trojan War.
4. **Athena:** Greek goddess of wisdom and war.
5. **Priam's empire:** Troy, of which Priam was king.
6. **Dolopes** [dō′lə pēz]: Greeks from Dolopians, a region bordering Thessaly on the southwest.

30 Here was beached their navy, and here the battle raged.
Some of us gaped at the gift—so deadly—the Greeks had left for
Minerva,[7] and its stupendous bulk. Thymoetes[8] first,
Either from treachery or because Troy's fate now was sealed,
Urged that the horse be brought through the walls and placed in
    our citadel.
35 But Capys[9] and all those of sounder views recommended
Hurling it into the sea or setting fire to it, as some
Booby-trap of the Greeks and not to be trusted—or else
Boring holes in its belly to see what might be inside it.
So the rank and file were violently torn between contraries.
40 Then out in front of them all, hundreds straggling behind him,
In a great temper Laocoon[10] came tearing down from the citadel,
Crying from far:

                    Citizens, are you all stark mad?
Do you really believe our foes are gone? Do you imagine
Any Greek gift is guileless? Is that your idea of Ulysses?
45 This thing of wood conceals Greek soldiers, or else it is
A mechanism designed against our walls—to pry into
Our homes and to bear down on the city; sure, some trick
Is there. No, you must never feel safe with the horse, Trojans.
Whatever it is, I distrust the Greeks, even when they are
    generous.
He spoke: he put forth his strength, and spun his huge great
50   spear
At the flank of the monster, right into its belly's rounded frame.
The spear stuck quivering; the hollow womb of the creature
Grunted at the concussion and rumbled hollowly.
If destiny, if our own will had not been so contrary,
Laocoon would have made us rip open that cache of Greek
55   troops—
There'd still be a Troy—O topless towers, you'd be standing
    now! . . .

"Bring the horse to Minerva's shrine! Pray for her goodwill!"
All of our people shouted.

---

7. **Minerva:** Roman goddess of wisdom, identified with the Greek goddess Athena.
8. **Thymoetes** [thī mē′tēz]: Trojan elder and adviser of Priam.
9. **Capys** [kap′is]: Trojan suspicious of the wooden horse; he later fled from Troy with Aeneas.
10. **Laocoon** [lā ok′ō on′]: After warning the Trojans against the wooden horse, Laocoon, a Trojan priest, was killed with his two sons by two enormous sea serpents.

We cut into our walls,[11] laid open the heart of the city.

60 Everyone set about the task: we inserted rollers
Under its hooves, put hawsers of hemp around its neck,
And strained. The disastrous engine[12] was jockeyed over our walls,
An army in its womb. Boys and unmarried maidens
Escorted it, singing psalms, joyfully gripping the traces.

65 The menace mounts, comes trundling into the city center.
O, my country! O Ilium,[13] home of the gods! O Troy town,
Famous through war! Four times the monster stopped, just where
    the entrance
Was, and every time the accouterments[14] clanged in its belly.
Yet we persevered, with never a thought—we were madly
    blind—

70 Until we had lodged the ominous thing in our holy place.
Then, to cap all, Cassandra[15] opened her mouth for prophecy—
She whom her god had doomed to be never believed by the
    Trojans.
But we poor fools, whose very last day it was, festooned
The shrines of the gods with holiday foliage all over the city.

75 So now the sky rolled round, and night raced up from the ocean
Voluminously shrouding the earth and heaven's vault
And the villainous scheme of the Greeks. Not a sound from the
    Trojans, supine
Along the walls, tired out, in the embrace of sleep.
And now the main Greek army was moving from Tenedos

80 In fleet formation, under the favoring silences
Of a quiet moon, toward the coast they knew so well.
Their leading galley had signaled with flame: Sinon, protected
By fate's injustice, stealthily unlocked the wooden horse
And let the Greeks out from its belly. The horse disgorged, the
    men

85 Burst reveling forth from its hollow flank into the fresh air—
Thessander and Sthenelus in the lead, with Ulysses the terrible,
Sliding down a rope they had lowered—Acamas, Thoas,
Neoptolemus son of Peleus, Machaon and Menelaus,
And Epeus—the man who had actually built the clever
    contraption.

---

11. **We . . . walls:** The Trojans had been convinced by Sinon [sī′nən], a
pretended Greek deserter, that if they could succeed in getting the huge horse
into their city, Troy would rule Europe.
12. **engine:** here, evil contrivance.
13. **Ilium** [il′ē əm]: another name for Troy.
14. **accouterments** [ə ko͞o′tər mənts]: arms and armor.
15. **Cassandra:** Trojan princess, sister of Hector; when she rejected the love of
Apollo, he punished her by giving her the gift of prophecy with the curse that
she would never be believed.

90 They broke out over a city drowned in drunken sleep;
They killed the sentries and then threw open the gates, admitting
Their main body, and joined in the prearranged plan of attack. . . .

*The Trojan Hector, bloodied and mutilated after being killed
by the Greek Achilles, appears to Aeneas in a dream. He advises
Aeneas to take his family and flee because the fall of Troy is inevitable and imminent. Awakening to find Troy in flames,
Aeneas arms himself and rushes out to fight. Following the Greek
soldiers to Priam's palace, he witnesses the destruction of the palace and the murder of Priam on his own altar by Pyrrhus,
Achilles' son. Before he dies, Priam reminds Aeneas of his father,
to whose house he now returns in an effort to save his family.*

When I reached the door of my father's house, the ancestral
Home, my father Anchises, whom first I looked for, wishing
95 To get him away first to the safety of the hills—Anchises
Flatly refused to prolong his life, now Troy was finished,
Or to endure exile. He said:

O you, whose blood
Is in the prime, who are strong enough to stand on your own
feet,
Do you try for escape!
100 But as for me, if the gods had meant me to go on living,
They'd have preserved this place. Enough, more than enough
To have seen Troy ruined once and once have survived her
capture.
Bid me farewell and leave, O leave this body of mine
Where it is! I shall find death in action. The foe will slay me
For pity, or spoils. And to bury me—that will not cost them
105   much.
For years now I have been lingering, obnoxious to heaven and
useless
To mankind, ever since the ruler of gods and men
Blasted me with the searing breath of his levin-flash.[16]

So he went on saying. We could not shift him, although
110 We implored him with floods of tears—I, and my wife Creusa,
Ascanius[17] and the whole household—not to ruin everything,
Not to add his weight to the doom which was heavy upon us.
He refused: obstinately he clung to his house and his purpose.
Once again I am moved to fight, yearning for death in my misery,
115 Since neither luck nor forethought offered a way out now.

———————
16. **levin-flash:** lightning-flash.
17. **Ascanius** [as kā′nē əs]: son of Aeneas and Creusa.

"Father," I said, "did you really think I could run away
And leave you? Did so shameful a notion escape your lips?
If it's the will of heaven that nothing be left of our city,
And if your mind's made up that you and your family
120 Shall perish, as well as Troy, a door to that death is wide open:
Pyrrhus is coming, all bathed in Priam's blood; he loves
Butchering sons in front of their fathers, fathers at the altar.
Was it for this, dear mother, you fetched me through fire and
        steel,
That I should witness the enemy right in our house, witness
125 Ascanius and my father and my Creusa beside them
Lying slaughtered here in one another's blood?
To arms, my men! To arms! Their last hour calls the conquered.
Send me back to the Greeks! Let me go back and renew
The fight! It must never be said we died unavenged this day!"

130 My sword was at my side again; I was fitting my left arm
Through the strap of my shield, and on my way out of the house,
When Creusa clung to me at the door, gripping my ankles,
Holding little Ascanius up to his father, and crying:

If it's deathwards you go, take us with you! O take us, and
        come what may!

135 But if your experience tells you that something is to be gained by
Fighting, protect this house first! Think what you're leaving
        us to—
Ascanius, your father, and me who loved to be called your wife
        once!

Loudly she cried these words, and filled the house with her crying.
Just then a miracle happened, a wonderful miracle.
140 Imagine it!—our hands and our sad eyes were upon
Ascanius, when we beheld a feathery tongue of flame
Luminously alight on his head, licking the soft curls
With fire that harmed them not, and playing about his temples.
Anxious, in great alarm, his mother and I hurried to
145 Beat out, put out with water, that holy blaze on his hair.
But father Anchises, greatly heartened, lifted his eyes up,
Stretched up his hands to heaven, with words of prayer, saying:

O god omnipotent, if any prayers can sway you,
Give ear to mine. One thing I ask: if by our goodness
150 We have deserved it, grant your aid, confirm this omen!

The old man had hardly spoken when from our left hand came
A sudden crash of thunder, and a shooting star slid down

The sky's dark face, drawing a trail of light behind it.
We watched that star as it glided high over the palace roof,
155 And blazing a path, buried its brightness deep in the woods of
Ida;[18] when it was gone, it left in its wake a long furrow
Of light, and a sulphurous smoke spread widely over the terrain.
That did convince my father. He drew himself upright,
Addressed the gods above, and worshipped the heaven-sent star:
No more, no more lingering! I follow, I'm there, where you guide
160   me!
Gods of our fathers, guard this family, guard my grandson!
This sign is yours, and Troy is still in your heavenly keeping.
Yea, I consent. I refuse no longer, my son, to go with you.

He had spoken; and now more clearly over the town the fire's roar
165 Was heard, and nearer rolled the tide of its conflagration.
"Quick, then, dear father," I said, "climb onto my back, and I will
Carry you on my shoulders—that's a burden will not be
    burdensome.
However things turn out, at least we shall share one danger,
One way of safety, both of us. Let little Ascanius walk
170 Beside me, and Creusa follow my steps at a distance.
And you, servants, pay careful attention to what I shall tell you.
As you go out of the city, you come to a mound with an ancient
Temple of Ceres[19] upon it, secluded; nearby, an old cypress
Stands, which for many years our fathers preserved in reverence.
175 Let this be our rendezvous: we'll get there by different routes.
Do you, my father, carry the sacred relics and home-gods:
Sinful for me to touch them, when I have just withdrawn
From battle, with blood on my hands, until in running water
I am purified.

180 With these words, I laid the pelt of a tawny lion
For covering over my broad shoulders and bowed neck;
Then stooped to lift my burden: Ascanius twined his fingers
In mine, hurrying to keep up with his father's longer stride.
My wife came on behind. We fared on, hugging the shadows.

185 I, who just now had faced the enemy volleys, the Greeks'
Concentrated attack, without turning a hair—I was scared by
Every breeze, alarmed by every sound, so strung up
Was I with anxiety for my burden and my companion.

---

18. **Ida** [ī′dä]: mountain in a region near Troy, from which Zeus, the king of the
gods, often watched and directed the progress of the Trojan War.
19. **Ceres** [sē′rēz]: Roman goddess of grain and harvest; associated with the
Greek goddess Demeter.

And now I was nearing the gates and thinking that we had made it,
190 When on a sudden there came to my ears the sound of many
Footsteps—or so it seemed. Then, peering into the gloom,
My father exclaimed:
                              Run! They're upon us! Run, Aeneas!
I can see the shine of their shields and the bronze accouterments winking.

Well, I panicked. My wits were fuddled, were snatched away
195 By some malignant prompting. For even as I darted off
Into byways, off my course among streets I knew not—O god,
The anguish of it!—my wife Creusa, fate took her—did she
Stop there? or lose her way? Did she sink down in exhaustion?
We never knew. We never set eyes on her again.
200 I did not look back for the lost one, I did not give her a thought
Until we had reached the mound, the ancient, hallowed place
Of Ceres. Here at last, when all were assembled, one was
Missing, one had denied husband and son her company.
I was out of my mind. What mortal, what god did I not curse?
205 In all the city's ruin what bitterer thing did I see?
Commending Ascanius, Anchises and the Teucrian[20] home-gods
To my friends' care, and hiding them deep in the hollow vale,
I put on my shining armor, I made for the city once more.
To reconstruct those events, to retrace our path through Troy
210 And expose my life to its perils again—that was my purpose.

For a start, I returned to the shadowed gate in the city wall
By which I had sallied forth, noting my tracks and following them
Back through the night, straining my eyes to scan them. Everywhere
Dread and the sheer silence reduced my courage to nothing.
215 Next, I went home, in case—just on the chance that she might have
Gone there. The Greeks had broken in, the whole house was occupied.
That instant, gluttonous fire was fanned by the draught right up to
The roof top; flames burst out there, the blast of the heat roared skywards.
I went on, to revisit Priam's house and the citadel.
220 Here, in the empty colonnades of Juno's[21] sanctuary,
Phoenix[22] and fell Ulysses were engaged on the duty allotted them,
Guarding the loot. To this point from all over Troy had plunder,
Salvaged from burning shrines, been brought: tables of gods,
Solid gold bowls and looted vestments were being piled up here
225 In heaps. Children and frightened mothers were standing about
In a long queue.

---

20. **Teucrian** [tōō′krē ən]: another name for *Trojan,* from Teucer, first king of Troy.
21. **Juno:** queen of the gods and enemy of the Trojans; she is a most appropriate guardian for the triumphant Greeks.
22. **Phoenix** [fē′niks]: Greek warrior and foster father of Achilles.

I dared (you will hardly believe it) to call out loud through the gloom
And fill the streets with shouting: sadly I cried "Creusa!"—
Called to her over and over again, but it was no good.

230 As I roamed on that endless, frenzied search through the city buildings,
There appeared before my eyes a piteous phantom, yes,
The very ghost of Creusa—a figure larger than life.
I was appalled: my hair stood on end, and my voice stuck
In my throat. It was she who spoke then, and thus relieved my pain:

235 Darling husband, it's madness of you to indulge your grief
Like this. These happenings are part of the divine
Purpose. It was not written that you should bring Creusa
Away with you; the great ruler of heaven does not allow it.
For you, long exile is destined, broad tracts of sea to be furrowed;
240 Then you will reach Hesperia,²³ where Lydian Tiber²⁴ flows
Gently through a land in good heart, and good men live.
There, your affairs will prosper; a kingdom, a royal bride
Await you. No more tears now for your heart's love, Creusa:
I shall not see the proud halls of the Myrmidons or Dolopes,
245 Nor work as a slave for Greek women—I, who am Dardan²⁵
And daughter-in-law to the goddess Venus.²⁶
No, the great Mother of the gods is going to keep me here.
Good-by, Aeneas. Cherish our love in the son it gave us.

With these words, though I wept and had so much to say
250 To her, she left me, fading out into thin air.
Three times I tried to put my arms round her neck, and three times
The phantom slipped my hands, my vain embrace: it was like
Grasping a wisp of wind or the wings of a fleeting dream.
So in the end I went back to my friends, the night being over.
255 I was astonished to find, when I got there, a great number
Of new arrivals come in, both women and men, a sorry
Concourse of refugees assembled for exile. From all sides
They'd rendezvous'd, their minds made up, their belongings ready
For me to lead them wherever I wished across the sea.
260 And now was the dawn star rising over the ridges of Ida,
Bringing another day. The Greeks were holding the gates of
The city in force. Troy was beyond all hope of aid.
I accepted defeat, picked up my father and made for the mountains.

---

23. **Hesperia** [hes pēr′ē ä]: land of the evening or land in the west; Italy.
24. **Lydian Tiber:** Tiber River, second longest in Italy. It bordered a territory
settled by people from ancient Lydia and was therefore often called *Lydian*.
25. **Dardan** [där′dən]: Trojan, that is, one of the race of Trojans begun by
Dardanus, founder of Troy.
26. **Venus:** Roman goddess of love, counterpart of the Greek goddess Aphrodite;
mother of Aeneas.

STUDY QUESTIONS

Recalling

1. Describe in detail how the Greeks used the wooden horse to defeat Troy.
2. List all the Trojan opinions in favor of and opposed to letting the wooden horse into Troy.
3. What two courses of action are open to Aeneas when he returns to his home? What decision does he finally make? What event sways him at the last moment?
4. What and whom does Aeneas take with him from Troy? Who is left behind? Why?

Interpreting

5. Why does the Greek strategy involving the wooden horse work?
6. How does fate influence Aeneas' departure?

Extending

7. When Aeneas again prepares to fight the Greeks on the night of Troy's fall, his wife, Creusa, begs him to consider first her and their young son, Ascanius. Compare this scene with the scene in the *Iliad* where Andromache pleads with Hector. What values and feelings do the two scenes have in common? How do they differ?

VIEWPOINT

The classics scholar Wendell Clausen argues that we are moved by the *Aeneid* in part because

> its larger structure . . . enlists our sympathy on the side of loneliness, suffering, and defeat. For it is the paradox of the *Aeneid,* the surprise of its greatness, that a poem which celebrates the achievement of an exemplary hero and the founding of Rome itself should be a long history of defeat and loss. Aeneas finally wins—for that is his fate—but he wins at a terrible cost. . . .

1. As Aeneas tells of the fall of Troy, do you feel sympathy for him? Why or why not?

2. Does your feeling change with the knowledge that Aeneas himself will live to found Rome?
3. Referring to particular details, tell how this selection supports the theme of ultimate victory through defeat and terrible loss.

VOCABULARY

Word Origins

Many words come to English from Latin, the language of the Romans who occupied Britain and, later, of the medieval church. Using a good dictionary, look up the following words from the translation of the *Aeneid,* and explain their origins. Also explain their meanings *as they are used in the selection.*

1. derelict
2. ferocious
3. concussion
4. voluminously
5. supine
6. obnoxious
7. obstinately
8. luminously
9. omnipotent
10. conflagration
11. malignant
12. sanctuary

COMPOSITION

Writing About Theme

■ Show how Virgil illuminates his theme in the excerpt from the *Aeneid.* First write a sentence that states the excerpt's theme. Then explain how Virgil develops that theme through characterization, setting, events, point of view, and tone. *For help with this assignment, see Lesson 6 in the Writing About Literature Handbook at the back of this book.*

Writing a First-Person Narrative

■ Tell a story from the point of view of one of the soldiers inside the wooden horse when it is dragged into Troy. Imagine that soldier's feelings as the Trojans debate whether to destroy the horse or to take it into Troy. Describe the atmosphere inside the horse as the soldiers feel the Trojans pulling them into the city, where the surprise attack will occur.

Ovid 43 B.C.–A.D. 17

Born into a wealthy landowning family, Publius Ovidius Naso (Ovid) studied law and rhetoric in Rome, where he later did considerable public service. Preferring society and poetry to politics and law, however, Ovid delighted the Roman socialites with his brilliant and forthright love poetry. The *Amores* and the *Art of Love* provided advice and described strategies for lovers' intrigues. The *Heroides,* fictitious love letters from legendary women, revealed Ovid's sensitivity to women's feelings and his sympathetic understanding of love. Ovid's auspicious career came to an abrupt halt in A.D. 8, when, for reasons that remain obscure, Emperor Augustus exiled him to the remote town of Tomis on the Black Sea.

At the time of his exile, Ovid was completing the *Metamorphoses* [met′ə môr′fə sēz], his great poem based on the Greek and Roman myths. He continued to write poetry, including some efforts to persuade Augustus to pardon him. In these he failed; he died in exile at the age of sixty without ever seeing his beloved Rome again.

Ovid said of himself at the end of the *Metamorphoses,* "I shall be read, and through all centuries,/If prophecies of bards are ever to be truthful,/I shall be living, always." The prophecy was correct: The *Metamorphoses* has been a source of inspiration for poets and painters from the Middle Ages to the present; Chaucer, Dante, Shakespeare, Milton, Dryden, and, more recently, modern poets such as Yeats and Eliot all acknowledge Ovid's influence. A poem of nearly twelve thousand lines, the *Metamorphoses* is a collection of stories about all kinds of transformations, or metamorphoses, that occur in the myths. These stories begin with the transformation of chaos into an ordered universe and end with Ovid's fanciful transformation of Julius Caesar into a blazing star. One of the most touching metamorphoses occurs in the story of Daedalus, which follows. Daedalus [ded′əl əs] is the legendary craftsman and architect who has been held prisoner with his son, Icarus, on the island of Crete in the Mediterranean. They are prisoners of King Minos, who wants to prevent them from revealing the secret of the labyrinth, or maze, that Daedalus had built for the king.

▨ Literature reminds us that people do not change; wars happen, discoveries are made, and through it all people change little. Think of a time when you failed to heed a parent's warning. What happened?

Ovid

from the **Metamorphoses**

Translated by Rolphe Humphries

from Book 8, The Story of Daedalus and Icarus

Homesick for homeland, Daedalus hated Crete
And his long exile there, but the sea held him.
"Though Minos blocks escape by land or water,"
Daedalus said, "surely the sky is open,
5 And that's the way we'll go. Minos' dominion
Does not include the air." He turned his thinking
Toward unknown arts, changing the laws of nature.
He laid out feathers in order, first the smallest,
A little larger next it, and so continued,
10 The way that panpipes[1] rise in gradual sequence.
He fastened them with twine and wax, at middle,
At bottom, so, and bent them, gently curving,
So that they looked like wings of birds, most surely.
And Icarus, his son, stood by and watched him,
15 Not knowing he was dealing with his downfall,
Stood by and watched and raised his shiny face
To let a feather, light as down, fall on it,
Or stuck his thumb into the yellow wax,

---

1. **panpipes:** primitive musical instruments consisting of a series of
reeds or pipes of increasing length.

Fooling around, the way a boy will, always,
20 Whenever a father tries to get some work done.
Still, it was done at last, and the father hovered,
Poised, in the moving air, and taught his son:
"I warn you, Icarus, fly a middle course:
Don't go too low, or water will weigh the wings down;
25 Don't go too high, or the sun's fire will burn them.
Keep to the middle way. And one more thing,
No fancy steering by star or constellation,
Follow my lead!" That was the flying lesson.
And now to fit the wings to the boy's shoulders.
30 Between the work and warning the father found
His cheeks were wet with tears, and his hands trembled.
He kissed his son (*Good-by,* if he had known it),
Rose on his wings, flew on ahead, as fearful
As any bird launching the little nestlings
35 Out of high nest into thin air. *Keep on,*
Keep on, he signals, *follow me!* He guides him
In flight—O fatal art!—and the wings move
And the father looks back to see the son's wings moving.
Far off, far down, some fisherman is watching
40 As the rod dips and trembles over the water,
Some shepherd rests his weight upon his crook,
Some plowman on the handles of the plowshare,
And all look up, in absolute amazement,
At those airborne above. They must be gods!
45 They were over Samos, Juno's² sacred island,
Delos and Paros toward the left, Lebinthus
Visible to the right, and another island,
Calymne,³ rich in honey. And the boy
Thought *This is wonderful!* and left his father,
50 Soared higher, higher, drawn to the vast heaven,
Nearer the sun, and the wax that held the wings
Melted in that fierce heat, and the bare arms
Beat up and down in air, and lacking oarage
Took hold of nothing. *Father!* he cried, and *Father!*
55 Until the blue sea hushed him, the dark water
Men call the Icarian now. And Daedalus,
Father no more, called "Icarus, where are you!
Where are you, Icarus? Tell me where to find you!"
And saw the wings on the waves and cursed his talents,
60 Buried the body in a tomb, and the land
Was named for Icarus.⁴

---

2. **Juno's:** referring to the Roman queen of the gods.
3. **Samos** [sā′mos], **Delos** [dē′los], **Paros** [pär′os], **Lebinthus** [leb in′thəs],
Calymne [kə lim′nē]: islands in the Aegean Sea.
4. **land . . . Icarus:** the Aegean island of Icaria.

STUDY QUESTIONS

Recalling

1. Why must Daedalus change the laws of nature? What means does he employ for his escape?
2. What warning does Daedalus give his son? What simile in lines 32–35 describes Daedalus' paternal feelings?
3. What does Icarus do in disobedience of his father? Why? What are the consequences of his disobedience?

Interpreting

4. What two transformations occur in this story?
5. What moral can be drawn from Daedalus' advice to "fly a middle course"?

Extending

6. The fisherman, the shepherd, and the plowman, seeing Daedalus and Icarus flying, think they must be gods. In what ways is Daedalus like a god? What price does he pay for these gifts? What does the myth imply about human pride and humility?

LITERARY FOCUS

Greek Mythology

A **myth** is an anonymous traditional story with its roots in cultural folk beliefs that rely on the supernatural to explain the mysteries of the world. While not attempting to be rational or scientific, myths do help us to grapple with our perceptions of humankind and the world. All mythologies revolve around ideas of cosmic creation, supernatural power, birth, death, and humanity's existence in the universe.

Greek mythology collects stories told by the ancient Greeks about their gods, ancestors, and legendary heroes. Reflecting the high-spirited and beauty-loving character of their creators, the Greek myths glorify the best in human beings. Although the gods, who are represented mainly as powerful and immortal men and women, may be capricious, they are seldom downright evil. Like mortals, they are susceptible to emotions and are capable of being flattered or enraged.

In their gallery of mythological characters and stories, the Greeks left a heritage that has been a source of artistic inspiration to succeeding generations. The first people influenced by the Greek myths were the Romans, who adopted the Greek gods and goddesses, changing many of their names.

Thinking About Greek Mythology

How does the myth of Daedalus reflect at the same time the classical admiration for spectacular human achievement and a wholesome respect for moderation in all things?

COMPOSITION

Applying a Statement About Literature

Ovid has been called a master storyteller. Show how that evaluation of Ovid applies to "Daedalus and Icarus." First explain what a master storyteller must be. Then show Ovid's mastery in this particular story. You might consider the plot (including the "hints" Ovid drops about its conclusion and the buildup to the climax) and the characters (including qualities that make Daedalus and Icarus seem human). *For help with this assignment, refer to Lesson 9 in the Writing About Literature Handbook at the back of this book.*

Writing Drama

Write a dramatic sketch about a person who has the opportunity to do something new. Examine the conflict that arises between being safe and taking a risk. How does one choose?

COMPARING WRITERS

Both Virgil and Ovid are concerned with the place and purpose of humanity in the universe and with overconfidence. How does each view the consequences of too much confidence? How do the contexts of their stories differ?

Omar Khayyám   *died 1123*

Born some time in the eleventh century in Naishápur, Persia (present-day Iran), Omar Khayyám is today among the most famous poets of the medieval Moslem world, yet in his own day he was known chiefly as a mathematician and an astronomer. The background of Omar Khayyám is somewhat obscure. The word *khayyám* is a nickname meaning "tent maker," probably his father's profession. (Since *Khayyám* is a nickname, the poet is referred to as *Omar,* not *Khayyám,* when the full name is not used.) Omar lived at a time when the Seljuk Turks ruled over Persia as well as Syria and Asia Minor (Asian Turkey). Legend has it that as a young man he was close friends with Nizam-ul-Mulk, later the respected and powerful vizier (minister) of two Seljuk sultans (rulers), and with Hasan-ben-Sabbah, who later founded the fanatical Persian sect called the Assassins. While this legend may or may not be true, Omar became a historical figure when he produced a major treatise on algebra, written in Arabic, then the chief language of scholarship in the Moslem world. This treatise brought him to the attention of Sultan Malik-shah, who in 1074 invited Omar to become court astronomer. In this position Omar revised the astronomical tables known as the *Zij* and also helped produce a new Moslem calendar.

Though Omar's poetry was not unknown, it was not really famous—even in Persia—until the Victorian poet Edward FitzGerald (1809–1883) created an English version of it. FitzGerald studied Persian for six years, yet he did not produce a word-for-word translation. Rather, he saw his effort as the reproduction of a work of art, and his aim was to capture the spirit and feelings of the original. His first version of *The Rubáiyát of Omar Khayyám* was published in 1859; thereafter he continued to polish it, publishing his final revised edition in 1879.

Omar Khayyám expressed his views of life, death, friendship, love, and fate in a series of quatrains, called *rubá'īyāt* in Arabic, the plural of *rubá'īyah* (from *rubá'i,* "composed of four"). He rhymed his quatrains *aaxa*—that is, the first, second, and fourth lines rhyme, while the third line can have any end sound. FitzGerald's English versions maintain this *aaxa* rhyme scheme and use iambic pentameter—a stanza form that, in testament to the work's popularity, has now become known as the **Rubáiyát stanza**.

The following selection is from FitzGerald's best-known version of *The Rubáiyát of Omar Khayyám,* the one published in 1879. The selection powerfully illustrates Omar Khayyám's vivid feeling for life and his strong but rarely gloomy fatalism.

▌ Which of life's simple pleasures do you most enjoy?

Omar Khayyám

from **The Rubáiyát**

translated by Edward FitzGerald

Wake! For the Sun, who scattered into flight
The Stars before him from the Field of Night,
   Drives Night along with them from Heaven
     and strikes
The Sultan's Turret with a Shaft of Light.

5 Come, fill the Cup, and in the fire of Spring
Your Winter-garment of Repentance fling;
   The Bird of Time has but a little way
To flutter—and the Bird is on the Wing.

Whether at Naishápur[1] or Babylon,[2]
10 Whether the Cup with sweet or bitter run,
   The Wine of Life keeps oozing drop by
     drop,
The Leaves of Life keep falling one by one.

Each Morn a thousand Roses brings, you say;
Yes, but where leaves the Rose of Yesterday?
15   And this first Summer month that brings
     the Rose
Shall take Jamshyd[3] and Kaikobád[4] away.

Well, let it take them! What have we to do
With Kaikobád the Great, or Kaikhosrú?[5]
   Let Zál[6] and Rustum[7] bluster as they will,
20 Or Hátim[8] call to Supper—heed not you.

With me along the strip of Herbage strown
That just divides the desert from the sown,
   Where name of Slave and Sultan is forgot—
And Peace to Mahmúd[9] on his golden Throne!

25 A Book of Verses underneath the Bough,
A Jug of Wine, a Loaf of Bread—and Thou
   Beside me singing in the Wilderness—
Oh, Wilderness were Paradise enow!

The Worldly Hope men set their Hearts upon
30 Turns Ashes—or it prospers; and anon,
   Like Snow upon the Desert's dusty Face,
Lighting a little hour or two—is gone.

Think, in this battered Caravanserai[10]
Whose Portals are alternate Night and Day,
35   How Sultan after Sultan with his Pomp
Abode his destined Hour, and went his way.

A Moment's Halt—a momentary taste
Of BEING from the Well amid the Waste—
   And Lo!—the phantom Caravan has reached
40 The NOTHING it set out from—Oh, make
     haste!

We are no other than a moving row
Of Magic Shadow-shapes that come and go
   Round with the Sun-illumined Lantern held
In Midnight by the Master of the Show;

45 But helpless Pieces of the Game He plays
Upon this Checkerboard of Nights and Days;
   Hither and thither moves, and checks, and
     slays,
And one by one back in the Closet lays.

---

1. **Naishápur** [nē shä′poor]: town in northeast Persia
(now Iran), birthplace of Omar Khayyám.
2. **Babylon** [bab′ə lon′]: ancient city of Mesopotamia
(now southern Iraq).
3. **Jamshyd** [jəm shēd′]: legendary Persian king.
4. **Kaikobád** [kā′kō bäd′]: pre-Islamic mythical Persian
king.
5. **Kaikhosrú** [kā′kōs roo′]: mythical Persian king.
6. **Zál** [zal]: Persian warrior hero.
7. **Rustum** [roos toom′]: Persian warrior hero.
8. **Hátim** [ha′tim]: pre-Islamic poet noted for his extreme generosity.
9. **Mahmúd** [mə mood′]: the prophet Mohammed,
founder of Islam.
10. **Caravanserai** [kar′ə van′sər ē]: in Eastern countries,
an inn with an enclosed court where caravans rest at
night.

The Ball no question makes of Ayes and Noes,
50 But Here or There as strikes the Player goes;
    And He that tossed you down into the Field,
He knows about it all—HE knows—HE knows!

The Moving Finger writes, and, having writ,
Moves on; nor all your Piety nor Wit
55   Shall lure it back to cancel half a Line,
Nor all your Tears wash out a Word of it.

Yet Ah, that Spring should vanish with the
    Rose!
That Youth's sweet-scented manuscript should
    close!
    The Nightingale that in the branches sang,
60 Ah whence, and whither flown again, who
    knows!

Would but the Desert of the Fountain yield
One glimpse—if dimly, yet indeed, revealed,
    To which the fainting Traveler might spring,
As springs the trampled herbage of the field.

65 Would but some wingèd Angel ere too late
Arrest the yet unfolded Roll of Fate,
    And make the stern Recorder otherwise
Enregister, or quite obliterate!

Ah, Love! could you and I with Him conspire
70 To grasp this sorry Scheme of Things entire,
    Would not we shatter it to bits—and then
Remold it nearer to the Heart's Desire!

Yon rising Moon that looks for us again—
How oft hereafter will she wax and wane;
75   How oft hereafter rising look for us
Through this same Garden—and for *one* in
    vain!

And when like her, O Sáki,[11] you shall pass
Among the Guests Star-scattered on the Grass,
    And in your joyous errand reach the spot
80 Where I made One—turn down an empty
    Glass!

                                        TAMÁM[12]

---

11. **Sákí** [sä′kē]: water or wine bearer.
12. TAMÁM [ta mäm′]: the end.

STUDY QUESTIONS

Recalling

1. What demands does the speaker make in the first two quatrains? In the third quatrain what does he say "keeps oozing"?
2. According to lines 25–28, what are the only four things needed to turn wilderness to paradise? According to lines 29–40, what are the two possible courses that worldly hope may take? What has happened to "Sultan after Sultan"?
3. To what do lines 45–48 compare human beings? According to lines 53–56, what does the "Moving Finger" do?
4. In lines 69–72, what does the speaker say he and his beloved would do if they could?
5. What does the speaker request in the final quatrain?

Interpreting

6. Identify five words or images used in the selection to symbolize life or time. What central message involving life and time does the selection convey?
7. To whom are the quatrains, or most of the quatrains, addressed? What do lines 25–28 suggest are the things that bring happiness in life? What do lines 13–23 and 29–36 suggest are not important in life?
8. What overall picture of humanity is presented in lines 41–56? Restate in your own words the human wish expressed in lines 69–72. Does the speaker think this wish can be fulfilled?
9. Examine the speaker's overall tone in the selection. Would you say his attitude toward life is negative or unhappy? Explain.

Extending

10. With which of the ideas about life expressed in this selection do you agree? With which do you disagree? Why?

VOCABULARY

Words from Middle Eastern Languages

Many English words have their origins in Middle Eastern languages such as Persian, Arabic, Hebrew, and Turkish. Use a dictionary to find the meanings and origins of the following words, some of which are used in the selection from *The Rubáiyát*. Then use each word in a sentence.

1. caravan
2. cummerbund
3. kismet
4. sultan
5. zenith

COMPARING WRITERS

1. Both *Gilgamesh* and *The Rubáiyát of Omar Khayyám* are products of Middle Eastern literature, though they are separated by thousands of years of change. Despite this passage of time, do the works have any ideas or attitudes in common? Cite details to support your answer.
2. Compare the selection from *The Rubáiyát* with Marvell's "To His Coy Mistress" (page 259) and Herrick's "To the Virgins" (page 267). What does *The Rubáiyát* have in common with the carpe-diem tradition? What other similarities do you detect between *The Rubáiyát* and one or both of the English poems?

Dante   *1265–1321*

Of all medieval literature Dante's epic poem, *The Divine Comedy,* is the best known and the most dearly loved. Few other poems of any time have had so much influence or have been the subject of such thorough study. The modern poet T. S. Eliot said, "Dante and Shakespeare divide the world between them; there is no third."

Born in Florence, Dante Alighieri received a traditional medieval education, spending some time at the University of Bologna and studying copiously on his own as well. As was customary, he was betrothed at the age of twelve to Gemma Donati, with whom he later had at least three children. However, when Dante was nine, he met the true love of his life, Beatrice Portinari, who would become the poet's lifelong inspiration.

Active in civil affairs as well as in letters, Dante fought at the battle of Campaldino in 1289. In 1295 he held public office, and in 1300 he served as an ambassador for Florence. During the same year, as one of the priors, or religious officials, of Florence, he was obliged to exile one of his best friends, the poet Guido Cavalcanti, for inciting a street riot—an exile that caused Guido's death. After further serving his city, Dante was himself exiled when a rival faction took power. He never returned to Florence, and for the next twenty years he moved all over Italy, spending time in Verona, particularly with Bartolomeo della Scala and his son Can Grande, who became his great friend and patron. In 1321 Dante died and was buried in Ravenna, where his remains still rest.

Dante's minor works alone would have assured him a place in literary history. His first work, *La Vita Nuova,* completed around 1293, tells of his great love for Beatrice in a series of poems with prose introductions. Beatrice is represented alternately as an ideal woman—an angel sent by God to comfort men—and as a very lovely, desirable human woman. *Il Convivio* and *De Monarchia,* written in order to inform and to persuade fellow Florentines of the virtues of knowledge and restraint of power, are works in which logic and reason prevail.

Introducing The Divine Comedy

Dante's supreme work and the masterpiece of the Middle Ages is his *Commedia*. Dante called his work *The Comedy* because it had a happy ending, not because it was humorous. The word *divine* was not added to the title until the sixteenth century. The poem, which begins in misery and ends in happiness, is divided into three parts of thirty-three cantos each—*Inferno* (Hell), *Purgatorio* (Purgatory), and *Paradiso* (Paradise). The poem is composed in the Italian vernacular in **terza rima**, a difficult verse form of three-line stanzas in which the first and third lines rhyme and the second line rhymes with the first line of the following stanza. The translation of a portion of Dante's work, which begins on the following page, is not in terza rima.

In a letter to Can Grande, Dante explained that the first meaning of *The Divine Comedy* was the literal one: The cantos tell the story, according to the beliefs of medieval Christianity, of the state of souls after death, brought to that point by choices made during life. *The Divine Comedy* may also be read on other levels; on an allegorical level its purpose is to turn the living to the path of salvation.

In the *Inferno* the damned souls occupy nine circles and are divided into three main groups: those lacking self-restraint; those committing violence against themselves, others, nature, or God; and those guilty of all types of fraudulence. Purgatory is divided into nine levels of the penitent and Paradise into nine heavens of the virtuous. *The Divine Comedy* ends with the vision of a human's attainable unity with God, which is the final destination of the entire journey of the soul.

Dante makes himself the central character who undertakes the soul's long and arduous journey. As his guide he takes Virgil, the poet he most loved, who was regarded in the Middle Ages as a magician of sorts. Since Virgil is not a Christian, he must abandon Dante at the end of the journey through Purgatory. Thereafter, it is Beatrice herself, who had sent Virgil to bring Dante to her, who becomes Dante's guide.

Dante's journey begins on the night before Good Friday in 1300, when he finds himself lost in a dark wood. As Dante struggles to find his way out, he meets three terrifying animals who refuse to let him leave the wood. Just as he is about to give up hope of ever escaping, Dante meets the poet Virgil, who leads him from the forest.

■ If you walked into a room and saw the words "abandon all hope ye who enter here," what would your reaction be?

Dante

from **The Divine Comedy**

Translated by John Ciardi

from **Canto I, Virgil**

Midway in our life's journey, I went astray
    from the straight road and woke to find myself
    alone in a dark wood. How shall I say

what wood that was! I never saw so drear,
5   so rank, so arduous a wilderness!
    Its very memory gives a shape to fear.

Death could scarce be more bitter than that place!
    But since it came to good, I will recount
    all that I found revealed there by God's grace.

10 How I came to it I cannot rightly say,
    so drugged and loose with sleep had I become
    when I first wandered there from the True Way.

But at the far end of that valley of evil
    whose maze had sapped my very heart with fear
15   I found myself before a little hill

and lifted up my eyes. Its shoulders glowed
    already with the sweet rays of that planet[1]
    whose virtue leads men straight on every road,

and the shining strengthened me against the fright
20   whose agony had wracked the lake of my heart
    through all the terrors of that piteous night.

Just as a swimmer, who with his last breath
    flounders ashore from perilous seas, might turn
    to memorize the wide water of his death—

25 so did I turn, my soul still fugitive
    from death's surviving image, to stare down
    that pass that none had ever left alive.

And there I lay to rest from my heart's race
    till calm and breath returned to me. Then rose
30   and pushed up that dead slope at such a pace

---

1. **that planet:** The sun, which symbolizes God, was considered
a planet in medieval astronomy.

each footfall rose above the last. And lo!
 almost at the beginning of the rise
 I faced a spotted Leopard,[2] all tremor and flow

and gaudy pelt. And it would not pass, but stood
35 so blocking my every turn that time and again
 I was on the verge of turning back to the wood.

This fell at the first widening of the dawn
 as the sun was climbing Aries[3] with those stars
 that rode with him to light the new creation.

40 Thus the holy hour and the sweet season
 of commemoration did much to arm my fear
 of that bright murderous beast with their good omen.

Yet not so much but what I shook with dread
 at sight of a great Lion that broke upon me
45 raging with hunger, its enormous head

held high as if to strike a mortal terror
 into the very air. And down his track,
 a She-Wolf drove upon me, a starved horror

ravening and wasted beyond all belief.
50 She seemed a rack for avarice, gaunt and craving.
 Oh many the souls she has brought to endless grief!

She brought such heaviness upon my spirit
 at sight of her savagery and desperation,
 I died from every hope of that high summit.

55 And like a miser—eager in acquisition
 but desperate in self-reproach when Fortune's wheel
 turns to the hour of his loss—all tears and attrition

I wavered back; and still the beast pursued,
 forcing herself against me bit by bit
60 till I slid back into the sunless wood.

And as I fell to my soul's ruin, a presence
 gathered before me on the discolored air,
 the figure of one who seemed hoarse from long silence.

---

2. **Leopard:** along with the Lion and the She-Wolf, one of three beasts
representing types of worldliness and sin: the Leopard represents
malice and greed; the Lion, violence and pride; and the She-Wolf,
self-indulgence.
3. **Aries:** the first sign of the zodiac, here representing spring, the Easter
season, and rebirth.

At sight of him in that friendless waste I cried:
65 "Have pity on me, whatever thing you are,
whether shade or living man." And it replied:

"Not man, though man I once was, and my blood
was Lombard, both my parents Mantuan.⁴
I was born, though late, *sub Julio,*⁵ and bred

70 in Rome under Augustus in the noon
of the false and lying gods. I was a poet
and sang of old Anchises' noble son⁶

who came to Rome after the burning of Troy.
But you—why do *you* return to these distresses
75 instead of climbing that shining Mount of Joy

which is the seat and first cause of man's bliss?"
"And are you then that Virgil and that fountain
of purest speech?" My voice grew tremulous:

"Glory and light of poets! now may that zeal
80 and love's apprenticeship that I poured out
on your heroic verses serve me well!

For you are my true master and first author,
the sole maker from whom I drew the breath
of that sweet style whose measures have brought me honor.

85 See there, immortal sage, the beast I flee.
For my soul's salvation, I beg you, guard me from her,
for she has struck a mortal tremor through me."

And he replied, seeing my soul in tears:
"He must go by another way who would escape
90 this wilderness, for that mad beast that fleers⁷

before you there, suffers no man to pass.
She tracks down all, kills all, and knows no glut,
but, feeding, she grows hungrier than she was. . . .

Therefore, for your own good, I think it well

95 you follow me and I will be your guide
and lead you forth through an eternal place.⁸
There you shall see the ancient spirits tried

---

4. **Lombard . . . Mantuan:** Virgil was born in Mantua, a city in the
region of Lombardy in northern Italy.
5. *sub Julio:* during the reign of Julius Caesar (100?–44 B.C.).
6. **Anchises'** [an kē′sēz] **. . . son:** Aeneas, hero of Virgil's *Aeneid.*
7. **fleers:** sneers at.
8. **an eternal place:** Hell.

in endless pain, and hear their lamentation
as each bemoans the second death of souls.
100 Next you shall see upon a burning mountain[9]

souls in fire and yet content in fire,
knowing that whensoever it may be
they yet will mount into the blessed choir.

To which, if it is still your wish to climb,
105 a worthier spirit shall be sent to guide you.
With her shall I leave you, for the King of Time,

who reigns on high, forbids me to come there[10]
since, living, I rebelled against his law.
He rules the waters and the land and air

110 and there holds court, his city and his throne.
Oh blessed are they he chooses!" And I to him:
"Poet, by that God to you unknown,

lead me this way. Beyond this present ill
and worse to dread, lead me to Peter's gate[11]
115 and be my guide through the sad halls of Hell."

And he then: "Follow." And he moved ahead
in silence, and I followed where he led.

---

9. **a burning mountain:** Purgatory, where souls may be redeemed.
10. **forbids . . . there:** Because Virgil lived before the Christian Era, he missed salvation through Christ, which, according to Dante's theology, was necessary for entry into Heaven.
11. **Peter's gate:** the gate of Purgatory.

Dante and Beatrice depicted in an illustration from a thirteenth-century manuscript of *The Divine Comedy.*

from **Canto III, The Gate of Hell**

Dante, after spending a whole day trying to climb the moun-
tain, gets discouraged and makes excuses to Virgil. Virgil then ex-
plains that Saint Lucy and the Virgin Mary sent Beatrice to Pur-
gatory to beg him to go to Dante's rescue. Thus encouraged,
Dante prepares to follow Virgil without further complaint. The
poets then arrive at the Gate of Hell, upon which they read an
ominous inscription.

I AM THE WAY INTO THE CITY OF WOE.
I AM THE WAY TO A FORSAKEN PEOPLE.
I AM THE WAY INTO ETERNAL SORROW.

SACRED JUSTICE MOVED MY ARCHITECT.
5 I WAS RAISED HERE BY DIVINE OMNIPOTENCE,
PRIMORDIAL LOVE AND ULTIMATE INTELLECT.

ONLY THOSE ELEMENTS TIME CANNOT WEAR[12]
WERE MADE BEFORE ME, AND BEYOND TIME I STAND.[13]
ABANDON ALL HOPE YE WHO ENTER HERE.[14]

10 These mysteries I read cut into stone
    above a gate. And turning I said: "Master,
    what is the meaning of this harsh inscription?"

And he then as initiate to novice:
    "Here must you put by all division of spirit
15   and gather your soul against all cowardice.

This is the place I told you to expect.
    Here you shall pass among the fallen people,
    souls who have lost the good of intellect."

So saying, he put forth his hand to me,
20   and with a gentle and encouraging smile
    he led me through the gate of mystery.

Here sighs and cries and wails coiled and recoiled
    on the starless air, spilling my soul to tears.
    A confusion of tongues and monstrous accents toiled

---

12. **ELEMENTS . . . WEAR:** the highest heavens, the first matter created, and
the angels.
13. **BEYOND . . . STAND:** Just punishment for sins is endless.
14. **ABANDON . . . HERE:** For the soul entering Hell there is no return. Dante is
naturally fearful; however, since he is still alive, he is entering not Hell itself but
the vision of Hell and may escape if he keeps his faith.

25 in pain and anger. Voices hoarse and shrill
    and sounds of blows, all intermingled, raised
    tumult and pandemonium that still

    whirls on the air forever dirty with it
    as if a whirlwind sucked at sand. And I,
30 holding my head in horror, cried: "Sweet Spirit,

    what souls are these who run through this black haze?"
    And he to me: "These are the nearly soulless
    whose lives concluded neither blame nor praise.

    They are mixed here with that despicable corps
35 of angels who were neither for God nor Satan,
    but only for themselves. The High Creator

    scourged them from Heaven for its perfect beauty,
    and Hell will not receive them since the wicked
    might feel some glory over them." And I:

40 "Master, what gnaws at them so hideously
    their lamentation stuns the very air?"
    "They have no hope of death," he answered me,

    "and in their blind and unattaining state
    their miserable lives have sunk so low
45 that they must envy every other fate.

    No word of them survives their living season.
    Mercy and Justice[15] deny them even a name.
    Let us not speak of them: look, and pass on."

from Canto XXVI, Ulysses

From here on Dante, guided by Virgil, proceeds to descend through the various levels of Hell. Despite the difficulties they encounter along the way, they eventually arrive in the Eighth Circle. With Virgil's instruction and encouragement, Dante overcomes the barriers to their passage, and the travelers enter the eighth chasm of the Eighth Circle, where evil counselors wrapped in tall flames are punished. Here the poets talk to Ulysses (the Latin form of Odysseus) and Diomede, the Greeks responsible for the treachery of the wooden horse.

As many fireflies as the peasant sees
    when he rests on a hill and looks into the valley
    (where he tills or gathers grapes or prunes his trees)

---

15. **Mercy and Justice:** Heaven and Hell.

in that sweet season when the face of him
5   who lights the world rides north, and at the hour
     when the fly yields to the gnat and the air grows dim—

such myriads of flames I saw shine through
     the gloom of the eighth abyss when I arrived
     at the rim from which its bed comes into view. . . .

10   I stood on the bridge, and leaned out from the edge;
     so far, that but for a jut of rock I held to
     I should have been sent hurtling from the ledge

without being pushed. And seeing me so intent,
     my Guide said: "There are souls within those flames;
15   each sinner swathes himself in his own torment."

"Master," I said, "your words make me more sure,
     but I had seen already that it was so
     and meant to ask what spirit must endure

the pains of that great flame which splits away
20   in two great horns, as if it rose from the pyre
     where Eteocles and Polynices lay?"[16]

He answered me: "Forever round this path
     Ulysses and Diomede[17] move in such dress,
     united in pain as once they were in wrath;

25   there they lament the ambush of the Horse
     which was the door through which the noble seed
     of the Romans issued from its holy source;

there they mourn that for Achilles slain
     sweet Deidamia weeps even in death;
30   there they recall the Palladium in their pain."

"Master," I cried, "I pray you and repray
     till my prayer becomes a thousand—if these souls
     can still speak from the fire, oh let me stay

16. **pyre . . . lay:** Sons of Oedipus, the brothers Eteocles and Polynices killed
each other in combat over who would rule Thebes. According to one version of
the legend, their mutual hatred was so great that even the flames of their funeral
pyre drew apart.
17. **Ulysses and Diomede:** in the war against Troy, Greek heroes who are being
punished for their joint guilt in three acts considered evil by Dante: devising the
stratagem of the Wooden Horse by which Troy was destroyed; coercing Achilles
into going to Troy, thus causing his love, Deidamia, to die of grief; and stealing
the Palladium, the sacred statue of Pallas Athena, on which the safety of Troy
depended.

until the flame draws near! Do not deny me:
35   You see how fervently I long for it!"
And he to me: "Since what you ask is worthy,

it shall be. But be still and let me speak;
for I know your mind already, and they perhaps
might scorn your manner of speaking, since they were Greek."[18]

40 And when the flame had come where time and place
seemed fitting to my Guide, I heard him say
these words to it: "O you two souls who pace

together in one flame!—if my days above
won favor in your eyes, if I have earned
45   however much or little of your love

in writing my High Verses, do not pass by,
but let one of you be pleased to tell where he,
having disappeared from the known world, went to die."

As if it fought the wind, the greater prong[19]
50   of the ancient flame began to quiver and hum;
then moving its tip as if it were the tongue

that spoke, gave out a voice above the roar.
"When I left Circe,"[20] it said, "who more than a year
detained me near Gaeta[21] long before

55 Aeneas came and gave the place that name,
not fondness for my son, nor reverence
for my aged father, nor Penelope's[22] claim

to the joys of love, could drive out of my mind
the lust to experience the far-flung world
60   and the failings and felicities of mankind.

I put out on the high and open sea
with a single ship and only those few souls
who stayed true when the rest deserted me.

As far as Morocco and as far as Spain
65   I saw both shores; and I saw Sardinia
and the other islands of the open main.

---

18. **since they were Greek:** The Greek heroes might have more respect for
Virgil, whose poetry commemorates their fame, than for Dante, who, as an
Italian, is a descendant of Aeneas and the conquered Trojans.
19. **the greater prong:** As both warrior and leader, Ulysses bore a greater guilt.
20. **Circe** [ser'sē]: enchantress who detained Ulysses on her island.
21. **Gaeta** [gä ä'tə]: coastal town in southeastern Italy, named for Aeneas' nurse.
22. **Penelope:** Ulysses' faithful wife.

I and my men were stiff and slow with age
    when we sailed at last into the narrow pass
    where, warning all men back from further voyage,

70 Hercules' Pillars[23] rose upon our sight.
    Already I had left Ceuta[24] on the left;
    Seville[25] now sank behind me on the right.

'Shipmates,' I said, 'who through a hundred thousand
    perils have reached the West, do not deny
75   to the brief remaining watch our senses stand

experience of the world beyond the sun.
    Greeks! You were not born to live like brutes,
    but to press on toward manhood and recognition!'

With this brief exhortation I made my crew
80   so eager for the voyage I could hardly
    have held them back from it when I was through;

and turning our stern toward morning, our bow toward night,
    we bore southwest out of the world of man;
    we made wings of our oars for our fool's flight.

85 That night we raised the other pole ahead[26]
    with all its stars, and ours had so declined
    it did not rise out of its ocean bed.

Five times since we had dipped our bending oars
    beyond the world, the light beneath the moon
90   had waxed and waned, when dead upon our course

we sighted, dark in space, a peak so tall[27]
    I doubted any man had seen the like.
    Our cheers were hardly sounded, when a squall

broke hard upon our bow from the new land:
95   three times it sucked the ship and the sea about
    as it pleased Another to order and command.

At the fourth, the poop rose and the bow went down
    till the sea closed over us and the light was gone."

---

23. **Hercules' Pillars:** now called the straits of Gibraltar, once presumed to
be the western limit beyond which no one could navigate.
24. **Ceuta** [soo′tä]: town on the African coast opposite Gibraltar.
25. **Seville:** region of southwestern Spain. With Seville and Ceuta behind
them, the sailors had passed into the Atlantic Ocean.
26. **raised . . . ahead:** had sailed south across the equator.
27. **a peak so tall:** the Mount of Purgatory, sighted after five months' sailing.

STUDY QUESTIONS

Recalling

1. In Canto I what three beasts does Dante encounter? How does he behave when he meets each? Which one threatens him most?
2. How does Dante come to recognize Virgil? What is Dante's reaction to Virgil's presence?
3. What does Dante ask of Virgil?
4. How far will Virgil be able to take Dante? Why will Dante later need "a worthier spirit" to take him further?
5. Where does Dante ask Virgil to lead him?
6. What does the inscription at the Gate of Hell mean, according to the "Master"?
7. What is the fault of those souls Dante first encounters after passing through the Gate of Hell? What is their fate?
8. Who are the sinners who share the dual flame? Who responds to Dante's questions?
9. How did Ulysses die, according to his own retelling of the story in Canto XXVI?

Interpreting

10. Given the description of the She-Wolf, why might Dante be fearful of her?
11. Considering the nature of their sin, why is the punishment accorded those souls just within the Gate of Hell appropriate?
12. What did Ulysses hope to achieve by his voyage? Would he have made the voyage if he had foreseen its end?

VIEWPOINT

Literary critic Erich Auerbach argues that Dante's vision of reality, in which the individual is important, provides a link between the medieval (God-centered) and the Renaissance (human-centered) views of the world.

In the history of modern European culture, there is, indeed, a constant . . . which is first discernible in Dante; namely, the idea (whatever its basis may be) that individual destiny is not meaningless, but is necessarily tragic and significant. . . .

■ How does *The Divine Comedy* embody a belief that individual destiny is important? Do these selections from Dante's work imply a tragic view of human destiny? Explain your answer.

LITERARY FOCUS

Allegory

Allegory is a form of extended metaphor in which the events, objects, and persons in a narrative represent moral qualities or specific abstract ideas, such as love, fear, and virtue. In Dante's allegory every element corresponds first to a literal reality; the allegorical reality then expresses a significance that is separate and coherent in itself.

For example, on the literal level Dante is the poet going on a journey, guided by Virgil, the poet of Rome. Beatrice is the beautiful woman adored by Dante. On the allegorical level, however, Dante represents the mortal soul experiencing after death the consequences of choices made in life. Virgil represents human reason and moral wisdom, and Beatrice at the end of the poem is an image of Christian wisdom illuminated by grace. Although *The Divine Comedy* is completely understandable on the literal level, Dante's purpose in writing it—to teach people the consequences of worldly actions in the hereafter—can best be appreciated through recognition of his masterful use of allegory.

Thinking About Allegory

■ As *The Divine Comedy* begins, Dante recounts being lost in a dark wood and is trying to climb up a hill toward the light. What do you think is the allegorical significance of this beginning?

COMPOSITION

Writing a Comparison/Contrast

■ In Canto XXVI ancient Greek values are juxtaposed against medieval Christian values. First define and then compare and contrast the values represented by Ulysses and by Dante, as you understand them. What is important to each? What kind of immortality does each seek? *For help with this assignment, refer to Lesson 2 in the Writing About Literature Handbook at the back of this book.*

Writing a Narrative

■ Compose a narrative in which you meet a favorite historical person who asks to spend the afternoon with you. First decide what you are going to do. Then describe your activities and the reactions of the person with you.

Miguel de Cervantes   *1547–1616*

The Spaniard Miguel de Cervantes [mē gel′ dä sər vän′tēz] created the best-known and best-loved knight who ever lived in the pages of a book, Don Quixote de la Mancha [don′ kē hō′tē dä lä män′chä]. Cervantes was born near Madrid to a family of minor nobility who moved from place to place in near poverty for most of Cervantes' childhood. In 1571, when he was twenty-four, Cervantes fought under Don John of Austria and was wounded at the Battle of Lepanto—"the battle of the century"—which drove the Turks from the eastern Mediterranean. On his journey back to Spain, Cervantes was captured by pirates, and he spent the next five years as a slave in North Africa. He made several futile efforts to escape, until at length he was ransomed and returned to Spain, where he found his family in severe financial difficulties. Cervantes never emerged from these financial misfortunes, and even the immediate success of *Don Quixote* did little to relieve his burdens. He died in poverty in 1616, the same year that England lost its greatest writer, William Shakespeare.

Author of the greatest work in Spanish literature, Cervantes showed only indifferent talent in the traditional literary forms of his time. He wrote a quantity of insignificant poetry, moderately good prose stories, and twenty or thirty plays, most of which have been lost. Yet *Don Quixote* was an instant best seller and has become an enduring classic. It is generally considered the world's first great novel.

Published in Madrid early in 1605, Part I of *Don Quixote* went through sixteen editions in Cervantes' lifetime and was translated into French and English. Along with Part II, which appeared in 1615, it became the world's most frequently published novel. Widely imitated, it spurred the English eighteenth-century vogue for **picaresque novels**, loosely strung satiric novels that recount episodes in the lives of adventurers or lovable rogues.

Yet *Don Quixote* is far more than a picaresque novel. Although it sets out to satirize the long and complicated medieval romances of chivalry, its title character soon transcends his role as a caricature. Along with his faithful squire, Sancho Panza, Don Quixote rides forth, carrying the improbable banner of right into a world full of probable wrongs. Cervantes allows the reader to decide whether it is better to accept life's injustices and appear sane or to attempt to battle life's various "windmills" and be considered crazy.

■ Someone once said that it is all right to daydream as long as you build foundations under your dream. Can you name some people who have done this?

Miguel de Cervantes

from **Don Quixote**

Translated by Samuel Putnam

Chapter 1

Which treats of the station in life and the pursuits of the famous gentleman, Don Quixote de la Mancha.

In a village of La Mancha,[1] the name of which I have no desire to recall, there lived not so long ago one of those gentlemen who always have a lance in the rack, an ancient buckler, a skinny nag, and a greyhound for the chase. A stew with more beef than mutton in it, chopped meat for his evening meal, scraps for a Saturday, lentils on Friday, and a young pigeon as a special delicacy for Sunday went to account for three quarters of his income. The rest of it he laid out on a broadcloth greatcoat and velvet stocking for feast days, with slippers to match, while the other days of the week he cut a figure in a suit of the finest homespun. Living with him were a housekeeper in her forties, a niece who was not yet twenty, and a lad of the field and market place who saddled his horse for him and wielded the pruning knife.

This gentleman of ours was close on to fifty, of a robust constitution but with little flesh on his bones and a face that was lean and gaunt. He was noted for his early rising, being very fond of the hunt. They will try to tell you that his surname was Quijada or Quesada—there is some difference of opinion among those who have written on the subject—but according to the most likely conjectures we are to understand that it was really Quejana. But all this means very little so far as our story is concerned, providing that in the telling of it we do not depart one iota from the truth.

You may know, then, that the aforesaid gentleman, on those occasions when he was at leisure, which was most of the year around, was in the habit of reading books of chivalry[2] with such pleasure and devotion as to lead him almost wholly to forget the life of a hunter and even the administration of his estate. So great was his curiosity and infatuation in this regard that he even sold many acres of tillable land in order to be able to buy and read the books that he loved, and he would carry home with him as many of them as he could obtain.

Of all those that he thus devoured, none pleased him so well as the ones that had been composed by the famous Feliciano de Silva, whose lucid prose style and involved conceits were as precious to him as pearls; especially when he came to read those tales of love and amorous challenges that are to be met with in many places, such a passage as the following, for example: "The reason of the unreason that afflicts my reason, in such a manner weakens my reason that I with reason lament me of your comeliness." And he was similarly affected when his eyes fell upon such lines as these: ". . . the high heaven of your divinity divinely fortifies you with the stars and renders you deserving of that desert your greatness doth deserve."

The poor fellow used to lie awake nights in an effort to disentangle the meaning and make sense out of passages such as these, although Aristotle[3] himself would not have been able to understand them, even if he had been resurrected for that sole purpose. He was not at ease in his mind over those wounds that Don

---

1. **La Mancha:** in Cervantes' time a poor and backward region of south-central Spain.

2. **books of chivalry:** medieval stories of knighthood and courtly love. Cervantes refers to many authors, characters, and events from such books.
3. **Aristotle:** Greek philosopher (384–322 B.C.).

Belianís gave and received; for no matter how great the surgeons who treated him, the poor fellow must have been left with his face and his entire body covered with marks and scars. Nevertheless, he was grateful to the author for closing the book with the promise of an interminable adventure to come; many a time he was tempted to take up his pen and literally finish the tale as had been promised, and he undoubtedly would have done so, and would have succeeded at it very well, if his thoughts had not been constantly occupied with other things of greater moment.

He often talked it over with the village curate, who was a learned man, a graduate of Sigüenza,[4] and they would hold long discussions as to who had been the better knight, Palmerin of England or Amadis of Gaul; but Master Nicholas, the barber of the same village, was in the habit of saying that no one could come up to the Knight of Phoebus, and that if anyone *could* compare with him it was Don Galaor, brother of Amadis of Gaul, for Galaor was ready for anything—he was none of your finical knights who went around whimpering as his brother did, and in point of valor he did not lag behind him.

In short, our gentleman became so immersed in his reading that he spent whole nights from sundown to sunup and his days from dawn to dusk in poring over his books, until, finally, from so little sleeping and so much reading, his brain dried up and he went completely out of his mind. He had filled his imagination with everything that he had read, with enchantments, knightly encounters, battles, challenges, wounds, with tales of love and its torments, and all sorts of impossible things, and as a result had come to believe that all these fictitious happenings were true; they were more real to him than anything else in the world. He would remark that the Cid Ruy Díaz had been a very good knight, but there was no comparison between him and the Knight of the Flaming Sword, who with a single backward stroke had cut in half two fierce and monstrous giants. He preferred Bernardo del Carpio, who at Roncesvalles had slain Roland despite the charm the latter bore, availing himself of the stratagem which Hercules employed when he strangled Antaeus, the son of Earth, in his arms.

He had much good to say for Morgante who, though he belonged to the haughty, overbearing race of giants, was of an affable disposition and well brought up. But, above all, he cherished an admiration for Rinaldo of Montalbán, especially as he beheld him sallying forth from his castle to rob all those that crossed his path, or when he thought of him overseas stealing the image of Mohammed which, so the story has it, was all of gold. And he would have liked very well to have had his fill of kicking that traitor Galalón, a privilege for which he would have given his housekeeper with his niece thrown into the bargain.

At last, when his wits were gone beyond repair, he came to conceive the strangest idea that ever occurred to any madman in this world. It now appeared to him fitting and necessary, in order to win a greater amount of honor for himself and serve his country at the same time, to become a knight errant[5] and roam the world on horseback, in a suit of armor; he would go in quest of adventures, by way of putting into practice all that he had read in his books; he would right every manner of wrong, placing himself in situations of the greatest peril such as would redound to the eternal glory of his name. As a reward for his valor and the might of his arm, the poor fellow could already see himself crowned Emperor of Trebizond at the very least; and so, carried away by the strange pleasure that he found in such thoughts as these, he at once set about putting his plan into effect.

The first thing he did was to burnish up some old pieces of armor, left him by his great-

---

4. **Sigüenza** [sē gwen′zä]: insignificant center of learning.

5. **knight errant:** wandering knight in search of adventures to add to his reputation.

grandfather, which for ages had lain in a corner, moldering and forgotten. He polished and adjusted them as best he could, and then he noticed that one very important thing was lacking: there was no closed helmet, but only a morion, or visorless headpiece, with turned-up brim of the kind foot soldiers wore. His ingenuity, however, enabled him to remedy this, and he proceeded to fashion out of cardboard a kind of half-helmet, which, when attached to the morion, gave the appearance of a whole one. True, when he went to see if it was strong enough to withstand a good slashing blow, he was somewhat disappointed; for when he drew his sword and gave it a couple of thrusts, he succeeded only in undoing a whole week's labor. The ease with which he had hewed it to bits disturbed him no little, and he decided to make it over. This time he placed a few strips of iron on the inside, and then, convinced that it was strong enough, refrained from putting it to any further test; instead, he adopted it then and there as the finest helmet ever made.

After this, he went out to have a look at his nag; and although the animal had more *cuartos,* or cracks, in its hoof than there are quarters in a real,[6] and more blemishes than Gonela's[7] steed which *tantum pellis et ossa fuit,*[8] it nonetheless looked to its master like a far better horse than Alexander's Bucephalus or the Babieca of the Cid. He spent all of four days in trying to think up a name for his mount; for—so he told himself—seeing that it belonged to so famous and worthy a knight, there was no reason why it should not have a name of equal renown. The kind of name he wanted was one that would at once indicate what the nag had been before it came to belong to a knight errant and what its present status was; for it stood to reason that, when the master's worldly condition changed, his

6. **real** [rä äl′]: old Spanish coin. There were eight quarters in a real.
7. **Gonela's:** referring to a court jester in Italy in the fifteenth century.
8. **tantum pellis et ossa fuit** [tän′tōōm pel′ is et′ ô′sä fōō′it]: Latin for "was just skin and bones."

horse also ought to have a famous, high-sounding appellation, one suited to the new order of things and the new profession that it was to follow.

After he in his memory and imagination had made up, struck out, and discarded many names, now adding to and now subtracting from the list, he finally hit upon "Rocinante,"[9] a name that impressed him as being sonorous and at the same time indicative of what the steed had been when it was but a hack, whereas now it was nothing other than the first and foremost of all the hacks in the world.

Having found a name for his horse that pleased his fancy, he then desired to do as much for himself, and this required another week, and by the end of that period he had made up his mind that he was henceforth to be known as Don Quixote,[10] which, as has been stated, has led the authors of this veracious history to assume that his real name must undoubtedly have been Quijada, and not Quesada as others would have it. But remembering that the valiant Amadis was not content to call himself that and nothing more, but added the name of his kingdom and fatherland that he might make it famous also, and thus came to take the name Amadis of Gaul, so our good knight chose to add his place of origin and become "Don Quixote de la Mancha"; for by this means, as he saw it, he was making very plain his lineage and was conferring honor upon his country by taking its name as his own.

And so, having polished up his armor and made the morion over into a closed helmet, and having given himself and his horse a name, he naturally found but one thing lacking still: he must seek out a lady of whom he could become enamored; for a knight errant without a ladylove was like a tree without leaves or fruit, a body without a soul.

"If," he said to himself, "as a punishment for my sins or by a stroke of fortune I should come upon some giant hereabouts, a thing that very commonly happens to knights errant, and if I should slay him in a hand-to-hand encounter or perhaps cut him in two, or, finally, if I should vanquish and subdue him, would it not be well to have someone to whom I may send him as a present, in order that he, if he is living, may come in, fall upon his knees in front of my sweet lady, and say in a humble and submissive tone of voice, 'I, lady, am the giant Caraculiambro, lord of the island Malindrania, who has been overcome in single combat by that knight who never can be praised enough, Don Quixote de la Mancha, the same who sent me to present myself before your Grace that your Highness may dispose of me as you see fit'?"

Oh, how our good knight reveled in this speech, and more than ever when he came to think of the name that he should give his lady! As the story goes, there was a very good-looking farm girl who lived near by, with whom he had once been smitten, although it is generally believed that she never knew or suspected it. Her name was Aldonza Lorenzo, and it seemed to him that she was the one upon whom he should bestow the title of mistress of his thoughts. For her he wished a name that should not be incongruous with his own and that would convey the suggestion of a princess or a great lady; and accordingly, he resolved to call her "Dulcinea[11] del Toboso," she being a native of that place. A musical name to his ears, out of the ordinary and significant, like the others he had chosen for himself and his appurtenances.

from **Chapter 2**
Which treats of the first sally that the ingenious Don Quixote made from his native heath.

Having, then, made all these preparations, he did not wish to lose any time in putting his plan into effect, for he could not but blame himself for what the world was losing by his delay, so many were the wrongs that were to

---

9. **Rocinante:** literally, a worn-out horse of little worth, originating from *rocín,* a nag.
10. **Quixote:** a piece of armor that protects the thigh.

11. **Dulcinea** [dळ्l'sē nā'ə]: a name meaning "the sweet or pleasing one."

be righted, the grievances to be redressed, the abuses to be done away with, and the duties to be performed. Accordingly, without informing anyone of his intention and without letting anyone see him, he set out one morning before daybreak on one of those very hot days in July. Donning all his armor, mounting Rocinante, adjusting his ill-contrived helmet, bracing his shield on his arm, and taking up his lance, he sallied forth by the back gate of his stable yard into the open countryside. It was with great contentment and joy that he saw how easily he had made a beginning toward the fulfillment of his desire.

No sooner was he out on the plain, however, than a terrible thought assailed him, one that all but caused him to abandon the enterprise he had undertaken. This occurred when he suddenly remembered that he had never formally been dubbed a knight, and so, in accordance with the law of knighthood, was not permitted to bear arms against one who had a right to that title. And even if he had been, as a novice knight he would have had to wear white armor, without any device on his shield, until he should have earned one by his exploits. These thoughts led him to waver in his purpose, but, madness prevailing over reason, he resolved to have himself knighted by the first person he met, as many others had done if what he had read in those books that he had at home was true. And so far as white armor was concerned, he would scour his own the first chance that offered until it shone whiter than any ermine. With this he became more tranquil and continued on his way, letting his horse take whatever path it chose, for he believed that therein lay the very essence of adventures. . . .

As his adventures continue, Don Quixote encounters a bewildered innkeeper and persuades the man to "knight" him. He also breaks his "helmet" in the course of his exploits. His travels are cut short by his friends, who trick him into returning home, where he is treated like a madman and not permitted to read his "dangerous" books about chivalry.

from Chapter 7

Of the second sally of our good knight, Don Quixote de la Mancha.

. . . He remained at home very tranquilly for a couple of weeks, without giving sign of any desire to repeat his former madness. During that time he had most pleasant conversations with his two old friends, the curate and the barber, on the point he had raised to the effect that what the world needed most was knights errant and a revival of chivalry. The curate would occasionally contradict him and again would give in, for it was only by means of this artifice that he could carry on a conversation with him at all.

In the meanwhile Don Quixote was bringing his powers of persuasion to bear upon a farmer who lived near by, a good man—if this title may be applied to one who is poor—but with very few wits in his head. The short of it is, by pleas and promises, he got the hapless rustic to agree to ride forth with him and serve him as his squire. Among other things, Don Quixote told him that he ought to be more than willing to go, because no telling what adventure might occur which would win them an island, and then he (the farmer) would be left to be the governor of it. As a result of these and other similar assurances, Sancho Panza forsook his wife and children and consented to take upon himself the duties of squire to his neighbor.

Next, Don Quixote set out to raise some money, and by selling this thing and pawning that and getting the worst of the bargain always, he finally scraped together a reasonable amount. He also asked a friend of his for the loan of a buckler and patched up his broken helmet as well as he could. He advised his squire, Sancho, of the day and hour when they were to take the road and told him to see to laying in a supply of those things that were most necessary, and, above all, not to forget the saddlebags. Sancho replied that he would see to all this and added that he was also thinking of taking along with him a very good ass that he had, as he was not much used to going on foot.

With regard to the ass, Don Quixote had to do a little thinking, trying to recall if any knight errant had ever had a squire thus asininely mounted. He could not think of any, but nevertheless he decided to take Sancho with the intention of providing him with a nobler steed as soon as occasion offered; he had but to appropriate the horse of the first discourteous knight he met. Having furnished himself with shirts and all the other things that the innkeeper had recommended, he and Panza rode forth one night unseen by anyone and without taking leave of wife and children, housekeeper or niece. They went so far that by the time morning came they were safe from discovery had a hunt been started for them.

Mounted on his ass, Sancho Panza rode along like a patriarch, with saddlebags and flask, his mind set upon becoming governor of that island that his master had promised him. Don Quixote determined to take the same route and road over the Campo de Montiel that he had followed on his first journey; but he was not so uncomfortable this time, for it was early morning and the sun's rays fell upon them slantingly and accordingly did not tire them too much.

"Look, Sir Knight errant," said Sancho, "your Grace should not forget that island you promised me; for no matter how big it is, I'll be able to govern it right enough."

"I would have you know, friend Sancho Panza," replied Don Quixote, "that among the knights errant of old it was a very common custom to make their squires governors of the islands or the kingdoms that they won, and I am resolved that in my case so pleasing a usage shall not fall into desuetude. I even mean to go them one better; for they very often, perhaps most of the time, waited until their squires were old men who had had their fill of serving their masters during bad days and worse nights, whereupon they would give them the title of count, or marquis at most, of some valley or province more or less. But if you live and I live, it well may be that within

a week I shall win some kingdom with others dependent upon it, and it will be the easiest thing in the world to crown you king of one of them. You need not marvel at this, for all sorts of unforeseen things happen to knights like me, and I may readily be able to give you even more than I have promised."

"In that case," said Sancho Panza, "if by one of those miracles of which your Grace was speaking I should become king, I would certainly send for Juana Gutiérrez,[12] my old lady, to come and be my queen, and the young ones could be infantes."[13]

"There is no doubt about it," Don Quixote assured him.

"Well, I doubt it," said Sancho, "for I think that even if God were to rain kingdoms upon the earth, no crown would sit well on the head of Mari Gutiérrez, for I am telling you, sir, as a queen she is not worth two maravedis.[14] She would do better as a countess, God help her."

"Leave everything to God, Sancho," said Don Quixote, "and he will give you whatever is most fitting; but I trust you will not be so pusillanimous as to be content with anything less than the title of viceroy."

"That I will not," said Sancho Panza, "especially seeing that I have in your Grace so illustrious a master who can give me all that is suitable to me and all that I can manage."

from Chapter 8

Of the good fortune which the valorous Don Quixote had in the terrifying and never-before-imagined adventure of the windmills, along with other events that deserve to be suitably recorded.

At this point they caught sight of thirty or forty windmills which were standing on the plain there, and no sooner had Don Quixote laid eyes upon them than he turned to his squire and said, "Fortune is guiding our affairs

---

12. **Juana Gutiérrez** [hwä′nä gōō tē är′ez]: Sancho's wife, also referred to as Mari Gutiérrez and other names.
13. **infantes** [ēn fän′tās]: Spanish princes and princesses.
14. **maravedis** [mä′rä vä′dēs]: copper coins of little value.

better than we could have wished; for you see there before you, friend Sancho Panza, some thirty or more lawless giants with whom I mean to do battle. I shall deprive them of their lives, and with the spoils from this encounter we shall begin to enrich ourselves; for this is righteous warfare, and it is a great service to God to remove so accursed a breed from the face of the earth.

"What giants?" said Sancho Panza.

"Those that you see there," replied his master, "those with the long arms, some of which are as much as two leagues in length."

"But look, your Grace, those are not giants but windmills, and what appear to be arms are their wings which, when whirled in the breeze, cause the millstone to go."

"It is plain to be seen," said Don Quixote, "that you have had little experience in this matter of adventures. If you are afraid, go off to one side and say your prayers while I am engaging them in fierce, unequal combat."

Saying this, he gave spurs to his steed Rocinante, without paying any heed to Sancho's warning that these were truly windmills and not giants that he was riding forth to attack. Nor even when he was close upon them did he perceive what they really were, but shouted at the top of his lungs, "Do not seek to flee, cowards and vile creatures that you are, for it is but a single knight with whom you have to deal!"

At that moment a little wind came up and the big wings began turning.

"Though you flourish as many arms as did the giant Briareus," said Don Quixote when he perceived this, "you still shall have to answer to me."

He thereupon commended himself with all his heart to his lady Dulcinea, beseeching her to succor him in this peril; and, being well covered with his shield and with his lance at rest, he bore down upon them at a full gallop and fell upon the first mill that stood in his way, giving a thrust at the wing, which was whirling at such a speed that his lance was broken into bits and both horse and horseman went rolling over the plain, very much battered indeed. Sancho upon his donkey came hurrying to his master's assistance as fast as he could, but when he reached the spot, the knight was unable to move, so great was the shock with which he and Rocinante had hit the ground.

"God help us!" exclaimed Sancho, "did I not tell your Grace to look well, that those were nothing but windmills, a fact which no one could fail to see unless he had other mills of the same sort in his head?"

"Be quiet, friend Sancho," said Don Quixote. "Such are the fortunes of war, which more than any other are subject to constant change. What is more, when I come to think of it, I am sure that this must be the work of that magician Frestón, the one who robbed me of my study and my books, and who has thus changed the giants into windmills in order to deprive me of the glory of overcoming them, so great is the enmity that he bears me; but in the end his evil arts shall not prevail against this trusty sword of mine."

"May God's will be done," was Sancho Panza's response. And with the aid of his squire the knight was once more mounted on Rocinante, who stood there with one shoulder half out of joint. And so, speaking of the adventure that had just befallen them, they continued along the Puerto Lápice highway; for there, Don Quixote said, they could not fail to find many and varied adventures, this being a much-traveled thoroughfare. The only thing was, the knight was exceedingly downcast over the loss of his lance.

"I remember," he said to his squire, "having read of a Spanish knight by the name of Diego Pérez de Vargas, who, having broken his sword in battle, tore from an oak a heavy bough or branch and with it did such feats of valor that day, and pounded so many Moors,[15] that he came to be known as Machuca, and he and his descendants from that day forth have been called Vargas y Machuca.[16] I tell you this because I, too, intend to provide myself with just such a bough as the one he wielded, and with it I propose to do such exploits that you shall deem yourself fortunate to have been found worthy to come with me and behold and witness things that are almost beyond belief."

"God's will be done," said Sancho. "I believe everything that your Grace says; but straighten yourself up in the saddle a little, for you seem to be slipping down on one side, owing, no doubt, to the shaking up that you received in your fall."

"Ah, that is the truth," replied Don Quixote, "and if I do not speak of my sufferings, it is for the reason that it is not permitted knights errant to complain of any wound whatsoever, even though their bowels may be dropping out."

"If that is the way it is," said Sancho, "I have nothing more to say; but, God knows, it would suit me better if your Grace did complain when something hurts him. I can assure you that I mean to do so, over the least little thing that ails me—that is, unless the same rule applies to squires as well."

Don Quixote laughed long and heartily over Sancho's simplicity, telling him that he might complain as much as he liked and where and when he liked, whether he had good cause or not; for he had read nothing to the contrary in the ordinances of chivalry. Sancho then called his master's attention to the fact that it was time to eat. The knight replied that he himself had no need of food at the moment, but his squire might eat whenever he chose. Having been granted this permission, Sancho seated himself as best he could upon his beast, and, taking out from his saddlebags the provisions that he had stored there, he rode along leisurely behind his master, munching his victuals and taking a good, hearty swig now and then at the leather flask in a manner that might well have caused the biggest-bellied tavernkeeper of Málaga to envy him. Between draughts he gave not so much as a thought to any promise that his master might have made him, nor did he look upon it as any hardship, but rather as good sport, to go in quest of adventures however hazardous they might be.

---

15. **Moors:** Moslems of North Africa who invaded Spain.
16. **Machuca** [mä chōō′kä]: the Hammerer.

STUDY QUESTIONS

Recalling

1. What physical description of Don Quixote is provided in the second paragraph of Chapter 1? What does he read in his leisure time?
2. What strange idea does Don Quixote conceive when his wits are "gone beyond repair"? What does he plan to "right"?
3. What does Don Quixote wear on his journey? What does he rename his horse, and why? What does he call himself?
4. Whom does Don Quixote choose as his lady? Why does he believe he needs a lady? What name does he give her?
5. How is Sancho Panza described in the second paragraph of Chapter 7? For what reason does he agree to accompany Don Quixote?
6. In Chapter 8 identify three phrases that Don Quixote uses to describe the windmills.
7. What does Sancho Panza exclaim after Don Quixote falls to the ground? How does Don Quixote explain the windmills after his fall?

Interpreting

8. What aspects of Don Quixote's character are mildly mocked in the first chapter? What else does the chapter criticize?
9. Compare Don Quixote and Sancho Panza with respect to their stations in life, their motives in sallying forth, and their general attitudes toward life.
10. What might the windmills represent?
11. What virtues does Don Quixote possess? What does the fact that he is considered mad suggest about his society?

Extending

12. What parallels can you draw between Don Quixote's time and today's society?

VIEWPOINT

Joseph Wood Krutch, a noted literary critic, explains the value of the developing relationship between Don Quixote and Sancho Panza:

Conceived at first as no more than a simple-minded foil to his extravagant master, the latter [Sancho Panza] grows wiser in one kind of wisdom as the Don grows wiser in another until, though the one is mad and the other a clown, they have come to represent the two types of human wisdom—that which knows how things really are and that which knows how they ought to be.

—*Five Masters*

■ Explain in your own words the two types of wisdom Krutch is talking about. Do you agree that Don Quixote and Sancho Panza each represents one of these types of wisdom? Support your answer using evidence from the selection.

LITERARY FOCUS

Caricature

A **caricature** is a humorous picture that exaggerates or distorts certain qualities of a person in order to create a ridiculous effect. In literature caricature is frequently associated with satire or parody. Its true intent is not to criticize just one individual but rather to ridicule a societal group or a social practice. The ultimate aim of caricature is to ridicule in order to correct a weakness.

Thinking About Caricature

1. In what sense is Don Quixote a caricature? What things is Cervantes parodying or satirizing in Don Quixote's character?
2. In what sense is Don Quixote not a caricature?

VOCABULARY STUDY

Words from Fictional Names

From the famous fictional character Don Quixote comes the English word *quixotic*, which means "idealistic but impractical." Using a good dictionary, explain the meanings and origins of the following words.

1. babbitt
2. braggadocio
3. chanticleer
4. ignoramus
5. knickerbocker
6. malapropism
7. pantaloons
8. ragamuffin
9. scrooge
10. yahoo

COMPARING WRITERS

■ Just as Shakespeare is frequently named the greatest writer in English, Cervantes is often cited as the most famous writer in Spanish. What do these two authors have in common that would warrant such evaluations? Consider especially the understanding of human nature that each author displays.

Molière *1622–1673*

The great comic playwright Molière took to task all that was false, affected, and excessive in his society. So inventive was Molière as a dramatist that present-day comedy has found little to improve upon in his work.

Born in Paris into an affluent bourgeois, or middle-class, family, Jean Baptiste Poquelin, who later took the stage name Molière, received a solid education from the liberal and scholarly Jesuits. He studied law for a time, but his early fascination with the theater led him to establish his own acting troupe at the age of twenty-one. With no experience, he soon went bankrupt and joined a company of traveling actors. Becoming director of the group in 1650, Molière wandered through France, learning the vast repertoire of tragedy and comedy and observing a great deal about human nature. Returning to Paris in 1658, Molière gained favor at the court of Louis XIV, the Sun King. For the next fifteen years he managed his company, acted leading roles, directed, and found time to write twenty-nine plays. Among Molière's greatest works are *Tartuffe, or The Imposter* (1664), *The Misanthrope* (1666), *The Miser* (1668), and *The Imaginary Invalid* (1673). On February 17, 1673, during the final scene of a performance of *The Imaginary Invalid,* Molière, long ailing, suffered a hemorrhage on stage; he finished the performance and died shortly thereafter.

The basis of Molière's comedy is realism, which portrays human nature on stage with all the little quirks, graces, flaws, and inconsistencies that can be observed in real life. Yet to gain dramatic effectiveness, Molière simplifies psychology, creating universal types and exaggerating the dominant characteristics of those whose behavior he exposes. Knowing that he could not openly attack the settled opinions of either noble or bourgeois audiences, Molière flattered his spectators by praising the common sense of the average individual while mocking stereotypical characters such as the miser. In several plays, including *The Flying Doctor,* he attacks the pretensions of physicians and of the learned, suggesting that nature may be the better and wiser healer.

■ You probably know someone who pretends to be smarter, richer, or more popular than he or she is. Describe your reaction to such a person.

Gorgibus, Sganarelle, Lucile, and Sabine, in a recent production of *The Flying Doctor*.

Molière

The Flying Doctor

Translated by Albert Bermel

CHARACTERS

GORGIBUS: respectable, comfortable, but simple-minded citizen
LUCILE: Gorgibus' daughter
SABINE [sa bēn´]: Gorbigus' niece

VALÈRE [va lär´]: young man in love with Lucile
SGANARELLE [sga´nə rel´]: servant to Valère
GROS-RENÉ [grō´rə nā´]: servant to Gorgibus
A LAWYER

A street in a small French town.

[VALÈRE, *a young man, is talking to* SABINE, *a young woman, in front of the house of* GORGIBUS, *her uncle.*]

VALÈRE. Sabine, what do you advise me to do?

SABINE: We'll have to work fast. My uncle is determined to make Lucile marry this rich man, Villebrequin, and he's pushed the preparations so far that the marriage would have taken place today if my cousin were not in love with you. But she is—she has told me so—and since my greedy uncle is forcing our hand, we've

come up with a device for putting off the wedding. Lucile is pretending to be ill, and the old man, who'll believe almost anything, has sent me for a doctor. If you have a friend we can trust, I'll take him to my uncle and he can suggest that Lucile is not getting nearly enough fresh air. The old boy will then let her live in the pavilion[1] at the end of our garden, and you can meet her secretly, marry her, and leave my uncle to take out his anger on Villebrequin.

VALÈRE. But where can I find a doctor who will

---

1. **pavilion:** summer house.

be sympathetic to me and risk his reputation? Frankly, I can't think of a single one.

SABINE. I was wondering if you could disguise your valet? It'll be easy for him to fool the old man.

VALÈRE. If you knew my valet as I do—He's so dense he'll ruin everything. Still, I can't think of anybody else. I'll try to find him. [SABINE *leaves.*] Where can I start to look for the half-wit? [SGANARELLE *comes in, playing intently with a yo-yo.*] Sganarelle, my dear boy, I'm delighted to see you. I need you for an important assignment. But I don't know what you can do—

SGANARELLE. Don't worry, Master, I can do anything. I can handle any assignment, especially important ones. Give me a difficult job. Ask me to find out what time it is. Or to check on the price of butter at the market. Or to water your horse. You'll soon see what I can do.

VALÈRE. This is more complicated. I want you to impersonate a doctor.

SGANARELLE. A doctor! You know I'll do anything you want, Master, but when it comes to impersonating a doctor, I couldn't do it if I tried—wouldn't know how to start. I think you're making fun of me.

VALÈRE. If you care to try, I'll give you one hundred francs.[2]

SGANARELLE. One hundred whole francs, just for pretending to be a doctor? No, Master, it's impossible. You see I don't have the brains for it. I'm not subtle enough; I'm not even bright. So that's settled. I impersonate a doctor. Where?

VALÈRE. You know Gorgibus? His daughter is lying in there ill—No, it's no use; you'll only confuse matters.

SGANARELLE. I bet I can confuse matters as well as all the doctors in this town put together. Or

kill patients as easily. You know the old saying, "After you're dead, the doctor comes." When I take a hand there'll be a new saying: "After the doctor comes, you're dead." Now I think it over, though, it's not that easy to play a doctor. What if something goes wrong?

VALÈRE. What can go wrong? Gorgibus is a simple man, not to say stupid, and you can dazzle him by talking about Hippocrates and Galen.[3] Put on a bold front.

SGANARELLE. In other words, talk about philosophy and mathematics and the like. Leave it to me, Master; if he's a fool, as you say, I think I can swing it. All I need is a doctor's cloak and a few instructions. And also my license to practice, or to put it another way, those hundred francs. [*They go out together.*]

[GORGIBUS *enters with his fat valet,* GROS-RENÉ.]

GORGIBUS. Hurry away and find a doctor. My daughter's sick. Hurry.

GROS-RENÉ. The trouble is you're trying to marry her off to an old man when she wants a young man; that's the only thing making her sick. Don't you see any connection between the appetite and the illness?

GORGIBUS. I can see that the illness will delay the wedding. Get a move on.

GROS-RENÉ. All this running about and my stomach's crying out for a new inner lining of food and now I have to wait for it. I need the doctor for myself as much as for your daughter. I'm in a desperate state. [*He lumbers off.*]

[SABINE *comes in with* SGANARELLE *behind her.*]

SABINE. Uncle, I have good news. I've brought a remarkably skilled doctor with me, a man who has traveled across the world and knows the medical secrets of Asia and Africa. He'll certainly be able to cure Lucile. As luck would

---

2. **francs:** A franc is the French monetary unit, now worth about twenty cents.

3. **Hippocrates** [hi pok′rə tēz] (460–370 B.C.) **and Galen** [gā′lən] (A.D. 130–200): Ancient Greek physicians.

have it, somebody pointed him out to me and I knew you'd want to meet him. He's so clever that I wish I were ill myself so that he could cure me.

GORGIBUS. Where is he?

SABINE. Standing right behind me. [*She moves away.*] There he is.

GORGIBUS. Thank you so much for coming, Doctor. I'll take you straight to my daughter, who is unwell. I'm putting all my trust in you.

SGANARELLE. Hippocrates has said—and Galen has confirmed it with many persuasive arguments—that when a girl is not in good health she must be sick. You are right to put your trust in me, for I am the greatest, the most brilliant, the most doctoral physician in the vegetable, mineral, and animal kingdoms.

GORGIBUS. I'm overjoyed to hear it.

SGANARELLE. No ordinary physician am I, no common medico. In my opinion, all others are quacks. I have peculiar talents. I have secrets. *Salamalec* and *shalom aleichem. Nil nisi bonum? Si, Signor. Nein, mein Herr. Para siempre.*[4] But let us begin. [*He takes* GORGIBUS' *pulse.*]

SABINE. He's not the patient. His daughter is. She may be up by now. I'll bring her out. [*She goes into the house and brings* LUCILE *back with her.*]

SGANARELLE. How do you do, Mademoiselle? So you are sick?

LUCILE. Yes, Doctor.

SGANARELLE. That is a striking sign that you are not well. Do you feel pains in your head, in your kidneys?

LUCILE. Yes, Doctor.

SGANARELLE. Very good. As one great physician has said in regard to the nature of animal life—

well—he said many things. We must attribute this to the interconnections between the humors and the vapors.[5] For example, since melancholy is the natural enemy of joy, and since the bile that spreads through the body makes us turn yellow, and since there is nothing more inimical to good health than sickness, we may conclude with that great man that your daughter is indisposed. Let me write you a prescription.

GORGIBUS. Quick! A table, paper, some ink—

SGANARELLE. Is there anybody here who knows how to write?

GORGIBUS. Don't you?

SGANARELLE. I have so many things to think of I forget half of them. Now it's obvious to me that your daughter needs fresh air and open prospects.

GORGIBUS. We have a very beautiful garden and a pavilion with some rooms that look out on it. If you agree, I can have her stay there.

SGANARELLE. Let us examine this dwelling. [*They start to go out. The* LAWYER *appears.*]

LAWYER. Monsieur Gorgibus—

GORGIBUS. Your servant, Monsieur.

LAWYER. I hear that your daughter is sick. May I offer my services, as a friend of the family?

GORGIBUS. I have the most scholarly doctor you ever met looking into this.

LAWYER. Really? I wonder if I might be able to meet him, however briefly?

[GORGIBUS *beckons to* SGANARELLE. LUCILE *and* SABINE *have moved offstage.*]

GORGIBUS. Doctor, I would like you to meet one of my dear friends, who is a lawyer and would like the privilege of conversing with you.

SGANARELLE. I wish I could spare the time,

---

4. *Salamalec . . . siempre:* series of unconnected phrases in Arabic, Hebrew, Latin, Italian, German, and Spanish.

5. **the humors and the vapors:** body fluids and gases once thought to control health and disposition.

Monsieur, but I dare not neglect my patients. Please forgive me.

[*He tries to go. The* LAWYER *holds his sleeve.*]

LAWYER. My friend Gorgibus has intimated, Monsieur, that your learning and abilities are formidable, and I am honored to make your acquaintance. I therefore take the liberty of saluting you in your noble work, and trust that it may resolve itself well. Those who excel in any branch of knowledge are worthy of all praise, but particularly those who practice medicine, not only because of its utility, but because it contains within itself other branches of knowledge, all of which render a perfect familiarity with it almost impossible to achieve. As Hippocrates so well observes in his first aphorism, "Life is short, art is long, opportunity fleeting, experiment perilous, judgment difficult: *Vita brevis, ars vero longa, occasio autem praeceps, experimentum periculosum, judicium difficile.*"[6]

SGANARELLE. [*Confidentially to* GORGIBUS.] Ficile, bicile, uptus, downtus, inandaboutus, wrigglo, gigolo.[7]

LAWYER. You are not one of those doctors who apply themselves to so-called rational or dogmatic medicine, and I am sure that you conduct your work with unusual success. Experience is the great teacher: *experientia magistra rerum.* The first men who practiced medicine were so esteemed that their daily cures earned them the status of gods on earth. One must not condemn a doctor who does not restore his patients to health, for healing may not be effected by his remedies and wisdom alone. Ovid[8] remarks, "Sometimes the ill is stronger than art and learning combined." Monsieur, I will not detain you longer. I have enjoyed this dialogue and am more impressed than before with your percipience and breadth of knowledge. I take my leave, hoping that I may have the pleasure of conversing with you further at your leisure. I am sure that your time is precious, and . . .

[*He goes off, walking backwards, still talking, waving good-bye.*]

GORGIBUS. How did he strike you?

SGANARELLE. He's moderately well informed. If I had more time I could engage him in a spirited discussion on some sublime and elevated topic. However, I must go. What is this?

[GORGIBUS *is tucking some money into his hand.*]

GORGIBUS. Believe me, Doctor, I know how much I owe you.

SGANARELLE. You must be joking, Monsieur Gorgibus. I am no mercenary. [*He takes the money.*] Thank you very much.

[GORGIBUS *goes off, and* SGANARELLE *drops his doctor's cloak and hat at the edge of the stage, just as* VALÈRE *reappears.*]

VALÈRE. Sganarelle, how did it go? I've been worried. I was looking for you. Did you ruin the plan?

SGANARELLE. Marvel of marvels. I played the part so well that Gorgibus thought I knew what I was talking about—and paid me. I looked at his home and told him that his daughter needed air, and he's moved her into the little house at the far end of his garden. You can visit her at your pleasure.

VALÈRE. You've made me very happy, Sganarelle. I'm going to her now. [*He rushes away.*]

SGANARELLE. That Gorgibus is a bigger dimwit than I am to let me get away with a trick like that. Save me—here he comes again. I'll have to talk fast.

[GORGIBUS *returns.*]

GORGIBUS. Good morning, Monsieur.

---

6. *Vita brevis . . . difficile:* translation in Latin of what the lawyer has just said.
7. **Ficile . . . gigolo:** Sganarelle's response to the lawyer is a series of nonsense words with Latin-sounding endings.
8. **Ovid** (43 B.C.–A.D. 17): classical Roman poet famous for his writings about love.

SGANARELLE. Monsieur, you see before you a poor lad in despair. Have you come across a doctor who arrived in town a short while ago and cures people miraculously?

GORGIBUS. Yes, I've met him. He just left my house.

SGANARELLE. I am his brother. We are identical twins and people sometimes take one of us for the other.

GORGIBUS. Heaven help me if I didn't nearly make the same mistake. What is your name?

SGANARELLE. Narcissus, Monsieur, at your service. I should explain that once, when I was in his study, I accidentally knocked over two containers perched on the edge of his table. He flew into such a rage that he threw me out and swore he never wanted to see me again. So here I am now, a poor boy without means or connections.

GORGIBUS. Don't worry; I'll put in a good word for you. I'm a friend of his; I promise to bring you together again. As soon as I see him, I'll speak to him about it.

SGANARELLE. I am very much obliged to you, Monsieur.

[*He goes out and reappears in the cloak and hat, playing the doctor again and talking to himself.*]

When patients refuse to follow their doctor's advice and abandon themselves to debauchery and—

GORGIBUS. Doctor, your humble servant. May I ask a favor of you?

SGANARELLE: What can I do for you, Monsieur Gorgibus?

GORGIBUS. I just happened to meet your brother, who is quite distressed—

SGANARELLE. He's a rascal, Monsieur Gorgibus.

GORGIBUS. But he truly regrets that he made you so angry, and—

SGANARELLE. He's a scoundrel, Monsieur Gorgibus.

GORGIBUS. But surely, Doctor, you're not going to give the poor boy up?

SGANARELLE. Not another word about him. The impudence of the rogue, seeking you out to intercede for him! I implore you not to mention him to me.

GORGIBUS. In God's name, Doctor, and out of respect for me, too, have pity on him. I'll do anything for you in return. I promised—

SGANARELLE. You plead so insistently that, even though I swore a violent oath never to forgive him—well, I'll shake your hand on it; I forgive him. You can be assured that I am doing myself a great injury and that I would not have consented to this for any other man. Good-bye, Monsieur Gorgibus.

GORGIBUS. Thank you, Doctor, thank you. I'll go off and look for the boy to tell him the glad news.

[*He walks off.* SGANARELLE *takes off the doctor's cloak and hat.* VALÈRE *appears.*]

VALÈRE. I never thought Sganarelle would do his duty so magnificently. Ah, my dear boy, I don't know how to repay you. I'm so happy I—

SGANARELLE. It's easy for you to talk. Gorgibus just ran into me without my doctor's outfit, and if I hadn't come up with a quick story we'd have been sunk. Here he comes again. Disappear.

[VALÈRE *runs away.* GORGIBUS *returns.*]

GORGIBUS. Narcissus, I've been looking everywhere for you. I spoke to your brother and he forgives you. But to be safe, I want to see the two of you patch up your quarrel in front of me. Wait here in my house, and I'll find him.

SGANARELLE. I don't think you'll find him, Monsieur. Anyhow, I wouldn't dare to wait; I'm terrified of him.

GORGIBUS. [*Pushing* SGANARELLE *inside.*] Yes, you will stay. I'm locking you in. Don't be afraid of your brother. I promise you that he's not angry now.

[*He slams the door and locks it, then goes off to look for the doctor.*]

SGANARELLE. [*At the upstairs window.*] Serves me right; I trapped myself and there's no way out. The weather in my future looks threatening, and if there's a storm I'm afraid I'll feel a rain of blows on my back. Or else they'll brand me across the shoulders with a whip—not exactly the brand of medicine any doctor ever prescribed. Yes, I'm in trouble. But why give up when we've come this far? Let's go the limit. I can still make a bid for freedom and prove that Sganarelle is the king of swindlers.

[*He holds his nose, closes his eyes, and jumps to the ground, just as* GROS-RENÉ *comes back. Then he darts away, picking up the cloak and hat.* GROS-RENÉ *stands staring.*]

GROS-RENÉ. A flying man! What a laugh! I'll wait around and see if there's another one.

[GORGIBUS *reenters with* SGANARELLE *following him in the doctor's outfit.*]

GORGIBUS. Can't find that doctor. Where the devil has he hidden himself?

[*He turns and* SGANARELLE *walks into him.*]

There you are. Now, Doctor, I know you said you forgive your brother, but that's not enough. I won't be satisfied until I see you embrace him. He's waiting here in my house.

SGANARELLE. You are joking, Monsieur Gorgibus. Have I not extended myself enough already? I wish never to see him again.

GORGIBUS. Please, Doctor, for me.

SGANARELLE. I cannot refuse when you ask me like that. Tell him to come down.

[*As* GORGIBUS *goes into the house,* SGANARELLE *drops the clothes, clambers swiftly up to the window again, and scrambles inside.*]

GORGIBUS. [*At the window.*] Your brother is waiting for you downstairs, Narcissus. He said he'd do what I asked.

SGANARELLE. [*At the window.*] Couldn't you please make him come up here? I beg of you— let me see him in private to ask his forgiveness, because if I go down there he'll show me up and say nasty things to me in front of everybody.

GORGIBUS. All right. Let me tell him.

[*He leaves the window, and* SGANARELLE *leaps out, swiftly puts on his outfit again, and stands waiting for* GORGIBUS *outside the door.*]

Doctor, he's so ashamed of himself he wants to beg your forgiveness in private, upstairs. Here's the key. Please don't refuse me.

SGANARELLE. There is nothing I would not do

for you, Monsieur Gorgibus. You will hear how I deal with him.

[*He walks into the house and soon appears at the window.* GORGIBUS *has his ear cocked at the door below.* SGANARELLE *alternates his voice, playing the characters one at a time.*]

SGANARELLE. So there you are, you scoundrel!
—Brother, listen to me, please. I'm sorry I knocked those containers over—
—You clumsy ox!
—It wasn't my fault, I swear it.
—Not your fault, you bumpkin? I'll teach you to destroy my work.
—Brother, no, please—
—I'll teach you to trade on Monsieur Gorgibus' good nature. How dare you ask him to ask me to forgive you!
—Brother, I'm sorry, but—
—Silence, you dog!
—I never wanted to hurt you or—
—Silence, I say—

GROS-RENÉ. What exactly do you think is going on up there?

GORGIBUS. It's the doctor and his brother, Narcissus. They had a little disagreement, but now they're making it up.

GROS-RENÉ. Doctor and his brother? But there's only one man.

SGANARELLE. [*At the window.*] Yes, you scoundrel, I'll thump some good behavior into you. [*Pretends to strike a blow.*] Ah, he's lowering his eyes; he knows what he's done wrong, the jailbird. And now this hypocrite wants to play the good apostle—

GROS-RENÉ. Just for fun, tell him to let his brother appear at the window.

GORGIBUS. I will. [*To* SGANARELLE.] Doctor, let me see your brother for a moment.

SGANARELLE. He is not fit to be seen by an honest gentleman like yourself. Besides, I cannot bear to have him next to me.

GORGIBUS. Please don't say no, after all you've done for me.

SGANARELLE. Monsieur Gorgibus, you have such power over me that I must grant whatever you wish. Show yourself, beast!

[*He appears at the window as Narcissus.*]

Monsieur Gorgibus, I thank you for your kindness.

[*He reappears as the doctor.*]

Well, Monsieur, did you take a good look at that image of impurity?

GROS-RENÉ. There's only one man there, Monsieur. We can prove it. Tell them to stand by the window together.

GORGIBUS. Doctor, I want to see you at the window embracing your brother, and then I'll be satisfied.

SGANARELLE. To any other man in the world I would return a swift and negative answer, but to you, Monsieur Gorgibus, I will yield, although not without much pain to myself. But first I want this knave to beg your pardon for all the trouble he has caused you.

[*He comes back as Narcissus.*]

Yes, Monsieur Gorgibus, I beg your pardon for having bothered you, and I promise you, brother, in front of Monsieur Gorgibus there, that I'll be so good from now on that you'll never be angry with me again. Please let bygones be bygones.

[*He embraces the cloak and hat.*]

GORGIBUS. There they are, the two of them together.

GROS-RENÉ. The man's a magician.

[*He hides;* SGANARELLE *comes out of the house, dressed as the doctor.*]

SGANARELLE. Here is your key, Monsieur. I have left my brother inside because I am ashamed of him. One does not wish to be seen in his company now that one has some reputation in this town. You may release him whenever you think fit. Good-bye, Monsieur.

[*He strides off, then as* GORGIBUS *goes into the house he wheels, dropping the cloak and hat, and climbs back through the window.*]

GORGIBUS. [*Upstairs.*] There you are, my boy, you're free. I am pleased that your brother forgave you, although I think he was rather hard on you.

SGANARELLE. Monsieur, I cannot thank you enough. A brother's blessing on you. I will remember you all my life.

[*While they are upstairs,* GROS-RENÉ *has picked up the cloak and hat, and stands waiting for them. They come out of the door.*]

GROS-RENÉ. Well, where do you think your doctor is now?

GORGIBUS. Gone, of course.

GROS-RENÉ. He's right here, under my arm. And by the way, while this fellow was getting in and out of the cloak, the hat, and the window, Valère ran off with your daughter and married her.

GORGIBUS. I'm ruined! I'll have you strung up, you dog, you knave! Yes, you deserve every name your brother called you—What am I saying?

SGANARELLE. You don't really want to string me up, do you, Monsieur? Please listen for one second. It's true that I was having a game with you while my master was with Mademoiselle Lucile. But in serving him I haven't done you any harm. He's a most suitable partner for her, by rank and by income. Believe me, if you make a row about this you'll only bring more confusion on your head. As for that porker there, let him get lost and take Villebrequin with him. Here come our loving couple.

[VALÈRE *enters contritely with* LUCILE. *They kneel to* GORGIBUS.]

VALÈRE. We apologize to you.

GORGIBUS. Well, perhaps it's lucky that I was tricked by Sganarelle; he's brought me a fine son-in-law. Let's go out to celebrate the marriage and drink a toast to the health of all the company.

[*They dance off in couples:* VALÈRE *with* LUCILE, GORGIBUS *with* GROS-RENÉ, *and* SGANARELLE *with* SABINE.]

STUDY QUESTIONS

Recalling

1. Why does Valère need advice, and what advice does Sabine give him?
2. Who is Sganarelle, and what does Valère think of him? Relate Sganarelle's conflicting opinions about his ability to impersonate a doctor.
3. Describe how Sganarelle deceives Gorgibus into believing that he is a doctor.
4. After his initial success what further trick does Sganarelle play on Gorgibus, and why?
5. Explain how Sganarelle is finally found out. What arguments does he then use to convince Gorgibus to condone the marriage?

Interpreting

6. What various character traits does Sganarelle reveal? Does he disprove Valère's opinion of him? Explain.
7. What aspects of the medical profession does Molière mock in this play, and how does he mock them?
8. Which characters represent exaggerations or stereotypes? What elements of society and human nature does Molière ridicule through these characters?
9. What makes *The Flying Doctor* funny? What truths about life might it make an audience remember?

Extending

10. What sorts of weaknesses and wrongs might lend themselves especially well to ridicule? Suggest one specific present-day problem that might be effectively satirized, and give two or three reasons for your choice.

VIEWPOINT

In his introduction to an English translation of Molière's comedies, Professor F. C. Green observes:

> The author [of comedy] must seize and fix the universal and eternal truth which lies at the roots of human conduct. This Molière achieved. He does more than just reflect life: he interprets its hidden significance.

■ What, in your opinion, is the "hidden significance" of Sganarelle's triumph over Gorgibus?

LITERARY FOCUS

Farce

Farce is a type of comedy that relies largely on improbable situations, broad characters, and slapstick action. The object of farce is to provoke the spectator to laugh through surprise and exaggeration. Farce usually includes broad physical "gags," such as pratfalls, fast action, and exaggerated facial expressions. The situations in farce often involve mistaken identity; characters frequently wear outrageous disguises that would fool no one in real life. The characters in a farce are simple and straightforward; generally they are either tricksters or fools.

Molière is a master of the art of farce. He uses the devices of farce for two purposes: to amuse his audience and, more important, to make his audience reflect on the absurdities of extreme social custom and human behavior.

Thinking About Farce

■ Identify three farcical elements in the situation, characters, and action of *The Flying Doctor*. Explain how these elements are both amusing and thought-provoking.

VOCABULARY

Antonyms

Antonyms are words that have opposite, or nearly opposite, meanings. *Gently* and *harshly* are antonyms. The words in capitals below are from *The Flying Doctor*. Choose the word that is most *nearly* the opposite of each word in capitals *as the word is used in the play*. Write the number of each item and the letter of your choice on a separate sheet.

1. CREDULOUS: (a) gullible (b) dangerous (c) skeptical (d) unimaginative
2. INIMICAL: (a) amazing (b) hostile (c) unbeatable (d) helpful
3. FORMIDABLE: (a) slight (b) formal (c) lovely (d) considerable
4. DOGMATIC: (a) traditional (b) feline (c) worldly (d) improvised
5. PERCIPIENCE: (a) keenness (b) dullness (c) wit (d) confusion
6. SUBLIME: (a) boring (b) low (c) intellectual (d) temperamental
7. MERCENARY: (a) volunteer (b) hostage (c) messenger (d) demigod
8. IMPUDENCE: (a) weakness (b) putridness (c) timidity (d) arrogance
9. INTERCEDE: (a) withdraw (b) separate (c) mix (d) forget
10. CONTRITELY: (a) sadly (b) clumsily (c) generously (d) defiantly

COMPOSITION

Writing a Comparison/Contrast

■ Compare and contrast Cervantes' use of humor in *Don Quixote* (page 895) with Molière's use of humor in *The Flying Doctor*. First point out the major similarities and differences between the comic circumstances created by each author. Then compare and contrast the satiric purposes to which both authors put humor. *For help with this assignment, refer to Lesson 2 in the Writing About Literature Handbook at the back of this book.*

Writing a Drama Review

■ Imagine that you have just attended the opening night performance of *The Flying Doctor*. Write a review of the play, either positive or negative. Your review should concentrate on evaluating the effectiveness of the farcical moments and the leading characters. End by telling your readers whether or not they should see the play, and why.

Bashō *1644–1694*

Just after centuries of fighting within Japan came to an end, Matsuo Bashō was born into a peaceful political and social climate conducive to the arts. The samurai, or warrior class, from which Bashō came, could now direct their energies away from fighting to more creative pursuits, and poetry flourished during this period. While still a boy, Bashō was sent to the south of Japan to serve a nobleman's son. From this young master, named Sengin, and from Sengin's teacher, Bashō was first formally instructed in the art of poetry. By the age of eight, he was writing his own poems. Devastated when his good friend and master died, Bashō entered a monastery. He later emerged to study haiku with a famous poet-teacher, first in Kyoto and later in what is now Tokyo. Soon Bashō was heading up his own poetry school, which continued to grow in size and reputation throughout his life.

Bashō's later poems became the model for future haiku writers. Each of these brief, classic **haiku** had seventeen syllables spread out over three lines with five syllables in the first line, seven in the second, and five in the third. In its original Japanese form, the first of Bashō's haiku, which appears on page 915, adheres strictly to this formula. Written in 1686, it is probably the most widely recognized haiku in Japan. The last haiku, which appears on page 916, is known as Bashō's "death poem" and was his final work. It is thought to sum up his views on life, illness, philosophy, and death.

▨ Have you ever focused on one or two small details in nature and had an unexplainably large and powerful emotional reaction to what you saw? When and where did this occur?

Bashō

Ten Haiku

Old pond—
    and a frog-jump-in
      water-sound.

The first day of the year:
    thoughts come—and there is loneliness;
      the autumn dusk is here.

Spring starts:
    new year; old rice,
      five quarts.

Summer grass:
    of stalwart warriors' splendid dreams
      the aftermath.

This road:
    with no man traveling on it,
      autumn darkness falls.

Snow that we two
    looked at together—this year
      has it fallen anew?

Around existence twine
    (Oh, bridge that hangs across the gorge!)
      ropes of twisted vine.

In Kyō[1] I am,
    and still I long for Kyō—
      oh, bird of time!

---

1. **Kyō** [kyō′]: Japanese for "today."

A Chinese hanging scroll depicting the
woods and valleys of Mount Yü, 1372.

The Great Wave off Kanagawa, a
Japanese print by Katsushika Hokusai
(1760–1849).

So wild a sea—
    and, stretching over Sado Isle,[2]
        the Galaxy . . .

On a journey, ill,
    and over fields all withered, dreams
        go wandering still.

---

2. **Sado** [Sa′dō] **Isle:** island in the Sea of Japan.

STUDY QUESTIONS

Recalling

1. In which of the haiku do you find direct references to the season? To the time of day or year? What are these references?
2. Scan all ten haiku, locating references to the following objects and phenomena: an animal, water, rice, snow, a gorge, fields, and dreams.

Interpreting

3. The concrete references you have just located are used as springboards for larger meanings. Examine one of the ten poems closely, looking beyond its simple, concrete surface. How does Bashō use condensed, concrete description to create subtle moods? A deep appreciation for nature?
4. In their original Japanese form, these haiku follow a strict three-line, seventeen-syllable format. In English, which of these haiku have the standard three lines? Which, if any, have seventeen syllables in a 5–7–5 pattern?
5. What does the tenth haiku, Bashō's "death poem," mean to you? Is it a poem of despair, hope, or both?

Extending

6. If you were to write your own "death poem," as Bashō has done, what basic elements of your philosophy of life would you want to include?

VIEWPOINT

One translator's words about a famous Bashō poem apply to others of his haiku as well:

First, the over-all mood or emotion is produced by a simple description, a plain statement of fact which makes a picture. Second, the two parts that make up the whole are compared to each other, not in simile or metaphor, but as two phenomena, each of which exists in its own right. This may be called "the principle of internal comparison" in which the differences are just as important as the likenesses.

—*An Introduction to Haiku*
Harold G. Henderson

1. Apply Henderson's quote to one of Bashō's ten haiku. What are the "two parts" of the haiku? How are these two parts different from one another? Alike?

2. What emotional effect is produced in the haiku by this "internal comparison"?

LITERARY FOCUS

Translation

All the world masterpieces presented in this book are English translations of works originally written in other languages, among them Sumerian, Greek, Latin, Italian, French, Japanese, Spanish, German, and Russian. The general elegance of style, beauty of expression, and power of communication in these selections prove that successful translations are possible.

The difficulty in translation, however, lies in avoiding the two extremes of being too literal or too liberal. Literal translations render the work word for word but ignore subtleties of language such as idiom, connotation, and imagery. As a result, every word is translated, but the spirit of the original work is damaged. On the other hand, liberal translations attempt to communicate only the essential spirit and meaning of a work and, therefore, often neglect the original language. The best translations must fall, as the Italian critic Benedetto Croce said, somewhere between "faithful ugliness and faithless beauty."

To see the differences that can exist between two translations of the same poem, compare the following Robert Bly translation with the fifth Bashō haiku on page 915, a Harold G. Henderson translation:

It's fall and dusk.
And no one is walking
along the road.

Next, compare the following Bly translation with another of Henderson's translations, the first haiku on page 916:

The sea grows rough.
the Milky Way reaches past
the island of Sado!

Thinking About Translations

■ Compare and contrast the two translations of the first haiku pair. In which is the word order most like that of standard speech? Which seems most "poetic"? Why? Explain how the difference in wording affects the mood of each translation.

Johann Wolfgang von Goethe
1749–1832

When he met Goethe in 1808, Napoleon exclaimed, "Voilà un homme!" (Behold a man!) Poet, playwright, scientist, philosopher, and statesman, Johann Wolfgang von Goethe [yō′hän vôlf′gäng′ von gur′tə] was indeed remarkable. He was born in Frankfurt in what is now West Germany, the son of a wealthy lawyer who supervised his son's education in art, literature, and language. Goethe wrote his first important poetry while studying law. As a student he met Johann Gottfried von Herder, a leader of the *Sturm und Drang* (Storm and Stress) literary movement, a forerunner to German Romanticism that emphasized nature and the emotions.

Goethe practiced law in Frankfurt until his novel *The Sorrows of Young Werther* (1774) became a best seller and made him a hero to young people throughout Europe. The book is a melancholy work about hopeless love and nature's destructive beauty. At the invitation of the duke of Weimar, Goethe moved to that city and became a counselor to the duke. In his new role Goethe studied science and technology, including anatomy, optics, geology, and botany. In 1786 he traveled to Italy for a two-year stay that inspired an admiration for the classical tradition of the Renaissance. When he returned to Weimar, he withdrew from political and social activity to concentrate on writing. His topics included folklore, natural science, philosophy, Oriental literature, and international events. He also composed short stories, plays, and poetry. Goethe once called all his writing "the fragments of a great confession," and he devoted his later years to autobiographical work. He died calling for "more light, more light!"

Goethe's work is massive in quantity and diversity, but his masterwork is *Faust,* a reader's play in verse. In twelve thousand lines *Faust* combines dramatic, epic, and lyrical elements and demonstrates Goethe's interest in theology, mythology, philosophy, economics, science, aesthetics, and music. Goethe worked on *Faust* from 1773, when he was twenty-four, until 1831, a year before his death. According to a legend that Goethe knew from his childhood, Faust is a scholar who trades his immortal soul to Mephistopheles [mef′ə stof′ə lēz′], the devil, in return for complete knowledge and experience. Goethe's version transforms the traditional ending, in which Faust is carried away by demons, into one of salvation. Goethe's Faust is redeemed by his dedication to perfection, a redemption available to all who devote themselves to selfless striving for fulfillment.

■ True or false: Continual striving gives meaning to life. Support your answer.

Johann Wolfgang von Goethe

from **Faust**

Translated by Louis MacNeice

The Prologue in Heaven

The Lord and the heavenly hosts[1] enter, with Mephistopheles following. After three archangels step forward to praise the Lord and his creations, Mephistopheles speaks.

MEPHISTOPHELES. Since you, O Lord, once more approach and ask
If business down with us be light or heavy—
And in the past you've usually welcomed me—
That's why you see me also at your levee.[2]
5 Excuse me, I can't manage lofty words—
Not though your whole court jeer and find me low;
My pathos certainly would make you laugh
Had you not left off laughing long ago.
Your suns and worlds mean nothing much to me;
10 How men torment themselves, that's all I see.
The little god of the world,[3] one can't reshape, reshade him;
He is as strange today as that first day you made him.
His life would be not so bad, not quite,
Had you not granted him a gleam of Heaven's light;
15 He calls it Reason, uses it not the least
Except to be more beastly than any beast.
He seems to me—if your Honor does not mind—
Like a grasshopper—the long-legged kind—
That's always in flight and leaps as it flies along
20 And then in the grass strikes up its same old song.
I could only wish he confined himself to the grass!
He thrusts his nose into every filth, alas.

LORD. Mephistopheles, have you no other news?
Do you always come here to accuse?
25 Is nothing ever right in your eyes on earth?

MEPHISTOPHELES. No, Lord! I find things there as downright bad as ever.
I am sorry for men's days of dread and dearth;
Poor things, *my* wish to plague 'em isn't fervent.

LORD. Do you know Faust?

MEPHISTOPHELES.   The Doctor?

---

1. ***hosts:*** multitudes; here, all the angels and saints.
2. **levee:** monarch's first reception of subjects in the morning.
3. **little . . . world:** man, who was created in God's image and who was given dominion over earthly creatures.

LORD.   Aye, my servant.

30 **MEPHISTOPHELES.** Indeed! He serves you oddly enough, I think.
   The fool has no earthly habits in meat and drink.
   The ferment in him drives him wide and far,
   That he is mad he too has almost guessed;
   He demands of heaven each fairest star

35 And of earth each highest joy and best,
   And all that is new and all that is far
   Can bring no calm to the deep-sea swell of his breast.

   LORD. Now he may serve me only gropingly,
   Soon I shall lead him into the light.

40 The gardener knows when the sapling first turns green
   That flowers and fruit will make the future bright.

   MEPHISTOPHELES. What do you wager? You will lose him yet,
   Provided *you* give *me* permission
   To steer him gently the course I set.

45 **LORD.** So long as he walks the earth alive,
   So long you may try what enters your head;
   Men make mistakes as long as they strive.

   MEPHISTOPHELES. I thank you for that; as regards the dead,
   The dead have never taken my fancy.

50 I favor cheeks that are full and rosy-red;
   No corpse is welcome to my house;
   I work as the cat does with the mouse.

   LORD. Very well; you have my full permission.
   Divert this soul from its primal source[4]

55 And carry it, if you can seize it,
   Down with you upon your course—
   And stand ashamed when you must needs admit;
   A good man with his groping intuitions
   Still knows the path that is true and fit.

60 **MEPHISTOPHELES.** All right—but it won't last for long.
   I'm not afraid my bet will turn out wrong.
   And, if my aim prove true and strong,
   Allow me to triumph wholeheartedly.
   Dust shall be eaten—and greedily—

65 Like my cousin the Snake[5] renowned in tale and song.

   LORD. That too you are free to give a trial;
   I have never hated the likes of you.
   Of all the spirits of denial
   The joker is the last that I eschew.

_____

4. **primal source:** origin; here, God and heaven.
5. **the Snake:** serpent that tempted Eve in the Garden of Eden.

70   Man finds relaxation too attractive—
     Too fond too soon of unconditional rest;
     Which is why I am pleased to give him a companion
     Who lures and thrusts and must, as devil, be active.
     But ye, true sons of Heaven, it is your duty
75   To take your joy in the living wealth of beauty.
     The changing Essence which ever works and lives
     Wall you around with love, serene, secure!
     And that which floats in flickering appearance
     Fix ye it firm in thoughts that must endure. . . .

     [*Heaven closes.*]

80 **MEPHISTOPHELES** [*alone*]. I like to see the Old One now and then
     And try to keep relations on the level.
     It's really decent of so great a person
     To talk so humanely even to the Devil.

     After "The Prologue in Heaven," the actual poem begins with a scene called "Night." Faust contemplates the limits of human understanding and concludes that complete knowledge is possible only after death. He considers suicide but is distracted by the life-affirming bells of Easter morning. Rushing outside, Faust is temporarily encouraged by the activity of the common people, but later, while the sun sets, he again gives in to despair. Back in his study, Faust is confronted by Mephistopheles. He resists the demon's temptations at first. Then as his despair deepens, he curses all things that humanity strives for—family, love, fame, wealth, hope, and faith. Mephistopheles, delighted that Faust is now more open to his temptation, returns.

The Pact with the Devil

MEPHISTOPHELES. Stop playing with your grief which battens[6]
     Like a vulture on your life, your mind!
     The worst of company would make you feel
     That you are a man among mankind,
5   Not that it's really my proposition
     To shove you among the common men;
     Though I'm not one of the Upper Ten,[7]
     If you would like a coalition
     With me for your career through life,
10   I am quite ready to fit in,
     I'm yours before you can say knife.
     I am your comrade;
     If you so crave,
     I am your servant, I am your slave.

---

6. **battens:** grows fat.
7. **Upper Ten:** ten most powerful spirits.

15 **FAUST.** And what have I to undertake in return?

MEPHISTOPHELES. Oh it's early days to discuss what that is.

FAUST. No, no, the devil is an egoist
And ready to do nothing gratis[8]
Which is to benefit a stranger.
20   Tell me your terms and don't prevaricate!
A servant like you in the house is a danger.

MEPHISTOPHELES. I will bind myself to your service in this world,
To be at your beck and never rest nor slack;
When we meet again on the other side,
25   In the same coin you shall pay me back.

FAUST. The other side gives me little trouble;
First batter this present world to rubble,
Then the other may rise—if that's the plan.
This earth is where my springs of joy have started,
30   And this sun shines on me when brokenhearted;
If I can first from them be parted,
Then let happen what will and can! . . .

MEPHISTOPHELES. With such an outlook you can risk it.
Sign on the line! In these next days you will get
35   Ravishing samples of my arts;
I am giving you what never man saw yet.

FAUST. Poor devil, can *you* give anything ever?
Was a human spirit in its high endeavor
Even once understood by one of your breed?
40   Have you got food which fails to feed?
Or red gold which, never at rest,
Like mercury runs away through the hand?
A game at which one never wins?
A girl who, even when on my breast,
45   Pledges herself to my neighbor with her eyes?
The divine and lovely delight of honor
Which falls like a falling star and dies?
Show me the fruits which, before they are plucked, decay
And the trees which day after day renew their green!

50 **MEPHISTOPHELES.** Such a commission doesn't alarm me,
I have such treasures to purvey.
But, my good friend, the time draws on when we
Should be glad to feast at our ease on something good.

FAUST. If ever I stretch myself on a bed of ease,
55   Then I am finished! Is that understood?
If ever your flatteries can coax me

---

8. **gratis:** Latin for "free of charge."

To be pleased with myself, if ever you cast
A spell of pleasure that can hoax me—
Then let *that* day be my last!
That's my wager!

MEPHISTOPHELES.   Done!

60 FAUST.   Let's shake!
If ever I say to the passing moment
"Linger a while! Thou art so fair!"
Then you may cast me into fetters,
I will gladly perish then and there! . . .

65 MEPHISTOPHELES. Think what you're saying, we shall not forget it.

FAUST. And you are fully within your rights;
I have made no mad or outrageous claim.
If I stay as I am, I am a slave—
Whether yours or another's, it's all the same.

70 MEPHISTOPHELES. I shall this very day at the College Banquet[9]
Enter your service with no more ado,
But just one point—As a life-and-death insurance
I must trouble you for a line or two.

FAUST. So you, you pedant, you too like things in writing?
75 Have you never known a man? Or a man's word? Never?
Is it not enough that my word of mouth
Puts all my days in bond for ever? . . .
What do you, evil spirit, require?
Bronze, marble, parchment, paper?
80 Quill or chisel or pencil of slate?
You may choose whichever you desire.

MEPHISTOPHELES. How can you so exaggerate
With such a hectic rhetoric?
Any little snippet is quite good—
85 And you sign it with one little drop of blood.

FAUST. If that is enough and is some use,
One may as well pander to your fad.

MEPHISTOPHELES. Blood is a very special juice.

FAUST. Only do not fear that I shall break this contract.
90 What I promise is nothing more
Than what all my powers are striving for. . . .
Let us cast ourselves into the torrent of time,
Into the whirl of eventfulness,
Where disappointment and success,
95 Pleasure and pain may chop and change

9. **College Banquet:** dinner to celebrate the awarding of a doctoral degree.

As chop and change they will and can;
It is restless action makes the man. . . .

MEPHISTOPHELES. You are in the end . . . what you are.
You can put on full-bottomed wigs with a million locks,
100　You can put on stilts[10] instead of your socks,
You remain forever what you are.

FAUST. I feel my endeavors have not been worth a pin
When I raked together the treasures of the human mind,
If at the end I but sit down to find
105　No new force welling up within.
I have not a hair's breadth more of height,
I am no nearer the Infinite.

MEPHISTOPHELES. My very good sir, you look at things
Just in the way that people do;
110　We must be cleverer than that
Or the joys of life will escape from you. . . .
So good-by to thinking! On your toes!
The world's before us. Quick! Here goes!
I tell you, a chap who's intellectual
115　Is like a beast on a blasted heath
Driven in circles by a demon
While a fine green meadow lies round beneath.

FAUST. How do we start?

MEPHISTOPHELES. 　　　　　We just say go—and skip.
But please get ready for this pleasure trip. [*Exit* FAUST.]
120　Only look down on knowledge and reason,
The highest gifts that men can prize,
Only allow the spirit of lies
To confirm you in magic and illusion,
And then I have you body and soul.
125　Fate has given this man a spirit
Which is always pressing onward, beyond control,
And whose mad striving overleaps
All joys of the earth between pole and pole.
Him shall I drag through the wilds of life
130　And through the flats of meaninglessness,
I shall make him flounder and gape and stick
And to tease his insatiableness
Hang meat and drink in the air before his watering lips;
In vain he will pray to slake his inner thirst,
135　And even had he not sold himself to the devil
He would be equally accursed.

---

10. **full-bottomed . . . stilts:** large curled wigs and elevated shoes worn
by actors in the seventeenth century.

STUDY QUESTIONS

Recalling

1. About what part of creation does Mephistopheles say, "that's all I see"?
2. In the prologue what wager do God and Mephistopheles make regarding Faust?
3. What permission does the Lord give Mephistopheles? What reason does the Lord give for sending humanity the devil as "a companion"?
4. What promise does Mephistopheles make Faust? What does he ask in return? According to Faust, when will he lose the wager?
5. Explain how Mephistopheles describes Faust's spirit in his final speech. What does he say he is planning to do with Faust?

Interpreting

6. Explain the relationship between the Lord and Mephistopheles in the prologue. Find two examples of the Lord's control over the devil.
7. What statements by the Lord and Faust reflect Goethe's belief that "restless action" gives life meaning? Explain how these statements suggest an outcome to Faust's wager.

VIEWPOINT

Writing about freedom, a concept that is central to much of his work, Goethe said:

Let a man but declare himself free, straightway he will feel himself limited. But let him be bold enough to declare himself limited, and he will experience a sense of freedom.

■ In what way does Faust declare himself free, and how does this actually limit him? What must he do to find true freedom?

VOCABULARY

Analogies

An **analogy** is a comparison. Analogy items appear on vocabulary tests as double comparisons between two pairs of words. You may be given the first pair and asked to find or complete a second pair of words that has the same relationship as the first pair. See the following example:

SMILE : GRIN :: laugh : chuckle

Here both pairs of words are synonyms.

Each numbered item below begins with two related words in capital letters, the first of which is from *Faust*. First decide how the two capitalized words relate to each other. Then choose the pair with the relationship most like the relationship between the pair in capital letters. Write the number of each item and the letter of your choice on a separate sheet.

1. FRENZY : TURMOIL ::
   (a) action : consequence
   (b) excitement : agitation
   (c) hope : loss
   (d) warmth : coolness

2. PATHOS : PATHETIC ::
   (a) minuscule : titanic
   (b) strength : power
   (c) humility : humble
   (d) stature : rank

3. TORRENT : TRICKLE ::
   (a) gust : wind
   (b) tornado : breeze
   (c) monsoon : hurricane
   (d) breath : sigh

4. TENACITY : STUBBORN ::
   (a) tradition : radical
   (b) exultation : aggressive
   (c) beauty : charismatic
   (d) ambition : farsighted

5. INSATIABLENESS : FOOD ::
   (a) boredom : exercise
   (b) studiousness : books
   (c) brilliance : dull
   (d) activity : apathy

Rabindranath Tagore   *1861–1941*

Born to an upper-class family in Calcutta, India, Rabindranath Tagore had a childhood of privilege. Tutored privately in India, he traveled to England at seventeen to study law. He later returned to India to concentrate on his writing and to open a progressive school whose aim was to combine the best of Indian and western culture. Today the school he founded, Visva-Bharati, is an international university.

Tagore's creative achievements are many and varied. He was an accomplished painter and musician, a well-known mystic, and a dedicated spokesman for Indian culture. His literary talents were equally broad, and he wrote poems, plays, novels, short stories, and essays on topics ranging from religion to Indian nationalism. Much of his work was written in his native Bengali, an Indian dialect, but Tagore also wrote fluently in English, sometimes even translating his own work.

Outside of India, Tagore is best known for his poems. His volumes of poetry include *The Gardener, Fireflies, Sheaves,* and *Gitanjali* (Song Offerings), excerpted here, for which he was awarded the Nobel Prize in 1913. This powerful literary tribute to God has been compared to the Psalms of the Bible as well as to William Blake's *Songs of Innocence.*

■ What aspects of existence give you the most and the deepest joy?

Indian tent panel made of red silk velvet with applied gold leaf, c. 1635.

Rabindranath Tagore

from **Gitanjali**

Thou hast made me endless, such is thy pleasure. This frail vessel thou emptiest again and again, and fillest it ever with fresh life.

This little flute of a reed thou hast carried over hills and dales, and hast breathed through it melodies eternally new.

At the immortal touch of thy hands my little heart loses its limits in joy and gives birth to utterance ineffable.

Thy infinite gifts come to me only on these very small hands of mine. Ages pass, and still thou pourest, and still there is room to fill.

The time that my journey takes is long, and the way of it long.

I came out on the chariot of the first gleam of light, and pursued my voyage through the wildernesses of worlds, leaving my track on many a star and planet.

It is the most distant course that comes nearest to thyself, and that training is the most intricate which leads to the utter simplicity of a tune.

The traveler has to knock at every alien door to come to his own, and one has to wander through all the outer worlds to reach the innermost shrine at the end.

My eyes strayed far and wide before I shut them and said, "Here art thou!"

The question and the cry, "Oh, where?" melt into tears of a thousand streams and deluge the world with the flood of the assurance, "I am!"

Where the mind is without fear and the head is held high;
Where knowledge is free;
Where the world has not been broken up into fragments by narrow domestic walls;
Where words come out from the depth of truth;
Where tireless striving stretches its arms toward perfection;
Where the clear stream of reason has not lost its way into the dreary desert sand of dead habit;
Where the mind is led forward by thee into ever-widening thought and action—
Into that heaven of freedom, my Father, let my country awake.

Light, my light, the world-filling light, the eye-kissing light, heart-sweetening light!
Ah, the light dances, my darling, at the center of my life; the light strikes, my darling, the chords of my love; the sky opens, the wind runs wild, laughter passes over the earth.
The butterflies spread their sails on the sea of light. Lilies and jasmines surge up on the crest of the waves of light.
The light is shattered into gold on every cloud, my darling, and it scatters gems in profusion.
Mirth spreads from leaf to leaf, my darling, and gladness without measure. The heaven's river has drowned its banks and the flood of joy is abroad.

The same stream of life that runs through my veins night and day runs through the world and dances in rhythmic measures.
It is the same life that shoots in joy through the dust of the earth in numberless blades of grass and breaks into tumultuous waves of leaves and flowers.
It is the same life that is rocked in the ocean-cradle of birth and of death, in ebb and in flow.
I feel my limbs are made glorious by the touch of this world of life. And my pride is from the life-throb of ages dancing in my blood this moment.

In one salutation to thee, my God, let all my senses spread out and touch this world at thy feet.
Like a rain-cloud of July hung low with its burden of unshed showers, let all my mind bend down at thy door in one salutation to thee.
Let all my songs gather together their diverse strains into a single current and flow to a sea of silence in one salutation to thee.
Like a flock of homesick cranes flying night and day back to their mountain nests let all my life take its voyage to its eternal home in one salutation to thee.

STUDY QUESTIONS

Recalling

1. What has God made the speaker? What kind of gifts came to him from God?
2. Why must the traveler knock at "every alien door" and "wander through all the outer worlds"?
3. The speaker asks God's help in awaking his country into what?
4. What does the speaker request that his senses do? His mind? His life?

Interpreting

5. Characterize the speaker's view of God, citing evidence from the poem. Does he view God as loving or vengeful? Accessible or distant? Generous or selfish? Constructive or destructive? Does he begrudgingly or willingly pay tribute?
6. The speaker contrasts himself with God. Which images in particular underscore this contrast?
7. How would you describe the overall emotional tone of the poem? Give examples from the text to support your answer.
8. Point to places in the poem where there are striking examples of repetition and parallelism. How do these techniques add to the poem's music and meaning?

Extending

9. For what reasons do you think light has been a central image in most world religions and their literature?

VOCABULARY

Synonyms

A synonym is a word that has the same or nearly the same meaning as another word. For example, *angry* and *mad* are synonyms. The words in capital letters come from *Gitanjali*. Choose the word that is *nearest* the meaning of the word in capitals as the word is used in the selection. Write the number of each item and the letter of your choice on a separate sheet.

1. INEFFABLE: (a) loud (b) unspeakable (c) limitless (d) secretive
2. DELUGE: (a) destroy (b) uplift (c) unsettle (d) fill
3. PROFUSION: (a) fragment (b) jest (c) disarray (d) abundance
4. MIRTH: (a) fungus (b) sunlight (c) gladness (d) sadness
5. DIVERSE: (a) varied (b) harmonious (c) liquid (d) angelic

COMPOSITION

Writing About an Author's Philosophy

Write a short essay in which you discuss Tagore's philosophy as presented in this poem, particularly his belief in the connectedness of things. First introduce the idea of connectedness and that it is central to "Gitanjali." In subsequent paragraphs, explore the different ways in which he finds himself connected to other aspects of existence (to God, nature, history and death). Use specific references from the text to support your views.

Writing a Salutation

Write a salutation, or goodwill greeting and tribute, of at least ten lines to a person from history or contemporary life whom you deem great. As Tagore does, use repetition, parallelism, and vivid imagery to express and reinforce your intense appreciation for the person and his or her effect on you. You might wish to begin with the person's name and then present the details of your appreciation.

Luigi Pirandello   *1867–1936*

Outside Italy Luigi Pirandello [lo͞o ē′jē pir′ən del′ō] may be his country's best-known modern author, and he is its most famous playwright. In fact, his plays, more than half of which are dramatizations of his own short stories, won for him the Nobel Prize for Literature in 1934. Pirandello's work—novels and poems as well as plays and short stories—is recognizable for the atmosphere of mystery and tension that he creates.

Pirandello was born in Sicily to a wealthy family. He studied in Rome and received a degree in philosophy from the University of Bonn in Germany. He taught for a while at a girls' high school in Rome. His wrote verse, essays, and novels, but his many volumes of short stories have established him as a master of that genre. He turned to playwrighting reluctantly when he was asked to dramatize one of the stories. His plays include *Six Characters in Search of an Author* (1918) and *Henry IV* (1922). He invented "grotesco," his own grotesque form of theatrical expressionism, a theatrical style that sacrifices realism in order to give expression to psychological experience. In 1925 Pirandello founded his own theater company, which then toured Europe.

A conflict between reality and illusion rages throughout Pirandello's plays, novels, and short stories. His characters often deceive themselves in an effort to avoid troublesome facts. Self-awareness is painful, and the characters survive by perpetuating illusions and ignoring reality. The tone is often mysterious or ironic, and when characters are forced to accept the truth, it becomes tragic.

"War" is a short story that also shows Pirandello's skill with dramatic dialogue. Like much of his work, it shows the ways people struggle to cope with unpleasant reality. Pirandello's own son was a prisoner of war during World War I, and Pirandello knew intimately the anguish he treats in this story.

■ Has a stranger sitting beside you on a train or plane ever begun to tell you of his problems? Why do you think people tell strangers things they might not tell friends?

Luigi Pirandello

War

Translated by Samuel Putnam

The passengers who had left Rome by the night express had to stop until dawn at the small station of Fabriano in order to continue their journey by the small old-fashioned "local" joining the main line with Sulmona.

At dawn, in a stuffy and smoky second-class carriage in which five people had already spent the night, a bulky woman in deep mourning was hoisted in—almost like a shapeless bundle. Behind her—puffing and moaning—followed her husband, a tiny man, thin and weakly, his face death-white, his eyes small and bright and looking shy and uneasy.

Having at last taken a seat, he politely thanked the passengers who had helped his wife and who had made room for her. Then he turned round to the woman trying to pull down the collar of her coat and politely inquired:

"Are you all right, dear?"

The wife, instead of answering, pulled up her collar again to her eyes, so as to hide her face.

"Nasty world," muttered the husband with a sad smile.

And he felt it his duty to explain to his traveling companions that the poor woman was to be pitied, for the war was taking away from her her only son. He was a boy of twenty to whom both had devoted their entire life, even breaking up their home at Sulmona to follow him to Rome, where he had to go as a student. Then they had allowed him to volunteer for war, with an assurance, however, that at least for six months he would not be sent to the front. And now, all of a sudden, they had received a wire that he was due to leave in three days' time and asking them to go and see him off.

The woman under the big coat was twisting and wriggling, at times growling like a wild an-imal, feeling certain that all those explanations would not have aroused even a shadow of sympathy from those people who—most likely—were in the same plight as herself. One of them, who had been listening with particular attention, said:

"You should thank God that your son is only leaving now for the front. Mine has been sent there the first day of the war. He has already come back twice wounded and been sent back again to the front."

"What about me? I have two sons and three nephews at the front," said another passenger.

"Maybe, but in our case it is our *only* son," ventured the husband.

"What difference can it make? You may spoil your only son with excessive attentions, but you cannot love him more than you would all your other children if you had any. Paternal love is not like bread that can be broken into pieces and split among the children in equal shares. A father gives *all* his love to each one of his children without discrimination, whether it be one or ten, and if I am suffering now for my two sons, I am not suffering half for each of them but double. . . ."

"True . . . true . . ." sighed the embarrassed husband, "but suppose (of course, we all hope it will never be your case) a father has two sons at the front and he loses one of them, there is still one left to console him . . . while . . ."

"Yes," answered the other, getting cross, "a son left to console him but also a son left for whom he must survive, while in the case of the father of an only son, if the son dies, the father can die, too, and put an end to his distress. Which of the two positions is the worse? Don't you see how my case would be worse than yours?"

"Nonsense," interrupted another traveler, a

fat, red-faced man with bloodshot eyes of the palest gray.

He was panting. From his bulging eyes seemed to spurt inner violence of an uncontrolled vitality which his weakened body could hardly contain.

"Nonsense," he repeated, trying to cover his mouth with his hand so as to hide the two missing front teeth. "Nonsense. Do we give life to our children for our own benefit?"

The other travelers stared at him in distress. The one who had had his son at the front since the first day of the war sighed: "You are right. Our children do not belong to us, they belong to the Country. . . ."

"Bosh," retorted the fat traveler. "Do we think of the Country when we give life to our children? Our sons are born because . . . well, because they must be born and when they come to life they take our own life with them. This is the truth. We belong to them but they never belong to us. And when they reach twenty, they are exactly what we were at their age. We, too, had a father and mother, but there were so many other things as well—girls, cigarettes, illusions, new ties—and the Country, of course, whose call we would have answered, when we were twenty, even if father and mother had said no. Now, at our age, the love of our Country is still great, of course, but stronger than it is the love for our children. Is there any one of us here who wouldn't gladly take his son's place at the front if he could?"

There was a silence all round, everybody nodding as to approve.

"Why, then," continued the fat man, "shouldn't we consider the feelings of our children when they are twenty? Isn't it natural that at their age they should consider the love for their Country (I am speaking of decent boys, of course) even greater than the love for us? Isn't it natural that it should be so, as after all they must look upon us as upon old boys who cannot move any more and must stay at home? If Country exists, if Country is a natural necessity like bread, of which each of us must eat in order not to die of hunger, somebody must go to defend it. And our sons go, when they are twenty, and they don't want tears, because if they die, they die inflamed and happy (I am speaking, of course, of decent boys). Now, if one dies young and happy, without having the ugly sides of life, the boredom of it, the pettiness, the bitterness of disillusion . . . what more can we ask for him? Everyone should stop crying: everyone should laugh, as I do . . . or at least thank God—as I do—because my son, before dying, sent me a message saying that he was dying satisfied at having ended his life in the best way he could have wished. That is why, as you see, I do not even wear mourning. . . ."

He shook his light fawn coat as to show it. His livid lip over his missing teeth was trembling, his eyes were watery and motionless and soon after, he ended with a shrill laugh which might well have been a sob.

"Quite so . . . quite so . . ." agreed the others.

The woman who, bundled in a corner under her coat, had been sitting and listening had—for the last three months—tried to find in the words of her husband and her friends something to console her in her deep sorrow, something that might show her how a mother should resign herself to send her son not even to death but to a probable danger of life. Yet not a word had she found among the many which had been said . . . and her grief had been greater in seeing that nobody—as she thought—could share her feelings.

But now the words of the traveler amazed and almost stunned her. She suddenly realized that it wasn't the others who were wrong and could not understand her but herself who could not rise up to the same height of those fathers and mothers willing to resign themselves, without crying, not only to the departure of their sons but even to their death.

She lifted her head, she bent over from her corner trying to listen with great attention to the details which the fat man was giving to his companions about the way his son had fallen as a hero, for his King and his Country, happy and without regrets. It seemed to her that she had stumbled into a world she had never dreamed of, a world so far unknown to her, and she was so pleased to hear everyone joining in congratulating that brave father who could so stoically speak of his child's death.

Then suddenly, just as if she had heard nothing of what had been said and almost as if waking up from a dream, she turned to the old man, asking him:

"Then . . . is your son really dead?"

Everybody stared at her. The old man, too, turned to look at her, fixing his great, bulging, horribly watery light gray eyes deep in her face. For some little time he tried to answer, but words failed him. He looked and looked at her, almost as if only then—at that silly, incongruous question—he had suddenly realized at last that his son was really dead . . . gone forever . . . forever. His face contracted, became horribly distorted, then he snatched in haste a handkerchief from his pocket and, to the amazement of everyone, broke into harrowing, heart-rending, uncontrollable sobs.

STUDY QUESTIONS

Recalling

1. Where are the tiny man and his grieving wife going? Give two examples of the woman's behavior from the beginning of the story.
2. Summarize the arguments of the two fathers who have sons at the front.
3. What reason does the father who lost his son give for not wearing mourning?
4. What is the man's reaction when the woman asks if his son is really dead?

Interpreting

5. Explain the following statement, and tell why the man who lost his son makes it: "We belong to them but they never belong to us."
6. What does the grieving mother think at first of the man's reason for not mourning his son? As a result, what does she think of herself?
7. Why does the man break down? Does his crying affect the strength of his earlier remarks?
8. What do you think is the theme of the story?

LITERARY FOCUS

Dialogue

Dialogue is conversation between characters in any form of writing. Dialogue helps to develop character; it indirectly informs the reader of characters' thoughts and opinions. Dialogue also enables an author to present an interplay of ideas among a number of characters.

What a character says must be appropriate to that character's personality, background, and intelligence. In addition, dialogue must sound like natural speech and still be free of the flaws of everyday conversation.

Thinking About Dialogue

1. What does their dialogue reveal about the personalities of the two men who have sons at the front? Is their dialogue natural? Explain.
2. In what sense does the dialogue in "War" provide an interplay of ideas?

COMPOSITION

Developing a Thesis Statement

■ Develop a thesis statement about "War," and write a brief essay to defend your thesis. First clearly state your thesis. Then use examples from the story to explain and defend it. You may want to consider one of the following for your thesis: (a) Pirandello's attitude toward war, (b) the attitudes about children, (c) the use of dialogue, or (d) the conflict between illusion and reality. *For help with this assignment, refer to Lesson 1 in the Writing About Literature Handbook at the back of this book.*

Writing Dialogue

■ Imagine three strangers who begin a conversation while riding on a train. They realize that they agree about some ideas and disagree about others. First describe each character. Then write a brief dialogue in which the three strangers come to know one another.

Rainer Maria Rilke   *1875–1926*

Rainer [rī′nər] Maria Rilke [ril′kə], the celebrated German lyric poet, is considered one of the guiding influences of modern poetry. He was born in Prague in what is now Czechoslovakia. Rilke's childhood was unhappy; he later described it as a "primer of horror." His father claimed to be an aristocrat even though he came from peasant stock; his mother, who wore only black, was a snobbish woman who abandoned her family when Rilke was only ten years old. Young Rilke was sent to military and business schools, none of which suited his artistic temperament, and later attended the universities of Prague, Munich, and Berlin.

As a young man Rilke traveled widely throughout Europe, associating with writers and artists wherever he went. In Paris he served as secretary to the famous sculptor Auguste Rodin [rō dan′]. Influenced by Rodin's ideas about art, Rilke became convinced that the artist could achieve perfection through hard work and careful craftsmanship rather than through inspiration, as the Romantics believed. Rilke later shared his theories about art in his influential *Letters to a Young Poet* (published in 1929). Plagued by leukemia in his later years, Rilke withdrew from public life and lived in a medieval tower in Switzerland. It was in Switzerland that he died.

Rilke's poetry evolved considerably over time. His early poems, represented in his *Book of Hours* (1905), are neo-Romantic—that is, sentimental and overstated. As his writing matured, it became increasingly complex, unpredictable, and searching. Rilke sought external symbols of his internal visions and became a leader in the Symbolist movement, which had begun in the nineteenth century. His concerns include love, death, childhood fears, and the search for God. Spiritual questions haunted his work more and more as the years passed; his *Duino Elegies* (1912–1920) and *Sonnets to Orpheus* (1923) are intensely mystical. The isolation and self-examination in his work have come to be characteristic of much modern poetry. In addition, Rilke's innovative use of language has had a profound effect on modern literature. Master of the nuance, he writes poems that shimmer with many meanings and rich images.

While working with Rodin, Rilke developed his idea of the *ding-Gedicht,* or "object poem," which aims to capture in poetry the vital, changeable essence of an object or creature. He once said, "If a thing is to speak to you, you must for a certain time regard it as the only thing that exists." In each of the following poems, Rilke devotes such attention to an animal, capturing its essence.

■ The setting of Rilke's "Panther" is a zoo. What is your reaction to caged animals?

Rainer Maria Rilke

The Gazelle

Translated by C. F. MacIntyre

Dorcas Gazelle[1]

Enchanted one: how shall two chosen words
achieve the harmony of the pure rhyme
which in you like a signal comes and goes?
From your forehead the leafy lyre[2] climbs,

5 and all your being moves in sure accord,[3]
like those love-lyrics whose words softly flow:
rose petals laid upon the closed eyelids
of one grown weary, who no longer reads

but shuts his eyes to see you—swiftly brought,
10 as though each leg were charged with leaps but not
fired, as long as the neck holds the head

quiet to listen: as when in a green place
a bather in the woods is interrupted . . .
with the lake's shine on her averted face.

---

1. **Dorcas** [dôr′kəs] **Gazelle:** light-brown gazelle less
than two feet high.
2. **lyre:** small, stringed musical instrument resembling a
harp.
3. **accord:** harmony.

Rainer Maria Rilke

The Panther

Translated by C. F. MacIntyre

Jardin des Plantes,[1] Paris

His sight from ever gazing through the bars
has grown so blunt that it sees nothing more.
It seems to him that thousands of bars are
before him, and behind them nothing merely.

5 The easy motion of his supple stride,
which turns about the very smallest circle,
is like a dance of strength about a center
in which a mighty will stands stupefied.

Only sometimes when the pupil's film
10 soundlessly opens . . . then one image fills
and glides through the quiet tension of the limbs
into the heart and ceases and is still.

---

1. **Jardin des Plantes** [zhär dan′ dä plänt]: famous botanical and zoological gardens in Paris.

STUDY QUESTIONS

The Gazelle

Recalling

1. With what two words does Rilke begin his description of the gazelle? What sort of "harmony" does he see in the gazelle?
2. In line 6 to what does Rilke compare the gazelle's movement?
3. How does Rilke describe the gazelle's legs in lines 10–11? In lines 11–14 what image does Rilke use to describe the way the gazelle holds its head?

Interpreting

4. Where in the poem does Rilke use images of motion? Where does he use images of stillness? What impression of the gazelle does he create by mixing these images?

5. Find two references to music and two to poetry in "The Gazelle." Why might these references to arts be appropriate in describing a gazelle?
6. In what ways is the poem musical? What effect does Rilke create by making lines 4–14 into a single sentence?
7. What qualities does this poem present as the "essence" of the gazelle? What might the gazelle come to symbolize in the poem?

Extending

8. Why might a creature like a gazelle be "enchanted" in a way that human beings are not?

The Panther

Recalling

1. According to line 1 why has the panther's sight grown "blunt"? What does he seem to see, according to lines 3–4?

2. In what terms does Rilke describe the panther's motion in lines 5–6? To what does he compare this motion in lines 7–8?
3. According to lines 9–12 what does "one image" do "sometimes"?

Interpreting
4. Describe in your own words the actual situation of the panther in the poem.
5. What contrasting images does the second stanza apply to the panther? Why are these images appropriate to this particular panther?
6. Describe the panther's state of mind at the end of the poem. How does the "one image" change the panther? Is he better or worse off at the end of the poem than at the beginning? Why?
7. How does the poet feel about the panther, and how do you know? In what ways might this panther resemble a poet writing a poem?

Extending
8. What similar responses might people and animals have to the lack of freedom? How might people differ from animals in their response to captivity?

VOCABULARY

Analogies
An **analogy** is a comparison. Analogy items appear on vocabulary tests as double comparisons between two pairs of words. You may be given the first pair of words and asked to find or complete a second pair that has the same or a similar relationship as the first pair. For example, you would complete the analogy POUND : OUNCE : : _____ : _____ with the pair FOOT : INCH, since the first word in each pair represents a whole and the second word a part.

Each of the items in the next column begins with two related words in capital letters; the first capitalized word in each pair comes from the translation of one of Rilke's poems.

1. LYRE : STRING : :
   (a) harp : violin
   (b) floor : board
   (c) music : poetry
   (d) window : door
2. PETALS : STEM : :
   (a) leaves : branch
   (b) fruit : vegetable
   (c) stem : stern
   (d) gazelle : panther
3. BLUNT : SHARP : :
   (a) boring : imaginative
   (b) rounded : curved
   (c) false : ambiguous
   (d) durable : old
4. STUPEFIED : DULLED : :
   (a) intense : moderate
   (b) excited : afraid
   (c) ignorant : wise
   (d) friendly : hostile
5. SOUNDLESSLY : QUIETLY : :
   (a) softly : loudly
   (b) dazzlingly : brightly
   (c) gently : kindly
   (d) rapidly : quickly

COMPOSITION

Writing a Comparison/Contrast
Compare and contrast Rilke's two object poems, "The Gazelle" and "The Panther." First make a general statement about the two poems. Then point out the similarities between them, both in their content and Rilke's use of literary techniques such as imagery and sound effects. Go on to identify the differences in the two poems' content and form. End by explaining the different aspects of life that seem to be presented in the two poems. *For help with this assignment, refer to Lesson 2 in the Writing About Literature Handbook at the back of this book.*

Writing Two Poems About Motion
Write two poems describing the motion of two different animals or people. Choose subjects that present a definite contrast: for example, a hummingbird and a bear, or a ballerina and a tap-dancer. In each poem use several different images to convey the distinct qualities of your subject's motion.

Franz Kafka *1883–1924*

Franz Kafka's [fränts käf′kə] fiction presents the most unusual events as completely commonplace. For example, in "The Metamorphosis" a young man wakes to discover his own transformation into an insect. Kafka's world is full of such occurrences, nightmares that capture what he saw as the particular anxiety of modern life. His characters—ordinary, rational beings—must cope with a world they no longer understand. They struggle unsuccessfully with the unknown, trying to make sense of events that are incomprehensible. Kafka's puzzling view of the world defies classification but contains elements of surrealism and existentialism. The nightmare vision, the illogical combination of events, and the seemingly realistic, detailed style create a verbal equivalent of surrealist art. Yet the fiction also pictures an existential world without meaningful order or pattern, a world in which human beings must live according to rules they cannot understand.

Franz Kafka was born in Prague, in what is now Czechoslovakia, to an affluent German-speaking Jewish family. He wrote part time while working as an insurance lawyer. Because his father disapproved of his literary interests and because of his own doubts about his talents, he published only a few works during his life and intended the rest to be destroyed after his death. A friend disobeyed instructions and published the remainder of the work after Kafka died of tuberculosis at forty-one.

Kafka's work is a series of variations on a recurring topic: the estrangement of the individual from society. In *The Trial* (1925) a man is arrested, tried, and executed for a crime he never understands. In *The Castle* (1926) a man struggles to enter the fortress home of a supreme authority. The atmosphere is one of futility, loneliness, and alienation. Meaning exists on different levels and is suggested through symbolism, descriptive detail, and concrete imagery. Like all Kafka's fiction, "First Sorrow" presents a puzzle for both hero and reader.

Have you ever been confused by something without knowing exactly why? What was your reaction to this state of confusion?

Franz Kafka

First Sorrow

Translated by Willa and Edwin Muir

A trapeze artist—this art, practiced high in the vaulted domes of the great variety theaters, is admittedly one of the most difficult humanity can achieve—had so arranged his life that, as long as he kept working in the same building, he never came down from his trapeze by night or day, at first only from a desire to perfect his skill, but later because custom was too strong for him. All his needs, very modest needs at that, were supplied by relays of attendants who watched from below and sent up and hauled down again in specially constructed containers whatever he required. This way of living caused no particular inconvenience to the theatrical people, except that, when other turns were on the stage, his being still up aloft, which could not be dissembled, proved somewhat distracting, as also the fact that, although at such times he mostly kept very still, he drew a stray glance here and there from the public. Yet the management overlooked this, because he was an extraordinary and unique artist. And of course they recognized that this mode of life was no mere prank, and that only in this way could he really keep himself in constant practice and his art at the pitch of its perfection.

Besides, it was quite healthful up there, and when in the warmer seasons of the year the side windows all around the dome of the theater were thrown open and sun and fresh air came pouring irresistibly into the dusky vault, it was even beautiful. True, his social life was somewhat limited, only sometimes a fellow acrobat swarmed up the ladder to him, and then they both sat on the trapeze, leaning left and right against the supporting ropes, and chatted, or builders' workmen repairing the roof exchanged a few words with him through an open window, or the fireman, inspecting the emergency lighting in the top gallery, called over to him something that sounded respectful but could hardly be made out. Otherwise nothing disturbed his seclusion; occasionally, perhaps, some theater hand straying through the empty theater of an afternoon gazed thoughtfully up into the great height of the roof, almost beyond eyeshot, where the trapeze artist, unaware that he was being observed, practiced his art or rested.

The trapeze artist could have gone on living peacefully like that, had it not been for the inevitable journeys from place to place, which he found extremely trying. Of course his manager saw to it that his sufferings were not prolonged one moment more than necessary; for town travel, racing automobiles were used, which whirled him, by night if possible or in the earliest hours of the morning, through the empty streets at breakneck speed, too slow all the same for the trapeze artist's impatience; for railways journeys, a whole compartment was reserved, in which the trapeze artist, as a possible though wretched alternative to his usual way of living, could pass the time up on the luggage rack; in the next town on their circuit, long before he arrived, the trapeze was already slung up in the theater and all the doors leading to the stage were flung wide open, all corridors kept free—yet the manager never knew a happy moment until the trapeze artist set his foot on the rope ladder and in a twinkling, at long last, hung aloft on his trapeze.

Despite so many journeys having been successfully arranged by the manager, each new one embarrassed him again, for the journeys, apart from everything else, got on the nerves of the artist a great deal.

Once when they were again traveling together, the trapeze artist lying on the luggage rack dreaming, the manager leaning back in the opposite window seat reading a book, the trapeze artist addressed his companion in a low voice. The manager was immediately all attention. The trapeze artist, biting his lips, said that he must always in future have two trapezes for his performance instead of only one, two trapezes opposite each other. The manager at once agreed. But the trapeze artist, as if to show that the manager's consent counted for as little as his refusal, said that never again would he perform on only one trapeze, in no circumstances whatever. The very idea that it might happen at all seemed to make him shudder. The manager, watchfully feeling his way, once more emphasized his entire agreement, two trapezes were better than one, besides it would be an advantage to have a second bar, more variety could be introduced into the performance. At that the trapeze artist suddenly burst into tears. Deeply distressed, the manager sprang to his feet and asked what was the matter, then getting no answer climbed up on the seat and caressed him, cheek to cheek, so that his own face was bedabbled by the trapeze artist's tears. Yet it took much questioning and soothing endearment until the trapeze artist sobbed: "Only the one bar in my hands—how can I go on living!" That made it somewhat easier for the manager to comfort him; he promised to wire from the very next station for a second trapeze to be installed in the first town on their circuit; reproached himself for having let the artist work so long on only one trapeze; and thanked and praised him warmly for having at last brought the mistake to his notice. And so he succeeded in reassuring the trapeze artist, little by little, and was able to go back to his corner. But he himself was far from reassured, with deep uneasiness he kept glancing secretly at the trapeze artist over the top of his book. Once such ideas began to torment him, would they ever quite leave him alone? Would they not rather increase in urgency? Would they not threaten his very existence? And indeed the manager believed he could see, during the apparently peaceful sleep which had succeeded the fit of tears, the first furrows of care engraving themselves upon the trapeze artist's smooth, childlike forehead.

STUDY QUESTIONS

Recalling

1. Why did the trapeze artist stay on his trapeze night and day? Why did the management permit him to do so?
2. Briefly describe the trapeze artist's manner of traveling.
3. What tearful request does the trapeze artist make of his manager? What is the manager's reaction?
4. What thought worries the manager at the end of the story?

Interpreting

5. In what sense do the trapeze artist's way of life and his request to the manager represent modern life in general? Explain.
6. What is the significance of the story's title?
7. Explain the significance of the story's last four sentences.

LITERARY FOCUS

Existentialism

Existentialism [eg′zis ten′shə liz′əm] is a modern European philosophy that is concerned with the nature of life, or existence. It developed as a highly pragmatic response to the alienation and confusion that defines the modern age. Existentialists consider life empty of any meaning, purpose, or value other than that which individuals give to their own lives. Existentialists believe that people must cope with the indifference of the world around them and define themselves entirely through their own actions. Although Kafka's fiction is not purely existential, his work influenced Jean-Paul Sartre and Albert Camus, leaders of the existentialist movement in France.

Thinking About Existentialism

■ Explain how the events of "First Sorrow" suggest an existentialist view of life.

Gabriela Mistral   *1889–1957*

In 1945 Gabriela Mistral became the first Latin American to receive the Nobel Prize for Literature. Raised in a small village in the north of Chile, her original goal was to become a teacher, not a writer. She taught at both the elementary and secondary levels and later served as a school principal. Her interest in education and its reform continued throughout her life, even long after she became a celebrated author. She labored for educational changes in Mexico, served in the Chilean Department of Education, and became a visiting professor at a variety of colleges and universities, from Middlebury in Vermont to the University of Puerto Rico.

Though Mistral's passion remained rural Chile and its landscape, she lived an international life, holding a position as delegate to the League of Nations, among other international posts. The last four years of her life were spent far from her native homeland, on Long Island, New York.

From the age of fifteen, Mistral contributed poems to local publications under various pseudonyms. In fear of losing her teaching job, she chose the name Gabriela Mistral for the Archangel Gabriel and the famous strong winds of southern France. In 1914, using this pen name, she submitted three sonnets to a national poetry contest and, winning, gained instant literary celebrity.

Mistral's poems are compact, passionate, and intense. Her themes include nature, womanhood, motherhood, children, and loss. She frequently uses the rural speech of her native region in her work. Her volumes of poetry include *Desolation* (*Desolación,* 1922); *Tenderness* (*Ternura,* 1924), a collection of children's poems; *Feeling* (*Tala,* 1938); and *Wine Press* (*Lagar,* 1954). In "Time" Mistral takes an emotional and energetic look at the unfolding of a single day.

■ Is there one particular portion of the day to which you feel the greatest affinity, or close relationship? If so, which one? Why?

Gabriela Mistral

Time

Daybreak

My heart swells that the Universe
like a fiery cascade may enter.
The new day comes. Its coming
leaves me breathless.
5 I sing. Like a cavern brimming
I sing my new day.

For grace lost and recovered
I stand humble. Not giving. Receiving.
Until the Gorgon[1] night,
10 vanquished, flees.

Morning

She has returned! She has returned!
Each morning the same and new.
Awaited every yesterday,
she must return this morning.

5 Mornings of empty hands
that promised and betrayed.
Behold this new morning unfold,
leap like a deer from the East,
awake, happy and new,
10 alert, eager and rich with deeds.

Brother, raise up your head
fallen to your breast. Receive her.
Be worthy of her who leaps up,
soars and darts like a halcyon,[2]
15 golden halcyon plunging earthward singing
Alleluia, alleluia, alleluia!

---

1. **Gorgon** [gôr′gən]: in Greek mythology, any of three sisters with snakes for hair whose appearance was so hideous that a glance turned the beholder to stone.
2. **halcyon** [hal′sē ən]: bird in ancient legend said to nest at sea and calm the waves during the winter solstice.

Detail, *Landscape, New Mexico*, Marsden Hartley, 1919–1920.

Afternoon

I feel my heart melt like wax
in this sweetness:
slow oil, not wine,
my veins,
5 I feel my life fleeting
silent and sweet as a gazelle.

Night

Mountain ranges dissolve,
cattle wander astray,
the sun returns to its forge,
all the world slips away.

5 Orchard and garden are fading,
the farmhouse already immersed.
My mountains submerge their crests
and their living cry.

All creatures are sliding aslant
10 down toward forgetfulness and sleep.
You and I, also, my baby,
tumble down toward night's keep.

Detail from *Landscape, New Mexico,*
Marsden Hartley, 1919-1920.

STUDY QUESTIONS

Recalling

1. In "Daybreak" how does the coming of the new day leave the speaker? The speaker stands humble until what flees?
2. Name three of the adjectives the poet uses in "Morning" to describe that time of day.
3. The speaker's heart melts like what in "Afternoon"? What does she feel fleeting?
4. What slips away in "Night"? Toward what do all creatures slide down?

Interpreting

5. Summarize the poet's emotional reactions to each of the times of day she describes.
6. Where in the poem does the poet advise the reader to be receptive to nature and the universe? In "Morning" what do you think she means when she advises, "Be worthy of her who leaps up"?
7. How does the reference to night in "Daybreak" contrast with the portrayal of night in the poem's last segment, particularly the poem's final line?

Extending

8. When in your life have you viewed time as an ally? An enemy?

VIEWPOINT

Though Mistral's work often describes nature, it usually simultaneously explores a state of mind, emotion, or spirit. According to one critic:

Her mind elaborates trenchant thoughts—of almost divine essence—which her pen clothes in the most natural, the most current, the most casual, the most soil-rooted, the most familiar of expressive garb. And this Gabriela is not forced . . . for it springs directly from her need of close contact with the earth, with reality, with the material, even when expressing the conceptual and the abstract.

—Sidonia Carmen Rosenbaum,
Modern Women Poets of Spanish America

■ In what ways does Mistral's poem "Time" reveal "divine essence"? In what ways is it "soil-rooted"?

COMPOSITION

Writing About Similes

■ In a few paragraphs discuss Mistral's use of similes in "Time." How often does she use them? What kinds of comparisons does she make? What do her similes add to the poem's overall emotion?

Writing About the Passage of Time

■ Write a poem comprised of four four-line stanzas describing, respectively, daybreak, morning, afternoon, and night. Through the use of vivid imagery, particularly similes, create a distinct mood for each of the times of day that you describe.

Boris Pasternak *1890–1960*

Perhaps the best-known writer of postrevolutionary Russia, Boris Pasternak has for fifty years been a poet without honor in his own country—at least as far as the Soviet government is concerned. He was born to an aristocratic, cultivated family in czarist Russia, with a well-known painter for a father and a pianist for a mother. Expecting to become a composer, the young Pasternak studied law and philosophy as well as music. After a trip to Italy in 1913, he expanded his interests to literature and began to write poetry.

When a leg injury prevented him from fighting in World War I, Pasternak went to the Ural Mountains to work in a factory. He returned to Moscow in 1917 and developed a reputation as a leading poet in the heady aftermath of the Russian Revolution. At first the Revolution sparked a great flurry of experimentation among poets, who hoped the new regime would create a better future. However, Pasternak refused to produce propaganda in the vein of "socialist realism" advocated by the government; he preferred instead to write searching, intellectual, and apolitical poetry. In retaliation, Soviet officials prevented his poems from being published during the 1930s and 1940s, and Pasternak was forced to translate the works of others. His most famous encounter with government censorship occurred over his novel *Dr. Zhivago* (1957), which presented a mixed view of the 1917 revolution. The novel was rejected for publication by Soviet censors and was subsequently smuggled into the West, where it became a best seller in many languages. When the Nobel Committee honored Pasternak with the Nobel Prize for Literature for this work in 1958, the Soviet government pressured him into refusing the award.

Despite the worldwide success of *Dr. Zhivago,* Pasternak is celebrated primarily as a poet. His poems often have religious overtones; like much nineteenth-century Russian literature, these poems return repeatedly to the ideas of faith, love, art, and human destiny. Pasternak's poems are marked by their use of many varied allusions as well as by their fresh imagery and fine coordination of sound and meaning. Pasternak's poetry has often been compared to Impressionist painting in that the perceiver must tie a number of seemingly disconnected parts into a unified whole. In "Winter Night" Pasternak creates a vivid winter scene while simultaneously exploring the themes of faith and human destiny.

■ In what ways can a snowstorm create a feeling of safety?

Boris Pasternak

Winter Night

It snowed and snowed, the whole world over,
Snow swept the world from end to end.
A candle burned on the table;
A candle burned.

5 As during summer midges swarm
To beat their wings against a flame,
Out in the yard the snowflakes swarmed
To beat against the windowpane.

The blizzard sculptured on the glass
10 Designs of arrows and of whorls.
A candle burned on the table;
A candle burned.

Distorted shadows fell
Upon the lighted ceiling:
15 Shadows of crossed arms, of crossed legs—
Of crossed destiny.

Two tiny shoes fell to the floor
And thudded.
A candle on a nightstand shed wax tears
20 Upon a dress.

All things vanished within
The snowy murk—white, hoary.
A candle burned on the table;
A candle burned.

25 A corner draft fluttered the flame
And the white fever of temptation
Upswept its angel wings that cast
A cruciform[1] shadow.

It snowed hard throughout the month
30 Of February, and almost constantly
A candle burned on the table;
A candle burned.

---

1. **cruciform** [krōo′sə form′]: forming or arranged in a cross.

STUDY QUESTIONS

Recalling

1. Where, according to the first stanza, did it snow? What burned on the table?
2. In stanza 4 what kinds of shadows fell? Where did they fall? In stanza 5 what fell to the floor?
3. According to the last stanza, how, when, and for how long did the snow fall?

Interpreting

4. How does Pasternak combine both the small and the large world view within a single poem? What categories of contrasting images does he present? What do these contrasts add to the poem's emotion?
5. The collapse of czarist Russia took place in March of 1917, but events leading to this downfall intensified the month before. What larger comment might Pasternak have been making about the events in his own country? What might the snow represent? The candle?
6. Where in the poem does Pasternak use religious references? How do these relate to the rest of the poem?
7. What do you suppose the poet means by the words "crossed destiny" in line 16?
8. Point to those words or phrases in "Winter Night" that Pasternak repeats. What effect does his use of repetition have on the poem?

VIEWPOINT

Russian critic Andrei Sinyavsky observes the way Pasternak's poetry fuses seemingly disconnected elements:

In Pasternak's poetry one must not separate man from his environment nor living feelings from dead matter. . . . Reality is depicted as a single unity in the blending of different components and in the intersecting of boundaries and contours.
—For Freedom of Imagination

■ What diverse components seem combined into a single unity in "Winter Night"? Where in the poem do inanimate objects seem to have human attributes?

LITERARY FOCUS

Style in Poetry

The *style* of a poem is the unique mode of expression that a poet or other artist chooses to convey emotions and ideas. It is the attempt by an author to match language and thoughts and to combine the two in an individualistic manner. In addition to the artist's individuality, style also conveys his or her theme or purpose.

The poetry of various authors whose work shares similar characteristics is often lumped together and described as having the same style. Though looking at literature this way can be useful, it is also important to remember that no two authors' writing, like no two fingerprints, is exactly the same.

Different characteristics of writing are highlighted when people discuss styles. A particular work may be referred to as having a realistic, scientific, or journalistic style, or it might be described as fanciful or imaginative. The style of a poem might be called elevated or plain, formal or informal, comic or serious, vivid or bland. Inevitably, though, a serious discussion of style should include the arrangement of ideas, diction, rhythm, imagery, sound devices, sentence structure, and variety.

Thinking About Style

1. Describe the style of "Winter Night." Would you describe it as realistic or fanciful, serious or comic, bland or vivid? Using examples, demonstrate how Pasternak's choice and arrangement of words, line length, sound effects, sentence structure, imagery, and theme work together to create his style.
2. Is the style of Pasternak's poem uniform throughout "Winter Night," or does it change?

Jorge Luis Borges   *1899–1986*

Jorge Luis Borges is one of the most outstanding and inventive literary figures of modern times. Born in Buenos Aires, Argentina, he had early exposure to the English language through his paternal grandmother, who was English. But his early exposure to other languages and cultures did not stop there. During World War I he and his family lived in Switzerland, where he became fluent in French and German, and he later moved to Spain. In 1921 Borges returned to Buenos Aires, not only well-read in world literature but also a dedicated student of philosophy.

At first Borges wrote only poetry, but he later expanded his writing interests to include essays, short fiction, and translations of others' works. Among the stories for which he is best known are *Ficciones* (1944), *Labyrinths* (1960), *The Aleph* (1970), and *El Informe de Brodie* (*Dr. Brodie's Report,* 1972). His *Selected Poems 1923–1967* was published in 1972, and *Borges: A Reader* (1981) is considered the most complete collection of his work.

From 1955 to 1973, Borges served as director of the National Library in Argentina, as a professor at the University of Buenos Aires, and as a visiting lecturer at many universities around the world. In 1961 he was awarded the International Publishers' Prize and in 1979 the Cervantes Prize, the most coveted literary award among Spanish-speaking nations.

Borges' works are difficult, inventive, intellectual, and metaphysical. Though he lost his sight in later life, his works provide the reader with a kind of x-ray look into the deepest meanings of existence. In a sense all of his work might be viewed as a vigorous attempt at inner vision. Among his recurrent themes are the identity of the self, the relationship of dreams to reality, and the disquieting conclusion that there are no complete, lasting answers to some of the bigger questions of existence. That is the basic contradiction of Borges' work—that he struggles intellectually to understand the nature of reality while at the same time recognizing that this attempt is futile. In "Borges and I" the author makes just such an attempt.

■ How can becoming famous make a person a stranger to him- or herself?

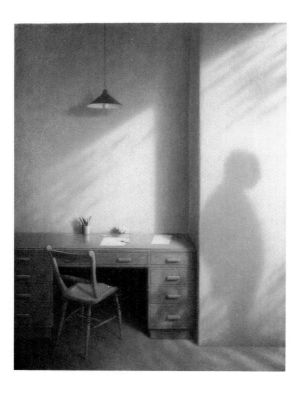

Jorge Luis Borges

Borges and I

The other one, the one called Borges, is the one things happen to. I walk through the streets of Buenos Aires and stop for a moment, perhaps mechanically now, to look at the arch of an entrance hall and the grillwork on the gate; I know of Borges from the mail and see his name on a list of professors or in a biographical dictionary. I like hourglasses, maps, eighteenth-century typography, the taste of coffee, and the prose of Stevenson[1]; he shares these preferences, but in a vain way that turns them into the attributes of an actor. It would be an exaggeration to say that ours is a hostile relationship; I live, let myself go on living, so that Borges may contrive his literature, and this literature justifies me. It is no effort for me to confess that he has achieved some valid pages, but those pages cannot save me, perhaps because what is good belongs to no one, not even to him, but rather to the language and to tradition. Besides, I am destined to perish, definitely, and only some instant of myself can survive in him. Little by little, I am giving over everything to him, though I am quite aware of his perverse custom of falsifying and magnifying things. Spinoza[2] knew that all things long to persist in their being; the stone eternally wants to be a stone and the tiger a tiger. I shall remain in Borges, not in myself (if it is true that I am someone), but I recognize myself less in his books than in many others or in the laborious strumming of a guitar. Years ago I tried to free myself from him and went from the mythologies of the suburbs to the games with time and infinity, but those games belong to Borges now and I shall have to imagine other things. Thus my life is a flight and I lose everything and everything belongs to oblivion, or to him.

I do not know which of us has written this page.

---

1. **Stevenson:** Robert Louis Stevenson (1850–1894), British essayist, novelist, and poet.
2. **Spinoza** [spi nō′zə]: Baruch Spinoza (1632–1677), Dutch philosopher.

STUDY QUESTIONS

Recalling

1. To which of the piece's characters do "things happen"? Where does he walk?
2. How does the speaker know Borges?
3. Why does the speaker live?
4. At the end of the work, what does the speaker "not know"?

Interpreting

5. Who is "the other one," the "I" of this selection?
6. In a few sentences summarize the dilemma of this person. How does he help to create the problem?
7. In what ways does the speaker resent and distrust Borges? Which sentences tell you this?
8. Where in the piece does the speaker suggest that Borges has produced some valuable writing?
9. In what ways is this short fiction like a short story? A philosophical essay? A poem? In what ways is it unlike any of these genres?

Extending

10. What does the speaker's last line suggest about his view of reality?

VIEWPOINT

In talking about some of his most famous fiction, one critic said of Borges:

Two ideas, two aspects of reality, two attributes or "beings" vie for the attention of the consciousness; one must be victorious over the other . . . and although the victory of one is necessary, it is nevertheless deplorable because the victor is only a perspective, a partial image of reality.

—Carter Wheelock,
*The Mythmaker: A Study
of Motif and Symbol in the
Short Stories of Jorge Luis Borges*

How is "Borges and I" about two aspects of reality? About two "beings vying for attention"? Which being seems to be the more victorious one? Despite this victory, how is the overall tone of the piece unvictorious?

COMPOSITION

Writing About Contrasted Characters

In a few paragraphs contrast the two characters, or two "beings," in Borges' short fictional piece. Contrast what the two characters like, what they accomplish, and how they live. Spotlight any additional character traits, giving evidence from the text to support your views.

Writing An Interior Monologue

Write an interior monologue, or first-person speech, in which the speaker thinks out loud. In this monologue the speaker should be the private, "real" you observing, describing, and commenting on the public, less real, or authentic, you. As Borges has done, entitle your piece with three words—your last name, followed by the words "and I."

Pablo Neruda   *1904–1973*

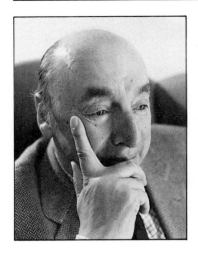

Born in Parral, Chile, the child of a railroad worker, Pablo Neruda went on to become an internationally known poet and winner of the Nobel Prize for Literature. At sixteen he left his hometown for Santiago, where he attended school and became president of the Temuco Literary Club. It was there that he often visited Gabriela Mistral, another Nobel laureate, who acted not only as his school's principal but as his literary mentor. At twenty he published his first volume of poems, *Twenty Poems of Love and One Ode of Desperation.*

Interested in politics, Neruda joined the Central Committee of the Chilean Party and later served as a Chilean consul in the Far East, Spain, Mexico, and Argentina. He traveled widely and toward the end of his life served as ambassador to Paris. It is no surprise, then, that for Neruda politics and poetry were closely intertwined.

Neruda was a prolific writer and a major influence on other modern Latin American authors. Among his works best known in the United States are *Selected Poems: A Bilingual Edition, Twenty Poems of Pablo Neruda,* and *The Heights of Macchu Pichu.*

Neruda's poems are varied in subject but frequently focus on the common person and the universals of human existence. His poems are lyrical, passionate, and vivid. They are both mystical and political. In addition, they often explore the relationship between people and nature.

Neruda has been called both the greatest Latin American poet and the Walt Whitman of Latin America. In "Poetry" he explores the mystical and miraculous process of becoming a poet.

▉ In what way do you think most people decide on a profession or vocation—by choice, accident, default, or a deep and mystical calling?

Pablo Neruda

Poetry

And it was at that age . . . Poetry arrived
in search of me. I don't know, I don't know where
it came from, from winter or a river.
I don't know how or when,
5 no, they were not voices, they were not
words, nor silence,
but from a street I was summoned,
from the branches of night,
abruptly from the others,
10 among violent fires
or returning alone,
there I was without a face
and it touched me.

I did not know what to say, my mouth
15 had no way
with names,
my eyes were blind,
and something started in my soul,
fever or forgotten wings,

20 and I made my own way,
    deciphering
    that fire,
    and I wrote the first faint line,
    faint, without substance, pure
25 nonsense,
    pure wisdom
    of someone who knows nothing,
    and suddenly I saw
    the heavens
30 unfastened
    and open,
    planets,
    palpitating plantations,
    shadow perforated,
35 riddled
    with arrows, fire and flowers,
    the winding night, the universe.

    And I, infinitesimal being,
    drunk with the great starry
40 void,
    likeness, image of
    mystery,
    felt myself a pure part
    of the abyss,
45 I wheeled with the stars,
    my heart broke loose on the wind.

Recalling

1. In stanza 1 what arrived in search of the speaker? From where was the speaker summoned?
2. According to stanza 2, what did his mouth have? How were his eyes? What did he decipher, or decode? What did he write?
3. Recall three of the items the speaker saw when the heavens opened.
4. In the final stanza, of what does the speaker feel a part? What happened to his heart?

Interpreting

5. In what sense does Neruda view his becoming a poet as a calling that came, quite by accident, from outside himself? Point to specific lines to support your answer.
6. For what might the images of fire, fever, and wings stand in stanza 2?
7. Explain the contradiction presented in lines 23–27.
8. What do the images in lines 32–37 suggest about the way Neruda's introduction to writing affected him?

VOCABULARY

Antonyms

Antonyms are words that have opposite or almost opposite meanings. For example, *hardy* and *frail* are antonyms. The words in capital letters are from Neruda's "Poetry." Choose the word that is most nearly the opposite of each word in capitals as the word is used in the selection.

1. DECIPHERING: (a) coding (b) extinguishing (c) entering (d) decoding
2. UNFASTENED: (a) closed (b) unlatched (c) expanded (d) slowed
3. PERFORATED: (a) pierced (b) brewed (c) harvested (d) unpunctured
4. INFINITESIMAL: (a) tiny (b) gargantuan (c) frightened (d) staggering
5. VOID: (a) heavens (b) constellation (c) wine (d) fullness

COMPOSITION

Writing About a Poem's Last Line

■ In a short essay discuss the last line of Neruda's poem "Poetry." Explain its meaning and how this meaning relates to the rest of the poem. Discuss its images and what they add to the poem's emotion. Finally, indicate whether or not you think the poem's final line provides a sense of closure, or final "wrapping up" of the poem's parts.

Writing a Poem by Image-Stacking

■ As Neruda does in "Poetry," write a free-verse poem of three stanzas. In each, respectively, describe poetry, painting, and music. Begin each stanza with one of these terms followed by vivid, imaginative images that suggest that genre's essence. Use only one image per line, creating an "image stack" in each stanza.

Gabriel García Márquez   *born 1928*

Gabriel García Márquez is a Colombian novelist and short story writer who has won international acclaim for his unusual, sometimes supernatural, tales. Born in the town of Aracataca, Colombia, García Márquez was one of twelve children born to a poor telegraph operator and his wife. He was raised by his mother's parents and inspired, in particular, by his grandmother, who was a masterful storyteller. In her home he was exposed to a wealth of folklore, legends, myths, and superstitions, the influence of which can be seen in his writing. At the age of eight, García Márquez was sent away to school and later began the study of law. However, when civil war closed down the University of Bogotá, where he was studying, he turned his full attention to writing. He first worked as a journalist and film critic for the newspaper *El espectador,* which was responsible for publishing his first stories. In addition, he worked as a correspondent in Italy and France and for a Cuban news agency in New York. In recent years García Márquez has spent much of his time living in Mexico. It was in Mexico that he first began writing film scripts and gained celebrity for his most famous book, *Cien años de soledad* (One Hundred Years of Solitude, 1967). The book was the culmination of a cycle, or related series of tales, including *La hojarasca* (Leaf Storm, 1955), *El coronel no tiene quien le escribe* (No One Writes to the Colonel and Other Stories, 1961), and *La Mala Hora* (The Evil Hour, 1966). Other well-known works include *El Otoño del Patriarca* (The Autumn of the Patriarch, 1976) and *Crónica de una muerte anunciada* (Chronicle of a Death Foretold, 1983). In 1982 García Márquez was awarded the Nobel Prize for Literature, and in 1984 his *Collected Stories* were published.

García Márquez's fiction is known for its use of "magical realism," the blending of both realistic and fantastic details. As you read "A Very Old Man with Enormous Wings," a piece that appeared in his first book of stories, think about the ways in which García Márquez combines these elements to create a sense of mystery.

■ Have you ever been in an unusual or catastrophic situation in which people acted like spectators at a carnival? Why do you think people do this?

Gabriel García Márquez

A Very Old Man with Enormous Wings

On the third day of rain they had killed so many crabs inside the house that Pelayo had to cross his drenched courtyard and throw them into the sea, because the newborn child had a temperature all night and they thought it was due to the stench. The world has been sad since Tuesday. Sea and sky were a single ash-gray thing and the sands of the beach, which on March nights glimmered like powdered light, had become a stew of mud and rotten shellfish. The light was so weak at noon that when Pelayo was coming back to the house after throwing away the crabs, it was hard for him to see what it was that was moving and groaning in the rear of the courtyard. He had to go very close to see that it was an old man, a very old man, lying face down in the mud, who, in spite of his tremendous efforts, couldn't get up, impeded by his enormous wings.

Frightened by that nightmare, Pelayo ran to get Elisenda, his wife, who was putting compresses on the sick child, and he took her to the rear of the courtyard. They both looked at the fallen body with mute stupor. He was dressed like a ragpicker.[1] There were only a few faded hairs left on his bald skull and very few teeth in his mouth, and his pitiful condition of a drenched great-grandfather had taken away any sense of grandeur he might have had. His huge buzzard wings, dirty and half-plucked, were forever entangled in the mud. They looked at him so long and so closely that Pelayo and Elisenda very soon overcame their surprise and in the end found him familiar. Then they dared speak to him, and he answered in an incomprehensible dialect with a strong sailor's voice. That was how they skipped over the inconvenience of the

wings and quite intelligently concluded that he was a lonely castaway from some foreign ship wrecked by the storm. And yet, they called in a neighbor woman who knew everything about life and death to see him, and all she needed was one look to show them their mistake.

"He's an angel," she told them. "He must have been coming for the child, but the poor fellow is so old that the rain knocked him down."

On the following day everyone knew that a flesh-and-blood angel was held captive in Pelayo's house. Against the judgment of the wise neighbor woman, for whom angels in those times were the fugitive survivors of a celestial conspiracy, they did not have the heart to club him to death. Pelayo watched over him all afternoon from the kitchen, armed with his bailiff's club, and before going to bed he dragged him out of the mud and locked him up with the hens in the wire chicken coop. In the middle of the night, when the rain stopped, Pelayo and Elisenda were still killing crabs. A short time afterward the child woke up without a fever and with a desire to eat. Then they felt magnanimous and decided to put the angel on a raft with fresh water and provisions for three days and leave him to his fate on the high seas. But when they went out into the courtyard with the first light of dawn, they found the whole neighborhood in front of the chicken coop having fun with the angel, without the slightest reverence, tossing him things to eat through the openings in the wire as if he weren't a supernatural creature but a circus animal.

Father Gonzaga arrived before seven o'clock, alarmed at the strange news. By that time onlookers less frivolous than those at dawn had already arrived and they were making all kinds of conjectures concerning the captive's future. The simplest among them thought that he should be

---

1. **ragpicker** [rag′pick er]: one who collects rags and junk for a livelihood.

named mayor of the world. Others of sterner mind felt that he should be promoted to the rank of five-star general in order to win all wars. Some visionaries hoped that he could be put to stud in order to implant on earth a race of winged wise men who could take charge of the universe. But Father Gonzaga, before becoming a priest, had been a robust woodcutter. Standing by the wire, he reviewed his catechism in an instant and asked them to open the door so that he could take a close look at that pitiful man who looked more like a huge decrepit hen among the fascinated chickens. He was lying in a corner drying his open wings in the sunlight among the fruit peels and breakfast leftovers that the early risers had thrown him. Alien to the impertinences of the world, he only lifted his antiquarian eyes and murmured something in his dialect when Father Gonzaga went into the chicken coop and said good morning to him in Latin. The parish priest had his first suspicion of an impostor when he saw that he did not understand the language of God or know how to greet His ministers. Then he noticed that seen close up he was much too human: he had an unbearable smell of the outdoors, the back side of his wings was strewn with parasites and his main feathers had been mistreated by terrestrial winds, and nothing about him measured up to the proud dignity of angels. Then he came out of the chicken coop and in a brief sermon warned the curious against the risks of being ingenuous. He reminded them that the devil had the bad habit of making use of carnival tricks in order to confuse the unwary. He argued that if wings were not the essential element in determining the difference between a hawk and an airplane, they were even less so in the recognition of angels. Nevertheless, he promised to write a letter to his bishop so that the latter would write to his primate so that the latter would write to the Supreme Pontiff[2] in order to get the final verdict from the highest courts.

His prudence fell on sterile hearts. The news of the captive angel spread with such rapidity that after a few hours the courtyard had the bustle of a marketplace and they had to call in troops with fixed bayonets to disperse the mob that was about to knock the house down. Elisenda, her spine all twisted from sweeping up so much marketplace trash, then got the idea of fencing in the yard and charging five cents admission to see the angel.

The curious came from far away. A traveling carnival arrived with a flying acrobat who buzzed over the crowd several times, but no one paid any attention to him because his wings were not those of an angel but, rather, those of a sidereal[3] bat. The most unfortunate invalids on earth came in search of health: a poor woman who since childhood had been counting her heartbeats and had run out of numbers; a Portuguese man who couldn't sleep because the noise of the stars disturbed him; a sleepwalker who got up at night to undo the things he had done while awake; and many others with less serious ailments. In the midst of that shipwreck disorder that made the earth tremble, Pelayo and Elisenda were happy with fatigue, for in less than a week they had crammed their rooms with money and the line of pilgrims waiting their turn to enter still reached beyond the horizon.

The angel was the only one who took no part in his own act. He spent his time trying to get comfortable in his borrowed nest, befuddled by the hellish heat of the oil lamps and sacramental candles that had been placed along the wire. At first they tried to make him eat some mothballs, which, according to the wisdom of the wise neighbor woman, were the food prescribed for angels. But he turned them down, just as he turned down the papal lunches that the penitents brought him, and they never found out whether it was because he was an angel or because he was an old man that in the end he ate nothing but eggplant mush. His only supernatural virtue seemed to be patience. Especially during the first days, when the hens pecked at him, searching for the stellar parasites that proliferated in his wings, and the cripples pulled out feathers to touch their defective parts with, and even the most merciful threw stones at him, trying to get him to rise so they could see him

---

2. **Supreme Pontiff** [sə prēm′ pon′tif]: the Pope.

3. **sidereal** [sī dē′rē əl]: relating to the stars.

standing. The only time they succeeded in arousing him was when they burned his side with an iron for branding steers, for he had been motionless for so many hours that they thought he was dead. He awoke with a start, ranting in his hermetic[4] language and with tears in his eyes, and he flapped his wings a couple of times, which brought on a whirlwind of chicken dung and lunar dust and a gale of panic that did not seem to be of this world. Although many thought that his reaction had been one not of rage but of pain, from then on they were careful not to annoy him, because the majority understood that his passivity was not that of a hero taking his ease but that of a cataclysm in repose.

Father Gonzaga held back the crowd's frivolity with formulas of maidservant inspiration while awaiting the arrival of a final judgment on the nature of the captive. But the mail from Rome showed no sense of urgency. They spent their time finding out if the prisoner had a navel, if his dialect had any connection with Aramaic,[5] how many times he could fit on the head of a pin, or whether he wasn't just a Norwegian with wings. Those meager letters might have come and gone until the end of time if a providential event had not put an end to the priest's tribulations.

It so happened that during those days, among so many other carnival attractions, there arrived in town the traveling show of the woman who had been changed into a spider for having disobeyed her parents. The admission to see her was not only less than the admission to see the angel, but people were permitted to ask her all manner of questions about her absurd state and to examine her up and down so that no one would ever doubt the truth of her horror. She was a frightful tarantula the size of a ram and with the head of a sad maiden. What was most heart-rending, however, was not her outlandish shape but the sincere affliction with which she recounted the details of her misfortune. While still practically a child she had sneaked out of her parents' house to go to a dance, and while she was coming back through the woods after having danced all night without permission, a fearful thunderclap rent the sky in two and through the crack came the lightning bolt of brimstone that changed her into a spider. Her only nourishment came from the meatballs that charitable souls chose to toss into her mouth. A spectacle like that, full of so much human truth and with such a fearful lesson, was bound to defeat without even trying that of a haughty angel who scarcely deigned to look at mortals. Besides, the few miracles attributed to the angel showed a certain mental disorder, like the blind man who didn't recover his sight but grew three new teeth, or the paralytic who didn't get to walk but almost won the lottery, and the leper whose sores sprouted sunflowers. Those consolation miracles, which were more like mocking fun, had already ruined the angel's reputation when the woman who had been changed into a spider finally crushed him completely. That was how Father Gonzaga was cured forever of his insomnia and Pelayo's courtyard went back to being as empty as during the time it had rained for three days and crabs walked through the bedrooms.

The owners of the house had no reason to lament. With the money they saved they built a two-story mansion with balconies and gardens and high netting so that crabs wouldn't get in during the winter, and with iron bars on the windows so that angels wouldn't get in. Pelayo also set up a rabbit warren close to town and gave up his job as bailiff for good, and Elisenda bought some satin pumps with high heels and many dresses of iridescent silk, the kind worn on Sunday by the most desirable women in those times. The chicken coop was the only thing that didn't receive any attention. If they washed it down with creolin and burned tears of myrrh[6] inside it every so often, it was not in homage to the angel but to drive away the dungheap stench that still hung everywhere like a ghost and was turning the new house into an old one. At first, when the child learned to walk, they were careful that he

---

4. **hermetic:** magical; incomprehensible.
5. **Aramaic** [ar′ə mā′ik]: ancient language of the Middle East.

6. **creolin . . . myrrh:** aromatic resins.

not get too close to the chicken coop. But then they began to lose their fears and got used to the smell, and before the child got his second teeth he'd gone inside the chicken coop to play, where the wires were falling apart. The angel was no less standoffish with him than with other mortals, but he tolerated the most ingenious infamies with the patience of a dog who had no illusions. They both came down with chicken pox at the same time. The doctor who took care of the child couldn't resist the temptation to listen to the angel's heart, and he found so much whistling in the heart and so many sounds in his kidneys that it seemed impossible for him to be alive. What surprised him most, however, was the logic of his wings. They seemed so natural on that completely human organism that he couldn't understand why other men didn't have them too.

When the child began school it had been some time since the sun and rain had caused the collapse of the chicken coop. The angel went dragging himself about here and there like a stray dying man. They would drive him out of the bedroom with a broom and a moment later find him in the kitchen. He seemed to be in so many places at the same time that they grew to think that he'd been duplicated, that he was reproducing himself all through the house, and the exasperated and unhinged Elisenda shouted that it was awful living in that hell full of angels. He could scarcely eat and his antiquarian eyes had also become so foggy that he went about bumping into posts. All he had left were the bare cannulae[7] of his last feathers. Pelayo threw a blanket over him and extended him the charity of letting him sleep in the shed, and only then did they notice that he had a temperature at night, and was delirious with the tongue twisters of an old Norwegian. That was one of the few times they became alarmed, for they thought he was going to die and not even the wise neighbor woman had been able to tell them what to do with dead angels.

And yet he not only survived his worst winter, but seemed improved with the first sunny days. He remained motionless for several days in the farthest corner of the courtyard, where no one would see him, and at the beginning of December some large, stiff feathers began to grow on his wings, the feathers of a scarecrow, which looked more like another misfortune of decrepitude. But he must have known the reason for those changes, for he was quite careful that no one should notice them, that no one should hear the sea chanteys that he sometimes sang under the stars. One morning Elisenda was cutting some bunches of onions for lunch when a wind that seemed to come from the high seas blew into the kitchen. Then she went to the window and caught the angel in his first attempts at flight. They were so clumsy that his fingernails opened a furrow in the vegetable patch and he was on the point of knocking the shed down with the ungainly flapping that slipped on the light and couldn't get a grip on the air. But he did manage to gain altitude. Elisenda let out a sigh of relief, for herself and for him, when she saw him pass over the last houses, holding himself up in some way with the risky flapping of a senile vulture. She kept watching him even when she was through cutting the onions and she kept on watching until it was no longer possible for her to see him, because then he was no longer an annoyance in her life but an imaginary dot on the horizon of the sea.

---

7. **cannulae** [kan′yo͞o lē′]: tubular bases of feathers.

STUDY QUESTIONS

Recalling

1. What are some of the outstanding physical characteristics of the man Pelayo finds groaning at the back of the courtyard? What does the wise neighbor, the woman "who knew everything about life," say about the man?
2. When the man is locked up, what suggestions do the onlookers make about what should happen to him? What is Father Gonzaga's suspicion about the man?
3. Who takes the place of the man in the onlookers' eyes? What is unusual about this person? What happened to her to make her this way?
4. What does Elisenda see at the end of the story?

Interpreting

5. If you were to reduce the mystery of this story into a single question that needs answering, what would it be? In what way is this question answered at the story's end?
6. In what ways do Pelayo and Elisenda profit from the intruder's stay? How do others in the story use or abuse him? What does García Márquez seem to be saying about human nature? Do you think he is totally cynical of the motives of human beings? Why or why not?
7. Reread the story's first paragraph. How does García Márquez use sensory detail to create a realistic setting? What details add a supernatural dimension to this setting? How does this opening setting add to the story's mystery?

Extending

8. If you had been one of the onlookers staring at the creature in the coop, what would you have concluded about his origins?

COMPARING WRITERS

1. Compare any two poems from this unit that describe night in detail. Which do you think is the most effective description? The most comforting? The most foreboding? In which nighttime setting would you most like to find yourself? Why? Relate your answers to specific lines and images from the pair of poems.
2. Compare the haiku of Bashō with the fragments of Sappho. How are they similar in length and imagery? In emotion? Which has the greater impact on you? Why?
3. Compare the attitudes toward and feelings for nature as they are described by any two authors from this unit. Which author seems most closely connected with nature? Most replenished by it? Most threatened by it? Most distant from it? In your opinion which of the two selections provides the more striking images of the natural world?
4. Compare the prose of Kafka, Borges, and García Márquez. How does each writer rely on the fantastic? The realistic? Which of these pieces seems most mysterious to you? Which has the most powerful emotional effect on you? Why? If you were to paint a mural spotlighting the highlights of each story, which do you think would be the most colorful and graphic? The most detailed?

Key to Illustrations on Pages 778–779.

1. Detail, Christopher Columbus at the Royal Court of Spain, American lithograph, 1892.
2. Detail, embarkation of Chevaliers du Saint-Esprit on a Crusade, fourteenth-century miniature.
3. Ruins of small temple at Delphi.
4. Miguel de Cervantes (1547–1616).
5. Detail, *View of Toledo,* El Greco, early 1600s.
6. Detail, thirteenth-century miniature depicting Dante composing the *Divine Comedy.*
7. Detail, French etching showing the storming of the Bastille, 1817.
8. Detail, *The Great Wave off Kanagawa,* a Japanese print by Katsushika Hokusai (1760–1849).
9. Silver kneeling bull holding a vessel, Iranian, c. 2900 B.C.
10. Detail, *Harlequin,* Pablo Picasso, 1901.

STUDENT'S RESOURCES
LESSONS IN ACTIVE LEARNING

SPEAKING AND LISTENING HANDBOOK

THINKING SKILLS HANDBOOK

WRITING ABOUT LITERATURE HANDBOOK

RESEARCH PAPER CASEBOOK

LITERARY TERMS HANDBOOK

SPEAKING AND LISTENING HANDBOOK

LESSON 1: *A Speech of Inquiry About Literature*

OVERVIEW

You will present a speech in which you raise an issue concerning one or more literary selections in this textbook. You will identify the issue, explain why it is a problem, and motivate your audience to examine the issue.

This kind of speech is referred to as a speech of inquiry because your major purpose is to ask questions and to offer alternatives rather than to come up with a final conclusion. In the course of putting together this speech, you will also *inform* your listeners about an issue and *persuade* them that the issue you raise is significant. In effect, then, this kind of speech demands that you practice all previous speechmaking skills that you have learned.

PREPARING THE SPEECH

1. **Find an issue.**
   Look through this book of literary selections, ask yourself questions, use your imagination, and write down all the things that arouse your curiosity. Perhaps you will brainstorm as a class to raise absorbing issues that may become the subjects of speeches. Here are some ideas to get you started:

   • So-called light literature such as Aesop's fables vs. more serious works
   • Relevance of older works of literature such as *Beowulf* and the *Aeneid* to today's problems
   • The influence one writer, such as Shakespeare, had on another, such as Ben Jonson

2. **Formulate the issue as a question.**
   For this kind of speech, your thesis should be stated as a question, not a statement. For example, rather than stating, "Someone else may have written Shakespeare's play," ask, "Did Shakespeare write his own plays?" Rather than stating, "Some literature is written in response to war," ask, "In what ways does war influence the writing of literature?"

3. **Establish the importance of the question.**
   You do not want to waste your own time and your audience's time exploring a question that is either not very significant or to which the answers are already known. For example, the question "Is *Macbeth* a great work of literature?" does not warrant investing time in preparing a speech of inquiry; the overwhelming amount of opinion and evidence indicates that the answer is indisputably *yes*. On the other hand, the following question is worth exploring because the answer is not immediately apparent: "Does Macbeth's 'Tomorrow and tomorrow and tomorrow' speech have just as much power when taken out of the context of the play as it has in the play?" There may be evidence on both sides of the question.

4. **Explore possible answers.**
   In your speech you will explore possible answers to the question under investigation. You do not have to—you should not—attempt to take sides or to provide a definite answer. The whole point is to present a speech that explores possibilities. You will examine all possible answers. You will present the opinions of critics and your own insights. This is probably the part of the preparation that will take the longest and require the most care on your part.

5. **Organize and outline your speech.**
   Begin by arousing your audience's interest in the issue. You might mention briefly what made you choose this particular issue—how and why you became interested in it. Or you may want to ask for a show of hands from those who have also wondered

about the same thing. Make sure that you have stated the question clearly.

The body of your speech will be concerned with presenting two or more views on the issue and supporting those views with references to the literary work or works in question.

In your conclusion you can draw some inferences about what you have found out and once again stress the importance of the issue. You may also want to challenge your audience to look into the matter further—or at least to give it some further thought.

A SAMPLE SPEECH

Suppose you want to inquire into the question "Does early poetry differ significantly from more recent poetry?" This question may have occurred to you as you read various poems from different chronological units of this book. You may note the similarities and differences you see between, say, "The Seafarer" (written in the tenth century) and "Dover Beach" (written in the nineteenth century). You may also note what literary critics have said about these poems. Here are questions to consider as you think about the larger question of early vs. recent poetry:

- Are the subjects the same?
- Are they written to the same kind of audience?
- Which do you enjoy reading more?
- What kind of language does each use?

An outline based on your inquiry might look like this:

I. Introduction
A. Get attention of audience.
B. State the question clearly.
C. Defend the importance of the question.

II. Body
A. Explain why you chose the examples you chose.
B. Identify what the critics and you see as the differences between the poems.
C. Identify what the critics and you see as the similarities between the poems.

III. Conclusion
A. State the question again.
B. Summarize what you have found through inquiry.
C. Show the implication of what you have learned. (E.g., perhaps you have learned that early poetry has more meaning for today than you previously thought.)

DELIVERING THE SPEECH

1. **Be clear.**
Make sure your audience understands that it is not your intention to resolve an issue but simply to make the audience appreciate the issue.

2. **Speak extemporaneously.**
Be familiar enough with your speech that you have only to glance at your outline or notes. You want to be able to look at your audience as much as possible. Practice enough so that you are so sure of your ideas that you can speak with confidence.

3. **Speak with enthusiasm.**
If you are genuinely excited about your ideas and want to share them with your classmates, your delivery will sound refreshing, and your audience will become interested and stay interested.

4. **Answer questions politely.**
Listen carefully to the questioner, look directly at him or her, and give a brief answer.

ASSIGNMENTS

1. Using the question posed under the head "A Sample Speech," read "The Seafarer" and "Dover Beach" so that you can complete the suggested outline. Then practice and deliver the speech.

2. Convert one of the literary issues listed on page 964 to a question. Proceed to develop that question into a speech of inquiry.

3. Develop a question on your own. Base the question on one or more pieces of literature in this anthology. Prepare and deliver a speech of inquiry in response to your question.

LESSON 2: *A Symposium About Literature*

OVERVIEW

A group of four to six students will present a symposium on a literature-based topic to the class. A **symposium** is a formal public discussion in which individuals present speeches giving their own views on a preselected topic or question, which is open to debate. The goal of the symposium is to explore the question and to consider various perspectives and possible answers.

A symposium differs from an informal discussion and a panel discussion in that the participants prepare and present formal speeches based on their independent research; in an informal discussion and a panel discussion the participants speak spontaneously in response to questions from the leader or moderator. A symposium also needs a moderator (see below).

PREPARING FOR A SYMPOSIUM

1. **Select a topic.**

   For this symposium the members of the group should select a topic that is of current interest. Suggestions include peace, leadership, the environment, the economy, and so on. The topic should contain some element that is debatable. Otherwise, all the opinions expressed will be similar, and the symposium will lack interest.

   Remember that the topic you select must be one that is touched upon by literature in this anthology. Ask yourself, What do the selections of literature included here have to say about this topic? What light can they shed on the topic?

   Although most literary works are not written to address a social issue, they concern themselves with these issues indirectly.

2. **Formulate the discussion question.**

   The symposium members as a group must formulate a question that demands more than a yes/no answer. Each individual's speech should take a stand on the question and attempt to provide *possible* answers.

The question can be a question of fact or a question of values. The former asks whether something is true or asks for identification of some kind or another. The latter asks whether something is good or bad.

Examples

QUESTION OF FACT: Throughout history what qualities have our great political leaders manifested?

QUESTION OF VALUE: What are the advantages and disadvantages of inherited leadership or leadership acquired through physical dominance?

To answer these questions, symposium members can refer to the following pieces of literature, among others, from this book:

- *Beowulf*
- *Macbeth*
- the *Iliad*
- *Le Morte d'Arthur*
- "Oyzmandias"
- *Antigone*

3. **Research the question.**

   Each member of the symposium must individually read about the issue, using books and articles from the school or local library. After using these outside sources you can turn to the literature in this book to find support for your position. You might cite the overall theme of a literary work, or you may want to quote a few specific lines from the work.

4. **Continue to work together as a group.**

   The symposium group must meet several times in advance of the symposium proper. In addition to dealing with the steps already enumerated, the group will profit from sharing research sources and then organizing the symposium proper:

   a. Decide who will deal with which piece or pieces of literature, and decide on the order of the speeches.

b. Agree on the stages of the symposium, which might follow this pattern: introduction by moderator; individual speeches; questioning by members of the symposium; questions from the audience; summary by moderator.

c. Share one another's insights and findings. It is especially important that the moderator know ahead of time the direction each speech will take.

GUIDELINES FOR THE MODERATOR

1. Set up the room to establish a good climate for discussion. Speakers can sit behind tables facing the audience, or they can stand in the center while they speak, returning to their seats afterward.

2. Introduce the symposium, identifying the question to be discussed, providing background on the question if necessary, and perhaps explaining why the group selected this question.

3. Introduce each speaker, and briefly tell what each speaker will talk about, noting how it fits into the total picture. Thus the moderator provides a transition from speaker to speaker and ties the entire symposium together.

4. Lead the discussion that follows the individual presentations. Here the moderator acts as a gatekeeper, calling on members of the symposium to ask one another questions or to comment on what one another has said. The moderator offers his or her own observations throughout and keeps the discussion moving forward.

5. Invite the audience to ask questions and offer comments.

6. Summarize the symposium so that everyone gets a sense of what has been covered and what consensus has developed. During this summary the moderator may recount each participant's contributions.

7. Monitor time allotments. The moderator is responsible for seeing that each speaker stays within the agreed-upon time frame. The moderator must also make sure there is enough time for questions and for a summary.

GUIDELINES FOR SYMPOSIUM SPEAKERS

1. Your speech must have an introduction, body, and conclusion. The introduction should make clear your position. The body should offer support for that position, including reference to one or more literary works in this book. The conclusion should relate your point to the overall discussion question.

2. Your delivery should be smooth and clear. You can either sit or stand, as the group decides. You can refer to notes or outline, but try to speak extemporaneously and practice eye contact.

3. Make sure that you refer to literature in this book as a way of supporting your ideas. If you quote from the literature, be sure to speak expressively (see Lesson 3), and quote exactly. Make sure your audience understands what is a quotation and what is your speech proper.

4. Listen attentively and with an open mind to other members of the symposium. They may have thought about the question in a way that you have not. You may be able to form good follow-up questions to help with an exciting discussion after each member has given his or her formal speech.

GUIDELINES FOR THE AUDIENCE

1. Do not speak until you are recognized by the moderator.

2. Be brief when you ask a question or make a comment.

3. Do not monopolize the discussion.

ASSIGNMENT

If you need help in coming up with a question that is current, debatable, and discussable in terms of literature in this book, you might consider the following:

- the effect of money
- insights into death
- life-style differences
- world peace

LESSON 3: *Oral Interpretation of Prose Fiction*

OVERVIEW

You will select a short story or an excerpt of one, and read it aloud to the class. The story or excerpt should contain some narration and some dialogue, even if just a few lines.

As an oral interpreter you will speak primarily as the narrator, or storyteller, but you will also present the various characters in the story and speak as those characters.

PREPARING AN ORAL INTERPRETATION OF PROSE FICTION

1. **Cutting and adapting a story**

   Your reading should be from five to six minutes in length. Some of the stories in this book may be able to be read aloud to the class in this time, but others will have to be cut. There are two ways to cut a work:

   a. Read an excerpt only. Find a good place to begin and a good place to end, so that the excerpt makes sense on its own.

   b. Eliminate portions of the story, resulting in an abridged version of the story. You will read the story to the class from the beginning to the end, but you will cut out portions, summarizing them in sentences of your own, so that the reading fits within the required time limits.

2. **Establishing a narrative tone**

   As you read from your selected story, you will want most of all to capture the right tone for the narrator. The narrator's tone is the most important element of the story for the oral interpreter. The oral interpreter's relationship with the audience depends on the narrator's tone:

   • Does the narrator seem to be superior to the audience, or readers?

   • Does the narrator adopt a tone of folksiness and come across as on the same level as the audience?

   • What is the degree of formality or informality established by the narrator?

   • What mood does the narrator establish—one of suspense, one of outlandish humor, one of mild criticism, or one of great sympathy?

   As an oral interpreter, you want to capture the narrative tone and make it clear to your audience from the very beginning of your reading. The audience should be able to tell what kind of story this will be from the very first sentences you utter. In other words, establish the narrative tone right away, and establish it firmly and strongly.

3. **Characterization**

   The narrator tells about the background, setting, characters, and action of the story. The narrator also allows the characters to talk, in first person, in the present tense, much as they would in a play. For example, in "The Singing Lesson" by Katherine Mansfield, the narrator tells us the following about Miss Meadows:

   > And she called to the girls, "I shall put you on your honor to talk quietly while I am away."

   In your reading you will want to say this line as Miss Meadows would say it—in her tone of voice (not the narrator's) with a sense of her character. Then you resume the voice of the narrator.

   When the narrator gives us two (or more) characters talking to each other in the story, we have what is referred to as a scene. The characters speak dialogue, just as they do in a play. As an interpreter you want to create a sense of each character through your voice, body, gestures, and facial expression. To make the characters believable, you want to create a sense of their inner worlds, too—of how they think, of why they are speaking, of their motivation, or intention. From a performance perspective you want to create, or establish, a focus: Where is each character looking at each moment as he or she speaks? Instead of reading dialogue that sounds stiff, wooden, or unnatural, you can bring the scene to life.

Unlike a play, however, the dialogue in a story will usually be interspersed with narration. There will be whole paragraphs, transitional sentences, or just a dialogue tag (e.g., "she called") before or after a character speaks. The skillful performer will blend the line of dialogue with the line of narration. Sometimes they are a part of the same sentence. In delivering these you do not want, necessarily, to pause between the narration and the dialogue (especially when they are a part of the same sentence gramatically). To do so would be to interrupt the reading and set up a boring rhythm. Rather, aim for smoothness. In the reading of prose fiction, you want to achieve both a sense of characters speaking to each other (as in drama) and a sense of a story being told. Listen to your own friends or family members telling stories naturally as they do every day. How do they handle presenting what other people have said? How do they blend dialogue and description? You can apply these techniques to your oral interpretation of fiction.

4. **Structure of the reading**
   You will need to know where the climax is—of the story and of the excerpt you are reading. You want to build up to this point—make this the high point of the reading. Along the way may be smaller climaxes, or tension points. You will want to emphasize these by raising your voice in pitch, quickening your rate, or even by pausing. Finally, there will be many transitions, or changes, in what is occurring. You want to realize these changes as you read the piece. Shift your tone as you turn your attention to something else—a new description, a new scene, another character. By thinking about the structure, or shape, of the reading, you will make it clear to your audience, and they will understand what is going on in the piece.

5. **Preparing an introduction**
   Finally, you want to prepare a few introductory remarks about your oral interpretation. The introduction should put the audience in the proper mood to hear the piece, explain any information that they might need to know (such as which piece it is, who wrote it, what your excerpt consists of, and why you chose it).

PRESENTING YOUR ORAL INTERPRETATION

1. Approach the front of the room slowly. Put your manuscript on the lectern or reading stand. Pause and look around your audience for a moment before beginning, rather than rushing.

2. Deliver your introduction to the reading as a brief extemporaneous speech.

3. Open your manuscript, and begin your reading firmly and clearly. Speak the first few words boldly, so the audience can key into what you are saying.

4. Use eye contact throughout the reading. As the narrator, or storyteller, you can look directly at your audience. Talk to different members of your audience, moving your eyes from person to person gradually, not staying on one person too long—only a few seconds. When you are reading a character's own words, establish a focal point, or image, of the other character being spoken to.

5. Develop strong concentration. Think about what you are saying; really see the events described and the characters spoken to.

6. Begin with and maintain (or increase) your energy as you perform. Be sure that you project your voice and speak clearly. Allow yourself to use gestures or other bodily movements if they seem to come naturally to you. Get involved in the reading, and develop an enthusiasm for it and for sharing it with your audience.

7. Conclude your reading firmly. Close your manuscript. Pause for a moment, and acknowledge any applause.

ASSIGNMENTS

The following stories or excerpts from them lend themselves to oral interpretation:

- "Araby" by James Joyce (page 707)
- "The Singing Lesson" by Katherine Mansfield (page 712)
- "The New Dress" by Virginia Woolf (page 726)
- excerpt from *Oliver Twist* by Charles Dickens (page 511)

LESSON 4: *A Literary Debate*

OVERVIEW

You will collaborate with another student on this assignment. Together you will choose a notable issue concerning one or more of the literary selections in this anthology. You will then take opposing points of view in relation to the topic and present persuasive speeches to the class. You will each go on to present a rebuttal speech in which you answer what your opponent said in his or her speech. The class will decide which point of view they agree with based on which one of you argued most persuasively.

DECIDING ON AN ISSUE

With your partner select an issue that is interesting, important, and arguable—much in the same way you selected an issue to examine in a speech of inquiry (see Lesson 1 of this handbook). If the issue you choose is interesting and important, it will hold the attention of your audience. If it is arguable, it will allow each of you to take a different point of view.

FORMULATING THE DEBATE QUESTION

Formulate the issue you decide upon as a question that can be answered simply by yes or no—even though you will go on to say considerably more in your speech.

Examples

- Was Thomas Hardy a better poet than novelist? Yes or no?
- Does the use of a first-person narrator draw the reader further into the literary work and create a greater sense of intimacy between speaker and reader? Yes or no?
- Does knowledge of the author's life help us to understand the literary work better? Yes or no?
- Is Lady Macbeth a stronger character than Macbeth? Yes or no?

SUPPORTING A POINT OF VIEW

You and your partner will have to decide who will argue which side of the issue. One of you will argue for an affirmative answer to the question, the other will argue for a negative answer. In the last question, for example, one of you would argue that, yes, Lady Macbeth is a stronger character than Macbeth, while the other would argue that Lady Macbeth is *not* stronger and might even argue further that Macbeth is actually stronger than Lady Macbeth.

In arguing your side of the issue you will want to refer to the play itself and perhaps even quote certain lines or speeches that defend your position.

ORGANIZING THE SPEECHES

When two people present speeches to the audience on the same topic, it is important to arrange the speeches in a proper order. Each of you will present an introductory speech; a persuasive speech; and a rebuttal speech, in which you answer the arguments of your opponent. The speeches should be arranged in the following order for maximum effect:

Speeches of introduction (one-half minute each)
- Speaker A: Present and explain the question.
- Speaker B: Justify the importance of the question.

Persuasive speeches (four minutes each)
- Speaker A: Affirmative speech in favor of the question
- Speaker B: Negative speech not in favor of the question

Rebuttal speeches (one minute each)
- Speaker A: Refute the arguments of Speaker B.
- Speaker B: Refute the arguments of Speaker A.

Organize the middle speech just as you would any other persuasive speech, except that the opening and closing can be much shorter because the speeches of introduction and rebuttal accomplish these tasks for you. Within a literary debate the persuasive speech itself is just the "body" of an ordinary persuasive speech. It presents the relevant arguments for your side of the question along with appropriate support materials.

The rebuttal speeches are given completely spontaneously, or impromptu. They are in response to the opponent's persuasive speech. Although the two of you decide on the issue, formulate the question, and establish its importance, you prepare your own sides of the question separately. You may share information and sources—and you may even discuss your views of the play with each other before presenting your speeches to the class, but you do not share your actual speeches with each other. You can anticipate what your opponent is going to say, but you do not know for sure. As a result, the rebuttals are often the most exciting part of a debate.

DELIVERING THE SPEECHES

When you are one of two people speaking to an audience, you have to decide where each of you will stand and sit. The two of you can sit on opposite sides of the front of the room but move to the center for speaking, or the two of you can speak from either side of the room.

You may want to stand while you are speaking and sit when the other person is speaking, or both of you can speak while sitting if you can be seen easily by everyone in the room.

You will want to outline your speech on either small index cards—one point on a card—or on one or two sheets of notebook paper. You will speak in an extemporaneous manner, glancing at your notes but maintaining strong eye contact with members of your audience.

As in all persuasive speeches you will want to speak with conviction and enthusiasm. You will want to demonstrate by your tone of voice, your intensity, firm eye contact, and gestures that you are genuinely excited about your topic and your arguments. If you quote from the literature at any length, you will want to use the principles of good oral interpretation (see Lesson 3).

ASSIGNMENT

With a partner debate one of the literary questions listed above. Alternatively, create your own debate question regarding one or more literary works in this book.

THINKING SKILLS HANDBOOK

LESSON 1: *Problem Solving*

■ DEFINITION

Problem solving is a way of thinking that involves a group of skills. Regardless of the type of problem, good problem solvers attack problems systematically rather than in a haphazard fashion. These are the basic steps in problem solving:

Stating the goal
Identifying the givens, the things that
   cannot be changed
Identifying the obstacles
Developing the plan, including consideration
   of all the options
Carrying out the plan
Checking the results

The good problem solver knows both the *specifics* of the problem and the *procedures* of problem solving. Problems are solved in specific contexts, and they are solved by orderly thinking.

■ EXAMPLE

Alice has been assigned the task of defending a statement made on page 108 of this book: "Nothing, not even the opening of the American frontier or our recent exploration of space, would ever match the explosion of energy in England in those days."

■ EXPLANATION

Alice first defines the problem. Her **goal** is a defense of the statement, a defense so convincing that the members of her class will all agree with the statement. The **given** in the situation is the statement itself. The **obstacles** are that Alice is not sure she knows exactly what the statement means, and she is not at all sure that the statement is true.

Alice develops a **plan,** a set of **methods,** to solve the problem. She will first make sure that she understands the terms of the statement. She will write out

specific definitions of "the opening of the American frontier," "recent exploration of space," "explosion of energy," and "England in those days." She will do the necessary library research to identify facts and details describing each part of the statement. This will overcome the first obstacle, that of not understanding the statement.

Alice then plans to make a comparison chart of the events she has listed under "American frontier" and "exploration of space" with the events she has listed under "England in those days." The comparison she plans will enable her to decide if the more recent events "would ever match" the older ones. This will overcome the second obstacle, that of not being sure of the truth of the statement.

Alice **carries out the plan** and presents her arguments to the class. She **checks the results** by noting that not only has she become sure of the truth of the statement but virtually every member of the class also agrees with her. She has solved the problem.

■ PROCEDURES

1. **State a goal.**
   Identify what you want to do or to achieve.

2. **List the givens.**
   What information is available to you as you start to think about reaching the goal? Are you looking at the problem in its full context, considering the situation completely?

3. **List the obstacles.**
   What will prevent you from reaching the goal? Obstacles are sometimes obvious and clearly stated, sometimes unstated or hidden.

4. **Identify the methods.**
   What will you do to reach a solution? What is your plan of attack? What specific steps will you follow to eliminate each obstacle?

5. **Carry out the plan.**

6. **Check the results.**
Have you solved the problem? How will you be sure? Did you follow the best plan? Was there a better way to solve the problem?

ACTIVITY I. APPLYING PROBLEM-SOLVING PROCEDURES

The purpose of this activity is to apply problem-solving procedures to a particular work of Anglo-Saxon, Medieval, or Elizabethan literature.

Choose one of the selections you have read in one of the first three units of this book—for example, *Beowulf* (page 10), *Le Morte d'Arthur* (page 99), or *Macbeth* (page 148). Describe how you would apply each step of the problem-solving process to a specific problem presented in the selection. For example, one problem might be how to slay Grendel.

1. What is the **goal?**

2. What are the **givens** of the situation, the conditions that cannot be changed? What is the context, the particular situation in which the problem exists?

3. What are the **obstacles?** Are all the obstacles obvious? Are some hidden?

4. What is the **plan** used to reach the goal? In the plan, what steps are to be followed and in what order?

5. Describe the actions involved in **carrying out the plan.** Be realistic. Have any new obstacles arisen?

6. **Check the results.** Does the plan solve the problem? If not, why not? Were the givens or the obstacles wrongly identified? Were the methods incorrectly chosen? Was the plan not carried out properly? Could the plan ever have been successful?

ACTIVITY II. IDENTIFYING OR APPLYING PROBLEM SOLVING TO ANY WORK OF LITERATURE

The purpose of this activity is to identify or apply the procedure of the problem-solving process to any work of literature in this book or any other work of literature you have read.

1. Select a work of literature, identify the **goal,** the problem to be solved, in the main action of the plot.

2. State the **givens** in the situation. Be sure to consider the full context of the problem.

3. State the **obstacles** to solving the problem. Consider any hidden obstacles as well as the most obvious ones.

4. Identify the **methods,** or the **plan,** used to solve the problem in the literary work, or develop your own plan for solving it.

5. Tell whether the **plan is carried out.**

6. Check the **results** by telling whether or not the problem is solved. If the problem is not solved, tell what change in the methods or plan you would make in order to solve it.

LESSON 2: *Evaluation*

DEFINITION

Evaluation is a thinking skill that involves judgment. Decisions about value, excellence, beauty, effectiveness, truthfulness, or reliability of something or someone, including yourself, are evaluations. Proper evaluation rests on the application of **appropriate criteria** for making judgments. Part of the process of maturing as a thinking person is learning how to apply appropriate criteria in a calm and deliberate way rather than by responding to emotion or following impulse.

EXAMPLE

Marsha, editor-in-chief of the yearbook, must recommend to the yearbook committee someone from her staff to be next year's editor-in-chief.

EXPLANATION

Marsha must establish criteria for judging the qualifications of her staff members. She decides on the following: number of years on the staff, reliability in completing assignments, ability to work with others successfully, and desire for the job. Marsha then interviews all members of her staff who wish to be considered for the position. She evaluates each candidate on the listed criteria. When her interviews are complete, Marsha reviews the ratings she has made and recommends the best-qualified person she has found in this process.

PROCEDURES

1. **Determine the reason or purpose** for evaluation.

2. **Identify the criteria**—the rules, tests, or standards to be applied in judging.

3. **Apply the criteria.**

4. **Draw a conclusion.** The result of this process is your evaluation. Did the criteria fit? Were they appropriate? Did the evaluation result in a favorable or an unfavorable outcome?

ACTIVITY I. EVALUATING MOTIVATIONS IN *MACBETH* AND *PARADISE LOST*

The purpose of this activity is to evaluate the motivations for evil as found in *Macbeth* (page 148) and *Paradise Lost* (page 278) by developing and applying criteria for judging evil motivations in literary works. Work with a partner.

Shakespeare and Milton intended that their audiences contemplate the motivations for evil in the world. Did Shakespeare and Milton share similar views of the motivations for evil?

1. From *Macbeth* **make a list of evil actions and events** that occur in the play. Beside each entry write the motivation for the evil action or event. The motivation may be from within or outside of the character. If it is outside the character, specify its source.

2. From *Paradise Lost* **make a list of evil actions or events.** Specify the motivations as you did for *Macbeth*.

3. **Compare the lists** of motivations. What criteria would you apply to judging these motivations? Are they true to human nature? Are they consistent? Are they dramatically impressive? **List the criteria** you believe to be most significant. You may want to set up a chart listing the motivations down one side and your criteria across the top. **Applying the criteria in this way enables you to draw a conclusion** in a calm and deliberate way rather than by following emotion or impulse as you think about motivations.

4. **Evaluate** the motivations for evil in Shakespeare and Milton. What conclusions do you reach about this subject? Did Shakespeare and Milton share similar views?

5. **Speculate** on what may have influenced Shakespeare's and Milton's views of the motivations for evil in the world.

ACTIVITY II. INFERRING JONSON'S CRITERIA FOR EVALUATING SHAKESPEARE'S WORK

Ben Jonson, in his poem "To the Memory of My Beloved Master, William Shakespeare" (page 262), evaluated the works of Shakespeare.

1. What were Jonson's qualifications for judging Shakespeare's works? Were there any areas of scholarship in which Jonson had knowledge superior to that of Shakespeare?

2. Does Jonson rate Shakespeare among poets and writers of his own time? Why or why not?

3. With whom does Jonson rank William Shakespeare?

4. What criteria do you think Jonson uses to evaluate Shakespeare's writing? **List the criteria** you think he probably had in mind.

5. **Applying** Jonson's criteria, **evaluate your favorite author.** How does your author rate according to Jonson's criteria?

6. **Speculate** on the prospect of another writer of the stature of William Shakespeare appearing in your lifetime.

LESSON 3: *Logical Reasoning*

DEFINITION
Logical reasoning is a way of organizing your ideas to support an explanation or to convince someone that you are correct. When you reason logically, you first identify for your audience the necessary conditions that are required for your claim to be accepted. Your audience must be willing to accept the assumptions you are making—that these conditions are appropriate to support your argument. Then you must demonstrate sufficient evidence that the necessary conditions have been met.

EXAMPLE
The relationship of governments to the governed was often the subject of English writers during the eighteenth century. Jonathan Swift, the greatest of the satirists, draws attention to the problems raised by warfare and general distrust of government. How can you demonstrate logically that any particular literary work is a satire?

EXPLANATION
In order to demonstrate that a literary work that purports to be a straightforward report of life is really a satire on contemporary society, you must establish that the necessary conditions for satire are present in sufficient quantity. Some elements of society must be presented in so exaggerated a way as to be ridiculous.

One way to support your contention that a literary work is a satire is to list the necessary conditions and see whether they do apply to the case in question. You may find a chart like this helpful:

Examination of the chart reveals that the necessary conditions are present in sufficient quantities for the item to be considered a satire. It would not be logical to say that a literary work that exaggerated all these elements was not a satire.

PROCEDURES
When you want to use logical reasoning to support your own position on a subject, you will find the following steps helpful:

1. **State what you believe** to be true.

2. **Identify the conditions** that are necessary for the situation to be true.

3. Show that the necessary conditions have been met in the situation you are explaining. **Give a sufficient number of specific examples.**

4. **Identify the assumptions** you and your audience must share if your position is to be convincing.

ACTIVITY I. REASONING LOGICALLY ABOUT HUMOR
There are many examples of humor and wit in eighteenth-century English literature. Select two examples that illustrate an important issue being addressed in a humorous manner.

1. For each example **state what you believe** to be the situation that is the object of the humor.

2. **List the conditions** that would be necessary if a particular statement or idea is to be considered

ELEMENT OF SOCIETY	EXAGGERATION EVIDENT
Communication	+
Relative size and importance	+
Education of ruling class	+
Ability and honesty of rulers	+
Lawyers and courts	+
Taxes and expenditures	+
Reasons for wars	+
Religious group membership	+

humorous. Identify your assumptions about what would make this situation humorous.

3. **Show that the two examples meet the necessary conditions** for humor.

4. **Write a brief statement** supporting your contention that these two examples are intended to be humorous.

ACTIVITY II. REASONING LOGICALLY ABOUT HUMANITY

Eighteenth-century English writers often focus on the foibles of mankind. How do these writers feel about the human race? Is their perspective optimistic or pessimistic? Do they appear to express the same attitude? Or do they see things differently?

1. **State your belief** about the positions of two writers regarding the human race. Use eighteenth-century English writers or any other writers you choose.

2. **List the necessary conditions** that would support your position regarding each writer's view.

3. **Demonstrate that there is sufficient evidence** in each writer's work to support your position. You may find it helpful to chart your findings.

4. Compare and contrast the positions of these two writers. How are they alike? How are they different? **Write a brief statement** of your findings.

LESSON 4: *Inductive Inquiry*

DEFINITION

Inductive inquiry is a way to *discover* meaning by observation. As you examine several examples of an idea, you discover which characteristics the examples share. Once you have discovered what is special, or characteristic, about the idea you are examining, you can also tell how that idea differs from similar ideas.

EXAMPLE

The unit in this book called "The Romantic Age" includes a variety of literary selections that differ in subject matter, form, and point of view. What makes all the selections Romantic?

EXPLANATION

In order to **inquire** deliberately into the idea of Romanticism in literature, you first need to **identify some examples** of Romanticism. Using literary selections you have read, you might list three examples—say, Wordsworth's "Tintern Abbey," Shelley's "Ozymandias," and Byron's *Don Juan.* Your next step is to consider each example carefully and **identify the general characteristics** found in each example. Then, after you have identified those characteristics, you **identify which characteristics are common** to all examples.

A chart will **display** all of the characteristics in a practical and efficient way to reveal the pattern you are looking for. A chart that displays the general characteristics might look like the one at the bottom of this page.

The plus and minus signs indicate whether or not a work has (+) or does not have (−) that characteristic. Observing the chart, you see that three characteristics—individualism, emotional tone, and natural diction—are common to all the examples you examined. Once you have identified these features, you are in a better position to consider a new example of literature and judge whether or not it is Romantic.

It is also useful to **test your findings** against examples that are not likely to share the characteristics. In this case, you might test your findings about Romanticism against an example from seventeenth-century English literature. Add one more column to your chart for a non-example (for instance, Milton's *Paradise Lost*).

Observing the chart at the top of the next page, you see that the non-example does not share enough of the characteristics to make it fit the pattern established by the examples. You will want to expand your list of characteristics and add more examples and non-examples to make the basis of your inquiry even stronger.

CHARACTERISTICS	EXAMPLE 1	EXAMPLE 2	EXAMPLE 3
Individualism	+	+	+
Theme of nature	+	−	−
Emotional tone	+	+	+
Exoticism	−	+	+
Natural diction	+	+	+
Nostalgia for past	+	+	−

CHARACTERISTICS	EXAMPLE 1	EXAMPLE 2	EXAMPLE 3	NON-EXAMPLE
Individualism	+	+	+	−
Theme of nature	+	−	−	−
Emotional tone	+	+	+	−
Exoticism	−	+	+	−
Natural diction	+	+	+	−
Nostalgia for past	+	+	−	−

PROCEDURES

1. In order to inquire into a particular idea, first **examine several familiar examples** of the idea.

2. **List all the general characteristics** you can think of that are true of each of the examples.

3. **Display the list** in a way that helps you see the pattern of common characteristics.

4. **Identify the pattern** of common characteristics.

5. **Test your findings** by comparing what you found to be true of the idea with the characteristics of a closely related non-example. You will find some combination of characteristics that is special to your idea and that does not occur in the non-example.

ACTIVITY I. INQUIRING INTO IMAGES IN LITERATURE

The purpose of this activity is to apply the steps of inductive inquiry to discover the characteristics of images in English literature from 1798 to 1837, *images removed in time and place from the immediate lives of the writers.*

1. Using selections you have read in the unit called "The Romantic Age" (page 387), **identify five examples** of images.

2. Look at each example separately, and **list all the general characteristics** of each example. You may find such characteristics to include Far Eastern setting, an unnamed mysterious setting, Greek mythological setting, supernatural elements, and use of non-English vocabulary.

3. **Display the list** in a way that helps you see the pattern of common characteristics.

4. **Identify the pattern** of common characteristics.

5. **Test your findings** by comparing what you found to be true of the examples with the characteristics of a closely related non-example. (Consider an image based on a writer's own time and place.)

6. **Write a brief summary** of the characteristics of images as you find them in the literature of this period. Support your findings with the specific examples you used as the basis for your inquiry. Would you conclude that the examples are exotic?

ACTIVITY II. INQUIRING INTO PATTERNS OF PERSONIFICATION

1. Using any English literature in this book or any other literature you have read, **identify at least seven examples** of personification.

2. **List the general characteristics** of each example—that is, list the object or animal that is being personified and *how* it is personified.

3. **Display the list** in a way that helps you see any pattern of common characteristics.

4. **Identify any patterns** of commonly occurring characteristics. For example, are many of the objects found in the countryside? Are many of them made by human hands? Are many of them animals?

5. **Test your findings** by comparing what you find to be true of the examples with a closely related non-example. (Try to find an example of personification that does not fit any pattern.)

6. **Write a brief summary** of the patterns you have discovered. Support your findings with the examples you used in your inquiry.

LESSON 5: *Representation*

▓ DEFINITION

Representation involves changing the way that you perceive information. If the information is in words, making pictures or diagrams of the meaning is a way of representing that information. This is called graphic representation. If the information is given in some type of picture or diagram, thinking about its meaning in words is another way of representing that information. Representations are usually developed by asking yourself what the important elements are and how they are related. In making graphic representations, different shapes may be used to represent different ideas.

▓ EXAMPLE

Some of the selections written in the nineteenth century both in England and on the Continent describe different social classes such as the very wealthy and the very poor. Judith thought of a way to represent the different classes.

▓ EXPLANATION

At first Judith represented the groups on a line, or continuum, according to the amount of wealth. However, as she thought about it, she realized that the amount of money a person had was related to his or her education and family background; the wealthy tended to be well educated and well placed socially, whereas the poor tended to have much less education and little social prestige. Also, the different classes seemed to have different occupations. She represented these understandings in the following diagram:

Scales such as the one below are also helpful to order people, places, things, ideas, or events in relation to a continuum of some sort. The concept of happiness is a continuum, and words describing a state of happiness can be scaled according to the degree of happiness.

HAPPINESS SCALE

Very happy   **Very unhappy**

exuberant	joyful	calm	depressed	grief-stricken

In the example above, the scale *topic* is happiness and the *end points* are very happy and very unhappy. The scale *items* are words that describe words or degrees of happiness: exuberant, joyful, calm, depressed, or grief-stricken.

Scaling is the process of placing items on a scale. Discrete objects, such as animals, may be scaled according to specific characteristics such as degree of furriness, length, complexity of brain functions, and so on. In such scales, scale end points might range from very furry to having little fur, from very long to very short, and from simple to complex. People and objects can be scaled on continua according to degrees of feelings, points of view, and the like. On such a scale, the end points might be conservative and liberal, and you would place each person in terms of the degree of conservatism or liberalism.

SOCIAL CLASSES IN NINETEENTH-CENTURY EUROPE			
CHARACTERISTIC	**LOWER CLASSES**	**MIDDLE CLASSES**	**UPPER CLASSES**
Amount of wealth Amount of education Family position Typical occupations	very little uneducated low prestige laborers	comfortable wealth having some education respectable position storekeepers	extreme wealth very well educated royalty, nobility bankers, land owners

PROCEDURES

1. **Define the scale topic** and end points. Be sure you understand the meaning of the end points. You may need to spend some time discussing specific behaviors, or criteria, for the end points.

2. **Select the items** to be scaled.

3. For each item, ask **yourself how it compares** to the end points in relation to the topic.

4. **Place it on the scale** according to your decision.

Note: In many scales the specific placement of items may be variable according to the individual person's perspective or rationale. On a temperature scale, for example, a person from a very warm climate might place the word *frigid* much closer to center than someone from a very cold climate. What is important is how the individual defends his or her choice.

ACTIVITY I. SCALING ITEMS ON ONE TOPIC

The purpose of this activity is to order items on a scale. By thinking about where to place the item, you will refine your understanding of the item and the topic. Prepare a scale for one of the following:

1. The topic of *social reform.* You may choose authors or specific characters. The end points might be "Strongly *for* Social Reform" and "Accepts Status Quo."

2. The topic of *literary experimentalism.* The end points might be "Traditional" and "Avant-Garde."

ACTIVITY II. DEFINING SCALE

The purpose of this activity is to gain more experience in scaling. Possible topics to consider are words relating to beauty, words relating to sorrow, words relating to love, or words relating to conflict.

ACTIVITY III. DEVELOPING A TIMELINE TABLE

The purpose of this activity is to develop a timeline table that represents historical events in four categories: political, economic, sociocultural, and literary.

Timeline tables are a special type of timeline that gives an added perspective on events. Generally, timelines in history books are single lines, and they contain all of the significant historical events. In a timeline table the events are *categorized* and placed in different locations according to the category, as in the example at the bottom of this page.

1. **Brainstorm to identify** key events for any period of history you choose.

2. Working through your list of items one by one, **decide** whether each item is truly important—worthy of including on your timeline table. Eliminate those that are less important.

3. Again working item by item, **decide** whether the event is political (P), economic (E), sociocultural (SC), or literary (L). Code each item on your list with a P, E, SC, or L.

4. **Construct a timeline table** with categories like the one below.

5. **Analyze your timeline** table to see if there are any patterns or connections between events. Questions to help your analysis might include the following:
   a. Are there any broad trends or patterns in political events? Economic events? Sociocultural events? Literary events?
   b. Examine several key literary events one by one. **Ask yourself:** Could this event be caused by or be related to events in other categories?

DATES	POLITICAL (P) EVENTS	ECONOMIC (E) EVENTS	SOCIOCULTURAL (SC) EVENTS	LITERARY (L) EVENTS

LESSON 6:   *Synthesis*

DEFINITION

Synthesis is the creation of something new, a pattern or perspective that was not present before you created it. Synthesis requires a complex combination of skills to organize ideas from different sources. This new pattern may be stated in various forms: an essay, a definition, a point of view, a play or poem, a work of art.

Note: An essay on one perspective is not a synthesis because it represents only one point of view. A synthesis must contain elements from more than one source or point of view.

EXAMPLE

Sally's class was asked to define the characteristics of English literature in the twentieth century, using the selections from this literature anthology. This task requires synthesis because in order to define the characteristics, the group must establish the characteristics from many different literary works and merge the characteristics into a single meaningful statement.

EXPLANATION

The task is to combine information from several different sources and organize it into a new statement. In other words, it is a task of synthesis. The *purpose* is clear—to examine a topic or a situation and clarify it for an audience by presenting a conclusion. The thinker must *identify the elements* that contribute to the situation. The thinker must *state a relationship* between the elements—tell how they are related or opposed or associated in some way. The thinker must *construct an original product*—a definition that expresses the relationship. The definition is a synthesis, a combining of information into something new that did not exist before.

The most helpful synthesis will act as a jumping-off point for further thought.

PROCEDURES

1. **Establish a purpose** for the product.

2. **Identify the elements** to be combined.

3. **State a relationship** among the elements, and represent the relationship in a graphic form if possible.

4. **Construct an original product** that expresses the relationship.

ACTIVITY I. DEFINING CHANGES IN ROLES SHOWN IN LITERATURE

There are important differences in the roles of men, women, and children in different areas of the world and in different periods of history. Often elements of these roles are revealed in literature. The purpose of this activity is to identify some of those changes and differences through literature.

1. **Review** selections you have read that provide good descriptions of the roles in society of men, women, and children.

2. Brainstorm to identify at least two historical periods and attributes of social roles that you would like to examine. This list is likely to change once you begin your study and uncover other attributes. However, it is useful to have some attributes in mind as you review the various selections.

3. Construct a chart such as the one below, leaving space to add new row categories.

MEN	VICTORIAN PERIOD	TWENTIETH CENTURY
Attribute 1 Attribute 2 Etc.		

Note: Use newsprint or butcher block paper because these charts will be shared with the class and used later on. Also, for each bit of information that is recorded on the chart, note the author in some way, such as using his or her initials.

4. **Construct** similar charts for women and children for the two periods.

5. Working in small groups, complete the charts, using your literary selections as sources. Each group should work with a different chart or segment of a chart, depending on the number and complexity of selections that pertain to each chart.

6. **Analyze** similarities and differences between periods (the columns information) and among the different age and sex groups (the row information) across charts.

7. Each analysis should be **reported** to the class.

8. **Analyze** the set of charts to answer at least two of the following questions.
   a. Are there *important* differences in social roles expressed by different authors?
   b. What does it mean to be "grown up" in different eras and different geographic regions?
   c. Identify what you think are the most important changes in social roles for the two periods and the causes of these changes.
   d. Using information from both periods and your knowledge of current realities, predict future trends in social roles for the next century.

9. Working as a whole group, **construct** an outline or essay discussing the role of men, women, and children in two periods of time as seen in literature. Use the charts to help organize your outline or essay. Give examples from literature for each generalization.

ACTIVITY II. PLANNING A POLITICAL SPEECH FOR AN AUTHOR OR CHARACTER

The purpose of this activity is to determine the general point of view of a given character or author and use it as the basis for developing a speech on a particular topic.

1. **Identify** a literary selection that makes a political statement (about war, property, social reform, individualism, freedom).

2. **Brainstorm** to **identify** the key political points about that topic.

3. **Discuss** which points are most important.

4. **Brainstorm** to **identify** current issues that might be the focus of a political speech today.
   Some example categories are the following:
   a. priorities for spending money
   b. tax increases
   c. education
   d. the armaments race

5. **Select** any *two* current political issues from your list for the focus of your political speech.

6. **Decide** what your chosen author or character would think about the two topics.

7. **Brainstorm** to **identify** elements or characteristics of a good political speech.

8. **Develop** an outline for the speech from the perspective of your chosen author or character.

WRITING ABOUT LITERATURE HANDBOOK

LESSON 1: Developing a Thesis Statement

The thesis statement of a composition states the topic of your composition and explains your purpose in writing about it. The thesis statement, which usually appears in the introductory paragraph, expresses the thesis, or proposition, that you will defend. For example, after reading James Joyce's "Araby" (page 707 in this book) you may want to write about the boy's attitudes toward the fair. "Appearance and reality," then, is your *topic*. What you will say about the topic is the *thesis,* and you will state the thesis in a *thesis statement.* Note that a thesis statement may contain more than one main clause and may even, at times, be two sentences long.

> *Example:* The boy in "Araby" initially expects the fair to be exotic and ablaze; when he reaches his goal of attending the fair, he confronts disappointment and darkness.

A thesis statement is *not* merely a fact; it is an opinion or interpretation based on the facts of the literary selection. In other words, " 'Araby' centers around a Dublin fair" would not qualify as a thesis statement. The sentence is not a thesis statement because it does not state a position based on the facts of the work.

CONCEPTS TO REMEMBER

A thesis statement is much more detailed and specific than a general topic. The topic is often just a single word or phrase. The thesis statement is one or more complete sentences that express your position and indicate the plan you will follow in the composition as a whole. Here are examples:

> *Beowulf*
> General Topic: Loyalty to lord and king
>
> Thesis Statement: In excerpts from *Beowulf* we can see the dominant role that loyalty to lord and king played in the life of Anglo-Saxon nobles.

The thesis statement should narrow and focus the general topic so that you can write a coherent composition within the limit of three to five paragraphs.

TYPICAL ESSAY QUESTION

The most challenging essay question may be the kind that asks you to create a thesis statement and to go on to support the thesis statement. Such an assignment may be worded as follows:

> Develop a thesis statement about a piece of literature, and in a brief essay defend your thesis with examples from the work.

PREWRITING

Assuming you have read a work carefully, ask yourself some or all of the following questions or other, similar questions. These questions will help you identify which aspect of the work you want to write about and then to create a thesis statement that will focus your area of concern narrowly enough so that you can handle the topic within a brief essay.

1. What is the most intriguing literary element or aspect of the work?

2. Why is this element or aspect of the work interesting? Is it central to understanding the work? Do other elements or aspects of the work support the one you plan to write about?

3. Can you support your idea about the element you have selected? What support can you find in the text itself? What evidence can you find in secondary sources, such as the author's biography or critics' writings?

4. What are some of the arguments against your thesis statement? How would you go about responding to these arguments?

The following example shows a thesis statement generated for the epic poem *Beowulf*.

> *Example:* In the epic poem *Beowulf* the monster Grendel and the fire-breathing dragon are symbols of absolute evil, and Beowulf's heroic battles with the two monsters represent the eternal, universal, and predestined struggle between good and evil.

WRITING AN ESSAY PARAGRAPH BY PARAGRAPH

1. Begin the introductory paragraph with the thesis statement. Fill out the introductory paragraph with definitions of terms or clarification of your thesis statement.

2. In the following paragraphs give at least two specific examples from *Beowulf* to support the thesis statement.

3. In your concluding paragraph repeat your thesis statement in different words, and indicate that the preceding paragraphs have shown that the thesis statement is defensible.

WRITING A ONE-PARAGRAPH ANSWER

All the preceding advice on structure applies as well to written responses that are only one paragraph long. If you are limited to one paragraph, begin with a strong topic sentence. Each of your following sentences should develop one aspect of the topic sentence. You can conclude this one-paragraph response with a **clincher** sentence, which sums up the evidence you have presented.

REVISING AND EDITING

Here are specific guidelines to follow as you review your first draft.

1. Read your writing aloud. Your ear has been responding to words longer than you have been writing.

2. Use the following checklist to revise your writing. If you can answer "yes" to each question on the list, you will submit an essay that your audience will find interesting and logical.

I. Organization
a. Does your thesis statement in the introductory paragraph relate directly to the assignment?
b. Are the ideas mentioned in the thesis statement then taken up in the following paragraphs with a topic sentence for each?
c. Is there clear movement from paragraph to paragraph by means of transitions?
d. Does the final paragraph offer a restatement of the thesis statement along with additional insights?

II. Content
a. Does the essay as a whole adequately answer the question posed in the assignment?
b. Is each idea adequately developed with supporting details from the literature rather than simply stated and restated in different ways without evidence?

III. Grammar, Usage, Mechanics
a. Is each sentence complete (no fragments, no run-ons)?
b. Have you avoided errors in the use of verbs (especially, subject-verb agreement), pronouns, and modifiers?
c. Have you correctly capitalized and punctuated all sentences?
d. Are all words spelled correctly?

IV. Word Choice, Style
a. Have you used words that are appropriate for your audience and your purpose?
b. Have you avoided slang and clichés unless (and this should be rare) you are using them for a very special purpose or effect?
c. Have you eliminated wordiness and vagueness?
d. Have you varied sentence length and structure while checking for parallelism?

ASSIGNMENTS

1. Write the composition that will support the thesis statement supplied here for *Beowulf*.
2. Do one of the assignments called "Developing a Thesis Statement" that appear after the folk ballads (page 55) or after the selections by Christopher Marlowe and Sir Walter Raleigh (page 131), Samuel Johnson (page 358), William Hazlitt (page 465), and Joseph Conrad (page 698).

LESSON 2: *Writing a Comparison/Contrast*

As you identify similarities and differences between two works of literature, you are examining the properties of each work in order to define its meaning. A comparison/contrast analysis of two works clarifies your understanding of how each author has approached the subject, what the meaning or theme is, and how each author feels about the subject.

▰▰ CONCEPTS TO REMEMBER

1. *To compare* in this lesson means "to examine two or more literary works for the purpose of noting similarities." *To contrast* means "to examine two or more literary works for the purpose of noting differences."

2. In stories and novels you can compare and contrast these elements: plot, characters, settings, points of view, tones, themes, symbols, and irony.

3. In poetry you can compare and contrast these elements: speakers, sound devices, rhythm, rhyme, imagery, and figurative speech.

▰▰ TYPICAL ESSAY QUESTION

When you are asked to compare and contrast two literary works, you will often have to answer an essay assignment like this one:

Select two pieces of literature that you have read. Compare and contrast the two by pointing out similarities and differences in content and literary techniques.

▰▰ PREWRITING

1. Use the following questions and others like them to compare and contrast two stories.
   a. What plot elements in each are similar?
   b. How are the characters similar or different? Do the characters change?
   c. From what point of view is each story told?
   d. What is the setting of each piece? In what period does it take place? Under what social conditions?
   e. Are the tones of the two pieces alike?

   f. What theme is each author expressing?
   g. What symbols are used? How?
   h. How is irony used in each piece?
   i. What is the total impact of each piece?

2. Use the following questions and others like them to compare and contrast two poems.
   a. Does each poem focus on the actions of a character? On a place? On a thing? On an event?
   b. Does each poem focus on an idea? A feeling?
   c. What is your emotional response to each?
   d. On what does each poem cause you to reflect?
   e. Who is the speaker in each poem?
   f. What sound devices are used in each?
   g. What kind of rhyme and rhythm is used?
   h. How does each poem use imagery to appeal to your five senses?
   i. What figures of speech are used in the poem?

3. Prepare a chart (see the opposite page) on which to record your answers to the questions.

▰▰ WRITING PARAGRAPH BY PARAGRAPH

1. Begin your introductory paragraph with a thesis statement that restates the main points of the assignment. State the major similarities and differences in meaning and technique.

   Example: The two Scottish folk ballads, "Sir Patrick Spens" and "The Wife of Usher's Well," tell different stories that, however, share common techniques and a common theme.

2. Use one of the following options for organizing the body of the essay.

Option A
Introductory paragraph
Next paragraph: Tell about one selection.
Next paragraph: Tell about the second one.
Next paragraph: Discuss similarities and differences based on two preceding paragraphs.
Concluding paragraph

SIMILARITIES AND DIFFERENCES IN POEMS

SELECTION: (1) "Sir Patrick Spens" and (2) "The Wife of Usher's Well"

	SPEAKER AND TONE	FOCUS	SOUND	THEME OR MEANING
SELECTION 1	Speaker tells story directly to audience. *Tone:* Foreboding, sad, somber	*Events:* Knight recommends Sir Patrick as the man to sail the king's ship. Shipwreck and drowning of all hands.	*Rhythm:* Ballad stanza *Rhyme:* Follows ballad rhyme scheme, *abcb* *Alliteration:* "A loud lauch lauched he." *Repetition of words and phrases:* "Haf owre, haf owre to Aberdour"	Death at sea as a result of the captain's ignoring his premonition to carry out his duty; loyalty of both captain and his men
SELECTION 2	Speaker tells story directly to audience. *Tone:* Sad, but not ominous	Drowning at sea of the three sons Visitation by ghosts of three sons to comfort mother and to say good-by to life	*Rhythm:* Ballad stanza *Rhyme:* Follows ballad rhyme scheme, *abcb* *Alliteration:* "And a wealthy wife was she." *Repetition of phrases and words:* "They hadna' been a week from her, /A week but barely ane."	*Disaster:* Death at sea; loyalty and love of mother and sons

Option B

Introductory paragraph
Next paragraph: Discuss the similarities in meaning and elements in each selection.
Next paragraph: Discuss the differences in meaning and elements in each selection.
Concluding paragraph

3. In the concluding paragraph use different words to remind readers of your thesis. Focus on whether the two selections are more alike or more different.

REVISING AND EDITING

See page 985 for detailed reminders about improving your writing.

ASSIGNMENTS

1. Use the chart for "Sir Patrick Spens" and "The Wife of Usher's Well" to write a comparison/contrast for the two folk ballads.

2. Do one of the "Writing a Comparison/Contrast" assignments that follow the selections by Robert Browning (page 507), William Butler Yeats (page 650), John Galsworthy (page 701), Dante (page 893), Molière (page 913), and Rainer Maria Rilke (page 937).

LESSON 3: *Citing Evidence*

Whether you write one paragraph or an entire essay of literary analysis, you must provide details—evidence— to support the generalization you have made in your topic sentence or thesis statement.

Sample

In the Prologue to *The Canterbury Tales*, Chaucer's portraits of the pilgrims not only tell us much about life and customs in medieval England but also show that human nature is the same, whatever the period. For example, his detailed descriptions of dress, which tell us much about daily life, include the heroic Knight's " . . . fustian tunic stained and dark / With smudges where his armor had left mark"; the Yeoman's " . . . coat and hood of green . . . A hunting-horn, well-slung and burnished clean, / That dangled from a baldric of bright green"; and the Woman from Bath's wimple, cloak, and hose of "the finest scarlet red." Chaucer helps us understand customs by showing us people at work: the Reeve, an overseer who was "Feared like the plague"; the Plowman, a hard-working farmer who did "as the gospel bade him." Demonstrating human nature, Chaucer shows us the Miller, who was a "wrangler and buffoon" and "a master-hand at stealing grain," and the Merchant, who worked hard concealing the fact that he was in debt. Chaucer's satiric and witty descriptions make the people of this long-ago period come alive.

CONCEPTS TO REMEMBER

Evidence may be in the form of a paraphrase or in the form of a direct quotation.

1. A **paraphrase** is a restatement in your own words of the sense of a piece of writing. When you paraphrase, you should indicate the source either within the context of your paraphrase or in a footnote or endnote.

Paraphrase

Pilgrims to Canterbury traveled as a group from London and may have passed the time by telling stories to one another as they journeyed. In one famous fictional account of such a pilgrimage, the pilgrims actually competed to see who would tell the most entertaining story.[1]

2. When you use a **direct quotation,** you use precisely the same words and the same word order as your source.

Direct Quotation

One of literature's classic monsters, Grendel, attacks the warriors at Herot:

He slipped through the door and there in the silence
Snatched up thirty men, smashed them
Unknowing in their beds and ran out with their bodies,
The blood dripping behind him, back
To his lair, delighted with his night's slaughter.

TYPICAL ESSAY QUESTION

You should always cite evidence in support of your thesis statement. Some essay questions make a particular point of reminding you to do so. The following essay assignment is an example.

Write a brief essay in which you give your opinion or make a generalization about a particular piece of literature. First clearly state your opinion.

PREWRITING

1. Gather material in support of your thesis by reading and rereading the piece of literature.

2. Prepare a chart on which you can list (on the left) the arguments you will present in support of your thesis. In the middle column add exact quotations that defend each argument you list. In the right-hand column, offer a paraphrase of the quotation. The chart on the opposite page served as preparation for the sample paragraph near the beginning of this lesson.

USING FOOTNOTES OR ENDNOTES AND BIBLIOGRAPHY ENTRIES

A **footnote** or **endnote** gives source information for a statement in your composition. It tells

CITING EVIDENCE

SELECTION: Prologue to *The Canterbury Tales*

THESIS: In the Prologue to *The Canterbury Tales,* Chaucer's portraits of the pilgrims not only tell us much about life and customs in medieval England but also show that human nature is the same, whatever the period.

ARGUMENT	SUPPORTING QUOTATION	SUPPORTING PARAPHRASE
Descriptions of dress	*Knight:* "He wore a fustian tunic stained and dark / With smudges where his armor had left mark."	The Knight was dressed simply in a heavy cotton tunic stained by his armor.
	Yeoman: "This Yeoman wore a coat and hood of green, / And peacock-feathered arrows, bright and keen / And neatly sheathed, hung at his belt the while . . . And in his hand he bore a mighty bow. . . . A medal of Saint Christopher he wore / Of shining silver on his breast, and bore / A hunting horn, well slung and burnished clean, / That dangled from a baldric of bright green."	The Yeoman was dressed in the costume of a forester—rather Robin Hood–like and very clean and neat. His arrows in a quiver hung from a belt; a horn, from a shoulder strap.
	Woman from Bath: "Her hose were of the finest scarlet red / And gartered tight; her shoes were soft and new. / . . . she sat / Well wimpled up, and on her head a hat / As broad as is a buckler or a shield; / She had a flowing mantle that concealed / Large hips, her heels spurred sharply under that."	She wore a long hood topped by a hat that looked like a shield, bright red stockings, long cloak, and spurs on her new shoes.
Descriptions of work customs	*Reeve:* "His master's sheep, his animals and hens, / Pigs, horses, dairies, stores and cattle pens / Were wholly trusted to his government. . . . No bailiff, serf or herdsman dared to kick, / He knew their dodges, knew their every trick; / Feared like the plague he was, by those beneath."	The overseer managed the estate for the land-owner, keeping all accounts.
	Plowman: "He was an honest worker, good and true, . . . / And, as the gospel bade him, so did he."	A hard-working farmer who tried to follow the teachings of the Bible
Examples of human nature	*Miller:* "A wrangler and buffoon, he had a store / Of tavern stories, filthy in the main. / His was a master-hand at stealing grain."	A boorish fellow who told off-color jokes and was very clever at stealing grain
	Merchant: "This estimable Merchant so had set / His wits to work, none knew he was in debt, / He was so stately in administration, / In loans and bargain and negotiation."	The merchant pursued his business in such a way as to keep people from suspecting that he was in debt.

who wrote the source, its title, where it was published, by whom, and when.

A **bibliography** is an alphabetical arrangement by last name of the authors of all the sources used in writing a composition. The bibliography appears at the end of the composition.

■ ASSIGNMENT

Do one of the assignments called "Citing Evidence" that appear after the selections by Geoffrey Chaucer (page 97), Samuel Pepys (page 305), James Boswell (page 365), and James Joyce (page 711).

LESSON 4: *Writing About Nonfiction*

Essays, biographies, autobiographies, diaries, and journals are all types of nonfiction. You can analyze all kinds of nonfiction, whether book length or just a few paragraphs long, in the same way. You can discuss the author's purpose in writing the piece and demonstrate with specific examples from the work how the author achieved that purpose.

CONCEPTS TO REMEMBER

1. The **purpose** of a piece of nonfiction is the central idea, or general statement about life, that the author wishes to make.

2. To communicate the purpose, the author uses various techniques such as sensory details, facts, statistics, examples, and opinions.

TYPICAL ESSAY QUESTION

When you are asked to write about a piece of nonfiction, you are often answering an assignment such as the following:

> Select a piece of nonfiction that you have read. An author always has a purpose in writing nonfiction. To accomplish this purpose, the author may use various techniques such as sensory details, facts, statistics, examples, and opinions.

What is the purpose of the piece of nonfiction you have read? Cite with examples the particular techniques that the author uses to accomplish the purpose of the piece.

PREWRITING

1. To determine the author's purpose in writing a work of nonfiction, ask yourself the following questions:

   a. What, if anything, does the title suggest about the author's opinion of the subject of the essay, diary, or journal or about the person in a biography or autobiography?
   b. What opinion about life in general is suggested by the experiences that the author relates?

   c. What opinion about the subject or about people in general is suggested by details (including sensory details, facts, statistics, examples, and opinions)?
   d. What ideas about the world in general are suggested by details of setting?
   e. What tone, or attitude, toward the subject is revealed by the author's style?

2. Based on your answers to the preceding questions, prepare a statement of the author's purpose, and, on a chart like the one on the opposite page, record the techniques that the author uses to achieve that purpose. The fill-in chart represents an analysis of the essay "Of Ambition" by Sir Francis Bacon (page 229).

WRITING PARAGRAPH BY PARAGRAPH

1. Begin the introductory paragraph with a thesis statement. It should specify the author's purpose and the techniques used to accomplish it.

   > *Example:* In his essay "Of Ambition" Sir Francis Bacon uses sensory detail, facts, examples, and opinion to advise rulers on when to employ ambitious men and how to protect themselves against the dangers of thwarted or unbridled ambition.

2. In each of the body paragraphs, show how the author uses one technique to make the purpose clear.

3. In the concluding paragraph restate in other words the thesis statement from the introductory paragraph. Here you might include briefly your own reaction to the author's efforts.

REVISING AND EDITING

See page 985 for detailed reminders about improving your writing.

PURPOSE AND TECHNIQUES

SELECTION: "Of Ambition"

PURPOSE: To state his opinion that ambitious men can be valuable to rulers but that they can also be very dangerous and, therefore, should be curbed.

SENSORY DETAILS	FACTS	STATISTICS
"But then there must be some middle counselors to keep things steady; for without that ballast the ship will roll too much."	". . . choler; which is a humor that maketh men active, earnest, full of alacrity, and stirring . . ." ("fact" in Bacon's day)	NONE

EXAMPLES	OPINION	
Examples of when to use ambitious men: "Good commanders in the wars must be taken, be they never so ambitious. . . ." "There is also great use of ambitious men in being screens to princes in matters of danger and envy. . . ." "There is use also of ambitious men in pulling down the greatness of any subject that overtops: as Tiberius used Macro in the pulling down of Sejanus." *Examples of how to protect against the dangers of ambition:* "It is counted by some a weakness in princes to have favorites; but it is of all others the best remedy against ambitious great ones." "Another means to curb them is to balance them by others as proud as they."	*Opinions on the value and danger of ambition:* "So ambitious men, if they find the way open for their rising, and still get forward, they are rather busy than dangerous; but if they be checked in their desires, they become secretly discontent, and look upon men and matters with an evil eye, and are best pleased when things go backward; which is the worst property in a servant of a prince or state." ". . . it is good not to use such natures at all." "He that seeketh to be eminent amongst able men hath a great task; but that is ever good for the public. But he that plots to be the only figure amongst ciphers is the decay of a whole age." "Generally, let princes and states choose such ministers as are more sensible of duty than of rising; and such as love business rather upon conscience than upon bravery: and let them discern a busy nature from a willing mind."	

ASSIGNMENTS

1. Use the chart for "Of Ambition" (Prewriting Step 2) to write an essay in which you discuss the author's purpose and the techniques he used to achieve that purpose.

2. Do the assignment called "Writing About Non-fiction" that follows the selections by Joseph Addison and Richard Steele (page 339) or about author's purpose in another selection of your choice.

LESSON 5:   Writing About a Quotation or a Symbol

Why does a quotation from a piece of literature stand out? In some fiction, poetry, nonfiction, or drama, a single line can at times sum up the meaning so vividly that the line itself comes to represent the entire work. In the same way, a symbol can create a vivid impression in the reader's mind. Just as a quotation can summarize an idea or opinion in a dramatic way, so a symbol may represent the message that the writer wishes to communicate. Because quotations and symbols express the writer's meaning so clearly and concisely, you should learn how to analyze them and relate them to a work as a whole.

▆▆ CONCEPTS TO REMEMBER

1. A powerful quotation may have vivid adjectives and strong action verbs. It may use strong parallel structure that gives dramatic rhythm to a sentence. It may use metaphorical language. It may appeal strongly to the reader's emotions or sense. It may have a universal meaning. It may use clever word play or state a paradox. It may occupy a prominent position in the work.

2. A **symbol** is something that stands for itself but also for something larger than itself. It may be a person, an animal, an inanimate object, or an action. A writer often uses a concrete object to express an abstract idea, a quality, or a belief. A symbol may also appeal to a reader's emotions and can provide a dramatic way to express an idea, communicate a message, or clarify meaning.

▆▆ TYPICAL ESSAY QUESTION

When you are asked to write about a quotation or a symbol, you may find an essay question such as this:

Identify a quotation [or symbol] from a piece of literature. Explain the specific meaning of the quotation [or symbol] in the work as a whole, explaining how it relates to a theme or main idea of the work.

▆▆ PREWRITING

For a quotation
1. Identify a quotation from a given work of literature. Ask yourself the following questions if you need help in selecting a quotation:

    a. Is there a sentence that has gained fame?

    b. Is there a sentence with strong parallel structure, emotional appeal, or notable simplicity?
    c. Does the work begin or end with a particularly impressive statement?

    For example, in considering Act I, Scene i, of Shakespeare's tragedy *Macbeth,* you might choose the line "Fair is foul, and foul is fair." The witches' observation is, like so many of Shakespeare's lines, quite well known. It is a good choice to write about because it contains strong parallelism, contradiction, alliteration: in addition, it commands a prominent position—the *end* of a scene.

2. Explain in your own words the meaning of the quotation. That is, translate any figurative language, and fill in any information your reader may need in order to understand the quotation. Make sure you explain when, where, and why the statement was made. For example, if you were working with the quotation "Fair is foul, and foul is fair," you could explain that in this scene, which introduces the play, the witches foreshadow the difference between appearance and reality. Macbeth, we will see, is not the loyal subject he appears to be.

For a symbol
1. Identify a symbol from a piece of literature. Look for a concrete object that seems to stand for something abstract above and beyond its concrete meaning. Ask yourself the following questions if you need help in selecting a symbol.

    a. Does the title for the selection alert you to symbolism? For example, titles such as "A Poison Tree" (page 380), "Sailing to Byzantium" (page 648), and "The New Dress" (page 726) might alert you to an object or place with symbolic meaning.
    b. Has the author given particular emphasis to one object or other detail, and thereby perhaps raised it to the level of a symbol? For example, in *Macbeth,* Act II, Scene iv, unnatural weather—perhaps an eclipse—accompanies the murder of Duncan.
    c. Does the object seem to be representative of something of *another kind?* Remember that you would not say that an ant symbolizes all insects;

an ant is merely representative of certain types of insects. However, you might say that an ant is symbolic of dogged, hard work. An ant is an insect, while hard work is an action, *something of another kind.*

2. Explain the meaning of the symbol. That is, tell what abstract idea, quality, or belief is called to mind by the given person, animal, object, or action. For example, the unnatural weather seems to symbolize the unnatural human behavior that hungry ambition has caused.

For both a quotation and a symbol
3. Identify a main idea or theme of the piece of literature by asking yourself questions such as the following. Remember that a main idea or theme should be stated in a complete sentence as a *general* truth.

   a. What ideas about life does the selection's *title* suggest?
   b. What do the particular *events* and *conflicts* reveal about life in general?
   c. What might these particular *people* or *characters* with these personality traits tell us about life in general?
   d. What view of the world do the *setting* and its details offer us?

For example, answers to these questions should help you see the following main ideas:

Appearances do not always reflect the truth; an honest face may mask a traitor.

—Witches, Act I, Scene i

The natural order can mirror any upset in the proper order of human society.

—Ross, Act II, Scene iv

4. Once you have identified the main idea or theme of the work, make notes on how the quotation or symbol relates to the work as a whole.

   a. Does the quotation or symbol *summarize* the theme or main idea?
   b. Does the quotation or symbol *illustrate* the theme or main idea?

▨ WRITING PARAGRAPH BY PARAGRAPH

1. Begin your introductory paragraph with a thesis statement that tells what quotation or symbol you are going to write about and that identifies a theme or main idea of the literary work.

   Examples
   For a quotation: The final comment of the witches in Act I, Scene i, of Shakespeare's tragedy *Macbeth,* "Fair is foul, and foul is fair," introduces the audience to the dominant theme of appearance versus reality.

   For a symbol: As described in Act II, Scene iv, of *Macbeth,* the unnatural weather that accompanies the murder of Duncan symbolizes the disruption of the proper order of human society. The play as a whole underscores the chaos that results from meddling with that order.

2. In the next paragraph tell the specific meaning of the quotation or the symbol. Explain, if necessary, how you arrived at your understanding.

3. In the next paragraph explain in what way the quotation or symbol fits into the literary work.

4. In your concluding paragraph you might tell how the analysis of the quotation or symbol has helped you to understand better the nature of the piece as a whole.

▨ REVISING AND EDITING

See page 985 for detailed reminders about improving your writing.

▨ ASSIGNMENTS

1. Using the information in this lesson, write an essay explaining the significance of the quotation from *Macbeth,* Act I, Scene i, or the symbol from Act II, Scene iv.

2. Do one of the assignments called "Writing About a Quotation" or "Writing About a Symbol" that appear after the pieces by John Donne (page 255), John Dryden (page 294), Samuel Taylor Coleridge (page 431), Alfred, Lord Tennyson (page 501), Rupert Brooke (page 662), Louis MacNeice (page 667), Geoffrey Hill (page 688), D. H. Lawrence (page 724), and Sophocles (page 861), or select another piece of literature from this book, and write about a symbol or quotation within the work.

LESSON 6: *Writing About Theme*

Authors usually have an underlying central idea, or **theme,** in mind when they write a literary work. A theme is more than just the specific topic or subject of the work. Whether the work is a novel, short story, poem, or play, its theme expresses an opinion or raises a question about human nature or the meaning of human experience. You may or may not agree with the theme, but if the selection is well written, it will provide a new and moving insight into the human condition, and you will be able to write about that. For example, one subject in *Beowulf* is the battle with Grendel. The theme might be stated as "The forces of good will triumph over the forces of evil."

■ CONCEPTS TO REMEMBER

1. Most pieces of literature have only one theme, although the theme can be worded in several ways. Some works, however, may contain several themes; such is the case with a long, complex novel.

2. Sometimes the theme may be clearly stated. Usually, however, the theme is implied or suggested through other elements. The author uses characterization, setting, events, point of view, and tone to develop the theme.

■ TYPICAL ESSAY QUESTION

When you are asked to write about the theme of a selection, you are often answering an essay assignment such as the following:

Identify the theme of a work of literature. Show how the author illuminates this theme through characterization, setting, events, point of view, and tone.

■ PREWRITING

1. Identify the subject of a selection that you have read. The selection may have more than one subject, but select only one. For example, the subject of "The Pardoner's Tale" (page 91) is three friends' secret plot to kill one another in order to keep the whole pile of gold coins they have found.

2. Keeping the subject in mind, ask yourself the following questions so that you can get beyond the subject of the selection to its theme.

a. What do various characters (or the main character) think, say, and do about the subject?

b. What are the character's key traits? Does the character change at all?

c. How do the time, place, clothing, and other details of setting serve as a suitable background for the work's subject?

d. What do the events and conflicts have to do with the subject matter?

e. What do the selection's climax and resolution have to do with the selection's subject matter?

f. From whose point of view is the story told and how does this point of view affect you?

g. What tone does the writer use, and how does that tone affect your reaction?

3. Prepare a chart to record your answers to the questions in Prewriting Step 2. The chart on the opposite page is a sample prepared for "The Pardoner's Tale."

4. Examine the completed chart, and try to develop a statement of the theme of the selection. For example, for "The Pardoner's Tale" you might state the theme as follows: Greed can lead to destruction.

■ WRITING PARAGRAPH BY PARAGRAPH

1. Begin your introductory paragraph with a thesis statement that restates the main ideas of the assignment. Indicate what the theme of the selection is, being certain to state the theme in terms of a generalization about human nature or experience. Then show how the theme is illuminated through the other elements of the selection.

> *Example:* The theme of "The Pardoner's Tale" is that greed can lead to destruction. All the elements in the story—particularly the characterization of the old man, the setting, and the ironic tone—contribute to the effective presentation of this moral lesson.

EVENTS ILLUMINATING THEME

SELECTION: "The Pardoner's Tale"

SUBJECT OF STORY: Three friends secretly plot to kill one another in order to keep all the gold they have found.

CHARACTERIZATION	SETTING	EVENTS
Old man's traits: Very, very old and wise; wants to die but cannot; might represent the Devil or Death	*Time:* Fourteenth century; Black Plague killing thousands *Place:* An English village and road leading to another village	*Events and Conflicts:* Rioters want to challenge "Death." When they find gold, they forget their vow and decide to share the wealth. One goes off for provisions, leaving the other two, who plot to stab him; the one who has gone off likewise plans to eliminate the remaining two. *Climax:* Upon his return the other two stab him according to plan. *Resolution:* The remaining two celebrate and drink the poisoned wine; they die an agonizing death.

POINT OF VIEW	TONE	
Omniscient: Narrator tells about all events and what characters think and feel; uses Publican to explain the setting (description of Black Death).	Author uses all three types of irony: *Verbal*—The boy says death is a "privy thief." Rioters think they are going off to fight a real person; *Situational*—Merrymaking as death is all around; *Dramatic*—Readers know that two are secretly plotting to kill the third, while the third is secretly plotting to kill the other two.	

2. In the next paragraph focus on how the characters, setting, and events reveal the generalization you feel the selection makes about life. Support your ideas with details from the work.

3. In the next paragraph focus on how the point of view helps to illustrate the theme.

4. In the next paragraph focus on how the tone clarifies the theme.

5. In the concluding paragraph restate your thesis statement. Explain whether the elements of the selection led you to understand a theme new to you, or whether they helped renew an awareness that you had.

▆▆ REVISING AND EDITING

See page 985 for detailed reminders about improving your writing.

▆▆ ASSIGNMENTS

1. Use the chart for "The Pardoner's Tale" to write about theme. How do characterization, setting, events, point of view, and tone show that greed can lead to destruction?

2. Choose one of the assignments called "Writing About Theme" that follow the selections by John Milton (page 286), Sean O'Faolain (page 756), and Virgil (page 873), or select another piece of literature from this book, and show how all the other elements illuminate its theme.

LESSON 7: Writing About Poetry

Poetry has much in common with both music and art. Musicians use techniques such as rhythm and sound to capture a mood or convey feeling; artists use color and line to create a beautiful painting. In the same way, poets use various literary techniques to convey the sense, or meaning, of a poem and to convey mood and feeling. These techniques include choice of the speaker, sound, imagery, and figurative language. You should learn to think about all these techniques so that when you write an essay about a poem you will be able to show the connection between the techniques of the poem and its meaning.

▇▇ CONCEPTS TO REMEMBER

1. The **speaker** of the poem is the voice of the poem. Sometimes the speaker is the poet himself or herself; sometimes the speaker is a character or thing created by the poet.

2. Among the sound devices that a poet may use are **onomatopoeia** (a word or phrase that actually imitates or suggests the sound of what it describes); **alliteration** (the repetition of initial consonant sounds); **consonance** (the repetition of similar consonant sounds preceded by different accented vowels); **assonance** (the repetition of vowel sounds).

3. Other aspects of sound in poetry are **rhyme** (the repetition at regular intervals of similar or identical sounds) and **rhythm** (the pattern created by arranging stressed and unstressed syllables).

4. A poem's images may appeal to one or more senses.

5. The most common kinds of figurative language available to a poet are metaphor, simile, and personification. (**Metaphor** is a figure of speech in which two unlike things are compared without the use of *like* or *as*; **simile** is a comparison using *like* or *as*; **personification** is a figure of speech in which an animal, object, or idea is described as having human form or characteristics.)

▇▇ TYPICAL ESSAY QUESTION

When you are asked to write about poetry, you are often answering an assignment such as the following:

Select a poem that you have read. What is the meaning of the poem? What techniques does the poet use to reveal this meaning? Techniques include the selection of speaker, sound, imagery, and figurative language.

▇▇ PREWRITING

1. Use the following questions to help you determine the meaning of the poem.

   a. Does the poem focus on the actions of a character?
   b. Does the poem describe something?
   c. Does the poem focus on an idea? A feeling?
   d. What emotional response does the poem seem to call up in you?
   e. After your immediate emotional response to the poem, on what does the poem cause you to reflect?

2. Prepare a chart on which to record your statement of the meaning of the poem. The chart opposite represents an analysis of John Donne's Sonnet 10 (page 251), which begins, "Death, be not proud. . . ."

▇▇ WRITING PARAGRAPH BY PARAGRAPH

1. Begin your introductory paragraph with a thesis statement, which should restate the main points of the assignment. Indicate that the various techniques used by the poet all serve to enhance and present effectively the underlying meaning.

   Example: In Sonnet 10 by John Donne, the poet uses the speaker, sound devices, imagery, and figurative language as he admonishes death not to be proud of its dreadful reputation; in the end, the speaker argues, eternal life will triumph.

THE MEANING AND TECHNIQUES OF A POEM

SELECTION: Sonnet 10

MEANING: Eternal life triumphs over death.

SELECTION OF SPEAKER	SOUND	IMAGERY	FIGURATIVE LANGUAGE
Narrator cautions Death. Proud speaker ("nor yet canst thou kill me")	*Rhythm:* generally iambic pentameter—i.e., very natural human speech *Alliteration* ("*D*ie not, poor *D*eath"; "*M*uch pleasure, then from thee *m*uch *m*ore *m*ust flow") and *assonance* ("slave to fate") give richness and smoothness to speaker's words.	Images paint a picture of limitations of death: men dying willingly, death as slave, death as dwelling with "poison, war, and sickness."	*Personification:* Narrator speaks to Death as if it were a person; attributes human quality of pride to be a state of Death as if it were a person; attributes human quality of pride to a state or condition.

2. In each of the following paragraphs, discuss one or two of the techniques that the poet uses to underscore the poem's meaning—choice of speaker, sound devices, imagery, and figurative language. Show how each technique enhances the meaning.

3. In the next paragraph discuss further the meaning of the poem.

4. In the concluding paragraph restate your thesis statement. You might here go into greater detail than you have earlier on the emotional impact of the poem on you—now that you have analyzed the elements used to create emotion in the poem.

███ REVISING AND EDITING

See page 985 for detailed reminders about improving your writing.

███ ASSIGNMENTS

1. Use the chart for Sonnet 10 to write an essay about poetry. What is the meaning of the poem? What techniques are used to reveal this meaning?

2. Do one of the assignments called "Writing About Poetry" that follows the selections by John Keats (page 452), Dylan Thomas (page 679), and Ted Hughes (page 685).

LESSON 8: *Writing About the Total Effect*

A theatrical director combines elements such as lighting, sets, costume, makeup, stage movement, timing, and music to help an audience understand and be moved by the meaning of a play. Similarly, writers use a variety of elements in creating a literary work. These elements include plot, characters, setting, point of view, tone, theme, symbol, and irony. A skillful writer combines these elements to create a total effect, or impact, on the reader. We can analyze this impact by studying the contribution of each element to the whole. Often you will see that, as in a play, one element dominates. However, all the elements are woven together to support that key element. In this way the author—or director—creates a unified effect.

▉ CONCEPTS TO REMEMBER

Review the lessons dealing with writing about the various literary elements individually. Review the definitions and important concepts in each lesson.

▉ TYPICAL ESSAY QUESTION

When you are asked to write about the total effect of a selection, you are often answering an essay question such as the following:

> Select a piece of literature that you have read. What is the total effect of the piece—that is, what is its impact on the reader? How does the author use the following literary elements to achieve this effect: plot, character, setting, point of view, tone, theme, symbol, and irony?

▉ PREWRITING

1. Ask yourself the following questions :

    a. What is the impact of the work? Specifically, does the work irritate you, delight you, sadden you? Does it surprise you, or does it support an opinion or impression you already had? Does the work remind you of something else or contrast greatly with something else?
    b. Which literary element dominates?
    c. How do the other literary elements support or relate to the dominant element?

2. Prepare a chart on which to record your answers to the questions in Step 1. The chart should have columns for the question, the answer, and the de-

tails that support your answer. For the excerpt from *Le Morte d'Arthur* on page 99, a chart might look like the one on the opposite page.

▉ WRITING PARAGRAPH BY PARAGRAPH

1. Begin the introductory paragraph with a thesis statement. The thesis statement should express the total effect of the work on the reader and note that all the key literary elements work together to create this impact.

    > *Example:* The dominant literary element in *Le Morte d'Arthur* is its theme, but all the elements are woven together to create the total effect that enchants the reader. The reader is transported into the life of a medieval court, with its pageantry, magic, and romantic code of honor and chivalry.

2. In the next paragraph focus on the dominant literary element, and show by the inclusion of details how it contributes to the total effect.

3. In the following paragraphs discuss additional literary elements, and show by the inclusion of details how each element supports or relates to the dominant element.

4. In the concluding paragraph remind your audience that the elements mentioned in the preceding paragraphs work together to produce the total impact on the reader.

▉ REVISING AND EDITING

See page 985 for detailed reminders about improving your writing.

▉ ASSIGNMENTS

1. Use the chart for *Le Morte d'Arthur* to write a brief multiparagraph essay about the total effect of the work.

2. Do the assignment called "Writing About the Total Effect" that appears after the selections by William Shakespeare (page 225) and George Bernard Shaw (page 640), or write about another piece of literature from this book.

ANALYSIS OF THE TOTAL EFFECT

SELECTION: *Le Morte d'Arthur*

QUESTION	ANSWER	DETAILS
A. WHAT IS THE IMPACT OF THE WORK?	Reader is transported into a romantic medieval world where magic flourishes.	*Setting:* "He found there a brilliantly decorated pavilion. . . . A multicolored shield hung from a tree, and resting against it was a spear." *Magic:* "That is the magic sword Excalibur . . . and it will be given to you by the Lady of the Lake, who is now crossing the water in her bark."
B. WHAT IS THE DOMINANT LITERARY ELEMENT?	*Theme:* The romantic ideals of loyalty, honor, respect for women, and skill in battle guide the behavior of a knight and are important in medieval feudal society.	*Loyalty:* "One of Arthur's knights should avenge [Sir Myles's] death." *Honor:* "King Pellinore is already tired. . . . To win would bring you no honor, to lose would be to increase your shame." *Respect for women:* "You must address her courteously. . . ." *Skill in battle:* "Arthur's knights rejoiced in the boldness of their king."
C. HOW DO THE OTHER ELEMENTS SUPPORT THE STORY?	*Plot:* The death of Sir Myles sets in motion the pursuit of revenge. *Characters:* Each character plays a specific role in presenting the values of a medieval court. Merlin also controls the events; Pellinore provides motive for revenge by killing Sir Myles; Gryfflette illustrates loyalty. *Setting:* Details of setting describe medieval England. *Tone:* Air of a fairy tale or ballad; imparts feeling of predestined events. *Symbol:* Excalibur, the magic sword, is the symbol of Arthur's power. *Irony:* There is a bit of situational irony in that Arthur's knights cheer him when actually Merlin prevented Arthur from making a possibly fatal mistake and continues to teach him how to be king.	"[Arthur] decided to avenge Sir Gryfflette secretly. . . ." *Merlin:* "Merlin adroitly put him to sleep with a magic spell." *King Pellinore:* ". . . it would seem that no knight can pass this well without your challenging him." *Gryfflette:* ". . . still I mean to joust with you." ". . . they found King Pellinore seated outside his pavilion." "She comes from her castle, which is hewn in the rock. . . ." "King Arthur," she replied, "Excalibur shall be yours, if you consent now to granting me whatever gift I shall ask of you in my own time." ". . . the hand grasped a finely jeweled sword and scabbard." "I cast a spell over him; had he done so [seen us], you would not have escaped so lightly."

LESSON 9:   *Applying a Statement About Literature*

Sometimes a statement about life or literature in general can provide deep insight into a particular work of literature. The statement seems to penetrate to the heart of a situation or illuminate the essential meaning of a literary work. It is your task to explain precisely why the general statement fits the specific piece of literature so well.

TYPICAL ESSAY QUESTION

A common essay question involves giving you a statement, asking you to explain the meaning of the statement, and then requesting you to show how the statement relates to a work you select or to a work specified in the essay question.

> *Example:* Contemplation of the timeless beauty of nature can inspire a dreamlike enchantment that temporarily transcends mortal cares or pain. Explain this statement, and show how it applies to "Ode to a Nightingale" by John Keats.

PREWRITING

1. To make sure you understand the general statement and can do the first part of the assignment, paraphrase the statement and define any key terms.

> *Example:* People may observe something so overwhelmingly beautiful in nature that they find themselves in a dreamlike trance. They are caught up in the eternal quality of nature and find a joy and peace in which they forget their problems—at least for a while.

2. Prepare a chart that helps you focus on the essay assignment and the piece of literature. The left column will contain questions to help you connect the essay assignment to specific literary elements in the work. In the middle column jot down quotations or other specifics from the work as answers to the questions. Cite specifics from *throughout* the work; remember that giving only one specific is not sufficient evidence to prove a point. In the right column explain more fully the relationship of evidence from the middle column to the essay question and to the particular piece of literature. The chart on the opposite page was filled in after rereading Keats's "Ode to a Nightingale" (page 453).

WRITING PARAGRAPH BY PARAGRAPH

1. Begin the introductory paragraph with a thesis statement that ties the given statement to a specific work.

> *Example:* The events, setting, point of view, and poetic techniques in John Keats's "Ode to a Nightingale" illustrate that contemplation of the timeless beauty of nature can inspire a dreamlike enchantment which, in turn, can temporarily transcend mortal cares or pain.

The rest of this paragraph might offer a quick summary of the work or a generalization about its main idea or theme.

2. In each of the following paragraphs, discuss how the given statement about the work connects with a specific literary element in the work. Be sure to cite examples.

3. In the concluding paragraph emphasize that the evidence presented from the work demonstrates the applicability of the statement to this particular piece of literature.

REVISING AND EDITING

See page 985 for detailed reminders about improving your writing.

ASSIGNMENTS

1. Use the preceding chart to write a well-developed essay about the application of the following statement to John Keats's "Ode to a Nightingale": Contemplation of the timeless beauty of nature can inspire a dreamlike enchantment that temporarily transcends mortal cares or pain.

2. Do one of the assignments called "Applying a Statement About Literature" that follow the selections by A. E. Housman (page 557) and Ovid (page 877). Or select another piece of literature from this book, and find a statement that applies to it. Then explain what the statement means and how it relates to the piece.

3. In the concluding paragraph reiterate that this author and the specific work being studied exemplify key characteristics of the particular literary period.

APPLICATION OF GENERAL STATEMENT TO SPECIFIC WORK

SELECTION: "Ode to a Nightingale"

GENERAL STATEMENT: Contemplation of the timeless beauty of nature can inspire a dreamlike enchantment that temporarily transcends mortal cares or pain.

LITERARY ASPECT	EVIDENCE FROM WORK	RELATIONSHIP OF EVIDENCE AND STATEMENT
WHAT *EVENTS* IN THE WORK DOES THE STATEMENT BRING TO MIND?	A nightingale sings ". . . of summer in full-throated ease." Poet imagines himself flying "on the viewless wings of Poesy" to be with the nightingale and "forget / What thou among the leaves hast never known, / The weariness, the fever, and the fret. . . ." When the nightingale flies off, "thy plaintive anthem fades / Past the near meadows, over the still stream. . . ." The poet wonders, "Was it a vision, or a waking dream? / Fled is that music:—Do I wake or sleep?"	The beautiful song of the nightingale enchants the poet. He wants to be with the bird and *imagines* himself flying to the woods at night, to a world free of pain. When the nightingale flies away, he is not sure whether what he heard and saw is a dream or real.
WHAT DETAILS ABOUT *SETTING* DOES THE STATEMENT BRING TO MIND?	"Here, where men sit and hear each other groan; Where palsy shakes a few, sad, last gray hairs, Where youth grows pale, and specter-thin, and dies; Where but to think is to be full of sorrow And leaden-eyed despairs. . . ."	The situation the speaker is in is one of mortal cares or "pain."
WHAT DOES THE *POINT OF VIEW* (OR, IF THE WORK IS A POEM, THE SPEAKER) HAVE TO DO WITH THE STATEMENT?	*Speaker addresses the nightingale:* "Thou wast not born for death, immortal Bird!" *Views bird as immortal:* "The voice I hear this passing night was heard / In ancient days by emperor and clown. . . ." *Wants to die:* "now more than ever seems it rich to die. . . ." *Changes mind:* "Still wouldst thou sing, and I have ears in vain— / To thy high requiem become a sod."	The poet speaks to the bird, reflecting on the *timelessness* of its beautiful song. At first, the speaker wishes to die with its music in his ears, but he realizes that if he dies, he will no longer hear its song.
IF THE WORK IS A POEM, WHAT *POETIC TECHNIQUES* HAVE TO DO WITH THE STATEMENT?	*Imagery:* "Through verdurous glooms and winding mossy ways"; "what soft incense hangs upon the boughs"; "The coming musk-rose, full of dewy wine." *Alliteration:* "Fast fading violets covered up in leaves"	The poet uses appeals especially to sight and smell to create a vivid picture of the woods *where he imagines himself to be with the nightingale.* Hearing the nightingale's song affected the poet so much that with poetic techniques he creates a song as lovely and as immortal as that of the nightingale he celebrates.

LESSON 10: *Writing About Literature and Its Period*

Researchers who study a particular period often turn to the great literature, fiction or nonfiction, of the time. Works of great writers reflect—indeed, sometimes anticipate—the religious, economic, social, and political developments of the period.

■ CONCEPTS TO REMEMBER

1. You learn about a period through literature (a primary source) or through analyses of the period such as history textbooks (secondary sources). Make sure that you look carefully at a literary work and do not "read more into" it than is really there. Some pieces of literature could have been created during any period; they do not specifically reflect one particular time.

2. When thinking about literature and its period, you must remember to pay particular attention to the writer's tone, or attitude. In order to understand how the work relates to the period, you must determine whether the author is being satiric, supportive, optimistic, or pessimistic—to mention just a few possible tones.

■ TYPICAL ESSAY QUESTION

When you are asked to write about literature and its period, you are often answering an essay question like this one:

Write an essay showing how an author exemplifies a given literary period. State each characteristic of the period, and for each give examples from the work under discussion.

■ PREWRITING

1. Identify the literary or historical period during which the piece of literature was created. List the major characteristics of the period.

2. Ask yourself the following questions:
   a. *Social Customs*   What manners and customs of the time does the work present? What seems to be the author's attitude toward them? What does the work say or imply about interpersonal relations?

   b. *Economy*   What attitude does the author seem to have toward the economic conditions of the age (toward trade and working conditions, toward agrarian or industrial pressures)?

   c. *Politics*   What is the author's reaction to the political situation? Specifically, what does the author seem to think about the ruling powers? The laws? Other political systems?

   d. *Religion and Philosophy*   Does the work present religious beliefs accepted during the period in question? Do scenes take place within traditional religious institutions? How are religious people characterized? What seems to be the author's attitude toward the human ability to do good or evil?

3. Prepare a chart that will help you to focus on the most important parts of the essay question. At the top of the chart, identify and define the period. In the left column list ideas about the period that you have been able to determine based on either secondary sources or answers to the questions in Prewriting Step 2. In the right column cite specifics, including direct quotations from the work, for each of the generalizations on the left. Such a chart for *The Rape of the Lock* by Alexander Pope (page 341) might look like the one on the opposite page.

■ WRITING PARAGRAPH BY PARARAPH

1. Begin the introductory paragraph with a thesis statement that will define the period. The thesis statement should also indicate that the work being analyzed exemplifies key characteristics of that period.

   Example: The Rape of the Lock by Alexander Pope is a classic example of the cutting and witty satire that deflated the vanity, silliness, and triviality that marked court life during the Age of Reason.

2. In each of the following paragraphs, discuss one or more of the major characteristics of the period, and cite examples from the work that illustrate that particular characteristic.

LITERATURE AND ITS PERIOD

SELECTION: *The Rape of the Lock*

PERIOD: The Age of Reason—a period during which reason and common sense were accepted as the only tests of truth. Neoclassicism became popular, as writers modeled their works on the classics of ancient Greece and Rome. It was also the age of satire, as writers in both prose and poetry mocked the social institutions of the time.

CHARACTERISTICS OF THE PERIOD	EXAMPLES FROM THE WORK
Social Customs The social life of drawing-room society was the target of much of the satire written during this period. The extravagant social intrigues of that society and the rising middle class offered plenty of material for the satirists' pens.	"Hither our nymphs and heroes did resort, To taste awhile the pleasures of a court; In various talk the cheerful hours they passed, Of, who was bitt, or who capotted last: This speaks the glory of the British Queen, And that describes a charming Indian screen; A third interprets motions, looks, and eyes; At every word a reputation dies." 　　　　　　　　　　　　—Canto I, lines 71–78
Economics While England was still largely agrarian, it was beginning to build foreign trade and an empire. The birth of the Industrial Revolution was well under way.	"When hungry judges soon the sentence sign, And wretches hang that jury men may dine; When merchants from th' Exchange return in peace . . ." 　　　　　　　　　　　　—Canto I, lines 83–85
Politics Under the British constitution, there was a combination of rule by monarchy, aristocracy, and democracy. The king or queen traditionally had the right to choose the ministers. The functions of government were the keeping of order, the protection of property, the conduct of commercial, financial, and foreign affairs, with the direction of whatever warlike operations these might unfortunately involve.	"Here Britain's statesmen oft the fall foredoom Of foreign tyrants, and of nymphs at home; Here thou, great Anna! whom three realms obey, Dost sometimes counsel take—and sometimes tea." 　　　　　　　　　　　　—Canto I, lines 67–70
Religion and Philosophy The Church of England was restored to power. Philosophers believed that God regulated nature; they often compared nature to a clock. Great thinkers such as John Locke, Addison and Steele, and others formulated ideals of human dignity and worth.	"With such a prize no mortal must be blessed, So Heaven decrees! with Heaven who can contest?" 　　　　　　　　　　　　—Canto II, lines 156–157

▄▄ REVISING AND EDITING

See page 985 for detailed reminders about improving your work.

▄▄ ASSIGNMENTS

1. Write a well-developed essay in which you identify the Age of Reason and show how Pope's *Rape of the Lock* exemplifies key characteristics of that period.

2. Do one of the assignments called "Writing About Literature and Its Period" that follow the selections by William Wordsworth (page 406), Charles Dickens (page 514), and Charles Tomlinson (page 683), or select another piece of literature from this book, and show how that piece exemplifies its literary period.

RESEARCH PAPER CASEBOOK

A literary research paper deals with a limited topic and draws on information found in print and nonprint sources. The paper should do more than just report information, however. A good research paper will include your own analysis of the information and will present the opinions that you form on the topic after you research it. For example, if you were writing a paper about Nathaniel Hawthorne's use of Puritan history, you could support and at times broaden your analysis with information found in critical books, articles, or film adaptations of his tales. However, the basis of your paper should be your *own* analysis of this history.

To write a literary research paper, you will follow a writing process, the details of which may vary. If your teacher wants you to employ a special method, follow his or her directions; otherwise you may use this casebook as a guide. The casebook is divided into two sections: The first describes a process for writing a literary research paper using Shakespeare's *Macbeth* as its example; the second presents a group of critical articles on *Macbeth*. Thus, the casebook gives you everything you need to write a fifteen-hundred-word research paper on the play. If you wish to write about other literature, however, you may follow the general guidance here and locate your own critical articles.

PREWRITING: SELECTING AND LIMITING A TOPIC

Literary research always begins with careful reading of literature. Begin by choosing a work (or works) that interests you and that will require you to do research. As you read, take notes on passages of particular interest. Your reading notes may suggest possible topics for your literary research paper. They may reveal, for example, that you are especially interested in examining a specific piece of literature, several works by an author, or works by two authors.

After you have decided on an area of interest (the single play *Macbeth*, for example), ask yourself what aspects of the play interest you the most. If you decide to limit your topic to the language of the play, your next step will be to read what others have written on the subject of Shakespeare's language. If you write on language in *Macbeth*, you may skim the articles in this casebook. Otherwise, consult the following types of sources:

- Encyclopedias: Look at general and readers' encyclopedias. Check author and text entries.
- Introductions: Paperback editions of literary works usually open with essays that discuss relevant critical issues. Read several for a range of opinion.
- Casebooks: Casebooks present the history of criticism on a work or an author. Skim the articles for an overview of critical thought.

After reading several sources you should be ready to further limit your topic.

In your broad reading about language in *Macbeth*, you may notice that critics often mention the play's imagery. At this point, skimming your original reading notes and critical articles may help you to narrow your focus even more. For example, you may decide to examine color imagery in *Macbeth*, which is a suitably narrow topic for a literary research paper.

GENERAL: *Macbeth*
LESS GENERAL: language of *Macbeth*
LIMITED: color imagery in *Macbeth*

Before you finalize your topic, visit the library to make sure that enough material is available for your research. A research paper of fifteen hundred words should be based on at least five sources of information (in addition to any encyclopedias); the longer your paper, the more sources you will probably find helpful. Do not make the mistake of thinking that library sources are your only sources of information, however. A **source** is anyone or anything that provides factual information on your topic. For some topics, interviewing an expert, watching a TV documentary, or conducting your own survey may provide valuable information.

PREWRITING: CONTROLLING IDEA

The next step in prewriting is to state your controlling idea. The **controlling idea**—or **working thesis statement**— is the central thought that you want to develop in your paper. State the controlling idea as precisely as possible in a single sentence. Your statement of the controlling idea performs three important tasks: (1) It states the main point of your paper; (2) it suggests your opinion or attitude about the topic; and (3) it indicates the path that your paper will follow. For instance, research into color imagery in *Macbeth* may begin with this controlling idea: "Through the repetition of certain color images in *Macbeth*, Shakespeare emphasizes the changes in Scotland that result from Duncan's murder."

Once you have established a controlling idea, you may find it helpful to develop a set of questions that will help you support your idea and guide your research. For example, in order to develop the idea that color images in *Macbeth* emphasize changes in Scotland resulting from Duncan's murder, you could gather notes that help you answer questions like the following:

- What state is Scotland in as the play opens?
- How does it change after Duncan's murder?
- What specific color imagery is repeated?
- How is imagery used before Duncan's murder?
- How is it used after Duncan's murder?
- How does the color imagery associated with Macbeth differ from that associated with Duncan's loyal followers?

When you are satisfied with your research questions, write each on its own 4″ × 6″ note card. Refer to these cards as you continue your research.

PREWRITING: PREPARING A WORKING BIBLIOGRAPHY

At this point in the process, you will create a working bibliography of sources on 3″ x 5″ note cards. Your working bibliography will consist of both primary and secondary sources. For a literary research paper, the primary source is the work of literature you are discussing (in this case, *Macbeth*); secondary sources are books, articles, or reviews written about *Macbeth*.

The following types of books will be useful:

- Various editions of the text(s) you are researching. Review their critical introductions or check for bibliographies and critical articles in the appendices.

- Critical books on the author, literary text(s), or topic. For a paper on color imagery in *Macbeth,* for example, Caroline Spurgeon's book *Shakespeare's Imagery and What It Tells Us,* will be of interest.

- Anthologies of critical articles or casebooks on the author, text(s), or topic. For instance, *Twentieth Century Interpretations of Macbeth*, edited by Terence Hawkes, is a useful collection of Shakespearean criticism.

- Bibliographies on the author or text(s) you are researching. For example, you will find bibliographies on Shakespearean criticism in general and on *Macbeth* in particular. Annotated bibliographies are most useful because they describe the sources.

Indexes

Use indexes to find articles on your author, text(s), or topic. Articles are usually more recent and, often, more closely related to your topic than book-length studies.

- *Humanities Index.* This index will be most useful. Find the entry for your author(s); then check the title of your text(s) and the specific topic. For example, under William Shakespeare, check entries for *Macbeth* and for "Symbolism and Imagery."

- *The Readers' Guide to Periodical Literature* or *The New York Times Index*. These indexes will help you locate special sources—reviews of stage, film, or video productions of *Macbeth,* for example.

Write the bibliographic information for each possible source on its own card (3″ × 5″ size). In that way, you will be able to sort and alphabetize the cards as necessary. Follow the samples on page 1006.

PREWRITING: TAKING NOTES

Take notes from your secondary sources.

Summarize by restating only the main points and important details. For example, here is a passage from

Bibliography Card: A Book-length Study

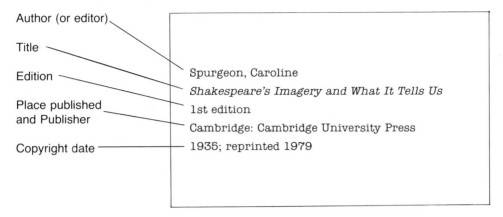

Author (or editor)

Title

Edition

Place published and Publisher

Copyright date

Spurgeon, Caroline
Shakespeare's Imagery and What It Tells Us
1st edition
Cambridge: Cambridge University Press
1935; reprinted 1979

Bibliography Card: A Section of a Book

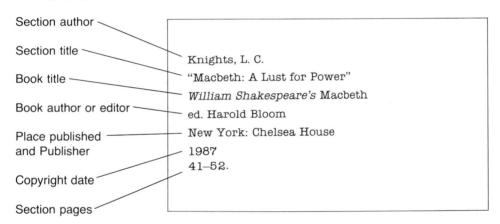

Section author

Section title

Book title

Book author or editor

Place published and Publisher

Copyright date

Section pages

Knights, L. C.
"Macbeth: A Lust for Power"
William Shakespeare's Macbeth
ed. Harold Bloom
New York: Chelsea House
1987
41–52.

Bibliography Card: An Article in a Magazine or Journal

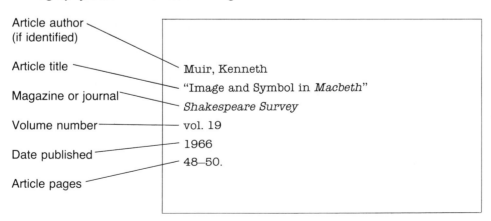

Article author (if identified)

Article title

Magazine or journal

Volume number

Date published

Article pages

Muir, Kenneth
"Image and Symbol in *Macbeth*"
Shakespeare Survey
vol. 19
1966
48–50.

Kenneth Muir's essay "Image and Symbol in *Macbeth*":

> Another important group of images is concerned with sickness and medicine, and it is significant that they all appear in the last three acts of the play after Macbeth has ascended the throne; for Scotland is suffering from the disease of tyranny, which can be cured, as fever was thought to be cured, only by bleeding or purgation.

One way to summarize the Muir passage follows:

> The images of sickness and medicine in the last three acts of the play point to the disease of Macbeth's tyranny, an illness that a bloodletting will cure.

The summary includes only the main points and most important details from Muir's passage. Most of the notes you take from secondary sources will be summaries.

Paraphrase by restating an author's ideas in your own words. Here is a sample paraphrase of the Muir passage you read above:

> All the images of sickness and medicine appear after Macbeth has become King of Scotland—in the last three acts of the play. These images are

significant because they reinforce the idea that Scotland is diseased or infected by Macbeth's tyranny. The cure for the country's illness—like the cure for fever—will be a purging or bloodletting.

Here all of Muir's thoughts are retained but translated into the researcher's own words.

Directly quote a source by presenting the writer's exact words. As you examine your secondary sources, you may come across an especially relevant or powerful phrase, sentence, or passage that you may want to include exactly in your paper. Copy the quotation carefully, and enclose it within quotation marks. Here is an example of a note that directly quotes the Muir passage:

> The images of sickness and medicine that appear after Macbeth has become king are important signals that "Scotland is suffering from the disease of tyranny." The disease will be cured by a bloodletting.

As you can see, the researcher quoted only Muir's striking phrase and summarized the remainder of the passage. An effective literary research paper highlights its writer's argument and the words of the literary text(s) being discussed. Therefore, direct quotation of secondary sources should not be overused.

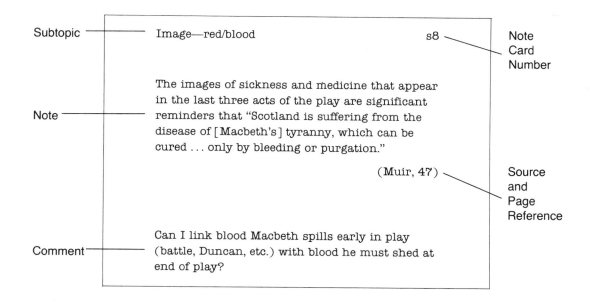

Use a note card (4″ × 6″ size) like the one above to record each of your summaries, paraphrases, or direct quotations. At the top, write the subtopic the note addresses, and number each card (s1, s2, s3, and so on) for easy reference. Under the note, write the name of the author and the source page number. If you are using more than one work by an author, include a brief title reference with the author's last name (Muir, "Image and Symbol" 47). At the bottom of the card, write any ideas that come to mind about how you may use the information in your paper.

Remember, whether you summarize, paraphrase, or directly quote your source, you will have to credit the author's ideas in your paper. If you do not properly credit your sources, you are **plagiarizing,** or stealing, the thoughts or words you use.

When you have finished taking notes from your secondary sources, review your note cards, grouping them with the research question each of the notes answers and putting aside any notes that do not address one of your questions. Review each question and the notes that address it. If you do not have notes for one or more of your research questions, you may (1) consult other secondary sources for information, (2) wait to search in your primary source for textual details that address the question, or (3) discard the question because it is no longer relevant to your research paper. Next, turn to the group of cards that address issues not covered by your questions. Decide whether you should revise your questions to include the notes in this group or whether you should add one or more new research questions to those you generated earlier.

Take notes from your primary source(s).

During this stage of the process, you will be employing the skills you practiced in "Lesson 3: Citing Evidence" of the "Writing About Literature Handbook." Before you begin to take notes, consider what you want to find in your primary source(s). Review your research questions and secondary-source note cards, paying particular attention to any comments you noted. For example, review the sample secondary-source note card above. The comment asks if one color image, the red of blood, can be traced through *Macbeth*. If you are writing about color imagery, you may want to note images of blood in the play.

Follow a procedure like the one you used for secondary sources. Decide whether summary, paraphrase, or direct quotation will make the most effective note. If you note a direct quotation, copy the passage exactly, making only the most necessary changes by inserting information in brackets or by omitting part of the passage by using ellipses. Use note cards (4″ × 6″) to record your notes. Number each card (p1, p2, p3, and so on) for easy reference (the *p* stands for *primary*); and record precisely where you find the note (page and chapter number for a novel; act, scene, and line numbers for a play; title and line numbers for a poem).

After arranging your primary-source notes effectively, review your controlling idea, research questions, and secondary-source notes to begin to understand how you can combine all of your research. Consider, for example, whether your primary-source notes are related to or different from the arguments put forward by other critics. As you compare and contrast your analysis with that offered in your secondary sources, you should begin to see your paper taking shape.

■ PREWRITING: ORGANIZING YOUR RESEARCH

A useful way to organize all of your notes is to make an outline. An effective outline, one that blends your analysis of primary source(s) with the arguments offered in secondary sources, will guide you as you write the first draft of your research paper. Let your purpose, audience, and controlling idea, as well as your notes, guide you.

If you are writing a research paper on different color imagery in *Macbeth*, you may consult your secondary-source notes to see what other critics have said about blood imagery in relation to light and dark, or white and black, imagery. As you review your notes, you may decide that the first major point of your outline will look at light and blood images in relation to the idea of order:

I. Daylight and blood as images of order
  A. Battle that opens play
    1. Bloody Captain reports that Macbeth conquers the rebels who want to overthrow Duncan (p 1)
    2. Blood shed to preserve order in Scotland

B. Battle that closes play
1. Macduff reports that Macbeth, the traitor who murdered Duncan, has been killed (p 29)
2. Blood shed to restore order in Scotland

The second major point of this outline would most likely be "Night and blood as images of disorder."

When you have drafted a complete outline, review your purpose, audience, controlling idea, and research questions to make sure that you have developed your thoughts fully. Make any necessary revisions, and then turn to your primary- and secondary-source notes. Group the note cards with the sections of the outline to which they pertain, and check to make sure that you have enough information to develop the points of your outline. Return to your primary and secondary sources for additional information if you find that some points need to be supported with more evidence. When you are satisfied with your outline, you may begin to write your first draft.

WRITING: DRAFTING YOUR RESEARCH PAPER

Your first draft will consist of the introduction, body, and conclusion to your research paper. These sections perform different tasks in the paper.

Introduction

Begin by considering how you are going to reword your controlling idea in order to make it an effective thesis statement. (You may want to review "Lesson 1: Developing a Thesis Statement" in the "Writing About Literature Handbook.") Then decide how you can best lead up to that statement with information that sets a context.

Body

The body is the major portion of your research paper. Follow the guidance of your outline as you discuss significant points and provide supporting evidence to develop your thesis statement effectively. As you write, keep your purpose squarely in mind, for it is in the body of your paper that you must provide the information that will help you achieve your goals.

When you use evidence from a primary or secondary source, simply follow the summary, paraphrase, or direct quotation with parentheses in which you write the number of the note card from which you took the reference (p1, s3, and so on). You will credit your sources fully as you revise.

Conclusion

Like the introduction, the conclusion to a 1500-word research paper will probably be one paragraph in length. In it you should restate your thesis in a way that will impress readers with the force of your argument. Do not simply repeat your thesis and major points. Instead, summarize your argument and emphasize it in a fresh way. Remember, this is the last paragraph your audience will read. Make it clear and convincing.

REVISING: CONTENT, STYLE, AND MECHANICS

You are about to begin the most important stage of the writing process: revising and polishing your paper. Concentrate on the content of your research paper by asking the following types of questions:

1. How effective is my introduction? Where have I clearly stated my thesis? Where have I set the context for my argument?

2. Did I omit any of the points or details of my formal outline?

3. What details and examples have I included to support general statements? Should I add details and examples from the note cards I did not use in my first draft?

4. Are my ideas clearly and logically presented? Do I need better transitions between sections of my paper?

5. How can I make my conclusion more effective? Does it sum up my main points? Does it reinforce my purpose?

6. Which sentences can I make clearer and easier to understand?

7. Where can I improve my word usage or vary my sentence structure to make the paper more interesting to read?

8. Is my paper free from errors in spelling, punctuation, capitalization, grammar, and usage?

When you have finished revising for style and correctness, make a final pass through your draft, checking the accuracy of your citations against your note cards and inserting parenthetical documentation.

▬ DOCUMENTATION

Parenthetical documentation provides brief source information in parentheses within the body of a research paper. For more complete source information, readers consult the alphabetized bibliography (titled "Works Cited") at the end of the paper.

Most parenthetical documentation will consist of the last name of the author(s) and a page number (Muir 48). There are several exceptions, however:

- If a book has no author, use the editor's name.
- If a book has no author or editor, use its title (*Collier's* 151).
- If two authors have the same last name, use their first initials and last name (L. C. Knights 41).
- If you are using more than one work by an author, include an abbreviated title in the parentheses (Spurgeon, *Shakespeare's Imagery* 324).
- If the wording of your draft makes clear the name of the author (and, where appropriate, the title of the work), omit the author's name (or the title of the work) from the parentheses.

EXAMPLES

As Caroline Spurgeon shows, in *Macbeth* images of light are associated with life while dark images signify death (329).

Images of light are good while dark images are evil (Spurgeon 329), as one can see in the following passage. . . .

Place parentheses before the punctuation mark that concludes the sentence, clause, or phrase containing the source you are crediting.

When the final act of the play begins, Scotland is a country that is "suffering from the disease of tyranny" (Muir 47).

Close quotation marks of a direct quotation before the parentheses; put concluding punctuation after the parentheses.

Macbeth associates the color white not with innocence and purity but with a fear that should be disguised in the color red, as he demonstrates in the command to a servant who announces Macduff's advance:

> Go prick thy face and over-red thy fear,
> Thou lily-livered boy. What soldiers, patch?
> Death of thy soul! Those linen cheeks of thine
> Are counselors to fear. (5.3.14–17)

Put the parentheses after the closing punctuation of set-off passages. Note act, scene, and line numbers of passages from drama.

In Edith Wharton's *False Dawn*, Lewis Raycie says Edgar Allan Poe is a "Great Poet" (13; pt. I, ch. 2).

In a novel, note page and chapter number, separated by a semicolon. Where necessary, include any part number with chapter number.

Like Robert Frost's speaker, the protagonist realizes that he took the road "less traveled by / And that has made all the difference" ("The Road Not Taken" 19–20).

Note title and line numbers in poetry.

As you insert parenthetical references, check the accuracy of your information and the form of each of your direct quotations.

Direct quotations

Unless you wish to give them special emphasis, direct quotations of four or fewer lines of prose (approximately fifty words) and three or fewer lines of poetry or drama are included in the body of the paper; longer quotations are indented ten spaces from the left margin and set off from the body. All quotations included in the body of the paper are marked with quotation marks; omit quotation marks from set-off passages. When lines of poetry and drama are included in the body of the paper, a slash (/) indicates line breaks, as in the Frost example above.

List of works cited

Finally, create your list of works cited, or list of texts to which your parenthetical documentation refers. Gather together the bibliography cards for the sources you have used in your paper, double-checking your final draft to make certain that you have not overlooked any sources. Arrange the cards in alphabetical order according to the last name of the author, and create your list from the cards.

Proofread the "Works Cited" section carefully, and place it at the end of your paper. You may now publish your research paper, or submit it to your teacher.

▨ SAMPLE BIBLIOGRAPHY
Works Cited

Grebanier, Bernard. "Macbeth." *Collier's Encyclopedia.* New York: Macmillan Ed. Co., 1984. Vol. 15: 151.

Jorgensen, Paul A. *William Shakespeare: The Tragedies.* Boston: Twayne, 1985.

Knights, L. C. "Macbeth: A Lust for Power." *Some Shakespearean Themes.* Palo Alto: Stanford UP, 1959. Rpt. in *William Shakespeare's Macbeth.* Ed. Harold Bloom. New York: Chelsea House, 1987.

Muir, Kenneth, "Image and Symbol in *Macbeth.*" *Shakespeare Survey* 19 (1966): 48–50.

Shakespeare, William. *The Tragedy of Macbeth. English Literature with World Masterpieces.* New York: Scribner Laidlaw, 1989. 149–223.

Spurgeon, Caroline. *Shakespeare's Imagery and What It Tells Us.* Cambridge: Cambridge UP, 1935, rpt. 1979.

SECONDARY SOURCES

The following five articles about *Macbeth* along with the play itself, on pages 148–223, form a resource bank for a research paper. Throughout the reprinted articles you will find italicized page numbers. Each number indicates that the text following it appears on that page in the book or journal from which the article is reprinted. You will need this page information when you cite a secondary source.

SOURCE: Grebanier, Bernard. "Macbeth." *Collier's Encyclopedia.* New York: Macmillan Ed. Co., 1984 ed. Vol. 15: 151

page 151

MACBETH, a tragedy by Shakespeare, probably written in 1606 for presentation before King James I. In its main outline the action follows the narrative in Holinshed's *Chronicle.* The brave but overly ambitious Scottish general, Macbeth, prodded to become king by his equally ambitious wife and encouraged by the prophecies of three witches whom he meets by chance in a forest, murders the gentle trusting Duncan, the king of Scotland, while Duncan is a guest in his castle. Ever insecure as king, Macbeth murders his former comrade-in-arms, Banquo. He also attempts to murder another threat to his status, the nobleman Macduff, but only succeeds in butchering Macduff's family. Lady Macbeth finally dies of remorse and the frustration of her hopes for happiness. The witches prophesy that only a man not born of woman can kill Macbeth and that only when Birnam wood moves to Macbeth's castle at Dunsinane will Macbeth be defeated. Both prophecies are fulfilled. Macduff and his supporters, camouflaged by branches taken from Birnam wood, successfully besiege Macbeth's castle; and Macduff, "untimely ripp'd" from his mother's womb, slays Macbeth in combat. Duncan's son, Malcolm, is then proclaimed king of Scotland. . . .

Macbeth's extraordinary power of speech reveals how greatly he was tempted and how terribly he suffered. In the last act, he sadly comprehends the tragic personal consequences of his ambition:

> I have lived long enough: my way of life
> Is fallen into the sear, the yellow leaf,

And that which should accompany old age,
As honour, love, obedience, troops of friends,
I must not look to have; but in their stead,
Curses not loud but deep, mouth-honor, breath,
Which the poor heart would fain deny, but dare
    not.

Lady Macbeth is one of Shakespeare's greatest creations. Holinshed calls her a woman of "insatiable ambition," but in the play her ambition is solely for her husband. In order to steel him to the task of murdering the king, she tries to crush all tenderness within herself.

Come, you spirits
That tend on mortal thoughts! Unsex me here,
And fill me from the crown to the toe top-full
Of direst cruelty . . .

But later, consumed by guilt, she begins to disintegrate. Her collapse is portrayed in the sleepwalking scene, where she tries to remove imaginary bloodstains from her hands.

Out damned spot! Out I say . . .
Yet who would have thought the old man to have
    had so much blood in him . . .
Here's the smell of blood still: all the perfumes of
    Arabia will not sweeten this little hand.

It is the magnificent poetry in *Macbeth* that gives it a particular distinction among Shakespeare's plays. Even minor characters speak in superb language; for example, the few lines uttered by one of the assassins employed by Macbeth:

The west yet glimmers with some streaks of day,
Now spurs the lated traveller apace
To gain the timely inn . . .

It is Shakespeare's poetry, in addition to the complex characterization of Macbeth, that converts what could have been mere bloody melodrama into great tragedy.

SOURCE: Spurgeon, Caroline. *Shakespeare's Imagery and What It Tells Us*. Cambridge: Cambridge University Press, 1935; reprint 1979. 324–333

page 324 begins

The imagery in *Macbeth* appears to me to be more rich and varied, more highly imaginative, more unapproachable by any other writer, than that of any other single [Shakespearean] play. It is particularly so, I think, in the continuous use made of the simplest, humblest, everyday things, drawn from the daily life in a small house, as a vehicle for sublime poetry. But that is beside our point here.

The ideas in the imagery are in themselves more imaginative, more subtle and complex than in other plays, and there are a greater number of them, interwoven the one with the other, recurring and repeating. . . .

page 329

Another constant idea in the play arises out of the symbolism that light stands for life, virtue, goodness; and darkness for evil and death. "Angels are bright" (4.3.22), the witches are "secret, black and midnight hags" (4.1.48), and, as Dowden says, the movement of the whole play might

page 330

be summed up in the words, "good things of day begin to droop and drowse" (3.2.32.)

This is, of course, very obvious, but out of it develops the further thought which is assumed throughout, that the evil which is being done is so horrible that it would blast the sight to look on it; so that darkness, or partial blinding, is necessary to carry it out.

Like so much in the play it is ironic that it should be Duncan who first starts this simile, the idea of which turns into a leading motive in the tragedy. When he is conferring the new honour on his son, he is careful to say that others, kinsmen and thanes, will also be rewarded:

signs of nobleness, like stars, shall shine
On all deservers. 1.4.41

No sooner has the king spoken, than Macbeth realises that Malcolm, now a prince of the realm, is an added obstacle in his path, and suddenly, shrinking from the blazing horror of the murderous thought which follows, he cries to himself,

Stars, hide your fires;
Let not light see my black and deep desires. 1.4.50

From now on, the idea that only in darkness can such evil deeds be done is ever present with both Macbeth and his wife, as is seen in their two different and most characteristic invocations to darkness: her blood-curdling cry,

Come, thick night,
And pall thee in the dunnest smoke of hell, 1.5.51

which takes added force when we hear later the poignant words, "She has light by her continually" (5.1.23); and his more gentle appeal in the language of falconry,

Come, seeling night,
Scarf up the tender eye of pitiful day. 3.2.46

page 331

And when Banquo, sleepless, uneasy, with heart heavy as lead, crosses the courtyard on the fateful night, with Fleance holding the flaring torch before him, and, looking up to the dark sky, mutters,

There's husbandry in heaven,
Their candles are all out, Mac. 2.1.4

we know the scene is set for treachery and murder.

So it is fitting that on the day following, "dark night strangles the travelling lamp" (2.4.7), and

darkness does the face of earth entomb,
When living light should kiss it. 2.4.9

The idea of deeds which are too terrible for human eyes to look on is also constant; Lady Macbeth scoffs it—"the sleeping and the dead," she argues, 'are but as pictures':

'tis the eye of childhood
That fears a painted devil; 2.2.53

but Macduff, having seen the slain king, rushes out, and cries to Lennox,

Approach the chamber, and destroy your sight
With a new Gorgon. 2.3.76

Macbeth boldly asserts he dare look on that "which might appal the devil" (3.4.60), and the bitterness of

defeat he realises on seeing one "too like the spirit of Banquo" in the procession of kings, is expressed in his agonised cry,

Thy crown does sear mine eye-balls; 4.1.113

while in his bitter and beautiful words at the close, the dominant thoughts and images are the quenching of light and the empty reverberation of "sound and fury signifying nothing" (5.5.28).

A final chief symbolic idea in the play is one which is very constant with Shakespeare, and is

page 332

to be found all through his work, that sin is a disease—Scotland is sick.

So Macbeth, while repudiating physic for himself, turns to the doctor and says if he could, by analysis, find Scotland's disease

And purge it to a sound and pristine health,
I would applaud thee to the very echo,
That should applaud again . . .
What rhubarb, senna, or what purgative drug,
Would scour these English hence? Mac. 5.3.52

Malcolm speaks of his country as weeping, bleeding and wounded, and later urges Macduff to

make us medicines of our great revenge,
To cure this deadly grief; 4.3.214

while Caithness calls Malcolm himself the "medicine of the sickly weal," "the country's purge" (5.2.27).

It is worth noting that all Macbeth's images of sickness are remedial or soothing in character: balm for a sore, sleep after fever, a purge, physic for pain, a "sweet oblivious antidote" (5.3.43); thus intensifying to the reader or audience his passionate and constant longing for well-being, rest, and, above all, peace of mind.

Other subsidiary motives in the imagery, which work in and out through the play, insensibly but deeply affect the reader's imagination. One of these is the idea of the *unnaturalness* of Macbeth's crime, that it is a convulsion of nature. This is brought out repeatedly and emphasised by imagery, as are also the terrible results of going against nature.

Macbeth himself says that Duncan's wounds

look'd like a breach in nature
For ruin's wasteful entrance, 2.3.118

and Macduff speaks of his murder as the sacrilege of

page 333

breaking open the Lord's anointed temple. The events which accompany and follow it are terrible because unnatural; an owl kills a falcon, horses eat each other, the earth was feverous and did shake, day becomes night; all this, says the old man, is unnatural,

Even like the deed that's done. Mac. 2.4.10

Macbeth's greatest trouble is the unnatural one that he has murdered sleep, and the whole feeling of dislocation is increased by such images as "let the frame of things disjoint" (3.2.16), or by Macbeth's conjuration to the witches with the terrible list of the convulsions of nature which may result from their answering him. Indeed, if from one angle the movement of the play may be summed up in Macbeth's words,

Good things of day begin to droop and drowse,
3.2.52

from another it is completely described by the doctor in his diagnosis of the doomed queen's malady as "a great perturbation in nature" (5.1.10).

SOURCE: Jorgensen, Paul A. *William Shakespeare: The Tragedies.* Boston: Twayne, 1985. 82–90.

page 82 begins

Led by prophecies of the Weird Sisters, by "vaulting ambition" (1.7.27), and by the "valor" (1.5.25) of his Lady's tongue, the fierce and loyal general Macbeth . . . reluctantly takes on a mission alien to his deepest nature: the murder of the king, "gracious Duncan" (3.1.66). For barely the first act are husband and wife together in spirit, first in the excitement of the "deed" (2.2.14) and then in unexpected profusion of blood. Lady Macbeth overcomes for only a while the moral scruples and terrible visions of her husband: "A little water clears us of this deed" (2.2.66); "how easy is it then" (2.2.67); "leave all the rest to me" (1.5.71). Regicide is ter-

page 83

rible, and all of Scotland is convulsed on the "unruly" (2.3.50) starless night of Duncan's murder. When the dead king is discovered in the morning in Macbeth's castle where he had been a guest, the loyal thanes, ultimately suspecting the murderer, unite in horror, but Macbeth becomes king. Banquo, a tempted but loyal thane, serves as foil to Macbeth. Macduff flees to England for military aid against the "tyrant, bloody sceptered" (4.3.104). But Banquo, who according to the Weird Sisters is "not so happy yet much happier" (1.3.66) because he will "get kings though [thou] be none" (1.3.67), is cut down by murderers suborned by Macbeth, who has become victim to paranoid fears. Consequently, when Banquo obligingly appears at Macbeth's banquet, he appears as a ghost, with twenty mortal gashes on his head, taking the chair before the tyrant. For one of Macbeth's punishments is that he can no longer be a part of humanity or break bread with his fellow man. "The table's full" (3.4.46). Driven still compulsively, Macbeth has Macduff's entire family slaughtered. Malcolm and Macduff succeed in leading an army from England and killing Macbeth. The queen who, like her husband, has known not a single moment of joy since Duncan's murder, goes mad, walks nightly in her sleep, and kills herself. The state, under the new reign of Duncan's rightful heir, Malcolm, is now "free" (5.8.55)—free from murderers and bloody banquets. And free from the horrors that raged within Macbeth's now severed head—horrors that had made of him more than the "dead butcher" (5.8.69) he is finally called. . . .

page 87

Much has been written supporting the thesis that Macbeth is a hapless victim of fate. . . . Evidence is nevertheless strong and ultimately attractive that a man of Macbeth's moral sensibility has a moral choice. Admittedly his Lady has a compelling influence upon him. And this power will be "fiendlike" (5.8.69) as well as human.

But even before they meet after news of the prophecy, he has, as we noted, been startled and fearful upon hearing it. On his own, moreover, he has virtually conjured evil after hearing that Malcolm is named Prince of Cumberland. His aside has what will become his habitual accent, a style solemn in ritual:

> Stars, hide your fires;
> Let not night see my black and deep desires.
> The eye wink at the hand; yet let that be
> Which the eye fears, when it is done, to see.
>   (1.4.50–53)

The speech is also characteristically at Macbeth's expense ironic. He asks for, and is granted in a juggling sense, a kind of moral anaesthesia. He will not see now, for fear, yet he will after "it is done" *see*. And the horrid sights will be a major part of his later "torture of the mind" (3.2.21). . . .

Murder . . . is not congenial to Macbeth. Beyond this, however, is a fair nature that abhors regicide. He may feebly explain to his Lady, in practical terms she might grasp, that he has won "golden opinions" (1.7.33) that he would enjoy. But privately he reveals, besides his fear of "the life to come" (1.7.7), that powerful Elizabethan passion: conscience. . . . Here we can look briefly only at his most

page 89

characteristic soliloquy of regret, the famous "If it were done when 'tis done" (1.7.1). Proceeding in it from fear of "Bloody instructions, which, being taught, return / To plauge th'inventor (1.7.9–10), he moves to a more sorrowful feeling: pity and horror at killing the virtuous Duncan. Even more to Macbeth's credit in this outcry is that it occurs after he has committed himself to the deed. Macbeth, with a still not dead moral sensitivity, deeply feels how evil it is to kill a man "here in double trust" (1.7.10). Then comes the most heartfelt agony of the soliloquy, aglow with imagery the likes of which Shakespeare had never essayed before:

> Besides, this Duncan
> Hath borne his faculties so meek, hath been
> So clear in his great office, that his virtues
> Will plead like angels, trumpet-tongued against
> The deep damnation of his taking-off,
> And pity, like a naked new-born babe
> Striding the blast, or heaven's cherubin horsed
> Upon the sightless couriers of the air,
> Shall blow the horrid deed in every eye
> That tears shall drown the wind. (1.7.16–25)

The images . . . come from the heated imagination and the wounded heart. And the heart . . . is bleeding for someone else. If Macbeth had been able to maintain this intensity of feeling, in which new-born babes stride the blast and tears drown the wind, he would not only have "lived a blessed time" (2.3.88), but also have taken a rightful place among those of Shakespeare's heroes who are redeemed by sorrow.

But, in perhaps his most crucial speech, he commits himself to Satan. Finally acceding to his Lady's pressure, he promises sadly and wearily: "I am settled, and bend up / Each corporal agent to this terrible feat" (1.7.79–80). . . .

page 90

By thus committing his members to Satan (as he could do only more luridly . . . if he were to write in blood), Macbeth becomes king. But the "settled" is deeply ironic, for he will be more driven in restless ecstasy to seek final security. This will require endless crime, but the killing of Banquo is most important, for in resolving upon it, he expresses his own great loss:

> For Banquo's issue have I filed my mind;
> For them the gracious Duncan have I murdered;
> Put rancors in the vessel of my peace
> Only for them, and mine eternal jewel
> Given to the common enemy of man
> To make them kings—the seeds of Banquo
>   kings. (3.1.65–70)

And the bending up of his members will further lead to the terrible "fits" (3.4.21) that will torment him until he has lost one of his most saving features, his moral imagination.

SOURCE: Knights, L. C. "Macbeth: A Lust for Power," from *Some Shakespearean Themes*, Palo Alto: Stanford University Press, 1959. Reprinted in *William Shakespeare's Macbeth*. Ed. Harold Bloom. New York: Chelsea House, 1987. 41–52.

page 41

In none of [Shakespeare's] tragedies is there anything superfluous, but it is perhaps *Macbeth* that gives the keenest impression of economy. The action moves directly and quickly to the crisis, and from the crisis to the full working out of plot and theme. . . . The main theme of the reversal of values is given out simply and clearly in the first scene, "Fair is foul, and foul is fair"; and with it are associated premonitions of the conflict, disorder and moral darkness into which Macbeth will plunge himself. Well before the end of the first act we are in possession not only of the positive values against which the Macbeth evil will be defined but of the related aspects of that evil, which is simultaneously felt as a strained and unnatural perversion of the will, an obfuscation of the clear light of reason, a principle of disorder (both in the "single state of man" and in his wider social relations), and a pursuit of illusions. All these impressions, which as the play proceeds assume the status of organizing ideas, are produced by the interaction of all the resources of poetic drama—action, contrast, statement, implication, imagery, and allusion. Thus the sense of the unnaturalness of evil is evoked not only by repeated explicit references ("nature's mischief," "nature seems dead," "'Tis unnatural, even like the deed that's done," and so on) but by the expression of unnatural sentiments and an unnatural violence of tone in such things as Lady Macbeth's invocation of the "spirits" who will "unsex" her, and her affirmation that she would murder the babe at her breast if she had sworn to do it. So too the theme of the false appearances inseparable from evil, of deceit recoiling on the deceiver, is not only the subject of explicit comment,

> —And be these juggling fiends no more believ'd,
> That palter with us in a double sense—
> (5.8.19–20)

it is embodied in the action, so that Macbeth's despairing recognition of mere "mouth-honour" among his remaining followers (5.3.27) echoes ironically his wife's advice to "look like th' innocent flower, But be the serpent under't" (1.5.64–65) and the hypocritical play of the welcoming of Duncan; and it is reinforced by—or indeed one with—the evoked sense of equivocation and evasiveness associated with the witches, and the cloud of uncertainty that settles on Scotland during Macbeth's despotism. It is fitting that the final movement of the reversal that takes place in the last act should open with

page 42

the command of Malcolm to the camouflaged soldiers, "Your leavy screens throw down, And show like those you are" (5.6.1–2).

page 49

The nature against which the "unnaturalness" of the Macbeth evil is defined and judged is human nature; and essential characteristics of that nature—its capacity for and intimate dependence on relationship—are powerfully evoked throughout the play. In act 3, scene 4, Macbeth, overcome by his vision of Banquo's ghost, glances back to a time

page 50

when murder was common. . . .

> Blood hath been shed ere now, i' th' olden time,
> Ere humane statute purg'd the gentle weal;
> Ay, and since too, murthers have been perform'd
> Too terrible for the ear: the time has been,
> That, when the brains were out, the main would
>   die,
> And there an end; but now, they rise again,
> With twenty mortal murthers on their crowns,
> And push us from our stools. This is more
>   strange
> Than such a murther is. (3.4.74–82)

This is a more profound version of the origins of society than is suggested by the notion of contract or expediency. What "purges" the supposed mere multitude and makes it into a "gentle" commonweal is a decree greater than any law in which it may be embodied, for it is what is dictated by the very fact of being human; if you accept your humanity then you can't murder with impunity. Nor is this simply a matter of judicial punishment: the murdered man "rises" again, in you. Killing may be common in wild nature, but it is not natural to man as man; it is a violation of his essential humanity. When Lady Macbeth describes her husband as "too full o' the milk of human kindness" she intends to be disparaging. . . . But what the phrase also says is that human kindness is natural to man as man, and, like his mother's milk, nourishes his manhood. When Malcolm accuses himself of imaginary crimes, and in so doing reflects the evil that Macbeth has brought on Scotland, the climax is,

> Nay, had I power, I should
> Pour the sweet milk of concord into Hell,
> Uproar the universal peace, confound
> All unity in earth. (4.3.97–100)

"Concord," "peace," "unity"—these are *active* words, signifying not a mere absence of disagreeables, a mere deliverance from "continual fear, and danger of violent death," but the condition of positive human living. We learn little about a play by making lists of words, but

page 51

it is a significant fact that *Macbeth* contains a very large number of words expressing the varied relations of life (not only "cousin," "children," "servants," "guest," "host," but "thanks," "payment," "service," "loyalty," "duties"), and that these sometimes, as in act 1, scenes 4 and 6, seem to be dwelt on with a special insistence. At the end of the play, when Macbeth thinks of what he has lost, it is

> "that which should accompany old age,
> As honour, love, obedience, troops of friends"
> (5.3.24–25)

That the man who breaks the bonds that tie him to other men, who "pours the sweet milk of concord into Hell," is at the same time violating his own nature and thwarting his own deepest needs, is something that the play dwells on with a special insistence.

It is only when the essential needs and characteristics of human nature are given an absolute, unconditional priority, that nature in its widest sense can be invoked as an order underlying, invigorating, and in a certain sense offering a pattern for, human nature. In Macbeth's apocalyptic soliloquy before the murder, the "Pity" that dominates the chaotic natural forces and rides the whirlwind appears as a newborn babe—an offspring of humanity, naked, vulnerable, and powerful. It is, we may say, because of the symbol of the babe, and all it stands for, that Shakespeare can invoke the powers of nature and associate them, as Professor Wilson Knight shows that he does, with all that is opposed to, and finally victorious over, the powers of destruction.

It is in the scene of Duncan's entry into Macbeth's castle (1.6.)—"a perfect contrast in microcosm to the Macbeth evil"—that we are most vividly aware of the energies of untaught nature in significant relation to the human order. The scene is set for full dramatic effect between Lady Macbeth's invocation of the powers of darkness ("The raven himself is hoarse, that croaks the fatal entrance") and Macbeth's final resolution, and Duncan's courtesy underlines the irony. But the contrast is not confined to the situation. The suggestion of a sweet fresh air, and the pleased contemplation of the birds that build and

page 52

breed affect us first as sensory contrasts to the smothering oppression ("Come, thick Night") so recently evoked; but like the images of darkness and disorder the presented scene is inseparable from the values it embodies and defines.

> This guest of summer,
> The temple-haunting martlet, does approve,
> By his lov'd mansionry, that the heaven's breath
> Smells wooingly here: no jutty, frieze,
> Buttress, nor coign of vantage, but this bird
> Hath made his pendent bed, and procreant
>   cradle:
> Where they most breed and haunt, I have
>   observ'd
> The air is delicate.

What we are contemplating here is a natural and wholesome *order*, of which the equivalent in the human sphere is to be found in those mutualities of loyalty, trust, and liking that Macbeth proposes to violate. And it is an order that is at one with the life it fosters. The opening lines of the scene, in short, are not only beautiful in themselves, they form an image of life delighting in life. It is in terms of destructive and self-destructive energies that Macbeth's power lust is defined; and it is from the "life" images of the play, which range from the temple-haunting martlets to Macduff's "babes," his "pretty ones," and include all the scattered references to man's natural goods—sleep and food and fellowship—that we take our bearings in the apprehension of evil. . . .

SOURCE: Muir, Kenneth. "Image and Symbol in 'Macbeth.'" *Shakespeare Survey* 19 (1966): 48–50.

Page 48 begins

The contrast between good and evil is brought out in a variety of ways. There is not merely the contrast between the good and bad kings, which becomes explicit in the scene where Malcolm falsely accuses himself of avarice, lechery, cruelty and all of Macbeth's vices, and disclaims the possession of the king-becoming graces. . . . There is also a contrast throughout the play between the powers of light and darkness. It has often been observed that many scenes are set in darkness. Duncan arrives at Inverness as night falls; he is murdered during the night; Banquo returns from his last ride as night is again falling; Lady Macbeth has light by her continually; and even the daylight scenes during the first part of the play are mostly gloomy in their setting—a blasted heath, wrapped in mist, a dark cavern. The murder of Duncan is followed by darkness at noon—'dark night strangles the travelling lamp.' Before the murder Macbeth prays to the stars to hide their fires and Lady Macbeth invokes the night to conceal their crime:

> Come, thick night,
> And pall thee in the dunnest smoke of hell,
> That my keen knife see not the wound it makes,
> Nor heaven peep through the blanket of the dark
> To cry 'Hold, hold'.

Macbeth, as he goes towards the chamber of the sleeping Duncan, describes how

> o'er the one half-world
> Nature seems dead, and wicked dreams abuse
> The curtain'd sleep.

The word 'night' echoes through the first two scenes of the third act; and Macbeth invokes night to conceal the murder of Banquo:

page 49 begins

> Come, seeling night,
> Scarf up the tender eye of pitiful day . . .

> Light thickens, and the crow
> Makes wing to th' rooky wood;
> Good things of day begin to droop and drowse,
> Whiles night's black agents to their preys do rouse.

In the scene in England and in the last act of the play—except for the sleep-walking scene—the darkness is replaced by light.

The symbolism is obvious. In many of these contexts night and darkness are associated with evil, and day and light are linked with good. The "good things of day" are contrasted with "night's black agents"; and, in the last act, day stands for the victory of the forces of liberation (v, iv, I; v, vii, 27; v, viii, 37). The "midnights hags" are "the instruments of darkness"; and some editors believe that when Malcolm (at the end of act IV) says that "The Powers above/Put on their instruments" he is referring to their human instruments—Malcolm, Macduff and their soldiers. Several critics have pointed out the opposition in the play between night and day, life and death, grace and evil, a contrast which is re-iterated more than four hundred times.

The evidence for this has gone beyond imagery proper and most modern imagistic critics have ex-tended their field to cover not merely metaphor and simile, but the visual symbols implied by the dialogue, which would be visible in performance, and even the iteration of key words. The Poet Laureate once re-marked that *Macbeth* is about blood; and from the ap-pearance of the bloody sergeant in the second scene of the play to the last scene of all, we have a continual vision of blood. Macbeth's sword in the battle "smok'd with bloody execution"; he and Banquo seemed to "bathe in recking wounds"; the Sergeant's "gashes cry for help." The Second Witch comes from the bloody task of killing swine. The visionary dagger is stained with "gouts of blood." Macbeth, after the murder, de-clares that not all great Neptune's ocean will cleanse his hands:

> this my hand will rather
> The multitudinous seas incarnadine,
> Making the green one red.

Duncan is spoken of as the fountain of his sons' blood; his wounds

> look'd like a breach in nature
> For ruin's wasteful entrance.

page 50 begins

The world had become a "bloody stage." Macbeth, be-fore the murder of Banquo, invokes the "bloody and invisible hand" of night. We are told of the twenty trenched gashes on Banquo's body and his ghost shakes his "gory locks" at Macbeth, who is convinced that "blood will have blood." At the end of the banquet scene, he confesses wearily that he is "stepp'd so far" in blood, that

> should I wade no more,
> Returning were as tedious as go o'er.

The Second Apparition, a bloody child, advises Mac-beth to be "bloody, bold, and resolute." Malcolm de-clares that Scotland bleeds,

> and each new day a gash
> Is added to her wounds.

Lady Macbeth, sleep-walking, tries in vain to remove the "damned spot" from her hands:

> Here's the smell of the blood still. All the perfumes of Arabia will not sweeten this little hand.

In the final scene, Macbeth's severed head is displayed on a pole. As Kott has recently reminded us, the subject of the play is murder, and the prevalence of blood en-sures that we shall never forget the physical realities in metaphysical overtones.

LITERARY TERMS HANDBOOK

ALEXANDRINE   *A line of poetry in iambic hexameter (six iambs).* The Spenserian stanza ends with an alexandrine, such as this one from *The Faerie Queene:*

His foes / have slain / themselves, / with whom / he should / contend.

See pages 124, 382–383, 438.

ALLEGORY   *A narrative work or a drama in which almost all the characters, settings, and events are symbols representing abstract ideas and in which the overall purpose is to teach a moral lesson.* Bunyan's *Pilgrim's Progress* is a famous prose allegory.

See pages 120, 290, 893.

ALLITERATION   *The repetition of nearby consonant sounds, usually at the beginnings of words.* Notice the repeated *s* sounds in this line from "The Seafarer":

Of smashing surf when I sweated in the cold

See pages 26, 430–431.

ALLITERATIVE VERSE   *Poetry that uses alliteration of a specific sound in each line.* In its original form, Old English poetry is alliterative verse.

See page 26.

ALLUSION   *A short reference in a work to something outside the work, usually to another piece of literature or to a well-known person, place, or event from history, religion, or mythology.* This epigram by Pope makes an allusion to the Pierian spring, Greek waters supposedly sacred to the Muses and an inspiration to creativity:

A little learning is a dangerous thing;
Drink deep, or taste not the Pierian spring.

ANAPEST   *A poetic foot consisting of two unstressed syllables followed by a stressed syllable (˘˘´); also called an **anapestic foot.*** In this line from Kipling's "Ballad of East and West," the first, second, third, fifth, and sixth feet are all anapests:

With the mouth / of a bell / and the heart / of Hell /
and the head / of the gal / lows tree.

See pages 382–383.

ANECDOTE   *A short written or oral account of an event in a real person's life.*

ANGLO-SAXON   See OLD ENGLISH.

ANTAGONIST   *In a work with an external conflict, the person or force that the protagonist must face.* In the selection from Spenser's *Faerie Queene,* the Knight's antagonist is the monster Error.

See page 701.

APHORISM   *A short, pointed statement expressing a wise or clever observation about life.* For example:

Fools rush in where angels fear to tread.
　　　　　　　　　　　　—Alexander Pope

APOSTROPHE   *A figure of speech in which an object, an animal, an idea, or an absent person is directly addressed as if capable of hearing.* For example, Donne's Holy Sonnet 10 uses apostrophe in addressing death:

Death, be not proud . . .

See page 448.

ART FOR ART'S SAKE   *An attitude that reacted to nineteenth-century realism by claiming that art is superior to nature, has no purpose other than to exist and be beautiful, and need not portray real life at all.* Oscar Wilde and others who held this attitude were sometimes called **Decadents.**

See pages 487, 546.

ASIDE   *In a play, a character's comment that is heard by the audience but not by other characters on stage.* The dramatist uses stage directions to indicate an aside:

MACBETH. [*Aside.*] Glamis, and Thane of Cawdor;
　　The greatest is behind.

An aside may also be spoken to one character with the others not hearing. Again, stage directions (for example, *Aside to Banquo*) will clarify such an aside.

See page 145.

ASSONANCE   *The repetition of nearby vowel sounds.* Notice the repeated long *i* sounds in these lines from Tennyson's *In Memoriam A. H. H.:*

Ring out, wild bells, to the wild sky,
　　The flying cloud, the frosty light.

See pages 430–431.

ATMOSPHERE   *The prevailing mood of a work of literature.* An author creates atmosphere chiefly through setting descriptions and tone. For example, Conrad's jungle setting and serious tone work together to create a tense atmosphere in "The Lagoon."

See pages 225, 756.

AUTOBIOGRAPHY   *A person's account of his or her own life.*

See page 365.
See also BIOGRAPHY, DIARY, JOURNAL.

BALLAD   *A usually simple narrative poem that recounts an exciting or dramatic episode and is composed to be sung or recited.* "Sir Patrick Spens" and Kipling's "Ballad of East and West" are examples.

See pages 52, 55.

BALLAD STANZA   *A quatrain in which the first and third lines have four stressed syllables, the second and fourth lines have three stressed syllables, and only the second and fourth lines rhyme.* Though the basic foot is the iamb, there tend to be many irregularities involving substitute feet, especially in the folk ballads that give this stanza form its name. In this stanza from "Sir Patrick Spens," notice the substitution of two anapests for iambs in line 3:

O wha / is this / has don / this deid
    And told / the king / o' me,
To send / us out / at this time / o' the yeir,
    To sail / upon / the sea!

See pages 55, 382–383, 438.

BIOGRAPHY   *A nonfiction account of a person's life and character, written by someone other than the subject.* Boswell's *Life of Samuel Johnson* is an example.

See page 365.
See also AUTOBIOGRAPHY, DIARY, JOURNAL.

BLANK VERSE   *Poetry or lines of verse drama written in unrhymed iambic pentameter.* Because blank verse attempts to sound like spoken English, its meter often is not perfectly regular. In these lines from *Macbeth,* for example, the second line is perfect iambic pentameter, but the first is not:

Life's but / a walk / ing shad / ow, a poor / player
That struts / and frets / his hour / upon / the stage.

See pages 165, 285, 382–383.

BYRONIC HERO   *The unconventional, brooding, Romantic character popularized by Lord Byron in some of his verse and, to a certain degree, his own life.* *Childe Harold's Pilgrimage* features such a character.

See pages 433, 436.

CAESURA   *A pronounced pause in a line of poetry, usually near the middle of the line.* For example:

I promise you this: // she'll find no shelter,
No hole in the ground, // no towering tree.
—*Beowulf*

See page 26.

CANTO   *A section or a division of a long poem.* Spenser's *Faerie Queene* is divided into books, which are further divided into cantos.

See page 120.

CARICATURE   *A humorous character portrayal that exaggerates or distorts certain qualities of the person in order to create a ridiculous effect.* Caricature is often used in satire and parody. Dryden's portrayal of Thomas Shadwell in *MacFlecknoe* is a caricature.

See page 903.

CARPE DIEM   *A term applied to literary works in which the theme suggests that life is short and that we must therefore enjoy life while we can.* Herrick's "To the Virgins, to Make Much of Time" is a famous example of a poem in the carpe-diem tradition, which goes back to ancient literature. (*Carpe diem* is Latin for "Seize the day.")

See page 269.

CATHARSIS   See TRAGEDY.

CHARACTER   *A person (or another creature given human qualities, such as Homer's Greek gods or Lewis Carroll's March Hare) who appears in a literary work.* A **flat character** reveals only one or two personality traits; the porter in Shakespeare's *Macbeth* is an example. A **round character** shows a variety of traits, often complex and contradictory; Macbeth is an example. A **static character** remains primarily the same throughout a work; the witches in *Macbeth* are examples. A **dynamic character** changes during the course of a work because of the influence of events or other characters; Macbeth and Lady Macbeth are examples.

See pages 78–79, 225, 724.

CHARACTERIZATION   *The personality of a character and the means by which it is revealed.* In **direct characterization** the narrator explicitly tells us something about a character's personality. For example, Chapter 1 of Austen's *Pride and Prejudice* explicitly states that Mrs. Bennet is "a woman of mean understanding, little information, and uncertain temper." In **indirect characterization** the character's personality is suggested by his or her actions, speech, thoughts, and physical appearance and by the reactions of other characters to him or her. For example, Mrs. Bennet's remarks and actions also reveal her to be a foolish, petty woman.

See pages 78–79, 476, 724.

CLASSICISM *A style that reflects the principles and concerns of the art and literature of ancient Greece and Rome.* The seventeenth- and eighteenth-century movement to imitate the balanced, orderly rationality of the ancients was called **neoclassicism.**

See pages 312–313, 389–390.

CLIMAX See PLOT.

CLOSET DRAMA See DRAMA.

COMEDY *A drama or another literary work that ends happily or that aims to amuse its audience.* Molière's *Flying Doctor* is a comedy.

See also FARCE, TRAGEDY.

COMEDY OF MANNERS *A realistic, satirical drama that pokes fun at the fashions, behavior, and outlook of sophisticated society.* Many of Molière's plays are comedies of manners, although *The Flying Doctor* is a bit less realistic than is typical.

See pages 242, 313.

CONCEIT *An elaborate or farfetched metaphor or simile.* The **Petrarchan conceit,** introduced by Italian poet Petrarch and popular among Elizabethan poets, captures the suffering of an unrequited lover or the magnificence of the beloved; the elaborate comparison of a lover to a ship in Wyatt's "My Galley" is an example. The **metaphysical conceit,** used by the metaphysical poets, presents a more intellectual, less typically "poetic" comparison and is used to capture a broader range of emotions; the farfetched comparison of the speaker to a usurped town in Donne's Holy Sonnet 14 is an example.

See page 249.

CONFLICT *The struggle between two opposing forces that is central to a plot and that involves the main character, or protagonist.* In an **external conflict** the protagonist struggles with an outside force, or *antagonist,* such as another character, nature, society, or fate; an example is Beowulf's struggle with the mon-

sters. In an **internal conflict** the struggle takes place within the protagonist's mind or conscience; an example is the conflict in O'Connor's "Masculine Protest," in which the narrator struggles for a more mature understanding of his parents. A work may have more than one conflict; sometimes an external conflict reflects an internal conflict taking place at the same time.

See pages 224, 698 701.

CONNOTATION *All the suggested meanings and associations that a word brings to mind beyond its denotation, or dictionary definition.* For example, in Byron's "She Walks in Beauty," which speaks of every "raven tress" of the woman's hair, both *raven* and *tress* have connotations of grace and beauty beyond their dictionary definition, "lock of black hair."

See page 679.

CONSONANCE *Repetition of consonant sounds at the ends of words or stressed syllables in order to create near rhyme.* For example, the near rhyme in these lines from Campion's "When to Her Lute" is based on consonance:

But if she doth of sorrow speak,
Even from my heart the strings do break.

See pages 430–431.

COUPLET *A two-line stanza, poem, or poetic saying.* The two lines of a couplet almost always rhyme; however, to stress that they do, the term **rhymed couplet** is sometimes used. A **heroic couplet** consists of two rhymed lines in iambic pentameter.

See pages 139, 291, 352, 438.
See also STANZA.

DACTYL *A poetic foot consisting of a stressed syllable followed by two unstressed syllables (′ ⌣ ⌣); also called a **dactylic foot.*** This line from Blake's "Infant Sorrow" opens with two dactyls:

$$\acute{ } \smile \smile \; / \; \acute{ } \smile \smile \; / \; \acute{ } \smile \; / \; \acute{ } \smile$$
Into the / dangerous / world I / leapt.

See pages 382–383.

DECADENTS See ART FOR ART'S SAKE.

DENOTATION *The basic meaning or dictionary definition of a word.*

See page 679.
See also CONNOTATION.

DENOUEMENT See PLOT.

DEVOTIONAL VERSE *Lyric poetry devoted to religion.* George Herbert was a noted writer of devotional verse.

See page 256.

DIALECT *A variety of a language spoken in a particular region or by a particular group of people.* Dialects differ in pronunciation, vocabulary, and sometimes grammar. Many of Robert Burns's poems are written in **Scottish,** a dialect of English spoken in parts of Scotland; Eliza Doolittle in Shaw's *Pygmalion* initially speaks in **cockney,** a dialect of London's East End.

See pages 372, 640.

DIALOGUE *The conversation between characters in a literary work.*

See pages 52, 476, 933.
See also DRAMA,
MONOLOGUE.

DIARY *An individual's personal, day-to-day account of impressions and events.* Diaries are usually more intimate than journals. Pepys' *Diary* is a famous example.

See page 305.

DICTION *The author's word choice, or use of appropriate words to convey a particular meaning.* Good writers choose their words carefully in order to express exactly what they intend. In particular, they consider denotations, connotations, and sounds of words.

See pages 285–286, 679, 752.

DRAMA *A story written to be performed—or as if to be performed—before an audience.* Drama is distinguished from poetry and prose by its format, which consists chiefly of **dialogue** labeled with the names of the characters who speak it and which also includes **stage directions** that give instructions about such things as scenery, costumes, lighting, sound effects, and the ways in which performers are to move or speak their lines. In a **verse drama,** this overall format is maintained, but the dialogue itself (or most of the dialogue) is in the form of poetry; *Macbeth* and *Antigone* are examples.

Though most dramas are written to be performed, authors have occasionally written verse dramas for reading only. Such dramas are sometimes called **closet dramas;** Goethe's *Faust* is an example.

See pages 49,
109–111, 242–243, 313,
391, 612.

DRAMATIC CONVENTIONS *Practices that audiences accept on stage as realistic but that differ from real-life behavior.* Quick shifts in time, soliloquies, and asides are examples of dramatic conventions.

See pages 145, 612.

DRAMATIC MONOLOGUE *A dramatic poem that consists of the speech of one character.* Tennyson's "Ulysses" is an example.

See pages 507, 557.
See also MONOLOGUE.

DRAMATIC POETRY *Poetry that reveals character through speech and that consists entirely of dialogue or monologue.* Robert Browning's "My Last Duchess" is a dramatic poem, for example.

See pages 507, 557.
See also LYRIC POETRY,
NARRATIVE POETRY.

ELEGIAC STANZA See HEROIC STANZA.

ELEGY *A serious poem of lament, usually mourning a death or another great loss.* "The Seafarer" and Tennyson's *In Memoriam A. H. H.* are examples.

See pages 38, 371.

EPIC *A long narrative poem that recounts, in grave and stately language, the exploits of a larger-than-life hero who usually embodies the ideals of the culture that produced him.* Epic poetry is sometimes called **heroic poetry.** *Gilgamesh* and *Beowulf* are epics.

See pages 8, 277, 351, 786.

EPIC CONVENTIONS *Elements that traditionally appear in epics and are imitated in mock-epics.* Among these elements are a brave hero who overcomes great trials, a major battle scene, gods involved in the action, and epithets and Homeric similes.

See pages 8–9, 351, 820.

EPIC SIMILE See HOMERIC SIMILE.

EPIGRAM *A brief, witty, often philosophical saying in prose or verse.* For example:

To err is human, to forgive divine.

—Alexander Pope

See page 352.

EPIGRAPH *A quotation at the beginning of a chapter, a poem, a book, or another literary work.* Eliot's "Hollow Men" opens with two epigraphs.

EPIPHANY   *A sudden realization, by the reader as well as a character, of the true nature of a person, an object, or a situation.* Epiphany, an innovation of James Joyce's, usually occurs near the end of a work. Joyce's "Araby" contains an epiphany.

See page 711.

EPITAPH   *A tombstone inscription or a brief poem composed in memory of someone who has died.* Gray's "Elegy Written in a Country Churchyard" ends with an epitaph.

EPITHET   *A characterizing nickname or adjective phrase; more specifically, in oral poetry or written epics modeled on oral ones, a formalized nickname or adjective phrase used to identify or describe a person, a place, an event, or an object that occurs again and again in the poem.* For example, "Higlac's follower" is an epithet often used to identify Beowulf; "rosy-fingered dawn" is often used in Homer's *Iliad.*

See pages 26, 820.

ESSAY   *A short prose composition that deals with a single topic.* A **formal essay** is a carefully structured attempt to instruct or persuade. It has a serious tone and presents its argument logically. Bacon's "Of Ambition" is an example. An **informal essay** aims to entertain or please the reader while it explores a given topic. Its tone is light, and its structure is somewhat sprawling. Steele's "Funeral of Thomas Betterton" is an example. When an informal essay includes personal references, as most informal essays do, it is sometimes called a **personal essay.**

See pages 228, 339.

EXEMPLUM   *A story that serves to illustrate the moral of the sermon in which it appears.* In the context of Chaucer's *Canterbury Tales,* "The Pardoner's Tale" appears as an exemplum illustrating the moral of a sermon about the folly of greed.

See page 91.

EXISTENTIALISM   *A modern European philosophy that considers life to be empty of any meaning, purpose, or value other than that which people give their own lives.* Kafka was influenced by existentialism.

See page 940.

EXPOSITION   See PLOT.

FABLE   *A short, usually simple tale that teaches a moral and often uses animal characters.*

FARCE   *A type of comedy that achieves humor largely through improbable situations, exaggerated* characters, and slapstick action. Molière's *Flying Doctor* contains many elements of farce.

See page 913.

FICTION   *Literature that focuses on invented characters and events, often in invented settings.*

See also NONFICTION.

FIGURATIVE LANGUAGE   *Language that is not meant to be interpreted literally.* In the following example, Chaucer uses *snowed* in a figurative sense:

It positively snowed with meat and drink.

Instances of figurative language, called **figures of speech,** include apostrophe, conceit, metaphor, paradox, personification, simile, symbol, and verbal irony.

See pages 139, 448.

FIGURE OF SPEECH   See FIGURATIVE LANGUAGE.

FLASHBACK   *In the plot of a narrative or a drama, an interruption in chronological order that jumps back to an earlier time.* Stream-of-consciousness stories, such as Woolf's "New Dress," contain many flashbacks.

See page 731.

FOIL   *A character created to contrast with another character.* Practical Sancho Panza is impractical Don Quixote's foil.

FOLK BALLAD   *An anonymous ballad composed, not by a professional poet or minstrel, but by simple, uneducated people and passed down by oral tradition.* "The Wife of Usher's Well" is an example.

See pages 52, 55.

FOOT   *The basic unit of meter in poetry.* The foot usually consists of one stressed syllable (marked ´) and one or two unstressed syllables (marked ˘). The four most frequently used kinds of feet are the **iamb** (˘´), the **trochee** (´˘), the **anapest** (˘˘´), and the **dactyl** (´˘˘). Two other kinds of feet that appear occasionally are the **spondee** (´´) and the **pyrrhic** (˘˘). This line from Lovelace's "To Althea, from Prison" opens with a spondee but otherwise uses iambs:

Stone walls / do not / a pri / son make.

See pages 382–383.

FORESHADOWING   *The use of clues by the author to prepare readers for events that will happen later in a narrative or a drama.* In *Macbeth,* for example, the witches' remark that "Fair is foul, and foul is fair" foreshadows the foul deeds that the seemingly noble Macbeth will perform later in the play.

See page 18.

FRAME STORY *A narrative within which one or more other narratives unfold.* In Chaucer's *Canterbury Tales,* for example, the narrative about the pilgrims heading for Canterbury is a frame story in which a series of other stories are told by the different pilgrims.

FREE VERSE *Poetry with no fixed rhythm, or meter.* Free verse has become especially popular among twentieth-century poets. Gunn's "Taylor Street," for example, is written in free verse.

See pages 232, 656.

GENRE *A type or a category of literature.* The term may refer to a broad literary category, such as the novel or short story, or to a specific literary type, such as the gothic novel or the novel of manners.

GOTHIC NOVEL *A novel that has a gloomy, foreboding setting and contains strong elements of horror, mystery, and the supernatural.* Mary Shelley's *Frankenstein* is a gothic novel.

See pages 313, 391.

HAIKU *An originally Japanese form of three-line poem with five syllables in the first and third lines and seven syllables in the middle line.* In the original Japanese, Bashō's haiku adhere to this pattern.

See page 914.

HERO See EPIC, PROTAGONIST, TRAGEDY.

HEROIC COUPLET *A pair of rhymed lines in iambic pentameter.* Heroic couplets were popular with the neoclassical poets, including Jonson, Dryden, and Pope.

To draw / no en / vy, Shake / speare, on / thy
  name,
Am I / thus am / ple to / thy book / and fame.
      —Jonson, "To the Memory of My Beloved Master,
                      William Shakespeare"

See pages 291, 352,
382–383, 438.
See also STANZA.

HEROIC POETRY See EPIC.

HEROIC STANZA *A quatrain that uses iambic pentameter and rhymes abab.* The heroic stanza is sometimes called the **elegiac stanza** after Gray's "Elegy Written in a Country Churchyard," which uses this stanza form.

See page 438.

HISTORICAL NOVEL *A novel that sets fictional characters against a backdrop of history and contains many details about the historical period in which it is set.* Defoe's *Journal of the Plague Year* is a historical novel in journal form.

See page 391.

HOMERIC SIMILE *An elaborate simile that extends over many lines; also called an* **epic simile.** Homer often used such similes; this one is from the *Iliad:*

Conspicuous as the evening star that comes,
amid the first in heaven, at fall of night,
and stands most lovely in the west, so shone
in sunlight the fine-pointed spear . . .

See page 820.

HYPERBOLE *A figure of speech that uses exaggeration not intended to be taken literally, usually for emphasis or to create humor.* For example, these lines from *Macbeth* use hyperbole for emphasis:

Will all great Neptune's ocean wash this blood
Clean from my hand?

IAMB *A poetic foot consisting of an unstressed syllable followed by a stressed syllable (˘ ′); also called an* **iambic foot.** This line from Marvell's "To His Coy Mistress" contains four iambs:

Had we / but world / enough, / and time

See pages 119, 165,
382–383.

IAMBIC PENTAMETER *A meter in which the predominant foot is the iamb (˘ ′) and there are five feet in a line.* One of the most popular meters in English poetry, iambic pentameter is used in blank verse, heroic couplets, and most sonnets, among other things. This iambic pentameter line is from one of Milton's sonnets:

They al / so serve / who on / ly stand / and wait.

See pages 119, 165,
291, 382–383, 438,
878.

IMAGE *Something that can be perceived by one or more of the five senses; something concrete, as opposed to abstract.*

See page 177.
See also IMAGERY.

IMAGERY *The use of words and phrases that evoke images in the reader's mind; the use of language that appeals to one or more of the five senses.* For example, this line from Tennyson's "Splendor Falls on Castle Walls" appeals to the senses of hearing and sight:

Blow, bugles, blow, set the wild echoes flying.

See pages 177, 286.

IN MEDIA RES *In the middle of the action.* A work is said to open *in media res* when it opens with action instead of exposition and reveals background information later, often gradually instead of in one section. (*In media res* is Latin for "in the midst of things.")

See also PLOT.

INTERLUDE *A brief comedy or dialogue of the late fifteenth and early sixteenth centuries.*

See page 111.

INVOCATION *A writer's call for aid or inspiration from a Muse or another spiritual force.* Milton's *Paradise Lost* opens with an invocation.

See page 277.

IRONY *The awareness—by author, character, or reader—of a contrast or an incongruity between appearance and reality.* Irony is achieved in one of three ways. In **verbal irony** words that appear to mean one thing really mean the opposite; the opening sentence of Austen's *Pride and Prejudice* is an example. In **dramatic irony** what appears true to a character is not what the audience or reader knows to be true; for example, Duncan's belief that the Macbeths are praiseworthy hosts creates irony because we know that the Macbeths are planning to kill Duncan. In **situational irony** what appears likely to happen is not what actually happens; for example, in Greene's "Shocking Accident," both the accident and Sally's unexpected reaction to it are ironic situations.

See page 225.

JOURNAL *A daily record of events kept by an individual who is a participant in or witness to the events.* Journals are usually less intimate than diaries, which contain more personal impressions. Defoe's *Journal of the Plague Year* is a novel in journal form.

See page 305.

KENNING *In Old English poetry, an imaginative metaphorical phrase used in place of a simple noun.* For example, "The Seafarer" uses the kenning "whales' home" to mean the sea.

See page 26.

LEGEND *A traditional tale believed to be based on history.* A legend usually celebrates the heroic qualities of a national or cultural hero. For example, many medieval legends revolve around the hero King Arthur.

See pages 103, 826–827.
See also MYTH.

LITERARY CRITICISM *The analysis or interpretation of one or more literary works in order to enlarge a reader's appreciation or comprehension.* Dryden's "Essay of Dramatic Poesy" is an early example.

See page 465.

LYRIC POETRY *Poetry in which a speaker expresses personal thoughts and feelings.* Lyric poems are usually short and can take many forms; for example, the sonnet and the ode are both lyric forms.

See pages 38, 557.
See also DRAMATIC POETRY, NARRATIVE POETRY.

MADRIGAL *A lyric poem designed to be sung without instrumental accompaniment.*

See page 143.

MASQUE *A stylized drama in which the focus is less on content than on elaborate staging, including song and dance.* Masques were popular in the Elizabethan Age.

See page 111.

METAPHOR *A figure of speech that compares one thing with another, seemingly different, thing generally to suggest a quality of the first thing or to help us perceive it in an unusual or more vivid way.* In these lines from "London, 1802," Wordsworth uses a metaphor to suggest the foulness and sluggishness he found in England and to help readers picture these qualities:

England hath need of thee: she is a fen
Of stagnant waters.

As distinguished from a simile, a metaphor implies the comparison instead of stating it directly. If Wordsworth had said "England . . . is *like* a fen of stagnant waters," he would have used a simile.

See pages 139, 448

METAPHYSICAL POETRY *A term now used for the profoundly or playfully intellectual poetry of John Donne and the younger mid-seventeenth-century poets whom he influenced.* Metaphysical poetry often makes clever use of paradox, conceit, and logical argument.

See pages 242, 246.

METER *In poetry, a regular, predictable pattern of stressed and unstressed syllables.* The basic unit of meter is the **foot**. In identifying meter, we identify the predominant kind of foot—**iamb** (˘ ´), **trochee** (´ ˘), **anapest** (˘ ˘ ´), or **dactyl** (´ ˘ ˘). We also identify the number of feet a line contains:

monometer = 1 foot	**pentameter** = 5 feet
dimeter = 2 feet	**hexameter** = 6 feet
trimeter = 3 feet	**heptameter** = 7 feet
tetrameter = 4 feet	**octameter** = 8 feet

For example, this line from Marlowe's "Passionate Shepherd" is in *iambic tetrameter*—it has four iambs:

˘ ´ / ˘ ´ / ˘ ´ / ˘ ´ /
Come live / with me / and be / my love.

> See pages 382–383, 501.
> See also FOOT, FREE
> VERSE, SPRUNG RHYTHM.

MIDDLE ENGLISH *The language that evolved from Old English as a result of the influence of Norman French after the Norman Conquest (1066) and that remained the language of England until about 1500.* Chaucer wrote *The Canterbury Tales* in Middle English.

> See pages 40–41, 96–97,
> 139–140.

MIRACLE PLAY *A medieval religious drama presenting a story from the Bible or the lives of the saints; also called a* **mystery play.**

> See page 49.

MOCK-EPIC *A poem that imitates epic style but makes fun of the hero or society it portrays.* By imitating a true epic, the mock-epic stresses that its hero or society cannot live up to the heroic standards of epics. Dryden's *MacFlecknoe* is a mock-epic.

> See page 351.
> See also PARODY.

MODERN ENGLISH *The English language spoken and written since about 1500.*

> See pages 40–41, 96–97,
> 139–140.

MODERNISM *An umbrella term for a variety of early twentieth-century movements that all had in common a desire to break with the past and to change the very structure of literature.* The use of free verse in poetry and the use of stream-of-consciousness technique in fiction are both typical of modernism. Among the British writers associated with modernism are Yeats, Eliot, Conrad, Joyce, Lawrence, and Woolf.

> See page 563.

MONOLOGUE *A speech by one character only.* An **interior monologue** is a monologue that takes place in a character's mind.

> See also DIALOGUE,
> DRAMATIC MONOLOGUE.

MORALITY PLAY *A medieval religious allegory in the form of a drama.*

> See page 49.

MOTIF *An event, an idea, or another element that occurs again and again in a particular type of literature.* For example, the Byronic hero is a motif of Romantic literature.

> See page 89.

MOTIVATION *The stated or implied reasons that characters in a literary work behave as they do.* In *Gilgamesh*, for example, Gilgamesh is motivated to seek the secret of eternal life because he is grief-stricken at the death of his friend Enkidu and hopes to revive him.

> See page 724.

MYSTERY PLAY See MIRACLE PLAY.

MYTH *An anonymous traditional story that relies on the supernatural to explain a natural phenomenon, an aspect of human behavior, or one of the universe's mysteries.* For example, the ancient Greeks explained the existence of evil with the myth of Pandora. According to that myth, the god Zeus had put all human evils into a box, and Pandora, prompted by curiosity, opened the box and released its contents into the world.

> See pages 103, 877.
> See also LEGEND.

NARRATIVE *Writing that tells a story, moving from event to event, usually in chronological order.* A narrative requires a **narrator**, or storyteller. Types of narrative include short stories, novels, narrative poetry, and narrative essays.

NARRATIVE HOOK See PLOT.

NARRATIVE POETRY *Poetry that tells a story.* Both the ballad and the epic are types of narrative poetry.

> See pages 553, 557.
> See also DRAMATIC
> POETRY,
> LYRIC POETRY.

NARRATOR See NARRATIVE, POINT OF VIEW.

NATURALISM *An outgrowth of nineteenth-century Realism that depicted nature and society as over-*

whelming forces completely indifferent to human misery. Although Naturalist literature is pessimistic, its aim is usually social reform. Both Hardy and Conrad were influenced by Naturalism.

> See pages 487, 545, 565.

NEOCLASSICISM *A literary movement of the seventeenth and eighteenth centuries that revived the orderly, rational, controlled style—or **Classicism**—of the literature of ancient Greece and Rome and stressed the importance of reason, order, harmony, and moderation.* Ben Jonson was the father of English neoclassicism.

> See pages 242–243, 261, 312–313, 389–390.
> See also RATIONALISM.

NONFICTION *Literature about real people and events or offering the opinions and theories of real people.*

> See also FICTION.

NOVEL *A book-length or longer work of prose fiction.* This loose definition is often further elaborated; for example, the *Oxford English Dictionary* defines a novel as "a fictitious prose narrative of considerable length, in which characters and actions representative of real life are portrayed in a plot of more or less complexity." Cervantes' *Don Quixote* was one of the first novels.

> See pages 313, 321, 391, 488–489, 514.

NOVEL OF MANNERS *A realistic, usually satirical novel that examines the behavior and outlook of a particular social class.* Austen's *Pride and Prejudice* is a novel of manners.

> See pages 313, 391.

NOVEL OF SENTIMENT *An unrealistic novel in which flat characters display excessive emotions and the protagonist faces misfortunes that bring tears to the reader's eyes; also called a **sentimental novel**.* The novel of sentiment usually includes a romance and contains a moral message.

> See page 313.

OCTAVE *An eight-line poem or stanza.*

> See pages 119, 438.
> See also STANZA.

ODE *A long lyric poem, serious and dignified in subject, tone, and style and usually written to celebrate an event or to honor someone or something.* An **irregular ode** has no set rhyme scheme or stanza pattern;

Dryden's "Song for St. Cecilia's Day" is an example. A **Horatian ode**, named for Roman poet Horace, follows a regular stanza pattern and rhyme scheme; Shelley's "Ode to the West Wind" is an example.

> See page 458.

OLD ENGLISH *The Germanic language spoken by the Angles, Saxons, and Jutes who invaded Britain in the fifth century; also called **Anglo-Saxon**.* Beowulf was originally composed in Old English.

> See pages 3, 40–41, 96–97.

ONOMATOPOEIA *The use of words with sounds that imitate or suggest their meanings.* This line from Hopkins' "God's Grandeur" uses onomatopoeia:

> It gathers to a greatness, like the ooze of oil.

> See page 431.

ORAL TRADITION *The process of passing literature by word of mouth from one generation to the next.* Folk ballads and many early epics, such as the *Iliad* and *Beowulf,* developed through the oral tradition.

OTTAVA RIMA *A stanza form using eight-line stanzas in iambic pentameter rhymed* abababcc. Byron uses ottava rima in *Don Juan*.

> See pages 438, 439.

OXYMORON *A type of paradox consisting of two seemingly contradictory terms.* "Sweet sorrow," "wise fool," and "cruel kindness" are examples.

PARABLE *An illustrative story answering a question or pointing to a moral or religious lesson.* The most famous parables are those told by Jesus, such as the parable of the Prodigal Son (Luke 15:11–32).

PARADOX *A statement or a situation that at first seems impossible or self-contradictory but that actually may be true, either in fact or in a figurative sense.* The statement "Stone walls do not a prison make," from Lovelace's "To Althea, from Prison," is an example.

> See pages 255, 671.
> See also OXYMORON.

PARALLELISM *The use of repeated structures in nearby phrases, clauses, sentences, or lines of poetry.* Parallelism gives emphasis to thoughts and can make them more memorable. This famous quotation from Donne's Meditation XVII uses parallelism:

> No man is an island, entire of itself; every man is a piece of the continent, a part of the main.

PARODY *A humorous imitation of another, usually serious work.* For example, a mock-epic, such as Pope's *Rape of the Lock,* is a parody of an epic.

See page 323.

PASTORAL *A work that depicts the simple pleasures of rural life.* Marlowe's "Passionate Shepherd to His Love" is a famous Elizabethan pastoral.

See page 131.

PERSONIFICATION *A figure of speech in which human qualities are given to objects, animals, or ideas.* For example, Surrey personifies a buck in this line from "Description of Spring":

The buck in brake his winter coat he flings.

See page 448.
See also APOSTROPHE.

PICARESQUE NOVEL *A humorous novel consisting of loosely strung episodes about an adventurer or a lovable rogue.* Cervantes' *Don Quixote* inspired many English picaresque novels.

See page 313.

PLOT *The sequence of events in a drama or a narrative work.* Each event usually causes or leads to the next and revolves around a **conflict,** the struggle that the main character undergoes. Usually a plot begins with **exposition,** or background information, that introduces the characters, settings, and situations. The **narrative hook** (sometimes called the **dramatic hook** in a play) draws readers (or the audience) into the story and is the point at which the conflict begins. Events that contribute to the conflict form the **rising action** that leads to the **climax,** or point of highest dramatic tension. The **falling action** presents the results of the climax and ends with the **resolution,** or final outcome, sometimes called the **denouement.** Modern literature often varies this traditional plot structure.

See pages 224, 514, 698, 711.
See also IN MEDIA RES, SUBPLOT, STREAM OF CONSCIOUSNESS.

POINT OF VIEW *The relationship of the narrator, or storyteller, to the narrative.* In the **first-person point of view** the narrator is a character in the plot who refers to himself or herself with first-person pronouns such as *I.* Charlotte Brontë's *Jane Eyre* is told from the first-person point of view. In **third-person points of view,** which may be **limited** or **omniscient,** the narrator is detached from the plot and refers to all characters with third-person pronouns such as *he* or *she.* In the **limited**

third-person point of view, the narrator limits the experiences being described to those of only one character and provides only that character's thoughts and feelings. Galsworthy's "Japanese Quince" uses this point of view, showing all the action through Mr. Nilson's eyes. In the **omniscient point of view,** the narrator reveals the thoughts and feelings of all the characters. Lawrence's "Goose Fair" uses an omniscient point of view.

See pages 698, 716.

PROSE *Literature that is neither poetry nor drama; literature written in sentence and paragraph form.* Prose may be fiction or nonfiction.

PROTAGONIST *The main character of a narrative work, a drama, or a dramatic poem; also called the* **hero.** Usually the action revolves around the protagonist, who undergoes the conflict. The protagonist of O'Connor's "Masculine Protest" is the narrator, Denis Halligan.

See page 701.
See also ANTAGONIST, CONFLICT.

PSYCHOLOGICAL REALISM *A type of realism that seeks to portray not outward reality but the inner realities of the human mind.* Psychological realism began in the nineteenth century and later incorporated new psychological theories of Freud and others. Stream-of-consciousness technique, used in Woolf's "New Dress," is typical of modern psychological realism.

See pages 487, 563, 731.

PUN *A humorous play on word meanings.* In Carroll's "Mad Tea Party," for example, the Dormouse makes a pun involving two meanings of the word *draw,* "to sketch a picture" and "to bring up from a well."

PYRRHIC *A poetic foot consisting of two unstressed syllables (˘ ˘); also called a* **pyrrhic foot** *or an* **empty foot.** The pyrrhic appears only as a substitute foot; it cannot determine meter. This line from Shakespeare's Sonnet 30 uses a pyrrhic in the third foot:

When to / the ses / sions of / sweet si / lent thought

See pages 382–383.

QUATRAIN *A four-line poem or stanza.*

See pages 55, 139, 438, 878.
See also STANZA.

RATIONALISM *A system of thought that places strong faith in the capacity of human reason and de-*

mands that scientific observation be used to ascertain all facts. Sir Francis Bacon is often called the father of rationalism, which became closely linked to neoclassicism.

REALISM *A literary manner that attempts to portray life as it really is lived; more specifically, a literary movement of the nineteenth century that had such an aim and that generally focused on everyday middle- or working-class characters.* Dickens' *Oliver Twist* shows the influence of Realism.

See pages 487, 545, 565.

REFRAIN *In a poem or a song, a line or lines repeated at regular intervals.* Villanelles include refrains; ballads often do.

See pages 55, 676.

REGIONALISM *A literary manner that focuses on the accurate depiction of a specific region.* Regionalism often went hand in hand with Realism during the Victorian Age and early twentieth century. A number of contemporary writers—Nadine Gordimer, for example, and V. S. Naipaul—can also be considered Regionalists.

See page 487.

RESOLUTION See PLOT.

RHYME *The repetition of the final stressed vowel and any succeeding sounds in a word or, sometimes, a phrase.* **Masculine rhyme** involves rhyming only stressed syllables: *be/see, bent/intent;* **feminine rhyme** involves rhyming both stressed and unstressed syllables: *being/seeing, begin it/minute/win it.* In **near rhyme** (also called **off rhyme, slant rhyme, approximate rhyme,** and **imperfect rhyme**) the rhyme is not exact: *time/fine, enchanted/haunted.* In **end rhyme** the rhyme occurs at the ends of lines; in **internal rhyme** it occurs within lines, as in this line from Coleridge's "Ancient Mariner":

> The ship was *cheered,* the harbor *cleared.*

See page 430.
See also CONSONANCE, RHYME SCHEME.

RHYME SCHEME *The pattern that end rhymes form in a stanza or a poem.* In identifying rhyme scheme, a different letter of the alphabet is assigned to each new rhyming sound. For example, this stanza from Suckling's "Why So Pale and Wan?" has an *ababb* rhyme scheme:

> Why so pale and wan, fond lover?
> Prithee, why so pale?
> Will, when looking well can't move her,
> Looking ill prevail?
> Prithee, why so pale?

See page 119.
See also RHYME.

RHYTHM *The alternation between stressed and unstressed syllables in poetry or other writing.*

See page 501.
See also FREE VERSE, METER.

ROMANCE *A medieval narrative that blends chivalry with adventure, love, and magic; also, a later work containing similar elements.* Malory's *Morte D'Arthur* is a prose romance.

See pages 49, 89, 321

ROMANTICISM *A literary manner that stresses feeling, originality, idealism, primitive nature, mystery or the supernatural, and the self; more specifically, a literary movement of the late eighteenth and early nineteenth centuries that emphasized these and related values.* The **Romantic Age** in Britain is usually said to begin with the publication of Coleridge's and Wordsworth's *Lyrical Ballads* in 1798.

See pages 313, 387–391, 487.

RUBÁIYÁT STANZA *A quatrain that uses iambic pentameter and rhymes aaxa.* The term comes from *The Rubáiyát of Omar Khayyám,* which uses this stanza form.

See page 878.

SATIRE *Literature that exposes to ridicule the vices or follies of people or societies.* Satire may take the form of poetry, drama, prose fiction, or nonfiction. Swift's *Gulliver's Travels* is a famous satire.

See pages 242, 295, 331.

SCANSION *The analysis of a poem to determine its meter; also called* ***scanning*** *the poem.* Scansion is done by marking the stressed (′) and unstressed (˘) syllables and by marking off the feet with a slash (/):

> At length / did cross / an Al / ba tross,
>
> Thorough / the fog / it came.
> —Coleridge, "The Rime of the Ancient Mariner"

See pages 382–383.
See also METER.

SCOP   An Anglo-Saxon traveling minstrel who composed or memorized oral literature and passed it down in the oral tradition.

> See pages 5, 6.

SESTET   A six-line poem or stanza.

> See pages 119, 438.
> See also STANZA.

SETTING   The time and place in which the events of a literary work occur. The overall setting of Macbeth is eleventh-century Scotland; its specific settings include a heath, a military camp, and various castles.

> See pages 225, 514, 698, 756.

SHORT STORY   A brief, fictional narrative that usually can be read in one sitting. The most important elements of a short story are usually plot, characterization, setting, point of view, and theme.

> See pages 489, 565, 698.

SIMILE   A figure of speech that compares one thing with another, seemingly different, thing and directly states that comparison by using a word such as like or as. For example:

> He was as fresh as is the month of May.
> —Chaucer, The Canterbury Tales

> See pages 139–140, 448.
> See also METAPHOR.

SOLILOQUY   In a play the speech of a character alone on stage, revealing his or her thoughts to the audience. Macbeth's line "Is this a dagger which I see before me?" begins a famous soliloquy.

> See page 145.

SONNET   A fourteen-line lyric poem with a fixed rhyme scheme and meter, usually iambic pentameter. The **Italian,** or **Petrarchan, sonnet** divides into an octave, usually rhymed abbaabba, and a sestet, usually rhymed cdecde, cdccdc, or cdedce; Milton's sonnets are examples. The **English,** or **Shakespearean, sonnet** divides into three quatrains, usually rhymed abab cdcd efef, and a rhymed couplet (usually gg); all of the sonnets by Shakespeare are examples. The **Spenserian sonnet,** a variation of the English sonnet, rhymes abab bcbc cdcd ee; all of the sonnets by Spenser are examples.

> See pages 119, 139.

SPEAKER   In a lyric poem the voice that communicates the poem's thoughts or feelings to the reader. The speaker may or may not be the poet. In Jonson's "On My First Son," the speaker clearly is the poet, for Jonson's own son died in 1603 of the plague. In Marvell's "To His Coy Mistress," the speaker is probably not the poet; rather, Marvell is probably adopting the conventional personality of the unrequited lover in order to express his own ideas about life, love, and the passage of time.

> See page 116.

SPENSERIAN STANZA   A nine-line stanza rhymed ababbcbcc, in which the first eight lines are iambic pentameter and the last line, called an **alexandrine,** is iambic hexameter. Spenser established this stanza form with The Faerie Queene; Byron's Childe Harold's Pilgrimage also uses it.

> See pages 124, 438.

SPONDEE   A poetic foot consisting of two stressed syllables (' '); also called a **spondaic foot.** The spondee appears only as a substitute foot; it cannot determine the meter. This line from Shakespeare's song opens with a spondee:

> ′   ′   ᵕ   ′   ᵕ   ′
> Blow, blow, / thou win / ter wind.

> See pages 382–383.

SPRUNG RHYTHM   A kind of meter in which each foot contains one stressed syllable, usually the first, and any number of unstressed syllables. Gerard Manley Hopkins, who coined the term, felt that sprung rhythm resembled natural speech. Consider, for example, this line from "God's Grandeur":

> ′   ᵕ   ᵕ   ′   ′   ᵕ   ᵕ   ′   ′
> And for all / this, / nature is / never / spent.

> See page 540.

STAGE DIRECTIONS   See DRAMA.

STANZA   In poetry a recurrent group of a definite number of lines, usually bound together by a rhyme scheme. Stanzas need not have space between them. Common stanzas include the **couplet** (two lines), the **triplet** (three lines), the **quatrain** (four lines), the sestet (six lines), and the **octave** (eight lines).

> See page 438.
> See also VERSE
> PARAGRAPH.

STREAM OF CONSCIOUSNESS   A technique of writing that imitates the way the human mind works by providing a continuous flow of thoughts, feelings, images, observations, and memories. Unlike stories with conventional plots, stream-of-consciousness stories may change topic suddenly in order to imitate the way the mind suddenly shifts from one thought to another.

Woolf's "New Dress" is a stream-of-consciousness story.

> See page 731.
> See also FLASHBACK.

STRUCTURE *The framework or general plan of a literary work; the units of thought by means of which a literary work is put together.* For example, the structure of a short story is its plot.

> See pages 285–286, 406, 752.

STYLE *An author's choice and arrangement of words to convey both an idea and the author's individuality.* An author uses a particular style in a particular work but also has a characteristic style that distinguishes his or her way of writing from that of another author. Elements of style include subject, tone, structure, diction, and use of literary or poetic devices such as imagery, figurative language, allusion, or rhyme and meter in poetry.

> See pages 285–286, 683, 752.

SUBJECT *The topic of a literary work; the experience or idea being written about.* The subject of the *Iliad*, for example, is the Trojan War.

> See pages 285, 752.

SUBPLOT *A less important or less developed plot that is in some way related to the main plot.* Novels often have subplots.

> See page 514.

SYMBOL *A person, a place, an object, or a situation that exists on a literal level within a work but also represents something on a figurative level, usually an abstract quality or range of qualities.* For example, the statue of Ozymandias literally exists in Shelley's poem—it stands in the desert, and things have happened to it. However, on the figurative level the statue represents abstract ideas such as kingship, vanity, ambition, and the desire for immortality. The use of symbols in a literary work is called **symbolism.**

> See pages 382, 650.

SYMBOLIST POETRY *Lyric poetry that uses vivid imagery, musical language, and, especially, symbols to imply emotions instead of stating those emotions directly.* The **Symbolist** movement, a reaction to nineteenth-century Realism, saw the communication of emotion as literature's chief aim and influenced Wilde and Yeats, among others.

> See pages 487, 546, 650.

TERCET *A three-line stanza or poem in which rhyme is employed.*

> See pages 438, 676, 883.
> See also STANZA, TRIPLET.

TERZA RIMA *A stanza form using three-line stanzas in which the first and third lines rhyme and the middle line rhymes with the first and third lines of the next stanza to form the rhyme scheme* aba bcb cdc *and so on.* Shelley's "Ode to the West Wind" uses terza rima.

> See pages 438, 883.

THEME *The main idea—usually a general statement about life—expressed or implied by a literary work.* A theme may be **stated** within the work but is usually **implied,** or suggested. Longer works, such as novels and plays, often have more than one theme.

> See pages 225, 514, 698, 764.
> See also THESIS.

THESIS *The main idea of a formal essay or another nonfiction work aimed at instruction or persuasion.*

TONE *The writer's or speaker's attitude toward his or her subject or audience.* The tone of a work may be formal, informal, puzzled, angry, sad, or mocking, among other things, and it may change in the course of the work. For example, the tone of Herrick's "Ode for Him" is admiring and nostalgic in the first stanza but unemotional and knowing in the second.

> See pages 265, 285.

TRAGEDY *A drama or another literary work that ends in the downfall of its main character.* According to Greek philosopher Aristotle, the function of tragedy is to arouse in the audience the emotions of fear and pity in order to produce a **catharsis,** or cleansing, of these emotions by the play's end. The protagonist, or **tragic hero,** is usually a high-ranking or respected person whose personality is marred by a fatal weakness, or **tragic flaw,** that causes his or her downfall. Macbeth, for example, is a tragic hero whose tragic flaw, excessive ambition, leads to his decline and destruction.

> See pages 146, 861.
> See also COMEDY.

TRAGICOMEDY *A drama or another literary work that blends tragedy and comedy.*

TRIPLET *A three-line stanza or poem.* Triplets that employ rhyme are often called **tercets.**

> See pages 438, 676, 883.
> See also STANZA.

TROCHEE *A poetic foot consisting of a stressed syllable followed by an unstressed syllable (´ ˘); also called a **trochaic foot**.* This line from Robert Browning's "Home-Thoughts, from Abroad" contains three trochees:

> ´ ˘   ´ ˘   ´ ˘
> Oh, to / be in / England

See pages 382–383.

VERISIMILITUDE *The achievement of a true-to-life quality in a work of fiction.*

See page 79.

VERNACULAR *In medieval Europe, the languages of the people (English, Italian, and so on), as opposed to Latin, the language of the Church.* Beowulf and Dante's *Divine Comedy* were important early works in the vernacular.

See pages 8–9, 781.

VERSE DRAMA See DRAMA.

VERSE PARAGRAPH *A grouping of lines in a poem that groups together lines of varying number based on units of thought.* The term is used for poems that do not employ stanzas; for example, Wordsworth's "Tintern Abbey" uses verse paragraphs. The term may also be used for poems that do employ a stanza form (such as the couplet) but then have larger line groupings of varying number, usually signaled by indenting. For example, Marvell's "To His Coy Mistress" is written in couplets, but those couplets are grouped into three verse paragraphs.

See also STANZA.

VILLANELLE *A poem of nineteen lines divided into five triplets and a final quatrain; using the rhyme scheme aba aba aba aba aba abaa; repeating line 1 in lines 6, 12, and 18; and repeating line 3 in lines 9, 15, and 18.* Thomas' "Do Not Go Gentle into That Good Night" is a contemporary example.

See page 676.

WIT *The display of cleverness.* Wit is an important ingredient of metaphysical poetry, where it is usually displayed through the use of conceit, paradox, and clever argument; and of neoclassical literature, where it is usually displayed through the use of satire, irony, and parody.

See page 312.

GLOSSARY

The following Glossary lists words that are from the selections but may be unfamiliar to you. Although many of the words have several different meanings, they are defined only as they are used in the selections. Some words may be familiar to you in other contexts but may have unusual meanings in the text.

Each Glossary entry contains a pronunciation, a part of speech, and a definition. Some words are used in more than one way in the textbook and therefore have more than one definition and occasionally more than one part of speech. Related words are often combined in one entry: The main form (for example, the verb *afflict*) is defined, and another form (for example, the noun *afflictor*) is run on after the main definition. Adverbs ending in *-ly* are usually run on after the definitions of the adjective form.

Some unusual words or meanings of words are labeled ARCHAIC (old-fashioned), OBSOLETE (no longer in use), RARE, or POETIC. Other special usage labels include COLLOQUIAL, SLANG, CHIEFLY BRITISH, MILITARY, and so on. Occasionally an unfamiliar idiomatic expression is used within a selection; in such cases the main word of the expression is listed, followed by a definition of the idiom.

The following abbreviations are used in this Glossary:

n.	noun	*conj.*	conjunction
v.	verb	*prep.*	preposition
adj.	adjective	*interj.*	interjection
adv.	adverb	*pl.*	plural
pron.	pronoun	*n.pl.*	plural noun

A key to pronunciations may be found in the lower right-hand corner of each right-hand page of the Glossary.

A

abate [ə bāt′] *v.* to lessen; reduce.

abortive [ə bôr′tiv] *adj.* unsuccessful; useless.

absolution [ab′sə lōō′shən] *n.* formal forgiveness for sins.

absolve [ab zolv′, -solv′] *v.* to free from responsibility or blame.

abysmal [ə biz′məl] *adj.* bottomless; immeasurable.

accrue [ə krōō′] *v.* to come as an increase or addition.

acme [ak′mē] *n.* the highest point.

admonish [ad mon′ish] *v.* to caution; warn.

adversary [ad′vər ser′ē] *n.* enemy; opponent.

adversity [ad vur′sə tē] *n.* misfortune; trouble.

advocate [ad′və kit, -kāt′] *n.* a person who pleads the cause of another; lawyer.

afflict [ə flikt′] *v.* to cause pain, distress, or suffering. —**afflictor**, *n.*

affliction [ə flik′shən] *n.* any cause of pain, distress, or suffering.

aggrandizement [ə gran′dīz mənt, -diz mənt] *n.* the act of making greater.

aggregate [ag′rə gāt′] *v.* to collect into a whole; total.

agronomy [ə gron′ə mē] *n.* the science of crop and farmland management.

alacrity [ə lak′rə tē] *n.* readiness; promptness; eagerness.

alien [āl′yən, ā′lē ən] *adj.* foreign; strange.

alliteration [ə lit′ə rā′shən] *n.* repetition of an initial consonant.

amenable [ə mē′nə bəl, ə men′ə-] *adj.* responsive; yielding.

amenity [ə men′ə tē, ə mē′nə-] *n.* courtesy; pleasant manner; polite behavior.

amphibious [am fib′ē əs] *adj.* capable of living on land and in water.

animate [an′ə māt′] *v.* to cause to act; inspire.

annals [an′əlz] *n.pl.* a written, chronological account of events recorded year by year; history.

annihilate [ə nī′ə lāt′] *v.* to destroy; wipe out.

annuity [ə nōō′ə tē, ə nū′-] *n.* an investment that pays a fixed amount of money at regular intervals.

anoint [ə noint′] *v.* to rub oil on.

antiquated [an′tə kwā′tid] *adj.* old-fashioned; outdated.

antiquity [an tik′wə tē] *n.* ancientness.

aphorism [af′ə riz′əm] *n.* a short statement expressing a basic truth or principle; saying.

aplomb [ə plom′, ə plum′] *n.* confidence; assurance.

apostle [ə pos′əl] *n.* one of the twelve disciples of Christ, sent out by him to preach his gospel.

apparition [ap′ə rish′ən] *n.* a ghost.

appellation [ap′ə lā′shən] *n.* a name.

application [ap′lə kā′shən] *n.* steady attention.

apprehension [ap′ri hen′shən] *n.* understanding.

apprise [ə prīz′] *v.* to tell; notify.

approbation [ap′rə bā′shən] *n.* official approval; praise.

appurtenances [ə purt′ən ən səz] *n.pl.* equipment; accessories.

arable [ar′ə bəl] *adj.* (of land) suitable for cultivation.

arbiter [är′bə tər] *n.* a person with complete power to make decisions; judge.

arbitrator [är′bə trā′tər] *n.* a person chosen to settle a dispute.

arbitress [är′bə tris] *n.* a female arbiter.

armorial [är môr′ē əl] *adj.* relating to or bearing a coat of arms, a design representing a family emblem.

arrears [ə rērz′] *n.pl.* unpaid debts or unfinished duties. —**in arrears** behind in paying a debt or fulfilling an obligation.

artifice [är′tə fis] *n.* something skillfully made.

ascension [ə sen′shən] *n.* the act of rising.

asinine [as′ə nīn′] *adj.* like a donkey; stupid, silly, or stubborn. —**asininely**, *adv.*

asperity [as per′ə tē, əs-] *n.* sharpness of temper; harshness.

aspire [əs pīr′] *v.* to seek ambitiously to achieve something.

assay [ə sā′] *v.* to try.

assiduous [ə sij′ōō əs] *adj.* careful and persistent; hardworking. —**assiduously**, *adv.*

assignation [as′ig nā′shən] *n.* an appointment; date; rendezvous.

asunder [ə sun′dər] *adv.* apart in direction or position.

atrophy [at′rə fē] *v.* to waste away.

attribute [at′rə būt′] *n.* a characteristic.

attrition [ə trish′ən] *n.* sorrow for one's sins that comes from shame or fear of punishment.

audacious [ô dā′shəs] *adj.* bold; daring.

audit [ô′dit] *n.* an examination of financial records.

auditor [ô′də tər] *n.* a person who examines financial records.

augment [ôg ment′] *v.* to increase.

auspicious [ôs pish′əs] *adj.* successful; prosperous.

avarice [av′ər is] *n.* greed.

aver [ə vur′] *v.* to state positively; affirm.

avocation [av′ə kā′shən] *n.* OBSOLETE. a distraction.

axiom [ak′sē əm] *n.* an established principle or rule.

B

ballast [bal′əst] *n.* something heavy carried in a ship to make it steady.

balm [bäm] *n.* a sweet-smelling ointment.

bane [bān] *n.* a cause of suffering or destruction.

banter [ban′tər] *v.* to tease; joke.

barren [bar′ən] *adj.* without vegetation.

barrow [bar′ō] *n.* a mound of earth or stones over a grave.

beaker [bē′kər] *n.* a large cup.

beck [bek] *n.* a summoning or commanding gesture.

beleaguer [bi lē′gər] *v.* to surround; torment.

bier [bēr] *n.* a platform for a coffin; a coffin.

bilingual [bī ling′gwəl] *adj.* able to speak two languages.

bilious [bil′yəs] *adj.* bad-tempered; cross.

blasé [blä zā′, blä′zā] *adj.* bored; indifferent.

blear [blēr] *v.* to blur.

blight [blīt] *n.* something that damages or destroys.

blunt [blunt] *adj.* perceiving slowly; dull.

bogey [bō′gē] *n.* a cause of excessive fear or anxiety.

bogus [bō′gəs] *adj.* not genuine.

boundless [bound′lis] *adj.* without limits.

brandish [bran′dish] *v.* to wave threateningly.

breach [brēch] *n.* a gap, opening, or break.

bridle [brīd′əl] *v.* to control or restrain, as if with a horse's harness.

buffoon [bə foon′] *n.* a clown; joker.

bulbous [bul′bəs] *adj.* shaped like a bulb; rounded or swollen.

bullion [bool′yən] *n.* gold or silver in the form of bars.

burnish [bur′nish] *v.* to polish.

C

cadence [kād′əns] *n.* a rhythmic pattern of sound or movement.

calligraphy [kə lig′rə fē] *n.* the art of beautiful handwriting.

camouflage [kam′ə fläzh′] *n.* a way of hiding by blending with the background; disguise.

capricious [kə prish′əs, -prē′shəs] *adj.* tending to change suddenly or unpredictably.

casuistry [kazh′oo is trē] *n.* a method for deciding questions of right and wrong by applying moral principles to concrete situations.

causeway [kôz′wā′] *n.* a highway.

cavalcade [kav′əl kād′, kav′əl kād′] *n.* a group of horseback riders moving along together.

censure [sen′shər] *n.* strong disapproval.

certitude [sur′tə tood′, -tūd′] *n.* sureness; certainty of events.

chalice [chal′is] *n.* a cup or goblet, especially one used in Holy Communion.

charlatanry [shär′lə tən rē] *n.* a pretending to have knowledge; fakery; trickery.

chivalry [shiv′əl rē] *n.* the qualities of a perfect knight, such as courtesy, bravery, helpfulness, respect for women.

choleric [kol′ər ik] *adj.* bad-tempered.

chronic [kron′ik] *adj.* constant; always present. —**chronically,** *adv.*

circumscribe [sur′kəm skrīb′] *v.* to encircle; limit; restrict.

citadel [sit′əd əl, -ə del′] *n.* a high fortress for defending a city.

cite [sīt] *v.* to refer to; quote.

civility [si vil′ə tē] *n.* politeness.

clandestine [klan des′tin] *adj.* secret.

clarion [klar′ē ən] *n.* a sound like a trumpet.

cleave [klēv] *v.* to divide; split.

clement [klem′ənt] *adj.* merciful; lenient.

cloy [kloi] *v.* to make weary by too much of anything pleasing; satiate.

coagulate [kō ag′yə lāt′] *v.* to form into a mass; thicken.

coalition [kō ə lish′ən] *n.* an alliance.

cogitate [koj′ə tāt′] *v.* to think deeply or seriously.

combustible [kəm bus′tə bəl] *adj.* burning easily.

comely [kum′lē] *adj.* pleasing in appearance; attractive.

commodity [kə mod′ə tē] *n.* a product that is bought and sold.

communal [kə mūn′əl, kom′yən əl] *adj.* shared; public.

compassion [kəm pash′ən] *n.* sympathy for a person's misfortune combined with a desire to help.

complier [kəm plī′ər] *n.* one who agrees or conforms.

composure [kəm pō′zhər] *n.* calmness; self-control.

compulsion [kəm pul′shən] *n.* the act of forcing or being forced.

compulsive [kəm pul′siv] *adj.* able to compel or force.

compulsory [kəm pul′sər ē] *adj.* mandatory; required.

computation [kom′pyə tā′shən] *n.* the act of counting or figuring mathematically; calculation.

concentrate [kon′sən trāt′] *n.* proportional content; strength.

concession [kən sesh′ən] *n.* something granted or yielded.

conchology [kong kol′ə jē] *n.* the study of shells and shellfish.

conciliate [kən sil′ē āt′] *v.* to win the friendliness or calm the anger of.

concourse [kon′kôrs, kong′-] *n.* a crowd.

concussion [kən kush′ən] *n.* the shock of a blow or collision.

conduce [kən doos′, -dūs′] *v.* to lead or help bring about a result.

confederate [kən fed′ə rāt′] *v.* to unite; ally; associate.

confiscation [kon′fis kā′shən] *n.* the seizing of private property for public use.

conflagration [kon′flə grā′shən] *n.* a large fire.

conjecture [kən jek′chər] *v.* to guess.

conjunction [kən jungk′shən] *n.* the state of being joined; association; combination.

connoisseur [kon′ə sur′] *n.* an expert.

consequential [kon′sə kwen′shəl] *adj.* RARE. conceited; pompous.

consign [kən sīn′] *v.* to give; deliver.

consort [kon′sort] *n.* a companion; wife or husband.

consummation [kon′sə mā′shən] *n.* fulfillment.

---

at; āpe; cär; end; mē; it; īce; hot; ōld; fôrk; wood; fool; oil; out; up; ūse; turn; ə in ago, taken, pencil, lemon, circus; bat; chin; dear; five; game; hit; hw in white; joke; kit; lid; man; not; singer; pail; ride; sat; shoe; tag; thin; this; very; wet; yes; zoo; zh in treasure; кн in loch, German ach; и in French bon; œ in French feu, German schön

contemporary [kən tem′pə rer′ē] *n.* a person of the same age.

contend [kən tend′] *v.* to struggle; compete.

contrite [kən trīt′, kon′trīt] *adj.* sorry or guilty for one's wrongdoing; regretful; repentant. —**contritely,** *adv.*

contrive [kən trīv′] *v.* to construct cleverly.

copious [kō′pē əs] *adj.* 1. abundant; lavish. 2. pouring out words; enthusiastically long-winded.

cordial [kôr′jəl] *n.* a sweet liqueur.

covert [kuv′ərt, kō′vərt] *n.* a hidden or protected place; a thick growth of bushes or trees where animals can hide.

croup [krōōp] *n.* the rear part of an animal's body; rump.

crystalline [krist′əl in, -īn′] *adj.* clear; transparent.

curfew [kur′fū] *n.* in the Middle Ages, a bell rung to indicate the time to put out lights and retire.

D

dale [dāl] *n.* a valley.

dappled [dap′əld] *adj.* spotted.

dearth [durth] *n.* scarcity; famine.

debauchery [di bô′chər ē] *n.* excessive indulgence in pleasure.

decanter [di kan′tər] *n.* a decorative bottle used for serving liquids.

declaim [di klām′] *v.* to recite or speak in a dramatic or artificial manner.

decree [di krē′] *v.* to make an official order or decision.

decry [di krī′] *v.* to speak out against; express disapproval of.

deem [dēm] *v.* to think; judge; consider.

defer [di fur′] *v.* to put off; delay.

deference [def′ər əns] *n.* respect.

defile [di fīl′] *v.* to stain; disgrace; dishonor.

deign [dān] *v.* to consider something good enough for oneself.

delusive [di lōō′siv] *adj.* misleading.

delve [delv] *v.* ARCHAIC. to dig.

demure [di myoor′] *adj.* proper; reserved; modest. —**demurely,** *adv.*

denounce [di nouns′] *v.* to accuse; criticize.

depict [di pikt′] *v.* to picture; portray.

deprecate [dep′rə kāt′] *v.* to criticize; belittle.

derision [di rizh′ən] *n.* mockery.

dervish [dur′vish] *n.* a member of a Moslem group among whom whirling and other movements are performed as religious exercises.

desolation [des′ə lā′shən] *n.* waste; ruin; destruction.

despoil [di spoil′] *v.* to rob; plunder.

desultory [des′əl tôr′ē] *adj.* not orderly; rambling; disconnected.

devastate [dev′əs tāt′] *v.* to destroy; ruin.

dexterity [deks ter′ə tē] *n.* skill in using one's hands, body, or mind.

didactic [dī dak′tik] *adj.* instructive.

differentiate [dif′ər en′shē āt′] *v.* to perceive as different; distinguish.

diligent [dil′ə jənt] *adj.* careful; persistent; hard-working.

diminution [dim′ə nū′shən, -nōō-] *n.* a lessening; decrease.

dirge [durj] *n.* a slow, mournful piece of music.

discourse [dis kôrs′] *v.* to talk; converse.

discreet [dis krēt′] *adj.* not showy; modest; unobtrusive. —**discreetly,** *adv.*

disinterested [dis in′tris tid, -in′tər is-, -in′tə res′-] *adj.* unconcerned; aloof.

disparage [dis par′ij] *v.* to speak of as having little value; belittle.

disperse [dis purs′] *v.* to scatter; cause to disappear.

disquisition [dis kwə zish′ən] *n.* a long, formal discussion of a topic.

dissemble [di sem′bəl] *v.* to disguise; conceal.

dissipate [dis′ə pāt] *v.* to scatter; disperse.

distracted [dis trak′tid] *adj.* OBSOLETE. crazy; insane.

ditty [dit′ē] *n.* a little song.

divert [di vurt′, dī-] *v.* to turn from a particular course.

dogmatic [dôg mat′ik] *adj.* relating to established beliefs or principles.

doughty [dou′tē] *adj.* brave.

drear [drēr] *adj.* POETIC. dreary; gloomy.

dregs [dregz] *n.pl.* the most unwanted or useless part.

E

ecclesiast [i klē′zē ast] *n.* a clergyman.

edict [ē′dikt] *n.* an official announcement.

effectual [i fek′chōō əl] *adj.* producing a result; effective. —**effectually,** *adv.*

effluence [ef′lōō əns] *n.* something that flows out.

effusion [i fū′zhən] *n.* emotional expression or outpouring.

egregious [i grē′jəs] *adj.* ARCHAIC. extraordinary.

eke [ēk] *v.* to make (a living, etc.) with great difficulty.

elemental [el′ə ment′əl] *adj.* relating to one of the four elements, earth, air, fire, and water.

elocution [el′ə kū′shən] *n.* a style of public speaking. —**elocutionary,** *adj.*

elongate [i lông′gāt] *v.* to lengthen.

elude [i lōōd′] *v.* to get away from or avoid skillfully.

elysium [i lizh′əm, i liz′ē əm] *n.* a place of great happiness; paradise.

emanate [em′ə nāt′] *v.* to come out; flow.

embolden [em bōld′ən] *v.* to make bold or courageous.

eminent [em′ə nənt] *adj.* famous; outstanding.

emolument [i mol′yə mənt] *n.* ARCHAIC. benefit.

encumber [en kum′bər] *v.* to hold back; hinder; burden.

enigma [i nig′mə] *n.* a mystery; puzzle. —**enigmatic** [en′ig mat′ik, ē′nig-] *adj.*

entreaty [en trē′tē] *n.* a humble request.

envisage [en viz′ij] *v.* to imagine; picture.

envoy [en′voi, än′-] *n.* a messenger.

equity [ek′wə tē] *n.* LAW. a set of general rules used to supplement specific laws.

estrange [es trānj′] *v.* to separate; keep away.

estuary [es′chōō er′ē] *n.* a place where a river widens and meets an arm of the sea.

etymology [et′ə mol′ə jē] *n.* 1. the history of a word. 2. the study of the history of words.

eunuch [ū′nək] *n.* a castrated man.

exaltation [eg′zôl tā′shən, ek′sôl-] *n.* a feeling of great joy or pride; elation.

exasperate [ig zas′pə rāt′] *v.* to annoy greatly; irritate; anger.

exemplify [eg zem′plə fī′] *v.* to give an example of.

exempt [ig zempt′] *v.* to release from a rule or requirement; excuse.

exhortation [eg′zôr tā′shən, ek′sôr-] *n.* an attempt to persuade; strong advice.

exonerate [ig zon′ə rāt′] *v.* to declare free of blame; pardon.

exorbitant [ig zôr′bə tənt] *adj.* higher or greater than is reasonable.

exorciser [ek′sôr sī′zər] *n.* one who frees a person or place from an evil spirit.

expatiate [eks pā′shē āt′] *v.* to speak or write in detail.

expedient [iks pē′dē ənt] *n.* something useful for achieving a purpose.

expiation [eks′pē ā′shən] *n.* an atonement or payment for a wrongdoing.

expletive [eks′plə tiv] *n.* an exclamation or curse.

expound [iks pound′] *v.* to state or explain in detail.

expunge [iks punj′] *v.* to erase.

extort [iks tôrt′] *v.* to take by force or threats.

extremity [iks trem′ə tē] *n.* the farthest part.

F

façade [fə säd′] *n.* the front of a building.

faction [fak′shən] *n.* quarreling between opposing groups. —**factious**, *adj.*

fallow [fal′ō] *n.* land that is plowed but left unplanted for a time. —**fallow,** *adj.*

farthing [fär′thing] *n.* an old British coin worth one-fourth of a penny.

faze [fāz] *v.*COLLOQUIAL. to disturb.

feasible [fē′zə bəl] *adj.* possible.

feign [fān] *v.* to pretend.

felicity [fi lis′ə tē] *n.* 1. happiness. 2. a source of happiness.

ferment [fur′ment] *n.* a state of great excitement or unrest.

fickle [fik′əl] *adj.* changeable.

finical [fin′i kəl] *adj.* overly careful or particular; finicky.

flaccid [flak′sid] *adj.* hanging loosely; limp.

flank [flangk] *n.* the side of a formation of soldiers.

flog [flog, flôg] *v.* to force; drive; urge.

florin [flôr′in, flor′-] *n.* a British coin worth two shillings.

flunkey [flung′kē] also **flunky** *n.* a person who does low, minor jobs; servant.

foliage [fō′lē ij] *n.* the leaves of a plant.

formidable [fôr′mi də bəl] *adj.* impressive.

freehold [frē′hōld′] *adj.* held for life or able to be passed on by inheritance.

frenzy [fren′zē] *n.* a wild outburst of activity.

friar [frī′ər] *n.* a member of any of several religious orders that survive mainly by begging.

G

gable [gā′bəl] *n.* a wall with a triangular top formed by a pointed roof that slopes down on both sides. —**gabled,** *adj.*

gantlet [gônt′lit, gant′-] *n.* a punishment in which two rows of men armed with clubs strike a person who runs between them.

garrulous [gar′ə ləs, gar′yə-] *adj.* talkative.

gelding [gel′ding] *n.* a castrated male horse.

gentry [jen′trē] *n.* people of a high social class.

genuflection [jen′yoo flek′shən] *n.* the bending of the knee, as in worship.

girdle [gurd′əl] *n.* a belt.

glade [glād] *n.* an open area within a forest.

glean [glēn] *v.* to examine or pick over for information.

granary [grā′nər ē, gran′ər ē] *n.* a place for storing grain.

gratuitous [grə tōo′ə təs, -tū′-] *adj.* unjustified; uncalled-for.

grisly [griz′lē] *adj.* horrible; ghastly.

guileless [gīl′lis] *adj.* candid; not sly or crafty.

gumption [gump′shən] *n.* initiative; daring.

guttural [gut′ər əl] *adj.* throaty; rasping.

H

habituate [hə bich′ōo āt′] *v.* to make used to; accustom.

harry [har′ē] *v.* to push along.

hawser [hô′zər] *n.* a heavy rope for moving or anchoring a ship.

heath [hēth] *n.* an area of open, uncultivated land.

herald [her′əld] *v.* to introduce; announce; publicize.

heraldic [he ral′dik] *adj.* relating to coats of arms.

hireling [hīr′ling] *n.* a person hired to perform an unpleasant or criminal act.

homage [hom′ij, om′-] *n.* a sign of honor or respect.

host [hōst] *n.* a crowd; multitude.

hostelry [host′əl rē] *n.* an inn.

hull [hul] *n.* the body of a ship.

I

imbue [im bū′] *v.* to fill; spread through.

imitable [im′ə tə bəl] *adj.* able to be imitated.

immoderate [i mod′ər it] *adj.* exceeding proper limits; excessive; unreasonable.

immutable [i mū′tə bəl] *adj.* unchanging. —**immutably,** *adv.*

impalpable [im pal′pə bəl] *adj.* not able to be touched or detected.

impart [im pärt′] *v.* to give; tell, reveal.

impassive [im pas′iv] *adj.* not showing any feelings.

impeccable [im pek′ə bəl] *adj.* without fault; perfect.

imperious [im pēr′ē əs] *adj.* ruling over harshly; overly proud and scornful.

imperturbable [im′pər tur′bə bəl] *adj.* not able to be upset; showing no feeling; calm.

impetuous [im pech′ōo əs] *adj.* rushing forcefully; violent.

impinge [im pinj′] *v.* to hit sharply; collide.

impious [im′pē əs] *adj.* disrespectful.

implacable [im plak′ə bəl, -plā′kə-] *adj.* without pity; not able to be won over.

impotence [im′pət əns] *n.* weakness; helplessness.

imprecation [im′pri kā′shən] *n.* a curse.

impudence [im′pyə dəns] *n.* sauciness; disrespectfulness.

impute [im pūt′] *v.* to place blame for; charge with.

inadvertency [in′əd vurt′ən sē] *n.* inattentiveness; carelessness.

incantation [in′kan tā′shən] *n.* the chanting of magical spells or charms.

incarnate [in kär′nit, -nāt] *adj.* given human form.

incarnation [in′kär nā′shən] *n.* the taking of human form.

incense [in′sens] *n.* 1. a substance that releases a pleasant smell when burned. 2. a pleasant smell; fragrance.

---

at; āpe; cär; end; mē; it; īce; hot; ōld; fôrk; wcod; fōol; oil; out; up; ūse; turn; ə in ago, taken, pencil, lemon, circus; bat; chin; dear; five; game; hit; hw in white; joke; kit; lid; man; not; singer; pail; ride; sat; shoe; tag; thin; <u>this</u>; very; wet; yes; zoo; zh in treasure; ᴋʜ in loch, German ach; ɴ in French bon; œ in French feu, German schön

incessant [in ses′ənt] *adj.* never stopping; constant.

incipient [in sip′ē ənt] *adj.* just beginning.

incommensurable [in′kə men′sər ə bəl, -shər-] *adj.* not measurable or comparable.

incommodious [in′kə mō′dē əs] *adj.* inconvenient; troublesome.

incongruity [in kən grōō′ə tē] *n.* lack of agreement or harmony.

inconsiderable [in′kən sid′ər ə bəl] *adj.* unimportant.

incredulous [in krej′ə ləs] *adj.* unbelieving.

incursion [in kur′zhən] *n.* the act of entering or intruding.

indefatigable [in′di fat′ə gə bəl] *adj.* not able to be made tired; untiring. —**indefatigably,** *adv.*

indignant [in dig′nənt] *adj.* angry because of injustice, meanness, or ingratitude.

ineffable [in ef′ə bəl] *adj.* too awesome to be put into words; indescribable.

ineptitude [i nep′tə tōōd, -tūd] *n.* awkwardness; clumsiness.

inexorable [i nek′sər ə bəl] *adj.* that cannot be changed or stopped.

inextricable [in eks′tri kə bəl, -iks trik′ə bəl] *adj.* that cannot be untangled or untied.

infamous [in′fə məs] *adj.* having a very bad reputation.

infectious [in fek′shəs] *adj.* spreading easily to others.

infest [in fest′] *v.* to fill; overrun.

ingress [in′gres] *n.* entrance.

inimical [in im′i kəl] *adj.* opposed; unfavorable; harmful.

iniquity [in ik′wə tē] *n.* wickedness.

inquisition [in′kwə zish′ən] *n.* an investigation or harsh questioning, often of those who do not conform.

insatiable [in sā′shə bəl] *adj.* not able to be satisfied. —**insatiableness,** *n.*

inscrutable [in skrōō′tə bəl] *adj.* difficult to understand; mysterious.

inseparable [in sep′ər ə bəl, -sep′rə-] *adj.* not able to be separated.

insolence [in′sə ləns] *n.* disrespectfulness; impertinence.

integrity [in teg′rə tē] *n.* honesty; sincerity; trustworthiness.

inter [in tur′] *v.* to bury.

intercede [in′tər sēd′] *v.* to plead in behalf of another person.

interfuse [in′tər fūz′] *v.* to spread through something; blend.

interminable [in tur′mi nə bəl] *adj.* endless.

intimation [in′tə mā′shən] *n.* a hint; suggestion.

intone [in tōn′] *v.* to say or recite in a singsong way or on a single note; chant.

introspection [in′trə spek′shən] *n.* the act of looking inward; examination of one's own thoughts and feelings.

intuition [in′tōō ish′ən, -tū-] *n.* something that is known or understood without the use of conscious thought.

inventory [in′vən tôr′ē] *n.* a list of items.

inverse [in vurs′, in′vurs′] *adj.* opposite; reverse.

inveterate [in vet′ər it] *adj.* fixed as a habit; established.

invoke [in vōk′] *v.* to request solemnly.

iridescent [ir′ə des′ənt] *adj.* showing shifting, rainbowlike colors.

irreducible [ir′i dōō′sə bəl, -dū′-] *adj.* not able to be reduced or lessened.

irremediable [ir′i mē′dē ə bəl] *adj.* not able to be remedied or fixed.

J

jackdaw [jak′dô′] *n.* a blackbird like a crow but smaller.

jocund [jok′ənd, jō′kənd] *adj.* cheerful; merry.

L

landed [lan′did] *adj.* possessing land.

languid [lang′gwid] *adj.* lacking liveliness and interest in things.

lateral [lat′ər əl] *adj.* relating to the side.

laudable [lô′də bəl] *adj.* worthy of praise.

lay [lā] *n.* a short poem.

legion [lē′jən] *n.* a large unit of soldiers; army.

lexicon [lek′sə kən, -kon′] *n.* a dictionary.

libellous [li′bə ləs] also **libelous** *adj.* containing damaging written or printed information about a person.

lichen [li′kən] *n.* a plant that grows in patches on rocks or other surfaces.

liege [lēj] *adj.* loyal.

ligature [lig′ə choor′, -chər] *n.* something used to tie.

lineage [lin′ē ij] *n.* family descent; ancestry.

listless [list′lis] *adj.* lacking energy and interest in things.

litany [lit′ən ē] *n.* a repetitive reciting or chanting.

lithograph [lith′ə graf′] *v.* to print from a stone or plate that has been treated to attract ink to certain areas and repel it from others.

livid [liv′id] *adj.* discolored; black-and-blue.

lucid [lōō′sid] *adj.* clear; transparent.

lugubrious [loo gōō′brē əs, -gū′-] *adj.* exaggeratedly sad or mournful.

lurid [loor′id] *adj.* pale or grayish; ghastly.

M

malign [mə līn′] *adj.* evil; harmful.

malignant [mə lig′nənt] *adj.* wishing evil; malicious.

mallow [mal′ō] *n.* any of a group of plants, usually having showy flowers and leaves with rounded divisions.

manifest [man′ə fest′] *adj.* clear; obvious. —**manifestly,** *adv.*

manor [man′ər] *n.* an estate or mansion.

mansion [man′shən] *n.* ARCHAIC. a dwelling; residence.

mantle [mant′əl] *n.* a cloak; cape.

mar [mär] *v.* to damage; spoil.

marrow [mar′ō] *n.* the soft, fatty tissue inside bones.

meander [mē an′dər] *v.* to wander; ramble.

mellifluous [me lif′lōō əs] *adj.* sweet; smooth; flowing.

melodious [mi lō′dē əs] *adj.* producing a melody; sweet-sounding.

mercenary [mur′sə ner′ē] *adj.* working only for money, as a soldier in a foreign army. —*n.* a person who works only in order to make money.

metaphysical [met′ə fiz′i kəl] *adj.* supernatural.

mindful [mīnd′fəl] *adj.* paying attention; aware.

ministry [min′is trē] *n.* the representatives of a government.

miscarriage [mis kar′ij] *n.* bad handling; failure.

modulation [moj′ə lā′shən] *n.* regulation of the tone or pitch of the voice.

molder [mōl′dər] *v.* to crumble; decay.

molest [mə lest′] *v.* to annoy; trouble.

molten [mōlt′ən] *adj.* glowing.

morose [mə rōs′] *adj.* bad-tempered and gloomy. —**morosely,** *adv.*

mortification [môr′tə fi kā′shən] *n.* shame; humiliation.

motley [mot′lē] *adj.* made up of many colors or varied elements.

muse [mūz] *v.* to think; ponder.

myriad [mir′ē əd] *n.* an extremely large number.

N

narcissistic [när′si sis′tic] *adj.* self-centered.

nimble [nim′bəl] *adj.* moving quickly and lightly. —**nimbly,** *adv.*

nocturnal [nok turn′əl] *adj.* of or occurring in the night.

nomenclature [nō′mən klā′chər] *n.* a system of names.

notary [nō′tər ē] *n.* an official who declares documents authentic, records statements made under oath, etc.: short for **notary public.**

O

obdurate [ob′dər it, ob′dyər-] *adj.* stubborn; unbending; hardened.

obese [ō bēs′] *adj.* very fat.

oblique [ə blēk′, ō blēk] *adj.* slanting; sloping. —**obliquely,** *adv.*

obliterate [ə blit′ə rāt] *v.* to wipe out; erase.

oblivion [ə bliv′ē ən] *n.* forgetfulness.

obsequies [ob′sə kwēz] *n.pl.* funeral rites.

obtuse [əb tōōs′, -tūs′] *adj.* slow in understanding; insensitive.

odious [ō′dē əs] *adj.* disgusting; hateful.

office [ô′fis, of′is] *n.* a religious ceremony.

officious [ə fish′əs] *adj.* impertinent; meddling.

ogle [ō′gəl] *v.* to eye flirtatiously.

opiate [ō′pē it, -āt′] *n.* a medication that relieves pain or brings on sleep or relaxation.

oppressive [ə pres′iv] *adj.* harsh; cruel.

opulence [op′yə ləns] *n.* wealth; luxury.

ordain [ôr dān′] *v.* to order; decree.

ornament [ôr′nə ment′] *v.* to decorate.

P

palatial [pə lā′shəl] *adj.* like a palace; large and stately.

pallor [pal′ər] *n.* paleness.

palpitation [pal′pə tā′shən] *n.* rapid beating.

palsy [pôl′zē] *n.* a condition marked by a shaking or trembling of a part of the body.

paltry [pôl′trē] *adj.* unimportant; worthless.

pandemonium [pan′də mō′nē əm] *n.* wild uproar or confusion.

pander [pan′dər] *v.* to satisfy or exploit someone's desires or weaknesses.

paraphernalia [par′ə fər nāl′yə] *n.pl.* equipment.

parley [pär′lē] *n.* conversation; conference.

partiality [pär′shē al′ə tē, pär shal′-] *n.* a certain fondness or taste.

passion [pash′ən] *n.* suffering or agony.

pathetic [pə thet′ik] *adj.* arousing pity, sadness, or sympathy.

pathos [pā′thos] *n.* a quality that causes a feeling of pity or compassion.

patriarch [pā′trē ärk′] *n.* a father, founder, or leader; respected old man.

pauper [pô′pər] *n.* a very poor person.

pecuniary [pi kū′nē er′ē] *adj.* relating to money.

pedant [ped′ənt] *n.* a person who overemphasizes minor details or points of knowledge. —**pedantic** [pi dan′tik], *adj.*

penitent [pen′ə tənt] *n.* a person who regrets and wants to make up for wrongdoing.

penury [pen′yər ē] *n.* severe poverty.

percipience [pər sip′ē əns] *n.* perception.

peremptory [pə remp′tər ē] *adj.* not permitting argument or delay; commanding. —**peremptorily,** *adv.*

perfidious [pər fid′ē əs] *adj.* not trustworthy; disloyal. —**perfidiousness,** *n.*

pernicious [pər nish′əs] *adj.* RARE. wicked.

perplex [pər pleks′] *v.* to puzzle; confuse.

personable [pur′sə nə bəl] *adj.* attractive.

peruse [pə rōōz′] *v.* to study; examine; read carefully.

pestilence [pes′tə ləns] *n.* a highly contagious and dangerous disease; plague.

petulance [pech′ə ləns] *n.* bad temper; crankiness.

philology [fi lol′ə jē] *n.* the study of language.

phonetic [fə net′ik] *adj.* relating to the study of speech sounds.

picket [pik′it] *n.* a soldier or group of soldiers stationed away from the main group to protect it from surprise attack; sentry.

piety [pī′ə tē] *n.* devotion to religion, family, etc.; faithfulness.

pipe [pīp] *n.* a tubelike musical instrument into which air is blown. —*v.* to play on a pipe.

pique [pēk] *v.* to offend; annoy.

plaintive [plān′tiv] *adj.* sad; sorrowful.

plaudits [plô′dits] *n.pl.* praise; applause.

ploy [ploi] *n.* a playful adventure.

plunder [plun′dər] *n.* things taken by force; loot.

podium [pō′dē əm] *n.* a platform for a speaker, orchestra conductor, etc.

polecat [pōl′kat′] *n.* a small animal like a weasel.

pomegranate [pom′gran′it, pom′ə-, pum′-] *n.* a reddish fruit with a thick skin and numerous small seeds, each covered with juicy pulp.

pompous [pom′pəs] *adj.* overly proud and dignified; pretentious.

ponderous [pon′dər əs] *adj.* heavy.

postillion [pōs til′yən, pos-] *n.* a person who rides on one of the horses drawing a carriage.

prate [prāt] *v.* to chatter foolishly.

precedent [pres′ə dənt] *n.* an earlier action, decision, etc., that serves as an example or rule.

precipitate [pri sip′ə tāt′] *v.* to cause; bring on.

precipitation [pri sip′ə tā′shən] *n.* hurriedness.

predestinate [prē des′tə nit, -nāt′] *adj.* having a certain destiny or fate.

prelate [prel′it] *n.* a high-ranking clergyman.

prevarication [pri var′ə kā′shən] *n.* the act of lying or avoiding the truth.

primordial [prī môr′dē əl] *adj.* existing from the earliest times.

probity [prō′bə tē, prob′ə-] *n.* honesty; honorableness.

procurement [prə kyoor′mənt] *n.* the act of getting or obtaining.

prodigious [prə dij′əs] *adj.* enormous.

prodigy [prod′ə jē] *n.* an unusually talented child.

---

at; āpe; cär; end; mē; it; īce; hot; ōld; fôrk; wood; fōōl; oil; out; up; ūse; turn; ə in ago, taken, pencil, lemon, circus; bat; chin; dear; five; game; hit; hw in white; joke; kit; lid; man; not; singer; pail; ride; sat; shoe; tag; thin; <u>th</u>is; very; wet; yes; zoo; zh in treasure; кн in loch, German ach; N in French bon; œ in French feu, German schön

profane [prō fān′, prə-] v. to treat with disrespect or contempt.

promontory [prom′ən tôr′ē] n. a high point of land that juts out into the water.

propagate [prop′ə gāt′] v. to spread widely. **—propagator,** n.

propensity [prə pen′sə tē] n. a tendency; inclination.

propitiate [prə pish′ē āt′] v. to win the favor of.

propitious [prə pish′əs] adj. favorably inclined; benevolent.

prospectus [prə spek′təs] n. a statement describing a proposed work or undertaking.

prostrate [pros′trāt] adj. lying flat or with the face down.

protract [prō trakt′] v. to draw out; lengthen.

provincial [prə vin′shəl] adj. of a province, or division of a country.

proximity [prok sim′ə tē] n. nearness.

pullet [pool′it] n. a young hen.

pulverize [pul′və rīz′] v. to pound into dust.

purvey [pur vā′] v. to supply.

R

rabid [rab′id] adj. overly enthusiastic or devoted.

radiate [rā′dē āt′] v. to send out; spread.

rafter [raf′tər] n. a beam that supports a roof.

rally [ral′ē] v. to recover; revive.

rapacious [rə pā′shəs] adj. taking by force; robbing.

recoil [ri koil′] v. to draw back.

redound [ri dound′] v. to lead; contribute.

regenerate [ri jen′ə rāt′] v. to form again; renew; reestablish.

rend [rend] v. to tear; split.

render [ren′dər] v. to cause to be; make.

rent [rent] past tense of **rend.**

repast [ri past′] n. a meal.

repository [ri poz′ə tôr′ē] n. a place in which something is stored.

repudiate [ri pū′dē āt′] v. to refuse; reject; disown.

requiem [rek′wē əm, rē′kwē-] n. a piece of music sung in honor of the dead.

resurrection [rez′ə rek′shən] n. a rising from the dead.

retraction [ri trak′shən] n. a taking back or withdrawing.

revel [rev′əl] n. a wild, noisy celebration.

rhetoric [ret′ər ik] n. showy language.

risible [riz′ə bəl] adj. making one laugh; funny.

robust [rō bust′, rō′bust] adj. strong and healthy.

rod [rod] n. a stick used for punishment, carried as a symbol of authority, etc.

rogue [rōg] n. a mischievous person. **—roguish,** adj.

rubicund [rōō′bi kənd] adj. reddish.

rustic [rus′tik] n. a person from the country. —adj. relating to the country.

rustle [rus′əl] n. a series of soft, fluttering sounds.

S

sacrilegious [sak′rə lij′əs, -lē′jəs] adj. showing disrespect toward something sacred.

saffron [saf′rən] adj. orange-yellow.

sagacity [sə gas′ə tē] n. sound judgment; shrewdness.

salvation [sal vā′shən] n. a saving from the punishment for sins; redemption.

sanctity [sangk′tə tē] n. sacredness; holiness.

sanctuary [sangk′chōō er′ē] n. a holy place, such as a church, temple, or part of a church.

sanguine [sang′gwin] adj. having a healthy, reddish complexion and a cheerful manner.

sate [sāt] v. to satisfy fully.

scabbard [skab′ərd] n. a case for the blade of a sword, etc.

scanty [skan′tē] adj. barely enough; small; meager.

scarab [skar′əb] n. a stone carved with the form of a beetle, used as a charm in ancient Egypt.

schism [siz′əm, skiz′-] n. a division in a church.

scope [skōp] n. the range of activity or thought.

scourge [skurj] n. a cause of trouble or suffering.

scrupulosity [skrōō′pyə los′ə tē] n. strict attention to what is proper or conventional.

sear [sēr] v. 1. to burn. 2. to dry up; wither.

sect [sekt] n. a religious or political group.

secular [sek′yə lər] adj. not relating to religion.

sensibility [sen′sə bil′ə tē] n. the tendency to be easily hurt or offended.

sensible [sen′sə bəl] adj. aware.

sententious [sen ten′shəs] adj. fond of using trite phrases or maxims. **—sententiously,** adv.

sepulcher [sep′əl kər] n. a grave or tomb.

sequestered [si kwes′tərd] adj. isolated; secluded.

sere [sēr] adj. POETIC. withered.

serf [surf] n. in the feudal system, a slavelike laborer bound to the land of a lord.

servile [sur′vil, -vīl] adj. lacking self-respect; timid and obedient. **—servilely,** adv.

shire [shīr] n. a country or region in England.

shrill [shril] adj. high-pitched and piercing.

shrivel [shriv′əl] v. to shrink; wrinkle up; wither.

sickle [sik′əl] n. a tool with a curved blade and short handle used for cutting grass, etc.

signal [sig′nəl] adj. noticeable; remarkable.

signification [sig′nə fi kā′shən] n. OBSOLETE. a sign; symbol.

sinew [sin′ū] n. a tough, cordlike tissue that connects a muscle to another part of the body; tendon.

sinuous [sin′ū əs] adj. winding.

slack [slak] v. to be careless or lazy.

slander [slan′dər] n. the spreading of false and harmful statements about a person.

slavish [slā′vish] adj. like a slave; overly humble and obedient.

slough [sluf] v. to shed; get rid of.

solemn [sol′əm] adj. serious; sacred.

solicitous [sə lis′ə təs] adj. full of concern.

sonorous [sə nôr′əs, son′ər əs] adj. impressive sounding.

spare [spār] adj. thin.

specter [spek′tər] n. a ghost.

splay [splā] v. to spread out.

sprightly [sprīt′lē] adj. lively.

staff [staf] n. a stick carried for support.

stagnant [stag′nənt] adj. not moving or flowing.

stave [stāv] n. a stick.

stealthy [stel′thē] adj. secret; sly; sneaky. **—stealthily,** adv.

stile [stīl] n. a set of steps leading over a wall or fence.

stint [stint] n. a holding back or limiting.

straiten [strāt′ən] v. to cause to be in distress or need, especially financially.

stratagem [strat′ə jəm] n. a clever plan or trick for achieving something.

strife [strīf] n. struggle; conflict.

stupefy [stōō′pə fī′, stū′-] v. to make dull; stun.

sublime [səb līm′] adj. noble; lofty.

submissive [səb mis′iv] *adj.* giving in easily to the power or control of another.

subsistence [səb sis′təns] *n.* means of living; livelihood.

succor [suk′ər] *v.* to help.

suffuse [sə fūz′] *v.* to spread over and fill with light or a liquid. —**suffusion,** *n.*

sullen [sul′ən] *adj.* gloomy; dull.

sulphurous [sul′fər əs, sul fūr′əs] *adj.* fiery; hellish.

sultry [sul′trē] *adj.* hot; fiery; passionate.

sundry [sun′drē] *adj.* various.

superfluous [soo pur′floo əs] *adj.* unnecessary; extra.

supine [soo pīn′] *adj.* lying on one's back.

supplant [sə plant′] *v.* to replace.

supple [sup′əl] *adj.* able to bend easily; limber; flexible.

surmise [sər mīz′, sur′mīz] *n.* a guess.

susceptible [sə sep′tə bəl] *adj.* easily affected or influenced; sensitive.

swain [swān] *n.* a country person.

swathe [swoth, swāth] *v.* to wrap; surround.

swound [swound] *n.* a swoon; faint.

symmetry [sim′ə trē] *n.* the matching of parts or opposite sides; balanced proportions.

syndicate [sin′di kit] *n.* a business that sells articles, etc., to be published at the same time to a number of newspapers or magazines.

syntax [sin′taks] *n.* the arrangement of words in sentences.

T

tally [tal′ē] *n.* something used for recording accounts.

tariff [tar′if] *n.* a list of taxes or prices.

tarry [tar′ē] *v.* to leave slowly; stay; linger.

tee [tē] *n.* the letter *t.* —**to a tee** exactly.

teem [tēm] *v.* to be full.

temerity [tə mer′ə tē] *n.* foolhardy boldness; recklessness.

temperate [tem′pər it, -prit] *adj.* not extreme; mild.

tenacity [ti nas′ə tē] *n.* persistence; stubbornness.

tenor [ten′ər] *n.* a continuing course or tendency.

terrestrial [tə res′trē əl] *adj.* earthly.

throes [thrōz] *n.pl.* a condition of pain or struggle.

titillation [tit′ə lā′shən] *n.* a reaction; feeling; thrill.

tome [tōm] *n.* a book, especially a large one.

torrent [tôr′ənt, tor′-] *n.* a rapid, violent stream.

tortuous [tôr′choo əs] *adj.* twisting; winding.

trace [trās] *n.* a strap or chain connecting an animal's harness to a vehicle being pulled.

transgress [trans gres′, tranz-] *v.* to violate; break.

tremulous [trem′yə ləs] *adj.* trembling; throbbing.

trepidation [trep′ə dā′shən] *n.* a shaking or trembling.

trestle [tres′əl] *n.* a framework for supporting something.

trick [trik] *v.* to ornament.

tumult [too′məlt, tū′-] *n.* violent motion; confusion.

turbid [tur′bid] *adj.* muddy; confusing.

U

unallayed [un′ə lād′] *adj.* not lessened or quieted.

unassailable [un′ə sā′lə bəl] *adj.* not able to be attacked or questioned.

unburnished [un bur′nisht] *adj.* unpolished.

unconditional [un′kən dish′ən əl] *adj.* unlimited; absolute.

unfledged [un flejd′] *adj.* not yet having all its feathers.

unkempt [un kempt′] *adj.* not well groomed; messy.

unravished [un rav′isht] *adj.* not violated.

unslaked [un slākt′] *adj.* not satisfied or quenched.

untrammeled [un tram′əld] *adj.* not restrained or tied up.

V

vacillate [vas′ə lāt′] *v.* to be unable to decide; hesitate.

valance [val′əns, vā′ləns] *n.* a decorative strip of wood or other material.

valediction [val′ə dik′shən] *n.* a farewell.

vanguard [van′gärd′] *n.* the front part of a moving army.

vantage [van′tij] **ground** a position giving an advantage.

velocity [vi los′ə tē] *n.* speed.

vend [vend] *v.* to sell.

venomous [ven′ə məs] *adj.* poisonous.

veracious [və rā′shəs] *adj.* honest; accurate.

verbatim [vər bā′tim] *adj.* word-for-word.

verisimilitude [vər′ə si mil′ə tood′, -tūd′] *n.* something having the appearance of truth or reality.

verity [ver′ə tē] *n.* truth.

vermin [vur′min] *n.* a small, harmful or disgusting animal.

vessel [ves′əl] *n.* a ship or boat.

vexatious [vek sā′shəs] *adj.* annoying; disturbing.

vicissitude [vi sis′ə tood′, -tūd′] *n.* changeableness.

victuals [vit′əlz] *n.pl.* food.

vie [vī] **vied, vying** *v.* to compete.

vigilance [vij′ə ləns] *n.* watchfulness; alertness.

vilify [vil′ə fī′] *v.* to say harmful and false things about.

vindication [vin′də kā′shən] *n.* the act of defending.

virtuosity [vur′choo os′ə tē] *n.* great skill in music, art, acting, etc.

visage [viz′ij] *n.* a person's face.

vivacious [vi vā′shəs, vī-] *adj.* lively; animated.

vociferous [vō sif′ər əs] *adj.* shouting forcefully.

voluble [vol′yə bəl] *adj.* speaking easily and rapidly; talkative.

voracious [vô rā′shəs, və-] *adj.* wanting large amounts of food; ravenous.

vouchsafe [vouch sāf′] *v.* to be nice enough to give.

W

warden [wôrd′ən] *n.* a person in charge of something.

weal [wēl] *n.* well-being.

wend [wend] *v.* ARCHAIC. to travel.

whet [hwet, wet] *v.* to sharpen.

wile [wīl] *n.* a trick.

wizened [wiz′ənd] *adj.* dried out; shriveled.

wrangler [rang′glər] *n.* a quarrelsome person.

wrest [rest] *v.* to take by force; wring.

Z

zealous [zel′əs] *adj.* extremely enthusiastic or devoted.

zenith [zē′nith] *n.* the point in the sky directly above the observer.

zephyr [zef′ər] *n.* a breeze.

---

at; āpe; cär; end; mē; it; īce; hot; ōld; fôrk; wood; fool; oil; out; up; ūse; turn; ə in ago, taken, pencil, lemon, circus; bat; chin; dear; five; game; hit; **hw** in white; joke; kit; lid; man; not; singer; pail; ride; **s**at; **sh**oe; tag; thin; **th**is; very; wet; yes; zoo; **zh** in treasure; кн in loch, German ach; N in French bon; œ in French feu, German schön

VOCABULARY REVIEW

In addition to the words listed in the Glossary and the words covered in the word study sections throughout this book, each of the following words is presented to help you prepare for standardized tests of verbal skills. The page numbers at the right tell where you can find these words treated in *English Literature with World Masterpieces*.

abyss	286
acme	469
acrid	764
alacrity	231
anarchy	650
animate	231
asperity	358
auspicious	861
averse	481
ballast	231
barren	501
bleared	540
blight	540
blunt	937
bridled	231
brimming	650
clamorous	650
conjecture	331
contritely	913
contrive	331
cosseted	89

covet	89
credulous	913
crone	89
dappled	540
deciphering	955
dejected	89
dilate	481
diminution	469
dissipated	469
dogmatic	913
eminent	231
encumbers	358
exasperating	764
felicity	331
fickle	540
formidable	913
frenzy	925
ignominy	286
impassively	861
impious	286
implacable	861
impudence	913
inadvertency	358
infinitesimal	955
infernal	286
inimical	913
insatiableness	925
intercede	913
invocations	481
lyre	937
mars	231
mercenary	913
mortifying	481
obdurate	286
odious	331
pathetic	469

pathos	925
percipience	913
perfidiousness	331
perforated	955
pernicious	331
petals	937
precipitate	231
prodigious	331
progeny	481
reprove	89
revelation	650
reverberating	764
risible	358
ruinous	764
sagacity	331
sanctity	331
scanty	469
seared	540
sententiously	861
serrated	764
slander	501
soundlessly	937
strife	501
stupefied	937
sublime	913
tenacity	925
torrent	925
transgress	861
tumult	650
unburnished	501
unfastened	955
venomous	231
vessel	501
vexatious	331
vigilance	358
void	955

INDEX OF TITLES BY THEME

INDEX OF TITLES BY GENRE

INDEX OF SKILLS

Page numbers in boldface italics indicate entries in the Writing About Literature Handbook.
Page numbers in italics indicate entries in the Literary Terms Handbook.

See the Table of Contents for list of complete *lessons* on Speaking and Listening Skills, Thinking Skills, Researching Skills, and Writing Skills.

LITERARY SKILLS

Action, 476
Age of Classicism, 311
Age of Elegance, 311
Age of Johnson, 312, 353, *1021*
Age of Pope, 312
Age of Reason, 311
Alexandrine, 127, 438, *1020*
Allegory, 120, 287, 290, 893, *1020*
Alliteration, 26, 430, **996,** *1020*
Alliterative verse, 26, *1020*
Allusion, 276, 286, 656, *1020*
Anapest, *1020, 1024*
Anecdote, *1020*
Anglo-Saxon, 3, 5, 40–41, *1020*
Antagonist, *1020*
Aphorism, *1020*
Apostrophe, 448, *1020*
Argument, logical, 260
Aside, 145, *1020*
Assonance, 430, **996,** *1020*
Atmosphere, 225, 756, *1021*
Audience, 236
Augustan Age, 312
Autobiography, 365, *1021*

Ballad stanza, 55, *1021*
Bibliography, **989**
Biography, 365, *1021*
Blank verse, 165, 277, 285, 286, *1021*

Caesura, 26, *1021*
Cantos, 120, *1021*
Caricature, 903, *1021*
Carpe-diem theme, 269, *1021*
Catharsis, 861, *1021, 1032*
Cavaliers, 242, 261, 267, 272
Character, 78, 225, 502, 510, 724, 904, *1021*
  complex, 724
  dynamic, 225, 724, *1021*
  flat, 225, 724, *1021*
  round, 78, 225, 724, *1021*
  static, 225, 724, *1021*

Characterization, 78, 79, 104, 698, 712, 724, *1021–1022*
  direct, 78, 79, 724, *1021, 1022*
  indirect, 78, 712, 724, *1021–1022*
  in short story, 698, 724
Chivalry, 47
Classicism, 311–313, *1022*
Climax, 224, 711, *1022*
Comedy, 242, 569, *1022*
  of ideas, 569, *1022*
  of manners, 242, *1022*
  satiric, 242
Conceit, 249, *1022*
  metaphysical, *1022*
  Petrarchan, *1022*
Conflict, 224, 701, *1022, 1029*
  external, 224, 701, *1022*
  internal, 224, 701, *1022*
Connotation, 679, *1022*
Consonance, 431, **996,** *1022*
Couplet, 139, 291, 352, 438, *1022, 1025*
  heroic, 291, 352, 438, *1025*
  rhymed, 139

Dactyl, *1022, 1024*
Denotation, 679, *1022*
Denouement, *1022, 1029*
Details, 42, 78, 79, 104
Dialect, *1023*
Dialogue, 52, 476, 933, *1023*
Diary, 305, *1023*
Diction, 286, 679, 683, 752, *1023*
Dirge, 143
Drama, 144–145, 236, 242, 391, 826, *1023*
  closet, 391
  Elizabethan, 144–145
  Greek, 826
  melodrama, 391
  Restoration, 242
  sound in, 236
Dramatic conventions, 145, 612, *1023*
Dramatic monologue, 502, 507, *1023*
Elegy, 38, 371, *1023*
Endnote, **988**
Epic, 5, 8, 120, 277, 285, 351, 786, 820, *1023, 1027*
Epigram, 352, *1023*
Epiphany, 711, *1024*
Epitaph, 370, *1024*
Epithet, 820, *1024*
Essay, 228, 332, 339, 461, *1024*
  expository, *1024*
  familiar, 466
  formal, 339, *1024*
  informal, 339, *1024*
Exemplum, 91, *1024*

Existentialism, 940, *1024*
Exposition, 224, 711, *1024, 1029*

Fable, *1024*
Falling action, 224, 711, *1029*
Farce, 913, *1024*
Figurative language, 139, 448, *1024–1025*
Figure of speech, *139,* 448, *1024*
Flashback, *1024*
Folk ballad, 49, 52, 55, 554, *1024, 1027*
Foot, 119, *1024*
Footnote, **988**
Foreshadowing, 18, *1024–1025*
Frame story, 57, *1025*
Free verse, 232, 563, 656, *1025*

Georgian poetry, 657, 658

Hero, 146, 433, 861, *1032*
  Byronic, 433, 436, *1021*
  tragic, 146, 861, *1032*
Homeric (epic) simile, 820, *1023, 1025*

Iamb, 119, *1025*
Iambic hexameter, 127
Iambic pentameter, 119, 165, *1025*
Imagery, 177, 286, *1026*
Imaginative reading, 558
Implication, 384
Inference, 384
Interior monologue, *1027*
Interludes, 111, *1026*
Invocation, 277, *1026*
Irish National Theatre, 564, 641
Irish Renaissance, 641
Irony, 225, *1026*
  dramatic, 225, *1026*
  situational, *1026*
  verbal, 225, *1026*

Journal, 305, *1026*

Kenning, 26, *1026*

Legend, 103, 826–827, *1026*
Literary criticism, 243, 465, 482, *1026*
Literature of conscience, 660

Madrigal, 143
Masque, 111
Metaphor, 139, 448, **996,** *1026*
Metaphysical poetry, 242, 246, 260, *1026*
Meter, 119, 501, *1027*

COMPOSITION SKILLS

Page numbers in boldface italics indicate entries in the Writing About Literature Handbook.

ANALYTICAL

INDEX OF AUTHORS AND TITLES